FOOTBALL MANAGERS

THE BREEDON BOOK OF

FOOTBALL MANAGERS

Dennis Turner and Alex White

The Breedon Books
Publishing Company
Derby

First published in Great Britain by
The Breedon Books Publishing Company Limited
44 Friar Gate, Derby, DE1 1DA
1993

ISBN 1 873626 32 0

Printed and bound by Hillmans Printers Limited of Frome.
Covers printed by BDC Printing Services Limited of Derby.

Contents

Photographic Acknowledgements

The overwhelming majority of the photographs in this book have been drawn from the EMPICS Agency of Nottingham and the Hulton-Deutsch Picture Library in London. For that research we are grateful to Neal Simpson and Kevin Allcock of Empics. A few other photographs are from Colorsport of London, and others from various private collections.

Authors' Introduction and Acknowledgements

FOLLOWING the publication of *Fulham: A Complete Record* in 1987, we thought it would be a good idea to attempt another book, but one with broader appeal. It was surprising to both of us that whilst there was a history of virtually every League club, little but the most general overviews existed on the men who have come to be regarded by the public as the most important influences on a club's playing record.

Several years of research later, it was apparent why nobody had tackled the subject. The idea was to produce a book in keeping with the spirit of the *Complete Record* series but to focus exclusively on the role of the manager at each club during their time in the Football League and FA Premier League. To add a bit of spice, we also devised a scoring system to rank managers, regardless of competition or dates.

This is the end product of that idea and in the following pages are sections which contain a 'Who's Who' of Football League and FA Premier League managers, a club-by-club analysis and the statistical rankings. In the annexes are the names of the successful managers for every season in each of the domestic competitions and the three European club cups.

We seriously underestimated the amount of work involved and in order to have got this far, we have tested the patience and goodwill of a number of people to the limit. The least we can offer in return is a public thank you for their contributions which, although not seperately identifiable, were absolutely vital. Jim Creasey has been an invaluable source of pre-1939 biographical data, whilst Bob Lilliman's marvellous library of club histories was generously put at our disposal.

As well as the references listed in the bibliography, we would also like to thank Steve Phillips, Doug Lamming, Malcolm Hartley, Michael Braham, Mike Davage, Chris McMenemy, Steve Beaglehole, Dick Bate, Colin Murphy, Stuart McIntosh, Gareth Davies, Peter Jones and Roger Triggs for supplying information and Barry Naisbitt for his help on the construction of the scoring system.

It is most unlikely that this book will be free of errors, factual or otherwise. The range of sources was so wide and the evidence often contradictory that we had to make (perhaps arbitary) judgements. Any such mistakes are entirely ours and we accept full responsibility. We hope, however, that there is enough in the pages which follow to interest the general supporter and history buff alike and that this book is viewed as having made an interesting and original contribution to football's growing literature.

Alex White
Dennis Turner
July 1993

Clubs and Their Managers

The role of the manager at a football club has evolved and developed over the last century. Shaped initially by the pioneers of the pre-World War One era like Tom Watson, Harry Bradshaw and Ernest Mangnall and extended by such inter-war figures as Herbert Chapman, Frank Buckley and George Jobey, the job has now become a mix of tactician, businessman, public relations consultant and personnel manager for which there is no adequate preparation or training. Perhaps the last 20 years have seen the position of the manager at its zenith. As the major football clubs become bigger and bigger commercial enterprises, the responsibilities of the manager may become more narrowly defined, and the autonomy assumed by or given to the best of the modern generation will be reined back.

Even though all clubs have had a person bearing the title of manager for many years, there have been marked differences between them in their attitudes to the person popularly regarded as the key figure at the club. In particular, there have been variations as to:

☐ when a manager was first appointed. Sunderland, for example, began in the 1890s, Everton not until 1939;

☐ the control an individual was allowed. At some First Division clubs, the manager still did not pick the team in the 1950s;

☐ the time a person was given to do the job, which has ranged from Bill Lambton's three days at Scunthorpe to the 35 years Fred Everiss spent at West Brom; and

☐ the background that was felt to be most appropriate. It is only relatively recently that a playing career was thought to be a necessary qualification.

Space constraints preclude an in-depth analysis of each club's managerial history, but an attempt has been made to summarize the key features in the following pages. The tables for the clubs have been constructed on a common basis, using the following guidelines:

• only those managers who were in the job during League seasons are included: those whose tenures covered pre-League or wartime competitions only have been omitted;

• caretaker managers have been excluded, other than where they were subsequently upgraded to permanent manager;

• the length of managerial careers are expressed in terms of League seasons rather than years and months to avoid distortions caused by the war and pre-League periods;

• the average managerial term for each club is shown using the season of the first appointment as the base year rather than the first season in the Football League. Everton, therefore, is based on the 47 seasons since Theo Kelly's debut season rather than the 94 the Toffees have spent in the League;

• the qualifying period for inclusion in this section is all clubs currently in the Premier/Football League (with the exception of very new boys Barnet) and any former League clubs which competed for at least 20 League seasons (ie Accrington Stanley, Aldershot, Barrow, Bradford, Gateshead, New Brighton, Newport, Southport and Workington). All the other former League clubs, plus Barnet, are shown in a summary table at the end of this section;

• the final column in each of the club tables shows a points tally for honours won, an attempt to identify on an objective basis the most successful manager. This is taken from the analysis in *The Scoring System*, which contains a full explanation of the methodology; and

• only managers in post at some stage up to the last game of 1992-93 have been included. Subsequent appointees may be shown on the tables, but they have been omitted from the statistical summaries.

Despite these stringent ground rules, there are still obvious areas of difficulty where the authors' judgement has been applied. The most obvious of these is the question of who was a manager rather than a secretary or caretaker. In most cases, reference has been made to the most up to date club history, and in this respect, the Breedon 'Complete Record' series has been indispensable. Where no history was available, contemporary sources were consulted. There are, nevertheless, still grey areas, and whilst the likes of Fred Everiss (West Brom) and Bill Tulip (Gateshead) have been included here as managers, there are persuasive reasons for regarding their roles as more secretarial or administrative and thus excluding them. In the final analysis, this was a matter of personal judgement rather than definitional certainty.

For each of the managers shown on the accompanying club tables, there is a full entry in the 'Who's Who' section, whilst the points tallies are aggregated in the section analysing managerial career performances.

General Conclusions

The table below summarizes some of the key managerial information on clubs' records. A cursory glance down the third column of figures reveals significant variations in the average life expectancy of managers at different clubs. Overall, the average for all 100 clubs is 3.3 seasons per manager, and the distribution within narrow bands is as follows:

Average managerial tenure of:
Up to 2.0 seasons: ....5 clubs
2.1 — 2.5 seasons: ....15 clubs
2.6 — 3.0 seasons: ....22 clubs
3.1 — 3.5 seasons: ....22 clubs
3.6 — 4.0 seasons: ....13 clubs
Over 4.0 seasons: ....23 clubs

None of the five with the fastest rate of turnover has ever played in the top flight, and three of them only gained League status in the post-1945 era. They are:
Scarborough ....1.5 seasons per manager
Workington...........................1.6 seasons per manager
Peterborough ....1.9 seasons per manager
Walsall ....2.0 seasons per manager
Barrow...............................2.0 seasons per manager

At the other end of the longevity spectrum, some of the biggest and longest established League clubs have the best records for managerial stability, perhaps implying a link between success and a low casualty rate. The top ten, all with an average managerial lifespan in excess of five seasons, are:

Seasons per manager
1. West Ham 9.6
2. Liverpool............................6.9
3. Sheffield United 6.4
4. Nottingham Forest 6.3
5. Manchester United....................5.6
6. Arsenal 5.3
6. Ipswich Town 5.3
6. Wolverhampton Wanderers 5.2
6. Stoke City 5.2
10. Derby County 5.1

Whilst these averages often reflect a tradition of low managerial turnover, they can also be heavily influenced by one long serving individual. Each club's longest serving manager is shown in the final column of the tables, and an examination of this list reveals 22 names which spent at least 15 League seasons at the helm of one club. In addition, there are two other clubs (Bolton and Wolves) whose second longest serving manager exceeded 15 years. They are shown separately below, and for those with an asterisk against their names, the years exceeded the seasons, for their periods in office included the World Wars or pre-League competitions. These most durable of men are:

Rank	Name	Club	Sns
1	Fred Everiss*	West Bromwich A (1902-48)	35
2	Jack Addenbrooke*	Wolves (1885-1922)	30
3	John Nicholson*	Sheffield Utd (1899-1932)	29
4	Matt Busby*	Manchester Utd (1945-71)	23.5
5	David Calderhead*	Chelsea (1907-33)	22
6	Charles Webb*	Brighton & HA (1919-47)	20
6	Charles Foweraker*	Bolton W (1919-44)	20
8	Tom Watson	Liverpool (1896-1915)	19
8	Bob Kyle*	Sunderland (1905-28)	19
10	Bill Anderson	Lincoln City (1947-65)	18
10	Bob Jack*	Plymouth Argyle (1910-38)	18
10	Bill Ridding	Bolton W (1950-68)	18
10	Bert Tann	Bristol Rovers (1950-68)	18
10	Ted Bates	Southampton (1955-73)	18
15	Brian Clough	Nottingham Forest (1975-93)	17.5
16	Tony Waddington	Stoke City (1960-77)	17
17	Joe Smith*	Blackpool (1935-58)	16
17	Bill Tulip*	Gateshead (1933-56)	16
17	Billy Lucas	Newport County (1953-74)	16
17	Bill Nicholson	Tottenham Hotspur(1958-74)	16
17	Harry Curtis*	Brentford (1926-49)	16
17	Jimmy Seed*	Charlton Athletic (1933-56)	16
17	Stan Cullis	Wolves (1948-64)	16
24	John Lyall	West Ham United (1974-89)	15

Given the rate at which chairmen seem prepared to change managers in modern times, it is not perhaps surprising that only two names on the above list have been involved with clubs in the last 15 years, Clough and Lyall. These two have much in common as managers, not least the way they both left the clubs they had served so well for so long.

That the pace of change has accelerated is undeniable. Currently, a club gives a manager about two and a half years in the job before presenting him with his P45, whereas in the 1920s, a manager could plan on about four years in one place before having to scan the 'Sits Vac' columns. From the information in the club tables, it is possible to track the increase in the rate of turnover. Using calender years as the basis, starting from 1919, and making no distinction between the various reasons for a change (ie dismissal, retirement, death, resignation, etc are all treated the same way), the graph moves inexorably upwards over time as follows:

Average number of managerial changes a year in the periods:

1919-24	18
1925-29	21
1930-34	20
1935-39	24
1946-50	21
1951-55	21
1956-60	27
1961-65	25
1966-70	33
1971-75	30
1976-80	34
1981-85	38
1986-90	35
Overall Average	
1919-90	27

These trends may well now have peaked. The 1990s could mark a watershed in British club football, with the emergence of the Premier League and satellite broadcasting highlighting the growing gap between the rich and the rest. As the commercial side becomes as important as the playing, the

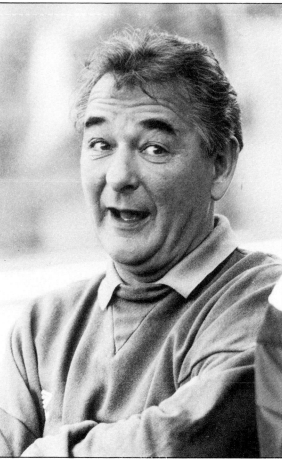

Fred Everiss (far left) spent 35 years with West Brom, whilst Brian Clough was Nottingham Forest manager for almost 18 seasons.

notion of one all-embracing manager could become redundant. The Continental model might be more appropriate in the future, an idea half embraced by Spurs with the ill-fated Chief Executive and Chief Coach arrangement. Or, perhaps, there will be a reversion to 19th-century practice, with an all-powerful chairman calling the shots and becoming the focus of attention to an even greater extent. Whatever the future, the following tables summarize the past, showing, club by club, a chronological listing of the occupants of the managers office.

Club	Sns*	No of Man	Ave† Term	Longest serving manager	Dates	No sns
Accrington Stanley	33	12	2.7	Ernest Blackburn	1924-32	7
AFC Bournemouth	63	22	2.9	Freddie Cox	1956-58 1965-70	7
Aldershot	53	13	4.1	Tom McAnearney	1972-81	9
Arsenal	85	16	5.3	Bertie Mee	1966-76	10
Aston Villa	52	17	3.1	Ron Saunders	1974-82	8
Barnsley	83	20	4.2	Johnny Steele	1960-71 1972-73	12
Barrow	36	18	2.0	Jack Hacking	1949-55	6
Birmingham City	72	23	3.1	George Liddell	1933-39	6
Blackburn Rovers	64	23	2.8	Jack Marshall	1960-67	7
Blackpool	73	20	3.7	Joe Smith	1935-58	16
Bolton Wanderers	74	16	4.6	Charlie Foweraker	1919-44	20
Bradford	51	22	2.3	Claude Ingram	1925-34	9
Bradford City	79	29	2.7	Peter O'Rourke	1905-21 1928-30	14
Brentford	66	20	3.3	Harry Curtis	1926-49	16
Brighton & HA	66	16	4.1	Charles Webb	1919-47	20
Bristol City	81	21	3.9	Alan Dicks	1967-80	13
Bristol Rovers	66	21	3.1	Bert Tann	1950-68	18
Burnley	89	25	3.6	Harry Potts	1958-70 1977-79	14
Bury	75	26	2.2	Archie Montgomery	1907-15	8
Cambridge United	23	8	2.9	John Docherty	1978-83	6
Cardiff City	66	20	3.3	Fred Stewart	1911-33	13
Carlisle United	58	24	2.4	Alan Ashman	1963-67 1972-75	7
Charlton Athletic	65	17	3.8	Jimmy Seed	1933-56	16
Chelsea	77	16	4.8	David Calderhead	1907-33	22
Chester City	55	15	3.7	Frank Brown	1938-53	8
Chesterfield	64	20	3.2	Teddy Davison	1927-32 1952-58	10.5
Colchester United	41	14	2.9	Benny Fenton	1955-63	8
Coventry City	67	26	2.6	Harry Storer	1931-45 1948-53	13.5
Crewe Alexandra	61	18	3.4	Tom Bailey	1925-38	13
Crystal Palace	66	25	2.6	Steve Coppell	1984-93	9
Darlington	64	27	2.4	Jack English	1919-28	7
Derby County	82	16	5.1	George Jobey	1925-41	14
Doncaster Rovers	63	22	2.9	Billy Bremner	1978-85 1989-91	9
Everton	47	10	4.7	Harry Catterick	1961-73	12
Exeter City	66	24	2.8	John Newman	1969-76	7.5
Fulham	75	23	3.3	Phil Kelso	1909-24	11
Gateshead	34	9	3.8	Bill Tulip	1933-56	16
Gillingham	61	18	3.4	Archie Clark	1939-58	8
Grimsby Town	66	23	2.9	Wilf Gillow	1924-32	8
Halifax Town	65	25	2.6	Joe McClelland	1911-30	9
Hartlepool United	65	27	2.4	Fred Westgarth	1943-57	11
Hereford United	21	10	2.1	John Sillett	1974-78 1991-92	4.5
Huddersfield Town	72	22	3.3	Clem Stephenson	1929-42	10
Hull City	77	26	3.0	Cliff Britton	1961-69	8
Ipswich Town	48	9	5.3	Bobby Robson	1969-82	13.5
Leeds United	77	20	3.9	Don Revie	1961-74	13
Leicester City	75	20	3.8	Matt Gillies	1958-68	10.5
Leyton Orient	77	25	3.1	Peter Proudfoot	1922-29 1930-31 1935-39	12
Lincoln City	78	22	3.5	Bill Anderson	1947-65	18
Liverpool	90	13	6.9	Tom Watson	1896-1915	19
Luton Town	61	21	2.9	Dally Duncan	1947-58	11
Manchester City	90	26	3.5	Leslie McDowell	1950-63	13
Manchester United	79	14	5.6	Matt Busby	1945-69 1970-71	23.5
Mansfield Town	55	24	2.3	Ian Greaves	1983-85	6
Middlesbrough	83	22	3.8	Bob Dennison	1954-63	8.5
Millwall	66	18	3.7	Robert Hunter	1918-33	13
New Brighton	21	5	4.2	Bill Sawyer	1933-40	6
Newcastle United	56	18	3.1	Joe Harvey	1962-75	13
Newport County	60	24	2.5	Billy Lucas	1953-61 1962-67 1970-74	16
Northampton Town	66	24	2.8	Dave Bowen	1959-67 1969-72	11
Norwich City	66	22	3.0	Ken Brown	1980-87	7
Nottingham Forest	50	8	6.3	Brian Clough	1975-93	17.5
Notts County	69	28	2.5	Jimmy Sirrel	1969-75 1977-82 1985-87	13
Oldham Athletic	75	22	3.4	Jimmy Frizzell	1970-82	12
Oxford United	31	10	3.1	Arthur Turner	1959-69	6.5
Peterborough United	33	17	1.9	Noel Cantwell	1972-77 1986-88	7
Plymouth Argyle	66	20	3.3	Bob Jack	1910-38	18
Portsmouth	66	16	4.1	Jack Tinn	1927-47	13
Port Vale	67	21	3.2	Joe Schofield John Rudge	1920-29 1983-93	9.5
Preston North End	67	24	2.8	Jimmy Milne	1961-67	6
Queen's Park R	66	23	2.9	Alec Stock	1959-68	9
Reading	66	17	3.9	Harry Johnston	1955-63	7.5
Rochdale	65	27	2.4	Jack Peart	1923-30	7.5
Rotherham United	67	20	3.4	Reg Freeman	1934-52	11.5
Scarborough	6	4	1.5	Ray McHale	1989-93	3.5
Scunthorpe United	43	18	2.4	Ron Ashman	1967-73 1976-81	11.5
Sheffield United	83	13	6.4	John Nicholson	1899-1932	29
Sheffield Wednesday	66	17	3.9	Rob Brown	1920-33	13
Shrewsbury Town	43	14	3.1	Arthur Rowley	1958-68	10
Southampton	66	13	5.1	Ted Bates	1955-73	18
Southend United	66	20	3.3	Edward Birnie	1921-34	13
Southport	46	21	2.2	Gordon Hunt	1937-58	14
Stockport County	81	34	2.4	Fred Stewart	1900-11	10
Stoke City	67	13	5.2	Tony Waddington	1960-77	17
Sunderland	92	19	4.8	Bob Kyle	1905-28	19
Swansea City	66	20	3.3	Billy McCandless	1947-55	8
Swindon Town	66	16	4.1	Sam Allen	1902-33	13
Torquay United	59	25	2.4	Eric Webber	1951-65	14
Tottenham Hotspur	70	16	4.4	Bill Nicholson	1958-74	14
Tranmere Rovers	65	15	4.3	Bert Cooke	1911-35	14
Walsall	65	33	2.0	Bill Moore	1957-63 1969-72	9
Watford	66	22	3.0	Graham Taylor	1977-87	10
West Bromwich A	80	21	3.8	Fred Everiss	1902-48	35
West Ham United	67	7	9.6	John Lyall	1974-89	15
Wigan Athletic	15	6	2.5	Bryan Hamilton	1985-86 1989-93	5
Wimbledon	16	7	2.3	Dave Bassett	1981-87	6.5
Wolverhampton W	94	18	5.2	Jack Addenbrooke	1885-1922	30
Workington	26	16	1.6	Joe Harvey	1957-62	5
Wrexham	62	22	2.8	John Neal	1968-77	9
York City	57	19	3.0	Tom Lockie	1960-67	7

*From the first managerial appointment. †Seasons per manager

The Scoring System

In the histories of individual clubs, the authors are usually able to identify the most successful manager, generally by counting the number of trophies or promotions won during a person's term in office. Something more ambitious is attempted in this book: to find the most successful managers in English football as a whole, taking into account all first-class League competitions, the FA Cup, League Cup and the three European trophies. To achieve this, a points-scoring system has been devised, which, even if it is not without its anomalies, does at least have the merit of consistency. Before looking at the results of this analysis, some explanation of the scoring framework is necessary.

The points awarded for each competition are shown in Table 1 below. In deciding on the relative weights, a number of criteria had to be satisfied.

a. The framework had to be simple and easily understood. Winning the First Division championship earned the same number of points in 1989 as in 1889, for example, even though the number of games played had increased.

b. The system had to reflect the fact that the First Division was assumed to be a bigger prize than the Second, the Second Division a more important title than the Third, and so on.

c. The distinction should not, however, be exaggerated, since in managerial terms, winning the Fourth Division championship with a team of free transfer players, part-timers and YTS apprentices is an achievement which compares favourably with winning the First Division with millions of pounds to spend.

d. Coming first was too narrow a definition of success. The points scoring system was widened to take into account the runners-up in each division, which was then modified to include promoted clubs when three or four sides went up from a particular division. Equal weight has been given to promoted clubs, regardless of their final League position.

Table 1: Framework For Scoring System

Competition*	Pts
DIVISION ONE	
Champions	18
Runners-up	12
DIVISION TWO	
Champions	16
Runners-up/promoted	10
DIVISION THREE (plus NORTH & SOUTH)	
Champions	14
Runners-up/promoted	8
DIVISION FOUR	
Champions	12
Runners-up/promoted	6
FA CUP/FOOTBALL LEAGUE CUP	
Winners	18
Finalists	12
Semi-finalists	6
EUROPEAN CUPS	
Winners	18
Finalists	12
Semi-finalists	6

*(NB: The League competitions are as defined pre-1992)

e. On the few occasions in the 1890s when a club finished runners-up in Division Two, but lost in the Test Matches and did not get promoted, points have still been awarded for coming second. Where, on the other hand, a club was only in contention for promotion via the modern play-offs, no points have been awarded if they missed out on promotion.

f. The relative weightings also recognize the fact that

winning a trophy should count for more than finishing runners-up. The winner of any competition was, therefore, automatically awarded five points, with extra points earned depending on the competition (eg 13 for Division One, 11 for Division Two, 9 for Division Three, etc.) The gap between first and second in each competition was then fixed at six points.

g. All cup competitions have been given the same points, equivalent to the First Division scores. No allowance has been made, for example, for the fact that not all clubs entered the League Cup when it started in 1960-61, the rationale being that the winners could do no more than beat all the opponents they met. The fact that others chose not to enter should not detract from the achievement of those who had.

h. Points are awarded to the winners, finalists and semi-finalists of all Cup competitions. The semi-finalists are included because more clubs are involved at the start of the FA and League Cups than in any one division of the League. Coming third/fourth, therefore, is an achievement which should be recognized.

No points scoring system can ever be absolutely fair, and different results can be obtained by applying different values to the competitions. What is attempted here is to establish a reasonable hierarchy of honours which tries to reflect the relative achievements of managing successful sides at every level. To give a greater bias to the higher divisions is to devalue the skills of men in charge of smaller clubs.

There are two qualifications or shortcomings to the methodology that are admitted at the outset.

j. Each manager's score reflects only the success he has achieved. No account has been taken of the occasions on which he may have managed a team which was relegated or which was knocked out of a cup in the first round.

k. A manager has been awarded all the available points if he was in office at the time the competition was won. There are instances of managers leaving or arriving half-way through a title or cup winning season. In fairness, they should have their points totals adjusted accordingly, but this would over-complicate the system.

Both of these adjustments are entirely logical and would provide a more balanced assessment of the most successful managers. Neither is attempted here, but are recommended to those who are interested in pursuing this line of enquiry further.

Overall Rankings

In Appendix 1, the managers who guided the clubs to points-winning positions in the various competitions are shown, season by season. As in previous sections of this book, the precise definition of 'manager' is at times an arbitrary one, particularly in the pre-1915 years. Here, an approach consistent with the club and 'Who's Who' sections is adopted, which means 'secretaries with managerial responsibilities' are included. The definition has generally been based on the latest or definitive club history, if available. In this context, Breedon's 'Complete Record' series has been an essential reference source.

Using the scoring system described above produces the overall managerial rankings shown in Table 2 (The clubs shown against each manager's name are only those with which he achieved some points success and not a complete list of his managerial appointments). Before discussing the results, it is only fair to acknowledge the achievement of a number of 'secretaries' in the early years who did not have managerial responsibilities and are thus excluded from the system. The principal points earners would have been:

George Ramsey — Aston Villa — 312 points
Frank Watt — Newcastle Utd — 172 points
Arthur Dickinson — The Wednesday — 118 points
Will Cuff — Everton — 114 points

Had they been included, Ramsey (six Division One Championships and five FA Cup victories) would have topped the rankings, Watt would have been in ninth place and Cuff would have shared 16th spot with Harry Catterick. Another 'victim' of the definition is Harry Newbould, who earned 30 points as Derby secretary between 1896 and 1899 before he was given managerial responsibilities. Added to the 40 points he subsequently collected, Newbould would have climbed to 39th slot from 86th.

It is not surprising that the analysis produces rankings which give the highest placings to modern managers and to those who have managed clubs at the top level. This is because the number of eligible competitions has doubled in recent times (to include the League Cup and the various European trophies) and because the top honours carry the most points (one League championship, for example, is worth three promotions from the Fourth Division). Of the managers in the top 20 positions (see Table 2), only three (Tom Watson, Herbert Chapman and Fred Everiss) are from the pre-war era. This is in spite of the higher rate of managerial turnover/shorter average tenure since 1945.

The careers of the top three managers, Matt Busby, Bob Paisley and Don Revie, span the first 40 years after World War Two, and each was associated with one particular club, Manchester United, Liverpool and Leeds respectively. Such loyalty is the exception rather than the rule, for only four others from the leading 20 achieved all their success with only one club, Bill Nicholson (Spurs), Fred Everiss (West Brom), Bertie Mee (Arsenal) and Alex Ferguson (Manchester United). The rest picked up their honours with at least two clubs but Ron Saunders had some success with four different clubs, and Ron Atkinson with five.

Ron Atkinson, success with five different clubs.

Whilst Busby comes out on top on points, Paisley is the 'champion' in terms of titles/cups won. As with Don Revie, Busby's ranking reflects consistency over a long period, with several runners-up positions, beaten finalists, etc. to add to the outright successes. Table 3 shows for the managers with at least five League titles/cup victories to their names, the spread of honours across the various competitions. (It includes only the Division One championship and not the Second Division titles won by Clough, Shankly, Mercer, Revie and Watson.)

It can be seen that only three men, Revie, Nicholson and Mercer, won the League, FA Cup, League Cup and a European trophy, and of these, Nicholson probably comes out ahead because he won two different Euro-titles, the Cup-winners Cup and the EUFA Cup. In modern times, Paisley and Clough share a failure to capture the FA Cup, something they have in common with Tom Watson from several generations earlier. Busby and Shankly both missed out on the League Cup (both did participate in the competition, albeit intermittently) whilst Cullis, Graham and Dalglish all failed to win a Euro cup, Cullis and Graham because their teams were not good enough, and Dalglish because his teams were ineligible.

To a certain extent, the number of points won reflects the number of attempts an individual made in a particular competition. Playing in the League, FA Cup, League Cup and in a Euro cup increases the probability of a modern manager winning something over his pre-1956 predecessors, who only had the League and FA Cup to go for each season. To make some allowance for this factor, the points won by the managers sharing the top 20 positions have been adjusted, by dividing the points total by the number of competitions in which they participated. The results of these adjustments are shown in Table 4.

Table 2: Overall Managerial Rankings 1888-1993

	Manager	Pts	Club(s)	Title/cup wins
1	Matt Busby	306	Manchester U	8
2	Bob Paisley	300	Liverpool	13
3	Don Revie	268	Leeds U	7
4	Brian Clough	248	Derby/Nottm Forest	9
5	Bill Shankly	198	Liverpool/Grimsby T	7
6	Bill Nicholson	192	Tottenham H	8
7	Tom Watson	190	Sunderland/Liverpool	6
8	Kenny Dalglish	166	Liverpool/Blackburn R	5
9	Herbert Chapman	162	Huddersfield T/Arsenal	6
10	Joe Mercer	152	Aston Villa/Manchester C	7
11	Stan Cullis	150	Wolves/Birmingham C	5
12	Howard Kendall	128	Blackburn R/Everton	4
13	George Graham	116	Millwall/Arsenal	5
14	Ron Saunders	114	Norwich/Man City/Aston Villa/Birmingham	4
15	Ron Atkinson	112	Oxford/Man Utd/West Brom/Sheff Wed/Aston Villa	4
	Harry Catterick	112	Sheff Wed/Everton	4
17	Tommy Docherty	110	Chelsea/Manchester U	3
	Fred Everiss	110	West Bromwich A	3
19	Alex Ferguson	108	Manchester U	4
	Bertie Mee	108	Arsenal	3
21	Graham Taylor	100	Lincoln/Watford/Aston Villa	2
22	John Lyall	98	West Ham U/Ipswich T	4
23	John Nicholson	96	Sheffield U	3
	Dave Sexton	96	Chelsea/QPR/Manchester U	2
25	Joe Fagan	84	Liverpool	3
	Peter McWilliam	84	Tottenham H/Middlesbro'	4
	Alec Stock	84	Leyton O/QPR/Luton/Fulham	3
28	Keith Burkinshaw	82	Tottenham H	3
	Ernest Mangnall	82	Man Utd/Man City	3
	Lawrie McMenemy	82	Doncaster/Grimsby/Southampton	3
31	Joe Smith	80	Reading/Blackpool	1
32	Jack Addenbrooke	78	Wolves	2
	Terry Neill	78	Tottenham H/Arsenal	1
	Bobby Robson	78	Ipswich T	2
35	Ron Greenwood	72	West Ham U	2
36	Cliff Britton	70	Burnley/Everton/Preston/Hull	1
	Charlie Foweraker	70	Bolton W	3
	John Haworth	70	Burnley	2
	Terry Venables	70	C Palace/QPR/Tottenham H	3
40	Alan Ashman	66	Carlisle U/West Brom A	2
	Jimmy Seed	66	Charlton A	2
	Harry Storer	66	Coventry C/Birmingham/Derby	3
	Tom Whittaker	66	Arsenal	3
44	Tom Maley	64	Manchester C/Bradford	2
	Jim Smith	64	Colchester/Oxford/Birmingham/QPR/Portsmouth	2
46	Bob Jack	62	Plymouth	1
47	Johnny Cochrane	60	Sunderland	2
	Dave Bassett	60	Wimbledon/Sheffield U	1
	Harry Potts	60	Burnley	1
	Arthur Turner	60	Birmingham/Oxford	2
	Billy Walker	60	Sheffield Wed/Nottm Forest	3
52	Rob Brown	58	Sheffield W	3
	Bill McGarry	58	Ipswich T/Wolves	2
	Arthur Rowe	58	Tottenham H/Millwall	2
	Fred Stewart	58	Cardiff C	1
	Tony Waddington	58	Stoke C	2
57	Gordon Lee	56	Blackburn/Port Vale/Everton/Newcastle	2
	Howard Wilkinson	56	Sheffield W/Leeds U	2
59	George Allison	54	Arsenal	3
	Reg Freeman	54	Rotherham U/Sheffield U	1
	Matt Gillies	54	Leicester C	1
	George Jobey	54	Wolves/Derby Co	1
	Bob Stokoe	54	Bury/Carlisle U/Sunderland	2
64	John Bond	52	Bournemouth/Norwich C/Man City	0
	Frank Buckley	52	Wolves	1
66	David Calderhead	50	Chelsea	0
67	Peter O'Rourke	48	Bradford C	3
	Alf Ramsey	48	Ipswich T	3
	Eric Taylor	48	Sheffield W	2
	Wilf Wild	48	Manchester C	2
71	Arthur Fairclough	46	Barnsley/Leeds U	2
	Joe Harvey	46	Newcastle U	2
	Graham Turner	46	Shrewsbury T/Wolves/Aston Villa	3
74	Ken Brown	44	Norwich C	2
	John Carey	44	Blackburn R/Leyton O/Nottm Forest	0
	Ian Greaves	44	Huddersfield/Bolton W/Mansfield T	2
	Peter Hodge	44	Leicester C/Manchester C	2
78	Jack Chaplin	42	Huddersfield T	0
	Jimmy Hagan	42	Peterborough U/West Brom A	2
	Bob Jackson	42	Portsmouth	2
	Robert Kyle	42	Sunderland	1
	Billy McCandless	42	Newport Co/Cardiff C/Swansea T	2
	Clem Stephenson	42	Huddersfield T	0
	Stan Seymour	42	Newcastle U	2
	Jack Tinn	42	Portsmouth	1
86	Leslie McDowall	40	Manchester C	1
	Harry Newbould	40	Derby Co/Manchester C	1
	David Pleat	40	Luton T/Tottenham H	1
	Harry Thickett	40	Bristol C	1
90	Jimmy Armfield	38	Bolton W/Leeds U	1
	Harry Curtis	38	Brentford	2
	Albert Fisher	38	Notts Co	2
	Jimmy Methven	38	Derby Co	1
	Dave Smith	38	Plymouth A/Mansfield T/Southend U	2
	Frank Womack	38	Grimsby T/Leicester C	2
96	Vic Buckingham	36	West Bromwich A	1
	Bobby Campbell	36	Portsmouth/Chelsea	2
	Jack Charlton	36	Middlesbro'/Sheffield W	1
	Ted Davison	36	Sheffield U/Chesterfield	1
	Maurice Evans	36	Reading/Oxford U	2
	Ray Harford	36	Luton T	1
	Charlie Hewitt	36	Millwall/Chester	2
	George Kay	36	Liverpool	1
	James McIntyre	36	Southampton/Fulham	2
	Alex Raisbeck	36	Bristol C/Halifax T	2
	Denis Smith	36	Sunderland/York C	2
	Freddie Steele	36	Port Vale/Mansfield T	1
108	David Ashworth	34	Liverpool/Oldham A	1
	Arthur Cox	34	Newcastle U/Derby Co	1
	Bob Crompton	34	Blackburn R	2
	Ted Drake	34	Reading/Chelsea	2
	Frank O'Farrell	34	Leicester C/Torquay U	1
	Ian Porterfield	34	Rotherham U/Sheffield U	2
	Joe Royle	34	Oldham A	1
	Lou Macari	34	Swindon T/Stoke C	2

The manager with the highest points per competition ratio is Joe Fagan, who had two seasons at the Anfield helm as Dalglish's predecessor. Of the eight competitions entered in these years, Fagan won three, finished runner-up twice and reached one semi-final. This yields 84 points, an average of 10.5 per competition. His overall total, however, does not earn Fagan a place in the top twenty and he is not included in Table 4. For most of the top twenty, the League was the principal source of points, and in the cases of Busby, Shankly, Watson, Chapman, Dalglish, Cullis, Catterick and Taylor, it accounted for over half of their totals. Taylor is unique amongst this group of leading managers in that he won points in all four divisions. His only challenger in this respect is Bill Shankly, who in addition to First and Second honours with Liverpool, finished runners-up in the Third North with Grimsby.

The largest contributions to Clough's and Saunders' totals came from the League Cup, whilst the FA Cup provided Docherty, Mee and Atkinson with more of their points than any other competition. The odd one out of this group is Spurs' Bill Nicholson. Although he was a winner of all three major domestic trophies, the biggest slice (31%) of his substantial points haul came from Europe, where he was at least a semi-finalist in all three cups. A more detailed analysis of the individual competitions follows this introduction.

When Arsenal won the FA Cup in 1993, manager George Graham set a new record: This was the third of the three major domestic trophies he had won as the Gunners' manager, thus making him the first person to play for and manage teams winning the First Division, FA Cup and League Cup. All his successes came with Arsenal apart from playing in a victorious League Cup side, which he achieved at Chelsea in 1964-65.

Looking at the spread of points in Table 2, it is hard not to be impressed by the career achievements of those managers who won around 200 points, down to say Tom Watson in seventh place. Although one or two of today's managers are young enough to add substantially to their present tallies, the likelihood of anyone getting close to Busby or Paisley, or even Revie or Clough, seems remote. George Graham, for instance, now has 116 points with the undoubted potential to gain more. If, however, he is to overtake Busby, he will need another 190 points, equivalent to winning at least another 11 League titles or cups. In modern football it is hard to see anyone achieving the consistency of a Busby over such a long period or the total domination established by Paisley in a shorter space of time. Their places at the top of the all-time managerial role of honour seem secure for a long time to come.

Table 3. Leading Managerial Trophy Winners

Manager	Divl	FACup	LCup	Euro	Total
Bob Paisley	6	-	3	4	13
Brian Clough	2	-	4	2	8
Bill Nicholson	1	3	2	2	8
Matt Busby	5	2	-	1	8
Don Revie	2	1	1	2	6
Herbert Chapman	4	2	-	-	6
Bill Shankly	3	2	-	1	6
Joe Mercer	1	1	2	1	5
Kenny Dalglish	3	2	-	-	5
Stan Cullis	3	2	-	-	5
Tom Watson	5	-	-	-	5
George Graham	2	1	2	-	5

Table 4. Adjusted Managerial Rankings

Manager	Pts	No of Comps	Average
Bob Paisley	300	36	8.3
Kenny Dalglish	166	21	7.9
Herbert Chapman	162	29	5.6
Don Revie	268	48	5.6
Matt Busby	306	58	5.3
Alex Ferguson	108	23	4.7
Bill Nicholson	192	46	4.2
George Graham	116	29	4.0
Tom Watson	190	51	3.7
Joe Mercer	152	43	3.5
Howard Kendall	128	37	3.5
Bertie Mee	108	33	3.3
Stan Cullis	150	49	3.1
Bill Shankly	198	65	3.0
Brian Clough	248	87	2.9
Tommy Docherty	110	49	2.2
Ron Saunders	114	54	2.1
Harry Catterick	112	60	1.9
Ron Atkinson	106	58	1.8
Fred Everiss	110	70	1.6

Division One

Since its inception 94 seasons ago in 1888, only 23 different clubs have won the Division One title. Of these, 71 of the championship winning teams have had managers (as defined above), with most of the gaps occurring in the pre-World War One era. Since 1919, only Newcastle (1926-27) and Everton (1927-28, 1931-32 and 1938-39) still retained the secretary as the main official (usually working in conjunction with the directors and trainer), while

Arsenal's triumph in 1933-34 was secured under the stewardship of a 'caretaker'. Joe Shaw, the assistant manager, who took over temporarily in January 1934, after the death of Herbert Chapman and reverted to the number-two spot when George Allison was appointed the following close season. The position is similar with clubs finishing runners-up: Aston Villa (1930-31 and 1932-33) came second (to Arsenal on both occasions) with secretary Billy Smith at the helm, the only club without a manager to finish second to the champions since 1919.

From Table 5, the managers of First Division clubs who have won at least 30 points are shown, that is those who have had more than one season in the top two. Together, these 28 managers account for almost two-thirds (60 out of 93) all championships, and for 85% of the titles won by clubs with managers. In addition, 49 of the 93 championships were won by managers who lifted the First Division on at least two occasions.

Although Bob Paisley has won more League Championships than any other manager, he has to accept second in the rankings behind Manchester United's Matt Busby. This is because Busby won 84 points for finishing second on seven occasions in addition to his five League titles, compared with Paisley's two runners-up positions and six championships. If, however, the points total is related to the number of seasons each manager had in charge (thus reflecting the attempts on the title), Paisley comes out ahead, an average of 14.7 points per season over nine seasons compared with Busby's 7.6 points over 23 seasons.

Ranked by this criterion, however, Kenny Dalglish rates more highly than Busby. In his five seasons at Anfield he never finished outside the top two, giving him an average of 15.6 points per season, just ahead of his predecessor at Liverpool, Joe Fagan, who picked up 15 points in each of his two seasons at the helm. Dalglish's most recent season in the top flight, with Blackburn, has reduced his points per season average to 13.

Table 5: Leading First Division Managers

Manager	Pts Club(s)	Div One wins
1 Matt Busby	174 Manchester U	5
2 Bob Paisley	132 Liverpool	6
3 Tom Watson	126 Sunderland/Liverpool	5
4 Herbert Chapman	96 Huddersfield T/Arsenal	4
Don Revie	96 Leeds U	2
6 Stan Cullis	90 Wolves	3
7 Kenny Dalglish	78 Liverpool	3
Bill Shankly	78 Liverpool	3
9 Harry Catterick	48 Sheffield W/Everton	2
Brian Clough	48 Derby C/Nottm Forest	2
Howard Kendall	48 Everton	2
Ernest Mangnall	48 Manchester U/City	2
13 Alex Ferguson	42 Manchester U	1
14 George Allison	36 Arsenal	2
Rob Brown	36 Sheffield W	2
George Graham	36 Arsenal	2
Bob Jackson	36 Portsmouth	2
Tom Whittaker	36 Arsenal	2
19 Johnny Cochrane	30 Sunderland	1
Fred Everiss	30 West Bromwich A	1
Joe Fagan	30 Liverpool	1
John Haworth	30 Burnley	1
Robert Kyle	30 Sunderland	1
Alex Mackie	30 Sunderland	1
Bertie Mee	30 Arsenal	1
Bill Nicholson	30 Tottenham H	1
Harry Potts	30 Burnley	1
Arthur Rowe	30 Tottenham H	1

Although, as Table 5 shows, 17 managers have had at least two championship successes, only three lifted the trophy with two different clubs. Tom Watson was the first in the early days of the League, three wins with Sunderland's 'Team of All The Talents' in the 1890s which he followed with the first two of Liverpool's 18 titles. On top of this, his sides finished runners-up three times (Sunderland once and Liverpool twice). Herbert Chapman came close to emulating Watson, winning two titles with Huddersfield in the 1920s and then two with Arsenal in the thirties. He may well have added to his tally but for his untimely death in January 1934. Chapman's side went on to retain the championship in 1933-34 and then complete the hat-trick 18 months after his demise. Since World War Two, only Brian

Clough has achieved the feat of First Division success at two clubs. His first triumph, with Derby in 1971-72, was secured in most unlikely circumstances. His team were on an end-of-season holiday in Majorca when Liverpool and Leeds failed to get the points they needed in overhaul the Rams. Clough's second victory was just as improbable. His Forest team scraped the third Second Division promotion spot in 1976-77 and then proceeded to take the top flight by storm, winning the League by the comfortable margin of seven points in the days when there were only two points for a win.

When Ted Drake steered Chelsea to their only championship in their jubilee season in 1954-55, he became the first person to win the League title as a player and as a manager. In the 1930s, Drake was a fearless and dynamic centre-forward, the leading scorer when Arsenal topped Division One in 1934-35 and 1937-38. This was Drake's only managerial success, but since then, eight others completed the player-manager championship double. Alf Ramsey (Ipswich 1961-62), Joe Mercer (Manchester City, 1967-68) and Dave Mackay (Derby 1974-75) all lifted the trophy after achieving playing honours with different clubs: Spurs, Everton and Arsenal, and Spurs respectively. The other five, Bill Nicholson (Spurs), Bob Paisley (Liverpool), Howard Kendall (Everton), Kenny Dalglish (Liverpool) and George Graham (Arsenal), all managed clubs to the top of the First Division having won a championship medal with those clubs as players. Alex Ferguson's success in the Premier League in 1992-93 made him the first man to manage winners of the top flight in England (Manchester United) and Scotland (Aberdeen).

No manager was able to win titles either side of the two World Wars: Ernest Mangnall came closest when his Manchester City side finished runners-up in 1920-21 after having won two championships with Manchester United in the first decade of the twentieth century. The longest period between title wins was the 15 years that separated Matt Busby's first and last successes, in 1951-52 and 1966-67. Tom Watson pushes him close, however: his first triumph was in 1891-92 and his last 14 years later, in 1905-06. There were, on the other hand, seven managers who won the League in consecutive seasons: Tom Watson (Sunderland, 1891-93), Herbert Chapman (Huddersfield, 1923-25), Rob Brown (Sheffield Wednesday, 1928-30), Bob Jackson (Portsmouth, 1948-50), Busby (1955-57), Stan Cullis (Wolves, 1957-59) and Bob Paisley (1975-77, 1978-80 and 1981-83).

Most of the managers shown in the table won other honours, usually at the highest level. There are, however, only 12 men who have won both the First and Second Division titles (Tom Watson, Fred Everiss, Rob Brown, Arthur Rowe, Harry Catterick, Alf Ramsey, Joe Mercer, Bill Shankly, Don Revie, Brian Clough, Ron Saunders and Howard Wilkinson) and only Alf Ramsey won the Third, Second and First Divisions, thus completing a divisional hat-trick.

Division Two

The manager who has accumulated most Second Division points, as Table 6 shows, is Peter McWilliam. The former Scottish international wing half in Newcastle's Edwardian heyday, McWilliam made his managerial mark when he steered Spurs to the Division Two title in 1919-20. After a period of some success at White Hart Lane, McWilliam left North London for Middlesbrough following a dispute about salary. During his time at Ayresome Park, the Teessiders won the Second Division title twice, although McWilliam can take little credit for the first, in 1926-27, apart from the fact he was there. The Boro board sacked Herbert Bamlett early in 1927, when promotion was already on the cards. McWilliam arrived the following month when First Division football was a virtual certainty. The following season, Boro finished at the foot of Division One, but in 1928-29, they again took the Second Division title, an honour McWilliam could legitimately claim as his own.

Table 6: Leading Second Division Managers

Manager	Pts Club(s)	Div Two wins
1 Peter McWilliam	48 Tottenham H/Middlesbro'	3
2 Eric Taylor	42 Sheffield W	2
3 Ron Saunders	36 Norwich C/Aston Villa/	
	Birmingham C	1

4 Albert Fisher	32 Notts Co		2
Ian Greaves	32 Huddersfield T/Bolton W	2
Peter Hodge	32 Leicester C/Man City	2
John Lyall	32 West Ham U/Ipswich T	2
Joe Mercer	32 Aston Villa/Man City	2
Jimmy Methven	32 Derby C	2
John McKenna	32 Liverpool	2
Terry Venables	32 Crystal P/QPR	2
Frank Womack	32 Grimsby T/Leicester C	2
13 Harry Bradshaw	26 Burnley/Arsenal	1
Ken Brown	26 Norwich C	1
Brian Clough	26 Derby C/Nottm Forest	1
Arthur Cox	26 Newcastle U/Derby C	1
Tommy Docherty	26 Chelsea/Manchester U	1
Fred Everiss	26 West Brom A	1
Tom Maley	26 Manchester C/Bradford	1
Sam Ormerod	26 Manchester C	1
Jim Smith	26 Birmingham C/Oxford U	1
Howard Wilkinson	26 Sheffield W/Leeds U	1

Given Sheffield Wednesday's record in the 15 years after World War Two, it is not surprising to see Eric Taylor in second place. The Owls' long-serving secretary-manager was involved in three promotions to Division One (two as champions) in the space of seven seasons. If points were deducted for relegation, however, Taylor would only have broken even. The three promotions were followed by three relegations and when Taylor handed over responsibility for team affairs to Harry Catterick in 1958, the club was back where it started under him.

In more recent times, Ron Saunders has one of the most interesting records. The FA Cup was the only major domestic honour to elude him, and he had success in the Second Division as well as winning the Football League and League Cup. What makes Saunders' achievements different is the number of clubs at which he enjoyed promotions or Cup wins. He took three different clubs to Wembley in consecutive years in the League Cup, while three clubs climbed into the First Division under his tutelage: Norwich (champions) and Aston Villa and Birmingham as runners-up. No other manager has achieved success in Division Two with three different clubs.

The list of promotion-winning managers with two Second Division clubs is quite a long one, but few were able to follow this by winning the First Division title. Tom Watson did it before Worldd War One with Liverpool, winning the Second and First Divisions in successive seasons between 1904 and 1906. This feat was emulated by Arthur Rowe's Spurs (1949-51) and Alf Ramsey's Ipswich (1960-62). Coincidentally, Ramsey was a member of Rowe's team a decade before his managerial success. Perhaps, predictably, Brian Clough can top most other managers. He took two clubs out of Division Two (Derby as champions in 1968-69 and Forest in 1976-77) and then on to the League title, at Derby within three years and at Forest after 12 months.

Overall, it is hard to escape the not very startling conclusion that the Second Division is a more 'open' competition than the First. In the 90 seasons since the competition began in 1892-93, there have been 43 different winners: Leicester and Manchester City head the list with six successes each, followed by Sheffield Wednesday on five. (By way of comparison, only 23 clubs have won the 94 First Division titles). This more even distribution is reflected in the managerial rankings.

Liverpool, under John McKenna, in 1893-94, were the first club with a manager to win the Second Division and Everton (where Tom McIntosh was secretary), the last to win it without a manager, in 1930-31. Altogether, all but 12 of the 90 champions had a person with managerial responsibilities at the helm, and these 78 winners shared 66 different managers. The 11 men who won more than one title acounted for only 29% of the 78 titles, where as the equivalent figure for the First Division was 69% (17 managers who won 49 titles between them). This clearly reveals the greater concentration of the spoils of the top flight amongst fewer hands.

For a number of these managers, winning the Second Division was the only success they had in any competition. For Norman Bullock, for example, winning Division Two in 1953-54 with Leicester came in his twentieth year of management in the League: before that, none of his sides had ever featured in promotion or got as far as the semi-final of the FA Cup. Sam Cowan, on the other hand, was appointed Manchester City manager in November 1946. By May 1947, the Second Division Championship was at Maine Road, yet Cowan left management the following month because the board was unhappy with him commuting from Brighton and he was reluctant to move north. Frank Osborne took Fulham to the Second Division title two years later, in 1949, only seven months after succeeding Jack Peart in the job. Although he remained at the Cottage in various capacities until 1964, he never won any further honours. Others for whom a lone Second Division championship was their sole success were Harry Evans (Blackpool honorary manager 1929-30), David Halliday (Leicester 1956-57), Ted Fenton (West Ham 1957-58) and Sammy Chung (Wolves 1976-77).

Divisions Three and Four

Every club apart from Reading in 1925-26 which has won one of the three Third Division titles (95 in all, 36 from Division Three, 30 from Division Three North and 29 from the South) has had a person acting in a managerial role, even if the duties performed would today be described as largely secretarial or administrative. Since seven of these managers won the title on more than one occasion, it means that 87 different individuals have steered a club to a Third Division championship.

Table 7: Leading Third Division Managers
(Division Three plus the Third South and North)

Manager	Pts Club(s)	Div Three wins
1 Bob Jack	62 Plymouth A	1
2 Alec Stock	44 Leyton O/QPR/Luton T	2
Harry Storer	44 Coventry C/Derby C	2
4 Billy McCandless	42 Newport C/Cardiff C/ Swansea T	3
5 Reg Freeman	38 Rotherham U	1
6 James McIntyre	36 Southampton/Fulham	2
Alex Raisbeck	36 Bristol C/Halifax T	2
8 Charlie Hewitt	30 Chester/Millwall	1
Billy Lane	30 Brighton & HA	1
Harry Parkes	30 Lincoln C	1
Freddie Steele	30 Mansfield T/Port Vale	1
Tim Ward	30 Barnsley/Grimsby T	1
13 Bill Anderson	28 Lincoln C	2
Graham Turner	28 Shrewsbury T/Wolves	2
Harry Curtis	22 Brentford	1
Jack English	22 Darlington	1
Bill Harvey	22 Chesterfield	1
Claude Ingram	22 Bradford	1
Ned Liddell	22 Luton T	1
Dave Mangnall	22 QPR	1
Ian Porterfield	22 Rotherham U/Sheffield U	1
David Wilson	22 Nelson	1
Lou Macari	22 Swindon T/Stoke C	1

In Division Four, it is the same story. Every one of the 35 winners, with the exception of Doncaster Rovers in 1965-66 (where Bill Leivers left a couple of months earlier) had a manager when the title was clinched. After allowing for the four managers who enjoyed two triumphs at this level, there are 30 different individuals who have managed Fourth Division champions. Tables 7 and 8 show the leading managers in these two divisions, and the qualification is again at least two seasons in the leading positions.

Top of the Third Division list is the remarkable Bob Jack, the long-time manager of Plymouth. Patriarch of a footballing clan that included the great David Jack, of Bolton, Arsenal and England fame, Jack senior had two spells in charge of the Pilgrims, 1905-06 and 1910-38, with a period at Southend in between. All his success came after World War One, yet he won only one title. He amassed 48 of his 62 points for the six consecutive seasons that Argyle finished runners-up in the Third South in the days when only one club was promoted. Finally, in 1929-30, Jack won the title he thoroughly deserved.

The first man to win the Third Division twice was James McIntyre. As Southampton manager, he was runner-up in the inaugural Third Division season of 1920-21, but the Saints made no mistake the following year, when it was the Third Division South. In 1928, he moved to Coventry, but missed out on any more honours until he went to Craven Cottage. In his first full season in west London, 1931-32, he steered Fulham to the first of only two

divisional titles they have won in their 75 season League history.

Some managers have a special skill for running smaller, unfashionable sides and were unable to repeat their success at a higher level with bigger clubs. Alec Stock is perhaps the best example of this phenomenon. He first came to prominence just after World War Two as player-manager of the Yeovil side which knocked mighty Sunderland out of the Cup. Between 1949 and 1959, he had three spells in charge of Third Division Leyton Orient, taking them to the title in 1956, 12 months after finishing runners-up. His stay at Brisbane Road was punctuated by brief sojourns with Roma and Arsenal, but he could not settle in such palatial surroundings. In the 1960s, Stock continued reviving lost causes, first taking QPR from the Third Division to the First Division (and to a League Cup victory at Wembley as a Third Division side) and helping Luton to runners-up spot in Division Three in 1969-70. He was not finished yet, however, for five years later, he led out Second Division Fulham at Wembley for their only FA Cup Final appearance. Stock had over 30 years continuous service in management and a marvellous record, but less than 18 months was at the highest level.

Only two men have won the Third Division title twice with the same club: Alex Raisbeck with Bristol City in 1922-23 and 1926-27 and Bill Anderson with Lincoln in 1947-48 and 1951-52. Anderson was at Sincil Bank from 1946 to 1966, and, like Stock, was a shrewd operator on the transfer market. He once defined success at Lincoln as finishing one point clear of relegation and with income £1 higher than expenditure. Raisbeck, an outstanding centre half for Liverpool and Scotland at the turn of the century, only ever managed Third Division clubs, Bristol City in the Third South and Halifax and Chester in the Northern section.

Graham Turner and Ian Porterfield have been involved more recently in League management, and both made their marks in the Third Division, Turner at Shrewsbury (champions in 1978-79) and Porterfield at Rotherham (1980-81). The two also had further Third Division successes, Turner with Wolves (1988-89) and Porterfield with Sheffield United (1983-84). Another with two Third Division championships to his credit is the legendary Harry Storer, the only man to win both the Northern section (Derby 1956-57) and the Southern (Coventry 1935-36). Alec Stock, on the other hand, is the only manager to win the Third Division as presently constituted (QPR 1966-67) having previously captured one of the regional variations (Leyton Orient 1955-56).

In addition, Stock is one of 15 managers who have taken the same club from the Third to the First Divisions, but only three others can match his achievement of adding one of the three major domestic trophies to their list of honours. In Stock's case, it was the League Cup in 1967 with QPR, but with Jimmy Seed and Billy Walker (both brilliant inside-forwards in the 1920s), it was the FA Cup. Seed took Charlton from the Third South to the First Division between 1934 and 1936, and was still at the Valley when they beat Burnley in the 1947 Cup Final. At Forest, Walker took from 1950 to 1957 to lift the club from the Third South to the top flight, but two years after that, they won the FA Cup, defeating Luton 2-1. The last of the four is Alf Ramsey, for whom the supreme honour was the League Championship in 1961-62, 12 months after his Ipswich side had won the Second Division and five after winning the Third South. Other managers have achieved the glittering prizes at the highest level after proving themselves in Division Three, notably Joe Smith, Bill Shankly, Ted Drake, George Graham and Terry Venables, but only Stock, Walker, Seed and Ramsey did it with one club.

Table 8: Leading Fourth Division Managers

Managers	Pts Club(s)	Div Four wins
1 Dave Smith	30 Mansfield T/Southend U	2
2 Jimmy McGuigan	24 Chesterfield/Crewe A/ Rotherham U	1
Lawrie McMenemy	24 Doncaster T/Grimsby T	2
Jimmy Meadows	24 Stockport C/Southport	2
Graham Taylor	24 Lincoln C/Watford	2
6 Dave Bassett	18 Wimbledon	1
Terry Cooper	18 Bristol C/Exeter C	1

There are two names which stand out on the Fourth

Graham Taylor, one of the leading Division Four managers, went on to manage England.

Division roll of honour, England manager Graham Taylor and his assistant, Lawrie McMenemy. They are two of only four managers who have won Division Four twice. Taylor first pulled it off with Lincoln in 1975-76 and two years later did it with Watford. This was the start of a climb for the Hornets which took them to Wembley and into Europe. McMenemy's first success was at Doncaster in 1968-69, and before he became a national figure, he won the Fourth Division a second time, with Grimsby in 1971-72. Both Swansea, under John Toshack, and Notts County, with Jimmy Sirrel at the helm, went from the Fourth to the First Divisions, as did Watford. Swansea did this without ever winning a title and Sirrel's tenure at Meadow Lane (and County's rise) was interrupted by a period at Sheffield United in the mid-1970s.

Most of the managers who enjoyed success in Division Four spent the bulk of their careers in the lower divisions. McMenemy was the second of a handful who went on to win one of the three major domestic competitions. Jimmy Hagan was the first, and he followed his 1960-61 Fourth Division win with Peterborough with a League Cup victory with West Brom in the last pre-Wembley final of 1966. Ron Atkinson, twice an FA Cup winner with Manchester United and once a League Cup winner with Sheffield Wednesday, won his first managerial honour with Fourth Division Cambridge in 1976-77 whilst Maurice Evans, in charge when Reading won Division Four in 1978-79, led Oxford to the League Cup at Wembley in 1986.

There are two managers who deserve special mention for their unique records with Third and Fourth Division clubs. In 1960-61, Northampton began a remarkable sequence which took them from the Fourth to the First Divisions and back again, all in nine seasons. Manager or general manager throughout the period was former Welsh international defender, Dave Bowen.

Finally, there is Billy McCandless, an Irishman who spent his best playing years in Scotland, with Glasgow Rangers in the inter-war period. He went into management when he retired and led three Welsh clubs, Newport, Cardiff and Swansea, to the Third Division South title in the space of four Football League seasons. This remarkable hat-trick spanned the years of World War Two, and McCandless was still managing Swansea when he died in August 1955.

FA Cup

The FA Cup is the oldest first-class competition, starting life in 1872, some 16 years before the Football League. There have been 111 Finals since then, won by 42 different clubs. In addition, another ten clubs have reached the Final without winning the Cup and 23 made it to the semi-finals but missed out on an appearance in the Final. The club with the most Cup wins is Spurs, who lifted the trophy for the eighth time in May 1991, once more than Aston Villa and Manchester United, and twice more than Blackburn, Arsenal and Newcastle. Arsenal lead the way in appearances in the Final (12), followed by Everton, Manchester United and Newcastle, and Everton (22), West Brom (19) and Liverpool (19) head those who have reached the last four most frequently.

In the period up to 1915, only ten of the Cup winners and 11 of the finalists had a man who could be described as a manager. Since 1920, however, only four clubs have lifted the trophy and three reached the Final without a manager. The last managerless club to win the Cup was Preston in 1937-38, while Luton were the last team to reach Wembley (in 1959) without a manager.

The table shows the list of managers who accumulated at least 36 points in the FA Cup and who between them account for 41 of the 112 Cup victories (37%), but the 46% of Cup-winning sides which had a manager. In addition, these managers appeared in a further 29 finals as runners-up: only eight of the 25 (Foweraker, Bill Nicholson, Cullis, Atkinson, Seymour, Burkinshaw, Lyall and Walker) were on the winning side in every Cup Final appearance.

Matt Busby comes out on top of these rankings, just as he did in the First Division table. Although other managers won the Cup more frequently, Busby's United appeared in two finals as losers and were beaten semi-finalists five times, as well as winning twice at Wembley. John Nicholson is one of two pre-World War One managers in this table. His Cup successes with Sheffield United spanned 23 years — the first at the Crystal Palace in 1902, the second at Old Trafford in 1915 and the third at Wembley in 1925. This was not the longest period between Cup wins, however. In 1935, Billy Walker was manager of Sheffield Wednesday when they beat West Brom at Wembley. His second and final triumph came 24 years later when his Nottingham Forest side defeated Luton.

Table 9: Leading FA Cup Managers

	Manager	Pts	Club(s)	FA Cup wins
1	Matt Busby	90	Manchester U	2
2	John Nicholson	84	Sheffield U	3
3	Jack Addenbrooke	78	Wolves	2
4	Herbert Chapman	66	Huddersfield T/Arsenal	2
	Don Revie	66	Leeds U	1
6	Charlie Foweraker	60	Bolton W	3
7	Kenny Dalglish	54	Liverpool	2
	Tommy Docherty	54	Chelsea/Man Utd	1
	Fred Everiss	54	West Brom A	1
	Bill Nicholson	54	Tottenham H	3
	Bill Shankly	54	Liverpool	2
12	Harry Catterick	48	Shefield W/Everton	1
	Stan Cullis	48	Wolves	2
	Terry Neill	48	Arsenal	1
	Tom Watson	48	Sunderland/Liverpool	0
16	Ron Atkinson	42	West Brom A/Man Utd	2
	Howard Kendall	42	Everton	1
	Stan Seymour	42	Newcastle U	2
	Joe Smith	42	Blackpool	1
	Jack Tinn	42	Portsmouth	1
21	Keith Burkinshaw	36	Tottenham H	2
	John Lyall	36	West Ham U	2
	Bertie Mee	36	Arsenal	1
	Fred Stewart	36	Cardiff C	1
	Billy Walker	36	Sheffield W/Nottm Forest	2

Walker was one of only two managers who have been Cup-winning managers with different clubs. The other, almost inevitably, was Herbert Chapman. He was in charge when Huddersfield beat Preston at Stamford Bridge in 1922, the last pre-Wembley Final. Then, in 1930, he had the satisfaction of seeing his new club, Arsenal, beat his old side 2-0. Chapman was also one of only three men who managed two different clubs to the First Division title. Curiously, neither of the other two, Tom Watson and Brian Clough, was ever a Cup winner.

The fact that Watson can make number 12 in the FA Cup rankings without winning the trophy is testimony to his remarkable consistency. He did make it to one Final, when Liverpool lost to Burnley in 1914, and also to six semi-finals. Clough's one Cup Final and two semi-final appearances do not qualify him for the rankings. Another notable omission is Bob Paisley, winner of a record six Football League titles — the best he could manage in the FA Cup was like Clough, one losing Final and two semi-finals.

The list of managers who won both the FA Cup and First Division title is lengthy. Ernest Mangnall was the first to achieve this double — he did it with Manchester United between 1907 and 1909. In the inter-war period, the feat was emulated by Fred Everiss (West Brom), Wilf Wild (Manchester City), George Allison (Arsenal) and Johnny Cochrane (Sunderland), together with Chapman, who pulled it off twice. Since 1945, Tom Whittaker (Arsenal), Stan Cullis (Wolves), Busby, Harry Catterick (Everton), Bill Nicholson (Spurs), Joe Mercer (Manchester City), Bertie Mee (Arsenal), Don Revie (Leeds), Bill Shankly (Liverpool), Howard Kendall (Everton), Kenny Dalglish (Liverpool), George Graham (Arsenal) and Alex Ferguson (Manchester United) have all added their names to the list.

In 1911, Newcastle won the Cup for the first time after dominating the Football League for seven seasons and losing in three Cup Finals. Exactly ten years later, Spurs won the Cup at Stamford Bridge. The link between these two victories was Peter McWilliam, left-half for Newcastle and manager of Spurs, the first person to play for and manage a Cup-winning side. A member of his Spurs side, inside-forward Jimmy Seed, also achieved the feat when he led Charlton to success over Burnley in 1947. Billy Walker (Aston Villa player and Sheffield Wednesday/Nottm Forest manager), Joe Mercer (Arsenal/Manchester City), Joe Smith (Bolton/Blackpool), Bill Shankly (Preston/Liverpool), Don Revie (Manchester City/Leeds), Matt Busby (Manchester City/United), Bob Stokoe (Newcastle/Sunderland), Kenny Dalglish (Liverpool), Graeme Souness (Liverpool) and George Graham (Arsenal) also achieved this dual success.

So also did Stan Seymour of Newcastle, first as a player in 1924 and then as a manager in 1951 and 1952. He thus became the first manager to lead a side to two successive Cup Final triumphs, something only Spurs' Bill Nicholson (1961 and 1962) and Keith Burkinshaw (1981 and 1982) have done since. There have been others who have made it through to the Final two years running, but left empty-handed on one of the occasions — John Nicholson of Sheffield United (1901 and 1902), Wilf Wild of Manchester City (1933 and 1934), Jimmy Seed Charlton (1946 and 1947), Manchester City's Leslie McDowall (1955 and 1956), Manchester United's Tommy Docherty (1976 and 1977), Arsenal's Terry Neill (1978 and 1979) and Liverpool's Kenny Dalglish (1988 and 1989) all returned and succeeded at the final hurdle 12 months after they had left as losers.

Bertie Mee (1971 and 1972), Don Revie (1972 and 1973), Terry Neill (1979 and 1980) and Howard Kendall (1984 and 1985), on the other hand, all reached Wembley to defend the trophy they had won the previous season (with Arsenal, Leeds, Arsenal and Everton respectively), only to suffer defeat in the attempt. For Kendall, there were to be two consecutive Cup Final defeats (1985 and 1986), a 'record' he shares with Matt Busby (1957 and 1958). Kendall also appeared in three consecutive Finals, a feat only Terry Neill had previously achieved.

League Cup

In its 33-season history, the League Cup, known variously as the League, Milk, Littlewoods or Rumbelows League and Coca-Cola Cup, has been won by 20 different clubs, with a further eight clubs reaching the Final without winning the trophy. Liverpool and Nottingham Forest head the list of winners, with four victories apiece, followed by Aston Villa with three. Forest's and Liverpool's six appearances in the Final is also a record, one ahead of Villa and Arsenal and two in front of Norwich. The highest number of times a club has reached the semi-finals is eight, by Tottenham, Villa and Liverpool, closely pursued by Arsenal and West Ham on seven.

Although founded in 1960-61, the League Cup was ignored by many First Division clubs for several years. It was not until 1966-67, when the Final was played at Wembley (it had previously been over two legs) and victory offered a passage to Europe, that most of the larger clubs decided to compete. Everton and Liverpool, however, waited until 1967-68, although Manchester United, who had taken part in the inaugural season, dropped out until 1966-77 and then again until 1969-70, since when they have participated continuously.

Joe Mercer was the manager of the first League Cup winners, Aston Villa. Just over 43,000 saw the two legs from which Villa emerged 3-2 victors over Second Division Rotherham, managed then by Tom Johnston. This was the first of three Final appearances for Mercer. He was there, again with Villa, two years later when they lost to neighbours Birmingham and he was in charge of Manchester City when they beat West Brom in 1970 to complete a hat-trick of domestic honours (League — FA Cup — League Cup) in consecutive seasons.

As Table 10 shows, however, there are managers with even better records. Brian Clough leads the list by a considerable distance. When Forest first won the League Cup in 1978, it was part of a double, with the Division One title, the first of its kind. By winning the trophy again the following year, Clough became the first manager to retain the League Cup. He could have made it a hat-trick but for a mix-up between Peter Shilton and David Needham which presented Wolves' Andy Gray with the easiest of chances to win the 1980 Final.

Table 10: Leading League Cup Managers

	Manager	Pts	Club(s)	League Cup wins
1	Brian Clough	102	Derby C/Nottm Forest	4
2	Bob Paisley	72	Liverpool	3
3	Ron Saunders	60	Norwich C/Man City/Aston Villa	2
4	Joe Mercer	48	Aston Villa/Man City	2
	George Graham	48	Arsenal	2
	Billy Nicholson	48	Tottenham H	2
7	Ron Atkinson	30	Man Utd/Sheff Wed	1
	Alex Ferguson	30	Manchester U	1
	Matt Gillies	30	Leicester C	1
	Ron Greenwood	30	West Ham U	0
	Ray Harford	30	Luton T	1
	Jimmy Hagan	30	West Brom A	1
	Tony Waddington	30	Stoke C	1
14	John Bond	24	Norwich C/Man City	0
	Tommy Docherty	24	Chelsea/Man Utd	1
	Maurice Evans	24	Oxford U	1
	Gordon Lee	24	Newcastle U/Everton	0
	Bill McGarry	24	Wolves	1
	Bertie Mee	24	Arsenal	0
	Dave Sexton	24	Chelsea/QPR	0

This left the way open for Bob Paisley to surpass Clough's record, with the first hat-trick of League Cup successes, between 1981 an 1983. In the last two of these seasons, Liverpool also won the League title, a feat Joe Fagan repeated in 1984 when he replaced Paisley. Clough, however, reclaimed his League Cup record when his Forest side beat Luton and Oldham in 1989 and 1990 respectively and were beaten finalists in 1992. To these six Final appearances with Forest, Clough can also add a run to the semi-finals with Second Division Derby in 1967-68, who lost 2-4 on aggregate to eventual winners Leeds.

Another manager closely identified with the League Cup is Ron Saunders. Not only did he appear in three consecutive Wembley Finals, but he did so with three different clubs. In 1973, he was in charge of the Norwich side which lost to Ralph Coates' goal for Spurs, and 12 months later was again a loser, this time as Manchester City manager when Wolves won 2-1. Saunders' luck changed in 1975 when his new club, Aston Villa, overcame one of his former clubs, Norwich, courtesy of Ray Graydon's lone goal. Just for good measure, Saunders tasted victory a second time with Villa two years later when they beat Everton 3-2 at the third attempt.

The League Cup has been kinder to clubs from the lower divisions than the FA Cup. In 1962, for example, Fourth Division Rochdale, managed by Tony Collins, made it all the way through to the Final, where they lost to Norwich, with an aggregate score of 0-4.

There have been few more dramatic Wembley Finals than in 1967, the first League Cup Final to be contested at the stadium. First Division West Brom, the holders of the trophy, appeared to be coasting against Queen's Park Rangers, a team two divisions lower. A Rodney Marsh-inspired comeback, however, turned the tables on Jimmy Hagan's side, and Rangers won 3-2. They were managed by Alec Stock, who was a formidable Cup fighter from his Yeovil days. Weeks later, the Loftus Road club clinched a marvellous double when they won the Third Division title.

Another stunning upset followed at Wembley two years later, when Swindon Town of the Third Division took on mighty Arsenal, who were to finish fourth in Division One. Still remembered as Don Rogers' match, the Wiltshire club won 3-1 on a quagmire of a pitch, a victory which thrust manager Danny Williams into the national spotlight and led him to management in the First Division with Sheffield Wednesday. Like Rangers, the Wiltshire Robins won promotion from the Third Division only weeks after they won the League Cup at Wembley.

Managing Arsenal that day was Bertie Mee, and for him it was a second League Cup Final defeat in 12 months — in 1968, the Gunners had gone down to Leeds. This was an experience Mee was to share with Saunders (Norwich 1973 and Manchester City 1974) and Gordon Lee (Newcastle 1976 and Everton 1977). Jimmy Hagan (West Bromwich 1966 and 1967), George Graham (Arsenal 1987 and 1988) and Ray Harford (Luton 1988 and 1989) all returned to the Final to defend the trophy they had won the previous year, but left empty-handed.

The League Cup has also signalled the emergence and the end of some famous managerial careers. When Plymouth Argyle got through to the semi-finals in 1965, it was the first mark Malcolm Allison made as a manager-coach and, shortly afterwards, he was to team up so successfully with Joe Mercer at Maine Road. In the 1970-71 competition, Manchester United were knocked out for the second consecutive season in the semi-finals by the odd goal, first by Manchester City and then by Aston Villa. This was as close as Wilf McGuinness came to winning anything at Old Trafford during his short stint as Matt Busby's successor. If just one of those games had gone his way, it might have all been so different.

For Harry Potts, Burnley's defeat in the semi-finals by Swindon (3-2 in a third match) in 1969, was the last successful run he enjoyed during his illustrious 12-year spell at Turf Moor, which included a League Championship and FA Cup Final appearance. It was a similar story with Stan Cullis. After achieving tremendous success with Wolves between 1949 and 1960 (three Championships and two FA Cup wins), his last serious attempt at national honours ended in the League Cup semi-finals in 1967, when his Birmingham City side were comprehensively beaten by QPR. Finally, it was success in the League Cup in 1987 that indicated George Graham was on the path that would lead Arsenal to two First Division titles, the FA Cup and another League Cup success in the next six years.

European Competitions

English clubs were slow to recognize the potential of European competitions. Chelsea gave in to the authorities request not to participate in the inaugural European Cup in 1955-56, although Scottish champions, Hibernian, did play, and made it to the semi-final. By the time the European Cup-winners Cup started in 1960-61, Europe was proving an attractive proposition, and Stan Cullis's Wolves were England's first representatives (losing to Glasgow Rangers in the semi-final). The EUFA Cup was only established in 1971, when two English clubs, Tottenham, managed by Bill Nicholson, and Wolves, under Bill McGarry, contested the first final. This competition was the successor to the Inter-City Fairs Cup. Initially, this was spread over several seasons, with Birmingham and London England's first representatives in 1955-58.

Despite the lukewarm welcome English clubs gave Europe, they have enjoyed considerable success in the three competitions. All told, they have won 23 of the Cups and, up to the time hooligans forced their suspension, English clubs had won each of the three trophies more often than sides from any other country. The 23 victories have been shared between

Sir Matt Busby, overall the most successful manager in the history of English club football.

17 managers, with Bob Paisley heading the list with four successes. As Table 11 shows, Brian Clough, Bill Nicholson and Don Revie were the others with more than one Eurotitle to their credit. In addition, English clubs have reached another 11 finals, which take in another six managers who are not amongst the 17 winners.

It was entirely appropriate that Matt Busby should have been the first English manager to lift the European Cup. His defiance of the authorities had paved the way for English participation, and after three losing semi-finals, and a tragic air crash, it was fitting that he and United should win the trophy in 1968. It proved to be his only success, however, and although it was the first English win in this competition, other managers had already done well in the other two.

Few people now remember that it was Birmingham City's Pat Beasley and Gil Merrick who were the first English club managers to make it to a Euro Final, the Fairs Cup in 1960 and again in 1961. They lost on both occasions, to Barcelona and Roma respectively. This was not the Blues' first taste of Euro success, however, for in 1957, under yet another manager, Arthur Turner, they went out to Barcelona in the semi-final of the same competition.

Table 11: Leading Managers In European Competitions

Manager	Pts	Club(s)	European wins
1 Bob Paisley	72	Liverpool	4
Don Revie	72	Leeds U	2
3 Bill Nicholson	60	Tottenham H	2
4 Brian Clough	48	Derby C/Nottm Forest	2
5 Matt Busby	42	Manchester U	1
Bill Shankly	42	Liverpool	1
7 Joe Fagan	30	Liverpool	1
8 Keith Burkinshaw	24	Tottenham T	1
Ron Greenwood	24	West Ham U	1
Joe Mercer	24	Manchester C	1

Bill Nicholson of Spurs was the first English manager to claim some Euro silverware. Following a narrow failure in the European Cup to Benfica

Don Revie, third in the all-time list behind Busby and Bob Paisley.

in the semi-final of 1962, his team went on to the Cup-winners Cup Final 12 months later, where they defeated Atlético Madrid. Don Revie in 1968 was the first to win the Fairs/UEFA Cup, the same year as Busby got his hands on the European Cup. From then until English clubs were suspended in 1985, there was a team from the Football League in at least one of the three Euro finals every season with the exception of 1983.

Of the trophy winners, Paisley (European and EUFA) and Nicholson (Cup-winners and EUFA) were the only managers to claim more than one of the cups, whilst Brian Clough (European Cup winners with Forest and semi-finalists with Derby) the only one to pick up Euro points with two clubs. (Alex Ferguson has, of course won the Cup-winners Cup twice with two different clubs, his success with Manchester United in 1991 following up his earlier triumph with Aberdeen).

For most of the managers who enjoyed Euro success, their achievements came 12 months after a triumph in one of the domestic competitions. The principal exceptions are the three Birmingham managers (Turner, Beasley and Merrick), who participated in Europe by invitation, and Jimmy Armfield and Tony Barton. These latter two took over Leeds and Aston Villa after their clubs had won the First Division (with Revie and Saunders at the helm respectively). The new managers took them to the European Cup final, and for both, it was the major achievement of their managerial careers.

Managers' Points Record

	Div1	Div2	Div3	Div4	3S	3N	FA	FL	Euro	Total
Jimmy Adamson		16					6	6		28
Jack Addenbrooke							78			78
Colin Addison				6						6
Ronnie Allen		10					6	6		22
Sam Allen							12			12
George Allison	36						18			54
Malcolm Allison							6	6		12
Bill Anderson						28				28
Jimmy Anderson	12						6			18
Stan Anderson			8							8
Jimmy Andrews			8							8
Colin Appleton				6						6
Ossie Ardiles			8							8
Jimmy Armfield			14				6	6	12	38
Alan Ashman		10	14	6			24	12		66
Ron Ashman				6						6
Len Ashurst			8	6				12		26
David Ashworth	18	10					6			34
Ron Atkinson	12	10		12			42	30	6	112
Billy Ayre				6						6
Mike Bailey			8							8
Alan Ball			14	6						20
Alan Ball (jnr)		10								10
Herbert Bamlett	12									12
Ken Barnes				6						6
John Barnwell							12	18		30
Tony Barton								6	18	24
Sam Bartram				6						6
Dave Bassett		20	16	18			6			60
Ted Bates		10	14				6			30
Pat Beasley					14			12		26
Andy Beattie		10								10
John Beck			14	6						20
Roy Bentley				6						6
Danny Bergara				6						6
Jackie Bestall						14	6			20
Billy Bingham				6						6
Billy Birrell							12			12
Ernie Blackburn						8				8
Jimmy Blessington		10								10
Jimmy Bloomfield			14				12			26
Frank Bluntstone				6						6
John Bond		10		6			12	24		52
Billy Bonds		20					6	6		32
Tony Book	12							18		30
Dave Bowen		10	14	6						30
Harry Bradshaw		26					6			32
Joe Bradshaw					14		6			20
Ian Branfoot			14	6						20
Billy Bremner			12				6			18
Cliff Britton	12	20	14				24			70
Bob Brocklebank			8				6			14
Tom Bromilow					8		6			14
Alan Brown		10					12	6		28
Allan Brown			12							12
Ken Brown		26						18		44
Rob Brown	36	16					6			58
Vic Buckingham	12						24			36
Alan Buckley			8	12			6			26
Frank Buckley	24	16					12			52
Norman Bullock		16								16
Ron Burgess				6						6
Keith Burkinshaw		10					36	12	24	82
Frank Burrows			12							12
Matt Busby	174						90		42	306
Mick Buxton			8	12						20
David Calderhead		20					30			50
John Cameron							18			18
Bobby Campbell		16	14					6		36
Robert Campbell	12									12
Noel Cantwell				12						12

	Div1	Div2	Div3	Div4	3S	3N	FA	FL	Euro	Total
John Carey	12	20					12			44
Graham Carr			12							12
Jack Carr							6			6
Raich Carter		10				14				24
Frank Casper*								6		6
Harry Catterick	48	16					48			112
Arthur Chadwick							6			6
Trevor Cherry			14							14
Allenby Chilton						14				14
Jack Chaplin	24						18			42
Herbert Chapman	96						66			162
John Chapman		10					6			16
Jack Charlton		16	8				6	6		36
Sammy Chung		16								16
Frank Clark			6							6
Gordon Clark								6		6
Paul Clark*			6							6
Allan Clarke			12							12
Brian Clough	48	26					24	102	48	248
Tommy Coakley			8							8
Johnny Cochrane	30						30			60
Tony Collins								12		12
Terry Cooper			8	18						26
Steve Coppell		10					12	6		28
Sam Cowan		16								16
Arthur Cox		26	8							34
Freddie Cox			12							12
Bob Crompton		16					18			34
Malcolm Crosby							12			12
Vic Crowe			14					12		26
Stan Cullis	90						48	6	6	150
Tommy Cummings			6							6
Andy Cunningham							18			18
George Curtis							18			18
Harry Curtis		16			22					38
Kenny Dalglish	78	10					54	24		166
Teddy Davison		10				14	12			36
Bob Dennison				8						8
Alan Dicks		10					6			16
Martin Dobson			6							6
John Docherty		16	8							24
Tommy Docherty		26					54	24	6	110
Bill Dodgin (jnr)			8	12						20
Peter Doherty						14				14
Ernie Douglass						8				8
Ted Drake	18				16					34
Archie Scott Duncan		16				14				30
Dally Duncan		10					12			22
John Duncan			12							12
Johnny Duncan							12			12
Alan Durban		10		6						16
Jack Edwards			6							6
Sam Ellis			6							6
Fred Emery						16				16
Jack English						22				22
Maurice Evans			12					24		36
Fred Everiss	30	26					54			110
Joe Fagan	30						6	18	30	84
Arthur Fairclough		16					30			46
Benny Fenton			6							6
Ted Fenton		16								16
Alex Ferguson	42						18	30	18	108
Bobby Ferguson								6		6
Albert Fisher		32					6			38
Brough Fletcher						14				14
Brian Flynn			6							6
Fred Ford			8							8
George Foster			6							6
Charlie Foweraker		10					60			70
Gerry Francis			14							14
Trevor Francis							12	12		24

	Div1	Div2	Div3	Div4	3S	3N	FA	FL	Euro	Total
Neil Franklin				6						6
Reg Freeman		16				38				54
Billy Frith				6						6
Jimmy Frizzell			14	6						20
Ken Furphy			14	6				6		26
Walter Galbraith						16				16
Johnny Giles		10								10
Matt Gillies							24	30		54
Wilf Gillow		10				14				24
Eddie Goodman					14					14
Freddie Goodwin		10					12			22
Bobby Gould							18			18
Dario Gradi			12							12
Dick Graham			8							8
George Graham	36		8				24	48		116
Billy Gray			8	6						14
Ron Gray			12							12
Ian Greaves		32	6					6		44
Hayden Green						14				14
Ron Greenwood							18	30	24	72
Arfon Griffiths			14							14
Jimmy Hagan			12					30		42
David Halliday		16								16
George Hardwick						14				14
Ray Harford							6	30		36
John Harris		20					6			26
Bill Harvey						22				22
Colin Harvey							12	6		18
Joe Harvey		16					12		18	46
Harry Haslam		10								10
Graham Hawkins		10								10
John Haworth	30	10					30			70
Vincent Hayes							18			18
Bert Head		10	8							18
Horace Henshall					14					14
Phil Henson			6							6
Bob Hewison			8							8
Charlie Hewitt					22	8	6			36
Frank Hill			6							6
Jimmy Hill		16	14							30
Peter Hodge		32					12			44
Glenn Hoddle		10								10
Jimmy Hogan		16					6			22
Phil Holder			14							14
John Hore							6			6
Brian Horton			8							8
Eric Houghton					14		18			32
Joe Hulme							6			6
Norman Hunter			8							8
Robert Hunter					14					14
Charlie Hurley			6							6
Lincoln Hyde						16				16
Claude Ingram						22				22
John Impey			6							6
Bob Jack					62					62
Bob Jackson	36						6			42
Gordon Jago		10	8							18
Bedford Jezzard		10					6			16
George Jobey	24	10				14	6			54
Tom Johnston			8	6				18		32
Bill Jones		10								10
Joe Jordan			8					6		14
George Kay	18						18			36
Kevin Keegan		16								16
Bob Kelly						14				14
Phil Kelso							12			12
Howard Kendall	48		8				42	12	18	128
Bobby Kennedy			6							6
George Kerr			14							14
Fred Kidd							6			6
John King			8	12						20
Syd King		10					12			22
Ken Knighton		10								10
Les Knighton							12			12

	Div1	Div2	Div3	Div4	3S	3N	FA	FL	Euro	Total
Cyril Knowles				6						6
Jim Knowles						14				14
Robert Kyle	30						12			42
Billy Lane				30						30
Ambrose Langley		10					12			22
Lennie Lawrence		20						6		26
Gordon Lee			14	6			12	24		56
Bill Leivers			6							6
Ned Liddell						14				14
Alan Little			6							6
Brian Little			12							12
Doug Livermore							6			6
Dug Livingstone							24			24
Barry Lloyd			8							8
Larry Lloyd			6							6
Tom Lockie			6							6
Norman Low			12	8						20
Harry Lowe				8						8
John Lyall		32					36	18	12	98
Tom McAnearney			6							6
Lou Macari		22	12							34
Archie Macaulay			8	12			6			26
Billy McCandless				42						42
John McCartney		10				14				24
Joe McClelland					8					8
Billy McCracken							6			6
Billy McDevitt				8						8
Malcolm McDonald			12	8						20
Malcolm Macdonald			8							8
Les McDowall		10					30			40
Don McEvoy			6							6
Billy McEwan			12							12
Roy McFarland			6							6
Alex McFarlane						14				14
Bill McGarry		16					6	24	12	58
John McGrath			12							12
Jimmy McGuigan			24							24
Wilf McGuinness							6	12		18
Mel Machin		10								10
James McIntyre					36					36
Dave Mackay	18						6			24
John McKenna		32								32
Alex Mackie	30									30
Angus McLean			6							6
Lawrie McMenemy	12	10		24			24	12		82
Stuart McMillan							24			24
Jimmy McMullan				8						8
Harry McNally			6							6
Billy McNeill		10								10
Matt McQueen	18									18
Peter McWilliam	12	48					24			84
Tom Maley	12	26				8	18			64
Dave Mangnall				22						22
Ernest Mangnall	48	10					24			82
Jack Marshall								6		6
George Martin		10								10
Tom Mather		16				14				30
Fred Maven				8						8
Eddie May			12							12
Jimmy Meadows			24							24
Bertie Mee	30						36	24	18	108
Don Megson			8							8
Jimmy Melia							12			12
David Menzies						14				14
Joe Mercer	18	32					30	48	24	152
Gil Merrick								18	12	30
Jimmy Methven		32					6			38
Brian Miller			14							14
Gordon Milne		10						6		16
Jimmy Milne							12			12
Bill Moore			8	12						20
Lol Morgan			6							6
Tom Morgan							14			14

	Div1	Div2	Div3	Div4	3S	3N	FA	FL	Euro	Total
Peter Morris			14							14
Trevor Morris							6			6
Tommy Muirhead							12			12
Jimmy Mullen				12						12
Alan Mullery		10	8							18
Colin Murphy				6						6
Alan Murray				6						6
Bill Murray							12			12
John Neal		16		6				6		28
Phil Neal				6						6
Terry Neill							48	18	12	78
Andy Nelson			8	6						14
Harry Newbould		16					24			40
John Newman				6						6
Chris Nicholl							6	6		12
Bill Nicholson	30						54	48	60	192
John Nicholson	12						84			96
Frank O'Farrell		16		6			12			34
Sam Ormerod		26								26
Willie Orr	12									12
Peter O'Rourke		16				14	18			48
Frank Osborne		16								16
Bob Paisley	132						24	72	72	300
Joe Palmer							6			6
Tom Parker				14						14
Harry Parkes						30				30
Charlie Paynter							6			6
Jack Peart				16			6			22
David Pleat		16					18	6		40
Ian Porterfield			22	12						34
Cecil Potter	18						6			24
Harry Potts	30						18	12		60
Ivor Powell				6						6
George Poyser								6		6
Jim Rae				14						14
Alex Raisbeck					28	8				36
Alf Ramsey	18	16			14					48
Dick Ray		20								20
Harry Rednapp			14							14
Willie Reid								18		18
Don Revie	96	16					66	18	72	268
Len Richley				6						6
Bill Ridding							30			30
Bruce Rioch		10	16							26
Bobby Roberts				6						6
Ken Roberts				6				6		12
Bobby Robson	24						30	6	18	78
John Robson		10								10
Arthur Rowe	30	16		6			6			58
Arthur Rowley				12				6		18
Jack Rowley			14	6						20
Walter Rowley							6			6
Joe Royle		16					6	12		34
John Rudge			8	6						14
Dave Russell			14	6						20
George Saunders							6			6
Ron Saunders	18	36						60		114
Pat Saward			8							8
Bobby Saxton				6						6
Will Scott		16								16
Jimmy Scoular				6				6	6	18
Angus Seed						14				14
Jimmy Seed	12	10			14		30			66
Will Settle		10					6			16
Dave Sexton	24						30	24	18	96
Stan Seymour							42			42
Arthur Shallcross		10								10
Bill Shankly	78	16				8	54		42	198
Les Shannon		10	8							18
Joe Shaw*	18									18
Peter Shreeves								6		6
John Sillett			14					6		20
Jimmy Sirrel		10	8	12						30
Bob Smith				6				6		12

	Div1	Div2	Div3	Div4	3S	3N	FA	FL	Euro	Total
Dave Smith			8	30						38
Denis Smith		10	14	12						36
George Smith			14							14
Jack Smith		10								10
Jim Smith		26	14	6			6	12		64
Joe Smith	12	10				16		42		80
Percy Smith		10								10
John Somerville		16								16
Graeme Souness	12							18		30
Charlie Spencer								6		6
Cyril Spiers		10								10
Freddie Steele						30	6			36
John Steele			6							6
Eddie Stein			6							6
Clem Stephenson	12							30		42
Fred Stewart	12	10						36		58
Nobby Stiles			8							8
Alec Stock		10	22			22	12	18		84
Bob Stokoe		16	8				18	12		54
Harry Storer		16			22	22	6			66
Dave Stringer							12			12
Ron Suart						14		6		20
Scot Symon	12							12		24
Ernie Tagg			6							6
Bert Tann						14				14
Dick Taylor								6		6
Eric Taylor		42					6			48
Graham Taylor	24	20	8	24			18	6		100
Harry Thickett	12	16					12			40
Jas Hunter Thompson		10								10
Jack Tinn							42			42
John Toshack		10	8	6						24
Jack Tresadern						16				16
Bill Tulip						8				8
Arthur Turner		16	14	6			18		6	60
Chris Turner			8	6						14
Graham Turner			28	12				6		46
Terry Venables		32	8				30			70
Tony Waddington		16					12	30		58
Tony Waiters			8					6		14
Billy Walker		10				14	36			60
Len Walker			6							6
Jock Wallace		16					6			22
Tim Ward			8		22					30
Neil Warnock		10	8							18
Tom Watson	126	16					48			190
Dave Webb			8	12						20
Eric Webber			6	8						14
Fred Westgarth						8				8
Jimmy Wheeler			6							6
Tom Whittaker	36							30		66
Wilf Wild	18							30		48
Howard Wilkinson	18	26					6	6		56
Albert Williams						14				14
Danny Williams			8						18	26
David Wilson				22						22
Frank Womack		32					6			38
Angus Wylie							6			6
Terry Yorath			6							6

*Caretaker manager

The Winning Managers

Appendix One

The tables below show for each division of the Football League, the FA Cup, League Cup and three European club competitions the managers of the clubs which finished in the leading positions. These schedules forms the basis of the points-scoring system used in *The Scoring System* to develop the rankings. The rationale for inclusion is explained in full in the introduction to *The Scoring System*, but in summary, the attached show:

FA Premier League: 1993: Football League Division One
1888-1992: Champions and runners-up
Football League Division One: 1992-1993: Division Two
1892-1992: Champions, runners-up and promoted clubs
Football League Division Two: 1992-1993: Division Three
1958-92: Champions and promoted clubs
Football League Division Three: 1992-1993: Division Four
1958-92 Champions and promoted clubs
Football League Division Three South: 1920-1958: Champions and runners-up
Football League Division Three North: 1921-1958: Champions and runners-up
FA Cup: 1888-1993: Winners, finalists and semi-finalists
Football League Cup: 1960-1993: Winners, finalists, semi-finalists
European competitions: 1956-1993: English winners, finalists and semi-finalists.

The names of the managers (or secretaries with managerial responsibilities) who qualify for the available points are shown in block capitals. Where the club was guided by a secretary whose duties were only administrative, the name is in lower case and highlighted with an asterisk. They have been excluded from the points scoring system and rankings.

DIVISION ONE

Season	Champions (18 pts) Manager	Club	Runners-up (12 pts) Manager	Club
1888-89	William Sudell*	Preston NE	George Ramsey*	Aston Villa
1889-90	William Sudell*	Preston NE	Dick Molyneux*	Everton
1890-91	Dick Molyneux*	Everton	William Sudell*	Preston NE
1891-92	Tom WATSON	Sunderland	William Sudell*	Preston NE
1892-93	Tom WATSON	Sunderland	William Sudell*	Preston NE
1893-94	George Ramsey*	Aston Villa	Tom WATSON	Sunderland
1894-95	Tom WATSON	Sunderland	Dick Molyneux*	Everton
1895-96	George Ramsey*	Aston Villa	W.D.Clark*	Derby Co
1896-97	George Ramsey*	Aston Villa	J.Wolstinholm*	Sheffield U
1897-98	J.Wolstinholm*	Sheffield U	Robert CAMPBELL	Sunderland
1898-99	George Ramsey*	Aston Villa	Tom WATSON	Liverpool
1899-1900	George Ramsey*	Aston Villa	John NICHOLSON	Sheffield U
1900-01	Tom WATSON	Liverpool	Alex MACKIE	Sunderland
1901-02	Alex MACKIE	Sunderland	Will Cuff*	Everton
1902-03	Arthur Dickinson*	Wednesday	George Ramsey*	Aston Villa
1903-04	Arthur Dickinson*	Wednesday	Tom MALEY	Manchester C
1904-05	Frank Watt*	Newcastle U	Will Cuff*	Everton
1905-06	Tom WATSON	Liverpool	Charlie Parker*	Preston NE
1906-07	Frank Watt*	Newcastle U	Harry THICKETT	Bristol C
1907-08	Ernest MANGNALL	Manchester U	George Ramsey*	Aston Villa
1908-09	Frank Watt*	Newcastle U	Will Cuff*	Everton
1909-10	George Ramsey*	Aston Villa	Tom WATSON	Liverpool
1910-11	Ernest MANGNALL	Manchester U	George Ramsey*	Aston Villa
1911-12	R.B.Middleton*	Blackburn R	Will Cuff*	Everton
1912-13	Robert KYLE	Sunderland	George Ramsey*	Aston Villa
1913-14	R.B.Middleton*	Blackburn R	George Ramsey*	Aston Villa
1914-15	Will Cuff*	Everton	Herbert BAMLETT	Oldham A
1919-20	Fred EVERISS	West Brom A	John HAWORTH	Burnley
1920-21	John HAWORTH	Burnley	Ernest MANGNALL	Manchester C
1921-22	David ASHWORTH	Liverpool	Peter McWILLIAM	Tottenham H
1922-23	Matt McQUEEN	Liverpool	Robert KYLE	Sunderland
1923-24	Herbert CHAPMAN	Huddersfield	Fred STEWART	Cardiff C
1924-25	Herbert CHAPMAN	Huddersfield	Fred EVERISS	West Brom A
1925-26	Cecil POTTER	Huddersfield	Herbert CHAPMAN	Arsenal
1926-27	Frank Watt*	Newcastle U	Jack CHAPLIN	Huddersfield
1927-28	Tom McIntosh*	Everton	Jack CHAPLIN	Huddersfield
1928-29	Rob BROWN	Sheffield W	Willie ORR	Leicester C
1929-30	Rob BROWN	Sheffield W	George JOBEY	Derby Co
1930-31	Herbert CHAPMAN	Arsenal	Billy Smith*	Aston Villa
1931-32	Tom McIntosh*	Everton	Herbert CHAPMAN	Arsenal
1932-33	Herbert CHAPMAN	Arsenal	Billy Smith*	Aston Villa
1933-34	Joe Shaw†	Arsenal	Clem STEPHENSON	Huddersfield
1934-35	George ALLISON	Arsenal	Johnny COCHRANE	Sunderland
1935-36	Johnny COCHRANE	Sunderland	George JOBEY	Derby Co

Season	Manager	Club	Manager	Club
1936-37	Wilf WILD	Manchester C	Jimmy SEED	Charlton A
1937-38	George ALLISON	Arsenal	Frank BUCKLEY	Wolves
1938-39	Theo Kelly*	Everton	Frank BUCKLEY	Wolves
1946-47	George KAY	Liverpool	Matt BUSBY	Manchester U
1947-48	Tom WHITTAKER	Arsenal	Matt BUSBY	Manchester U
1948-49	Bob JACKSON	Portsmouth	Matt BUSBY	Manchester U
1949-50	Bob JACKSON	Portsmouth	Stan CULLIS	Wolves
1950-51	Arthur ROWE	Tottenham H	Matt BUSBY	Manchester U
1951-52	Matt BUSBY	Manchester U	Arthur ROWE	Tottenham H
1952-53	Tom WHITTAKER	Arsenal	Scot SYMON	Preston NE
1953-54	Stan CULLIS	Wolves	Vic BUCKINGHAM	West Brom A
1954-55	Ted DRAKE	Chelsea	Stan CULLIS	Wolves
1955-56	Matt BUSBY	Manchester U	Joe SMITH	Blackpool
1956-57	Matt BUSBY	Manchester U	Jimmy ANDERSON	Tottenham H
1957-58	Stan CULLIS	Wolves	Cliff BRITTON	Preston NE
1958-59	Stan CULLIS	Wolves	Matt BUSBY	Manchester U
1959-60	Harry POTTS	Burnley	Stan CULLIS	Wolves
1960-61	Bill NICHOLSON	Tottenham H	Harry CATTERICK	Sheffield W
1961-62	Alf RAMSEY	Ipswich T	Harry POTTS	Burnley
1962-63	Harry CATTERICK	Everton	Bill NICHOLSON	Tottenham H
1963-64	Bill SHANKLY	Liverpool	Matt BUSBY	Manchester U
1964-65	Matt BUSBY	Manchester U	Don REVIE	Leeds U
1965-66	Bill SHANKLY	Liverpool	Don REVIE	Leeds U
1966-67	Matt BUSBY	Manchester U	John CAREY	Nottm Forest
1967-68	Joe MERCER	Manchester C	Matt BUSBY	Manchester U
1968-69	Don REVIE	Leeds U	Bill SHANKLY	Liverpool
1969-70	Harry CATTERICK	Everton	Don REVIE	Leeds U
1970-71	Bertie MEE	Arsenal	Don REVIE	Leeds U
1971-72	Brian CLOUGH	Derby Co	Don REVIE	Leeds U
1972-73	Bill SHANKLY	Liverpool	Bertie MEE	Arsenal
1973-74	Don REVIE	Leeds U	Bill SHANKLY	Liverpool
1974-75	Dave MACKAY	Derby Co	Bob PAISLEY	Liverpool
1975-76	Bob PAISLEY	Liverpool	Dave SEXTON	QPR
1976-77	Bob PAISLEY	Liverpool	Tony BOOK	Manchester C
1977-78	Brian CLOUGH	Nottm Forest	Bob PAISLEY	Liverpool
1978-79	Bob PAISLEY	Liverpool	Brian CLOUGH	Nottm Forest
1979-80	Bob PAISLEY	Liverpool	Dave SEXTON	Manchester U
1980-81	Ron SAUNDERS	Aston Villa	Bobby ROBSON	Ipswich T
1981-82	Bob PAISLEY	Liverpool	Bobby ROBSON	Ipswich T
1982-83	Bob PAISLEY	Liverpool	Graham TAYLOR	Watford
1983-84	Joe FAGAN	Liverpool	Lawrie McMENEMY	Southampton
1984-85	Howard KENDALL	Everton	Joe FAGAN	Liverpool
1985-86	Kenny DALGLISH	Liverpool	Howard KENDALL	Everton
1986-87	Howard KENDALL	Everton	Kenny DALGLISH	Liverpool
1987-88	Kenny DALGLISH	Liverpool	Alex FERGUSON	Manchester U
1988-89	George GRAHAM	Arsenal	Kenny DALGLISH	Liverpool
1989-90	Kenny DALGLISH	Liverpool	Graham TAYLOR	Aston Villa
1990-91	George GRAHAM	Arsenal	Graeme SOUNESS	Liverpool
1991-92	Howard WILKINSON	Leeds U	Alex FERGUSON	Manchester U
1992-93	Alex FERGUSON	Manchester U	Ron ATKINSON	Aston Villa

†Joe Shaw was caretaker-manager of Arsenal from January 1934, following Herbert Chapman's death, until George Allison's appointment five months later.

DIVISION TWO

Season	Champions (16 pts) Manager	Club	Runners-up (10 pts) Manager	Club
1892-93	Alfred Jones*	Small Heath	J.Wolstinholm*	Sheffield U
1893-94	John McKENNA	Liverpool	Alfred Jones*	Small Heath
1894-95	H.S.Hamer*	Bury	Tom Harris*	Notts Co
1895-96	John McKENNA	Liverpool	Sam ORMEROD	Manchester C
1896-97	Tom Harris*	Notts Co	A.H.Albut*	Newton Heath
1897-98	Harry BRADSHAW	Burnley	Frank Watt*	Newcastle U
1898-99	Sam ORMEROD	Manchester C	Mark Elliott*	Glossop
1899-1900	Arthur Dickinson*	Wednesday	John Somerville*	Bolton W
1900-01	H.N.Hickson*	Grimsby T	Alfred Jones*	Small Heath
1901-02	Frank Heaven*	WBA	John ROBSON	Middlesbro'
1902-03	Tom MALEY	Manchester C	Alfred Jones*	Small Heath
1903-04	E.H.Bahr*	Preston NE	Harry BRADSHAW	Arsenal
1904-05	Tom WATSON	Liverpool	John Somerville*	Bolton W
1905-06	Harry THICKETT	Bristol C	Ernest MANGNALL	Manchester U
1906-07	Harry Hallam*	Nottm Forest	William Lewis*	Chelsea
1907-08	Peter O'ROURKE	Bradford C	Jas BLESSINGTON	Leicester F
1908-09	John SOMERVILLE	Bolton W	No Manager*	Tottenham H
1909-10	Harry NEWBOULD	Manchester C	David ASHWORTH	Oldham A
1910-11	Fred EVERISS	West Brom A	Will SETTLE	Bolton W
1911-12	Jimmy METHVEN	Derby Co	David CALDERHEAD	Chelsea
1912-13	Charlie Parker*	Preston NE	John HAWORTH	Burnley
1913-14	Albert FISHER	Notts Co	Tom MALEY	Bradford
1914-15	Jimmy METHVEN	Derby Co	Charlie Parker*	Preston NE
1919-20	Peter McWILLIAM	Tottenham H	Ambrose LANGLEY	Huddersfield
1920-21	Frank Richards*	Birmingham	Fred STEWART	Cardiff C
1921-22	Bob Masters*	Nottm Forest	Arthur SHALLCROSS	Stoke

Season	Manager	Club	Manager	Club
1922-23	Albert FISHER	Notts Co	Syd KING	West Ham U
1923-24	Arthur FAIRCLOUGH	Leeds U	Jas HUNTER	Bury
			THOMPSON	
1924-25	Peter HODGE	Leicester C	John CHAPMAN	Manchester U
1925-26	Rob BROWN	Sheffield W	George JOBEY	Derby Co
1926-27	Peter McWILLIAM	Middlesbro'	John McCARTNEY	Portsmouth
1927-28	Peter HODGE	Manchester C	Dick RAY	Leeds
1928-29	Peter McWILLIAM	Middlesbro'	Wilf GILLOW	Grimsby
1929-30	Harry Evans*	Blackpool	David CALDERHEAD	Chelsea
1930-31	Tom McIntosh*	Everton	Fred EVERISS	WBA
1931-32	Frank BUCKLEY	Wolves	Dick RAY	Leeds U
1932-33	Tom MATHER	Stoke C	Percy SMITH	Tottenham H
1933-34	Frank WOMACK	Grimsby T	No Manager*	Preston NE
1934-35	Harry CURTIS	Brentford	Charlie FOWERAKER	Bolton W
1935-36	Archie SCOTT	Manchester U	Jimmy SEED	Charlton A
	DUNCAN			
1936-37	Frank WOMACK	Leicester C	Joe SMITH	Blackpool
1937-38	Jimmy HOGAN	Aston Villa	Walter Crickmer*	Manchester U
1938-39	Bob CROMPTON	Blackburn R	Ted DAVISON	Sheffield U
1946-47	Sam COWAN	Manchester C	Cliff BRITTON	Burnley
1947-48	Harry STORER	Birmingham	George MARTIN	Newcastle U
1948-49	Frank OSBORNE	Fulham	Jack SMITH	WBA
1949-50	Arthur ROWE	Tottenham H	Eric TAYLOR	Sheffield W
1950-51	Will SCOTT	Preston NE	Les McDOWALL	Manchester C
1951-52	Eric TAYLOR	Sheffield W	Cyril SPIERS	Cardiff C
1952-53	Reg FREEMAN	Sheffield U	Andy BEATTIE	Huddersfield
1953-54	Norman BULLOCK	Leicester C	Cliff BRITTON	Everton
1954-55	Arthur TURNER	Birmingham	Dally DUNCAN	Luton T
1955-56	Eric TAYLOR	Sheffield W	Raich CARTER	Leeds U
1956-57	David HALLIDAY	Leicester C	Billy WALKER	Nottm Forest
1957-58	Ted FENTON	West Ham U	John CAREY	Blackburn R
1958-59	Harry CATTERICK	Sheffield W	Bedford JEZZARD	Fulham
1959-60	Joe MERCER	Aston Villa	Bill JONES	Cardiff C
1960-61	Alf RAMSEY	Ipswich T	John HARRIS	Sheffield U
1961-62	Bill SHANKLY	Liverpool	John CAREY	Leyton O
1962-63	Tony WADDINGTON	Stoke C	Tommy DOCHERTY	Chelsea
1963-64	Don REVIE	Leeds U	Alan BROWN	Sunderland
1964-65	Joe HARVEY	Newcastle U	Dave BOWEN	Northampton
1965-66	Joe MERCER	Manchester C	Ted BATES	Southampton
1966-67	Jimmy HILL	Coventry C	Ronnie ALLEN	Wolves
1967-68	Bill McGARRY	Ipswich T	Alec STOCK	QPR
1968-69	Brian CLOUGH	Derby Co	Bert HEAD	Crystal Pal
1969-70	Ian GREAVES	Huddersfield	Les SHANNON	Blackpool
1970-71	Frank O'FARRELL	Leicester C	John HARRIS	Sheffield U
1971-72	Ron SAUNDERS	Norwich C	Freddie GOODWIN	Birmingham
1972-73	Jimmy ADAMSON	Burnley	Gordon JAGO	QPR
1973-74	Jack CHARLTON	Middlesbro'	Harry HASLAM	Luton T
	PROMOTED —		Alan ASHMAN	Carlisle U
1974-75	Tommy DOCHERTY	Manchester U	Ron SAUNDERS	Aston Villa
	PROMOTED —		John BOND	Norwich C
1975-76	Bob STOKOE	Sunderland	Alan DICKS	Bristol C
	PROMOTED —		Johnny GILES	WBA
1976-77	Sammy CHUNG	Wolves	Eddie McCREADIE	Chelsea
	PROMOTED —		Brian CLOUGH	Nottm Forest
1977-78	Ian GREAVES	Bolton W	Lawrie McMENEMY	Southampton
	PROMOTED —		Keith BURKINSHAW	Tottenham H
1978-79	Terry VENABLES	Crystal Pal	Alan MULLERY	Brighton
	PROMOTED —		Alan DURBAN	Stoke C
1979-80	Jock WALLACE	Leicester C	Ken KNIGHTON	Sunderland
	PROMOTED —		Jim SMITH	Birmingham
1980-81	John LYALL	West Ham U	Jimmy SIRREL	Notts Co
	PROMOTED —		John TOSHACK	Swansea C
1981-82	David PLEAT	Luton T	Graham TAYLOR	Watford
	PROMOTED —		Ken BROWN	Norwich C
1982-83	Terry VENABLES	QPR	Graham HAWKINS	Wolves
	PROMOTED —		Gordon MILNE	Leicester C
1983-84	John NEAL	Chelsea	Howard WILKINSON	Sheffield W
	PROMOTED —		Arthur COX	Newcastle U
1984-85	Jim SMITH	Oxford U	Ron SAUNDERS	Birmingham
	PROMOTED —		Billy McNEILL	Manchester C
1985-86	Ken BROWN	Norwich C	Lennie LAWRENCE	Charlton A
	PROMOTED —		Dave BASSETT	Wimbledon
1986-87	Arthur COX	Derby Co	Alan BALL	Portsmouth
1987-88	John DOCHERTY	Millwall	Graham TAYLOR	Aston Villa
	PROMOTED —		Bruce RIOCH	Middlesbro'
1988-89	Bobby CAMPBELL	Chelsea	Mel MACHIN	Manchester C
	PROMOTED —		Steve COPPELL	Crystal Pal
1989-90	Howard WILKINSON	Leeds U	Dave BASSETT	Sheffield U
	PROMOTED —		Denis SMITH	Sunderland
1990-91*	Joe ROYLE	Oldham A	Billy BONDS	West Ham U
	PROMOTED —		Ron ATKINSON	Sheffield W
1991-92	John LYALL	Ipswich T	Lennie LAWRENCE	Middlesbro'
	PROMOTED —		Kenny DALGLISH	Blackburn R
1992-93	Kevin KEEGAN	Newcastle U	Billy BONDS	West Ham U
	PROMOTED —		Glenn HODDLE	Swindon T

*In 1990-91, Neil Warnock (Notts Co) also gained promotion to Division One.

DIVISION THREE

	Champions (14 pts)		Promoted (8 pts)	
Season	Manager	Club	Manager	Club
1958-59	Jack ROWLEY	Plymouth A	Bob BROCKLEBANK	Hull C
1959-60	Ted BATES	Southampton	Archie MACAULAY	Norwich C
1960-61	Dave RUSSELL	Bury	Bill MOORE	Walsall
1961-62	George SMITH	Portsmouth	Tim WARD	Grimsby T
1962-63	Dave BOWEN	Northampton	Bert HEAD	Swindon T
1963-64	Jimmy HILL	Coventry C	Dick GRAHAM	Crystal Pal
1964-65	Alan ASHMAN	Carlisle U	Fred FORD	Bristol C
1965-66	Cliff BRITTON	Hull C	Billy GRAY	Millwall
1966-67	Alec STOCK	QPR	Stan ANDERSON	Middlesbro'
1967-68	Arthur TURNER	Oxford U	Les SHANNON	Bury
1968-69	Ken FURPHY	Watford	Danny WILLIAMS	Swindon T
1969-70	Jimmy BLOOMFIELD	Orient	Alec STOCK	Luton T
1970-71	Alan BALL (snr)	Preston NE	Bill DODGIN (jnr)	Fulham
1971-72	Vic CROWE	Aston Villa	Pat SAWARD	Brighton
1972-73	Jimmy ARMFIELD	Bolton W	Jimmy SIRREL	Notts Co
1973-74	Jimmy FRIZZELL	Oldham A	Don MEGSON	Bristol R
	PROMOTED —		Tom JOHNSTON	York C
1974-75	Gordon LEE	Blackburn R	Tony WAITERS	Plymouth A
	PROMOTED —		Andy NELSON	Charlton A
1975-76	John SILLETT	Hereford U	Jimmy ANDREWS	Cardiff C
	PROMOTED —		Gordon JAGO	Millwall
1976-77	Peter MORRIS	Mansfield T	Alan MULLERY	Brighton
	PROMOTED —		Terry VENABLES	Crystal Pal
1977-78	Arfon GRIFFITHS	Wrexham	John DOCHERTY	Cambridge
	PROMOTED —		Nobby STILES	Preston NE
1978-79	Graham TURNER	Shrewsbury T	Graham TAYLOR	Watford
	PROMOTED —		John TOSHACK	Swansea C
1979-80	George KERR	Grimsby T	Howard KENDALL	Blackburn R
	PROMOTED —		Jack CHARLTON	Sheffield W
1980-81	Ian PORTERFIELD	Rotherham U	Norman HUNTER	Burnley
	PROMOTED —		Mike BAILEY	Charlton A
1981-82	Brian MILLER	Burnley	Bob STOKOE	Carlisle U
	PROMOTED —		Malcolm	Fulham
			MACDONALD	
1982-83	Bobby CAMPBELL	Portsmouth	Len ASHURST	Cardiff C
	PROMOTED —		Mick BUXTON	Huddersfield
1983-84	Jim SMITH	Oxford U	Dave BASSETT	Wimbledon
	PROMOTED —		Ian PORTERFIELD	Sheffield U
1984-85	Trevor CHERRY	Bradford C	George GRAHAM	Millwall
	PROMOTED —		Brian HORTON	Hull C
1985-86	Ian BRANFOOT	Reading	Dave SMITH	Plymouth A
	PROMOTED —		Arthur COX	Derby Co
1986-87	Harry REDKNAPP	Bournemouth	Bruce RIOCH	Middlesbro'
	PROMOTED —		Lou MACARI	Swindon T
1987-88	Denis SMITH	Sunderland	Barry LLOYD	Brighton
	PROMOTED —		Tommy COAKLEY	Walsall
1988-89	Graham TURNER	Wolves	Dave BASSETT	Sheffield U
	PROMOTED —		John RUDGE	Port Vale
1989-90	Gerry FRANCIS	Bristol R	Joe JORDAN	Bristol C
	PROMOTED —		Neil WARNOCK	Notts Co
1990-91*	John BECK	Cambridge	Dave WEBB	Southend U
	PROMOTED —		Alan BUCKLEY	Grimsby T
1991-92	Phil HOLDER	Brentford	Terry COOPER	Birmingham
	PROMOTED —		Chris TURNER	Peterborough
1992-93	Lou MACARI	Stoke C	Bruce RIOCH	Bolton W
	PROMOTED —		Ossie ARDILES	WBA

*In addition, John King (Tranmere) won promotion to Division Two

DIVISION THREE SOUTH

	Champions (14 pts)		Runners-up (8 pts)	
Season	Manager	Club	Manager	Club
1920-21†	Eddie GOODMAN	Crystal Pal	James McINTYRE	Southampton
1921-22	James McINTYRE	Southampton	Bob JACK	Plymouth A
1922-23	Alex RAISBECK	Bristol C	Bob JACK	Plymouth A
1923-24	John McCARTNEY	Portsmouth	Bob JACK	Plymouth A
1924-25	Joe BRADSHAW	Swansea T	Bob JACK	Plymouth A
1925-26	H.F.Bray*	Reading	Bob JACK	Plymouth A
1926-27	Alex RAISBECK	Bristol C	Bob JACK	Plymouth A
1927-28	Robert HUNTER	Millwall	Jack TRESADERN	Northampton
1928-29	Alex McFARLANE	Charlton A	Fred MAVEN	Crystal Pal
1929-30	Bob JACK	Plymouth A	Harry CURTIS	Brentford
1930-31	Horace HENSHALL	Notts Co	Jack TRESADERN	Crystal Pal
1931-32	James McINTYRE	Fulham	Joe SMITH	Reading
1932-33	Harry CURTIS	Brentford	Billy McDEVITT	Exeter C
1933-34	Tom PARKER	Norwich C	Harry STORER	Coventry C
1934-35	Jimmy SEED	Charlton A	Joe SMITH	Reading
1935-36	Harry STORER	Coventry C	No Manager	Luton T
1936-37	Ned LIDDELL	Luton T	Jimmy McMULLAN	Notts Co
1937-38	Charlie HEWITT	Millwall	Bob HEWISON	Bristol C
1938-39	Billy McCANDLESS	Newport Co	Tom BROMILOW	Crystal Pal
1946-47	Billy McCANDLESS	Cardiff C	Dave MANGNALL	QPR
1947-48	Dave MANGNALL	QPR	Harry LOWE	Bournemouth
1948-49	Billy McCANDLESS	Swansea T	Ted DRAKE	Reading
1949-50	Eric HOUGHTON	Notts Co	Bob DENNISON	Northampton
1950-51	Billy WALKER	Nottm Forest	Norman LOW	Norwich C

Season	Manager	Club	Manager	Club
1951-52	Jim RAE	Plymouth A	Ted DRAKE	Reading
1952-53	Bert TANN	Bristol R	Charlie HEWITT	Millwall
1953-54	Archie SCOTT DUNCAN	Ipswich T	Billy LANE	Brighton
1954-55	Pat BEASLEY	Bristol C	Alec STOCK	Leyton O
1955-56	Alec STOCK	Leyton O	Billy LANE	Brighton
1956-57	Alf RAMSEY	Ipswich T	Eric WEBBER	Torquay U
1957-58	Billy LANE	Brighton	Malcolm McDONALD	Brentford

†In 1920-21 a Third Division was created and 12 months later a second followed, divided on regional lines. The original Third Division formed the new Third Division South.

DIVISION THREE NORTH

Season	Champions (14 pts) Manager	Club	Runners-up (8 pts) Manager	Club
1921-22	Albert WILLIAMS	Stockport Co	Jack ENGLISH	Darlington
1922-23	David WILSON	Nelson	Tom MALEY	Bradford
1923-24	George JOBEY	Wolves	Jack PEART	Rochdale
1924-25	Jack ENGLISH	Darlington	David WILSON	Nelson
1925-26	Wilf GILLOW	Grimsby T	Claude INGRAM	Bradford
1926-27	Tom MATHER	Stoke	Jack PEART	Rochdale
1927-28	Claude INGRAM	Bradford	Harry PARKES	Lincoln C
1928-29	Peter O'ROURKE	Bradford C	Lincoln HYDE	Stockport Co
1929-30	Tom MORGAN	Port Vale	Lincoln HYDE	Stockport Co
1930-31	Ted DAVISON	Chesterfield	Harry PARKES	Lincoln C
1931-32	Harry PARKES	Lincoln C	Ernest DOUGLAS	Gateshead
1932-33	Haydn GREEN	Hull C	Ernest BLACKBURN	Wrexham
1933-34	Brough FLETCHER	Barnsley	Bill HARVEY	Chesterfield
1934-35	David MENZIES	Doncaster R	Alex RAISBECK	Halifax T
1935-36	Bill HARVEY	Chestefield	Charlie HEWITT	Chester
1936-37	Bob KELLY	Stockport Co	Joe McCLELLAND	Lincoln C
1937-38	Jim KNOWLES	Tranmere R	Fred EMERY	Doncaster R
1938-39	Angus SEED	Barnsley	Fred EMERY	Doncaster R
1946-47	Jack BESTALL	Doncaster R	Reg FREEMAN	Rotherham U
1947-48	Bill ANDERSON	Lincoln C	Reg FREEMAN	Rotherham U
1948-49	Raich CARTER	Hull C	Reg FREEMAN	Rotherham U
1949-50	Peter DOHERTY	Doncaster R	Bill TULIP	Gateshead
1950-51	Reg FREEMAN	Rotherham U	Freddie STEELE	Mansfield T
1951-52	Bill ANDERSON	Lincoln C	Bill SHANKLY	Grimsby T
1952-53	George HARDWICK	Oldham A	Freddie STEELE	Port Vale
1953-54	Freddie STEELE	Port Vale	Tim WARD	Barnsley
1954-55	Tim WARD	Barnsley	Walter GALBRAITH	Accrington
1955-56	Allenby CHILTON	Grimsby T	Harry STORER	Derby Co
1956-57	Harry STORER	Derby Co	Fred WESTGARTH	Hartlepools
1957-58	Ron SUART	Scunthorpe U	Walter GALBRAITH	Accrington

Tim Ward, took Barnsley out of the Third Division North after they finished runners-up the previous season. Ward later managed Grimsby, Derby and Carlisle without any success, although they were difficult jobs with hardly any money to spend on team building.

DIVISION FOUR

Season	Champions (12 pts) Manager	Club	Promoted (6 pts) Manager	Club	Promoted (6 pts) Manager	Club	Promoted (6 pts) Manager	Club
1958-59	Norman LOW	Port Vale	Billy FRITH	Coventry C	Arthur ROWLEY	Shrewsbury	Sam BARTRAM	York C
1959-60	Bill MOORE	Walsall	Frank HILL	Notts Co	Ron BURGESS	Watford	Eric WEBBER	Torquay U
1960-61	Jimmy HAGAN	Peterborough	Jimmy SCOULAR	Bradford	Arthur ROWE	Crystal Pal	Dave BOWEN	Northampton
1961-62	Ron GRAY	Millwall	Ivor POWELL	Carlisle U	Ken BARNES	Wrexham	Benny FENTON	Colchester
1962-63	Malcolm McDONALD	Brentford	Tom CUMMINGS	Mansfield T	Jimmy McGUIGAN	Crewe A	Jack ROWLEY	Oldham A
1963-64	Freddie COX	Gillingham	Jack EDWARDS	Exeter C	Alan ASHMAN	Carlisle U	Ken FURPHY	Workington
1964-65	Archie MACAULAY	Brighton	Billy GRAY	Millwall	Arthur TURNER	Oxford U	Tom LOCKIE	York C
1965-66	No Manager*	Doncaster R	Lol MORGAN	Darlington	Frank O'FARRELL	Torquay U	Neil FRANKLIN	Colchester
1966-67	Jimmy MEADOWS	Stockport Co	Dave RUSSELL	Tranmere R	Billy BINGHAM	Southport	Don McEVOY	Barrow
1967-68	Allan BROWN	Luton T	John STEELE	Barnsley	Angus McLEAN	Hartlepools	Ernie TAGG	Crewe A
1968-69	Lawrie McMENEMY	Doncaster R	Jimmy WHEELER	Bradford C	Alan BALL (snr)	Halifax T	Len RICHLEY	Rochdale
1969-70	Jimmy McGUIGAN	Chesterfield	Gordon LEE	Port Vale	Roy BENTLEY	Swansea T	John NEAL	Wrexham
1970-71	Jimmy SIRREL	Notts Co	John BOND	Bournemouth	Jimmy FRIZZELL	Oldham A	Tom JOHNSTON	York C
1971-72	Lawrie McMENEMY	Grimsby T	Frank BLUNSTONE	Brentford	Arthur ROWLEY	Southend U	Ron ASHMAN	Scunthorpe U
1972-73	Jimmy MEADOWS	Southport	Tom McANEARNEY	Aldershot	Colin ADDISON	Hereford U	Bill LEIVERS	Cambridge
1973-74	Noel CANTWELL	Peterborough	Andy NELSON	Gillingham	Jim SMITH	Colchester	Bobby SMITH	Bury
1974-75	Dave SMITH	Mansfield T	Ken ROBERTS	Chester	Jimmy McGUIGAN	Rotherham U	Alan DURBAN	Shrewsbury
1975-76	Graham TAYLOR	Lincoln C	Bill DODGIN (jnr)	Northampton	Charlie HURLEY	Reading	John KING	Tranmere R
1976-77	Ron ATKINSON	Cambridge	Robert KENNEDY	Bradford	Bobby SAXTON	Exeter C	Bobby ROBERTS	Colchester
1977-78	Graham TAYLOR	Watford	Bill DODGIN (jnr)	Brentford	Dave SMITH	Southend U	John TOSHACK	Swansea C
1978-79	Maurice EVANS	Reading	Allan CLARKE	Barnsley	John NEWMAN	Grimsby T	Dario GRADI	Wimbledon
1979-80	Mick BUXTON	Huddersfield	Frank BURROWS	Portsmouth	Len ASHURST	Newport Co	Alan BUCKLEY	Walsall
1980-81	Dave SMITH	Southend U	Dave BASSETT	Wimbledon	Colin MURPHY	Lincoln C	Billy BREMNER	Doncaster R
1981-82	Ian PORTERFIELD	Sheffield U	Dave WEBB	Bournemouth	Roy McFARLAND	Bradford C	Larry LLOYD	Wigan A
1982-83	Dave BASSETT	Wimbledon	Colin APPLETON	Hull C	John McGRATH	Port Vale	Allan CLARKE	Scunthorpe U
1983-84	Denis SMITH	York C	Terry COOPER	Bristol C	Ian BRANFOOT	Reading	Billy BREMNER	Doncaster R
1984-85	John DUNCAN	Chesterfield	Sam ELLIS	Blackpool	Cyril KNOWLES	Darlington	Martin DOBSON	Bury
1985-86	Lou MACARI	Swindon T	Ian GREAVES	Mansfield T	John RUDGE	Port Vale	Harry McNALLY	Chester C
1986-87	Graham CARR	Northampton	Len WALKER	Aldershot	John McGRATH	Preston NE	Paul Clark†	Southend U
1987-88	Graham TURNER	Wolves	Phil NEAL	Bolton	Frank BURROWS	Cardiff C	Terry YORATH	Swansea C
1988-89	Billy McEWAN	Rotherham U	John KING	Tranmere R	Dario GRADI	Crewe A	Frank CLARK	Leyton O
1989-90	Terry COOPER	Exeter C	Alan BUCKLEY	Grimsby T	Dave WEBB	Southend U	John BECK	Cambridge
1990-91*	Brian LITTLE	Darlington	Danny BERGARA	Stockport Co	Alan MURRAY	Hartlepool	Chris TURNER	Peterborough
1991-92	Jimmy MULLEN	Burnley	Phil HENSON	Rotherham U	George FOSTER	Mansfield T	Billy AYRE	Blackpool
1992-93	Eddie MAY	Cardiff C	Brian FLYNN	Wrexham	Eddie STEIN	Barnet	Alan LITTLE	York C

*In addition John Impey (Torquay) gained promotion to Division Three. †Caretaker manager.

FA CUP

Season	Winners (18 pts) Manager	Club	Finalists (12 pts) Manager	Club	Semi-finalists (6 pts) Manager	Club	Semi-finalists (6 pts) Manager	Club
1888-89	William Sudell*	Preston NE	Jack ADDENBROOKE	Wolves	Louis Ford*	WBA	Thomas Mitchell*	Blackburn R
1889-90	Thomas Mitchell*	Blackburn R	Arthur Dickinson*	Wednesday	John Bentley*	Bolton W	Jack ADDENBROOKE	Wolves
1890-91	Thomas Mitchell*	Blackburn R	Edwin Browne*	Notts Co	Tom WATSON	Sunderland	Louis Ford*	WBA
1891-92	Louis Ford*	WBA	George Ramsey*	Aston Villa	Harry Radford*	Nottm Forest	Tom WATSON	Sunderland
1892-93	Jack ADDENBROOKE	Wolves	Dick Molyneux*	Everton	William Sudell*	Preston NE	Thomas Mitchell*	Blackburn R
1893-94	Tom Harris*	Notts Co	John Bentley*	Bolton	Thomas Mitchell*	Blackburn R	Arthur Dickinson*	Wednesday
1894-95	George Ramsey*	Aston Villa	Edward Stephenson*	WBA	Tom WATSON	Sunderland	Arthur Dickinson*	Wednesday
1895-96	Arthur Dickinson*	Wednesday	Jack ADDENBROOKE	Wolves	W.D.Clark*	Derby Co	Harry Downs*	Bolton W
1896-97	George Ramsey*	Aston Villa	Dick Molyneux*	Everton	Tom WATSON	Liverpool	Harry Newbould*	Derby Co
1897-98	Harry Hallam*	Nottm Forest	Harry Newbould*	Derby Co	E.Arnfield	Southampton	Dick Molyneux*	Everton
1898-99	J.B.Wolstinholm*	Sheffield U	Harry Newbould*	Derby Co	Tom WATSON	Liverpool	H.D.Austerbury*	Stoke
1899-1900	H.S.Hamer*	Bury	E.Arnfield*	Southampton	Harry Hallam*	Nottm Forest	Fred KIDD	Millwall
1900-01	John CAMERON	Tottenham H	John NICHOLSON	Sheffield U	Frank Heaven*	WBA	George Ramsey*	Aston Villa
1901-02	John NICHOLSON	Sheffield U	E.Arnfield*	Southampton	Harry Hallam*	Nottm Forest	Harry NEWBOULD	Derby Co
1902-03	H.S.Hamer*	Bury	Harry NEWBOULD	Derby Co	George Ramsey*	Aston Villa	George SAUNDERS	Millwall
1903-04	Tom MALEY	Manchester C	John Somerville*	Bolton W	Harry NEWBOULD	Derby Co	Arthur Dickinson*	Wednesday
1904-05	George Ramsey*	Aston Villa	Frank Watt*	Newcastle U	Will Cuff*	Everton	Arthur Dickinson*	Wednesday
1905-06	Will Cuff*	Everton	Frank Watt*	Newcastle U	Tom WATSON	Liverpool	Phil KELSO	Arsenal
1906-07	Arthur Dickinson*	Wednesday	Will Cuff*	Everton	Fred EVERISS	WBA	Phil KELSO	Arsenal
1907-08	Jack ADDENBROOKE	Wolves	Frank Watt*	Newcastle U	Harry BRADSHAW	Fulham	E.Arnfield*	Southampton
1908-09	Ernest MANGNALL	Manchester U	Harry THICKETT	Bristol C	Jimmy METHVEN	Derby Co	Frank Watt*	Newcastle U
1909-10	Frank Watt*	Newcastle	Arthur FAIRCLOUGH	Barnsley	Sam ALLEN	Swindon T	Will Cuff*	Everton
1910-11	Peter O'ROURKE	Bradford C	Frank Watt*	Newcastle U	David CALDERHEAD	Chelsea	R.B.Middleton*	Blackburn R
1911-12	Arthur FAIRCLOUGH	Barnsley	Fred EVERISS	WBA	R.B.Middleton*	Blackburn R	Sam ALLEN	Swindon T
1912-13	George Ramsey*	Aston Villa	Robert KYLE	Sunderland	David ASHWORTH	Oldham A	John HAWORTH	Burnley
1913-14	John HAWORTH	Burnley	Tom WATSON	Liverpool	John NICHOLSON	Sheffield U	George Ramsey*	Aston Villa
1914-15	John NICHOLSON	Sheffield U	David CALDERHEAD	Chelsea	Will SETTLE	Bolton	Will Cuff*	Everton
1919-20	George Ramsey*	Aston Villa	Ambrose LANGLEY	Huddersfield	Joe PALMER	Bristol C	David CALDERHEAD	Chelsea
1920-21	Peter McWILLIAM	Tottenham H	Jack ADDENBROOKE	Wolves	Fred STEWART	Cardiff C	Vincent HAYES	Preston NE
1921-22	Herbert CHAPMAN	Huddersfield	Vincent HAYES	Preston NE	Peter McWILLIAM	Tottenham H	Albert FISHER	Notts Co
1922-23	Charlie FOWERAKER	Bolton W	Syd KING	West Ham U	Cecil POTTER	Derby Co	John NICHOLSON	Sheffield U
1923-24	Frank Watt*	Newcastle U	George Ramsey*	Aston Villa	Ernest MANGNALL	Manchester C	John HAWORTH	Burnley
1924-25	John NICHOLSON	Sheffield U	Fred STEWART	Cardiff C	Jack CARR	Blackburn R	No Manager*	Southampton
1925-26	Charlie FOWERAKER	Bolton W	No Manager*	Manchester C	Joe BRADSHAW	Swansea T	John CHAPMAN	Manchester U
1926-27	Fred STEWART	Cardiff C	Herbert CHAPMAN	Arsenal	Angus WYLIE	Reading	Arthur CHADWICK	Southampton
1927-28	Bob CROMPTON	Blackburn R	Jack CHAPLIN	Huddersfield	Herbert CHAPMAN	Arsenal	John NICHOLSON	Sheffield U
1928-29	Charlie FOWERAKER	Bolton W	Jack TINN	Portsmouth	Jack CHAPLIN	Huddersfield	Billy Smith*	Aston Villa
1929-30	Herbert CHAPMAN	Arsenal	Clem STEPHENSON	Huddersfield	Rob BROWN	Sheffield W	Bill McCRACKEN	Hull C
1930-31	Fred EVERISS	WBA	Leslie KNIGHTON	Birmingham	Johnny COCHRANE	Sunderland	Tom McIntosh*	Everton
1931-32	Andy CUNNINGHAM	Newcastle U	Herbert CHAPMAN	Arsenal	Peter HODGE	Manchester C	David CALDERHEAD	Chelsea
1932-33	Tom McIntosh*	Everton	Wilf WILD	Manchester C	Charlie PAYNTER	West Ham U	George JOBEY	Derby Co
1933-34	Wilf WILD	Manchester C	Jack TINN	Portsmouth	Peter HODGE	Leicester C	Billy Smith*	Aston Villa
1934-35	Billy WALKER	Sheffield W	Fred EVERISS	WBA	Charlie FOWERAKER	Bolton W	Tom BROMILOW	Burnley
1935-36	George ALLISON	Arsenal	Ted DAVISON	Sheffield U	Jack PEART	Fulham	Frank WOMACK	Grimsby T
1936-37	Johnny COCHRANE	Sunderland	Tommy MUIRHEAD	Preston NE	Fred EVERISS	WBA	Charlie HEWITT	Millwall
1937-38	No Manager*	Preston NE	Clem STEPHENSON	Huddersfield	Johnny COCHRANE	Sunderland	Jimmy HOGAN	Aston Villa
1938-39	Jack TINN	Portsmouth	Frank BUCKLEY	Wolves	Charlie SPENCER	Grimsby T	Clem STEPHENSON	Huddersfield
1945-46	Stuart McMILLAN	Derby Co	Jimmy SEED	Charlton A	Walter ROWLEY	Bolton W	Harry STORER	Birmingham
1946-47	Jimmy SEED	Charlton A	Cliff BRITTON	Burnley	George KAY	Liverpool	Stan SEYMOUR	Newcastle U
1947-48	Matt BUSBY	Manchester U	Joe SMITH	Blackpool	Joe HULME	Tottenham H	Stuart McMILLAN	Derby Co
1948-49	Stan CULLIS	Wolves	John DUNCAN	Leicester C	Matt BUSBY	Manchester U	Bob JACKSON	Portsmouth
1949-50	Tom WHITTAKER	Arsenal	George KAY	Liverpool	Cliff BRITTON	Everton	Billy BIRRELL	Chelsea
1950-51	Stan SEYMOUR	Newcastle U	Joe SMITH	Blackpool	Stan CULLIS	Wolves	Bob BROCKLEBANK	Birmingham
1951-52	Stan SEYMOUR	Newcastle U	Tom WHITTAKER	Arsenal	Jack BESTALL	Blackburn R	Billy BIRRELL	Chelsea
1952-53	Joe SMITH	Blackpool	Bill RIDDING	Bolton W	Cliff BRITTON	Everton	Arthur ROWE	Tottenham H
1953-54	Vic BUCKINGHAM	WBA	Scott SYMON	Preston NE	Eric TAYLOR	Sheffield W	Freddie STEELE	Port Vale
1954-55	Dug LIVINGSTONE	Newcastle U	Leslie McDOWALL	Manchester C	Bill MURRAY	Sunderland	Bill SHERRINGTON	York C
1955-56	Leslie McDOWALL	Manchester C	Arthur TURNER	Birmingham	Bill MURRAY	Sunderland	Jimmy ANDERSON	Tottenham H
1956-57	Eric HOUGHTON	Aston Villa	Matt BUSBY	Manchester U	Vic BUCKINGHAM	WBA	Arthur TURNER	Birmingham
1957-58	Bill RIDDING	Bolton W	Matt BUSBY	Manchester U	Dug LIVINGSTONE	Fulham	John CAREY	Blackburn R
1958-59	Billy WALKER	Nottm Forest	No Manager*	Luton T	Archie MACAULAY	Norwich C	Joe MERCER	Aston Villa
1959-60	Stan CULLIS	Wolves	Dally DUNCAN	Blackburn R	Harry CATTERICK	Sheffield W	Joe MERCER	Aston Villa
1960-61	Bill NICHOLSON	Tottenham H	Matt GILLIES	Leicester C	John HARRIS	Sheffield U	Harry POTTS	Burnley
1961-62	Bill NICHOLSON	Tottenham H	Harry POTTS	Burnley	Matt BUSBY	Manchester U	Bedford JEZZARD	Fulham
1962-63	Matt BUSBY	Manchester U	Matt GILLIES	Leicester C	Bill SHANKLY	Liverpool	Ted BATES	Southampton
1963-64	Ron GREENWOOD	West Ham U	Jimmy MILNE	Preston NE	Matt BUSBY	Manchester U	Trevor MORRIS	Swansea T
1964-65	Bill SHANKLY	Liverpool	Don REVIE	Leeds U	Matt BUSBY	Manchester U	Tommy DOCHERTY	Chelsea
1965-66	Harry CATTERICK	Everton	Alan BROWN	Sheffield W	Matt BUSBY	Manchester U	Tommy DOCHERTY	Chelsea
1966-67	Bill NICHOLSON	Tottenham H	Tommy DOCHERTY	Chelsea	Don REVIE	Leeds U	John CAREY	Nottm Forest
1967-68	Alan ASHMAN	WBA	Harry CATTERICK	Everton	Don REVIE	Leeds U	Stan CULLIS	Birmingham
1968-69	Joe MERCER	Manchester C	Frank O'FARRELL	Leicester C	Harry CATTERICK	Everton	Alan ASHMAN	WBA
1969-70	Dave SEXTON	Chelsea	Don REVIE	Leeds U	Wilf McGUINESS	Manchester U	Ken FURPHY	Watford
1970-71	Bertie MEE	Arsenal	Bill SHANKLY	Liverpool	Harry CATTERICK	Everton	Tony WADDINGTON	Stoke C
1971-72	Don REVIE	Leeds U	Bertie MEE	Arsenal	Freddie GOODWIN	Birmingham	Tony WADDINGTON	Stoke C
1972-73	Bob STOKOE	Sunderland	Don REVIE	Leeds U	Bertie MEE	Arsenal	Bill McGARRY	Wolves
1973-74	Bill SHANKLY	Liverpool	Joe HARVEY	Newcastle U	Jimmy BLOOMFIELD	Leicester C	Jimmy ADAMSON	Burnley
1974-75	John LYALL	West Ham U	Alec STOCK	Fulham	Bobby ROBSON	Ipswich T	Freddie GOODWIN	Birmingham
1975-76	Lawrie McMENEMY	Southampton	Tommy DOCHERTY	Manchester U	Malcolm ALLISON	Crystal Pal	Dave MACKAY	Derby Co
1976-77	Tommy DOCHERTY	Manchester U	Bob PAISLEY	Liverpool	Jimmy ARMFIELD	Leeds U	Gordon LEE	Everton
1977-78	Bobby ROBSON	Ipswich T	Terry NEILL	Arsenal	Ron ATKINSON	WBA	Jimmy BLOOMFIELD	Orient
1978-79	Terry NEILL	Arsenal	Dave SEXTON	Manchester U	Bob PAISLEY	Liverpool	John BARNWELL	Wolves
1979-80	John LYALL	West Ham U	Terry NEILL	Arsenal	Bob PAISLEY	Liverpool	Gordon LEE	Everton
1980-81	Keith BURKINSHAW	Tottenham H	John BOND	Manchester C	John BARNWELL	Wolves	Bobby ROBSON	Ipswich T
1981-82	Keith BURKINSHAW	Tottenham H	Terry VENABLES	QPR	Jock WALLACE	Leicester C	Ronnie ALLEN	WBA
1982-83	Ron ATKINSON	Manchester U	Jimmy MELIA	Brighton	Jack CHARLTON	Sheffield W	Terry NEILL	Arsenal
1983-84	Howard KENDALL	Everton	Graham TAYLOR	Watford	Lawrie McMENEMY	Southampton	John HORE	Plymouth A
1984-85	Ron ATKINSON	Manchester U	Howard KENDALL	Everton	Joe FAGAN	Liverpool	David PLEAT	Luton T

Season	Manager	Club	Manager	Club	Manager	Club	Manager	Club
1985-86	Kenny DALGLISH	Liverpool	Howard KENDALL	Everton	Chris NICHOLL	Southampton	Howard WILKINSON	Sheffield W
1986-87	George CURTIS	Coventry C	David PLEAT	Tottenham H	Billy BREMNER	Leeds U	Graham TAYLOR	Watford
1987-88	Bobby GOULD	Wimbledon	Kenny DALGLISH	Liverpool	Ray HARFORD	Luton T	Brian CLOUGH	Nottm Forest
1988-89	Kenny DALGLISH	Liverpool	Colin HARVEY	Everton	Dave STRINGER	Norwich C	Brian CLOUGH	Nottm Forest
1989-90	Alex FERGUSON	Manchester U	Steve COPPELL	Crystal Pal	Joe ROYLE	Oldham A	Kenny DALGLISH	Liverpool
1990-91	Terry VENABLES	Tottenham H	Brian CLOUGH	Nottm Forest	Billy BONDS	West Ham U	George GRAHAM	Arsenal
1991-92	Graeme SOUNESS	Liverpool	Malcolm CROSBY	Sunderland	Dave STRINGER	Norwich C	Jim SMITH	Portsmouth
1992-93	George GRAHAM	Arsenal	Trevor FRANCIS	Sheffield W	Doug LIVERMORE	Tottenham H	Dave BASSETT	Sheffield U

FOOTBALL LEAGUE CUP

	Winners (18 pts)		Finalists (12 pts)		Semi-finalists (6 pts)		Semi-finalists (6 pts)	
Season	Manager	Club	Manager	Club	Manager	Club	Manager	Club
1960-61	Joe MERCER	Aston Villa	Tom JOHNSTON	Rotherham U	Arthur ROWLEY	Shrewsbury	Harry POTTS	Burnley
1961-62	Willie REID	Norwich C	Tony COLLINS	Rochdale	Ron SUART	Blackpool	Jack MARSHALL	Blackburn R
1962-63	Gil MERRICK	Birmingham	Joe MERCER	Aston Villa	Alan BROWN	Sunderland	Bob STOKOE	Bury
1963-64	Matt GILLIES	Leicester C	Tony WADDINGTON	Stoke C	George POYSER	Manchester C	Ron GREENWOOD	West Ham U
1964-65	Tommy DOCHERTY	Chelsea	Matt GILLIES	Leicester C	Dick TAYLOR	Aston Villa	Malcolm ALLISON	Plymouth A
1965-66	Jimmy HAGAN	WBA	Ron GREENWOOD	West Ham U	Jimmy SCOULAR	Cardiff C	Gordon CLARK	Peterborough
1966-67	Alec STOCK	QPR	Jimmy HAGAN	WBA	Ron GREENWOOD	West Ham U	Stan CULLIS	Birmingham
1967-68	Don REVIE	Leeds U	Bertie MEE	Arsenal	Brian CLOUGH	Derby Co	Tom JOHNSTON	Huddersfield
1968-69	Danny WILLIAMS	Swindon T	Bertie MEE	Arsenal	Bill NICHOLSON	Tottenham H	Harry POTTS	Burnley
1969-70	Joe MERCER	Manchester C	Alan ASHMAN	WBA	Wilf McGUINNESS	Manchester U	Bob STOKOE	Carlisle U
1970-71	Bill NICHOLSON	Tottenham H	Vic CROWE	Aston Villa	Wilf McGUINNESS	Manchester U	Alan DICKS	Bristol C
1971-72	Tony WADDINGTON	Stoke C	Dave SEXTON	Chelsea	Bill NICHOLSON	Tottenham H	Ron GREENWOOD	West Ham U
1972-73	Bill NICHOLSON	Tottenham H	Ron SAUNDERS	Norwich C	Bill McGARRY	Wolves	Dave SEXTON	Chelsea
1973-74	Bill McGARRY	Wolves	Ron SAUNDERS	Manchester C	John BOND	Norwich C	Tony WAITERS	Plymouth A
1974-75	Ron SAUNDERS	Aston Villa	John BOND	Norwich C	Tommy DOCHERTY	Manchester U	Ken ROBERTS	Chester
1975-76	Tony BOOK	Manchester C	Gordon LEE	Newcastle U	Terry NEILL	Tottenham H	Jack CHARLTON	Middlesbro'
1976-77	Ron SAUNDERS	Aston Villa	Gordon LEE	Everton	Ian GREAVES	Bolton W	Dave SEXTON	QPR
1977-78	Brian CLOUGH	Nottm Forest	Bob PAISLEY	Liverpool	Terry NEILL	Arsenal	Jimmy ARMFIELD	Leeds U
1978-79	Brian CLOUGH	Nottm Forest	Lawrie McMENEMY	Southampton	Graham TAYLOR	Watford	Jimmy ADAMSON	Leeds U
1979-80	John BARNWELL	Wolves	Brian CLOUGH	Nottm Forest	Bob PAISLEY	Liverpool	Bob SMITH	Swindon T
1980-81	Bob PAISLEY	Liverpool	John LYALL	West Ham U	Gordon MILNE	Coventry C	John BOND	Manchester C
1981-82	Bob PAISLEY	Liverpool	Keith BURKINSHAW	Tottenham H	Bobby ROBSON	Ipswich T	Ronnie ALLEN	WBA
1982-83	Bob PAISLEY	Liverpool	Ron ATKINSON	Manchester U	Terry NEILL	Arsenal	Frank CASPER	Burnley
1983-84	Joe FAGAN	Liverpool	Howard KENDALL	Everton	Tony BARTON	Aston Villa	Alan BUCKLEY	Walsall
1984-85	Ken BROWN	Norwich C	Len ASHURST	Sunderland	John NEAL	Chelsea	Bobby FERGUSON	Ipswich T
1985-86	Maurice EVANS	Oxford U	Jim SMITH	QPR	Kenny DALGLISH	Liverpool	Graham TURNER	Aston Villa
1986-87	George GRAHAM	Arsenal	Kenny DALGLISH	Liverpool	David PLEAT	Tottenham H	Chris NICHOLL	Southampton
1987-88	Ray HARFORD	Luton T	George GRAHAM	Arsenal	Colin HARVEY	Everton	Maurice EVANS	Oxford U
1988-89	Brian CLOUGH	Nottm Forest	Ray HARFORD	Luton T	Joe JORDAN	Bristol C	John LYALL	West Ham U
1989-90	Brian CLOUGH	Nottm Forest	Joe ROYLE	Oldham A	John SILLETT	Coventry C	Billy BONDS	West Ham U
1990-91	Ron ATKINSON	Sheffield W	Alex FERGUSON	Manchester U	Howard WILKINSON	Leeds U	Bobby CAMPBELL	Chelsea
1991-92	Alex FERGUSON	Manchester U	Brian CLOUGH	Nottm Forest	Lennie LAWRENCE	Middlesbro'	Peter SHREEVES	Tottenham H
1992-93	George GRAHAM	Arsenal	Trevor FRANCIS	Sheffield W	Steve COPPELL	Crystal Pal	Kenny DALGLISH	Blackburn R

EUROPEAN COMPETITIONS

	European Cup		Cup-winners Cup		Fairs/UEFA Cup	
Season	Manager	Rd/Pts	Manager	Rd/Pts	Manager	Rd/Pts
1956-57	Matt BUSBY	SF/6			Arthur TURNER	SF/6
1957-58	Matt BUSBY	SF/6				
1958-59						
1959-60					Pat BEASLEY	F/12
1960-61			Stan CULLIS	SF/6	Gil MERRICK	F/12
1961-62	Bill NICHOLSON	SF/6				
1962-63			Bill NICHOLSON	W/18		
1963-64						
1964-65	Bill SHANKLY	SF/6	Ron GREENWOOD	W/18		
1965-66	Matt BUSBY	SF/6	Bill SHANKLY	F/12	Don REVIE	SF/6
			Ron GREENWOOD	SF/6	Tommy DOCHERTY	SF/6
1966-67					Don REVIE	F/12
1967-68	Matt BUSBY	W/18	Jimmy SCOULAR	SF/6	Don REVIE	W/18
1968-69	Matt BUSBY	SF/6			Joe HARVEY	W/18
1969-70	Don REVIE	SF/6	Joe MERCER	W/18	Bertie MEE	W/18
1970-71			Dave SEXTON	W/18	Don REVIE	W/18
			Joe MERCER	SF/6	Bill SHANKLY	SF/6
1971-72					Bill NICHOLSON	W/18
					Bill McGARRY	F/12
1972-73	Brian CLOUGH	SF/6	Don REVIE	F/12	Bill SHANKLY	W/18
					Bill NICHOLSON	SF/6
1973-74					Bill NICHOLSON	F/12
1974-75	Jimmy ARMFIELD	F/12				
1975-76			John LYALL	F/12	Bob PAISLEY	W/18
1976-77	Bob PAISLEY	W/18				
1977-78	Bob PAISLEY	W/18				
1978-79	Brian CLOUGH	W/18				
1979-80	Brian CLOUGH	W/18	Terry NEILL	F/12		
1980-81	Bob PAISLEY	W/18			Bobby ROBSON	W/18
1981-82	Tony BARTON	W/18	Keith BURKINSHAW	SF/6		
1982-83						
1983-84	Joe FAGAN	W/18	Ron ATKINSON	SF/6	Keith BURKINSHAW	W/18
					Brian CLOUGH	SF/6
1984-85	Joe FAGAN	F/12	Howard KENDALL	W/18		
1990-91			Alex FERGUSON	W/18		

Alex Ferguson, won the Cup-winners' Cup with Manchester United, then steered United to their first championship since 1967.

The Clubs — Manager by Manager

Accrington Stanley

The first of only two post-war clubs to resign from the Football League in mid-season, Stanley's Third and Fourth Division life lasted 33 complete seasons. At the time they were forced out of the League, the club was in the hands of two joint caretaker managers, Bill Smith and Harry Hubbick. They had taken over at the start of 1962, but within three months the axe fell.

These two were the successors to 12 permanent managers, making the average tenure a little under three years. Jack Hacking, a former England goalkeeper, had the longest reign at Peel Park, but half of his 14-year stay was accounted for by World War Two. This puts Ernest Blackburn, with just over seven years in office, on top of the longevity table, although no individual was more closely identified with the club than Samuel Pilkington. Joining Stanley first as a player in the non-League days of 1906, he went on to become secretary (with team responsibilities in the early League seasons), director, chairman and honorary vice-president. Whilst Pilkington served the club throughout its entire League existence, managers Curtis Booth and Harold Bodle had less than a season at the helm, and James Porter, Walter Crook, George Eastham and Jimmy Harrower were gone after two.

This underestimates the total contribution some of their managers made to Stanley, since more than half the job holders also played for the club. Booth, Hacking and Galbraith were all player-managers, Bodle and Harrower were former players before taking on the manager's job, whilst Pilkington had played for Stanley in pre-League days. Galbraith

was the only one of the 11 individuals to have managed a League club before going to Peel Park, and he, along with Blackburn (Wrexham, Hull and Tranmere) and Hacking (Barrow) went on to managerial jobs elsewhere in the League.

Nobody came closer to bringing some success to Accrington than Galbraith. Under his guidance, the club twice finished runners-up in the Third Division North. A man whose managerial career was spent in the lower divisions, Galbraith was also associated with New Brighton and Bradford, making a hat-trick of clubs which left the Football League.

Manager	Start/Date	End/Date	Pts/Total
Samuel Pilkington	cs 1919	Jan 1923	-
Curtis Booth	June 1923	May 1924	-
Samuel Pilkington	May 1924	Oct 1924	-
Ernest Blackburn	Oct 1924	Jan 1932	-
Amos Wade	Jan 1932	May 1935	-
Jack Hacking	May 1935	May 1949	-
Jimmy Porter	June 1949	March 1951	-
Walter Crook	June 1951	March 1953	-
Walter Galbraith	June 1953	Aug 1958	16
George Eastham	Oct 1958	June 1959	-
Harry Bodle	June 1959	April 1960	-
Jim Harrower	April 1960	Jan 1962	-

Aldershot

Aldershot's demise in March 1992, towards the end of their 53rd League season, had been on the cards for several years. Their achievements were at best modest, two promotions from Division Four, both of which ended in relegation a couple of years later. For all their lack of success, however, Aldershot had a tradition of managerial stability. There were just 13 managers at the Recreation Ground, which gave each of them on average four years in the job. The first two managers put in 22 years between them, but for Angus Seed and Bill McCracken, this amounted to about five Third Division South seasons apiece, because of pre-League competitions and the war. This makes Tom McAnearney's nine-year second term the longest period of unbroken service. His two spells at the club totalled 10.5 years, about a year more than Len Walker's two terms. The last two managers were amongst the shortest serving, Brian Talbot on eight months and Ian McDonald on four, whilst Ron Harris held on for seven.

There is little in common between the 11 men who held the office. Harry Evans and Walker were the only former Shots players to manage the club, although both McAnearney and Jimmy Melia were players for short periods immediately prior to taking over the top job. Walker was also one of only four who had managerial experience in the League before assuming control at the Recreation Ground. He had been in charge at Darlington, whilst McCracken was at Hull and Gateshead, David Smith at Northampton and Talbot player-manager at West Brom. This means that for Seed, Gordon Clark, Harris and McDonald, this appointment was their first involvement with Aldershot and League management.

Working at Aldershot was rarely a step on the way to bigger and better things. Melia was the only one to go on to high honours, an FA Cup Final appearance as Brighton manager. There were only three of the Shots other ten managers who went on to similar jobs elsewhere in the League, McCracken to Millwall, Seed to Barnsley and Clark to West Brom and Peterborough.

At the end of their Football League career, Aldershot had little to show for their 53 years of effort. They went out of the League in the way that they had spent most of their time in it, quietly and unobtrusively, a modest little club with much to be modest about.

Manager	Start/Date	End/Date	Pts/Total
Angus Seed	1927	Feb 1937	-
Bill McCracken	Feb 1937	Nov 1949	-
Gordon Clark	May 1950	Aug 1955	-
Harry Evans	1955	cs 1959	-
David Smith	July 1959	March 1967	-
Tom McAnearney	April 1967	Oct 1968	-
Jimmy Melia	April 1969	Jan 1972	-
Tom McAnearney	May 1972	March 1981	6
Len Walker	April 1981	Nov 1984	-
Ron Harris	Nov 1984	June 1985	-
Len Walker	June 1985	March 1991	6
Brian Talbot	March 1991	Nov 1991	-
Ian McDonald	Nov 1991	March 1992	-

Arsenal

Herbert Chapman's appointment to Highbury in 1925 changed not only the course of the Gunners' history but also redefined the role of the football manager. Chapman was the seventh holder of the job at Arsenal, but set the standards by which his nine successors have been judged. Caretakers apart, Arsenal have had 16 managers over a period of 85 League seasons, each lasting therefore an average of 5.3 seasons. Before Chapman, Harry Bradshaw was probably the most influential, taking the Gunners into the First Division, and George Morrell the most unfortunate. Although he was in charge when the club moved from Woolwich to Highbury, he was also the only Arsenal manager to experience relegation.

The Chapman era, which began in 1925, effectively ended in October 1956 with the death of Tom Whittaker, who, like his predecessor, George Allison, had been a part of the Highbury heirarchy since the 1920s. When Whittaker died, he was replaced by his assistant Jack Crayston, and thus the job was kept 'in the family' for over 30 years. Whittaker was the first former Arsenal player to be given the manager's job, since when Crayston, Swindin, Neill, Howe and Graham have followed in his footsteps. None succeeded to the job directly from playing, however: all served apprenticeships as trainers, coaches or assistant managers at Highbury or as managers at other clubs.

In terms of sustained success, Arsenal's record is one of the most admirable in the Football League, yet until George Graham's arrival, it was probably fair to say that the most successful managers were the least successful as players. Chapman, Allison, Whittaker and Bertie Mee all won the League title and FA Cup whilst in charge at Highbury, but there was not a single top-class medal or cap between them. Crayston, George Swindin, Billy Wright and Don Howe, on the other hand, had long and successful careers as players but were considered unsuccessful as Arsenal managers,

all failing to win any trophies. Graham changed all this, for he is the only manager ever to win League Championship, FA Cup and League Cup winners' medals as a player and as a manager. All were gained with Arsenal, except for the League Cup which came when he was a Chelsea player.

The 'missing' honour from the list is the 1933-34 Division One championship. Following Chapman's death in January 1934, and before Allison stepped down from the board the following close season, assistant manager Joe Shaw took over the reins temporarily and steered his charges to the second title on their way to a hat-trick of wins.

Manager	Start/Date	End/Date	Pts/Total
Thomas Mitchell	cs 1897	March 1898	-
George Elcoat	1898	1899	-
Harry Bradshaw	cs 1899	May 1904	10
Phil Kelso	cs 1904	Feb 1908	12
George Morrell	Feb 1908	cs 1915	-
Leslie Knighton	May 1919	June 1925	-
Herbert Chapman	June 1925	Jan 1934	108
George Allison	June 1934	May 1947	54
Tom Whittaker	June 1947	Oct 1956	66
Jack Crayston	Nov 1956	May 1958	-
George Swindin	July 1958	May 1962	-
Billy Wright	May 1962	June 1966	-
Bertie Mee	June 1966	March 1976	108
Terry Neill	July 1976	Dec 1983	72
Don Howe	Dec 1983	March 1986	-
George Graham	May 1986	-	108

Aston Villa

During the early days of the Football League, Aston Villa were one of the dominant clubs, winning six First Division titles and five FA Cup Finals before 1915. All this was achieved under the aegis of secretary George Ramsey, and it was not until the summer of 1934, after 42 seasons in the top flight, that Villa took the plunge and appointed a manager. In the 52 seasons which followed, Villa have had 17 managers, each lasting an average of over three seasons. The most successful was Ron Saunders, who was also the longest serving, staying over seven and a half years. Only Alex Massie and Joe Mercer, with around five years apiece, come close to that. The battle for shortest serving manager is more closely contested: Billy McNeill (eight months) just shades it from Josef Venglos (nine months), Tommy Docherty (13 months) and Tommy Cummings (16 months).

In selecting their managers, Villa do not seem to have been impressed by earlier connections with the club. Amongst 17 managers, only Massie, Eric Houghton and Vic Crowe played for Villa, although Dick Taylor and Tony Barton were promoted from the number-two job. Villa have, on the other hand, shown considerable vision in twice going overseas for their managers. In 1936, they went to Austria to bring the legendary coach Jimmy Hogan back to England. He ended the club's first sojourn in Division Two and took them to the FA Cup semi-finals. Less successful was the experiment in 1990-91 with the Czechoslovakian, Dr Josef Venglos, who took over when Graham Taylor got the England job.

The League Cup has thrown up some interesting points about Villa managers. In 1961, Joe Mercer was the first manager of a League Cup winning side, and, ten years later, Vic Crowe became only the third Division Three manager to take a club to Wembley. Finally, when Ron Saunders' Villa side won the League Cup in 1975, it was his third appearance in the Final in three seasons, and with his third club. Saunders was Villa's most successful manager, but he resigned just months before his team lifted the European Cup. This gave Barton the opportunity to steer Villa to their biggest success, only three months into his managerial career. It was Barton's only success as a manager.

Manager	Start/Date	End/Date	Pts/Total
Jimmy McMullan	June 1934	Oct 1936	-
Jimmy Hogan	Nov 1936	Sept 1939	22
Alex Massie	Sept 1945	Aug 1950	-
George Martin	Dec 1950	Aug 1953	-
Eric Houghton	Sept 1953	Nov 1958	18
Joe Mercer	Dec 1958	July 1964	58
Dick Taylor	July 1964	May 1967	6
Tommy Cummings	July 1967	Nov 1968	-
Tommy Docherty	Dec 1968	Jan 1970	-
Vic Crowe	Jan 1970	May 1974	26
Ron Saunders	June 1974	Feb 1982	64
Tony Barton	Feb 1982	May 1984	24
Graham Turner	Jul 1984	Sept 1986	6
Billy McNeill	Sept 1986	May 1987	-
Graham Taylor	July 1987	July 1990	22
Josef Venglos	July 1990	May 1991	-
Ron Atkinson	June 1991	-	12

Barnsley

Barnsley, elected to Division Two in 1898, hold the record for the longest continuous membership of the League without having played in the top flight. Over the last 83 seasons, Oakwell has been home to 16 individuals who between them have shared 20 managerial terms: Arthur Fairclough had three separate spells at the helm, whilst Johnny Steele and Allan Clarke had two apiece.

There are marked variations around the 4.2 seasons average for each manager. Angus Seed was the longest serving, but seven of his 16 years were lost to World War Two. This puts Steele's 12 years at the top of the long-serving list, followed by Fairclough (11 seasons), Seed, Peter Sant (seven) and Tim Ward (seven). Bobby Collins and Harry Lewis, on the other hand, had only one season in charge, and John McSeveney held on for just 15 months.

A spell as a Barnsley player does not feature on the CVs of many of the Tykes' managers. John McCartney, Brough Fletcher, Ward and Steele were the only ones amongst the 16 to have played for the club before becoming managers. Fairclough, in an interval between two of his three terms, was also a director, whilst Fletcher and Steele, together with Norman Hunter and Bobby Collins, were involved on the coaching side.

Recruiting a manager with previous experience at League level is a relatively modern practice for Barnsley. Before 1939, only Lewis (Stockport) and Seed (Aldershot) went to Oakwell after managing other clubs. Since Seed's death in 1953, Jim Iley (Peterborough), Collins (Huddersfield and Hull) and Mel Machin (Manchester City) arrived at Oakwell having made their managerial debuts elsewhere. (Tim Ward's five days at Exeter hardly counts). Until Machin's appointment in 1989, the Revie influence at Oakwell was strong, since Clarke, Hunter and Collins, who held the managerial reins at Barnsley for 11 years after 1978, were all graduates of Elland Road.

The most successful (and most interesting) of the Tykes' managers is the first, Arthur Fairclough. Barnsley-born, his playing days were ended by injury before he was 20. He took to refereeing and was elected to the Barnsley committee in 1896, becoming secretary-manager in 1899. He steered Barnsley to two FA Cup Finals, managed Huddersfield and Leeds and began his third term at Oakwell when he was nearly 60. His final move came five years later when he was elected to the Barnsley board.

Manager	Start/Date	End/Date	Pts/Total
Arthur Fairclough	cs 1899	April 1901	-
John McCartney	April 1901	cs 1904	-
Arthur Fairclough	cs 1904	cs 1912	30
Jack Hastie	cs 1912	April 1914	-
Percy Lewis	April 1914	April 1919	-
Peter Sant	April 1919	cs 1926	-
John Commins	cs 1926	May 1928	-
Arthur Fairclough	May 1928	May 1930	-
Brough Fletcher	May 1930	Feb 1937	14
Angus Seed	Feb 1937	Feb 1953	14
Tim Ward	March 1953	Feb 1960	22
Johnny Steele	March 1960	Sept 1971	6
John McSeveney	Sept 1971	Nov 1972	-
Johnny Steele	Nov 1972	April 1973	-
Jim Iley	April 1973	April 1978	-
Allan Clarke	May 1978	Oct 1980	6
Norman Hunter	Oct 1980	Feb 1984	8
Bobby Collins	Feb 1984	June 1985	-
Allan Clarke	June 1985	Nov 1989	-
Mel Machin	Dec 1989	May 1993	-

Barrow

It was 11th time unlucky for Barrow at the League's AGM in 1972. After 44 seasons of first-class football at Holker Street, stretching back to the formation of the Third Division North, the Bluebirds failed to gain re-election after ten previous applications had succeeded. Although a League club from 1921, they did not appoint a manager until 1929, preferring to rely of the services of secretary William Dickinson.

Between Andy Walker and Jack Crompton, Barrow had 16 managers, making an average stay of exactly two seasons per manager. This relatively high turnover was defied only by Jack Hacking (six years), Tom Lowes (five years) and Don McEvoy, whose two terms amounted to four months less than five years. With these three accounting for nearly half of Barrow's managerial history, it is not surprising that a number of others hardly had time to get their feet under the table. Thomas Miller (four months), James Blissett (eight months), Colin Appleton (five months) and Jack Crompton (the final six months) were the principal short-term casualties of the club's lack of success.

Very few knew what they were letting themselves in for when they took over at Holker Street, lacking familiarity with both Barrow and management. Only Walker (Middlesbrough), John Commins (Barnsley), Hacking (Accrington), Norman Dodgin (Exeter) and Crompton (one week in charge at Luton) had any previous experience of League management, although Fred Pentland had coached the Spanish national side. No former Barrow player managed the club, and only Lowes (trainer), McEvoy (player-coach) and Crompton (coach) could be classed as internal appointments.

Several Barrow old boys moved to similar jobs elsewhere, with Andy Beattie and Joe Harvey the most notable. Commins, Lowes, Dodgin, McEvoy and Appleton all found new employment at League level after their spells with Barrow ended. In the 1960s and 1970s, Barrow were one of six clubs once in the Third Division North to lose their League status. It is something of a coincidence that four of their managers were associated with one of the other victims: Commins (Southport), Hacking (Accrington), Harvey (Workington) and McEvoy (Southport).

Manager	Start/Date	End/Date	Pts/Total
Andy Walker	1929	cs 1930	-
Thomas Miller	cs 1930	Nov 1930	-
John Commins	Nov 1930	April 1931	-
Tom Lowes	1932	April 1937	-
James Blissett	April 1937	Dec 1937	-
Fred Pentland	Feb 1938	1939	-
John Commins	June 1945	Dec 1946	-
Andy Beattie	March 1947	March 1949	-
Jack Hacking	May 1949	June 1955	-
Joe Harvey	July 1955	June 1957	-
Norman Dodgin	July 1957	July 1958	-
Bill Brown	July 1958	Aug 1959	-
Ron Staniforth	Oct 1959	July 1964	-
Don McEvoy	Aug 1964	July 1967	6
Colin Appleton	Aug 1967	Jan 1969	-
Norman Bodell	Feb 1969	Feb 1970	-
Don McEvoy	Feb 1970	Nov 1971	-
Jack Crompton	Dec 1971	June 1972	-

Aston Villa in 1978, pictured with the Football League Cup. Back row (left to right): Young, Findlay, Burridge, Spink, A.Evans, Linton. Middle row: Roy McLaren (coach), D.Evans, Buttress, Gregory, Gray, Smith, Hughes, Cowans, Peter Downs (physiotherpist). Front row: Deehan, Cropley, Phillips, Gidman, Ron Saunders (manager), Robson, Little, Mortimer, Carrodus.

Barnsley, FA Cup winners in 1912. Seated (players only, left to right): Glendinning, Downs, Cooper (behind trophy), Taylor, Bratley, Utley. On ground: Bartrop, Tufnell, Lillycrop, Travers, Moore.

Birmingham City

Birmingham City have recently sailed close to extinction — the latest rescue package being implemented in March 1993 —and financial uncertainty has taken its toll. In the last ten seasons, the Blues have played in three divisions and had six managers. Overall they have had 23 managers in 72 seasons since the first appointment in 1910, before which they had a five-man committee, including the secretary, treasurer and captain.

As the 1980s indicate, there are variations in the average tenure of a little over three seasons. In particular, Lou Macari (three months) and John Bond (16 months) were on their way shortly after arriving. The 1970s saw Sir Alf Ramsey come and go inside four months, but of his 15 predecessors, only Frank Richards and Joe Mallett had less than two seasons at the helm. The longest serving was George Liddell in the 1930s, for six seasons, a little longer than Bob McRoberts, Leslie Knighton, Bob Brocklebank and Freddie Goodwin.

A previous connection with the Blues was a help for McRoberts, Billy Beer, Liddell, Arthur Turner, Gil Merrick and Gary Pendrey (ex-players), Willie Bell and Mallett (coaches) and Ramsey (director). A route from management of other clubs was followed by virtually all the other 14. The pedigree of some is impressive. Stan Cullis was a League Championship and FA Cup winner at Wolves, Ron Saunders and Dave Mackay also managed League champions, as did Ramsey, who could also boast a World Cup success. There were some promotion successes, too, (Beasley, Harry Storer, Ramsey, Jim Smith, Saunders, Bond, Macari and Terry Cooper) and Wembley appearances (Bond and Saunders). At Birmingham, few repeated their earlier success or achieved much after leaving. With the problems the club has had of late, it is easy to overlook the success of the first 30 post-war years when every manager other than Mallett achieved something in the League or Cups. Between 1946 and 1975, the Blues won two divisional titles,

reached four Cup Finals (including the first in Europe by an English club) and five semi-finals, shared amongst seven managers. Before that there was one Final appearance and three promotions between 15 managers.

Manager	Start/Date	End/Date	Pts/Total
Bob McRoberts	July 1910	May 1915	-
Frank Richards	May 1915	May 1923	-
Billy Beer	May 1923	March 1927	-
William Harvey	March 1927	May 1928	-
Leslie Knighton	July 1928	Aug 1933	12
George Liddell	Aug 1933	Sept 1939	-
Harry Storer	June 1945	Nov 1948	22
Bob Brocklebank	Jan 1949	Oct 1954	6
Arthur Turner	Nov 1954	Sept 1958	40
Pat Beasley	Jan 1958	May 1960	12
Gil Merrick	June 1960	April 1964	30
Joe Mallett	July 1964	Dec 1965	-
Stan Cullis	Dec 1965	March 1970	12
Freddie Goodwin	June 1970	Sept 1975	22
Willie Bell	Oct 1975	Sept 1977	-
Sir Alf Ramsey	Nov 1977	March 1978	-
Jim Smith	March 1978	Feb 1982	10
Ron Saunders	Feb 1982	Jan 1986	10
John Bond	Jan 1986	May 1987	-
Gary Pendrey	May 1987	April 1989	-
Dave Mackay	April 1989	Jan 1991	-
Lou Macari	Feb 1991	May 1991	-
Terry Cooper	Aug 1991	-	8

Blackburn Rovers

The high-profile appointment of Kenny Dalglish in 1991 was an attempt by Rovers to restore the position of prominence they had not experienced since World War One. Up to 1915, they won the FA Cup five times and the First Division twice, all without a manager. Secretaries Mitchell, Walmsley and Middleton held the reins until Jack Carr's arrival in 1922, during Rovers 30th League season. In the ensuing 64 campaigns, Ewood Park has been home to 23 managers (21 individuals since Crompton and Carey both had two spells), an average job expectancy of 2.8 seasons.

No individual has stamped himself on Blackburn's managerial history. Legendary full-back Bob Crompton spent seven years as manager, but they were spread over two terms (the first as 'honorary' manager) and included two seasons of wartime football. 'Jolly Jack' Marshall's six and a half years in the 1960s was the longest anyone has spent at the Ewood helm in peacetime. John Carey, Bobby Saxton and Arthur Barritt are the only others to last more than five years. There were several short-term tenants, particularly Jim Iley (seven months) John Pickering (seven months) and Will Scott (eight months). Eddie Hapgood, like Carey and Crompton an illustrious international full back, could not match their longevity in management: his stay lasted eight months.

Blackburn have shown a reluctance to appoint former players as manager. Other than Crompton, only Jack Bruton and Eddie Quigley had worn the famous blue and white halved shirts, although Howard Kendall played for Blackburn, but as player-manager. Crompton and Bruton also served the club in other capacities, as director and assistant trainer/assistant secretary respectively. Barritt and Reg Taylor from the 1930s were 'promoted' from secretary to manager, whilst in the 1970s Pickering was Iley's assistant before stepping up.

For Kendall, Carr, Hapgood and Carey, the appointment to Ewood was their first exposure to Blackburn and League management. None left Rovers to enjoy greater success than Kendall at Everton, and none arrived at Ewood

having won more honours than his Merseyside rival Dalglish at Liverpool. Coincidentally, Carey and Gordon Lee also found their way to Goodison after Blackburn, but neither had the impact of Kendall.

Manager	Start/Date	End/Date	Pts/Total
Jack Carr	Feb 1922	Dec 1926	6
Bob Crompton	Dec 1926	Feb 1931	18
Arthur Barritt	Feb 1931	April 1936	-
Reg Taylor	Oct 1936	April 1938	-
Bob Crompton	April 1938	March 1941	16
Eddie Hapgood	June 1946	Feb 1947	-
Will Scott	April 1947	Dec 1947	-
Jack Bruton	Dec 1947	May 1949	-
Jackie Bestall	June 1949	May 1953	6
Johnny Carey	June 1953	Oct 1958	16
Dally Duncan	Oct 1958	June 1960	12
Jack Marshall	June 1960	Feb 1967	6
Eddie Quigley	Feb 1967	Oct 1970	-
John Carey	Oct 1970	June 1971	-
Ken Furphy	Aug 1971	Dec 1973	-
Gordon Lee	Jan 1974	June 1975	14
Jim Smith	June 1975	March 1978	-
Jim Iley	April 1978	Nov 1978	-
John Pickering	Nov 1978	May 1979	-
Howard Kendall	June 1979	May 1981	8
Bobby Saxton	May 1981	Dec 1986	-
Don Mackay	Feb 1987	Sept 1991	-
Kenny Dalglish	Oct 1991	-	16

Blackpool

Blackpool have a curious managerial history. There is nothing exceptional about 20 managers in the 73 seasons since the first appointment, but the club has had two lengthy spells without an official manager, winning promotion during the second of these. In addition, Blackpool were one of the first clubs to try a player-manager (Jack Cox), and in Joe Smith (23 years at Bloomfield Road) they had one of the longest serving in the League. It was also Blackpool who lured Major Frank Buckley back to football after three years as a commercial traveller, thereby re-starting the career of one of the inter-war periods most influential managers.

Although each of the 20 managers stayed on average 3.7 seasons, this conceals wide variations. Smith's record has never been seriously challenged, his successor, Ron Suart (nine years) and Sam Ellis (seven years in the 1980s) coming closest. Graham Carr (five months) and Stan Ternant (six months) are at the other extreme, alongside Sid Beaumont, Alan Ball and Jimmy Mullen, each of whom spent about a year at Bloomfield Road.

Jack Cox appears to have been the first manager. A former player, he returned to Blackpool from Liverpool in 1909, effectively as player-manager, an unusual appointment for the time. Since then, only Suart, Stan Mortensen, Allan Brown and Ball both played for and managed Blackpool, although Ternant and Billy Ayre were coaches/assistant-managers when the top job became available. Most of the others went to Bloomfield Road with a track record in management. Bill Norman (Barnsley), Alex McFarlane (Charlton), Suart (Scunthorpe), Bob Stokoe (Sunderland), Les Shannon (Bury), Brown (Luton) and Carr (Northampton) had all won honours before joining the Seasiders. Harry Potts at Burnley was the most successful, leading the Clarets to the League championship and an FA Cup Final.

After Blackpool, Norman (Leeds), Suart (Chelsea), Stokoe (Carlisle) and Mullen (Burnley) all enjoyed success elsewhere, but none could match

Buckley's post-Bloomfield Road career at Wolves. Smith stands out, not only for his durability but for his success: three FA Cup Finals, and all but his first two seasons with Blackpool in Division One. When Blackpool won the Cup in 1953, Harry Evans was chairman. He was one of Smith's predecessors, as honorary manager between 1928 and 1933, when the club won the Second Division.

Manager	Start/Date	End/Date	Pts/Total
Jack Cox	cs 1909	Dec 1911	-
Bill Norman	cs 1919	cs 1923	-
Frank Buckley	July 1923	May 1927	-
Sidney Beaumont	cs 1927	May 1928	-
Alex McFarlane	July 1933	July 1935	-
Joe Smith	Aug 1935	April 1958	64
Ron Suart	May 1958	Feb 1967	6
Stan Mortenson	Feb 1967	April 1969	-
Les Shannon	May 1969	Oct 1970	10
Bob Stokoe	Dec 1970	Nov 1972	-
Harry Potts	Jan 1973	May 1976	-
Allan Brown	May 1976	Feb 1978	-
Bob Stokoe	May 1978	Aug 1979	-
Stan Ternant	Aug 1979	Feb 1980	-
Alan Ball (jnr)	July 1980	Feb 1981	-
Allan Brown	March 1981	April 1982	-
Sam Ellis	June 1982	April 1989	6
Jimmy Mullen	May 1989	April 1990	-
Graham Carr	June 1990	Nov 1990	-
Billy Ayre	Nov 1990	-	6

Bolton Wanderers

For a club which has only been on nodding terms with major success, Bolton have a remarkable record of managerial stability. Founder members of the Football League, they have had just 16 managers (excluding caretakers and Tom Mather's four-year stint during World War One) in the 74 seasons since they made their first appointment. This means that the Trotters have changed managers every 4.6 seasons. Included in this average, however, are four men who between them accummulated just over two years service, Jimmy McIlroy, Jimmy Meadows, Charlie Wright and George Mulhall.

The relatively high average period of office is accounted for by two men, who shared over 40 years at Burnden Park. Charlie Foweraker put in 25 years (including four in wartime) during which Bolton won the FA Cup three times (a record he shares with John Nicholson of Sheffield United and Bill Nicholson of Spurs). The second was Bill Ridding, whose term stretched for nearly 18 years. In fact, up to the time of Ridding's departure in 1968, the Trotters had just five managers in 60 years.

It is also apparent that the Bolton board has had a preference for selecting people who had served the club in some other capacity. Each of the first seven appointments, up to and including McIlroy in 1970, was in effect an internal promotion. Mather, in charge during World War One, can be added to the list as can the later choices of Ian Greaves, Stan Anderson, George Mulhall and Charlie Wright. The only managers who were strangers to Burnden Park, therefore, were Meadows, Jimmy Armfield, John McGovern, Phil Neal and Bruce Rioch.

This means of course that few could claim to have had much managerial experience before accepting the Bolton job. Ridding, Meadows, Greaves, Anderson, Mulhall and Rioch were the exceptions, but none had achieved much in terms of League or Cup honours. Equally, only four of the 15 former Bolton managers, Walter Rowley, Meadows, Armfield and Greaves, took over at other clubs after leaving Burnden Park, with Armfield's European Cup Final appearance with Leeds the major achievement. Although Neal went to Coventry as number two from Bolton, he was also part of Graham Taylor's England management set-up, the first Trotters' manager to win international recognition since Ridding was trainer to England's 1950 World Cup squad in Brazil.

Manager	Start/Date	End/Date	Pts/Total
John Somerville	cs 1908	Jan 1910	16
Will Settle	Jan 1910	cs 1915	16
Charlie Foweraker	July 1919	Aug 1944	70
Walter Rowley	Aug 1944	Oct 1950	6
Bill Ridding	Oct 1950	Aug 1968	30
Nat Lofthouse	Dec 1968	Nov 1970	-
Jimmy McIlroy	Nov 1970	Nov 1970	-
Jimmy Meadows	Jan 1971	April 1971	-
Jimmy Armfield	May 1971	Oct 1974	14
Ian Greaves	Oct 1974	Jan 1980	22
Stan Anderson	Feb 1980	May 1981	-
George Mulhall	June 1981	June 1982	-
John McGovern	June 1982	Jan 1985	-
Charlie Wright	Feb 1985	Dec 1985	-
Phil Neal	Dec 1985	May 1992	6
Bruce Rioch	May 1992	-	8

AFC Bournemouth

For long the poor relations of the south coast clubs, it took Bournemouth until their 57th season to climb out of the two lower divisions, and then it was only temporary. Harry Redknapp alone amongst the Cherries 22 managers has competed in Division Two during the club's 63 League seasons. He is the club's longest serving manager, his nine-year tenure more than three times longer than the 2.8 seasons average. When Bournemouth joined the Third Division South in 1923, Harry Kinghorn was at the helm, as he was just after World War Two. This service was not unbroken, however, but he spent 27 years at Dean Court in a variety of capacities, including a long period as trainer under a series of other managers. Kinghorn was only in charge for three League seasons. Freddie Cox had two spells with the Cherries, which totalled seven years, and Billy Birrell in the 1930s and Jack Bruton in the 1950s, with 11 years between them, were the other two with a stay well above the average. Don Megson (six months), Bob Crompton (nine months) and Trevor Hartley (15 months) head the list of short-term appointments.

When Hartley, the Cherries' 16th manager, got the job in 1973, he was the first former Bournemouth player to get the chance to run the club. More recently, John Benson, Redknapp and Tony Pullis worked up to the manager's office from the Dean Court playing staff. The board's preference has been much more for experienced managers. Amongst the recruits were Leslie Knighton (once of Arsenal), Bob Crompton (Blackburn), Don Welsh (Liverpool) and Alec Stock (Orient, QPR, Luton and Fulham), all of whom had managed at the highest level. In addition, Frank Richards, Charles Bell, Jack Bruton, Reg Furness and Don Megson went to Bournemouth from similar jobs at other clubs, generally in the lower divsion.

A spell with the Cherries apparently looks good on a curriculum vitae since most of the managers moved on to other jobs in the League, with Knighton, Birrell, Richards, Crompton, Bill McGarry, John Bond and David Webb all finding their way to First Division/Premier League clubs.

Manager	Start/Date	End/Date	Pts/Total
Harry Kinghorn	cs 1920	cs 1925	-
Leslie Knighton	July 1925	July 1928	-
Frank Richards	July 1928	cs 1930	-
Billy Birrell	cs 1930	April 1935	-
Bob Crompton	June 1935	Feb 1936	-
Charles Bell	Feb 1936	cs 1939	-
Harry Kinghorn	cs 1939	cs 1947	-
Harry Lowe	cs 1947	Feb 1950	8
Jack Bruton	March 1950	March 1956	-
Freddie Cox	April 1956	July 1958	-
Don Welsh	July 1958	Feb 1961	-
Bill McGarry	March 1961	July 1963	-
Reg Flewin	Sept 1963	April 1965	-
Freddie Cox	April 1965	April 1970	-
John Bond	May 1970	Nov 1973	6
Trevor Hartley	Nov 1973	Jan 1975	-
John Benson	Jan 1975	Jan 1979	-
Alec Stock	Jan 1979	Dec 1980	-
David Webb	Dec 1980	Dec 1982	6
Don Megson	March 1983	Oct 1983	-
Harry Redknapp	Nov 1983	June 1992	14
Tony Pullis	June 1992	-	-

Bradford (Park Avenue)

Of the 27 now largely forgotten 'former Football League clubs', Bradford were one of the longest surviving and the only one to play in all four divisions. Their 51 season participation in the League ended in 1970 and they had virtually no other existence, for they were elected to Division Two just 12 months after their formation and they folded two seasons after failing to gain re-election.

In their 51 seasons, the Park Avenue club had 21 managers, an average life span of 2.4 seasons. Not surprisingly, the turnover rate accelerated towards the end of their career, as financial pressures intensified. After just eight managers in the 27 seasons up to 1939, it fell to nine in 21 seasons after the war and finally to five in the last three seasons. There were, however, three men who survived for periods well in excess of the average. Tom Maley spent 13 years at Park Avenue, four of which were covered by World War One, which means Claude Ingram's nine seasons were the longest. After 1945, Fred Emery added five years service to his three in wartime competitions. These three alone account for 45% of Bradford's time in the League. At the other end of the spectrum were eight managers who had less than a season each in the job (O'Rourke, Howie, Breedon, Young, McCalman, Brown and Tomlinson) which made this one of the least secure posts in football.

For a club which spent such a high proportion of their League history outside the top divisions, Park Avenue were nevertheless able to attract managers with experience and a proven track record. For ten of the 20 individuals, this was at least the second League managerial appointment, and in O'Rourke the board selected a man who had earlier had long spells with neighbours Bradford City, where he had been an FA Cup winner. Maley was another early jobholder. He went to Bradford after doing so much to put Manchester City on the map, and after having a suspension for financial irregularities lifted.

Almost as many, nine of the 20, went on to similar jobs elsewhere, although only Vic Buckingham made it to the highest level. For Walter Galbraith, managing Park Avenue completed a unique hat-trick. His earlier managerial jobs included New Brighton and Accrington, clubs who also lost their League status, although he was not at Accrington or Bradford when the axe fell.

Manager	Start/Date	End/Date	Pts/Total
George Gillies	May 1908	Feb 1911	-
Tom Maley	Feb 1911	Feb 1924	18
Peter O'Rourke	April 1924	Feb 1925	-
David Howie	Feb 1925	Aug 1925	-
Claude Ingram	Aug 1925	March 1934	22
Billy Hardy	May 1934	April 1936	-
David Steele	May 1936	Sept 1943	-
Fred Emery	Oct 1943	June 1951	-
Vic Buckingham	June 1951	Jan 1953	-
Norman Kirkman	March 1953	Jan 1955	-
Jack Breedon	Jan 1955	Oct 1955	-
Billy Corkhill	May 1956	Nov 1957	-
Alf Young	Dec 1957	Nov 1958	-
Walter Galbraith	Nov 1958	Jan 1961	-
Jimmy Scoular	Jan 1961	May 1964	6
Jock Buchanan	May 1964	March 1967	-
Jack Rowley	March 1967	Oct 1968	-
Don McCalman	Oct 1968	Dec 1968	-
Laurie Brown	Dec 1968	Oct 1969	-
Don McCalman	Oct 1969	Feb 1970	-
Frank Tomlinson	Feb 1970	Dec 1970	-

Bradford City

The job of managing Bradford City has been one of the riskier posts in the Football League. Since being elected to Division Two in 1903, there have been 29 managers, a change on average every 2.7 seasons. The survival rate was rather higher in the period up to 1939 (four seasons per manager) than in recent times (less than two seasons per manager since 1975) as the side experienced five changes of League status.

Only one man seemed able to defy this trend. Peter O'Rourke spent over 17 years in charge in two separate spells stretching from 1905 to 1930. His tenure included winning the FA Cup and the Second and Third Divisions, making him the most successful, as well as longest serving, City manager. Peter Jackson (six years), David Menzies (five years) and Jack Peart (five years) were the only others whose terms were about twice the average. The Bantams, on the other hand, had four managers who held the job for less than a year (Grenville Hair, 'honorary' manager Albert Harris, Jack Barker and John Napier) and seven others (Veitch, Milburn, Harris, Watson, McFarland, Yorath and Docherty) who failed to complete two seasons.

In seeking the right man, the City board have recruited from all sources. The last four managers have been an Englishman, Welshman, Scotsman and Irishman. Just under half of the managers (13 out of 28) went to Valley Parade with some experience of running a League club under their belts. There have also been nine former or current City players who were given the job, including six who were player-managers. In addition, four others served the club in other non-playing capacities before becoming manager.

Although one or two of City's managers had, or were to, work in the top flight, none was to win major domestic honours as managers. For the most part, they spent their careers in the lower divisions, with an occasional promotion. In Dick Ray and Terry Yorath, the Bantams had two men who won 'international' recognition as managers, for the Football League and Wales respectively, and in O'Rourke and David Steele, the only two who managed both Bradford City and Park Avenue.

Manager	Start/Date	End/Date	Pts/Total
Robert Campbell	June 1903	Oct 1905	-
Peter O'Rourke	Nov 1905	June 1921	34
David Menzies	July 1921	June 1926	-
Colin Veitch	Aug 1926	Jan 1928	-
Peter O'Rourke	May 1928	May 1930	14
Jack Peart	July 1930	March 1935	-
Dick Ray	April 1935	Feb 1938	-
Fred Westgarth	March 1938	July 1943	-
Jack Barker	May 1946	Jan 1947	-
Jack Milburn	Jan 1947	July 1948	-
David Steele	July 1948	Feb 1952	-
Albert Harris	Feb 1952	May 1952	-
Ivor Powell	May 1952	Feb 1955	-
Peter Jackson	Feb 1955	March 1961	-
Bob Brocklebank	May 1961	Oct 1964	-
Bill Harris	March 1965	March 1966	-
Willie Watson	April 1966	Jan 1968	-
Grenville Hair	Jan 1968	March 1968	-
Jimmy Wheeler	June 1968	Sept 1971	6
Bryan Edwards	Nov 1971	Jan 1975	-
Bobby Kennedy	Jan 1975	Jan 1978	6
John Napier	Feb 1978	Oct 1978	-
George Mulhall	Nov 1978	March 1981	-
Roy McFarland	May 1981	Nov 1982	6
Trevor Cherry	Dec 1982	Jan 1987	14
Terry Dolan	Jan 1987	Jan 1989	-
Terry Yorath	Feb 1989	March 1990	-
John Docherty	March 1990	Nov 1991	-
Frank Stapleton	Dec 1991	-	-

Brentford

Until winning promotion from the Third Division in 1992, Brentford had been the poor relations of West London football, the only one of the five clubs in the area not to have played in the top two divisions and reached the Cup Final in the last 25 years. The Bees, however, had their period in the spotlight when they were amongst the top half dozen clubs in the country in the 1930s. This was during Harry Curtis' long regime at Griffin Park. He was in the job for 23 years, seven of which were in wartime, and took the club from the Third to the First Division in three seasons.

Curtis is the key figure on the list of Bees managers. There have been 20 in 66 seasons, an average stint of 3.3 seasons per manager. The closest challenger but a poor second to Curtis is Malcolm McDonald's eight years in the 1950s/1960s. A number of others barely had time to familiarise themselves with the surroundings. Jim Bain's six months as manager was a sad end to 25 years service at Griffin Park in a variety of roles, and the shortest term of office. Tommy Lawton and Billy Gray, who each lasted about a year, and Tommy Cavanagh and John Docherty, in the job for 18 months, were the other short-term appointments.

Of the 20, six were former Bees (Jackie Gibbons, Bain, Lawton, McDonald, Docherty and Steve Perryman), whilst Tommy Cavanagh, Jimmy Sirrel, Frank Blunstone and Phil Holder were promoted from trainer-assistant manager to the top job. Fred Halliday had only three League seasons at the Griffin Park helm, but he had three spells as Bees manager, the first starting in 1908. His career ended 20 years later, and most of his time was spent as secretary or as a non-League manager. Halliday (Bradford), along with Curtis (Gillingham), Bill Dodgin senior (Southampton and Fulham) and junior (Fulham and Northampton), Billy Gray (Millwall) and Frank McLintock (Leicester) went to Griffin Park with some managerial experience to their name. This leaves just three men, Archie Mitchell, Mike Everitt and Fred Callaghan, who had no previous connection with the Bees and who were new to management.

A common link between many of the Bees managers is that most included at least one other London club on their curriculum vitae. The exceptions were Halliday, Curtis, Bain, McDonald, Cavanagh and Sirrel, the last four of whom were internal appointments when they became managers.

Manager	Start/Date	End/Date	Pts/Total
Fred Halliday	1915	Aug 1921	-
Archie Mitchell	Aug 1921	Dec 1924	-
Fred Halliday	Dec 1924	May 1926	-
Harry Curtis	May 1926	Feb 1949	38
Jackie Gibbons	Feb 1949	Aug 1952	-
Jim Bain	Aug 1952	Jan 1953	-
Tommy Lawton	Jan 1953	Sept 1953	-
Bill Dodgin (snr)	Oct 1953	May 1957	-
Malcolm McDonald	May 1957	Jan 1965	20
Tommy Cavanagh	Jan 1965	March 1966	-
Billy Gray	cs 1966	Sept 1967	-
Jimmy Sirrel	Sept 1967	Nov 1969	-
Frank Blunstone	Dec 1969	June 1973	6
Mike Everitt	Sept 1973	Jan 1975	-
John Docherty	Jan 1975	Sept 1976	-
Bill Dodgin (jnr)	Sept 1976	March 1980	6
Fred Callaghan	March 1980	Feb 1984	-
Frank McLintock	Feb 1984	Jan 1987	-
Steve Perryman	Jan 1987	Aug 1990	-
Phil Holder	Aug 1990	May 1993	14

Brighton and Hove Albion

For the first 31 years of their Football League life, Brighton were members of the old Third Division South. With Billy Lane as manager, they were the last club to win this competition, and, after the stability of the first period, the Seagulls' League status has since changed frequently. During 11 promotions/relegations, which took them into all four divisions over the last 35 seasons, Brighton have had 13 managers, to add to the four they had in the years up to 1958. Altogether, there have been 16 managers at the Goldstone Ground in 66 League seasons, an average of a little more than one every four seasons.

The list is dominated by Charles Webb, who spent 28 years at the helm, of which 20 were in the Football League. As a player, manager and then general manager, Webb was involved with Brighton for 40 years. His only challenger in the longevity stakes was Billy Lane, who came a poor second with 10 years service from 1951. The tragic Tommy Cook (an England international with Brighton, a Sussex county cricketer and structural engineer, he committed suicide a couple of years after leaving the Goldstone), Brian Clough and Jimmy Melia, on the other hand, were in and out in less than a season, whilst George Curtis, Peter Taylor, Freddie Goodwin and Mike Bailey lasted less than two.

Webb and Cook, together with Chris Cattlin, were the only former Seagulls to move into the manager's office at the Goldstone, excluding Lane's solitary war-time guest appearance. Lane had, however, been assistant manager for 12 months, whilst Melia was upgraded from chief scout to caretaker-manager and then manager. Archie Macaulay, the architect of Third Division Norwich's Cup run in 1959, was the first manager recruited by Brighton who had had similar experiences elsewhere. Clough, already a championship winner, spent a few months on the Sussex coast between jobs at Derby and Leeds, but for the most part, Brighton have not been afraid to give newcomers a start in management.

For Clough, there were major triumphs still to come, but at Forest not Brighton. Peter Taylor shared in many of these, but also had a spell as manager in his own right at Derby. Mullery and Goodwin both went on to First Division clubs in their post-Goldstone careers, as did Don Welsh. He went to Anfield, as George Kay's successor in 1951, and has the dubious distinction of being the last man to manage a relegated Liverpool team.

Manager	Start/Date	End/Date	Pts/Total
Charles Webb	cs 1919	May 1947	-
Tommy Cook	May 1947	Nov 1947	-
Don Welsh	Nov 1947	March 1951	-
Billy Lane	March 1951	May 1961	30
George Curtis	June 1961	Feb 1963	-
Archie Macaulay	April 1963	Oct 1968	12
Freddie Goodwin	Oct 1968	May 1970	-
Pat Saward	July 1970	Oct 1973	8
Brian Clough	Nov 1973	June 1974	-
Peter Taylor	Aug 1974	July 1976	-
Alan Mullery	July 1976	June 1981	18
Mike Bailey	June 1981	Dec 1982	-
Jimmy Melia	Jan 1983	Oct 1983	12
Chris Cattlin	Oct 1983	April 1986	-
Alan Mullery	May 1986	Jan 1987	-
Barry Lloyd	Jan 1987	-	8

Bradford City in 1911, pictured with the FA Cup. Back row (left to right): Peter O'Rourke (manager), Torrance, F.O'Rourke, Mellors, McDonald, Devine, C.Harper (trainer). Middle row: Gildea, Campbell, Speirs, Robinson, Taylor, Thompson. Front row: P.Logan, R.Bond.

Brighton & Hove Albion, 1983-84. Back row (left top right): Connor, Howlett, Ryan, Sille, Pearce, O'Reagan, Ramsey. Middle row: Mike Yaxley (physiotherpist), George Aitken (reserve-team coach), Smith, Moseley, Digweed, Nelson, Chris Cattlin (first-team coach), Glen Wilson (kit manager). Front row: Foster, Case, Grealish, Jimmy Melia (manager), Gatting, Robinson, Smillie.

Bristol City, 1904-05. Back row (left to right): W.P.Kingston, Thickett, Tuft, Clay, Hargett, Demmery, Sam Hollis. Middle row: D.Thomas, Gilson, Jones, Hosie, Fisher, Chambers, Fenton, Frank Bacon, R.Batten (trainer). Front row: Dean, Corbett, Gilligan, Capes, Wombwell. Hollis and Bacon later managed the club.

Bristol Rovers in 1983-84. Back row (left to right): Adams, Sherwood, Curle, Bailey. Second row: Wayne Jones (assistant manager), Tony Pulis (youth-team coach), Hughes, Parkin, Chashley, Randall, Kite, Barrett, Stevens, Roy Dolling (youth development officer). Seated: Barnes, Waited, Holloway, G.Williams, Dave Williams (manager), McCaffery, B.Williams, Slatter, Showering. Front row: Noble, Portch, Harding, Brain, Morris, Vassall, Hare, Metcalfe.

Bristol City

Elected to the League 20 years before neighbours Rovers, City have had 21 managers in 81 seasons, excluding the 19-day spells of Collins, Wimshurst and Sharpe (in the difficult early 1980s). Bourton's temporary period as player-manager during Hewison's suspension in 1938-39 is also omitted. Amongst the Robins' long-serving managers, Dicks, whose 13 years is the longest, and Hewison, whose 17 years were interrupted by seven years of war and one of suspension stand out. In addition Raisbeck, Beasley and Ford each stayed more than seven years. The years between Dicks and Cooper, when extinction was a real threat, saw the greatest upheaval. Hodgson was given only three months, much less than predecessors Bacon (15 months) and Wright (14 months) and successors Lumsden (17 months) and Smith (11 months).

Few City managers also played for the club. Thickett, Cooper, and Jordan were the only former players, although Osman was promoted to player-manager. Several managed League clubs before going to Ashton Gate: Bradshaw (Swansea and Fulham), Hewison (Northampton and QPR), Doherty (Doncaster), Cooper (Bristol Rovers) and Smith (York and Sunderland). The most successful in his pre-Robins career was, however, Houghton, who led Swedish club Malmö to the 1979 European Cup Final. Raisbeck, who twice took City to the Third Division South title, later managed Halifax and Chester, Beasley stepped up to the First Division with Birmingham and Fred Ford moved across the city to Eastville. Ford, along with Palmer and Cooper, managed both Bristol clubs. Like Beasley, Cooper also went to Birmingham, but it was to a Third Division club and via Exeter.

Manager	Start/Date	End/Date	Pts/Total
Sam Collis	1901	March 1905	
Harry Thickett	March 1905	Oct 1910	40
Frank Bacon	Oct 1910	Jan 1911	-
Sam Hollis	Jan 1911	April 1913	-
George Hedley	April 1913	May 1915	-
Joe Palmer	Aug 1919	Dec 1921	6
Alex Raisbeck	Dec 1921	June 1929	28
Joe Bradshaw	Aug 1929	Feb 1932	-
Bob Hewison	March 1932	March 1949	8
Bob Wright	April 1949	June 1950	-
Pat Beasley	July 1950	Jan 1958	14
Peter Doherty	Jan 1958	March 1960	-
Fred Ford	July 1960	Sept 1967	8
Alan Dicks	Oct 1967	Sept 1980	16
Bob Houghton	Oct 1980	Jan 1982	-
Roy Hodgson	Jan 1982	April 1982	-
Terry Cooper	May 1982	March 1988	6
Joe Jordan	March 1988	Sept 1990	14
Jimmy Lumsden	Sept 1990	Feb 1992	-
Denis Smith	March 1992	Feb 1993	-
Russell Osman	March 1993	-	-

Bristol Rovers

In 66 League seasons, covering 21 managers, Rovers have played in only the Second and Third Divisions, promoted and relegated three times. Each manager has had, on average, 3.1 seasons to improve on this meagre haul, although in the 21 years since 1972, each of 11 managers has been allowed only about 22 months. Had it not been for Bert Tann's 18 years to 1968, the average would have been much lower. He was at Eastville three times longer than the man in second place in the durability table. Although Brough Fletcher was with the Pirates almost 12 years, seven were lost to the World War Two. In terms of League campaigns, therefore, the quaintly named Captain Albert Prince-Cox (who previously had spells in the theatre, the RFC, as a meteorologist, a League referee and boxing administrator) came closest to Tann with six seasons. Those who were still relative newcomers to Bristol when they left were far more numerous, a list headed by Martin Dobson (three months), Harold Jarman (three months), Ben Hall (ten months), Percy Smith (12 months), Dennis Rofe (13 months) and David McLean (17 months).

Jarman is one of only three Rovers managers who previously were established players at the club: David Williams and Bill Dodgin were the others. Terry Cooper, Bobby Gould and Don Megson were Rovers player-coaches prior to becoming managers, whilst Gerry Francis' appearances were to help recovery from long-term injury. Bobby Campbell and Fred Ford had been trainer and coach. It has been difficult for the Pirates to attract experienced managers. Only six had managed other League clubs: Joe Palmer, Percy Smith (with Spurs in Division One), Fletcher, Ford, Dodgin (with Fulham in Division One and Sampdoria in Italy) and Gould. (Perhaps the most illustrious creditials were those of Malcolm Allison, a consultant for four months in 1992-93, and not included on the table.)

Fletcher was one of four Rovers managers (along with Andrew Wilson, McLean and Megson) previously with Sheffield Wednesday. Tann, Ford and Dodgin, who were in control continuously from 1950 to 1972, were teammates at Charlton in the 1930s. Francis left Rovers for First Division QPR and Gould for Wimbledon and an FA Cup victory, the most successful of Rovers' former managers.

Manager	Start/Date	End/Date	Pts/Total
Ben Hall	July 1920	May 1921	-
Andrew Wilson	June 1921	May 1926	-
Joe Palmer	May 1926	May 1929	-
David McLean	May 1929	Oct 1930	-
Capt Albert Prince-Cox	Nov 1930	Oct 1936	-
Percy Smith	Nov 1936	Nov 1937	-
Brough Fletcher	Jan 1938	Dec 1949	-
Bert Tann	Jan 1950	April 1968	14
Fred Ford	April 1968	Aug 1969	-
Bill Dodgin (snr)	Aug 1969	July 1972	-
Don Megson	July 1972	Nov 1977	8
Bobby Campbell	Nov 1977	Dec 1979	-
Harold Jarman	Jan 1980	April 1980	-
Terry Cooper	April 1980	Oct 1981	-
Bobby Gould	Oct 1981	May 1983	-
David Williams	May 1983	May 1985	-
Bobby Gould	May 1985	July 1987	-
Gerry Francis	July 1987	May 1991	14
Martin Dobson	July 1991	Oct 1991	-
Dennis Rofe	Oct 1991	Nov 1992	-
John Ward	March 1993	-	-

Burnley

When Jimmy Mullen led Burnley out of the Fourth Division wilderness in 1992, they became only the second club (after Wolves) to win all four divisions of the League. Founder members in 1888, the Clarets first appointed a manager after their fifth season, since when they have tried 25 in 89 seasons. Although the mortality rate is a moderate 3.6 seasons, it has accelerated over time. In the period up to 1939, each Burnley manager lasted over five years, but since 1976, job expectancy has dropped to 1.5 years.

For much of their early history, Burnley had a preference for professional administrators. Tom Bromilow, the seventh job holder in 1932, was the first to have played League football, whilst Alan Brown more than 20 years later, was the first former Burnley player to manage the Clarets. Since then, however, six of the 11 managers (Billy Dougall, Harry Potts, Jimmy Adamson, Joe Brown, Brian Miller and Frank Casper) were ex-Burnley players, and of the five who were not former players, four (John Bond, John Benson, Martin Buchan and Tommy Cavanagh) were amongst the shortest serving, none lasting much more than a year. Dougall in the 1950s and Joe Brown in the 1970s were the other members of the short-stay group.

The Clarets' most successful manager, John Haworth, was also one of the longest serving. Amongst a handful of managers who won both the Division One title and the FA Cup, only his death in 1924 prevented him adding to his 14-year stay (ten League seasons) at Turf Moor. Potts was the other championship winner at Burnley, his two terms of 12 and two years making him the most durable of Clarets managers. Amongst the early managers were two football's pioneers, Harry Bradshaw and Ernest Mangnall, who went on to lay the foundations for later glories at Arsenal and Manchester United respectively. Cliff Britton, in his first managerial job after a distinguished playing career, achieved a special double at Turf Moor, FA Cup finalists and Second Division promotion in the same season. Finally, Brian Miller carved a niche for himself in Burnley history. He was a player in Potts' Division One championship side in 1959-60, coach when Adamson took the Second Division title in 1972-73, manager of the Third Division winning line-up in 1981-82, and a chief scout under Mullen in 1991-92, when the Fourth Division title was won. Thus, he was associated with winning all four divisions at the same club, in different capacities and in reverse order of status.

Manager	Start/Date	End/Date	Pts/Total
Arthur Sutcliffe	1893	1896	
Harry Bradshaw	1896	1899	16
Ernest Mangnall	Jan 1900	Sept 1903	-
Spen Whittaker	Sep 1903	April 1910	-
John Haworth	July 1910	Dec 1924	70
Albert Pickles	Jan 1925	Sep 1932	-
Tom Bromilow	Oct 1932	July 1935	6
Alf Boland	Aug 1935	1940	-
Cliff Britton	Oct 1945	Sep 1948	22
Frank Hill	Sep 1948	Aug 1954	-
Alan Brown	Aug 1954	July 1957	-
Billy Dougall	July 1957	Feb 1958	-
Harry Potts	Feb 1958	Feb 1970	60
Jimmy Adamson	Feb 1970	Jan 1976	22
Joe Brown	Jan 1976	Feb 1977	-
Harry Potts	Feb 1977	Oct 1979	-
Brian Miller	Oct 1979	Jan 1983	14
Frank Casper‡	Jan 1983	June 1983	6
John Bond	June 1983	Aug 1984	-
John Benson	Aug 1984	May 1985	-
Martin Buchan	June 1985	Oct 1985	-
Tommy Cavanagh‡	Oct 1985	June 1986	-
Brian Miller	June 1986	Jan 1989	-
Frank Casper	Jan 1989	Oct 1991	-
Jimmy Mullen	Oct 1991	-	12

‡Technically, they were both caretakers, but over an extended period.

Bury

Amongst the pioneers of professional football in the late 19th century, Bury have competed in 87 of the League's 94 seasons. They had won the FA Cup twice and promotion to Division One before the first manager arrived at Gigg Lane in 1907. Altogether, the Shakers have tried 26 managers in the last 75 seasons, an average life span of 2.9 seasons per manager. From a cursory glance at the table, it is apparent that the rate of turnover has accelerated sharply in modern times. Up to 1965, there was a change every 4.3 seasons, but since then, it has dropped to 1.7 seasons.

Not surprisingly, the last quarter of a century is littered with managerial casualties who were out of office almost before they had time to reorganise the filing system. Jack Marshall, Colin McDonald, Dave Hatton and David Connor, all post-1968 appointees, came and went in less than a year, whilst Bert Head, Les Hart, Tom McAnearney, Allan Brown and Sam Ellis were at Gigg Lane for between 12 and 24 months. There are few serious challengers to Archie Montgomery's eight-year reign as the Shakers' longest-serving manager. He was the first job holder, and only Norman Bullock (two terms amounting to seven years) and Dave Russell (just eight years) subsequently came within touching distance.

An unusually high proportion (two thirds) had been with Bury in some capacity before being promoted to the manager's office. Most (Montgomery, William Cameron, James Thompson, Bullock, Bob Stokoe, Head, Hart, Hatton and Mike Walsh) were former players, whilst Russell, Marshall, Bobby Smith and Connor were coaches, McDonald was a scout and administrator, Arthur Paine was the secretary and Charlie Dean chairman. Of the other eight, all but two (Les Shannon and Martin Dobson) went to Gigg Lane with some management experience to offer, and 14 of the 23 former managers had yet further opportunities when their time at Gigg Lane ended.

The most notable progress was made by Percy Smith, who went to Spurs, Bullock, who guided Leicester to promotion, Stokoe was an FA Cup winner at Sunderland, whilst Shannon (Blackpool) and Head (Palace) both took their new clubs into Division One. The most ignominious exit from Gigg Lane was by Cameron in 1923. He was suspended for

his part in a match-fixing scandal in a game against Coventry three years earlier. The ban was, however, later lifted and Smith made a comeback with Rochdale.

Manager	Start/Date	End/Date	Pts/Total
Archie Montgomery	Feb 1907	April 1915	-
William Cameron	May 1919	May 1923	-
James Thompson	May 1923	Feb 1927	10
Percy Smith	May 1927	Jan 1930	-
Arthur Paine	Jan 1930	May 1934	-
Norman Bullock	June 1934	June 1938	-
Charlie Dean	June 1938	March 1944	-
Norman Bullock	July 1945	Nov 1949	-
John McNeil	March 1950	Nov 1953	-
Dave Russell	Nov 1953	Dec 1961	14
Bob Stokoe	Dec 1961	Aug 1965	6
Bert Head	Aug 1965	April 1966	-
Les Shannon	July 1966	May 1969	8
Jack Marshall	May 1969	Sept 1969	-
Les Hart	Sept 1969	Sept 1970	-
Colin McDonald	Sept 1970	Nov 1970	-
Tom McAnearney	Nov 1970	May 1972	-
Allan Brown	April 1972	Nov 1973	-
Bobby Smith	Nov 1973	Oct 1977	6
Bob Stokoe	Nov 1977	May 1978	-
Dave Hatton	May 1978	Oct 1979	-
David Connor	Nov 1979	June 1980	-
Jim Iley	July 1980	Feb 1984	-
Martin Dobson	March 1984	March 1989	6
Sam Ellis	April 1989	Dec 1990	-
Mike Walsh	Dec 1990	-	-

Cambridge United

Although they have competed in three divisions, and had eight changes of status, Cambridge are still amongst the League's 'new boys'. United have now had 23 seasons as League members, during which they have had eight managers. A turnover rate of one new manager every 34 months shows Cambridge quickly acquired the habit of many longer-established League clubs. John Docherty, who was at the Abbey Stadium for virtually six years, is the only one to have outperformed the average to any significant extent. At the other end of the spectrum are John Ryan and Ken Shellito, who between them cover the two calender years of 1984 and 1985, the most difficult period in United's League history.

When Ian Atkins was appointed to the job in December 1992, his background was typical of most of his predecessors. Like Ron Atkinson, John Ryan, Chris Turner and John Beck, he had no previous League management experience, and, in common with all the other seven apart from Turner and Beck, he had no prior connection with Cambridge. Both of these were former players, Turner returning to the Abbey after finishing his career elsewhere, Beck being upgraded from the staff at the time.

It was Beck who revitalised United's playing fortunes, lifting them from the Fourth Division to the verge of the FA Premier League in a little under three seasons. They also got to the quarter finals of the

FA Cup in consecutive seasons playing a style of football that made Wimbledon look sophisticated. Beck's management philosophy, which owes much to the SAS, was undoubtedly effective if short on aesthetics. His predecessor, Turner, resigned in 1990, but returned to management with Peterborough, and had the strange experience of seeing his new and his old club promoted from the same division in the same season. Ron Atkinson and John Docherty are two other Cambridge graduates who made good elsewhere, Atkinson with four top flight clubs and Docherty with Millwall, taking the Lions into the League's highest division for the first time in their history.

Manager	Start/Date	End/Date	Pts/Total
Bill Leivers	Dec 1967	Oct 1974	6
Ron Atkinson	Nov 1974	Jan 1978	12
John Docherty	Jan 1978	Dec 1983	8
John Ryan	Jan 1984	Jan 1985	-
Ken Shellito	March 1985	Dec 1985	-
Chris Turner	Jan 1986	Jan 1990	-
John Beck	Jan 1990	Oct 1992	20
Ian Atkins	Dec 1992	-	-

Cardiff City

Although it is over 30 years since they last played in the top flight, Cardiff City have been the most successful of the six clubs from Wales that have competed in the Football League. Winners of the FA Cup in 1927, the Bluebirds lost in another Final and were one penalty-kick away from the League championship in 1924. In their 66 seasons, Cardiff have had 20 managers, one every 3.3 seasons. Up to 1973, the turnover rate was much lower, but as financial problems started to emerge (as they did for Swansea and Newport), the pace of managerial change accelerated. In the 20 years since then, each of the 11 job holders has stayed on average just 22 months.

It was the club's first manager, Fred Stewart, who set the standards for longevity and success, and none of his successors has been able to match his record. He had 22 years in office, 13 of them in the Football League. Only Jimmy Scoular on 9.5 years came close to matching Stewart's contribution, with Cyril Spiers on six years a poor third. For Graham Williams, Frank O'Farrell and Jimmy Goodfellow, Ninian Park proved a very temporary home, none lasting more than six months, whilst Bartley Wilson was in and out of the manager's office inside nine months.

Only two of the 19 individuals who have managed the Bluebirds (Len Ashurst had two spells) once played for the club, Ritchie Morgan (who was also involved on the commercial side) and Alan Durban. Wilson and Trevor Morris were initially administrators at Ninian Park, whilst Bill Jennings, Bill Jones, Jimmy Andrews and Goodfellow were all promoted after serving as coaches or assistants. Most of the rest offered managerial experience rather than Cardiff connections: the exceptions were Spiers and Williams, who were new to both Ninian Park and management at the time of their appointment. This previous experience was largely managerial (although Ben Watts-Jones was a former Swansea chairman) and generally in the lower divisions, with George Swindin (Arsenal), O'Farrell (Manchester United), Ashurst (Sunderland) and Durban (Stoke) the four with a pre-Cardiff First Division pedigree.

There was little that any of the Bluebirds' managers achieved after leaving Ninian. McCandless went on to complete a hat-trick of Third Division titles with three clubs from South Wales, Morris was to become secretary to the Welsh FA and, after his first spell with Cardiff, Ashurst took Sunderland to the League Cup Final at Wembley. For most of the rest, Ninian was the end of the League road.

Manager	Start/Date	End/Date	Pts/Total
Fred Stewart	May 1911	May 1933	58
Bartley Wilson	May 1933	Feb 1934	-
Ben-Watts Jones	Feb 1934	April 1937	-
Bill Jennings	April 1937	April 1939	-
Billy McCandless	June 1946	Nov 1947	14
Cyril Spiers	April 1948	April 1954	10
Trevor Morris	April 1954	Aug 1958	-
Bill Jones	Sept 1958	Sept 1962	10
George Swindin	Oct 1962	April 1964	-
Jimmy Scoular	June 1964	Nov 1973	12
Frank O'Farrell	Nov 1973	April 1974	-
Jimmy Andrews	May 1974	Nov 1978	8
Ritchie Morgan	Nov 1978	Nov 1981	-
Graham Williams	Nov 1981	Feb 1982	-
Len Ashurst	March 1982	March 1984	8
Jimmy Goodfellow	March 1984	Sept 1984	-
Alan Durban	Sept 1984	May 1986	-
Frank Burrows	May 1986	Aug 1989	6
Len Ashurst	Sept 1989	May 1991	-
Eddie May	July 1991	-	12

Carlisle United

For 58 seasons, England's most northerly club has survived on small gates and limited funds. Although they have competed in all four divisions of the League (and done so in the last 20 years), Carlisle have won just one divisional title and never played in a major cup final. Incumbent David McCreery is the 24th manager to try his luck at Brunton Park since they were elected to the League in 1928, although for five seasons United had no manager. In these years, responsibility was shouldered by secretary Bill Clarke, helped by trainer Tom Curry, who was later to serve Manchester United in a similar capacity. On average, therefore, Carlisle managers have lasted about four months more than two years.

Unusually, the longest serving managers are relatively recent job holders, Bob Stokoe and Alan Ashman, with seven and eight years respectively. In both cases, however, it was the aggregate of at least two terms, with longest unbroken spell being Fred Emery's seven years in the 1950s. This was longer than the combined stays of David Taylor, Tim Ward, Dick Young, Martin Harvey and Bryan 'Pop' Robson, all of whom were in and out in less than a season. Bob Kelly, Fred Westgarth and Harry Gregg did not fare much better, hanging on for around 18 months.

The first former United player to manage the club was Bill Shankly in 1949, and of his successors, only Ashman, Robson and McCreery followed a similar path: Young was an internal appointment from the coaching staff. A rather more common route to the manager's office at Brunton Park was via managing another League club, the approach taken by Westgarth, Emery, Ivor Powell, Ward, Stokoe and Gregg, whilst Taylor had previously been in charge at Scottish club St Johnstone.

A spell at Brunton Park stood some of the club's managers in good stead. Between their first and second terms with Carlisle, both Ashman (West Brom) and Stokoe (Sunderland) were to be FA Cup winners, whilst Shankly's post-Cumbrian career is one of the most illustrious of modern times. His old Preston team-mate, Andy Beattie, had a lengthy but more varied subsequent career which included a period as Scotland's team manager, whilst the club's first manager, Billy Hampson, was later in charge at Elland Road for 12 years.

Manager	Start/Date	End/Date	Pts/Total
Billy Hampson	March 1930	May 1932	-
Robert Kelly	March 1935	Nov 1936	-
Fred Westgarth	Dec 1936	March 1938	-
David Taylor	April 1938	Sept 1939	-
Ivor Broadis	Aug 1946	Jan 1949	-
Bill Shankly	March 1949	July 1951	-
Fred Emery	July 1951	April 1958	-
Andy Beattie	May 1958	March 1960	-
Ivor Powell	May 1960	Feb 1963	6
Alan Ashman	Feb 1963	June 1967	20
Tim Ward	Sept 1967	Sept 1968	-
Bob Stokoe	Oct 1968	Jan 1970	6
Ian McFarlane	Jan 1970	July 1972	-
Alan Ashman	Aug 1972	Oct 1975	10
Dick Young	Nov 1975	Nov 1976	-
Bobby Moncur	Nov 1976	Feb 1980	-
Martin Harvey	Feb 1980	Sept 1980	-
Bob Stokoe	Sept 1980	Aug 1985	8
Bryan Robson	Aug 1985	Oct 1985	-
Bob Stokoe	Oct 1985	May 1986	-
Harry Gregg	May 1986	Nov 1987	-
Clive Middlemass	Nov 1987	March 1991	-
Aiden McCaffrey	April 1991	Sept 1992	-
David McCreery	Sept 1992	-	-

Charlton Athletic

Since joining the League in 1921, Charlton have made 17 managerial appointments, which involve 16 individuals: two men, Alex McFarlane and Albert Lindon had two spells, and since the 1991 close season, the team duties have been shared between two individuals, Alan Curbishley and Steve Gritt.

Although on average each Charlton manager has lasted 3.8 seasons, four men account for almost 60% of the clubs 65 seasons in the Football League. Lennie Lawrence (nine seasons), McFarlane (a total of six seasons in two terms) and Andy Nelson (six seasons) all held the job longer than the average, but none could match Jimmy Seed's remarkable record. He was at the Valley from 1933 to 1956, seven of which years were accounted for by World War Two. Seed was also the Valiants' most successful manager, leading them from the Third Division to runners-up spot in Division One in consecutive seasons and to two FA Cup Finals in twelve months. Others were less fortunate. Ken Craggs, for example, survived just six months, Lindon's two spells amounted to a little under a year, about the length of time Mike Bailey and Alan Mullery were given in the job.

Some famous names are amongst the list of Charlton managers, including six international players, although none was capped whilst at the Valley. Only six of 16 individuals who have managed the club (Lindon, Eddie Firmani, Theo Foley, Bailey, Gritt and Curbishley) were former Valiants players, whilst Jimmy Trotter was Seed's assistant before replacing him, as was Craggs with Mullery. Most arrived at the Valley with some managerial experience under their belts, the exceptions being Walter Raynor, Trotter, Firmani, Foley and Craggs.

Just under half of Charlton's 14 former managers moved on to other League clubs after leaving the Valley, including McFarlane, Seed, Foley, Bailey and Mullery. The two who enjoyed the most success, however, were Bob Stokoe, an FA Cup winner with Sunderland in 1973, and Lawrence, who took Middlesbrough into the Premier League in 1992.

Manager	Start/Date	End/Date	Pts/Total
Walter Raynor	June 1920	May 1925	-
Alex McFarlane	May 1925	Jan 1928	-
Albert Lindon	Jan 1928	May 1928	-
Alex McFarlane	May 1928	Dec 1932	14
Albert Lindon	Dec 1932	May 1933	-
Jimmy Seed	May 1933	Sept 1956	66
Jimmy Trotter	Sept 1956	Oct 1961	-
Frank Hill	Nov 1961	Aug 1965	-
Bob Stokoe	Aug 1965	Sept 1967	-
Eddie Firmani	Sept 1967	March 1970	-
Theo Foley	March 1970	April 1974	-
Andy Nelson	May 1974	March 1980	8
Mike Bailey	March 1980	June 1981	8
Alan Mullery	July 1981	June 1982	-
Ken Craggs	June 1982	Nov 1982	-
Lennie Lawrence	Nov 1982	July 1991	10
Alan Curbishley/Steve Gritt	July 1991	-	-

Chelsea

The longest serving manager in Chelsea's history was their second boss, David Calderhead. Arriving in the 1907 close season, after promotion to the First Division had been won (without a manager), he stayed at Stamford Bridge until his retirement 26 years later. It was a record for longevity which none of his successors could challenge, although until Dave Sexton's departure in the autumn of 1974, the Chelsea job seemed one of the safest in football. In their first 58 seasons in the League, the Blues used only seven managers. In the 19 seasons which followed, however, the pace of change accelerated, with Ian Porterfield the ninth job holder since Sexton left.

True to their image, Chelsea's choice has often been unpredictable, and occasionally eccentric (such as Danny Blanchflower, out of football for 15 years and working as a journalist). The early selections betrayed a bias in favour of managerial experience, after which the pendulum swung towards previous Chelsea connections. From Tommy Docherty through to Bobby Campbell, only Danny Blanchflower and John Neal had no prior experience at the Bridge. Coaching rather than playing was the route to the top at Chelsea, and it should be noted that the club's first manager, John Tait Robertson in 1905 was, very untypically for the period, a player-manager.

It was at Stamford Bridge that Docherty began his turbulent career in management, and he started as he meant to continue, once sending a number of players home following a breach of club discipline before a match. As he was to do again later at Old Trafford, Docherty gave youth its chance at Chelsea, benefiting from his predecessor's policy. When Ted Drake took the Blues to the League Championship in 1955, he became the first man to play for and then manage a title-winning team. Docherty's successor was his former assistant, Dave Sexton, who returned to the Bridge after a spell as coach at Highbury. Coincidently, Sexton was to go to Queen's Park Rangers after Chelsea, as Docherty did, and was the Doc's successor at Old Trafford in 1977.

Chelsea fans have to go back over 20 years to the last time their club won a major honour. Too often, the potential has failed to be realised but in view of the financial burdens that have constrained managers from Sexton onwards, and the uncertainty over the ground, many supporters are grateful they are still there at all.

Manager	Start/Date	End/Date	Pts/Total
John Tait Robertson	April 1905	Oct 1906	-
David Calderhead (snr)	Aug 1907	June 1933	50
Leslie Knighton	Aug 1933	April 1939	-
Billy Birrell	May 1939	May 1952	12
Ted Drake	June 1952	Sept 1961	18
Tommy Docherty	Oct 1961	Oct 1967	58
Dave Sexton	Oct 1967	Oct 1974	54
Ron Suart	Oct 1974	April 1975	-
Eddie McCreadie	April 1975	July 1977	10
Ken Shellito	July 1977	Dec 1978	-
Danny Blanchflower	Dec 1978	Sept 1979	-
Geoff Hurst	Sept 1979	April 1981	-
John Neal	May 1981	June 1985	22
John Hollins	June 1985	March 1988	-
Bobby Campbell	March 1988	May 1991	22
Ian Porterfield	June 1991	Feb 1993	-

Chester City

For most of their 55 seasons in the League, Chester have struggled in the basement area. The Seals' have never played outside the Third and Fourth Division, and a single Cup run, to the semi-final of the League Cup, is the sole moment of national attention. Yet for all the lack of success, the club has had just 15 managers since joining the League in 1931, which implies each manager has been given a little over three and a half years in the job. This average would have been even higher but for a particularly fraught period in the early 1980s when there were three managers in three years at Sealand Road.

The longest serving Chester manager is Frank Brown, although his 15 year tenure spanned the years of World War Two, which reduced his League duty for the Seals to eight seasons. This puts him on a par with Ken Roberts in the 1970s. All of the shortest serving were in the 1980s. Cliff Sear (six months), John Sainty (13 months) and John McGrath (16 months), who followed each other into the job, head the list.

When appointing a manager, the Chester board has tried all types of background, with an equal lack of success. There have been former Seals' players (Stan Pearson, Alan Oakes and Sear), club coaches promoted to manager (Sear and Sainty) and those with some managerial experience gained at other League clubs, such as Charlie Hewitt (Wrexham), Alex Raisbeck (Bristol City and Halifax), Brown (Torquay), Bill Lambton (Leeds), McGrath (Port Vale) and Harry McNally (Wigan). The magic formula eluded them all at Sealand Road, although Hewitt, who took Millwall to the FA Cup semi-final and the Third Division South championship, John Harris, later a long-time manager of Sheffield United, and McGrath,

a promotion winner at Preston, all enjoyed a measure of success in their post-Chester careers.

Success is, however, all relative, and Hewitt's achievement in steering the Seals into the top four of the Third Division North four times in five seasons makes him the club's most successful League manager. His only serious challenger is Ken Roberts, who took Chester to promotion from Division Four and the League Cup semi-final in the same season, where they lost to Aston Villa.

Manager	Start/Date	End/Date	Pts/Total
Charlie Hewitt	1930	April 1936	8
Alex Raisbeck	May 1936	April 1938	-
Frank Brown	May 1938	May 1953	-
Louis Page	June 1953	June 1956	-
John Harris	July 1956	April 1959	-
Stan Pearson	April 1959	Nov 1961	-
Bill Lambton	Nov 1961	July 1963	-
Peter Hauser	Aug 1963	March 1968	-
Ken Roberts	March 1968	Sept 1976	12
Alan Oakes	Sept 1976	March 1982	-
Cliff Sear	June 1982	Nov 1982	-
John Sainty	Nov 1982	Dec 1983	-
John McGrath	Jan 1984	May 1985	-
Harry McNally	June 1985	Oct 1992	6
Graham Barrow	Oct 1992	-	-

Chesterfield

The Spireites have had 75 seasons of League football since 1899, with an eight-year intermission from 1909. They are currently on their 20th manager but since the first job holder, Harry Hadley, did not get on board until the Third North days in the 1920s, they have been spread across only 64 seasons. This works out at an average managerial term of 3.2 seasons. A cursory glance down the Spireites managerial table reveals that no one individual dominates in terms of length of service and that most were given at least two years in the job. The exceptions were the early appointments of Hadley and Alec Campbell, both out in under a year, and Kevin Randall's 15 months in the 1980s. Teddy Davison was at Saltergate for over ten seasons as manager, the longest of all, but this was split between two terms 20 years apart. When he returned in 1952, he was 64 and ending a career in football that covered most of the first half of the 20th century.

Not until Frank Barlow was given the job in 1980 was anyone who had a previous connection with Chesterfield offered the opportunity to manage the club (apart from Davison's return). Only Randall and Chris McMenemy since then also fell into this category (apart from Duncans return!). More important has been some evidence of managerial experience, which, up to the time of Barlow's appointment, most of the 13 offered (the exceptions were Campbell, Bob Brocklebank and Arthur Cox).

A spell at Saltergate has not harmed the longer-term career prospects of a number of the club's managers. Davison left for a long stay at Sheffield United (where Dug Livingstone, his successor at Chesterfield in 1958, was coach) which included a Cup Final appearance, Cox later took Newcastle and Derby into the First Division, and John Duncan found his way to Ipswich and back. Brocklebank and Norman Bullock also had

many years ahead of them in management after their tenure at Chesterfield ended. When the Fourth Division title was won by the Spireites in 1970, it was under Jimmy McGuigan, a manager who spent most of his working life in the lower divisions, winning promotion from Division Four three times with three different clubs.

Manager	Start/Date	End/Date	Pts/Total
Harry Hadley	April 1922	Aug 1922	-
Harry Parkes	Aug 1922	April 1927	-
Alec Campbell	April 1927	Dec 1927	-
Teddy Davison	Dec 1927	June 1932	14
Bill Harvey	June 1932	June 1938	22
Norman Bullock	June 1938	July 1945	-
Bob Brocklebank	Sept 1945	Jan 1949	-
Bob Marshall	Feb 1949	July 1952	-
Teddy Davison	Aug 1952	May 1958	-
Dug Livingstone	May 1958	May 1962	-
Tony McShane	May 1962	May 1967	-
Jimmy McGuigan	July 1967	May 1973	12
Joe Shaw	Sept 1973	Oct 1976	-
Arthur Cox	Oct 1976	Sept 1980	-
Frank Barlow	Sept 1980	June 1983	-
John Duncan	June 1983	June 1987	12
Kevin Randall	June 1987	Oct 1988	-
Paul Hart	Nov 1988	Jan 1991	-
Chris McMenemy	April 1991	Feb 1993	-
John Duncan	Feb 1993	-	-

Colchester United

One of the first clubs to be elected to the Football League after World War Two, Colchester became one of the first to drop out when relegation to the GM Vauxhall Conference League became the penalty for finishing bottom of Division Four. They returned after a two year interval, winning automatic promotion, which means there have been 41 seasons of League football at Layer Road. The Us have needed 14 managers to guide them in this period, giving each a little under three seasons to ply their trade. Allan Hunter, Roger Brown, Jock Wallace and Mick Mills all had less than a year, however, but Benny Fenton (whose brother Ted had managed the Us in their Southern League days) and Bobby Roberts had the best part of nine and seven years respectively.

Inexperience of both League management and Colchester are the most striking characteristics of the club's 14 managers. Roberts and Mike Walker were the only two who had been at Layer Road in any capacity prior to their appointments as manager, whilst just Jack Butler (Torquay and Palace), Dick Graham (Palace), Wallace (Leicester) and Mills (Stoke) knew what was involved at first hand in running a League club.

Sadly, most of the careers ended at Layer Road. Benny Fenton (Orient and Millwall) and Bobby Roberts (Wrexham and Grimsby) were obvious exceptions. So also was Jim Smith. When his undistinguished playing career ended at Lincoln in 1968, he tried non-League management at Boston, before breaking into the League with Colchester. Subsequently, Smith managed six other League clubs, and his 20 years is one of the longest unbroken periods of managerial employment in modern football. Mike Walker was sacked the week he won the divisional manager of the

month award, but his record at Norwich since then has dispelled any doubts about his ability.

Smith was one of only four Colchester managers to win anything, and in each case it was promotion from Division Four. As well as promotion, Smith had to endure the humiliation of re-election, whilst all the other three promotion winners, Fenton, Neil Franklin and Roberts had to cope with relegation first.

Manager	Start/Date	End/Date	Pts/Total
Jimmy Allen	July 1948	April 1953	-
Jack Butler	June 1953	Jan 1955	-
Benny Fenton	Feb 1955	Oct 1963	6
Neil Franklin	Nov 1963	May 1968	6
Dick Graham	July 1968	Sept 1972	-
Jim Smith	Oct 1972	June 1975	6
Bobby Roberts	June 1975	April 1982	6
Allan Hunter	May 1982	Jan 1983	-
Cyril Lea	Feb 1983	April 1986	-
Mike Walker	April 1986	Nov 1987	-
Roger Brown	Nov 1987	Oct 1988	-
Jock Wallace	Jan 1989	Dec 1989	-
Mick Mills	Jan 1990	May 1990	-
Ian Atkins (Non-League)	June 1990	June 1991	-
Roy McDonough	July 1991	-	-

Coventry City

Although winning few honours, Coventry claim two League records: the first club to play in all seven divisions and the club which has spent longest in Division One without being relegated. They needed 26 managers to achieve all this, spread over 67 seasons, each staying an average 2.6 seasons. The most fraught period was the 15 seasons after the war until Jimmy Hill's arrival in 1961. Coventry tried nine managers in this time, giving each on average 20 months. The tempo quickened again after Gordon Milne's departure in 1981, since when eight managers lasted on average 18 months each.

Harry Storer is Coventry's longest serving manager, his two terms totalling 13 seasons. He also spent six of the seven World War Two years at Highfield Road, and his is the only tenure which exceeds ten years. The combined service of the next two, Milne (nine years) and Hill (six) was less than Storer's total. At the other end of the spectrum, Jesse Carver and George Raynor, both highly regarded coaches in Europe, between them lasted only 12 months at Coventry. Neither Dick Bayliss nor Jack Fairbrother managed to complete a year of League football in the job, and by the time Coventry began their second League season, they were on their third manager, having disposed with the services of William Clayton and Harry Pollitt. There are, amongst the 23 Coventry managers (Storer, Billy Frith and Bobby Gould all had two terms), former Sky Blues in James McIntyre, Frith, Charlie Elliott, John Sillett, George Curtis and Gould, whilst Bayliss and Don Howe stepped up from coaching. Only a handful had previous managerial experience. Dave Sexton, Howe and Gould managed at the highest level with some success in their pre-Coventry days, whilst McIntyre and Sillett made their marks in the lower divisions, as had Raynor and Carver in Europe. The fortunes of the 23 varied after leaving Coventry. Raynor took Sweden to the World Cup Final, Hill went into TV and Elliott became a Test cricket umpire. Some others stayed in football, usually managing lower division sides, with McIntyre (Fulham), Storer (Derby) and Milne (Leicester) most successful. For Pollitt, implicated in a notorious bribery scandal of 1920 involving Bury and Coventry, there was only suspension. Bayliss died 18 months into the job after a long illness.

Manager	Start/Date	End/Date	Pts/Total
William Clayton	Jan 1919	Oct 1919	-
Harry Pollitt	Nov 1919	May 1920	-
Albert Evans	June 1920	Nov 1924	-
James Kerr	July 1925	Feb 1928	-
James McIntyre	June 1928	Feb 1931	-
Harry Storer	June 1931	June 1945	22
Dick Bayliss	June 1945	Feb 1947	-
Billy Frith	Feb 1947	Nov 1948	-
Harry Storer	Nov 1948	Dec 1953	-
Jack Fairbrother	Dec 1953	Oct 1954	-
Charlie Elliott	Oct 1954	April 1955	-
Jesse Carver	June 1955	Dec 1955	-
George Raynor	Jan 1956	June 1956	-
Harry Warren	June 1956	Sept 1957	-
Billy Frith	Sept 1957	Nov 1961	6
Jimmy Hill	Nov 1961	Sept 1967	30
Noel Cantwell	Oct 1967	March 1972	-
Gordon Milne	June 1972	May 1981	6
Dave Sexton	May 1981	May 1983	-
Bobby Gould	May 1983	Dec 1984	-
Don Mackay	Dec 1984	April 1986	-
George Curtis	April 1986	May 1987	18
John Sillett	May 1987	Nov 1990	6
Terry Butcher	Nov 1990	Jan 1992	-
Don Howe	Jan 1992	July 1992	-
Bobby Gould	July 1992	-	-

Crewe Alexandra

Amongst the smallest of small clubs, Crewe were ever-present members of the Third Division North, since when they have played only four seasons outside Division Four. Re-election (ten times) has been more common than promotion (three). The Railwaymen have spent 69 seasons in the League, the first manager coming in the ninth season. The 18 managers therefore cover 61 seasons, an average stay at Gresty Road of just under 3.5 seasons. Over 35 per cent of Crewe's League career has been spent under just two managers, the first and then the current job holder. Tom Bailey, whose links with the club went back to 1906, was manager from 1925 for 13 years. Incumbent Dario Gradi was appointed in June 1983 and is within sight of Bailey's record. There have also been some very short tenures, notably Dennis Viollet (four months), Peter Morris (seven months) and Arfon Griffiths (14 months).

Inside knowledge has been a help in getting the job. Almost half played for the Railwaymen (Ralph Ward, Jimmy McGuigan, Ernie Tagg, Jimmy Melia, Warwick Rimmer and Tony Waddington) or like Bailey (secretary) and Viollet (coach) were already on the staff. Melia, in 1972, was the first to arrive at Crewe with previous managerial experience, since when it has been almost obligatory. Harry Gregg, Waddington, Griffiths, Morris and Gradi learned something of their trade at other League clubs. Amongst Crewe managers are some famous names, whose records showed that the Railwaymen's lowly status belies the impact they have had on English football. Tony Waddington, for example, started his career playing with Crewe in 1945 and ended it as manager in 1981. In between, he had 17 years at Stoke, making them one of the most attractive sides in the country. Similarly, Harry Catterick cut his managerial teeth at Gresty Road before taking Everton to the heights in the 1960s. Arthur Turner (Birmingham and Oxford) and Frank Hill (Burnley, Preston, Charlton and Notts County) had long careers after getting a break at Crewe, whilst Maurice Lindley was an important part of Don Revie's Leeds staff in the 1960s. If anyone, however, deserves the title 'Mr Crewe', it is Ernie Tagg, a player in the 1930s and, after the war, assistant manager, manager, secretary and finally a director in the 1980s.

Manager	Start/Date	End/Date	Pts/Total
Tom Bailey	1925	1938	-
George Lillycrop	1938	July 1944	-
Frank Hill	July 1944	Sept 1948	-
Arthur Turner	Oct 1948	Dec 1951	-
Harry Catterick	Dec 1951	June 1953	-
Ralph Ward	June 1953	1955	-
Maurice Lindley	1955	1958	-
Harry Ware	1958	May 1960	-
Jimmy McGuigan	June 1960	Nov 1964	6
Ernie Tagg	Nov 1964	cs 1971	6
Dennis Viollet	cs 1971	Nov 1971	-
Jimmy Melia	May 1972	Dec 1974	-
Harry Gregg	Jan 1975	1978	-
Warwick Rimmer	1978	May 1979	-
Tony Waddington	June 1979	July 1981	-
Arfon Griffiths	Aug 1981	Oct 1982	-
Peter Morris	Nov 1982	June 1983	-
Dario Gradi	June 1983	-	6

Crystal Palace

Steve Coppell did much to correct the impression that managing Palace is one of the least secure jobs in football. Until his appointment in 1984, they had tried 24 managers in 57 seasons, averaging one per 2.7 seasons. The nine seasons Coppell spent at Selhurst Park made him Palace's longest serving manager in League football, although he had some way to go to match Edmund Goodman's total of 18 plus years (only five were in the Football League, though, the rest accounted for by the Southern League or World War One). He was, nevertheless, the first manager to win the Third Division championship. (Goodman's service did not stop with Alex Maley's appointment: he continued as secretary until 1933). The nearest challenger to Coppell is Bert Head, who was in charge for seven years from 1966. Short-term appointments have been more common. In the 1980s, neither Dario Gradi nor Steve Kember lasted more than a season, following the example set by Tom Bromilow and R.S.Moyes in the 1930s. An experiment with joint managers (Fred Dawes and Charlie Slade) foundered within 11 months, whilst Malcolm Allison on his return to Selhurst Park in 1980 stayed for only 13 months. The champion, however, is Dave Bassett, whose two days in the job before going back to Wimbledon is the shortest for any League club. It was not until George Irwin took over in 1939 that Palace appointed a former player as manager, although director R.S.Moyes held the reins briefly in 1936. Since 1945, internal promotions have continued to be the exception. Ronnie Rooke and Dick Graham returned as managers after spending the best parts of their playing careers elsewhere, Dawes, Kember and Terry Venables were all Palace players, then coaches before taking over as manager, and Slade became manager via coaching and scouting for Palace. The rest were outsiders, most of whom were experienced managers. Only Goodman, Laurie Scott, George Smith and Coppell were new to both Palace and management. Of the 12 who had managed other clubs, the most illustrious were Arthur Rowe (Spurs) and Allison (Manchester City), whilst for Bromilow (Leicester), Tresadern (Spurs) and Venables (QPR, Barcelona and Spurs), the Palace job led to bigger and better things. For Goodman, Moyes, Rooke, Dawes, Slade, Scott and Kember, however, this was their only stab at League management.

Manager	Start/Date	End/Date	Pts/Total
Edmund Goodman	April 1907	Nov 1925	14
Alex Maley	Nov 1925	Oct 1927	-
Fred Maven	Nov 1927	Oct 1930	8
Jack Tresadern	Oct 1930	June 1935	8
Tom Bromilow	July 1935	June 1936	-
R Moyes	July 1936	Dec 1936	-
Tom Bromilow	Dec 1936	July 1939	8
George Irwin	July 1939	May 1947	-
Jack Butler	May 1947	May 1949	-
Ronnie Rooke	June 1949	Nov 1950	-
Fred Dawes/Charlie Slade	Nov 1950	Oct 1951	-
Laurie Scott	Oct 1951	Oct 1954	-
Cyril Spiers	Oct 1954	June 1958	-
George Smith	July 1958	April 1960	-
Arthur Rowe	April 1960	Nov 1962	6
Dick Graham	March 1963	Jan 1966	8
Bert Head	April 1966	March 1973	10
Malcolm Allison	March 1973	May 1976	6
Terry Venables	June 1976	Oct 1980	24
Malcolm Allison	Dec 1980	Feb 1981	-
Dario Gradi	Feb 1981	Nov 1981	-
Steve Kember	Nov 1981	June 1982	-
Alan Mullery	June 1982	May 1984	-
Dave Bassett	May 1984	May 1984	-
Steve Coppell	June 1984	May 1993	18

Darlington

Along with Hartlepool and Gateshead, Darlington have been the poor relations of professional football in the North-East, two Second Division seasons in the 1920s the peak of their achievements and the fifth round the furthest they have progressed in the FA Cup. That precarious existence is reflected in the fact that in 64 seasons of League football there have been 27 managers at Feethams, implying a change every 2.4 seasons. Since 1966, however, life has been tougher still, for in those 26 seasons, there have been 16 job holders, each lasting about 20 months, one of the highest turnover rates of any club.

The Quakers' first manager, Jack English, was also the longest serving, spending nine years at Feethams, all but the first two in the Football League. He was followed by Jack Fairless' five-year stint, and since then, only Bob Gurney in the 1950s has come close to matching the early managers' record for durability. In the 1970s, on the other hand, Darlington managers were almost as numerous as supporters. Frank Brennan, Allan Jones and Ralph Brand were around for just a few months (as was Frank Gray in the 1990s), whilst Dick Connor, Billy Horner and Len Walker were at Feethams for about a year. Only seven of the 27 had earlier links with the club. Fairless and George Collins were once directors, Eddie Carr was both a player and trainer, Ray Yeoman a former player and Peter Madden, Walker and Gray were all promoted from the coaching staff. Fewer still (Jackie Carr, George Irwin, Dick Duckworth, Len Richley, Connor, Dave Booth and Billy McEwan) had any previous League management experience. The road to Darlington led nowhere for most of the club's former managers: Brian Little (Leicester) and Lol Morgan (Norwich) alone managed to step up a division or two after their spells with the Quakers. The influence of the North-East is apparent in the club's choice of manager. Jackie Carr, Gurney, Billy Horner and Cyril Knowles, for example, managed Hartlepools as well as Darlington, whilst Collins, Bill Forrest, Brennan, Brand, Billy Elliott, Gray, Yeoman, Knowles, Carr and Horner all played for one of the 'Big Three' in the region.

Manager	Start/Date	End/Date	Pts/Total
Jack English	1919	May 1928	22
Jack Fairless	cs 1928	cs 1933	-
George Collins	cs 1933	Oct 1936	-
George Brown	Oct 1936	Oct 1938	-
Jackie Carr	Oct 1938	May 1942	-
Bill Forrest	1946	April 1950	-
George Irwin	April 1950	March 1952	-
Bob Gurney	March 1952	Oct 1957	-
Dick Duckworth	Oct 1957	May 1960	-
Eddie Carr	June 1960	June 1964	-
Lol Morgan	July 1964	June 1966	6
Jimmy Greenhalgh	July 1966	Feb 1968	-
Ray Yeoman	March 1968	cs 1970	-
Len Richley	cs 1970	July 1971	-
Frank Brennan	Aug 1971	Jan 1972	-
Allan Jones	April 1972	Dec 1972	-
Ralph Brand	Dec 1972	June 1973	-
Dick Connor	July 1973	May 1974	-
Billy Horner	cs 1974	cs 1975	-
Peter Madden	cs 1975	Oct 1978	-
Len Walker	Oct 1978	June 1979	-
Billy Elliott	June 1979	June 1983	-
Cyril Knowles	July 1983	March 1987	6
David Booth	March 1987	Feb 1989	-
Brian Little	Feb 1989	May 1991	12
Frank Gray	June 1991	Feb 1992	-
Billy McEwan	May 1992	-	

Derby County

The Rams' decision to appoint a manager in 1900 came after they had reached two FA Cup Finals, a semi-final and finished third in Division One. In the 82 seasons that have elapsed since then, the Baseball Ground has been home to 16 managers (excluding Ted Magner in wartime and Roy McFarland as caretaker), giving the relatively high average of 5.1 seasons per manager. The period between Brian Clough's departure and Arthur Cox's arrival was the most unstable. With financial pressures almost destroying the club and the uncertainty associated with six managers in 11 years, Derby slipped from League champions to the Third Division.

The tradition of managerial stability goes back to the turn of the century. Harry Newbould had four years as secretary before his six as manager, and he was followed by Jimmy Methven's 16-year tenure, of which four were accounted for by World War One. The inter-war period was dominated by George Jobey, who reigned for 14 League seasons and two more in wartime. Methven and Jobey are the two longest serving Derby managers, although incumbent Arthur Cox is staking his claim with nine seasons. For John Newman and Colin Murphy, however, the stay at the Baseball Ground was shorter and more traumatic (10 and 11 months respectively), whilst neither Peter Taylor (on his own) nor Tommy Docherty made it to their second anniversaries. In selecting their managers, Derby have tended to opt for experience. Only four of the 16 had not previously managed a League club. These, not surprisingly, include the first two appointees, who were in office when the general practice was for a secretary to do the board's bidding in team matters: the others were Stuart McMillan and Colin Murphy. A previous Derby connection was also a help. Methven, McMillan, Jack Barker, Harry Storer, Tim Ward and Dave Mackay were all former Rams, whilst Newbould (secretary) and Murphy,

Newman and Taylor (all assistant managers) had served the club in other capacities. For most of the job holders, Derby marked the summit of their managerial achievements. The exceptions were Docherty, who was a Cup winner with Manchester United before his destructive term at the Baseball Ground, Storer, who was closely identified with Coventry and Birmingham, and Clough and Cecil Potter, both of whom had managed Hartlepools before going to Derby and who both won the Division One championship later in their careers, with Nottingham Forest and Huddersfield respectively.

Manager	Start/Date	End/Date	Pts/Total
Harry Newbould	1900	July 1906	24
Jimmy Methven	Aug 1906	June 1922	38
Cecil Potter	July 1922	July 1925	6
George Jobey	Aug 1925	May 1941	40
Stuart McMillan	Jan 1946	Nov 1953	24
Jack Barker	Nov 1953	April 1955	-
Harry Storer	June 1955	May 1962	22
Tim Ward	June 1962	May 1967	-
Brian Clough	June 1967	Oct 1973	46
Dave Mackay	Oct 1973	Nov 1976	24
Colin Murphy	Nov 1976	Sept 1977	-
Tommy Docherty	Sept 1977	May 1979	-
Colin Addison	July 1979	Jan 1982	-
John Newman	Jan 1982	Nov 1982	-
Peter Taylor	Nov 1982	April 1984	-
Arthur Cox	May 1984	-	24

Doncaster Rovers

The 66 seasons Rovers have spent in the League have been spread over three separate spells, two short periods before World War One and an unbroken 63-season term beginning in 1923. This is when the first of the 22 managerial reigns began, each lasting a little under three seasons. Over 40 per cent of the time, however, is accounted for by just three men. Billy Bremner's two tours of duty lasted more than nine years, David Menzies (the longest continuous spell) was at Belle Vue for eight years and nine months, whilst the mercurial Peter Doherty might have stayed longer than 8.5 years had he not resigned on a matter of (allegedly religious) principle. It follows, therefore, that there were a few shorter-term appointments, none more so than the Bycroft/Hodgson duopoly (four months), Keith Kettleborough's six months and Danny Malloy's seven months.

The credentials of the 21 job holders have been mixed. Fred Emery, Syd Bycroft, John Hodgson and Dave Cusack were all former Rovers, whilst incumbent Steve Beaglehole worked his way up from youth coach to assistant manager before succeeding Bremner. A number went to Belle Vue with considerable managerial experience, like Jack Crayston (Arsenal), Dave Mackay (a championship winner at Derby), Dick Ray (Leeds), Stan Anderson (Middlesbrough) and David Menzies (Hull and Bradford City). As Rovers manager, Jack Bestall was a record breaker, steering them to the Third Division North title in 1947 with a record number of points and goals: 12 months later they were relegated. In 1966, Rovers again won promotion, this time from Division Four. They did it without a manager, however, for months earlier, Bill Leivers had left after a dispute with the board and he was not replaced for ten months. Promotion has proved a mixed blessing for the club. They went up in 1935 (Menzies), 1947 (Bestall), 1966, 1969 (McMenemy) and 1981 (Bremner), but within 24 months they had been relegated again. For a club that has never played in Division One and never got beyond round five of the FA Cup, Rovers

have a remarkable managerial pedigree. Of their old boys, five served national sides: Ray (Football League), Doherty (Northern Ireland), Raynor (Sweden), McMenemy (England) and Setters (Republic of Ireland).

Manager	Start/Date	End/Date	Pts/Total
Dick Ray	1923	July 1927	-
David Menzies	July 1927	March 1936	14
Fred Emery	March 1936	1940	16
Jack Bestall	March 1946	April 1949	14
Peter Doherty	June 1949	Jan 1958	14
Sydney Bycroft/John Hodgson	Feb 1958	cs 1958	-
Jack Crayston	June 1958	March 1959	-
Jack Bestall	March 1959	Aug 1960	-
Norman Curtis	Aug 1960	Aug 1961	-
Danny Malloy	Aug 1961	March 1962	-
Oscar Hold	March 1962	cs 1964	-
Bill Leivers	July 1964	Feb 1966	-
Keith Kettleborough	Dec 1966	May 1967	-
George Raynor	May 1967	Dec 1968	-
Lawrie McMenemy	Dec 1968	May 1971	12
Maurice Setters	May 1971	Nov 1974	-
Stan Anderson	Feb 1975	Nov 1978	-
Billy Bremner	Nov 1978	Oct 1985	12
Dave Cusack	Oct 1985	Dec 1987	-
Dave Mackay	Dec 1987	March 1989	-
Billy Bremner	July 1989	Nov 1991	-
Steve Beaglehole	Nov 1991	-	

Derby County, 1974-75, League champions for the second time. Back row (left to right): Des Anderson (assistant manager), Webster, Daniel, Todd, Boulton, Moseley, Bourne, Powell, Thomas, Newton, Hector, Gordon Guthrie (physiotherapist). Front row: Lee, George, Rioch, McFarland, Dave Mackay (manager), Gemmill, Nish, Davies, Hinton.

Doncaster Rovers, 1970-71. Back row (left to right): Haselden, Regan, Bird, Usher, Clish. Middle row: Gray, Rabjohn, Johnson, Ogston, Briggs, Branfoot. Front row: Gilfillan, Marsden, Johnson, Irvine, Lawrie McMenemy (manager), Robertson, Watson, Sheffield.

Everton

The last of the major clubs to become convinced of the need for a manager was Everton. They chose the end of what proved to be the final inter-war season, which they had finished as League Champions, to add managerial duties to secretary Theo Kelly's responsibilities. No club has since won the First Division without a manager, a feat the Toffees achieved three times between the wars. In 47 seasons since Kelly's promotion, there have only been ten managers at Goodison, Harry Catterick (12 years) and Cliff Britton (7.5 years) the longest serving and Kelly (only one full season because of the war) the shortest. The present incumbent, Howard Kendall, is in his second term in the job, and has added two and a half years to the six years of his first spell.

Of the nine individuals, five were former Everton players, and Kelly an internal appointment. Although only John Carey and Gordon Lee were new to Goodison when they got the job, both had a proven track record in League management before they went to Merseyside. The odd one out was the curious choice of Ian Buchan to succeed Cliff Britton in 1956. A former Loughborough College lecturer in physical education, Buchan was given the title of club coach rather than manager, and his principal contribution to the Toffees was to make them the fittest side in the League. It was alleged that after the domineering Britton, the Everton board was seeking somebody more pliable as manager.

Although Everton have never had the series of internal appointments that characterised Liverpool's selection of managers since Shankly, there are still obvious connections. Britton, for example, was a member of Kelly's successful side of the late 1930s, Catterick played for the Toffees during Britton's reign and Billy Bingham, Kendall and Colin Harvey all won championship medals at Goodison under Catterick. Each, however, had to leave Merseyside to do their managerial/coaching apprenticeships elsewhere before returning to the club in the top job.

Manager	Start/Date	End/Date	Pts/Total
Theo Kelly	May 1939	Sept 1948	-
Cliff Britton	Sept 1948	Feb 1956	22
Ian Buchan	Feb 1956	Oct 1958	-
John Carey	Oct 1958	April 1961	-
Harry Catterick	April 1961	April 1973	78
Billy Bingham	May 1973	Jan 1977	-
Gordon Lee	Feb 1977	May 1981	24
Howard Kendall	May 1981	June 1987	120
Colin Harvey	June 1987	Nov 1990	18
Howard Kendall	Nov 1990	-	-

Exeter City

Winning the Fourth Division in 1990 was the only title that went to Exeter in 66 seasons of League competition. The Grecians' time has been divided between the Third and Fourth Divisions and 24 managers have tried to improve their status. There have, of course, been variations around the average tenure of 2.8 seasons. At the long end of the range is John Newman, who spent seven and a half years in Exeter in the 1970s, about a year more than Billy McDevitt and two more than George Roughton. Although Arthur Chadwick was at the helm for 14 years, only 15 months were in the League, the remainder being in the Southern League and World War One. At the short end, were David Wilson, Bill Thompson, Cyril Spiers, Jock Basford, Gerry Francis and Jim Iley, all of whose heads rolled after less than a season.

With survival a higher priority than success at St James', the Grecians have not been a magnet for big names as their managers. Very few of the 24 had previous experience of management before joining Exeter, and then that tended to be from other Third or Fourth Division clubs. Spiers (Cardiff, Norwich and Palace) Iley (Barnsley, Bury and Blackburn) and Colin Appleton (Swansea, Barrow and Hull) were the most experienced, although Alan Ball had previously taken Portsmouth into the First Division for 12 months.

Only three of the 23 individuals (Frank Broome had two spells) were former Exeter players, McDevitt, Newman and Bobby Saxton, although Jack Edwards, Ellis Stuttard and Basford were on the training or scouting staff when the managerial vacancy arose. Just about half of the 22 former Exeter managers went on to manage other League clubs after leaving St James,' with Chadwick and Roughton (both Southampton), Stuttard (Plymouth), Newman (Derby), Saxton (Blackburn), Francis (Queen's Park Rangers) and Cooper (Birmingham) moving up to the First or Second Divisions.

The first Exeter manager to win promotion was Jack Edwards in 1963-4, a feat Bobby Saxton emulated in 1976-7. These were the major successes until Cooper's title win in 1990. On the other side of the coin, Stuttard and Francis were at the helm when the Grecians were relegated and Jack English has the misfortune to have suffered two of the club's eight re-election applications, these coming in successive seasons in the late 1930s.

Manager	Start/Date	End/Date	Pts/Total
Arthur Chadwick	April 1908	Dec 1922	-
Fred Maven	Jan 1923	Nov 1927	-
David Wilson	March 1928	Feb 1929	-
Billy McDevitt	Feb 1929	Sept 1935	8
Jack English	Oct 1935	1940	-
George Roughton	Oct 1945	March 1952	-
Norman Kirkman	March 1952	March 1953	-
Norman Dodgin	April 1953	April 1957	-
Bill Thompson	May 1957	Jan 1958	-
Frank Broome	Jan 1958	May 1960	-
Glen Wilson	June 1960	April 1962	-
Cyril Spiers	May 1962	Feb 1963	-
Jack Edwards	Feb 1963	Jan 1965	6
Ellis Stuttard	Feb 1965	June 1966	-
Jock Basford	June 1966	April 1967	-
Frank Broome	May 1967	Feb 1969	-
John Newman	April 1969	Dec 1976	-
Bobby Saxton	Jan 1977	Jan 1979	6
Brian Godfrey	Jan 1979	June 1983	-
Gerry Francis	June 1983	May 1984	-
Jim Iley	June 1984	April 1985	-
Colin Appleton	May 1985	Dec 1987	-
Terry Cooper	May 1988	Aug 1991	12
Alan Ball	Aug 1991	-	-

Fulham

London's oldest League club, Fulham, have had 23 managers in 75 League campaigns, a change on average every 3.3 seasons. There are, however, two managers whose combined service to the Cottagers totalled 28 years (but only 17 League seasons because of wars). Phil Kelso held the reins from 1909 until retirement in May 1924, his departure hastened by a bribery scandal a couple of years earlier. Jack Peart's term of office, from 1935 to 1948, was ended only by the manager's death. There are, however, two famous names on the list who were each given less than 12 months in the job. Jimmy Hogan, whose coaching skills had done so much to promote football in continental Europe, was sacked whilst recovering in hospital from appendicitis, after eight months at the Cottage. Bobby Robson, brought back from Canada, got the red card after ten months, and later went on to manage England.

Hogan and Robson were both former Fulham players, as were Andy Ducat, Joe Bradshaw, Frank Osborne, Bedford Jezzard, Bill Dodgin (jnr), Malcolm Macdonald and Ray Lewington. In addition, Ned Liddell had been Fulham's chief scout before he became manager and Bobby Campbell and Ray Harford were coaches. This lengthy roster of old boys turned managers is completed by Joe Edelston, Johnny Haynes and Arthur Stevens, who all had periods in charge as caretakers. Another link between the managers, curious in view of the fact that a Fulham chairman at the turn of the century, Henry Norris, wanted to merge Fulham and Arsenal, is the number of Cottagers' managers who had some links with the Gunners: Harry Bradshaw and Kelso managed both, Campbell coached both, Ducat, Dodgin jnr and Macdonald played for both, Stock was assistant at Highbury and Liddell an Arsenal player and Fulham manager.

A unique feature of Fulham's past managers is that there have been two father-and-son pairings. Harry Bradshaw's son, Joe, was a player at the Cottage during his father's term, and himself returned 20 years later as manager. Likewise, the Dodgins: Bill jnr was brought to Fulham by

father Bill snr and then sold to Arsenal by him. Young Bill returned later, first as a player, then as manager. Finally, a special mention for Frank Osborne, whose service to Fulham spanned almost 45 years as a player, director, manager, general manager and secretary, in that order.

Manager	Start/Date	End/Date	Pts/Total
Harry Bradshaw	April 1904	April 1909	6
Phil Kelso	cs 1909	May 1924	-
Andy Ducat	May 1924	May 1926	-
Joe Bradshaw	cs 1926	May 1929	-
Ned Liddell	May 1929	April 1931	-
James McIntyre	April 1931	Feb 1934	14
Jimmy Hogan	cs 1934	Feb 1935	-
Jack Peart	May 1935	Sept 1948	6
Frank Osborne	Sept 1948	June 1949	16
Bill Dodgin (snr)	cs 1949	Oct 1953	-
Frank Osborne	Oct 1953	Jan 1956	-
Dug Livingstone	Jan 1956	May 1958	6
Bedford Jezzard	June 1958	Dec 1964	16
Vic Buckingham	Jan 1965	Jan 1968	-
Bobby Robson	Jan 1968	Nov 1968	-
Bill Dodgin (jnr)	Dec 1968	May 1972	8
Alec Stock	June 1972	Dec 1976	12
Bobby Campbell	Dec 1976	Oct 1980	-
Malcolm Macdonald	Nov 1980	April 1984	8
Ray Harford	April 1984	June 1986	-
Ray Lewington	July 1986	June 1990	-
Alan Dicks	June 1990	Dec 1991	-
Don Mackay	Jan 1992	-	-

Gateshead

There was genuine surprise when Gateshead (once South Shields) lost their League status in 1960. The Laides had not finished bottom of Division Four that season, and they were making their first re-election application for 23 years. They were less frequent applicants than many of their divisional colleagues and it was felt at the time that the decision owed much to geography.

In their 34-season membership of the League, Gateshead used eight managers, with Jack Tinn having two spells. The average tenure, a relatively high 3.8 seasons, owes much to the remarkable contribution of Bill Tulip, generally known as 'Mr Gateshead'. One of the original directors of the club, he was honorary manager for 23 years (including seven during World War Two) and then became club president. He was almost 80 when he relinquished control of the managerial reins. The next longest unbroken period of office was Ernest Douglass', like Tulip a one-time director (he was chairman) who was honorary manager for five years, which covered the transition from South Shields to Gateshead.

These terms were in marked contrast to the rapidity with which two former Newcastle stalwarts, goalkeeper James Lawrence and full-back Bill McCracken, joined and left the club: neither stayed for a complete season. Charles Ferguson had even less time at the Gateshead helm, but he was appointed during the closing weeks of the Laides' League career. Like all his predecessors bar one, Ferguson had no previous experience of managing a League club. The exception was McCracken, whose introduction to the role had occurred at Hull in the 1920s. A quarter of a century later, another former Newcastle full-back, Ron Batty, stepped up to the manager's office at Redheugh Park, the one and only former Laides' player to be given the job.

Of the eight, only three moved on to other jobs in the Football League. Lawrence had a brief time in charge at Preston before returning to Scotland, whilst McCracken's long career took in managerial stop-overs at Millwall and Aldershot. The most successful was undoubtedly Jack Tinn, who spent 20 years with First Division Portsmouth and took them to three FA Cup Finals.

Manager	Start/Date	End/Date	Pts/Total
Jack Tinn	1920	May 1922	-
James Lawrence	May 1922	Jan 1923	-
Jack Tinn	Jan 1923	July 1927	-
Ernest Douglass	cs 1927	Sept 1932	8
Bill McCracken	Sept 1932	May 1933	-
Bill Tulip	May 1933	cs 1956	8
Bob Keen	cs 1956	cs 1958	-
Ron Batty	Oct 1958	March 1960	-
Charles Ferguson	April 1960	June 1960	-

Gillingham

With the exception of Maidstone's brief interlude in the Fourth Division, Gillingham have been the only Kent club in the Football League. Founder members of Division Three in 1920, their membership lapsed for 12 years when they failed to gain re-election in 1938. There have therefore, been 61 seasons of League football at Priestfield, during which there have been 18 managers, a survival rate of 3.4 seasons per manager. This average would have been much lower had it not been for the durability of Archie Clark, whose tenure lasted 19 years and covered eight League seasons. Gerry Summers and Keith Peacock in the 1970s and 1980s had a combined service in excess of 12 years, well above the average, whilst Keith Burkinshaw, Paul Taylor and Alan Ure counted their terms in months rather than years.

To have played for Gillingham seems to have counted for little in picking the club's manager. Although recent job holder Damien Richardson made over 400 appearances for the Gills, he was only the third former player to be given a chance as manager. Dick Hendrie, in the inter-war period, was the first, and Fred Maven also qualifies, although his playing experience was in the pre-League era before World War One when the Gills were known as New Brompton. Paul Taylor was, however, on the staff, as assistant manager/coach, at the time of his appointment in 1987, and Alan Ure was trainer when he was upgraded in 1937.

There are also surprisingly few of the 18 who went to Priestfield with some League management experience. Before the war, there was Albert Hoskins (Wolves) and Maven (Exeter and Palace) and since 1946, only Freddie Cox (Bournemouth and Portsmouth), Gerry Summers (Oxford), and Burkinshaw (Workington and Spurs). This means that five of the 18 were new both to League management and Gillingham, James McMillan, Hendrie, Clark, Harry Barratt and Basil Hayward.

Of the 18, none could challenge Burkinshaw's pre-Priestfield record of Cup and European success with Spurs, but in their post-Priestfield incarnations, Harry Curtis (at Brentford), Andy Nelson (Charlton) and Len Ashurst (Newport and Sunderland) achieved more than they had with Gillingham. The only Gills manager to make any impression on the honours were Cox (Fourth Division Champions) and Nelson (Fourth Division promotion), a meagre haul for 61 seasons effort.

Manager	Start/Date	End/Date	Pts/Total
John McMillan	July 1920	Aug 1922	-
Harry Curtis	May 1923	May 1926	-
Albert Hoskins	May 1926	May 1929	-
Dick Hendrie	May 1929	Dec 1931	-
Fred Maven	Jan 1932	May 1937	-
Alan Ure	May 1937	May 1938	-
Archie Clark	cs 1939	June 1958	-
Harry Barratt	July 1958	May 1962	-
Freddie Cox	June 1962	April 1965	12
Basil Hayward	Jan 1966	May 1971	-
Andy Nelson	June 1971	May 1974	6
Len Ashurst	June 1974	Oct 1975	-
Gerry Summers	Oct 1975	May 1981	-
Keith Peacock	July 1981	Dec 1987	-
Paul Taylor	Dec 1987	Oct 1988	-
Keith Burkinshaw	Oct 1988	April 1989	-
Damien Richardson	May 1989	Sept 1992	-
Glenn Roeder	Oct 1992	-	-

Grimsby Town

Founder members of Division Two in 1892, and missing just one Football League season since then (1910-11), Grimsby appointed the first of their 23 managers at the start of their 25th campaign. This means that the average managerial term at Blundell Park is 2.9 seasons. For longevity, two men stand out. Charlie Spencer arrived from non-League Wigan in 1937 and stayed until illness forced him out in 1951, but half of his 14 year tenure was accounted for by World War Two. This makes Wilf Gillow's eight-year reign, from 1924 to 1932, the longest in the Mariners' history. Their early years were characterised by managerial stability, for in the 24 seasons up to Spencer's departure there were just five job holders.

The most turbulent phase was the 1960s and 1970s, 19 seasons that saw ten managers go to and leave Cleethorpes. These included Don McEvoy, who stayed just six months in the job, and Bill Harvey, Ron Ashman and Tom Casey, who were each given about 18 months to prove themselves. In previous generations, Haydn Price was gone after four months and Billy Walsh after 13 months, whilst more recently, Bobby Roberts was in and out in 10 months.

A striking feature of Grimsby's choice of managers is that few were former Mariners. Only Wilf Gillow and David Booth previously played for the club before becoming manager. Although Allenby Chilton, Bobby Kennedy and Mike Lyons all played for Grimsby, they were appointed as player-managers and were not connected with the club before taking on the dual role. Of the remaining 18 managers, 15 had management experience with a League club prior to taking over at Blundell Park. The exceptions were Spencer and Billy Walsh, whose training had been in non-League football, and Tommy Casey, a well known coach at League level.

None had achieved much before going to Blundell Park, apart from lower division promotions (Tim Ward at Barnsley, Jimmy McGuigan at Crewe and Lawrie McMenemy at Doncaster). Several, however, used the Mariners as a stepping stone to higher level clubs, in particular McMenemy and Bill Shankly who won major domestic honours with Southampton and Liverpool respectively. Incumbent Alan Buckley has won two promotions for the Mariners (from the Fourth to the Second Divisions), equalling Gillow's achievement (the Third to the First) in the 1920s.

Manager	Start/Date	End/Date	Pts/Total
Haydn Price	July 1920	Nov 1920	-
George Fraser	March 1921	March 1924	-
Wilf Gillow	June 1924	April 1932	24
Frank Womack	May 1932	Oct 1936	22
Charles Spencer	March 1937	May 1951	6
Bill Shankly	July 1951	Jan 1954	8
Billy Walsh	Feb 1954	March 1955	-
Allenby Chilton	March 1955	April 1959	14
Tim Ward	Feb 1960	June 1962	8
Tom Johnston	July 1962	Oct 1964	-
Jimmy McGuigan	Nov 1964	July 1967	-
Don McEvoy	July 1967	Jan 1968	-
Bill Harvey	Jan 1968	Jan 1969	-
Bobby Kennedy	March 1969	May 1971	-
Lawrie McMenemy	May 1971	July 1973	12
Ron Ashman	July 1973	Feb 1975	-
Tom Casey	Feb 1975	Nov 1976	-
John Newman	Dec 1976	July 1979	6
George Kerr	July 1979	Jan 1982	14
Dave Booth	Jan 1982	Oct 1985	-
Mike Lyons	Nov 1985	June 1987	-
Bobby Roberts	July 1987	May 1988	-
Alan Buckley	June 1988	-	14

Halifax Town

The demise of Halifax as a League club in 1993 was sad but unsurprising. In six of the last nine seasons, the Yorkshire side had the unenviable record of being the worst supported club in the League. This gives a flavour of the financial constraints at the Shay and helps explain why the rate of managerial turnover accelerated after 1970. Overall, the club had 25 managers in 65 League seasons, an average tenure of 2.6 seasons. Up to 1962, however, it was over four seasons per manager, but after 1970, the average fell to around 20 months. Survival had the highest priority at the Shay, and this was the criterion of success.

By far and away the longest serving manager was the first, Joe McClelland, who had nearly 20 years with the club. Although this covered only nine League seasons, it was still longer than his successor, Alex Raisbeck (six years) in second place. The other long-time manager was James Thompson, but seven of his 11 years at the Shay were accounted for by World War Two. Only three managers, Jimmy Lawson, Ray Henderson and the last, Mick Rathbone, failed to complete a year at Halifax, although several others (Billy Wootton, Vic Metcalfe, John Quinn and Jim McCalliog) did not make it to their second anniversaries.

To have played for Halifax seemed to have counted for more in the last 20 years than previously. Before Quinn got the job in 1974, only Gerry Henry in the 1950s had played for the club. More recently, Lawson, Micky Bullock and Mick Jones were all former players, whilst Don McEvoy, George Mulhall, George Kirby and Metcalfe were promoted from the coaching staff and Rathbone from being the physio. It is unlikely that the Halifax job was regarded as one of football's glittering prizes, and it has been hard to attract men with a long managerial pedigree. Only Raisbeck, Thompson, Wootton, Jones and John McGrath had previous experience of managing at a League club before going to the Shay, and even then, it was in the lower divisions. For 10 of the 21 managers (three individuals had two spells) there was life after Halifax, but none made it beyond the Second Division.

This indicates that there was a sort of 'class' system amongst managers.

Men like Raisbeck and Thompson, who spent several seasons at Halifax, had long careers as managers, but were never given the chance at the highest level. As with players, perhaps there were managers who only operated effectively in the lower divisions.

Manager	Start/Date	End/Date	Pts/Total
Joe McClelland	May 1911	July 1930	-
Alex Raisbeck	July 1930	May 1936	8
James Thompson	May 1936	May 1947	-
Jack Breedon	Aug 1947	Nov 1950	-
Billy Wootton	Nov 1950	Feb 1952	-
Gerry Henry	Feb 1952	Oct 1954	-
Willie Watson	Nov 1954	April 1956	-
Harry Hooper	Oct 1957	April 1962	-
Don McEvoy	May 1962	Aug 1964	-
Willie Watson	Sept 1964	April 1966	-
Vic Metcalfe	June 1966	Nov 1967	-
Alan Ball (snr)	Dec 1967	cs 1970	6
George Kirby	cs 1970	Aug 1971	-
Ray Henderson	Aug 1971	May 1972	-
George Mulhall	June 1972	Sept 1974	-
John Quinn	Sept 1974	Feb 1976	-
Alan Ball (snr)	Feb 1976	Nov 1977	-
Jimmy Lawson	Nov 1977	Oct 1978	-
George Kirby	Nov 1978	June 1981	-
Micky Bullock	July 1981	Oct 1984	-
Mick Jones	Nov 1984	Dec 1986	-
Bill Ayre	Dec 1986	Mar 1990	-
Jim McCalliog	Apr 1990	Oct 1991	-
John McGrath	Oct 1991	Dec 1992	-
Mick Rathbone	Dec 1992	May 1993	-

Hartlepool United

Perhaps the Football League's definitive Cinderella club, Hartlepool had unbroken membership of the Third North between 1921 and 1958, and just three seasons outside Division Four since then. In the same period, they have made a record 14 re-election applications, and only four times since 1908 have they made it beyond Round Three of the FA Cup. Ironically, the manager who last took them to Round Four and who accounts for two of the three seasons outside Division Four was sacked in February 1993.

The unfortunate Alan Murray was United's 26th manager in 65 League seasons. Around the average stay of 29 months, Fred Westgarth's 13 years (10 League seasons) stands out for its length, which was ended only by his death in 1957. More recently, Billy Horner's two spells amounted to nine years, and these two are by far the club's longest serving managers. Competition for the shortest serving was more intense, with most of the challengers coming in the post-1963 period, when the average tenure dropped to 1.8 seasons. In particular, Allenby Chilton, Bob Gurney, Geoff Twentyman, John Simpson, John Duncan and Michael Docherty all failed to complete a season at the Victoria Ground. In the calender year 1983 alone, Hartlepool had four different managers.

With little to offer by way of tradition or resources, United have not found it easy to attract people with a proven managerial pedigree to the Victoria Ground. Only seven of the 26 individuals had had control of a League club in their pre-Hartlepool incarnations (Bill Norman, Westgarth, Gurney, Horner, Duncan, Bobby Moncur and Cyril Knowles), although several had been assistants, caretakers or coaches elsewhere. For many, moreover, the Victoria Ground was the end of the managerial road, for only a handful moved on to other clubs in a similar capacity.

Although life at the bottom appears not to have been an apprenticeship for anything other than further periods of life at the bottom (or even football oblivion), two of the Pool's old boys did go on to win the Football League Championship. Cecil Potter, Hartlepool's manager when they joined the League, was Herbert Chapman's successor at Huddersfield in 1925, and steered them to the third of their hat-trick of title wins. He

went to Leeds Road via Derby and 45 years later, Brian Clough also left the Victoria Ground for the Baseball Ground, and his glorious reign saw the Rams win the League title.

Manager	Start/Date	End/Date	Pts/Total
Cecil Potter	May 1920	July 1922	-
David Gordon	July 1922	cs 1924	-
Jack Manners	June 1924	July 1927	-
Will Norman	Aug 1927	April 1932	-
Jack Carr	April 1932	April 1935	-
Jimmy Hamilton	July 1935	Sept 1939	-
Fred Westgarth	Aug 1943	Feb 1957	8
Ray Middleton	May 1957	Nov 1959	-
Bill Robinson	Nov 1959	June 1962	-
Allenby Chilton	July 1962	April 1963	-
Bob Gurney	April 1963	Jan 1964	-
Alvan Williams	Feb 1964	May 1965	-
Geoff Twentyman	June 1965	Oct 1965	-
Brian Clough	Oct 1965	May 1967	-
Angus McLean	May 1967	April 1970	6
John Simpson	May 1970	March 1971	-
Len Ashurst	March 1971	June 1974	-
Ken Hale	June 1974	Oct 1976	-
Billy Horner	Oct 1976	March 1983	-
John Duncan	April 1983	June 1983	-
Michael Docherty	June 1983	Dec 1983	-
Billy Horner	Dec 1983	Nov 1986	-
John Bird	Nov 1986	Oct 1988	-
Bobby Moncur	Oct 1988	Nov 1989	-
Cyril Knowles	Nov 1989	March 1991	-
Alan Murray	March 1991	Feb 1993	6
Viv Busby	Feb 1993	-	

Hereford United

Hereford's best years in the League came shortly after they were elected to Division Four in 1972. Within four seasons, they were in the Second Division, but two seasons after that, they were back where they started. The first three of these four changes in League status occurred under the first two of the 10 managers United have had in 21 seasons of League football. A turnover rate of one manager every two seasons is on the high side, although John Sillett's two spells amounted to double the average, as did John Newman's tenure in the 1980s. For Tommy Hughes (five months) and Mike Bailey (16 months), however, Edgar Street proved to be a very temporary residence. When Colin Addison and John Sillett, United's first two managers in the League, returned 20 years later for second terms, both found it tougher second time around, neither surviving for more than a year.

It seems that United are a club where managers begin their careers, hoping it will lead to other opportunities. When he first arrived at Edgar Street, John Newman was the only one of the eight to have managed another League club, his experience being gained at Exeter, Grimsby and Derby. Other opportunities arose for one or two of Hereford's former managers, notably Addison (at Derby and Atlético Madrid), Sillett (Coventry) and Mike Bailey (Charlton and Brighton). As well as managerial beginners, the Hereford board has tended to look outside the club for its managers. Until the return of Addison and Sillett in the 1990s, only Tommy Hughes had

a prior connection with Hereford before taking on the top job. Even then, however, the former United goalkeeper's appointment was very much a holding operation, following Frank Lord's abrupt departure.

As interesting as the post-1972 list of managers is the pedigree of those United attracted to Edgar Street in their Southern League days. These included former Aston Villa manager Alex Massie, Ray Daniel, the Arsenal, Sunderland and Wales defender, Bob Dennison, who as Middlesbrough manager introduced Clough and Taylor to League football, and John Charles, of Leeds, Juventus and Wales fame.

Manager	Start/Date	End/Date	Pts/Total
Colin Addison	Oct 1971	cs 1974	6
John Sillett	July 1974	Jan 1978	14
Mike Bailey	June 1978	Oct 1979	-
Frank Lord	Dec 1979	Sept 1982	-
Tommy Hughes	Oct 1982	March 1983	-
John Newman	March 1983	Sept 1987	-
Ian Bowyer	Oct 1987	May 1990	-
Colin Addison	July 1990	May 1991	-
John Sillett	May 1991	May 1992	-
Greg Downs	May 1992	-	

Huddersfield Town

It is now almost 20 years since Huddersfield Town last played in the First Division, but in the 1920s, they dominated English football in a way that only Arsenal and Liverpool have since matched. This golden period occurred during the reign of the fourth of the Town's 22 managers in a 72-season League career.

There were several Leeds Road managers whose periods in office were markedly higher than the average of 3.3 seasons. Clem Stephenson spent 13 years in the job, although the last three were during World War Two. More recently were Mick Buxton's eight years at the helm and Ian Greaves' six. Although Arthur Fairclough was in his eighth year when he left for Elland Road, he had lost four years to World War One. If, on the other hand, the tenure of Malcolm Macdonald (seven months), Steve Smith (ten months), Ambrose Langley (15 months) and Bobby Collins (17 months) are combined, they barely exceed the average.

Managers at Leeds Road generally could claim some previous connection with Huddersfield or they had gained managerial experience elsewhere: the exceptions to this were Dick Pudan, George Stephenson and Bobby Collins. From the ranks of former players came Clem Stephenson, David Steele, Eddie Boot and Steve Smith, whilst Jack Chaplin, Ian Greaves, Mick Buxton and Eoin Hand all served the club as trainers or coaches prior to becoming managers. The remaining eight, therefore, (Arthur Fairclough, Ambrose Langley, Herbert Chapman, Cecil Potter, Andy Beattie, Bill Shankly, Tom Johnston and Malcolm Macdonald) all brought acknowledge of management with them to Leeds Road. The most successful in his pre-Huddersfield incarnation was Ambrose Langley, who had taken Barnsley to two FA Cup Finals before World War One.

The list of names who have managed Huddersfield is impressive. In Chapman and Shankly they had two of the outstanding managers of all time, although they are both largely remembered for their achievements elsewhere. Beattie went on to manage the Scottish national side whilst Pudan later became director and chairman of Leicester City. Ian Greaves had an eventful six years at Leeds Road. He took over a Second Division side, led them into the First and left when the Terriers were in Division Three.

Manager	Start/Date	End/Date	Pts/Total
Dick Pudan	Sept 1910	April 1912	-
Arthur Fairclough	April 1912	Dec 1919	-
Ambrose Langley	Dec 1919	March 1921	22
Herbert Chapman	March 1921	June 1925	54
Cecil Potter	July 1925	Aug 1926	18
Jack Chaplin	Aug 1926	May 1929	42
Clem Stephenson	May 1929	May 1942	42
David Steele	Sept 1943	June 1947	-
George Stephenson	Aug 1947	March 1952	-
Andy Beattie	April 1952	Nov 1956	10
Bill Shankly	Nov 1956	Nov 1959	-
Eddie Boot	Jan 1960	Sept 1964	-
Tom Johnston	Oct 1964	May 1968	6
Ian Greaves	June 1968	June 1974	16
Bobby Collins	July 1974	Dec 1975	-
Tom Johnston	Dec 1975	April 1977	-
Tom Johnston	Sept 1977	Aug 1978	-
Mick Buxton	Oct 1978	Dec 1986	20
Steve Smith	Jan 1987	Oct 1987	-
Malcolm Macdonald	Oct 1987	April 1988	-
Eoin Hand	June 1988	March 1992	-
Ian Ross	March 1992	-	-

Hull City

When Terry Dolan succeeded Stan Ternent in February 1991, he became Hull's 26th manager in 71 League seasons, giving each about three seasons at the helm. As ever, the average marks wide variations, with Cliff Britton, Billy McCracken and Ambrose Langley, with around eight years apiece, at one extreme, and Bobby Collins (four months), Eddie Gray (11 months) and Harry Chapman, Fred Stringer, Harry Lewis, Jack Hill, Ken Houghton and Ternent (between one and two seasons) at the other. The longest stay at Boothferry Park was Ernest Blackburn's nine years, but seven of these were during World War Two.

A number of Tigers managers were well known at the club before moving into the manager's office. Chapman, Hill, John Kaye and Ken Houghton were all former Hull players, Fred Stringer was on the board, David Menzies the trainer, Raich Carter player-assistant manager and Collins the coach. Most of the other 16 had some managerial experience under their belt, the exceptions being Langley, McCracken, Haydn Green, Terry Neill, Colin Appleton, Brian Horton and Ternent. For these men, the Hull appointment was their first exposure to both Boothferry Park and Football League management.

Despite the fact that the Tigers have only once got as far as the semi-final of the FA Cup and never been higher than the Second Division, they have attracted some men with very impressive reputations. There were few bigger managerial names in 1946 than Frank Buckley, whose long tenure at Wolverhampton had ended mysteriously 18 months earlier. Bob Jackson went to Boothferry Park just two years after he had led Portsmouth to the second of two League Championships in 12 months. When Cliff Britton was given a 10 year contract by Hull, it created a minor sensation, but he had proved his pedigree at the highest level with Burnley, Preston and Everton, whilst Mike Smith had been in charge of the Welsh national side before joining Hull. Others enjoyed more success after leaving the Tigers, especially Langley (Huddersfield and Leeds), Carter (Leeds) and Neill (Spurs and Arsenal).

For Menzies, the return to Hull in 1936 proved fatal, and Chapman, a more talented player than brother Herbert, never had the chance to prove himself as a manager, as ill-health (and early death) forced him out of office.

Manager	Start/Date	End/Date	Pts/Total
Ambrose Langley	April 1905	April 1913	-
Harry Chapman	April 1913	Sept 1914	-
Fred Stringer	Sept 1914	July 1916	-
David Menzies	July 1916	June 1921	-
Percy Lewis	July 1921	Jan 1923	-
Bill McCracken	Feb 1923	May 1931	6
Haydn Green	May 1931	March 1934	14
Jack Hill	March 1934	Jan 1936	-
David Menzies	Feb 1936	Oct 1936	-
Ernie Blackburn	Dec 1936	Jan 1946	-
Frank Buckley	May 1946	March 1948	-
Raich Carter	March 1948	Sept 1951	14
Bob Jackson	June 1952	March 1955	-
Bob Brocklebank	March 1955	May 1961	8
Cliff Britton	July 1961	Nov 1969	14
Terry Neill	June 1970	Sept 1974	-
John Kaye	Sept 1974	Oct 1977	-
Bobby Collins	Oct 1977	Feb 1978	-
Ken Houghton	April 1978	Dec 1979	-
Mike Smith	Jan 1980	March 1982	-
Colin Appleton	June 1982	May 1984	6
Brian Horton	June 1984	April 1988	8
Eddie Gray	June 1988	May 1989	-
Colin Appleton	May 1989	Oct 1989	-
Stan Ternent	Nov 1989	Jan 1991	-
Terry Dolan	Feb 1991	-	-

Ipswich Town

Few clubs can match Ipswich's record for managerial stability. In the 48 seasons they have been competing in the League, Town have had nine managers, each therefore lasting on average 5.3 seasons. Almost two thirds of the club's League career, however (31 seasons) were accounted for by just one third of the managers, Archie Scott Duncan (ten seasons), Alf Ramsey (eight seasons) and Bobby Robson (13 seasons). Although Scott Duncan spent 18 years at Portman Road, seven were lost to World War Two and the first was in the Southern League.

Of the rest, Jackie Milburn's 20 month tenure was the shortest and least successful. Lyall spent two years in charge of team affairs, won the Second Division title and then handed over to his coach Mick McGiven whilst he took on the title of general manager. The other three Ipswich managers, Bill McGarry, Bobby Ferguson and John Duncan, all had at least three seasons in the job before parting company with the club.

Not one of Town's managers had ever played for the club, and only Ferguson (Robson's coach) and McGiven (Lyall's coach) had any previous Portman Road connection. Most, however, had gained managerial experience with other clubs before moving to East Anglia. Lyall was the most successful (at West Ham), although Scott Duncan had won the Second Division championship with Manchester United. McGarry (Bournemouth and Watford), Robson (Fulham) and Duncan (Scunthorpe, Hartlepool and Chesterfield) had done their apprenticeships in more difficult circumstances.

For three of Ipswich's former managers, the Portman Road job was their last at this level, Scott Duncan (who gave up managing at the age of 66 but stayed another three years as secretary), Milburn (who turned to journalism) and Ferguson (who reverted to coaching). McGarry and Duncan went on to other League clubs whilst Ipswich's two most successful managers were destined for greater things. Both left Portman Road for the same job, managing England, and the two were the most successful managers England have had.

Manager	Start/Date	End/Date	Pts/Total
Archie Scott Duncan	Nov 1937	Aug 1955	14
Alf Ramsey	Aug 1955	April 1963	48
Jackie Milburn	April 1963	Sept 1964	-
Bill McGarry	Oct 1964	Nov 1968	16
Bobby Robson	Jan 1969	July 1982	78
Bobby Ferguson	Aug 1982	May 1987	6
John Duncan	June 1987	May 1990	-
John Lyall	May 1990	Aug 1992	16
Mick McGiven	Aug 1992	-	-

Howard Wilkinson with his Leeds United squad after they won the Second Division championship in 1990. Two years later, Leeds lifted the League championship under Wilkinson.

Leyton Orient, 1983-84. Back row (left to right): Pat Holland (player-coach), Kitchen, Houchen, Foster, Shoemake, Sussex, Roffey, Bill Songhurst (physiotherapist). Front row: Godfrey, Cornwall, Osgood, Cunningham, Frank Clark (manager), Silkman, Hales, Corbett, McNeill.

Leeds United

Until the appointment of Don Revie at Elland Road in 1961, Leeds main achievements in 44 seasons of League football were to win promotion from Division Two four times, and to have been suspended and then re-formed after a financial scandal. When Revie departed for the England job in 1974, Leeds were one of the most successful, if controversial and unpopular, sides in the country, and Revie one of the most successful managers. He was the club's 12th manager in 44 seasons, and following him, have been eight managers in 19 years. The pre-Revie average was a new manager every four seasons, which post-Revie, dropped to 2.4 seasons: Revie himself stayed for 13 years. This was easily the longest term, whilst two of his successors, Brian Clough and Jock Stein, both spent just 44 days in charge at Elland Road.

The list of Leeds managers contains some of the most famous names in football, although few made their major contribution whilst at United. Clough and Stein were both amongst the dominant managerial figures of the post war era, as were Herbert Chapman and Frank Buckley in the inter-war period. Leeds did not see the best of these four. There does seem to have been something of a preference for Elland Road old boys. Dick Ray, Billy Hampson and Willis Edwards were all former Leeds players before 1939, whilst Revie ended his playing days at Elland Road. In the 1980s, three of his former players, Allan Clarke, Eddie Gray and Billy Bremner, all tried to lift the club back to its former glories, but without success. Overall, however, the Leeds board have looked primarily for experience, for 16 of the 20 had managed at League club level before being given control at Elland Road. The exceptions were Edwards and Bill Lambton, who were both upgraded from the training staff, and Revie and Gray, who made the jump from Leeds player to manager in one go.

Whilst Chapman, Revie and Stein were given responsibility for looking after national sides in their post-Leeds careers, Dick Ray took on the role during his Leeds tenure. When he accompanied the Football League side to play the Scottish League at Ibrox in February 1934, he was the first man to 'manage' an England team.

Manager	Start/Date	End/Date	Pts/Total
Gilbert Gillies	March 1905	March 1908	-
Frank Scott Walford	March 1908	May 1912	-
Herbert Chapman	June 1912	Oct 1919	-
Arthur Fairclough	Feb 1920	May 1927	16
Dick Ray	July 1927	March 1935	20
Billy Hampson	July 1935	May 1947	-
Willis Edwards	May 1947	April 1948	-
Frank Buckley	May 1948	April 1953	-
Raich Carter	May 1953	June 1958	10
Bill Lambton	Dec 1958	April 1959	-
Jack Taylor	May 1959	March 1961	-
Don Revie	March 1961	April 1974	268
Brian Clough	Aug 1974	Oct 1974	-
Jimmy Armfield	Oct 1974	Aug 1978	24
Jock Stein	Aug 1978	Oct 1978	-
Jimmy Adamson	Nov 1978	Oct 1980	6
Allan Clarke	Oct 1980	June 1982	-
Eddie Gray	July 1982	Oct 1985	-
Billy Bremner	Oct 1985	Sept 1988	6
Howard Wilkinson	Oct 1988	-	40

Leicester City

A club from Leicester has been a member of the League since 1894, initially bearing the suffix of Fosse, but after World War One, City. James Blessington got on board in 1907, 75 seasons ago, and he was the first of three Fosse managers, who were followed by 17 for City. (This excludes the experienced Tom Mather and Tom Bromilow who presided over affairs during World War Two.)

By far the manager with the longest period of service at Filbert Street was Matt Gillies. His ten years in the job was more than twice the average of 3.8 seasons. Peter Hodge, on nine years, was not far behind, but his term was split into two, separated by six years. There are in addition, three other managers whose reigns at Leicester were well above the average, Willie Orr (5.5 years), Norman Bullock (5 years 2 months) and Jimmy Bloomfield (six years). The list of short serving managers is headed by two relatively recent appointees, Frank McLintock and Bryan Hamilton, who lasted nine and 18 months respectively.

Only four former Foxes have had the chance to manage the club, Arthur Lochhead before the war and John Duncan, Gillies and McLintock after it. Blessington had been a player with Fosse since 1903 before he was upgraded to manager. For all five, it was their first experience of League management. Of the others, all but four had previously worked at this level before going to Filbert Street. The exceptions were Hodge, Orr, David Halliday and Jock Wallace, all of whom had made their marks in Scotland first. Hodge had managed Stoke, but this was during a season the Potters were outside the League. Wallace and Halliday had particularly impressive records at Rangers and Aberdeen respectively.

Despite the experience of Leicester's recruits, none had won major national honours in their previous incarnations. Frank Womack (Grimsby), Frank O'Farrell (Torquay), Bloomfield (Orient), David Pleat (Luton) and Brian Little (Darlington) had been promotion winners, but from the lower divisions, whilst Pleat (Spurs) had been a losing FA Cup Finalist. In the Filbert Street after-life, Hodge had a successful spell at Manchester City, Gillies went to Forest, O'Farrell to Manchester United and McLintock to Brentford, whilst Bloomfield (Orient), Hamilton (Wigan) and Pleat (Luton) returned to their former clubs.

Manager	Start/Date	End/Date	Pts/Total
James Blessington	Jan 1907	Feb 1909	10
Andy Aitken	Feb 1909	May 1911	-
John Bartlett	March 1912	March 1914	-
Peter Hodge	May 1919	May 1926	16
Willie Orr	July 1926	Jan 1932	12
Peter Hodge	March 1932	July 1934	6
Arthur Lochhead	Aug 1934	Oct 1936	-
Frank Womack	Oct 1936	May 1939	16
Johnny Duncan	March 1946	Oct 1949	12
Norman Bullock	Dec 1949	Feb 1955	16
David Halliday	July 1955	Oct 1958	16
Matt Gillies	Nov 1958	Dec 1968	54
Frank O'Farrell	Dec 1968	June 1971	28
Jimmy Bloomfield	June 1971	May 1977	6
Frank McLintock	June 1977	April 1978	-
Jock Wallace	May 1978	July 1982	22
Gordon Milne	Aug 1982	June 1986	10
Bryan Hamilton	June 1986	Dec 1987	-
David Pleat	Dec 1987	Jan 1991	-
Brian Little	May 1991	-	-

Leyton Orient

The official history of the Os reveals that in 77 seasons of League football they have had 25 managers, a change once every three seasons. This simple statistic conceals a remarkable feature of the club's managerial personnel, that both Alec Stock and Peter Proudfoot had three separate spells in charge, and Jimmy Bloomfield two. Les Gore, moreover, who never held the job of manager, took over as caretaker no less than six times. Between August 1949 and May 1966, there were 12 managerial changes at Brisbane Road, but only five individuals were involved, John Carey, Benny Fenton and Dave Sexton along with Stock and Gore.

Not surprisingly, Proudfoot's three terms, which totalled 12 years, puts him top of Orient's list of long-serving managers, although Billy Holmes wins it for unbroken service, even though four of his 16 years were taken up by World War One. Stock (nearly nine years), Frank Clark (eight years), Bloomfield (seven years) and George Petchey (six years) also lasted well above the club's average. These men, in fact, account for 71% of the O's League career. Paul Went, on the other hand, was in and out in a month, whilst Sam Ormerod, Tom Halsey, Arthur Grimsdell and Dave Sexton had under a year in the job.

Just seven of the 20 men who have managed Orient had any previous connection with the club before moving into the manager's office. Holmes, Proudfoot, Sexton and Went were all former players, whilst Halsey, Neil McBain and Clark were on the secretarial side or assistant managers. There was not a greater bias in favour of managerial experience. Sam Ormerod had led Manchester City to the Second Division title in his pre-Orient days, Charlie Hewitt had made his (controversial) reputation at Millwall, Carey arrived from Everton, whilst Dick Graham and Ken Knighton had learned their trades at Crystal Palace and Sunderland respectively.

In Jimmy Seed, Stock and Sexton, the Os had three of the finest managers of their generations, but sadly for the East Londoners, these men did their best work elsewhere, at Charlton, QPR, Luton, Fulham and Chelsea. Carey also enjoyed a measure of success at Forest after leaving Brisbane Road (the route followed by Clark 30 years later), although Carey's principal managerial achievement was to have guided Leyton Orient into Division One for the only time in their history.

Manager	Start/Date	End/Date	Pts/Total
Sam Ormerod	April 1905	Jan 1906	-
Billy Holmes	March 1906	Feb 1922	-
Peter Proudfoot	April 1922	April 1929	-
Arthur Grimsdell	May 1929	March 1930	-
Peter Proudfoot	April 1930	April 1931	-
Jimmy Seed	April 1931	May 1933	-
David Pratt	May 1933	Dec 1934	-
Peter Proudfoot	Jan 1935	Jan 1939	-
Tom Halsey	Jan 1939	Dec 1939	-
Charlie Hewitt	Jan 1946	April 1948	-
Neil McBain	April 1948	Aug 1949	-
Alec Stock	Aug 1949	Feb 1956	8
Alec Stock	April 1956	Aug 1957	14
Alec Stock	Feb 1958	Feb 1959	-
John Carey	Aug 1961	Aug 1963	10
Benny Fenton	Nov 1963	Dec 1964	-
Dave Sexton	Jan 1965	Dec 1965	-
Dick Graham	June 1966	Feb 1968	-
Jimmy Bloomfield	June 1968	May 1971	14
George Petchey	July 1971	Aug 1977	-
Jimmy Bloomfield	Sept 1977	Aug 1981	6
Paul Went	Aug 1981	Oct 1981	-
Ken Knighton	Oct 1981	May 1983	-
Frank Clark	May 1983	July 1991	6
Peter Eustace	July 1991	-	-

Liverpool celebrate their 1982 Milk Cup Final victory over Tottenham Hotspur at Wembley. Manager Bob Paisley (extreme right) comes second in the overall rankings list of English club managers.

Luton Town, 1976-77. Back row (left to right): Gregory, Buckley, Smith, Wassell, Deans, Hill, Simon. Middle row: Jones, Futcher, Faulkner, Knight, Barber, Ryan, Price, McNichol, Reg Game (trainer). Front row: Fuccillo, Chambers, Carr, Roy McCrohan (coach), Harry Haslam (manager), Husband, Aston, Mead.

Lincoln City

The Imps of Lincoln have a unique Football League membership record. Founder members of the Second Division in 1892, they are now in their fifth spell in the League, having failed on four occasions to hold on to their place. Remarkably, however, their exiles, including the most recent, have never lasted more than 12 months, which means The Imps have competed in 86 of the 90 seasons since the formation of Division Two.

It was eight years later that a manager was first appointed, and in total, Lincoln have tried 22 managers in 78 seasons, a new one every three and a half season. Stability was much greater in the years up to 1965, when there was a change every 6.2 seasons. Since 1970, managers came and went at the rate of one every 1.9 seasons. The early post World War Two period belonged to Bill Anderson, whose 18 year reign is unlikely ever to be challenged. Joe McClelland spent ten years at Sincil Bank, but lost seven to the war, whilst David Calderhead (senior) stayed for seven years and Colin Murphy for a total nine years (including one non-League season) spread over two terms. In the troubled times of the mid-late 1980s, John Pickering, Peter Daniel and Allan Clarke were in and out inside six months and in both the calender years 1985 and 1990, the Imps had three different managers.

There has been a tendency to draw on people who had some prior connection with the club. A number (George Fraser, Calderhead jnr, Roy Chapman, Bert Loxley, Graham Taylor, Daniel and Steve Thompson) had all been on the playing staff at Sincil Bank, whilst Strawson (secretary), Anderson (trainer), Kerr (coach) and Pickering (coach) were members of the backroom staff. Of the rest, most could offer League management experience on their CV. Harry Parkes (Newport and Chesterfield), McClelland (Halifax), Ron Gray (Watford and Millwall), Willie Bell (Birmingham), Murphy (Derby) and Clarke (Barnsley, Leeds and Scunthorpe) all fall into this category although none had won any major trophy.

Only eight of the club's 20 former managers graduated to other jobs. Calderhead went on to become Chelsea's longest serving manager and Henshall had eight years at Notts County. Neither could match the success of Graham Taylor, who after cutting his managerial teeth at Sincil Bank, progressed to Watford, Aston Villa and England.

Manager	Start/Date	End/Date	Pts/Total
David Calderhead (snr)	1900	Aug 1907	
John Strawson	Aug 1907	1914	-
George Fraser	July 1919	March 1921	-
David Calderhead (jnr)	April 1921	cs 1924	-
Horace Henshall	cs 1924	cs 1927	-
Harry Parkes	May 1927	May 1936	30
Joe McClelland	May 1936	Jan 1946	8
Bill Anderson	Jan 1947	Jan 1965	28
Roy Chapman	Jan 1965	1966	-
Ron Gray	1966	July 1970	-
Bert Loxley	July 1970	March 1971	-
David Herd	March 1971	Dec 1972	-
Graham Taylor	Dec 1972	June 1977	12
George Kerr	June 1977	Dec 1977	-
Willie Bell	Dec 1977	Oct 1978	-
Colin Murphy	Nov 1978	May 1985	6
John Pickering	July 1985	Dec 1985	-
George Kerr	Dec 1985	March 1987	-
Peter Daniel	March 1987	May 1987	-
Colin Murphy	May 1987	May 1990	-
Allan Clarke	June 1990	Nov 1990	-
Steve Thompson	Nov 1990	May 1993	-

Liverpool

Such has been Liverpool's success since Bill Shankly's appointment in 1959, that it is easy to overlook the fact that they were amongst the premier clubs in the pre-1939 period as well. In 90 seasons, there have been just 13 managers at Anfield, a record for managerial stability (a change about once every seven seasons) which has surely contributed to the success. The first great manager at Liverpool, and probably the first great manager in English football, Tom Watson, was in the job for 19 seasons, the longest term of any of the 13, and it was ended only by his death. Although George Kay was in his 15th year at Anfield when he retired, he lost seven seasons to the war, which puts Shankly, with 14.5 years at the helm, in second place. Remarkably, no manager has had less than three years in the job, apart from Joe Fagan, who retired out of choice after two remarkably successful seasons.

The practice of promoting internally at Anfield did not begin with Shankly's successor. Only five of Liverpool's managers had no previous connection with the club before taking over the top job, Shankly himself, Watson, David Ashworth, Kay and Don Welsh, although Welsh had been a popular guest player in wartime. Only Matt McQueen, Phil Taylor, Bob Paisley, Kenny Dalglish and Graeme Souness were, however, former players: the rest had served in a variety of behind-the-scenes roles. Every Liverpool manager apart from George Patterson, Welsh (the last manager of a relegated Liverpool side) and Taylor had some silverware to show for their endeavours, and Paisley won more trophies than any manager in the history of English football. Whilst several enjoyed a measure of success before going to Anfield (for example, Tom Watson at Sunderland

and Souness at Rangers), Dalglish is the first to achieve promotion or Cup honours in the Liverpool after-life. For nine of the Reds' 12 former managers, their managerial careers ended at Anfield.

When Dalglish resigned in February 1991, it caused something of a sensation, but it was not a new experience for the club. In February 1923, David Ashworth, who had taken the Reds to the Division One title the previous campaign, resigned to go to struggling Oldham when Liverpool were poised for another championship win. The reasons for Ashworth's departure have never been fully explained.

Manager	Start/Date	End/Date	Pts/Total
John McKenna	1892	Aug 1896	32
Tom Watson	Aug 1896	May 1915	106
David Ashworth	Dec 1919	Feb 1923	18
Matt McQueen	Feb 1923	Feb 1928	18
George Patterson	Feb 1928	May 1936	-
George Kay	May 1936	Feb 1951	36
Don Welsh	March 1951	May 1956	-
Phil Taylor	May 1956	Nov 1959	-
Bill Shankly	Dec 1959	July 1974	190
Bob Paisley	July 1974	June 1983	300
Joe Fagan	June 1983	May 1985	84
Kenny Dalglish	June 1985	Feb 1991	150
Graeme Souness	April 1991	-	30

Luton Town

Although they were founder members of the Third Division in 1920, Luton had earlier spent three seasons in the Second Division before losing their League status. The Hatters made their first managerial appointment in 1925, during their eighth first-class season, and in 61 seasons have tried 21 managers (19 individuals since George Martin and David Pleat both had two spells). There have, however, been several periods since 1925 when Luton chose to be without a manager, including much of the 1958-59 season when they reached their only FA Cup Final. The Hatters were the last team to reach Wembley without a manager (they were led out by director Tom Hodgson).

Of the 19, two stand out for service well in excess of the average of 2.9 seasons. Dally Duncan was in his 12th year when he left for Blackburn in October 1958, whilst incumbent David Pleat's two spells amount to over 10 years. George Martin was at Kenilworth Road for a total of nine and a half years, but seven of these were accounted for by World War Two. In stark contrast was Jack Crompton's tenure of just one week and George Thompson's eight months. Similarly, Neil McBain, Syd Owen and John Moore each had just one season at the helm.

Well over half the 19 had worked at Luton in some other capacity before becoming manager (John McCartney, George Kay, Martin, Duncan, Owen, Crompton, Allan Brown, Harry Haslam, Pleat, Moore, Jimmy Ryan and Ray Harford), usually as player but occasionally as coach, trainer or scout. A few went to Kenilworth Road with some managerial experience under their belts, McCartney (Barnsley and Portsmouth), Liddell (Fulham), McBain (Watford), Sam Bartram (York), Alec Stock (Leyton Orient and QPR) and Harford (Fulham). In addition, of course, both Martin and Pleat held jobs at the highest level in between their two terms at Kenilworth Road, with Newcastle, Aston Villa and Spurs respectively.

A period in Bedfordshire enhanced the career prospects of a number

of Luton managers, for half the 19 went on to other jobs in League management, usually at the highest level. Kay was a conspicuous success, leading Liverpool to the League title and FA Cup Final. Duncan, Stock and Pleat all took their new clubs (Blackburn, Fulham and Spurs) to FA Cup Finals, whilst Martin steered Newcastle to promotion from Division Two.

Manager	Start/Date	End/Date	Pts/Total
George Thompson	Feb 1925	Oct 1925	-
John McCartney	Sept 1927	Dec 1929	-
George Kay	Dec 1929	May 1931	-
Harold Wightman	June 1931	Oct 1935	-
Ned Liddell	Aug 1936	Feb 1938	14
Neil McBain	June 1938	June 1939	-
George Martin	Aug 1939	May 1947	-
Dally Duncan	June 1947	Oct 1958	10
Syd Owen	May 1959	April 1960	-
Sam Bartram	July 1960	June 1962	-
Jack Crompton	June 1962	June 1962	-
Bill Harvey	July 1962	Nov 1964	-
George Martin	Feb 1965	Nov 1966	-
Allan Brown	Nov 1966	Dec 1968	12
Alec Stock	Dec 1968	April 1972	8
Harry Haslam	May 1972	Jan 1978	10
David Pleat	Jan 1978	May 1986	22
John Moore	May 1986	June 1987	-
Ray Harford	June 1987	Jan 1990	36
Jimmy Ryan	Jan 1990	May 1991	-
David Pleat	June 1991	-	-

Manchester City

From their days as Ardwick, founder members of Division Two in 1892, Manchester City have had an official who has had or assumed managerial responsibilities. In 90 League seasons there have been 26 managers, half coming in the last 22 campaigns. From a modest rate of 5.2 seasons per manager up to 1971, turnover accelerated to 1.7 seasons thereafter. Nobody seems likely to challenge Les McDowall's 13 years at Maine Road. Although Wilf Wild had over 14 years, half of those were lost to World War Two, just as four of Ernest Mangnall's 12 years were in World War One. Sam Cowan, Johnny Hart, Ron Saunders, John Benson and Jimmy Frizzell, on the other hand, managed less than 30 months between them. Only six of the 25 individuals (Allison had two spells) were former City players (Lawrence Furniss, Cowan, McDowall, Hart, Tony Book and Peter Reid), although Wild, George Poyser, Allison, Benson and Frizzell were internal promotions. Of the rest, City have tended to go for someone with a proven record.

In terms of success, Joe Mercer easily comes out on top, winning the three major domestic honours (in consecutive seasons), the Second Division title and a European trophy, all within six years. Yet in the 12 months prior to his appointment, he was out of football recovering from a heart attack. Much earlier, Tom Maley, brother of Celtic's long serving manager, Willie, put City on the football map. He might have gone even higher had not his involvement in an illegal payments scandal led to his suspension *sine die* in 1906 (subsequently lifted). Secretary Wilf Wild was a reluctant manager in 1932, but steered City to First Division and FA Cup success, although relegation followed 12 months after the League championship win. His successor, Sam Cowan, reclaimed City's position in the top flight following World War Two after only seven months at the helm, but resigned immediately thereafter. He was not prepared to move to Manchester, and the board were unhappy about him commuting from Brighton. Ernest Mangnall has a special place in the history of Manchester football as the only man to manage both City and United. In the early 1920s he came within a whisker of emulating the success he had had at Old Trafford before the war but had to settle for Division Onew runners-up and FA Cup semi-finalists.

Manager	Start/Date	End/Date	Pts/Total
Lawrence Furniss	1889	1893	-
Joshua Parlby	1893	1895	-
Sam Ormerod	1895	July 1902	26
Tom Maley	July 1902	July 1906	46
Harry Newbould	July 1906	July 1912	16
Ernest Mangnall	Aug 1912	May 1924	18
David Ashworth	July 1924	Nov 1925	-
Peter Hodge	May 1926	March 1932	22
Wilf Wild	March 1932	Nov 1946	48
Sam Cowan	Nov 1946	June 1947	16
Jock Thomson	June 1947	Feb 1950	-
Les McDowall	June 1950	May 1963	40
George Poyser	May 1963	April 1965	6
Joe Mercer	July 1965	Oct 1971	94
Malcolm Allison	Oct 1971	March 1973	-
Johnny Hart	May 1973	Nov 1973	-
Ron Saunders	Nov 1973	April 1974	12
Tony Book	April 1974	Jan 1979	30
Malcolm Allison	Jan 1979	Oct 1980	-
John Bond	Oct 1980	Feb 1983	18
John Benson	Feb 1983	June 1983	-
Billy McNeill	June 1983	Sept 1986	10
Jimmy Frizzell	Oct 1986	May 1987	-
Mel Machin	May 1987	Nov 1989	-
Howard Kendall	Dec 1989	Nov 1990	-
Peter Reid	Nov 1990	-	-

Manchester United

It was in their 12th season as a League club, in 1903-04, that United first appointed a manager and in the 78 seasons that have elapsed since then, there have been only 13 successors to Ernest Mangnall. This produces the rather high average term of 5.6 years, although there were three periods totalling five seasons when United had no manager.

Almost everything about the club's managerial record is dominated by Matt Busby, a Cup winner as a player with Manchester City. In his quarter of a century at the helm, he became the most successful manager in English football (see *Overall Managers' Ranking*) and created the modern Manchester United. This was, however, the second great phase in the club's history. Mangnall, recruited from Burnley, stands alongside the likes of Tom Watson as one of the outstanding pre-World War One managers. He built a hugely successful United side in the Edwardian era, and almost repeated his success with neighbours Manchester City in the 1920s. The years between Mangnall and Busby, primarily the inter-war era, were short on success and long on uncertainty. John Chapman was suspended for undisclosed irregularities and United's only player-manager, Clarrie Hilditch, held the job for less than a season. During the two periods in the 1930s without a manager, secretary Walter Crickmer, who was to lose his life in the Munich air crash in 1958, was given selection duties. He guided United to promotion to Division One in 1937-38 at the same time as Manchester City were being relegated.

Busby proved an almost impossible act to follow. His two successors, Wilf McGuinness (apart from Hilditch, the only one of the 13 to have played League football for United) and Frank O'Farrell lasted 18 months each, and Tommy Docherty saw his side relegated before being re-established in the top flight. Docherty is one of only four United managers to have experienced relegation (Chapman, Herbert Bamlett and Archie Scott Duncan are the others). In the last 15 years, there have been only three managers and Dave Sexton, Ron Atkinson and Alex Ferguson have records that put them in the top rank amongst their contemporaries. Only Ferguson, who has won all three main domestic trophies and a European title, has been accepted as Busby's heir for his success in bringing the League title back to Old Trafford after a 26-year gap. He also became the only manager to win both the English and Scottish championships.

Manager	Start/Date	End/Date	Pts/Total
Ernest Mangnall	Sept 1903	Sept 1912	64
John Robson	Dec 1914	Oct 1921	-
John Chapman	Oct 1921	Oct 1926	16
Clarence Hilditch	Oct 1926	April 1927	-
Herbert Bamlett	April 1927	April 1931	-
Archie Scott Duncan	June 1932	Sept 1937	16
Matt Busby	Feb 1945	June 1969	306
Wilf McGuinness	June 1969	Dec 1970	18
Sir Matt Busby	Dec 1970	June 1971	-
Frank O'Farrell	June 1971	Dec 1972	-
Tommy Docherty	Dec 1972	July 1977	52
Dave Sexton	July 1977	April 1981	24
Ron Atkinson	June 1981	Nov 1986	54
Alex Ferguson	Nov 1986	-	108

Mansfield Town

Relative newcomers to the Football League (1931), Mansfield have been the poor relations of the East Midlands clubs, one Second Division season the summit of their achievements. In 55 League seasons, the Stags have had 24 managers — a change once every 2.3 seasons, a relatively high turnover rate which perhaps reflects the board's impatience with the lack of success.

One of the most recent job holders, Ian Greaves, had the greatest staying power, lasting six years. Jack Poole was at Field Mill for a similar length of time, although five years were during wartime. The only others to last more than four years were Tommy Cummings, in the 1960s, and incumbent George Foster. Greaves and Foster provided some much needed stability after the tensions of the 13 years between 1970 and 1983, when seven managers came and went as Mansfield rose from the Fourth to Second Divisions and fell back again. This matches the uncertainty of the early League seasons in the 1930s, when the Stags had six managers in eight seasons, including the reigns of Charles Bell and Harold Wightman (the first to manage all three Notts clubs), both of which lasted less than nine months, the shortest in the club's history.

Few had much prior managerial experience, regarding it as a stepping stone to bigger things. Fewer still were former players, only Stan Mercer, Stuart Boam and George Foster. Harry Martin, Bell, Poole, Sam Weaver and Jock Basford were all, moreover, previously involved in Stags' training or coaching roles before taking on the top job.

There were few big names. George Jobey had an illustrious career at Derby between the wars, but was a spent force at Mansfield. For Danny Williams, manager of Swindon's League Cup winning side, Mansfield offered the chance to re-establish his career, which he did not take, and Raich Carter (Hull and Leeds) and Ian Greaves (Huddersfield, Bolton and Oxford) were past their peaks. Billy Bingham had been in charge at Everton, but was to concentrate on the Irish national side. For a few, Mansfield led to something bigger, particularly Charlie Mitten (Newcastle), Cummings (Aston Villa), Dave Smith, who completed a hat-trick of Fourth Division promotions with Southend, and Freddie Steele who took Port Vale to the Third Division North title and an FA Cup semi-final.

Manager	Start/Date	End/Date	Pts/Total
Jack Hickling	Jan 1928	Dec 1933	-
Harry Martin	Dec 1933	March 1935	-
Charles Bell	April 1935	Dec 1935	-
Harold Wightman	Jan 1936	May 1936	-
Harry Parkes	May 1936	Jan 1938	-
Jack Poole	May 1938	Aug 1944	-
Roy Goodall	May 1945	June 1949	-
Freddie Steele	Aug 1949	Dec 1951	8
George Jobey	Jan 1952	May 1953	-
Stan Mercer	Aug 1953	Jan 1956	-
Charlie Mitten	Feb 1956	June 1958	-
Sam Weaver	June 1958	Jan 1960	-
Raich Carter	Jan 1960	Jan 1963	-
Tommy Cummings	July 1963	July 1967	6
Tommy Eggleston	Aug 1967	July 1970	-
Jock Basford	July 1970	Nov 1971	-
Danny Williams	Nov 1971	March 1974	-
Dave Smith	April 1974	April 1976	12
Peter Morris	July 1976	Feb 1978	14
Billy Bingham	March 1978	July 1979	-
Mick Jones	Aug 1979	May 1981	-
Stuart Boam	July 1981	Jan 1983	-
Ian Greaves	Jan 1983	Feb 1989	6
George Foster	Feb 1989	-	6

Manchester City, the 1956 FA Cup winners. Back row (left to right): W.Griffiths (secretary), directors messrs A.Douglas, R.Smith, W.Smith, F.Jolly and E.Gill. Middle row: L.H.Barnett (trainer), Barnes, Leivers, Trautmann, Ewing, Little, Les McDowall (manager). Front row: Johnstone, Hayes, Paul, Revie, Dyson, Clarke.

Manchester United in 1957, before the Munich air crash. Back row (left to right): Duncan Edwards (died), Billy Foulkes, Mark Jones (died), Ray Woods, Eddie Colman (died), David Pegg (died). Front row: John Berry, Bill Whelan (died), Roger Byrne (died), Tommy Taylor (died), Dennis Viollet.

Middlesbrough

In Boro's 83-season League history, major honours have been few and far between. In 47 First Division campaigns, they have never finished higher than third, and two appearances in the Football League Cup semi-final their major achievement in knock-out competitions. In spite of this, there have only been 22 managers at Ayresome Park, one every 3.8 seasons. Bob Dennison, who reigned in the early postwar period, was the longest serving. He was well into his ninth year when he left. Peter McWilliam had seven years during the inter-war period and Stan Anderson six years ending in 1972. Although both Tom McIntosh and Wilf Gillow stayed longer than Dennison, both lost a significant proportion of their terms to wartime disruption.

When choosing their manager, the Boro board appears to have been reluctant to give their former players a chance at the job. Anderson, the 14th office holder, was the first, and that was in 1966. Since then, only Bobby Murdoch and Willie Maddren have come to the job with similar backgrounds. For five of the first six managers (Alex Mackie was the exception), the Middlesbrough job was their first in the Football League, but since James Howie's departure in 1923, most of the appointees have had managerial experience at other League clubs: the three former players, Jack Charlton and Colin Todd (who was coach at Ayresome Park) were the odd ones out.

Some went to Teesside with established managerial reputations, none more so than Mackie (Sunderland), McWilliam (Spurs), Raich Carter (Hull, Leeds) and Malcolm Allison (Manchester City). Others went on to greater success in their post-Ayresome careers. Tom McIntosh, although only secretary, was a key figure in Everton's successes in the 1920s and Jack Charlton (Sheffield Wednesday, Newcastle and the Republic of Ireland) were two cases in point.

A national reputation did not help at Middlesbrough. Mackie, along with Andy Walker, both survived for less than a season and their departures were related to financial irregularities. In the post-war period, Allison was one of four managers whose tenures lasted between one and two seasons. They included his predecessor (Murdoch) and his successor (Maddren), when the club was on the slide and financial pressures mounting. The other was the ageing Walter Rowley in the 1950s.

Manager	Start/Date	End/Date	Pts/Total
John Robson	May 1899	May 1905	10
Alex Mackie	June 1905	Nov 1906	-
Andy Aitken	Nov 1906	Feb 1909	-
Andy Walker	June 1910	Jan 1911	-
Tom McIntosh	Aug 1911	Dec 1919	-
James Howie	May 1920	July 1923	-
Herbert Bamlett	Aug 1923	Jan 1927	-
Peter McWilliam	Jan 1927	March 1934	32
Wilf Gillow	March 1934	March 1944	-
David Jack	Sept 1944	April 1952	-
Walter Rowley	June 1952	Feb 1954	-
Bob Dennison	July 1954	Jan 1963	-
Raich Carter	Jan 1963	Feb 1966	-
Stan Anderson	April 1966	Dec 1972	8
Jack Charlton	May 1973	April 1977	22
John Neal	May 1977	May 1981	-
Bobby Murdoch	May 1981	Sept 1982	-
Malcolm Allison	Oct 1982	March 1984	-
Willie Maddren	June 1984	Feb 1986	-
Bruce Rioch	March 1986	March 1990	18
Colin Todd	March 1990	May 1991	-
Lennie Lawrence	July 1991	-	16

Millwall

Although they had been a professional club since 1894, and had reached two FA Cup semi-finals at the turn of the century, the Lions of South London did not get their first taste of League football until the formation of the Third Division in 1920. During the ensuing 66 seasons, Millwall have tried only 18 managers. For a club that has won few honours, the average stay of 3.7 seasons per manager is relatively high.

This is largely attributable to the fact that during the inter-war period, there were just three managers at the Den. The first of these, Robert Hunter, set the record nobody has come close to challenging. He had 14 years in the job to add to the 23 he had previously spent as trainer. Benny Fenton's 8.5 years between 1966 and 1974 is the second longest unbroken stint, although Charlie Hewitt's two terms (the first was ended by the authorities' investigation into financial irregularities) either side of World War Two amounted to 10.5 League seasons. To balance this, Jimmy Seed, Jimmy Smith and Peter Anderson were all at the helm for less than two seasons.

To have played for Millwall has counted for little in securing the Millwall job. Only Jack Cock, Smith, Fenton and Mick McCarthy were former Lions players, although Hunter had served the club as trainer. Previous managerial experience was a more important qualification, and only Cock, Billy Gray, Anderson, George Graham and McCarthy were making their debuts at this level. None went to the Den with a more illustrious past than Jimmy Seed, but he was 62 years of age when he got the job and his best years were given to Charlton. Gordon Jago had an impressive track record at Queen's Park Rangers whilst Bill McCracken had taken Hull City to within minutes of an FA Cup final. Perhaps the most colourful was Hewitt. Modelling himself on Herbert Chapman, he led the Lions to the Division Three title and the FA Cup semi-final. An accountant by training, and learning his trade at Wrexham and Chester, he had a flair for publicity.

For most, a spell at the Den was the end of the managerial road. McCracken went on to Aldershot, Ron Gray to Lincoln, Billy Gray to Brentford and Notts County, John Docherty to Bradford City and Bruce Rioch to Bolton. The star graduate, however, is George Graham, who did his managerial apprenticeship with the Lions before revitalising the Gunners on the other side of London.

Manager	Start/Date	End/Date	Pts/Total
Robert Hunter	1918	March 1933	14
Bill McCracken	May 1933	March 1936	-
Charlie Hewitt	April 1936	April 1940	20
Jack Cock	Nov 1944	Aug 1948	-
Charlie Hewitt	Aug 1948	Jan 1956	8
Ron Gray	Jan 1956	Jan 1958	-
Jimmy Seed	Jan 1958	July 1959	-
Jimmy Smith	July 1959	Jan 1961	-
Ron Gray	Feb 1961	Nov 1963	12
Billy Gray	Nov 1963	May 1966	14
Benny Fenton	May 1966	Oct 1974	-
Gordon Jago	Oct 1974	Dec 1977	8
George Petchey	Jan 1978	Nov 1980	-
Peter Anderson	Dec 1980	Nov 1982	-
George Graham	Dec 1982	May 1986	8
John Docherty	July 1986	Feb 1990	16
Bruce Rioch	April 1990	March 1992	-
Mick McCarthy	March 1992	-	-

New Brighton

Anyone who can recall watching New Brighton play in the Football League must now be in their late forties at least, for it was in 1951 that the club failed to gain re-election after finishing bottom of Division Three North. Although now largely forgotten, the Rakers spent 21 seasons in the League, all in the same division, and they played in more League fixtures than half a dozen of the current membership and more than all but eight of the 27 former League clubs.

In their 21 seasons, New Brighton had just five managers, each therefore lasting just over four seasons. The longest serving was the first, Bert Pelham, whose nine-year tenure included one pre-League season. Pelham was secretary from 1922 and secretary-manager after 1927. His successor, Bill Sawyer, was in his eighth year in office when he died, a year into wartime competition. The other three barely managed five seasons between them. Only one of the five, the much travelled Neil McBain, had any previous League management experience (with Watford and Luton), although three of them, Pelham, Walter Galbraith and McBain went on to similar posts elsewhere. Galbraith, who was in charge at the time of the Rakers'

demotion was also later in charge at Accrington Stanley and Bradford, also to leave the League, although Galbraith had moved on by the time the axe fell. Similarly, Pelham's only other managerial appointment was at Southport, another club which bit the dust, but not until much later.

Although mid-table was a good position for the Rakers, and despite the fact that they finished in the bottom three in five of their 21 seasons, it was still a surprise when they lost their League status. After 1951, a return to first-class football was never likely. In 1976, New Brighton lost their Tower Grounds home and in 1983, what was left of the club folded.

Manager	Start/Date	End/Date	Pts/Total
Bert Pelham	Aug 1927	April 1931	-
Bill Sawyer	March 1933	June 1940	-
Neil McBain	June 1946	Feb 1948	-
Jack Atkinson	July 1948	July 1950	-
Walter Galbraith	Aug 1950	Aug 1951	-

Newcastle United

It was not until January 1930, during their 33rd League season when their really great days were behind them, that Newcastle appointed a manager. The man at the helm from 1895 until Andy Cunningham's appointment was secretary Frank Watt, during whose tenure the Magpies won four Division One titles and made six Cup Final appearances. In the 56 complete seasons since 1930, there have been 18 managers (17 individuals, since Stan Seymour had two spells), each lasting an average of around three seasons. The longest serving was Joe Harvey (13 years); at the other end of the spectrum, Dug Livingstone, Norman Smith, Richard Dinnis, Jack Charlton and Ossie Ardiles had little more than a season apiece.

Traditionally, Newcastle's board has always been influential in playing as well as financial and administrative affairs. The fact that no manager was appointed until 1930 is evidence of this, as is the role played by Stan Seymour, a former player and a director from 1938 until his death in 1978. He was in charge of team matters for two periods, and twice led the Magpies out at Wembley as 'honorary manager'. His successor, Dug Livingstone, guided Newcastle to another FA Cup success months after he had taken over, and was rewarded with having team selection taken away from him.

Despite being one of the glamour jobs in football, managing Newcastle has also been one of the most precarious in modern times, for which boardroom divisions are partly responsible. Since Harvey stepped aside in 1975, United have changed managers on average every two years and all the club had to show for it before Kevin Keegan's triumphant return to Tyneside was one promotion from Division Two (under Arthur Cox). Of the eight who came and went before Keegan, half (Gordon Lee, Cox, Charlton and Jim Smith) resigned, and at a time when the Magpies seemed poised for some success.

The first and most recent appointees were both former Newcastle players, but between Cunningham and Keegan, only Seymour, Harvey and Willie McFaul also wore the famous colours. Trainer Smith and coach Dinnis were the others who had previous experience at St James'. The rest got the job on the basis of their previous managerial record, but none has come close to recapturing glories enjoyed in the pre-manager days of Frank Watt.

Manager	Start/Date	End/Date	Pts/Total
Andy Cunningham	Jan 1930	May 1935	18
Tom Mather	June 1935	Sept 1939	-
Stan Seymour	Sept 1939	March 1947	6
George Martin	May 1947	Dec 1950	10
Stan Seymour	Dec 1950	Dec 1954	36
Dug Livingstone	Dec 1954	Jan 1956	18
Charlie Mitten	June 1958	Oct 1961	-
Norman Smith	Oct 1961	June 1962	-
Joe Harvey	June 1962	June 1975	46
Gordon Lee	June 1975	Feb 1977	12
Richard Dinnis	Feb 1977	Nov 1977	-
Bill McGarry	Nov 1977	Aug 1980	-
Arthur Cox	Sept 1980	May 1984	10
Jack Charlton	May 1984	Aug 1985	-
Willie McFaul	Sept 1985	Oct 1988	-
Jim Smith	Dec 1988	March 1991	-
Ossie Ardiles	March 1991	Feb 1992	-
Kevin Keegan	Feb 1992	-	16

Newport County

When Newport left the Football League in 1988 after finishing at the bottom of Division Four, a fate that had been threatening for years at last became reality. Their departure was automatic, but they had been living a precarious existence for most of the 1980s because of dire financial difficulties. The last rites were read by David Williams, the club's 24th manager in 60 League seasons. This gave each of the job holders 2.5 seasons to try to lift County's fortunes, although the average reflects the rapidity with which changes were made in the final decade (eight managers in ten years). In the 18 years between the wars, though, the club had only four managers, and in the early post-war period, Billy Lucas' three terms amounted to 15 years, two more than Jimmy Hindmarsh 30 years earlier. In the 1980s, it was easier to count the length of stay in months rather than years, a reflection more of the financial circumstances than the ability of the individual.

Unlike South Wales neighbours Cardiff and Swansea, who competed in all four divisions, Newport had only one Second Division season outside the lower echelons. The club, therefore, lacked both the traditions and resources to attract big names or experienced managers to Somerton Park. Tom Bromilow, Jimmy Scoular, Len Ashurst and Bobby Smith, all post-war appointees, were the only individuals with previous experience of League management. The ranks of former players was not an especially fruitful source for the Ironsides, only Hindmarsh, Fred Stansfield, Leslie Graham and Brian Harris coming via that route. Although his father played for Newport, Lucas did not progress beyond the Reserves.

Of the club's old boys, Billy McCandless made the biggest splash, winning promotion from Division Three with three clubs from South Wales, starting with Newport. Harry Parkes, Louis Page and Colin Addison also got managerial jobs elsewhere in the League, whilst Jimmy Mullen took Burnley to the Division Four title in 1992. The only other promotion

success at Newport was under Ashurst, who took County into Europe via the Welsh Cup. He later managed Sunderland.

Manager	Start/Date	End/Date	Pts/Total
Harry Parkes	June 1919	May 1922	-
Jimmy Hindmarsh	May 1922	May 1935	-
Louis Page	June 1935	Sept 1937	-
Billy McCandless	Sept 1937	April 1946	14
Tom Bromilow	May 1946	Jan 1950	-
Fred Stansfield	March 1950	Dec 1953	-
Billy Lucas	Dec 1953	April 1961	-
Bobby Evans	May 1961	March 1962	-
Billy Lucas	March 1962	Feb 1967	-
Leslie Graham	March 1967	May 1969	-
Bobby Ferguson	July 1969	Nov 1970	-
Billy Lucas	Nov 1970	Jan 1974	-
Brian Harris	Jan 1974	March 1975	-
Dave Elliott	April 1975	Feb 1976	-
Jimmy Scoular	Feb 1976	Jan 1977	-
Colin Addison	Feb 1977	May 1978	-
Len Ashurst	June 1978	Feb 1982	6
Colin Addison	Jan 1982	May 1985	-
Bobby Smith	June 1985	March 1986	-
John Relish	March 1986	May 1986	-
Jimmy Mullen	June 1986	Feb 1987	-
John Lewis	Feb 1987	Oct 1987	-
Brian Eastick	Oct 1987	March 1988	-
David Williams	March 1988	May 1988	-

Northampton Town

Few jobs in football have been as precarious over the last 25 years as managing Northampton. Until 1967, the Cobblers' record compared favourably with most clubs, nine managers in 40 seasons. Since then, however, each new appointee seems to have received his P45 almost as soon as the ink on his contract had dried. In 26 years, there have been 15 job holders, a change every 21 months or so. The confusion off the field reflects the lack of achievement on it, which has since become a fight for financial survival.

The Cobblers' most successful phase came during the reign of the club's longest serving manager, Dave Bowen. He had two spells in charge, the first of over eight years, the longest unbroken period of service, and the second of three seasons. Bill Dodgin (jnr) and Clive Walker also had two terms, but neither lasted more than five years. This seemed to be as much as anyone could take: for Bob Hewison, Jack Tresadern, Bob Dennison and Graham Carr, this was also their limit. Less fortunate were Tom Smith, Bill Baxter, Mike Keen and John Petts, all of whom were gone before their second anniversaries, and Tony Marchi, Ron Flowers, Bill Baxter, Pat Crerand and Tony Barton, who did not make it to their first.

Incumbent Phil Chard is the ninth Northampton manager to have been with the club earlier. He, Dennison, Tom and Dave Smith, Bowen, Walker, Carr and Theo Foley were players, and Flowers was promoted from player-coach. Only six (Jack English, Warney Cresswell, Dodgin, Keen, Barton and Foley) had managed elsewhere in the League, so for Hewison, Tresadern, Syd Puddefoot, Marchi, Baxter and Crerand it was their introduction to management and Northampton. Getting another job was easier for the club's earlier managers. Hewison (QPR and Bristol City), Tresadern (Spurs, Palace and Plymouth), English (Exeter and Darlington), Dennison (Middlesbrough) and Dave Smith (Aldershot) continued in management after leaving Northampton. More recently, only Dodgin (Brentford) and Carr (Blackpool) landed comparable posts elsewhere. In the 1960s, the Cobblers rose from the Fourth to the First Division, and fell back again even more quickly. Through these six changes in League status

in nine seasons, Bowen was involved. Although it was not always as team manager, this was a remarkable record. In their Southern League days before World War One, Northampton were the club which gave Herbert Chapman his managerial start: he repaid them with the Southern League title.

Manager	Start/Date	End/Date	Pts/Total
Bob Hewison	May 1920	May 1925	-
Jack Tresadern	May 1925	Oct 1930	8
Jack English	Feb 1931	March 1935	-
Syd Puddefoot	March 1935	March 1937	-
Warney Cresswell	April 1937	Sept 1939	-
Tom Smith	Sept 1939	March 1949	-
Bob Dennison	March 1949	July 1954	8
David Smith	July 1954	July 1959	-
Dave Bowen	July 1959	Sept 1967	30
Tony Marchi	Sept 1967	May 1968	-
Ron Flowers	May 1968	May 1969	-
Dave Bowen	May 1969	May 1972	-
Bill Baxter	May 1972	May 1973	-
Bill Dodgin (jnr)	June 1973	June 1976	6
Pat Crerand	July 1976	Jan 1977	-
John Petts	Jan 1977	Jan 1978	-
Mike Keen	Feb 1978	March 1979	-
Clive Walker	May 1979	Oct 1980	-
Bill Dodgin (jnr)	Oct 1980	Feb 1982	-
Clive Walker	May 1982	May 1984	-
Tony Barton	July 1984	April 1985	-
Graham Carr	April 1985	May 1990	12
Theo Foley	May 1990	April 1992	-
Phil Chard	April 1992	-	-

Norwich City

For a club located in a quiet East Anglian city, Norwich have been surprisingly active on the managerial front. Since becoming founder members of the Third Division 66 seasons ago, the Canaries have tried 22 different managers, a turnover rate of one manager every three seasons. Contrary to most other clubs, the rate of change was higher in the earlier part of their League career. The average managerial term between the wars was 2.4 seasons but since 1969 has doubled, to 4.8 seasons.

Not surprisingly, the longest serving have been amongst the most modern, John Bond and his successor Ken Brown each clocking up seven years service at Carrow Road. Tom Parker, whose two spells either side of World War Two amounted to six years, was the only other manager to come close to these two. Equally unsurprising is the fact that a number of job holders barely had time to re-arrange the office furniture before they were on their way. Charles O'Hagan, James Stansfield, Jimmy Jewell, Willie Reid and George Swindin had less than three years service between them, Swindin's tenure covering just 20 games.

Less than half the appointees could claim managerial experience before going to Carrow Road. Swindin (Arsenal) and Cecil Potter (a championship winner at Huddersfield) had the most impressive track record, but James Kerr, Cyril Spiers, Lol Morgan, Ron Saunders, Bond and Mike Walker had all cut their managerial teeth elswhere, if only in the lower divisions. Ron Ashman, Norman Low, Doug Lochhead, Potter and Dave Stringer were all former Canaries, although Stansfield (a pre-League manager), Robert Young (trainer), Brown (coach) and Walker (coach) all had a prior connection with the club.

For some of the 19 former managers (Lochhead, Jewell, O'Hagan, Albert Gosnell, Robert Young, Reid and Dave Stringer), Carrow Road marked the start and end of their careers at this level, but nine others went on to new League clubs. Archie Macaulay (West Brom) and Bond (Manchester City) moved to First Division clubs, as did Saunders, whose haul of honours at Aston Villa included the League Cup and First Division Championship. Perhaps the most famous of the Norfolk club's former managers is Frank Buckley. His first job was at Norwich in Southern League days and then he went on to help redefine the manager's job during his stay with Wolves.

Manager	Start/Date	End/Date	Pts/Total
Charles O'Hagan	July 1920	Jan 1921	-
Albert Gosnell	Jan 1921	Feb 1926	-
James Stansfield	March 1926	Nov 1926	-
Cecil Potter	Nov 1926	Jan 1929	-
James Kerr	April 1929	Feb 1933	-
Tom Parker	March 1933	Feb 1937	14
Robert Young	Feb 1937	Dec 1938	-
Jimmy Jewell	Jan 1939	Sept 1939	-
Cyril Spiers	June 1946	Dec 1947	-
Doug Lochhead	Dec 1947	March 1950	-
Norman Low	May 1950	April 1955	8
Tom Parker	May 1955	March 1957	-
Archie Macaulay	April 1957	Oct 1961	14
Willie Reid	Dec 1961	May 1962	18
George Swindin	May 1962	Nov 1962	-
Ron Ashman	Dec 1962	May 1966	-
Lol Morgan	June 1966	May 1969	-
Ron Saunders	July 1969	Nov 1973	28
John Bond	Nov 1973	Oct 1980	28
Ken Brown	Nov 1980	Nov 1987	44
Dave Stringer	Nov 1987	May 1992	12
Mike Walker	June 1992	-	-

Nottingham Forest

The recently-retired City Ground legend, Brian Clough, was, until May 1993, the longest-serving manager at one club. His 18 years with Forest, however, still fell short of Billy Walker's 21 years in charge, although this amounted to only 14 League seasons because of the war. Managerial stability is therefore nothing new at the City Ground. Dave Mackay's tenure lasted a little less than a year, but he left of his own accord to succeed Clough at Derby. Since Harold Wightman's appointment in the 1936 close season, Forest had only eight managers in 50 seasons, each lasting on average just over six seasons.

Curiously, none of the eight had ever previously played for Forest, and none had any other previous connection with the club. All were, however, experienced League club managers. Wightman, in a relatively short career, was the only man to manage all three clubs in Nottinghamshire (Forest, County and Mansfield), whilst Gillies' much longer career was spent entirely in the East Midlands. He took Leicester to two FA Cup Finals before his sojourn at Forest. Both Clough and Mackay were League Championship winners with Derby, Forest's near neighbours, Clough before going to Forest and Mackay afterwards.

When Billy Walker steered Forest to the FA Cup in 1959, he became only the second man to manage two clubs to the trophy: Herbert Chapman was the first. The gap of 24 years between Walker's two successes moreover, with Wednesday in 1935 and Forest in 1959, is a record. A final point about Walker's long tenure is that he is one of a small band who have managed the same club in three divisions of the League.

Equally original is Brian Clough's record. His Championship success with Forest in 1978 followed the title win with Derby in 1972, and he thus joins Tom Watson and Chapman as the only men to manage two different clubs to Division One success. He was also the first to retain the League Cup and to do the double of League Championship and League Cup, and he has more League Cup successes to his name than any other manager.

Manager	Start/Date	End/Date	Pts/Total
Harold Wightman	July 1936	March 1939	-
Billy Walker	March 1939	June 1960	42
Andy Beattie	Sept 1960	July 1963	-
John Carey	July 1963	Dec 1968	18
Matt Gillies	Jan 1969	Oct 1972	-
Dave Mackay	Nov 1972	Oct 1973	-
Allan Brown	Nov 1973	Jan 1975	-
Brian Clough	Jan 1975	May 1993	202

Notts County

Participants in the FA Cup from the late 1870s and founder members of the Football League, Notts County have a legitimate claim to the title of the 'oldest club in the world.' It was not, however, until they had completed 26 League seasons that the Magpies gave responsibility for team affairs to a manager rather than a secretary. Albert Fisher was the first of 28 permanent managers in the following 69 seasons, although there have also been three caretakers whose combined service exceeds two years.

This turnover rate of a new manager every 2.5 seasons has varied only slightly over time, with the eight managers in 11 seasons between 1957 and 1968 the most frenetic period. Fisher, who spent 14 years at Meadow Lane, was the longest serving, although his reign was interrupted by four years of World War One. The three times that Jimmy Sirrel had at County's helm amounted to 13 years and spanned all four divisions of the League. Horace Henshall is the only other manager whose tenure exceeded five years. There were, on the other hand, eight managers who lasted a season or less (Charlie Jones, David Pratt, Tommy Lawton, Jack Burkitt, Andy Beattie, Billy Gray, Howard Wilkinson and Ritchie Barker), whilst Percy Smith, Jimmy McMullan, Harry Parkes, Ronnie Fenton, Larry Lloyd and John Barnwell were gone inside two seasons. These 14 men account for half of the number of managers but for only 21% of the League seasons.

Surprisingly, just four of County's managers (Henshall, Eric Houghton, Lawton and Barker) once played for the Magpies, although Tim Coleman, Beattie and Fenton had served the club in various other capacities before taking on the top job. Most went to Meadow Lane with some previous League management experience (Fenton and Wilkinson are the exceptions in the last 25 years), but none other than Smith, McMullan, Frank Hill and Barnwell had managed in the First Division (with Spurs, Aston Villa, Preston/Burnley and Wolves respectively). After leaving County, just eight went on to other jobs at the same level in the League, with Houghton (a Cup winner at Villa) and Wilkinson (the League Championship at Leeds) the biggest successes.

Manager	Start/Date	End/Date	Pts/Total
Albert Fisher	cs 1913	cs 1927	38
Horace Henshall	cs 1927	May 1934	14
Charlie Jones	May 1934	Dec 1934	-
David Pratt	April 1935	June 1935	-
Percy Smith	June 1935	Oct 1936	-
Jimmy McMullan	Nov 1936	Dec 1937	8
Harry Parkes	Jan 1938	July 1939	-
Arthur Stollery	June 1946	Feb 1949	-
Eric Houghton	April 1949	Aug 1953	14
George Poyser	Oct 1953	Jan 1957	-
Tommy Lawton	May 1957	July 1958	-
Frank Hill	Oct 1958	Nov 1961	6
Tim Coleman	Nov 1961	July 1963	-
Eddie Lowe	July 1963	April 1965	-
Tim Coleman	April 1965	March 1966	-
Jack Burkitt	April 1966	Feb 1967	-
Andy Beattie	Feb 1967	Sept 1967	-
Billy Gray	Sept 1967	Sept 1968	-
Jimmy Sirrel	Nov 1969	Sept 1975	20
Ronnie Fenton	Sept 1975	Oct 1977	-
Jimmy Sirrel	Oct 1977	July 1982	10
Howard Wilkinson	July 1982	June 1983	-
Larry Lloyd	July 1983	Oct 1984	-
Ritchie Barker	Nov 1984	April 1985	-
Jimmy Sirrel	May 1985	May 1987	-
John Barnwell	June 1987	Dec 1988	-
Neil Warnock	Jan 1989	Jan 1993	18
Mick Walker	Jan 1993	-	-

Norwich City, 1976-77. Back row (left to right): Jones, Forbes, Machin, Hansbury, Keelan, Peters, Powell, MacDougall. Front row: Boyer, Grapes, Steele, Sullivan, Suggett, McGuire, Stringer.

Nottingham Forest, 1977-78. Back row (left to right): Bowyer, Anderson, Woodcock, Burns, Gordon, Clarke, Lloyd, Woods, Shilton, Barrett, Brian Clough (manager). Front row: Withe, Chapman, McGovern, O'Neil, Robertson.

Oldham Athletic, 1974-75. Back row (left to right): Buckley, Blair, Whittle, McNeil, Edwards. Middle row: Jimmy McGregor (physiotherapist), Hicks, Platt, Jones, Ogden, Mulvaney, Jimmy Frizzell (manager). Front row: McVite, Bailey, Groves, Sweeney, Garwood.

Oxford United, 1986 with the Second Division trophy. Back row (left to right): Thomas, Hicks, Hardwick, Briggs, Judge, Charles, Dreyer. Middle row: Ken Fish (trainer), Hamilton, Barnett, Langan, Reck, Fogg, Jones, Slatter, Hebberd, Rhoades-Brown, Aldridge, Ray Graydon (assistant manager). Front row: Trewick, McDonald, Shotton, Maurice Evans (acting manager), Brock, Phillips, McDermott.

Oldham Athletic

In Joe Royle, who was appointed in the summer of 1982, the Latics now have the longest-serving manager at one club in the League today. He is by no means a unique example of loyalty amongst Oldham's managerial roll call. The 22 separate appointments involve only 18 men, since David Ashworth (two terms), Robert Mellor (three) and Jack Rowley (two) all returned for another crack at the job. It is Jimmy Frizzell, however, who holds the Boundary Park longevity record. Of his 22 years with the club, over 12 were as manager, ahead of Royle's 11, Ashworth's nine and Mellors' nine (plus six years of World War Two). These four accumulated 39 League seasons between them, over half of Oldham's entire history.

Since 1970, the Latics have had just two managers (Frizzell and Royle), a marked contrast to the previous 24 years, between 1946 and 1970, when 11 managers came and went. Amongst them were Danny McLennan, who, since he was in office for just a month during a close season, never picked a team, and Gordon Hurst, who saw active service (eight months), but not much. They join Jimmy McMullan (12 months) and Charlie Roberts (17 months) from the inter-war period as the shortest-term appointments.

Only five of 18 were former Latics players, Roberts, Jimmy McIlroy and Frizzell stepping up straight from the dressing room, whilst Ted Goodier and Hurst returned to Boundary Park after spending parts of their career elswhere. George Hardwick also played for Oldham, but he was appointed player-manager. Much of the club's time was spent in the lower divisions during the 1950s and 1960's and therefore it was not easy to attract big names or experienced managers. Just seven of the 18 could claim to have managed at League level before joining the Latics (Ashworth, Andrew Wilson, Frank Womack, Goodier, Norman Dodgin, Les McDowall and Rowley). The most impressive CV belonged to McDowall, who had taken Manchester City into Division One and to consecutive FA Cup Finals in the 1950s. Ashworth, in between spells at Boundary Park, led Liverpool to the League title in 1922.

The Manchester link is clearly very strong. In addition to McDowall, Ashworth left Oldham for City and Herbert Bamlett was to manage United, whilst Roberts, McMullan, Rowley, Frizzell and Royle were all at one time connected with Maine Road or Old Trafford. Bamlett also made a Cup Final appearance in his pre-Oldham days, in 1914, when, just weeks before succeeding Ashworth, he refereed the Liverpool-Burnley Final.

Manager	Start/Date	End/Date	Pts/Total
David Ashworth	1906	April 1914	16
Herbert Bamlett	June 1914	May 1921	12
Charlie Roberts	July 1921	Dec 1922	-
David Ashworth	Jan 1923	July 1924	-
Robert Mellor	July 1924	July 1927	-
Andrew Wilson	July 1927	July 1932	-
Robert Mellor	July 1932	May 1933	-
Jimmy McMullan	May 1933	May 1934	-
Robert Mellor	May 1934	Feb 1945	-
Frank Womack	Feb 1945	April 1947	-
Billy Wootton	June 1947	Sept 1950	-
George Hardwick	Nov 1950	May 1956	14
Ted Goodier	May 1956	June 1958	-
Norman Dodgin	July 1958	May 1960	-
Danny McLennan	May 1960	June 1960	-
Jack Rowley	July 1960	May 1963	6
Les McDowall	June 1963	March 1965	-
Gordon Hurst	May 1965	Jan 1966	-
Jimmy McIlroy	Jan 1966	Aug 1968	-
Jack Rowley	Oct 1968	Dec 1969	-
Jimmy Frizzell	March 1970	June 1982	20
Joe Royle	July 1982	-	34

Oxford United

Oxford United's 31-year stay in the Football League has not been lacking in excitement or change. They have won promotion four times and been relegated twice, and in the process played in all four divisions of the League and made a victorious appearance in a Wembley Final. Team responsibilities have been shared over this period between ten men, each lasting, on average, three seasons. The man who took the club into the League, Arthur Turner, was the longest occupant of the manager's office at the Manor Ground. He guided United through their first six and a half seasons of senior football as well as the final three and a half in the Southern League. Gerry Summers was at the helm for six League seasons, just a few months less than Turner, but Ron Saunders and Mark Lawrenson, on the other hand, both lasted less than six months.

Exactly half the United managerial squad had gained previous experience of the job elswhere in the League before going to the Manor Ground. Turner had taken Birmingham to an FA Cup Final, whilst Ian Greaves and Jim Smith were two of the most experienced managers on the circuit, with a number of promotion successes between them. For both Maurice Evans and Brian Horton, it was a second post, after apprenticeships with Reading and Hull respectively. Although none of the ten ever played for Oxford, Mick Brown, Bill Asprey and Horton were all on the coaching staff when they were offered the chance to manage the club.

Of the nine former managers, five went on to similar appointments with other league clubs. Turner called it a day when he was nearly 60, and Lawrenson, who resigned on a matter of principle (not being consulted about the transfer of Dean Saunders), has yet to resume his managerial career. Brown was to team up with a former Oxford player, Ron Atkinson, first at West Brom and then Manchester United, whilst Evans, always a reluctant manager, never returned after his resignation from Oxford. Summers (Gillingham), Asprey (Stoke) and Greaves (Wolves and Mansfield) continued to ply their trade after leaving the Manor Ground, but had little success compared with Smith (at QPR and Portsmouth in particular) and especially Ron Saunders, who was to make his mark at Norwich, Manchester City and Aston Villa.

Manager	Start/Date	End/Date	Pts/Total
Arthur Turner	Jan 1959	Feb 1969	20
Ron Saunders	March 1969	June 1969	-
Gerry Summers	July 1969	Sept 1975	-
Mick Brown	Sept 1975	July 1979	-
Bill Asprey	July 1979	Dec 1980	-
Ian Greaves	Dec 1980	Feb 1982	-
Jim Smith	March 1982	June 1985	30
Maurice Evans	June 1985	March 1988	24
Mark Lawrenson	April 1988	Oct 1988	-
Brian Horton	Oct 1988	-	-

Peterborough United

For a club which ranks amongst the newest in the League, Peterborough have had a remarkably large number of managers, 17 in the 33 seasons since they were elected in 1960. There are wide variations around the average tenure of 1.9 seasons per manager, which is one of the highest turnover rates of any club. Noel Cantwell had over six years in charge at London Road, split into two terms, and he is by far the longest-serving manager. Only four others, Jim Iley, John Wile, Gordon Clark and Peter Morris, lasted more than three seasons. There are, on the other hand, several managers who barely had time to re-arrange the office furniture before they were on their way again. Both Billy Hails and David Booth were in and out inside a couple of months, Mick Jones and Martin Wilkinson lasted a season or so, and Jack Fairbrother, Norman Rigby, John Barnwell and Mark Lawrenson had less than two seasons in the job.

Although the Posh have spent 19 of their 33 seasons in Division Four, they have been able to attract managers with good pedigrees to London Road. Of the 16 individuals who tried their hands at running the club, seven (Fairbrother, Clark, Cantwell, Morris, Jones, Booth and Chris Turner) had all gained managerial experience elsewhere in the League, whilst Wilkinson had been assistant at two clubs. Only a couple went on to better things in their post-Peterborough careers, namely Jimmy Hagan at West Brom and Barnwell at Wolves, although in the club's Midland League days of the 1950s, their managers included George Swindin, Jack Fairbrother and Bob Gurney, all former top-class players who subsequently went on to League club management.

Not until Wile's appointment in 1983 did anyone who had played League

football for Peterborough get the chance to manage the club. Fairbrother, Rigby and Hails had all played in the Midland League days, and Barnwell, Jones and Booth won internal promotions. Since Wile, only Turner was also a former player. He returned to London Road in 1991 after a 14-year interval, which included managing Cambridge, and liked the club so much, he bought it. He started 1993 as chairman.

Manager	Start/Date	End/Date	Pts/Total
Jimmy Hagan	Aug 1958	Oct 1962	12
Jack Fairbrother	Dec 1962	Feb 1964	-
Gordon Clark	April 1964	Sept 1967	6
Norman Rigby	Sept 1967	Jan 1969	-
Jim Iley	Jan 1969	Sept 1972	-
Noel Cantwell	Oct 1972	May 1977	12
John Barnwell	May 1977	Nov 1978	-
Billy Hails	Nov 1978	Jan 1979	-
Peter Morris	Feb 1979	May 1982	-
Martin Wilkinson	June 1982	Feb 1983	-
John Wile	May 1983	Nov 1986	-
Noel Cantwell	Nov 1986	July 1988	-
Mick Jones	July 1988	Aug 1989	-
Mark Lawrenson	Sept 1989	Nov 1990	-
David Booth	Nov 1990	Jan 1991	-
Chris Turner	Jan 1991	Dec 1992	14
Lil Fuccillo	Dec 1992	-	-

Plymouth Argyle

Although Argyle have had 19 individuals who have shared 20 managerial appointments (two men had two spells — Ellis Stuttard and Malcolm Allison — and, on one occasion, two split the one job), one person dominates the list in terms of success and longevity. Altogether, Bob Jack, patriarch of a famous footballing family, spent the best part of 30 years as Argyle manager (in two periods separated by four years at Southend), 12 years prior to the club's entry to the League, and 18 in the inter-war period.

Each managerial term has lasted on average four months more than three years, but other than Jack, only Jimmy Rae (six and a bit years), Jack Rowley (five years) and Tony Waiters (four and a half years) were much above this average. Many were gone before they completed two years, such as the George Taylor/Neil Dougall duopoly, Allison (twice), Mike Kelly, John Hore and David Kemp. The pace of change has quickened in recent years and fell to 1.7 seasons per manager in the 1960s, and was 2.2 seasons in the 1970s and 1980s.

Half of the job holders were former Argyle players or had other connections with the club. Jack, Rae, Dougall, Stuttard, Taylor, Bobby Saxton, Hore and Kemp were once Plymouth players, whilst Derek Ufton and Kelly were on the coaching staff. When they were appointed, most of the club's managers had no previous experience when they first arrived at Home Park. The exceptions were Jack Tresadern (Crystal Palace and Spurs), Saxton (Exeter), Bobby Moncur (Carlisle), Dave Smith (Mansfield and Southend) and Ken Brown (Norwich).

After Home Park, few of the Argyle managers achieved much, other than Malcolm Allison, who was one of the most influential figures in English football in the 1960s and 1970s. Billy Bingham made it to Everton and then the Irish national side, Saxton went to Blackburn and Mike Kelly became one of the England national team's coaches. Amongst several caretakers at Plymouth were the nomadic Andy Beattie towards the end of his career, and a young Lennie Lawrence before his move to Charlton.

Manager	Start/Date	End/Date	Pts/Total
Bob Jack	cs 1910	April 1938	62
Jack Tresadern	April 1938	Nov 1947	-
Jimmy Rae	Sept 1948	Jan 1955	14
Jack Rowley	Feb 1955	March 1960	14
Neil Dougall/George Taylor	March 1960	Nov 1961	-
Ellis Stuttard	Nov 1961	Oct 1963	-
Malcolm Allison	May 1964	April 1965	6
Derek Ufton	May 1965	Feb 1968	-
Billy Bingham	Feb 1968	March 1970	-
Ellis Stuttard	March 1970	Oct 1972	-
Tony Waiters	Oct 1972	April 1977	14
Mike Kelly	May 1977	Feb 1978	-
Malcolm Allison	April 1978	Jan 1979	-
Bobby Saxton	Jan 1979	May 1981	-
Bobby Moncur	June 1981	Sept 1983	-
John Hore	Oct 1983	Nov 1984	6
Dave Smith	Nov 1984	June 1988	8
Ken Brown	July 1988	Feb 1990	-
David Kemp	March 1990	Feb 1992	-
Peter Shilton	March 1992	-	-

Portsmouth

The pace of managerial change at Fratton Park has accelerated sharply in recent times. In Pompey's 43 seasons between being founder members of the Third Division in 1920 and 1970, they used just six managers, giving each over seven years in office. Since then, however, as the club dropped to the Fourth Division and climbed back to the top flight, they tried ten managers in 23 seasons, which means that the modern generation has had less than one third of the time to prove themselves than their predecessors.

Not surprisingly, the longest serving Portsmouth managers are to be found during the early stages of League membership. The flamboyant Jack Tinn spent 20 years at Fratton Park, seven of which were during World War Two. His closest challengers for durability are George Smith, nine years during the 1960s, and John McCartney, seven years in the 1920s. A recent jobholder, John Gregory, has the dubious distinction of being the shortest serving (12 months), with John Mortimore not far behind on 16 months.

The Portsmouth board has shown a preference for experience when selecting their managers, never more so than in the choice of incumbent Jim Smith, who had counted Oxford, Queen's Park Rangers and Newcastle amongst his previous six clubs. He was certainly Pompey's unluckiest manager, losing an FA cup semi-final on a penalty competition and missing automatic promotion to the Premier League by just two goals, all in the space of 12 months. Before him, McCartney, Tinn, Freddie Cox, Smith, Bobby Campbell, Alan Ball and Frank Burrows (second time around) had all managed League clubs elsewhere before going down to the Hampshire coast. Bob Jackson, who twice led Pompey to the League title, and Mortimore had coached extensively, moreover, and Ian St John had managed in Scotland. A prior Pompey connection is less common. Eddie Lever, Ron Tindall, Jimmy Dickinson and Bobby Campbell were all former players and Burrows had been club coach. This leaves the unfortunate Gregory as the only one of the 15 individuals (Burrows held the job twice) who was new to management and Fratton Park at the time of his appointment.

A few of Pompey's former managers found similar employment elsewhere when their term at Fratton ended (McCartney at Luton, Jackson at Hull, Cox at Bournemouth, Campbell at Chelsea and Ball at Stoke and later Exeter), but the most famous Portsmouth old boy was Rob Brown. He left Hampshire for Sheffield and the Wednesday just before Pompey joined the League and took his new club to the heights of English football in the late 1920s.

Manager	Start/Date	End/Date	Pts/Total
John McCartney	May 1920	May 1927	24
Jack Tinn	May 1927	May 1947	42
Bob Jackson	May 1947	June 1952	42
Eddie Lever	Aug 1952	April 1958	-
Freddie Cox	Aug 1958	Feb 1961	-
George Smith	April 1961	April 1970	14
Ron Tindall	April 1970	May 1973	-
John Mortimore	May 1973	Sept 1974	-
Ian St John	Sept 1974	May 1977	-
Jimmy Dickinson	May 1977	May 1979	-
Frank Burrows	May 1979	March 1982	6
Bobby Campbell	March 1982	May 1984	14
Alan Ball (jnr)	May 1984	Jan 1989	10
John Gregory	Jan 1989	Jan 1990	-
Frank Burrows	Jan 1990	March 1991	-
Jim Smith	June 1991	-	6

Port Vale

Currently in their third spell as a Football League club, Port Vale's managerial history effectively dates from 1919 when they replaced the banned Leeds City in Division Two. In their 13 pre-World War One seasons, there was a manager for just 12 months, former player and coach Tom Clare. In the 67 seasons since 1919, the Valiants have employed 21 managers, giving each, on average, a little over three seasons to prove themselves.

Contrary to the experience of most clubs, one of the longest-serving managers at Vale Park is the incumbent John Rudge. His nine and a half years (up to May 1993) puts him on a par with Joe Schofield in the 1920s. Vale seem to be a club which encourage loyalty, for eight of the managers account for over three quarters of the League history. In addition to Rudge and Schofield, Freddie Steele (7.5 years), Norman Low (5.75 years), Gordon Lee (5.5 years), Gordon Hodgson (5 years) Tom Morgan (4 years) and John McGrath (4 years) all stayed for longer than the average term. At the other end of the spectrum are Alan Bloor (three months), Bobby Smith (six months) and Ivor Powell (six months), who barely had time to change the headed notepaper before they and Vale parted company.

Bloor was one of only three post-1919 Vale managers to have played for the club, along with Jackie Mudie and Roy Sproson. Tom Morgan (secretary) and Dennis Butler (coach) both were internal appointments, but the rest were newcomers to Vale Park. All but Steele (Mansfield), Low (Norwich) and Smith (Bury) were also newcomers to League management when they got the Port Vale job.

In retrospect, it was not a job that led to bigger and better things. Schofield and Hodgson both died in office, whilst Holford stayed with the club as a trainer and then scout. Most of the rest who went on to manage other clubs spent their time in the lower divisions, such as Morgan (Wrexham), Warney Cresswell (Northampton), Billy Frith (Coventry), Powell (Bradford City and Carlisle), Low (Workington), Smith (Swindon) and McGrath (Chester and Preston). Only Gordon Lee made it to the top flight, with Everton and Newcastle, before he too went to Third Division Preston.

Manager	Start/Date	End/Date	Pts/Total
Tom Clare	cs 1905	cs 1906	-
Tom Holford	cs 1914	March 1920	-
Joe Schofield	March 1920	Sept 1929	-
Tom Morgan	Sept 1929	June 1932	14
Tom Holford	June 1932	Sept 1935	-
Warney Cresswell	May 1936	April 1937	-
Tom Morgan	Dec 1937	April 1939	-
Billy Frith	Aug 1945	Oct 1946	-
Gordon Hodgson	Oct 1946	June 1951	-
Ivor Powell	June 1951	Dec 1951	-
Freddie Steele	Dec 1951	Jan 1957	28
Norman Low	Feb 1957	Oct 1962	12
Freddie Steele	Oct 1962	Feb 1965	-
Jackie Mudie	March 1965	May 1967	-
Sir Stanley Matthews	May 1967	April 1968	-
Gordon Lee	May 1968	Jan 1974	6
Roy Sproson	Jan 1974	Oct 1977	-
Bobby Smith	Nov 1977	May 1978	-
Dennis Butler	May 1978	Sept 1979	-
Alan Bloor	Sept 1979	Dec 1979	-
John McGrath	Dec 1979	Dec 1983	6
John Rudge	Dec 1983	-	14

Portsmouth, 1983-84. Back row (left to right): Tait, Hateley, Howe, Dillon. Middle row: Ellis, Doyle, Aizlewood, Knight, Gosney, Webb, Morgan, Ball. Front row: Bobby Campbell (manager), Sullivan, McLaughlin, Biley, Rogers, Thomas, Gordon Neave (physiotherapist).

Port Vale, 1982-83. Back row (left to right): Tartt, Cegielski, Moss, Harrison, Lawrence, Ridley, Sprosan. Front row: Shankland, Hunter, Waddington, N.Chamberlain, Bromage, M.Chamberlain, Armstrong, Greenhoff.

Preston North End

Although one of the dominant clubs in the opening years of League competition, it was not until 1919 that Preston appointed their first manager. Even then, the board's commitment to the principle of a manager was often less than 100%. In the 17 years between 1932 and 1949, there was a manager for just one of the 10 League seasons. The 24 jobholders at Deepdale, therefore, cover just 58 of the club's 94 League seasons, an average of 2.4 seasons each.

No one manager has really dominated at Preston, and the greatest success has been achieved under a chairman. Jimmy Milne, with six and a half years, and Cliff Britton, with five, are the longest serving, whilst Brian Kidd, who lasted just two months, 'tops' the list of those with least time in the job. The 1980s were a particularly fraught period. In the 12 seasons since Nobby Stiles departed, the Lillywhites have tried eight managers, only two of whom made it beyond their second anniversaries.

Playing for Preston counts for little in the board's choice of manager. Milne, the 11th manager, was the first former player to get the job, and only Stiles, Tommy Docherty, Alan Kelly, Tommy Booth and Les Chapman since have counted North End amongst their clubs. Some, however, served the club in other capacities before being made manager, most notably Frank Hill, Will Scott and Kidd who were trainers/coaches. Far more important has been evidence of management experience, and with the appointment of the likes of Britton, Harry Catterick, Docherty and Gordon Lee, Preston attracted managers who had previously enjoyed League or Cup success at the highest level. All them, however, had passed their sell-by date when they went to Deepdale. Only Scott Symon, who left Deepdale for a 13-year stint with Glasgow Rangers, went on to win major honours. There are two chairmen who have played key roles in Preston's history. The colourful Major William Suddell, a successful textile businessman, made Preston the outstanding side in the country in the late 1880s/early 1890s. His methods were controversial, and he was later found guilty of embezzlement and was thought to have committed suicide in South Africa. Between the wars, J.I.Taylor (a director and chairman) was an indimidating figure, who was involved on a day-to-day basis, leaving little room for a manager. He found in trainer Will Scott a loyal staff man and they guided the Lillywhites to promotion from Division Two and FA Cup success in 1938. Preston were the last club to win the cup without a manager.

Manager	Start/Date	End/Date	Pts/Total
Vincent Hayes	1919	Jan 1923	18
James Lawrence	Jan 1923	May 1925	-
Frank Richards	May 1925	cs 1927	-
Alex Gibson	cs 1927	April 1931	-
Lincoln Hyde	April 1931	Feb 1932	-
Tommy Muirhead	April 1936	May 1937	12
Will Scott	June 1949	March 1953	16
Scott Symon	March 1953	Aug 1954	24
Frank Hill	Aug 1954	May 1956	-
Cliff Britton	Aug 1956	April 1961	12
Jimmy Milne	April 1961	Nov 1967	12
Bobby Seith	Nov 1967	cs 1970	-
Alan Ball (snr)	cs 1970	Feb 1973	14
Bobby Charlton	March 1973	Aug 1975	-
Harry Catterick	Aug 1975	May 1977	-
Nobby Stiles	July 1977	June 1981	8
Tommy Docherty	June 1981	Dec 1981	-
Gordon Lee	Dec 1981	Dec 1983	-
Alan Kelly	Dec 1983	April 1985	-
Tommy Booth	April 1985	Jan 1986	-
Brian Kidd	Jan 1986	March 1986	-
John McGrath	May 1986	Jan 1990	6
Les Chapman	Jan 1990	Sept 1992	-
John Beck	Dec 1992	-	-

Queen's Park Rangers

As founder members of the Third Division in 1920, Rangers were amongst the second wave of London clubs to achieve League status. During their 66 seasons, Rangers have used the services of 23 managers, excluding caretakers, Ted Vizard's wartime tenure and Gordon Jago's bizarre return in 1984, which lasted days. Their managers have, however, been very unevenly distributed across the club's League career, and the average duration of 2.9 seasons per manager conceals wide variations. Up to 1968, Rangers, had just nine managers in 41 seasons (an average of 4.6 seasons) but in the 25 seasons since, Loftus Road has been home to 14 managers (1.8 seasons average), a remarkable change.

A prior QPR connection has been a help in getting the Rangers job, right up to the present day. Of the 22 individuals who have managed the club (Tommy Docherty had two spells), ten were former players (John Bowman, Archie Mitchell, Michael O'Brien, Dave Mangnall, Alec Stock, Les Allen, Frank Sibley, Terry Venables, Trevor Francis and Gerry Francis) whilst two others (Steve Burtenshaw and Don Howe) were on the coaching staff when the managerial vacancy arose. Most of the appointees (the exceptions were O'Brien, Mangnall, Jack Taylor, Allen, Jago, Sibley and Trevor Francis) had managed other League clubs before moving to Shepherds Bush. Several had impressive pedigrees, particularly amongst the more recent intakes as Rangers became established amongst the country's leading clubs.

Nobody did more than Alec Stock, their longest-serving manager, to put Queen's Park Rangers on the map, but he had established his credentials earlier at Brisbane Road. Similarly Tommy Docherty, the club's shortest-serving manager, had a good track record at Chelsea as had Dave Sexton (also at Chelsea), Venables (Crystal Palace), Alan Mullery (Brighton) and Jim Smith and Don Howe at several clubs. Perhaps the most obvious connection between Rangers managers is that most had experience of London, either as players or managers at clubs other than Queen's Park Rangers.

Most of the 20 former Rangers jobholders went on to similar posts elsewhere, some to top-flight positions, like Docherty, Sexton, Venables, Jim Smith and Trevor Francis in recent times and Billy Birrell (Chelsea) and Jack Taylor (Leeds) earlier. Ned Liddell (Luton), Alec Stock (Luton and Fulham) and Bill Dodgin (Fulham, Northampton and Brentford) also enjoyed League and Cup success, but with lower division clubs. Final points to note are that Queen's Park Rangers were the second of three clubs (after Chelsea and before Manchester United) to which Sexton had followed Docherty, and at Loftus Road, Mullery succeeded his old Spurs colleague Venables just as he had at Selhurst Park.

Manager	Start/Date	End/Date	Pts/Total
Ned Liddell	April 1920	1924	-
Bob Hewison	cs 1925	May 1931	-
John Bowman	May 1931	Nov 1931	-
Archie Mitchell	Nov 1931	May 1933	-
Michael O'Brien	May 1933	April 1935	-
Billy Birrell	April 1935	May 1939	-
Dave Mangnall	April 1944	May 1952	22
Jack Taylor	June 1952	May 1959	-
Alec Stock	Aug 1959	Aug 1968	42
Bill Dodgin (jnr)	Aug 1968	Nov 1968	-
Tommy Docherty	Nov 1968	Nov 1968	-
Les Allen	Dec 1968	Jan 1971	-
Gordon Jago	Jan 1971	Oct 1974	10
Dave Sexton	Oct 1974	July 1977	18
Frank Sibley	July 1977	July 1978	-
Steve Burtenshaw	Aug 1978	May 1979	-
Tommy Docherty	May 1979	Oct 1980	-
Terry Venables	Oct 1980	May 1984	28
Alan Mullery	June 1984	Dec 1984	-
Jim Smith	June 1985	Dec 1988	12
Trevor Francis	Dec 1988	Nov 1989	-
Don Howe	Nov 1989	May 1991	-
Gerry Francis	June 1991	-	-

Reading

Berkshire's sole representatives in the Football League, Reading, rank amongst the oldest clubs in the country, tracing their origins back to 1871. It was not, however, until their 50th year that they won admittance to the League, on the formation of the Third Division. The Royals had a manager in 1921, and in the 66 seasons since, there have been 16 successors, virtually one manager every four seasons. Harry Matthews, the first, was the longest serving, but he had only one League campaign in his 20 years, the rest were in the Southern League or wartime football. This leaves Harry Johnston's seven years as the longest tenure at Elm Park, followed by Roy Bentley and Maurice Evans with six years. Johnny Cochrane's term of just one month was not only the shortest in Reading's history, but it was amongst the shortest anywhere. Only two of the club's 17 managers played for Reading, Billy Butler and Maurice Evans (also coach before becoming manager). The rest, with the exception of Matthews who had been with the club for years before they joined the League, were new to Elm Park when they were appointed. Although a few (Arthur Chadwick, Cochrane, Joe Edelston, Jack Smith, Jack Mansell and Ian Porterfield) had some managerial background before taking over at Reading, the club has seemed more prepared than most to give new managers a start.

Several of the Royals managers enjoyed national success, but not with Reading. Joe Smith and Cochrane were FA Cup winners with Bolton and Sunderland respectively, Cochrane (Sunderland again) and Ted Drake (Chelsea) helped teams to the First Division title and, whilst at Oxford, Maurice Evans managed the League Cup winners. With the exception of Cochrane, all achievements came in the managers' post-Reading career.

Honours have been sparse. The Fourth Division title has been won under Evans and Branfoot, promotion from this division secured under Hurley. Branfoot took them to the Third Division title, the second time they had won this. The first occasion was without a manager, for Chadwick left for Southampton in October 1925, and secretary H.S.Bray held the reins for the rest of that season.

Manager	Start/Date	End/Date	Pts/Total
Harry Matthews	May 1902	Nov 1922	-
Arthur Chadwick	Jan 1923	Oct 1925	-
Andrew 'Angus' Wylie	cs 1926	June 1931	6
Joe Smith	July 1931	Aug 1935	16
Billy Butler	Aug 1935	Feb 1939	-
Johnny Cochrane	Mar 1939	April 1939	-
Joe Edelston	Apr 1939	May 1947	-
Ted Drake	Jun 1947	June 1952	16
Arthur Smith	June 1952	Oct 1955	-
Harry Johnston	Nov 1955	Jan 1963	-
Roy Bentley	Jan 1963	Feb 1969	-
Jack Mansell	April 1969	Jan 1972	-
Charlie Hurley	Jan 1972	May 1977	6
Maurice Evans	May 1977	Jan 1984	12
Ian Branfoot	Jan 1984	Oct 1989	20
Ian Porterfield	Nov 1989	March 1991	-
Mark McGhee	May 1991	-	-

Rochdale

Founder members of the Third Division North, Rochdale have some claim to being the least successful side in the Football League. After 65 seasons of trying, Dale can boast just one promotion (from Division Four under Len Richley) and an appearance in the 1961-2 League Cup Final under Tony Collins in the days when the competition was in its infancy and largely ignored by the top clubs. This is more than offset by 10 applications for re-election and the fact that in only 14 of the 65 seasons did they finish in the top half of the division in which they were competing.

Not surprisingly, the manager's job at Spotland has been a fraught one. There have been 26 individuals (27 managerial terms) brave enough to try, together with three caretaker managers and two periods totalling two years without a manager. Turnover amongst managers at Spotland has been amongst the highest of any League club, 27 in 65 seasons on a change every 2.4 seasons. Of the 26, six came and went within a year (Bob Stokoe and Thomas Wilson with seven months apiece the shortest) and 12 more who were gone in under two years. Just six of the 25 former managers spent more than three years at Spotland with Jack Peart in the 1920s, Ted Goodier either side of World War Two and Tony Collins, in 1960s, all around the seven-season mark.

For nine of the 26, the Spotland job was their first taste of management and of Rochdale. There were six who had managed other clubs (most notably Stokoe and Eddie Gray), seven were former Dale players, Peart had been a wartime guest whilst four others moved up from administrative or coaching capacities with Rochdale. For 15 of the 26, the road to Rochdale led nowhere and marked the end of their managerial career.

The list contains some interesting names. Harry Catterick learned his trade at the grass roots with Crewe and Dale before moving to the highest level with Sheffield Wednesday and Everton. William Smith Cameron was making his comeback in football after a suspension for his part in the Bury (where he was manager) — Coventry bribery scandal of 1920. Perhaps the most interesting was Thomas Wilson, their first League manager. He was club chairman, who had also played on the wing for Swindon, Millwall,

Villa, QPR, Bolton, Leeds and Manchester United. He was running a pub in the town centre when he was elected chairman in 1919 and three years later he was manager.

Manager	Start/Date	End/Date	Pts/Total
Thomas Wilson	July 1922	Feb 1923	-
Jack Peart	Feb 1923	July 1930	16
William Smith Cameron	Aug 1930	Dec 1931	-
Herbert Hopkinson	April 1932	Jan 1934	-
Billy Smith	July 1934	Nov 1935	-
Ernest Nixon	Nov 1935	Oct 1937	-
Sam Jennings	Oct 1937	Sept 1938	-
Ted Goodier	Sept 1938	June 1952	-
Jack Warner	July 1952	May 1953	-
Harry Catterick	June 1953	May 1958	-
Jack Marshall	Oct 1958	June 1960	-
Tony Collins	June 1960	Sept 1967	12
Bob Stokoe	Oct 1967	Oct 1968	-
Len Richley	Oct 1968	Feb 1970	6
Dick Connor	Feb 1970	May 1973	-
Walter Joyce	July 1973	May 1976	-
Brian Green	June 1976	Sept 1977	-
Mike Ferguson	Sept 1977	Nov 1978	-
Doug Collins	Jan 1979	Nov 1979	-
Bob Stokoe	Nov 1979	June 1980	-
Peter Madden	June 1980	March 1983	-
Jimmy Greenhoff	March 1983	March 1984	-
Vic Halom	May 1984	Dec 1986	-
Eddie Gray	Dec 1986	June 1988	-
Danny Bergera	July 1988	March 1989	-
Terry Dolan	March 1989	Jan 1991	-
Dave Sutton	Feb 1991	-	-

Rotherham United

In the 67 seasons they have been in the League (ignoring the three seasons of Rotherham Town in the 1890s), Rotherham have found success elusive. The 20 managers (19 individuals) they have used since 1919 have brought two Third Division and one Fourth Division championship to Millmoor, plus two other Division Four promotions and one appearance in a League Cup Final (the very first in 1960-61). The 3.2 seasons per manager is broadly in line with the average for League clubs as a whole, and, in common with many other clubs, this turnover rate has been faster in the most recent period, 1.8 seasons per manager since 1979, compared with 4.6 seasons up to 1958.

The Merry Millers most successful manager, Reg Freeman, is also the longest serving. He spent over 18 years in the job before being tempted away by Sheffield United. His successor, Andrew Smailes, who had also been trainer under Freeman, put in seven years (bringing his total service to the club of 29 years), about the same as Billy Heald's two terms in the inter-war period. That the modern average is so low is accounted for by the speed with which Dave Cusack (four months), Ian Porterfield (18 months) and Emlyn Hughes (20 months) went to and left Millmoor. In the club's earlier days, only Stanley Davies (15 months) failed to establish himself at Rotherham.

Another of Freeman's distinctions is that he was the first former Rotherham player to move into the manager's office. Of his successors, only Smailes, Danny Williams and incumbent Phil Henson can make the same claim, although Jimmy McAnearney was coach before being promoted. Not until the surprise and controversial appointment of Tommy Docherty in 1967 did anyone with previous experience of managing a League club take over at Millmoor. This route was subsequently followed Jimmy McGuigan, George Kerr, Norman Hunter, Cusack and Billy McEwan.

Looking at the post Millmoor records of the club's 18 former managers,

it is hard to claim Rotherham was a stepping stone to bigger and better things. Freeman (Sheffield United), Porterfield (Chelsea) and Docherty (too numerous to mention) managed at the highest level, whilst Williams found momentary fame leading Swindon to League Cup success. McGuigan deserves a special mention. He spent most of his long career as a player and manager in the lower divisions, but steered Crewe, Chesterfield and Rotherham to promotion from Division Four, a unique achievement.

Manager	Start/Date	End/Date	Pts/Total
Maurice Parry	Oct 1921	cs 1923	-
J Briggs	cs 1923	cs 1925	-
Billy Heald	1925	March 1929	-
Stanley Davies	March 1929	cs 1930	-
Billy Heald	cs 1930	1933	-
Reg Freeman	Jan 1934	Aug 1952	38
Andy Smailes	Aug 1952	Oct 1958	-
Tommy Johnston	Nov 1958	July 1962	12
Danny Williams	July 1962	Feb 1965	-
Jack Mansell	cs 1965	cs 1967	-
Tommy Docherty	Nov 1967	Nov 1968	-
Jimmy McAnearney	Dec 1968	May 1973	-
Jimmy McGuigan	May 1973	Nov 1979	6
Ian Porterfield	Dec 1979	June 1981	14
Emlyn Hughes	July 1981	March 1983	-
George Kerr	March 1983	May 1985	-
Norman Hunter	June 1985	Dec 1987	-
Dave Cusack	Dec 1987	April 1988	-
Billy McEwan	April 1988	Jan 1991	12
Phil Henson	Jan 1991	-	6

Scarborough

After years of being denied a place in the Football League, Scarborough became the first beneficiaries of the automatic promotion rule for the winners of the GM Conference League, introduced in 1987. In their pre-League days, the club counted Andrew Smailes, once Rotherham manager, and Colin Appleton, who went on to Hull and Swansea, amongst their managers.

'Boro have had four managers in their six League seasons. Neil Warnock, who guided the club into the League, left midway through the second season, to be succeeded by his coach, Colin Morris. Like Warnock, he was making his managerial debut at League level, but it lasted just 10 months. When he lost the job, it was his assistant/coach, Ray McHale who stepped up. Like his two predecessors, he is in his first managerial post. It was obvious what would happen on McHale's departure in the spring of 1993. In keeping with past, Phil Chambers, on the club's coaching staff, stepped up for his managerial debut.

Manager	Start/Date	End/Date	Pts/Total
Neil Warnock	1986	Jan 1989	-
Colin Morris	Jan 1989	Nov 1989	-
Ray McHale	Nov 1989	April 1993	-
Phil Chambers	April 1993	-	-

Scarborough, 1988-89. Back row (left to right): Graham, Cook, Bennyworth, Richards, Ironside, Craig Short, Thompson, Christian Short. Front row: Olsson, Dobson, Brook, Ray McHale (assistant manager), Colin Morris (player-manager), Norris, Kamara, Russell.

Scunthorpe United

The extension of the Third Divisions to 24 clubs in 1950 gave Scunthorpe the opportunity to bring League football to North Lincolnshire. In their 43 season League career, the Iron have tried 18 managers. Each has lasted on average, therefore, 2.4 seasons, a relatively high turnover rate. This was especially true in the early years (a change every 1.7 seasons between 1951 and 1960) and, although it slowed (to 4.3 seasons) between 1960 and 1973, it has since accelerated (to 2.2 seasons).

Few managerial terms in League history were as brief as Bill Lambton's at the Old Show Ground. His verbal contract was ended after just three days. In this early period, Tony McShane and Frank Soo (a Liverpudlian whose real name was Hong Y) bit the dust after barely a season. Not only was Ron Ashman the longest-serving United manager, a total tenure of over 11 years in his two separate spells but, if the two terms are counted individually, he ranks first and second. Dick Duckworth's 4.5 years (the end of 40 years in football) comes closest to the shortest of Ashman's stints.

In selecting their managers, the Scunthorpe board seem to have worked on the principle of 'better the devil you don't know!' Only the latest appointee, Richard Money, had ever played for the Iron, although Ron Bradley, Frank Barlow and Bill Green had served the club in other capacities before ascending to the top job. Managerial experience has been given a larger weight. Other than the unfortunate Lambton, who went to the Old Show Ground after a spell as Leeds manager, Duckworth (York, Stockport and Darlington), Ashman (Norwich), Allan Clarke (Barnsley and Leeds), Frank Barlow (Chesterfield) and Mick Buxton (Huddersfield) had all done apprenticeships in League club management before taking on the Scunthorpe job.

For some (Billy Corkhill, Suart, McShane, Lambton, Freddie Goodwin, John Duncan and Clarke), a sojourn at the Old Show Ground enhanced their career prospects. Suart (Blackpool and Chelsea) and Goodwin (Birmingham) made the most progress, spending some of their careers in the First Division. In Suart's case, it was well earned, for he was the only Scunthorpe manager to win an honour, the Third Division North in 1957-58, the last-ever winner of that competition.

Manager	Start/Date	End/Date	Pts/Total
Leslie Jones	June 1950	1951	-
Billy Corkhill	1952	May 1956	-
Ron Suart	May 1956	May 1958	14
Tony McShane	May 1958	April 1959	-
Bill Lambton	April 1959	April 1959	-
Frank Soo	June 1959	May 1960	-
Dick Duckworth	May 1960	Nov 1964	-
Freddie Goodwin	Dec 1964	Oct 1967	-
Ron Ashman	Oct 1967	June 1973	6
Ron Bradley	June 1973	Nov 1974	-
Dickie Rooks	Nov 1974	Jan 1976	-
Ron Ashman	Jan 1976	May 1981	-
John Duncan	June 1981	Feb 1983	-
Allan Clarke	Feb 1983	Aug 1984	6
Frank Barlow	Aug 1984	March 1987	-
Mick Buxton	April 1987	Jan 1991	-
Bill Green	Feb 1991	Jan 1993	-
Richard Money	Jan 1993	-	-

Sheffield United

In spite of some of the uncertainty that existed at Bramall Lane in the late 1960s and 1970s, Sheffield United have a record for managerial stability few clubs can match. In the first half of this century, just two men had responsibility for team affairs, and over the next 20 years, there were only five office holders, having two spells in the job. All told, since the first appointment in 1899, the Blades have employed 13 managers, each lasting, on average, just under six and a half seasons.

There are three of the 12 individuals whose service to United dwarfs the others. John Nicholson spent 33 years at the helm, a period ended only by his untimely death. It was followed by Teddy Davison, whose reign lasted 20 years and later still came John Harris, whose two terms amounted to over 13 years. Between them, these three account for two thirds of United's League career since a manager was first appointed. The average tenure comes down because Arthur Rowley, Jimmy Sirrel and Billy McEwan were each at Bramall Lane for under two seasons.

Although the board seems to have chosen wisely, it has shown a preference for men who had little previous experience with the Blades. None of the club's managers had ever played for United or had any prior connection, other than McEwan, who had been Porterfield's coach and assistant manager. More important in securing the United job appears to have been managerial experience. Since Nicholson's time, only Joe Mercer and McEwan were newcomers to management, the other nine all having previously been in charge of League clubs.

The fortunes of United's managers in their post-Bramall Lane careers were very mixed. For Nicholson and Freeman, there was nothing after the Blades, for both died in office. Davison, Rowley and McEwan stayed in management, but at a lower level, Sirrel returned to Notts County and took them into Division One, Haslam retired, Furphy went to the States and Porterfield went on to manage briefly in the Premier League with Chelsea. Harris stayed in the city, but switched to Hillsborough, where he was general manager for many years, right into the 1980s, whilst Joe Mercer, having won nothing at Bramall Lane in his first job, went on to become one of the most successful managers of all time, crowning his career with a short spell in charge of the England team.

Manager	Start/Date	End/Date	Pts/Total
John Nicholson	May 1899	April 1932	96
Teddy Davison	June 1932	Aug 1952	22
Reg Freeman	Aug 1952	Aug 1955	16
Joe Mercer	Aug 1955	Dec 1958	-
John Harris	April 1959	July 1968	16
Arthur Rowley	July 1968	Aug 1969	-
John Harris	Aug 1969	Dec 1973	10
Ken Furphy	Dec 1973	Sept 1975	-
Jimmy Sirrel	Oct 1975	Sept 1977	-
Harry Haslam	Jan 1978	May 1981	-
Ian Porterfield	June 1981	March 1986	20
Billy McEwan	March 1986	Jan 1988	-
Dave Bassett	Feb 1988	-	24

Sheffield Wednesday

For the entire pre-World War One period, Wednesday resisted the temptation to appoint a manager, preferring to have their affairs in the hands of secretary Arthur Dickinson, working with the board. It was a policy that served the club well, for in 23 seasons, they won the First Division title twice, the Second Division once and reached two FA Cup Finals. When, in 1919-20, the Owls finished at the foot of Division One, their attitude changed, and Rob Brown was appointed the 'first professional secretary-manager.'

It was a good start. Brown lasted 13 years in the job and restored the club's playing fortunes. Only Eric Taylor stopped longer, 16 years, but, because of the war, this amounted to 12 League seasons. Overall, in 66 seasons since Rob Brown's arrival, Wednesday have had 17 job holders, an average of 3.9 seasons per manager. The period between Alan Brown's departure in 1968 and Jack Charlton's arrival in 1977 was the most frenetic, with four managers coming and going. Yet it was a later manager, Peter Eustace, who was the shortest serving, surviving just four months in the 1988-89 season.

Eustace was one of only four men to have both played for and managed Wednesday: the unfortunate Derek Dooley was the first, and more recently Howard Wilkinson and Trevor Francis have followed. Rob Brown and Taylor had, however, both served the club in an administrative capacity before taking on the manager's role, while Alan Brown had been a coach and Jack Marshall the number two at Hillsborough.

When necessary, the Wednesday board have never hesitated to act decisively, even brutally. The Christmas Eve sacking of Hillsborough folk hero Dooley drew a great deal of criticism, Walker's services were disposed of two years after he had taken the club to FA Cup success, and even the ageing Brown was despatched with unseemly haste, his outstanding record counting for little. Walker, however, went on to further triumphs, with Forest, whilst Harry Catterick (Everton), Charlton (Republic of Ireland) and Wilkinson (Leeds) left Hillsborough of their own volition and scaled new heights in their next incarnations.

Manager	Start/Date	End/Date	Pts/Total
Rob Brown	June 1920	Dec 1933	58
Billy Walker	Dec 1933	Nov 1937	18
Jimmy McMullan	Dec 1937	April 1942	-
Eric Taylor	April 1942	July 1958	48
Harry Catterick	Aug 1958	April 1961	34
Vic Buckingham	May 1961	March 1964	-
Alan Brown	cs 1964	Feb 1968	12
Jack Marshall	Feb 1968	April 1969	-
Danny Williams	July 1969	Jan 1971	-
Derek Dooley	Jan 1971	Dec 1973	-
Steve Burtenshaw	Jan 1974	Oct 1975	-
Len Ashurst	Oct 1975	Oct 1977	-
Jack Charlton	Oct 1977	May 1983	14
Howard Wilkinson	June 1983	Oct 1988	16
Peter Eustace	Oct 1988	Feb 1989	-
Ron Atkinson	Feb 1989	May 1991	28
Trevor Francis	June 1991	-	24

Sheffield United, 1976. Back row (left to right): Jimmy Sirrel (manager), Colquhoun, Brown, Faulkner, Franks, Guthrie, Cec Coldwell (trainer). Front row: McGeadie, Garner, Ludlam, Currie, Bradford, Woodward, Flynn.

Sheffield Wednesday, 1974-75. Back row (left to right): Shaw, Coyle, Craig, Cameron. Middle row: Steve Burtenshaw (manager), Mullen, Dowd, Paterson, Springett, Sunley, Potts, Gerry Young. Front row: Thompson, Prudham, Knighton, Joicey, Rodrigues, Eustace, Holsgrove.

Shrewsbury Town

Although founded as long ago as 1876, it was not until 1950 that Shrewsbury were elected to the Football League when the Third Divisions were extended to 24 clubs. Still comparative newcomers, the Shrews have had 14 managers in 43 seasons, a change, on average, once every three seasons or so. This is a relatively high rate of turnover in view of the fact that Arthur Rowley alone accounts for almost a quarter of the total and Graham Turner spent over five years at the Gay Meadow helm. This clearly implies that several managers spent very little time in the job, in particular Johnny Spuhler (four months), Ritchie Barker (ten months) and Asa Hartford, who had about a year each.

Only three of the 14 (Alan Durban, Turner and Chic Bates) were former Shrews' players, but Maurice Evans and Hartford were coaches and Barker assistant manager before they took on the top job. Town's board do not seem to have been impressed by previous management experience. The recently departed John Bond was by far the most experienced (Gay Meadow was his seventh appointment, more than all Shrewsbury's previous managers combined). Of the rest, Walter Rowley had been with Bolton and Middlesbrough, Hartford with Stockport. By deduction, therefore, when Sammy Crooks, Harry Potts, Spuhler, Arthur Rowley, Harry Gregg and Ian McNeill arrived in Shropshire, it was their first taste of management and first contact with the Shrews.

For Walter Rowley and Bond, this post came towards the end of lengthy managerial careers, but for one or two others, the best was still to come when they left Gay Meadow. Potts was the most successful, taking Burnley to the League title and a Wembley Cup Final. Evans also went to Wembley, steering Oxford to the League Cup whilst Turner, after an unhappy spell at Villa Park, has helped revive the fortunes of Wolves. Finally, although they have not made their marks as managers, both Barker and McNeill are highly regarded coaches who have rarely been short of work.

The three managers who have taken Shrewsbury to promotion were all tempted away by bigger clubs, Arthur Rowley by Sheffield United, Durban by Stoke and Turner by Villa. None, however, was to enjoy the success at their new club that they had at Gay Meadow.

Manager	Start/Date	End/Date	Pts/Total
Sammy Crooks	May 1950	June 1954	-
Walter Rowley	July 1954	June 1957	-
Harry Potts	cs 1957	Feb 1958	-
John Spuhler	Feb 1958	June 1958	-
Arthur Rowley	June 1958	July 1968	12
Harry Gregg	July 1968	Oct 1972	-
Maurice Evans	Oct 1972	Feb 1974	-
Alan Durban	Feb 1974	Feb 1978	6
Ritchie Barker	Feb 1978	Nov 1978	-
Graham Turner	Nov 1978	July 1984	14
Chic Bates	July 1984	Nov 1987	-
Ian McNeill	Dec 1987	Jan 1990	-
Asa Hartford	Jan 1990	Jan 1991	-
John Bond	Jan 1991	May 1993	-

Southampton

Although the Saints' League career did not start until the formation of Division Three in 1920, they had enjoyed a taste of national fame 20 years earlier when they were twice beaten FA Cup Finalists. These appearances at the Crystal Palace occurred during secretary E.Arnfield's tenure, but by the time League status was achieved, former trainer James McIntyre was installed in a managerial role. During the 66 seasons that have elapsed since then, Southampton have had 13 managers, giving a relatively long average lifespan of a fraction over five years per manager. Ted Bates leads the way on 18 years, with his successor, Lawrie McMenemy, behind him on 11.5 years. During the 30 years from 1955, therefore, when most clubs were increasing their hiring and firing rate, the Saints had just two managers. To achieve the average, of course, means that others were less durable, particularly George Cross (10 months) and Syd Cann (28 months).

The appointment of Ian Branfoot in May 1991 was untypical of the club's usual practice. He was only the fourth of the 13 to have had no previous connections with the Dell, the others being George Kay, George Roughton and McMenemy. Amongst the other nine, Arthur Chadwick, Tom Parker, Bill Dodgin, Bates and Chris Nicholl were once Saints players, McIntyre and Cann ex-trainers, Cross a secretary and J.R.Sarjantson, one-time chairman.

It was during McMenemy's stewardship that the Saints enjoyed their greatest success. Not only did they finish second in the First Division, but they were also the first Second Division club since the war to win the FA Cup. It might have been very different had the Saints not surrendered a seemingly unassailable lead at the top of the Second Division in 1949. For manager Bill Dodgin, the frustration was eased when he left the Dell that summer to take over at Fulham, who had pipped Southampton for promotion. He was the second Saints manager to go on to Craven Cottage. McIntyre went to West London (albeit via Coventry) and when he guided them to the Third Division South title in 1932, he became the first manager to win the division twice with different clubs. (Southampton were the first ever winners in 1922.)

Manager	Start/Date	End/Date	Pts/Total
James McIntyre	Aug 1919	Dec 1924	22
Arthur Chadwick	Oct 1925	May 1931	6
George Kay	May 1931	May 1936	-
George Cross	May 1936	March 1937	-
Tom Parker	March 1937	June 1943	-
J.R.Sarjantson	June 1943	June 1947	-
Bill Dodgin (snr)	Jan 1946	Aug 1949	-
Syd Cann	Aug 1949	Dec 1951	-
George Roughton	March 1952	Sept 1955	-
Ted Bates	Sept 1955	Dec 1973	30
Lawrie McMenemy	Dec 1973	June 1985	58
Chris Nicholl	Aug 1985	May 1991	12
Ian Branfoot	May 1991	-	-

Southend United

After 60 seasons of League football, the pace of life at Southend accelerated. In the space of five seasons, the Shrimpers had four changes of status, and in the summer of 1991, reached the Second Division for the very first time. The rise was achieved under the 18th of Southend's 20 managers in their 66-seasons League career. This average tenure of 3.3 seasons per manager has varied markedly over time, from over seven seasons in the period up to 1956 to 15 months in the last ten seasons. There are two of the 19 individuals (Dave Webb had two spells at Roots Hall) who stand out for their durability, Harry Warren, whose 16 years covered ten League seasons, and Edward Birnie, who was at the helm for 13 years between the wars. Since Warren's departure in 1956, only Dave Smith and Arthur Rowley had an above-average stay, in marked contrast to Dick Bate, Peter Morris, Geoff Hudson and Frank Broome, four managers whose combined service came to less than two seasons.

When caretaker Paul Clark took temporary charge in 1987 (and helped win promotion), he became the first former Southend player to manage the Shrimpers. There does appear to have been some resistance to anyone previously connected with the club, for only Ernie Shepherd, who was trainer and assistant manager before he succeeded Alvan Williams in the 1960s, had any earlier association with the Shrimpers. The board's preference seems to have been for managerial experience rather than links with Southend, for eight of the 17 went to Essex from other League clubs, with Ted Fenton the most illustrious after his years in the top flight with West Ham. For most of Southend's former managers, this job was the end of the managerial line. The principal exceptions were Tom Mather and David Jack, both of whom went on to First Division clubs later in their careers.

In the Shrimpers' pre-League days, Bob Jack was in charge, and his son David followed the same route almost 30 years later. Amongst the other pre-League managers at Southend were Joe Bradshaw (1912-19) and Ned Liddell (1919-20), both later to manage Fulham, Liddell succeeding Bradshaw at the Cottage in 1929. This Fulham connection runs right through Southend's history. In later years, Eddie Perry, Ernie Shepherd, Arthur Rowley and Bobby Moore all spent part of their playing careers with the Cottagers and subsequently managed with Shrimpers.

Manager	Start/Date	End/Date	Pts/Total
Tom Mather	cs 1920	1921	-
Edward Birnie	1921	May 1934	-
David Jack	May 1934	Aug 1940	-
Harry Warren	Aug 1940	June 1956	-
Eddie Perry	cs 1956	May 1960	-
Frank Broome	May 1960	Dec 1960	-
Ted Fenton	March 1961	April 1965	-
Alvan Williams	May 1965	March 1967	-
Ernie Shepherd	April 1967	Oct 1969	-
Geoff Hudson	Oct 1969	1970	-
Arthur Rowley	March 1970	May 1976	6
Dave Smith	May 1976	June 1983	18
Peter Morris	July 1983	Feb 1984	-
Bobby Moore	Feb 1984	April 1986	-
Dave Webb	June 1986	March 1987	-
Dick Bate	June 1987	Sept 1987	-
Paul Clark	Sept 1987	May 1988	-
Dave Webb	Nov 1988	May 1992	14
Colin Murphy	May 1992	April 1993	-
Barry Fry	April 1993	-	-

Southport

It was in 1978 that Haig Avenue ceased to host Football League fixtures when Southport's 12th re-election application proved to be one too many. This came after 50 seasons of League membership, for the Sandgrounders were founder members of the Third Division North. Their managerial history began in 1925, the fifth season, after which there were 20 changes before the curtain came down.

There was, however, one manager whose reign extended well beyond the average 2.3 seasons for the club. Gordon Hunt had two spells at the Southport helm either side of World War Two. All but two of his 16 years were Football League seasons. The only other man whose stay at Haig Avenue was much above the average was John Commins, although, like Hunt, his contribution (around five years) was spread over two terms. Starting with the first manager, Tom Maley, there were several whose service to Southport was measured in months rather than years. Even Maley's five months and Trevor Hitchen's seven months, however, compare favourably with the two months of Arthur Peat and Jimmy Melia's and Allan Brown's four months.

Peat, along with Len Newcomb, Alex Parker, Jimmy Meadows and Alan Ball (snr), was one of a handful of Southport players who went on to manage their old club. The long-serving Hunt, who was with the club from 1923 to 1976, worked his way to manager (and back again) via the administrative route. Few of the appointees could boast previous managerial experience before taking over at Haig Avenue. Maley had the most impressive credentials, having worked at the highest level with Manchester City. Commins (Barnsley), Don McEvoy (Grimsby), Jimmy Meadows (Stockport and Bolton), Ball (Halifax and Preston), Melia (Aldershot and Crewe), Brown (Luton, Torquay, Bury and Forest) and Ray Henderson (Halfiax) had all cut their managerial teeth elsewhere. Still fewer went on to other clubs (Brown to Blackpool and Meadows to Stockport), with the most successful Haig Road graduate being Billy Bingham, who numbered Everton and the Northern Ireland FA amongst his future employers, and Melia, manager of Brighton's 1984 Cup Final side.

There are four of the 19 who were involved with other clubs which left the Football League, Commins (Barrow), McEvoy (Barrow), Pelham (New Brighton) and Maley (Bradford), although none was in charge when the axe fell.

Manager	Start/Date	End/Date	Pts/Total
Tom Maley	May 1925	Oct 1925	-
Charles Porter	May 1926	Jan 1929	-
John Commins	March 1929	Nov 1930	-
Bert Pelham	April 1931	March 1933	-
John Commins	March 1933	1936	-
Gordon Hunt	April 1937	Sept 1940	-
Gordon Hunt	1945	June 1958	-
Trevor Hitchen	June 1958	Jan 1959	-
Wally Fielding	Jan 1959	May 1960	-
Len Newcomb	July 1960	March 1964	-
Willie Cunningham	March 1964	April 1965	-
Billy Bingham	Dec 1965	Feb 1968	6
Don McEvoy	March 1968	Jan 1970	-
Arthur Peat	Feb 1970	April 1970	-
Alex Parker	May 1970	May 1971	-
Jimmy Meadows	May 1971	Dec 1973	12
Alan Ball (snr)	Jan 1974	July 1975	-
Jimmy Melia	July 1975	Sept 1975	-
Allan Brown	Jan 1976	May 1976	-
Ray Henderson	May 1976	March 1977	-
Hugh Fisher	March 1977	May 1978	-

Stockport County

In reaching the Third Division play-offs in 1992 and 1993, Stockport enjoyed the most successful period of their post-war history. Most of the time since 1945 has been spent in the lower reaches of the League, and it has been a Uruguayan who played his football in Europe who has lifted County. The years of obscurity took a heavy toll on Stockport managers. In their 81 League seasons, they have had the remarkably high number of 34 managers (31 individuals, since three came back for a second helping). This includes three lengthy spells in the 1930s when there was no manager. Up to 1939, County had nine managers in 34 seasons (average of 3.9 seasons per manager), but from 1946 to 1970, the pace of change quickened, with 10 managers in 24 seasons. Since then, however, it has accelerated further, with 16 managers in the last 24 seasons, the average tumbling to just 1.5 seasons.

No one has come close to challenging Fred Stewart's 11 year-reign as County's manager in the opening decade of the century. Albert Williams' five years in the 1920s is a distant second. Several of the 34, on the other hand, hardly had time to get to know the names of the squad. Colin Murphy, for example, was twice in charge and still only lasted a total of eight months. This was, nevertheless, twice the length of Jimmy Melia's tenure at Edgeley Park, and about the same as Les Chapman's term, all in the 1980s.

The 31 men have a variety of backgrounds. A handful (Lincoln Hyde, Willie Moir, Reg Flewin, Trevor Porteous, Matt Woods, Alan Thompson, Mike Summerbee, Jimmy McGuigan and Les Chapman) had played for County prior to becoming manager, and Albert Williams,

Fred Westgarth and Jimmy Meadows were once trainers/coaches. Most unusually, Eric Webster started at Edgeley Park as groundsman. Some (11 of the 31) went to Cheshire with League management experience behind them; Andrew Wilson, Walter Galbraith, McGuigan and Melia were the most experienced, with 14 clubs between them, but many were hoping to use it as a stepping stone to bigger and better things. This policy worked only for a few, most notably Stewart (FA Cup winner with Cardiff), David Ashworth (League championship with Liverpool), Hyde (Preston), Andy Beattie (five higher grade clubs), Eddie Quigley (Blackburn) and Meadows (Bolton).

Manager	Start/Date	End/Date	Pts/Total
Fred Stewart	Aug 1900	May 1911	-
Percy Lewis	June 1911	April 1914	-
David Ashworth	April 1914	Dec 1919	-
Albert Williams	Dec 1919	Nov 1924	14
Fred Scotchbrook	Nov 1924	Feb 1926	-
Lincoln Hyde	April 1926	April 1931	16
Andrew Wilson	July 1932	May 1933	-
Fred Westgarth	May 1934	Sept 1936	-
Robert Kelly	Nov 1936	Jan 1939	14
Bob Marshall	March 1939	Feb 1949	-
Andy Beattie	March 1949	April 1952	-
Dick Duckworth	Oct 1952	May 1956	-
Willie Moir	June 1956	July 1960	-
Reg Flewin	Oct 1960	Sept 1963	-
Trevor Porteous	Sept 1963	Oct 1965	-
Bert Trautmann	Oct 1965	April 1966	-
Eddie Quigley	April 1966	Oct 1966	-
Jimmy Meadows	Oct 1966	April 1969	12
Walter Galbraith	Aug 1969	April 1970	-
Matt Woods	April 1970	Dec 1971	-
Brian Doyle	March 1972	May 1974	-
Jimmy Meadows	May 1974	Aug 1975	-
Roy Chapman	Sept 1975	May 1976	-
Eddie Quigley	May 1976	April 1977	-
Alan Thompson	April 1977	March 1978	-
Mike Summerbee	March 1978	Oct 1979	-
Jimmy McGuigan	Nov 1979	April 1982	-
Eric Webster	May 1982	May 1985	-
Colin Murphy	Aug 1985	Oct 1985	-
Les Chapman	Oct 1985	July 1986	-
Jimmy Melia	July 1986	Nov 1986	-
Colin Murphy	Nov 1986	May 1987	-
Asa Hartford	June 1987	April 1989	-
Danny Bergera	April 1989	-	6

Stockport County, 1921-22, Third Division North champions. Players only, back row (left to right): Tarbuck, Walmsley, Hardy, Reid, Richardson, Critchley. Middle row: Gault, Layton, Woodcock, Jones. Front row: Crossthwaite, Heath, Waterall, Griffiths.

Stoke City

Although they were founder members of the Football League in 1888, Stoke have dropped out on three occasions, playing in 86 of the 94 seasons. Since 1919, however, participation has been unbroken, and the managerial history dates from the Potters last re-entry. The club's record up to 1977 was remarkable for its stability, just six managers in 51 seasons, with the last 47 of these campaigns covered by just four men. Since then, turnover has picked up, seven managers in 16 years, producing an overall average of an impressive five seasons per manager.

The last of the four who shared the 47 seasons, Tony Waddington, was the longest serving. He was at the Victoria Ground helm for almost 17 years. Although Bob McGrory's stint covered a similar period, he lost seven seasons to World World Two. This therefore puts Tom Mather, with nearly 12 years at the club, second behind Waddington. Others found the going tougher, particularly Jock Rutherford, George Eastham, Bill Asprey and Alan Ball, four men whose combined stay amounted to less than four years.

Eastham and Asprey moreover, were two of only three Stoke managers who had once played for the club. The third was McGrory, although both Rutherford and Mick Mills were appointed as player-managers. McGrory was also the number two (to Mather) at the time he was offered the manager's job, as were Waddington, Eastham, Asprey and Ball. When Ball arrived at the Victoria Ground, he could boast managerial experience at other clubs (Blackpool and Portsmouth), something he had in common with Mather, Alan Durban, Ritchie Barker and Lou Macari. Mather was the first of the 12 former managers to go on to another club as manager (Newcastle and Leicester), since when Waddington (Crewe), Durban

(Sunderland and Cardiff), Barker (Notts County) and Ball (Exeter) followed suit.

Winning the League Cup under Waddington in 1971 was the Potters first major honour, but it was during Mather's reign that the club gained national prominence. He took Stoke from the Third to First Divisions but only after surviving a severe financial crisis. This forced pay cuts on the players, some of whom responded by smashing up the dressing rooms and offices at the Victoria Ground. A final point to note is that Stoke's first secretary in their pre-League days was Harry Lockett. Appointed in 1884, he left in 1890 to become the first secretary of the Football League.

Manager	Start/Date	End/Date	Pts/Total
Arthur Shallcross	cs 1919	March 1923	10
Jock Rutherford	March 1923	Aug 1923	-
Tom Mather	Oct 1923	May 1935	30
Bob McGrory	June 1935	May 1952	-
Frank Taylor	June 1952	May 1960	-
Tony Waddington	June 1960	March 1977	58
George Eastham	March 1977	Jan 1978	-
Alan Durban	Feb 1978	June 1981	10
Ritchie Barker	June 1981	Dec 1983	-
Bill Asprey	Dec 1983	May 1985	-
Mick Mills	May 1985	Nov 1989	-
Alan Ball (jnr)	Nov 1989	Feb 1991	-
Lou Macari	May 1991	-	14

Sunderland

It was during the reign of the first of their 19 managers that Sunderland's claim to a place amongst the top tier of British clubs was established. Tom Watson was not only the Wearsiders' most successful manager, but he was also the most successful in England in the period up to World War One. Roker Park has been one of the more stable managerial territories over the last 92 seasons, with each of the 19 job holders being given, on average two months less than five years to prove themselves.

For 52 of these seasons (57 per cent of the time) four men were responsible for club affairs, the four holding office continuously between 1905 and 1957. Bob Kyle was the longest serving, although four of his 23 years were accounted for by World War One, whilst three others each clocked up 11 seasons at the Roker helm, Johnny Cochrane, Bill Murray (who was also in office throughout World War Two) and Alan Brown (whose 11 seasons were split over two terms). Others found the Wearside environment less benign. George Hardwick failed to make it through a season, whilst Jimmy Adamson, Ken Knighton, Len Ashurst (despite reaching a League Cup Final) and Malcolm Crosby (despite reaching an FA Cup Final) only lasted between one and two seasons.

Another short-term casualty was the high-profile Lawrie McMenemy, one of ten Sunderland managers to have gained experience of the job at other League clubs (Ian McColl had been in charge of the Scottish national side and one or two others had managed in Scotland at club level). For a club as big as Sunderland, it is surprising how few of their managers had won major domestic honours before going to Roker: McMenemy's FA Cup win with Southampton in 1976 and Brown's Wembley appearance with Wednesday in 1966 were the exceptions. Only three of the 19 had previously played for Sunderland (Murray, Ashurst and incumbent Terry Butcher), although Robert Campbell ('A' team secretary) Knighton (coach)

and Crosby (coach) made it to the position of manager via the internal route. There was not much of a Roker after-life for former Sunderland managers. Both Mackie and Murray lost their jobs through suspensions following financial irregularities (it happened a second time to Mackie at Middlesbrough) and, whilst a few found employment with other league clubs, only Watson went on to further honours (with Liverpool), although McMenemy landed the number two job on the England team with Graham Taylor.

Manager	Start/Date	End/Date	Pts/Total
Tom Watson	1889	Aug 1896	84
Robert Campbell	Aug 1896	April 1899	12
Alex Mackie	cs 1899	June 1905	30
Robert Kyle	Aug 1905	March 1928	42
Johnny Cochrane	May 1928	March 1939	60
Bill Murray	April 1939	June 1957	12
Alan Brown	June 1957	cs 1964	16
George Hardwick	Nov 1964	May 1965	-
Ian McColl	June 1965	Feb 1968	-
Alan Brown	Feb 1968	Nov 1972	-
Bob Stokoe	Nov 1972	Oct 1976	34
Jimmy Adamson	Nov 1976	Nov 1978	-
Ken Knighton	June 1979	April 1981	10
Alan Durban	June 1981	March 1984	-
Len Ashurst	March 1984	May 1985	12
Lawrie McMenemy	June 1985	April 1987	-
Denis Smith	June 1987	Dec 1991	24
Malcolm Crosby	Dec 1991	Feb 1993	12
Terry Butcher	Feb 1993	-	-

Swansea City

League football in South Wales has been through a turbulent period over the last 15 years, and life at the Vetch has been typical of the experience elsewhere in the Principality. Promoted from the Fourth to the First Division, and back again, the Swans have tried seven managers since 1984. This compares with just six managers in the 31 seasons up to 1958. Overall, Swansea have had 20 managers in 66 League campaigns and the average of 3 years 4 months per manager is close to the average for all clubs.

Not surprisingly, the long service award goes to one of the earlier job holders, Billy McCandless. He was approaching his eighth anniversary at the Vetch when he died on the eve of the 1955-6 season, Trevor Morris is the only other person to run him close, with a seven season term in the late 1950s/early 1960s although John Toshack spent a little over six years during the Swans meteoric rise. The list of those whose grip on the job was more precarious is much longer: Glyn Davies, Colin Appleton, John Bond, Tommy Hutchison and Ian Evans all survived for less than two seasons.

Being Welsh or a former Swansea player has not been an important qualification for the manager's job at the Vetch. Only five (Ron Burgess, Davies, Billy Lucas, Harry Griffiths, and Hutchison) of the 19 individuals (Terry Yorath had two spells in charge) had previously played for the Swans, and it was not until 1955, with Burgess' accession, that a Welshman was given the job. There were just four of the appointees (Yorath, Neil Harris, Toshack and Evans) who were new to both Swansea and League management when they went to the Vetch, whilst all but five of the 18 former managers moved on to other League management jobs after their spells at Swansea ended.

Although Toshack is the most successful of the Swans managers, McCandless set a record when he guided the club to the Third Division

title in his first full season at the helm, 1948-49. An Irishman, whose best playing days were spent with Glasgow Rangers, had previously won the Third South championship with Newport and Cardiff. He thus became the only man to win this title three times, and he did it with three different clubs, all in South Wales, in four League seasons.

Manager	Start/Date	End/Date	Pts/Total
Joe Bradshaw	cs 1919	May 1926	20
James Thompson	Feb 1927	1931	-
Neil Harris	July 1934	May 1939	-
Haydn Green	May 1939	Sept 1947	-
Billy McCandless	Nov 1947	July 1955	14
Ron Burgess	July 1955	1958	-
Trevor Morris	Aug 1958	May 1965	6
Glyn Davies	June 1965	Oct 1966	-
Billy Lucas	Feb 1967	March 1969	-
Roy Bentley	Aug 1969	Oct 1972	6
Harry Gregg	Nov 1972	Jan 1975	-
Harry Griffiths	Jan 1975	Feb 1978	-
John Toshack	Feb 1978	March 1984	24
Colin Appleton	May 1984	Dec 1984	-
John Bond	Dec 1984	Dec 1985	-
Tommy Hutchison	Dec 1985	May 1986	-
Terry Yorath	July 1986	Feb 1989	6
Ian Evans	Feb 1989	March 1990	-
Terry Yorath	March 1990	March 1991	-
Frank Burrows	March 1991		

Swindon Town

Although founded in 1881, Swindon had to wait until the formation of the Third Division in 1920 to achieve Football League status. Under their long-serving manager, Sam Allen, however, they had already made their mark nationally, with two appearances in the FA Cup semi finals as a non-League side. Although Allen held the job for 31 years, he had just 13 League seasons at the helm, the rest accounted for by the Southern League and World War One. None of his 15 successors has come anywhere near to matching his service to the Robins, apart perhaps from Bert Head, who was at the County Ground for almost ten years. Overall, each manager has lasted on average a little over four seasons, but this owes much to the stability of the pre-1970 period. In the 24 seasons since Fred Ford took over in 1969, Swindon have had 10 managers, with Dave Mackay, Les Allen, Bobby Smith, Ken Beamish and Ossie Ardiles standing out for the brevity of their association with the Wiltshire club.

Playing for Swindon does not seem to have been a necesary qualification for the job, for only John Trollope, Beamish and Maurice Lindley were former Robins. Less than half arrived at the County Ground with any management experience under their belts: Louis Page, Danny Williams, Ford, Les Allen and Smith were the only ones not to be making their debuts at this level. Swindon proved a good training ground, for all but the remarkable Sam Allen, Les Allen and Beamish went on to other jobs elsewhere in the League. There are two of the 16 who can claim special records. Williams led the Robins to the League Cup in 1969, only the second team from Division Three to win one of the two major Cup competitions. Under Lou Macari's guidance, the club climbed from the Fourth to the Second Division, then won a place in Division One,

only to be denied the prize because of financial irregularities. Swindon, therefore, were relegated from Division One without playing a game. It took three years to recapture that place, under Glenn Hoddle, who then promptly left for Chelsea.

An interesting point to note is that in the early 1970s, Dave Mackay and Les Allen, teammates in Spurs 1961 Cup winning side, were both managers at the County Ground. They were followed 20 years later by Ossie Ardiles and Hoddle, who both played in Spurs Cup winning side of 1981.

Manager	Start/Date	End/Date	Pts/Total
Sam Allen	July 1902	April 1933	12
Ted Vizard	April 1933	May 1939	-
Louis Page	July 1945	May 1953	-
Maurice Lindley	May 1953	May 1955	-
Bert Head	Oct 1955	Aug 1965	8
Danny Williams	Aug 1965	July 1969	26
Fred Ford	Oct 1969	May 1971	-
Dave Mackay	May 1971	Nov 1972	-
Les Allen	Nov 1972	Feb 1974	-
Danny Williams	March 1974	May 1978	-
Bobby Smith	May 1978	Oct 1980	6
John Trollope	Nov 1980	March 1983	-
Ken Beamish	March 1983	June 1984	-
Lou Macari	July 1984	July 1989	20
Ossie Ardiles	July 1989	March 1991	-
Glenn Hoddle	April 1991	June 1993	10

Torquay United

With just three promotions from Division Four to their name after 59 seasons of League football, Torquay's past is modest even by the undemanding standards of other West County clubs. If ambition is in some way indicated by a willingness to change managers, however, United have at least aimed high. Plainmoor has been home to 25 managers since the club joined the League in 1927, a change once every 2.4 seasons on average. In recent times, heads have rolled much faster. From an average tenure of 3.4 seasons up to 1965, the life span of a Torquay manager has fallen to about 13 months since 1981.

If it was not for Eric Webber's lengthy reign beginning in 1951, the turnover rate would have been the highest in League. He was in charge for 14 years, more than twice as long as Frank Brown in second place on six. Although John Sims' (33 days) stay was excessively short, there were five others who were at Plainmoor for less than a year, Ivan Golac (three months), John Impey (five months), Bob John (eight months), Alex Massie (ten months) and Jack Butler (11 months), plus nine others who were gone after two seasons or less. Since 1981, in fact, Cyril Knowles has been the only Torquay manager to have celebrated his second anniversary in the job.

The board has cast the net widely in their search for the right person to bring success to the club. They have given a try to seven former players (Frank Brown, Jack Butler, Mike Green, Sims, Stuart Morgan, Impey and Paul Compton) and promoted John (trainer) and Bruce Rioch (player coach) from inside. In addition, Jack Edwards had briefly been caretaker-manager almost three years before he was given the job permanently. It was not until 1950, with the appointment of the club's eighth manager, Massie, that Torquay employed someone with previous League management experience. This still remains the exception rather than the rule, with only Allan Brown (Luton), Edwards (Exeter), Dave Webb (Bournemouth), Knowles (Darlington) and Dave Smith (Mansfield, Southend and Plymouth) in the same category.

Several of the selections were to prove excellent managers, but not with Torquay. Frank Womack left Plainmoor for a four club career that lasted

until the 1950s. Butler (Crystal Palace and Colchester), John McNeil (Bury) and Knowles (Hartlepool) continued in the lower divisions, whilst Frank O'Farrell, three times Torquay manager, made it to the top flight with Leicester and Manchester United, as did Rioch (Middlesbrough) and Webb (Chelsea).

Manager	Start/Date	End/Date	Pts/Total
Percy Mackrill	1927	March 1929	-
Frank Womack	July 1930	May 1932	-
Frank Brown	May 1932	May 1938	-
Alf Steward	May 1938	May 1940	-
Jack Butler	June 1946	May 1947	-
John McNeil	June 1947	March 1950	-
Bob John	March 1950	Nov 1950	-
Alex Massie	Nov 1950	Sept 1951	-
Eric Webber	Oct 1951	May 1965	14
Frank O'Farrell	May 1965	Dec 1968	6
Allan Brown	Jan 1969	Oct 1971	-
Jack Edwards	Oct 1971	Jan 1973	-
Malcolm Musgrove	Jan 1973	Nov 1976	-
Frank O'Farrell	Nov 1976	March 1977	-
Mike Green	March 1977	May 1981	-
Frank O'Farrell	June 1981	June 1982	-
Bruce Rioch	July 1982	Jan 1984	-
Dave Webb	Feb 1984	Aug 1985	-
John Sims	Aug 1985	Sept 1985	-
Stuart Morgan	Sept 1985	May 1987	-
Cyril Knowles	June 1987	Oct 1989	-
Dave Smith	Oct 1989	April 1991	-
John Impey	May 1991	Oct 1991	6
Ivan Golac	Feb 1992	May 1992	-
Paul Compton	May 1992	March 1993	-

Tottenham Hotspur

Tottenham's League career did not begin until 1908, by which time they had already won the FA Cup (the last non-League club to do so) and had three managers. Ironically, their first League honour, promotion to Division One in 1908-09, came during a period when the directors (with secretary Arthur Turner) had control of team affairs. Since joining the League 74 seasons ago, there have been 16 managers (14 individuals since Peter McWilliam and Peter Shreeves had two spells), an average of one manager about every four and a half seasons. McWilliam was at White Hart Lane the longest, his two terms lasting 18 years. They were, however, both interrupted by wars, and he was at the helm for only 11 seasons, five fewer than Bill Nicholson over 40 years later. The shortest reigns were McWilliam's and Shreeves' second, a mere season each, whilst David Pleat had a little over a year in the job despite taking the club to Wembley.

When Spurs won the Cup in 1901, they counted manager John Cameron amongst the players. This has been the exception rather than the rule, for of his successors, only Billy Minter, Arthur Rowe, Bill Nicholson and Terry Venables were former Spurs, although Jimmy Anderson, Keith Burkinshaw and Peter Shreeves were all promoted from assistant manager or coaching roles.

In Bill Nicholson, Spurs had one of the most successful managers of all times, the winner of all three major domestic honours and two different European trophies. He was also the first 20th century manager of a 'Double' winning side. There were, however, two of his predecessors, equally noted for their commitment to classic football and individual flair, who carved for themselves a niche in managerial history. Peter McWilliam was laden with honours as a player with Newcastle in Edwardian times, and when he guided Spurs to the FA Cup in 1921, he became the first man to play for and manage a Cup winning side. Arthur Rowe, on the other hand, was one of only three men

to win the Second and First Division Championships in successive seasons (1949-51). The next, and last, man to achieve this feat was Alf Ramsey with Ipswich a decade later. Ramsey was, of course, a key member of Rowe's 'push and run' team at White Hart Lane, as was Nicholson, and Ipswich succeeded Spurs as League champions in 1962. In recent years, the club's financial difficulties have led to the development of a new management structure, with coaches assuming responsibility for the team and Venables fulfilling the role of chief executive. Although this experiment ended in tears, it may be the way other clubs go in the future, as the financial demands of the Premier League raise the stakes and make football clubs more like businesses.

Manager	Start/Date	End/Date	Pts/Total
Peter McWilliam	Jan 1913	Feb 1927	52
Billy Minter	Feb 1927	Nov 1929	-
Percy Smith	Jan 1930	April 1935	10
Jack Tresadern	June 1935	April 1938	-
Peter McWilliam	May 1938	June 1942	-
Joe Hulme	Jan 1946	May 1949	6
Arthur Rowe	May 1949	July 1955	52
Jimmy Anderson	July 1955	Oct 1958	18
Bill Nicholson	Oct 1958	Aug 1974	192
Terry Neill	Sept 1974	June 1976	6
Keith Burkinshaw	July 1976	May 1984	82
Peter Shreeves	June 1984	May 1986	-
David Pleat	May 1986	Oct 1987	18
Terry Venables	Nov 1987	June 1991	18
Peter Shreeves	July 1991	May 1992	6
Doug Livermore	May 1992	-	6

Tranmere Rovers

A few seasons after being within ten minutes of losing their League status, Tranmere were serious contenders for a place in the Premier League, a remarkable transformation which has taken place under John King, the 15th manager in Rovers' 65 League seasons. In their history, Rovers have won five promotions and King has been associated with all but one (three as manager and one as player). Now in his second spell at Tranmere, King has accumulated ten seasons as Rovers' manager, rather less than Bert Cooke's 24 years in the club's early days. Of those, however, ten were accounted for by World War One and pre-League football. There are two other managers whose terms are well above the club's average (of 4.3 seasons per manager), Ernie Blackburn, with nine years just after World War Two, and Dave Russell, in office for eight years during the 1960s. These four were in charge for two-thirds of Rovers' League career. A smaller contribution came from Ronnie Moore (three months, although he is still at Prenton as coach) and also from Walter Galbraith, Jack Carr, Jim Knowles, Noel Kelly and Frank Worthington, none of whom made it to their second anniversaries.

Since Tranmere have usually been Merseyside's poor relations, they have lacked the tradition and resources to attract established managerial names. Carr, Blackburn and Galbraith gained previous League management experience, but only in the Third Division. Russell — several years with Second Division Bury — was the only one to have managed at a higher level. Just under half the 14 individuals (King having had two spells in the job) had a previous connection with the club before becoming manager. Kelly, Ron Yeats, King and Moore were all former players, Jim Knowles

(a one-time film extra at Elstree) had five years administrative experience at Prenton before succeeding Carr, and Jackie Wright was promoted from trainer-assistant manager. Only Bryan Hamilton (Leicester and Wigan) and Galbraith went to manage other League clubs, although several remained at Prenton in other roles. Perhaps the most successful managerial old boy was Bill Ridding, in charge between Knowles and Blackburn during the war. He spent 18 years in charge of First Division Bolton.

Manager	Start/Date	End/Date	Pts/Total
Bert Cooke	1911	April 1935	-
Jack Carr	May 1935	Nov 1936	-
Jim Knowles	Nov 1936	Jan 1939	14
Ernie Blackburn	Sept 1946	May 1955	-
Noel Kelly	July 1955	Oct 1957	-
Peter Farrell	Oct 1957	Dec 1960	-
Walter Galbraith	Jan 1961	Dec 1961	-
Dave Russell	Dec 1961	Dec 1969	6
Jackie Wright	Dec 1969	April 1972	-
Ron Yeats	April 1972	April 1975	-
John King	May 1975	Sept 1980	6
Bryan Hamilton	Oct 1980	Feb 1985	-
Frank Worthington	July 1985	Feb 1987	-
Ronnie Moore	Feb 1987	April 1987	-
John King	April 1987	-	14

Walsall

The managerial history of Walsall is amongst the most convoluted and confusing of any League club. Founder members of Division Three North in 1921, the Saddlers have tried the relatively high number of 33 managers in 65 seasons. (This excludes the pre-1915 League career of Walsall Swifts). The average tenure, of two seasons per manager, has not varied much over time, and the Walsall job has always been one of the least secure in football.

A few men were at Fellows Park long enough to make an impression. Bill Moore's two spells lasted almost ten years, well ahead of Harry Hibbs, two of whose seven years were accounted for by wartime football. Another who had two terms at the helm was Alan Buckley. He spent six years in the job in sole command and another six months sharing responsibilities with Neil Martin. The only other man to have put in more than four years service as Walsall manager was Joe Burchell, the first jobholder. There are, on the other hand, nine of the 30 individuals who were out after less than a year, a list headed by Frank Sibley (one month) and Dick Graham (two months), with Neil Martin, John Smith, Ronnie Allen, Tony McPhee and Alan Ashman not far behind.

Although the Saddlers began in Division Three with a former player holding the reins (Joe Burchell), this was to prove the exception in subsequent years, only Jimmy Torrance, Jack Love, Smith, Doug Fraser and Buckley following suit. Burchell had, in addition, been secretary, and Sid Scholey (trainer) also came from a backroom role to the manager's office.

Despite the lack of success, Walsall have been able to attract managers with established reputations. In David Ashworth (Liverpool) and Dave Mackay (Derby), they selected men who had won the First Division title, whilst Peter O'Rourke (Bradford City) and Alan Ashman (West Brom) were past FA Cup winners. John Barnwell (Wolves) was a League Cup winner and the legendary Frank Buckley (Wolves) had almost won everything.

After Walsall, few achieved very much. For Frank Buckley, it was hardly surprising, as he was 72-years-of-age. Of the rest, Jimmy Kerr found his way to Norwich, Love to Wrexham, Graham to Colchester, Allen to West Brom, Mackay to Doncaster and Birmingham and Sibley back to Queen's Park Rangers. None, however, won any major honours, and only Alan Buckley, who took Grimsby from the Fourth to Second Divisions, had any measure of success.

Manager	Start/Date	End/Date	Pts/Total
Joe Burchell	Aug 1921	Feb 1926	-
David Ashworth	Feb 1926	Feb 1927	-
Jimmy Torrance	Feb 1927	May 1928	-
Jimmy Kerr	May 1928	April 1929	-
Sid Scholey	April 1929	Oct 1930	-
Peter O'Rourke	Oct 1930	Feb 1932	-
Bill Slade	Feb 1932	Oct 1934	-
Andy Wilson	Oct 1934	April 1937	-
Tommy Lowes	April 1937	Sept 1939	-
Harry Hibbs	Aug 1944	June 1951	-
Tony McPhee	July 1951	Dec 1951	-
Brough Fletcher	March 1952	April 1953	-
Frank Buckley	April 1953	Sept 1955	-
Jack Love	Sept 1955	Dec 1957	-
Bill Moore	Dec 1957	Nov 1963	20
Alf Wood	Nov 1963	Oct 1964	-
Reg Shaw	Oct 1964	March 1968	-
Dick Graham	March 1968	May 1968	-
Ron Lewin	July 1968	Feb 1969	-
Bill Moore	Feb 1969	Oct 1972	-
John Smith	Oct 1972	March 1973	-
Ronnie Allen	July 1973	Dec 1973	-
Doug Fraser	Jan 1974	March 1977	-
Dave Mackay	March 1977	May 1978	-
Alan Ashman	Aug 1978	Feb 1979	-
Frank Sibley	March 1979	April 1979	-
Alan Buckley	July 1979	July 1981	6
Alan Buckley/Neil Martin	July 1981	Jan 1982	-
Neil Martin	Jan 1982	May 1982	-
Alan Buckley	May 1982	June 1986	6
Tommy Coakley	Aug 1986	Dec 1988	8
John Barnwell	Jan 1989	March 1990	-
Kenny Hibbitt	May 1990	-	-

Watford

Watford's rise from the Fourth Division to runners-up in the First in six seasons was one of the more remarkable stories of modern football. It was achieved under the 18th of the 22 managers the Hornets have had in 66 seasons of League football. Graham Taylor, architect of the club's greatest triumphs, spent ten seasons at Vicarage Road, well above the average of three, but this was not the longest. Harry Kent was there for 16 years (only six in the League), whilst Neil McBain's two terms lasted almost 11 years. Other than Ken Furphy, who clocked up seven years, no one else lasted much more than the average, and Jack Bray, John Paton, Dave Bassett and Colin Lee measured their service in months — Paton Lee and Bassett not getting into double-figures. Of the 20 individuals who have managed the Hornets (McBain and Len Goulden were appointed twice), eight were former Watford players, Fred Pagnam, McBain, Bill Findlay, Ron Gray, Paton, Mike Keen and Steve Harrison, whilst Lee had been coach. Since nine had had previous League management experience, it was only Jack Bray and Goulden who were new to both managing and Watford. None of the Hornets old boys can match the post-Vicarage Road career of Graham Taylor. After a short, successful spell with Aston Villa, he took over the England team in 1990. His Watford successor, Dave Bassett had a traumatic time, but succeeded with Sheffield United, whilst in the 1960s, Bill McGarry achieved little in the early days of his managerial career, but subsequently took Ipswich to promotion and in the 1970s, Wolves to League Cup honours. Age has never been a barrier to appointment. Haydn Green had been in football for 40 years before he went to Watford. Even older was Neil McBain when he returned for a second term in 1956. He was then in his 60s. He began with Ayr United before World War One, and his League managerial career started at Watford in the 1920s and ended there 30 years later.

Manager	Start/Date	End/Date	Pts/Total
Harry Kent	1910	1926	-
Fred Pagnam	1926	1929	-
Neil McBain	1929	Aug 1937	-
Bill Findlay	Jan 1938	Feb 1947	-
Jack Bray	March 1947	Jan 1948	-
Eddie Hapgood	Feb 1948	March 1950	-
Ron Gray	June 1950	Aug 1951	-
Haydn Green	Aug 1951	Oct 1952	-
Len Goulden	Nov 1952	Oct 1955	-
John Paton	Oct 1955	Feb 1956	-
Len Goulden	Feb 1956	July 1956	-
Neil McBain	Aug 1956	Feb 1959	-
Ron Burgess	March 1959	May 1963	6
Bill McGarry	July 1963	Oct 1964	-
Ken Furphy	Nov 1964	Aug 1971	20
George Kirby	Aug 1971	May 1973	-
Mike Keen	June 1973	April 1977	-
Graham Taylor	June 1977	July 1987	66
Dave Bassett	May 1987	Jan 1988	-
Steve Harrison	Jan 1988	March 1990	-
Colin Lee	March 1990	Nov 1990	-
Steve Perryman	Nov 1990	-	-

West Bromwich Albion

Although not classed as a manager in Breedon's *West Brom: A Complete Record* by Tony Matthews with Colin MacKenzie (1987), it is hard to exclude Fred Everiss from the secretaries with managerial responsibilities. For almost 50 years (35 League seasons), he was the Albion official in day-to-day charge at The Hawthorns, and in his reign, the club enjoyed success in both League and Cup. Everiss' longevity is in marked contrast to the experience of some of his successors. After Don Howe's departure in 1975, the club had 12 managers in 18 seasons, a change every 18 months. If Everiss is included, Albion managers survived, on average, 3.8 seasons each, but discounting Everiss, the average falls to 2.3 seasons.

Not until Howe's appointment in 1971 did the board give a former Albion player the chance to manage the club (although both Jack Smith and Jimmy Hagan had been schoolboy trialists). After Howe, Ronnie Allen, Brian Talbot and Bobby Gould have all tried managing the club for which they once used to play. The earlier choices of managers, particularly Smith, Jesse Carver and Vic Buckingham, reveal an unusual preference for those breed of men with good coaching credentials. Of the various clubs he managed, Ron Saunders had least success at The Hawthorns, but his sojourn with the Baggies enabled him to complete a unique hat-trick of managing three major West Midlands clubs, Villa, Birmingham and Albion. Ron Wylie was also associated with the three but as a coach (Villa) and player (Birmingham), as well as manager (Albion). For good measure, he was also coach at Coventry. Although Albion went a long time without winning anything, from the 1968 FA Cup triumph to play-off victory in 1993 under Ardiles (who subsequently left for Spurs) it is easy to overlook how close they came to doing the Double under Buckingham in 1953-54 and to forget Everiss' unique 'double' in 1930-31, winning the FA Cup and promotion from Division Two. Cup competitions have offered the Baggies most encouragement in the last 30 years. There were two Wembley appearances in three years under Ashman, whilst Hagan was the first manager to take a club to the League Cup Final in consecutive seasons. If either of the two semi-finals Albion played under Ronnie Allen in 1981-82 had gone their way, the club's subsequent history may have been very different.

Manager	Start/Date	End/Date	Pts/Total
Fred Everiss	Aug 1902	cs 1948	110
Jack Smith	July 1948	April 1952	10
Jesse Carver	May 1952	Feb 1953	-
Vic Buckingham	Feb 1953	May 1959	36
Gordon Clark	June 1959	Oct 1961	-
Archie Macaulay	Oct 1961	April 1963	-
Jimmy Hagan	April 1963	May 1967	30
Alan Ashman	June 1967	June 1971	36
Don Howe	July 1971	April 1975	-
Johnny Giles	July 1975	May 1977	10
Ronnie Allen	June 1977	Dec 1977	-
Ron Atkinson	Jan 1978	June 1981	6
Ronnie Allen	July 1981	May 1982	12
Ron Wylie	July 1982	Feb 1984	-
Johnny Giles	Feb 1984	Sept 1985	-
Nobby Stiles	Oct 1985	Feb 1986	-
Ron Saunders	Feb 1986	Sept 1987	-
Ron Atkinson	Sept 1987	Oct 1988	-
Brian Talbot	Nov 1988	Jan 1991	-
Bobby Gould	Feb 1991	May 1992	-
Ossie Ardiles	May 1992	June 1993	8

West Ham United

West Ham's record for managerial stability is unparalleled in the history of the Football League. In 63 seasons up to John Lyall's departure in the 1989 close season, there had been only five occupants of the manager's office at Upton Park. Ted Fenton, with a mere 11 years' service, was the club's shortest-serving manager. Syd King, the first to hold the job, had over 31 years at the Hammers' helm, although it was not until his 15th season that League status was won. The appointment of Lou Macari to succeed Lyall marked a sharp break with the past traditions of the club, but he did not stay long, and with Billy Bonds taking over seven months later, normal service was resumed.

Throughout their history, the Hammers have favoured internal candidates to fill their managerial vacancies, Ron Greenwood and Macari being the exceptions. Lyall and Fenton, along with King and Bonds, also played for the club, whilst Charlie Paynter's route was via the training staff. There is, however, more variety about the manner in which the various managers relinquished the job. King's fondness for drink led to his suspension and then suicide, whilst Paynter chose his own time to retire. When Fenton left, the reasons were never fully explained, and still remain unclear, although it was assumed he had been dismissed. There was no way to dress up Lyall's departure after relegation in 1988-89. The failure to renew his contract amounted to dismissal. His successor, Macari, was the 'victim' of a colourful past, when allegations of financial irregularities with a previous club led him to court. Finally, Ron Greenwood stepped aside as team manager in 1974 to become general manager, but then left Upton Park to succeed Don Revie as England manager.

During Fenton's reign, the Hammers became a breeding ground for future managers. Although Fenton himself was not one of football's original thinkers, the Upton Park atmosphere encouraged others to discuss new ideas, and led to the development of what later became known as 'the Academy'. At one time in 1955-56, a West Ham side could include half a dozen or more future managers, such as Dave Sexton, Malcolm Allison, John Bond, Frank O'Farrell, Ken Brown, Jimmy Andrews, Noel Cantwell and Malcolm Musgrove.

Manager	Start/Date	End/Date	Pts/Total
Syd King	April 1901	Nov 1932	22
Charlie Paynter	Nov 1932	Aug 1950	6
Ted Fenton	Aug 1950	March 1961	16
Ron Greenwood	April 1961	Aug 1974	72
John Lyall	Aug 1974	June 1989	82
Lou Macari	July 1989	Feb 1990	-
Billy Bonds	Feb 1990	-	32

Wigan Athletic

When Wigan Athletic were elected to Division Four to replace Southport in 1978, it was almost 50 years after another club from the same town, Wigan Borough, had been forced by huge debts to resign from the League. The current club was founded a year after Borough's demise, and elected to the Fourth Division after an outstanding record in the Northern Premier League. As a non-League club, the Latics had been able to attract some impressive names to Springfield Park as manager. These included men who were former and future League managers, such as Jimmy Milne (Preston), his son Gordon (Coventry and Leicester), Ted Goodier (Derby), Allenby Chilton (Grimsby) and Allan Brown (Luton, Forest and Blackpool).

It was, therefore, by no means a footballing backwater. At the time of entry to the League, Ian McNeill was in charge, a vastly experienced player in England and Scotland. Since he left in 1981, the Latics have had four other managers, including Bryan Hamilton whose second spell ended with the team floundering in the spring of 1993. It was left to caretaker Dave Philpotts to preside over the club's first relegation months later. A change of manager every two and a half years suggests that the Wigan board soon acquired the habits of their more experienced League colleagues.

Each of the managerial terms has lasted a minimum of 15 months (Hamilton's first stint), with Hamilton's second stay (of four years) the longest. The backgrounds of the five have been very varied. Larry Lloyd had played at the highest level, for Liverpool, Forest and England among others, whilst all Harry McNally's pre-Wigan experience had been in non-League football, playing for Skelmersdale and managing Altrincham and the deposed Southport. Hamilton was an articulate Irishman, and his club coach (and then successor) was Roy Mathias, a tough northerner who had over 600 games for Tranmere under his belt.

There was a brief, uncharacteristic splash of glamour at Springfield Park for a few months in 1983 following Lloyd's departure. The unlikely figure of Bobby Charlton took over as caretaker manager, but he stepped aside that close season when McNally was appointed.

Manager	Start/Date	End/Date	Pts/Total
Ian McNeill	May 1976	Feb 1981	-
Larry Lloyd	March 1981	April 1983	6
Harry McNally	July 1983	March 1985	-
Bryan Hamilton	March 1985	June 1986	-
Ray Mathias	June 1986	March 1989	-
Bryan Hamilton	March 1989	March 1993	-

Wimbledon

Since joining the League as recently as 1977, Wimbledon have confounded most of the experts. Promoted five times, relegated twice, one of only two current First Division clubs never to have been relegated from the top flight, FA Cup winners and presently tenants of a club miles from their own home base, the Dons and controversy are never very far apart. Their style rather than their achievements tends to be the focus of attention. Since joining the League's elite in 1986, Wimbledon have shown themselves to be remarkably resilent to any polish or sophistication the top tier has to offer. Their character, formed in Southern League days, has remained basically unchanged through a succession of managers.

In 16 League seasons, the Dons have had seven managers, about one new jobholder every two seasons. The six-year tenure (broken by a three day stint with Crystal Palace in 1984) of Dave Bassett was probably the most influential. He took them from the Fourth to First Divisions (not always in the same direction) before moving on, with Watford and Sheffield United. Bobby Gould and Dario Gradi, both with three years service at Plough Lane, were the other two whose stays were above the club average. Both subsequently went on to other jobs in management in the League, Gradi with Crewe and Gould with West Brom and Coventry.

Gould was the first 'outsider' to manage the club, although he was faithful to its traditions during his term of office. Gradi had been Allen Batsford's assistant, the role that Bassett performed for Gradi when his playing days with the Dons ended. Both Ray Harford and Peter Withe were strangers to the club on their appointments, but with Joe Kinnear, the Wimbledon board went back to their previous practice of promoting internally. Only Gould (Bristol Rovers) and Harford (Fulham and Luton) went to Plough Lane with a track record in League management, Harford having steered the Hatters to two League Cup Finals in 12 months. For the rest, Wimbledon marked their managerial debut.

Despite the cynicism shown by the purists to the Dons, which is reciprocated in full by the club, they continue to survive, but on the lowest-ever attendances for a club in the top flight. It is doubtful if they will prosper in the long term.

Manager	Start/Date	End/Date	Pts/Total
Allen Batsford	cs 1974	Dec 1977	-
Dario Gradi	Jan 1978	Jan 1981	6
Dave Bassett	Jan 1981	July 1987	36
Bobby Gould	July 1987	May 1990	18
Ray Harford	June 1990	Oct 1991	-
Peter Withe	Oct 1991	Feb 1992	-
Joe Kinnear	Feb 1992	-	-

Wolverhampton Wanderers

According to the latest and most comprehensive history of the club, *The Wolves* by Tony Matthews (with Les Smith) Paper Plane Publishing (1989), Wolves have had a manager since their earliest days. Jack Addenbrooke took office in 1885, led the club to three FA Cup Finals and stepped down almost 37 years later on health grounds. None of his 17 successors came close to matching that length of time in office, but Stan Cullis' 16 years and Frank Buckley's 17 years (12 seasons) are impressive by the standards of most clubs. In fact these three account for almost two thirds (62 seasons out of 94) of Wolves' League career. Overall, the average life of a Wolves manager is a little over five years, but in the 1980s, Ian Greaves, Graham Hawkins, Tommy Docherty, Bill McGarry and Sammy Chapman could manage only four years between them.

The club's most successful manager, and one of the leading managers of his generation, was Stan Cullis. He had captained Buckley's successful young side in the 1930s, one of only two Wolves managers to have played League football for the club. Hawkins was the other, although Addenbrooke played in the pre-League days. Albert Hoskins (secretary), Ronnie Allen (coach), Sammy Chung (coach) and Chapman (scout) rose to the managerial position from inside the club, although they were from non-playing roles.

Wolves decline following Cullis' brutal dismissal in the autumn of 1964 and that of Ronnie Allen, sacked following a promotion, was all the more marked because of their previous triumphs. The downward trend lasted until the late 1980s, punctuated only by the occasional League Cup success (under McGarry, in his first spell, and Barnwell) and an isolated European (UEFA) final appearance (again under McGarry). The upturn in League status began with Graham Turner, and when he steered Wolves to the Fourth Division title in 1987-88, they became the first club to win all four divisions in the Football League.

Although criticised by purists, overshadowed by Busby and unsuccessful in Europe, the Cullis style in the 1950s was effective. In 16 seasons his record was remarkable: three League titles, three runners-up spots and three times finishing third. On top of this, there were two FA Cup wins, and one semi-final and two quarter-final appearances. By converting just one draw to a victory in 1959-60, Wolves under Cullis would have achieved the first League and Cup Double this century and a hat-trick of Championships.

Manager	Start/Date	End/Date	Pts/Total
Jack Addenbrooke	Aug 1885	June 1922	78
George Jobey	June 1922	May 1924	14
Albert Hoskins	June 1924	March 1926	-
Fred Scotchbrook	March 1926	June 1927	-
Frank Buckley	July 1927	March 1944	52
Ted Vizard	April 1944	May 1948	-
Stan Cullis	June 1948	Sept 1964	138
Andy Beattie	Sept 1964	Sept 1965	-
Ronnie Allen	Sept 1965	Nov 1968	10
Bill McGarry	Nov 1968	May 1976	42
Sammy Chung	June 1976	Nov 1978	16
John Barnwell	Nov 1978	Nov 1981	30
Ian Greaves	Feb 1982	Aug 1982	-
Graham Hawkins	Aug 1982	April 1984	10
Tommy Docherty	June 1984	July 1985	-
Bill McGarry	Sep 1985	Nov 1985	-
Sammy Chapman	Nov 1985	Aug 1986	-
Graham Turner	Oct 1986	-	26

Workington

For a club which spent only 26 seasons in the Football League before failing in their seventh re-election application in 1977, Workington had some impressive names pass through the Borough Park manager's office. Since, however, they had 16 managers in their 26 years, an average reign of just 1.6 seasons, it is not surprising that these individuals gained their successes elsewhere.

The Reds longest-serving manager was Joe Harvey, who spent five years at Borough Park before going back to Newcastle. (Harvey also managed Barrow, another club which lost its League status in the 1970s.) George Aitken, with three years, and Ken Furphy (the only Workington manager to win promotion) with two years and four months, were the only other two managers whose terms exceeded a modest two years. For several others, their association with Borough Park was considerably briefer, none more so than Keith Burkinshaw's four months. Frank Upton and John McNamee did not fare much better, surviving for just six months.

Burkinshaw and Aitken (who was also the club's trainer) were the only two of 15 individuals (Colin Meldrum went back for seconds) who had previously played for the club. Experience of League management was never a prerequisite for the Workington board, although it was a qualification that Bill Shankly (Grimsby and Carlisle), Norman Low (Norwich), Harvey (Barrow), Bill Leivers (Doncaster) and Alan Ashman (Carlisle and West Brom) could offer. Ted Smith, whilst having no League management training, was able to point to his time in charge of the Portuguese national side.

Most interest in the Workington managerial roll-call has been the subsequent achievements of some of the individuals. Low was to lead Port Vale to the first Fourth Division title, Furphy took Watford to the Third Division championship and Cambridge won promotion from Division Four under Leivers. Even more impressive were the post-Workington successes of Shankly, Harvey and Burkinshaw, who won an assortment of League titles, FA Cups and European trophies at Liverpool, Newcastle and Spurs respectively. Only Ashman went to Borough Park with a national honour behind him, an FA Cup success at West Brom in 1968.

Manager	Start/Date	End/Date	Pts/Total
Albert Flatley	Aug 1950	May 1952	-
Ted Smith	June 1952	Sept 1953	-
Bill Shankly	Jan 1954	Nov 1955	-
Norman Low	Jan 1956	Feb 1957	-
Joe Harvey	June 1957	June 1962	-
Ken Furphy	July 1962	Nov 1964	6
Keith Burkinshaw	Nov 1964	March 1965	-
George Ainsley	Jun 1965	Nov 1966	-
Bill Leivers	Nov 1966	Dec 1967	-
Frank Upton	Jan 1968	July 1968	-
Brian Doyle	July 1968	1969	-
George Aitken	1971	May 1974	-
Colin Meldrum	July 1974	April 1975	-
John McNamee	June 1975	Dec 1975	-
Alan Ashman	Dec 1975	Feb 1977	-
Colin Meldrum	Feb 1977	May 1977	-

Wrexham

Although they are one of the oldest clubs in Wales, founded in 1873, Wrexham's progress to the League was painfully slow, taking until the formation of the Third Division North in 1921 to attain senior status. Even then, it was not for another three years that a manager was appointed to the Racecourse Ground, and in the 62 seasons which have followed, the Robins have tried 22 alternatives, giving each two months less than three seasons in the job. As well as the 22, there have been various caretaker managers and a period of almost three years in the late 1920s without a manager. All this chopping and changing has yielded a mere three promotions from the Fourth Division and one championship of the Third, not a very heroic haul.

Contrary to the general trend, Wrexham have not been more inclined to change managers in the modern era: the turnover rate was high even in the early days. The longest-serving manager, moreover, is John Neal, who had nine years ending as recently as 1977. His nearest challenger is Ernest Blackburn on five years. The outbreak of war in 1939, just a few months into Tom Morgan's reign, makes him the shortest-serving manager, since he had been replaced by the time League football was resumed. Almost as short in terms of League games was the tenure of Morgan's predecessor, Arthur Cowell. In his three months at the Racecourse Ground, he was in charge for just seven games, before a disagreement with the board ended his only managerial post.

Until Alvan Williams' appointment in 1967, only one former Wrexham player (Cliff Lloyd) had been given the job of manager. Since then however, four of the six appointees had previously played for the Robins (Neal and Bobby Roberts were the exceptions). Several before Alvan Williams had served the club in other capacities, most notably Cowell (trainer), Tony Williams (scout and assistant manager) and Lloyd (secretary and caretaker manager). It is not surprising that few of Wrexham's managers could offer previous League management experience when they applied.

The exceptions were Blackburn (Accrington), Morgan (Port Vale), John Love (Walsall), Jack Rowley (Plymouth and Oldham), Alvan Williams (Hartlpool and Southend) and Roberts (Colchester). After leaving the Racecourse, Les McDowall, who took Manchester City to two FA Cup Finals, enjoyed the most success, although John Neal (Middlesbrough and Chelsea) managed in Division One and Charlie Hewitt recorded League and Cup success at Millwall.

Manager	Start/Date	End/Date	Pts/Total
Charlie Hewitt	Nov 1924	Dec 1926	-
Jack Baynes	Oct 1929	Dec 1931	-
Ernest Blackburn	Jan 1932	Jan 1937	8
Capt James Logan	Jan 1937	May 1938	-
Arthur Cowell	June 1938	Sept 1938	-
Tom Morgan	April 1939	April 1942	-
Tom Williams	April 1942	Feb 1949	-
Les McDowall	May 1949	May 1950	-
Peter Jackson	Nov 1950	Feb 1955	-
Cliff Lloyd	Feb 1955	Dec 1957	-
John Love	Dec 1957	Oct 1959	-
Cliff Lloyd	Oct 1959	May 1960	-
Billy Morris	June 1960	May 1961	-
Ken Barnes	May 1961	Feb 1965	6
Jack Rowley	Jan 1966	April 1967	-
Alvan Williams	April 1967	Sept 1968	-
John Neal	Sept 1968	May 1977	6
Arfon Griffiths	May 1977	June 1981	14
Mel Sutton	June 1981	May 1982	-
Bobby Roberts	June 1982	March 1985	-
Dixie McNeil	April 1985	Oct 1989	-
Brian Flynn	Nov 1989	-	6

York City

Founded in 1922 and elected to the Third Division North in 1929, the present York club have had 19 managers (18 individuals) in 57 seasons, an average tenure of three years per person. Tom Mitchell was at Bootham Crescent four times longer than this, but seven of his years were covered by World War Two. In terms of League matches played, Tom Lockie, at the helm for over seven years, comes out on top, followed by Tom Johnston with a six-year reign. York's shortest-serving manager was also the unluckiest, the experienced Charlie Spencer, who died three months after taking over the controls. Joe Shaw was only there for ten months before he resigned, whilst Jim McCormick, Barry Lyons and Bobby Saxton came and went inside two seasons.

With just five exceptions, the 18 men who have managed the Minster Men were either former League club managers or had some previous connection with York. The exceptions were John Collier, McCormick, Shaw, Charlie Wright and John Ward. The rest comprised six former York players, Mitchell, Dick Duckworth, Lockie and Lyons, together with Sam Bartram, a wartime guest, and Denis Smith, who as a Stoke player, had a period on loan at Bootham Crescent. In addition, George 'Billy' Sherrington was the long-time secretary turned manager on occasion and incumbent Alan Little was Ward's coach. Of the five who had previous managerial experience at League level under their belts, the most impressive pedigree belonged to Wilf McGuinness, Matt Busby's successor at Old Trafford. He, however, presided over the fastest decline in City's history, from the Second to the Fourth Divisions. McGuinness succeeded Johnston, once of Rotherham, Grimsby and Huddersfield, who was the architect of York's most rapid ascent, from Fourth Division re-election to Division Two. The other three with managerial experience were Spencer (Grimsby), Saxton (Exeter, Plymouth and Blackburn) and John Bird (Hartlepool).

Life after York had little to offer most of City's former managers. Bartram went to Luton, Johnston back to Huddersfield and Ward to Bristol Rovers,

all in higher divisions than York, whilst Smith took Sunderland from the Third to the First Division. There were periods in York's history when there was no manager, and on a number of occasions, Sherrington stepped into the breach. Originally a civil servant, he was one of the original five directors of the club in 1922, and then from 1924 until his retirement in 1961, served the club as secretary. This sometimes meant taking on team duties, as between 1930 and 1933, but in 1954-55, he shared responsibilities with trainer Tom Lockie when York reached the FA Cup semi-finals, only the second Third Division club to get within one round of the Final.

Manager	Start/Date	End/Date	Pts/Total
John Collier	July 1928	May 1930	-
George 'Billy' Sherrington	May 1930	May 1933	-
John Collier	May 1933	March 1937	-
Tom Mitchell	March 1937	Feb 1950	-
Dick Duckworth	March 1950	Oct 1952	-
Charlie Spencer	Nov 1952	Feb 1953	-
Jim McCormick	June 1953	Sept 1954	-
Sam Bartram	March 1956	July 1960	6
Tom Lockie	July 1960	Oct 1967	6
Joe Shaw	Nov 1967	Aug 1968	-
Tom Johnston	Oct 1968	Jan 1975	14
Wilf McGuinness	Feb 1975	Oct 1977	-
Charlie Wright	Nov 1977	March 1980	-
Barry Lyons	March 1980	Dec 1981	-
Denis Smith	May 1982	June 1987	12
Bobby Saxton	June 1987	Sept 1988	-
John Bird	Oct 1988	Oct 1991	-
John Ward	Oct 1991	March 1993	-
Alan Little	March 1993	-	6

Nelson's 1926 line-up. Back row (left to right): E.Jacques (trainer), Broadhurst, Baker, Abbot, Sharpe, Rigg, Harris. Front row: Brown, Stevenson, Hampson, Wilson, Mitchell, Keers.

Other League Clubs

ABERDARE ATHLETIC (1921-1927)

Manager	Start/Date	End/Date
William Lot	Jun 1920	Mar 1922
Frank Bradshaw	May 1923	Apr 1924
Sydney Beaumont	cs 1924	cs 1927
Harry Hadley	Nov 1927	Apr 1928

ASHINGTON (1921-1929)

Manager	Start/Date	End/Date
Pat O'Connell	1921	–

BARNET (1991-1993)

Manager	Start/Date	End/Date
Barry Fry		Mar 1993
Eddie Stein	Mar 1993	

BOOTLE (1892-1893)

BURTON SWIFTS (1892-1901)

BURTON UNITED (1901-1907)

BURTON WANDERERS (1894-1897)

DARWEN (1891-1899)

DURHAM CITY (1921-1928)

Manager	Start/Date	End/Date
J.W.Sowerby	1919	1923
Jackie Mordue	Feb 1923	Feb 1924
Richard Jackson	Jul 1926	1927
J.W.Sowerby	cs 1927	cs 1928

GAINSBOROUGH TRINITY (1896-1912)

GLOSSOP NORTH END (1898-1915)
(Dropped 'North End' in 1899)

Manager	Start/Date	End/Date
John Tait Robertson	Oct 1906	1909
David Weir	1909	Apr 1911
James McEwan	Mar 1911	Feb 1914

LOUGHBOROUGH TOWN (1895-1900)

MAIDSTONE UNITED (1989-1992)

Manager	Start/Date	End/Date
Keith Peacock	May 1989	Jan 1991
Graham Carr	Jan 1991	Oct 1991
Bill Williams	Oct 1991	Jan 1992
Clive Walker	Jan 1992	May 1992

MERTHYR TOWN (1920-1930)

Manager	Start/Date	End/Date
Harry Hadley	May 1919	Apr 1922
Thomas Jones	cs 1923	cs 1924
Albert Lindon	Aug 1924	Jan 1928
Harry Hadley	Apr 1928	Nov 1928
Tom McKenna	Nov 1928	May 1929
Harry Hadley	1930	Sep 1931

MIDDLESBROUGH IRONOPOLIS (1893-1894)

NELSON (1921-1931)

Manager	Start/Date	End/Date
David Wilson	May 1921	May 1925
Percy Smith	cs 1925	May 1927
Jack English	cs 1928	Jan 1931

NORTHWICH VICTORIA (1892-1894)

STALYBRIDGE CELTIC (1921-1923)

THAMES (1930-1932)

Manager	Start/Date	End/Date
David Buchanan	cs 1928	cs 1931

WIGAN BOROUGH (1921-1931)

Manager	Start/Date	End/Date
Herbert Bamlett	May 1921	Aug 1923
Charles Bell	Aug 1923	Feb 1924
Walter Raynor	cs 1925	Feb 1926
Angus McKinnon	May 1926	Jan 1930
Leslie Aldred	cs 1930	Oct 1931

About the Who's Who

ONE of the problems inherent in undertaking any Who's Who is to decide who appears in the book and who does not. In this case, where the definition of 'manager' changes over time, the difficulties are compounded. Below is a guide to explain how we made decisions on who to include. As with any research, there is often some conflicting information about particular individuals, but we have attempted to track the true facts by reference to contemporary sources.

Scope of the Who's Who

All managers are included in the Who's Who except those who were only ever caretaker managers, secretaries, or were managers before the club joined the Football League, or in wartime competition only. Three caretaker managers have been included in the book: Les Gore, Clarrie Bourton and Norman Smith, who were in charge for long periods.

If a manager was a caretaker prior to being appointed permanently, then the date used is the one on which he was initially appointed as caretaker manager. Clubs such as Newcastle United, Aston Villa and Everton did not appoint their first managers until the 1930s and were previously run by secretaries. These secretaries were not in charge of team affairs and so are not included in the Who's Who unless they were managers at other clubs. The position of honorary manager (usually club directors in a temporary capacity) is less clear cut. There are one or two (eg Bill Tulip at Gateshead) who proved to be the club's longest-serving manager. Consequently, the club section rather than the Who's Who will refer to these individuals.

We have included some chief coaches such as Doug Livermore, Eddie May and Greg Downs who were in charge of team affairs but called the chief coach. In the absence of any other appropriate official, these men's jobs were regarded as analagous to the managers.

Abbreviations:

Only two are used:
cs — close season; sub — substitute.

Honours List

All the various forms of the League Cup — ie Milk, Littlewoods, Rumbelows and Coca-Cola Cup — are referred to as the League Cup in the text. In 1992-93, the previous divisional names/points allocation have been retained, so the FA Premier League is still referred to as the First Division, and the new Third Division is still the Fourth for this purpose.

We have only included honours when a particular person has achieved promotion as a manager, NOT as a player. If a man wins promotion with his club as a player, it is not included in the honours list, but if he gets a club promoted when their manager, then it is included. All honours are included together whether achieved as a player or a manager.

A player must have played in at least a third of all matches in a championship season (eg 14 appearances in a 42-match season) for the honour to appear in his list.

Malcolm Allison's name appears in the Who's Who but the points in the club section have also been credited to Joe Mercer. The rationale for this is that he was seen as being in joint charge of the club, and an equal partner in the success.

Heights and Weights

The height and weight of a player is given with a date in brackets. This is the date when, as a player, these details were actually recorded.

Club Titles

Clubs are given the titles used at the time when a transfer or other event took place. For example, Clapton Orient became Leyton Orient in 1946, then Orient in 1966 and Leyton Orient again in 1987. Bradford refers to the now defunct Bradford Park Avenue as opposed to Bradford City which is a separate club. The headings in the club section, however, refer to the latest (or last name) of each club.

Transfer Fees

Transfer fees are those quoted in the press or various football histories and not necessarily accurate as fees are generally not made public.

BILLY WALKER

JOHN HARRIS

HARRY BRADSHAW

TOM MALEY

STAN SEYMOUR

JIMMY McINTYRE

MANAGERS

ADAMSON, James

Born: Ashington, 4 April 1929.
Right-half 5ft 8in; 11st 9lb (1964).
Career: Ashington YMCA; East Chevington (Ashington); Burnley January 1947, coach 1964 then manager February 1970-January 1976; Sparta Rotterdam manager May-June 1976; Sunderland manager November 1976-November 1978; Leeds United manager November 1978-October 1980.

Honours: England 'B' international (1 cap); Football League representative; Football League champions 1960; Division Two champions 1973; FA Cup runners-up 1962.

Adamson was a miner when he signed for Burnley as a professional in January 1947. He joined the club as an inside-forward but was soon off on National Service with the RAF. On his return, Adamson was tried at wing-half and soon made his debut, at Bolton, in 1950-51. He developed into one of the finest wing-halves in the country, regularly turning in sound performances without attracting a great deal of publicity. This probably accounted for him never gaining full England honours. He was ever-present in Burnley's championship-winning side in 1960 and two years later led the club to the FA Cup Final, where they lost to Spurs. His consistency was duly acknowledged when he was voted Footballer of the Year in 1962.

Adamson retired in 1964, after over 400 games for Burnley, and was appointed coach at the club. He had qualified as an FA coach in 1957 and in his early days coached Lancashire FA junior clubs. In 1962 he was appointed coach to the England World Cup side in Chile and was considered for the England manager's job when Walter Winterbottom left the post. When Harry Potts was made general manager at Turf Moor, Adamson was appointed team manager of Burnley in February 1970. He described his side as 'the Team of the 70s' with talented youngsters such as Dave Thomas, Leighton James, Steve Kindon and Alan West. However, Burnley were relegated to Division Two at the end of 1970-71. After an initial policy of selling to survive, Adamson was given money to invest in new players. He signed Keith Newton from Everton, Alan Stevenson from Chesterfield and Peter Noble from Swindon.

Burnley won the Second Division title in 1973 after re-establishing their self-confidence and after Adamson had re-organised the club. After another relegation in 1976, Adamson had a brief spell with Sparta Rotterdam, then moved to Sunderland. Alas, he was unable to steer them from relegation and was thus in charge of relegated

clubs for the second consecutive season. Adamson was the surprise choice to take over from Jock Stein at Leeds United in November 1978. Initially he was successful, taking Leeds into Europe and to a League Cup semi-final, but he was ultimately unable to stop the club's slide from the pinnacle of British soccer and left Elland Road in 1980.

ADDENBROOKE, John Henry 'Jack'

Born: Wolverhampton, 1865; Died: 7 September 1922.
Career: St Luke's School (Blakenhall) 1875-1877; Saltley College (Birmingham) 1879; Wolverhampton Wanderers Reserves c.1883, then secretary-manager August 1885-June 1922; also Staffordshire FA vice-president and served on committee for 28 years.

Honours: FA Cup winners 1893, 1908, runners-up 1889, 1896, 1921; Football League long-service medal 1909.

Addenbrooke was associated with Wolves for almost 40 years, joining the club as a reserve player in the 1880s, whilst working as a teacher in a local school. Although officially the club's secretary-manager, he did not have full powers of team selection nor complete control over which players were signed. Wolves had an excellent FA Cup record during Addenbrooke's period at Molineux. They lost 3-0 to Preston in the 1889 Final at The Oval, then won the trophy for the first time in 1893, when they beat Everton at Manchester's Fallowfield. Two years later they lost 2-1 to Sheffield Wednesday in another Final, but in 1908 again won the FA Cup, beating Newcastle United 3-1. In 1921, Wolves reached their fifth FA Cup Final under Addenbrooke, losing 1-0 to Tottenham at Stamford Bridge. By this time, though, the Midlands club were struggling in the bottom half of the Second Division. Their highest position was third in Division One in 1897-98 but they were relegated in 1906 and failed to regain their place.

ADDISON, Colin

Born: Taunton, 18 May 1940
Inside-forward 5ft 9½in; 10st 10lb (1964).
Career: Cliftonville (York); York City May 1957; Nottingham Forest January 1961 (£12,000); Arsenal September 1966 (£45,000); Sheffield United December 1967 (£40,000); Hereford United player-manager October 1971-1974; Durban City (South Africa) manager January 1975; Notts County assistant manager December 1975-October 1976; Newport County manager January 1977-May 1978; West Bromwich Albion assistant manager July 1978-1979; Derby County manager May 1979-January 1982; Newport County manager January 1982-May 1985; coaching in Kuwait and Qatar; Celta Vigo (Spain) manager April 1986-August 1987; West Bromwich Albion assistant manager September 1987-October 1988; Atlético Madrid assistant manager October 1988, then manager December 1988-June 1989; Cadiz (Spain) March-July 1990; Hereford United manager July 1990-May 1991; Al Arabi coach.

Honours: Division Four runners-up 1973.

In his playing days, Addison was a versatile forward, appearing in every front-line position whilst at York City. He scored 61 goals in 159 League appearances for Forest, but after his move to Arsenal he did not prove one of Bertie Mee's best buys. Addison never

fitted smoothly into the Highbury style, although he did admire Mee's methods. He found his form again at Bramall Lane before a move to Southern League Hereford United as player-manager. The club had ambitions for League status and it was Addison who was to help them achieve it after a famous run to the FA Cup fourth round which included a 2-1 victory over First Division Newcastle United in February 1972. When Hereford joined the League later that year, he sold Dudley Tyler to West Ham for £25,000 and bought seven new players with the money.

Addison had to retire from playing after breaking his leg in November 1973 and Hereford seemed to pick up after a poor start when he was able to concentrate on management full time. Promotion to the Third Division was achieved at the end of 1972-73. He left Edgar Street to manage Durban City in South Africa in 1974 but soon returned to become assistant manager at Notts County. After periods at Newport County and West Brom, Addison took over at Derby County. It was a hard slog at the Baseball Ground and the Rams were relegated, despite Addison spending £1 million on new players. After another mediocre season he was sacked in January 1982 but soon returned to the game for a second period at Newport. Addison had two spells in Spain. First as manager of Celta Vigo, who he took into the Spanish First Division, then as assistant to Ron Atkinson at Atlético Madrid. Atkinson lasted only two months in charge and Addison took over for a while after his dismissal. The two had worked together in Addison's two previous spells at The Hawthorns.

AINSLEY, George Edward

Born: South Shields, 15 April 1915; Died: Leeds, April 1985.
Centre-forward 6ft 1in; 13st (1936).
Career: Durham Schoolboys; South Shields St Andrew's; Sunderland April 1932; Bolton Wanderers August 1936; Leeds United December 1936; Bradford November 1947; wartime guest for Blackpool, Manchester United, Huddersfield Town, Liverpool, Birmingham, Southport, Crewe Alexandra, Bradford City; coached Cambridge University early 1950s; coached in India in 1950; Pakistan national coach until autumn 1962; Highland Park (Johannesburg) player-coach November 1962; Israel national coach late 1963-December 1964; Workington manager June 1965-November 1966.

Honours: FA XI tour to South Africa 1939.

Ainsley managed only one Football League club, Workington. In July 1965 he was appointed their boss from 30 applicants. He helped steer the club to fifth position in Division Three in 1965-66, although they were 13 points behind promoted Hull City and Millwall. This was Workington's best-ever season. However, the following season, Workington finished bottom and were relegated. Soon afterwards Ainsley was dismissed.

As a player he did not find much success until he joined Leeds United in December 1936. He led the attack and was an aerial 'ace', using his head to good purpose. Never a regular at Elland Road, his career was interrupted by the war. In 1939 he had won some unofficial caps whilst touring South Africa with an FA XI. He guested for many clubs during the wartime period. After the war he scored 30 goals in 47 appearances for Bradford before retiring in 1949, whereupon he proceeded to travel all over the world as a coach.

AITKEN, Andrew

Born: Ayr, 27 April 1877; Died: Ponteland, 15 February 1955.
Half-back 5ft 8in; 11st 9lb (1904)
Career: Ayr Thistle; Ayr Parkhouse; Newcastle United July 1895; Kilmarnock (loan) February-March 1898; Middlesbrough player-manager November 1906-February 1909; Leicester Fosse player-manager February 1909-May 1911; Dundee May 1911; Kilmarnock June 1912; Gateshead Town player-manager June 1913; Arsenal scout in 1930s, based in Manchester area.

Honours: Scotland international (14 caps); Football League champions 1905; FA Cup runners-up 1906.

Aitken was one of Newcastle United's all-time great wing-halves, who made 345 appearances and scored 41 goals for the club. Often used as the 'sixth forward', his versatility, attacking and heading ability were his main strengths. He was remembered as supreme in tackling and distribution, seldom wasting a ball. Aitken is one of the few player-managers to represent his country. He also gained many League and Cup medals whilst at St James' Park. He cost Middlesbrough £500 when he joined them as player-manager. In his first season, Aitken lifted 'Boro from bottom of the League at Christmas to a safe mid-table position at the close. The following season 'Boro finished sixth, their best-ever position. His next club, Leicester Fosse, were relegated at the end of his first season in charge. Things were even worse the following season and in May 1911, Aitken moved back to being just a player, with Dundee. His retirement from playing was forced upon him by a groin injury.

AITKEN, George B.

Born: Dalkeith, 13 August 1928.
Centre-half 5ft 10in; 12st 7lb (1959).
Career: Edinburgh Thistle; Hibernian (amateur); Middlesbrough June 1946; Workington July 1953 (£5,000), retired to become trainer 1960-1964; Watford trainer 1964-1971; Workington manager 1971-May 1974; Grimsby Town assistant manager 1975-1976; Brighton & Hove Albion coach 1976-1986; Watford scout 1986-1987; Aston Villa scout 1989-1990; England scout 1990.

Unable to break regularly into Middlesbrough's first team, Aitken moved to Workington for a fee of £5,000 in the summer of 1953, after only 17 appearances for 'Boro. A commanding centre-half, he had more success at Workington, quickly dispelling worries about his fitness to embark on a career which saw him make 262 League appearances (three goals) for the club. After retiring from playing he assisted Joe Harvey and Ken Furphy as trainer at Borough Park. Aitken moved with Furphy to Watford, who won the Third Division championship and reached an FA Cup semi-final, before he returned to Workington as manager in the 1970s. As always it was a constant struggle for Workington to avoid having to seek re-election and with such poor attendances, Aitken had to function on a shoe-string budget during his spell in charge. He worked under Peter Taylor, Alan Mullery and Jimmy Melia at Brighton and they reached the First Division and an FA Cup Final. In recent years, Aitken has worked with Graham Taylor at Watford, Aston Villa and in the England set-up.

ALDRED, Leslie

Career: Wigan Borough secretary-manager cs 1930-October 1931.

Leslie Aldred was appointed secretary-manager of Wigan Borough as an economy measure, for the jobs had previously been kept separate at Springfield Park. Nothing is known about Aldred or his credentials for the position but when he took over, hard-up Wigan had retained only five players from the previous season and he had to make several new signings. They included the former Aston Villa, Manchester United and England centre-half Frank Barson, and the ex-Fulham player Jim Scullion, who the previous season had been Crewe Alexandra's leading scorer with 29 goals. In 1930-31, Borough had a better season than anyone expected, finishing tenth in the Third Division North thanks mainly to an excellent home record. However, they still conceded 86 goals all told and on 26 October 1931, after 12 games of the new season, they resigned from the Football League with mounting debts. They had only seven points and had lost all six away games, conceding 24 goals in the process. Aldred, of course, lost his job with the demise of the club.

ALLEN, James Phillips.

Born: Poole, 16 October 1909.
Centre-half   6ft 1in; 11st 12lb (1933).
Career: Longfleet St Mary's School; Poole Central; Poole Town August 1927; Portsmouth February 1930; Aston Villa June 1934 (£10,775) (retired in 1944); wartime guest for Fulham, Portsmouth and Birmingham; sports and welfare officer in a Birmingham firm in mid-1940s; Colchester United manager July 1948-April 1953; licensee in Southsea in 1950s.

Honours: England international (2 caps); Football League representative; Division Two champions 1938; FA Cup runners-up 1934.

After joining Portsmouth from Poole Town, Allen soon established himself as one of the outstanding defenders in the country. He played for Pompey in the 1934 FA Cup Final defeat by Manchester City. Portsmouth were leading 1-0 when Allen was injured and he was off the field receiving attention when Tilson equalised for City. In June 1934 his transfer to Aston Villa was a sensation, when he moved for a British record fee of £10,775. It was a controversial move with Villa fans, who were

used to attacking centre-halves. Fair-haired Allen was a tall man who was ideally built for the 'stopper' duties dictated by the tactics of the time. However, he could not adapt himself to Villa's style and for months the crowd believed good money had been wasted. Allen, a great sportsman and most modest character, stayed long enough to prove his critics wrong. He was captain of the Second Division championship side of 1937-38, revealing form which had won him England caps whilst at Pompey.

After appearing for a number of sides in wartime soccer, Allen retired before the resumption of peacetime football. After a spell as sports and welfare officer in a Birmingham firm, Allen was offered the managership of non-League Colchester United. After finishing runners-up to Merthyr Tydfil in the Southern League in 1949-50, United were elected to the Football League when it was extended to 92 clubs. After moderate success in the Third Division South, Allen left the club in April 1953 to run a pub in Southsea.

ALLEN, Leslie W.

Born: Dagenham, 4 September 1937.
Centre-forward 5ft 10in; 11st 3lb (1964).
Career: Briggs Sports; Chelsea September 1954; Tottenham Hotspur December 1959; Queen's Park Rangers July 1965 (£20,000), then manager December 1968-January 1971; Woodford Town manager 1971-72; Swindon Town manager November 1972-February 1974.

Honours: England Under-23 international (1 cap); Football League champions 1961; Division Three champions 1967; FA Cup winners 1961; Football League Cup winners 1967; Division Two. runners-up 1968

Never able to establish himself in the Chelsea side, Allen moved to Spurs in exchange for Johnny Brooks in December 1959. His career picked up immensely at White Hart Lane and he won fame in Spurs double side of 1960-61. He was ever-present that season and scored 27 goals. He also scored five in Spurs' 13-2 victory over Crewe the previous season. With the arrival of Jimmy Greaves, his first-team place was under threat. He moved from inside-left to centre-forward but had to rely on injuries to others to get a game.

After his £21,000 move to Queen's Park Rangers in July 1965, Allen helped them to another double, this time the Third Division championship and League Cup in 1967. He eventually helped Rangers into Division One. With QPR struggling in the First Division, Les was made player-manager of the club in December 1968 after the premature departure of Alec Stock and the brief and stormy 28-day appointment of Tommy Docherty.

Relegation was a certainty long before

the end of the season. Allen was not a great success as a manager at either Queen's Park Rangers or later with Swindon Town. With chairman Jim Gregory apparently losing much of his interest in the club and the indifferent form of some players, Allen resigned in January 1971. He had a tough time at Swindon, which ended with the club's relegation to Division Three in 1974. His son, Clive, was later an England international and played for all three of his father's clubs, QPR, Spurs and Chelsea.

ALLEN, Ronald.

Born: Fenton, Staffs, 15 January 1929.
Inside-left   5ft 8in; 11st 3lb (1964).

Career: Bucknall Boys' Brigade; Wellington Scouts; Northwood Mission; Port Vale amateur March 1944: professional April 1946; West Bromwich Albion March 1950 (£15,000); Crystal Palace May 1961 (£4,500); retired 1965; Wolves coach 1965, then manager January 1966-November 1968; Athletic Bilbao manager March 1969-November 1971; Sporting Lisbon manager April 1972-May 1973; Walsall manager June-December 1973; West Bromwich Albion scouting advisor January-June 1977, then manager June-December 1977; Saudi Arabia national team coach December 1977; Panathinaikos (Greece) manager June-September 1980; West Bromwich Albion manager again July 1981-May 1982, then general manager until 1983; sales director of Black Country engineering firm specialising in oil rigs after 1983.

Honours: England international (5 caps); 'B' internationals (2 caps); Football League representative; Division Two runners-up 1967; FA Cup winners 1954.

Ronnie Allen was soon finding the net regularly for his first League club, Port Vale, and attracted the attention of West Brom, who signed him for £18,000 in 1950. Quick-thinking, allied with speed off the mark made him one of the most dangerous centre-forwards in the country when in his prime. He also played in deep-lying positions, creating chances for his fellow forwards as well as scoring regularly himself. He possessed a powerful shot in both feet, was a superb volleyer of the ball and reliable penalty-taker. In 457 appearances for Albion he scored 231 goals, he also played another 109 games for Palace in which he scored 37 goals before retirement in 1965.

In the spring of 1965, Allen joined Wolves as coach and when Andy Beattie was sacked he took over as manager in January 1966. He bought shrewdly. His

signings including Derek Dougan and Mike Bailey. Wolves were a struggling Second Division side when Allen took over but they won promotion back to the First Division in 1967. When things started to go wrong, Allen was sacked in November 1968. He was attracted to Spain to manage Athletic Bilbao but was able to sign only Basque players at the club which limited his choice. He quickly learned Spanish which helped him to develop relationships with the players.

After an initial struggle, Allen never looked back after taking Bilbao to a Spanish Cup victory over Elche and the following season just missing out on the championship as runners-up on goal-average to Athletic Madrid. He then moved to Portugal to manage Sporting Lisbon before returning to England to manage Walsall briefly in 1973. He later returned to The Hawthorns, first as scouting advisor, then as manager. Allen was then offered a lucrative post as manager to the Saudi Arabian national team. He next managed Panathinaikos of Athens, before a second spell in charge at West Brom, taking them to the semi-final of the FA and League Cups, although his stay was short-lived and tempestuous.

ALLEN, Samuel

Born: West Bromwich; Died: 1 January 1946
Career: Birmingham & District League referee; Swindon Town director 1895-1902; clerical worker in GWR offices until 1902; Swindon Town secretary-manager July 1902-April 1933, then secretary 1933-1946.

Honours: Southern League champions 1911, 1914.

Allen served Swindon Town from 1895 until his death in 1946. He spent two years as a member of the old committee, five years as a director, 31 years as secretary-manager and 13 as secretary. In July 1902, Allen became Swindon's first full-time secretary-manager and was in charge of team affairs, carrying this role through much of the club's most successful period. He became very well known and respected in the football world.

A shrewd judge of a good player, he also persuaded many fine footballers to come to Swindon over the years. His initial salary was ten shillings (50p) a week. Swindon enjoyed fine FA Cup runs in 1908, 1910 and 1912, losing to Newcastle United in the semi-final in 1910 and Barnsley at the same stage in 1912. They also won the Southern League championship in seasons 1910-11 and 1913-14.

Samuel Allen was still secretary-manager when the club joined the Football League in 1920. He was a pioneer of pooling gate money, the pooling of referee's and linesmen's expenses and, as a member of the select committee of Division Three South clubs, was striving for amended promotion and relegation rules.

ALLISON, George Frederick

Born: Hurworth-on-Tees, 24 October 1883; Died: Golders Green, 13 March 1957.
Career: Broadcaster and journalist, starting as a journalist on Teesside; Arsenal secretary-manager June 1934-May 1947.

Honours: Football League champions 1935, 1938; FA Cup winners 1936; War League Cup runners-up 1941; Football League South Cup winners 1943.

George Allison became secretary-manager of Arsenal on 1 June 1934, following the death of the legendary Herbert Chapman. He was to maintain the Gunners' great success of his predecessor, including winning the League championship at the end of his first season in charge to complete three titles in successive seasons for Arsenal.

Allison was born at Hurworth-on-Tees on 24 October 1883 and started his journalistic career in 1903 at Stockton-on-Tees, where he reported local games. He had experienced limited success as a player, appearing as a wing-half in local parks football.

His first job in the world of soccer was at Middlesbrough, where he became assistant secretary in 1905. A year later he moved to London to carry on his journalistic career, often reporting on Woolwich Arsenal matches. In the 1920s he became editor of the club's programme, writing under the *nom de plume* of Gunners' Mate. He joined the board of directors in 1926 and relinquished his position as managing director to take over as secretary-manager. Under his managership, Arsenal won the League championship in 1934-35 and 1937-38 and the FA Cup in 1936, beating Sheffield United in the Final. He broke the British transfer record when he paid Wolves £14,500 for Bryn Jones in 1938. One of his first signings was Ted Drake but, like most managers, he also made some mistakes and considered Len Shackleton too frail for top-class football.

Allison's readiness to spend money earned Arsenal the nickname of the 'Bank of England Team'. He let things go on very much as they had under Chapman and interfered as little as possible on the playing side. Indeed, he left the management of the players to Tom Whittaker and Joe Shaw.

Allison's brain child was Highbury's East Stand, built in 1936 and considered one of the finest stands in existence at that time. It has five floors, seating for 15,000 and also houses the administrative offices, boardroom, players' quarters and modern treatment rooms. This was built at a massive cost of £120,000. During World War Two, Allison practically ran Arsenal on his own and this probably took its toll as he retired in May 1947.

He maintained his links with the media, being London correspondent of the *New York Herald* for over 35 years, and was a pioneer broadcaster of football on both radio and television. He commentated on the first TV programme about football called *Soccer at Arsenal* which was broadcast in September 1937 and also appeared in the film *The Arsenal Stadium Mystery* in 1939.

Tom Whittaker, who succeeded him

as the manager of Arsenal, said of him: "Under the surface of the showman was a shrewd knowledge of the game, culled from long experience with Arsenal. He had an easy disposition, a ready sense of humour and was quick to praise and slow to condemn. He kept Arsenal in the headlines by continued success and flamboyant methods and no reporter lacked help in getting a story." George Allison died following a heart attack at his Golders Green home in 1957 and was sadly missed by his former friends and colleagues.

ALLISON, Malcolm Alexander

Born: Dartford, 5 September 1927.
Centre-half   6ft; 12st (1951).
Career: Welling Civic; Danson Boys' Club; Erith & Belvedere; Charlton Rovers; Charlton Athletic amateur 1944, professional December 1945; West Ham United February 1951, retired 1958 due to illness; Romford August 1960-May 1962; Cambridge University coach; Sutton United coach from November 1958; Wembley coach from May 1962; Bath City manager April 1963-May 1964; Plymouth Argyle manager May 1964-April 1965; Manchester City assistant manager and coach July 1965, then manager 1971-March 1973; Crystal Palace manager March 1973-May 1976; Galatasaray (Turkey) coach 1976-1978; also Memphis (Tennessee) coach November 1977-February 1978; Plymouth Argyle manager May 1978-January 1979; Manchester City coach January 1979, then manager July 1979-1980; Crystal Palace manager December 1980-February 1981; Sporting Lisbon manager February 1981-1982; Middlesbrough manager October 1982-March 1984; Willington manager October 1984; to Turkey as coach; Kuwait national coach until March 1986; Vitória Setúbal (Portugal) manager February 1988; Farense (Portugal) manager January-March 1989; Fisher Athletic manager June-November 1989; Bristol Rovers consultant November 1992.

Honours: Football League champions 1968; Division Two champions 1966; FA Cup winners 1969; Football League Cup winners 1970; European Cup-winners' Cup winners 1970.

Malcolm Allison's coaching and management days overshadowed his playing career with Charlton and West Ham. One of the best-known coaches in British football, Allison still works in the soccer industry, even though he is now in his 60s. He started his professional career at The Valley, where he arrived from Charlton Rovers in 1944, but made only two League appearances before his move

to Upton Park in February 1951 to replace the ageing Dick Walker at centre-half.

Considered a 'character' on the pitch, Big Mal had a highly individual style as a central defender. He played in 255 League and Cup games for the Hammers, scoring ten goals before being struck down with tuberculosis at the beginning of United's promotion season of 1957-58. Allison lost a lung as a result of this illness but carried on playing for Romford in the Southern League, ignoring medical advice. He was obviously disappointed never to have realised his ambition to play in the First Division.

Due to disillusionment with training methods at both Charlton and West Ham, Allison went to Lilleshall to sample Walter Winterbottom's coaching schemes. He was so inspired that he went back every summer for the next ten years and began to devote his spare time to coaching. His first jobs were with Cambridge University and Sutton United. Allison soon took up his first management post at Southern League Bath City in October 1962. In May 1964, he became Plymouth Argyle's manager and stayed until the following April, accepting the assistant manager's post at Manchester City three months later.

At Maine Road, Allison combined with Joe Mercer to form one of the most successful partnerships in English football. One of the best coaches in the game, Allison was also one of the most explosive. In October 1965 he was suspended for a month following a series of outbursts. Yet Mercer and Allison revived the City club, combining an attractive style of play with sustained success. The Second Division championship was won in 1965-66. Two years later, the League title was gained and other trophies soon followed. City won the FA Cup in 1969 and the European Cup-winners' Cup and Football League Cup the following year.

The men's strength as a pair was all the more apparent after Allison became the sole manager in 1971. There was now no cool judgement to temper Allison's driving determination to achieve the impossible and his close involvement with the players became a handicap. In his final spell with City, Big Mal paid huge transfer fees for some quite ordinary players and the club suffered financially. He left Maine Road in 1973, with the team in disarray and the supporters disenchanted, to join Crystal Palace.

Just relegated from the First Division, at the end of his first season in charge, Palace were a Third Division club. After losing his job at Selhurst Park in 1976, Allison moved abroad to coach Galatasaray of Turkey. In May 1978 he returned to English football for a second spell as manager of Plymouth Argyle, but following January he moved back to Maine Road as 'coaching overlord', uniting with general manager Tony Book. Plymouth received £35,000 as compensation.

After a number of disastrous million-pound signings he lost his job but returned to Crystal Palace in December 1980. When Ron Noades took over the club two months later, Allison was replaced by Wimbledon's manager, Dario Gradi.

Allison moved abroad again, after a short spell at Yeovil, to manage Sporting Lisbon and took them to the Portuguese League and Cup double in 1981-82. He was back in England in October 1982 to manage Middlesbrough, bottom of the Second Division

at the time. Allison had the job of reviving morale and creating a team which believed in itself. They eventually pulled themselves off the bottom to finish 16th, but his period at Ayresome Park ended in controversy in March 1984 after he blocked the £100,000 transfer of Darren Wood to Chelsea. Chairman Mike McCullough said, "As Mr Allison can no longer be relied upon to co-operate in trying to save the club, I have dismissed him." 'Boro were on the brink of bankruptcy at the time.

Malcolm Allison has since become a wanderer, from one football outpost to another. Willington, a North-East non-League club, was his first port of call, followed by a spell as Kuwait's national coach until March 1986. He re-emerged in Portugal as Vitória Setúbal's manager in February 1988 and became Farense's manager in January 1989 but was sacked after only two months. Fisher Athletic were his next club, where he took over in July 1989 with promises of getting the club into the Football League within a couple of seasons. In November 1992 he returned to Bath City's Twerton Park, albeit to take over as 'consultant' to Second Division strugglers Bristol Rovers, who were tenants there. By then he was saying that he wanted to work part-time and delegate to his own coaching team, a move which suited hard-up Rovers. Allison was dogged by ill health during his four months as caretaker manager at Twerton Park and was unable to turn around Rovers' poor form and was replaced by John Ward. Rovers were eventually relegated to Division Two at the end of the season.

Malcolm Allison will long be remembered as one of the outstanding coaches in English football. A dogmatic, demanding man with no doubts about what he wanted from his players, he never accepted the popular idea that basic skills are learnt at the apprentice stage. He believed in strength through dedication, skill through repetition. He is a great believer in a player constantly improving his techniques and Allison himself is an unrivalled demonstrator of footballing techniques.

ANDERSON, James

Died: 23 August 1970.
Career: Tottenham Hotspur coach and youth team manager for many years, then manager July 1955-October 1958.

Having been at White Hart Lane since 1908, originally as a groundstaff boy, Anderson capped a 50-year career with Spurs when he succeeded Arthur Rowe as manager in 1955. He already knew the players well, having taken charge when Rowe was absent, and if a little old for the job he was a perfect stopgap whilst player-coach Bill Nicholson was being groomed as the full-time manager. Spurs, though, were in need of new blood and although they reached an FA Cup semi-final under Anderson in 1956, they also struggled to avoid relegation. Ill-health, which had already dogged his two predecessors, Rowe and Joe Hulme, eventually saw Anderson resign after just over three years in the job.

ANDERSON, Peter T.

Born: Hendon, London, 31 May 1949.
Midfield   5ft 10in; 11st 3lb (1972).
Career: Hendon; Luton Town February 1971; Antwerp (Belgium), autumn 1975 (£62,500); San Diego Sockers

(NASL) April 1978; Sheffield United September 1978; Tampa Bay Rowdies (NASL) May 1978; Millwall player-manager December 1980-November 1982.

Honours: NASL Soccer Bowl runners-up 1979.

Peter Anderson was a skilled, wiry, tenacious and competitive midfielder with an eye for goal and a penchant for the unexpected. When he left Luton to join Antwerp late in 1975, the fee was used to ensure that the Kenilworth Road club did not go into liquidation. It was perhaps ironic that he was used as a financial pawn in the Hatters' survival because he had trained as a chartered accountant. Anderson's talent had been a prominent springboard for Luton's ambitious attacking team which won promotion to Division One in 1974. After his period in the Belgian First Division, he went to play in the North American Soccer League.

When he was appointed player-manager of Millwall, it was a surprise choice. He had been a player under former Lions manager, Gordon Jago, at Tampa Bay Rowdies. He concentrated on improving Millwall's defence at the start, but they ended his first season in charge with three defeats to finish 16th, only two points above relegated Sheffield United. A new chairman brought new funds for Anderson to purchase Alan West from Luton for £45,000, Sam Allardyce for £90,000 and Trevor Aylott for £150,000. In November 1982, Anderson was told that he had been suspended by the club and soon afterwards he was sacked. He had spent a lot of money at The Den but with little success to show for it on the field.

ANDERSON, Stanley

Born: Horden, 27 February 1934
Wing-half   5ft 9in; 11st 12lb (1964).

Career: East Durham Schools; Horden Colliery; Sunderland amateur June 1949, professional March 1951; Newcastle United November 1963 (£19,000); Middlesbrough player-coach November 1965 (£11,500), then manager April 1966-December 1972; AEK Athens manager December 1972-April 1974; Queen's Park Rangers assistant manager June 1974; Manchester City scout December 1974; Doncaster Rovers manager February 1975-November 1978; Bolton Wanderers assistant manager and coach November 1978-February 1980, then manager February 1980-May 1981.

Honours: England international (2 caps); Under-23 international (4 caps); Schoolboy international (2 caps);

Division Two champions 1955; Division Three runners-up 1967.

Stan Anderson had the distinction of skippering all three major North-East clubs, Sunderland, Newcastle United and Middlesbrough. He made his debut for Sunderland in October 1952, against Portsmouth, and went on to play in 402 League games, scoring 31 goals for the club. Sunderland reached two FA Cup semi-finals, in 1955 and 1956, but lost to Manchester City and Birmingham City respectively. A tough-tackling, dependable wing-half who could also be constructive, he moved to Newcastle in November 1963 and played an important role in their Second Division championship side of 1965. His full England career was probably hampered by a sending off received in an Under-23 international against Bulgaria in 1957 as his consistency probably deserved greater recognition.

After joining Middlesbrough as player-coach in 1965, he found things difficult at first and had trouble maintaining his form due to his responsibilities off the field. Anderson retired from playing when he was appointed manager in April 1966 and brought about a revival at Ayresome Park, greatly improving the team spirit.

His appointment had come too late to save the club from relegation to Division Three but he soon devised new training schedules, bringing greater interest and enjoyment to these day-to-day tasks. Promotion was achieved back to Division Two in 1967, after a great run from November, and after twice going close to further promotion, he decided to accept an offer to manage AEK Athens in December 1972. After spells with QPR, Manchester City and Doncaster Rovers, he joined Bolton Wanderers as coach under manager Ian Greaves. When Greaves was dismissed, Anderson took over as manager. He did not have a happy time at Burnden Park and was sacked in May 1981.

ANDERSON, William

Born: High Westwood, near Newcastle upon Tyne, 12 January 1913; Died: Radcliffe-on-Trent, Notts, 19 February 1986.
Left-back   5ft 10½in; 12st 6lb (1933).
Career: Medomsley Juniors; Chopwell Institute; Nottingham Forest August 1931; Sheffield United February 1932; Barnsley May 1935, retired through injury November 1935; Lincoln City trainer 1945-1947, then manager January 1947-January 1965, then general manager to October 1966; Nottingham Forest assistant manager October 1966.

Honours: Division Three North champions 1948, 1952.

Bill Anderson is Lincoln's most successful manager, steering the club to two championships of the Third Division North in 1948 and 1952. He is also their longest-serving manager, being in charge for almost 20 years. He did not have much success as a player, though, rarely playing first-team football for his League clubs.

He was more successful as a manager. Lincoln's 1948 title side was put together for £2,000 and in a close finish they just pipped Rotherham United to clinch the only promotion place. Their jubilation was short-lived, however, as the Imps were relegated after one season. In 1952, Anderson again produced a championship-winning side which gained a massive 69 points and scored 121 goals. This time Lincoln established themselves in the higher

division, albeit narrowly avoiding relegation on a number of occasions, and their best position was eighth.

After a financial crisis in 1960, Anderson was forced to sell a number of players and City had slumped to 22nd position in the Fourth Division by 1963. He left Sincil Bank in 1966, after a year as general manager.

Anderson had stayed loyal to Lincoln despite a number of lucrative offers to manage at a higher level, but the club was so hard-up most of his time there that sometimes they could not even afford apprentices and had to rely on useful amateurs.

ANDREWS, James P.

Born: Invergordon, 1 February 1927.
Outside-left   5ft 5in; 10st 10lb (1959).
Career: Dundee; West Ham United November 1951; Leyton Orient June 1956; Queen's Park Rangers June 1959-1963, then coach 1963-cs 1965, caretaker manager for a while in 1965; Chelsea chief coach August 1965-January 1967; Luton Town coach and assistant manager until March 1972; Coventry City coach; Tottenham Hotspur coach; Cardiff City coach 1973-1974, then manager May 1974-November 1978; Southampton scout 1978.

Honours: Division Three runners-up 1976.

A small, quick dribbling left winger, Jimmy Andrews cost West Ham £4,750 from Dundee in November 1951 and proved a worthwhile investment. He played for three London clubs, scoring 44 goals in 232 appearances between 1951 and 1963.

Andrews built a good reputation as a coach with Queen's Park Rangers (he was in charge of the club for a while in 1965), Chelsea, Luton Town, Coventry City, Spurs and Cardiff before taking over at Cardiff City from Frank O'Farrell in May 1974.

A quiet but positive Scot who made his name in football as one of the game's finest coaches, his advice and knowledge of coaching techniques were sought by several clubs. It was former Manchester United boss Frank O'Farrell who brought him to Ninian Park. Initially he was only caretaker manager but when City avoided relegation, he was appointed permanently. He had been offered managers' jobs in the past but had turned them down as he loved coaching so much.

The following season, City dropped into Division Three but Andrews brought them straight back again in 1976, playing brilliant football and with a new board of directors. He had put the club back on its feet again and there was a harvest of goals from

Adrian Alston and Tony Evans, a defence led by Mike England and a midfield directed by the experienced Doug Livermore and Alan Campbell. Back in Division Two, Cardiff struggled, narrowly avoiding relegation in 1976-77. They also had a run in the European Cup-winners' Cup, beating Servette Geneva and Dynamo Tbilisi.

But there was a high turnover of players and in 1978, following the unsuccessful coaching appointment of Micky Burns, Andrews felt the wrath of the City fans when results went against him and he was sacked in October 1978. After this he scouted in Wales for Southampton.

APPLETON, Colin Harry

Born: Scarborough, 7 March 1936.
Wing-half   5ft 9in; 11st 11lb (1964).
Career: Scarborough 1951; Leicester City March 1954; Charlton Athletic June 1966 (£7,500); Barrow player-manager August 1967-January 1969 (£4,000); Scarborough player-manager cs 1969-1973; Grimsby Town coach October 1973-1974; Scarborough manager 1975-1981; Hull City manager June 1982-May 1984; Swansea City manager May-December 1984; Exeter City manager May 1985-December 1987; Bridlington Town manager 1988-1989; Hull City manager May-October 1989.

Honours: Football League representative; Division Four runners-up 1983; FA Cup runners-up 1961, 1963; Football League Cup winners 1964, runners-up 1965; FA Challenge Trophy winners 1973, 1976, 1977.

Colin Appleton was a hard-tackling wing-half who served Leicester City well, captaining the side in the FA Cup Final defeats of 1961 and 1963 and scoring in the first leg of the 1965 League Cup Final against Chelsea, which was eventually lost. Appleton also represented the Football League versus Irish League in 1963. He appeared for City in 328 League and Cup games, scoring 22 goals before his move to Charlton.

His first managerial post was as player-manager of Barrow from August 1967. In his two seasons at the club, he managed to keep them in the Third Division, but left in January 1969 due to ill health. Appleton returned to his first club, Scarborough, as player-manager and helped them win the FA Challenge Trophy in 1973, playing at full-back. They won the trophy twice more in his second spell at the club.

Appleton returned to the Football League in 1982, as manager of Hull

City. With little money to spend, Hull somehow gained promotion to Division Three in 1983 and came very close to further promotion the following season. Appleton immediately resigned and joined Swansea City but lasted only seven months at Vetch Field before being dismissed. He had little success at Exeter City and after a spell with Bridlington Town, returned to manage Hull City again in May 1989. After only five months he was sacked, with the club at the bottom of the Second Division.

ARDILES, Osvaldo Cesar

Born: Cordoba, Argentina, 3 August 1952.
Midfield   5ft 6in; 9st 10lb (1980).
Career: Instituto de Cordoba; Huracan (Buenos Aires) 1974; Tottenham Hotspur July 1978 (£325,000); Paris St Germain (loan) January 1983; Blackburn Rovers (loan) March-May 1988; Queen's Park Rangers May 1988; Swindon Town manager July 1989-March 1991; Newcastle United manager March 1991-February 1992; West Bromwich Albion manager May 1992-June 1993. Tottenham Hotspur manager June 1993.

Honours: Argentina international; World Cup winners 1978; FA Cup winners 1981, runners-up 1987; League Cup runners-up 1982; UEFA Cup winners 1984. Division Three promotion 1993.

Ossie Ardiles signed for Tottenham after winning a World Cup winners' medal with Argentina in 1978 and became a great favourite with the Spurs fans. A midfield dynamo, his short-passing game was a delight to watch and although only small in frame, he was a terrier in the midfield, giving his opponents little time to dwell on the ball.

He was signed from Huracan for £325,000 by manager Keith Burkenshaw and Spurs won the FA Cup twice, and also gained the UEFA Cup with Ardiles in their ranks. Ardiles had to miss the 1982 FA Cup Final due to the Falklands conflict and moved to Paris St Germain on loan until the animosity against Argentina subsided. His later career was dogged by injury and he saw out his playing days with Blackburn Rovers and Queen's Park Rangers. In July 1989, Ardiles became the manager of Swindon Town and completely transformed their style of play. They won the Second Division play-offs in 1989-90 but were denied their place in the First Division after an illegal payments scandal at the club. Ardiles lasted just 11 months in charge

of Newcastle's playing fortunes and was sacked as the Magpies faced the possibility of relegation to Division Three for the first time in their history.

West Brom played attractive football under Ardiles but could only reach the new Second Division play-offs in 1993 rather than gaining instant promotion. Nevertheless, they beat Swansea City over two legs to meet Port Vale in the Wembley Final where they won 3-0 to gain a place in the First Division (formerly the Second). Then Ardiles controversially quit to take over at Spurs.

ARMFIELD, James Christopher

Born: Denton, 21 September 1935.
Right-back   5ft 11in; 12st 2lb (1964).
Career: Rovoe School and Arnold Grammar School (Blackpool); St Peter's Youth Club (Blackpool); Highfield Youth Club (Blackpool); Blackpool amateur 1952, signed professional September 1954, player-coach February-May 1971; Bolton Wanderers manager May 1971-October 1974; Leeds United manager October 1974-August 1978; full-time journalist and broadcaster from 1978.

Honours: England international (43 caps); Under-23 international (9 caps); Football League representative; Division Three champions 1973; European Cup runners-up 1975.

'Gentleman Jim' won fame as Blackpool and England's full-back and later as manager of Bolton Wanderers and Leeds United. Born at Denton, near Manchester, his family moved to Blackpool when he was young. Armfield was a star pupil at Rovoe and Arnold grammar schools in Blackpool where he gained 'A' levels, won representative honours playing rugby for Lancashire, was captain of the cricket team, athletic champion and a member of the swimming and rifle teams.

He was spotted by Blackpool playing for St Peter's Youth Club and signed for the Seasiders as an amateur. Armfield wanted to go to university and become a teacher, but when he finished his National Service in the King's Own Regiment, he was persuaded to sign professional forms for the Seasiders in September 1954. He made his debut over Christmas that year, against Portsmouth, and became a regular first-teamer in 1955-56 after an injury to Eddie Shimwell.

Armfield became one of Blackpool's greatest-ever servants, appearing in 568 League games for the club before retiring in 1971. He was one of the first full-backs to use the overlap to good purpose and his build and speed made him dangerous in such incursions.

A fine tackler, he won an Under-23 cap against Bulgaria in 1957 and Football League representative honours, appearing 11 times in all. He won his first full cap on a South American tour in the summer of 1959, against Brazil before 150,000 spectators, and eventually gained 43 caps including 37 in consecutive matches. Following brilliant displays in the 1962 World Cup finals, he was voted the finest right-back in the world by the Chilean press. Armfield took over the England captaincy after Johnny Haynes had been involved a car crash. After Blackpool were relegated from the First Division in 1967, Armfield led them back again in 1970. When they were relegated back again the following season, he retired to become Bolton Wanderers' manager.

Critics claimed that Armfield was

often 'too much of a gentleman', but his admirers could counter that he was able to be such a gentleman on the pitch as his ability and temperament enabled him to control himself as well as his opponent. It was England manager Walter Winterbottom who encouraged him to take an interest in coaching. Armfield gained his full FA coaching badge and was appointed player-manager of an FA touring party to the Far East in 1969.

He was appointed manager of Bolton Wanderers in May 1971, immediately after the club had been relegated into the Third Division, and immediately bought some experienced players including Henry Mowbray from Blackpool and Charlie Wright from Charlton. In his first season, the Trotters conceded only 41 goals but did not gain promotion. Two good Cup runs laid the foundation to reap the benefits of his hard work in the 1972-73 season, when Bolton won the Third Division championship.

At Burnden Park, Armfield put his reliance on youth and ran four teams. He discovered some fine young players including Paul Jones and Don McAllister. This, mixed with some shrewd signings such as Tony Dunne and Peter Thompson, led to success on the field. Armfield believed in attacking sides and used specialist wingers and adventurous defenders. Attendances soon quadrupled as the crowds were attracted back to watch the exciting football his teams played.

After many offers, Armfield finally gave way and moved to Leeds United in October 1974. He never reached the heights of Don Revie, but he did steer the club to the 1975 European Cup Final, where they lost to Bayern Munich in Paris. He bought some order to Elland Road after Brian Clough's whirlwind stay and he made some fine signings to replace ageing stars like Billy Bremner and Norman Hunter. These included Tony Currie from Sheffield United for £250,000, Ray Hankin and Bryan Flynn from Burnley and Arthur Graham from Aberdeen. But, although good players, they never helped to put Leeds back in their higher status of the early 1970s. Leeds just missed out on an FA Cup Final appearance in 1977, when they lost to Manchester United in the semi-final. In August 1978, Armfield left Elland Road to concentrate on his journalistic career with the BBC and the Daily Express.

ASHMAN, George Alan

Born: Rotherham, 30 May 1928.
Centre-forward
Career: Sheffield United amateur in wartime; Nottingham Forest in wartime; Carlisle United June 1951 (£5,050), retired 1958; Penrith manager until February 1963; Carlisle United manager February 1963-cs 1967; West Bromwich Albion manager 1967-1971; Olympiakos (Greece) coach 1971-1972;

Carlisle United manager August 1972-October 1975; Workington manager 1976; Walsall manager 1978; Walsall scout c.1977; Derby County chief scout and assistant manager; Hereford United assistant manager.

Honours: Division Two Promotion 1974; Division Three Champions 1965; Division Four runners-up 1964; FA Cup winners 1968.

Alan Ashman made his name as manager of Carlisle United and West Bromwich Albion. However, what should have been a long and successful career seemed to fade after he left Carlisle in 1975. Ashman represented West Riding Schools before playing for Sheffield United as an amateur in 1945, as a 16-year-old. In 1946 he signed for Nottingham Forest but was soon called up for National Service where he remained for the next three years. Unable to gain a regular first-team place in the Forest side on his return, he moved to Carlisle in June 1951 for a fee of £5,500.

A centre-forward with plenty of dash and shooting power, Ashman never looked back after scoring a hat-trick on his debut for Carlisle. He scored 98 goals in 207 League appearances for the Brunton Park club before being transfer-listed at £2,000 in 1958. He thereupon decided to retire as a player as he was also suffering from knee problems.

Ashman went to work on a poultry farm run by future Carlisle director, Mr Monkhouse, and in his spare time he managed the local club, Penrith, for four years. In February 1963, he was asked by his employer to take over as manager at Carlisle. The club were bottom of the Third Division at the time and were eventually relegated. In his first full season in charge, though, Carlisle won promotion back to Division Three and this was followed by the Third Division championship in 1964-65. Two seasons later, United finished third in Division Two. His achievements had been all the more creditable as attendances were so low and therefore the club was unable to buy new players.

His success attracted West Brom, who made him their manager in the close season of 1967. In his first season in charge, Ashman transformed a talented but inconsistent bunch of players into a strong unit and Jeff Astle scored the only goal to win the FA Cup against Everton at Wembley in 1968. The following season Albion reached the quarter-final of the European Cup-winners' Cup but lost to Dunfermline. They also lost an FA Cup semi-final against Leicester City at Hillsborough.

After a disappointing season in 1970-71, the Albion board replaced Ashman with Don Howe. He found out that he had lost his job when a journalist told him whilst he was on holiday in Greece. His next move was to manage Olympiakos Piraeus in that country and they finished runners-up in the Greek League in 1971-72.

Ashman returned to manage Carlisle for a second spell in August 1972. He had a poor season but the directors kept faith in him and the following season, United gained promotion to Division One for their one and only season in the top flight. This was managed on average crowds of just 8,270. Like several newly-promoted sides, they shot to the top of the First Division for a while but eventually fell off to be relegated at the end of the season. They also lost to Second Division Fulham in a quarter-final FA Cup tie at Brunton Park.

Ashman resigned in October 1975, after a poor start. The following year he returned to Football League management with lowly Workington but left without managing to lift them off the bottom of the Fourth Division. Ashman became a scout with Manchester United before a brief spell as manager of Walsall in 1978. He was later chief scout and assistant manager at Derby County and also assistant manager at Hereford United.

ASHMAN, Ronald G.

Born: Whittlesey, 19 May 1926.
Wing-half   6ft; 12st 8lb (1959)
Career: Whittlesey; Norwich City amateur 1944, professional January 1946, then manager December 1962-May 1966; Scunthorpe United manager October 1967-June 1973; Grimsby Town manager July 1973-February 1975; Scunthorpe United manager January 1976-May 1981; retired from football in 1981 to open a travel agency in Scunthorpe.

Honours: Division Three runners-up 1960; Division Four promotion 1972; Football League Cup winners 1962.

A great club man, Ron Ashman made a record 662 appearance for Norwich City between 1946 and 1963. At first he was loudly barracked by the crowd, but settled down to make the left-half position his own. He captained Norwich to an FA Cup semi-final in 1959, when they narrowly lost to Luton Town after a replay, and when they won promotion to the Second Division the following season.

In December 1962, Ashman became the club's manager and retired from playing in October 1963. One of his first actions was to sign Ron Davies from Luton Town. Davies developed into one of the best centre-forwards of the 1960s. In 1966, Ashman, who had found it difficult to make the transition from player to manager, was sacked. He returned to soccer the following year as manager of Scunthorpe and had two spells at the Old Show Ground. The club won promotion to Division Three in 1972 but finished bottom of the table twice, in 1968 and 1973. Scunthorpe also reached the fifth round of the FA Cup in 1970, during Ashman's spell as manager. Most of his years at the Old Show Ground were spent in the bottom half of the Fourth Division. A reserved, cultured man, he always treated his players with respect and consideration, but some of them perhaps took advantage of this gentlemanly approach from their boss.

ASHURST, Len

Born: Liverpool, 10 March 1939.
Full-back   5ft 9in; 11st 5lb (1964)
Career: Wolverhampton Wanderers
amateur; Prescot Cables; Sunderland December 1957; Hartlepool United player-manager March 1971-June 1974 (retired as a player 1973); Gillingham manager June 1974-October 1975; Sheffield Wednesday manager October 1975-October 1977; Newport County manager June 1978-March 1982; Cardiff City manager March 1982-March 1984; Sunderland manager March 1984-May 1985; Kuwait national coach 1985; Qatar coach; Blackpool assistant manager; Cardiff City manager September 1989-May 1991.*

Honours: England Under-23 international (1 cap); Youth international; Division Three runners-up 1983; Division Four promotion 1980; Football League Cup runners-up 1985; Welsh Cup winners 1980.

A steady, constructive full-back with good recovery, Len Ashurst made 410 League appearances for Sunderland before moving to Hartlepool in March 1971 as player-manager. The high spot of his Roker Park career was helping the club back to the First Division in 1964. His Under-23 cap came against West Germany in 1961.

Ashurst had spells as manager at Gillingham and Sheffield Wednesday, where he built the foundations for future successes. Even though he was unable to get the Owls promoted out of the Third Division, he made a number of important signings which were of long-term benefit to the club, and he also developed some fine youngsters. When Ashurst took over at Newport County in June 1978, they were near the bottom of the Fourth Division. He soon pulled them round and in 1980 Newport won promotion and, in lifting the Welsh Cup, entry into Europe. They failed by the narrowest of margins in reaching the semi-final of the European Cup-winners' Cup.

Ashurst was unable to prevent Cardiff dropping into the Third Division when he took over there in March 1982, but the following season they won promotion back again. He then had an unhappy spell at his former club, Sunderland, who lost in the League Cup Final at Wembley and were also relegated to the Second Division. He was sacked soon afterwards. After spells in Kuwait and Qatar, Ashurst returned to England to become assistant manager at Blackpool before taking full charge at Cardiff City. They were relegated to the Fourth Division in 1990 and after another poor season he was sacked.

ASHWORTH, David George 'Little Dave'

Born: Waterford, Ireland; Died: Blackpool, 23 March 1947 (age 79 years).
Career: Newchurch Rovers; then a referee on Football League lists; Oldham Athletic manager 1906-April 1914; Stockport County manager April 1914-December 1919; Liverpool manager December 1919-January 1923; Oldham Athletic manager January 1923-July 1924; Manchester City manager July 1924-November 1925; Walsall manager February 1926-February 1927; Caernarfon manager June 1927-May 1930; Llanelli manager early 1930s; Blackpool scout from January 1938.

Honours: Football League champions 1922; Division Two runners-up 1910.

Ashworth was one of the smallest-ever managers, for he stood just five feet tall. He was well known for his bowler hat and a waxed moustache and his nickname was 'Little Dave'. A first-class referee, he came originally from Waterford in Ireland. Ashworth did not play League football but turned out for Newchurch Rovers before joining the Football League list as a referee.

His first managerial post was with Oldham Athletic, who had just moved to a new ground at Boundary Park. He guided the club from the Lancashire Combination into the Football League in 1907, when they replaced Burslem Port Vale who had resigned from the League. The Latics' first four seasons in the League brought only five home defeats. The club won promotion to Division One at the end of the 1909-10 season, when they won 14 of the last 16 games.

The years leading up to World War One were glorious ones for the Latics. There was a backroom staff stability with David Ashworth as manager, Jimmy Harrison as trainer and Bob Mellor as secretary and there was an abundance of players of international calibre. The Latics were able to attract established professionals like Charlie Roberts from Manchester United, Finlay Speedie from Newcastle United and George Hunter from Aston Villa.

After the club had finished fourth in Division One in season 1913-14, Ashworth left for Stockport County in April to manage the club through the wartime period. The club finished 14th in Division Two in 1914-15. In December 1919, Ashworth became Liverpool's manager and took the club to the League Championship in 1921-22.

His time at Anfield coincided with one of the club's best periods. With the acquisition of Harold Beadles, Danny Shone and Fred Hopkins and the presence of many other fine players, he managed to produce one of Liverpool's greatest-ever sides which also included Elisha Scott, Tom Bromilow, Dick Forshaw and Ephraim Longworth. In January 1923, with Liverpool well on the way to another Championship, Ashworth suddenly left Anfield for a second spell at Boundary Park.

His actions have never been properly explained but he arrived too late to save Oldham from relegation and the club finished seventh in Division Two the following season. In July 1924 'Little Dave' joined Manchester City as manager but stayed for only 16 months. He was the first manager with secretarial responsibilities at City.

The club had just moved to a new ground at Maine Road and this restricted the amount of money he had to spend on new players. After a poor start to the 1925-26 season he was sacked in November 1925. The club was eventually relegated to Division Two but reached the FA Cup Final. City spent £3,000 on Phil McCloy from Ayr United in the summer of 1925 but it was not enough and Ashworth really
needed money to replace the ageing Eli Fletcher and Horace Barnes.

His next club was Walsall, whom he took over in February 1926. They had to seek re-election at the end of the season and with things little better the following season, Ashworth was sacked in February 1927. He then managed Caernarfon from June 1927 until May 1930 followed by another non-League side, Llanelli, in the 1930s. Here he signed a number of useful former Football League players. From January 1938 he scouted for Blackpool until his death in the town, aged 79.

ASPREY, William

Born: Wolverhampton, 11 September 1936.
Full-back   6ft 1in; 12st 11lb (1964).
Career: Stoke City September 1953; Oldham Athletic January 1966; Port Vale December 1967; Sheffield Wednesday coach February 1969; Coventry City assistant manager February 1970; Wolverhampton Wanderers coach; West Bromwich Albion coach; Rhodesian FA director of coaching 1975-78; Oxford United coach May 1978, then manager July 1979-December 1980; Stoke City assistant manager February 1982, then manager December 1983-May 1985.

Honours: Division Two champions 1963; Football League Cup runners-up 1964.

Converted from wing-half to full-back in his Stoke days, Bill Asprey was a tall, powerfully-built defender who made over 300 appearances for the club. The versatile Asprey played in eight different positions during his 13 years at Stoke and won promotion with the Potters. Asprey was assistant manager to Noel Cantwell at Coventry and was also a coach at Sheffield Wednesday, Wolves and West Brom, before joining Oxford United, where he made little impact as their manager. In February 1982, Asprey joined his former club, Stoke City, as assistant manager before taking over from Richie Barker, initially as caretaker boss.

Stoke just missed relegation after an Asprey-inspired revival and at the end of the season he was then appointed permanently to the post. However, with little money to spend and with the club in financial difficulties, Stoke finished rock bottom of the First Division in 1985 with their fewest points and goals totals ever. The traumatic season affected Asprey's health and he was sacked in May 1985.

ATKINS, Ian Leslie,

Born: Sheldon, Birmingham, 16 January 1957.
Midfield   6ft; 11st 13lb (1988).

Career: Sheldon Heath School; Leafield Athletic; Shrewsbury Town apprentice June 1973, professional January 1975; Sunderland August 1982 (£80,000); Everton November 1984 (£70,000); Ipswich Town September 1985 (£100,000); Birmingham City March 1988 (£50,000); Colchester United player-manager cs 1990-June 1991; Birmingham City player-assistant manager June 1991-December 1992; Cambridge United manager December 1992. Cambridge United manager December 1992-May 1993.

Honours: Division Three champions 1979; Welsh Cup Winners 1979.

Ian Atkins was captain at all his clubs except Everton. A competitive player with a fierce tackle, Atkins played 314 games, scoring 64 goals, for Shrewsbury before his move to Sunderland in 1982. He had helped the Shrews to the Third Division title in 1978-79. Atkins was a regular at each club he played except Everton and played over 600 games before his retirement.

Colchester United had just lost their Football League status when he took over as manager. Despite a full-time squad and Atkins making signings such as Mario Walsh and Scott Barrett for £25,000 each, United could finish only runners-up to Barnet in the Conference League. Atkins moved to St Andrew's as Terry Cooper's assistant manager before being appointed as Cambridge United's boss. They were struggling near the bottom of the First Division when he took over.

Atkins resigned at the end of the 1992-93 season, after only five months in charge, which ended with Cambridge's relegation after losing their final game of the season at promotion-chasing West Ham.

ATKINSON, John Edward 'Jack'

Born: New Washington, County Durham, 20 December 1913.
Centre-half.
Career: Durham Schoolboys; Washington Colliery; Bolton Wanderers August 1931; guest for Everton, Bury, Bolton Wanderers and Blackpool in World War Two: also served as NCO in Lancashire Fusilliers in Africa, Italy and Austria; New Brighton player-manager July 1948-July 1950; later a licensee in Bolton.

Honours: England Schoolboy international; Football League representative.

Tall and powerful, Jack Atkinson made 240 appearances for Bolton Wanderers, despite losing seven seasons to the war. He helped the Trotters back to Division One in 1934-35 and played in an FA Cup semi-final the following season when Bolton were beaten by West Brom in a replay. He was in charge of football whilst serving with the British Army in Austria at the end of the war. Atkinson produced a workmanlike team when player-manager of New Brighton. He brought Alf Lees and Les Barton from his old club but was unable to persuade Bert Trautmann to join the Rakers. Atkinson achieved some good results, despite the club having to fight for its very survival. Indeed, after he was dismissed for financial reasons, it perhaps proved an unwise decision because a year later, New Brighton were voted out of the Football League.

ATKINSON, Ronald F.

Born: Liverpool, 18 March 1939.
Wing-half   6ft; 13st 4lb (1964).

Career: Lea Village School; BSA Tools; Aston Villa May 1956; Oxford United July 1959; Witney Town 1971; Kettering Town player-manager late 1971-November 1974; Cambridge United manager November 1974-January 1978; West Bromwich Albion manager January 1978-June 1981; Manchester United manager June 1981-November 1986; West Bromwich Albion manager again September 1987-October 1988; Atlético Madrid manager October 1988-January 1989; Sheffield Wednesday manager February 1989-May 1991; Aston Villa manager June 1991.

Honours: Division Two promotion 1991; Division Three champions 1968; Division Four champions 1977; Southern League champions 1961, 1962; FA Cup winners 1983, 1985; Football League Cup winners 1991, runners-up 1983.

Outspoken Ron Atkinson likes to show off the wealth he has gained from football — gold jewellery and a taste for expensive cigars and champagne — and in the past, he was perhaps distrusted in some circles for this outward show. However, deep down, Atkinson is an intense man who has made a successful career as a manager.

He was born in Liverpool just before the war but brought up in the West Midlands area. After rejection from Wolves, he was signed by Aston Villa in May 1956 after being spotted playing as an inside-forward for BSA Tools.

Unable to make the first team at Villa Park, he was given a free transfer and joined Headington United in 1959. They changed their name to Oxford United the following year and here he was converted to wing-half and captained the side to great success. Big Ron was the driving force which took the club from the Southern League to Division Two in the 1960s. The Southern League championship was gained in both the 1960-61 and 1961-62 seasons, after which Oxford replaced the defunct Accrington Stanley in the Football League.

The 1964-65 season saw promotion to Division Three and the championship was gained in 1967-68. Nicknamed 'the Tank' on account of his sturdy build, Atkinson left the Manor Ground club, who were now established in the Second Division, after over 500 appearances for them.

He began his managerial career with Kettering Town in late 1971. In his first season he took them to the Southern League North Division championship and promotion to the Premier League. He obviously impressed Cambridge United officials and became their manager in 1974. They won the Fourth Division championship in 1977 and

were on their way to Division Two the following season when West Brom swooped in January 1978, appointing Atkinson to succeed Ronnie Allen.

Atkinson had an immediate impact. His flamboyant approach rubbed off on the players and coaching staff and Albion were soon winning matches again. He signed Brendon Batson from his former club and also had a number of useful attacking players on his books. These included Cyrille Regis, Bryan Robson, Laurie Cunningham and Willie Johnston. Albion reached the FA Cup semi-final in 1978, beating Blackpool, Manchester United, Derby County and Nottingham Forest on the way. In the last four they met Ipswich Town at Highbury but lost 3-1 in a disappointing performance, which was not helped by an injury to John Wile and the sending off of Mick Martin. The club finished sixth in Division One at the end of the season. They also reached the quarter-final of the UEFA Cup in 1978-79 before losing to Red Star on away goals.

After Albion had finished third in 1979-80, Atkinson moved to Old Trafford in June 1981 with his assistant Mick Brown. He immediately went back to his former club to sign Bryan Robson and Remi Moses for £2.4m and over the next five years he spent £7m on new players. These included Frank Stapleton, Alan Brazil, Gordon Strachan and Peter Davenport as well as overseas players such as John Sivebaek and Jesper Olsen.

Often United would start the season looking like potential champions but after injuries to key players, their season would peter out. However, United did win the FA Cup twice, in 1983 and 1985, beating Brighton and Everton respectively in the Final. However, the club really desired success in the League, which they had not won since 1967. Big Ron was sacked in November 1986, receiving £100,000 compensation.

Atkinson returned to The Hawthorns in September 1987 for a second spell as manager. By now the club was a struggling Second Division team and just missed the Third Division play-offs at the end of the 1987-88 season. In October 1988, Atkinson was enticed to join Atlético Madrid as manager with a contract worth half a million pounds over two years. He lasted just 96 days before being sacked, despite taking the club to third position.

Rather disillusioned, Big Ron returned to the Football League as caretaker manager of Sheffield Wednesday who were threatened with relegation after a disastrous spell under the managership of Peter Eustace. Atkinson saved the club from relegation and was persuaded to take the post permanently in the summer. The Owls were relegated, rather unluckily, at the end of the 1989-90 season though they swiftly returned to the First Division the following season. The Owls also won the League Cup, beating Manchester United 1-0 in the Final. Before he could enjoy the triumph Atkinson moved to Villa Park. He soon built a fine young side which looked as though it would soon be winning major honours.

Villa ended the 1992-93 season without any honours, which was disappointing as they had looked like winning the first Premier League title at one time. They ran out of steam near the end of the season and Manchester United eventually won the title by ten points. Atkinson had put together a very useful side but luck was not on their side.

AYRE, William

Born: Crookhill, 7 May 1952.
Defender   5ft 10in; 11st 4lb (1984).
Career: Scarborough; Hartlepool United August 1977; Halifax Town January 1981; Mansfield Town August 1982; Halifax Town July 1984, assistant manager 1985, then manager, December 1986-March 1990; Blackpool assistant manager May 1990, then manager November 1990.

Honours: Division Four promotion 1992.

Billy Ayre was a popular choice to succeed Mick Jones as Halifax's manager. He had played for the club in two separate spells and knew all about lower division soccer as he had spent much of his career there. The club were on the brink of bankruptcy when Ayre took over and he could not have had a tougher baptism into football management. Halifax endured a constant struggle for survival, a position made even more perilous by the introduction of the automatic drop into the Conference League. Whilst Halifax's manager, Ayre won a reputation as a team boss who could produce good young players. He resigned in March 1990 with the club in imminent danger of dropping out of the Football League. Billy Ayre enjoyed success at Blackpool, who reached the Fourth Division play-offs in 1991 and 1992, clinching promotion in the latter by beating Torquay after a penalty shoot-out at Wembley. Blackpool just managed to avoid relegation in 1992-93.

BACON, Frank

Died: 25 January 1918.
Career: Bristol City manager October 1910-January 1911, also director.

Director Frank Bacon took over at Bristol City in October 1910. He stayed in office until a shock 3-0 home defeat by non-League Crewe Alexandra in the FA Cup in January 1911. Bacon was essentially a stop-gap between managers Harry Thickett and Sam Hollis, but he proved a key figure in the signing of one of City's best-ever players, Billy Wedlock, who went on to play for England.

BAILEY, Michael Alfred.

Born: Wisbech, 27 February 1942.
Right-half   5ft 8in; 11st (1964).
Career: Gorleston; Charlton Athletic amateur June 1958, professional March 1959; Wolverhampton Wanderers March 1966 (£40,000); Minnesota Kicks (USA) player-coach summer 1977 (£15,000); Hereford United player-manager June 1978-October 1979; Charlton Athletic coach 1979, then manager March 1980-June 1981; Brighton & Hove Albion manager June 1981-December 1982; Fisher Athletic manager December 1989-January 1991; Portsmouth Reserve-team manager 1991.

Honours: England international (2 caps); Under-23 international (5 caps); Football League representative; Division Three promotion 1981; Football League Cup winners 1974; UEFA Cup runners-up 1972 (sub).

A midfield dynamo who was tough in the tackle and a driving force in attack, Mike Bailey was the ideal captain at both Charlton and Wolves and inspired with his own dynamic example. He gained England Under-23 and full caps before his move to Wolves and led the Molineux club to promotion from Division Two in 1966. His caps were against the USA, a game which

England won 10-0 in May 1964, and against Wales later that year. Bailey went to The Valley, thanks to Gorleston manager Joe Jobling, a former Charlton wing-half. He had played for Gorleston's first team at only 15.

Bailey made 528 League appearances in his career and, for Wolves alone, a total of 420 appearances in all games. After leaving Molineux in February 1977, he tried his luck as player-coach with Minnesota Kicks in the NASL. Within 18 months, though, he was back in England with Hereford United, where he got his first taste of management, and remained playing until his appointment as manager of Charlton Athletic in March 1980.

He employed Benny Fenton as his assistant but it was too late for the Valiants to avoid relegation to Division Three that season. The following season they bounced straight back again, promoted in third place. After his move to Brighton he helped to steer the club to 13th in the First Division in season 1981-82, but a poor start to the following season saw Bailey out of a job. He has not managed a League club since.

BAILEY, Thomas

Career: Local football; Crewe Alexandra manager 1925-1938.

Tom Bailey had been associated with Crewe since 1906 and served the club as secretary-manager for 13 years, having previously been assistant secretary for a number of years. The club usually held a comfortable mid-table position in the Third Division North but finished sixth in 1931-32 and again in 1935-36. Their worst season under Bailey was 1936-37, when the club just avoided having to seek re-election on goal-average. Under him Crewe also reached the fourth round of the FA Cup in 1927-28 before losing to Aston Villa.

BAIN, James.

Born: Rutherglen, 6 February 1902.
Centre-half   5ft 9½in; 11st 7lb (1933).
Career: Rutherglen Glencairn; Strathclyde; Manchester United October 1922; Manchester Central July 1928; Brentford November 1928, assistant manager May 1934-August 1952, then manager until January 1953.

Honours: Division Three South champions 1933.

Bain was assistant manager to Harry Curtis at Brentford during their First Division days in the 1930s. He had made only four appearances for Manchester United before moving to Manchester Central in July 1928 but six months later was rescued from non-League soccer by Brentford, for whom he made 191 League appearances and gained a good reputation at centre-half before retiring to become assistant manager. When Harry Curtis left Griffin Park in 1949, many expected Bain to take over as manager. Instead, Jackie Gibbons was appointed but Bain got his chance in 1952, although the club continued to struggle in Division Two.

BALL Alan (junior)

Born: Farnworth, 12 May 1945.
Midfield   5ft 8in; 10st 4lb (1971).
Career: Bolton Wanderers amateur; Blackpool apprentice September 1961, professional May 1962; Everton August 1966 (£110,000); Arsenal December 1971 (£220,000); Southampton December 1976 (£60,000); Philadelphia Fury player-coach May 1978; Vancouver Whitecaps June 1979; Blackpool

player-manager July 1980-February 1981; Southampton March 1981; Bulova (Hong Kong) October 1982; Bristol Rovers January 1983; Portsmouth manager May 1984-January 1989; Colchester United assistant manager February-October 1989; Stoke City assistant manager October-November 1989, then manager November 1989-February 1991; Exeter City manager August 1991-; England coach February-August 1992.

Honours: England international (72 caps); Under-23 international (8 caps); Football League representative; World Cup winners 1966; Football League champions 1970; Division Two runners-up 1987; FA Cup runners-up 1968, 1972.

Alan Ball played a major role in England's World Cup triumph of 1966. His tremendous work-rate was an inspiration for his teammates and more than made up for his temperamental outbursts. He was also a fine passer and was one of the best players of the 1960s and '70s. Ball played 72 times for England but it was not a vintage period for English soccer with little success after the 1970 World Cup. His transfers broke the British record twice: when he moved to Everton from Blackpool in 1966, he cost his new club £110,000; and when he moved from Everton to Arsenal in 1971, he cost a new record £220,000 fee.

Captaining the Gunners, his enthusiasm and experience had a big influence on the youngsters during a rebuilding period at Highbury. Ball gained a League championship medal with Everton in the 1969-70 season and ended on the losing side in two FA Cup Finals, in 1968 and 1972. After further spells with Southampton, Blackpool and Bristol Rovers, he retired in 1984 with 743 League appearances under his belt. In May that year he was appointed manager of Portsmouth and steered them into the First Division. Alas, Pompey were relegated straight back the following season.

He had previously been in charge at Blackpool in a disastrous spell in during 1980-81. With Pompey again struggling in Division Two, Ball was sacked in January 1989. He joined Colchester United as assistant to Jock Wallace. Ball moved to Stoke City as assistant to Mick Mills in October 1989, but within two weeks he was made caretaker manager when the man who appointed him was fired.

Ball's period as Stoke's manager was not a great success. Despite spending heavily on new players the club sunk to the bottom of the Second Division and stayed there. Goals were hard to

come by and they scored just 35 all season. Things did not improve the following season and City eventually ended the season in their lowest-ever position of 14th in the Third Division. It did not come as much of a surprise when Ball lost his job in February. He was not out of work for long and was soon offered the managers job at Exeter City. They narrowly avoided relegation from the Third Division in 1991-92 when they gained just one point from their last eight games.

Exeter avoided relegation on the last day of the 1992-93 campaign after struggling all season. They did reach the Southern Final of the Autoglass Trophy, though, before losing narrowly to Port Vale, 3-2 on aggregate.

BALL, James Alan (senior)

Born: Farnworth, Lancs, 23 September 1924; Died: Cyprus, 2 January 1982.
Inside-forward   5ft 8in; 10st 6lb (1951).
Career: Southport amateur October 1945, professional March 1946; Birmingham City May 1947; Southport February 1948 (£500); Oldham Athletic July 1950; Rochdale February 1952; Oswestry Town player-manager 1952-1953; Borough United; Ashton United manager 1959-1960; Nantwich manager; Stoke City coach; Halifax Town manager December 1967-summer 1970; Preston North End manager summer 1970-February 1973; Southport manager January 1974-July 1975; Halifax Town manager February 1976-November 1977; Blackpool scout 1980-1981; Saab, Sirius, Uppsala and two other Swedish sides as manager.

Honours: Division Three champions 1971; Division Four runners-up 1969; Birmingham League champions; Shropshire Senior Cup.

Alan Ball senior was a hard-working linkman with good ball control and was effective, despite his light build, appearing for a number of clubs just after the war. He was still in his 20s when he took up management in non-League soccer with Oswestry Town. Here, he gained Birmingham League honours and also lifted the Shropshire Senior Cup for the club.

Ball won a reputation for his coaching skills, securing a job in League management with Halifax Town in 1967 after many years in non-League soccer. At the end of Ball's first full season in charge, Halifax won promotion for the first time in their history, as runners-up in Division Four to champions Doncaster Rovers.

A most outspoken character, Ball had proved himself a fine manager by the time he moved to Preston in the close season of 1970. He had the ability to manipulate the transfer market and made large profits for the club with his dealings, including Chris Nichol whom he sold for £30,000. Ball took Preston to the Third Division championship in his first season at Deepdale and managed to keep North End in the higher division until losing his job in February 1973.

After a season at Southport, Ball returned to Halifax but things did not go so well in his second spell at The Shay and the club had to seek re-election at the end of the 1976-77 season. He died in a motoring accident in West Cyprus, where he had accepted a short-term coaching post prior to resuming with Vester Haringer of Sweden. His son is Alan Ball, the former England star and himself a League manager.

BAMLETT, Herbert

Born: Gateshead, 1 March 1882; Died: October 1941.

Career: Referee on Football League lists; Oldham Athletic manager June 1914-May 1921; Wigan Borough manager May 1921-August 1923; Middlesbrough manager August 1923-January 1927; Manchester United manager April 1927-April 1931.

Bamlett made his name as a referee rather than as a player before managing Oldham Athletic, Wigan Borough, Middlesbrough and Manchester United. The pinnacle of his refereeing career also marked his retirement before moving into management. He was in charge of the 1914 FA Cup Final between Burnley and Liverpool, the last Final to be played at Crystal Palace. Bamlett played at local league level but never for a League club.

His first managerial post was at Oldham Athletic, who he joined just after the outbreak of World War One. He soon had a crisis on his hands as attendances plummeted because of the war. Gate receipts were often under £100, even for the visits of Manchester United. However, the 1914-15 season was to prove Athletic's greatest in their history, when they finished runners-up in the First Division. They needed two points from their last two games, against Burnley and Liverpool, for the championship but lost both. Everton, their nearest rivals, won their last two games to clinch the title. Bamlett was called up for military service in the summer of 1916. After demobilisation in February 1919 he had the difficult task of rebuilding the side at Boundary Park. The club had lost the services of some great players and they proved difficult to replace. Oldham struggled for the next two seasons but maintained their First Division status.

Bamlett resigned in May 1921 to take charge of Wigan Borough, who had just been elected to the Football League's Division Three North. During the close season the club obtained Springfield Park and set to work on getting the ground ready for the start of the season. The dressing-rooms were improved and a temporary grandstand was built. Bamlett signed a number of useful players but the side struggled in the 1921-22 season, eventually finishing fourth from bottom. The following season they showed much improvement and finished fifth.

In August 1923, Bamlett received an offer to manage Middlesbrough. He did not endear himself to the club's supporters when he sold star striker Andy Wilson to Chelsea and also let George Carr move to Leicester City. 'Boro lost their only regular goalscorer in Wilson and ended the season relegated to the Second Division. During that season, Bamlett received £11,000 from selling players and bought players to the value of £20,000, thus making a loss of £9,000. The club experienced a terrible run from January 1924 with only one win in 19 games.

Middlesbrough bounced back in 1926-27 and broke all records in the process. The star was George Camsell, signed from Durham City by Bamlett. Camsell scored 59 goals in only 37 League appearances and the side netted 122 in all. Bamlett left the club in January 1927 before he could see his side win its place back in the First Division.

Three months later he joined Manchester United as manager. They were in the doldrums and finished in the bottom half of Division One in his first three seasons in charge. The 1930-31 season was a disaster with the Reds finishing bottom of the table and conceding 115 goals. His new signings had proved unsuccessful and included James Bullock, a prolific goalscorer, from Chesterfield. On 5 April 1931, Bamlett's unhappy reign came to an end.

BARKE, John Lloyd

Born: Nuncargate, 16 December 1912; Died: Kirkby-in-Ashfield, 7 March 1976.
Right-half   5ft 10in; 10st 7lb (1938).
Career: Nottingham Schools; Annesley Colliery; Chesterfield Reserves; East Kirkby Welfare; Bleakhall United; Scunthorpe & Lindsey United; Sheffield United May 1933; Mansfield Town player June 1937-1947, player-manager August 1944-May 1945; Denaby United 1947-1950; Sutton Town player-manager 1950; Heanor Town manager; Ilkeston Town manager; Belper Town manager; Derby County scout.

Signed as a player by Mansfield in June 1937, Barke was made the Stags' manager on the departure of Jack Poole in August 1944. After only six appearances for Sheffield United, Barke played regularly for Mansfield from 1937 until 1947 when he retired. He made 113 League appearances and 210 wartime appearances for the club, rarely missing a game for the Stags. Barke also appeared for Notts County as a guest in the war years. He made his farewell performance for Mansfield against Ipswich Town in April 1947. He was unlucky to miss Sheffield United's appearance in the 1936 FA Cup Final due to an ulcerated leg. He discovered Phil Boyer whilst scouting for Derby County.

BARKER, John William

Born: Denaby, 27 February 1907; Died: Derby, 20 January 1982.
Centre-half   5ft 11in; 12st 7lb (1933).
Career: Denaby Rovers (Rawmarsh League); Denaby United (Midland League); Derby County April 1928 (£200); Bradford City manager May 1946-January 1947; Dundalk manager January 1947; Oldham Athletic coach November 1948-January 1949; Derby County manager November 1953-April 1955.

Honours: England international (11 caps); Football League representative.

One of Derby County's best-ever centre-halves, Jack Barker made 353 appearances for the Rams and won 11 England caps, captaining both club and country. Barker had survived a pit disaster in his younger days and a thigh injury sustained at this time almost ended his playing career before it had began. He was appointed Bradford City's manager after serving in the Army Physical Training Corp during the war, but resigned after only eight months in charge, despite the club being in the top half of the Third Division North.

After managing Dundalk and coaching at Oldham Athletic, he joined his former club, Derby County, as manager. Despite spending £40,000 on new players, the Rams were relegated to the Third Division North in 1955. He resigned soon afterwards and the experience had left him bitter with football. He vowed never to manage again, 'not even for £10,000 a week'. He went to work as a fitter's mate at the Carriage & Wagon railway works in Derby. He suffered ill health later in life, including a spinal problem and cancer, and died in 1982, just before his 75th birthday. His son, also Jack, played in the Burton Albion team which scored an FA Cup giantkilling act over Halifax Town in 1955.

BARKER, Richie

Born: Derby, 23 November 1939.
Inside-forward   6ft; 12st 8lb (1970).
Career: Morris Sports; Burton Albion October 1960; Loughborough United May 1962; Matlock Town July 1963; Burton Albion November 1963; Primo Hamilton (Canada) (loan) April 1963; Derby County October 1967; Notts County December 1968; Peterborough United September 1971; Shrewsbury Town coach February 1974, then manager February-November 1978; Wolverhampton Wanderers assistant manager November 1978-1981; Stoke City manager June 1981-December 1983; Notts County manager November 1984-April 1985; Ethnikos (Greece) manager 1985; Zamalek (Egypt) manager 1986; Sheffield Wednesday assistant manager February 1989.

Honours: Division Four champions 1971.

A draughtsman by profession, Richie Barker was an experienced non-League player when he entered League football at the age of almost 28. Barker had played under Peter Taylor when he was manager of Southern League Burton Albion and it was Taylor, then assistant to Brian Clough, who took him to the Baseball Ground. He made 11 appearances in Derby's Second Division championship season of 1968-69 but was transferred to Notts County midway through that campaign.

Barker helped Notts County win the Fourth Division title in 1970-71 but broke his leg whilst with Peterborough and soon moved into management as

assistant to his former Derby colleague Alan Durban at Shrewsbury Town. They combined to take Shrewsbury from the Fourth to the Second Division and when Durban moved to Stoke City, Barker took control at Gay Meadow for ten months before moving to Wolves as assistant manager.

There was tension behind the scenes at Stoke during his first season as manager there. The Potters were struggling near the bottom of the First Division and he fell out with players Ray Evans and Mike Doyle and also sold Adrian Heath to Everton for £700,000. There was a huge turnover of players in the close season of 1982 and Barker was sacked after a disastrous start to the 1983-84 season. He had converted Stoke to a long-ball game and the players never came to terms with it. A poor season with Notts County ended with the sack again in April 1985 after the club were relegated to the Third Division. After working in Greece and Egypt, Barker returned to England as assistant manager at Sheffield Wednesday in 1989.

BARLOW, Frank

Born: Mexborough, 15 October 1946.
Wing-half   5ft 10in; 11st 9lb (1970).

Career: Sheffield United September 1965; Chesterfield August 1972 (£15,000), later coach, then manager September 1980-June 1983; Boston Minute Men (USA) (loan) April 1974; Scunthorpe United manager August 1984-March 1987; Barnsley assistant manager February 1989.

Honours: England Schoolboy international; Anglo Scottish Cup winners 1981.

Barlow was a player and a coach at Saltergate before taking over as manager in September 1980. After gaining three 'A' levels, he turned down the chance to go to university to become a professional footballer. A forceful midfield player, Barlow made 121

League appearances for Sheffield United before moving to Chesterfield in August 1972 for a club record fee of £15,000. But after receiving a terrible injury in the home game against Southend United in December 1975, he was forced to retire from playing at the age of 27.

He worked as a coach under manager Arthur Cox and took over as manager when Cox moved on to manage Newcastle United. Barlow lost his job when Chesterfield were relegated to Division Four in 1983. After three seasons with Scunthorpe United, he was unable to get the club out of the Fourth Division and was sacked in March 1987.

BARNES, Kenneth H.

Born: Birmingham, 6 March 1929.
Wing-half   5ft 11in; 10st 13lb (1964).
Career: Stafford Rangers; Manchester City May 1950; Wrexham player-manager May 1961-February 1965; Witton Albion player-manager 1965; Bangor City manager until 1970; Manchester City coach August 1970-1980, later chief scout.

Honours: Football League representative; Division Four promotion 1962; FA Cup winners 1956, runners-up 1955.

In his first season in charge at the Racecourse, Ken Barnes steered Wrexham into the Third Division, only to see them relegated after two years in the higher sphere. The crunch came in February 1965, when Wrexham lost 6-1 to arch-rivals Chester and a few days later Barnes was replaced by Billy Morris.

Unfortunate never to play for England — Denis Law described him as 'the finest uncapped wing-half who ever played English football' — Barnes was a great favourite of the Maine Road fans during his playing days. Whilst with Manchester City he gained both FA Cup winners' and runners-up medals and also represented the Football League. He also performed an integral role which enabled Don Revie to play his unique deep-lying centre-forward style for City. Both skilful and consistent, he gave the Wrexham sides he managed a touch of class whenever he played.

As an amateur he attracted the attentions of Birmingham City, West Brom and Sheffield Wednesday but it was Manchester City who snapped him up. He made 283 first-team appearances for City, scoring 19 goals, and played in 132 League games for Wrexham. He was awarded a testimonial at Maine Road in 1975 and is still involved with the club as chief scout. His son, Peter Barnes, played for Manchester City and England.

BARNWELL, John

Newcastle upon Tyne, 24 December 1938.
Wing-half 5ft 7in; 12st 3lb (1963).
Career: Bishop Auckland; Arsenal November 1956; Nottingham Forest March 1964; Sheffield United April 1970, retired June 1971; Hereford United coach summer 1972 (for 13 weeks); Peterborough United coach 1974, then manager May 1977-November 1978; Wolverhampton Wanderers manager November 1979-January 1982; Notts County manager June 1987-December 1988; Walsall manager January 1989-March 1990.

Honours: England Under-23 international (1 cap); Youth international; Football League Cup winners 1980.

John Barnwell won fame as a midfield schemer for Arsenal, Nottingham Forest and Sheffield United and as the manager of Peterborough United, Wolves, Notts County and Walsall. Barnwell was spotted by Arsenal playing as an amateur for Bishop Auckland, where he had won England Youth international honours.

Barnwell played for Arsenal during an uneventful period in their history with the club usually suffering mid-table mediocrity. After scoring 24 goals in 151 appearances for the Highbury club, he moved to Nottingham Forest in March 1964 after a difference of opinion over his playing position. He had gained England Under-23 caps at Highbury.

Forest were runners-up to Manchester United in 1966-67, but after 182 League games for Forest, Barnwell moved to Sheffield United in April 1970. He ended his playing career in June 1971 with a total of 327 League appearances and 47 goals.

Barnwell was Hereford United's coach for 13 weeks in 1972 and then moved on to be coach with Peterborough United. In May 1977 he became the manager of the club. United just missed promotion to Division Two on goal-average at the end of his first season in charge but on 9 November 1978, Barnwell walked out on Peterborough, saying that the club was not ambitious enough and put in applications for the vacant manager's jobs at Wolves and Sunderland.

After a week of speculation he was named as the new manager of Wolves on 20 November. Wolves almost made it to Wembley that season but lost to his former club, Arsenal, in the semi-final of the FA Cup. Barnwell almost lost his life in a horrific car crash in

which he suffered a fractured skull. He returned to Molineux just after the start of the 1979-80 season and set the soccer world talking when he was involved in two £1m plus transfers. He sold Steve Daley to Manchester City for £1,150,000 and then spent £1,465,000 on Andy Gray from Aston Villa. It was Gray who scored the winning goal in Wolves' League Cup Final success in 1980, when they beat Nottingham Forest. Barnwell also bought Emlyn Hughes, Dave Thomas and Rafael Villazen from Uruquay.

The following season was a big let down for the Wolves fans. They finished 18th and were knocked out of the FA Cup in the semi-final against Spurs. Wolves were bottom of the First Division when chariman Harry Marshall gave John Barnwell an ultimatum in January 1982: accept the terms of a new contract or resign. It came as no surprise when Barnwell terminated his contract after legal advice.

After a short spell out of the game, Barnwell coached in Saudi Arabia for a spell. He then became the manager at AEK Athens but was banned from Greek soccer after making deflamatory remarks about its standards. In June 1983 he became manager at Notts County and took them to the Third Division play-offs but was sacked in December 1988 after only 18 months in the job. The following month he took over at Walsall, then bottom of the Second Division, but could not prevent their relegation. Barnwell was sacked in March 1990 with the club heading towards relegation again.

BARRATT, Harry

Born: Headington, 25 December 1918; Died: Coventry, 23 September 1989.
Utility 5ft 9½in; 10st 2lb (1951).
Career: Herbert's Athletic; Coventry City December 1935; Cheltenham, on loan 1936; guest for Leicester City in World War Two; retired through injury in early 1952 and appointed club trainer in May 1952; Rugby Town manager; Snowdon Colliery (Kent) manager; Coventry City chief scout 1955; Gillingham manager July 1958-May 1962; Tunbridge Wells secretary-manager May 1962.

Barratt was a utility player who appeared in most positions for Coventry City. He joined the club when his father, Josiah, helped with the running of the youth team. Josiah had played as a full-back with Southampton, Leicester Fosse and Birmingham. Harry made his League debut in a 3-2 victory over Blackburn Rovers at Highfield Road in April 1938. He joined the Royal Warwickshire Regiment when the war began in 1939, thereafter he only made spasmodic appearances for City.

However, he was ever-present in 1945-46 and scored 27 goals. Barratt spent his last four seasons at Coventry as club captain and made a total of 178 appearances, scoring 27 goals for the club. At Snowdon Colliery, Barratt discovered George Curits, Alf Bentley and Eric Jones, all of whom later played League soccer. He was invited to become Coventry's chief scout based on the reputation gained at Snowdon. Barratt had four seasons as manager of Gillingham. His best season was 1959-60, when the Gills finished seventh in Division Four.

BARRITT, Arthur

Born: Burnley.
Career: North-East Lancashire League secretary until 1919; Burnley office staff

1919; Blackburn Rovers assistant secretary October 1925, then secretary December 1926, then secretary-manager February 1931-April 1936.

When he took over at Blackburn, Arthur Barritt had many years of administrative experience, but little of management. Barritt had been appointed secretary when Jack Carr resigned the manager's job. Bob Crompton had been in charge of team affairs but when he left Ewood Park, Barritt assumed full control. Rovers struggled in the lower reaches of the First Division until they were finally relegated in 1935-36. A rift had developed between Barritt and the directors and he resigned before the end of the season.

BARROW, Graham

Born: Chorley, 13 June 1954.
Midfield 6ft 2in; 13st 7lb (1983).
Career: Altrincham; Wigan Athletic July 1981 (£12,000); Chester City player-coach July 1986, assistant manager 1988, then manager October 1992.

A long-time friend of Harry McNally, Graham Barrow played under him at Altrincham, Wigan Athletic and Chester City. He joined Chester for a tribunal-fixed fee of £6,000 and was employed as player-coach. In 1988, Barrow became assistant manager and took over from McNally after a poor start to 1992-93.

Chester had remained in the Third Division, despite losing their Sealand Road ground and having to play at Macclesfield for two seasons. With little money to spend due to the cost of their new Deva Stadium, Barrow had a real struggle on his hands to prevent the club's relegation. In his Wigan days, Barrow helped Athletic to promotion to Division Three in 1982, and scored 36 goals in 179 League appearances for the club and has also played over 200 games for Chester City to date.

Things did not improve much after he took over from Harry McNally at Chester in October 1992. City finished the season cemented to the bottom of Division Two and the first season at a new ground ended on a sour note. The team's performance was not helped by the sale of Brian Croft to Queen's Park Rangers and the club may have overstretched themselves whilst acquiring a new ground. Chester also lost to Altrincham in the FA Cup first round.

BARTLETT, John William

Born: Forest Gate, 1878.
Career: Croydon Adults' School; Bensham Manor; St James United; Croydon Common secretary 1903-1912, secretary-manager cs 1907-December 1909, cs 1911-March 1912; Leicester Fosse manager March 1912-March 1914; Swansea Town manager May 1914-1915.

Honours: Southern League Division Two champions 1909.

When Bartlett became the secretary of Croydon Common they were an amateur club playing in minor local competitions. In 1907 he played a leading role when the club decided to become a professional outfit and join the Southern League Second Division. Bartlett quickly put together a squad of players and they finished third in their first season. Croydon gained promotion to the First Division in 1909 after finishing as champions. In December 1909, Bartlett was replaced as team manager by Nat Whittaker and he settled for the single role of secretary.

The Robins were relegated at the end of the 1909-10 season. Bartlett returned as team manager and secretary in the summer of 1911, replacing Sandy Tait who had himself replaced Whittaker the previous summer. Croydon had a poor season in the Second Division in 1911-12 and Bartlett departed for Leicester Fosse before the season's end. At 34, he was the youngest manager in the Football League. His two seasons in charge at Filbert Street were fraught with problems both on and off the pitch. The club was hugely in debt and Bartlett had little success in the players that he bought as Leicester struggled near the foot of the Second Division. Bartlett resigned shortly after the club was fined for making an illegal approach to an Ilford player called Blake.

He joined Swansea Town as manager in May 1914, after turning down an offer to coach in Germany. With war just around the corner, that was a wise decision for many other British coaches, including England internationals Steve Bloomer, Fred Pentland and Sam Wolstenholme, found themselves interned when hostilities began.

BARTON, Anthony Edward

Born: Sutton, 8 April 1937.
Outside-right 5ft 9in; 11st (1963).
Career: Surrey County FA; London Schools; Sutton United; Fulham May 1954; Nottingham Forest December 1959; Portsmouth December 1961, then player-coach; Aston Villa coach and assistant manager, then manager February 1982-May 1984; Northampton Town manager July 1984-April 1985; Southampton assistant manager September 1985-May 1988; Portsmouth assistant manager, then caretaker manager February 1991.

Honours: England Schoolboy international (1 cap); Youth international (5 caps); European Cup winners 1982.

One of a family of nine, Tony Barton represented London Boys and the Surrey County FA. He also gained England Schoolboy and Youth honours. After a loan period with Sutton United, he signed professional forms for Fulham in May 1954. Barton never settled with Nottingham Forest after his move to that club and joined Pompey in 1961 for a fee of £5,000. After retiring he joined their coaching staff.

He made his first big impact in management with Aston Villa, whom he joined as assistant manager in 1980. Promoted to team manager in February 1982, after Ron Saunders left, Barton guided the Midlands club to a European Cup Final victory four months later. After his sacking in May 1984, he moved to Northampton Town as manager but was forced to leave after a heart attack a year later. Barton was assistant manager to Chris Nichol at Southampton from September 1985 and was caretaker manager of Portsmouth after the sacking of Alan Ball, he is currently scouting for a number of clubs.

BARTRAM, Samuel

Born: Simonside, 22 January 1914; Died: Harpenden, 17 July 1981.
Goalkeeper   6ft ½in; 12st 5lb (1937).
Career: Sunderland Schools; Bolden Colliery School; Bolden Villa; North Shields; Chester le Street; Jarrow; Reading (trial at half-back) March 1933; Bolden Villa; Easington Colliery; Boldon Colliery Welfare; Charlton Athletic September 1934-1956; guest for Birmingham, Bournemouth, Bradford City, Crewe Alexandra, Crystal Palace, Liverpool, Millwall, Notts County, West Ham United and York City in World War Two; York City manager March 1956-July 1960; Luton Town manager July 1960-June 1962.

Honours: Durham County cap; England wartime international (3 caps); Division Three South champions 1935; Division Four promotion 1959; FA Cup winners 1947, runners-up 1946; League South Cup winners 1944, runners-up 1945 (guest with Millwall); FA Tours to South Africa (1949) and Australia (1951).

The name of Sam Bartram was synonymous with Charlton Athletic's great days and was a brave and agile goalkeeper. He had a reputation for loyalty — 22 years at The Valley — and as the finest goalkeeper never to have played for England apart from wartime appearances. He played in 613 peacetime games for Charlton — 582 in the League — and gained FA Cup medals just after the war.

He was unemployed when signed by Charlton's manager Jimmy Seed, this after an unsuccessful trial with Reading as a wing-half. Bartram went on a couple of FA tours to Australia and South Africa, but these did not make up for the disappointment of never being capped for England.

He played in four Cup Finals at Wembley between 1944 and 1947, for as well as his FA Cup Final appearances, he also won a League South Cup winners' medal with Charlton in 1944 and a losers' medal as a guest for Millwall the following year in the same competition.

With York City, another club for whom he had guested in wartime, Bartram experienced the realities of management in the lower divisions, although there were good times as well as bad. York failed only on goal-average to become members of the new national Third Division in 1958 and the following the season they gained promotion for the first time in their history, only to suffer immediate relegation in 1959-60.

Sadly, he did not have the managerial ability to get Luton Town back into Division One and, despite valiant efforts to make changes, he eventually departed in a cloud of controversy and publicity after a disagreement with the directors. He covered soccer for the *People* Sunday newspaper.

BASFORD, Walter John 'Jock'

Born: Crewe, 24 July 1925; Died: Mansfield, March 1982.
Inside-forward
Career: Wolverhampton Wanderers staff pre-war; Crewe Alexandra April 1948; Chester January 1954; Guildford City; Margate; Charlton Athletic trainer-coach; Exeter City assistant manager and trainer November 1965, then manager June 1966-April 1967; Charlton Athletic chief coach 1967-1968; Mansfield Town coach 1968-1970, then manager July 1970-November 1971; Mansfield Town youth team coach 1972-1982

Jock Basford scored 52 goals in 146 Third Division North games for Crewe before his transfer to Chester in January 1954. However, he lost his form at Chester and after only one goal in ten games for them, he entered non-League soccer.

He was promoted at Exeter too late to save the club from relegation and even though he made sweeping changes in the summer of 1966, it brought little success. At Charlton he discovered Billy Bonds, who was playing for Kent Schools at the time. Indeed, Bonds was one of several fine players whom Basford unearthed over the years.

He moved to Mansfield as coach in 1968 and was appointed manager two years later. Basford sold Malcolm Partridge to Leicester City for £50,000 and Stuart Boam to Middlesbrough for a similar fee in the close season of 1971 and by the time he left the Stags, they were £50,000 in the black. However, the players' departure had a big impact on the club's potential and the following season saw a terrible run which resulted in the demise of Basford and his assistant John Quigley. How different it had been at the start of his reign, with magnificent performances against Liverpool in the League Cup and seventh place in the League. He returned to the club a year later, as youth coach under Danny Williams, and despite several managerial changes thereafter, he stayed until his sudden death in March 1982.

BASSETT, David

Born: Watford, 4 September 1944.
Midfield   5ft 8in; 11st 2lb (1978).
Career: Watford Juniors; Chelsea

Juniors; Walton & Hersham; Wimbledon 1974, coach 1979, then manager January 1981-July 1987; Crystal Palace manager August 1984 (briefly); Watford manager May 1987-January 1988; Sheffield United manager February 1988.

Honours: England amateur international; Division Two runners-up 1990, promotion 1986; Division Three runners-up 1984, 1989; Division Four champions 1983, promotion 1981; Southern League champions 1975, 1976, 1977; FA Amateur Cup winners 1973.

A chirpy, cockney character, Bassett made a name for himself by developing a breed of soccer which did not impress the purists but proved very successful. The ball spends most of the time in the air as it is hoofed up to the tall strikers as quickly as possible, and they stampede the opposing goal. Not very good to watch but it is a method of play which has brought rewards for Bassett and his teams.

He failed to make the grade at both Watford and Chelsea before moving into non-League soccer with Walton & Hersham. He played at Wembley in 1973 in the FA Amateur Cup Final which Walton won 1-0 against Slough Town before a 41,000 crowd. The following season Walton had a fine FA Cup run in which they beat Brian Clough's Brighton 4-0 at the Goldstone.

In 1974 he moved to Wimbledon, who were then playing in the Southern League. They went on to win the Premier League title in the next three seasons and in 1977 were elected to the Football League in place of Workington. Bassett played in another famous FA Cup run with the Dons in 1974-75. They beat First Division Burnley 1-0 at Turf Moor, then held the mighty Leeds United 0-0 at Elland Road. Unfortunately it was Bassett's own-goal which won the tie for Leeds in the replay at Selhurst Park. Bassett played 35 times for the Dons in League soccer before retiring to become the club coach in 1979.

He took over as manager in January 1981 and his presence soon had an effect as the Dons lost only three of their last 20 games to clinch fourth place and promotion to the Third Division. They did not last long, however, and were relegated back again the following season. However, the 1982-83 season was a glorious one for Wimbledon. They won the Fourth Division championship with 98 points and scored 96 goals. The success continued the following season and Bassett's Dons finished runners-up to Oxford United to enter the Second Division for the first time.

The 1984-85 season was one of consolidation but the following season the Dons won promotion again, this time to the First Division. They finished third with an average attendance of only 4,578. Bassett had created a miracle by taking Wimbledon from the Fourth to the First Division on a shoestring budget. He made a number of shrewd signings during his years at Plough Lane, including Lawrie Sanchez from Reading, John Fashanu from Millwall and Nigel Winterburn from Oxford. He also made a number of discoveries where he paid little or no transfer fee. These included Dave Beasant from Edgware Town, Andy Thorn and Brian Gayle.

In May 1984, Bassett followed his chairman, Ron Noades, to Crystal Palace to become the manager. However, he changed his mind after only a week and returned to Plough Lane. After taking Wimbledon to sixth place in the First Division in 1986-87, Elton John, the Watford chairman, persuaded Bassett to become their manager in May 1987. It was an unhappy spell for Bassett and he left Vicarage Road in January 1988 with Watford struggling at the foot of the First Division. The club had not responded to Bassett's style and had shown little patience.

Within a month Bassett was the manager of Sheffield United and the success story was back on the road again. He made two inspired signings in Tony Agana from Watford and Brian Deane from Doncaster Rovers. They scored regularly over the next few seasons as United rose from the Third to the First Division. Bassett arrived too late to prevent the Blades' relegation to the Third Division at the end of the 1987-88 season but they bounced straight back the following season as runners-up. Both Agana and Deane scored over 20 goals each. United went up again at the end of the 1989-90 season, as runners-up behind champions Leeds United.

By Christmas 1990, the Blades were rock bottom of the First Division but a marvellous recovery led them to a final mid-table spot. Bassett never lost faith in his side and he maintained his reputation as a motivator of the highest order who manages to get the best out of moderate players with the instillation of team spirit and self belief.

Bassett's Blades struggled against relegation all season in the Premier Division and saved themselves only after a late run. However, they did reach the semi-finals of the FA Cup in 1993, where they lost to their great local rivals Sheffield Wednesday at Wembley in an exciting game.

BATE, Richard

Career: Sheffield Wednesday amateur 1963; York City amateur 1965; Alfreton Town 1968; Boston United 1971; Frickley Athletic 1976-1978; FA staff and qualified coach, PE teacher 1965-1979; Sheffield United youth coach 1978-1980; FA North West Regional coach 1980-1985; England Youth team assistant 1985; Notts County head coach 1985-1987; Southend United manager June-September 1987; Lincoln City assistant manager 1987-1988; Malaysian FA 1988-1990; Leeds United reserve/youth coach January 1990.

Bate was a surprise choice when he was selected to become Southend United's manager in 1987. He had failed to make the grade as a player and spent the majority of his career in non-League soccer. He used his FA qualifications and PE teaching experience to find a job with Sheffield United as their youth-team coach in 1978 and he also had Football League coaching experience with Notts County prior to joining Southend. His stay at Roots Hall was brief and later in 1987 he became assistant manager at Lincoln City. After two years in Malaysia, he returned to work for Leeds United.

BATES, Edric Thornton 'Ted'

Born: Thetford, 3 May 1918.
Inside-forward   5ft 9in; 10st 2lb (1936).
Career: Norwich City September 1936; Southampton May 1937, coach October 1952, then manager September 1955-December 1973.

Honours: Division Two runners-up 1966; Division Three champions 1960.

Any football manager who can keep his job and good humour for nearly 20 years has special assets as well as a level-headed chairman. Ted Bates' great love for football and for one club in particular made him synonymous with Southampton. Bates came from a sporting family. His grandfather, Willie, played cricket for Yorkshire and England and also represented his country at rugby, and his father, Billy, also played cricket for Yorkshire and for Glamorgan and Cheshire, as well as football for Leeds United and Bolton Wanderers. Ted joined Norwich City from school and when his manager Tom Parker moved to Southampton, one of the players he took with him was Bates.

Ted soon forced his way into the Saints' first team, only to have a promising career interrupted by the war. Whilst serving in the Army, he still managed to turn out for the Saints and on his demob returned to full-time football. Bates was particularly good in the air and, together with Charlie Wayman, terrorised Second Division defences. Before retirement he scored 64 goals in 202 appearances (not including wartime games) for the Saints. He had played in every position for the club, even as a goalkeeper when he took over once when Hugh Kelly was injured.

In October 1952, Bates was appointed coach and assistant trainer. He did well as a reserve-team coach and was the logical choice as the new manager to take over from George Roughton. When Ted took control at The Dell, Southampton had a £60,000 overdraft. He was soon wheeling and dealing on the transfer market and one of his best signings was George O'Brien from Leeds for just £8,000. O'Brien went on to score over 150 goals for Southamp-

ton. Within five years, Bates had sorted out the finances and the club was back in the Second Division. Their side was a blend of youth and experience and they finished as champions of the Third Division in 1959-60. Bates then set to work on getting into the top flight. It was Terry Paine, one of Bates' best discoveries, who headed the goal which brought First Division football to The Dell for the first time, in 1966 after a 1-1 draw at Leyton Orient.

A soccer workaholic, Bates was rarely at home and worked a seven-day week. His office was more a footballer's than a manager's with piles of boots stuffed in cabinets and shorts and shirts drying on the radiators. Bates had a happy knack of soothing unsettled footballers and making them feel happy at The Dell and also helped his players reach their full potential.

The Saints found it difficult holding on to their First Division status. It took all Bates' guile and knowledge and some astute work on the transfer market to consolidate the club's position. Amongst his signings were Ron Davies, a snip of a signing at £55,000, and he also signed a youthful Mick Channon. He balanced the books by selling Martin Chivers to Spurs for £86,000. Bates had the advantage of having George Reader as his chairman. Reader took over in 1963 and had played for the Saints in the 1920s. He never interfered with the buying or selling of players and Bates always knew exactly how much money was available for transfers. Besides getting to the First Division, the Saints also just missed out on a Wembley appearance when they lost to Manchester United in the FA Cup semi-finals. They also qualified for Europe in 1969, playing in the Fairs Cup. When Ted retired to become a director in 1973, he was the longest-serving manager in the League.

BATES, Philip 'Chic'

Born: West Bromwich, 28 November 1949.
Forward   6ft; 11st 12lb (1979).
Career: Stourbridge; Shrewsbury Town May 1974; (£5,000) Swindon Town January 1978 (£40,000); Bristol City March 1980 (£50,000); Shrewsbury Town December 1980 (£10,000), then player-manager July 1984-November 1987; Swindon Town coach 1989, assistant manager 1990. Shrewsbury Town assistant manager in 1992.

Chic Bates took over from Graham Turner as manager of Shrewsbury in

the summer of 1984 and retired from playing in the close season of 1986. He was sacked in November 1987 with the club bottom of Division Two, although Shrewsbury had previously maintained a respectable mid-table position during Bates' tenure of office. He played almost 300 games for the Shrews during his two periods at the club. Bates was assistant manager to Ossie Ardiles at Swindon Town.

BATSFORD, Allen

Career: Arsenal Reserves (for five seasons); Folkestone; Feltham Town manager 1963-1967; Walton & Hersham manager May 1967-1974; Wimbledon manager 1974-December 1977; Hillingdon Borough manager; Wealdstone manager November 1980; Queen's Park Rangers coach; Dulwich Hamlet general manager 1986. Millwall Youth team manager 1991.

Honours: Southern League champions 1975, 1976, 1977, 1982; Athenian League champions 1969; FA Amateur Cup winners 1973; Surrey Senior Cup winners 1971, 1973; Southern League Cup winners 1982.

Batsford was a regular for Arsenal's reserve team during his five years at Highbury but was unable to make the first team. After managing Feltham Town of the Surrey Senior League for four years, he took over at Walton & Hersham in May 1967. The club won the Athenian League in 1969 and were runners-up twice. They also won the Surrey Senior Cup twice in 1971 and 1973. He took Walton & Hersham to an FA Amateur Cup Final victory over Slough Town in 1973 and that same season the club finished as runners-up to Hendon in the Isthmian League. The following season Walton won 4-0 at Brighton (then managed by Brian Clough) in the first round of the FA Cup.

Batsford enjoyed an unprecedented run of success when he moved to Wimbledon as manager in 1974. The Dons won the Southern League championship three seasons on the trot from 1974-77 and the club performed great feats in the FA Cup including winning at First Division Burnley and holding mighty Leeds United to a draw at Elland Road. Shortly after Wimbledon had been elected to the Football League, Batsford fell out with the directors and left to manage Hillingdon Borough. After a comparatively lean spell, he bounced back taking over at Wealdstone. He steered that club to the Southern League championship and the League Cup in his first season.

BATTY, Ronald Robson

Born: West Sankey, 5 October 1925; Died: Lanchester summer 1971.
Left-back   5ft 9in; 12st 5lb (1954).
Career: East Tanfield Colliery; Newcastle United October 1945; Gateshead March 1958 (£510), then player-manager October 1958-March 1960; Bury scout.

Honours: FA Cup winners 1955.

A loyal clubman, Batty was a sound defender who was at his most impressive when under pressure. He had a reputation as a fierce defender and was dreaded by many a winger. He played in Newcastle United's FA Cup Final victory over Manchester City in 1955 and made 181 appearances for the Magpies altogether. Batty was appointed as manager of Gateshead when they were bottom of the Fourth Division in October 1958 but they eventually finished the season in a safe

position, fifth from bottom. He lost his job just before the club was voted out of the Football League in 1960. Gateshead then had the lowest average home support in the Football League, only 3,412 per game.

BAXTER, William A.

Born: Edinburgh, 23 April 1939.
Centre-half   5ft 8in; 10st 2lb (1970).
Career: Broxburn Athletic; Ipswich Town June 1960; Hull City March 1971; Watford October 1971; Northampton Town player-manager May 1972-May 1973.

Honours: Football League champions 1962; Division Two champions 1960, 1968.

Bill Baxter started his career as a right-half but was later converted to a pivot, even though he was small for the job. Made the Ipswich skipper by manager Alf Ramsey, Baxter won a League championship medal at Portman Road when the Suffolk club surprisingly lifted the title. He was a tenacious player with an attacking flair who scored a number of headed goals in his 409 League appearances for Town. Baxter made up for his lack of inches with skill. He left Ipswich after a clash with manager Bobby Robson over a minor club regulation. His one season as a manager at Northampton was a disaster when the club finished 91st in the Football League with only 31 points and had to seek re-election.

BAYLISS, Leonard Richard

Born: Alfreton, Derbyshire, 28 April 1899; Died: Coventry, 5 April 1947.
Left-half   5ft 9in; 13st (1925).
Career: Alfreton Town; Luton Town September 1920; Mansfield Town; Southend United May 1925; Coventry City, coach 1931, later chief scout, then manager June 1945-February 1947.

Dick Bayliss had worked as coach and chief scout under Harry Storer since 1931 and was the obvious choice to take over at Highfield Road when Storer left for Birmingham City. He had an unspectacular playing career — one game for Luton Town and eight for Southend United — but was considered to be an excellent judge of a player and brought a constant stream of talented footballers to Coventry before the war. When League soccer resumed in 1946, Coventry had a talented but ageing side. Bayliss' health deteriorated and he became ill after a nightmare drive back from Southend during the big freeze of 1947. Soon afterwards he died of kidney failure. Bayliss had been popular with the players, who mourned his passing.

BAYNES John Henly 'Jack'

Born: 18 February 1888; Died: Wrexham, 14 December 1931.
Career: Rotherham County; Mansfield Town coach 1922-1925; Nottingham Forest secretary June 1925-June 1929; Wrexham manager October 1929-December 1931.

Honours: Welsh Cup winners 1931.

Jack Baynes succeeded Charles Hewitt as Wrexham's manager, although the team had been selected by the directors after Hewitt's departure three years earlier. Baynes was very popular with the fans at the Racecourse and, but for his untimely death, could have produced a side capable of making the Second Division before World War Two. He kept the club in the higher reaches of the Third Division North and had some good runs in the FA Cup. Wrexham also won the Welsh Cup in 1931, when they beat Shrewsbury Town 7-0 in the Final.

Baynes began his League career with Rotherham County and then coached at non-League Mansfield, taking them to two Midland League championships and to the first round of the FA Cup in his time at Field Mill.

At Nottingham Forest he was in charge of team affairs — although the club had no official manager until Harold Wightman in July 1936 — during an undistinguished period of their history. Mainly a mid-table Second Division side, Forest had a good run in the FA Cup in 1925-26, but lost in the quarter-finals to Bolton Wanderers in a second replay. They also had another good run to the same stage in 1927-28, this time losing to Sheffield United 3-0 at Bramall Lane.

In September 1931, he was admitted to Chester Royal Infirmary for 'operative treatment' on a cancer and although allowed to return home, three months later he suffered a relapse and died in Croesnewydd Hospital, Wrexham, just before Christmas.

BEAGLEHOLE, Steven

Born: Doncaster, 17 October 1960.
Midfield
Career: British Colleges; FA full coaching badge; Doncaster Rovers youth coach 1985-1986, then reserve/youth coach 1986-1987; Middlesbrough youth coach 1988; Doncaster Rovers assistant manager 1989, then manager November 1991.
Honours: England Schoolboy international.

Despite representing his country at schoolboy level, Steve Beaglehole never made the grade in senior football. But he soon gained his full coaching badge and was given his first job in the Football League by Billy Bremner, in 1985 during Bremner's first spell as Doncaster manager. Beaglehole later worked under Bruce Rioch at Middlesbrough and when Bremner returned to Belle Vue for a second spell in charge, Beaglehole was appointed as his assistant manager. When Bremner was sacked, it was Beaglehole who stepped up for his first managerial job in the Football League.

BEAMISH, Kenneth

Born: Bebbington, 25 August 1947.
Forward   6ft; 12st 6lb (1970).
Career: Tranmere Rovers July 1966; Brighton & Hove Albion March 1972; Blackburn Rovers May 1974; Port Vale September 1976; Bury September 1978; Tranmere Rovers November 1979; Swindon Town August 1981, later coach, then manager March 1983-June 1984; Blackburn Rovers commercial manager 1990.
Honours: Division Three champions 1975.

A journeyman striker who scored goals wherever he went, Ken Beamish played in three promotion sides: Tranmere in 1967, Brighton in 1972 and Blackburn Rovers in 1975. In his career he scored 160 goals in 554 League appearances.

Initially taking over as caretaker manager of Swindon Town, he saw the team take 18 points from their last 12 games of the 1982-83 season to finish in eighth position. Beamish was then offered the job permanently. His period in control got off to a controversial start, though, when young striker Paul Rideout was sold over his head to Aston

Villa for £175,000, a move seen as essential if the club was to stay alive.

Swindon finished 17th in Division Four with Beamish in charge and he soon lost his post to Lou Macari. He was offered a coaching post but declined the offer and later became commercial manager at Blackburn Rovers.

BEASLEY, Albert 'Pat'

Born: Stourbridge, 17 July 1913; Died: Taunton, 27 February 1986.
Outside-left/Wing-half   5ft 7½in; 10st 7lb (1937).
Career: Brierley Hill Schools; Cookley; Stourbridge; Arsenal May 1931 (£550); Huddersfield Town May 1936; Fulham December 1945; Bristol City player-manager July 1950-January 1958 (retired from playing 1952); Birmingham City manager January 1958-May 1960; Fulham scout 1960; Dover manager cs 1961-April 1964.
Honours: England international (1 cap); Football League champions 1934, 1935; Division Two champions 1949; Division Three South champions 1955; FA Cup runners-up 1938; Inter-Cities Fairs Cup runners-up 1960.

Although only small and slight, Pat Beasley tackled with enthusiasm and was a constant inspiration after he had converted to wing-half with Fulham after the war. Before hostilities he had played as a left winger with Arsenal and Huddersfield Town. Beasley missed two FA Cup Finals with Arsenal when he was dropped to accommodate other players. He finally played in a Cup Final in 1938, when Huddersfield lost to Preston.

Beasley was an astute captain with Fulham, helping to weld the side into a cohesive and winning unit. He retired from playing with Bristol City just before his 40th birthday. City won the Third Division South championship under his managership in 1955, with 70 points, but his contract was terminated by mutual agreement in January 1958 after two steady seasons of Second Division soccer. He initially joined Birmingham City as joint manager with Arthur Turner, became acting manager from September 1958 and then team manager in January 1959. After three seasons as Dover's manager, Beasley retired to live in Chard, Somerset.

BEATTIE, Andrew

Kintore, Aberdeenshire, 11 August 1913; Died: Rushcliffe, 20 September 1983.
Full-back   5ft 8in; 11st (1937).
Career: Inverurie Loco; Preston North End March 1935 (£150), retired March 1947; guested for Leicester City, Notts County, Aldershot, Northampton Town, Derby County, Bradford City, Manchester City and Clapton Orient in World War Two; Barrow secretary-manager March 1947-March 1949; Stockport County manager March 1949-April 1952; Huddersfield Town manager April 1952-November 1956; Carlisle United manager May 1958-March 1960; Nottingham Forest manager September 1960-July 1963; Plymouth Argyle caretaker manager October 1963-March 1964; Wolverhampton Wanderers caretaker manager November 1964-September 1965; Notts County professional advisor and later general manager December 1965-September 1967; Sheffield United assistant manager October 1967; also Scotland national manager February-June 1954 and March 1959-October 1960; also coached or scouted at Brent-

ford, Wolves, Walsall, Liverpool and Notts County at various times.
Honours: Scottish international (7 caps); Wartime international (4 caps); Division Two runners-up 1953; FA Cup winners 1938, runners-up 1937.

Scottish international Andy Beattie has probably been involved with more clubs than any other person in the history of English football. As well as managing seven clubs, he has also been in charge of the Scottish national side, been assistant manager at Sheffield United, coached and scouted for four clubs and appeared for nine different teams during wartime soccer. The one thing that is not complex about Beattie's career is his loyalty to Preston North End, his one and only professional club, throughout his playing days.

Beattie played for the local clubs Inverurie Rovers and Locos whilst working as a quarryman in the town. It was from the latter that he joined Preston in March 1935. He appeared in the 1937 FA Cup Final, when North End lost 3-1 to Sunderland, but gained a winners' medal the following year when Huddersfield were beaten thanks to a last-minute penalty by George Mutch. A stylish defender, noted for his coolness and crisp tackling, Beattie had joined Preston as a wing-half but after being converted to full-back he represented his country in that position, against England in 1937. He gained another six Scottish caps before 1939 plus four wartime caps. Due to the seven years lost to the war, he made only 125 League appearances for the Lilywhites before retiring in March 1947.

As well as a few games for Preston in the war years, Andy also turned out for a number of other clubs. He appeared for Preston in a Cup Final at Wembley in May 1941, against Arsenal, but only just. Beattie had experienced problems with his release from the RAF and his deputy, Cliff Mansley, had already changed into his kit when Andy arrived. Poor Mansley didn't get a game but Preston won the Final 2-1 in a replay at Ewood Park.

On retirement from playing, Beattie's first managerial position was with lowly Barrow. He produced a new-found team spirit which quickly paid dividends and the team was heading the table by Boxing Day 1947. They were unable to maintain their form, though, and eventually finished seventh but attracted a record crowd to Holker Street of 14,801 for the FA Cup visit of local rivals, Carlisle United.

After a disagreement with the club's chairman in August 1948, Beattie resigned but this was not accepted by

the other directors. As a consequence the chairman left instead and Beattie was reinstated. In March 1949 he moved to Stockport County as manager. After a moderately successful season in 1951-52, he was on the move again, to Huddersfield Town in April 1952. Beattie soon found success at Leeds Road as the club won promotion back to Division One at the end of his first season and finished third in Division One in 1953-54. However, they were relegated in 1956 and Beattie was sacked the following November.

Beattie was in charge of the Scottish national side on two occasions, in 1954 and from 1959 to 1960. The first period was short-lived as he resigned in the middle of the 1954 World Cup, claiming that he had neither received direction or support. He was surprisingly reappointed in 1959 but when he had to choose between watching Nottingham Forest play Blackpool or Scotland play at Cardiff, he chose his club rather than his country and was sacked soon afterwards.

In May 1958 he returned to football management with Carlisle United. They had just dropped into the newly-formed Fourth Division and things did not improve much over the next few months. One improvement he did make was to buy new houses as accommodation for the players, which had been non-existent before. In March 1960, he left Brunton Park and six months later succeeded Billy Walker as manager at Nottingham Forest.

His three years at the City Ground were not outstanding and he left the club in July 1963. A month later he joined Plymouth Argyle as caretaker manager and steered them from relegation by the slimmest of margins, on goal-average. Beattie was next caretaker manager at Molineux from November 1964 for ten months, taking over from the legendary Stan Cullis. He failed in his attempt to restore pride to the Wolves. In 1964-65, he used 28 players and the season ended in relegation to Division Two. After a 9-3 defeat at Southampton and the illness of his wife, Beattie decided that he had had enough and resigned in September 1965.

In December 1965, he joined Notts County as a professional advisor and general manager and was in charge of team affairs when Jack Burkitt was taken ill in December 1966. After resigning in September 1967, he joined Sheffield United as assistant manager to John Harris for a period. Beattie also coached or scouted at Brentford, Wolves, Walsall and Liverpool at various times. When he died in September 1983, at the age of 70, he enjoyed a long and relatively successful career in the game and left his mark on many clubs in the Football League.

BEAUMONT, Sidney

Born: Biggleswade.
Half back/Left Winger   5ft 8in; 11st 4lb (1911)
Career: Watford 1909-1911; Preston North End 1911-1912; Merthyr Town cs 1912; Troedyrhiw cs 1913; Llanelli; Aberdare Athletic manager cs 1924-cs 1927; Blackpool manager cs 1927-May 1928..

Syd Beaumont had an undistinguished playing career, making only one League appearance for Preston and just 25 appearances for Watford and 15 for Merthyr Town. His first managerial post at Aberdare Athletic was fraught with financial problems and ended with the club being voted out of the Football League in 1927.

His best season was 1925-26, when the club made the first round of the FA Cup and finished ninth in the Third Division South. The financial circumstances were aggravated, first by unemployment in the town and then by industrial action down the mines, both of which affected attendances. And things were not helped when the wooden grandstand burnt down — such is the lot of a football club manager.

Beaumont's spell as manager of Blackpool lasted less than a year. He lost his job mainly due to the shortage of money at the club. Blackpool did without a paid manager for five years after this as club director Harry Evans became honorary manager, helped by trainers Jackie Charles and Allan Ure.

BECK, John Alexander

Born: Edmonton, 25 May 1954.
Midfield   5ft 10½in; 11st 9lb (1978).
Career: Queen's Park Rangers apprentice 1970, professional May 1972; Coventry City June 1976 (£40,000); Fulham October 1978 (£80,000); Bournemouth & Boscombe Athletic (loan) September 1982, permanently February 1983; Cambridge United July 1986, assistant manager 1988, manager January 1990-October 1992; Preston North End manager December 1992.

Honours: Division Three champions 1991; Division Four promotion 1990; Associate Members' Cup winners 1984.

John Beck gained a reputation as a dead-ball specialist and was also a fine crosser of the ball. In 1988, Beck took over as assistant manager at Cambridge United, under the managership of Chris Turner. When Turner resigned in January 1990, Beck took over as caretaker manager. He became the first caretaker boss to win the divisional manager of the month award twice in succession. He took full control as Cambridge reached the quarter-finals of the FA Cup before losing to Crystal Palace and gained promotion to Division Three via winning the Fourth Division play-offs at Wembley at the end of the season. Beck's initial impact as a manager can only be described as stunning as United then won the Third Division championship in 1990-91. However, their style of play was not appreciated by the football purists.

Beck was in charge at two clubs in 1992-93 which were eventually relegated: Cambridge United lost their place in the First Division; and his new club, Preston, also went down from the Second Division when they lost their final game of the season at Bolton.

BEER, William John

Born: Poolsbrook, near Chesterfield, 4 January 1879; Died: March 1941.
Right-half
Career: Staveley Town; Chesterfield Town; Sheffield United August 1898; Small Heath January 1902-1910, retired 1910; then sheep farmer in Australia 1910-20; Licensee in Birmingham 1920; Birmingham manager May 1923-March 1927 (secretary-manager 1925-1927).

Honours: FA Cup winners 1899.

Usually a right-half, Beer showed his versatility by also appearing at inside-forward and centre-half. He moved from Sheffield United to Small Heath with inside-left Charlie Field for a fee of £1,000 and made 260 appearances for the newly-named Birmingham, scoring 35 goals mainly from the penalty spot.

As well as playing football he was also an accomplished musician and composer. After spending ten years in Australia working as a sheep farmer, Beer returned to Birmingham to run a pub near Villa Park. He teamed up with Frank Richards at St Andrew's, managing team affairs whilst Richards carried out secretarial duties. Beer was famous for his rigorous training routines and the Blues remained a mid-table First Division club during his term of office.

BELL, Charles

Born: Dumfries, 1884
Centre-forward 5ft 8in; 11st 4lb (1921).
Career: Dumfries Amateurs; Dumfries Wanderers; Douglas Wanderers; Carlisle City; Arsenal September 1913; Chesterfield July 1914; Barrow 1920; Queen's Park Rangers May 1921; Reading trainer-coach; Notts County trainer cs 1922-August 1923; Wigan Borough manager August 1923-February 1924; Mansfield Town trainer July 1934, then manager March-December 1935; Bournemouth & Boscombe Athletic manager February 1936-1939; also coached in Italy, Portugal, Brazil and France (with Marseilles for three years).

Charles Bell made only one senior appearance for Arsenal, but managed two goals for the Gunners, against Leicester Fosse at Filbert Street in December 1913. During World War One he attained the rank of captain in the Footballers' Battalion of the Middlesex Regiment. In 1920-21 he was Barrow's top scorer when they won the Lancashire Combination and in 1923 he steered Notts County into Division One.

At Mansfield, Bell was less than successful and the minutes of a board meeting held on 19 December 1935 show that he had admitted he was losing control of the players. He said he would resign if the club paid him £450, to which they agreed. He made one major contribution to the Stags' fortunes, though, in signing Ted Harston from Bristol City for £250 in October 1935. Harston went on to score 85 goals in only 75 League and Cup appearances for the Stags.

BELL, William John

Born: Johnston, 3 September 1937.
Full-back   5ft 10in; 11st 2lb (1964)
Career: Neilston Juniors; Queen's Park 1957; Leeds United July 1960; Leicester City September 1967 (£40,000); Brighton & Hove Albion player-coach July 1969, retired June 1970; Birmingham City coach 1970, then manager October 1975-September 1977; Lincoln City manager December 1977-

October 1978; joined Liberty Baptist College, Virginia, USA, in 1978 as a soccer coach.

Honours: Scotland international (2 caps); Amateur international (2 caps); Division Two champions 1964; FA Cup runners-up 1965; Inter-Cities Fairs Cup runners-up 1967.

As a youngster Willie Bell turned down the chance to join Stoke City as he wished to finish his Clydeside engineering apprenticeship. He started his career as a half-back with Queen's Park, where he won Scottish amateur international honours, but Don Revie converted him into a full-back when he moved to Leeds United.

Bell won two full caps for Scotland, against Brazil and Portugal in 1966, and played 260 games for Leeds, scoring 18 goals, before his move to Leicester City in 1967. He became player-coach under Freddie Goodwin at Brighton and moved with him to Birmingham City as coach, when Goodwin became manager at St Andrew's. When Goodwin was sacked in October 1975, Bell took over. The Blues just missed relegation in 1975-76. After a poor start to the 1977-78 season, Bell was sacked. Two months later he took over at Lincoln City. In October 1978, after a poor start to the season, he left to join a religious sect in the USA.

BENSON, John Harvey

Born: Arbroath, 23 December 1942
Defender   5ft 9in; 11st 13lb (1964)
Career: Stockport Boys; Manchester City July 1961; Torquay United June 1964; Bournemouth & Boscombe Athletic October 1970; Exeter City (loan) March 1973; Norwich City December 1973; Bournemouth & Boscombe Athletic player-manager January 1975-January 1979; Manchester City assistant manager October 1980, then manager February-June 1983; Burnley manager August 1984-May 1985; Barnsley chief scout 1990.

A colourful personality with a strong sense of humour off the field and a sense of duty on it, John Benson was a busy player who got through a great deal of work in a quite efficient manner. He was made skipper at Bournemouth by manager John Bond and, indeed, seemed to spend most of his career following Bond about. He played alongside him at Torquay, played under him at Bournemouth and Norwich City and coached under him at Manchester City and Burnley. Benson made 240 appearances for Torquay and 469 in all during his career.

He jumped up three divisions when he moved from Exeter to Norwich in 1973 and surprised a lot of people by his displays in the First Division. He won promotion with Torquay in 1966 and went with Bournemouth to the Third Division in 1971. He was player-manager at Bournemouth but was unable to get the club out of the Fourth Division. Taking over at both Manchester City and Burnley from John Bond, he lost his job at both clubs after relegation seasons. He was probably a better coach than a manager.

BENTLEY, Roy Thomas Frank

Born: Bristol, 17 May 1924
Centre-forward/Centre-half
5ft 10in; 12st (1950).
Career: Bristol Schools; Portway; Bristol Rovers amateur 1937; Bristol City amateur 1938, professional August 1941; Newcastle United June 1946

(£8,500); Chelsea January 1948 (£12,500); Fulham September 1956 (£8,600); Queen's Park Rangers June 1961; Reading manager January 1963-February 1969; Bradford City scout 1969; Swansea City manager August 1969-October 1972; Thatcham Town manager; Reading secretary 1977-February 1984; Aldershot secretary January 1985-1986.

Honours: England international (12 caps); 'B' international(1) cap; Football League representative; Great Britain representative; Football League champions 1955; Division Four promotion 1970.

Roy Bentley played an unorthodox centre-forward role. Beginning his career as an inside-forward, he was tried at centre-forward by Chelsea with great success. He scored nine goals in his 12 games for England and altogether hit 172 in the League, 26 in the FA Cup and five for the Football League representative side. He appeared in the 1950 World Cup in Brazil and captained Chelsea to their only First Division title in 1955. He was converted to centre-half when he moved to Fulham, a position which he also mastered with great success.

Bentley was appointed Reading's manager during the big freeze of 1963. He soon reorganised the club and experimented on new methods of play. The club finished consecutive seasons in fourth and fifth position in Division Three, in 1967 and 1968, but after a poor season in 1968-69 he left the club. Bentley next took over at Swansea City, who won promotion to Division Three after his first season in charge. He was sacked after a poor start to the 1972-73 season. Later secretary at Reading and Aldershot, he ran a newsagent at Littlewick Green whilst managing Thatcham Town.

BERGERA, Daniel Alberto

Born: Uruguay, 1943.
Position: Midfield
Career: Uruguayan junior football; Racing Club (Montevideo); Real Majorca 1962; Seville 1967; Tenerife 1972; Luton Town coach c.1973; Sheffield United assistant manager 1978-1981; England youth coach 1980-1981; coaching in Brunei; Sheffield FC coach c.1984; Sheffield United coach 1987-1988; Rochdale manager July 1988-March 1989; Stockport County manager March 1989.

Honours: Uruguay Youth international; Spanish League Division Two champions 1965, 1969; Division Four runners-up 1991; Autoglass Trophy runners-up 1992. Autoglass trophy runners up 1993.

Danny Bergera played in Spanish soccer after moving to that country in his teens. Eventually he carved out for himself a coaching career in England and it was Harry Haslam who first employed him, initially as a coach at Luton and then as his assistant at Sheffield United. Later, Bergera had a spell as caretaker boss at Bramall Lane between Billy McEwan and Dave Bassett.

In his season as manager of Rochdale he impressed quite a few people and in March 1989, Stockport County appointed him. Bergera has done well at Edgeley Park. County reached the Fourth Division play-offs in 1989-90, albeit losing 6-0 on aggregate to Chesterfield. The following season, however, they went straight up as runners-up to Darlington after a run of eight wins in their last nine matches. They also scored 84 goals, the highest tally in the League. Bergera built a sound team, using several of the men who had played under him at Spotland.

Stockport were very unlucky not to be promoted again the following season. After finishing fifth they reached the play-off Final at Wembley where they lost to Peterborough United 2-1. The week before they had lost again at Wembley, this time 1-0 to Stoke City, in the final of the Autoglass Trophy.

Stockport had another good season under Bergera in 1992-93. They reached the play-offs but lost on aggregate 2-1 to Port Vale. Four days later they met each other again in the Final of the Autoglass Trophy at Wembley and County lost again, 2-1.

BESTALL, John Gilbert 'Jackie'

Born: Beighton, 24 June 1900; Died: Doncaster, 11 April 1985.
Inside-forward   5ft 5in; 9st 6lb (1933).
Career: Sheffield Schoolboys; Beighton Miners Welfare; Rotherham United 1925; Grimsby Town (£700) November 1926-May 1938; Birmingham coach-chief scout June 1938; Doncaster Rovers manager March 1946-April 1949; Blackburn Rovers manager June 1949-May 1953; Nelson manager cs 1953-November 1954; Doncaster Rovers chief scout August 1958-March 1959, then manager March 1959-August 1960.
Honours: England international (1 cap); Football League representative (3 caps); Division Two champions 1934; Division Three North champions 1947.

One of Grimsby Town greatest players and captain, Jackie Bestall was their star during the Mariners' First Division days in the 1930s. He was described as 'a diminutive craftsman, full of guile and possessing outstanding constructive qualities'. For a long period he held Grimsby's appearance record with 427 games for the club, in which he scored 76 goals. There is a street in Cleethorpes, near to Blundell Park, named after him. His one full cap for England was against Ireland in a 2-1 victory at Goodison Park in February 1935.

He took over as manager at Doncaster Rovers just after the war and ended his first season in charge of the club by winning the Third Division North title with 72 points as Rovers scored 123 goals. Sadly, the club were relegated after only one season. In 1952, he took Blackburn Rovers to an FA Cup semi-final, where they lost to Newcastle United 2-1 in a replay, the winning goal a fortuitous penalty. Bestall made a comeback to management with Doncaster again in 1959 but stepped down after a poor season.

BINGHAM, William L.

Born: Belfast, 5 August 1931.
Outside-right   5ft 7½in; 10st 5lb (1964).
Career: Glentoran 1949; Sunderland November 1950 (£7,000); Luton Town July 1958 (£15,000); Everton, October 1960 (£20,000); Port Vale, August 1963, retired 1965; Southport trainer-coach July 1965, then manager December 1965-February 1968; Plymouth Argyle manager February 1968-March 1970; Northern Ireland national team manager 1968-August 1970; Linfield manager June 1970-1971; Greece national coach 1971; Everton manager May 1973-January 1977; PAOK Salonika (Greece) manager April-October 1977; Mansfield Town manager March 1978-July 1979; Northern Ireland team manager.
Honours: Northern Ireland international (56 caps); Schoolboy international; Youth international; Irish League representative; Football League champions 1963; Division Four runners-up 1967; FA Cup runners-up 1959.

Sunderland paid a large fee for Billy Bingham after an outstanding display for the Irish League against the Football League in 1950 and he went on to make 42 consecutive appearances for Northern Ireland in the 1950s. A likeable man with a sense of humour, Bingham was a superb dribbler and crosser of the ball. His playing days ended after a broken leg in 1965 but before then he had played in the 1958 World Cup finals. He also managed Northern Ireland to some success in the 1982 and 1986 finals. They had a great win over hosts Spain in 1982, thanks to a memorable goal by Gerry Armstrong, to reach the second stage.

Bingham's first managerial post was at lowly Southport in December 1965. They had a good run to the fifth round of the FA Cup that season and Bingham embarked on a youth campaign which paid off when the club won promotion to Division Three in 1967, as runners-up. Indeed, there was great sadness at Haig Avenue when Bingham moved to Plymouth.

He was not very successful at Home Park, however, and when he was unable to get the club out of the Third Division the fans began to voice their discontent and Bingham was sacked. After spells with Linfield and the Greek national side, he returned to England as manager of Everton in 1973. The team was badly in need of reconstruction and with neighbours Liverpool doing so well, it was always going to be a struggle. He bought some useful players but when honours did not come he was sacked in January 1977. Bingham had just one season as Mansfield's manager when they finished 18th in the Third Division.

BIRD, John Charles

Born: Doncaster, 9 June 1948.
Defender   6ft; 12st (1970)
Career: Doncaster United; Doncaster Rovers March 1967; Preston North End March 1971 (£6,000); Newcastle United August 1975 (£60,000); Hartlepool United July 1980, coach 1985, then manager November 1986-October 1988; York City manager October 1988-October 1991; Doncaster Rovers coach 1992.

A strongly-built pivot, whose career was often hindered by injury, John Bird's transfer from Preston eventually led to Bobby Charlton resigning as that club's manager. Newcastle paid £60,000 for his services and Bird retired in the summer of 1986 after 444 appearances and 32 goals for his four clubs. He was assistant manager and coach before taking charge at Hartlepool. Bird was unable to lift United to a challenge for promotion and he resigned to join York City in October 1988. Bird had little success at Bootham Crescent as well and, in 1992, he returned to Doncaster Rovers as coach.

BIRNIE, Edward Lawson

Born: Sunderland, 25 August 1878; Died: Southend, 22 December 1935.
Left-half
5ft 10†in; 12st 9lb (1910)
Career: Sunderland Seaburn; Newcastle United June 1898; Crystal Palace May 1905; Chelsea (£100) August 1906-May 1910; Tottenham Hotspur July 1910; Mulheim (Germany) player-coach August 1911; Sunderland assistant trainer August 1919; Rochdale trainer cs 1921; Southend United manager 1921-May 1934, then retired.

A commanding defender with speed, heading ability and also an intelligent reader of the game, Birnie played in Chelsea's first promotion side of 1906-07 and appeared in over 100 games for the Blues. A leisurely ball player, he represented Northumberland County. A respected coach and manager, Birnie was in charge at Southend United for 13 years. The club twice finished bottom of the Third Division South in his early days but were just below the promoted club in the early 1930s. Their best season was 1931-32 when they finished in third spot, four points behind champions Fulham. Southend also reached the fifth round of the FA Cup in 1926, their best-ever run.

BIRRELL, William

Born: Cellardyke, Fife, 13 March 1897; Died: November 1968.
Outside/Inside-right
5ft 9in; 11st 3lb (1926).
Career: Inverkeithing United; Raith Rovers; Middlesbrough February 1921; Raith Rovers player-manager November 1927-1930; Bournemouth & Boscombe Athletic manager 1930-April 1935; Queen's Park Rangers secretary-manager April 1935-May 1939; Chelsea manager May 1939-May 1952.
Honours: Division Two champions 1927.

A great favourite with the 'Boro crowd as a player, Billy Birrell captained the side to promotion to Division One in 1927 and, although he had years of struggle at Bournemouth, who finished bottom and had to seek re-election in 1934, things changed when he moved the Queen's Park Rangers in 1935. The Shepherds Bush club enjoyed four seasons of relative success, just missing out on promotion to Division Two.

In 1939, just after QPR had sold

prolific scorer Tommy Cheetham to Brentford, Birrell became the Chelsea manager and after the war much of his time was spent trying to keep a struggling side in the First Division. They had a miraculous escape in 1951, winning their last three games to stay up. Chelsea also reached the semi-finals of the FA Cup in 1950 and 1952.

Birrell launched a prolific youth scheme at Stamford Bridge. A kindly, well-loved man, he had also steered Chelsea through the difficult war years and two Wartime Cup Final appearances at Wembley. After the war he signed a number of fine players including Tommy Walker, Len Goulden, Tommy Lawton and Roy Bentley. After leaving soccer, Birrell worked as a clerk in Kenton where his son was a solicitor.

BISSETT, James Thompson

Born: Lochee, near Dundee, 19 June 1898
Right-back   5ft 11in; 12st (1924).
Career: Dundee local football; Dundee; Everton Reserves, Ebbw Vale; Southend United cs 1922; Rochdale cs 1923; Middlesbrough May 1924; Lincoln City July 1926; Dundee manager cs 1928; Barrow secretary-manager April-December 1937.

After spells with his home-town club, Dundee, and on Everton's staff, Jimmy Bissett played for Ebbw Vale before returning to a League club with Southend United. He was ever-present for Rochdale in 1922-23 and attracted the attentions of Middlesbrough where he made 33 appearances before ending his career at Lincoln City.

Bissett returned to his home town to manage Dundee in succession to Alex McFarland. They were mainly an average First Division side under Bissett but he did steer them to the Scottish Cup quarter-finals in 1929-30. Alas, he had a disastrous spell as manager of Barrow, who scored only eight goals in the 17 games he was in charge of the Holker Street club.

BLACKBURN, Robert Ernest

Born: Crawshaw Booth, near Rawtenshaw, 23 April 1892; Died: Birkenhead, 13 July 1964.
Right-back   5ft 10in; 12st (1919).
Career: Loveclough FC; Manchester Youth Club; Army football (Royal Medical Corp); Aston Villa April 1919; Bradford City May 1922, retired due to injury 1923; Accrington Stanley trainer August 1924, then manager October 1924-January 1932; Wrexham manager January 1932-January 1936; Hull City manager December 1936-January 1946;

Tranmere Rovers manager September 1946- May 1955 and secretary 1955-1959 when he retired.

Ernest Blackburn spent seven and a half years in charge at Accrington Stanley and had to work under the burden of financial problems at the club. Blackburn had charge of the day-to-day running of the club but the directors picked the team. When he moved to Wrexham they came very close to promotion in 1932-33 when they finished as runners-up to Hull City, the club he later moved to. Financially astute, he helped reduce the Tigers' debts and transformed non-League recruits into quality players. In 1938, Hull City just missed out on promotion to Division Two.

Blackburn recruited 14 new players in the summer of 1939 in an attempt to find success for the club. After keeping City going during the war years, the directors decided not to retain him after the end of hostilities and was thus the first manager to lose his job after the war. When Blackburn took over at Tranmere, he welded together a successful and entertaining side. He brought some fine players to Prenton Park. In 1955 Blackburn became the secretary at the club, relinquishing team duties. He won a reputation as a hard worker, a fine judge of player and good at balancing the books.

BLANCHFLOWER, Robert Dennis 'Danny'

Born: Belfast, 10 February 1926.
Right-half   5ft 9ins; 11st 1lb (1964).
Career: Belfast Technical College; Bloomfield United 1939; Glentoran amateur 1945, professional January 1946; Swindon Town guest in World War Two; Barnsley April 1949 (£6,000); Aston Villa March 1951 (£15,000); Tottenham Hotspur December 1954-November 1963 (£30,000); Showbiz XI; Northern Ireland manager June 1976-November 1978; Chelsea manager December 1978-September 1979; sports journalist with the Sunday Express 1964-1988.

Honours: Northern Ireland international (56 caps); Irish and Football League representative; Footballer of the Year 1958, 1961; Great Britain representative; Football League champions 1961; FA Cup winners 1961, 1962; European Cup-winners' Cup winners 1963.

Not very quick nor a good tackler, Danny Blanchflower excelled as a reader of the game, as a beautiful passer and at his ability to change tactics in the process of a match. Blanchflower was a thinker, not just a footballer, and was a master tactician with an ability to spot

weaknesses in the opposition and exploit them, or to plug any deficiencies in his own side.

Although it was Aston Villa who took him into the First Division, club honours did not come his way until he joined Spurs in December 1954 for a large fee of £30,000. When Bill Nicholson became manager, he reinstated Blanchflower as captain and as Danny's ideas of inventive, attacking football matched Nicholson's, it was not long before Spurs were the supreme team in English football. Honours came thick and fast. Blanchflower captained the side to the League and Cup double in 1960-61, the first time it had been achieved this century.

A witty, rational and intelligent man, Blanchflower started a career as a journalist for the *Sunday Express*. He gained a reputation for being outspoken and openly attacking the football establishment. His brief excursion into Football League management came in December 1978, when he took charge, reluctantly, at Chelsea, but resigned after only nine months. He felt so alienated by present-day values and what he saw as the absence of loyalty and integrity in the game. Also, it has to be said that he had been out of contact with day-to-day football for some 15 years and his appointment had looked doomed to failure from the start. Also, Chelsea had a poor team, with some players past their best and others never Division One quality in the first place. And one senior player confided: "He's fascinating to listen to, but we're never quite sure what he's trying to say."

He is the brother of Jackie Blanchflower, the Northern Ireland and Manchester United centre-half who was seriously injured in the Munich air disaster.

BLESSINGTON, James

Born: Linlithgow, West Lothian, 28 February 1874; Died: Newton Abbot, 18 April 1939.
Inside/Outside-right   5ft 7ins; 11st 6lb (1896).
Career: Leith Hibernian 1890; Hibernian amateur; Leith Athletic 1891; Glasgow Celtic cs 1892; Preston North End March 1898; Derby County June 1899; Bristol City October 1899; Luton Town August August 1900; Leicester Fosse May 1903, player-manager January 1907-February 1909; Belfast Celtic coach 1913.

Honours: Scotland international (4 caps); Scottish League representative (5 caps); Scottish League champions 1893, 1894, 1896; Division Two runners-up 1908; Scottish Cup runners-up 1893, 1894.

Jimmy Blessington was a leading forward of the 1890s, who was accomplished in dribbling and distribution skills. A tough, thoughtful and skilled Scot, he was one of the players who did a great deal to change the face of early English professional soccer. His Derby career was short — only two League appearances — but he was still a valuable player when he became the player-manager of Leicester Fosse and they won promotion to the First Division in 1908. Unfortunately, the club was relegated the following season. Blessington had the habit of taking players away to seaside resorts before important matches. He was also an athletics handicapper in Ireland and a Newton Abbot licensee in the inter-war years.

BLOOMFIELD, James Henry

Born: Kensington, 15 February 1934;

Died: Chingford, Essex, 3 April 1983.
Inside-forward 5ft 9ins; 10st 11lb (1964).

Career: Middlesex County Youth; Hayes; Brentford October 1952; Arsenal July 1954; Birmingham City November 1960 (£30,000); Brentford June 1964; West Ham United October 1965; Plymouth Argyle September 1966; Orient player-manager March 1968-June 1971; Leicester City manager June 1971-May 1977; Orient manager September 1977-August 1981; Luton Town scout 1981-1983.

Honours: England Under-23 international (2 caps); Football League representative; Division Three champions 1970; Football League Cup winners 1963; Inter-Cities Fairs Cup runners-up 1960.

A skilful, ball-playing inside-forward, Jimmy Bloomfield made 227 appearances for Arsenal, scoring 56 goals. His early games for the Gunners were on the wing as part of a young and enthusiastic forward line. He represented the Football League against the Scottish League in March 1960 but after George Eastham came to Highbury, Bloomfield lost his place and moved to Birmingham City.

His first managerial post was with Orient, where he was initially player-manager before retiring in the summer of 1969. The following season Orient went on to win the Third Division championship. Bloomfield sold Tommy Taylor to West Ham for £78,000 and the team struggled the following season in the Second Division. Leicester City saw his potential as a manager and appointed him in June 1971. At Filbert Street he spent large sums on a number of players including Keith Weller and Frank Worthington. Bloomfield produced entertaining sides but never gained much success. In his second spell at Orient he took the club to their first-ever FA Cup semi-final in 1978 before losing to his former club, Arsenal. He left Orient by mutual consent due to ill health and died at the early age of 49, from a heart condition.

BLOOR, Alan

Born: Stoke-on-Trent, 16 March 1943.
Defender   6ft; 13st (1970).
Career: Stoke City March 1960; Port Vale June 1978, then manager September-December 1979.

Honours: England Youth international; Football League Cup winners 1972.

Bloor was in charge at Port Vale for only a few weeks, resigning in early

December after a string of poor results. Bloor and his assistant Gordon Banks blamed the players due to lack of effort. As a player he made 388 appearances for Stoke City after taking over the centre-half berth from Maurice Setters, who was transferred to Coventry City. He also scored some important goals for the Potters. He played in Stoke's Football League Cup Final victory in 1972 which brought the club it's first major trophy. Chelsea were beaten 2-1 in the Final at Wembley

BLUNSTONE, Frank

Crewe, 17 October 1934.
Left winger   5ft 7ins; 11st 7lb (1964).
Career: Crewe Alexandra January 1952; Chelsea March 1953, youth-team coach 1964; Brentford manager December 1969-June 1973; Manchester United youth-team manager January 1973-June 1977; Derby County assistant manager September 1977-May 1979; Ethnikos (Greece) coach August 1979; Aris Salonika (Greece) coach March-July 1980; Brentford youth-team manager 1980s; Sheffield Wednesday youth-team manager-coach 1982-1984, then caretaker manager February 1984.

Honours: England international (5 caps); Under-23 international (5 caps); Youth international; Football League representative; Football League champions 1955; Division Four promotion 1972.

Frank Blunstone broke his leg twice in seven months whilst playing for Chelsea and had to miss the whole of the 1957-58 season. He had gained his first full cap back in 1954 and also won a Football League championship medal with Chelsea in 1955. Blunstone helped the Blues back to Division One in 1962-63.

He was a classic left-winger with dribbling skills and the ability to centre with pinpoint accuracy. His career ended prematurely due to injury after scoring 54 goals in his 347 games for Chelsea. He took over as youth-team coach at Stamford Bridge and as manager at Brentford he worked financial miracles, running the club on a shoestring budget. He did most of the jobs himself and bought and sold players wisely. He never managed a club again after Brentford, preferring to work as assistant boss or youth-team manager at Manchester United, Derby County and Sheffield Wednesday.

BLYTHE, Robert

Born: Glenbuck, Ayrshire, 1870.

Wing-half   5ft 10in; 12st (1903).
Career: Glenbuck Athletic; Middles-brough Ironopolis; Glasgow Rangers; Dundee; Preston North End 1894-1899; Portsmouth 1899, then player-manager July 1901-August 1904, director 1909 and chairman from August 1924.
Honours: Southern League champions 1902.

Bob Blythe made over 100 appearances for both Preston and Portsmouth. A very neat half-back, he had gained an excellent reputation by the time he was signed for Pompey by manager Frank Brettell in 1899. He took over as player-manager in July 1901 and guided the club to the Southern League championship in his first season in charge. But there was controversy after the signing of three players from Liverpool, Raybould, Goldie and Glover. An FA commission was set up to investigate the dealings and Blythe was suspended until January 1903 without wages and the club was fined £100. When he retired from playing, he also relinquished the managership. He later served Pompey as a director and chairman. Blythe was an uncle of the great Bill Shankly.

BOAM, Stuart
Born: Kirkby-in-Ashfield, 28 January 1948.
Defender   6ft ½in; 11st 3lb (1970).
Career: Kirkby Boys' Club; Mansfield Town July 1966; Middlesbrough June 1971 (£50,000); Newcastle United August 1979 (£140,000); Mansfield Town player-manager July 1981-January 1983; Hartlepool United non-contract March 1983; Guisborough Town player-manager 1984
Honours: Division Two champions 1974.

A rugged defender with some good skills, Boam missed only ten games in his four seasons at Mansfield. He formed a fine partnership with Willie Maddren at 'Boro and helped the club back to the First Division in 1974. Boam made over 300 appearances for 'Boro and almost 600 in all during his career. He managed Mansfield for just a season and a half. In 1981-82 they missed re-election by only one point and the following season were in a mid-table spot when Boam was sacked in January 1983. They had only 31 points from 21 games and on 17 December 1982, suffered their lowest League attendance ever when only 1,293 fans watched the game against Torquay.

BODELL, Norman
Born: Manchester, 29 January 1938.
Forward   5ft 9in; 11st 8lb (1959).

Career: Rochdale September 1956; Crewe Alexandra May 1963; Halifax

Town October 1966; Barrow coach 1968, then manager February 1969-February 1970; Preston North End coach 1974; Birmingham City coach 1979-1981, then chief scout until 1983; West Bromwich Albion chief scout in 1990. Blackburn Rovers coach until March 1978; Birmingham City coach march 1978.

Norman Bodell was the youngest manager in the Football League when he took charge at Barrow. His first full season was a disaster, though, with the club finishing second from bottom of the Third Division. It was the beginning of the end as Barrow lost their Football League status soon afterwards. Bodell played regularly for Rochdale and Crewe during his playing days. A qualified FA coach, Bodell worked with Bobby Charlton at Preston and Jim Smith at Birmingham City. He has organised the scouting systems at the Hawthorns and St Andrew's in recent years.

BODLE, Harold
Born: Woodlands, Doncaster, 4 January 1920.
Inside-forward   5ft 10in; 11st 10lb.
Career: Doncaster Schools; Silverwood Colliery; Rotherham United May 1938; Birmingham December 1938 (£3,000); wartime guest with Rotherham United and Doncaster Rovers; Bury March 1949; Stockport County October 1952; Accrington Stanley August 1953, then trainer and manager June 1959-June 1960; ran grocery store in Manchester 1960; ran sub-post office and also ran boys' team in Derby; Burton Albion trainer and manager 1962-1964.
Honours: Football League South champions 1946; Division Two champions 1948.

Harold Bodle helped Birmingham City to the Football League South title in 1945-46, when he scored 16 goals in 40 games. He was also the top scorer, with 14 goals, when the Blues won the Second Division title in 1947-48. Bodle, who scored 90 goals in 337 League appearances during his career, came near to a Wembley Cup Final when Birmingham lost to Derby in the 1946 semi-final replay. He scored on his debut for Accrington Stanley and was an inspiring captain at Peel Park as the club just missed out on the Northern Section title three years on the trot. When he became manager of Stanley, they had already begun the downward spiral which eventually saw them go out of business. Just when things seemed to be getting better, he was forced to sell striker Harvey McCreadie to Luton Town for £5,500. With the club hurtling towards Division Four and a financial crisis, Bodle was sacked.

BOLAND Alfred
Born: Burnley.
Career: Burnley 'A' team 1930; Burnley assistant secretary July 1932, secretary November 1932, then secretary-manager August 1935-1940.

Alf Boland was the youngest secretary in the Football League when he was appointed by Burnley in November 1932. Born and educated locally, Boland had played for the club's junior sides in the 1930s whilst working in the office of a textile mill in the Lancashire cotton town. He shared team responsibilities with the board and was never in sole charge at Turf Moor. Burnley were developing an excellent youth scheme and discovered a number of players including Harry Potts. Boland was more administrator

than out-and-out football man. He was also a regular contributor the the club's programme. He left the club just after the Football League closed down at the start of World War Two.

BOND, John F.
Born: Colchester, 17 December 1932.
Right-back   6ft 1in; 13st 4lb (1964).
Career: Colchester Casuals; West Ham United amateur 1949, professional March 1950; Torquay United January 1966; Gillingham coach 1969; Bournemouth & Boscombe Athletic manager May 1970-November 1973; Norwich City manager November 1973-October 1980; Manchester City manager October 1980-February 1983; Burnley manager June 1983-August 1984; Swansea City manager December 1984-December 1985; Birmingham City manager January 1986-May 1987; Shrewsbury Town assistant manager 1989, then manager January 1990. Shrewsbury Town manager January 1991-May 1993.
Honours: Football League representative; Division Two champions 1958, promotion 1975; Division Four runners-up 1971; FA Cup winners 1964, runners-up 1981; Football League Cup runners-up 1975.

John Bond made his name as an outspoken manager who brought glamour to ordinary clubs after a career as a full-back for West Ham United and Torquay United. A native of Colchester, he played for Essex Schools as a centre-forward and also appeared for Essex Army Cadets and Colchester Casuals before joining West Ham as an amateur in 1949, making his debut for the 'A' team at Great Yarmouth in the Eastern Counties League.

In 1950-51 he was converted to right-back in the Hammers' reserve team and made his League debut at Coventry in February 1952, becoming a regular after his demob from National Service in March 1953. He had represented the Army whilst in the services.

Bond developed into a steady, skilful defender who could read the game well and was a dead-ball expert, especially from the penalty spot. He played for the Football League on two occasions and toured South Africa with the FA in 1956. He scored eight goals in the Hammers' Second Division championship side of 1958-59 and also played in the club's 1964 FA Cup Final victory over Preston. Bond made 428 League and Cup appearances and scored 35 goals before moving to Torquay United

in January 1966. He helped them to promotion to Division Three in 1966 and went on to play 130 League games for the Plainmoor club before his retirement in 1969.

Bond joined Gillingham as coach and was on the point of moving to Plymouth Argyle in a similar capacity in 1970 but accepted the offer of the manager's job at Bournemouth instead. He quickly transformed the club and they won promotion to Division Three at the end of his first season in charge. Bournemouth almost went up again the following season but missed out in the last game of the season. Bond made Bournemouth a more democratic club, allowing the players to have their say about team affairs and tactics. He also introduced a radically new training policy. It was not long before the bigger clubs came knocking on the door.

After days of haggling, Bond left Bournemouth to join Norwich City and took his chief coach Ken Brown with him. The Dean Court club received £10,000 in compensation and Bond stayed at Carrow Road for seven years. After relegation in 1973-74, he took the Canaries back to Division One the following season. They were also losing Finalists in the Football League Cup in 1975.

In October 1980, John Bond accepted an offer to join Manchester City, replacing Malcolm Allison and Tony Book after City had made a dreadful start to the season. He made three major new signings, Tommy Hutchinson, Bobby McDonald and Gerry Gow, and City recovered to finish 12th after a spell of ten wins in 15 matches. They also reached the League Cup semi-finals and the FA Cup Final, where they lost to Spurs in a replay. Bond paid £1.2m for Trevor Francis in August 1981 but after looking championship contenders before Christmas, they finished tenth. After a 4-0 FA Cup defeat at Brighton, Bond resigned in February 1983 and City were eventually relegated.

After the glamour of Maine Road, he next managed three struggling clubs. In June 1983 he took over at Burnley, who had a disappointing season to finish 12th in Division Three. Bond was unpopular at Turf Moor and, indeed, in December 1992 he heeded police advice to stay away from Shrewsbury Town's game there. He joined Swansea City in December 1984 and they just avoided relegation at the end of that season. In October 1985, with the Swans on the brink of bankruptcy, Bond lost his job and was out of soccer for a while before returning as manager of Birmingham City in January 1986.

By now he seemed to have lost his magic touch. The Blues were in dire straits, having gone 18 games without a win and been put out of the FA Cup by non-League Altrincham. Bond was unable to halt their slide into the Second Division and after another season of struggle it came as no surprise when he was sacked in May 1987. He made a comeback as assistant manager to Asa Hartford at Shrewsbury Town and when Hartford was sacked in January 1990, Bond was made the caretaker manager, a position that was eventually made permanent. The Shrews had a great run at the end of the season to avoid relegation but the following season, 1991-92, they went down to the Fourth Division.

Sixty-year-old Bond resigned in May 1993 after Shrewsbury failed to make the Third Division play-offs after losing their last game of the season to relegation-threatened Northampton Town, 3-2 after being two goals up.

BONDS, William Arthur MBE

Born: Woolwich, 17 September 1946.
Defender   6ft ½in; 12st 10lb (1970).
Career: Eltham Green School; Moatbridge FC; Charlton Athletic amateur April 1962, professional September 1964; West Ham United May 1967 (£47,000), retired July 1988 to become youth team coach, then manager February 1990.

Honours: England Under-23 international (2 caps); Division Two champions 1981, runners-up 1991; FA Cup winners 1975, 1980; Football League Cup runners-up 1981; European Cupwinners' Cup runners-up 1976. Division One runners up 1993.

Billy Bonds gave West Ham wonderful service in his 21 years as a player at Upton Park and, indeed, to mark his loyalty to the game and to one club, he was awarded the MBE in the 1987 New Year's Honours List. He made a record 816 appearances for the Hammers from 1967 until he retired in the summer of 1988 to become youth team coach. Bonds had also made 100 appearances for Charlton prior to coming to Upton Park. He was unlucky never to have been capped for England at full international level and was an unused substitute in one game against Italy. An inspirational player, biting in the tackle and dynamic when making runs from midfield, Bonds captained the Hammers to two FA Cup Final victories. He took over as manager when Lou Macari resigned, re-establishing the Hammers' tradition for promoting from within. Bonds was 42 years old when he retired from playing. Bonds took West Ham back to Division One in 1991 but they were relegated straight back again. The Hammers also reached the FA Cup semi-final that season but lost 4-0 to Nottingham Forest after the controversial sending off of Tony Gale. They reached the semi-final of the Football League Cup in 1990 where they lost 6-3 on aggregate to Oldham Athletic.

The Hammers had looked promotion certainties for much of the 1992-93 season but nearly missed out after a late run from Portsmouth. Bonds will have to strengthen his squad if they are to stay in the Premier League as it is virtually the same as the one which was relegated the previous season.

BOOK, Anthony

Born: Bath, 4 September 1935.
Full-back   5ft 11in; 11st 2lb (1971).
Career: Bath City; Plymouth Argyle August 1964; Manchester City July 1966

(£17,000), retired November 1973 to become assistant manager, then manager April 1974-July 1979, then general manager, then coach to 1989 and caretaker manager November-December 1989, then coach again.

Honours: Footballer of the Year (joint with Dave Mackay) 1969; Football League champions 1968; FA Cup winners 1969; Football League Cup winners 1970, 1976; European Cupwinners' Cup winners 1970.

Tony Book was a latecomer to full-time football and did not kick his first ball in League soccer until just before his 29th birthday. It was Malcolm Allison who discovered Book when he was the manager of Southern League Bath City.

Book, though, could have joined Preston North End as a youngster but was advised to finish his apprenticeship as a bricklayer rather than take a risk with full-time professional soccer. When Allison moved to Plymouth Argyle, he took Book with him, signing him for £1,500 in August 1964. Book missed only three games in two seasons at Home Park, where he became a great success. He had poise, assurance, more than enough pace and the ability to size up a situation and act accordingly. And he was a revelation when he stepped into the First Division with Manchester City in July 1966.

Allison, now Joe Mercer's assistant at Maine Road, persuaded his boss to sign Book for £17,000. His greatest asset, from the club's point of view, was that he was a natural captain and he led City to some of their greatest triumphs. The League championship was won in 1967-68, but Book was hurt during the club's post-season tour of the USA and an Achilles tendon injury kept him out of the side until the turn of the year. It was reckoned that his absence was one of the main reasons for City's slump that season. Upon his return, they had a great run which ended when they beat Leicester City at Wembley in the 1969 FA Cup Final. Book was voted Footballer of the Year with Derby's Dave Mackay at the end of the season.

He was back at Wembley the following year, carrying off the Football League Cup after City had beaten West Bromwich Albion. Seven weeks later, in a Viennese downpour, they beat Gornik Zabrze 2-1 to bring home the European Cup-winners' Cup, their fourth major trophy in three seasons.

Book retired from playing in 1973 and joined City's coaching staff. Passed over as manager when Malcolm Allison left in 1973, he was first assistant manager to Johnny Hart and then Ron Saunders. When Saunders was dismissed, the directors turned to Book in an attempt to stabilise the situation at Maine Road after three managers in little over a year. He soon found some success as a manager when City won

the Football League Cup in 1976 and were runners-up in the League in 1976-77. During his spell as manager he signed some outstanding players, including Asa Hartford, Joe Royle, Dave Watson, Brain Kidd and Mick Channon.

In the summer of 1979, Book was made general manager with Allison returning as team manager, and he later had an important behind-the-scenes role. This included a spell as youthteam manager, where he found some outstanding youngsters to win the FA Youth Cup in 1986. When Mel Machin was sacked in November 1989, Tony Book returned as the caretaker manager until the appointment of Howard Kendall. Book reverted to his coaching post after this.

BOOT, Edmund

Born: Aughton, near Sheffield, 13 October 1915.
Wing-half   5ft 11in; 11st (1937).
Career: Aughton; Denaby United cs 1934; Sheffield United October 1935; Huddersfield Town March 1937-1952, coach December 1953, then manager January 1960-September 1964.

Honours: FA Cup runners-up 1938.

Eddie Boot gave Huddersfield Town many years of service and from 1937 until 1964 served the Terriers as a player, then coach and finally manager. He made over 300 appearances for Huddersfield, despite the war years, and played in the 1938 FA Cup Final for the club. He took over from Bill Shankly as manager in January 1960 and Huddersfield managed to stay in a healthy mid-table position during his tenure of office, except in 1960-61 when they had to fight against relegation.

His period in charge coincided with the abolition of the maximum wage and this put an increased burden on the club to produce their own players and Boot rose to the challenge. He also made some inspired signings including Pat Saward from Aston Villa. The Terriers reached the fifth round of the FA Cup in 1964 but Boot surprised everybody when he resigned after an inept performance by the team. There must have been more reasons behind his departure as it was said that he had become disillusioned with football.

BOOTH, Curtis 'Tommy'

Born: Gateshead, 12 October 1891.
Died: Amsterdam, 29 October 1949.
Centre-forward   5ft 9½in; 11st 5lb (1921).
Career: Wallsend Elm Villa; Newcastle United November 1913 (£15); Leeds City guest in wartime soccer; Norwich City September 1920-1923 (£800); Accrington Stanley player-manager

June 1923-May 1924; Erfurt FC (Germany) coach June 1925; coach Turkey (head coach to Turkish FA), Egypt and Holland in 1920s; Racing Club de Paris (France) 1930s.

Curtis Booth was a strong and able forward who was unable to obtain a regular first-team spot with the Magpies. Between 1920 and 1923 he made 62 appearances for Norwich scoring 11 goals. As the player-manager of Accrington Stanley he made only one appearance, suffering a knee ligament injury in the first match of the season which prevented him from playing again. He returned to take up his managerial duties for the last two months of the season before losing his job due to the financial problems at the club. They finished 13th in Division Three North in 1923-24 and made it to the first round of the FA Cup for the first time, losing to Charlton Athletic in a replay. Booth worked abroad in the late-1920s.

BOOTH, David

Born: Kexborough, Barnsley, 2 October 1948.
Left-back   5ft 10in; 11st 7lb (1970).
Career: Higham Rovers; Barnsley May 1967; Grimsby Town June 1972 (£6,000), retired through injury 1978 to become coach of juniors 1978-1979, assistant manager August 1979, then manager January 1982-October 1985; ran a property business in Tenerife 1985-1987; Darlington manager March 1987-February 1989; Peterborough United assistant manager 1989, then manager November 1990-January 1991.

A thoughtful and constructive defender, Booth made 161 League appearances for Barnsley before moving to Grimsby Town in June 1972. He was forced to retire at only 29, due to a knee injury, after playing in a further 199 games for the Mariners. Booth joined the coaching staff and in August 1979 became assistant manager under George Kerr. When Kerr departed, David Booth became the manager. The club finished fifth in Division Two in 1982-83, but after selling many of the best players and not investing the money received very successfully, the club went into decline. Later at Darlington, he lost the job with the Feethams club heading out of the Football League. Booth took over at Peterborough United from Mark Lawrenson, to whom he had been assistant manager, but lasted for just three months (16 games). The Posh still managed to gain promotion after Booth's departure, despite having three different managers during 1990-91.

BOOTH, Thomas

Born: Langley, Lancashire, 9 November 1949.
Centre-half   6ft 1in; 11st 12½lb (1970).
Career: Middleton Boys; Manchester City apprentice September 1965, professional August 1967; Preston North End October 1981 (£30,000), coach 1984, then manager April 1985-January 1986.

Honours: England Under-23 international (4 caps); FA Cup winners 1968; Football League Cup winners 1970, 1976, runners-up 1974; European Cupwinners' Cup winners 1970.

Tommy Booth had a meteoric rise to fame with Manchester City, scoring the winning goal in an FA Cup semi-final victory over Everton in 1969 five months after his debut for the club. He went on to gain a winners' medal. Once described by his manager Joe Mercer as 'a cross between Stan Cullis and Neil Franklin all rolled into one,' he lost his pivotal spot to Dave Watson but was a success when he moved to midfield to cover for the injured Colin Bell.

Booth first played for and then managed Preston. He was not a great success as a manager and was sacked after Preston entered one of the worst spells in their history. They were heading towards relegation to Division Four but the end came after a 4-1 FA Cup defeat at home to non-League Telford United.

BOURTON, Clarence Frederick Thomas

Born: Paulton, Bristol, 30 September 1908; Died: Bath, 20 April 1981.
Centre-forward 5ft 10in; 11st 7lb (1933).
Career: Paulton United (Bristol District League) 1926; Bristol City cs 1927; Blackburn Rovers May 1928 (£3,650 & a player); Coventry City 1931 (£750); Plymouth Argyle October 1937; Coventry City 1938-1944, player-manager October 1938-May 1939.

Honours: Division Three South champions 1936.

Clarrie Bourton was signed by Bristol City after scoring 30 goals for Paulton Rovers in the 1926-27 season. After only four appearances for the club, he was sold to Blackburn Rovers along with Albert Keeting for £3,630. It was a big outlay for an inexperienced player but he soon made a name for himself, scoring four goals for his new club against Manchester United at Old Trafford. He left his apprenticeship as a linotype operator when he moved north.

Bourton later scored 171 goals in 228 games for Coventry City and held the Third Division South goalscoring record for some time with 49 goals in 1931-32. In 1938, when Bob Hewison was suspended by the FA for illegal payments to amateurs, the club captain Clarrie Bourton was made the temporary player-manager. He reverted back to a player again at the end of Hewison's suspension.

BOWEN, David Lloyd

Born: Maesteg, Wales, 7 June 1928.
Wing-half 5ft 10in; 11st 1lb (1959).
Career: Northampton Town July 1947; Arsenal July 1950; Northampton Town manager July 1959-September 1967, and May 1969-May 1972, then general manager and secretary until 1986, then joined the board of directors; Wales team manager September 1964-1974.

Honours: Wales international (19 caps); Division Two runners-up 1965; Division Three champions 1963; Division Four promotion 1961.

Dave Bowen will always be remembered as the first manager to take a club from the Fourth to the First Division and back again. In fact, Bowen was not completely involved in Northampton's decline, as at the time they re-entered the Fourth Division he was the general manager and not in charge of team affairs.

He was born in Wales and played Rugby Union at school but his family moved to Northampton whilst he was still a boy and he was signed as a wing-half by the local club. There was an abundance of wing halves at the County Ground at this time and after only 12 appearances in two seasons, he was placed on the 'open-to-offers' list.

Bowen was serving in the RAF at the time and met the son of the Arsenal manager, Tom Whittaker, who recommended Dave to his father. Bowen signed for Arsenal in July 1950 but did not become a first-team regular until the retirement of Joe Mercer, due to a broken leg, in 1954. Bowen was to later captain both club and country. He gained a London Challenge Cup winners' medal in 1954, a Southern Floodlit Cup medal in 1959 and a Football Combination championship medal. He made 162 first-team appearances for the Gunners and also won 19 caps for Wales. In fact, Bowen made his international debut in September 1954, against Yugoslavia, before he commanded a regular first-team place at Highbury.

His greatest moment as a player was at the Solna Stadium in Stockholm in June 1958, when Wales qualified for the quarter-finals of the World Cup for the only time in their history. Bowen was captain in the play-off victory over Hungary and had an outstanding game.

He left Arsenal to return to the Cobblers in July 1959 as the club's new player-manager. They were struggling in the Fourth Division when he took over but within six years they were a First Division club, although that progress probably happened too quickly to allow for the development of the resources to sustain it. Under Bowen's leadership, promotion to Division Three was achieved in 1961. Two seasons later the Third Division championship was won and the Cobblers moved into Division Two for the first time in their history.

In 1965 they achieved a near-miracle when they won promotion to Division One and, for one season, the Fourth Division upstarts were playing hosts to Manchester United and Tottenham Hotspur. It was only a home defeat by nearest rivals Fulham, before a record crowd, which cost the Cobblers their First Division place and they were relegated despite gaining 33 points.

With the club's relegation into the Third Division in 1967, Bowen moved 'upstairs' to become general manager and this allowed Tony Marchi to take charge of team affairs. After relegation again to Division Four, Bowen was reinstated as manager in May 1969. Things did not improve and the club faced re-election problems in 1972. He resumed secretary-general manager duties in May 1972 and did not leave the club until 1988 to take up business interests outside football.

Bowen had won a reputation for wheeling and dealing on the transfer market and made some shrewd signings. He also made numerous finds such as Phil Neal and John Gregory, both of whom later played for England. Bowen also managed the Welsh national side from September 1964 until 1971. Things were always tough for him with only a small pool of players to call upon. He was in charge for 40 internationals of which Wales won only eight. The players did not always put a high priority on playing for their country and the side which actually appeared was rarely the one he had originally selected.

BOWMAN, John William

Born: Middlesbrough, 23 April 1879; Died: Sudbury, 26 January 1943.
Right-half 5ft 8½in; 12st (1904).
Career: Staffs junior football; Sheldon Juniors; Burslem Port Vale; Stoke August 1899; Queen's Park Rangers 1901-1905; Norwich City manager May 1905-June 1907; Croydon Common manager April 1912-cs 1916; Queen's Park Rangers director 1920s, then manager March-November 1931.

John Bowman became Norwich City's first-ever manager in 1905, when the club became a limited company and joined the Southern League. He was given a three-year contract but left after two years. He bought a number of players from northern clubs and seemed to have a special preference for Bury players. Norwich enjoyed their most successful spell in the Southern League during Bowman's time in office, finishing seventh and eighth. He made only four appearances for Stoke but played over 100 games for Queen's Park Rangers. He returned to that club as a director in the 1920s and had a period in charge of the team in his last year at the club. He also ran a sports shop in Harlesden at this time, supplying a number of League clubs with their kits. A member of Burslem Water Polo Club which won the Northern Counties championship, he was also captain of the North Staffordshire Harriers and excelled at sprinting.

BOWYER, Ian

Born: Ellesmere Port, 6 June 1951.
Midfield 5ft 10in; 11st 11lb (1984).
Career: Mid-Cheshire Boys; Little Sutton; Manchester City apprentice July 1966, professional August 1968; Orient June 1971 (£25,000); Nottingham Forest October 1973 (£40,000); Sunderland January 1981 (£50,000); Nottingham Forest January 1982 (£50,000); Hereford United July 1987, then player-manager October 1987-May 1990; Cheltenham coach February 1991.

Honours: Football League champions 1978; Football League Cup winners 1978, runners-up 1980; European Cup winners 1979, 1980; European Super Cup runners-up 1981.

Ian Bowyer played almost 800 games for his five clubs before his retirement in 1990. He played for Nottingham Forest for 13 years, over two periods, and made over 500 appearances for the Reds, appearing in two European Cup Finals for Forest with 1-0 victories over Malmö FF and Hamburger SV, in Munich and Madrid respectively, and also gained a European Super Cup runners-up medal against Valencia CF. He won a League championship medal in 1977-78, making 29 appearances, and a League Cup winners' medal in 1978, although he missed the 1979 League Cup Final and also missed the World Club Champions game in 1981.

Bowyer made a little bit of history on 21 April 1990 when he played in the same Hereford United side as his son, the first time this had happened since 1951 when father and son Alec and David Herd appeared in the same line-up. Bowyer's son was the cause of his sacking at Edgar Street. He refused to sign him as a professional for the club so that they could obtain a fee for him when he moved to Nottingham Forest in the summer of 1990. For this he was sacked. Hereford had not achieved a great deal during his three seasons in charge. Survival was the name of the game.

BRADLEY, Ronald John

Born: Ellingshall, near Wolverhampton, 24 April 1939.
Wing-half 5ft 10in; 12st 2lb (1964).
Career: South-East Staffordshire Boys; West Bromwich Albion amateur April 1954, professional June 1956; Norwich City July 1964; Wolverhampton Wanderers coach October 1966; Olympiakos (Greece) manager-coach 1970-1972; Scunthorpe United coach 1972, then manager June 1973-November 1974; Lybia national coach 1975; coached at Scunthorpe United and Derby County; Wolverhampton Wanderers coach October 1982; ran soccer camps in USA 1981-1987; FA coach August 1986.

Honours: England Youth international; Greek FA Cup winners 1971.

Despite gaining England youth international honours, Bradley had a moderate playing career. He made only 13 appearances for West Bromwich Albion and only four for Norwich. Later he gained a good reputation as a coach and was at Wolves when they won promotion to the First Division in 1967. Olympiakos won the Greek Cup under his management. In 1973-74, Scunthorpe United reached the fourth round of the FA Cup before going out to Newcastle United after a replay, but Bradley left the Old Show Ground with the Iron in 23rd position.

BRADSHAW, Francis

Born: Sheffield, 31 May 1885; Died: Deceased but details unknown.
Inside-left 5ft 9in; 12st 2lb (1922).
Career: Oxford Street Sunday School; Sheffield Schools; Sheffield Wednesday amateur 1904, professional cs 1904; Northampton Town cs 1910 (£250); Everton November 1911; Arsenal August 1914, retired May 1923; Aberdare Athletic manager May 1923-April 1924.

Honours: England international (1 cap); Football League representative; FA Cup winners 1907; London Challenge Cup winners 1923.

Frank Bradshaw was a strong and dangerous inside-left who was considered potent and brainy. A member of Sheffield Wednesday's 1907 FA Cup winning side, Bradshaw got his chance due to an injury to regular Harry Davis. He scored a hat-trick in his only England game, against Austria in Vienna in June 1908. He suffered from frequent knee trouble after this and moved to Northampton. Later sold to Everton for a big profit, Bradshaw then moved to Woolwich Arsenal, playing 132 times for them and ending his playing days as a full-back. He remained for just 11 months as Aberdare Athletic's manager and they finished 12th in the Third Division South in 1923-24. The club was in a poor financial state.

BRADSHAW, Harry

Died: 1921.
Career: Burnley player 1891-1899 (secretary 1896-1899); Arsenal manager June 1899-March 1904; Fulham manager April 1904-May 1909; Secretary of the Southern League May 1990-1921.

Honours: Division Two champions 1898, runners-up 1904; Southern League champions 1906, 1907.

Harry Bradshaw was Fulham's first full-time manager, taking the club to two Southern League titles and eventually into the Football League. The Cottagers also reached an FA Cup semi-final and narrowly missed promotion to the First Division in 1908. Bradshaw was also instrumental in re-developing Craven Cottage into a modern stadium.

When his contract expired in 1909, he chose to become the secretary of the Southern League. A good administrator, shrewd businessman and clever tactician, Bradshaw had previously been in charge of Woolwich Arsenal. The club was in bad way when he took over but he quickly transformed it, to win promotion back to Division One just as he decided to become Fulham's manager in 1904.

BRADSHAW, Joseph

Born: Burnley, c.1880.
Outside Right 5ft 7in; 10st 7lb (1910).
Career: Woolwich Polytechnic; West Norwood; Southampton; Woolwich Arsenal; Fulham March 1904; Chelsea May 1909; Queen's Park Rangers cs 1910; Southend United player-manager 1912-1919; Swansea Town manager cs 1919-May 1926; Fulham manager May 1926-May 1929; Bristol City manager August 1929-February 1932.

Honours: Division Three South champions 1925; Southern League Division Two promotion 1913.

Joe Bradshaw, who had played for Fulham when his father was the manager, followed in his father's footsteps by becoming manager of the Cottagers in 1926. An average winger, he rarely made the first team at either Fulham or Chelsea but helped Southend United back to Division One of the Southern League in 1913. He left that club for Swansea Town in 1919, piloting them into the Football League and to the Third Division South championship in 1925. The following season the Swans reached the semi-final of the FA Cup before losing to Bolton Wanderers at White Hart Lane. They also finished fifth in the Second Division.

Bradshaw had a difficult time at Fulham. A number of established players were past their best and the replacements that he obtained performed, overall, quite poorly. The Cottagers were relegated for the first time in 1928 and although they scored over 100 goals in 1928-29, Bradshaw was not able to save his job. Things did not improve much at Bristol City. With only three wins in 32 games in 1931-32, he was sacked with the club in a desperate financial position. Brother of Will and son of Harry, he later worked in insurance.

BRAND, Ralph Laidlaw.

Born: Edinburgh, 8 December 1936.
Centre-forward 5ft 7in; 10st (1964).
Career: Carricknowe School; Slateford Athletic; Broxburn Athletic 1952; Glasgow Rangers June 1952; Manchester City August 1965 (£25,000); Sunderland August 1967 (£5,000); Raith Rovers June 1969-1970; Hamilton Academical 1971; Darlington player December 1972-June 1973; Albion Rovers coach 1971-1972, manager August 1973-May 1974; Dunfermline Athletic coach cs 1974.

Honours: Scotland international (8 caps); Under-23 international (10 caps); Scottish League representative (5 caps); Scottish League champions 1959, 1961, 1963, 1964; Football League Division

Two champions 1966; Scottish Cup winners 1962, 1963, 1964; Scottish League Cup 1961, 1962, 1964, 1965.
Ralph Brand was a smart, tricky player who had good ball control. He was capped eight times for Scotland and won many medals with Glasgow Rangers, including four Scottish League championship titles and three Scottish Cup winners triumphs. He scored in Rangers' 2-0 triumph over Kilmarnock in 1961 and their 3-1 win over Hearts in the following year's Final. He also played in the European Cup-winners' Cup Final defeat against Fiorentina in 1961. After he moved south to join Manchester City, Brand helped them back to the First Division in 1966. He was briefly in charge at Darlington, who, under his management in 1972-73, experienced one of their worst-ever campaigns, winning only seven games all season. Brand resigned after they had only narrowly defeated Yeovil Town in the re-election poll.

BRANFOOT, Ian

Born: Gateshead, 26 January 1947.
Defender 5ft 10in; 12st 2lb (1970).

Career: Gateshead; Sheffield Wednesday July 1965; Doncaster Rovers December 1969; Lincoln City July 1973, coach 1978; Southampton coach; Reading assistant manager 1983, then manager January 1984-October 1989; Crystal Palace assistant manager November 1989; Southampton manager June 1991.

Honours: Division Three champions 1986; Division Four champions 1976, promotion 1984; Zenith Data Systems Cup runners-up 1992.

Ian Branfoot played occasionally for Sheffield Wednesday as a wing-half or full-back before moving to Doncaster Rovers in 1969. He made 156 League appearances at Belle Vue and 166 for Lincoln City, being an ever-present when Lincoln were Fourth Division champions in 1976. As a manager at Reading, he initially found great success but this was followed by a steady decline in the club's fortunes. The 1983-84 season saw promotion to Division Three and two seasons later, Reading walked away with the Third Division championship with 94 points to reach the Second Division for the first time since 1926. They were relegated after only one season, however, and after a struggle to avoid relegation again, Branfoot was sacked in October 1989 with the crowd calling for his head. Southampton struggled in the League under Branfoot but did well in Cup competitions. They reached the quarter-finals of the FA Cup and the Final of the Zenith Data Systems Cup where they lost 3-2 to Nottingham Forest at Wembley.

Branfoot had a difficult season in

1992-93. He was barracked by the fans early in the season as the Saints struggled near the foot of the Premier League. Their form came in fits and starts but they eventually avoided the drop.

BRAY, Jack

Born: Oswaldtwistle, 22 April 1909; Died: Blackburn 20 November 1982.
Left-half 5ft 9ins; 10st 9lb (1937).
Career: St Andrew's School; Oswaldtwistle; Clayton Olympia; Manchester Central 1928; Manchester City October 1929 (£1,000), retired during the war; Watford manager March 1947-January 1948; Nelson coach February-September 1948.

Honours: England international (6 caps); Football League representative (5 caps); Football League champions 1937; FA Cup winners 1934, runners-up 1933.

Jack Bray was a fast, clever wing-half who was an imaginative and consistent player. He made over 350 appearances for Manchester City in League, FA Cup and wartime games before retiring at the end of hostilities. Bray was an elegant figure, who danced through 90 minutes of football, rarely becoming ruffled. He gained losers' and winners' medal in the FA Cup, in 1933 finishing on the losing side 3-0 to Everton and the following year played in City's 2-1 victory over Portsmouth at Wembley. He also appeared in City's First Division championship side of 1936-37. During his brief stay as Watford's manager, the side struggled near the foot of the Third Division South.

BREEDON, John Norman, 'Jack'

Born: South Hindley, near Barnsley, 29 December 1907.
Goalkeeper 5ft 9in; 11st 6lb (1933).
Career: South Hindley; Barnsley September 1928; Sheffield Wednesday November 1930; Manchester United July 1935-1945; Halifax Town manager August 1947-November 1950; Bradford manager January-October 1955; Leeds United scout in early 1960s.

Jack Breedon was a former miner who developed into a spectacular goalkeeper during wartime soccer with Manchester United, although in peacetime he was mainly a reserve at Old Trafford and with Sheffield Wednesday. He made 47 appearances for the Owls as reserve to Jack Brown and 35 for United before 1939, but made 160 appearances in the regional wartime competitions.

As manager of Halifax Town after the war, Breedon experienced three years of struggle. Twice in this period, Halifax had to seek re-election to the Third Division North and, despite wholesale changes, he was unable to find a winning combination. When relieved of his duties, Breedon stayed at The Shay until they could find a replacement. He had just nine months at Bradford and after a poor start to the 1955-56 season, he resigned.

BREMNER, William John

Born: Stirling, 9 December 1942.
Right-half 5ft 5in; 9st 10lb (1964).
Career: Stirling Schoolboys; Gowanhill Juniors (Stirling); Leeds United amateur cs 1958, professional December 1959; Hull City September 1976 (£35,000), retired May 1978; Doncaster Rovers manager November 1978-October 1985 (played two games in emergency); Leeds United manager October 1985-September 1988; Doncas-

ter Rovers manager July 1989-November 1991.

Honours: Scotland international (54 caps); Under-23 international (4 caps); Schoolboy international; Footballer of the Year 1970; Football League champions 1969, 1974; Division Two champions 1964; Division Four runners-up 1984, promotion 1981; FA Cup winners 1972, runners-up 1965, 1970, 1973; Football League Cup winners 1968; European Cup runners-up 1975; Inter-Cities Fairs Cup winners 1968.

Billy Bremner skippered Leeds United during their greatest era and also led his country. This small red-haired player was highly skilled, determined and brave and also had an eye for goal, scoring 115 in 773 appearances for Leeds. In his early days at Elland Road, Bremner regularly had brushes with soccer's authorities but he matured to collect many honours with the club and had the knack of scoring goals which turned big games.

Totally dedicated and single-minded, he made up for lack of height and weight with determination and a never-say-die spirit. As a manager at Doncaster Rovers, he built teams on the basis of hard-workers rather than experienced talent due to cash constraints. Rovers had languished for years in the Fourth Division but Bremner soon found a winning formation and promotion. After relegation in 1983, they were back again in the Third Division the year after. He sold a number of youngsters for good fees including Ian Snodin to Leeds for £200,000.

Bremner took over at Elland Road in October 1985 and two years later guided the club to the semi-finals of the FA Cup, where they lost 3-2 to Coventry City at Hillsborough. They also just missed out on promotion to Division One after losing to two extra-time goals from Charlton Athletic in the Second Division play-off final. He was sacked in September 1988, after a poor start to the season, taking over at Doncaster again in July 1989. The highspot of Bremner's second spell in charge at Belle Vue came when Rovers went top of the Fourth Division at the turn of the year in 1991. Thereafter the club's form slumped and Bremner was sacked with the club at the bottom of the League.

BRENNAN, Frank

Born: Annathill, 23 April 1924.
Centre-half 6ft 2in; 13st 13lb (1950).
Career: Coatbridge St Patrick's; Airdrie amateur February 1941, later professional; Newcastle United May 1946 (£7,500); North Shields player-coach

March 1956; coach in Singapore and Trinidad from 1962; North Shields trainer-coach April 1967; Darlington trainer 1970, then manager August 1971-January 1972; North Shields trainer-coach February-October 1972

Honours: Scotland international (7 caps); Wartime international (2 caps); FA Cup winners 1951, 1952; FA Amateur Cup winners 1969.

Frank Brennan was the backbone of the Magpies defence for many years. Cool, steady and a tough no-nonsense player, Brennan was a legendary figure on Tyneside. He played in the fine Newcastle United sides of the early-1950s and won FA Cup winners' medals in 1951 and 1952. After one of his many battles with the club's hierarchy, he left St James' Park to join North Shields whilst still at his peak. He later coached that club to their FA Amateur Cup victory in 1969. His short spell as Darlington's manager brought little success with the club near the foot of the Fourth Division. He ran sports outfitters in Newcastle before retiring to live in Whitley Bay.

BRETTELL, Frank

Career: St Domingo (Liverpool) player-secretary; Everton player, assistant secretary and finally secretary; Bolton Wanderers secretary 1896-1897; Tottenham Hotspur secretary-manager February 1897-February 1898; Portsmouth manager May 1898-June 1901; Plymouth Argyle manager 1903-1905.

Frank Brettell was a universally respected manager who started as a football administrator in 1875. He seemed to specialise in setting up new professional clubs and was employed by both Portsmouth and Plymouth Argyle in this capacity as well as being one of the founder-members of Everton. In his playing days, he was a sturdy full-back and assistant secretary of the Goodison club, playing in nearly every position for Everton in their early days.

He joined the *Liverpool Mercury* as a reporter when he retired from playing. As Spurs' manager he introduced the club to the Southern League and persuaded many northern stars to join the club. He left when offered a substantial rise to manage Pompey and built the club from scratch to finish as runners-up in their first season in the Southern League. He later did a similar job for Plymouth Argyle.

BRIGGS J.

Career: Sheffield United; possibly Attercliffe secretary 1902 and honorary secretary of Sheffield and Hallamshire FA executive; Rotherham United manager cs 1923-1925.

In Briggs' first season in charge at Rotherham they finished fourth in the Northern Section after relegation the previous season. However, fortunes waned the following season and financial problems accumulated rapidly as the team plunged to the foot of the table. They finished bottom with only 21 points and only seven wins all season. At the end of the season, County amalgamated with Rotherham Town to become Rotherham United and Briggs was replaced by Billy Heald.

BRITTON, Clifford Samuel

Born: Hanham, 27 August 1909; Died: 1 December 1975.
Right-half   5ft 11in; 11st 2lb (1937).
Career: Hanham Athletic; Hanham United Methodists; Bristol St George's; Bristol Rovers amateur 1926, professional cs 1928; Everton June 1930,

retired October 1945 after guesting for Bristol Rovers and Aldershot in the war; Burnley manager October 1945-September 1948; Everton manager September 1948-February 1956; Preston North End manager August 1956-April 1961; Hull City manager July 1961-November 1969, then general manager until October 1971 when he retired.

Honours: England international (9 caps); Wartime international (12 caps); Football League representative (4 caps); Division Two runners-up 1947, 1954; Division Three champions 1966; FA Cup winners 1933.

Cliff Britton was well-known as a strict disciplinarian and it was said that his ideal team would consist of 11 tee-total bachelors.

Tommy Docherty, who played for him whilst Britton was manager of Preston, described him as strict and tense. He said: "I don't think I have ever seen a man who appears less able to relax in my life. He demanded great discipline and we would never dare to be late for training. He was a cold man, difficult to approach and lacked a sense of humour."

Pre-match talks were very detailed and he surveyed the opposition's strength and weaknesses. Britton's ways paid with results as he was successful at Burnley, Everton, Preston and Hull City.

After 55 appearances for Bristol Rovers he joined Everton for a four-figure fee and made 221 League appearances for the Toffees before the outbreak of war. Britton gained an FA Cup winners' medal in 1933 but made only one appearance in Everton's League championship season of 1938-39. He was, however, a member of a famous wartime England half-back line along with Joe Mercer and Stan Cullis and won a reputation as a wing-half with great style and polish, with precision passes and clear thinking.

Britton became Burnley's manager in October 1945 and in the first proper post-war season, the Clarets won promotion to Division One and lost in the FA Cup Final to Charlton Athletic as Burnley came to be noted as a team of dour defence.

In September 1948, Britton became Everton's manager at the age of 39. He fought to keep the club in Division One but wished to avoid being drawn into the inflationary transfer market. Britton persisted in developing home-grown talent but after a gradual slide, Everton dropped into the Second Division in 1951. It took three years for the Toffees to return to the top flight and he was in conflict with the directors who wanted him to buy success.

Britton left Goodison Park in unhappy circumstances in February 1956. Everton were planning a six-weeks tour of North America and the club wanted to appoint a caretaker manager whilst he was away. He took exception to this and resigned. Mud was thrown around in public about his acrimonious departure, leading to the resignation of the chairman. Britton had become disillusioned at being unable to manage the club with what he considered was the necessary freedom to do the job satisfactorily.

Six months later, Preston managed to persuade Britton back into football as their new manager. During his five-year stay at Deepdale, Preston went close to the League championship twice, in 1956-57 and 1957-58. With the retirement of Tom Finney in April 1960, however, the club went into decline and although there was reason for some optimism with the youth side reaching the FA Youth Cup Final in 1960, sadly, they had not developed in time for Preston to avoid relegation to Division Two and Britton resigned in April 1961.

Two months later he was back in football in charge at Hull City. Progress at Boothferry Park was slow with financial constraints within the club plus the abolition of the maximum wage hindering player recruitment. Britton therefore developed a highly successful youth policy. In January 1963, he was offered a ten-year contract and then given money to spend on team building.

The ground was improved with a new cantilever stand and a new sports complex. After the acquisition of three new forwards, Ken Houghton, Ken Wagstaffe and Ian Butler, the Tigers won the Third Division championship in 1965-66 and then held their own in the higher division. In November 1969, though, the board decided to appoint a younger man and Britton became general manager.

BROADIS, Ivan Arthur 'Ivor'

Born: Poplar, 18 December 1922.
Inside-forward   5ft 9in; 11st (1950).
Career: Cooper's Company School (Bow); Finchley; Northfleet; Finchley; Tottenham Hotspur and Millwall as guest in wartime soccer; Carlisle United player-manager August 1946-January 1949; Sunderland January 1949 (£8,000); Manchester City October 1951 (£25,000); Newcastle United October 1953 (£20,000); Carlisle United player-coach July 1955 (£3,500); Queen of the South June 1959-1960, coach until 1962; sports journalist 1960-1980s on Carlisle Evening News and Star.

Honours: England international (14 caps); Football League representative (3 caps).

Ivor Broadis was the first manager to transfer himself, although William Rowley, who was Stoke's secretary, also transferred himself to Leicester City back in August 1898. Rowley was suspended two months later when the FA rejected his registration. Broadis was only 23 and without Football League experience when he became Carlisle's player-manager after guesting for the club during World War Two. He sold himself to Sunderland for £18,000, leaving the club in a healthier state than when he took over.

Surprisingly, he never managed again. In his two spells at Brunton Park, Broadis scored 84 goals in 250 games. A creative, old-fashioned inside-

forward, he possessed a lethal shot. He played in the 1954 World Cup finals but missed the FA Cup Final the following year with Manchester City due to loss of form.

BROCKLEBANK, Robert Edward

Born: Finchley, 23 May 1908; Died: Brixham, September 1981.
Inside-forward   6ft; 12st (1933).
Career: Finchley Boys; Finchley August 1925; Aston Villa May 1929; Burnley March 1936; Chesterfield manager September 1945-January 1949; Birmingham City manager January 1949-October 1954; West Bromwich Albion coach/scout October 1954-March 1955; Hull City manager March 1955-May 1961; Bradford City manager May 1961-October 1964; retired to Brixham in 1964.

Honours: Division Three runners-up 1959.

Brocklebank was one of eight brothers and was one of Finchley's most illustrious players before joining Aston Villa. His chances were limited at Villa Park but he developed as an inside-forward when he moved to Burnley and earned the nickname 'The Toff' because of his gentlemanly approach to life and football. He scored 33 goals in 121 League games for Burnley and also starred in wartime football for the club.

After the war he became the manager of Chesterfield, establishing them as a Second Division side, then joined Birmingham City during difficult times and the club was relegated to Division Two. The Blues reached the semi-final of the FA Cup in 1951, losing to Blackpool 2-1 in a replay, as Brocklebank rebuilt the club who were on the brink of honours when he left in 1954. Hull City were relegated the season after he took over at Boothferry Park but the Tigers entered the newly-formed Third Division in 1958. He resigned to take over at Bradford City. Twice the Bantams just missed promotion from the Fourth Division, finishing fifth on both occasions, and after an average start to the 1964-65 season, Brocklebank resigned.

BROMILOW, Thomas George

Born: Liverpool, 7 October 1894; Died: Nuneaton, 4 March 1959.
Left-half   5ft 7in; 10st 8lb (1922).
Career: West Dingle (Liverpool & District); United West Dingle Presbyterian Club (Liverpool); Liverpool 1919, retired May 1930; Amsterdam as coach cs 1931; Burnley manager October 1932-July 1935; Crystal Palace manager July 1935-June 1936, reappointed December 1936-July 1939; Leicester City manager July 1939-May 1945; coach in Holland 1945; Newport County manager May 1946-January 1950; Leicester City chief scout and trainer July 1950 until his death.

Honours: England international (5 caps); Football League representative (6 caps); Football League champions 1922, 1923.

A constructive left-half, who was a crisp tackler and fine passer, Tommy Bromilow was the brains behind Liverpool's League championship titles of 1922 and 1923. Invalided out of the Army due to septic poisoning, he recovered to become a fine servant to Liverpool, playing in 341 games for the club. When he took over as manager of Burnley, they just missed out on relegation to the Third Division in 1933.

Thereafter they were a mid-table side but did reach the quarter-finals of the FA Cup in 1933 and the semi-finals in 1935, when they lost 3-0 to Sheffield Wednesday at Villa Park. At Crystal Palace he resigned in June 1936 after a row with the directors but was reappointed six months later. Palace finished as runners-up in the Third Division South in 1938-39.

Disappointed, he moved to Leicester City where his sides won the Midland Cup in 1941 and the War League South in 1942. He was not a great success at Newport after the war. The club finished bottom of the Second Division in 1947, conceding 133 goals, and they was heading for re-election when he left in 1950. He died on a train in Nuneaton, returning from watching a game.

BROOME, Frank Henry

Born: Berkhampstead, 11 June 1915.
Centre-forward   5ft 7in; 9st 8lb (1937).
Career: Boxmoor United; Berkhampstead Town; Aston Villa November 1934; Derby County September 1946; Notts County October 1949; Brentford July 1953; Crewe Alexandra October 1953; Shelbourne February 1955; Notts County assistant trainer cs 1955, caretaker manager January-May 1957; Exeter City manager January 1958-May 1960; Southend United manager May-December 1960; Bankstown (New South Wales) manager-coach July 1961-October 1962; Corinthians (Sydney) manager-coach 1962; Exeter City manager May 1967-February 1969; Middle East coaching in 1970s.
Honours: England international (7 caps); Wartime international (1 cap); FA Tour of Australia 1951; Division Two champions 1938; Division Three South champions 1950; Football League North Cup winners 1944; Football League Cup winners 1942.

A leading scorer for Aston Villa before the war, Frank Broome was often played as a thrustful winger for Derby and was adept at switching to the centre-forward berth. In 1938 he played in the infamous England-Germany game in Berlin when the players were forced to give the Nazi salute. Broome played for England in four different positions in his seven appearances. Despite being small, Broome was extremely dangerous with his remarkable speed and marksmanship.

As the caretaker manager of Notts County he helped the club through a transitional period to avoid relegation to the Third Division. He found himself in a difficult position as assistant to Tommy Lawton and resigned in December 1957. He had two periods in charge at Exeter and was briefly the manager of Southend.

BROWN, Alan Winston

Born: Corbridge, 26 August 1914.

Centre-half   5ft 11in; 11st 11lb (1937).
Career: Spen Black & White; Huddersfield Town April 1933; Burnley February 1946; Notts County October 1948 (£15,000); Burnley manager August 1954-July 1957; Sheffield Wednesday coach 1957 (briefly); Sunderland manager July 1957-cs 1964; Sheffield Wednesday manager cs 1964-February 1968; Sunderland manager February 1968-November 1972; coach in Norway.
Honours: Football League representative; Division Two runners-up 1964; FA Cup runners-up 1947-1966.

Alan Brown made his name as a manager through his ability to discover fine young players and develop them and his seemingly magic touch as a finder and developer of players was shown at all the clubs that he managed.

Never a first-team regular for Huddersfield, he managed only 38 appearances in five seasons before the war came in 1939. It was not until after the war that Brown made a name for himself in a Burnley side which won promotion to the First Division in 1946-47. Brown was a dominant figure in a defence which conceded only 29 goals. The following season, Burnley reached the FA Cup Final at Wembley but lost 1-0 to Charlton Athletic. In October 1948, he moved to Notts County for a £15,000 fee but made only 13 appearances for the Meadow Lane club.

Brown's first managerial post was at Burnley in August 1954. Due to their small attendances, they could not afford to compete on the transfer market with their bigger neighbours. So, with the backing of chairman Bob Lord, Brown developed Burnley's youth policy in his three seasons at Turf Moor. He also gained a reputation for his innovative thinking on set-pieces. Free-kicks in range of goal became a Burnley speciality and a pattern for others to follow, especially ideas for kicks that worked the ball around the defensive wall.

After a short spell as Sheffield Wednesday's coach in 1957, Brown became Sunderland's manager in July of that year. The Wearsiders were struggling to maintain their First Division status and the board knew they needed a young, enterprising manager to rebuild them up to their former glory. The club had over spent on star names without much success. Unfortunately, at the end of the 1957-58 season Sunderland were relegated for the first time in their history.

Brown was a tracksuit manager who could often be found leading the players on a four-lap race around the ground rather than sitting behind a desk. He unearthed a number of future stars with the help of ace scout Charlie Ferguson. One of the best was the big Irish centre-half Charlie Hurley, who was signed from Millwall. Sunderland finally made it back to the First Division in 1964 after going close on a number of occasions.

Rather than enjoy his new success, Brown moved on to manage Sheffield Wednesday in the close season of 1964. His period at Hillsborough saw the Owls reach the 1966 FA Cup Final. From being two goals up they threw away victory to lose 3-2. It was Brown's second defeat in a Final. Wednesday maintained good positions in Division One but struggled near the bottom in 1967-68 and Brown received an offer to return to Sunderland.

As with his first spell, the club was relegated to Division Two in 1969-70. Brown was criticised for being more interested in developing young players

than dealing with the more complex problems of mature, established professionals. Sunderland challenged for promotion for much of 1971-72 but when they looked like missing out again the following season, Brown was sacked in November 1972. His cousin, Austen Campbell, played for Huddersfield Town.

BROWN, Allan Duncan

Born: Kennoway, Fife, 12 October 1926.
Inside-forward   5ft 10in; 11st 11lb (1964).
Career: Kennoway; East Fife 1944; Blackpool December 1950 (£27,000); Luton Town Feburary 1957 (£8,000); Portsmouth March 1961; Wigan Athletic player-manager 1963-1966; Luton Town manager November 1966-December 1968; Torquay United manager January 1969-October 1971; Bury manager April 1972-November 1973; Nottingham Forest manager November 1973-January 1975; Southport manager January-May 1976; Blackpool manager May 1976-February 1978; Quadsia (Kuwait) coach 1978; Blackpool manager March 1981-April 1982.
Honours: Scotland international (14 caps); Scottish League representative (1 cap); Division Three champions 1962; Division Four champions 1968; FA Cup runners-up 1959; Scottish Cup runners-up 1950.

Allan Brown was unfortunate with injuries, twice having to miss FA Cup Finals for Blackpool. He eventually appeared in a Wembley Final for Luton Town in 1959. Brown played in one of East Fife's most successful sides, appearing in two Scottish Cup Finals for the club in 1950. He cost Blackpool £25,000 in December 1950.

A fine inside-forward, 'Bomber' Brown packed a stunning shot and used his strength and pace to great effect. He played in the 1954 World Cup for Scotland and but for injuries would have won more than 14 caps. Brown twice broke his leg and had two cartilage operations during his career.

He started in management with Cheshire League side Wigan Athletic. They won that competition once and also finished as runners-up. Wigan won four cups in a season and once went 53 games without defeat. Luton Town saw his potential and appointed him as manager when the Hatters were at their lowest ebb, 91st in the Football League.

An isolated but dedicated man, Brown's single-mindedness soon brought Luton success. A strict disciplinarian and fitness fanatic, he saw them win the Fourth Division cham-

pionship in 1968 and they were on the way to promotion again when he was sacked after applying for a vacant post at Leicester City. At Bury he got the club out of debt for the first time in years by selling players for big fees after having previously bought them for a song. Brown could not get Forest out of the Second Division, though, and was not too successful at Southport or Blackpool. The Seasiders were relegated in each of his two spells at the club.

BROWN, Frank

Born: Rotherham, autumn 1890.
Centre-half   5ft 11in; 12st (1920).
Career: Barnsley 1910; Rotherham County 1914; Huddersfield Town 1915; Blackpool August 1919; Exeter City May 1921; Pontypridd June 1922; Torquay United 1923, trainer on retiring from playing, then manager May 1932-May 1938; Chester manager May 1938-May 1953.

As a manager, Frank Brown had a fine eye for raw, young talent. As a player he had found it difficult to break into the Blackpool side after the war but after joining Torquay United 1923 his career took an upturn. He became the club's trainer and in 1926-27 they won the Southern League title and were runners-up in the Western League. Torquay were elected to the Third Division South in 1927 and as manager he helped establish the side as a Football League club. At Chester he saw the club mainly hover near the foot of the Third Division North but they did finish third in 1946-47. He achieved miracles keeping both Torquay and Chester going during difficult times.

BROWN, George

Born: Mickley, Northumberland, 22 June 1903; Died: Birmingham, 10 June 1948.
Centre-forward 5ft 9in; 10st 7lb (1923).
Career: Mickley Colliery; Huddersfield Town April 1921; Aston Villa August 1929 (£5,000); Burnley September 1934 (£1,400); Leeds United, September 1935 (£3,100); Darlington manager October 1936-October 1938; licensee in Aston.
Honours: England international (9 caps); Football League representative (3 caps); Football League champions 1924, 1925, 1926; FA Cup runners-up 1928.

George Brown was a pit boy who was on strike when he signed for Huddersfield Town in 1921. He scored 143 goals in 214 League games for the Town and gained three League championship medals at the club. Brown was a skilful dribbler with a hard shot and a good eye for an opening. In January 1932 he scored five goals for Aston Villa in an 8-3 win at Leicester City. As the manager of Darlington, he saw the club avoid having to apply for re-election only on goal-average in 1937-38 and also lose at home to non-League Scarborough in the FA Cup. He was sacked in October 1938.

BROWN, Joseph

Born: Crumlington, 26 April 1929.
Wing-half   5ft 9in; 10st 7lb (1923).
Career: Middlesbrough April 1946; Burnley August 1952; Bournemouth June 1954; Aldershot July 1960; Burnley coach 1961, senior coach from 1969, also chief scout then manager January 1976-February 1977.

Joe Brown was Jimmy Adamson's assistant at Burnley before taking over as manager on Adamson's departure.

Brown had worked at Turf Moor for many years prior to becoming the manager. He had become the senior coach in 1969 and also chief scout for a period. The 1975-76 season ended with relegation to Division Two and he was unable to stop the slide the following season. He had made six appearances for Burnley in the 1950s and played 215 games for Bournemouth after leaving Turf Moor, plus a handful of games for Middlesbrough and Aldershot.

BROWN, Kenneth

Born: Forest Gate, 16 February 1934.
Centre-half   6ft; 13st 9lb (1964).
Career: Dagenham Schools; Neville United; West Ham United October 1951; Torquay United May 1967; Hereford United cs 1969; Bournemouth & Boscombe Athletic coach May 1970-November 1973; Norwich City assistant manager November 1973-1980, then manager November 1980-November 1987; Shrewsbury Town caretaker manager November-December 1987; Plymouth Argyle manager July 1988-February 1990.

Honours: England international (1 cap); Division Two champions 1958, 1986, promotion 1982; FA Cup winners 1964; Football League Cup winners 1966, 1985; European Cup-winners' Cup winners 1965.

Ken Brown is one of life's most affable characters whose infectious humour brings pleasure to all around him and was a product of the West Ham 'academy' along with John Bond, Frank O'Farrell, Malcolm Allison and Malcolm Musgrove. Brown made his name as a centre-half with West Ham and as assistant manager to John Bond at Bournemouth and Norwich City, whom he later managed.

His family lived in Dagenham, where Brown attended Lymington Secondary Modern School. He represented Dagenham Boys and was spotted by a West Ham scout playing for Neville United in the Dagenham League. He signed professional for the Hammers in October 1951 and made his debut at Rotherham United in February 1953. Brown found it difficult to become a first-team regular and spent much of his early career playing for the Reserves. But when regular centre-half, Malcolm Allison, became ill in 1957, Brown took over the pivotal position and was one of the stars in the Hammers' march to promotion to Division One in 1957-58. Brown made one appearance for England, in 1959 against Northern Ireland at Wembley.

A quiet, competent defender who was creative but seldom drawn out of position, Brown was always cool, calm and collected. He went on to play 453 League and Cup matches for the Hammers. In 1964 he appeared in their FA Cup winning side, which beat Second Division Preston, and the following season picked up a European Cup-winners' Cup winners medal when the Hammers beat Munich 1860, 2-0 in the Final at Wembley. In 1966 Brown played in West Ham' Football League Cup winning side which beat West Bromwich Albion 5-3 on aggregate in a two-legged final.

In May 1967, he moved to Torquay United to team up with his former Upton Park teammate John Bond. After a short spell at Hereford United in 1969-70, Brown rejoined Bond at Dean Court as trainer-coach in 1970. Bournemouth won promotion to Division Four in 1971-72, finishing runners-

up. The following season they just missed out on promotion again. He helped turn Ted McDougall into one of the most sought after strikers in the League.

When Bond moved on to manager Norwich City, Brown followed him in November 1973 to become assistant manager at Carrow Road. After relegation at the end of 1973-74, Norwich soon bounced back as runners-up behind Manchester United the following season. Norwich also appeared in a League Cup Final in 1975, where they lost 1-0 to Aston Villa. Brown took over as manager of the Canaries when Bond joined Manchester City in November 1980. During his seven years as manager at Carrow Road, he was even more successful than Bond. Norwich won promotion to Division One in 1982 and 1986 and also won the League Cup in 1985, beating Sunderland 1-0 in the Final but also being relegated to the Second Division.

In November 1987, Brown was sacked after 14 years at Carrow Road, a victim of boardroom changes. Later that month he took over as caretaker manager at Shrewsbury Town but resigned after only two weeks, fuelling speculation that a move back to Norwich was on the cards. It was not to be and in July 1988, Brown took over as manager at Plymouth Argyle. They finished 18th in Division Two in his first season at Home Park but the following season, having won only one of their last 15 games, Brown was sacked by Argyle on 6 February 1990.

BROWN, Laurence

Born: Shildon, 22 August 1937.
Centre-half   5ft 11in; 12st 5lb (1964).
Career: Timothy Hackworth School; Shildon; Shildon Workers Juniors FC; All Saints' Rovers; Shildon Town; Woking; Bishop Auckland; Fulham amateur March 1957; Darlington amateur March 1959; Bishop Auckland; Northampton Town October 1960; Arsenal August 1961; Tottenham Hotspur February 1964; Norwich City September 1966; Bradford player-manager December 1968-October 1969, when he became asistant manager; King's Lynn player-manager December 1970, later general manager; Altrincham player-manager in 1970s.

Honours: England Amateur international.

Laurie Brown left school at 15 and took a job as an apprentice shopfitter-cabinet maker. He joined Woking as a centre-half after being posted to the area whilst on National Service. Spotted by Fulham manager Duggie Livingstone, he signed amateur forms and

played a full season for the club being unable to break into the first team. Brown made his Football League debut as an amateur with Darlington. He later played First Division football with Spurs and Arsenal, occasionally appearing at centre-forward at White Hart Lane. He also played for Great Britain in the 1960 Olympic Games in Rome.

Brown had a difficult time as manager of Bradford. The Park Avenue club was on the way out of the League, having finishing bottom of the Fourth Division for the third successive season. The club's attendances had reached rock bottom by the end of Brown's first season in charge. In October 1969, the director Mr Metcalfe took matters into his own hands and picked the team. Brown immediately resigned and 19 players handed in transfer requests.

BROWN, Michael John

Born: Walsall, 11 July 1939.
Full-back   5ft 10in; 11st 9lb (1960).
Career: Hull City amateur 1954, professional October 1958; Lincoln City July 1967; Cambridge United player-coach 1968-1969; Oxford United coach January 1970, then manager September 1975-July 1979; West Bromwich Albion assistant manager July 1979; Manchester United assistant manager June 1981-November 1986; Bolton Wanderers assistant manager 1989-May 1992.

Honours: Division Three champions 1965.

Mick Brown made only eight appearances for Hull City in nine years at the club, but he was a regular at Lincoln City. He became much better known as a manager, following Ron Atkinson as his assistant at West Brom and Manchester United. When he managed Oxford United, they were relegated to Division Three in 1976 and struggled in the lower half of the table until his departure to The Hawthorns in 1979. Brown and Atkinson enjoyed much success at Old Trafford but Mick lost his job when Atkinson was dismissed.

BROWN, Robert

Died: March 1935.
Career: Hebburn Argyle and many other non-League sides; Portsmouth manager June 1911-April 1920; Gillingham manager May-June 1920; Sheffield Wednesday manager June 1920-December 1933.

Honours: Football League champions 1929, 1930; Division Two champions 1926; Southern League champions 1920; Southern League Division Two champions 1912.

Robert Brown never played professional football but gained some fame as manager of Portsmouth and Sheffield Wednesday and he led his sides to five championships, two in the Southern League and three in the Football League.

After leaving school, Brown served an apprenticeship in a shipyard and played for local sides including Hebburn Argyle. Around the turn of the century he joined Sheffield Wednesday for the first time, scouting in the North-East, and he later worked in the club's offices at Owlerton.

In June 1911, Brown was appointed secretary-manager of Southern League Portsmouth. Pompey had just been relegated and faced financial ruin if they did not regain their First Division status quickly, for the Second Division meant a great deal of travelling and smaller attendances. At the end of his

first season at the club, Pompey won the championship, much to the relief of the board and fans.

Brown signed a number of Scottish players to help boost the club's flagging fortunes and in 1912, Portsmouth were re-constituted and this gave the club a firmer financial base. Brown also took them to the First Division championship in season 1919-20 but left in April 1920 when he resigned with chairman George Lewin-Oliver over a difference of opinion about future policy.

After a brief spell as manager of Gillingham, Brown rejoined the Owls in the close season of 1920 as their first professional secretary-manager. He was probably Wednesday's most successful manager. Brown had a useful eye for talent and had the ability to mould individuals into successful sides, although he was decidedly distant from publicity and the Press.

Success took some time to come to Wednesday. The club struggled in Brown's first season in charge and went from mid-October to mid-January with only one win in 15 matches. The tide finally turned in 1925-26 when the Owls won the Second Division championship with 60 points. They looked set for relegation in 1928 but made a remarkable recovery with 17 points from the last ten games to escape the drop.

The following two seasons brought nothing but success. The League championship was won in both 1928-29 and 1929-30 and the club almost won the double but for a controversial goal in an FA Cup semi-final against Huddersfield Town. The Owls took the lead but Alex Jackson equalized when it appeared he was both offside and using his hands. Town went on to win after this fillip.

Brown's secret was an ability to choose the right staff to train and look after the players. He was more of an administrator and did not always have a say in who the club bought. It is claimed that he signed Ernie Blenkinsop in January 1923, as well as many other famous names. However, it is more likely that the directors of the club had more say in who was transferred. His masterstroke was making Jimmy Seed captain in 1927. This proved a major turning point in the club's fortunes.

After the death of his wife in 1932, the team struggled for the first time in years. Brown seemed to lose interest in the job and resigned a year later due to ill health. When he recovered, he returned to scout for Chelsea. Whilst on a scouting mission in March 1935, he collapsed while boarding a train and died in hospital the next day.

BROWN, Roger William

Born: Tamworth, 12 December 1952.
Centre-half   6ft 1in; 11st 10lb (1980).
Career: Walsall apprentice; Paget Rangers; AP Leamington; Bournemouth & Boscombe Athletic February 1978; Norwich City July 1979 (£85,000); Fulham March 1980 (£100,000); Bournemouth & Boscombe Athletic December 1983 (£35,000); Weymouth player-coach; Colchester United manager November 1987-October 1988.

Honours: Associate Members' Cup winners 1984.

Roger Brown holds Fulham's goalscoring record for a defender with 12 goals in their promotion season of 1981-82. He had failed to make the grade at Walsall and drifted into non-League soccer whilst working his way up to production manager in an engineering firm in Leamington, whilst playing for the local club. A powerful, dominant central defender, Bournemouth persuaded him back into the Football League at the age of 25. A popular figure with the Fulham crowd he moved back to Bournemouth after falling out with the club's manager Malcolm Macdonald. Colchester United finished ninth in his first season as their manager but he resigned after an 8-0 defeat at Orient with the club in 21st spot in Division Four.

BROWN, William F.

Born: Larkhill, Lanarkshire, 20 October 1922; Died: 27 May 1978.
Right-back   5ft 11in; 11st 3lb (1953).
Career: Larkhill Thistle; Preston North End January 1942; Queen of the South November 1949; Elgin City 1950, then player-manager 1951; Grimsby Town June 1951 (£1,350), retired July 1958; Barrow manager July 1958-August 1959; Bridgewater Town manager.
Honours: Division Three North champions 1956.

A mature defender who was reliable and able to maintain a high level of performance, Bill Brown made 264 appearances for Grimsby Town from 1951 to 1958, winning a Third Division championship medal in 1956. A tough tackler he often brought upon himself the wrath of away supporters for his uncompromising style. When he took over at Barrow, they had just been relegated to Division Four. Poor form in the New Year meant the club had to seek re-election at the end of the season. Brown resigned four days before the start of the following season.

BRUTON, Jack

Born: Westhoughton, Lancashire, 21 November 1903; Died: Bournemouth, 13 March 1986.
Outside-right   5ft 7in; 11st 1lb (1933).
Career: Hindley Green; Horwich RMI 1924; Wigan Borough amateur 1925; Burnley March 1925; Blackburn Rovers December 1929 (£56,500), retired during the war; Blackburn Rovers assistant secretary September-December 1947, then manager December 1947-May 1949; Bournemouth & Boscombe Athletic manager March 1950-March 1956, then coach 1956-1960, coach and scout for Portsmouth; Blackburn Rovers scout August 1961.
Honours: England international (3 caps); Football League representative (2 caps); Division Two champions 1939.

A former miner, Jack Bruton signed for Burnley on an overturned pit tub in 1925. Outstandingly fast and with good ball control and artistry, he was one of the best wingers of the day. He won three caps, against France and Belgium in 1928 and against Scotland in 1929. Bruton scored 150 goals in 491 League appearances in his career. This included 104 goals in 304 appearances for Blackburn Rovers. As the Blackburn manager, he saw the club relegated to Division Two in 1948. Bruton was never given a free hand to run the club the way that he wanted and he was eventually sacked. At Dean Court, Bournemouth were usually in a comfortable mid-table position during his ten years at the club.

BUCHAN, Ian

Died: Glasgow, 1965 (aged 45) in car accident.
Career: Everton manager February 1956-October 1958.

Honours: Scotland amateur international.

Ian Buchan had a difficult time as Everton's manager. The previous boss, Cliff Britton, had fought against the board's meddling in team affairs and Buchan, an insider, went along with their wishes to the detriment of the team. A courteous and intensely loyal man, Buchan never enjoyed the full trappings of the position of manager. Everton were probably the fittest side in Division One, but Buchan did not have players of sufficient quality to win honours.

BUCHAN, Martin McLean

Born: Aberdeen, 6 March 1949.
Defender   5ft 10in; 11st 11lb (1978).
Career: Banks O'Dee; Aberdeen August 1966; Manchester United March 1972 (£125,000); Oldham Athletic August 1983-October 1984; Burnley manager June-October 1985.
Honours: Scotland international (34 caps); Under-23 international (3 caps); Youth international; Scottish Player of the Year 1971; Division Two champions 1975; FA Cup winners 1977, runners-up 1976, 1979; Scottish Cup winners 1970.

Martin Buchan was Aberdeen's youngest captain (21) when he led the side to a convincing victory over Celtic in the 1970 Scottish Cup Final. His father had also played for Aberdeen before the war.

When he joined the Old Trafford club from Aberdeen, Buchan's fee was a record for Manchester United and Scottish football and he was an immediate steadying influence on the team, bringing strength and calm to the middle of the defence. A superb reader of the game and a great influence on the side, he was also made skipper at United. He gained 34 caps for Scotland and appeared in the 1974 and 1978 World Cup finals for the Scots and also played in three FA Cup Finals for United. Buchan had a very brief spell as Burnley's manager and left after only four months in charge.

BUCHANAN, David M.

Born: c.1874.
Half-back   5ft 6½in; 11st (1909).
Career: Middlesbrough; Brentford 1903; Plymouth Argyle cs 1905; Clapton Orient 1906; Leyton player-manager 1908-1911; Charlton Athletic assistant manager and coach 1925-1928; Thames Association manager cs 1928-cs 1931.

David Buchanan never appeared in Middlesbrough's first team but performed regularly for all his other clubs. He made 65 appearances for Clapton Orient in the Football League and scored eight goals in 78 games for Southern League Leyton. He worked as assistant manager to Alex McFarlane at The Valley and took over at newly-formed Thames Association in 1928. The club were surprisingly elected to the Football League in 1930 after finishing fifth in the Southern League the previous season. But they struggled in the Third Division South with poor attendances and performances, and Buchanan was relieved of his duties in the close season of 1931. Financial constraints had made his job virtually impossible.

BUCHANAN, John 'Jock'

Born: Underwood, near Stirling, 9 June 1928.
Forward   5ft 10in; 12st 10lb (1959).
Career: Kilsyth Rangers; Clyde 1946;

Derby County February 1955; Bradford November 1957, retired May 1963 and worked as a Bradford pools promoter; Bradford manager May 1964-March 1967.
Honours: Scottish League Division Two champions 1952.

Jock Buchanan helped Clyde to win the Scottish Second Division in 1951-52 and was one of the players signed by Derby manager Jack Barker in a vain attempt to avoid relegation to the Third Division in 1955. Buchanan scored 12 goals in his 32 appearances for the Rams but did not collect a Third Division North championship medal in 1956-57 as he played in only six games. He scored 75 goals in 173 appearances for Bradford before retiring in May 1963 to work as a pools promoter with the Park Avenue club. A year later he was back as their manager. They finished seventh and 11th in his first two seasons in charge but were heading for re-election when he lost his job in March 1967.

BUCKINGHAM, Victor Frederick

Born: Greenwich, 23 October 1915.
Wing-half   5ft 10in; 11st 2lb (1937).
Career: Greenwich Schoolboys; Northfleet; Tottenham Hotspur May 1935-1949; Middlesex County FA chief scout; Oxford University coach; Pegasus AFC coach 1950; Bradford manager June 1951-January 1953; West Bromwich Albion manager February 1953-May 1959; Ajax (Amsterdam) manager May 1959-May 1961; Sheffield Wednesday manager May 1961-March 1964; Fulham manager January 1965-January 1968; Ethnikos (Greece) manager 1968; Barcelona (Spain) coach 1970; Seville (Spain) coach March 1972.
Honours: England wartime international (2 caps); FA Cup winners 1954; Netherlands League champions 1960, Cup winners 1961; Spanish Cup winners 1971.

Vic Buckingham was acknowledged as one of the most capable soccer coaches in the country and also one of the most respected managers in the 1950s and '60s. He graduated through Tottenham's nursery side at Northfleet but had barely established himself in the League side when war took him away to join the RAF.

A stylish wing-half, Buckingham often guested for Fulham during the war and after being demobbed, he resumed as a full-back for Spurs, eventually making 234 appearances before retiring in 1949 having never played First Division football for the club. On retirement he turned to coaching and was chief scout to the Middlesex County FA, followed by a

spell coaching at Oxford University. In 1950, Buckingham took over as coach to Pegasus, the Oxbridge club who won the FA Amateur Cup the following year. Debonair, happy-go-lucky and articulate, he was the ideal man to motivate a university side.

In June 1951, his coaching talents widely recognised, he was appointed manager of Bradford and the Park Avenue club finished eighth in the Third Division North in his first season in charge. He introduced Derek Kevan to the Football League and later signed him for West Brom.

In February 1953, Buckingham moved to The Hawthorns as manager and almost immediately found success. Albion won the FA Cup in 1954 and were also runners-up in the League that year. Although not quite so successful afterwards, he got Albion to an FA Cup semi-final in 1957, when they lost to Aston Villa after a replay. He also arranged some attractive fixtures against the leading European sides and there were many memorable nights at The Hawthorns during his tenure of office. When he left the club in May 1959, he left a huge gap which proved hard to fill. His sides were successful and played with style and he set the pattern of play for the club for practically the whole of the decade.

Buckingham moved abroad to coach Ajax of Amsterdam and is said to be the man who 'discovered' Johann Cruyff. Ajax were Dutch champions in 1959-60 and won their national cup the following year. He agreed to become Plymouth Argyle's manager in March 1961, but due to contractual difficulties was unable to take up the post immediately. When he was free of his contract, he decided to accept an offer to manage Sheffield Wednesday instead. In each of his three seasons at Hillsborough the Owls finished in the top half of the First Division and also reached the quarter-finals of the Fairs Cup. Yet he was not considered a great success as the board demanded more trophies and he was sacked in March 1964. Buckingham was Wednesday's manager during the bribery scandal which saw Tony Kay, Peter Swan and 'Bronco' Layne banned for life. He must have been devastated that his players could sabotage his efforts to win matches.

Buckingham was appointed Fulham's manager in January 1965 and immediately appointed former Spurs colleagues Ronnie Burgess and Eddie Gibbons in coaching posts at the Cottage. Buckingham was given a three-year contract and completely overhauled many aspects of the club's affairs. Unfortunately, results were poor and when his contract came up for renewal in January 1968, his services were dispensed with. His tenure was not a happy one and he let too many experienced players leave the club. Relegation from Division One was a constant threat which finally materialised a few months after his departure.

He tried too many changes too quickly and succeeded only in upsetting almost everyone. Unable to tolerate the attitude of the flamboyant Rodney Marsh, he sold him for a paltry £15,000, although he did buy Allan Clarke from Walsall for £35,000. The players found Buckingham distant and difficult to approach and this affected team spirit.

After this, he moved abroad to manage Ethnikos of Greece and proved very popular in that country where his flamboyance and generous character was appreciated by the Greek people.

He then took Barcelona to the Spanish Cup in 1971 and from March 1972, managed Seville.

BUCKLEY, Alan P.

Born: Mansfield, 20 April 1951.
Forward   5ft 5in; 9st 11lb (1970).
Career: Nottingham Forest apprentice June 1967, professional April 1968; Walsall August 1973 (£20,000); Birmingham City October 1978 (£175,000); Walsall (£175,000) player-manager July 1979-August 1986; Stourbridge September 1986; Tamworth 1986; Kettering Town manager November 1986-June 1988; Grimsby Town manager June 1988.

Honours: Division Four runners-up 1980, 1990; Division Three promotion 1991.

After only 16 games for Nottingham Forest, Alan Buckley moved to Fellows Park and scored 125 goals in 241 League appearances over the next five seasons. He was made caretaker manager at Walsall in 1978 but when Alan Ashman took over he was sold to Birmingham City for a large fee. When the Blues were relegated to the Second Division, he moved back to Fellows Park, for a record £175,000 fee, as player-manager. The club finished as runners up in Division Four in his first season in charge.

In 1981, Neil Martin was made joint manager and later took over completely until 1982, when Buckley was re-appointed. He lost his job in 1986 when millionaire businessman Terry Ramsden took over the club. Under Buckley's management, Kettering won the Bob Lord Trophy in 1987, the Northamptonshire Senior Cup in 1987 and 1988 and finished third in the Conference League in 1987-88. After two years in charge at Rockingham Road, he joined Grimsby Town as manager in June 1988. The Mariners reached the fifth round of the FA Cup in 1988-89 and were Fourth Division runners-up the following season. Buckley took them to promotion for the second successive season and they returned to the Second Division in 1992. His policy of playing entertaining football brought its just rewards. He is the brother of Steve Buckley and a cousin of Ambrose Buckley.

BUCKLEY
'Major' Franklin Charles

Born: Urmston, Manchester, 9 November 1883; Died: Walsall, 22 December 1964.
Centre-half   5ft 11in; 13st (1914).
Career: Aston Villa April 1903; Brighton & Hove Albion May 1905; Manchester United June 1906; Manchester City September 1907; Birmingham July 1909; Derby County May 1911; Bradford City May 1914; CO

of the Footballers' Battalion (Middlesex Regiment) in World War One; Norwich City player-manager March 1919-July 1920; commercial traveller 1920-1923; Blackpool manager July 1923-May 1927; Wolverhampton Wanderers manager May 1927-March 1944; Notts County manager March 1944-May 1946; Hull City manager May 1946-March 1948; Leeds United manager May 1948-April 1953; Walsall manager April 1953-September 1955.

Honours: England international (1 cap); Division Two champions 1912; FA Cup runners-up 1939; Football League War Cup winners 1942.

Frank Buckley's sides never won a major honour — Wolves came close to the League and Cup double in 1939 but just missed out on both — yet he is one of the most famous managers of all time. Buckley gained fame as a shrewd dealer on the transfer market, especially during his 17 years at Molineux. In many ways he was ahead of his time but his patriarchal, disciplined approach seemed to suit the era in which he managed.

In 1898, he enlisted in the Army and served in the Boer War. On his return he became a professional footballer with Aston Villa. A vigorous attacking centre-half, Buckley was skilled in the tackle and a glutton for work. He reached the peak of his playing career when he moved to the Baseball Ground and won his only England cap, against Ireland in 1914 when his side suffered a humiliating 3-0 defeat at Middlesbrough.

Buckley moved around as a player with Brighton, Manchester United, Manchester City, Birmingham, Derby and Bradford City, and he made one appearance for Norwich City after the war whilst their manager. He was one of six sons and his brother Chris played for Arsenal and Aston Villa and was later the Villa chairman. With the outbreak of World War One, Buckley joined the 17th Battalion (Footballers' Battalion) of the Middlesex Regiment and was eventually promoted to major, a rank he proudly used for the rest of his life.

After the war he became manager of Norwich City, who were then in the Southern League. He steered them to 12th position but they also lost 5-0 to Darlington in the FA Cup. He sold Sam Jennings to Middlesbrough for a record £2,250 in April 1920, the first of many such transactions he was to be involved in over the next 35 years. After a crisis at the club, six directors resigned, many players left the club and Buckley also resigned.

He was out of the game for three years, working as a commercial traveller, until Blackpool persuaded him

back into soccer as their manager. For the first time the public could see some of his new methods and for years to come he was the most controversial manager in League football — and also the highest paid.

A commanding figure, Buckley was well educated and well spoken, six feet tall and with a distinct military bearing. He wore plus-fours and could easily be mistaken for a farmer. Buckley had a strong self discipline, was a non-drinker and non-smoker and demanded dedication from his players. He arranged informal discussions on tactics and had a far-sighted youth policy.

Blackpool never really threatened to win promotion to the First Division in his four years at the club but did finish fourth in 1923-24 and sixth two seasons later. They also reached the quarter-finals of the FA Cup in 1925.

In May 1927, Buckley became manager of Wolves and at Molineux his unique ability to turn young unknowns into stars was allowed to flourish for the next 17 years. By the time war came, Wolves had risen from a moderate Second Division side to runners-up in the League and FA Cup. The Major enjoyed a period as a media star, freely communicating his progressive and ambitious views to the local and national newspapers. In his early years at Molineux he dabbled in the transfer market and signed some excellent players such as Dai Richards, Alf Tootill, Walter Bottrill and Charlie Phillips. He also sold a number of players, making a fair profit for the club. In 1931-32, Wolves arrived back in the First Division for the first time since 1906.

In the 1930s, Buckley signed other famous names including Stan Cullis, Billy Wright, Jimmy Mullen, Dennis Westcott and Bryn Jones. It never pleased the fans to see their favourites sold but he always had a replacement ready. Honours would surely have come if he had kept some of these star players but Buckley always kept the directors happy by making vast amounts of money for the club between 1935 and 1939. Wolves received a massive £110,658 in transfer fees in this period, a huge sum in those days. They were just about to reach their peak when the war came. They were surprisingly beaten 4-1 by Second Division Portsmouth in the 1939 FA Cup Final and they also were runners-up in the First Division.

Some of Buckley's methods were controversial like his 'monkey-gland injections', which in reality were just innoculations against colds. He also sent some players to see a psychologist in his search for the elusive confidence so important to footballers. With the retirement of his greatest ally, chairman Ben Matthews, Buckley was left feeling vulnerable and in March 1944, never being one to take orders, he resigned.

Thereafter, his career seemed to go downhill. He joined Notts County straight from Wolves but soon resigned to join Hull City. He was 62 years old by this time and wanted to bring First Division soccer to the city. In his experimentations to blend a successful side, he used a record number of players in the first peacetime season of 1946-47. Over 170 Hull City players were registered with the League that season. Some were given only one League outing, only to disappear back into obscurity afterwards.

His experimentations the following season seemed to cost the Tigers

promotion and the public concern began to grow, as did that of the board of directors. A rift appeared in October 1947 but was soon patched up. However, after the signing of Raich Carter as player-assistant manager, Buckley resigned two days later.

Two months later the Major became Leeds United's manager. It was here that he discovered what was, he felt, his greatest find. He built up John Charles into a versatile all-round player who fitted nicely into the manager's coaching theory, which was that every player should be equally competent in all departments. Buckley spent five seasons at Elland Road but was unable to get the club out of the Second Division.

Towards the end of 1952-53 he moved to manage his final club, Walsall. The following season was a disaster with Walsall at the bottom of the Third Division South. The next campaign was little better and Buckley decided to retire from football in June 1955 at the age of 71. He had spent almost 50 years in the game.

BULLOCK, Michael E.

Born: Stoke-on-Trent, 2 October 1946.
Forward   5ft 10½in; 12st 10lb (1970).
Career: North Staffordshire Schools; Stoke Boys; Birmingham City apprentice July 1962, professional October 1963; Oxford United June 1967; Orient October 1968; Halifax Town February 1976, retired in 1979 to become coach, then manager July 1981-October 1984; Goole Town manager 1986; Ossett Town manager 1989.

Honours: England Schoolboy international; Division Three champions 1968, 1970.

Micky Bullock was a cool, clever forward who was a fine header of the ball. He made 277 appearances for Orient, scoring 64 goals, and was the leading scorer with 19 goals in their Third Division championship season. Altogether he scored 108 goals in 469 League appearances before retiring in 1979. When he was manager of Halifax Town it was always a struggle and he had to constantly sell his best players to survive. The club had massive debts when he took over and therefore he did very well in 1982-83 when the club finished 11th in the Fourth Division. Halifax had to seek re-election at the end of the following season and when the club had a poor start the next season, Bullock was sacked after nine years at the club. He left football disillusioned but re-emerged as manager of Goole Town in 1986. He is the brother of Peter and uncle of Simon.

BULLOCK, Norman

Born: Monton Green, 8 September 1900; Died: Bushby, Leicestershire, 27 October 1970.
Centre-half-Forward   5ft 9in; 11st 1lb (1933).
Career: Salford Schools; Broughton St Johns; Sedgeley Park Amateurs; Prestwich Amateurs; Bury September 1920 (£10), then manager June 1934-June 1938; Chesterfield manager June 1938-July 1945; Bury manager again July 1945-November 1949; Leicester City manager December 1949-February 1955.
Honours: England international (3 caps); Football League representative (1 cap); Division Two champions 1954.

Norman Bullock scored 124 goals in 506 games for Bury from 1920 to 1935 and he still holds the appearances record for the club. He led the Shakers to promotion in 1924 and to fourth in Division One two years later. He showed speed and staying power and shooting ability as a centre-forward and was later converted to a dependable pivot later on in his playing career.

When he became the manager at Bury, his authority was limited by the directors, who had responsibility for team matters. Criticism from supporters over poor team selection and a run of bad results prompted the board to give Bullock more control in December 1935. Bury finished third in the Second Division in 1936-37, but in June 1938, when he requested, but was refused, complete control of the team, he left for Chesterfield. After the war he rejoined Bury, who struggled in the Second Division but with increased crowds. At Leicester he sold Don Revie to Hull City and bought Arthur Rowley from Fulham for £12,500, Rowley proved a great goalscoring success for City. Bullock took City to the Second Division title in 1954, but the team struggled in the higher grade. After player indiscipline at a Whitley Bay hotel brought things to a head, Bullock was sacked and decided to leave the game.

BURCHELL, Joseph

Born: Walsall April 1873; Died: Hednesford, 19 October 1932.
Career: Walsall Unity FC; Walsall part-time secretary 1914, secretary-manager August 1921-February 1926, then secretary until October 1930; licensee of the Vine Inn, Rugeley, May 1930; Hednesford Town director in 1930s.

Joe Burchell was a keen cyclist in his younger days and was president and secretary of Walsall Polytechnic Cycling Club. He first became involved with Walsall FC at the start of World War One and as secretary helped guide the Saddlers into the Football League in March 1921. They finished eighth in their first season, then third in 1922-23, only five points behind champions Nelson.

Then their form took a turn for the worse and they finished in the re-election zone in 1925-26 when they gained only 26 points. Walsall also had a poor record in the FA Cup and made the first round only in 1921-22 and 1925-26, otherwise losing to fellow League clubs in the qualifying rounds. Burchell remained as secretary until 1930, when he took a pub at Rugeley. He died at the Crosskey Hotel in Hednesford.

BURGESS, William Arthur Ronald

Born: Cwm, Wales, 9 April 1917.
Left-half

Career: Cwm Villa; Tottenham Hotspur May 1936; Northfleet; guest for Notts County in World War Two; Swansea Town August 1954, player-manager July 1955-1958; Watford coach 1958, then manager March 1959-May 1963; Hendon manager 1963; Fulham coach summer 1965.
Honours: Wales international (32 caps); Wartime international; Football League representative; Great Britain representative; Football League champions 1951; Division Two champions 1950; Division Four promotion 1960; FA Amateur Cup winners 1965.

Ronnie Burgess learned his football kicking around the slagheaps above the River Ebbw in South Wales, Burgess was a miner when he joined Spurs and developed in their nursery side at Northfleet before making his League debut just before the outbreak of war. He played his first game for Wales in November 1939, in a wartime game. After serving in the RAF during hostilities, he captained Spurs for eight seasons afterwards, leading the club to the Second Division championship and the League championship in successive seasons.

Much of Arthur Rowe's 'push and run' system revolved around this energetic, attacking wing-half. He had incredible stamina and was a human dynamo. Burgess was the first Welshman to play for the Football League XI and he made 328 League appearances for Spurs before departing to Swansea Town. He was also an automatic choice for Wales.

Swansea maintained their Second Division status during his term of office. At Watford he discovered Pat Jennings and sold him to his former club, Tottenham. He took the side to promotion to Division Three in 1960 and also the fifth round of the FA Cup. At Hendon, he took the club to a 3-1 FA Amateur Cup Final victory over Whitby Town at Wembley.

BURKINSHAW, Keith H.

Born: Higham, 23 June 1935.
Wing-half   5ft 11in; 12st 6lb (1964).
Career: Denaby United; Wolverhampton Wanderers amateur; Liverpool November 1953; Workington December 1957 (£3,000), then manager November 1964-March 1965; Scunthorpe United May 1965, retired cs 1968; coaching in Zambia May 1968; Newcastle United assistant coach 1968, first-team coach 1971-May 1975; Tottenham Hotspur coach May 1975, then manager July 1976-May 1984; Bahrain national coach June 1984; Sporting Lisbon (Portugal); Gillingham manager October 1988-

April 1989; Swindon Town chief scout March 1991; West Bromwich Albion assistant manager May 1992, then manger June 1993.*
Honours: Division Two promotion 1978; FA Cup winners 1981, 1982; Football League Cup runners-up 1982; UEFA Cup winners 1984.

Keith Burkinshaw made his name as manager of Tottenham Hotspur where, with two FA Cup Final victories and an exciting triumph in the UEFA Cup, he was the club's second most successful boss after Bill Nicholson

A South Yorkshireman, Burkinshaw first worked at Dodworth Colliery, transporting tubs of coal from the pit face, and had a spell with Wolves' junior side whilst playing for Denaby United in the Midland League. Then Liverpool signed him and at last he had escaped from the pits.

Burkinshaw played only one game for Liverpool's first team, in April 1955 at Port Vale, before his transfer to Workington. He made 293 League appearances for the Cumbrian club over the next seven and a half seasons, at Borough Park linking up with team manager Joe Harvey, whom he later rejoined at Newcastle United as coach. During his final season at Workington, Burkinshaw became player-manager and then moved to Scunthorpe United, playing 108 League games for the Iron.

In his three-year spell at the Old Show Ground, he was caretaker manager for a spell and when he was released by Scunthorpe, he retired from playing and went to coach in Zambia. He soon returned to England, however, to take up a coaching job at Newcastle, where he was in charge of the Reserves. In 1971 he was made first-team coach and the Magpies reached the 1974 FA Cup Final before he was controversially sacked a year later.

A much respected and well-liked coach, he was not out of work for long before joining Spurs in a similar capacity. Extremely popular with the players, Burkinshaw had their full support when he became manager at White Hart Lane. At the time he insisted that the club's greatest-ever manager, Bill Nicholson, rejoined the club's staff. Nicholson became a positive presence, always supporting Burkinshaw to the hilt.

Burkinshaw, though, was relatively unknown at the time and faced an enormous task as Spurs were relegated at the end of his first season. Fortunately, chairman Sidney Wale and the board kept their faith in him, although Burkinshaw did not endear himself to Tottenham's fans when he sold Pat Jennings to arch-rivals Arsenal, thinking — wrongly as it turned out — that the Irish international goalkeeper was nearing the end of his career. Indeed,

Spurs had goalkeeping problems during the whole of Burkinshaw's reign.

Tottenham bounced back into the First Division at the first attempt, promoted in third place, but Burkinshaw felt that the players at his disposal were not quite good enough for the First Division, so he sensationally signed two stars of Argentina's 1978 World Cup winning side, Osvaldo Ardiles from Huracan and Ricardo Villa from Racing Club Buenos Aires. They proved great buys, helping Spurs to FA Cup Final successes in 1981 and 1982.

However, midway through the 1983-84 season, Burkinshaw became disillusioned after a boardroom takeover and announced that he would resign at the end of the season. As a farewell present, Spurs won the UEFA Cup in the emotion-charged atmosphere of White Hart Lane, beating Anderlecht on penalties in the Final.

Burkinshaw moved to the Middle East to manage the Bahrain national side and afterwards managed Sporting Lisbon of Portugal. He returned to England to take charge of Gillingham but it was an unhappy time for him and he resigned, complaining of lack of commitment by the club and its players, as the Gills sank towards relegation to the Fourth Division. Burkinshaw worked with Glenn Hoddle at Swindon and Ossie Ardiles at the Hawthorns, both of whom played under him at Spurs, succeeding Ardiles as Albion manager in June 1993.

BURKITT, Jack Orgill

Born: Wednesbury, 19 January 1926.
Wing-half   5ft 9½in; 11st 8lb (1959).
Career: Darlaston; Nottingham Forest May 1947-1961, then coach; Notts County manager April 1966-February 1967; Derby County trainer September 1967-1969.
Honours: FA Cup winners 1959.

Originally signed by Nottingham Forest as a centre-half, Jack Burkitt settled down at wing-half and was one of the most consistent players in the club's history. A top-class, constructive player, he probably would have played for his country had he been with a more fashionable club. As captain, he led the club into the First Division and to an FA Cup Final victory in 1959.

Shortly after taking over at Notts County, they had their lowest-ever post-war crowd of 1,927 against Chesterfield. With the Magpies near the bottom of the Fourth Division, he was offered a leave of absence due to ill health in December 1966 and he resigned in February 1967. He was suffering from nervous strain due to overwork. He returned to the game as trainer at Derby County and worked with Brian Clough and Peter Taylor when the Rams stormed to the Second Division title in 1968-69.

BURROWS, Frank

Born: Larkhill, 30 January 1944.
Defender   6ft 1in; 12st 8lb (1970).
Career: Raith Rovers; Scunthorpe United June 1965; Swindon Town July 1968 (£12,000); Mansfield Town (loan) March 1974; Swindon Town assistant manager; Portsmouth coach 1978-1979, then manager May 1979-March 1982; Southampton coach August 1983; Sunderland coach 1986; Cardiff City manager May 1986-August 1989; Portsmouth assistant manager September 1989, then manager January 1990-March 1991; Swansea March 1991-.
Honours: Division Four runners-up 1988, promotion 1980; Football League Cup winners 1969.

A tough, uncompromising defender, Frank Burrows made over 500 appearances in his career. He helped Swindon to promotion to Division Two as runners-up and to a shock League Cup Final victory over Arsenal in 1969. His playing career ended in October 1976, when he became Swindon's assistant manager. Burrows succeeded Jimmy Dickinson as Pompey's manager and the club won promotion to the Third Division after his first season in charge at Fratton Park. Burrows left after the club had consolidated their Third Division status. He took over at Cardiff as they entered the Fourth Division for the first time. The Bluebirds finished runners-up in 1987-88 and he left to work as assistant to John Gregory at Portsmouth in 1989. When Gregory moved on, Burrows took control at the club for a second time. Lack of good results and general disenchantment throughout the club led to Burrows resigning as manager and Tony Barton took over as caretaker until the end of the season.

Swansea reached the Second Division play-offs in 1993 after a late run. However, they lost to West Bromwich Albion 3-2 on aggregate at the semi-final stage.

BURTENSHAW, Stephen

Born: Portslade, 23 November 1935
Wing-half   5ft 11in; 12st 2lb (1964).
Career: Sussex Boys; Brighton & Hove Albion November 1952-1966; Arsenal reserve-team coach 1966, then chief coach July 1971; Queen's Park Rangers chief coach August 1973; Sheffield Wednesday manager January 1974-October 1975; Everton caretaker manager January-February 1977; Queen's Park Rangers manager August 1978-May 1979; Arsenal chief scout and caretaker manager March 1986.

Honours: Division Three champions 1958.

Steve Burtenshaw served Brighton as a wing-half for 14 seasons, making 237 League appearances and winning a Third Division championship medal in 1957-58. He was encouraged to take up coaching by Brighton boss George Curtis and when he retired, secured a job with Arsenal as reserve-team coach. He took over as the chief coach when Don Howe left Highbury. In 1973, Burtenshaw swopped jobs with Bobby Campbell at Queen's Park Rangers and later worked under Billy Bingham and Gordon Lee at Everton. As the boss at Hillsborough, Burtenshaw experienced only 14 victories in over 70 games in charge at the club. They just missed relegation in April 1974 by winning their last game but went down the following season. The Owls won only five games all season and collected just 21 points to finish bottom of the Second Division. After a poor start to the

1975-76 season, his contract was terminated. His only season in charge at Loftus Road was also a disaster with Rangers being relegated at the end of the season. Chairman Jim Gregory sacked him after only ten months of his three-year contact. He is the brother of William and Charles Burtenshaw.

BUSBY, Sir Matthew, CBE

Born: Orbiston, near Bellshill, Lanarkshire, 26 May 1909.
Right-half   5ft 10in; 11st 4lb (1933).

Career: Alpine Villa; Denny Hibernian; Manchester City February 1928; Liverpool March 1936 (£8,000); guest for Chelsea, Middlesbrough, Reading, Brentford, Bournemouth and Hibernian in World War Two; retired October 1945; Manchester United manager February 1945-June 1969, administration manager June 1969, caretaker manager December 1970-July 1971, director June 1971-August 1982, club president March 1980; also Football League Management member June 1973; Football League vice president February July 1982; Scotland team manager 1958-1959.

Honours: Scotland international (1 cap); Wartime international (7 caps); Football League champions 1952, 1956, 1957, 1965, 1967; FA Cup winners 1934, 1948, 1963, runners-up 1933, 1957, 1958; European Cup winners 1968.

Sir Matt Busby is undoubtedly one of the greatest managers, not only in British soccer, but in the history of the world game. For almost a quarter of a century he managed Manchester United with such enthusiasm, shrewdness and skill, that he turned them into one of football's most outstanding clubs. His ability to spot real talent when still in its infancy and his success with unknown youngsters has been phenomenal.

Busby combined all the assets of a successful manager. He possessed great abilities in setting up networks to find youngsters, he made many shrewd signings and was able to teach, reach and mould players to the United style. He was also an able administrator who had imagination and a clear vision on how the game should be played and also implemented his theories. Entertainment came first with Busby and his sides won most of their honours with a brand of exciting soccer. Yet he always remained a modest, kindly and compassionate man who could also be ruthless if the situation demanded it.

Busby has humble origins. His father was killed whilst on active service in World War One and his mother struggled to bring up a family during the poverty of the 1920s. Busby was forced to work down the mines for a while, much to his dislike, and in later years he would often recall his humble beginnings when the star adoration became too much for him.

He started playing football for his

local village side and then progressed to a local junior club called Alpine Villa, from whom he signed semi-professional forms for Denny Hibernian. He played only six games before being snapped up by Manchester City but was on the point of emigrating to the USA with his mother when he signed for the Maine Road club. Thus, football nearly lost one of its greatest-ever personalities.

Originally a moderate inside-forward, Busby moved to right-half in 1931 and never looked back. A classic half-back, composed, skilled in footwork and tackling, he stamped his influence more as a reader of the game who preferred to make his killing with one pass rather than over-elaboration. The pinnacle of his playing career was City's 2-1 victory over Portsmouth in the 1934 FA Cup Final. A year earlier they had lost disappointingly to Everton 3-0 in the Final.

Busby won a Scottish cap in 1934, against Wales, and went on to captain his country in seven wartime internationals whilst serving as a physical-training instructor in the services. In March 1936 he had moved to Liverpool for an £8,000 fee and overall had made 317 League appearances, scoring 14 goals, when war broke out in 1939.

Busby appeared for several clubs in wartime soccer and when he retired in October 1945 he was offered a coaching post by Liverpool. However, a better offer came along — to manage Manchester United. He took over at a club whose ground had been badly damaged by wartime bombing and although Old Trafford eventually became one of the finest stadiums in Britain, Busby had the difficult task of motivating his early teams to play their home games at Maine Road, the home of United's deadliest rivals, Manchester City.

Over the next 24 years, United were to win almost every honour but also to experience a disaster which would have crushed a lesser man than Matt Busby. The dreadful air disaster at Munich in February 1958, which wiped out most of the 'Busby Babes', was a blow from which the club inevitably took some time to recover.

United's honours list was remarkable under Busby: five times Football League champions, seven times runners-up, FA Cup winners and runners-up twice each, and European Cup semi-finalists on three occasions and winners once in 1968. After taking over as United's boss, Busby soon demonstrated his gift for producing fine footballing sides. The 1948 and 1952 FA Cup and League-winning sides possessed some great players such as defender Johnny Carey and a forward line of Jimmy Delaney, Johnny Morris, Jack Rowley, Stan Pearson and Charlie Mitten. They were First Division runners-up four times before winning the title in 1951-52.

United had a formidable scouting system run by Joe Armstrong and Jimmy Murphy, probably the finest such set-up of the 1950s. They gradually built the 'Busby Babes' with the emergence of Duncan Edwards, Dave Pegg, Johnny Berry, Tommy Taylor, Liam Whelan and Dennis Violett. United won the League championship again in 1956, with a side whose average age was only 22, and won it again the following year.

They were the first club to enter European competition, against the advice of the English ruling body. Reinforced with a young Bobby Charlton, they reached the 1957 European

Cup semi-finals, only to lose to Real Madrid; a year later, decimated by Munich, they went out to AC Milan in the last four.

United were riding high and promised to dominate English soccer for the next decade when tragedy struck in February 1958. The 'Busby Babes' were cut down in their prime, their bodies scattered with the wreckage of their Elizabethan aircraft in the snow of a Munich airport. Eight players died and two others never played again. Busby was also seriously injured and took some time to recover.

It also took a great deal of courage to start again and rebuild the United side. This he achieved slowly but surely, blooding home-grown youngsters such as George Best and Nobby Stiles and with big buys such as Paddy Crerand and Denis Law. United won the FA Cup in 1963 and the League championship in 1965 and 1967. They gained their biggest prize, the European Cup, in 1968 when they beat Benfica 4-1 after extra-time at Wembley in the Final. After three semi-final defeats, it had become Matt Busby's last great obsession to win this competition.

In June 1969, Busby decided to retire and selected former Busby Babe, Wilf McGuiness, as his successor. Busby became the administrative and general manager of the club but McGuiness was not a success — what a difficult task he had — and Busby took over team affairs again from December 1970 until July 1971. When Frank O'Farrell was appointed as manager, Sir Matt joined United's board.

He had been made a CBE in 1958 and knighted ten years later. He remained on the board of directors until August 1982. He has also been club president since March 1980 and served as Scotland's national team manager for a time as well as on the Football League Management Committee. Today, Sir Matt Busby continues his involvement with his greatest love, Manchester United.

BUSBY, Vivian Dennis

Born: High Wycombe, 19 June 1949.
Centre-forward   5ft 11½in; 11st 6lb (1976)
Career: Wycombe Wanderers 1966; Fulham (trial) 1969; Luton Town January 1970; Newcastle United (loan) December 1971-February 1972; Fulham August 1973 (£25,000); Norwich City September 1976 (£50,000); Stoke City November 1977 (£50,000); Sheffield United (loan) January 1980; Tulsa Roughnecks (NASL) (loan) March-August 1980; Blackburn Rovers February 1981 (£40,000); York City August 1982, assistant manager 1984; Sunderland assistant manager May 1987-December 1991; Hartlepool United manager February 1993.

Honours: FA Cup Finalist 1975.

An excellent forward who should have scored more often than he did, Viv Busby possessed fine ball skills and usually entertained the crowds. He scored some vital goals in Fulham's run to the FA Cup Final in 1975, including two in the quarter-final at Everton. Busby had played as a trialist for Fulham in 1969 and had not been given a contract but joined Luton Town from Wycombe Wanderers in January 1970. Soon afterwards he went to Newcastle United for a loan period with Malcolm Macdonald but, unlike 'Supermac', was not signed permanently. He was signed for a second time by Alec Stock, his former boss at Kenilworth Road, for

Fulham in August 1973. After losing his place to Rodney Marsh, Busby moved to Norwich City. He later played for Stoke City, Tulsa Roughnecks, Sheffield United, Blackburn Rovers and York City, then at Sunderland until December 1991 when he was sacked. Busby was out of football for over a year before returning as manager of Hartlepool United as a replacement for Alan Murray. The club were in the middle of a poor run when he took over. The run continued but eventually United managed to win a couple of games near the end of the season to avoid relegation.

BUTCHER, Terence Ian

Born: Singapore, 28 December 1958.
Central defender   6ft 4½in; 14st 5lb (1984).
Career: Lowestoft Schools; Ipswich Town August 1976; Glasgow Rangers July 1986 (£725,000); Coventry City player-manager November 1990-January 1992 (£300,000); Halesowen Town player-coach January 1992; Sheffield Wednesday reserves April 1992; Sunderland player August 1992, player-manager February 1993. Sunderland manager February 1993.

Honours: England international (77 caps); 'B' international; Under-21 international (7 caps); First Division runners-up 1981, 1982; Scottish Premier Division winners 1987, 1989, 1990; Scottish Cup runners-up 1989; Scottish League Cup winners 1987, 1988, 1989; UEFA Cup winners 1981.

A very competitive and commanding central defender, Terry Butcher has played in three World Cup finals for England including skippering them to the semi-final against West Germany in 1990.

Butcher was born in Singapore where his father was in the Royal Navy. He was a major influence at both Ipswich and Glasgow Rangers, making over 300 appearances for the Suffolk club and helping them to a UEFA Cup Final victory over AZ67 Alkmaar in 1981, in a season where they also finished as runners-up in the First Division. After Town's relegation in 1986, Butcher moved to Rangers and helped them to dominate the Scottish scene, gaining three Scottish League championship medals and three Skol Cup medals.

But he fell out with manager Graeme Souness and was tempted to join Coventry City as player-manager to replace John Sillett, who had announced that he would retire at the end of the season. In Butcher's first season in charge, City struggled against relegation but eventually pulled away to safety. In October 1991, Butcher was

forced to sack his right-hand men, Mick Mills and Brian Eastick, by new chairman Peter Robins. Robins then objected to Butcher's high wages and felt that he should negotiate a new 'manager only' contract as he was suffering from a long-term injury. Butcher was sacked when he refused to do this. He made a comeback with Sunderland in 1992 after it had looked as though his playing career would come to an end because of his injury. Butcher was appointed player-manager following the sacking of Malcom Crosby in February 1993.

Butcher took over from Malcolm Crosby at Roker Park after the team struggled find their form after their appearance in the FA Cup Final in 1992. In the end they were lucky to avoid relegation and Butcher had a lot to do before the start of a new season if they were not to struggle again.

BUTLER, Jack Dennis

Born: Colombo, Ceylon, 14 August 1894; Died: South East London, 5 January 1961.
Centre-half   5ft 11çin; 11st 5lb (1925).
Career: West London Schools; Fulham Thursday; Fulham 1913; Dartford 1913-1914; Arsenal March 1914; Torquay United May 1930 £1,000), retired 1932; Daring (Brussels) coach 1932-1939; Leicester City coach October 1940; Copenhagen coach 1946; Torquay United manager June 1946-May 1947; Crystal Palace manager May 1947-May 1949; Daring (Brussels) manager May 1949; coached in Denmark; Colchester United manager June 1953-January 1955.

Honours: England international (1 cap); FA Cup runners-up 1927; London Challenge Cup winners 1922.

Jack Butler was a centre-half of willowy build, who was a commanding defender. Cool in action and a fine distributor, he became the Gunners' first 'stopper' centre-half, although he had joined the club as a centre-forward in March 1914. Butler served in the Royal Field Artillery during World War Two and reverted to half-back in peacetime and made his debut in November 1919.

He made 296 appearances for Arsenal and played in their 1927 FA Cup Final defeat against Cardiff City. Butler also played once for England, against Belgium at West Bromwich in December 1924. When he became a manager at Torquay United and then Crystal Palace, his assistant was Bob John, a colleague in the Gunners side. He was not a great success at any of his clubs. Palace and Colchester both had to seek re-election during his terms of office.

BUTLER, Dennis A.

Born: Macclesfield, 24 June 1944.
Winger   5ft 6in; 9st 8lb (1964).
Career: Atherton; Bolton Wanderers June 1961; Rochdale, February 1968, retired 1973, then youth team coach 1973; Bury coach; Port Vale coach, then manager May 1978-September 1979.

Dennis Butler made his debut for Bolton Wanderers in December 1963 but lost his place the following season after cartilage problems. Thereafter, he struggled to gain regular first-team soccer at Burnden Park. With the arrival of Terry Wharton, Butler moved to Rochdale, where he scored 39 goals in 156 appearances. He was assistant manager to Bob Smith at Port Vale but when Smith moved to Swindon Town,

Butler took over. The club finished 16th in Division Four in 1978-79 and he was sacked after a poor start to the following season. He is the nephew of William Butler.

BUTLER, William

Born: Atherton, 27 March 1900; Died: 11 July 1966.
Outside-right   5ft 7in; 10st 9lb (1933).
Career: Howe Bridge; Atherton Colliery; Bolton Wanderers May 1921; Reading June 1933, then manager August 1935-February 1939 and caretaker manager April-May 1939; Guildford City manager June 1939; Torquay United manager cs 1945-May 1946; Johannesburg Rangers (South Africa) manager; Pietermaritzburg & District FA coach; Rhodesian FA coach.

Honours: England international (1 cap); FA Cup winners 1923, 1926, 1929.

Billy Butler was an outside-right who possessed a fine turn of speed and expertise at dribbling. He gained one cap for England, against Scotland in 1924, and later had two benefit matches for Bolton. The son of a rugby player, he joined the Army as a boy and became prominent in his local North Lancashire Regiment. As a centre-forward for Atherton, Butler once scored nine goals in a match.

One of Wanderers' best-ever wingers, he scored the opening goal in their 1929 FA Cup Final victory and had popped in another four goals in their run to the Final. Butler scored 74 goals in his 449 appearances for Bolton and asked for a transfer when the club was relegated in 1933. He was reunited with his former teammate, Joe Smith, who was the Reading manager. Butler took over as manager of Reading when Smith left the club. He was a PT instructor in the RAF during World War Two.

BUXTON, Michael

Born: Corbridge, 29 May 1943.
Full-back   5ft 10½in; 11st (1970).
Career: Burnley June 1960; Halifax Town player-coach June 1969-1971; Southend coach cs 1971-1978; Huddersfield Town coach 1978, then manager October 1978-December 1986; Scunthorpe United manager April 1987-January 1991.

Honours: Division Three promotion 1983; Division Four champions 1980.

Mick Buxton had a very brief Football League career, playing 19 games for Burnley and 35 times for Halifax Town. He is better known as a manager. His first post was at Huddersfield Town where he succeeded Tom John-

ston. In his first full season in charge he led the Terriers to the Fourth Division championship as the team failed to score in only six games out of 46 and hit a century of goals. The following season the club missed promotion again by only three points. The Terriers eventually went up into the Second Division in 1983 after finishing third. The club then held their own until Buxton's departure in 1986. At Scunthorpe he took over from caretaker manager Richard Money and guided the side to the Fourth Division play-offs in 1988 and 1989, but they failed to win promotion each time. The fans became discontent in 1990-91 and called for the resignation of both chairman Graham Pearson and Mick Buxton. Pearson went in September 1990 followed by Buxton four months later.

BYCROFT, Sydney

Born: Lincoln, 19 February 1912.
Centre-half   6ft 1in; 14st (1938).
Career: Grantham; Newark Town; Doncaster Rovers January 1936-1952, then various staff jobs including manager February-June 1958 (joint with Jack Hodgson)

Honours: Division Three North champions 1947, 1950.

Syd Bycroft is one of the most famous names in Doncaster Rovers' history and served the club for almost 25 years as player, trainer and manager. Despite losing seven seasons to the war, Bycroft made 333 League appearances for the club and also played in 150 wartime games. He continued to work for Rovers after retirement in various capacities, including being the joint manager with Jack Hodgson in 1958. They were unable to prevent the club from finishing bottom of the Second Division. Bycroft played in Rovers' Third Division North championship sides in 1947 and 1950.

CALDERHEAD,
David (senior)

Born: Hurlford, Ayrshire, 19 June 1864; Died: 9 January 1938.
Centre-half
Career: Wishaw Swifts; Wishaw Thistle; Queen of the South Wanderers cs 1881; Notts County 1889; Lincoln City secretary-manager 1900-August 1907 (retired as a player 1901); Chelsea manager cs August 1907-June 1933, when he retired from football.

Honours: Scottish international (1 cap); Football League representative (1 cap); Division Two champions 1897, runners-up 1912, 1930; FA Cup winners 1894, runners-up 1891, 1915.

David Calderhead served Chelsea as manager for 26 years. He was a quiet, reserved man who played a conspicuous part in setting Stamford Bridge football on its feet. A man of action rather than words, Calderhead never sought the spotlight and rarely gave an interview to the Press.

He played in Scottish junior football before joining Queen of the South Wanderers and in 1889, he was capped for Scotland against Ireland before moving south later that year to join Notts County. He gained no more caps due to the Scottish selection committee's stand against using Anglo-Scots in their sides, which was unfortunate, as Calderhead was one of the best centre-halves of the 1890s.

He maintained a high level of performance and was an inspired leader as Notts County's skipper from 1893 to 1900. He appeared in two FA Cup

Finals for the Magpies, picking up a winners' medal in 1894 and a losers' medal three years earlier. County also won the Second Division championship in 1896-97 and finished fifth in the First Division two seasons later. He made 285 League appearances for County scoring 12 goals in 11 seasons at the club. Whilst at County he also played for the Football League v the Football Alliance, the Rest of the League v Aston Villa and captained the Anglo-Scots against England in a fundraising match in aid of the Langton Explosion Fund.

In 1900, Calderhead became the secretary-manager of Lincoln City. In 1901-02 he took them to their highest-ever position in the Football League when they finished in fifth place in Division Two. It was always a struggle during his seven seasons at Sincil Bank, the Imps usually finishing in the bottom half of the table.

Calderhead became Chelsea's manager in the close season of 1907. He was to remain with the club until 1933. During this time, Chelsea had their ups and downs but were mainly a First Division club. During his first season at Stamford Bridge he paid the first-ever four figure transfer fee for the club, £1,000 to Stoke for Fred Rouse. Chelsea appeared in the 1915 FA Cup Final where they lost to Sheffield United 3-0 in the game now known as the 'Khaki Cup Final' due to there being so many men in uniform at the game in the early days of World War One.

The club beat Swindon Town, Arsenal, Manchester City, Newcastle United and Everton on the way to the Final. Chelsea also reached the semi-finals in 1910 and 1932, losing to Newcastle United on both occasions. The Blues were relegated to Division Two in 1910 and 1924, winning promotion as runners-up in Division Two in 1912 and 1930. With Chelsea second from bottom of the First Division, Calderhead announced he would be retiring at the end of the 1932-33 season. His son, also David, played for Chelsea and also managed Lincoln City.

CALDERHEAD,
David (Junior)

Born: Scotland.
Centre-half   5ft 9in; 12st 10lb (1919).
Career: Lincoln City; Chelsea September 1907; Motherwell April 1914; Leicester Fosse as guest in World War One; Clapton Orient 1919; Lincoln City secretary-manager April 1921-1924.

Not as successful as his father as a player, this David Calderhead played 43 games for Chelsea, eight for Leicester in wartime soccer and just one for Clapton Orient. His father was manager when he appeared at centre-half for Chelsea, but he was unable to claim a regular first-team place. At Lincoln, Caldershead was the secretary who was also in charge of team affairs. His best season was 1923-24, when the club finished eighth in the Third Division North.

CALLAGHAN,
Frederick John

Born: Parsons Green, 19 December 1944.
Left-back   5ft 9¾in; 11st 8lb (1970).
Career: West London Schools; Fulham August 1962, retired through injury 1974; Enfield manager cs 1974-1977; Woking manager 1977-March 1980; Brentford manager March 1980-February 1984; Sunderland scout 1985; Woking assistant manager November 1988-cs 1991; Kingstonian assistant manager cs 1991; Basingstoke manager November 1991. Basingstoke manager until January 1993.

A wholehearted player who was affectionately known as the 'Tank' by the Fulham crowd due to his surging runs up the wing to turn defence into attack, Fred Callaghan started as a right-half but was later converted to left-back. He survived Fulham's plummet from the First to the Third Division in the late 1960s but a slipped disc ended his career at the age of 29, after 326 appearances for Fulham, in which he scored 12 goals.

Whilst managing Woking and Enfield he worked also as a taxi driver. When he managed Brentford, the club finished in mid-table positions in each of his first three seasons in charge but he was sacked in February 1984 with the Bees in 21st place in Division Three. Callaghan went back to taxi driving before renewing his acquaintance with Woking, who won promotion to the Vauxhall League Premier Division in 1990.

CAMERON, John

Born: Ayr, 13 April 1872; Died: 20 April 1935.
Inside-forward   5ft 10in; 11st 6lb (1901).
Career: Ayr Grammar School; Ayr Parkhouse; Queen's Park; Everton September 1895; Tottenham Hotspur May 1898, then player-manager February 1899-March 1907; coached in Germany in 1914, interned during the war; Ayr United manager 1919; sports journalist.

Honours: Southern League champions 1900; FA Cup winners 1901.

One of the many Scottish players signed for Spurs by his predecessor, Frank Brettell, John Cameron took over as player-manager after Brettell's departure in 1899. Cameron played as an amateur until just before he left Everton. A goalscoring inside-forward, he led Spurs to an FA Cup Final victory over Sheffield United in 1901 and also to the Southern League championship in 1900 and runners-up in 1902 and 1904.

Cameron gradually took a less active role on the pitch to concentrate on his managerial responsibilities. He resigned in March 1907 after a difference of opinion with the directors. He managed his home-town club, Ayr United, just after World War One.

CAMERON,
William Smith 'Kilty'

Born: Mossend, Lanarkshire 1884; Died: 15 October 1958.
Inside-right   5ft 8in; 12st (1908).
Career: Burnbank Athletic 1902-1903; Albion Rovers 1903; Renton 1904; Glossop 1904; Bolton Wanderers cs 1906; Blackburn 1907; Bury 1912; Hull City January 1914; guest for Hamilton Academical in World War One; Bury player-manager May 1919-May 1923, then suspended for fixing games; Rochdale manager August 1930-December 1931; after retirement he became a licensee and firm's representative.

Honours: Football League champions 1912.

'Kilty' Cameron was banned for life for his involvement in a big bribery scandal which came to light in March 1923, three years after the events took place. For the fixture between Bury and Coventry City in April 1920, Bury players had paid the opposition £750 to square the match. His life suspension was revoked in 1929, along with the players and directors involved, and he returned to League management with Rochdale in August 1930. As Bury's manager, the club finished fifth in Division Two in 1919-20. He made a number of shrewd signings but as the Shakers were in debt, he was forced to sell to survive. Under his management Rochdale had to seek re-election in both seasons 1930-31 and 1931-32. He was sacked during a run of 26 games with only one point gained.

CAMPBELL,
Alistair Kenyon 'Alec'

Born: South Stoneham, Southampton, 29 May 1890; Died: Cosham, Hants, 16 June 1943.
Centre-half   6ft 3in; 12st (1925).
Career: King Edward VI Grammar School (Southampton); Southampton 1908; Glossop cs 1909; West Ham United 1913; Southampton January 1914; guest for West Ham United during World War One; Poole Town June 1926; Chesterfield April-December 1927; director of a Southampton fruit importers; also played seven first-class games for Hampshire CCC.

Honours: England Amateur international; Division Three South champions 1922.

Whilst at school, Campbell played for England in an Amateur international against Holland and is one of the few schoolboys to represent his country at this level. He made just three appearances in his first spell at The Dell before moving to Glossop, where he was again mainly a reserve. He did not make the first team at West Ham before returning to The Dell just before the outbreak of World War One. Campbell was the Saints' captain after the war and played in their first-ever Football League game, against Gillingham in August 1920. They finished runners-up that season but the following season gained the Third Division South championship, Campbell scoring eight goals in 37 appearances as an attacking centre-half. He just missed out on a Wembley appearance in 1925, when the Saints lost to Sheffield United in a semi-final at Stamford Bridge. He made a total of 176 appearances for the Saints and spent just eight months as manager of Chesterfield, in which they did relatively well.

CAMPBELL, Robert

Born: Renton.
Career: Sunderland manager August 1896-April 1899; Bristol City manager April 1899-1901; Bradford City manager June 1903-October 1905; secretary of Southern League and Referee Selection Committee.

Bristol City were elected to the Football League under Campbell's managership but he left the club after a disagreement with the directors over a huge wage bill. He won the job from 30 applicants and his brief had been to mould a team from the players acquired by the committee and he had no secretarial duties. Earlier in his career he had piloted Sunderland through a series of Test matches to retain their First Division status and the club were runners-up in 1897-98. At Bradford City he put the club on a firm footing and they finished in the top half of the Second Division in his two seasons at the club. He moved to Scotland, leaving the club by mutual consent in 1905. Campbell made a name for himself lecturing on football.

CAMPBELL, Robert

Born: Liverpool, 23 April 1937.
Wing-half   5ft 9in; 12st 4lb (1964).
Career: Liverpool Schools; Liverpool May 1954; Wigan Athletic cs 1961; Portsmouth November 1961 (£1,000); Aldershot, July 1966, retired through injury 1967; Portsmouth coach 1967-1972; Queen's Park Rangers coach 1972-1973; Arsenal coach September 1973-1976; Fulham chief coach July 1976, then manager December 1976-October 1980; Aldershot assistant manager 1980-1982; Portsmouth manager March 1982-May 1984; Arsenal assistant manager cs 1984; Queen's Park Rangers reserve-team coach; Chelsea manager March 1988-May 1991.

Honours: England Youth international; Division Two champions 1989; Division Three champions 1983; Simod Cup winners 1990.

Bobby Campbell won more fame as a manager than a player. He built a reputation as a coach with Pompey, Queen's Park Rangers and Arsenal. At

Queen's Park Rangers he worked with Gordon Jago to get the club back into the First Division. He moved to Highbury to work with Bertie Mee and joined Fulham as coach under Alec Stock but was promoted to manager when Stock was forced to leave by boardroom pressure.

A tough no-nonsense character, he made almost £1 million in profit on transfer fees during his period at the Cottage but greatly weakened the side which ended in relegation to the Third Division in 1980 and his sacking after a poor start to the 1980-81 season. Campbell took Pompey to the Third Division championship in 1983 but was surprisingly sacked in May 1984 after a season of consolidation in the Second. He enjoyed a successful spell at Stamford Bridge from March 1988, taking the club to the Second Division title in 1989 with a 17-point margin over runners-up Manchester City. Chelsea finished in a creditable fifth the following season. But despite spending nearly £4 million on players, Chelsea's fortunes faded and it was no surprise when he was replaced by Ian Porterfield. After this Campbell worked as chairman Ken Bates' personal assistant.

CAMPBELL, Robert Inglis

Born: Glasgow, 28 June 1922.
Winger   5ft 9in; 11st 7lb (1950).

Career: Glasgow Perthshire; Falkirk 1941; guest player for Queen's Park Rangers in World War Two; Chelsea May 1947 (£9,000); Reading player-coach August 1954; retired 1957; Reading coach until 1961; Dumbarton manager April 1961-1962; Bristol Rovers coach and trainer May 1962-November 1977, then manager November 1977-December 1979; Gloucester City manager November 1980-1982; Bristol City Council football coach.

Honours: Scotland international (5 caps).

Campbell lost some his best playing years to the war. He was an immediate success after joining Chelsea as a fast, direct winger and later played as an inside-forward. In his 213 games for the Blues, he scored 40 goals. He was a typical Scottish winger with natural ball skills and a good turn of speed. After coaching at Reading and a year in charge at Dumbarton, Campbell joined Bristol Rovers as coach under Bert Tann in 1962.

He stayed with the club for 17 years, the last two as manager. When he took over from Don Megson as manager, he was 55 years old but showed the

enthusiasm of a younger man. He bought and sold well on the transfer market but after a poor start to the 1979-80 season, he was sacked. Campbell was employed by Bristol City Council to arrange soccer matches for unemployed men.

CANN, Sydney Thomas

Born: Torquay, 30 October 1911.
Right-back/centre-half   5ft 8in; 11st 3lb (1933).

Career: Babbicombe School; Torquay United November 1928; Manchester City March 1930; Charlton Athletic June 1935-1939; guest for Torquay United, Aldershot and Bristol City in World War Two; Southampton assistant manager June 1946-1949, then manager August 1949-December 1951; FA coaching post 1951-1952; Wycombe Wanderers manager-coach July 1952-June 1961; Norwich City coach June 1961-March 1962; Sutton United manager-coach July 1962-September 1973.

Honours: England Schoolboy international (2 caps); FA Cup runners-up 1933; Football League War Cup 1943; FA Amateur Cup runners-up 1963, 1969.

Although not a first-team regular, Cann appeared for Manchester City in their 1933 Cup Final defeat against Everton but missed the following year's Final. Cann played only 42 games for City in his five seasons at Maine Road. He made just 15 appearances at The Valley, whilst Charlton were marching from the Third to the First Division. At Charlton, he met Bill Dodgin senior and became his assistant at The Dell after the war.

Cann joined the Army Physical Training Corps in World War Two and reached the rank of warrant officer. He qualified as a masseur at the Bristol College of Physiotherapy, joining the Saints in that capacity in the war. When Dodgin moved to Fulham as manager, Cann was promoted to the vacant manager's job at The Dell. In his first season in charge, the Saints missed promotion on goal-average. He resigned in 1951 after disagreements with the board and later took Sutton United to two FA Amateur Cup Finals, losing to Wimbledon in 1963 and to North Shields in 1969.

CANTWELL, Noel

Born: Cork, 28 February 1932.
Left-back   6ft; 12st 9lb (1964).
Career: Cork United; West Ham United September 1952; Manchester United November 1960 (£29,500); PFA chairman 1966-October 1967; Coventry City manager October 1967-March 1972 and Republic of Ireland team manager October 1967-September 1968; New England Tea Men manager March-October 1972 and 1978-1982; Peterborough United manager October 1972-May 1977 and November 1986-July 1988, general manager until April 1989.

Honours: Republic of Ireland international (36 caps); Division Two champions 1958; Division Four champions 1974; FA Cup winners 1963; also represented Ireland at cricket.

An attacking full-back, Noel Cantwell formed a fine partnership with John Bond and helped West Ham to the Second Division title in 1958. He made 263 appearances for the Hammers before moving to Manchester United for £29,500, a record for a full-back at the time. He played in United's 1963 FA Cup Final side which beat Leicester

City 3-1 but made only a couple of appearances in their League championship side of 1965.

Cantwell started his managerial career in the First Division with Coventry City, which he later admitted was a tough baptism. He managed to keep the Bantams in the First Division and after finishing sixth in 1970 they took part in the Fairs Cup. Along with chief scout Bob Dennison, he produced a long line of talented players from the club's youth scheme. When he left Highfield Road he was given a £30,000 golden handshake. When he joined Peterborough, the club were rock bottom of the Football League. He rejuvenated the Posh and they finished as Fourth Division champions in 1974. In November 1986 he returned to manage Peterborough for a second time and was later general manager until sacked in April 1989.

CAREY, John James

Born: Dublin, 23 February 1919.
Full-back/Wing-half   5ft 10½in; 11st (1937).
Career: St James' Gate (Ireland); Manchester United November 1936-1953; Blackburn Rovers manager June 1953-October 1958; Everton manager October 1958-April 1961; Leyton Orient manager August 1961-August 1963; Nottingham Forest manager July 1963-December 1968; Blackburn Rovers general manager January 1969, then manager October 1970-June 1971; also Republic of Ireland manager for a spell.

Honours: Republic of Ireland international (29 caps); Northern Ireland international (7 caps); Rest of Europe v Great Britain; Footballer of the Year 1949; Football League champions 1952; Division Two runners-up 1958, 1962; FA Cup winners 1948.

As well as being the outstanding captain of Manchester United and the Republic of Ireland, Johnny Carey also managed five clubs after his retirement as a player in 1953. He was spotted by Manchester United scout, Louis Rocca, by chance, playing for the Dublin club, St James' Gate. Rocca had gone over to Ireland to watch another player but had been more impressed by Carey.

He joined United in November 1936 for a small fee of £240 and made his debut in September 1937 at inside-left, helping United to promotion that season. Six weeks after his League debut, Carey made his international debut for the Republic of Ireland against Norway in a World Cup qualifying match in Dublin which was drawn 3-3. Instead of returning home at the outbreak of war, he joined the

British Army and served in Italy. He was nicknamed 'Cario' by the local fans when he found himself playing for a number of Italian professional sides with considerable success.

Carey played an intelligent, constructive game, his skill augmented by an excellent physique. He was also a versatile player, appearing in nearly every position for United including goalkeeper in an emergency. His influence was incalculable. Carey was a commanding presence, a natural leader of men who possessed matchless ability to read the game. Matt Busby appointed him captain after the war and was seen as being able to transmit his wishes on to the field.

Carey started as an inside-forward, was later converted to wing-half and finally, most successfully to full-back. His positional play allowed him to appear unhurried.

He led United to a remarkable FA Cup Final success over Blackpool in 1948, when the team came from 2-1 down to win 4-2. United also won the League championship in 1951-52 after finishing as runners-up in four of the previous five seasons. As well as representing both the Republic of Ireland and Northern Ireland, Carey also captained the Rest of Europe side against Great Britain in 1947 and was voted Footballer of the Year in 1949.

He led the Republic of Ireland to a shock 2-0 victory over England at Goodison Park in 1949 and had the unusual distinction of representing both Irelands against England in the space of three days in September 1946.

When Carey retired in 1953, he was still at the top and could have probably played on for another two seasons. Despite the lost war years, he still made 306 League appearances for United. Carey became the manager at Blackburn Rovers in June 1953. He changed the fortunes of the club after years of struggle and they finally won promotion to Division One in 1958 after a number of near-misses. Carey built a fine forward line at Ewood Park around winger Bryan Douglas and centre-forward Tommy Briggs.

The success established Carey's reputation as a manager and in October 1958 he accepted a lucrative offer to manage Everton. At Goodison he inherited a promising squad which included Bobby Collins, Derek Temple and Brian Labone. He was also fortunate to arrive when lifelong Everton supporter John Moores moved in to become the club's benefactor. With his arrival came a massive financial backing.

Carey went into the transfer market to buy some of the most talented players available including Roy Vernon, Billy Bingham, Alex Young and Jimmy Gabriel. He took Everton to their highest post-war position of fifth in 1960-61, after two largely disappointing seasons. Ironically, he was sacked by Moores in April 1961, whilst attending a Football League meeting in London. He must be the only manager ever sacked in a London taxi.

Although stunned and saddened, he made no fuss, accepting the decision with dignity. Carey gave two reasons for his sacking. Moores wanted a man he had appointed himself and Carey had been there before him; also he wanted a tough manager, someone to crack the whip. But Carey's sacking angered the fans.

Carey was soon employed again, two months later by Leyton Orient, and managed the club through what was probably their greatest era. His first season ended in promotion to the First Division for the first time in the club's history. They left it to the last match against Bury to clinch their promotion place. Carey gave the same side a chance to prove themselves in the top flight, although with no money available and the directors, not prepared to put the club in debt, he had little choice. Defeat followed defeat as Orient dropped back down again after only one season. His only major signing had been Malcolm Musgrove, signed from West Ham for £11,000.

Carey decided to leave the club and joined Nottingham Forest as manager in July 1963. He also managed the Republic of Ireland side for a while. Forest reached a peak in 1966-67, when they finished runners-up in the League and reached the last four in the FA Cup. Carey bought wisely. His signings included Terry Hennessey for £50,000 from Birmingham City, Joe Baker and John Barnwell, for less than £100,000 from Arsenal, and Alan Hinton from Wolves.

Forest's success was not enough and after dropping into the relegation zone, the club committee fired Carey in December 1968. One of the reasons he left was his inability to make any effective use of Jim Baxter, for whom the club had paid £100,000 in 1967. Baxter made only 48 appearances for the club before being given a free transfer.

In January 1969, after no other offer, Carey returned to Blackburn Rovers as general manager. They were struggling near the bottom of the Second Division with Eddie Quigley as team manager. In October 1970, he became team manager but when the club went down to the Third Division he was sacked in June 1971. He left football to work for a tile company and did not seem to miss football as he rarely attended a game.

Carey eventually retired in February 1984 from a post in the treasurer's office of Trafford Borough Council. Carey had never been a manager in the style of Revie, Doherty or Clough. He was a 'front man', the genial father-figure who presented the right image for a club, perhaps surviving more on respect than on ability. Although sacked three times, usually without warning, he publicly accepted his fate with a dignified and philosophical calmness of a truly wise man.

CARR, Edward Miller

Born: Wheatley Hill, 3 October 1917.
Centre-forward   5ft 6in; 10st 6lb.
Career: Wheatley Hill Colliery; Arsenal February 1935; Margate; guest for Bradford, Darlington and Newcastle United in World War Two; Huddersfield Town July 1945; Newport County October 1946; Bradford City October 1949; Darlington August 1953, trainer July 1954-1960, then manager June 1960-1964; Tow Law Town manager 1964-1969; Newcastle United scout 1969.

Eddie Carr played in Arsenal's nursery side, Margate, before making the big breakthrough in 1937-38, when he scored seven goals in 11 games for the Gunners after Ted Drake was injured. Alas, this was not enough appearances to pick up a League championship medal that season. In 1946-47 he scored 19 goals for Newport County, despite them finishing bottom of the Second Division. He scored 47 goals in 98 League appearances for Newport before joining Bradford City, where he scored 56 goals in 98 appearances.

After six years as the Darlington trainer, Carr became the caretaker manager in June 1960 and his job was made permanent five months later. He had an eventful start as manager with the opening of floodlights, followed by the West Stand at Feethams burning down. Successes were rare and although Darlington did beat West Ham 3-2 in the League Cup, after a 10-0 defeat at Doncaster and an FA Cup defeat against non-League Gateshead, Carr was sacked. As manager of Tow Law Town in the late 1960s, he saw that club have a memorable FA Cup victory over Mansfield Town, by 5-1.

CARR, John

Born: Seaton Burn, Newcastle Spring 1876; Died: 17 March 1948.
Left-back   5ft 9½in; 12st 4lb (1903).
Career: Seaton Burn; Newcastle United December 1899, retired cs 1912, then assistant trainer 1912-1922; Blackburn Rovers manager February 1922-December 1926; also played cricket for Northumberland;

Honours: England international (2 caps); Football League representative (1 cap); Football League champions 1905, 1907, 1909; FA Cup winners 1910, runners-up 1905, 1906.

Originally a half-back but converted to left-back by Newcastle United, Jack Carr often kept Billy McCracken in the Reserves for long periods. Well built, Carr used his physical advantages with brilliant judgement. After two losers' medals in the FA Cup, he finally gained a winners' medal in the 1910 replay against Barnsley when he replaced Whitsun in the side after the first drawn match.

Carr won League championship medals on three occasions with 27, 26 and 11 appearances respectively in seasons 1904-05, 1906-07 and 1908-09. In February 1922, after ten years as the Magpies' trainer, he took control at Ewood Park. The club maintained a mid-table position in Division One during his four years at Blackburn. The highlight was an FA Cup semi-final appearance in 1925, but Rovers lost 3-1 to Cardiff City. Carr was team manager until September 1925, when he became the secretary-manager.

CARR, John 'Jackie'

Born: South Bank, 26 November 1892; Died: 10 May 1942.
Outside-right   5ft 9in; 11st 4lb (1914).
Career: South Bank; Middlesbrough February 1911; guest for Fulham in World War One; Blackpool May 1930; Hartlepools United player-coach July 1931, then manager April 1932-April 1935; Tranmere Rovers manager July 1935-November 1936; Darlington manager October 1938-May 1942.

Honours: England international (2 caps); Division Two champions 1927,

1929; FA Amateur Cup runners-up 1910.

A tee-totaller and non-smoker, Jackie Carr was still playing at the age of 40. He made 449 appearnaces for 'Boro after beginning his career as a right-winger with South Bank where he gained an Amateur Cup runners-up medal when they lost to RMLI Gosport in the 1910 Final. Carr was a subtle schemer and provider of goal chances. He played alongside his brothers, Willie and George, at Ayresome Park.

Jackie lost his first job at Hartlepools after a cost-cutting exercise but was selected from 60 applicants for the Tranmere post. He developed a great knowledge of the game, had a sound understanding of the players and also possessed a great sense of humour. Tranmere led the Third Division North for much of the 1935-36 season but collapsed to finish third. He left the club the following season after a further slump in form.

CARR, William Graham

Born: Newcastle upon Tyne, 25 October 1944.
Half-back
Career: Corinthians (Newcastle junior soccer); Northampton Town August 1962; York City June 1968; Bradford July 1969; Altrincham; Telford United; Dartford player-manager; Tonbridge; Weymouth player-manager; Nuneaton Borough manager until 1985; Northampton Town manager April 1985-May 1990; Blackpool manager June-November 1990; Maidstone United manager February-October 1991; Kettering Town manager September 1992.

Honours: England Youth international; Division Four champions 1987; FA Trophy winners 1971.

Graham Carr captained Northampton Town Reserves before breaking into the Football League with the Cobblers. He made 27 appearances at wing-half or full-back in their only season in the First Division and played in 160 League games before retirement. Carr then spent ten years in non-League management before returning to manage Northampton in 1985. The 1986-87 season saw the club as outstanding Fourth Division champions with Richard Hill scoring 32 goals. Hill was later sold to Watford for £258,000 and Trevor Morley went to Manchester City for £200,000. Carr thereafter produced a series of dull, negative sides which relied heavily on the offside trap. The Cobblers suffered crippling ground problems and Carr was sacked after their relegation to Division Four in 1990. He then took over at fellow relegated club, Blackpool, soon afterwards.

His reign at Bloomfield Road was as short as it was unsuccessful, for he arrived in the close season and left the following November, thus making him the Seasiders' shortest-serving manager ever. He was never popular with the fans, especially after selling Player of the Year Colin Methven to Carlisle United, and was dismissed after Blackpool lost 4-0 at Tranmere in the Leyland Daf Cup. He spell at Maidstone was also short and he left for 'personal reasons'.

CARTER, Horatio Stratton 'Raich'

Born: Hendon, Sunderland, 21 December 1913.

Inside-forward   5ft 8in; 10st 6lb (1937).
Career: Sunderland Schools; Whitburn St Mary; Esh Winning; Sunderland Forge; Leicester City on trial; Esh Winning; Sunderland amateur November 1930, professional November 1931; Derby County December 1945 (£8,000); Hull City player-assistant manager March 1948 (£6,000), then manager March 1948-September 1951; Cork Athletic January-May 1953; Leeds United manager May 1953-June 1958; Mansfield Town manager January 1960-January 1963; Middlesbrough manager January 1963-February 1966; then returned to Hull to run a sports outfitting department in a local store.

Honours: England international (13 caps); Wartime international; Schoolboy international (4 caps); Football League representative (4 caps); Football League champions 1936; Division Two runners-up 1956; Division Three North champions 1949; FA Cup winners 1937, 1946; FA of Ireland Cup winners 1953.

Raich Carter was one of the greatest inside-forwards ever produced by England, an ice-cool player who always seemed in control of the game. Carter was the complete inside-forward who could create and take chances with equal flair. He had a fine footballing brain and could shoot fiercely with either foot. He was an arrogant performer, strutting around the midfield and dictating the flow of play as he saw fit.

And whilst he was not as great a manager as he was a player, he had varied amounts of success with Hull City, Leeds United, Mansfield Town and Middlesbrough. As a manager his biggest problem was that he could not suffer fools gladly, usually because he was such a perfectionist. Carter was unable to come to terms with footballers who were infinitely less talented than himself and he gained a reputation as a sound rather than spectacular manager.

He first came to be noticed in England's Schoolboy side in 1927, when he gained four caps in company with Len Goulden and Cliff Bastin. Carter had an unsuccessful trial with Leicester City but Sunderland soon saw his potential. He was capped for the first time by England in 1934, against Scotland at Wembley, but thereafter was only spasmodically recalled to the international side and, of course, the war robbed him of many caps.

In 1935-36, Carter's enthusiasm and arrogance lifted a bunch of largely ageing players to win the League championship title and a year later he skippered Sunderland to an FA Cup Final success over Preston. So, by the time he was 23, he had won every major honour then open to an English footballer.

During the war he served in the RAF and appeared for Derby County whilst helping to rehabilitate injured airmen at RAF Loughborough. Unsettled at Sunderland, who after a disagreement had put Carter on the transfer list, he moved on to Derby County permanently for a fee of £6,000. "Sunderland were silly to sell me for that price and Derby were lucky to get me," he once said. At Derby, he formed a dynamic partnership with Irish international Peter Doherty, who was serving with him at Loughborough, and they helped the Rams to an FA Cup Final success over Charlton Athletic in 1946.

In March 1948, Carter joined Hull City as player-assistant manager, but within two months he was made the manager in succession to Major Frank Buckley. Carter's now famous silver-grey hair was to become a familiar sight in football as the Tigers experienced something of a renaissance under his management. He believed in the minimum amount of change in a side and used only 12 players for the bulk in the Northern Section championship season of 1948-49. Hull set a record of nine successive wins from the start of the season and also reached the quarter-finals of the FA Cup as the Tigers played before huge home attendances, for the Third Division, several topping the 40,000 mark.

Carter was a quiet man off the field and a calming influence in the dressing-room and he was as surprised as anyone by his instant success. When he resigned in September 1951, after failing to get the Tigers into First Division, despite signing such players as Don Revie and Neil Franklin, he said he was leaving because of 'disagreements on matters of a general nature in the conduct of the club's affairs'. Without him, Hull plummeted down the table and he was persuaded to finish the season as a player. With Carter back in the side, the Tigers avoided relegation.

Carter retired from playing in 1952, after scoring 216 goals in 451 League appearances for his three clubs. As well as his 13 international caps, he also won eight wartime caps and made four Football League representative appearances. In January 1953, at the age of 40, he made a comeback with Cork Athletic, winning an FA of Ireland Cup medal that season. He flew to Dublin every match-day and was then driven to wherever Cork were playing.

In May 1953, Carter returned to football management in charge of Leeds United. He steered the club into the First Division in 1955-56 and it came as a surprise when Leeds decided not to renew his contract in June 1958, although his authoritarian approach seemed less productive off the field than on it at Elland Road. There were times when players rubbed him up the wrong way.

Carter was out of football for a while before returning to manage Mansfield Town in January 1960, but the Stags were relegated to Division Four at the end of the season. After two seasons of struggle, Mansfield returned to the Third Division in 1963 after finishing fourth.

In January 1963, Carter's success at Field Mill brought an offer from Middlesbrough to manage them. But it was a constant struggle at Ayresome Park as 'Boro fought against relegation

to Division Three and, when the drop came, Carter was dismissed. His dealings on the transfer market were disappointing. He allowed promising players like Alan Peacock and Cyril Knowles to leave the club and did not buy wisely with the money from these transfer fees.

Raich Carter finished with soccer after this and returned to Hull to run a sports department of a local store. He later ran a credit business in Hull and today lives in nearby Willerby, sadly now suffering from poor health.

CARVER, Jesse

Born: Liverpool, 7 July 1911.
Centre-half   5ft 10in; 13st (1937).
Career: Blackburn Rovers 1929; Newcastle United June 1936 (£2,000); Bury April 1939 (£850); Huddersfield Town assistant trainer 1946-1947; Dutch FA coach 1947; Lazio, Juventus and Valdagho coach; Torino coach 1952; West Bromwich Albion manager May 1952-February 1953; AS Roma manager 1953; Coventry City manager June-December 1955; Lazio manager January 1956-1958; Genoa manager; Internazionale manager; Tottenham Hotspur coach October 1958-March 1959; then to Portugal and USA as coach.

Honours: Italian League champions 1950 (with Juventus).

Jesse Carver was a butcher's assistant when he joined Blackburn Rovers, the club for whom he made 146 League and Cup appearances at centre-half before the emergence of Bob Pryde and a dispute over a benefit payment soured his relationship with the Ewood Park club. He later made 76 appearances for Newcastle but gained more fame as a coach after the war with his revolutionary ideas. He was very successful in Italy and guided Juventus to the League championship at his first attempt and later coached Roma, Lazio, Internazionale, Torino and Genoa. West Brom finished fourth in the First Division in the season that he managed the Throstles but when he returned from Italy to manage Coventry City with George Raynor they found disillusionment. A highly regarded coach and manager on the continent, he was under-used in England.

CASEY, Thomas

Born: Camber, East Belfast, 11 March 1930.
Wing-half   5ft 8½in; 11st 4lb (1950).
Career: Camber School; Second Argyle School (Belfast); Belfast YMCA; Bangor; East Belfast; Leeds United May 1949; Bournemouth August 1950; Newcastle United August 1952 (£7,500); Portsmouth June 1958; (£8,500); Bristol City March 1959; Gloucester City player-manager cs 1963; Swansea Town trainer c.1964-October 1966; Distillery manager cs 1967; Everton assistant coach July 1972; Coventry City coach 1974-1975; Grimsby Town manager February 1975-November 1976.

Honours: Northern Ireland international (12 caps); Youth international; FA Cup winners 1955.

Tommy Casey was a human dynamo, a tough tackler who was the workhorse of the side. In all he made 332 League appearances for his five League clubs and played for the Northern Ireland side which reached the quarter-finals of the World Cup in 1958. His first chance of Football League management came at Grimsby in 1975. Resources were limited at Blundell Park and he was able to buy only three players

during his 21 months in charge. Casey established a sound youth policy which was his greatest legacy. He was sacked with the Mariners third from bottom of the Third Division, ironically on the day he moved into a newly-purchased house.

CASPER, Frank

Born: Barnsley, 9 December 1944.
Centre-forward   5ft 10in; 10st 7lb (1971).
Career: Rotherham United July 1962; Burnley June 1967 (£27,000), retired cs 1976; Burnley chief trainer, then caretaker manager January-June 1983; Bury coach 1984; assistant manager 1988-1989; Burnley manager January 1989-October 1991.

Honours: Football League representative; Division Two champions 1973.

Burnley paid a club record fee when they signed Frank Casper from Rotherham United. A slimly built player who could play in any forward position, he was best known as a centre-forward. He played for the Football League against the Scottish League at Hampden Park in March 1969 and scored 100 goals in 338 League appearances for Rotherham and Burnley.

Casper had been ever-present in Burnley's Second Division championship side of 1972-73 and also appeared in their Football League Cup semi-final defeat against Swindon Town in 1969. He joined Burnley's training staff on retirement and was made caretaker manager briefly in 1983. After five seasons at Bury, Casper returned to Turf Moor as the manager in January 1989. Casper spent a great deal of money on the transfer market but Burnley finished in a disappointing 16th spot in Division Four in 1989-90. The following season they lost to Torquay United in the play-offs after finishing sixth. Casper lost his job in October 1991 after which Burnley's form improved enormously and they eventually took the Fourth Division championship

CATTERICK, Harry

Born: Darlington, 26 November 1919.
Died: Goodison Park, 9 March 1985.
Centre-forward   5ft 9in; 10st 10lb (1937).
Career: Stockport County amateur; Cheadle Heath Nomads; Everton March 1937; guest for Manchester United in World War Two; retired 1952; Crewe Alexandra manager December 1951-June 1953; Rochdale manager June 1953-August 1958; Sheffield Wednesday manager August 1958-April 1961; Everton manager April 1961-April 1973; Preston North End manager August 1975-May 1977.

Honours: Football League champions 1963, 1970; Division Two champions 1959; FA Cup winners 1966, runners-up 1968.

Harry Catterick was one of the greatest managers of the post-war years, reaching the pinnacle of his success with Everton in the 1960s and '70s.

As a player at Goodison Park, Catterick was understudy to Tommy Lawton, then Jock Dodds, and his appearances were also limited by the intervention of the war and a couple of serious injuries. When peacetime soccer returned, he broke his arm twice in a short space of time. But, despite some tempting offers, he remained loyal to Everton until becoming player-manager of Crewe Alexandra in December 1951. He retired from playing the following year to concentrate on management.

Catterick learned his trade in the hard proving grounds of lower division soccer and after moving to Rochdale he brought the Spotland club their first successful side for many years, building a team from free-transfer players. In his five seasons at Rochdale, the club was always in a healthy mid-table position and in his last season at the club they finished tenth to enter the newly-formed Third Division.

Catterick joined Sheffield Wednesday in August 1958 and established his reputation as the Owls won promotion from Division Two in his first season at Hillsborough, followed by a run to the FA Cup semi-finals in 1960 and runners-up position behind Spurs in Division One in 1960-61. His departure disappointed the fans but Catterick was possibly frustrated by the lack of money to buy new players. He also had an uneasy relationship with club secretary Eric Taylor.

Catterick resigned due to interference from the board, but was out of work for only ten days before being offered the Everton job. Everton was Catterick's first love and whilst he was with them as a player, he had taken time to learn from secretary Theo Kelly all about the administrative aspects of running a football club. Whilst other players spent time playing cards, golf or snooker, Catterick would read books on the laws, organisation and control of the game. He shunned publicity, never openly criticising his players, his opponents or referees. Indeed, Harry Catterick earned the reputation as the silent gentleman of football.

The Everton directors allowed him to buy and sell whom he wished, within an agreed spending limit, and he also had a flair for finding and developing young players.

Thus, Catterick built two League championship teams at Everton, transforming them into a great side after a period of mediocrity. He was a tough task-master and a strict disciplinarian, who ruled his staff with a rod of iron whilst managing to retain the human touch when getting the best out of his players. He also gained a fine reputation for his wheeling and dealing on the transfer market and brought a succession of top quality players to Goodison Park, including Gordon West, Tony Kay, Ray Wilson, Fred Pickering, Alan Ball and Howard Kendall.

The League championship was won with style in 1962-63 before the bitter blow of one of his signings, Tony Kay, being banned for life and imprisoned for fixing games whilst with his — and

Catterick's — former club, Sheffield Wednesday. Everton soon recovered from this blow to win the FA Cup Final in 1966, beating the Owls 3-2 after being two goals down.

Catterick had taken a gamble by dropping star striker Fred Pickering and selecting the hitherto unknown Cornishman Mike Trebilcock. It paid off handsomely when Trebilcock scored two of Everton's Wembley goals.

Catterick signed Alan Ball for a record fee and his youth policy also began to pay dividends, producing Jimmy Husband, Joe Royle and John Hurst amongst others. He also signed Howard Kendall in March 1967 and the Toffees reached the FA Cup Final again in 1968 before losing to West Brom by a single goal.

The 1969-70 season proved to be one of triumph for Everton with another League championship. With Colin Harvey, Kendall and Ball now running the midfield, and Royle hitting the target regularly, they regained the title with style.

After a disappointing couple of seasons. Catterick suffered from two illnesses, one of which was a mild heart attack in January 1972, which reduced his ability to carry on as a 'tracksuit' manager. He became Everton's general manager in April 1973, but two years later made a comeback as team manager of Preston North End, where he stayed two years before retiring from soccer in 1977. Harry Catterick collapsed and died after watching an Everton v Ipswich FA Cup tie at his beloved Goodison Park on 9 March 1985.

CATTLIN, Christopher
Born: Milnrow, 25 June 1946.
Defender   5ft 11in; 12st 6lb (1971).
Career: Burnley amateur; Huddersfield Town August 1964; Coventry City March 1968 (£70,000); Brighton & Hove Albion June 1976, retired cs 1980, coach 1978, then manager October 1983-April 1986.

Honours: England Under-23 internationals (2 caps).

One of a long line of top class full-backs produced by the Terriers, Chris Cattlin played in 217 League games for Coventry City before his move to Brighton. Very popular with the fans at Highfield Road, he was affectionately known as Spider. He managed just two goals in his career.

Cattlin helped Brighton to promotion to Division One in 1979, as runners-up, but was unable to make the first team in the higher bracket. In his first season in charge at Brighton they finished ninth in Division Two. Maintaining mid-table positions was not

considered good enough and, despite getting to the sixth round of the FA Cup, he was sacked shortly afterwards.

CAVANAGH, Thomas H.
Born: Liverpool, 29 June 1928.
Inside-forward   5ft 8in; 11st (1959).

Career: Preston North End August 1949; Stockport County January 1950; Huddersfield Town May 1952; Doncaster Rovers May 1956; Bristol City July 1959; Carlisle United June 1960; Cheltenham Town player-manager April 1961; Brentford trainer, then manager January 1965-March 1966; Nottingham Forest trainer-coach 1966; Hull City coach July 1971; Manchester United trainer December 1972, assistant manager 1977-1980; Newcastle United assistant manager 1981-1982; Burnley manager October 1985-June 1986; Wigan Athletic coach 1988-1989.

Tommy Cavanagh made a total of 302 League appearances, scoring 57 goals, for his six clubs. His first experience as a manager was as player-boss of Southern League Cheltenham Town. At Brentford he lasted barely a season which ended in relegation to Division Four. He worked with Johnny Carey at Forest, who reached an FA Cup semi-final and were runners-up in the First Division in 1967. At Hull and Manchester United he teamed up with his old mate from his Preston days, Tommy Docherty, and with his training schedules he gained a reputation as a 'slave driver' who was totally committed to football. United won the FA Cup in 1977 and were Finalists twice and also won the Second Division championship during his time at the club. He was only briefly in charge at Burnley, who finished 14th in Division Four during that season.

CHADWICK, Arthur
Born: Church, Lancashire, summer 1875; Died: Exeter, 21 March 1936.
Half-back   5ft 8in; 12st (1904).
Career: Church; Accrington; Burton Swifts 1894; Southampton cs 1897; Portsmouth cs 1901; Northampton Town cs 1904; Accrington cs 1906; Exeter City player-manager April 1908-December 1922, retired from playing in 1910; Reading manager January 1923-October 1925; Southampton October 1925-May 1931.

Honours: England international (2 caps); Southern League champions 1898, 1899, 1901, 1902; FA Cup runners-up 1900.

Edgar Chadwick, who had a reputation

as a fine penalty-taker, was converted to centre-half at Southampton. He gained two England caps in that position and played in the Saints' 1900 FA Cup Final defeat against Bury. Chadwick scored six goals in 81 appearances at The Dell before moving to Fratton Park, where he made 80 appearances, scoring 14 goals in all competitions. He was in charge at Exeter City when they joined the Football League in 1920. Reading had three mediocre seasons with Chadwick in charge and he resigned to take over at Southampton. He took the Saints to the semi-finals of the FA Cup in 1927 but had to sell Saints' best players for the club to survive. He died in 1936, whilst watching Exeter City from the stands.

CHAMBERS, Philip Martin
Born: Barnsley, 10 November 1953.
Left back   5ft 7¼in; 11st 1lb (1982).
Career: Worsborough High School; Barnsley apprentice 1969, professional November 1971; Rochdale August 1985; Hartlepool United November 1985; Scarborough youth-team coach, assistant manager 1991, then manager April 1993.

Honours: England Schoolboy International 6 caps.

A great club servant to Barnsley, Phil Chambers played over 400 games for the club and helped them to two promotions. In 1978-79, Chambers helped Barnsley to promotion from Division Four and was ever-present. Two seasons later he was captain as they finished as runners up in the Third Division. He made his debut in April 1971 whilst still an apprentice against Reading and established himself at left-back in season 1972-73. Phil made 170 consecutive appearances before missing a game. After a number of years, first as youth-team coach, then assistant manager, Chambers took over from Ray McHale as Scarborough's manager near the end of the 1992-93 season. His brother, David, played for Rotherham United, Southend United and York City.

CHAPLIN, John Fowler
Born: Dundee, 10 October 1882; Died: Doncaster, 15 April 1952.
Right-back   5ft 8†; 12st 10lb (1911).
Career: Dundee Arnot; Dundee Wanderers; Tottenham Hotspur 1905; Dundee 1908; Manchester City November 1910; Leeds City November 1913; career ended by knee injury; Leeds City assistant manager-trainer; Sheffield Wednesday assistant trainer; Bristol Rovers assistant trainer; Huddersfield Town trainer 1921-1926 and May 1929-1935, manager August 1926-May 1929.

Honours: Scottish League representative; FA Cup runners-up 1928.

Jack Chaplin was Herbert Chapman's assistant during the great man's days at Leeds City and Huddersfield Town. In fact, Chaplin served the Town for 14 years, first as trainer, then as manager before reverting to trainer again.

The oldest of three footballing brothers — Alec of Fulham and George of Bradford City — Chaplin made 67 Southern League and FA Cup appearances at full-back for Tottenham and won a Southern Charity Cup winners' medal in 1907, leaving Spurs just as they were joining the Football League. Another player at the club at this time was Herbert Chapman.

Chaplin moved back to his home town to play for Dundee, where he won two Scottish League representative

honours against the Irish League in October 1909, but returned to England to join Manchester City in November 1910. After a knee injury ended his playing career, he joined Leeds City as assistant trainer under Herbert Chapman in November 1913 and later became Chapman's assistant manager. When the club was wound-up in October 1919, Chaplin became assistant trainer at Sheffield Wednesday for a period and later held a similar post at Bristol Rovers.

Chaplin was reunited with Herbert Chapman at Huddersfield Town, where he was the trainer during a golden period in the club's history. In 1922 they beat Preston 1-0 to win the FA Cup at Stamford Bridge. This was followed by three League titles in successive seasons, 1923-24, 1924-25 and 1925-26. Chapman moved to Highbury as manager in 1925 and after Cecil Potter's brief period in charge at Leeds Road, Chaplin took over in August 1926.

It was a hard act to follow but the Town finished runners-up in the next two seasons — five points behind Newcastle United in 1926-27 and two points behind Everton the following season. They also reached the FA Cup Final again in 1928, losing 3-1 to Blackburn Rovers at Wembley.

The 1928-29 season saw the start of Huddersfield's decline when they reached the FA Cup semi-finals again but finished 16th in the First Division. Chaplin reverted to trainer again in May 1929 and stayed with the club until 1935.

CHAPMAN, Henry 'Harry'
Born: Kiveton Park, Sheffield 1879;
Died: 29 April 1916.
Outside/inside-right   5ft 8in; 11st 7lb (1911).
Career: Kiveton; Worksop Town; Attercliffe; Sheffield Wednesday 1900; Hull City April 1911, retired March 1913; Hull City manager April 1913 September 1914.

Honours: Football League champions 1903, 1904; FA Cup winners 1907.

A better player than Herbert, his more famous brother, Harry Chapman was described as 'the finest inside-forward of his day not to be capped'. A great favourite with the crowd due to his dynamic making and taking of goals, Chapman was a tremendous worker, extremely fast and imaginative with an acute tactical brain. He scored 102 goals in 298 games for the Owls before moving to Hull but in September 1912 he broke a knee cap in a reserve match and was never able to play again.

He became the manager a month after his official retirement and his side topped the Second Division in January 1914 before falling away. Chapman was forced to retire in September 1914 due to ill health and died 19 months later of tuberculosis without really having a chance to prove himself as a manager.

CHAPMAN, Herbert
Born: Kiveton Park, Sheffield, 19 January 1878; Died: London, 6 January 1934.
Inside-forward 5ft 7in; 12st 2lb (1903).
Career: Kiveton Park; Ashton North End; Stalybridge Rovers; Rochdale 1897; Grimsby Town May 1898; Swindon Town 1899; Sheppey United November 1899; Worksop cs 1900; Northampton Town 1901; Sheffield United May 1902; Notts County May 1903 (£300); Northampton Town cs 1904; Tottenham Hotspur March 1905;

Northampton Town player-manager April 1907-June 1912; Leeds City manager June 1912-October 1919; Huddersfield Town manager September 1921-June 1925; Arsenal June 1925-January 1934.

Honours: Football League champions 1924, 1925, 1931, 1933; Southern League champions 1909; FA Cup winners 1922, 1930, runners-up 1927, 1932.

One of the most successful and influential managers in the history of the game, Herbert Chapman was a great innovator who changed the face of football on and off the field in the 1920s and '30s. He created two great sides, at Huddersfield Town and Arsenal, and introduced tactical methods and many other new ideas which had a far-reaching effect on the game.

Chapman's most important legacy was to establish the manager as the man who mattered at a football club. Before his day the manager's authority was often undermined by club directors or else the secretary was in the control of team selection, pay and signing of players. Chapman always insisted on complete control of all team and administrative matters.

A native of South Yorkshire, he was an inside-forward who perhaps should have scored more goals. Sturdily built but limited in skill, he seemed forever on the move, eventually turning professional with Northampton Town in 1901. More moves followed and played 65 games for Spurs, scoring 21 goals, before returning to Northampton Town for a third spell, this time as player-manager. He soon weaved his magic and Northampton were Southern League champions in 1908-09. By the time he left for Leeds City in 1912, the Cobblers had won 102 of their 196 games under his managership.

Chapman did not find much success at Leeds City until World War One, during which he worked in munitions and so was not often at the club. There was an illegal payments scandal at Elland Road and in October 1919, Leeds City were thrown out of the Football League. Chapman was suspended in December 1919 for his alleged part in this but he always strenuously denied his complicity, claiming that he had not been in office when the illegal payments were made.

He worked as an industrial manager of an oil and coke firm in Selby for a while until his appeal was upheld and he was able to return to football management.

In September 1921, Chapman was invited to become manager of Huddersfield Town. He brought success to the club despite a lack of finance and relatively poor attendances. The Town won the FA Cup in 1922 against Preston, thanks to a controversial penalty by Billy Smith, and they won the first of three consecutive League championships in 1923-24, when they edged out nearest rivals Cardiff City on goal-average in a dramatic finale to the season.

The following season they conceded just 26 goals when they took the title again. Before the start of the next season, Chapman had moved to Arsenal but the Town won the League again after his departure. Their side consisted of few outstanding players but they worked exceedingly well as a team. However, they did include Scottish international Alex Jackson, and Clem Stephenson and Sam Wadsworth in their line-up.

Chapman always wanted to create a great club in London and when the Arsenal job became available he jumped at the chance to manage the club. It took him some time to achieve success but when he did, Arsenal became almost invincible in the 1930s. He spent huge amounts on the transfer market.

His first signing was Charles Buchan from Sunderland and between them they devised the third-back game, a new strategy used to counter the new offside law introduced in 1925. This tactical switch of holding the centre-half to block the middle was not particularly complex, but it helped counteract the effectiveness of the centre-forward. The first 'stopper' was Jack Butler but Chapman selected just the right man for the job when he brought Herbert Roberts to Highbury. Roberts used his great heading ability to marvellous effect.

Chapman later signed David Jack for almost £11,000 and Alex James for £9,000, two players who were to become great performers at Highbury. Chapman was able to make ordinary players into internationals and good players into great ones.

At Highbury, Chapman became unequalled as an all-rounder — a tactical theoriser, shrewd businessman, motivator of players and builder of teams. He had developed a golden touch through the whole range of the manager's duties.

In 1927, Arsenal reached the FA Cup Final but lost 1-0 to Cardiff City, when goalkeeper Don Lewis let the ball slide underneath his body for the Welshmen's winning goal. The Gunners made amends in 1930 when they beat Chapman's old club, Huddersfield Town, 2-0 in the Final. They lost to Newcastle United in the 1932 Final. United were one down when Jack Allen scored an equalizer when the ball had appeared to go over the byline. The Gunners were not happy when United scored the winning goal, claiming they had been robbed.

In 1930-31, Arsenal won the League championship for the first time with a record 66 points. The Gunners, like Huddersfield Town in the 1920s, lifted the title three seasons in succession from 1932 to 1935. Sadly, Chapman died halfway through the second season but many still gave him the credit for these successes.

Chapman could be ruthless with his footballers. When Arsenal lost to Walsall in the FA Cup in 1933, in one of the biggest Cup upsets of all time, one of the Arsenal players, Tommy Black, was responsible for the winning goal. He had given the ball away after feuding with a forward. Chapman sent him home and ordered him to keep away from the ground. Soon afterwards he was transferred to Plymouth. Chapman also once sacked a coach for undermining his instructions.

Not only did Herbert Chapman build a great side, he also converted Highbury into one of the best grounds in Britain. He even had the name of the local underground station changed to 'Arsenal'. He encouraged his coach, Tom Whittaker, to become the first of the true physiotherapist/trainers and also introduced savings schemes for the players and held regular team meetings. Many of his ideas for improving the game were blocked by the Football Association but most of these were later implemented in the years ahead. These ideas included numbers on shirts, white footballs, weather-proof pitches, floodlights and many others.

Chapman always subjected himself to the utmost limits in the interests of his work and following a hectic spell of attending matches, he returned home with what was initially thought to be a bad cold. Within days it had developed into pneumonia and Chapman died in early 1934. Today, a bust of Herbert Chapman stands in the main entrance hall at Arsenal Stadium as an epitaph to one of the greatest managers in football.

CHAPMAN, John Adam

Born: c.1882. Died: 31 December 1948.
Career: Airdrieonians manager until 1921; Manchester United manager October 1921 until suspended from secretarial duties in October 1926; Greyhound Stadium management; director of Plymouth Argyle.

Honours: Division Two runners-up 1925.

When John Robson resigned as the manager of Manchester United in October 1921, Chapman took control with Robson as his assistant. In his first 15 games in charge, United won only once and finished bottom of the table. It took him three years to get the Reds back into the top division as runners-up in 1925. They conceded only 23 goals that season. Chapman took United to an FA Cup semi-final in 1926, where they lost 3-0 to local rivals, City. In October 1926, United were advised that Chapman had been suspended by the end of the season but he never returned to Old Trafford. The full details of the charges against him were never made public.

CHAPMAN, Leslie

Born: Oldham, 27 September 1948.
Midfield   5ft 7in; 10st 4lb (1970).

Career: High Barn; Huddersfield Town amateur; Oldham Athletic trialist September 1966, professional January

1967; Huddersfield Town September 1969; Oldham Athletic December 1974; San Jose Earthquakes (NASL) (loan) May-August 1978; Stockport County May 1979; Bradford City February 1980 (£10,000); Rochdale June 1983; Stockport County player-manager October 1985-July 1986; Preston North End player-assistant manager August 1986, then manager January 1990-September 1992.

A durable player Les Chapman made over 700 appearances over 22 seasons for his various clubs. By January 1988, he was the second-longest serving player in action after Frank Worthington. When he was signed by Oldham as an amateur, he was also a trainee accountant. Chapman moved to Huddersfield Town and played in their Second Division championship side but missed out on a medal as he had not made enough appearances.

He appeared in all four divisions of the Football League plus the NASL with San Jose Earthquakes. Chapman had a terrible season as player-manager of Stockport, who finished 91st in the League during his season in control. He steered Preston away from relegation in 1989-90 and was permanently appointed in the summer of 1990. The club continued to struggle at the wrong end of Division Three and the director's patience eventually ran out and Chapman was sacked.

CHAPMAN, Roy Clifford

Born: Kingstanding, Birmingham, 18 March 1934; Died: Birmingham, March 1983.
Inside-forward 6ft 2in; 12st 9lb (1969).
Career: Kingstanding Youths; Kynoch Works; Birmingham FA; Aston Villa amateur November 1951, professional February 1952; Lincoln City November 1957; Mansfield Town August 1961 (£7,000); Lincoln City player-manager January 1965-1966; Port Vale August 1967; Chester June 1969; Stafford Rangers manager October 1969-September 1975; Stockport County manager September 1975-May 1976; Stafford Rangers manager August 1977-February 1980; Walsall Sports Co FC manager.

Honours: Northern Premier League champions 1972, runners-up 1971; FA Challenge Trophy winners 1972; Staffordshire Senior Cup (3 times); FA XI v South Africa.

Roy Chapman scored over 200 goals in his career and was on the target regularly at all his clubs. He struggled to keep Lincoln out of the re-election zone and Stockport County faired little better. Chapman enjoyed most success with Stafford Rangers, who won the FA Trophy twice, beating Barnet 3-0 in the 1972 Final and Kettering Town 2-0 in 1979. Their Northern Premier League championship in 1972 was a fine achievement in which they scored 91 goals and lost only five times. He is the father of Lee Chapman of Leeds United.

CHAPMAN, Samuel E.C.

Born: Belfast, 16 February 1938.
Wing-half   5ft 9in; 12st (1963).
Career: Glenavon; Manchester United amateur; Shamrock Rovers; Mansfield Town October 1956; Portsmouth February 1958; Mansfield Town December 1961, retired May 1964; Crewe Alexandra coach 1983; Wolverhampton Wanderers chief scout, caretaker manager August-September 1985, then manager November 1985-August 1986; Leicester City chief scout 1989.

Honours: Northern Ireland 'B' international (1 cap).

Sammy Chapman was a surprise choice as the manager of Wolves, who had just been relegated to the Third Division for the first time since 1924 when he took over. Initially, Chapman was the

caretaker manager until the arrival of Bill McGarry in September 1985, but he left after just 61 days and Chapman was put in charge again. He was never really cut out to be a manager, though, as he appeared too easy-going and was unable to stop the sinking ship. Wolves were relegated again at the end of the season after using 34 different players, including 18 debutants. Relieved of his duties in August 1986, he was replaced by caretaker Brian Little, who was later succeeded by Graham Turner. As a player, Chapman was an attacking wing-half who was a great favourite at Mansfield Town where he scored 41 goals in 168 games. Chapman gained a 'B' international cap for Northern Ireland against Romania in 1958. He is the father of Campbell and Cavan of Wolves.

CHARD, Phillip J.

Born: Corby, 16 October 1960.
Midfield   5ft 8in; 11st 3lb (1991).
Career: Corby Town; Nottingham Forest juniors; Peterborough United January 1979; Northampton Town August 1985 (£10,000); Wolverhampton Wanderers March 1988; Northampton Town October 1989 (£50,000), then player-manager April 1992.

Honours: Division Three champions 1989; Division Four champions 1987.

A versatile player, Chard is equally effective in defence or midfield. He went close to promotion twice with Peterborough United but after 197 appearances (21 as sub) and 21 goals for the club, he moved to Northampton Town. He helped them to the Fourth Division title in 1986-87, making 40 appearances and scoring 12 goals. He played the last nine games when Wolves were Fourth Division champions a year later and gained a Third Division championship medal in 1988-89 after 19 appearances for Wolves. Chard had started the season as first choice but when he was unable to win back his first-team place, he moved back to the Cobblers. Chard took over as manager at the County Ground near the end of the 1991-92 season after the departure of Theo Foley.

Chard had a tough baptism into League management but the 1992-93 eventually had a happy ending. The Cobblers had to win their last game of the season to ensure that they retained

their League status. They achieved this with an excellent 3-2 victory at Shrewsbury Town after being two goals down at one stage. The drop into the Conference League could have proved the end for the club due their poor ground and their terrible financial position.

CHARLTON, Jack OBE

Born: Ashington, 8 May 1935.
Centre-half   6ft 2in; 12st 3lb (1964).
Career: Ashington YMCA; Leeds United May 1952; Middlesbrough manager May 1973-April 1977; Sheffield Wednesday manager October 1977-May 1983; Newcastle United manager June 1984-August 1985; Middlesbrough caretaker manager March 1984 for short period; Republic of Ireland manager February 1986.

Honours: England international (35 caps); England 'B' international (1 cap); Football League representative (6 caps); World Cup winners 1966; Footballer of the Year 1967; Manager of the Year 1974; Football League champions 1969; Division Two champions 1964, 1974; Division Three promotion 1980; FA Cup winners 1972, runners-up 1965, 1970; Football League Cup winners 1968; Inter-Cities Fairs Cup winners 1968, runners-up 1967, 1971.

Jack Charlton has always been an earthy, uncomplicated man who believes simply in speaking his mind. Indeed, the articulate Charlton has become as famous for his forthright comments as a manager as he ever was for his build and style as a player.

He made 629 appearances for Leeds United from 1953 to 1973, scoring 70 goals, mainly at free-kicks and corners. He has also successfully managed Middlesbrough, Sheffield Wednesday and the Republic of Ireland national side. But football is not the only thing in his life, for he became involved in field sports and has presented a TV series on the subject. He likes nothing better than to head off to some remote tract of the rural north in pursuit of a day's fishing. His home is in Ponteland on the outskirts of Newcastle and there he walks his dog in the local countryside.

He worked down the pits as a 15-year-old and when he had a chance of a trial with Leeds United, Jack initially turned it down due to homesickness. His chance came again just as he was about to be interviewed for a job as a police cadet at Morpeth and he signed professional forms for the Elland Road club in May 1952, making his debut at the age of 17, against Doncaster Rovers in April 1953.

Shortly afterwards, he was called up to do his National Service in the Horse Guards, helping them win the Cavalry Cup for the first time, whilst serving in Germany. His early career was overshadowed by his brother, Bobby,

at Manchester United, but after the departure of John Charles to Juventus, his career came into its own as he gained a regular first-team place at centre-half, only injuries keeping him out of the side. Leeds were relegated to Division Two after Charles' departure and Charlton worked under a steady succession of managers.

He soon became the official union leader in the dressing-room with his constant urge to speak out and when Don Revie became the manager, the two soon fell out. Charlton was given an ultimatum by Revie — either to do it his way or leave the club. Charlton backed down and Revie developed him into to a much better centre-half who would eventually play alongside brother Bobby for England. Jack represented the Football League and England 'B' in 1958, but it was not until April 1965 that he made his full international debut against Scotland at Wembley. He and Bobby became the first brothers to play for England in the 20th century and Jack went on to gain 35 caps, winning a World Cup winners' medal in 1966.

After Leeds gained promotion as champions in 1964, honours came thick and fast (*see above*). The icing on the cake was probably being voted Footballer of the Year in 1967, but Charlton blotted his copybook just before he retired when he revealed that he kept a little black book in which he entered the names of troublesome opponents on which he intended to exact retribution. For this he was suspended for a while.

Known as 'Giraffe' because of his height and style of play, he decided to retire from playing when he was offered the manager's job at Middlesbrough. This was in May 1973 and at the end of his first season in charge, 'Boro ran away with the Second Division championship. The only change he made to the squad was to sell the ageing Nobby Stiles to Preston and replace him with Bobby Murdoch from Celtic.

As early as 23 March, with eight games still to play, Middlesbrough ensured promotion back to the First Division for the first time since 1954. They then established themselves as a First Division club, mostly finishing in mid-table. In 1975 they reached the quarter-finals of the FA Cup and the following year lost to Manchester City in a League Cup semi-final. 'Boro did win the Anglo-Scottish Cup, beating Fulham in a two-legged Final in 1975.

Charlton resigned on 21 April 1977 after four years at Ayresome Park. He felt he needed a six-month break from football. When he resigned Charlton said, "I have not known anything but football and felt that I needed a change, made my decision and went."

In October 1977, Jack returned to the game as manager of Sheffield Wednesday. The club's fortunes were at a low ebb, for they had gone ten games without a win and Fourth Division football stared them in the face. But Charlton led the Owls to respectable mid-table position. It took him two years to transform the club but with signings such as Terry Curran and Andy McCullough, he created a team which won promotion to Division Two in 1980. Two years later they missed further promotion by only one point. However, Jack resigned in 1983, just after the Owls had reached the FA Cup semi-finals.

His strength has been his ability to assemble a fine backroom staff of John Harris, Maurice Setters and Frank

Blunstone, all former managers themselves. After a brief spell as caretaker manager at Middlesbrough, Charlton took control at Newcastle United. It was an unhappy time and he resigned at the start of the 1985-86 season after being barracked by the crowd. The directors had also attempted to sign a player he did not want. After this, Charlton said that there was no way that he would return to full-time club management.

In February 1986, he was approached by the FA of Ireland to take over the running of the national side on a part time basis. This was just the job for Jack Charlton. He got together a squad, most of whom had rather tenuous links with Ireland — a grandmother or some even more remote relative. His sides included scouser John Aldridge, Glaswegian Ray Houghton and Londoner Chris Hughton, and most of the players appeared in the Football League. In 1988, Ireland reached the European Championship finals for the first time, beating England 1-0, drawing 1-1 with the USSR and losing narrowly to the Dutch. They also reached the 1990 World Cup finals where they lost to Italy in the quarter-finals.

Charlton is held in high regard by the Irish people and must also be one of the few managers who can claim never to have suffered the humiliation of the sack or the experience of relegation.

CHARLTON, Robert, OBE

Born: Ashington, 11 October 1937.
Forward   5ft 9in; 12st (1964).
Career: East Northumberland Schools; Manchester United October 1954, retired April 1973; Preston North End manager June 1973-August 1975, re-registered as a player May 1974; Wigan Athletic director and caretaker manager April 1983; Manchester United director June 1984.

Honours: England international (106 caps); Under-23 international (6 caps); Youth international; Schoolboy international; Football League representative; World Cup winners 1966; Footballer of the Year 1966; European Footballer of the Year 1966; Football League champions 1957, 1965, 1967; FA Cup winners 1963, runners-up 1957, 1958; European Cup winners 1968.

A survivor of the Munich air disaster of 1958, Bobby Charlton went on to break Billy Wright's record for England caps and still holds the record for goalscoring for his country with 49 goals. He played an important role in United's recovery after Munich.

Charlton was admired and respected as a player all over the world. Alongside his brother, Jack, he was a member of the 1966 World Cup winning side, having had an outstanding game in the semi-final against Portugal in which he scored two fine goals. He also played in the 1962 and 1970 tournaments.

When he retired in 1973, Charlton had played in more than 750 games for United and scored 198 goals in 606 League appearances, both club records. A model sportsman, he possessed a rocket of a shot in both feet and his gazelle-like running and dazzling body swerve made him one of the finest players in the world.

Unfortunately, he was not such a successful manager. Relegated to Division Three at the end of the 1973-74 season, Preston were struggling again when Charlton resigned in August 1975, after a dispute with the directors over a deal involving John Bird's transfer to Newcastle which was made without his knowledge. Charlton took over briefly as caretaker manager at Wigan Athletic in April 1983, after the sacking of Larry Lloyd. He also ran a football school from February 1982.

CHERRY, Trevor

Born: Huddersfield, 23 February 1948.
Left-back   5ft 10in; 11st 6lb (1977).

Career: Huddersfield YMCA; Huddersfield Town apprentice July 1963, professional July 1965; Leeds United June 1972 (£100,000); Bradford City player-manager December 1982-January 1987 (£10,000); promotions and marketing director of a sports equipment firm and worked for local radio from January 1987.
Honours: England international (27 caps); Football League representative; Football League champions 1974; Division Two champions 1970; Division Three champions 1985; FA Cup runners-up 1973; European Cup-winners' Cup runners-up 1973.

Trevor Cherry steered Bradford City through traumatic times including a receivership and the disastrous fire which claimed over 50 lives at Valley Parade. City won the Third Division championship but the fire at the ground on the day they were supposed to celebrate this meant that the club led a nomadic existence over the next year and a half whilst their home was rebuilt. There was also, of course, the terrible trauma of those times. Cherry was unsympathetically sacked only ten days after the club's emotional return to Valley Parade.

As a player he captained Huddersfield Town to the Second Division title in 1970, but when the Terriers were relegated back again, Don Revie, the Leeds manager, paid £100,000 for him as a replacement for the injured Terry

Cooper. Cherry played in two Cup Final defeats in 1973, against Sunderland in the FA Cup and against AC Milan in the European Cup-winners' Cup. He played in 482 games for Leeds before his move to Bradford City.

CHILTON, Allenby C.

Born: South Hylton, 16 September 1918.
Centre-half   6ft 1in; 13st.
Career: Seaham Colliery; Manchester United November 1938; Charlton Athletic guest in World War Two; Grimsby Town player-manager March 1955-April 1959, retired from playing October 1956; publican in York 1959-1960; Wigan Athletic manager May 1960-1961; Hartlepools United scout 1961-1962, then manager July 1962-April 1963; ran a shop for five years then worked at a steelworks for 14 years; retired to Sunderland 1981.
Honours: England international (2 caps); Football League champions 1952; Division Three North champions 1956; FA Cup winners 1948; Football League South winners 1944; Football League North Cup runners-up 1945.

A dominant pivot with aerial power and meticulous ground passing, Chilton was a key figure in Manchester United's post-war teams. He made 353 appearances for the Reds before his move to Grimsby Town on a free transfer and won a Cup medal when United beat Blackpool in the splendid 1948 Final. Four years later he gained a League championship medal after the Reds had finished runners-up on four previous occasions. He was regarded by Matt Busby as his best-ever centre-half.

Grimsby were in dire trouble when he took control and they were unable to avoid re-election in 1955. In a year, however, he had transformed the club into Third Division North champions with himself in a revamped defence. Chilton retired just after the start of the 1956-57 season. He left the game after a disastrous spell at Hartlepool, who finished 92nd in the Football League.

CHUNG, Cyril 'Sammy'

Born: Abingdon, 16 July 1932.
Inside-forward 5ft 9in; 11st 6lb (1964).

Career: Headington United; Reading amateur August 1949, professional November 1951; Norwich City January 1955 (£6,000); Watford June 1957, then player-coach July 1963-1964; Ipswich Town coach 1964; Wolverhampton Wanderers trainer-coach c.1967-1970, assistant manager 1972, then manager June 1976-November 1978; IFK Vastern (Sweden) 1970-1972; United Arab Emirates coach; Stoke City assistant manager cs 1985-October 1989; Colchester

United assistant manager 1990; Tamworth manager 1991; Sacked Jan 1993.
Honours: Division Two champions 1977.

Sammy Chung, whose father was Chinese and mother English, was a valuable utility player who started his career as a part-time centre-forward with Headington United whilst doing a carpentry apprenticeship. He joined Reading as a wing-half but did not sign professional forms until he had finished his National Service. Chung played 240 games for Watford and gained his FA coaching badge whilst at that club.

At Vicarage Road, he became player-coach under Bill McGarry and was with McGarry when he took Ipswich into Division One and later did the same as a manager with Wolves, when he succeeded McGarry as boss at Molineux. After struggling in the First Division, Chung was sacked with the fans calling for his head.

CLARE, Thomas

Born: Congleton, Cheshire 1865; Died: Ladysmith, Vancouver, 27 December 1929.
Right-back   6ft; 13st (1902).
Career: Talke FC (Staffs); Goldenhill Wanderers; Stoke 1883; Manchester City May 1897; Burslem Port Vale player-coach cs 1899, then manager cs 1905-cs 1906; emigrated to Canada in 1910s.
Honours: England international (4 caps); Football League representative (1 cap); Football Alliance champions 1891.

Tom Clare never showed his true form when playing for England. A steady full-back, he was reliable and hardworking and also quick, resolute and a good header of the ball. When Stoke lost their League status in 1890, he helped them to the Football Alliance title in 1891 and they were re-elected back again to the League. He formed an excellent defence at Stoke with Rowley and Underwood and made over 250 appearances before his move to Burslem.

Clare had just one season in charge, taking over from Sam Gleaves who became a director. Burslem Port Vale struggled in the Second Division and there was talk of the club being wound-up. They lost £451 over the 1905-06 season and Clare lost his job due to the club's financial problems. Gleaves returned to replace him, but was not in charge of team affairs.

CLARK, Archibald

Born: Maidstone, 4 April 1902; Died: Sheffield, 14 January 1967.
Centre-half 5ft 11in; 12st 10lb (1937).
Career: Aylesford Paper Mills FC; Brentford March 1927; Arsenal May 1927; Luton Town November 1928 (£1,000); Everton May 1931; Tranmere Rovers March 1936; Gillingham manager cs 1939-June 1958; Sheffield United assistant manager in 1965.
Honours: Football League champions 1932; Kent League champions 1945, 1946; Southern League champions 1947, 1949; Kent Senior Cup winners 1947.

Clark was discovered by Brentford scout Dick Hendrie playing for Aylesford Paper Mills, but his stay at Griffin Park was short and after only seven weeks

he moved to Highbury. This was after impressing the visiting chairman Sir Henry Norris in a London Combination match for the Bees' reserve team against Arsenal.

Clark never got on well with Herbert Chapman and was unhappy at Highbury. Clark wanted regular first-team football and so moved to Luton. He later won a League championship medal at Everton.

He was the driving force behind Gillingham's post-war success as they won just about every honour going in non-League soccer. In 1950 they won back their Football League place when the competition was extended by four clubs. Two Southern League titles had helped sway opinion in their favour. Things did not go so well in the League, however, where Clark produced exciting but less successful sides. He left in 1958, after 19 years at the club.

CLARK, Frank Albert

Born: Highfield, County Durham, 9 September 1943.
Left-back   6ft; 12st 2lb (1971).
Career: Highfield; Crook Town; Newcastle United October 1962; Nottingham Forest May 1975; Sunderland assistant manager July 1979-August 1981; Nottingham Forest assistant trainer August 1981; Orient assistant manager October 1981, then manager May 1983-July 1991, remaining at the club as managing director. Nottingham Forest manager 1993.
Honours: England Youth international; Football League representative (1 cap); Football League champions 1978; Division Two champions 1965; Division Four promotion 1989; FA Cup runners-up 1974; Football League Cup winners 1978, 1979, runners-up 1980; European Cup winners 1979; Inter-Cities Fairs Cup winners 1969; FA Amateur Cup winners 1962.

Frank Clark broke his leg early in his career but fought back to win just about every honour in the game except international recognition. A sound defender rather than a spectacular one, he obtained a new lease of life when he joined Brian Clough at Nottingham Forest.

A qualified laboratory technician, Clark appeared at Wembley at the age of 19 when he played in Crook Town's 4-0 FA Amateur Cup Final replay win over Hounslow Town. After he moved to Newcastle, Clark was ever-present in their Second Division championship season of 1964-65 and also played in their FA Cup Final against Liverpool in 1974, when they lost 3-0. He won plenty of honours with Forest, including a European Cup winners' medal against Malmö FF in Munich and three League Cup medals.

Clark had difficult early years as manager of Orient. They were relegated to Division Four at the end of the 1984-85 season but the board stood by him and Orient twice went close to the play-offs. Eventually the Os made it to the play-offs in 1988-89 and beat Scarborough and Wrexham to enter the Third Division. In November 1986 he became managing director and was given a seat on the board. In July 1991, Clark moved into an administrative role with the club and Peter Eustace took on responsibility for team affairs.

Clark left his managing director's job at Leyton Orient to take over as manager at Nottingham Forest, replacing his former boss Brian Clough.

CLARK, Gordon Vincent

Born: Gainsborough, 15 June 1944.
Right-back   5ft 7in; 11st 10lb (1937).
Career: Goldthorpe United; Denaby United; Southend United; Manchester City January 1936; Hyde United April 1947; Waterford player-manager November 1947; Distillery manager until 1950; Aldershot manager May 1950-August 1955; West Bromwich Albion chief scout and assistant manager August 1955-1959, then manager June 1959-October 1961; Sheffield Wednesday assistant manager 1961-1964; Peterborough United manager April 1964-September 1967; Arsenal chief scout until February 1977; Fulham assistant manager April 1977; Philadelphia Fury (NASL) coach 1977-1978; Queen's Park Rangers assistant manager 1979.

Gordon Clark came to Aldershot after managerial experience with Irish clubs Waterford and Distillery. At the Recreation ground he had little money to buy new talent and depended on unearthing talent and selling his best players to survive. Clark surprisingly resigned early in 1955-56 to become Albion's chief scout. He gained a reputation as a great judge of ability and his enthusiasm for football took him to more than seven matches a week as a scout.

When he took over at The Hawthorns, the fans were mourning the departure of Vic Buckingham and it proved a hard act to follow. Albion finished fifth at the end of his first season in charge and tenth the next after an early struggle. He resigned halfway through the 1961-62 season. Peterborough reached the quarter-finals of the FA Cup in 1965. Their run included a 2-1 victory over Arsenal. They also reached the semi-final of the League Cup in 1966 where they lost to West Bromwich Albion on aggregate. This run included a 4-3 victory at Newcastle and a 4-0 thumping of Burnley. After his walk-out in 1967, Peterborough were demoted for making illegal payments to players. Clark then went back to what he knew best, discovering young talent.

CLARK, Paul P.

Born: Benfleet, 14 September 1958.
Midfield   5ft 10in; 12st 5lb (1978).
Career: Southend United July 1976; Brighton & Hove Albion November 1977; Reading (loan) October 1981; Southend United August 1982, caretaker manager March-June 1987, player-manager September 1987-May 1988, then player-assistant manager until 1991; Gillingham July 1991.

Honours: England Youth international; Schoolboy international.

Paul Clark helped Brighton into the First Division. A midfield dynamo, his all-action style was best appreciated at Southend, where he made almost 300 appearances. He returned to Roots Hall after losing his place in Brighton's first team and was appointed Southend's player-manager in 1987, the club finishing 17th in Division Three during his season in charge. He was caretaker manager when Southend clinched promotion to Division Three that year. He was demoted to assistant manager after a poor start to the following season. Clark moved to Gillingham after being given a free transfer in the summer of 1991.

CLARK, William D.

Career: Burton Wanderers secretary-manager 1894-1897; Leicester Fosse secretary-manager July 1897-September 1898 when suspended from the game; Burton United secretary-manager 1901-1904.

William Clark was secretary-manager of Second Division Burton Wanderers for three seasons. Their best campaign was in 1895-96 when they finished fourth. Appointed manager of Leicester Fosse when the club became a limited company, Clark had an eye for gimmickry but did not take much notice of Football League regulations and was suspended in September 1898 for making illegal payments and poaching players. This was later rescinded and he returned to Burton to take over the new United club after the Swifts and Wanderers amalgamated in 1901.

CLARKE, Allan John

Born: Willenhall, 31 July 1946.
Centre-forward 6ft 2in; 11st 11lb (1972).

Career: Birmingham Schools; South-East Staffordshire Boys; Walsall apprentice 1961, professional August 1963; Fulham March 1966 (£35,000);

Leicester City June 1968 (£150,000); Leeds United July 1969 (£165,000); Barnsley player-manager May 1978-October 1980; Leeds United manager October 1980-June 1982; Scunthorpe United manager February 1983-August 1984; Barnsley manager July 1985-November 1989; Lincoln City manager June-November 1990.

Honours: England international (19 caps); Under-23 international (6 caps); Football League representative (2 caps); Football League champions 1974; Division Four promotion 1979, 1983; FA Cup winners 1972, runners-up 1969, 1970, 1973; European Cup winners 1971.

Allan Clarke came from a footballing family, his brothers Frank, Derek, Kelvin and Wayne all playing League soccer. 'Sniffer' Clarke had a instinctive nose for goals and scored 223 in his 513 League appearances. Paradoxically, the sides he managed had a reputation for their lack of goals.

Twice Clarke was involved in record transfers, first when he moved from Fulham to Leicester, then when he moved on to Leeds United. Clarke played in four FA Cup Finals but was on the winning side only once, when he scored the winning goal for Leeds against Arsenal in a dull 1972 Final. His powerful diving header was easily the highlight of the match. He scored 151 goals in 366 appearances for Leeds and formed a great goalscoring partnership with Mick Jones.

As Barnsley's manager, he saw the Colliers win promotion in his first season in charge but he had a turbulent time at Leeds and he was sacked after their relegation to Division Two in 1982. Leeds scored only 78 goals in the League during his two seasons in charge. Scunthorpe won promotion to the Third Division in 1983 but were relegated back straight away. His best season back at Oakwell was 1988-89, when Barnsley just missed the play-offs in finishing in seventh position. He was sacked after seven defeats in nine games in November 1989. Clarke lasted just five months at Lincoln City departing after a run of poor results.

CLOUGH, Brian Howard

Born: Middlesbrough, 21 March 1935.
Centre-forward 5ft 10½in; 11st 1lb (1960).
Career: Great Broughton; Middlesbrough amateur November 1951, professional May 1953; Sunderland July 1961 (£45,000), retired through injury November 1964; Hartlepools United manager October 1965-June 1967; Derby County manager June 1967-October 1973; Brighton & Hove Albion manager November 1973-June 1974; Leeds United manager August-October 1974; Nottingham Forest manager January 1975-May 1993.

Honours: England international (2 caps); 'B' international (1 cap); Football League representative (2 caps); Under-23 international (3 caps); Football League champions 1972, 1978; Division Two champions 1969, promotion 1977; FA Cup runners-up 1991; Football League Cup winners 1978, 1979, 1989, 1990, runners-up 1980, 1992; European Cup winners 1979, 1980; European Super Cup winners 1980, runners-up 1981; World Club championship runners-up 1981; Zenith Data Systems Cup winners 1992.

Brian Clough rates alongside the greats of British football management with the likes of Matt Busby, Bill Shankly, Jock Stein and Herbert Chapman. He

has won just about everything there is to win and one either loves him or hates him.

But Clough's earnest, abrasive and honest approach to the job are the major factors in his success. Many in the game are impressed by his sincerity, clarity of thought and his approach to football. And if he appears a little eccentric at times — planting a kiss on the cheek of a journalist at the end of a televised football match in front of millions of viewers — then that is Brian Clough.

No one has an easy passage with him due to his tough, uncompromising approach and the tongue that can be cuttingly cruel. His strict disciplinarian approach has been the undoing of many a player who has not given Clough 100 per cent effort. Yet one international player — perhaps typical of many who have played under Clough — once said, "He can be an absolute bastard, but you'd give him your last penny." The side of Clough which loses him friends is his forthright and often outrageous opinions which he has expressed through the television and the media.

Clough was one of nine children. He worked as a clerk with ICI whilst playing for Billingham Synthonia and Great Broughton before joining Middlesbrough. He was one of the great marksmen of his — or any — era, with 204 goals in 222 appearances for 'Boro before moving to Sunderland in July 1961 for a fee of £45,000. Clough was the leading goalscorer in the Second Division for three seasons on the trot and scored 40 goals or more every season from 1956 to 1960.

He netted 63 goals in 74 appearances for Sunderland before an injury received against Bury on Boxing Day 1962 virtually ended his career. He tried to make a comeback but when he realised it was a hopeless cause, he retired from playing. Clough failed to score in either of his two internationals for England but hc would probably have won more caps with a fashionable southern club.

Initially he took the premature ending of his career very badly. However, after accepting the manager's job at Hartlepools United in October 1965, he found a new fulfilment to his life. He persuaded his former 'Boro teammate, Peter Taylor, to give up the manager's job at Southern League Burton Albion to join him at the Victoria Ground.

Hartlepools had sought re-election in five of the previous six seasons and it was not going to be an easy task to turn the club's fortunes around. But Clough did everything — mended a leaking roof at the ground, drove the team coach, went around local working men's clubs asking for donations and, most important of all, building and motivating a useful team from virtually nothing. Hartlepools finished eighth at the end of the 1966-7 season, but Clough and Taylor departed for Derby County in June 1967.

With Taylor, he transformed Derby from a modest Second Division side into League champions. They made three major signings in John O'Hare, Roy McFarland and Alan Hinton, at a combined fee of £75,000. Dave Mackay and Willie Carlin also arrived for the start of the 1968-69 season, in which Derby stormed to the Second Division championship, and more major signings were made including Archie Gemmill, Colin Todd and David Nish. Derby won the League championship in 1971-72, for the first time in their history, and the following season the Rams reached the semi-finals of the European Cup before losing to Juventus, 3-1 on aggregate. Clough and Taylor seemed to have an excellent partnership and their talents and moods complimented each other.

After this, there were lots of rumours that Clough was about to leave Derby. His outspoken comments were worrying his chairman and the football authorities. Disputes between the board and management became bitter and in October 1973, Clough and Taylor resigned. The players threatened to go on strike if he was not reinstated and the Derby fans held a series of public meetings in a bid to have their favourite restored.

But Clough had left the Baseball Ground for good, although in 1993 he still lives in Derby, and the following month he and Taylor accepted an offer to manage Third Division Brighton. This seemed a very strange decision. To go from a leading First Division club to one with only limited potential appeared the height of folly. Clough, though, did not take long to assert his authority on the club as players came and went in quick succession. But Brighton were beaten 8-2 at home by Bristol Rovers and 4-0 by non-League Walton & Hersham in the FA Cup. Clough left Brighton in July 1974 and took over at Leeds United the following month. Taylor was left to run Brighton.

Clough arrived at Elland Road as the man to replace the much-respected Don Revie, who had become the England manager. Leeds were in need of a major overhaul as many of their star players were now reaching the end of their careers. Clough was soon making major changes and signed Duncan McKenzie and John O'Hare. Early results were disappointing, though, and there were rumours of an unhappy dressing-room atmosphere. The Press blamed 'player power' when Clough was sacked after only 44 days in charge. He later received £20,000 compensation and it was a decision that Leeds probably lived to regret as they suffered years of mediocrity after this. Clough, it appeared, had tried to change tried and trusted methods too quickly and alienated almost everybody in the process.

He was not out of work for long, though, and became the manager of Nottingham Forest in January 1975. Over the next 16 years he was to produce some golden moments for the Reds, including a League championship and two European Cup successes. It was marvellous for their fans, for Forest had won very little in their history before Clough's arrival.

He persuaded Peter Taylor to leave Brighton and team up with him again. Sadly, they fell out in 1982 and apparently never spoke to each other again before Taylor's death in 1990.

In 1977, Forest won promotion to the First Division and a year later clinched the League title. In 1979, they beat Malmö FF, thanks to a Trevor Francis goal. Clough had been the first British manager to spend a million pounds on one player when he signed Trevor Francis. A year later, they confounded the critics and won the European trophy again, this time beating Hamburg 1-0 in Madrid. Forest then played for the World Club Championship against Naçional of Uruquay in Tokyo but lost 1-0.

Forest played in six League Cup Finals between 1978 and 1992, winning four of them. However, Clough did not have much success in the FA Cup until 1991, when they reached the Final, only to lose to Spurs after taking the lead. His son, Nigel, is one of the stars of the game today. Brian Clough has signed some brilliant players over the years but not all of his deals have come off. Notable failures have been Justin Fashanu, Ian Wallace and Gary Megson, but Clough achieved so much success at provincial clubs, one wonders what he could have achieved with a major club side.

Unfortunately, he was never offered the England job as his views were far too outspoken for the Football Association. He was offered the Welsh national team manager's job, but Forest would not release him to carry out his duties on a part-time basis. Few can now argue that Brian Clough is not one of the greatest managers of all time and that judgement is not dimmed by Forest's poor performance in 1992-93, when they fell to the foot of the new Premier League.

Brian Clough sadly decided to retire in May 1993 amidst a lot of bad publicity. Forest finished rock bottom of the Premier League which brought an unfortunate end to a great career. Many felt that he should have retired on a high note after Forest's FA Cup Final appearance in 1991. Forest's main problem had been with scoring goals and Clough had refused to pay inflated transfer fees for a striker to replace Teddy Sheringham, who he had sold to Spurs for £2m. His legacy was a virtually rebuilt ground and lots of great memories for the Forest fans.

COAKLEY, Thomas

Born: Bellshill, 2 May 1947.
Outside-right
Career: Motherwell; Arsenal May 1966; Morton 1968; Detroit Cougars April 1968; Chelmsford City player-coach; Maldon Town manager; Bishop's Stortford manager 1983-1986; Walsall manager August 1986-December 1988; Blackenhall manager February-October 1989; Telford United coach January 1992.

Honours: Division Three promotion 1988.

Tommy Coakley made only nine appearances for Arsenal before returning to Scotland to play for Morton. His first managerial post had been at Essex Senior League club Maldon Town, from whom he moved to Isthmian League club Bishops Stortford. Surprise choice as manager of Walsall, he moulded a very attacking side at Fellows Park. He took Walsall to the fifth round of the FA Cup in 1987 and the following season they won promotion to the Second Division after finishing third and beating Bristol City 4-0 in the play-offs. Coakley had a tough time in the higher division and was sacked after 11 successive defeats.

COCHRANE, John

Born: Paisley.
Career: Paisley Grammar School; Johnston Thistle; Elderslie Amateurs; St Johnstone, then secretary 1912; St Mirren manager 1916; Sunderland manager May 1928-March 1939; Reading manager March-April 1939.

Honours: Football League champions 1936; FA Cup winners 1937; Scottish Cup winners 1926.

Under Johnny Cochrane's management, Sunderland were to win the FA Cup and the League championship during his 11 years in charge. He had been the club's third choice to take over from the retiring Bob Kyle in May 1928. They had failed to secure the services of both George Jobey and Major Frank Buckley.

Cochrane had been in charge at St Mirren from 1916, and they had won the Scottish Cup for the first time in 1926, beating Celtic 2-0 in the Final. They also finished fourth in the Scottish League that season. In his younger days, Cochrane had played for Paisley Grammar School, Johnston Thistle, Elderslie Amateurs and St Johnstone before taking up secretarial duties with the latter in 1912.

On his arrival at Roker Park, Cochrane was soon active in the transfer market and signed two Scottish internationals, Adam McClean and Tom McInally. This immediately boosted the team and they finished fourth in the First Division in 1928-29. In 1931 they reached the semi-finals of the FA Cup but lost 2-0 to Birmingham. Cochrane's teams were always entertaining and scored plenty of goals.

Gradually he produced a side which was capable of challenging for the League title. In 1934-35, Sunderland finished runners-up, four points behind champions Arsenal. The following season they lifted the title outright to break the hold that Arsenal had over it. They scored 109 goals and were eight points clear of their nearest rivals. A year later and Sunderland won the FA Cup, beating Preston 3-1 in the Final. They nearly reached the Final again the following year but lost to Huddersfield Town in the semis. Cochrane lasted only 13 days as manager of Reading.

Johnny Cochrane was well known for his laid-back approach and his team talks were legendary. Casual and brief, he could hardly be accused of being a brilliant technician. Raich Carter recalled: "Just before a game, this man wearing a bowler hat, smoking a cigar and drinking a whisky would pop his head round the dressing-room door. He'd ask, 'Who are we playing today?' We would chorus, 'Arsenal, boss.'' Johnny would just say, 'Oh, we'll piss that lot,' before shutting the door and leaving us to it."

COCK, Jack Gilbert

Born: Hayle, Cornwall, 14 November 1893; Died: Kensington, London, 19 April 1966.
Centre-forward 5ft 11½in; 11st 4lb (1914).
Career: West Kensington United 1908; Forest Gate; Old Kingstonian December 1912; Brentford amateur March 1914; Huddersfield Town April 1914; Chelsea October 1919 (£2,500); Everton January 1923; Plymouth Argyle March 1925; Millwall November 1927; Folkestone July 1931; Walton October 1932; Millwall manager November 1944-August 1948.

Honours: England international (2 caps); Wartime international (1 cap); Football League representative; Division Three South champions 1928; Football League South Cup runners-up 1945.

A naturally gifted centre-forward, Jack Cock gave the impression that he played the game for laughs. A typically robust target man, he could score with both feet and his head. Indeed, Cock netted over 200 League goals during his career. He also made a name for himself in the music-halls and cinemas as a singer. Described as a sophisticated socialite who dressed in expensive clothes, in reality he came from a poor family of ten with a humble background in Cornwall. He was reported 'missing presumed dead' during World War One, when he won a Military Medal and rose to the rank of sergeant-major. He made his England debut in 1919 against Ireland and scored a goal.

Cock scored goals for all his clubs and helped Millwall to the Third Division South championship in season 1927-28. In November 1944, he became the Lions' manager and took them to the Football League South Cup Final at Wembley, where they lost 2-0 to Chelsea. He was relieved of his duties after their relegation to Division Three in 1948. He is a brother of Donald and Herbert Cock.

COLEMAN, Ernest 'Tim'

Born: Blidworth, Notts, 4 January 1908; Died: Nottingham, 20 January 1984.
Centre-forward/Inside-left 5ft 8in; 11st 2lb (1930).
Career: Hucknall Church Boys' Brigade; Hucknall Colliery; Halifax Town July 1926; Grimsby Town February 1929 (£1,250); Arsenal March 1932 (£5,000 & a player); Middlesbrough August 1934 (£4,000); Norwich City February 1937; Linby Colliery player-manager; Notts County caretaker manager July-October 1957, in various capacities 1958-1966, then manager November 1961-July 1963 and April 1965-March 1966.

Honours: Football League champions 1933.

An incisive goalscorer, Tim Coleman scored 57 goals in 87 appearances for Grimsby Town and 142 goals altogether in his career total of 324 League appearances. He scored 35 goals for Grimsby in 1930-31 and also netted 24 in 27 games in Arsenal's League championship season of 1932-33. Later he played at wing-half for Norwich. At Notts County he was assistant manager to Frank Hill and when he took control, he introduced Jeff Astle to the side. In 1965 there was rumours that County would fold, but with the unpaid assistance of Andy Beattie and Peter Doherty, Coleman steered the club out of the crisis.

COLLIER, John C.

Born: Dysart, Fife, 1 February 1897; Died: 28 December 1940.
Right-half 5ft 9in; 11st 10lb (1923).
Career: Victoria Hawthorn; Denbeith Star; Inverkeithing United; Raith

Rovers 1919; Hull City cs 1920; Queen's Park Rangers July 1926; York City player-manager July 1928-May 1930 and May 1933-March 1937, trainer coach March 1937; licensee in York 1930-33.

A canny Scot, Collier was a fine tackler who played with vigour and also commanded respect from opponents. He was a regular at Grimsby for five seasons and made 169 appearances for the club. Collier was manager of York City when they were elected to the Football League in 1929 and they finished sixth in their first season in the League.

Collier had joined York City as player-manager but a broken ankle ended his career. He left the club in 1930 to run a pub and managerial duties were carried by Bill Sherrington until his return in 1933. York reached the fourth round of the FA Cup in 1937 but he left the club soon afterwards to go into business with his brothers in Scotland. He was troubled by ill health and died at the early age of 43.

COLLINS, Anthony Norman

Born: Kensington, 19 March 1926.
Outside-left   5ft 11in; 11st 3lb (1955).
Career: Brentford amateur; Sheffield Wednesday November 1947; York City July 1949; Watford August 1950; Norwich City July 1953; Torquay United July 1955; Watford July 1957; Crystal Palace November 1957; Rochdale June 1959, then manager June 1960-September 1967; Bristol City chief scout December 1967-1972, assistant manager 1976-1980, caretaker manager September 1980 (for 19 days).
Honours: Football League Cup runners-up 1962.

Rochdale gave Collins a five-year contract in January 1963 and, working on a shoestring budget, he improved the outlook at Spotland in a very short time. This included steering the club to a Football League Cup Final in 1962, where they lost to Norwich City in a two-legged Final. Of course, the competition did not have the glamour of today's Wembley Final competition and, indeed, most of the top sides did not take part. After Rochdale had to seek re-election twice, Collins resigned in September 1967. For many years he worked with Alan Dicks at Bristol City.

COLLINS, George

Born: Felling, c.1880; Died: 1958 (aged 78).
Outside-left
Career: Gateshead junior football; Newcastle United Reserves; Darlington 1904, reserve-team manager 1919-1933, then manager cs 1933-October 1936.
Honours: Division Three North Cup winners 1934, runners-up 1936.

George Collins did not make the first team with Newcastle United and was reinstated as an amateur to play for Darlington. After World War One he moved back to Darlington for business reasons and developed a keen interest in the local club. Collins was a director as well as reserve-team manager from 1919. They won the North Cup shortly after he took charge of the first team in 1934, when they beat Stockport County 4-3 at Old Trafford before only 4,640, and in 1936 they lost to Chester in the Final. He was known as 'genial George' by the Feethams fans.

COLLINS, John Douglas

Born: Newton, near Doncaster, 28 August 1945.

Midfield   5ft 9in; 10st 6lb (1966).
Career: Pinxton Miners' Welfare; Rotherham United apprentice; Grimsby Town amateur March 1963, professional June 1963; Burnley September 1963 (£27,000); Plymouth Argyle May 1976; Sunderland March 1977; Tulsa Roughnecks (NASL) April 1978; Derby County coach 1978; Rochdale player-manager January-November 1979.
Honours: Division Two champions 1973.

Slight in physique, Doug Collins compensated with brain power and subtlety. A provider rather than a goalscorer, he gained a reputation as a tricky winger with Burnley and the step up to First Division soccer at Turf Moor posed no problems for him. At Rochdale, Collins dragged the club off the bottom of the Fourth Division and they won the last game of the season to avoid having to seek re-election at a time when there was a good chance that they would have been voted out of the League. But Rochdale struggled again the following season and Collins was sacked in November 1979 after just ten months in charge.

COLLINS, Robert Young

Born: Govanhill, Glasgow, 16 February 1931.
Inside-forward   5ft 4in; 10st 3lb (1963).
Career: Polmadie; Hawthorn Juveniles; Glasgow Pollok; Glasgow Celtic April 1948; Everton September 1958 (£23,500); Leeds United March 1962 (£22,500); Bury February 1967; Greenock Morton player-coach April 1969-April 1971; Ringwood City (Melbourne); Hakoah (Sydney) manager October 1971; Shamrock Rovers; Oldham Athletic player-coach September 1972, assistant manager June 1973; Huddersfield Town manager July 1974-December 1975; Leeds United youth coach 1976; Hull City coach July 1977, then manager October 1977-February 1978; Blackpool coach March-May 1978; Barnsley youth coach October 1980, then manager February 1984-June 1985; Guiseley manager November 1987.

Honours: Scotland international (31 caps); Scottish League representative (15 caps); Division Two champions 1964; Scottish League champions 1954; FA Cup runners-up 1965; Scottish Cup winners 1951, runners-up 1955; Scottish League Cup winners 1957, 1958.

Don Revie built his early teams at Leeds around the pocket general, Bobby Collins. Revie described him as a teacher on the field and he was indeed a real captain and leader. "The example he set others in his dedication and attitude

was his greatest attribute," Revie commented. Leeds just missed the League and FA Cup double in 1965 and Collins was voted Footballer of the Year and was also recalled to the Scotland side after an absence of six years.

He had won many honours with Celtic and scored a hat trick of penalties against Aberdeen in September 1953. Collins broke his thigh in a bruising Fairs Cup match for Leeds, in Turin, but fought his way back again. He helped Bury to promotion in 1968 and was in his 43rd year when he made his final League appearance for Oldham. Collins scored 154 goals in his 639 Scottish and Football League games.

As a manager Collins was far less successful. He had an unhappy spell as manager of Huddersfield, who were relegated to Division Four in May 1975. He also had a disappointing season in charge at Barnsley.

COMMINS, John James

Born: County Kildare, Ireland. Died: Southport, March 1955
Career: Clyde player-manager 1912-1926; Barnsley manager cs 1926-May 1928; Southport secretary-manager March 1929-November 1930 and March 1933-1936; Barrow manager November 1930-April 1932 and June 1945-December 1946; Shelbourne (Ireland) manager 1932-33; Cork United (Ireland) August-October 1948; scouted for Aston Villa and Wolverhamptom Wanderers in 1930s.

Commins joined Barnsley from Clyde and had a constant struggle to keep the club going. He had to sell his best players, Fred Tilson and Eric Brook, to Manchester City during 1928-29 to keep the club solvent. Both went on to fine careers in the First Division. At Barrow, this genial Irishman assembled a fine side at no cost. They went on to achieve some excellent Cup runs and also finished sixth in the Third Division North in 1931-32. He moved to work in Ireland in 1932 but returned a year later for a second spell as manager of Southport, leaving Haig Avenue in 1936 after the club had sought re-election two seasons running. He returned to management in 1945 for a second spell at Barrow, but resigned after a disagreement with both the board and the supporters.

COMPTON, Paul D.

Born: Stroud, 6 June 1961.
Defender   6ft 1½in; 13st 1lb (1983).
Career: Cardiff City trialist 1977; Trowbridge Town 1978; Bournemouth & Boscombe Athletic October 1980 (£10,000); Aldershot December 1983; Torquay United February 1984; Newport County December 1986; Weymouth cs 1987, then manager 1990-91; Bashley February 1991; Torquay United August 1991 and youth development officer until May 1992, then manager May 1992. Torquay United manager May 1992-March 1993.
Honours: Welsh Cup runners-up 1987.

A big central defender, Paul Compton was useful in the air but a little slow on the ground. After helping Bournemouth to promotion in 1981-82, he experienced playing for sides which finished bottom of their division, three seasons on the trot from 1984 to 1987. The first two were with Torquay, who finished bottom of Division Four, and with Newport, who finished bottom of Division Three.

Compton played in County's Welsh Cup Final defeat against Merthyr

Tydfil in 1987. He had a disastrous time as manager of Weymouth, who finished at the bottom of the Premier Division of the Southern League during his season in charge and won only four matches all season. When Compton took over at Torquay he was their fifth manager in 13 months. They struggled near the bottom of Division Three and were also knocked out of the FA Cup by Yeovil, 5-2 at Plainmoor.

Compton was sacked in March 1993 to be replaced by Neil Warnock as caretaker manager. After Compton's departure, Warnock steered the club away from relegation to the Conference League, then gave way as manager to Don O'Riordan.

CONNER, Richard J.

Born: Jarrow, 13 August 1931.
Right-half   5ft 8in; 11st (1957).
Career: Newcastle United January 1950; South Shields c.1951; Grimsby Town August 1952; Southampton July 1959; Tranmere Rovers July 1961 (£3,000); Aldershot July 1962, retired cs 1963 to become trainer, then caretaker manager October 1968-April 1969; Rochdale coach-assistant manager April 1969, then manager February 1970-May 1973; Darlington July 1973-May 1974; Grimsby Town coach 1977-1978.
Honours: Division Three champions 1960; Division Three North champions 1956;.

An excellent wing-half, neat in style and strong in the tackle, Conner failed to make the first team at St James' Park and moved to non-League South Shields before enjoying seven successful years at Grimsby and also helping Southampton to promotion to Division Two in 1959-60.

He was caretaker manager at Aldershot between Tom McAnearney and Jimmy Melia and left for Rochdale after the latter's appointment. Rochdale finished in their highest ever position, ninth in Division Three in 1969-70, just after Conner's appointment. They also beat Coventry in the FA Cup, 2-1, and Conner sold David Cross to Norwich for a record fee. Darlington had a poor season with Conner in charge. They just avoided re-election by winning their last game of the season, against Barnsley.

CONNOR, David

Born: Wythenshawe, 27 October 1945.
Full-back   5ft 7in; 11st 6lb (1970).
Career: Manchester Boys; Manchester City amateur August 1962, professional November 1962; Preston North End January 1972 (£40,000); Manchester City March 1974; Macclesfield Town 1975, then manager 1976-77; Bury coach, then manager November 1979-June 1980.
Honours: FA Cup winners 1969 (sub).

During his ten years at the club, David Connor made 152 full appearances for (plus 11 as a sub) for Manchester City, turning down several moves to other clubs to stay at Maine Road. A utility player, he appeared in ten games in City's League championship winning season of 1967-68. Connor played in every position except goalkeeper and centre-half. At Bury he tried a host of unknown teenagers in the side. They had a good FA Cup run before defeat at Anfield in the fifth round, but he was sacked after the Shakers were relegated to Division Four.

COOK, Thomas Edwin Reed

Born: Cuckfield, Sussex, 4 January 1901; Died: 15 January 1950.
Centre-forward 5ft 8in; 11st 4lb (1925).
Career: Brighton Municipal School;

Royal Navy 1917; Cuckfield; Brighton & Hove Albion 1921-cs 1929; Sussex cricketer 1922-1937 and cricket coach in South Africa 1929-1930; Northfleet September 1930; Bristol Rovers October 1931, retired cs 1933; managed the Prince Alfred hotel in Simonstown, South Africa, 1937; Brighton & Hove Albion manager May-November 1947.

Honours: England international (1 cap).

Cook joined the Royal Navy as a 16-year-old and saw active service during World War One. He later became a qualified structural engineer at the Crystal Palace School of Engineering. He made his name as a Sussex cricketer and scored 20,206 runs including 31 centuries for the county. Cook won his England cap against Wales in 1925, whilst playing in the Third Division for Brighton. He scored 114 goals in 190 League appearances for the south coast club. As their manager, Cook was not a great success and left after only six months in charge. Cook served in the South African Air Force in World War Two.

COOKE, Albert

Career: Tranmere Rovers office staff 1909, then secretary-manager 1911-April 1935.

Albert Cooke was secretary-manager at Tranmere Rovers for 26 years before he was suddenly sacked on 30 April 1935 following boardroom wrangles over illegal payments to directors and players. Cooke was made the scapegoat and banned by an FA Commission. He signed some fine players during his time at Prenton Park including 'Dixie' Dean and 'Pongo' Waring. He sowed the seeds which enabled the club to join the Football League in 1920. His best season in charge was 1930-31, when Tranmere finished third.

COOPER, Terence

Born: Castleford, 12 July 1944.
Left-back   5ft 7½in; 10st 9lb (1970).

Career: Brotherton School; Wath Wanderers; Ferrybridge Amateurs; Leeds United apprentice May 1961, professional July 1962; Middlesbrough March 1975 (£50,000); Bristol City July 1978 (£20,000); Bristol Rovers player-coach August 1979, then player-manager April 1980-October 1981; Doncaster Rovers November 1981; Bristol City player-manager May 1982-March 1988 (retired from playing 1984), director 1983-1988; Exeter City manager May 1988-August 1991; Birmingham City manager August 1991.

Honours: England international (20 caps); Football League champions 1969; Division Three runners-up 1992; Division Four champions 1990, promotion 1984; FA Cup runners-up 1970; Football League Cup winners 1968;

Inter-Cities Fairs Cup winners 1968, 1971, runners-up 1967; Freight/Rover Trophy winners 1986, runners-up 1987. Terry Cooper won a reputation as a fine attacking left-back with Leeds United in the 1960s. He was the master of the attacking overlap and his speed of recovery was also a great asset when getting back to defend. Cooper went on to make 350 appearances for the club, scoring 11 goals before departing to Middlesbrough. He won a League championship medal in 1968-69 and played in 1970 FA Cup Final defeat against Chelsea. Cooper scored the winning goal in the 1968 Football League Cup victory over Arsenal. Cooper also gained 20 England caps and played in the 1970 World Cup finals. He broke his leg at Stoke in April 1972 but fought back to earn an England recall in November 1974. Cooper missed almost two seasons due to this injury.

In his first season in management, Bristol Rovers were relegated and the main stand burnt down. Dismissed in October 1981, Cooper played briefly for Doncaster Rovers before rejoining Bristol City as player-manager. He took them to promotion to Division Three and to the Freight/Rover Final in 1986 and 1987. After joining City's board, Cooper became the first player-manager director since Vivian Woodward in the early years of the century. He joined Exeter City as manager in May 1988 and took the club to the Fourth Division championship in 1990 and the fourth round of the League Cup in 1989-90. When he moved to St Andrew's, Cooper took Birmingham to runners-up spot in Division Three at the end of his first season.

In 1992-93, Birmingham were lucky not to be relegated. The club had new owners and an injection of cash for Cooper to use on the transfer market but still the club struggled. They saved themselves with a win over Charlton Athletic in the last game of the season.

COPPELL, Stephen James

Born: Liverpool, 9 July 1955.
Midfield   5ft 6in; 10st 3lb (1978).
Career: Liverpool University; Tranmere Rovers amateur June 1973, professional January 1974; Manchester United February 1975 (£60,000), retired through injury October 1983; PFA chairman; Crystal Palace manager June 1984-May 1993.

Honours: England international (42 caps); Under-23 international (1 cap); Football League representative; Division Two promotion 1989; FA Cup winners 1977, runners-up 1976, 1978, 1990; Football League Cup runners-up 1983; Zenith Data Systems Cup winners 1991.

Steve Coppell was a winger-cum-midfielder with his prodigious work-rate and old fashioned winger's skills. He was a late developer as football took second place to his academic studies at Liverpool University. He was snapped up by Manchester United, for £60,000 from Tranmere, and went on to play in four Cup Finals for United and also play in the final stages of two World Cup finals for England. His only winners' medal came when United beat Liverpool 2-1 in the 1977 FA Cup Final.

Coppell made 320 (plus 2 as a sub) League appearances, scoring 53 goals, before injury ended his career at only 28 years old. When he took over at Crystal Palace, Coppell became the youngest manager in the League. He steered Palace to Division One in 1989,

via the play-offs, and also to an FA Cup Final replay defeat against his former club, Manchester United the following year. Palace finished in third position in the First Division in 1990-91 and won the Zenith Data Systems Cup, beating Everton 4-1 in the Final at Wembley.

Palace never recovered from a poor start to the 1992-93 season and went down after a defeat by 3-0 at Arsenal in the last game of the campaign. They had looked safe after beating rivals Ipswich Town a week earlier, but Oldham won their last three games of the season to survive the drop. Palace did reach the semi-finals of the League Cup where they lost to their bogey club Arsenal, again to miss out on another Wembley Final. Coppell decided to resign in May 1993.

CORKHILL, William Grant

Born: Belfast, 23 April 1910; Died: Nottingham, 9 August 1978.
Wing-half   5ft 10in; 11st 4lb (1937).
Career: Northern Nomads; Marine; Notts County May 1931; Cardiff City May 1938; Notts County November 1945-1951; Scunthorpe United manager 1952-May 1956; Bradford manager May 1956-November 1957; licensee in Nottingham.

Honours: FA XI v Combined Universities 1930.

Spotted playing for Marine, Corkhill played his first and last matches for Notts County against Barnsley, 19½ years apart. Despite playing for County for most of this long period, he made only 264 appearances for the club, due to the seven seasons lost to the war. He is the oldest player, apart from Albert Iremonger, to play for Notts County, being 40 when he played his last game. Under his management, Scunthorpe twice finished third in the Third Division North, in 1953-54 and 1954-55, but they were unable to gain promotion. At Bradford he had a constant struggle and left after a poor start to the 1957-58 season.

COWAN, Samuel

Born: Chesterfield, 10 May 1901; Died: Haywards Heath, 4 October 1964.
Centre-half   5ft 11in; 13st 2lb (1935).
Career: Ardwick Juniors; Bullcroft Colliery; Denaby United; Doncaster Rovers cs 1923; Manchester City December 1924; Bradford City October 1935 (£2,000); Mossley July 1937; Brighton & Hove Albion coach June 1938; Manchester City manager November 1946-June 1947; physiotherapist in Brighton; masseur to Sussex CCC and to MCC on tour of Australia in 1962-63.

Honours: England international (3 caps); Football League representative (1 cap); Division Two champions 1928, 1947; FA Cup winners 1934, runners-up 1926, 1933.

A hefty pivot who was happiest in an attacking role, Sam Cowan was a resourceful and enthusiastic player. He once scored a hat-trick of headers, for Doncaster against Halifax in March 1924. Cowan captained Manchester City to three FA Cup Finals and as well as winning three England caps from 1926 to 1931 and representing the Football League and the Irish League in 1934. Cowan scored 24 goals in 407 games for City.

As manager of Manchester City, he led the side to the Second Division championship during his only season in charge. He continued to live in Hove and in June 1947, when the City directors expressed concern at his commuting, he decided to leave Maine Road and concentrate on his physiotherapy business in the Sussex town. He died in 1964 whilst refereeing a charity match in Haywards Heath.

COWELL, Arthur

Born: Blackburn, 20 May 1886; Died: 12 February 1959.
Career: Blackburn St Peters; Nelson 1904; Blackburn Rovers May 1905, retired cs 1920 to become club trainer until May 1937; Wrexham trainer May 1937, then manager June-September 1938; ran newsagents in Kirkham and Darwen after this.

Honours: England international (1 cap); Football League representative (1 cap); Football League champions 1912, 1914.

Along with Bob Crompton, Arthur Cowell was part of one of the best full-back partnerships in Blackburn Rovers' history. Crompton was capped many times for England, but Cowell played only once, against Ireland in Belfast in February 1910 when he did not partner Crompton. He helped Rovers to two League titles, appearing 31 times in their 1911-12 success and being ever-present when they easily took the championship again two seasons later. He made a total of 306 League and FA Cup appearances for Blackburn but the last few years of his career were blighted, first by the war and then injury. He made only one appearance after the war.

A relentless tackler who possessed speed and had good distribution, Cowell became trainer at Ewood Park after his retirement. He had a short spell as manager of Wrexham just before World War Two but under him they struggled near the foot of the Third Division North. At the beginning of 1938-39 he fell out with the board and resigned after a home win over Rochdale after only seven matches in charge.

COX, Arthur

Born: Southall, Warwickshire, 14 December 1939.
Career: Coventry City 1955-1958, retired through injury to become youth-team coach; Walsall coach; Aston Villa coach July 1968-January 1970, caretaker manager briefly in December 1968; Preston North End coach 1970; Halifax Town coach; Blackpool assistant manager; Sunderland assistant manager 1973-1976; Galatasaray (Turkey) coach 1976; Chesterfield manager October 1976-September 1980; Newcastle United manager September 1980-May 1984; Derby County manager May 1984.

Honours: Division Two promotion 1984, Division Two champions 1987; Division Three promotion 1986.

Arthur Cox is a tough, dour man who has made a name for himself despite keeping a relatively low profile. He has successfully managed Chesterfield, Newcastle United and Derby County, despite having to work with some difficult directors and chairmen. He is a disciplinarian with a non-stop approach to his job and has always enjoyed the respect of his players.

Cox looked to have a bright future ahead of him as a player before being forced to give up the game after only three seasons at Highfield Road after his leg was shattered so badly that his playing career was at an end. He joined the club's coaching staff and later ran the youth team. He moved to Walsall as a coach and also served Aston Villa in a similar capacity from July 1968 until January 1970. He was caretaker manager of Villa briefly in December 1968.

Midway through the 1969-70 season he moved to Preston as coach and they went on to clinch the Third Division title that season. He later coached at Halifax Town before becoming assistant manager at Blackpool. Then Cox moved to Roker Park as assistant manager to Bob Stokoe and he was there when Second Division Sunderland won the FA Cup in 1973, sensationally beating giants Leeds United. They also gained the Second Division title in 1975-76.

Cox took up the challenge of his first managerial post at Chesterfield in October 1976. He did well at Saltergate and, although lucky to avoid relegation to Division Four by just one point in 1978-79, the following season he was equally unlucky not to obtain promotion when Chesterfield finished fourth, one point behind promoted Sheffield Wednesday.

Cox was the surprise choice to take over at Newcastle United in September 1980. His appointment was criticized by Brian Clough, who suggested that the Newcastle board had taken the easy way out in choosing Cox to change the club's fortunes. Cox saw this as the greatest possible motivation to do well. He took the Magpies back to the First Division in 1984, then surprisingly resigned over the duration of his contract.

One of the youngsters who was making a name for himself during Cox's first season at St James' Park was Chris Waddle, a signing from Tow Law Town. Newcastle were gradually improving their position every season

in the Second Division. They finished fifth in 1982-83 but were never in with a real chance of gaining promotion. However, the following season, they finished third and returned to the First Division. Cox pulled off a masterstroke when he persuaded Kevin Keegan to join the club in 1982, Terry McDermott also returned from Liverpool and Peter Beardsley completed the jigsaw when signing from Vancouver Whitecaps in September 1983 for just £120,000. This was an inspired signing by Cox, as he was later sold to Liverpool for £1.8m.

Cox rocked the Gallowgate fans when he resigned days after achieving promotion and moved, apparently at a reduced wage, to manage Third Division Derby County, who had only just ensured their survival after being on the point of liquidation.

Former Rams star Roy McFarland was caretaker manager following the sacking of Peter Taylor and he accepted an invitation to be Cox's assistant at the Baseball Ground. The Rams were in a mess when Cox arrived and he had to rely on free-transfer signings and also had to sell striker Kevin Wilson — who later became a Northern Ireland international — to Ipswich to raise funds for other players.

But Cox signed some good players, built a more than useful side, and after a tense finish, Derby were promoted to Division Two in 1986. The following year they were celebrating the Second Division title, thus moving from the Third to the First in successive seasons. Cox restored Derby's dignity and then signed England internationals Mark Wright and Peter Shilton from Southampton to boost the Rams' chances of staying in the top division. The signings were made possible by Robert Maxwell, but if Derby fans thought that this would be the start of great things under the chairmanship of the man who was later to be dubbed 'the world's biggest crook', then, like a lot of people who dealt with Maxwell, they were to be sadly disappointed.

The Rams' first year back in Division One was spent worrying about relegation, but then Maxwell moved some money from one pocket to another and for a club record £1 million Derby signed Welsh international striker Dean Saunders from Oxford United, who were also controlled by the Maxwell family. Derby went on to finish fifth but then the money dried up and that, coupled with an appalling list of injuries, eventually saw the Rams relegated in 1990-91.

It had been a difficult time and if Derby fans wondered why Maxwell had inexplicably lost all interest in their club, events after his death revealed why. Cox, meanwhile, had taken little blame for Derby's decline and maintained his dignity throughout the whole unhappy episode. Aston Villa were said to want him as their manager but Derby refused to let him speak to them.

Remarkably, hard-up Derby began their first season back in the Second Division by storming into the promotion places. Then local newspaper millionaire Lionel Pickering bought the club and suddenly Cox had millions to spend. Big-money strikers Marco Gabbiadini, Paul Kitson, Paul Simpson and Tommy Johnson joined Derby who just lost out to Blackburn in the end-of-season play-offs. For 1992-93, Cox signed more big-money players — midfielders Martin Kuhl and Mark Pembridge and defenders Darren Wassell and Craig Short.

But despite spending millions on new players, Derby County were unable to even get into the play-offs in 1992-93 and Cox's job was on the line at the turn of the year with the Rams looking more likely to struggle against relegation than gain promotion. He survived but the fans' patience was wearing thin with the man who was once their hero.

COX, Frederick James Arthur

Born: Reading, 1 November 1920; Died: Bournemouth, 17 August 1973.
Outside-right   5ft 7in; 11st 7lb (1954).
Career: Redlands School; St Georges' Boys Club (Reading); Northfleet; Tottenham Hotspur professional August 1938; guest for Fulham, Manchester City, Reading and Swindon Town in World War Two; Arsenal September 1949; West Bromwich Albion July 1953 as player-coach and assistant manager until April 1956; Bournemouth & Boscombe Athletic manager April 1956-July 1958; Portsmouth August 1958-February 1961; Gillingham manager June 1962-April 1965; Bournemouth & Boscombe Athletic manager April 1965-June 1970; ran newsagent in Bournemouth.

Honours: Division Four champions 1964; FA Cup winners 1950, runners-up 1952.

A winger who was noted for his courageous, stop-at-nothing attitude, Freddie Cox lost his best years to the war. He spent much of those years flying transport planes in the Far East. He later played an important role in getting Arsenal to two FA Cup Finals, scoring valuable goals in the 1950 and 1952 semi-finals. At Bournemouth he steered the club to an excellent FA Cup run in 1957, in which they beat Wolves and Spurs.

Whilst in charge at Portsmouth, Cox had a difficult time with Pompey being relegated from the First Division in 1959 and heading for the Third when he was sacked in February 1961. At Gillingham he took the club to the Fourth Division championship in 1963-64. Cox later concentrated on his newsagent's business in Bournemouth.

COX, John 'Jack'

Born: Blackpool, 21 November 1876.
Winger   5ft 9in; 11st (1904).
Career: South Shore Standard; South Shore; Blackpool cs 1897; Liverpool February 1898 (£150); Blackpool player-manager cs 1909-1911, also retired as a player 1911.

Honours: England international (3 caps); Football League representative (3 caps); Football League champions 1901, 1906; Division Two champions 1905.

Jack Cox could play on either wing for Liverpool and made 360 appearances, scoring 60 goals for the Reds. Extremely fast, Cox sometimes overdid the trickery. A noted athlete, he won several handicap races. He missed only two games in Liverpool's League championship season of 1900-01, scoring ten goals. He also made 28 appearances, scoring eight goals, in 1905-06 when they won the title again. Cox had two mediocre seasons as player-manager of Blackpool, when they finished in mid-table positions in Division Two.

CRAGGS, Kenneth

Born: Ferryhill, c.1936.
5ft 11in; 12st 1lb (1958).
Career: Fulham amateur 1954, professional 1958; King's Lynn cs 1960;

Folkestone 1961; Tunbridge Wells United cs 1961; Dartford 1963; Hounslow player-coach in 1960s; Fulham part-time coach September 1968, full-time cs 1976, later assistant manager; Brighton & Hove Albion assistant manager 1978-1981; Charlton Athletic assistant manager 1981, then manager June-November 1982.

Ken Craggs joined Fulham as an amateur in 1954 and turned professional four years later. He moved to King's Lynn in the summer of 1960 and later played for Folkestone, Tunbridge Wells United, Dartford and Hounslow, where he was the player-coach. He joined Fulham on a part-time basis in September 1968, as youth-team coach and scout, and became a full-time member of staff in the summer of 1976, running the youth team for a while. Craggs was then assistant manager to Alan Mullery at both Brighton and Charlton and succeeded him as manager at The Valley in June 1982. He was involved in the on-off signing of Alan Simonsen, the Danish international, but in November 1982 Craggs was rather shabbily sacked by the Charlton board.

CRAYSTON, William John

Born: Grange over Sands, 9 October 1910 Died: Streetly, 26 December 1992.
Right-half   6ft; 13st 5lb (1935).
Career: Barrow Schools; Ulverston Town; Barrow August 1928; Bradford May 1930; Arsenal May 1934 (£5,250), retired through injury 1943; Arsenal training staff 1946, assistant manager 1947-1956, then manager November 1956-May 1958; Doncaster Rovers manager June 1958-March 1959 and secretary until June 1961; ran a newsagent's and general store in Streetly near Birmingham.

Honours: England international (8 caps); Football League champions 1935, 1938; FA Cup winners 1936; Football League War Cup runners-up 1941; Football League South Cup winners 1943.

Tall, elegant and fast, Crayston was good in the air and also one of the first long-throw specialists. Crayston was a utility player when he was with Bradford, playing at inside and centre-forward as well in the half-back line. He preferred to play at centre-half but settled at right-half, where his pace and control captivated the Park Avenue crowd. He broke a bone in his ankle and wrist in 1933-34. Crayston made over 70 appearances for Barrow and 102 for Bradford, in which he scored 15 goals, before moving to Highbury.

He won two League championship and an FA Cup winners' medal at Arsenal. His playing career came to an end during the war because of severe varicose veins. He served in the RAF during hostilities.

Crayston joined Arsenal's training staff after the war and was appointed to succeed Tom Whittaker as manager in 1956. In his first season in charge, Arsenal finished fifth and reached the sixth round of the FA Cup but things did not go so well after this. He was given little money to improve the side and, out of frustration, he resigned in May 1958.

CRERAND, Patrick Timothy

Born: Glasgow, 19 February 1939.
Right-half   5ft 11in; 11st 10lb (1964).
Career: Duntocher Hibs; Glasgow Celtic cs 1958; Manchester United February 1963 (£56,000), then coach August 1971, later assistant manager 1974; Northampton Town manager July 1976-January 1977; Professional to a Manchester engineering company.

Honours: Scotland international (16 caps); Under-23 international (1 cap); Scottish League representative (7 caps); Football League champions 1965, 1967; FA Cup winners 1963; Scottish Cup runners-up 1961; European Cup winners 1968.

Paddy Crerand was brought up in the Gorbals area of Glasgow and made 91 appearances for Celtic before his move to Manchester United. This included Celtic's Scottish Cup Final defeat against Dunfermline in 1961.

Although he lacked pace, Crerand was the master of the defence-splitting pass and had a piledriver of a shot. He had a lot to do with United's success in the 1960s and helped them to an FA Cup Final victory over Leicester City shortly after joining the Reds in 1963. There were also two League championships, and a European Cup Final victory over Benfica at Wembley by 4-1 in 1968.

Crerand had a hot temper and was sent off six times in his career, including once whilst playing for Scotland against the Czechs in Bratislava. His involvement in football was passionate to the point of fanaticism. Surprisingly, football club management did not suit him and Crerand was in charge at Northampton Town for only six months in a season where the Cobblers were eventually relegated after he had left the County Ground.

CRESSWELL, Warneford

Born: South Shields, 5 November 1894; Died: 20 October 1973.
Full-back   5ft 10in; 10st 10lb (1935).
Career: Stanhope School; South Shields Schools; South Shields junior soccer; Hearts and Hibernian as guest in World War One; South Shields cs 1919; Sunderland March 1922 (£5,500); Everton February 1927 (£7,000); Port Vale manager May 1936-April 1937; Northampton Town manager April 1937-September 1939; licensee after the war.

Honours: England international (7 caps); Schoolboy international; Football League representative (5 caps); Football League champions 1928, 1932; Division Two champions 1931; FA Cup winners 1933.

A classy defender who was the forerunner to the modern full-back, Warney Cresswell had a fine sense of positioning and timing and was composed and

elegant, allowing him to stroll through a game. Nicknamed 'The Iceberg' by his teammates, he played over 500 games for his three clubs, including 306 appearances for Everton. His £5,500 move to Sunderland was a British record at the time. He had a fine game in Everton's 3-0 win over Manchester City in the 1933 FA Cup Final and probably should have won more than seven caps for England. However, he did not have such a distinguished career as a manager. Both Port Vale and Northampton could achieve only mid-table positions under him.

CROMPTON, John 'Jack'

Born: Chorlton, Manchester, 18 December 1921.
Goalkeeper
Career: Oldham Athletic amateur in wartime soccer; Goslings FC; Manchester United amateur June 1943, professional November 1945-1956; Luton Town coach 1956-1958; Manchester United coach 1958-1971; Luton Town manager June 1962 (one week); Barrow coach 1971, then manager December 1971-June 1972; Bury assistant manager 1972; Preston North End coach 1973-1974; Manchester United reserve-team manager 1974, caretaker manager April-June 1981.

Honours: Football League champions 1952; FA Cup winners 1948.

Jack Crompton was Manchester United's regular goalkeeper from 1945-50 and made 191 appearances in all for the Reds. His finest game was against Blackpool in the 1948 FA Cup Final, in which he made a number of fine saves to help his side to a 4-2 victory. After coaching at Luton, Crompton returned to Old Trafford as coach after the Munich air disaster in 1958. He stayed at United for 13 years, except for a one-week spell as Luton's manager, which he left for 'health' reasons. United won many honours in this period, including the European Cup.

He left Old Trafford in 1971, when Matt Busby retired, and worked as a coach and then manager at Barrow. Injury problems and bad luck took the Holker Street club from a healthy mid-table position to the bottom of the Fourth Division and Crompton resigned after Barrow were voted out of the League at the end of the season.

Crompton coached under Bobby Charlton at Preston, then returned again to Manchester United as coach to Tommy Docherty. He was caretaker manager in the summer of 1981, between the management of Dave Sexton and Ron Atkinson. In recent years he has been the president of the

Manchester Alliance Sunday League, although he now lives in Majorca.

CROMPTON, Robert

Born: Blackburn, 26 September 1879; Died: 16 March 1941.
Right-back   5ft 11in; 13st (1901).
Career: Moss Street School (Blackburn); Rose and Thistle; Blackburn Trinity; Blackburn Rovers September 1896-May 1920, when he retired, then director June 1921-March 1931 and manager December 1926-February 1931; Bournemouth & Boscombe Athletic manager June 1935-February 1936; Blackburn Rovers manager April 1938-March 1941; director of contracting firm in Blackburn.

Honours: England international (41 caps); Football League representative (17 caps); Football League champions 1912, 1914; Division Two champions 1939; FA Cup winners 1928.

A superbly-equipped full-back, Bob Crompton was robust but scrupulously fair and quick in recovery. He made 528 appearances for Rovers in almost 24 years with the club. Crompton made his debut against Stoke in April 1897 and played his last game in the spring of 1920. He held the long-service record with one club until it was beaten by Ted Sagar in the 1950s. He also held the appearance record for England with 41 caps (including 12 caps against Scotland) until Billy Wright passed it in 1952.

Crompton gained two League championship medals as a player for Rovers and a FA Cup winners' medal in 1928 as the manager at Ewood Park when they beat Huddersfield 3-1 at Wembley. He spent his entire career at Rovers except for an eight-month spell as manager of Bournemouth.

CROOK, Walter.

Born: Whittle-le-Woods, 28 April 1913; Died: Mellor, near Blackburn, 27 December 1988.
Wing-half   5ft 10in; 10st 4lb (1935).
Career: Blackburn Nomads; Blackburn Rovers March 1932; Bolton Wanderers May 1947, retired 1948; Accrington Stanley manager June 1951-March 1953; Ajax Amsterdam manager in 1950s.

Popular with the Ewood Park crowd, Walter Crook was a consistent defender who made 218 League appearances for the Ewood Park club and later played 28 games for Bolton. When he was manager of Accrington Stanley, the club's fortunes sunk to almost the lowest possible depths as they plunged into a financial crisis.

Stanley won only 59 points from 92 games during Crook's two seasons in charge at Peel Park and he resigned after the club had finished bottom of the Third Division North in 1953-54. He is definitely a candidate for the manager with the worst-ever record in the Football League. He went on to manage Ajax of Amsterdam, who had just turned professional in 1954. Here, he had more success and helped establish Ajax as the club we know today.

CROOKS, Samuel Dickinson

Born: Bearpark, County Durham, 16 January 1908; Died: Belper, Derbyshire, 3 February 1981.
Right winger   5ft 8in; 10st 9lb (1935).
Career: Bearpark Colliery; Brandon Juniors; Tow Law Town; Durham City May 1926; chairman of the PFA until 1939; Derby County April 1927 (£300), retired 1947, chief scout February 1946-

August 1949; Retford Town manager December 1949; Shrewsbury Town secretary-manager May 1950-June 1954; Gresley Rovers player December 1954, then player-manager January 1955-May 1957; Burton Albion manager May-November 1957; Gresley Rovers manager June 1958; Heanor Town manager-coach April 1959; Derby County chief scout June 1960-May 1967.

Honours: England international (26 caps); Football League representative (4 caps).

Despite his frail physique, Sammy Crooks had pace, a bundle of tricks and a sharp football brain. He started as an inside-forward in the Third Division North at Durham City but was considered too small for the hurly-burly of midfield and was converted to outside-right. Crooks still worked down the coal pit until he was signed by Derby County, for whom he went on to score 111 goals in 445 appearances between 1927 and 1947. After Eddie Hapgood, he was England's most capped player between the wars and would have played more, but for the presence of Stanley Matthews.

It was so sad that he had to miss Derby's FA Cup Final victory over Charlton in 1946, due to injury, for it would have capped a fine career. By this time he had also become the club's chief scout, a position he was to fill for ten years in two separate periods. Crooks was secretary-manager of Shrewsbury Town when they entered the Football League in 1950 but they struggled near the bottom of the table during his years in charge, rarely being out of the bottom four. Crooks had served Derby for a total of 30 years when he retired in 1967 and he was still playing in charity matches well past his 60th birthday. Indeed, such was his enthusiasm for the game that he always carried a pair of football boots in his car and would often join in kick-about games with local lads.

CROSBY, Malcolm

Born: South Shields, 4 July 1954.
Midfield   5ft 9in; 11st (1981).
Career: Aldershot July 1972; York City November 1981-1987 (player exchange); Wrexham (loan) September-October 1984; Sunderland youth-team coach 1987, then manager December 1991-February 1993; York City player-youth team trainer 1985; coaching in Kuwait August 1986; Sunderland manager December 1991-February 1993.

Honours: England Youth international; Division Four champions 1984; FA Cup runners-up 1992.

Malcolm Crosby took Second Division Sunderland to an FA Cup Final in May

1992, despite their struggles against relegation to Division Three. He was initially the caretaker manager after the sacking of Denis Smith and it was not until just before the Cup Final that the Sunderland board stopped it's dithering and offered Crosby the job permanently. Sunderland lost the Final to Liverpool but stayed in the Second Division. Sacked 1993, hearing the news over telephone.

Crosby had previously been the youth-team coach at Sunderland. He made 301 (plus 23 sub) appearances for Aldershot, scoring 27 goals and helping the Shots to promotion in 1972-73. Crosby played six games whilst on loan to Wrexham and 103 League games for York City, scoring four goals. York were Division Four champions in 1983-84 with an enormous 101 points. Crosby made 33 appearances that season.

CROWE, Victor Herbert

Born: Abercynon, Wales, 31 January 1932.
Wing-half   5ft 10in; 11st 8lb (1964).
Career: Handsworth Schools; Erdington Albion; West Bromwich Albion amateur; Aston Villa June 1952; Peterborough United July 1964; Atlanta Chiefs (NASL) 1967-1969; Aston Villa assistant coach August 1969-1970, then manager January 1970-May 1974; Portland Timbers (NASL) manager 1975-1976; coached in non-League football; advisory manager of Bilston Town in 1988.
Honours: Wales international (16 caps); Division Two champions 1960; Division Three champions 1972; Football League Cup winners 1961, 1963, runners-up 1971.

Vic Crowe left Wales at the age of two to be brought up in the Handsworth area of Birmingham. He went on to serve Aston Villa for 18 years as player, coach and manager. Crowe captained Villa to the Second Division championship in 1959-60, and also to two losing FA Cup semi-final appearances, against Forest in 1959 and Wolves the following year, and to two League Cup Final victories. When he skippered Wales for the first time against Scotland at Ninian Park in October 1960, Crowe was the only person in the side who did not speak with a Welsh accent.

He won a reputation as a great battler in midfield and as the manager of Villa, Crowe took the club back to the Second Division as champions in 1972. This followed a League Cup Final defeat, whilst a Third Division victory, against Spurs a year earlier. He moved to the USA to manage Portland Timbers in the North American Soccer League in 1974.

CULLIS, Stanley

Born: Ellesmere Port, 25 October 1915.
Centre-half   5ft 10in; 11st 7lb (1937).
Career: Bolton Wanderers amateur;

Ellesmere Port Wednesday; Wolverhampton Wanderers February 1934, then assistant manager August 1947, manager June 1948-September 1964; Birmingham City manager December 1965-March 1970.

Honours: England international (12 caps); Wartime international (20 caps); Football League representative (3 caps); Football League champions 1954, 1958, 1959; FA Cup winners 1949, 1960, runners-up 1939;

Over the years, Wolves probably owe more to Stan Cullis for their success than to any other personality in the club's history. Cullis served the Molineux club as player and manager for 30 years. At wing-half he was a powerful tackler and supreme in the air as well as being a fine ball player. He had the ability to hold the ball until he could use it well, making one of his famous long through passes or perhaps taking it through with his ungainly, crouching, dribbling style. As a manager he instilled a fighting quality into his players and built a side which thrived on the quick, long pass and played a brand of direct robust football, stretching opposing defenders with wing-to-wing crosses.

After Bolton had failed to capture him on professional forms, Cullis joined Wolves in February 1934 and gave the club splendid service before retiring in May 1947, when he found himself prone to concussive injuries. Wolves' defeat against Portsmouth in the 1939 FA Cup Final was one of the greatest disappointments of his career and during his playing career they also twice missed League championships by narrow margins, although Cullis more than made up for these disappointments when he became manager.

He was made skipper of the Wolves side when he was only 19 and later captained England, taking over for a fiery game in Bucharest in May 1939, when his calming influence was a major factor in a 2-0 victory over Romania. With Cliff Britton and Joe Mercer he also formed a fine England half-back line in wartime internationals and played in several inter-services matches during hostilities. Whilst appearing in only 171 peacetime League and FA Cup games for Wolves, he played regularly in wartime football whilst serving in the Army as a physical training instructor.

On retirement, Cullis became assistant to Ted Vizard at Molineux before being appointed manager in June 1948. Under his guidance, Wolves won three League titles, in 1953-54, 1957-58 and 1958-59. They also lifted the FA Cup

twice, in 1949 and 1960, the FA Charity Shield and the FA Youth Cup, and they entered European competiton in the late 1950s.

Cullis signed and developed some brilliant footballers and pioneered floodlit friendlies against some of the top sides in Europe, including memorable games against Russian and Hungarian sides.

He drove his players on with relentless, impassioned determination. To be near him at a match was to experience total involvement, although his torrent of words was often just a meaningless chant to ease his tension.

Alas, after 1961 things began to go wrong and attendances at Molineux declined. Wolves were often at the wrong end of the First Division and Cullis was finally sacked in September 1964. In many ways, the football style he used so successfully had been copied by several sides and he was apparently unable to 'modernise' his football thinking. His dismissal led to bitter recriminations from fans and media alike. How could Cullis, who had served his club so well for so long, be so shabbily treated?

For the next 15 months he worked for Coventry City chairman Derrick Robins, trying to boost the sales of sports pavilions and grandstands, and did some football reporting before returning to manage Birmingham City at the age of 50.

City hoped that his experience would guide them back into the First Division but it was not to be. Performances and crowds improved and the players appreciated his coaching methods and good humour, but the Blues never finished higher than fifth in Division Two before his departure in March 1970 with the team struggling at the wrong end of the table. Two excellent Cup runs were achieved, though. In the League Cup, Birmingham reached the semi-finals in 1967, and in the FA Cup they reached the same stage a year later.

Cullis left football to work for a travel agent and write for a Midlands sports paper. Today, he lives in retirement in Malvern, Worcestershire.

CUMMINGS, Thomas S.

Born: Sunderland, 12 September 1928.
Centre-half   5ft 10½in; 11st 9lb (1959).

Career: Stanley United; Hylton Colliery Welfare; Burnley October 1947; Mansfield Town March 1963, then manager July 1963-July 1967; Aston Villa manager July 1967-November 1968; later scout for Burnley and Sunderland.

Honours: England 'B' international (3 caps); Football League representative; Football League champions 1960; Division Four promotion 1963; FA Cup runners-up 1962.

Tommy Cummings made 434 appearances for Burnley after succeeding Alan Brown as the Clarets' regular pivot in 1949-50. Cummings relied on positional skill and judgement and played a leading role in Burnley's second League championship success in 1959-60. Cummings also gained an FA Cup runners-up medal when the Clarets lost 3-1 to Spurs in the 1962 FA Final. He also represented the Football League against the Irish League in 1951.

Before taking over as player-manager of Mansfield, Cummings was the chairman of the PFA for two years. In 1964-65 the Stags just missed promotion to the Second Division on goal-average thus finishing third. This was followed by 16 largely undistinguished months in charge at Villa Park. He was sacked in November 1968 with Villa at the bottom of the Second Division. Cummings had been given little money to spend so therefore was unable to rebuild the side after relegation.

CUNNINGHAM, Andrew N.

Born: Galston, near Kilmarnock 30 January 1891; Died: 8 May 1973.
Inside-right   6ft; 12st 8lb (1922).
Career: Galston Riverside Rangers 1906; Newmilns 1907; Kilmarnock June 1909; Rangers April 1915 (£800); Newcastle United February 1929 (£2,300), then manager January 1930-May 1935, retired from playing May 1930; Dundee manager June 1937-May 1940; sports journalist with the Scottish Sunday Express.

Honours: Scotland international (12 caps); Scottish League representative (10 caps); Scottish League champions 1920, 1921, 1923, 1924, 1925, 1927, 1928; Scottish Cup winners 1928, runners-up 1920, 1922; FA Cup winners 1932.

One of the greats of Scottish football in the 1920s. A tall, well-built and commanding forward, this massive six-footer was as light on his feet as a ballet dancer. He could shoot with tremendous power with both feet, had good ball control, a fine long-passing game and excellent positional sense.

Cunningham played almost 450 times for Rangers, winning seven Scottish League championship medals. He was probably the oldest player to make his Football League debut when joining Newcastle at the age of 38. He became the Magpies' first manager and took them to victory in the 1932 FA Cup Final but United were relegated to the Second Division two years later. He resigned at the end of the 1934-35 season. Dundee were relegated to the Scottish Second Division at the end of his first season in charge. Cunningham seemed a lot happier as a journalist than as a manager.

CUNNINGHAM, William Carruthers

Born: Hill of Beath, Fife, 22 February 1925.
Full-back   5ft 9in; 12st (1955).
Career: Crossgates Primrose; Dunfermline Athletic 1944; Airdrie 1945; Preston North End June 1949 (£5,000), then assistant trainer; Southport player-manager March 1964-April 1965; sports outfitter in Preston.

Honours: Scotland international (8 caps); 'B' international (1 cap); Schoolboy international; Division Two champions 1951; FA Cup runners-up 1954.

Cunningham was a stalwart for Preston for 14 years. A sturdy compact player who defended stoutly, Cunningham

made 440 League appearances for the Deepdale club, scoring just three goals. He was captain of Scotland when they played in the 1954 World Cup finals and also played in Preston's FA Cup Final defeat by West Brom in 1954. Cunningham was still playing when he turned 40 and was player-manager of Southport, for whom he made 12 appearances. Southport finished 20th in Division Four in his season in charge. He returned to Preston afterwards as assistant trainer for a period. He is the cousin of the Preston player Jim Baxter.

CURBISHLEY, Llewellyin Charles 'Alan'

Born: Forest Gate, London, 8 November 1957.
Midfield   5ft 9in; 11st 6lb (1983).
Career: Forest Gate Schools 1972; West Ham United apprentice July 1973, professional July 1975; Birmingham City July 1979 (£225,000); Aston Villa March 1983 (£100,000 & player); Charlton Athletic December 1984 (£40,000); Brighton & Hove Albion August 1987 (£32,000); Charlton Athletic player-coach July 1990 (£5,000), assistant manager October 1990, then joint manager with Steve Gritt July 1991.

Honours: Under-21 international; England Schoolboys international; Youth international; FA Youth Cup runners-up 1975.

For the 1991-92 season, Alan Curbishley was appointed joint manager of Charl-

ton Athletic along with Steve Gritt. Despite problems with grounds and injuries, the Valiants narrowly missed the Second Division play-offs. They played the whole season at Upton Park, when it had been hoped they would return to The Valley. Charlton finally made an emotional return to The Valley in December 1992, after great efforts by the directors and supporters of the club to make their dream come true. As a player, Curbishley has made over 600 senior appearances. A determined, all-action player, Curbishly also possesses a lot of skill. He was a member of West Ham's side which reached the FA Youth Cup Final in 1975, but lost to Ipswich Town 2-0. He was reluctantly allowed to leave Upton Park for a large fee after a dispute over his role in the side. He helped Birmingham City to promotion to Division One in 1979-80 and in May 1981 gained an Under-21 cap against Switzerland in Neuenburg.

CURTIS, George Frederick

Born: Orsett, 3 December 1919.
Inside-forward
Career: Anglo (Purfleet); Arsenal April 1937; Southampton August 1947; Valenciens (France) player-coach 1952; Cambridge University coach for two years; England Youth team coach for two years; Sunderland coach 1957-1961; Brighton & Hove Albion manager June 1961-February 1963; Stevenage Town manager 1964-cs 1967; Hull City coach 1967; San Diego Toros (USA) manager-coach in 1968; Norway national coach in 1970s; Rosenburg Trondeim (Norway) coach; Qatar coach 1978; FIFA instructor; Hitchin Town manager in 1980s.

A much-travelled coach and manager, George Curtis began his career at Highbury as an inside-forward. His early career was badly affected by the war in which he spent six years in the RAF, including two and a half years in India as a physical training instructor. He made only the occasional appearance for Arsenal but was a regular for Southampton, playing 174 games until he moved to play in France in 1952. Curtis qualified as an FA coach in 1947 and became an FA staff coach in 1952.

The only League club that Curtis managed was Brighton, where he had an unhappy time. Brighton sunk from the Second to the Fourth Division from 1961 to 1963. His teams were based on defence, which did not endear him to the Goldstone fans. After a spell at Stevenage, he was coach under Cliff Britton at Hull and moved to the United States to manage San Diego Toros, who reached the national finals of the first NASL.

· He then spent five years in Norway, three as national coach, and took Rosenburg Trondheim into Europe for the first time. After being involved in a motor accident, Curtis spent two years in Qatar in the Arabian Gulf. He then he worked as a FIFA instructor in Japan, South Korea and other Far East countries.

CURTIS, George W.

Born: Dover, 5 May 1939.
Centre-half   5ft 11in; 13st 9lb (1964).
Career: Snowdon Colliery; Coventry City amateur May 1954, professional May 1956; Aston Villa December 1969 (£25,000), retired cs 1972; Coventry City commercial staff 1974, then managing director from September 1983, team manager April 1986-May 1987 (with John Sillett).

Honours: England Youth international (4 caps); Division Two champions 1967; Division Three champions 1964; FA Cup winners 1987.

A tough uncompromising defender who was the foundation stone to Coventry City's success in the 1960s, George Curtis holds the record for appearances at Highfield Road with 483 (plus three as a sub) and played in five different divisions for the club. He went up to the First Division with the Sky Blues, winning two championships on the way. Curtis was a stop-gap signing for Villa near the end of his career. In partnership with John Sillett, he took City to their first-ever FA Cup Final appearance in 1987, when they beat Spurs.

CURTIS, Harry

Born: Holloway, 1890; Died: 31 January 1966.
Career: Shernhall United (Walthamstow League); Romford; Walthamstow Grange; Gnomes Athletic manager c.1919; Football League referee; possibly Charlton Athletic secretary for a short spell; Gillingham manager May 1923-May 1926; Brentford manager May 1926-February 1949.

Honours: Division Two champions 1935; Division Three South champions 1933.

The most successful manager in Brentford's history is undoubtedly Harry Curtis, who managed the club from 1926 until 1949. Not only did he bring First Division football to Griffin Park, but after it was achieved, the Bees became one of the most formidable sides of the late 1930s.

Curtis never played professional football, although he gained a reputation as an inside-right in amateur soccer before giving up the game at a relatively early age to concentrate on refereeing on Hackney Marshes. He graduated to the Southern League and during World War One officiated in the London Combination. After the war, Curtis joined the Football League list and often refereed at Griffin Park.

In 1919 he managed a sports club belonging to a large firm in the Walthamstow area and ran a team called Gnomes Athletic FC, made up from the sports section of the company for whom he worked. They won many trophies and some of their players went on to play in League soccer. In 1919-20, the Gnomes had a fine run in the FA Cup, reaching the final qualifying round before losing 3-0 at home to Hednesford Town when victory could have meant a visit to a League club. Curtis introduced methods and amenities which made the Gnomes the envy of other clubs with far more resources than themselves.

After leaving the Gnomes, Curtis ran a private club in Rayleigh, Essex, arranging dances, concerts and whist drives etc. He then had a spell with Charlton Athletic, followed by three seasons as manager of Gillingham from the close season of 1923. Lack of funds made his task difficult and after three mediocre seasons, in which the Gills finished in the bottom half of the Third Division South, he accepted an offer to manage Brentford.

The Bees were also a struggling Third Division side with a ground which was in poor condition and clearly unable to hold very large crowds. Curtis immediately set to work in improving the set-up at Griffin Park. Fortunately, the club had a good FA Cup run in his first season, which

helped raise funds. Nearly all the ties went to replays before the Bees lost 1-0 at Reading in the fifth round.

Curtis used the money wisely. A new stand was built at Griffin Park and support for the team improved. New dressing-rooms and a treatment room were also included in the refurbishment.

Curtis made a sensational deal with Middlesbrough in bringing three of their young cast-offs to Griffin Park. It cost Brentford in the region of £1,500 to bring Jack Halliday, Billy Scott and Bert Watson from Ayresome Park. All three did valiant work for the Bees as Curtis won a reputation as one of the best judges of latent talent in the country. In 1932-33, within a year of their signings, Brentford won the Third Division South title with 62 points, four clear of runners-up Exeter City.

The Bees had come close to promotion in 1929-30 and 1930-31 but the new men made all the difference.

Two seasons later, First Division status was achieved and Curtis felt it necessary to import a few star players to Griffin Park. He paid a club record, £6,000 for Hearts' centre-forward Dave McCullough and it proved money well spent as McCullough scored regularly for the Bees.

The Second Division title had been gained in 1934-35, with 61 points, and for the next three years Brentford were genuine challengers for the League championship, finishing fifth, sixth and sixth respectively. They also reached the quarter-finals of the FA Cup, where they lost 3-0 to Preston in 1938.

After war broke out in 1939, the club lost many of their leading players, mainly through retirement, and after the war they struggled to re-establish themselves. In 1942, the Bees won the London Cup Final at Wembley, beating Portsmouth by 2-0, but relegation to the Second Division came in 1947, when they gained only 25 points.

After this, Brentford held their own in the lower division until Curtis retired in February 1949. His talents had been in man management and he had little to do with training and coaching. He was essentially a wheeler and dealer and Brentford greatly missed his ability to balance the books. Indeed, since his departure, the Bees have struggled unsuccessfully to retain their former status until 1992.

CURTIS, Norman W.

Born: Darlington, 10 September 1924.
Full-back   5ft 8in; 13lb (1939).
Career: Gainsborough Trinity; Sheffield Wednesday January 1950; Doncaster Rovers player-manager August 1960-August 1961; Buxton August 1961.

Honours: Division Two champions 1952, 1959.

'Cannonball' Curtis was a character on the field but quiet and studious off it. A fearless bundle of energy, Curtis was a positive terror to opposing wingers. He had a reputation as a penalty-taker and ran all the way from defence to hit the ball after somebody else had placed it. As an emergency goalkeeper he once saved two penalties for the Owls at Preston. Ever-present in Wednesday's Second Division championship side of 1958-59, Curtis played 324 games for the Owls in all, scoring 21 goals. Doncaster Rovers finished 11th in Division Four in his only season in charge.

CUSACK, David Stephen

Born: Rotherham, 6 June 1956.
Defender   6ft 1½in; 13st 13lb (1979).

Career: Sheffield Wednesday June 1974; Southend United September 1978; Millwall March 1983; Boston United player-coach 1988; Doncaster Rovers July 1985, then player-manager October 1985-December 1987; Rotherham United player-manager December 1987-April 1988; Boston United cs 1988; Doncaster Rovers August 1989; Boston United caretaker manager January 1990-May 1992; Kettering Town manager June-September 1992.

A rugged centre-half, Cusack played 106/3 games for the Owls before his move to Southend, for whom he made 186 League appearances. He also played 98 games for Millwall and 83 for Doncaster Rovers. He was one of the younger managers in League football when, at the age of 30, he took control at Doncaster. After two satisfactory seasons at Belle Vue, Cusack was sacked with Rovers at the bottom of the Third Division in December 1987. He took over at fellow strugglers Rotherham United, who were also relegated at the end of the season. Cusack was sacked for the second time in four months, having been in charge of two relegated clubs in one season. He took over from George Kerr as the manager of Boston United. Cusack swapped jobs with Peter Morris in May 1992 but lasted just three months in charge at Kettering. He lost his job when the club went into receivership

DALGLISH,
Kenneth Mathieson, MBE

Born: Dalmarnock, Glasgow, 4 March 1951.
Forward   5ft 8in; 11st 13lb (1983).
Career: Glasgow Schools; Drumchapel Amateurs; Glasgow United; Glasgow Celtic August 1967; Cumbernauld United for a spell; Liverpool August 1977 (£440,000), then player-manager June 1985-February 1991, retired from playing February 1991; Blackburn Rovers manager October 1991.

Honours: Scotland international (102 caps); Under-23 international (4 caps); Youth international; Schoolboy international; Football League champions 1979, 1980, 1982, 1983, 1984, 1986, 1988, 1990; Second Division promotion 1992; Scottish League champions 1972, 1973, 1974, 1977; FA Cup winners 1986, 1989, runners-up 1988; Football League Cup winners 1981, 1982, 1983, 1984, runners-up 1978 and 1987; Scottish Cup winners 1972, 1974, 1975, 1977, runners-up 1973; Scottish League Cup winners 1975, runners-up 1972, 1973, 1974, 1977; European Cup winners 1978, 1981, 1984, runners-up 1985; European Super Cup winners 1977, runners-up 1978, 1985.

A dour personality who is always careful about what he says to the media, Kenny Dalglish is known for his sense of humour by those who work with him, although that side of him is rarely seen in public.

As a player, Dalglish had a remarkable career. He holds the Scottish international appearances and joint goalscoring records and is the only player to reach 100 goals in both Scottish and English League football.

Determined, disciplined, unselfish and razor sharp, he won just about every honour in the game with his ability to twist and turn and to hold and shield the ball in the tightest situations in opponents' goalmouths. He helped win four Scottish League titles and eight Football League titles. He scored the winning goal in Liverpool's European Cup Final victory over Bruges and

also played in two losing Finals of the World Club Championships, against Flamengo and Independiente.

Dalglish apppeared in his first Scottish Cup Final in 1972, when Celtic beat Hibs 6-1 although he did not appear on the scoresheet. In his early days at Parkhead, he often played in a midfield position rather than his more familiar striking role. He appeared in five Scottish Cup Finals for Celtic and was on the losing side only once. He also played in five League Cup Finals but was on the winning side just once.

Succeeding Kevin Keegan as 'king' of the Liverpool Kop, Dalglish had scored 112 goals in 204 League games for Celtic and went on to play almost 500 games for Liverpool, scoring over 160 goals. He picked up five Football League championship medals as a player and another three as a manager at Anfield. He was ever-present in four of those seasons and scored 21 goals in his first League championship campaign of 1978-79. After three defeats in the semi-finals, Dalglish did not play in an FA Cup Final until 1986, when Liverpool beat their great rivals, Everton, 3-1. He also played in six League Cup Finals for the Reds, picking up four winners' medals and two losers'. On top of all this, Dalglish played in four European Cup Finals including the tragic match against Juventus in the Heysel Stadium in 1985. All in all, Dalglish won an amazing 39 medals during his playing career.

He became Liverpool's player-manager in June 1985 and the Reds won the League and FA Cup double at the end of his first season in charge to make him the only player-manager ever to achieve this feat. Dalglish played in the last seven games of the 1985-86 season, all of which were won, and scored the winner in the title-decider against Chelsea. Liverpool narrowly missed out on another double in 1988, when they clinched the title by nine points but lost to Wimbledon in the FA Cup Final. The following year they beat neighbours Everton in the Final, but lost 2-0 to Arsenal at Anfield in the championship-deciding match. In 1990, Liverpool again won the title by nine points but lost to Crystal Palace in the semi-final of the FA Cup.

In February 1991, Dalglish shocked the football world by resigning due to the stress of the job, saying he needed a complete rest from the game. After a break he returned to football as manager of free-spending Blackburn Rovers and in 1992 steered them into

the new FA Premier League via a play-off victory over Leicester City. Once in what was effectively the old First Division, Blackburn went into the championship-chasing places whilst under Graeme Souness, his former club, Liverpool, struggled to maintain their former glories.

Under Dalglish, Blackburn got off to a great start on their return to the top flight, but their form dipped after a long-term injury to Alan Shearer. They eventually finished fourth and also reached the semi-finals of the League Cup, losing to Sheffield Wednesday. They lost to the other Sheffield club, United, in the quarter-finals of the FA Cup.

DANIEL, Peter William

Born: Hull, 12 December 1955.
Right-back   5ft 9in; 10st 10lb (1975).
Career: Hull City apprentice 1971, professional September 1973; Wolverhampton Wanderers May 1978 (£182,000); Minnesota Kicks (NASL) May 1984; Sunderland August 1984 (£15,000); Lincoln City November 1985, then manager March-May 1987; Burnley July 1987-1989.

Honours: England Under-21 international (7 caps); Football League Cup winners 1980.

A full-back with Hull, Peter Daniel was converted to a defensive midfield role with Wolves. Daniel was neat, intelligent and mobile in style. A sharp tackling and adventurous full-back, Wolves offered him the chance to show off his skills in the First Division. His career went off the rails a little at Molineux when injury, followed by a change in position, made life difficult for him. But he helped Wolves through a difficult spell in their history. He missed England 'B' honours through injury and never got a second opportunity. His short spell as Lincoln's manager was a disaster with the club becoming the first to automatically drop out of the Fourth Division into the Conference League. They were seventh in January but finished bottom of the table after a terrible run and defeat in the final game at Swansea. Daniel reverted to just playing again at Turf Moor.

DAVIES, Glyn

Born: Swansea, 31 May 1932.
Wing-half   5ft 8in; 10st 8lb (1959).
Career: Derby County amateur May 1949, professional July 1949; Swansea Town July 1962; Yeovil Town player-manager April 1964-1965; Swansea City manager June 1965-October 1966.

Honours: Wales Schoolboy international; Division Three North champions 1957.

After signing professional forms in 1949, Glyn Davies had to wait four years for his Derby debut, at Rotherham in December 1953. A ferocious tackler, he had limited skill but an abundance of effort and tireless leadership. Davies was unquestionably committed to the game. A wing-half or a full-back at the Baseball Ground, he made a total of 213 appearances for Derby, scoring five goals. He was not a regular until season 1956-57. As the manager of Yeovil, he steered the club to fourth in the Southern League in 1964-65. At Swansea, the club struggled for most of the time in the Third Division.

DAVIES, Stanley Charles

Born: Chirk, 24 March 1898; Died: Birmingham, 17 January 1972.

Right winger/Centre-forward 5ft 11in; 11st 7lb (1922).
Career: Chirk Schools; Rochdale 1915; Manchester United trialist 1918; Preston North End April 1919; Everton January 1921; West Bromwich Albion November 1921 (£3,300); Birmingham November 1927 (£1,500); Cardiff City May 1928; Rotherham United player-manager March 1929-1930; Barnsley September 1930; Manchester Central October 1930; Dudley Town 1933, retired from playing in 1936; Chelmsford City trainer April 1938-1941; publican in West Bromwich 1937-1946; Shorts (Rochester) manager during the war.

Honours: Wales international (18 caps); Military Medal and Croix de Guerre in World War One.

Stanley Davies was known as 'Mr Versatility' and gained 18 caps for Wales in six different positions. He cost West Brom £3,300, a lot of money in those days, and went on to score 83 goals in 159 games for Albion. Davies could head a ball hard and had lots of stamina. He was mercurial and enthusiastic but inconsistent later in his career. In 1929, he toured Canada with the Welsh international side. He had recently become the Millers' first player-manager, one of the youngest in the League at 32. He did well on limited resources at Millmoor but the club just missed having to ask for re-election at the end of the 1929-30 season. A hero during the First World War, he won the Military Medal and the Croix de Guerre. Stan's son, John Davies, is now a sports writer with the *Daily Express*.

DAVISON,
John Edward 'Teddy'

Born: Gateshead, 2 September 1887; Died: Wortley, Sheffield, early 1971.
Goalkeeper   5ft 7in; 11st 10lb (1922).
Career: Gateshead St Chads; Gateshead Town; Sheffield Wednesday April 1908, retired cs 1926; Mansfield Town manager June 1926-December 1927; Chesterfield manager December 1927-June 1932; Sheffield United manager June 1932-August 1952; Chesterfield manager August 1952-May 1958, then chief scout.

Honours: England international (1 cap); FA tour of Australia (3 caps); Division Two runners-up 1939; Division Three North champions 1931; FA Cup runners-up 1936.

Teddy Davison served Sheffield soccer well, spending 18 years as a player with the Wednesday and 20 years as secretary-manager of rivals, United. The rest of his life in professional football was spent a few miles south of Sheffield, with two spells at Chesterfield.

A placid, gentle person, it was difficult to imagine Davison in the highly-charged world of professional football, but after joining Sheffield Wednesday he eventually displaced regular goalkeeper Jack Lyall and made 102 consecutive appearances for the Owls up until 1913. Probably the smallest goalkeeper ever to play for England, Davison possessed courage and determination and a fine sense of anticipation. His razor-sharp reflexes made up for his lack of height and his speciality was saving penalties.

Sadly, Davison won no club honours with the Owls, despite making 424 appearances for the club, but he played for England against Wales in March 1922 in Liverpool, winning his chance by making difficult saves look easy, using his strength to make brave, acrobatic saves.

In his book "Football in Sheffield" Percy Young says of Davison that he expressed his concern for society through participation in religious organisations and appreciated football less as an end in itself than a means to some more general end.

After retiring from playing, Davison became manager of non-League Mansfield Town before moving to Chesterfield. They finished fourth in Division Three North in 1929-30, albeit 17 points behind the champions. The following season, though, they won the title, one point clear of Lincoln City.

Chesterfield struggled in the higher division but in June 1932, Davison received a lucrative offer to manage Sheffield United, where he was to stay for the next two decades. The Blades were relegated from Division One in 1934, but two years later they reached the FA Cup Final by beating Burnley, Preston, Leeds, Spurs and, rather fortunately, Fulham in the semi-final. At Wembley they gave the mighty Arsenal a run for their money before losing to a lone goal from Ted Drake.

United went close to promotion in 1935-36 and 1937-38, in the latter season missing out only on goal-average. The following season, though, they were runners-up and returned to the First Division. Relegation came again in 1948-49 as they finished bottom of the First Division. The Blades failed to achieve an immediate return when they lost out to local rivals Wednesday on goal-average the following season. After United reached the FA Cup quarter-finals but had a mediocre season in the Second Division, Davison lost his job in August 1952 and went back to Saltergate to manage Chesterfield again.

At all the clubs he managed, Davison developed successful youth schemes and his return to Chesterfield produced one of the finest moments in their history when the youth team battled their way through to the FA Youth Cup Final. Here they lost to Manchester United, but attracted a crowd of 26,000 to Saltergate for the home leg. In goal for Chesterfield that day was a young Gordon Banks, whom former 'keeper Teddy Davison helped to develop before selling to Leicester City.

Chesterfield finished sixth in the Northern Section four seasons on the trot between 1953 and 1957. Davison became their chief scout in May 1958, at the age of 71. He died in early 1971 at Wortley near Sheffield, after having spent virtually the whole of his life in football.

DAWES, Frederick William

Born: Frimley Green, 2 May 1911; Died: Shirley, near Croyden, 12 August 1989.
Left-back   5ft 9in; 11st 8lb (1929).
Career: Frimley Green; Aldershot; Northampton Town March 1930; Crystal Palace February 1936-1950 (assistant manager 1949), then manager November 1950-October 1951 (joint with Charlie Slade); Beckenham as player 1951.

Fred Dawes' career was linked with that of his brother Albert, who also appeared for Aldershot, Northampton Town and Crystal Palace. Fred was signed by the Cobblers with his brother in 1930 and followed him to Palace in February 1936. Fred Dawes made 235 peacetime appearances for Palace and also played in 157 wartime games for the club. He became assistant manager to Ronnie Rooke in October 1949 and then joint manager with Charlie Slade in

November 1950. He initially retired from playing due to injury in 1949 but made a comeback with Beckenham after being reinstated as an amateur in 1951 and also ran a grocery shop in the area.

DENNISON, Robert Smith

Born: Amble, 6 March 1912.
Utility   6ft; 11st 4lb (1935).

Career: Radcliffe United; Newcastle United May 1929; Nottingham Forest May 1934; Fulham June 1935; Northampton Town May 1939-1948, then manager March 1949-July 1954; Middlesbrough manager July 1954-January 1963; Hereford United manager December 1963-December 1967; Coventry City chief scout December 1967, assistant manager December 1969, caretaker manager March-June 1972, retired in 1978 but remained a scout for the club.

Honours: Southern League Division One champions 1965.

Bob Dennison is today still involved in professional soccer over 60 years after he first turned professional with Newcastle United. Dennison has had a whole range of roles and has been involved from First Division to non-League.

One of a family of ten, he began his career as an inside-forward with the Magpies but made only 11 appearances in five years at St James' Park. He was a utility player with Fulham, but settled at centre-half with Northampton Town.

His first managerial post was with Northampton — he had previously worked in the timber business in the town — but wanted to manage teams on his own terms, which was a bit too much for some directors.

Released from his contract at the County Ground, Dennison joined Middlesbrough for the start of the club's first season back in Division Two after relegation, and from August 1955 until 1961 he also assumed secretarial duties at the club.

He spent nine eventful years at Ayresome Park and if he was unable to get 'Boro back into the First Division, he still produced some fine players including Mick McNeil, Alan Peacock, Eddie Holliday and Brian Clough. He also signed goalkeeper Peter Taylor, thus bringing together the men who would one day form one of the most successful managerial partnerships in football.

On 10 January 1963, Dennison was told that his contract, which still had 19 months to run, would be terminated, and although a Press conference was told that this was 'by mutual consent', Dennison later sued Middlesbrough for

unfair dismissal and was eventually awarded £3,200 damages.

Initially, he had a tough time at Hereford United, who nearly went out of business after their relegation to the lower division of the Southern League in 1964. A year later, though, they bounced back as champions, 11 points ahead of Wimbledon, and to third in the Premier Division the year after. Dennison moved to Coventry City in December 1967, as chief scout. He was later the assistant manager and caretaker manager between the reigns of Noel Cantwell and Gordon Milne. Bob Dennison enjoyed working with the juniors most of all. Today, he lives in Kent and still works for Coventry as a part-time scout after officially retiring in 1978.

DICKINSON, James William MBE

Born: Alton, Hants, 24 April 1925; Died: 8 November 1982.
Wing-half   5ft 10in; 11st 12lb (1963).
Career: Alton Schools; Alton Youth Club; Portsmouth amateur 1943, professional January 1944-April 1965, then public relations officer and scout until July 1968 when he became club secretary, then manager May 1977-May 1979 when he retired on medical advise.

Honours: England international (48 caps); 'B' international (3 caps); Football League representative (11 caps); Football League champions 1949, 1950; Division Three champions 1962.

An automatic choice for England for many years, Jimmy Dickinson was known as a gentleman on and off the field. He was not spectacular but was elegant, sure-footed, industrious and quietly efficient. He won two League championship medals in consecutive seasons for Pompey but in later years the club sunk down into the Third Division, despite Dickinson's presence. They made a comeback as champions of the Third Division in 1961-62 and he ended his playing career on his 40th birthday in April 1965, in a 1-1 draw with Northampton.

Dickinson was never cautioned or spoken to by a referee throughout his career, a remarkable feat considering that he made 764 appearances for Pompey, which was then a Football League record for one club. He played in England's shock defeat by the USA in the 1950 World Cup finals in Brazil, but also had many great moments playing for his club and country.

Alas, he did not have a happy time as Portsmouth's manager and was

probably too much of a gentleman for a job which he was most reluctant to take in the first place. Pompey were in financial difficulties, so it came as no surprise when they were relegated to Division Four in 1978. They could finish only seventh the following season after leading the table in January, and Dickinson left the club soon afterwards after 36 years at Fratton Park. He died following a second heart attack.

DICKINSON, William

Born: Walsall, 31 December 1872.
Career: Barrow secretary in charge of team affairs in 1921; Founder and chairman of North Western Association Football League; chairman of Barrow Trade's Charity Cup Competition; honorary secretary and treasurer of North Western Referees' and Linesmens' Association; former referee.

Dickinson was in charge when Barrow joined the Football League's new Third Division North. Officially the secretary in charge of team affairs, in reality he had two trainers to organise coaching whilst the directors sought new players. A well-known local football administrator, he was a Class 1 referee with the Lancashire FA and officiated at many local Cup Finals and representative games.

DICKS, Alan V.

Born: Kennington, London, 29 August 1934.
Centre-half   5ft 10in; 11st 7lb (1953).
Career: Kennington Secondary School; London Schools; Dulwich Hamlet; Rainham Town; Millwall amateur; Chelsea Sepember 1951; Southend United November 1958 (£12,000); Coventry City February 1962-1967 and assistant manager; Bristol City manager October 1967-September 1980; Ethnikos (Greece) coach 1982-1983; Limassol (Cyprus) coach 1984; coaching in Qatar for three years; coaching in Cyprus again; coaching in USA until 1990; Fulham assistant manager April 1990, then manager June 1990-November 1991.

Honours: Division Two runners-up 1976.

By his own admission an average player, Alan Dicks made only one appearance during Chelsea's League championship season of 1954-55, but he worked hard and took an interest in all aspects of the game, obtaining a coaching badge at the age of 23. Dicks was assistant manager to Jimmy Hill at Coventry City as the Sky Blues went from the Third to the First Division, but left Highfield Road after Hill's resignation and joined Bristol City as manager.

Dicks survived at Ashton Gate for 13 years. City lost to Spurs in the semi-final of the League Cup in 1971 and also reached the quarter-final two years later. As runners-up to Sunderland they won promotion to the First Division in 1975-76, for the first time in 65 years, but that almost bankrupted the club — too many players on big wages — and Dicks left shortly after their relegation in 1980.

He had a break from soccer, working for a promotions company involved in golf and snooker and was also a director of a travel agency. After a season in Greek soccer, he worked for the BBC for a short while in 1983, but after ten years away from English soccer, he was reunited with Jimmy Hill, who was now the chairman of Fulham. Initially, Dicks was assistant to Ray Lewington, but it was clear that he would succeed him and they reversed roles in the summer of 1990. Dicks lost full control of team affairs in the 1990-91 season when Hill took on a more active role. He was sacked after a string of poor results. His brother, Ronnie, played for Middlesbrough.

DINNIS, Richard R.

Born: Blackburn.
Career: Burnley amateur; Blackburn Rovers 1969, then coach 1971; Newcastle United coach cs 1975, then manager February-November 1977; Philadelphia Furies (NASL) coach January-June 1978; Blackburn Rovers coach March-October 1979; Bristol City scout; Middlesbrough coach 1985-1987; Barrow manager December 1992.

Richard Dinnis never made a Football League appearance but he was the players' choice to succeed Gordon Lee at Newcastle United. The players had threatened to strike after Lee's departure and Dinnis' spell as manager was a controversial time for the club. He took the Magpies into Europe but they lost to French club Bastia in the early rounds and with the club at the bottom of the First Division, he was sacked. A qualified coach and PE instructor, Dinnis worked as a schoolteacher before joining his first League club at a relatively late age and did not make the grade as a player. Originally he had joined Newcastle as Lee's assistant after following him from Ewood Park.

DOBSON, John Martin

Born: Blackburn, 14 February 1948.
Midfield   5ft 9in; 11st 7lb (1983).

Career: Lancashire Youth; Bolton Wanderers July 1966; Burnley August 1967; Everton August 1974 (£300,000); Burnley August 1979 (£100,000); Bury

player-manager March 1984-March 1989, retiring as a player 1986; Northwich Victoria manager June 1991 (39 days); Bristol Rovers manager July-October 1991.

Honours: England international (5 caps); Under-23 international (1 cap); Football League representative (1 cap); Division Two champions 1973; Division Three champions 1982; Division Four promotion 1985; Football League Cup runners-up 1977.

Martin Dobson made 252 appearances for Burnley (four as sub), scoring 50 goals in his two spells at the club, and won four of his England caps whilst at Turf Moor. He helped Burnley to the Second Division championship in 1972-73.

Dobson took a considerable time to settle at Goodison Park due to his enormous price tag, but went on to make 230 appearances, scoring 40 goals for the Toffees. He began his career as a centre-forward with Bolton Wanderers but was given a free transfer by the Trotters and it was his father who persuaded him to continue in soccer after he contemplated giving up the game. Switched to midfield at Burnley, Dobson became a highly skilful player with the ability to drift forward to create openings and goals out of nothing. In his second spell at Turf Moor, he helped the club to promotion from Division Three and as manager of Bury steered the Shakers to promotion from the Fourth Division in 1984-85. He had a constant struggle to keep the club going on low attendances, however, and was sacked in March 1989 after a dispute over a new contract. Dobson was in charge at Bristol Rovers for just eleven games before leaving by 'mutual consent'.

DOCHERTY, John

Born: Glasgow, 29 April 1940.
Outside-right   5ft 5in; 9st 9lb (1963).

Career: St Rochs; Brentford July 1959; Sheffield United March 1961; Brentford December 1965; Reading February 1968; Brentford March 1970; Queen's Park Rangers player-coach July 1974-February 1975; Brentford manager January 1975-September 1976; Cambridge United manager January 1978-December 1983; Brentford assistant manager February 1984-July 1986; Millwall manager July 1986-February 1990; Bradford City manager March 1990-November 1991.

Honours: Division Two champions 1988; Division Three runners-up 1978.

A small but effective lower division player, John Docherty had three spells

at Griffin Park in which he made 255 appearances and scored 67 goals. Docherty had an outstanding reputation for building teams on a shoestring budget. A forceful character, who instilled discipline into most of his players, he managed to keep Cambridge United in the Second Division for his first five seasons in charge but with the club heading for relegation he was sacked in December 1983.

At Millwall, Docherty made a number of useful signings including Jimmy Carter from Queen's Park Rangers for only £15,000. The 1987-88 season was the greatest in the club's history when they won the Second Division championship and entered the First Division for the first time. The Lions finished ninth in their first season but struggled in 1989-90. Docherty signed Derby's Paul Goddard for £800,000, but within a year Goddard had left Millwall on a free transfer. Docherty was sacked in March 1990, but was not out of work for long, taking over at Bradford City who were heading for relegation to the Third Division. He was unable to prevent the drop. Docherty was sacked when he failed to bring success again to Valley Parade.

DOCHERTY, Michael

Born: Preston, 29 October 1950.
Defender   5ft 7in; 9st 9lb (1971).
Career: Burnley April 1967; Manchester City April 1976; Sunderland December 1976, retired through injury September 1979; Sunderland coach and caretaker manager April-June 1981; Hartlepool United manager June-December 1983; Wolverhampton Wanderers coach; Blackpool coach 1988; Burnley assistant manager January 1989; Hull City assistant manager cs 1990-January 1991; Rochdale coach 1991.

Honours: England Youth international; FA Youth Cup winners 1968. Division Two Champions 1973.

The son of Tommy Docherty, as a youngster Mick Docherty was sent by his father to Burnley where he believed Mick would receive the best preparation for professional soccer. He captained Burnley to the FA Youth Cup in 1968 and was the Clarets' youngest-ever League captain at 19, when he skippered them against Everton in November 1969. A quick-tackling full-back, Docherty made 35 appearances in the Turf Moor club's Second Division championship season of 1972-73 but then missed two and a half seasons due to ligament trouble. He did not have a happy spell as manager of Hartlepool, being sacked with the club at the bottom of the Fourth Division, after only one win in 23 games.

DOCHERTY, Thomas Henderson

Born: Pershaw, Glasgow, 24 August 1928.
Wing-half   5ft 6in; 10st 10lb (1955).
Career: Shettleston Juniors; Glasgow Celtic July 1948; Preston North End November 1949 (£4,000); Arsenal August 1958 (£28,000); Chelsea player-coach February 1961, retired cs 1961, then manager September 1961-October 1967; Rotherham United manager November 1967-November 1968; Queen's Park Rangers manager November 1968; Aston Villa manager December 1968-January 1970; FC Oporto manager February 1970-June 1971; Hull City assistant manager July-September 1971; Scotland national manager September 1971-December

1972; Manchester United manager December 1972-July 1977; Derby County manager September 1977-May 1979; Queen's Park Rangers manager May 1979-October 1980; Preston North End manager June-December 1981; Sydney Olympic manager twice, quit July 1983; South Melbourne manager July 1982; Wolverhampton Wanderers manager June 1984-July 1985; Altrincham manager October 1987-February 1988.

Honours: Scotland international (25 caps); 'B' international (1 cap); Division Two champions 1951, 1975, runners-up 1963; FA Cup winners 1977, runners-up 1954, 1967, 1976; Football League Cup winners 1965.

The irrepresible Tommy Docherty, one of the best known managers in soccer, now seems to have come to the end of his career in football, but in his day, he was dedicated, dynamic, reckless, ruthless, seldom predictable and always controversial.

He started life in Glasgow's notorious Gorbals and after junior football and National Service with the Highland Light Infantry — he played for the regiment in Palestine — he signed for Glasgow Celtic in June 1948. In the shadow of the great Bobby Evans at Parkhead, he soon moved to Preston, where he developed into a fine wing-half, making more than 350 League and FA Cup games for the Deepdale club, including their FA Cup Final defeat by West Brom in 1954. After gaining a Scottish 'B' cap, he went on to win 25 full caps for Scotland and gained a Second Division Championship medal with Preston in 1951.

In August 1958, Docherty moved to Arsenal for £28,000 after Preston had refused him permission to play in that summer's World Cup finals in Sweden, insisting that he went on a club tour of Switzerland instead.

Stamford Bridge was his next port of call but when he was signed as player-coach in February 1961, it was without the knowledge of the manager Ted Drake. When Drake left in September, Docherty became caretaker manager and was given the job permanently in January 1962. He could not prevent Chelsea's relegation that season, but they bounced straight back again the following term. The League Cup was won in 1965 and the Doc also took Chelsea to their first Wembley FA Cup Final, where they lost 2-1 to Spurs. This was after consecutive semi-final defeats in the two previous seasons.

Four times, he broke Chelsea's transfer record with signings such as Graham Moore, Derek Kevan, Charlie Cooke and Tony Hateley. He also sold many favourites, including future managers Terry Venables and George Graham. Both men had strong opinions on the game, but there could only ever be one manager at Docherty's club.

It was never boring when the Doc was around. He once shocked the soccer world by sending home eight Chelsea first-teamers from their training headquarters in Blackpool, for staying out too late at night. He was also fined £100 for ungentlemanly remarks to a referee and quipped afterwards that it was worth every penny.

He once rebelled against the Chelsea directors over the players' allocation of tickets for an FA Cup tie and also threatened to call off a tour to Bermuda after Tony Hateley was sent off. He later received a 28-day suspension.

Docherty resigned as manager of Chelsea in October 1967. Things had not been the same since the death of chairman Joe Mears and Docherty found that he was unable to work with the new chairman.

There was talk of him managing Panathinaikos of Greece but he became manager of Rotherham United from November 1967. With the exception of the captain and the goalkeeper, he scrapped the entire team and gave Rotherham one of the youngest sides in the League. He sold 14 players for a total of £70,000 and replaced them with four new faces within weeks of making his decision. Rotherham were still relegated to Division Three at the close of the season but had a fine FA Cup run to the quarter-final, beating Wolves and Aston Villa on the way. One of his successes at Millmoor was to pick up future England centre-half Dave Watson for next to nothing from Notts County.

In November 1968, Docherty was lured to Queen's Park Rangers. He wanted to move back to London and wished for First Division football again, but he soon realised that he had made a mistake and sensationally quit after only 29 days. He resented the influence of chairman Jim Gregory, who wanted control over the signing of players, and was refused permission to sign Brian Tiler from his former club, Rotherham.

Docherty was not out of work for long, however, joining Aston Villa as manager the following month. Villa were struggling in the Second Division and he ordered a backs-to-the-wall defensive policy. They avoided relegation by losing only five of their last 23 games and Docherty became a great favourite with the fans as attendances doubled at Villa Park. However, he was soon courting controversy again, being accused of poaching Rotherham's backroom staff and then arguing with Carlisle manager Bob Stokoe over his team's negative tactics.

The following season was one of the worst in Villa's history and Docherty was sacked in January 1970 with the club rock bottom of the Second Division. He complained that four players with drinking problems had been a bad influence on the rest of the team, but the board had not let him sell them.

The following month he was off to manage Porto of Portugal, seeking to get away from the glare of publicity in England. His side just missed the Portuguese championship by two points from Benfica and his stay lasted 15 months before, missing his family and England, he returned to become Terry Neill's assistant at Hull City in July 1971. This arrangement was never going to last and two months later, the Doc became Scotland's national team manager.

The Scots made a remarkable recovery when he took over the reins and he restored the team's pride. But in December 1972 he accepted the offer to manage Manchester United.

Docherty always seemed more at home managing the bigger clubs and had little or no success with any of his smaller outfits. Certainly, the United job seemed to suit him and he assembled some exciting sides during his four and a half years at Old Trafford. United were trying, unsuccessfully, to fill the gulf left by the retirement of Matt Busby and although Docherty steered them clear of relegation, they dropped into Division Two in 1974. It did them little harm as attendances were increased (by 5,000 on average) and they swept to the Second Division title the following season. Docherty signed some promising young players including Stuart Pearson, Gerry Daly, Sammy McIlroy, Steve Coppell and Gordon Hill.

In 1975-76, the Reds finished third in the First Division and reached the FA Cup Final, only to lose to Second Division Southampton. They won the trophy the following year, beating Liverpool 2-1 in the Final, but it was Docherty's final achievement at Old Trafford. He lost his job as the result of an affair with the wife of United's physiotherapist Laurie Brown. He was then in and out of court, suffering a major setback with the collapse of his libel action against Willie Morgan and Granada TV.

In September 1977, Docherty took over at Derby County and managed to keep them in the First Division but was heavily criticised for allowing talented players to leave the Baseball Ground. His replacements were not a great success. Players came and went at an alarming rate and Derby fans still smart at what they felt was the virtual dismantling of their club by the controversial Scotsman.

In May 1979, he resigned to become manager of Queen's Park Rangers. It was a surprise that he should rejoin a club he had left so acrimoniously 11 years earlier and history seemed to repeat itself when he was sacked almost immediately, although he was reinstated nine days later. The axe finally fell in October 1980. In the meantime, he had been arrested and brought back to Derby to be questioned over the transfers of Rams players to clubs in the North American Soccer League. Eventually he was released and no charges were brought.

His next move was to Australia to manage Sydney Olympic but in June 1981 he returned to manage his old club, Preston, for just six months. Returning to Australia again, he managed both Sydney Olympic and South Melbourne for a spell. In June 1984 he returned again, this time to manage Wolves who had a very depressing campaign in season 1984-85, ending in relegation to Division Three. The club was in crisis and Docherty tried his best to save them, but after a run of 21 League and Cup games without a win, the situation could not be saved and he was sacked in July 1985.

Except for a brief spell in charge at Altrincham in 1988, Tommy Docherty has not been employed in football since and now earns his money as an after-dinner speaker with engagements all over the world.

DODGIN, Norman

Born: Sheriff Hill, Gateshead, 1 November 1921.

Left-half 5ft 11in.
Career: Whitehall; Newcastle United August 1940; Reading, June 1950 (£5,000); Northampton Town September 1951; Exeter City player-manager August 1953-April 1957, retired as a player 1955; Yeovil Town manager June 1957; Barrow manager September 1957-July 1958; Oldham Athletic manager July 1958-May 1960.

A sound player who gained a lot of experience in overseas wartime soccer, Norman Dodgin — brother of Bill senior — was a grafter and team man. He made 86 appearances for Newcastle, including playing in their 1948 promotion side, and was 31 when he took over at Exeter City.

Dodgin gained a reputation for catching players young and moulding them. At Barrow things went well until the New Year of 1958, when the club was in fourth position but won only two more games to finish 18th and were consigned to play in the newly-formed Fourth Division. He resigned after a row with the directors over his retained list. At Oldham, Dodgin had to use a lot of untried youngsters in a struggling side and after successive applications for re-election he left football to run a newsagent's in Exeter.

DODGIN, William (senior)

Born: Gateshead 17 April 1909.
Wing-half 5ft 6½in; 11st 7lb (1930).
Career: Kirkley & Waveney; Gateshead; High Fell; Wallsend; Lowestoft; Huddersfield Town October 1929; Lincoln City March 1933; Charlton Athletic cs 1934; Bristol Rovers May 1936; Clapton Orient July 1937; Southampton 1939-1945, coach 1945, then manager June 1946-May 1949; Fulham manager June 1949-October 1953; Brentford manager October 1953-May 1957; Sampdoria (Italy) manager 1957-1959; Yiewsley manager 1959-1961; Bristol Rovers chief scout 1961-1969, became manager August 1969-July 1972, then chief scout again until 1983 when he retired.

Honours: Division Three South champions 1935.

A workmanlike player who helped Charlton Athletic rise from the Third to the First Division in two seasons, Bill Dodgin surprisingly left for Bristol Rovers before he could taste top-level soccer. He gained more fame as a manager than as a player, although at his first post, at The Dell, he did not have much luck. Twice it looked as though the Saints would go up to the First Division and twice they blew it. They finished third in 1947-48 and in April 1949 led the table by three points before a host of misfortunes cost them dear.

An attractive offer enticed him to Craven Cottage in June 1949, where he was in charge of team affairs with Frank

Osborne as the general manager. Fulham had just been promoted to the First Division as the Saints missed out. The Cottagers remained in the top flight for only three seasons but reached the sixth round of the FA Cup in 1951. Dodgin was given one season to get Fulham back again and, when he failed, he was sacked in October 1953. The best thing he did for Fulham was to discover their greatest-ever player, Johnny Haynes.

After a spell with Brentford, some time in Italy and a period in charge at Yiewsley, Dodgin joined Bristol Rovers as chief scout in 1961. He was 58 when he took charge at Eastville. He produced a series of exciting, attacking sides and when his team came to Fulham for an FA Cup tie in November 1969, the opposition manager was his son, also Bill. He retired at the age of 72.

DODGIN, William (junior)

Born: Durham, 4 November 1931.
Centre-half 6ft 1in; 12st 3lb (1963).

Career: Southampton amateur; Fulham September 1949; Arsenal December 1952; Fulham March 1961; Millwall coach 1965; Queen's Park Rangers coach, then manager January-August 1968; Fulham manager December 1968-May 1972; Leicester City coach 1972-1973; Northampton Town manager June 1973-June 1976; Brentford manager September 1976-March 1980; Northampton Town manager October 1980-February 1982; Woking manager 1982-September 1984; Brighton & Hove Albion scout 1990.

Honours: England Under-23 international (1 cap); Division Three runners-up 1971; Division Four runners-up 1976, promotion 1978.

When Bill Dodgin became the manager of Fulham, it was the second father-son succession, the first being the Bradshaws, Harry and Joe. Like his father, Bill junior's teams played with attacking flair and were always a pleasure to watch.

Dodgin was an apprentice draughtsman in an aircraft factory when he was playing as an amateur under his father at The Dell. He followed him to Craven Cottage, making his debut as a right-back but later playing at centre-half. Dodgin bore the brunt of the dissatisfaction with his father's handling of a struggling side and he left for Arsenal, where he made 210 appearances before returning to Fulham in the early 1960s. He played in Fulham's FA Cup semi-final defeat against Burnley, thus missing out on a Wembley appearance. A broken leg sustained shortly afterwards virtually ended his playing career.

Dodgin was unable to prevent

Queen's Park Rangers' relegation from the First Division and also joined Fulham too late to prevent their slide into the Third Division. He remoulded the Cottagers' side which won promotion in 1971 but was sacked a year later, after Fulham had struggled to avoid instant relegation. At Northampton, Dodgin led the club to promotion to Division Three in 1976 and did the same with Brentford two years later. He had a second spell with the Cobblers which ended with the sack after the club had to seek re-election.

DOHERTY, Peter Dermont

Born: Magherafelt, 5 June 1913; Died: Fleetwood, 6 April 1990.
Inside-foward 5ft 10in; 11st 6lb (1936).
Career: Station United (Coleraine); Coleraine; Glentoran June 1930; Blackpool November 1933 (£1,500); Manchester City June 1936 (£10,000); Derby County wartime guest, then signed permanently December 1945 (£6,000); Huddersfield Town December 1946; Doncaster Rovers player-manager June 1949-January 1958, retired as a player 1953; Northern Ireland national manager October 1951-February 1962; Bristol City manager January 1958-March 1960; Notts County joint advisor (with Andy Beattie) December 1965; Aston Villa chief scout July 1968; Preston North End assistant manager October 1970-June 1973; Sunderland assistant manager; Blackpool scout.
Honours: Northern Ireland international (16 caps); Football League champions 1937; Division Three North champions 1950; FA Cup winners 1946; Irish Cup winners 1932.

Peter Doherty was one of the finest players of his era. He had immaculate ball control, an elusive swerve and fine heading ability. Doherty also had speed, stamina, versatility and the ability to score spectacular goals and was probably the most exciting and innovative footballer of his time, and certainly one of the most complete footballers of all time.

Doherty was discontented with the system in football and took on the role of football trade unionist, which did not please all his employers. He won a League championship medal with Manchester City in 1936-37, yet the following year the club was relegated. During the war he guested for Derby County, and, alongside another great inside-forward, Raich Carter, helped the Rams win the FA Cup in 1946. Shortly afterwards, though, he left Derby after a row with the board, who refused him permission to run a hotel near the Baseball Ground.

"If they thought it would affect my game, then they didn't know me and I had to leave, although I loved the club and the town," he said in later years.

On Boxing Day 1946, the Derby programme announced that Doherty had been transferred to Huddersfield but the forms had not been completed and Rams supporters were pleasantly surprised when he ran out against Everton and signed off with two goals in a 5-1 win.

As player-manager, Doherty helped Doncaster Rovers to the Third Division North title in 1949-50, when he scored 26 goals. He ended his career after 403 League appearances and 197 goals, a large total despite the seven years lost to the war.

As a manager he was probably at his best in charge of the Northern Ireland team. He had the ability to infect his players with his boundless energy and enthusiasm and the perception he had shown as a player. He took his country to the quarter-final of the World Cup in 1958, working well with his skipper, Danny Blanchflower who took his ideas on to the pitch. Alas, Doherty did not have a such happy time at Ashton Gate and was sacked in March 1960 with the club heading towards relegation to the Third Division. After retiring he lived near Blackpool, largely shunning publicity. His son, Paul, worked as a television sports journalist in Manchester.

DOLAN, Terence

Born: Bradford, 11 June 1950.
Forward 6ft 1in; 11st 3lb (1980).
Career: Bradford City amateur June 1967; Bradford amateur December 1968, professional April 1969; Huddersfield Town October 1970 (£7,000); Bradford City August 1976 (£10,000); Rochdale August 1981; Thackley August 1982; Harrogate Town player-coach; Bradford City youth-team coach January 1985, first-team coach August 1986, then manager January 1987-January 1989; Rochdale manager March 1989-January 1991; Hull City manager February 1991.

Terry Dolan was a commanding midfield player with a fierce shot from dead-ball kicks, gaining a great reputation as a penalty taker. When Bradford dropped out of the Football League, Dolan moved to Huddersfield. They dropped from the First to the Fourth Division during his time at the club but he had more luck at Bradford City, who won promotion from Division Four in 1977, although they were relegated straight back again. He played in 217 games for City (five as sub), scoring 49 goals, before his move to Rochdale in 1981. Dolan made 448 League appearances in all, scoring 58 goals. He returned to Valley Parade as manager in January 1987 and steered the club clear of relegation with seven wins in the last ten games of the season. The 1987-88 season ended with City losing to Middlesbrough in the play-offs for promotion to Division One. He guided Rochdale to the fifth round of the FA Cup in 1990 where they lost to the eventual runners-up, Crystal Palace. Dolan accepted a more lucrative post at Hull City in early 1991, but they eventually finished at the bottom of Division Two.

Hull City just avoided relegation in 1992-93 in a rather forgettable season for the Tigers.

DOMINY, Arthur A.

Born: Southampton, 11 February 1893; Died: 23 September 1974.

Inside-forward 5ft 8in; 11st (1927).
Career: Peartree Green; Bitterne Guild; Southampton March 1913; Everton May 1926; Gillingham March 1928; Clapton Orient 1929; Newport (Isle of Wight) 1930; Southampton manager June 1943-January 1946; licensee in Southampton.

Southampton were attracted to Arthur Dominy after he had scored 50 goals for Bittern Guild in 1911-12. He was employed by Harland & Wolf shipyard in the war years and was the mainstay of the Saints attack in the early 1920s. An England trailist who never won a full cap, Dominy made 222 appearances, scoring 68 goals for the Saints. He was an inspirational captain and the Saints received many offers for his services but resisted them all until Everton made an offer they could not refuse in 1926. Dominy played only one game in their League championship season of 1927-28, then moved to Gillingham in 1928, where he was the club's leading scorer in 1928-29 with 14 goals.

Dominy was the manager at The Dell in the final years of World War Two and as the club had no training facilities, he saw his team only on match days. Their best season under his control was in 1944-45, when they finished fifth in the Football League South.

DONNELLY, James

Born: Mayo, Ireland, 18 December 1899.
Left-back 5ft 10in; 12st 2lb (1924).
Career: Army; Blackburn Rovers November 1919; Accrington Stanley May 1922; Southend United May 1924; Brentford August 1925; Thames Association July 1928, then player-manager cs 1931-cs 1932; Grajanski (Yugoslavia) coach; Gunes (Turkey) coach.

Jim Donnelly was a much-travelled player who, after failing to make the grade at Blackburn, moved around the lower division clubs. His best season was 1924-25, when he ever-present for Southend United. He also made 79 appearances for Brentford. Donnelly served in the Royal Artillery in France in World War One. He was a powerful and dashing back who was sometimes too adventurous.

At Thames he really had his work cut out to find success. He signed the ageing Jimmy Dimmock from Spurs and Len Davies from Cardiff, but a series of heavy defeats meant that Thames were soon bottom of the Third Division South and there they stayed for the rest of the season, at the end of which they folded with massive debts. This was not the fault of Donnelly, rather a set of unhappy circumstances for this club with the briefest of League careers.

DOOLEY, Derek

Born: Sheffield, 13 December 1929.
Centre-forward.
Career: Lincoln City amateur September 1946; Sheffield Wednesday June 1947, retired through injury 1953; journalist in the mid-1950s; returned to Sheffield Wednesday to take charge of development fund from 1962, then manager January 1971-December 1973; Sheffield United commercial manager 1977-late 1980s and also a director.

Red-haired with fiery courage and an instinct for goals, Derek Dooley had his career tragically cut short by a terrible accident. At Preston in February 1953, Dooley broke his leg in a collision with goalkeeper George Thompson. The limb became infected with gangrene and had to be amputated to save his life. Dooley's sensational scoring in 1951-52 had made him a folk hero. Big and ungainly, he netted 46 goals in only 30 games as the Owls won the Second Division championship. His benefit game raised £15,000.

As Wednesday's manager, he was a reflective, pipe-smoking man, who believed that football was a game of adventure and attack. Although Wednesday were briefly at the top of Division Two in 1972-73, results fell away and he was unable to lift the Owls from the malaise that had enveloped the club. He left Hillsborough after a poor run, although he felt that his side had turned the corner. It was a bitter parting, for he was sacked on Christmas Eve.

Despite the lack of success, Dooley had made some useful signings for Wednesday, including Clements, Joicey, Holsgrove, Knighton and Henderson. Had he been given the job sooner and been able to work under happier circumstances, then he might have achieved more for the club where he had been an idol.

Dooley switched his allegiance to neighbours United and in recent years has worked in many roles for the Bramall Lane club, including commercial manager, director and managing director.

DOUGALL, Cornelius 'Neil'

Born: Falkirk, 7 November 1921.
Inside-forward 5ft 10in; 12st (1951).
Career: Burnley July 1940; wartime guest for Oldham Athletic, Watford, Walsall and Coventry City; Birmingham City October 1945 (£2,750); Plymouth Argyle March 1949 (£12,000), retired January 1959 to become assistant trainer and head trainer 1959-March 1968, then manager March 1960-November 1961 (joint with George Taylor).

Honours: Scotland international (1 cap); Wartime international; Division Two champions 1948; Division Three South champions 1952; Division Three champions 1959; Football League South champions 1946.

A versatile player, Neil Dougall was at his best at right-half but played in every position except goalkeeper and outside-left. He appeared in the Birmingham City side which lost to Derby County in the 1946 FA Cup semi-final and was also an important member of their 1948 promotion side. His one Scottish cap was against Wales at Wrexham in 1946.

After 18 goals in 108 appearances for the Blues, Dougall moved to Plymouth, where he made a further 289 appearances, scoring 26 goals. Fast and able to exploit openings with some fine passes, he gained two Third Division championship medals with Argyle. From March 1960, Dougall shared the managerial tasks with George Taylor at Home Park. This proved difficult to implement and he took sole charge in June 1961. He left in November that year, after the team had conceded five goals in each of three consecutive matches. He was the son of William Dougall of Falkirk and Bury.

DOUGALL, William

Born: Denny, 25 October 1895; Died: Burnley, 15 November 1966.
Left-half   5ft 10in; 12st 1lb (1926).
Career: Denny Hibernian; Falkirk cs 1921; Burnley February 1926 (£3,000), training staff cs 1929; Thames Association trainer July 1930-1931; Burnley training staff c.1931, then manager July 1957-January 1958 before retiring through ill health and becoming physiotherapist.

Billy Dougall joined Burnley's training staff after being forced to give up the game through injury. Except for a brief spell as Thames Association's trainer, he was involved at Turf Moor for almost 40 years. He started the youth development scheme at Burnley in the 1930s, when the Clarets were one of the first clubs to set up such an organisation. Manager briefly between Alan Brown and Harry Potts, he held the post for less than a season, at the end of which Burnley were sixth in Division One. His brother Peter played for Arsenal.

DOWNS, Gregory

Born: Carlton, Nottingham, 13 December 1958.
Full-back   5ft 9½in; 10st 7lb (1983).
Career: Weavers School; Norwich City apprentice March 1975, professional December 1976; Connecticut Bicentennials (NASL), loan March-August 1977; Torquay United, loan November-December 1977; Coventry City August 1985 (£50,000); Birmingham City August 1990; Hereford United player-coach July 1991, then chief coach-manager May 1992.

Honours: FA Cup winners 1987.

The greatest moment of Greg Down's career was probably helping Coventry beat Spurs 3-2 in the 1987 FA Cup Final to bring the club its first major trophy. This made up for the disappointment of not being selected for Norwich City's League Cup Final appearance at Wembley in 1985.

Downs was converted from a striker to full-back by the Canaries' reserve-team manager Mel Machin. He made his League debut whilst on loan to Torquay United. Downs helped Norwich into the First Division in 1982 and played over 200 games for the club.

A free-kick expert, Downs loved to attack down the flanks. He took some time to settle at Coventry but eventually won over the fans. He joined Hereford United as player-coach and took over from John Sillett in 1992. Hereford lost to Yeovil Town in the second round of the FA Cup and struggled at the bottom of Division Three in 1992-93. But they managed to avoid the drop to the Conference League, finishing 16th. They sent Halifax out of the League when they won their last game of the season at The Shay. United also lost to Yeovil Town in the second round of the FA Cup in what was a disappointing season.

DOYLE, J.Brian

Born: Manchester, 15 July 1930; Died: 22 December 1992.
Full-back   5ft 9in; 12st (1959).
Career: Lostock Green; Stoke City March 1951; Exeter City April 1954; Bristol Rovers August 1957-1959, retired through injury; Carlisle United coach; Workington manager July 1968-1969; Blackpool coach 1971; Stockport County manager March 1972-May 1974.

A fast moving defender who enjoyed most success at Exeter City, where he made 104 appearances, John Doyle joined Stoke City from Mid-Cheshire League club, Lostock Green in March 1951 but made only 17 League appearances before his move to St James' Park. He ended his playing career at Eastville, where he played 43 games for the club. Workington finished 12th in Division Four during his season in charge and at Stockport the club finished at the bottom of the Football League in the 1973-74 season.

DRAKE, Edward Joseph

Born: Southampton, 16 August 1912.
Centre-forward   5ft 10in; 12st 7lb (1936).
Career: Southampton Schools; Winchester City; Southampton November 1931; Arsenal March 1934, retired through injury 1945; Hendon manager 1946; Reading manager June 1947-June 1952; Chelsea manager June 1952-September 1961; turf accountant 1962; Barcelona assistant manager January-June 1970; then commercial salesman in London; Fulham reserve-team manager November 1972, chief scout cs 1975 until mid-1980s, then club president; also cricket for Hampshire CCC 1931-1936.

Honours: England international (5 caps); Football League champions 1935, 1938, 1955; London League champions 1941; Football League South champions 1943; FA Cup winners 1936; Football League War Cup runners-up 1941; Football League South Cup winners 1943.

Ted Drake is one of the few men to have won League championship medals as a player and as a manager, with different clubs. In his playing days, Drake gained a reputation as a brave, strong centre-forward with Southampton and Arsenal, and as an expert at developing young players as the manager of Chelsea.

He showed his goalscoring ability early in his career with Southampton Schoolboys and Winchester City. When he was spotted by Southampton, Drake was working in the local gas company

works as a meter inspector's apprentice. He scored 48 goals in 72 League appearances for the Saints before his £6,500 transfer to Arsenal. His sale prevented a financial crisis at The Dell, but it was a huge blow to Saints' supporters.

Drake proved equally successful at Highbury, winning League championship medals in 1934-35 and 1937-38 and an FA Cup winners' medal in 1936, when he scored the only goal in the Gunners' victory over Sheffield United. He scored 42 goals in only 41 appearances in 1934-35 and netted all seven goals in the win at Villa Park in December 1935, equalling James Ross' feat 47 years earlier. Remarkably, Drake was not completely fit that day, nor had he been in particularly good form.

A brave centre-forward, he was speedy, had fine ball-control and a great shot in either foot. His never-say-die attitude won him the respect of fellow players and supporters all over the country. Arsenal secretary Bob Wall said of his play, "There was no finesse about him on the field. He went for the ball and the goal in a blunt and uncompromising way. He was a buccaneer, opening a vivid red path through the middle with broad shoulders, speed and courage."

Drake scored 150 goals in 197 appearances for Arsenal before war was declared in 1939. During the war he served in the RAF as a flight-lieutenant and played for Arsenal when service duties permitted, appearing in two Wartime Cup Finals, in 1941 and 1943. He also appeared for Hampshire in the County Cricket Championship from 1931 to 1936.

It was inevitable that injury would shorten Ted Drake's career, as his brave style had made him injury prone. He damaged his back in performing a high dive, on a course as a physical fitness officer during the war, and aggravated the injury in a wartime match at Reading. This led to his premature retirement. He won five England caps, making his debut in the notorious 'Battle of Highbury' against Italy in November 1934 when there were seven Arsenal players in the line-up. And he would have won more caps but for playing in an era of great English centre-forwards.

After a short spell as the manager of amateurs Hendon in 1946, Drake took over from Joe Edelston at Reading in June 1947. In 1948-49 and 1951-52, they narrowly missed promotion from the Third Division South, finishing runners-up both times with only one team going up. Reading scored 112 goals and gained 61 points in 1951-52 and Drake's clever and imaginative handling of affairs at Elm Park attracted the attention of Chelsea.

He took over from Billy Birrell, as manager at Stamford Bridge, in June 1952, when Chelsea were £63,000 in debt, still known as the Pensioners and a music-hall joke due to their being the experts at brinkmanship. Drake made some shrewd signings, including John McNichol from Brighton, Les Stubbs from Southend United, Frank Blunstone from Crewe and Ron Greenwood from Brentford, and he gave the club a more purposeful image.

In 1954-55, Chelsea gained their only League championship in their Jubilee year. Drake put together a team which came from nowhere to clinch the title from the teams that dominated the 1950s, Wolves and Manchester United. His key players in that success were Stan Wicks, a centre-half signed from his

former club Reading, and Roy Bentley, a most intelligent footballer. He also used two amateurs in his sides, unimaginable today. These were Seamus O'Connell from Bishop Auckland and Jim Lewis from Walthamstow Avenue. Drake used his experiences at Highbury to create a family atmosphere at Stamford Bridge, which proved important in Chelsea's success.

His teams became known as 'Drake's Ducklings' as more and more of his players were developed through his newly set-up youth scheme. They included Peter Bonetti, Jimmy Greaves, Barry Bridges, Ken Shellito, Bobby Tambling and Terry Venables. The club also won every other league in which they competed during their First Division championship season.

Chelsea struggled somewhat after 1955 and Drake did not survive their only really bad season, leaving Stamford Bridge in September 1961 after an altercation over the appointment, against his wishes, of Tommy Docherty as coach.

This left him bitterly disappointed and he temporarily left the game. It was Vic Buckingham, Fulham's manager, who persuaded him to make a comeback with his backroom staff at Craven Cottage in 1965. Ted's son, Bobby, played occasionally in Fulham's first team at full-back. When Buckingham was sacked, Drake followed him out of the game, returning to turf accountancy.

He came back into football again as Buckingham's assistant manager at Barcelona in 1970. From November 1972, Drake combined his job as a insurance company representative with a post as part-time reserve-team manager at Craven Cottage. He became chief scout in the summer of 1975 and joined Fulham's board on retirement from the game, later becoming the club's president. Ted Drake still occasionally attends games at Craven Cottage today, travelling from his home in Wimbledon.

DUCAT, Andrew

Born: Brixton, London, 16 February 1886; Died: Lord's Cricket Ground, London, 23 July 1942.
Right-half   5ft 9in; 12st 7lb (1920).
Career: Brewery Road School and Compton House School in Southend; Westcliffe Athletic; Southend Athletic; Woolwich Arsenal February 1905; Aston Villa June 1912 (£1,500)); Fulham May 1921 (£2,000), retired May 1924; Fulham manager May 1924-May 1926; Casuals July 1926; also Surrey CCC 1906-1931 coached cricket at Eton College; later a hotel manager and journalist; ran sports outfitters shop in Birmingham during his Villa days.

Honours: England international (2 caps); FA Cup winners 1920; England cricket international (1 Test).

Andy Ducat is one of only 17 men this century to win caps for England at both football and cricket. He made his Football League debut for Woolwich Arsenal against Blackburn Rovers at centre-forward, but established himself as a wing-half. Ducat was sold to Aston Villa, due to a financial crisis at Plumstead, for £1,500. A master of positional play, good in the air and a gentleman on the pitch, he was very graceful despite his bulky frame. After only four games for Aston Villa, he missed almost two complete seasons due to a broken leg, but captained Villa when they beat Huddersfield Town in the 1920 FA Cup Final.

His spell as Fulham's manager was

an unhappy one. For most of the time he was in charge, they struggled against relegation from Division Two but did manage a good run to the quarter-finals of the FA Cup in 1926. After leaving Fulham, Ducat was reinstated as an amateur and played for the Casuals.

As a cricketer, he scored 23,000 runs for Surrey from 1906 to 1931, including 52 centuries. His 305 against Oxford University is the highest score by an active professional footballer in the first-class game. His one Test appearance was against Australia in 1921, where he had a rather unfortunate dismissal. He died whilst batting at Lord's for the Surrey Home Guard during a wartime game.

DUCKWORTH, Richard

Born: Bacup, 6 June 1906; Died: Sheffield, 9 April 1983.
Utility   5ft 9in; 12st 8lb (1935).
Career: Carlisle United; Rochdale 1926; Oldham Athletic June 1927; Chester-field June 1929; Southport September 1932; Chester February 1933; Rother-ham United August 1934; York City July 1936-1939; Newark Town man-ager until 1950; scouting for Bir-mingham City and Sheffield United; York City manager March 1950-October 1952; Stockport County man-ager October 1952-May 1956; Sheffield United chief scout 1956-1957; Darling-ton manager October 1957-May 1960; Scunthorpe United manager May 1960-November 1964.

Honours: Division Three North cham-pions 1931.

A very experienced manager around lower division circles, Dick Duckworth did not have an outstanding record on the pitch but was able to keep his clubs solvent with shrewd dealings on the transfer market. Duckworth also played all of his League football in the Third Division North, after starting his career at non-League Carlisle United. He did not make his League debut until he joined Chesterfield in 1929 but helped them to the Third North championship in 1931, moving on to Southport after 89 League appearances at Saltergate. At Rotherham, Duckworth was converted from full-back to wing-half. He fin-ished his playing career at Bootham Crescent and retired after 278 League appearances altogether.

Duckworth returned to Bootham Crescent in 1950 and was York's manager when they met Stockport County on 18 October 1952. Three days earlier he had been appointed to the Stockport post with the arrangement that he should begin his new duties immediately after that match. At Stockport had finished in their highest position for some years, seventh in the Third North, he left to become chief scout at Bramall Lane. At Darlington, his side reached the last 16 of the FA Cup in 1957-58 before losing 6-1 at Wolves in front of 55,778 spectators, although they finished 20th in the Third North that season. Duckworth moved to Scunthorpe in May 1960. The Iron were in Division Two and finished fourth in 1961-62, only five points off promotion to the First Division. Things went wrong in 1963-64, how-ever, and with Scunthorpe bottom of Division Two and heading for relega-tion, Duckworth left the Old Show Ground.

DUNCAN,
Adam Scott Mattewson 'Archie'

Born: Dumbarton, 2 November 1888; Died: 3 October 1975.

Outside-right   5ft 7½in; 10st 10lb (1907).
Career: Dumbarton c.1906; law clerk in 1907; Newcastle United March 1908; Glasgow Rangers May 1913; Dumbar-ton c.1918; Cowdenbeath cs 1920; Hamilton Academical secretary-manager cs 1923-25; Cowdenbeath secretary-manager October 1925; Man-chester United secretary-manager June 1932-September 1937; Ipswich Town manager September 1937-August 1955, then general manager for a while.

Honours: Football League champions 1909; Division Two champions 1936; Division Three South champions 1954.

Archie Duncan was a fast ball-playing winger with intricate dribbling skills, who played for the Anglo-Scots in an international trial game in 1911. Duncan was able to play in every position in the forward line and made 81 appearances scoring 12 goals for Newcastle. After managing Hamilton and Cowdenbeath, he arrived at Old Trafford in June 1932 on a salary of £300 per annum plus bonuses.

Duncan spent a great deal of money in his first two years at the club, buying several players from Scotland, but failed to produce good results. United nar-rowly escaped relegation to the Third Division in 1934, but two years later Duncan steered them to the Second Division title. However, United were relegated again the following season and he was asked to be released from his five-year contract to manage Southern League Ipswich Town.

With average attendances of 10,000, the Suffolk club had great potential and a year later were elected to the Football League. Duncan stayed at Portman Road for 18 years. Ipswich won the Third South title in 1953-54 but were relegated the following year and he left the club soon afterwards.

DUNCAN, Douglas 'Dally'

Born: Aberdeen, 14 October 1909; Died Brighton, 2 January 1990.
Outside-left   5ft 6in; 11st 2lb (1929).
Career: Aberdeen Richmond 1927; Hull City August 1928; Derby County March 1932 (£2,000)); guest for Notts County, Reading and Nottingham Forest in World War Two; Luton Town player-coach October 1946, then player-manager June 1947-October 1958, retired cs 1948; Blackburn Rovers manager October 1958-June 1960; coached Brighton Schoolboys for a year; ran guest house in Brighton; Luton Town scout.

Honours: Scotland international (14 caps); Schoolboy international; Div-ision Two runners-up 1955; FA Cup winners 1946, runners-up 1960.

One of the most modest, loyal and best-loved managers in Luton Town's history, 'Dally' Duncan steered the Hatters to promotion to Division One

in 1955. His technical excellence as a coach and his commonsense led to his success and Luton reached a peak when they finished eighth in the First Division. Their players were young, keen and talented and it was practically the only time in the Hatters' history that the club has not been in financial difficulties.

As a player, Duncan's nonchalant approach was deceptive and he was known for trying the unexpected. Nicknamed 'Dally' due to his unhur-ried, unflurred play, Duncan was the natural successor to the great Alan Morton in the Scotland team and his friendly rivalry with England's Sammy Crooks as to who would be Derby's highest-scoring winger, helped the Rams become a First Division force in the 1930s. Duncan worked at the Derby Carriage & Wagon works during the war and helped the Rams win the FA Cup in 1946. Altogether he made 289 appearances for Derby, scoring 69 goals, but missed many more due to the war.

Duncan took Blackburn Rovers to the 1960 FA Cup Final, when they lost 3-0 to Wolves after being reduced to ten men after full-back Dave Whelan suffered a broken leg. Despite their Wembley appearance, those were unhappy times at Ewood Park — Derek Dougan had asked for a transfer before the Cup Final and Duncan had suffered an uneasy relationship with Welsh international Roy Vernon which ended with the player being transferred to Everton. Between Boxing Day 1959 and the end of the season, Blackburn collected only six points and narrowly missed relegation. The board asked Duncan to resign and when he refused, they sacked him. Thereafter he ran a boarding house in Brighton.

DUNCAN, John Pearson

Born: Lochee, 22 February 1949.
Forward   5ft 11in; 11st 4lb (1980).
Career: Clepington Road School; Morgan Academy; Dundee Schools; Broughty Athletic; Dundee April 1966; Tottenham Hotspur October 1974 (£125,000); Derby County September 1978 (£150,000); Scunthorpe United player-manager June 1981-February 1983; Hartlepool United manager April-June 1983; Chesterfield manager June 1983-June 1987; Ipswich Town manager June 1987-May 1990; England team 'observer' August 1992. Chester-field manager February 1993.

Honours: Scottish League represen-tative; Division Four champions 1985; Scottish League Cup winners 1974.

John Duncan won a Scottish League Cup winners' medal with Dundee when they beat Celtic 1-0 in the 1974 Final. He also played for the Scottish League against the Football League in 1973 and was leading scorer when Spurs were promoted to Division One in 1978. He

had scored 62 goals in 124 appearances for Dundee (three as sub) and scored 62 goals in 120 games (two as sub) for Spurs. His appearances were curtailed by a back injury which forced him to miss most of the 1976-77 season. Tommy Docherty signed him for Derby for £150,000, despite his suspect back, but he managed only 39 first-team appearances for the Rams, although he did score 12 goals.

Duncan was poorly treated by Scun-thorpe, who sacked him in February 1983 with the side well on the way to promotion from Division Four. In 1985 he steered Chesterfield to the Fourth Division championship with 91 points and although they struggled in the higher division, in 1987 Duncan received a better offer and became the manager of Ipswich Town. After three seasons of mid-table positions in the Second Division, Duncan was sacked to make way for John Lyall. He went into radio journalism, then into teach-ing, and Graham Taylor appointed him as one of his 'observers' for the England team. In February 1993, Duncan was once again appointed manager of Chesterfield, Duncan returning to management after a gap of nearly three years when he took over from Chris McMenemy at Saltergate in February 1993.

DUNCAN, John 'Tokey'

Born: Lochgelly, Fife, 14 February 1896; Died: 14 March 1966.
Inside-right/Right-half
5ft 8in; 11st 4lb (1925).

Career: Lochgelly United; Raith Rovers 1920; Leicester City July 1922, retired August 1930; licensee from 1930; Leicester City manager March 1946-October 1949, later scout.

Honours: Scotland international (1 cap); Division Two champions 1925; FA Cup runners-up 1949.

A forceful forward and later a classy wing-half, Duncan made 357 appear-ances, scoring 79 goals in his career in the Scottish and Football Leagues. He scored six against Port Vale on Christ-mas Day 1924 and netted 30 goals in Leicester's Second Division champion-ship season of 1924-25. Duncan won his only Scottish cap against Wales in October 1925, scoring the first goal. As the manager at Filbert Street, he was careful with spending and missed out on some useful players because of this. In January 1948 he sold four players to one club, Watford, at the same time. In 1949, Leicester lost 3-1 to Wolves in the FA Cup Final but narrowly missed relegation to the Third Division.

DURBAN, William Alan

Born: Port Talbot, 7 July 1941.
Midfield   5ft 9in; 10st 11lb (1963).

Career: Cardiff City juniors; Derby County July 1963 (£10,000); Shrewsbury Town September 1973, then player-manager February 1974-February 1978; Stoke City manager February 1978-June 1981; Sunderland manager June 1981-March 1984; Cardiff City manager September 1984-May 1986; Telford indoor tennis centre manager.

Honours: Wales international (27 caps); Under-23 international (14 caps); Football League champions 1972; Division Two champions 1969, promotion 1979; Division Four runners-up 1975.

A skilful midfield player with precise passing ability, Alan Durban joined Derby County when they were a moderate Second Division side but was one of the players whose careers blossomed following the arrival of Brian Clough as manager at the Baseball Ground. Under Clough he won a Second Division championship medal in 1969 and a League championship medal in 1972.

Durban was 22 when Tim Ward signed him for £10,000 and as a goalscoring inside-forward he netted 24 goals (Eddie Thomas, his partner, also scored 24) in 1964-65 and went on to score 112 in 388/15 appearances for the Rams overall. Under Clough he developed more into a constructive midfield player with a real feel for the game as Derby became one of the leading teams of the early 1970s.

As manager of Shrewsbury, Durban steered the club out of the Fourth Division in 1975 and later into the Second Division and to Welsh Cup success. At Stoke, he introduced more discipline into the club and appointed Howard Kendall as his chief coach. Stoke won promotion to Division One in 1979 and Durban made quite a few new signings in the summer but Stoke still struggled to avoid relegation the following season.

He left for Sunderland after a more tempting offer but was sacked after three troubled years a Roker Park. Six months later he moved back to his first club, Cardiff City, as manager but it was a bad move. His spell at Ninian Park was a disaster with the club plummeting from the Second to the Fourth Division. In 1986, Durban left football to run an indoor tennis club in Telford. He also played cricket for Glamorgan 2nd XI.

EASTHAM, George Edward OBE

Born: Blackpool, 23 September 1936.
Inside-forward   5ft 8in; 10st 2lb (1963).

Career: Ards; Newcastle United May 1956 (£9,000); Arsenal November 1960 (£47,500)); Stoke City August 1966, £30,000); Hellenic (Cape Town) player-manager February-October 1971; Stoke City October 1971, assistant manager from December 1972, then manager March 1977-January 1978, retired from playing February 1975.

Honours: England international (19 caps); Under-23 international (6 caps); Football League representative (3 caps); Irish League representative; Football League Cup winners 1972; Irish Gold Cup winners 1955.

When George Eastham played for England against Brazil at Wembley in May 1963, it was the first time that a father and son had gained caps for their country. Eastham had played alongside his father at Ards before signing for Newcastle United. He went on strike when Newcastle refused to transfer list him after he asked for a move and won a celebrated High Court case, in the process helping to change the almost feudal retain-and-transfer system in British football.

He was a member of England's 1966 World Cup squad — but did not play — and also appeared in Stoke City's first Wembley Cup Final, in 1972 when they beat Chelsea in the League Cup. Eastham was initially the caretaker manager of Stoke in March 1977, and was appointed permanently two months later. He had little money to spend and the stars that were still there wished to get away. He was sacked after a 3-2 defeat at the hands of non-League Blyth Spartans in the FA Cup.

EASTHAM, George Richard

Born: Blackpool, 13 September 1913.
Inside-forward   5ft 8in; 9st 9lb (1935).
Career: Cambridge Juniors (Blackpool); South Shore Wednesday; Bolton Wanderers August 1932; Brentford June 1937; Blackpool November 1938 (£7,000); Swansea Town August 1947; Rochdale June 1948; Lincoln City January 1949; Hyde United cs 1950; Ards player-manager July 1953-October 1958, retired as a player 1955; Accrington Stanley manager October 1958-June 1959; Distillery manager June 1959-March 1964; Ards manager late 1964-March 1970; Stoke City scout; Hellenic (South Africa) manager 1971; Glentoran manager briefly in 1972.

Honours: England international (1 cap).

George Eastham started his working life in a bakery before signing for Bolton and helping the Trotters to an FA Cup semi-final and promotion to Division One in 1935. Eastham was a fine close dribbler and a master of the delayed pass and was sometimes called the 'Diddler' by the Press because of his ball wizardry. He gained his England cap against Holland in 1935 and left Burnden Park for Griffin Park after 131 appearances. He made just under 250 appearances in a career that was interrupted by war. His older brother, Harry, played for Liverpool and Tranmere and his son, also George, was with Newcastle, Arsenal and Stoke and was also a manager.

George senior spent most of his career managing in Ireland. He took Ards to their only Irish League championship in 1958 and also guided Distillery to a rare championship success in 1963. Eastham also managed two Irish Cup Final sides: Distillery, who lost to Linfield in 1963; and Ards, who beat his former club in 1969. His brief spell at Peel Park saw

Stanley finish 19th in the Third Division and reach the fourth round of the FA Cup.

EASTICK, Brian

Born: Balham, London, 1949.
Goalkeeper.
Career: Crystal Palace juniors; Plymouth Argyle Reserves for 18 months; Queen's Park Rangers youth-team coach 1975; Chelsea reserve-team coach 1980; Brighton & Hove Albion coach 1980; Sporting Club (Kuwait) coach; Charlton Athletic coach 1987; Newport County manager October 1987-March 1988; Leyton Orient assistant manager 1988-December 1990; Coventry City reserve-team manager December 1990.

Brian Eastick's first managerial post at Newport could not have been tougher. The club was in terrible financial straits and heading out of the Football League and towards its final demise when Eastick took over. He was forced to fill his sides with loan players, cast-offs and youngsters and had to battle against adversity. Nevertheless, he impressed with his integrity and dignity in such trying circumstances. Eastick was sacked simply because Newport could not afford his wages but one of his signings, Paul Bodin, went on to better things with Swindon Town and Crystal Palace.

EDELSTON, Joseph

Born: Appleby Bridge, near Wigan, 27 April 1891; Died: London, 10 March 1970.
Wing-half   5ft 9in; 11st 6lb (1923).
Career: St Helen's Recreation; Hull City March 1913; Manchester City June 1920; Fulham November 1920, reserve-team player-coach 1925, retired to become assistant manager 1927-November 1937, also caretaker manager February 1934 and February 1935; Brentford coach and scout 1937-1939; Reading manager April 1939-May 1947; Leyton Orient assistant manager 1947-1951; also coach to Oxford and Cambridge Universities.

Honours: FA tour of South Africa 1920.

Joe Edelston is probably the only player ever to be transferred on the high seas. When on board a ship to South Africa with the FA in 1920, he was transferred from Hull to Manchester City. As a coach and manager, Edelston had fine organisational abilities and a good knowledge of the game. He served six different managers at the Cottage and was caretaker manager twice. Many felt that he would get the job after Jimmy Hogan but the Fulham board plumped for Jack Peart instead.

One of the first FA qualified coaches, Joe was to fall out with Peart in 1937. With the Reserves at the top of the Combination and the first team at the bottom of the Second Division, Edelston was accused of counter-manding Peart's tactical instructions and was sacked. He took his son, Maurice, with him and he later played for England in wartime and amateur internationals and was also a BBC radio commentator. Joe was in charge at Elm Park in the war years and when in 1945 he fell ill with pneumonia and was hospitalised, Maurice took over his secretarial duties. Joe managed a club for one peacetime season, when Reading finished ninth in the Third Division South in 1946-47.

EDWARDS, George Bryan

Born: Woodlesford, Leeds, 27 October 1930.
Wing-half   5ft 11in; 11st 10lb (1963).
Career: Oulton Youth Club (Leeds);

Bolton Wanderers October 1947; Blackpool assistant coach autumn 1965; Preston North End coach March 1969; Plymouth Argyle chief coach and assistant manager; Bradford City manager November 1971-January 1975; Huddersfield Town coach and physiotherapist; Leeds United youth-team coach and manager; Bradford City coach July 1977, general manager May 1978, assistant manager and physiotherapist November 1978-1986.

Honours: FA Cup winners 1958.

Edwards made 518 appearances for Bolton and, but for two games, was ever-present from 1956 to 1959. He made his debut in a 3-3 draw at Liverpool in September 1950 and played his last game in April 1965. He would have beaten the club's appearances record but for missing most of 1953-54 due to being on National Service. Edwards gained an FA Cup winners' medal in 1958, when Manchester United, shattered by the Munich air disaster, were beaten in the Final.

As Bradford City's manager, Edwards could not prevent their relegation in 1972 and introduced a strict disciplinary code for the players. He resigned after failing to get the club back up again. He returned to Valley Parade in 1977 and stayed until 1986 working as the club's physiotherapist.

EDWARDS, John William 'Jack'

Born: Risca, Monmouthshire, 6 July 1929.
Full-back   5ft 9in; 11st (1959).
Career: Cardiff City amateur; Lovell's Athletic; Crystal Palace September 1949; Rochdale June 1959; Ashford Town player-coach cs 1961; Exeter City trainer cs 1962, then manager February 1963-January 1965; Torquay United trainer 1965-1973, and caretaker manager December 1968-January 1969, manager October 1971-January 1973; Exeter City trainer January 1973; Plymouth Argyle assistant manager late 1973; Leeds United scout.

Honours: Division Four promotion 1964.

Jack Edwards played in the 1948 Army Cup Final, when two players were killed by lightning at Aldershot. He was the skipper at Selhurst Park and made 239 appearances during years of struggle for Palace. After 68 games for Rochdale, Edwards moved to Southern League Ashford Town. Employed at Exeter City by Cyril Spiers as trainer in 1962, he replaced him the following February as caretaker.

When he steered the team from 22nd to 17th to avoid relegation, Edwards was offered the job permanently in May. Exeter won promotion at the end of his first full season in charge, finishing fourth in Division Four, but he resigned when Ellis Stuttard was appointed chief scout without his knowledge. When he was at Torquay, they were relegated to Division Four in 1972 and struggled the following season. Edwards was a Leeds United scout for many years.

EDWARDS, Willis

Born: Newton, near Alfreton, 28 April 1903; Died: Leeds, 27 September 1988.
Right-half   5ft 7in; 11st 7lb (1935).
Career: Newton Rangers; Chesterfield 1919; Leeds United March 1925 (£1,500), retired to become club trainer 1942-1947 and 1948-June 1960, and manager May 1947-April 1948.

Honours: England international (16

caps); *Football League representative
(11 caps).*

Willis Edwards was working down the pits and was about to set off for a trial with Blackburn Rovers when he was signed by Chesterfield. Edwards developed into one of the best wing-halves of the inter-war period. Calm with superb control and positional play, he was exceptionally quick and reduced tackling to a fine art. He helped Leeds to promotion twice, in 1928 and 1932, both times as runners-up in Division Two, and played in 444 games before war broke out. He was a trainer at Elland Road from 1942 to 1960, except for an 11-month spell as manager. Leeds United struggled against relegation in 1948-49, eventually finishing 18th in Division Two. In all he spent 35 years at Elland Road.

EGGLESTON, Thomas

Born: Mitcham, 21 February 1920.
Wing-half
Career: Derby County amateur December 1936, professional February 1937; Royal Navy; guest for Southampton in the war; Leicester City July 1946; Watford February 1948; Brentford trainer September 1954; Watford coach May 1957; Sheffield Wednesday coach October 1958; Everton coach June 1961; Mansfield Town manager August 1967-July 1970; Ethnikos (Greece) manager July 1970; Panahaiki (Greece) manager 1971; Everton youth-team coach February 1972, assistant manager May 1972-June 1973; Plymouth Argyle physiotherapist; Ipswich Town physiotherapist December 1978 until retirement.

Tommy Eggleston's best playing days were at Watford, where he made 177 League appearances after being part of a remarkable five-man transfer from Leicester to Vicarage Road in 1948. Eggleston began his coaching career at Brentford and returned to Watford before teaming up with Harry Catterick at Sheffield Wednesday. He followed Catterick to Goodison Park and worked there for six years until he was offered the manager's job at Mansfield in 1967.

In his first season at Field Mill the Stags avoided relegation on goal-average and were also helped by Peterborough United's demotion due to irregular payments. The 1968-69 season was a good one with Mansfield reaching the quarter-finals of the FA Cup before narrowly losing to Leicester City at Field Mill. After Mansfield finished sixth in Division Three in 1969-70, Eggleston was lured away to manage

Ethnikos in Greece. He returned to Goodison Park to team up with Catterick again in 1971 and trained to become a physiotherapist. He later had a private practice in Ipswich and helped out the local club, before retiring to live in Tockwith, Yorkshire.

ELCOAT, George

Born: Stockton-on-Tees.
Career: Woolwich Arsenal manager May 1898-May 1899.

George Elcoat had one season in charge at Woolwich Arsenal, in which they finished seventh in Division Two. The club was in a poor financial position and players had to be sold to keep the Gunners solvent. Attendances at Plumstead were poor, averaging only around 4,000, but Elcoat made one excellent signing in John Dick, who developed into an excellent wing-half.

ELLIOTT, Charles Standish

Born: Bolsover, 24 April 1912.
Full-back   5ft 10in; 12st (1933).
Career: Sheffield Wednesday amateur cs 1930; Chesterfield November 1930; Coventry City July 1931; Birmingham as guest in World War Two; retired cs 1948; Coventry City chief scout 1948-1953, and caretaker manager October 1954-April 1955; also Derbyshire cricketer and Test panel umpire.

Normally a full-back who occasionally turned out at centre-half, Charlie Elliott helped Coventry to promotion to the Second Division, making only 12 appearances but appearing as an emergency stopper in some vital games. Unable to win a first-team place at either Sheffield Wednesday or Chesterfield, Elliott went on to make 98 appearances for Coventry before the war and 101 overall.

Coventry's caretaker manager between Jack Fairbrother and Jesse Carver, Elliott was also the club's chief scout, discovering amongst others, Ray Sambrook, who was later sold to Manchester City for £15,000. Elliott was a fine opening batsman for Derbyshire, scoring over 11,000 runs in seven seasons, and was later a Test umpire. More recently he was chairman of Derbyshire's cricket committee. He was in the same Derbyshire team as Harry Storer, who also managed Coventry City, Birmingham City and Derby County.

ELLIOTT, David

Born: Tantobie, County Durham, 10 February 1945.
Midfield   5ft 8in; 12st 3lb (1970).
Career: Gateshead; Sunderland February 1962; Newcastle United December 1966 (£10,000); Southend United January 1971; Newport County player-manager April 1975-February 1976; Bangor City player-manager 1977-1978 and 1978-1984; Newport County November 1978 (briefly); coached at Cardiff City, Caernarfon and Bangor.

Honours: Northern Premier League champions 1982; Welsh Cup runners-up 1978.

A strongly-built midfielder, Dave Elliott was never a regular at Sunderland or Newcastle but found first-team football at Southend United, making 177 appearances (four as sub) for the Roots Hall club. Newport County finished 16th in Division Four after he was sacked after only ten months as their player-manager. He found more success as manager of Bangor City, who just missed out on European football when they lost 3-1 on aggregate to

Wrexham in the 1978 Welsh Cup Final. Bangor also reached the 1981 FA Trophy semi-final and won the Northern Premier League championship in 1982. After two seasons in the Alliance, however, they were relegated.

ELLIOTT, William Henry

Born: Bradford, 20 March 1925.
Outside-left   5ft 7in; 10st 7lb (1951).
Career: Thornbury Boys; Bradford amateur 1939, professional March 1942; Burnley August 1951 (£23,000); Sunderland June 1953 (£26,000); Wisbech Town July 1961-1963; Sheffield Wednesday scout 1963-1964; US Forces (Germany) coach 1964-1966; Daring FC (Brussels) trainer-manager July 1966-January 1968; Sunderland trainer-coach January 1968-June 1973; Brann (Norway) coach 1974-78; Sunderland caretaker manager December 1978-May 1979; Darlington manager June 1979-June 1983.

Honours: England international (5 caps); Football League representative (4 caps).

Billy Elliott made his reputation as a left winger but later played at left-half and left-back. He scored 58 goals in 443 League appearances in his career and played in two losing FA Cup semi-final sides for Sunderland, in 1955 and 1956. He was also with the Wearsiders in 1958, when they were relegated for the first time in their history. In that year he was also implicated in an illegal payments scandal at Roker Park.

After a variety of jobs at home and abroad, Elliott was made Sunderland's caretaker manager in 1978. He was unlucky not to be offered the job permanently after taking them to the brink of promotion in 1979. He moved to Darlington, who had to seek re-election at the end of the 1979-80 season. In January 1982 the Feethams club almost went bankrupt after they had no home games for two months. Elliott later sold David Speedie to Chelsea for a club record £65,000.

ELLIS, Samuel

Born: Ashton-under-Lyne, 12 September 1946.
Centre-half   6ft; 13st 5lb (1970).
Career: Audenshaw Grammar School; Snipe Wanderers; W.H.Smith FC; Sheffield Wednesday September 1964; Mansfield Town January 1972; Lincoln City May 1973; Watford player-coach August 1977; Blackpool manager June 1982-April 1989; Bury manager May 1989-December 1990; Manchester City assistant manager December 1990.

Honours: England Under-23 international (3 caps); FA Cup runners-up 1966; Division Four runners-up 1985.

Sam Ellis made his debut for the Owls in April 1966 and after only ten games was selected for an FA Cup Final appearance against Everton, which Wednesday lost 3-2 after being two goals up. An awkward-looking player, he went on to make 181 appearances for Wednesday, mainly at centre-half.

Ellis linked up with Graham Taylor at Lincoln in May 1973. The Imps won the Fourth Division championship in 1976 and he followed Taylor to Watford in August 1977, where they repeated the feat in 1978. Ellis retired in the summer of 1979 to become the club coach, his first step towards management. He had scored 45 goals in 428 League appearances during his career.

In the summer of 1982, he applied

for the Blackpool job and spent seven years at Bloomfield Road. His first season in charge was not a happy one with the Seasiders having to seek re-election. Two years later, however, Blackpool won promotion to the Third Division, finishing runners-up behind Chesterfield. But they struggled against relegation in 1988-89 and Ellis was dismissed in the spring of that season.

In his first two years he had spent only £60,000 on new players, making some excellent free-transfer signings such as Mike Walsh and Ian Britton. He also signed Paul Stewart, who was later sold to Manchester City for £250,000, and for most of his time at Bloomfield Road had been a highly popular manager. Certainly he had done well with limited resources, often having to sell players to survive. One star, Colin Greenhall, had to be transferred to Sheffield United so that the taxman could be paid.

Taking over from Martin Dobson as Bury's manager in May 1989, in his first season the Shakers finished 13th in Division Three and Ellis brought a number of talented newcomers. Bury reached the Third Division play-offs in 1990 but lost to Tranmere Rovers. When financial problems arose at Gigg Lane and the whole of the first-team squad were put on the transfer list, Ellis accepted an offer to join Peter Reid at Maine Road.

EMERY, Frederick David

Born: Lincoln, 19 May 1900; Died: Carlisle, 8 May 1959.
Right-back/Left-half   5ft 8in; 11st 8lb (1936).
Career: Lincoln City; Wibsey; Bradford City September 1923; Doncaster Rovers July 1924, then manager March 1936-1940; Bradford manager October 1943-June 1951; Carlisle United manager July 1951-April 1958.

Honours: Division Three North champions 1935.

Fred Emery played 417 League games (a club record), scoring 26 goals, for Doncaster Rovers between 1924 and 1936, when he became the club's manager. He had captained Doncaster to the Third Division North championship in 1934-35 and as manager he managed to keep them in Division Two for two seasons before they were relegated. Thereafter the club finished as runners-up in the next two seasons but missed out on promotion as only the champions of each Third Division section went up in those days. Bradford were in the Second Division when he took over and he managed to maintain this status until 1950. Emery had only limited success at Carlisle.

ENGLISH, Jack

Born: Hebburn c.1887; Died: Darlington, December 1985.

Left-back   5ft 8in; 11st 7lb (1914).
Career: Hebburn Argyle; Walls End Park Villa; Preston North End cs 1910; Watford cs 1912; Sheffield United April 1913; Darlington player-manager 1919-May 1928, retired as a player 1921; Nelson manager cs 1928-January 1931; Northampton Town manager January 1931-October 1935; Exeter City manager October 1935-1940; Darlington manager 1940-1944.

Honours: Football League representative (1 cap); Division Three North champions 1925; North-Eastern League champions 1921; FA Cup winners 1915.

Jack English played in the so-called Khaki Cup Final of 1915, when Sheffield United beat Chelsea 3-0 at Old Trafford to win the only FA Cup Final ever played in wartime. He joined Darlington as player-manager in 1919 and steered the club to the North-Eastern League championship in 1920-21. They joined the newly-formed Third Division North in 1921 and finished runners-up in its first season.

Darlington were champions in 1925 and were promoted to the Second Division. However, English had to sell two of his best players, Jack O'Donnell to Everton for £2,700 and Tom Scott to Liverpool for £1,300, and the club struggled to survive in the higher division before being relegated in 1927. He was not a great success at Nelson and left for Northampton with the club heading for their worst-ever season.

Emery took the Cobblers to the fifth round of the FA Cup in 1934 but otherwise they were a mid-table side. At Exeter he signed 60 new players in four years but was unable to find success and succeeded only in creating an unhappy atmosphere at the club. A phlegmatic character, though, he was apparently able to cope with all the ups and downs that professional soccer had to offer.

EUSTACE, Peter

Born: Stocksbridge, 31 July 1944.
Midfield   5ft 10in; 11st (1963).
Career: Stockbridge Works; Sheffield Wednesday apprentice 1960, professional June 1962; West Ham United January 1970 (£90,000); Rotherham United (loan) March 1972; Sheffield Wednesday August 1972 (£12,000); Peterborough United July 1975-76; Sunderland coach 1983; Sheffield Wednesday assistant manager 1984, then manager October 1988-February 1989; Leyton Orient assistant manager December 1990, then team manager July 1991.

Honours: FA Cup runners-up 1966.

Peter Eustace played exceptionally well in the Owls' run to the 1966 FA Cup Final. Tall and elegant, Eustace was initially a wing-half but later became a midfield player with flare and grace. He also had a spell as a sweeper with Wednesday and appeared 268/12 games for them in his two spells at Hillsborough. Eustace was unable to reproduce his form after joining West Ham for a record £90,000 fee and returned to Wednesday for a much reduced fee. He had a difficult time in charge at the club, winning only two games in 19 matches and being sacked after only four months in charge. Eustace took over from Frank Clark as team manager at Orient in July 1991. In 1992 the O's just missed the play-offs despite

many injuries and having to sell players like Chris Bart-Williams to Sheffield Wednesday.

In 1992-93, Orient missed the Second Division play-offs after a poor run near the end of the season. Eustace took full control of the club after the departure of managing director Frank Clark to Nottingham Forest.

EVANS, Albert James

Born: Barnard Castle, March 1874; Died: Warwick, 24 March 1966.
Full-back   5ft 11in; 11st 6lb (1907).
Career: Stortforth & West Auckland Schools; Egglestone Abbey Boys; Barnard Castle 1891; Aston Villa August 1896; West Bromwich Albion October 1907, retired to become trainer June 1909; briefly coached in Norway; Coventry City manager June 1920-November 1924; after this he travelled the world doing many different jobs including gold prospecting in the Yukon and sheep farming in Canada and the USA; Aston Villa scout in 1950s.

Honours: Football League representative 1900; Football League champions 1897, 1899, 1900; FA Cup winners 1897.

A clean-tackling full-back who won three League championship medals during his time at Villa Park and played in Villa's double-winning side of 1896-97, Albert Evans did not play in Villa's 1905 FA Cup success and suffered five broken legs during his career, three whilst at Villa, one with West Brom and one in a charity match in 1915. He made 206 appearances for Villa and 40 for Albion.

When he took over at Coventry City, Evans was their third manager in three months. It was a constant struggle at Highfield Road and the club were lucky to survive relegation during his four years in charge. City were struggling under a mountain of debt and he inherited a moderate team. Even after strengthening it, he never took the Bantams above 18th place in Division Two but the players and the fans were loyal to him and support was always relatively good considering the club's plight.

When he died at the age of 92, he was the last survivor of Villa's double-winning side.

EVANS, Harry A.

Born: Lambeth, 17 April 1919; Died: 1962.
Centre-forward.
Career: Woking; Fulham; Southampton October 1943; Exeter City April 1947; Aldershot March 1949; Tottenham Hotspur assistant manager; Aldershot manager 1955-1959.

Harry Evans joined Fulham from Woking during the war, when he was still in the RAF, but did not appear in the Cottagers' first team, although he later played for Southampton, Exeter City and Aldershot. He was also assistant manager at Tottenham Hotspur and manager of Aldershot, where he took over from Gordon Clark. After Aldershot had to seek re-election in 1958-59, Evans' contract was terminated.

EVANS, Ian Peter

Born: Egham, 30 January 1952.
Centre-half   6ft 2½in; 11st 2lb (1973).
Career: Queen's Park Rangers apprentice May 1968, professional January 1970; Crystal Palace September 1974 (£40,000); Barnsley December 1979 (£95,000), then coach September 1980-August 1983; Exeter City (loan) August

1983; Cambridge United (loan) October-December 1983; Crystal Palace assistant manager June 1984-February 1989; Swansea City manager February 1989-March 1990.

Honours: Wales international (13 caps); Under-23 international (2 caps).

A tall and physically strong central defender, Evans was ever-present in Palace's promotion season of 1976-77, when the club went up to Division Two. In October 1977 he suffered a badly broken leg after a tackle from George Best and was out of the game for two years. When he recovered, Evans moved to Barnsley and helped the Colliers to promotion in 1980-81. He also helped QPR to runners-up spot in Division One in 1972-73 but could not win a regular place in the side in the higher division. Evans had a long spell as assistant manager to Steve Coppell at Palace and then replaced Terry Yorath as manager of Swansea City. He had a difficult time at Vetch Field and was sacked after only a year in charge.

EVANS, Maurice G.

Born: Didcot, 22 September 1936.
Wing-half   5ft 7in; 10st 10lb (1964).
Career: Reading September 1953-1966; Shrewsbury Town coach 1968, then manager October 1972-February 1974; Reading coach 1974, then manager May 1977-January 1984; Oxford United youth development officer and chief scout 1984, then manager June 1985-March 1988.

Honours: Division Three South representative side; Division Four champions 1979; Football League Cup winners 1986.

Maurice Evans was a favourite of the Elm Park fans as a player, making 407 League appearances for the club. He played representative games for the Army and the Third Division South and was well known for his honesty and his knowledge of the game. Indeed, he was a widely respected figure in football. He left Gay Meadow in 1974, after the Shrews were relegated, but had more success at Reading. Initially he caretaker manager, he was officially appointed in May 1977. Evans went about the job quietly and methodically and in 1978-79 steered Reading to their first championship for 53 years, breaking several records on the way, despite spending only £30,000 on new players.

Evans was very disillusioned after his sacking, along with secretary Roy Bentley, in January 1984 by new Reading chairman Roger Smee. Evans

was reluctant to take over at Oxford because of this and was initially caretaker manager until August 1985, when he accepted the post permanently. Oxford won the League Cup in 1986, beating Queen's Park Rangers 3-0 in the Final. It was a great achievement for such a small club, who until relatively recently had been in the Southern League. Ironically, Evans may have become the manager of both Oxford and Reading when Robert Maxwell mooted an amalgamation between the clubs to form something called Thames Valley Royals, a move which both sets of fans were dead against. Evans reluctantly stepped down as manager in March 1988, with Oxford heading for relegation to Division Two.

EVANS, Robert

Born: Glasgow, 16 July 1927.
Right-half   5ft 8in; 12st (1950).
Career: Thornliebank Methodist FC; St Anthony's (Glasgow); guest for Motherwell and Aberaman Athletic during World War Two; Glasgow Celtic 1944; Chelsea May 1960 (£12,500); Newport County player-manager May 1961-March 1962; Morton July 1962; Third Lanark player-trainer-coach cs 1963, then player-manager June 1964-June 1965; Raith Rovers (player only) cs 1965, retired 1967.

Honours: Scotland international (48 caps); Scottish League representative (24 caps); Scottish League champions 1954; Scottish Cup winners 1951, 1954; runners-up 1955, 1956; Scottish League Cup winners 1957, 1958.

Bobby Evans was one of Scotland's best half-backs after the war, well-known for his heading and tackling. He began his career as an inside-forward but soon reverted to wing-half. A sturdily built player who retained an attacking flair, Evans won 18 Scottish caps at wing-half but when George Young retired, he took over at centre-half and won a further 30 caps in this position. He made 385 League appearances for Celtic and gained many honours with the club. He was still playing regularly for Raith Rovers in 1967, at the age of 40. Evans made 564 appearances, in all, in Scottish and English League soccer. Newport finished at the bottom of the Third Division at the end of his only season in charge, with just 22 points. He did little better at Third Lanark, who were relegated to the Scottish Second Division in 1964-65.

EVERISS, Frederick JP

Born: Spon Lane, May 1882; Died: 1951.

Career: West Bromwich Albion office boy September 1896, secretary-manager 1902-1948, director 1948-1951; Football League Secretaries' and Managers' Association secretary from 1927, later chairman.

Honours: Football League champions

1920; Division Two champions 1911, runners-up 1931; FA Cup winners 1931, runners-up 1912, 1935.

Fred Everiss was associated with West Bromwich Albion from 1896 until his death in 1951 and was was secretary-manager of the club for a remarkable 46 years until 1948, when he was succeeded by his son-in-law, Ephraim Smith, who was in turn replaced by Fred's son, Alan, as secretary from 1960 to 1980 — a family record of service to West Brom which lasted for a remarkable 84 years.

When Fred Everiss joined Albion as an office boy in September 1896, he was put in charge of programmes and also did general clerical duties. He impressed the directors so much that when Frank Heaven resigned as secretary in 1902, Everiss was appointed the club's new secretary-manager. He became a much-loved and respected figure at The Hawthorns and in 1926 was presented with an illuminated address as a tangible token of the high regard in which he was held by players, past and present. The following year, he became secretary of the Football League Secretaries' and Managers' Association, a post he held for many years, eventually becoming chairman.

During the war years, Everiss took over most of the jobs at The Hawthorns — even that of ARP nightwatchman — and virtually ran the club by himself. Upon his retirement as secretary-manager in 1948, he joined the board and was a director until his death.

Although strictly not in control of team affairs, he served on selection committees and controlled the club's training staff during his years as secretary-manager. And if he cannot be given direct credit for Albion's successes during his period in the post, he was obviously a great influence at the club.

His early years in the job were not always easy. A boardroom split in 1904 was quickly followed by the main stand burning down on Bonfire Night, but the turning point came in 1910, after Everiss helped gather Albion's youngest-ever side and the season ended in triumph with the Second Division title.

They lost the 1912 FA Cup Final to Barnsley after a replay and the League championship was gained in 1919-20 with one of the club's greatest-ever sides. The Throstles finished runners-up in 1924-25, but were relegated back to Division Two in 1927.

Four years later, however, Albion regained their First Division status and also won the FA Cup that year, beating Birmingham at Wembley. They again reached the Final in 1935, losing 4-2 to Sheffield Wednesday.

West Brom were relegated again in 1938 and had not regained First Division status when Everiss resigned in 1948, the year that Albion appointed Jack Smith as their first team manager with the secretarial duties being taken over by Eph Smith. The name of Fred Everiss will long be remembered in the history of West Bromwich Albion Football Club.

EVERITT, Michael Dennis

Born: Clacton, 16 January 1941.
Utility   5ft 10in; 11st (1964).
Career: Arsenal February 1958; Northampton Town February 1961; Plymouth Argyle March 1967; Brighton & Hove Albion July 1968; Wimbledon player-manager June 1971-September 1973; Brentford manager September 1973-January 1975; Leicester City coach 1975-1977.

Honours: Division Three champions 1963.

A versatile player, Everitt appeared in both defence and attack for Northampton. He had made nine appearances for Arsenal in the First Division before moving to the Cobblers and developed into a utility player, appearing at full-back, wing-half, outside-right and centre-forward for Northampton.

Everitt went from Division Four to Division One with the Cobblers as runners-up in Division Four in 1961, Third Division champions in 1963 and runners-up in the Second Division in 1965. They were relegated after one season in the top flight and altogether Everitt made 207 appearances for Northampton (one as sub) before moving to Plymouth, and then to Brighton. As manager of Wimbledon, he saw the club finished in mid-table positions in the Southern League and was unable to get Brentford out of Division Four before joining Leicester City as a coach.

FAGAN, Joseph Francis

Born: Liverpool, 12 March 1921.
Centre-half   5ft 10in; 12st (1951).

Career: Earlestown Bohemians; Manchester City October 1938; Bradford August 1953; Altrincham; Nelson player-manager August 1951-1953; Rochdale trainer 1953; Liverpool coach, assistant manager July 1974, then manager June 1983-May 1985.

Honours: Football League champions 1984; Division Two champions 1947; Football League Cup winners 1984; European Cup winners 1984, runners-up 1985.

Joe Fagan managed Liverpool between Bob Paisley and Kenny Dalglish, carrying on the tradition of promoting from within at Anfield.

As a player, Fagan joined Manchester City as a solid, dependable centre-half from Earlestown Bohemians in October 1938, but due to the war he did not make his League debut until New Year's Day 1947, against Fulham.

Fagan was ever-present for City from January 1947 until November 1949 and helped establish them in Division One. He made 148 appearances for the Maine Road club before joining Altrincham in 1950 and moved back briefly into the Football League in August 1953 to make three appearances for Bradford. There followed a move to Nelson as player-manager and he later he took up a trainer's post with Rochdale.

In the early 1960s, Bill Shankly persuaded Fagan to join Liverpool in a similar capacity and he became assistant manager to Bob Paisley when

Shankly resigned in 1974, stepping into the manager's job after Paisley's retirement in June 1983.

Fagan inherited a young side which again looked like dominating soccer in Britain in the 1980s. He made some signings of his own, including Paul Walsh from Luton, John Wark from Ipswich and Michael Robinson from Brighton, and Liverpool went on to win their third successive League championship in 1983-84, equalling the feats of Huddersfield Town in the 1920s and Arsenal in the '30s.

The Reds had already beaten Everton in the League Cup Final and they also gained their fourth European Cup Final victory, beating AS Roma on penalties in Rome. Fagan thus became the first English club manager to achieve three major trophies in one season, although a major blow was Graeme Souness' transfer to Sampdoria.

The 1984-85 season was an anticlimax. At one stage Liverpool were 18th in the table but eventually finished runners-up behind Everton. They did not do much better in Cup competitions, losing in third round of the League Cup, in the semi-final of the FA Cup and going down to Juventus in the tragic European Cup Final in Brussels.

Fagan obviously found the death of over 30 people during crowd trouble before the match, too much to bear. He had offered his resignation before the game but was now extremely upset by what he had seen and returned to Liverpool tearful and tight-lipped. The implications of this disaster led to a ban for all English clubs in European competitions — Liverpool were to be banned the longest — and it was a great pity that Fagan's retirement from the game should have been overshadowed thus.

FAIRBROTHER, John 'Jack'

Born: Burton, 16 August 1917.
Goalkeeper.
Career: Burton Town, Preston North End March 1937; Newcastle United July 1947 (£6,500); Peterborough United player-manager June 1952-December 1953; Coventry City manager December 1953-October 1954; Israel team coach c.1955; Consett manager June 1962; Peterborough United manager again December 1962-February 1964.

Honours: FA Cup winners 1951; Football League War Cup winners 1941; Football League North champions 1941.

Jack Fairbrother was a well-built goalkeeper who was stylish and confident. He did not make his League

debut until the age of 30, due to the war, but played in 145 games for Newcastle United, appearing in their 1951 FA Cup Final victory over Blackpool. He was manager at Peterborough United during their great Midland League days, when they shone as FA Cup giantkillers, and his success at London Road led to his appointment at Coventry City.

Fairbrother stayed at Highfield Road for only ten months and the club finished in 14th position in the Third Division South. He managed the Posh for a second spell in the early 1960s and they finished sixth in Division Three in 1962-63. He was the nephew of George Harrison, who played for England and Everton.

FAIRCLOUGH, Arthur

Born: Redbrook, Barnsley, March 1873; Died: Sheffield, 19 March 1947.
Career: Barnsley Reserves 1891, retired due to serious illness; referee 1896; Barnsley director 1896-1898; then secretary, then manager cs 1899-May 1901; elected to the executive of Sheffield FA July 1902; Barnsley manager cs 1904-cs 1912; Huddersfield Town manager April 1912-December 1919; Leeds United manager February 1920-May 1927; Barnsley manager yet again May 1928-May 1930, director 1935.

Honours: Division Two champions 1924; FA Cup winners 1912, runners-up 1910.

Arthur Fairclough guided Barnsley to great times between 1910 and 1912, when they appeared in two FA Cup Finals. These were probably the greatest days in their history. He also played a major role in the history of Huddersfield Town and took the newly-formed Leeds United into the First Division.

As a player he was unfortunate in having to retire after only one game for Barnsley Reserves, due to a serious injury. He took up refereeing and his most important games were in the FA Cup qualifying rounds, the Midland League and Sheffield FA competitions. He became a director of Barnsley FC in 1896 and was appointed secretary-manager in the close season of 1899. He vacated the post in May 1901, but returned as manager in the summer of 1904. In July 1902, Fairclough was elected to the executive of the Sheffield FA.

He helped with the transformation of Barnsley into a limited company in July 1900 but soon financial problems forced him to sell players to more wealthier clubs. Fairclough discovered Jackie Mordue in non-League football and upset the Barnsley fans by selling him to Woolwich Arsenal for £600 in 1908. He got the same reaction when he sold George Reeves to Aston Villa for almost £1,000. Attendances at Oakwell were affected by these two sales due to the disillusionment of the supporters.

In 1910, Barnsley reached the FA Cup Final but lost to Newcastle United in a replay after coming so close to victory in the first game. The following season Barnsley had to seek re-election and to keep the club going, Fairclough was forced to sell star player Tommy Boyle to Burnley for £1,250.

Somehow, Barnsley reached the FA Cup Final again in 1912. Fairclough took the players away before the big match and they won the trophy thanks to Tufnell's 118th-minute winner in the replay against West Brom.

In April 1912, he accepted an offer to join Huddersfield Town and steered the Town through many difficult periods, but did not endear himself with the fans in 1919 when the club was on the point of folding and he supported a proposed move to Elland Road to replace the expelled Leeds City. Attendances had plummeted at Leeds Road and the club was heavily in debt. Circumstances surrounding this led to his resignation in December 1919 after he had put Huddersfield in an embarrassing position by indicating that he would act as a receiver if such an application was successful.

When former Town chairman John Hilton Crowther was appointed to head the board of directors at the newly-formed Leeds United, he persuaded Arthur Fairclough to become the first manager at the club. Fairclough and his assistant, Dick Ray, scoured the country looking for talent to establish United in the Second Division.

From June 1923 he had a new assistant in Dick Norman, the former Blackpool manager, with whom he had worked at Barnsley. In 1923-24, Leeds won the Second Division championship but, despite signing a number of talented players, they were relegated back again in 1927. Fairclough resigned in May that year.

In May 1928, he returned to Barnsley for a third spell as manager, resigning after two years but returning to the club as a director in 1935. Arthur Fairclough was 74 when he died in a Sheffield nursing home.

FAIRLESS, Jack

Career: Darlington manager cs 1928-cs 1933, and director 1919-33.

Jack Fairless took control of team affairs at Darlington as an economic measure when he was also a director of the club. In 1928-29 the team slumped to near the bottom of the Third Division North with only three points won away from home. Fairless was forced to sell players to keep the club afloat, Frank Wrightson going to Manchester City for £2,000. It was not a very successful period for the club and they had to apply for re-election in 1932-33.

FARRELL, Peter Desmond

Born: Dalkey, Dublin, 16 August 1922.
Wing-half   5ft 8½in; 12st 1lb (1959).
Career: Cabinteely United; Shamrock Rovers 1940; Everton August 1946 (£10,000); Tranmere Rovers player-manager October 1957-December 1960; Sligo Rovers February 1961; Holywell Town player-manager 1961; management in Ireland.

Honours: Republic of Ireland international (28 caps); Northern Ireland international (7 caps); FA of Ireland Cup winners 1942.

A sturdy wing-half who never shirked a tackle and was popular on and off the field, mixing freely with the supporters, Peter Farrell made 453 appearances for Everton, scoring 17 goals, and later played 114 games for Tranmere. He was capped by both the Republic of Ireland and Northern Ireland before the rules were changed in 1949, allowing him to be capped by only one country. He gained his first cap whilst still at Shamrock Rovers and captained the Republic in their first international after the war. Playing as an inside-right, Farrell scored one of the goals in Ireland's 2-0 win over England at Goodison Park in 1949.

He appeared in two losing FA Cup semi-finals and experienced relegation to the Second Division with Everton but helped the Toffees to clinch

promotion back again as runners-up in 1953-54. When Farrell became the manager at Prenton Park, the crowds flocked back to see the brand of pure football produced by his sides. Alas, he was sacked on 12 December 1960, as the team slid towards relegation to Division Four. After a spell as manager of Holywell Town, he returned to Dublin to open an insurance business.

FENTON, Benjamin Robert Vincent

Born: West Ham, 28 October 1918.
Wing-half/Outside-left
5ft 11in; 11st 6lb (1951).
Career: Essex, London and West Ham Schoolboys; Colchester Town 1934; West Ham United October 1935; Millwall March 1939; guest for Charlton Athletic, West Ham United, York City, Cardiff City and Manchester City in World War Two; Charlton Athletic 1947 (£6,000); Colchester United player-manager February 1955-October 1963, retired as a player 1958; Leyton Orient manager October 1963-December 1964; Millwall manager May 1966-October 1974; Charlton Athletic secretary January 1977-July 1979, assistant manager March 1980, general manager June 1981-June 1982.

Honours: FA tour to South Africa of 1939 (3 caps); Division Four runners-up 1962.

Benny Fenton followed in his brother Ted's footsteps and played alongside him in the Hammers' first team just before the war. Given a free transfer in 1939, he joined Millwall and played regularly at The Den during the war years. He had started his career as an inside-forward but was converted to wing-half at Charlton Athletic, helping them to maintain their First Division status. Fenton made 275 League appearances for Charlton but missed their 1947 FA Cup Final victory due to being cup-tied. Like brother Ted, he also managed Colchester United. Benny revitalised a mediocre side and also inspired the team to better things as skipper.

He was unlucky at Leyton Orient, given barely a year to work a miracle and being sacked when he did not achieve one. He took over at The Den just as the Lions were achieving promotion to the Second Division. His sides were quite negative as Millwall's best players were defenders and he built the team around them. The club went agonisingly close to promotion to Division One in 1971-72 but missed out

to Birmingham City. The side broke up after this disappointment and Fenton resigned after a poor start to the 1974-75 season.

FENTON, Edward Benjamin Ambrose 'Ted'

Born: Forest Gate, 7 November 1914;
Died: 12 July 1992.
Wing-half   5ft 11in; 12st (1935).

Career: West Ham Boys; Ilford, Colchester Town; West Ham United November 1933; Colchester United player-manager 1946-June 1948; West Ham United assistant manager June 1948, then manager August 1950-March 1961; Southend United manager March 1961-April 1965; licensee from 1965 and ran sports shop in Brentwood; retired to live in Gloucestershire.

Honours: England Wartime international (1 cap); Schoolboy international; Division Two champions 1958; Football League War Cup winners 1940.

Ted Fenton made his debut for West Ham as a centre-half but usually played at wing-half and appeared for the Hammers 176 times, scoring 18 goals, before the outbreak of the war in 1939. Fenton played in the 1940 War Cup Final, won wartime international honours and served as a PT instructor in North Africa and Burma.

When he became manager of Colchester United after the war they were a Southern League club. He guided them to the fifth round of the FA Cup in 1947-48 but left at the end of that season to return to Upton Park as assistant manager to Charlie Paynter. Fenton took over in 1950 and his best achievement as West Ham manager was winning the Second Division championship in 1958 to regain the Hammers' First Division status for the first time in 26 years. They finished sixth the following season.

He also set up a fine youth scheme and the club reached the FA Youth Cup Final in 1954. He left Upton Park for reasons that were never explained and moved to Southend United. Fenton never had much success at Roots Hall and was sacked in 1965.

FENTON, Ronald

Born: South Shields, 2 September 1940.
Inside-forward   5ft 8in; 10st 4lb (1963).
Career: South Shields Schools; Durham Boys; West Bromwich Albion trial 1955; South Shields; Burnley apprentice April 1956, professional September 1957; West Bromwich Albion November 1962 (£18,000); Birmingham City January 1965 (£7,500); Brentford January 1968; Notts County youth coach July 1970, then manager September 1975-October 1977; Nottingham Forest assistant manager October 1977-May 1993.

Only ever a first-team regular at Brentford, Ronnie Fenton's best season at West Brom was when he made 31 appearances and scored eight goals in 1963-64, playing at inside-right. He moved to Notts County as youth-team coach in 1970 and later helped manager Jimmy Sirrell get the Magpies from the Fourth to the Second Division. When he became manager in 1975, Fenton appointed Colin Addison as his coach. County challenged for promotion in his first two seasons in charge at Meadow Lane but he was sacked in October 1977, with the team at the bottom of the Second Division. Since that time he has worked as assistant manager to Brian Clough at Nottingham Forest, but left when Clough resigned in May 1993.

FERGUSON, Alex OBE

Born: Govan, 31 December 1941.
Centre-forward.
Career: Queen's Park; St Johnstone 1960; Dunfermline 1964; Glasgow Rangers July 1967 (£65,000); Falkirk player-coach November 1969 (£20,000); Ayr United 1973; East Stirling player-manager July-October 1974; St Mirren manager October 1974-1978, retired as a player in 1975; Scottish PFA secretary early 1970s; Aberdeen manager June 1978-November 1986; Scotland national manager September 1985-July 1986 (had been Jock Stein's assistant for the previous 12 months); Manchester United manager November 1986.

Honours: Scotland Schoolboy international; Youth international; Amateur international; Scottish Premier champions 1980, 1984, 1985; Scottish League Division One champions 1977; Scottish League Cup winners 1986, runners-up 1979, 1980; Scottish Cup winners 1982, 1983, 1984, 1986; FA Cup winners 1990; Football League Cup winners, 1992, runners-up 1991; European Cup-winners' Cup winners 1983, 1991. Premier League Champions 1993.

Alex Ferguson has an excellent record as a manager in both Scottish and English football. He has taken two clubs to success in the European Cup-winners' Cup, Aberdeen in 1983 and Manchester United in 1991. He has now won every honour on both sides of the border.

Yet until United won the FA Cup in 1990, it looked as though Ferguson was on the point of being sacked as he had found little success at Old Trafford up until that point. Since then, however, the Old Trafford club have hardly looked back under his shrewd management.

As a rumbustuous centre-forward, Ferguson signed for amateurs Queen's Park in the late 1950s and moved to St Johnstone in 1960. Four years later, he joined Dunfermline where his goalscoring exploits led Rangers to pay £65,000 for his services in July 1967. However, he did not have a happy time at Ibrox. His style upset opposing players but his short temper sometimes landed him in trouble. In November 1969, he moved to Falkirk as player-coach for a £20,000 fee and then on to Ayr United in 1973. He finally hung up his boots in 1975.

In July 1974, he took on his first managerial position, at East Stirling, but after only three months in charge was enticed away to become manager of St Mirren. At Love Street, he transformed a mid-table Second Division club into one going for honours in the Premier Division. Yet after all this new-found success for the club, he was surprisingly dismissed after a behind-the-scenes row.

He was soon snapped up by ambitious Aberdeen and led the Pittodrie club to one of their most successful periods. They were Scottish Premier League champions in 1979-80, 1983-84 and 1984-85, they also won the Scottish Cup in 1982, 1983, 1984 and 1986 and the Scottish League Cup in 1985 as well as playing in losing Finals in 1979 and 1980. In 1983, Aberdeen won the European Cup-winners' Cup, beating Real Madrid 2-1 in the Final in Gothenburg. The following year they lifted the League and Cup double, a fine achievement for a club outside of Glasgow's 'Big Two'.

After the death of Jock Stein, Ferguson reluctantly took over as Scotland's team manager, agreeing to lead the side until after the 1986 World Cup finals.

His record at Pittodrie attracted the attention of Manchester United and he became their manager in November 1986. United were runners-up in the First Division in 1987-88, but were nine points behind champions Liverpool, and boardroom struggles at the beginning of the 1989-90 season hardly helped. Lack of success looked to have put his job in jeopardy by the New Year of 1990, but after a great run, United beat Crystal Palace in an FA Cup Final replay.

More success soon followed for Ferguson. United won the European Cup-winners' Cup in 1991, beating Barcelona 2-1 in the Final in Rotterdam. That season they also reached the League Cup Final but lost 1-0 to Sheffield Wednesday. In 1992, however, United reached the League Cup Final again, this time beating Nottingham Forest at Wembley. They should have also won the League championship, but after leading the table for much of the season blew their chances in the final run-in to let Leeds United overtake them.

Manchester United won the League Championship in 1992-93 for the first time in 26 years after a long struggle for supremacy with Aston Villa and Norwich City. Ferguson deserved his success and his great buy of the season was obtaining the brilliant Frenchman Eric Cantona from Leeds United for just over £1m. It was Cantona's second championship medal in successive seasons, having won a medal with Leeds United the previous season. The stars of the side were Paul Ince and the young Ryan Giggs and the whole United side played with great flair and entertained the crowds throughout the country.

FERGUSON, Charles

Born: Dunfermline (possibly), 22 November 1910.
Inside-forward 5ft 8in; 10st 7lb (1933).
Career (possibly): Yoker; Glasgow Benburg; Middlesbrough May 1932; Notts County May 1936; Sunderland chief scout; Corinthian (Newcastle) manager-coach; Gateshead manager April 1960-August 1961.

Charlie Ferguson was appointed the manager of Gateshead just before they were voted out of the Football League in 1960. He had been given a three-year contract and soldiered on with the club in the newly-formed Northern Counties League for a while. If it is the same person, then Ferguson played just over 20 games for both Middlesbrough and Notts County just before World War Two. He had previously been an apprentice plater in the shipyards. Corinthian were the youth team of Newcastle United and here Ferguson gained a reputation for discovering young talent.

FERGUSON, Michael K.

Born: Burnley, 9 March 1943.
Midfield 5ft 11in; 10st 9lb (1964).
Career: Burnley Schools; Plymouth Argyle amateur March 1959; Accrington Stanley July 1960; Blackburn Rovers March 1962 (£1,500); Aston Villa May 1968 (£55,000); Queen's Park Rangers November 1969 (£11,500); Cambridge United July 1973; Rochdale July 1974; Los Angeles Aztecs (NASL) April-August 1975; IA Akranes (Iceland) 1975; Halifax Town December 1976, retired 1977; Rochdale manager September 1977-November 1978; coached around the world in the 1980s; Enfield manager 1989.

Honours: Iceland League championship 1976.

Blackburn Rovers got a bargain when they paid £1,500 to the Football League for Mike Ferguson's transfer after the winding-up of Accrington Stanley in 1962, for he had been a regular in the Stanley side before their demise. Ferguson was later sold to Aston Villa for £55,000 but made only 38 appearances for Villa before moving to Loftus Road for a much reduced fee. This well-built, strong-running midfielder played his best soccer at Blackburn Rovers, for whom he appeared 220 times, scoring 29 goals. IA Akranes won the Icelandic championship under his guidance. At Rochdale, though, he had a difficult time, the Spotland club finishing bottom of the Fourth Division and losing to non-League Scarborough in the FA Cup in 1977-78. Following an even more humiliating Cup defeat at the hands of Droylesden, he was sacked in November 1978.

FERGUSON, Robert Burnitt

Born: Dudley, Northumberland, 8 January 1938.
Full-back 5ft 10in; 11st 7lb (1965).
Career: Dudley; Newcastle United May 1955; Derby County October 1962 (£4,000); Cardiff City December 1965 (£5,000); Barry Town player-manager December 1968; Newport County player-manager July 1969-November 1970, player until cs 1971; Ipswich Town youth coach July 1971, reserve-team coach 1973, then manager August 1982-May 1987; Al-Arabi (Kuwait) manager June 1987; Birmingham City assistant manager June 1989-January 1991; Colchester United coach March 1991; Coventry City coach late 1991; Sunderland coach June 1992.

Bobby Ferguson came from a footballing family, his father played for West Bromwich Albion and his uncle for Chelsea. A hard, determined left-back, Ferguson proved to be a bargain buy when Derby County paid £4,000 for his services and he made 123 appearances for the Rams. He had made only 11 League appearances in seven seasons at St James' Park before moving to the Baseball Ground. He made a further 87/1 appearances for Cardiff and 71 for Newport County as player-manager.

Ferguson had a difficult time at Somerton Park with the club having to seek re-election in 1969-70. He moved to Ipswich Town as coach under Bobby Robson and took over as boss when Robson became the England manager. In 1984-85, Ipswich reached the sixth round of the FA Cup and also the semi-final of the League Cup. The following season, though, they were relegated to the Second Division and Ferguson was unfortunate to lose his job when Ipswich finished fifth in Division Two and lost to Charlton in the play-offs for promotion in 1986-87. More recently he was assistant manager to Dave Mackay at Birmingham City and then moved to Sunderland.

FIELDING, Alfred Walter

Born: Edmonton, 26 November 1919.
Inside-forward 5ft 7in; 10st 11lb (1959).
Career: Walthamstow Avenue; Charlton Athletic; Everton September 1945; Southport player-manager January 1959-May 1960, retired as a player early in 1960.

Wally Fielding was at the centre of a row when he signed for Everton in 1945. Charlton Athletic claimed that he had signed amateur forms for them before joining the Army. He served in the Middle East and won Army representative honours during this spell. A brilliant ball player and strategist, Fielding was the engine-room of the 1offees. He played for England in the 1946 Bolton Disaster Fund match against Scotland in Manchester, which was an unofficial international. Fielding appeared in 410 games, scoring 54 goals, for Everton. He was not a great success as player-manager of Southport, the club having to seek re-election in 1959-60. In financial difficulties, they were lucky not to be voted out of the League instead of Gateshead.

FINDLEY, William

Born: Musselburgh, c.1900; Died: Braunstone, Leicestershire, 11 June 1949.
Utlity 5ft 9in; 11st 10lb (1925).
Career: Musselburgh Brutonians 1922; Third Lanark cs 1923; Liverpool Reserves 1924; Leicester City May 1925; Watford June 1932, then manager January 1938-February 1947; Edgware Town manager 1947-1949.

Honours: Scottish Junior Cup winners 1923.

Bill Findley played in Musselburgh's Scottish Junior Cup winning side of 1923. He was unable to break into Liverpool's first team before his move to Leicester City and although he made 104 appearances for City, he was never a regular, often called upon to cover for injuries. He did, however, manage 28 games when Leicester finished third in the First Division in 1927-28. Findley almost single-handedly kept Watford going in the war years and it was useful that he was also a qualified physiotherapist. Watford were on the brink

of being a good side when war broke out, having finished fourth in the Third Division South in 1938-39. Findley was manager of Edgware Town at the time of his death.

FIRMANI, Edward Ronald

Born: Cape Town, South Africa, 7 August 1933.
Centre-forward 5ft 11in; 12st 2lb (1963).
Career: Clyde (South Africa); Charlton Athletic February 1950; Sampdoria (Genoa) 1955 (£35,000); Internazionale June 1958 (£88,000); Genoa cs 1961 (£66,000); Charlton Athletic October 1963 (£12,000); Southend United June 1965 (£8,500); Charlton Athletic March 1967 (£2,000), then player-manager September 1967-March 1970; Crystal Palace chief scout May 1970; Bromley manager November 1973-January 1974; Tampa Bay Rowdies (NASL) coach 1974-1977; New York Cosmos (NASL) coach 1977-June 1979; New Jersey Americans manager June 1979; Philadelphia Fury (NASL) coach October 1979; Montreal Manic (NASL) coach 1981-1982; New York Cosmos (NASL) coach 1984; from 1985 was manager of Kazma, Shabab, Arabi and Kaiten August 1990 in Kuwait.

Honours: Italy international (3 caps); NASL Soccer Bowl winners 1975, 1976, 1977.

Eddie Firmani was a great favourite with The Valley faithful, who must have been saddened when their hero was sold to Sampdoria for a British record fee of £35,000 in 1955. Firmani had scored five goals in a match against Aston Villa just before his departure. Despite being born in South Africa, Firmani won his three caps due to birthright, his grandfather being Italian. He managed to score 100 goals in defence-dominated Italian soccer before returning to Charlton Athletic in 1963. It was not such a happy time for him on his return, often playing out of position at wing-half. Firmani won fame for his cool and sportsmanlike demeanor.

This model professional tried to take his high moral stance into management. He demanded that his players did not swear or retaliate and threatened them with punishments if they did. He left The Valley rather disillusioned with soccer, the game at that time being too cynical for Firmani's values to survive. He was revitalised by his involvement with the North American Soccer League and Tampa Bay Rowdies won the Soccer Bowl at the end of his first season in charge. He was then lured away to New York Cosmos and took them to two more titles, in 1976 and 1977.

FISHER, Hugh

Born: Glasgow, 9 January 1944.
Midfield   5ft 8½in; 10st 3lb (1970).
Career: Blackpool August 1962; Southampton March 1967 (£35,000); Southport player-manager March 1977-May 1978; sales representative in Southampton.

An intelligent midfield player, Hugh Fisher added some steel to Southampton's midfield after joining the club in March 1967 from Blackpool. He was a substitute when the Saints won the FA Cup in 1976 as a Second Division side. Fisher made over 300 appearances for the Saints and perhaps should have scored more than the seven goals he netted for them.

They had not retained their higher status when he joined Southport as player-manager in 1977. The Haig Avenue club had massive financial worries and he was unable to lift them out of the gloom. Fisher left soon after Southport were voted out of the Football League. He had wanted to get away earlier, but the board had held him to his contract.

FISHER, James Albert

Born: Glasgow, June 1879; Died: 4 December 1937.
Career: East Stirlingshire; St Bernard's; Glasgow Celtic 1901; Aston Villa 1902; Fulham August 1903; Bristol City July 1904; Brighton & Hove Albion August 1905; Manchester City June 1906; Bradford June 1907; non-League football in Scotland; Merthyr Town manager cs 1912-cs 1913; Notts County secretary-manager cs 1913-cs 1927.
Honours: Division Two champions 1914, 1923.

Fisher was Notts County's first secretary-manager and was in charge of the club for 14 years, taking them to two Second Division championships.

After moving to England from Celtic he made only one League appearance for Aston Villa but was top scorer for their Reserves in the Birmingham League. Fisher possessed a good shot, was clever with the ball and had plenty of pluck near goal. Never able to settle, he was soon on the move and played for Fulham in the first Southern League game of 1903-04, against Spurs, but was dropped. He did appear in four more games, in the early qualifying rounds of the FA Cup in a side made up mostly of reserve-teamers. He scored two goals in these Cup games, against Crouch End Vampires and the Civil Service.

In 1904-05 Fisher was Bristol City's top scorer, with 13 goals in 26 League games and, after seven appearances for Brighton he moved to Manchester City and then to Bradford, playing mainly in the Reserves at Park Avenue before switching to non-League soccer in Scotland.

In the summer of 1912, Merthyr Town became a limited company after their promotion to the First Division of the Southern League and Albert Fisher was appointed secretary-manager. They finished 12th in their first season in the top flight but Fisher was then enticed away to become the first secretary-manager of Notts County.

At the end of his first season in charge, Notts won promotion to the First Division as champions by four clear points. The following season, however, they were saved from relegation when they beat Chelsea 2-0 in their last game. They were relegated, though, in the first season after World War One but bounced back again as Second Division champions in 1922-23. County were relegated again in 1925-26 and did not return to the First Division again until 1981.

Only 4,715 spectators turned up to see their last game of the season, against League champions Huddersfield Town. Notts County had reached the semi-final of the FA Cup in 1921-22, every match having been replayed up to the last four. In a first-round replay they beat Grimsby Town 3-0. Then Bradford City were beaten 1-0 in a second replay at Bramall Lane with a goal from Widdowson. In round three West Brom were knocked out 2-0 in a replay, then in the quarter-final Aston Villa were defeated 4-3 in an exciting replay at Villa Park. The semi-final ended in a disappointing defeat by 3-1 against Huddersfield Town at Turf Moor.

Fisher left Meadow Lane at the end of a disappointing 1926-27 season when he felt it was time to quit the pressures of club management.

FLATLEY, Albert Austin

Born: Bradford, 5 September 1919; Died: Yeadon, near Leeds, 9 April 1987.
Inside-forward.
Career: York City February 1934; Port Vale June 1939; Bradford July 1944; Bury December 1946; Alessandria (Italy) 1948-1950; Workington player-manager August 1950-May 1952.

Bert Flatley's career was ruined by World War Two. He had just broken into the York City side in 1938-39 but never played for them again and, indeed, rarely turned out for anyone until the latter stages of the war, when he joined Bradford in 1944. He appeared 23 times in their first team but was unable to gain a place in peacetime and moved to Bury, where he had a similar experience. After two seasons in Italy he returned to England as player-manager of Workington. A 'track suit' boss, he was a full FA coach and he took Workington from non-League soccer into the Third Division North in 1950. Their first season in the Football League was a traumatic one and Flatley resigned just after they had been re-elected after finishing bottom of the table. Flatley was popular with the Press, always willing to speak to journalists.

FLETCHER, Brough

Born: Shildon, County Durham, 9 March 1893; Died: Bristol, 12 May 1972.
Right-half   5ft 8in; 12st 4lb (1920).

Career: Shildon Athletic; Chilton Colliery; Barnsley November 1914; Sheffield Wednesday January 1922; Barnsley December 1926, coach 1929, then manager cs 1930-February 1937; Bristol Rovers manager January 1938-December 1949; Walsall manager March 1952-April 1953.
Honours: Division Three North champions 1934.

A small and robust forward, Fletcher played over 300 games, scoring 73 goals, for Barnsley. In contrast, he made just two appearances for the Owls in almost four years at Hillsborough. In 1929 he became a coach at Oakwell and a year later was promoted to manager.

Fletcher was the first man to hold the job at Oakwell without secretarial responsibilities. He had little money to spend and Barnsley struggled, being relegated from the Second Division in 1931-32 after 34 years in that division. They were soon back as Third Division North champions in 1933-34 and the inspired signing of Abe Blight produced 31 goals. Fletcher sold Dick Spence to Chelsea for £4,000, much to the chagrin of the fans but he did take the club to the quarter-finals of the FA Cup in 1936 before losing to Arsenal.

Fletcher is not fondly remembered at Bristol Rovers as he was responsible for selling Eastville to a greyhound racing company. However, he did discover a number of talented players. He was dismissed in 1949 after an FA inquiry into the club's involvement with the greyhound company.

FLEWIN, Reginald

Born: Portsmouth, 28 November 1920.
Centre-half
Career: Ryde Sports (IoW); Portsmouth November 1937, retired 1953, then youth-team coach and assistant manager 1953-1960; Stockport County manager October 1960-September 1963; Bournemouth & Boscombe Athletic manager September 1963-1965.

Honours: England Wartime international (1 cap); Football League champions 1949, 1950; FA tours to Canada and Australia.

Reg Flewin's playing career was badly affected by the war and he made only 167 appearances for Pompey in 18 years at the club. After the war, he was the club's regular centre-half and although a serious injury put him out of the side in January 1951, he had gained two League championship medals as captain. Flewin also went on two FA tours, to Canada 1950 and Australia 1951. He had three seasons of struggle as manager of Stockport County, but some success at Bournemouth, who just missed promotion to Division Two in 1964 when they finished fourth.

FLOWERS, Ronald

Born: Edlington, near Doncaster, 28 July 1934.
Left-half   5ft 11in; 12st 12lb (1964).
Career: Yorkshire Schools; Edlington Grammar School; Doncaster Rovers juniors; Wath Wanderers July 1950; Wolverhampton Wanderers July 1952; Northampton Town player-coach September 1967, then player-manager May 1968-May 1969; Telford United player-coach July 1969-October 1971; then ran a sports shop in Wolverhampton.

Honours: England international (49 caps); Under-23 international (2 caps); Football League representative (13 caps); Football League champions 1954, 1958, 1959; FA Cup winners 1960; FA Trophy runners-up 1970.

A fair-haired, well-built and strong player who was solid and industrious with a crisp tackle and boundless energy, Ron Flowers scored in four consecutive internationals for England and also played in 40 consecutive games for his country. Flowers enjoyed wonderful years with Wolves during the 1950s, when they were the toast of English soccer. Later in his career, he was hindered by a back injury. He played in Wolves' 1960 FA Cup Final victory over Blackburn and also gained three League championship medals.

As Wolves went into decline in the 1960s, Flowers struggled to find his form and after 467 appearances (32 goals) for the Molineux club, he joined Northampton Town as player-coach. In 1968 he became player-manager of the club but was sacked when the Cobblers were relegated to the Fourth Division in 1969. Flowers played in the 1970 FA Trophy Final when Telford United lost to Macclesfield, but did not select himself when they won the trophy the following year. His father and brother both played for Doncaster Rovers.

FLYNN, Brian

Born: Port Talbot, 12 October 1955.
Midfield   5ft 3in; 9st (1978).
Career: Sandfields Comprehensive School; Neath Schools; Afon Lido; Burnley apprentice 1970, professional October 1972; Leeds United November 1977 (£175,000); Burnley, (loan) March 1982, permanently November 1982 (£60,000); Cardiff City November 1984 (£15,000); Doncaster Rovers November 1985; Bury July 1986; Limerick player-coach January 1987; Doncaster Rovers August 1987; working for PFA in 1988; Wrexham February 1988, then manager November 1989.

Honours: Wales international (66 caps); Under-23 international (2 caps); Schoolboy international; Welsh Cup runners-up 1988. Division Three runners up 1993.

Although small in stature, Brian Flynn was a real battler on the field. A product of Burnley's youth scheme after Cardiff

City let him slip through their fingers, he formed a fine partnership with Tony Currie after he moved to Leeds United. Flynn scored a memorable goal on his full international debut for Wales, against Scotland in 1975, and altogether made 174/3 appearances for Leeds and 242/11 in his two spells at Turf Moor.

At Limerick in the League of Ireland he was player-coach under former teammate Billy Hamilton. His days at Wrexham have sometimes been difficult and in 1990 they were saved from dropping into the Conference only because no team was relegated from the Fourth Division that year, Wrexham having finished rock bottom.

It was hardly Flynn's fault and he did well with some very young players. In 1991-92, though, he saw his side improve to finish 14th and score a sensational FA Cup victory over League champions Arsenal, a feat which earned Flynn his first Manager of the Month award. Still playing occasionally — six games in 1991-92. Wrexham made it a Welsh double when they finished as runners-up in Division Three to Cardiff City in 1992-93. Flynn's young side which had done so well in the FA Cup the previous season had developed into a useful combination.

FOLEY, Theo Cornelius
Born: Dublin, 2 April 1937.
Full-back   5ft 10in; 11st 9lb (1964).
Career: Bulfin United; Ormeau FC; Home Farm (Dublin); Exeter City March 1955; Northampton Town May 1961; Charlton Athletic August 1967, chief coach December 1967, then manager March 1970-April 1974; Dulwich Hamlet manager September 1974 briefly; Millwall assistant manager April 1975, caretaker manager December 1977; Queen's Park Rangers coach December 1977; Millwall assistant manager December 1982; Arsenal assistant manager April 1986; Northampton Town manager May 1990-April 1992; Fulham Youth team manager March 1993.

Honours: Republic of Ireland international (9 caps); Division Three champions 1963.

Theo Foley was a fast full-back who won a reputation as a firm tackler. Foley was a regular in the Exeter side from 1957-58 and made 159 appearances for the club, and was one of the stars of the Northampton Town side which went from the Third to the First Division.

He became the manager at The Valley in 1970 and the club narrowly avoided relegation from Division Two

at the end of his first season in charge, but went down the following season after a neck-and-neck struggle with Fulham. He left The Valley after two seasons of struggle in the Third Division.

Foley had discovered a number of talented players during his time at The Valley, including Mike Flanagan, Derek Hales and Colin Powell. He won a reputation as a coach at Loftus Road and in 1982 teamed up with George Graham at Millwall. This successful combination moved on to Highbury in 1986 and found even more success, including the League championship. In May 1990, Foley decided to try his luck again as manager at Northampton Town. They finished in a mid-table position at the end of his first season in charge but struggled the following season and flirted with bankruptcy on many occasions. The administrators in charge of the debt-ridden club sacked Theo Foley in April 1992 along with nine players and two other staff members.

FORD, Frederick George Luther
Born: Dartford, 10 February 1916; Died: Oxford, 16 October 1981.
Centre-half.

Career: Erith & Belvedere; Arsenal amateur December 1934; Charlton Athletic March 1936; Millwall November 1945; Carlisle United July 1947, then trainer-coach 1949-1955 after knee injury ended his career; Bristol Rovers chief coach 1955-1960; England Under-23 and 'B' team coach 1958-1960; Bristol City manager July 1960-September 1967; Swindon Town coach 1967-1968; Bristol Rovers manager April 1968-October 1969; Swindon Town manager October 1969-May 1971; Torquay United coach and assistant manager 1972; Oxford United youth coach 1974 until his death.

Honours: Division Three runners-up 1965.

Fred Ford was a constructive, hard-working defender whose career was dogged by a knee injury. He worked with Bill Shankly at Carlisle United and they became close friends. Ford joined Bert Tann at Bristol Rovers as coach in 1955 and moved to neighbours City as manager in 1960.

In 1965 they returned to the Second Division as runners-up but struggled in the higher division and Ford was dismissed after a poor start to the 1967-68 season. He returned to Eastville as manager in April 1968 and discovered a number of talented youngsters includ-

ing Larry Lloyd, who was later sold to Liverpool for £50,000. Ford took Swindon to fifth place in the Second Division in 1969-70 and they also reached the quarter-final of the FA Cup. He won a reputation as a talent scout, discovering several useful youngsters, and also did sterling work at Oxford in the 1970s.

FORREST, William
Born: Trament, Edinburgh, 28 February 1908; Died: Middlesbrough, February 1965.
Left-half   5ft 9in; 11st (1930).
Career: Haddington; Musselbrough juniors; Trament; St Bernard's; Middlesbrough March 1929, retired in 1945 to become juniors coach; Darlington manager 1946-1950.

Honours: Scottish Schoolboy international.

A stylish wing-half, Forrest was a regular at Ayresome Park except for a period in the 1933-34 season when he had a serious injury. This former miner went on to play 307 League appearances for 'Boro and the club finished fourth in Division One in the last pre-war season. When he was Darlington's manager, the club had record crowds after a good start to the 1948-49 season and they eventually finished fourth in the Third Division North and reached the third round of the FA Cup, their best season for years. Later ran a hotel in Billingham but in 1956 was partially paralysed after an accident which led to his death.

FOSTER, George William
Born: Plymouth, 26 September 1956.
Defender   5ft 10in; 11st 2lb (1983).
Career: Plymouth Argyle September 1974; Torquay United (loan) October 1976; Exeter City (loan) December 1981; Derby County June 1982 (£40,000); Mansfield Town August 1983, then player-manager February 1989-May 1993.

Honours: Division Four promotion 1992; Freight/Rover Trophy winners 1987.

George Foster played for all three West Country sides in the Football League and has made over 639 League appearances up to 1991-2 in his career after being advised to give up the game as a teenager, due to injury. Slightly on the small side for a centre-half, Foster was a vigorous footballer who gave the opposition little room to play. He captained Mansfield to promotion from Division Three in 1986 and to victory in Freight/Rover Trophy Final the following year. When he took over from the long-serving Ian Greaves in February 1989, he inherited a side which was struggling against relegation. They were relegated back to Division Four in 1991, but bounced straight back again, promoted in third place. Foster helped the cause by signing Phil Stant from Fulham for £55,000 and he scored 26 goals for the Stags. Stant was surprisingly sold to Cardiff City for £150,000 and Mansfield's goal power dried up alarmingly in 1992-93.

Foster's job was on the line when Mansfield were relegated at the end of the 1992-93 season. Goals were difficult to come by and this was not helped by the sale of Phil Stant to Cardiff City for £150,000 during the season, and he parted company with the club at the end of the season.

FOWERAKER, Charles E.
Died: Bolton, July 1950.
Career: Bolton Wanderers gateman

1895, assistant secretary cs 1915-1919, then secretary-manager July 1919-August 1944.

Honours: Division Two runners-up 1935; FA Cup winners 1923, 1926, 1929; Football League long-service medal 1938;

Charles Foweraker served Bolton Wanderers as secretary and manager for 25 years and was the most successful manager in the club's history. Entering football in 1895, he worked as a gateman and checker at Burnden Park whilst also being employed by the Lancashire & Yorkshire Railway Company. When the Bolton manager Tom Mather was called up to join the Royal Navy in the summer of 1915, Foweraker filled in and guided the club through the war years. He was appointed secretary-manager on a permanent basis in July 1919 and was given a five-year contract worth £400 per annum with annual increase of £25 over that period.

During the 1920s, The Trotters won the FA Cup on three occasions at Wembley. In fact they won the Cup in its inaugural Final at the stadium. The club also went close to the League championship on a number of occasions and with fame and success came travel throughout Europe for the Trotters.

Foweraker was awarded the Football League's long service medal in July 1938 in recognition of more than 21 years service to the Wanderers. He also served as vice-president of the Lancashire FA for many years.

Bolton suffered some lean spells in the early 1930s but Foweraker soon steered them to promotion back to Division One in 1935. He gained a reputation for the way he handled his players in the days when it did not seem so important for a manager to have played the game at a professional level.

After war was declared in September 1939, he worked for the club voluntarily and kept them going during his second spell in charge during the hostilities. Bolton disbanded the playing staff from the summer of 1940 until January 1941, when Foweraker reopened the club. In his final years he discovered and developed one of the greatest players to appear for the Trotters, Nat Lofthouse. In August 1944, Foweraker retired through ill health, having worked for the club for almost 50 years.

FRANCIS, Gerry Charles James
Born: Chiswick, 6 December 1951.
Midfield   5ft 9in; 12st 4lb (1983).
Career: Queen's Park Rangers June 1969; Crystal Palace July 1979 (£465,000); Queen's Park Rangers, February 1981 (£150,000); Coventry City February 1982 (£165,000); Exeter City player-manager June 1983-May 1984; Cardiff City September 1984; Swansea City October 1984; Portsmouth November 1984; Wimbledon player-coach 1985; Bristol Rovers September 1985, then manager July 1987-May 1991 (also director); Queen's Park Rangers manager June 1991.

Honours: England international (12 caps); Under-23 international (6 caps); Division Three champions 1990; Leyland Daf Cup runners-up 1990.

Gerry Francis captained England in eight of his 12 internationals and also made 493 appearances and scored 63 goals in a career which was often dogged by injury. He was only 32 when he became player-manager of Exeter City and experienced a nightmare start to management.

Exeter had one of their worst-ever seasons during his year in charge and finished bottom of the Third Division, with Francis sacked soon afterwards. He had a great deal of success, though, as manager of Bristol Rovers.

In 1989 they lost to Port Vale 2-1 in the final of the Third Division play-offs but were promoted the following season as champions with 93 points. He produced a winning side despite Rovers losing their Eastville ground and the manager having to work from a temporary office at the club's training ground. His sides did not please the purists with their 'up and at them' style, but they got results. After four extraordinary years at Bristol Rovers, Gerry Francis accepted an offer to manage Queen's Park Rangers in the summer of 1991. One of his first actions was to sell England defender Paul Parker to Manchester United for £2 million. With a huge injury list, Rangers struggled initially but ended the season in a comfortable 11th place to enter the newly formed Premier League in 1992.

Queens Park Rangers finished as the top London side in 1992-93, fifth in the Premier League. Francis' future at the club was in some doubt after talk of the possibility of selling his stars Les Ferdinand and Andy Sinton to balance the books. Francis was reluctant to sell, despite pressure from the board. His father, George Francis, played for Brentford.

FRANCIS, Trevor John

Born: Plymouth, 19 April 1954.
Forward   5ft 10in; 11st 7lb (1980).
Career: Plymouth Schools; Birmingham City apprentice June 1969, professional May 1971; Detroit Express (NASL) May-August 1978 and June-August 1979; Nottingham Forest February 1979 (£1.1m); Manchester City September 1981 (£1m); Sampdoria (Italy) July 1982 (£700,000); Atalanta (Bergamo) July 1986 (£800,000); Glasgow Rangers August 1987 (£75,000); Queen's Park Rangers March 1988, then player-manager December 1988-November 1989; Sheffield Wednesday January 1990, then player-manager June 1991.

Honours: England international (52 caps); Under-23 international (5 caps); Youth international; Football League Cup runners-up 1980; Scottish League Cup winners 1988; Italian Cup winners 1985; European Cup winners 1979, 1980. FA Cup runners-up 1993; Football League Cup runners-up 1993.

A striker with acceleration and style in

tight situations, Trevor Francis was very dangerous around the penalty area. He was the first 16-year-old to score four goals in a League match, at Bolton in February 1971, and later became Britain's first £1 million player when moving from Nottingham Forest in February 1979. He also had a great record when playing for Detroit Express, where he scored 36 goals in 33 matches. He had previously scored 128 goals for Birmingham City before his move to Forest.

At Forest, Francis scored the winning goal in the 1979 European Cup victory over Malmö and gained another winners' medal the following year. Amazingly, he did not win his first cap until he was 23. He had some successful years in Italian soccer before returning to Britain to play for Rangers.

Francis had an unhappy spell as player-manager of Queen's Park Rangers, who struggled in the First Division during his time in charge. He tried to be a disciplinarian, which did not really suit his temperament, and the players did not respond. He also received some adverse publicity after fining a player who decided to attend the birth of his first child rather than appear for the first team. It was an error of judgement on Francis' part and he was sacked shortly afterwards.

Francis joined Sheffield Wednesday as a player and they were unlucky to be relegated to the Second Division in 1990. However, they bounced straight back the following season when they finished third. He also helped the club reach the Final of the League Cup where they beat Manchester United 1-0 at Wembley, although he was a non-playing substitute that day. With the departure of Ron Atkinson to Aston Villa, Francis took over as player-manager but his appearances in the first team were now becoming rare. The Owls had an excellent first season under Francis, finishing third in the First Division.

Francis' managerial career took a huge upturn in 1992-93 with the Owls reaching two domestic Finals and finishing in a respectable league position. Sadly, they lost to Arsenal 2-1 in both Finals, the Gunners' negative tactics stifling the Owls' natural attacking skills. The FA Cup Final was especially heart-breaking for Francis when Arsenal scored the winning goal in the last minute of extra-time in a replay.

FRANKLIN, Cornelius F. 'Neil'

Born: Stoke-on-Trent, 24 January 1922.
Centre-half   5ft 11in; 11st 4lb (1950).
Career: Stoke Schools; Stoke Old Boys;

Stoke City amateur 1936, professional January 1939; guest for Gainsborough Trinity in World War Two; Sante Fé (Bogota) May 1950; suspended until February 1951; Hull City February 1951 (£22,500); Crewe Alexandra February 1956 (£1,250); Stockport County October 1957 (£1,250); Macclesfield 1958; Wellington Town player-coach July 1959; Sankeys (Wellington) player-manager July 1960-January 1961 and July 1961-1962; retired December 1962; Apoel (Cyprus) February-November 1963; Colchester United manager November 1963-May 1968; licensee in Oswaldtwistle.

Honours: England international (27 caps); Wartime international (3 caps); 'B' international (2 caps); Football League representative (5 caps); Division Four promotion 1966.

One of the stars of the post war era, Neil Franklin had so much skill that he was probably wasted at centre-half. An excellent header with a superb positional sense, he also had a mastery of the ball. Franklin became dissatisfied with his wages in the Football League and along with other British stars moved to play in Bogata, Colombia, in May 1950. It did not work out and upon his return, Franklin was banned from the game for a while and never represented his country again. Damaged knee ligaments at Hull made it impossible for him to retain his best form.

Franklin had some up and down years as the manager of Colchester United. After relegation to Division Four in 1965, the club bounced straight back the following season in fourth place. He was sacked in May 1968 after another relegation season, United having won only one game from the turn of the year.

FRASER, Douglas Michael

Born: Eaglesham, Renfrewshire 8 December 1941.
Wing-half/Right-back
5ft 10in; 11st 8lb (1964).
Career: Busby Senior School; Rolls-Royce works side; Eaglesham Amateurs; Blantyre Celtic 1956; Aberdeen December 1959; West Bromwich Albion September 1963 (£25,000); Nottingham Forest January 1971 (£35,000); Walsall July 1973, then player-manager January 1974-March 1977 (£8,000); entered the prison service in 1977.

Honours: Scotland international (2 caps); FA Cup winners 1968; Football League Cup winners 1966, runners-up 1967, 1970.

An uncompromising defender, Doug Fraser was a compact player who, despite being a hard tackler, was a stylish player with fine ball control. He had started his career as a centre-forward with Aberdeen but switched to

wing-half and also played at right-back near the end of his career. He played in three Football League Cup Finals for Albion and was also in their 1968 FA Cup Final side which beat Everton.

He made 325 appearances for Albion and another 120 for Forest and Walsall. As well as his two caps for Scotland, Fraser also toured Australia with the Scotland side in 1967. As the manager of Walsall, they were constantly a mid-table Third Division side during his years in control, although they did reach the fifth round of the FA Cup in 1975.

FRASER, George

Born: Edinburgh 1880.
Wing-half   5ft 8¾in; 11st 9lb (1910).
Career: Elgin; Sunderland cs 1899; Lincoln City cs 1901-1910; Lincoln City secretary-manager July 1919-March 1921; Grimsby Town manager March 1921-March 1924.

Fraser made 253 League appearances for the Imps as a wing-half before retiring at the outbreak of World War One. He had been unable to make the Sunderland first team during his time at Roker Park. He was not a success as manager of Lincoln City after the war, the club finishing in 21st place in Division Two and then losing their League place. Grimsby Town finished third in Third Division North at the end of his first season in charge but managed little success after this. The relationship between Fraser and the board became fraught as they did not allow him a free reign in the selection of the side or the acquisition of players and he left in March 1924.

FREEMAN, Reginald Vincent

Born: Birkenhead, 20 December 1897; Died: Wickersley, near Rotherham, 4 August 1955.
Right-back   5ft 10in; 12st 4lb (1933).
Career: Wallasey Rovers; Harrowby; Northern Nomads 1919; Oldham Athletic January 1921; Middlesbrough April 1923 (£4,000); Rotherham United August 1930, then manager January 1934-August 1952; Sheffield United manager August 1952-August 1955.

Honours: Division Two champions 1927, 1929, 1953; Division Three North champions 1951.

Reg Freeman managed Rotherham United for 18 years and Sheffield United for three after making his name as a gentlemanly full-back for Oldham Athletic, Middlesbrough and Rotherham.

He stepped straight from amateur soccer into Oldham Athletic's First

Division side in January 1921, making his debut against Bolton Wanderers at Boundary Park. A stylish, graceful and skilful full-back, Freeman was immediately an automatic choice for Oldham. On 23 April 1923, he moved to Middlesbrough for a £4,000 fee and went on to win two Second Division championship medals at Ayresome Park.

'Boro romped to the title in 1926-27, scoring 122 goals. The star of the side was George Camsell, signed from Durham City, who scored 59 goals that season. They were relegated straight back the following season but won the title again in 1928-29 scoring 105 goals this time.

Freeman joined Rotherham United on 30 August 1930 and he was to give the club 22 years service as a player and manager. Playing at left-back for United Reserves versus Wombwell in December 1931, he scored a second-half hat-trick, the first goal from a free-kick after 65 minutes, followed by two penalties.

He became player-manager on 9 January 1934. The club was £15,000 in the red and threatened with closure. With the help of trainer Andy Smailes and secretary Billy Heald, he piloted the club away from their dark and penniless days and although he could not prevent Rotherham having to seek re-election in 1933-34, when they finished 21st, the following year they finished in the top half of the Northern Section for the first time in eleven years. They managed to beat Sheffield Wednesday 1-0 to win the County Cup Final. After a couple of seasons of struggle, United finished sixth in 1937-38.

In the years up to World War Two, Reg Freeman brought about a consistency not seen before at Millmoor. He rarely changed the side unless forced to; and he signed a number of excellent players in this period including goalscorer Arnie Bromham and Dick Duckworth who later become a manager.

During the war years, United joined the Northern Regional League and Freeman made a great discovery in Wally Ardron, who went on to score prolifically throughout the war. After the war, Rotherham were unfortunate to be runners-up in the Northern Section three seasons on the trot when only the champions were promoted. Promotion to Division Two was achieved at last in 1951 and Freeman reaped the rewards for all his hard work.

He enjoyed a very settled side throughout the season as Rotherham broke records galore. They obtained 71 points in all, 36 away from home, and lost only twice all season. In 1951-52 they finished in a respectable ninth

position but Freeman left for Bramall Lane in August 1952.

Sheffield United won the Second Division championship at the end of his first season in charge. They hit the top of the table in November 1952 and stayed there for the rest of the season. The strength of the side was in attack. In the next two seasons, though, the Blades struggled in the First Division and finished bottom in 1954-55. Freeman was still their manager when he died.

FRITH, William

Born: Sheffield, 9 June 1912.
Half-back   5ft 9in; 11st 6lb (1935).
Career: Worksop Town 1929; Mansfield Town April 1930; Chesterfield May 1931; Coventry City May 1932; guest for Leicester City in World War Two; Port Vale player-manager August 1945-October 1946; Coventry City manager February 1947-November 1948; Stafford Rangers manager August 1948-May 1950; Rugby Town manager; Chelmsford City manager; Coventry City manager again September 1957-November 1961; Hinckley Athletic manager June 1965; Chesterfield scout in 1980.
Honours: Division Three South champions 1936; Division Four runners-up 1959.

Billy Frith joined Midland League club Worksop at the age of 17 and was soon a regular in the first team. Frith was an inside-right when he moved to Coventry City and was converted to right-half. He came from a footballing family with his grandfather being the trainer of Sheffield Wednesday and his father playing at full-back for Rotherham and Rochdale.

He had two spells as manager of Coventry City. They finished tenth in Division Two in his first spell and were struggling in the Third North when he returned in 1957. They entered the newly-formed Fourth Division but gained promotion to the Third as runners-up in 1958-59. He was replaced by Jimmy Hill after a mediocre season in 1960-61. Later he worked as a PE teacher in Coventry from 1961 to 1977.

FRIZZELL, James Letson

Born: Greenock, 16 February 1937.
Utility   5ft 9in; 11st 10lb (1963).

Career: Largs Thistle; Morton 1955; Oldham Athletic May 1960 (£1,500), coach September 1968, then manager December 1969-June 1982; Manchester City assistant manager July 1983, manager October 1986-May 1987, when he became general manager for a while.
Honours: Division Three champions

1974; Division Four promotion 1971.
Jimmy Frizzell spent 22 years at Boundary Park as player, coach and manager. Originally an inside-right, scoring 24 goals in 1961-62, he later played at wing-half and full-back. Frizzell became the club coach in 1968 and took over as caretaker manager in December 1969 and was permanently appointed in March 1970.

He took Oldham to promotion to Division Three in 1971, when they also won the Ford Sporting League and with it, £70,000. A new stand was built with the prize money.

Oldham made steady progress and were Third Division champions in 1973-74, but with the club maintaining their Second Division status he was surprisingly sacked in June 1982, after he had laid the foundations for future successes at Boundary Park. He was the second-longest serving manager in the League at this time. A year out of work ended when he was appointed assistant at Maine Road to Billy McNeil. Frizzell took over himself when McNeil moved to Aston Villa.

FRY, Barry F.

Born: Bedford, 7 April 1945.
Inside-forward
Career: Manchester United April 1962; Bolton Wanderers May 1964; Luton Town July 1965; Gravesend & Northfleet; Orient December 1966; Romford 1968; Bedford Town July 1969-May 1972; Dunstable manager until September 1976; Hillingdon Borough manager September 1976-August 1977; Bedford Town manager August 1977-August 1978; Barnet manager August 1978-January 1985; Maidstone United manager January 1985-July 1986; Barnet manager again July 1986-April 1993; Southend United manager April 1993.
Honours: England Schoolboy international; Vauxhall Conference League champions 1991.

Barry Fry never made the grade at Old Trafford and only had a handful of appearances at his other League clubs. A tricky attacking midfield player, Fry had more success in non-League soccer and was a legend at Bedford Town for his over-elaborate free kicks. He took Dunstable to runners-up position in the Southern League North in 1974-75 but has had most success at Barnet.

Under Fry, they developed from a side struggling for existence to a club with very good attendances, a steady stream of talented players and entry into the Football League. After finishing runners-up in the Conference League three seasons out of four, Fry finally achieved his ultimate desire when the club won the title in 1990-91 to enter the Fourth Division. In their first season they led the table for a long time but dropped away to enter the play-offs where they lost to Blackpool. This ended with a bust-up with chairman Stan Flashman and Fry's resignation, although he was soon reinstated. Fry has sold a number of useful players to League clubs, including Andy Clarke to Wimbledon.

Fry and Flashman clashed again when Barnet were brought before an FA commission for keeping their books incorrectly in November 1992. The club received a heavy fine and Fry and the club's supporters became very critical about the way that Flashman was running the club. Fry was sacked yet again but reinstated after a week. Despite all of the internal problems Barnet continued to do well on the pitch. In April 1993, Fry moved on to manage Southend.

FUCCILLO, Pasquale 'Lil'

Born: Bedford, 2 May 1956.
Midfield   5ft 9in; 11st 4lb (1982).
Career: Luton Town July 1974; Tulsa Roughnecks (NASL) April 1983; Southend United December 1983; Peterborough United August 1985; Cambridge United January 1988; Peterborough United assistant manager January 1991, then manager December 1992.
Honours: Division Two champions 1982.

Son of Italian parents who settled in Bedford, 'Lil' Fuccillo was a hardworking and skilful midfield player who liked to join the attack and score goals. He broke his leg when only 19, playing for Luton at Brighton, and did not appear at all in 1979-80 due to injury.

He scored 24 goals in 153/7 League appearances for Luton and helped the Hatters to the Second Division championship in 1981-82, when they finished eight points clear of their great rivals, Watford. Fuccillo was appointed assistant manager at Peterborough United shortly after Chris Turner was employed as manager. When Turner was part of a consortium which took over the Posh, Fuccillo was appointed the new manager as Turner took over as chairman. Peterborough United finished tenth, their highest ever position, in the Football League in 1992-93.

FURNISS, Lawrence

Forward.
Career: Gorton until a knee injury ended his career; Manchester City manager 1889-1893, director 1903-1905 and 1915-1921, chairman 1921-1928, later club president; possibly Chesterfield secretary 1906-1907.

Lawrence Furness was involved in the formation of Gorton FC when two clubs in the town amalgamated in 1883. A serious knee injury ended his playing career. He was involved in Ardwick's early formation and growth and their later transformation into Manchester City. He was the man who brought Billy Meredith to the club after spotting him play for Northwich when refereeing a match involving the club. Furness signed a number of players from Scotland during his spell as manager at Hyde Road. He was possibly the secretary of Chesterfield after being a director at City.

FURPHY, Kenneth

Born: Stockton, 28 May 1931.
Wing-half   5ft 10½in; 11st (1959).
Career: Everton November 1950; Runcorn December 1951; Darlington August 1953, player-youth-team coach in late 1950s, retired 1965; FA staff coach 1963; Workington player-manager July 1962-November 1964; Watford player-manager November 1964-August 1971; Blackburn Rovers manager August 1971-December 1973; Sheffield United manager December 1973-October 1975; New York Cosmos (NASL) coach January 1976; Detroit Express (NASL) coach 1978-1980; Washington Diplomats (NASL) coach 1981.
Honours: Division Three champions 1969; Division Four promotion 1964; NASL Soccer Bowl winners 1977.

Ken Furphy never made the grade at Goodison Park before going into the Cheshire League with Runcorn. Darlington spotted his potential and signed him as a professional in August 1953.

Furphy became one of the youngest

player-managers in the Football League when he took charge at Workington, being only 31. He took the club to promotion in 1962-63 and to fourth in Division Three the following season. He transferred himself to Watford to work in a similar capacity and became known as one of the new brand of 'tracksuit' managers. He took Watford to the Third Division championship in 1969 and to the semi-final of the FA Cup in 1970 after a quarter-final victory over mighty Liverpool at Vicarage Road.

His reward was a higher-paid job at Ewood Park. Furphy had to go down a division to join Blackburn and undertook a massive rebuilding programme, but success did not come until after he left the club. He had an indifferent spell at Bramall Lane and was sacked in October 1975.

Next, he managed New York Cosmos, where he signed Chinaglia to team up with Pelé. Cosmos won the Soccer Bowl in 1977, beating Seattle Sounders 2-1 in the Final. He moved to manage Washington Diplomats when Detroit Express folded. In recent years Furphy has worked for local radio in the West Country.

GALBRAITH, Walter McMurray

Born: Glasgow, 26 May 1918.
Left-back   5ft 9½in; 11st 4lb (1950).
Career: Strathclyde Juniors; Clyde 1939; Queen's Park 1941; guest for Glasgow Rangers in World War Two; Clyde 1945; New Brighton September 1948, then player-manager August 1950-August 1951; Grimsby Town August 1951; Accrington Stanley player-manager June 1953-August 1958, retired as a player May 1954; Bradford manager November 1958-January 1961; Tranmere Rovers manager January-December 1961; Hibernian manager December 1961-March 1964; Bradford general manager 1965-March 1967; Stockport County chief scout July 1968, then trainer-coach, then manager March 1969-April 1970.

Walter Galbraith spent most of his managerial career in the lower reaches of the Football League and was in charge at three clubs which have since gone out of business. That is not to say that this had anything to do with him, rather that he enjoyed an impossible challenge.

He became the player-manager at New Brighton in August 1950 and lasted just a year with the club who failed to gain re-election and were replaced by Workington. The Rakers went 17 games without a win during that season. After a spell playing for Grimsby Town, Galbraith became manager of Accrington Stanley. This

coincided with one of the best spells in their history. They were twice runners-up and twice third in the Third Division North in the next five seasons. He had a policy of recruiting players from Scotland and earned the tag of 'Mr McStanley'.

At Park Avenue, he stopped the rot after Bradford had five managers in six seasons and the club improved their position in the newly-formed Fourth Division.

His next move was to Tranmere Rovers for an 11-month spell in charge, but he could not prevent their relegation to Division Four and soon received a better offer to manage Hibernian. Galbraith discovered some fine players for the Edinburgh club, including Neil Martin, John Parke and Willie Hamilton, who were later sold for substantial fees to English clubs. It is estimated that this long-striding and pleasant soccer assessor, groomed and sold almost £300,000 worth of talent in his career.

GIBBONS, Albert Henry 'Jackie'

Born: Fulham, 10 April 1914.
Centre-forward
Career: RAF; Hayes; Kingstonian; Tottenham Hotspur amateur July 1937; Brentford amateur August 1938; Tottenham Hotspur; Bradford amateur 1945, professional May 1946; Brentford August 1947, then manager February 1949-August 1952; later coached in Israel, Belgium and South Africa.
Honours: England Amateur international; Wartime international (1 cap); FA tour to South Africa 1939 (2 caps).
Jackie Gibbons represented the Royal Air Force on a number of occasions and also appeared for Hayes and Kingstonian. He signed amateur forms with Spurs in 1937 and scored 18 goals in 33 appearances, including five in their FA Cup run to the quarter-finals in 1938. Gibbons moved to Brentford in the summer of 1938 and made 11 appearances for the Bees, scoring one goal, before the war broke out. He then played mostly for Spurs, scoring 91 goals in 115 games in the regional competitions.

Upon leaving the RAF, Gibbons turned professional for Bradford after the war and then moved to Brentford in August 1947. He finished his first season at Griffin Park as leading scorer with 13 goals and replaced the long-serving Harry Curtis as manager in February 1949, combining this task with the equally difficult one of trying to inject punch into the attack. Brentford remained a mid-table Second Division side during his three and a half years in charge.

GIBSON, Alex

Career: Preston North End manager cs 1927-April 1931.
Alex Gibson's best year in charge at Deepdale was his first when the club finished fourth in the Second Division, scoring 100 goals. They blew their chances of promotion over Easter with two defeats including a 6-2 reverse against Notts County. This was followed by three seasons of mediocrity and limited Cup success. His actions over the use of Alec James led to the player's discontent with the club, when he decided to play James in a League match rather than release him to play for Scotland. He was soon sold for a record fee to Arsenal, for £8,000 in June 1929. If Gibson had been a little more shrewd, he would have probably got more for the Scottish star. He left Deepdale with Preston feeling gloomy about their prolonged stay in Division Two.

GILES, Michael John

Born: Cabra, Dublin, 6 January 1940.
Midfield   5ft 6in; 11st 2lb (1964).
Career: St Columbus; Dublin Schools; Dublin City; The Leprechauns; Stella Maris; Home Farm 1954; Manchester United amateur July 1956, professional November 1957; Leeds United August 1963 (£37,500); West Bromwich Albion (£48,000), then player-manager July 1975-May 1977; Philadelphia Fury (NASL) January-August 1978; Shamrock Rovers player-manager June 1977-February 1983, executive director July 1977; Republic of Ireland manager December 1977-April 1980; Vancouver Whitecaps (NASL) general manager and coach November 1980-December 1983; West Bromwich Albion manager February 1984-September 1985.
Honours: Republic of Ireland international (60 caps); Schoolboy international; Football League champions 1969, 1974; Division Two champions 1964, promotion 1976; FA Cup winners 1963, 1972, runners-up 1970, 1973; Football League Cup winners 1968; Inter-Cities Fairs Cup winners 1968, 1971, runners-up 1967; European Cup runners-up 1975; FA of Ireland Cup winners 1978.

One of the most complete midfield players of the era in which he played, Johnny Giles' patience, guile and hidden aggression, linked with excellent positional play, made him a wonderful player for his colleagues. He was always there to help them out of trouble and was almost impossible to dispossess. With his superb passing

ability and one-touch play, it was inevitable that he would become one of the most-capped players for the Republic of Ireland.

Giles scored many vital goals for Leeds after joining them for a bargain fee of £37,500 from Manchester United. He went on to score 115 goals in 521/4 games for the Elland Road club. He played in 11 FA Cup semi-finals in his career, a record, and gained two winners' medals and two losers' medals. His last game for Leeds was in the 1975 European Cup Final, the last of many medals he won with the club.

After he joined West Brom as player-manager, the Throstles won promotion to Division One after finishing third in 1975-76. He then helped to establish them as a First Division club. In 1977, Giles bought a part-share in Shamrock Rovers and became their executive director and player-manager. He also ran the national side at the same time. His second spell at The Hawthorns was not so successful and he left with the team near the bottom of the First Division. In recent years, Giles has become a successful businessman and journalist.

GILLIES, Gilbert

Born: Scotland
Career: Chesterfield manager in 1890s; Leeds City manager March 1905-May 1908; Bradford manager May 1908-February 1911; Was running a hotel in Matlock in 1914.

As secretary-manager of Chesterfield, Gillies helped the club into the Football League and consolidated them in the Second Division. He got the job at Leeds City from 100 applicants and became their first manager, on 16 March 1905. He was working as a journalist at the time. Gillies had exceptional organisational abilities and was not scared to experiment with his line-ups. However, when his contract expired it was not renewed and he immediately moved to Bradford as manager. The Park Avenue club were a mid-table Second Division side in his three seasons with them.

GILLIES, Matt Muirhead

Born: Loganlea, 12 August 1921.
Centre-half.
Career: Motherwell amateur; RAF Weaton; Bolton Wanderers October 1942; guest for Arsenal, Queen's Park Rangers and Chelsea in World War Two; Leicester City January 1952 (£10,000), retired April 1956 to become coach, then manager November 1958-December 1968; Nottingham Forest manager January 1969-October 1972.
Honours: Division Two champions 1954; FA Cup runners-up 1961, 1963; Football League Cup winners 1964, runners-up 1965.

Matt Gillies won his reputation as the manager of Leicester City in the 1960s, transforming the fortunes of the Filbert Street club by finding just the right blend of personality, temperament and skill.

Gillies had decided on a medical career but war ended his studies in 1939. He joined RAF Bomber Command as a navigator and also played soccer for his unit. In 1942, when stationed at RAF Weaton, he signed for nearby Bolton Wanderers, having previously been on Motherwell's books as an amateur. During the war he also guested for Arsenal, QPR and Chelsea.

In January 1952, after 145 League appearances for the Trotters, Gillies moved to Leicester City, for a £10,000 fee, to bolster their central defensive positions. He had a steadying influence on the defence, using thoughtful but solid play to good advantage. He won a Second Division championship medal in 1953-54 and retired two years later, after 111 appearances for City.

His original aim was to become a physiotherapist but he was appointed as a coach at Filbert Street instead. He became caretaker manager in November 1958, when David Halliday resigned, and was given full managerial duties on a permanent basis in January 1959.

An intelligent man, Gillies' deep thinking about the game produced sides to play to his own concept of soccer. After two seasons of mediocrity, City turned the corner in 1961 when they finished sixth in Division One and reached the FA Cup Final, only to lose to double-chasing Spurs. When his team slumped the following season, Gillies blamed it on that Cup Final defeat. Things changed for the better when Hibernian's reserve Dave Gibson was signed, along with striker Mike Stringfellow from Mansfield Town, for a combined fee of £50,000. They made all the difference and Leicester again reached the FA Cup Final in 1963, this time losing to Manchester United. Gillies also developed players such as Gordon Banks, Graham Cross, Colin Appleton and Frank McLintock.

Because Spurs had also won the League title, City played in the European Cup-winners' Cup in 1961-62 and reached yet another Cup Final in 1964, when they beat Stoke City 4-3 on aggregate in the League Cup. Twelve months later they were in the Final again, this time being beaten on aggregate by Chelsea.

Gillies, who became a JP whilst in office at Filbert Street, won a reputation over his dealings on the transfer market but suffered ill health due to stress towards the end of his period as manager. After breaking the British transfer record to sign Allan Clarke from Fulham for £150,000, he resigned in December 1968, shortly after his trusted coach, Bert Johnson, had been sacked.

Gillies was out of work for only a short period and the following month he was appointed manager of Nottingham Forest. However, over the next three and a half seasons at the City Ground he enjoyed little success. Forest finished in the bottom half of Division One in each of his seasons before being relegated in 1972. The Reds also had no success in Cup competitions. After a poor start to the 1972-73 season, with

Gillies being booed by the fans, and the club in the lower reaches of the Second Division, he was sacked and turned his back on the game after this bitter blow.

GILLOW, Wilfred Bernard

Born: Preston, 8 July 1892; Died: 12 March 1944.
Right-half   5ft 8in; 10st 7lb (1919).
Career: Lancaster Town; Preston North End; Fleetwood; Blackpool 1912; Preston North End 1914; Grimsby Town February 1920; Lancaster Town cs 1922; Grimsby Town May 1923, then player-manager June 1924-April 1932; Middlesbrough manager March 1934-March 1944.

Honours: Division Two runners-up 1929; Division Three North champions 1926.

A capable, skilled, ball player who also appeared occasionally at inside-right, Wilf Gillow was also a good cricketer and was on Lancashire's books just after World War One. He also played for Middlesbrough in the North Yorkshire League. Gillow made just under 200 Football League appearances before retiring and built the foundations for future success at Blundell Park. When he took over, the Mariners were a moderately placed Third Division North side. Five years later they were in the First Division.

He liked to develop the skills of the players but had to sell them regularly to balance the books. A quietly spoken pipe smoker, Gillow was firm but fair and respected by the players. He found life in Division One a struggle, however, and resigned in April 1932 but remained in office until the end of the season when Grimsby Town were relegated.

Two years later, Gillow joined Middlesbrough as manager. They were on the point of great things when the war came along and in 1938-39 had finished fourth in the First Division. Gillow was too old for active service and so worked in Middlesbrough Council's treasury department during the day and for 'Boro part-time in the evening and at weekends. He died whilst still in office.

GODFREY, Brian Cameron

Born: Flint, 1 May 1940.
Inside-forward 5ft 8in; 10st 2lb (1964).
Career: Flint Alexandra 1955; Everton amateur June 1957, professional May 1958; Scunthorpe United June 1960; Preston North End October 1963 (£8,000); Aston Villa September 1967; Bristol Rovers May 1971; Newport County June 1973 (£10,000); Portland Timbers (NASL) March 1975-1976, retired May 1976; Bath City manager 1976-1979; Exeter City manager January 1979-June 1983; Weymouth manager 1983-1987; Gloucester City manager cs 1987.

Honours: Wales international (3 caps); Under-23 international (1 cap); Football League Cup runners-up 1971; Southern League champions 1978; Southern League Midland Division champions 1989.

Brian Godfrey played in Villa's Football League Cup Final defeat against Spurs at Wembley in 1971. He made only one appearance for Everton before joining Scunthorpe United but made over 100 appearances each for Preston, Villa and Newport and also scored 128 goals in a career total of 544/8 League games for his six clubs. He was bitterly disappointed to miss Preston's FA Cup Final appearance in 1964.

As manager of Bath City, Godfrey took the club to the Southern League championship in 1977-78. Exeter City finished eighth and ninth in his first two seasons at the club and also reached the sixth round of the FA Cup for only the second time in their history in 1981. He quit with a year of his contract still to go. Weymouth finished fifth in the Conference in 1985-86 with Godfrey in charge, but he left in the summer of 1987 when they finished in a lowly position. Recently, Godfrey has brought about something of a revival at Gloucester City. After winning the Midland Division of the Southern League in 1988-89, with 92 points, they finished in a respectable ninth position in the Premier Division the following season.

GOLAC, Ivan

Born: Yugoslavia, 15 June 1950
Right-back   5ft 10in; 12st 10lb (1980).
Career: Partizan Belgrade; Southampton November 1978 (£50,000); Bournemouth & Boscombe Athletic November 1982; Manchester City (loan) March 1983; Bjelascia (Yugoslavia) 1983; Southampton March 1984-1986; Portsmouth (loan) January 1985; Torquay United manager February-May 1992.

Honours: Yugoslavia international; Football League Cup runners-up 1979.

Golac had a short and unhappy spell as manager of Torquay United in the second half of the 1991-92 season, being unable to prevent their relegation to Division Four. In May 1992 he was replaced by the club's youth development officer Paul Compton, Torquay's fifth manager in a year. Golac had to wait until he was 28 before he could leave Yugoslavia to play in the West.

He joined Southampton and proved one of the most successful soccer imports. A hard tackler who liked to attack, his swashbuckling style made him very popular at The Dell. He played in the Saints' Football League Cup Final side which lost 3-2 to Nottingham Forest at Wembley. A disagreement over terms led to his departure to Bournemouth but he returned to The Dell, helping the club to runners-up spot in Division One in 1983-84. He made 167/1 appearances for the Saints, scoring four goals.

GOODALL, Frederick Roy

Born: Dronfield, Derbyshire, 31 December 1902; Died: Huddersfield, 19 January 1982.
Right-back   5ft 11½in; 12st 5lb (1935).
Career: Dronfield Grammar School; Dronfield Woodhouse; Huddersfield Town 1921 (£20); Nottingham Forest training staff May 1937-1944; Mansfield Town manager August 1945-June 1949; Huddersfield Town training staff August 1949 and youth-team manager October 1964-July 1965.

Honours: England international (25 caps); Football League representative (8 caps); Football League champions 1924, 1925, 1926; FA Cup runners-up 1928, 1930.

Roy Goodall formed an excellent full-back partnership with Sam Wadsworth at Huddersfield Town. A master of positional tactics and with a magnificent first-time tackle, Goodall was the England skipper in his later international appearances. He was discovered by Ambrose Langley whilst playing for his home-town club and gave up his accountancy studies to become a footballer. He was a member of the Huddersfield side which won three League championships on the trot and was runners-up the two following seasons.

During the war he served in the Army as a company quartermaster and was an instructor at a local hospital when appointed manager of Mansfield. They had their worst-ever season in his first campaign in charge, finishing bottom of the Third Division South with only 28 points. The following season they joined the Northern Section and finished eighth. In 1949, Goodall returned to his first love Huddersfield Town and stayed there to the mid-1960s.

GOODFELLOW, James

Born: Bishop Auckland, 16 September 1943.
Forward   5ft 8in; 10st 7lb (1974).
Career: Crook Town; Bishop Auckland; Port Vale June 1966; Workington July 1969; Rotherham United January 1974; Stockport County August 1978; Newport County assistant manager until November 1981; Cardiff City assistant manager July 1982, then manager March-September 1984, returned as physiotherapist 1986.

Honours: FA Amateur Cup winners 1964.

Jimmy Goodfellow had won a reputation as a goalscorer with Bishop Auckland when he was signed by Port Vale in 1966 but was converted into a more defensive role at Vale Park. He made almost 200 appearances for Workington and Rotherham United and altogether made 470/9 League appearances, scoring 34 goals in his career. He was assistant manager to Len Ashurst at Newport and followed him to Cardiff City in 1982. Goodfellow was made caretaker manager after Ashurst's departure in 1984 and had a very short period officially in charge at the club at the start of 1984-85. With little backing from the board of directors he was eventually replaced by Alan Durban. Two years later Goodfellow returned to Ninian Park as physiotherapist.

GOODIER, Edward

Born: Farnworth, Lancs, 15 October 1902; Died: Farnworth 4 November 1967.
Half-back   6ft 1in; 12st 8lb (1935).
Career: Brookhouse United; Huddersfield Town May 1922; Lancaster Town cs 1923; Oldham Athletic June 1925; Queen's Park Rangers November 1931; Watford June 1935 (£1,000); Crewe Alexandra June 1936; Rochdale June 1937, then player-manager September 1938-June 1952; Birmingham caretaker manager November 1944-May 1945; Wigan Athletic manager June 1952-1954; Oldham Athletic manager May 1956-June 1958.

A tall fair-haired wing-half who spent a long time in reserve-team soccer before becoming a first-team regular at Oldham, Ted Goodier left Boundary Park after a row over benefit payments and joined Queen's Park Rangers. He had a lengthy spell at Rochdale, helping the club to find its feet during his 14 years in charge. They won the Lancashire Senior Cup in 1949, beating Blackpool 1-0 in the Final at Oldham.

A legendary figure on the transfer market, he knew a good player when he saw one. He had a six-month spell in charge at St Andrew's in the war years, before Birmingham added the 'City' tag. At Wigan, his side held mighty Newcastle United 2-2 at St James' Park in the FA Cup in 1954. In 1956, Goodier moved back into Football League management with Oldham Athletic, but he did not have a happy time at Boundary Park and left after the club entered the newly-formed Fourth Division.

GOODMAN, Edmund F.

Born: Birmingham, 8 October 1873.
Career: Aston Villa Reserves, retired after losing his leg after a football accident; Aston Villa assistant secretary until 1905; Crystal Palace secretary 1905, secretary-manager April 1907-November 1925, then secretary again until May 1933; ran grocery store in Anerley from 1933.

Honours: Division Three South champions 1921.

Goodman was a promising reserve with Aston Villa when he broke his leg and when complications set in, he had to have the limb amputated. He was only 19 at the time. He joined Villa's office staff in 1892 and gradually rose to become assistant secretary. Joining the newly-formed Crystal Palace as secretary in 1905, two years later he also took charge of the team.

Palace narrowly missed the Southern League championship in 1913-14, finishing behind Swindon Town on goal-average, but were the first champions of the newly-formed Third Division. However, they were relegated in 1925 after several poor seasons. Results did not improve much and Goodman reverted to secretarial duties only. He had a far-reaching effect on Palace's progress and the club played at four different grounds during his time with them. He supervised many improvements at Selhurst Park, including a new gymnasium and players' recreation room.

GOODWIN, Frederick J.

Born: Heywood, Lancashire, 28 June 1933.
Wing-half   6ft 1½in; 13st 4lb (1966).

Career: Chorlton County Secondary Schools; Manchester United October 1953; Leeds United March 1960; Scunthorpe United player-manager December 1964-October 1967, retired as a player 1966; New York Generals coach November 1967-October 1968; Brighton & Hove Albion manager October 1968-May 1970; Birmingham City manager June 1970-September 1975; Minnesota Kicks (NASL) coach 1976-1979 and 1980-1981; also cricket for Lancashire.

Honours: Division Two runners-up 1972.

One of the Busby Babes, Freddie Goodwin was a reserve at Old Trafford until after the Munich air disaster in 1958. He played in that year's FA Cup Final, which was lost to Bolton 2-0. His Leeds United career ended with a triple fracture of his leg, although he made a brief comeback with Scunthorpe. He was also a fine cricketer and played 11 first-class matches for Lancashire, taking 27 wickets.

At Scunthorpe, he discovered Ray Clemence before moving to manage New York Generals in the USA. It was a unique post as he was the manager of a team which did not exist and did not have a ground. He was given an air ticket to travel the world in search of a team.

In 1968, he returned to England to manage Brighton. After two good seasons at the Goldstone, Goodwin accepted a offer to manage Birmingham City. He took the Blues into the First Division in 1972 and to two losing FA Cup semi-finals, in 1973 and 1975. Goodwin was full of new ideas and introduced yoga, psychological tests and a variety of new training techniques at St Andrew's. He also introduced Trevor Francis to League football.

Goodwin switched players around and also implemented new tactics and formations. but Birmingham constantly struggled against relegation and he finally lost his job five months after they went down to Fulham in the semi-final of the FA Cup. He returned to the United States to coach Minnesota Kicks and in the 1980s recruited players for the American Major Indoor Soccer League.

GORDON, David S.

Born: Leith 1883.
Left-half   5ft 9in; 12st (1910).
Career: Leith Athletic; Hull City June 1905; Leith Athletic again 1914; Hibernian secretary-manager 1919-1922; Hartlepools United manager July 1922-cs 1924; St Bernard's manager 1924-c.1930.

Feared by many a forward for his grim 'never-say-die' persistence, Gordon played 275 games for Hull City, winning a reputation as a very consistent player. He had a brother who played for Middlesbrough Ironopolis and Preston and another was on Hull's books but did not make the first team. Hibernian did not achieve much with Gordon in charge and although they managed to finish sixth in the table in 1921-22, they had a poor record in the Cup.

He moved south to take control at Hartlepools United but they failed to win an away match in 1922-23 and had to seek re-election at the end of the following season. Hartlepools lost a great deal of money as they employed far too many professionals for the attendances they attracted.

GORE, Leslie F.

Born: Coventry 1914; Died: Coventry, 21 January 1991.
Right winger   5ft 7in; 11st 7lb (1935).
Career: Morris Motors Works (Birmingham); Fulham June 1933; Stockport County July 1936; Carlisle United 1937; Bradford City February 1938; Clapton Orient May 1939, retired in war; Yeovil player-coach 1946; Gillingham; Gravesend & Northfleet August 1949; Leyton Orient trainer 1951-November 1966 and caretaker manager February-April 1956, August 1957-March 1958, February 1959-May 1961, September-November 1963, December 1964-January 1965 and January-June 1966; Charlton Athletic scout until his death.

Les Gore was caretaker manager of Leyton Orient on no less than six occasions. He moved to Yeovil in 1946, where he teamed up with Alex Stock, whom Gore had played alongside in wartime soccer for Orient. Stock appointed him assistant trainer at Brisbane Road in 1951 and he became head trainer in 1954. His first spell as

caretaker manager was in January 1956, for just 53 days when Alec Stock, Orient's manager, went to Highbury as assistant manager but did not like it so returned to Brisbane Road. His second spell in charge came from the close season of 1957 until February 1958 when Stock moved to Italy to manage AS Roma.

The third spell was from March 1959 until the summer of 1961, between the resignation of Stock and the appointment of Johnny Carey as manager. When Carey resigned in the summer of 1963, Gore was caretaker again until the arrival of Benny Fenton in November. His fifth spell came between the sacking of Fenton in December 1964 and the appointment of Dave Sexton a month later; and his sixth and final spell in charge came from January to June 1966 between the resignation of Sexton and the arrival of Dick Graham. Gore was dismissed in November 1966 after a disagreement with Graham and possibly also due to Orient's perilous financial state. He joined Charlton Athletic as a scout soon afterwards and worked for them until his death.

GOSNELL, Albert Arthur

Born: Colchester, 10 February 1880; Died: Norwich, 30 Janaury 1972.
Outside-left   5ft 11in; 12st 3lb (1910).
Career: The Albion (Colchester) cs 1898; Colchester Town; Essex County; New Brompton cs 1901; Chatham cs 1902; Newcastle United May 1904; Tottenham Hotspur cs 1910; Darlington cs 1911; Port Vale c.1912; Newcastle United staff 1919, Norwich City manager January 1921-February 1926; Colchester Town coach cs 1926; later publican in Norwich.

Honours: England international (1 cap); Football League champions 1905, 1907; FA Cup runners-up 1905, 1906.

Tall for a left winger but very lively and a possessor of an excellent shot, Gosnell was never a regular at Gallowgate and had to compete with the skills of Scot Bobby Templeton. He often got the bird from the fans as his passing ability was not his strong point and he was eventually driven away from the club by the crowd. He had appeared in 124 games for United, scoring 17 goals, and managed to gain two League championship medals and two FA Cup losers' medals. His England cap was against Ireland in Belfast, a game which England won 5-0.

He took control at Norwich City just after they had joined the League but had very limited success although the club had a whole host of colourful characters in the side. The Canaries had massive financial problems at this time and Gosnell had to ask the fans to help the club out of their predicament. Things seemed, at long last, to be getting better when Gosnell left the club in 1926.

GOSS, George

Career: Royal Navy 1916-1921; Southampton assistant secretary 1921-May 1936, secretary-manager May 1936-March 1937; ran pub in St Denys 1938; rejoined Navy in war and took command of a mine sweeper in 1939; emigrated to Australia.

Goss served in the Royal Navy in World War One and played for Naval sides from 1916 until he left the services to join the staff at The Dell as assistant secretary in 1921. When the incumbent secretary retired, Goss succeeded him. He served three managers and when George Kay resigned at the end of

1935-36, he took on the job of manager and secretary. He was, in reality, the caretaker until Tom Parker came to manage the Saints in March 1937. Goss left in the summer of 1937 to run the Railway Hotel at St Denys. In 1939 he took command of a minesweeper and later emigrated to Australia.

GOULD, Robert Anthony

Born: Coventry, 12 June 1946.
Forward   5ft 10in; 11st 5lb (1974).

Career: Coventry Schools; Coventry City apprentice July 1962, professional June 1964; Arsenal February 1968 (£90,000); Wolverhampton Wanderers June 1970 (£55,000); West Bromwich Albion September 1971 (£60,000); Bristol City December 1972 (£69,000); West Ham United November 1973 (£70,000); Wolverhampton Wanderers December 1975 (£30,000); Bristol Rovers player-coach October 1977 (£10,000); Aalsund (Norway) coach 1977-1978; Hereford United player-coach September 1978 (£10,000); Charlton Athletic coach 1979; Chelsea assistant manager October 1979; Wimbledon coach August 1981; Aldershot coach September-October 1981; Bristol Rovers manager October 1981-May 1983; Coventry City manager May 1983-January 1985; TV presenter January-May 1985; Bristol Rovers manager May 1985-July 1987; Wimbledon manager July 1987-May 1990; Queen's Park Rangers coach December 1990; West Bromwich Albion manager February 1991-May 1992; Coventry City manager July 1992.

Honours: Division Two champions 1967, 1977; FA Cup winners 1988; Football League Cup runners-up 1969.

A great-hearted competitor and much-travelled striker, Bobby Gould had the ability to make and score goals and his unselfish running created many chances for his teammates at his various clubs. Gould appeared in the Arsenal side which sensationally lost to Third Division Swindon Town in the League Cup Final in 1969 and had previously been a member of Coventry's side which won promotion to Division One in 1967. Gould was unfortunate to miss out on a place in West Ham's 1975 FA Cup Final side after playing in the semi-final. He scored 160 goals in 408/31 League appearances in his career.

He began his coaching career at Bristol Rovers in 1977 and became manager at Eastville four years later. He recruited star names such as Mick Channon and Alan Ball, who were near the end of their careers but stimulated interest in the club. Gould impressed at Eastville and was offered the post of manager at First Division Coventry City, one of his many former clubs.

He made massive changes in the playing staff at Highfield Road and completely reconstructed the side. Another spell at Bristol Rovers was followed by his greatest moments, at Wimbledon. The Dons beat mighty Liverpool 1-0 in the 1987 FA Cup Final with a goal from Lawrie Sanchez and a penalty save by Dave Beasant. Gould surprisingly resigned in January 1990 and was unable to work again until his contract ran out 11 months later.

Then he took over at The Hawthorns after Albion had suffered a humiliating FA Cup defeat at the hands of non-League Woking. Gould could not prevent Albion from being relegated to the Third Division for the first time in their history in May 1991. The following season, Albion looked promotion candidates until March but, after winning just three of their last 13 games, they finished seventh. Gould had become very unpopular with the fans who hated the long-ball game that he had introduced to the club. He was sacked and chairman John Silk also resigned. He was hated so much by the fans that when he turned up at the Hawthorns as a match commentator for Sky TV he was advised to stay away from the ground as it was felt that his presence could cause crowd problems.

Within a couple of weeks of his departure from the Hawthorns, Gould was appointed joint manager of Coventry City with Don Howe. Howe soon left for Chelsea and Gould was put in sole charge. Coventry showed some excellent form after the inspired signing of Mick Quinn from Newcastle United.

GOULDEN, Leonard Arthur

Born: Hackney, London, 16 July 1912.
Inside-left   5ft 9in; 10st 4lb (1945).
Career: West Ham Schools; Chelmsford; Leyton cs 1932; Dagenham; West Ham United amateur 1931, professional April 1933; Chelsea as guest in World War Two; Chelsea August 1945 (£4,500), retired as a player cs 1950, then coach 1950-1952; Watford manager November 1952, then general manager October 1955-February 1956; worked as a sub-postmaster 1956-1959; Watford coach July 1959-cs 1962; coaching in Libya for two years; Banbury Town manager 1965-March 1967; Oxford United Reserves coach January 1969; worked in US Air Force base in Northamptonshire; retired to Cornwall.
Honours: England international (14 caps); Wartime international (5 caps); Schoolboy international (2 caps); Football League representative (2 caps); Football League War Cup 1940; Football League South Cup winners 1945.

Although West Ham were a mid-table Second Division side, Len Goulden played regularly for England before the war. He had midfield mastery and the ability to change the focus of an attack with devastating cross-field passes and he developed a fine partnership with Jimmy Ruffell on the Hammers' left wing. Goulden, who served in the police force during the war, was a member of West Ham's side which won the War Cup Final at Wembley in 1940. After the war he moved to Stamford Bridge and First Division football. Goulden had scored 55 goals in 253 peacetime appearances for the Hammers and he played a further 111 games for the Blues, scoring 19 goals before retiring. He appeared in an FA cup semi-final for Chelsea in 1950.

His best season as manager of Watford was when they finished fourth in the Third Division South in 1953-54. He was made general manager after a poor start to the 1955-56 season. He later took Banbury United from the West Midlands League into the Southern League. His son, Roy, played for Arsenal and Southend United.

GRADI, Dario

Born: Milan, Italy, 1942.
Career: Fulham Juniors; Tooting & Mitcham United; Sutton United; PE teacher; FA's London regional staff coach 1968-1971; Chelsea assistant coach January 1971; Sutton United manager 1976-1977; Derby County assistant manager September 1977; Wimbledon manager January 1978-January 1981; Crystal Palace manager February-November 1981; Orient youth-team coach November 1981; Crewe Alexandra manager June 1983.
Honours: England Amateur international (1 cap); Division Four promotion 1979, 1989; FA Amateur Cup runners-up 1969.

Whilst at Sutton United, Dario Gradi won an England Amateur international cap and appeared in their losing FA Amateur Cup Final side in 1969. He is one of the few managers to make it as a League manager without having played League football. He started his coaching career at Chelsea and developed a number of useful youngsters such as Ray Wilkins and Kenny Swain, who later became his assistant at Crewe.

Gradi's first managerial post in the Football League was with Wimbledon, who won promotion to Division Three but were relegated again soon afterwards. He was in charge at Selhurst Park during one of the most traumatic times in their history and he lost his job shortly after they were relegated.

Gradi has really made a name for himself since he joined Crewe Alexandra in 1983. They struggled at first and at one time the fans barracked him and he threatened to leave. However, in 1988-89 Crewe won promotion to Division Three for only the third time in their history, vindicating the faith shown in Gradi by the board of directors. He has changed Crewe from a soccer wasteland to a club with an excellent youth policy which enabled him to rescue future England international David Platt from the soccer scrapheap. Gradi was rewarded with a ten-year contract and more recently he has seen another Crewe youngster, Rob Jones, move to Liverpool and win his first full England cap.

Crewe continued to play cultured, entertaining soccer and were unlucky

to be relegated in 1991. They did reach the fifth round of the FA Cup that season for the first time since 1887 before narrowly losing to West Ham. Crewe finished sixth in the Fourth Division in 1991-92, but lost to Scunthorpe United in the play-offs. Gradi sold yet another discovery, Craig Hignett, to Middlesbrough for £600,000 in late 1992.

After the departure of Brian Clough from Nottingham Forest, Gradi became the longest-serving manager after Joe Royle in the Football League. Crewe reached the Third Division play-offs in 1993 and easily beat Walsall 9-3 over two legs to meet York City in the Final at Wembley, which they lost on penalties.

GRAHAM, Douglas Richard

Born: Corby, 6 May 1922.
Goalkeeper.
Career: Corby Town; Northampton Town; guest for Southport, Crewe Alexandra and Crystal Palace in World War Two; Leicester City November 1944; Crystal Palace December 1945, retired through injury 1951; licensee in Croydon; brewers' representative; part-time reporter; coach to Surrey FA; West Bromwich Albion assistant trainer November 1956; Crystal Palace assistant manager November 1960, then manager March 1963-January 1966; Charlton Athletic advisor January-June 1966; Orient manager June 1966-February 1968; Walsall manager March-May 1968, then assistant coach May-July 1968; Colchester United manager July 1968-September 1972; Cambridge United chief scout 1972-1973; Wimbledon manager September 1973-March 1974; Wills Faber sports centre (Ipswich) manager 1974-1987; Maidstone Bowls Club manager 1987.
Honours: Division Three runners-up 1964; Watney Cup winners 1971.

Despite letting in ten goals in a match at Reading in September 1946, Graham was a regular for Palace after the war until injury ended his career. His eldest brother, Jim, also played League football with Clapton Orient and Nottingham Forest. Graham was assistant to Arthur Rowe at Selhurst Park in the early 1960s, taking over when Rowe left.

A strict disciplinarian, he took Palace to promotion to Division Two in 1963-64, as runners-up to Coventry City, before unrest amongst the supporters spread to the dressing-room and the club cancelled his contract. He did well as manager at Brisbane Road, despite lack of cash, and was forced to sell Paul Went to Charlton for £26,000 to keep the club alive. He proved a popular manager at Layer Road, especially when Colchester beat mighty Leeds United in the FA Cup.

GRAHAM, George

Born: Bargeddle, Lanark, 30 November 1944.
Midfield   5ft 11in; 12st 3lb (1976).
Career: Coatbridge Schools; Aston Villa December 1961; Chelsea July 1964 (£5,950); Arsenal September 1966 (£50,000 and a player); Manchester United December 1972 (£120,000); Portsmouth November 1974; Crystal Palace November 1976; California Surf (NASL) March-July 1978; retired as a player cs 1980; Queen's Park Rangers coach 1980; Millwall manager December 1982-May 1986; Arsenal manager May 1986.

Honours: Scotland international (12 caps); Under-23 international (2 caps); Schoolboy international; Youth international; Football League champions 1971, 1989, 1991; Division Three promotion 1985; FA Cup winners 1971, runners-up 1972; Football League Cup winners 1987, runners-up 1965, 1968, 1969, 1988; Inter-Cities Fairs Cup winners 1970; Football League Trophy winners 1983. FA Cup Winners 1993; Football League Cup Winners 1993.

Under the astute management of George Graham, Arsenal have again become one of the leading clubs in Britain as two League championships in three years have put the Gunners back in the big-time.

Never flashy, and very careful how he spends his money on transfers, Graham has gradually built an excellent squad at Highbury. He has a record of going for long-term investments in young players who have great potential, and his shrewd judgement has usually proved right.

Graham made only ten appearances for Aston Villa, scoring twice, but they included playing in the side which lost on aggregate to Birmingham City in the 1963 Football League Cup Final. Two seasons later, Graham gained a winners' medal with Chelsea when they beat Leicester City 3-2 on aggregate. He had joined Chelsea in July 1964, for a £5,950 fee, and at Stamford Bridge struck up a fruitful partnership with Barry Bridges, over 80 goals coming from the duo over the next two seasons. Graham was developing into a stylish, elegant player and in 1966-67 he helped Chelsea reach the Fairs Cup semi-finals, where they lost to Barcelona. Then, after 102 games (46 goals) for the Blues, he moved to Highbury.

Graham joined Arsenal for £50,000 plus Tommy Baldwin and he was new manager Bertie Mee's first signing for the Gunners. Playing alongside John Radford, he scored 21 goals in 1967-68 but thereafter appeared more in a midfield role with his casual style earning him the nickname 'Stroller'. He played in two losing League Cup Finals, in 1968 (1-0 to Leeds United) and in 1969 (3-1 to Third Division Swindon Town), but in April 1970, Arsenal beat Anderlecht 4-3 over two legs to win the Fairs Cup with Graham in their side.

The following season they clinched the double and Graham was in superb form. After winning the League title in the final game of the season, at Spurs of all places, the Gunners beat Liverpool 2-1 in the FA Cup Final at Wembley five days later. In 1972, Graham again played at Wembley when Arsenal lost to Leeds United in another FA Cup Final.

He made 332/15 appearances for the Gunners in League and Cup competitions and scored 82 goals for them before moving to Manchester United in December 1972, for £120,000. United were in decline and struggled to avoid relegation in 1972-73. The following season they were relegated, Graham losing his place midway through the season. In November 1974, he was on the move again, this time to Portsmouth. Again he experienced relegation, in 1975-76 when Pompey dropped into Division Three, and, unable to find a regular first-team place, moved again, this time to Crystal Palace in November 1976. He helped Palace to promotion from Division Three in 1976-77 but never played in the first team after March 1978, when he went to the USA to play for California Surf for four months. After 50/1 appearances for Palace, he retired in 1980.

Graham had done some coaching whilst at Selhurst Park but at Queen's Park Rangers he was officially appointed as coach in 1980 and in December 1982 he became manager of Millwall. Immediately he appointed Theo Foley his assistant and Foley remained with him in his early years at Highbury. In his first season at The Den, the Lions won the Football League Trophy, a competiton for lower division clubs, by beating Lincoln City in the Final. However, that season they just avoided relegation to the Fourth Division by winning their last three games.

In 1984-85, Millwall gained promotion to Division Two as runners-up but the season was marred when they lost 1-0 to Luton Town on the sixth round of the FA Cup at Kenilworth Road. What followed were some of the worst scenes ever witnessed at a British ground as Millwall fans fought running battles with the police on the pitch and wrecked one of the stands.

After another good season in which Millwall consolidated their position in Division Two, Graham was offered the manager's job at Highbury. This maintained a tradition with Arsenal appointing an old boy as their manager. Soon afterwards, Millwall won promotion to Division One for the first time in their history, a success based on the foundations laid by George Graham.

Arsenal tasted success at the end of Graham's first season in charge. Liverpool were beaten 2-1, thanks to two goals from Charlie Nicholas, to lift the League Cup at Wembley. The following season, the Gunners lost 3-2 in the Final to Luton Town.

The 1988-89 season was a marvellous one for Arsenal, who clinched the League championship in a never-to-beforgotten final league match of the season at Anfield. Needing to win by two clear goals, Arsenal led 1-0 with

the minutes ticking away. Right at the end, Michael Thomas scored to thrill the travelling Arsenal support and clinch the title in one of the most exciting finishes ever. Two seasons later, Arsenal won the championship again, this time leading Liverpool by seven points. However, the season was spoiled a little when they lost 3-1 to Tottenham Hotspur in the first FA Cup semi-final to be staged at Wembley.

The ban on English clubs now over, the Gunners' championship success saw them compete in the European Cup for the first time since 1972 and Graham seemed on course to bring even more trophies to Highbury, although there was a nasty shock in 1992 when they were beaten at lowly Wrexham in the FA Cup.

Arsenal reached the Finals of both major domestic cups in 1992-93 and met Sheffield Wednesday in both. They won the League Cup Final 2-1, then repeated the scoreline in a replayed FA Cup Final in which the brave Andy Linighan scored the winning goal in the last minute of extra-time. Graham had therefore won all three domestic honours as both a player and a manager.

GRAHAM, Leslie

Born: Manchester, 14 May 1924.
Inside-forward   5ft 8in; 10st 6lb (1954).
Career: Flixton; Blackburn Rovers April 1947; Newport County February 1953; Watford July 1955; Newport County September 1957 (£1,250); Cambridge United July 1959; Merthyr Tydfil player-manager 1959-1960; Cwmbran manager and coach; Tottenham Hotspur scout; Newport County manager March 1967-May 1969.

A talented inside-forward, Les Graham had two spells as a player with Newport County, the club he also managed. Graham scored 62 goals in 179 appearances for Newport and owed his chance of a career in football to an Army major in India, who recommended him to Blackburn Rovers when Graham was serving there. Graham played First Division soccer for the Ewood Park club, making 151 League appearances altogether (scoring 42 goals) including some games at wing-half. He also had an enjoyable playing career at Watford. His two and a bit seasons as Newport's manager were not as happy, the Somerton Park club finishing 12th and 22nd respectively in Division Four.

GRAY, Edwin MBE

Born: Glasgow, 17 January 1948.
Left-winger   5ft 10in; 11st 5lb (1976).

Career: Glasgow Schools; Leeds United amateur 1962, professional January 1965, then player-manager July 1982-October 1985; Whitby Town November 1985; Middlesbrough reserve and youth-team coach 1986; Rochdale manager December 1986-June 1988;

Hull City manager June 1988-May 1989; Whitby Town manager cs 1989.
Honours: Scotland international (12 caps); Under-23 international (2 caps); Schoolboy international; Football League champions 1969, 1974; FA Cup winners 1972, runners-up 1970, 1973; Football League Cup winners 1968; European Cup runners-up 1975 (sub); European Cup-winners' Cup runners-up 1973; Inter-Cities Fairs Cup winners 1968, runners-up 1967.

Eddie Gray was an extremely skilful player for such a tall man. He loved to dribble past defenders and did so with ease. Indeed, Gray was a graceful player with plenty of tricks up his sleeve. He won his first Scottish cap against England at Wembley in 1969 and gave a virtuoso performance in the first FA Cup Final match against Chelsea the following year. Later in his career, he lost some of his speed after a succession of injuries. Gray won many medals with Leeds in his 559/18 appearances for the club, also scoring 69 goals in his career.

He rebuilt the side during his spell as manager of Leeds United, bringing back old favourite Peter Lorimer, but was unable to bring First Division soccer back to Elland Road, Leeds just missing out on three occasions. When he was sacked in 1985, it brought to an end a 22-year association with the club. Gray did not achieve any success at Rochdale or Hull City. He is the brother of Frank Gray.

GRAY, Francis Tierney

Born: Castlemilk, Glasgow, 27 October 1954.
Left-back   5ft 9½in; 11st 10in (1981).
Career: Glasgow Schools; Leeds United apprentice cs 1970, professional November 1971; Nottingham Forest July 1979 (£475,000); Leeds United May 1981 (£300,000); Sunderland July 1985 (£100,000); Darlington player-coach cs 1989, retired as a player 1991, then manager June 1991-February 1992.

Honours: Scotland international (32 caps); Under-23 international (5 caps); Schoolboy international; Division Three champions 1988; Football League Cup runners-up 1980; European Cup winners 1980, runners-up 1975; European Cup-winners' Cup runners-up 1973.

Frank Gray had a tough baptism into football management when he took over from Brian Little after Darlington lifted the Fourth Division title in 1990-91 and Little moved to Leicester City. Unfortunately Darlington were out of their depth in the Third Division and Gray was sacked with the club struggling at the bottom of the table.

He had followed his brother Eddie to Leeds United and his early career was spent in midfield, although he had most success when he converted to left-back and played in the same side as Eddie. Frank's best years were at Nottingham Forest, where he gained European Cup winners' medal in 1980 to go with his losers' medal gained with Leeds in 1975. He also collected a League Cup runners-up medal in 1980, when Forest lost to Wolves. Gray made a total of 396/9 appearances, scoring 35 goals, in his two spells at Leeds United before being sold to Sunderland by his brother, who was then boss at Elland Road. Frank helped Sunderland to the Third Division title in 1988 before moving to Conference side Darlington and helping them back into the Football League as player-coach.

GRAY, Roland 'Ron'

Born: North Shields, 25 June 1920.
Left-half.
Career: Sheffield United May 1938; Watford 1946, retired 1947, then trainer 1947, manager June 1950-August 1951; Millwall trainer October 1951, head trainer January 1954, then manager January 1956-January 1958; Millwall manager again January 1961-November 1963; Lincoln City manager 1966-July 1970; Ipswich Town chief scout September 1970 until 1980s.

Honours: Division Four champions 1962.

Although a fine judge of a player, Ron Gray was not always able to get the best out of his men. He did not have a very successful start in management with Watford, who finished second-to-bottom of the Third Division South in 1950-51. Initially a trainer under Charlie Hewitt at The Den, he was made head trainer, then manager after Hewitt's departure. Millwall just avoided re-election in his first season in charge by winning their last three games, but he resigned after a run of poor results including a 6-1 thrashing by bottom club Gillingham in the FA Cup.

Gray returned to The Den three years later and took the club to the Fourth Division championship in 1961-62, but then surprised the fans by selling his leading scorer Peter Burridge to Crystal Palace. He was sacked after another humiliating Cup defeat, 3-2 against non-League Kettering. At Lincoln he found more trouble and the club ended his first season in control having to seek re-election. However things later improved and the Imps finished eighth in the Fourth Division in 1969-70.

GRAY, William Patrick

Born: Dinnington, County Durham, 24 May 1927.
Outside-left/Winger
5ft 7in; 11st 3lb (1959).

Career: Dinnington Colliery; Wolverhampton Wanderers amateur; Gateshead amateur; Leyton Orient May 1947; Chelsea March 1949; Burnley August 1953 (£16,000); Nottingham Forest June 1957; Millwall player-manager November 1963-May 1966; Brentford manager cs 1966-September 1967; Notts County manager September 1967-September 1968; Fulham coach January 1969; Notts County groundsman.

Honours: England 'B' international (1 cap); FA Cup winners 1959; Division Three runners-up 1966; Division Four runners-up 1965.

A fast and clever winger, Billy Gray

appeared in two losing FA Cup semi-finals for Chelsea before playing in the winning side for Forest at Wembley in the 1959 Final. He made many appearances for Chelsea, Burnley and Forest and also played for England 'B' against Switzerland in 1950.

When he took over at Millwall, the situation at The Den was so bad that he had to bring himself out of virtual retirement to play again, but his energy and enthusiasm soon rubbed off on the other players and the 1964-65 season was very successful for the Lions, who finished runners-up in the Fourth Division and knocked First Division Fulham out of the FA Cup. They were assured of promotion again the following season when Gray resigned over comments made by directors about his team.

During his time at Griffin Park, Brentford nearly went out of business due to financial problems. Notts County were bottom of the Fourth Division when he resigned, but he had made a number of useful signings for the future including Les Bradd and future Scottish international Don Masson. Gray was coach to Bill Dodgin at Fulham, thus reversing roles they had filled at Millwall.

GREAVES, Ian Denzil

Born: Oldham, 26 May 1932.
Full-back   6ft; 12st 4lb (1959).
Career: St Joseph's; Buxton United; Manchester United May 1953; Lincoln City December 1960; Oldham Athletic May 1961 (£2,000); Altrincham June 1963; Huddersfield Town coach August 1964, then manager June 1968-June 1974; Bolton Wanderers assistant manager August 1974, then manager October 1974-January 1980; Hereford United assistant manager cs-December 1980; Oxford United manager December 1980-February 1982; Wolverhampton Wanderers manager February-August 1982; Mansfield Town manager January 1983-February 1989.

Honours: Football League champions 1956; Division Two champions 1970, 1978; Division Four promotion 1986; FA Cup runners-up 1958; Freight/Rover Trophy winners 1987.

Ian Greaves gained a reputation for producing dull, dour sides whose defensive tactics were disliked on away grounds throughout the country. He had his moments of success and was greatly appreciated by his players, but many people also saw him as being responsible for creating many of English football's negative tactics of the 1970s and '80s.

As a player, though, he was a sturdy full-back who believed in turning defence into attack by calm, constructive use of the ball. Signing professional forms for Manchester United just before his 21st birthday, Greaves went on to win a League championship medal and an FA Cup runners-up medal. He picked up his championship medal by appearing in the last 14 games of the 1955-56 season, in which ten games were won and four drawn. And he helped United to recover from the Munich air disaster and reach the 1958 FA Cup Final. Altogether, he made 75 League and Cup appearances for the Reds before moving to Lincoln City on 17 December 1960.

In May 1961, after only 11 games for the Imps, Greaves moved to his home-town club, Oldham Athletic, but, never a regular at Boundary Park, he joined Altrincham in June 1963.

Retiring in August 1964, he became a coach at Huddersfield Town and four years later took over as manager. He took Town to Division Two title in 1970 and spent two seasons in the top bracket before relegation in successive seasons down to Division Three, walking out of Leeds Road in June 1974 after a boardroom power struggle.

After two months of unemployment, Greaves joined Bolton Wanderers as assistant manager to Jimmy Armfield. When Armfield left for Leeds United, Greaves was appointed manager in October 1974. He used 20 different players in his first ten weeks in charge as the Trotters slumped. However the club finished in a mid-table position at the end of his first season in charge. He took Bolton to a League Cup semi-final in 1976-77 and the following season they clinched Division Two championship, when he was named Division Two's Manager of the Year. The club failed to establish themselves in the top division, though, and Greaves was sacked in January 1980 with the Trotters at the bottom of the table.

From the summer of 1980, Greaves was assistant manager at Hereford United and in December of that year became the manager at Oxford United who were near the bottom of Division Three. They won their first match under Greaves, beating the leaders Charlton Athletic, then lost just three of their remaining 21 games to finish 14th. The following season United had good runs in both Cup competitions before Greaves departed in February 1992 to become manager at Wolves. Although highly regarded by the supporters, he could not halt the club's decline. After only five wins in his six months at Molineux, he was sacked by the new regime led by former player Derek Dougan.

In January 1983, after a period out of the game, Greaves became manager of Mansfield Town and led them to promotion to Division Three in 1986 and to the Freight/Rover Trophy at Wembley, the following year. In February 1989, he left Field Mill by mutual consent and has been out of football ever since.

GREEN, Brian G.

Born: Heywood, 5 June 1935.
Centre-forward 5ft 11in; 12st 4lb (1959).
Career: Haggate Boys; Rochdale August 1955; Southport March 1959; Colwyn Bay 1960; Barrow September 1960; Altrincham 1961; Exeter City

August 1962; Chesterfield February 1963; Prague (Australia) 1964; Barrow coach 1968; Halifax Town coach 1970; coaching in Kuwait 1971; Southport coach 1972; Chester coach 1973; Australia national coach 1974; Rochdale manager June 1976-September 1977; Leeds United coach September 1977; Stockport County assistant manager 1979.

An experienced and well-liked coach, Brian Green worked with his former clubs, Barrow and Southport, and managed Rochdale, for whom he played in the 1950s. He did not have a happy time in charge at Spotland and Rochdale were bottom of the Football League when he was sacked. Never a first-team regular at any of his clubs, Green made only 80 League appearances, scoring 16 goals in his playing career.

GREEN, Haydn

Born: South Kirkby, Yorkshire; Died: February 1957.
Inside-forward 5ft 7½in; 11st 2lb (1914).
Career: Stanton Hill Victoria; Nottingham Forest cs 1907; Manchester United cs 1910; Aston Villa 1912; Newport County 1913; Reading cs 1914; Lincoln City assistant manager 1920s, Ebbw Vale manager; Hull City manager May 1931-March 1934; Bangor manager; Guildford City manager until 1939; Swansea Town manager May 1939-September 1947; Watford manager August 1951-October 1952.

Honours: Division Three North champions 1933; Southern League champions 1938.

Haydn Green went for experienced players at Hull City and quickly found success in 1932-33, as the Tigers lifted the Third Division North championship. However, he found problems in the higher division as his ageing team struggled to find its form. Green had to start rebuilding but surprisingly resigned in March 1934 before completing the job.

He took Guildford City to the Southern League title in 1937-38, with a four-point advantage over runners-up Plymouth Argyle Reserves.

At Swansea, Green had a constant struggle to find players during the war years but willingly gave up his Christmas dinner one year to sign future star centre-forward Trevor Ford. His family could not have been too pleased when he arrived back for his dinner at midnight. After selling Ford, the Swans struggled to score goals and were relegated in the first season after the war. Green had constant clashes with the board over money to sign new players and this finally led to his resignation. He found little success at Watford during his 14 months in charge.

GREEN, Michael Clive

Born: Carlisle, 8 September 1946.
Defender   6ft 1in; 12st 4lb (1976).
Career: Cumbria Schools; Carlisle United September 1964; Gillingham July 1968; Bristol Rovers July 1971; Plymouth Argyle July 1974 (£20,000); Torquay United player-manager March 1977-May 1981; Newton Abbott.
Honours: Watney Cup winners 1972.

Green played in two promotion sides, first with Bristol Rovers in 1973-74 and the following season captained Plymouth Argyle to runners-up in the Third Division. He made over 100 appearances at both Gillingham and Argyle and gained a Watney Cup winners' medal in 1972, when Bristol

Rovers beat Sheffield United 7-6 on penalties after a 0-0 draw.

He survived as Torquay's manager for over four years. His best season being 1977-78 when they finished ninth in the Fourth Division. He retired from playing in April 1980 and was replaced by Frank O'Farrell as manager in May 1981. O'Farrell had formerly been his consultant.

GREEN, William

Born: Newcastle upon Tyne, 22 December 1950.
Central defender 6ft 3in; 12st 8lb (1984).
Career: Hartlepool United June 1969; Carlisle United July 1973 (£15,000); West Ham United June 1976 (£100,000); Peterborough United July 1978 (£90,000); Chesterfield player-coach June 1979; Doncaster Rovers June 1983; Scunthorpe United assistant manager October 1984, then manager February 1991-January 1993. Scunthorpe United manager February 1991-January 1993.

Bill Green joined Hartlepool from school and gained a reputation at Brunton Park where he helped Carlisle United into Division One for the first and only time in 1974. He captained the side to the quarter-finals of the FA Cup in 1975 but after a good start they were relegated after only one season in the top flight. The Hammers paid a large fee for his services but Green suffered a badly broken leg shortly after moving south, an injury from which it took him a great deal of time to fully recover. He went on to make 482/5 League appearances in his career before retirement in 1984. For six and a half years, Green was assistant manager to Frank Barlow and Mick Buxton at Scunthorpe before taking control in February 1991. Despite taking United to the Fourth Division play-offs in 1992, he lost his job the following January.

GREENHALGH, James Radcliffe

Born: Manchester, 25 August 1923.
Wing-half   5ft 9in; 11st 4lb (1947).
Career: Newton Heath Loco (Manchester); Hull City August 1946; Bury November 1950 (£13,000); Wigan Athletic cs 1955; Gillingham player-coach July 1956; Lincoln City trainer February 1959; Newcastle United trainer June 1962; Darlington manager July 1966-February 1968; Middlesbrough trainer March 1968-December 1979; Sunderland chief scout December 1979-cs 1982.

Honours: Division Three North champions 1949.

Jimmy Greenhalgh was a fine tackler, popular with the fans, but his distribution prevented him from becoming an even better player. He was appointed by Joe Harvey as trainer at St James' Park, where his astute tactical appraisal and knowledge of the game helped Newcastle's development. Greenhalgh was known as 'a bit of a character' and was also a well-respected coach. When he took control at Darlington, they had just been promoted to the Third Division. At the end of his first season in charge, however, they were relegated, mainly due to a crippling injury list. They finished 16th the following season but did have a good run in the League Cup before losing 5-4 to Brian Clough's Derby County in a thriller.

GREENHOFF, James

Born: Barnsley, 19 June 1946.
Forward   5ft 10in; 11st 2lb (1968).

Career: Barnsley Boys; Leeds United apprentice June 1961, professional August 1963; Birmingham City August 1968 (£75,000); Stoke City August 1969 (£100,000); Manchester United November 1976 (£120,000); Crewe Alexandra December 1980; Toronto Blizzard (NASL) March 1981; Port Vale August 1981; Rochdale March 1983, then player-manager December 1983-March 1984; Port Vale coach March 1984; later coached at holiday camps and worked in insurance.

Honours: England Under-23 international (5 caps); Football League representative; FA Cup winners 1977, runners-up 1979; Football League Cup winners 1968, 1972; Inter-Cities Fairs Cup winners 1968, runners-up 1967; English Schools Trophy winners 1961.

Jimmy Greenhoff moved from Leeds to Birmingham in the middle of a Cup Final. This was the two-legged Fairs Cup Final against Ferencváros in August 1968, in which Greenhoff played in the first leg. Unlucky never to win a full England cap, especially during his Stoke days when he scored 76 goals in 274 League appearances, he played in the Potters' League Cup Final victory at Wembley against Chelsea in 1972 and for Leeds against Arsenal in the 1968 Final.

Greenhoff, who netted 146 League goals during his career, was adept at finding space for himself and he also set up many scoring opportunities for his colleagues. He played alongside his brother, Brian, during his Old Trafford days and signed Brian when he was manager at Rochdale. Jimmy had a four-month spell in charge at Spotland but the club struggled near the bottom of the Fourth Division and the board did not really give him a chance to prove himself in management.

GREENWOOD, Ronald

Born: Burnley 11 November 1921.
Centre-half   5ft 10in; 10st (1951).
Career: Chelsea October 1943; guest for Belfast Celtic in World War Two; Bradford December 1945; Brentford March 1949; Chelsea October 1952; Fulham February 1955; Oxford University coach for three years in 1950s; Walthamstow Avenue 1955-1957; Eastbourne United manager 1957; Arsenal assistant manager November 1958; England Youth and Under-23 manager; West Ham United manager April 1961-August 1974, then general manager until December 1977; England manager December 1977-July 1982; Brighton & Hove Albion director November 1983; technical advisor to FIFA 1966 and 1970 World Cup Finals.

Honours: England 'B' international; Football League champions 1955; FA Cup winners 1964; Football League Cup runners-up 1966; European Cup-winners' Cup winners 1965.

As manager of West Ham United, Ron Greenwood gained an enormous reputation for his tactical genius and knowledge of the game. He believed in the encouragement of skill, even when fighting against relegation. He studied the game in depth, communicating it well to others, and made a number of innovations to the game. His sides played with attacking flair and if they weren't always as successful as they could have been, they were always a delight to watch.

Greenwood made his debut in senior soccer as a wartime guest, for Chelsea against Crystal Palace in December 1940 before just 940 spectators at Stamford Bridge. He moved to Bradford in December 1945, as he was not assured of a regular first-team spot at Chelsea, but made only 59 League appearances in his three seasons at Park Avenue. In March 1949, he moved back to London to join Brentford, who were then in Division Two.

Greenwood had his best playing days at Griffin Park and won an England 'B' cap in 1949. He also played in representative matches for the FA, the London Combination and the London FA.

A stylish, unflappable centre-half, Greenwood was also an intelligent footballer and an ideal captain. After 142 League appearances for the Bees, he returned to Chelsea in October 1952 and made 21 appearances in their League title season of 1954-55. But after losing his place he switched to Fulham on a free transfer in February 1955. Greenwood was past his best at Craven Cottage and the Fulham defence continued to leak goals galore, despite his presence.

He qualified as a coach whilst still a player and coached Oxford University for three years and Walthamstow Avenue from 1955-57. His first managerial post was with Eastbourne United in 1957.

A close friend of England manager, Walter Winterbottom, Greenwood got many of his ideas from him and he ran England's Youth and Under-23 sides for two and a half years in the late 1950s. In November 1958, Greenwood became assistant manager to George Swindin at Arsenal and stayed there until April 1961, when he was given the manager's job at West Ham United, only the fourth such appointment in the Hammers' history.

West Ham won the FA Cup in 1964, beating Second Division Preston 3-2 with a last-minute Wembley goal from Ronnie Boyce to bring the trophy to Upton Park for the first time. The following year they were back at Wembley, this time to lift the European Cup-winners' Cup. They beat La Gantoise, Sparta Prague, Lausanne and Real Zarragosa to reach the Final against Munich 1860. The teams produced a marvellous Final which the Hammers won 2-0.

Ron Greenwood developed England's World Cup-winning trio Bobby Moore, Geoff Hurst and Martin Peters (who Alf Ramsey described as 'ten years ahead of his time') and had converted Hurst from a struggling wing-half into a deadly striker as well as bringing Johnny Byrne from Crystal Palace as his striking partner.

West Ham lost the 1966 Football League Cup Final when they went down 4-1 to West Brom at The Hawthorns to lose 5-3 on aggregate. Thereafter, the Hammers suffered some lean years and Greenwood did not endear himself to Hammers' fans when he sold Peters to Spurs for £200,000 and Jimmy Greaves moved in the opposite direction. Greaves proved a flop at Upton Park and retired soon afterwards.

Despite his outward appearance, Greenwood could be tough at times. In 1971, after West Ham lost 4-0 to Blackpool in an FA Cup tie, it was reported that Bobby Moore and three other players had been seen at a night club the night before the game. Greenwood imposed a heavy fine on each one and suspended them for a number of weeks.

Greenwood had a reputation for attacking sides but not for producing good defences. He has been heavily criticised for what he did to Alan Stephenson, a promising signing from Crystal Palace. Bobby Moore, no less, accused Greenwood of ruining a good player by taking away his fighting spirit.

The Hammers nearly reached Wembley in 1972, but lost 3-2 to Stoke City in a League Cup semi-final second replay. After a poor season in 1973-74, Greenwood became general manager at Upton Park and John Lyall took over as team manager. Success returned when the Hammers won the FA Cup in 1975 and reached the European Cup-winners' Cup Final the following year.

In December 1977, Ron Greenwood was selected to take over from Don Revie as the England manager and, compared with what had gone before in the 1970s, he was relatively successful. England reached the European Championship finals in 1980, albeit failing to get through their group after losing to the host nation, Italy. And in the 1982 World Cup finals in Spain, they started well by gaining maximum points in their group and went on to meet Spain and West Germany in a quarter-final group but failed to beat either. Greenwood retired from soccer after this but in November 1983, he became a director of Brighton & Hove Albion.

GREGG, Harold

Born: Derry, Northern Ireland, 25 October 1932.
Goalkeeper   6ft 1in; 13st 3lb (1964).
Career: Coleraine; Doncaster Rovers October 1952; Manchester United December 1957 (£23,000); Stoke City player-coach December 1966; Shrewsbury Town manager July 1968-October 1972; Swansea Town manager November 1972-January 1975; Crewe Alexandra manager January 1975-78; Swansea City coach February 1982-February 1983; Swansea Town assistant manager July 1984; Carlisle United manager May 1986-November 1987.

Honours: Northern Ireland (international) 24 caps; Irish League representative; Amateur and Schoolboy international; Football League

champions 1965; FA Cup runners-up 1958.

It caused quite a stir when Matt Busby paid a record fee of £23,000 for a goalkeeper, when Harry Gregg was transferred from Doncaster Rovers to Manchester United. Gregg survived the Munich air disaster of 1958 — he emerged as a hero after going back into the crashed aircraft to rescue others — to appear in the FA Cup Final later that year. At Wembley, he was knocked out by Nat Lofthouse as the Bolton centre-forward scored his second goal.

Acclaimed by the Press as the best goalkeeper in the 1958 World Cup finals in Sweden, Gregg was dropped by Ireland when he refused to fly to Spain for a match. It was a rather harsh decision bearing in mind his previous experience of flying.

He made 210 League appearances for United before moving to Stoke as player-coach. At Gay Meadow he steered the club away from relegation in 1968-69 with the inspired use of Alf Wood at centre-forward. At Shrewsbury and Swansea he produced some fine young players but as soon as they showed potential he was forced to sell them. He resigned from Swansea for this reason out of frustration.

Gregg gained a reputation as a make-do-and-mend sort of manager. His main role at all his clubs was to keep them alive rather than to find success. He experienced having to seek re-election at both Swansea and Carlisle.

GREGORY, John Charles

Born: Scunthorpe, 11 May 1954.
Midfield   6ft 1in; 11st 5lb (1983).

Career: Northampton Town apprentice June 1969, professional May 1973; Aston Villa June 1977 (£40,000); Brighton & Hove Albion July 1979 (£250,000); Queen's Park Rangers June 1981 (£300,000); Derby County November 1985 (£100,000); Portsmouth player-coach August 1988, then manager January 1989-January 1990 (playing registration from Derby to Portsmouth August 1989); Plymouth Argyle January 1990, player-caretaker manager February 1990; Bolton Wanderers March 1990; Leicester City coach June 1991; football expert on Sky TV News during 1991.

Honours: England international (6 caps); FA Cup runners-up 1982; Division Two champions 1983, 1987; Division Three promotion 1986.

John Gregory was known as 'Mr Versatility' at Villa Park, where he played in nine different positions. Gregory was a quality midfielder with plenty of aggression and was good enough to play six times for England. He appeared in Queen's Park Rangers' losing FA Cup Final against Spurs in 1982 and was ever-present in Rangers' Second Division title side of 1982-83. He later helped Derby from the Third to Division One and won a Second Division championship medal at the Baseball ground, scoring some vital goals for the Rams. Gregory was in charge at Fratton Park for 50 weeks before being sacked after a poor run, and he was caretaker manager at Plymouth between Ken Brown and David Kemp. His father, also John, played for West Ham, Scunthorpe and Aldershot.

GRIFFITHS, Arfon Trevor MBE

Born: Wrexham, 23 August 1941.
Midfield   5ft 6in; 9st 10lb (1964).

Career: Wrexham amateur May 1957, professional May 1959; Arsenal February 1961 (£14,000); Wrexham September 1962, assistant manager, player-manager May 1977-June 1981 (£12,000) (retired as a player 1979); Seattle Sounders (NASL) (loan) May-August 1978; Crewe Alexandra manager August 1981-October 1982.

Honours: Wales international (17 caps), Under-23 international (4 caps); Division Three champions 1978; Welsh Cup winners 1960, 1965, 1972, 1978, runners-up 1967.

A tricky ball-player, Arfon Griffiths was sold to Arsenal for a large fee by his home-town club, Wrexham, but never settled at Highbury and returned to North Wales for a slightly reduced fee. Surprisingly, he did not win a Welsh cap until he was 30. He scored 141 goals in 713 appearances for Wrexham.

Griffiths was the mastermind behind Wrexham's promotion to Division Three in 1970 and their Third Division championship in 1977-78. He was awarded the MBE for services to football. He managed to keep Wrexham in Division Two during his spell in charge and won the Welsh Cup during his first season at the Racecourse Ground. But Crewe finished bottom of the Football League in 1981-82 and were still bottom when he was sacked in October 1982. He returned to Wrexham to open a newsagent's shop and has not been involved in football since.

GRIFFITHS, Harold James

Born: Swansea, 4 January 1931; Died: Swansea, 24 April 1978.
Outside-right/Left-back   5ft 7in; 10st 9lb (1964).
Career: Swansea Town June 1949-1964; Merthyr Tydfil player-manager April

1964-1967; Swansea Town chief scout 1967, assistant manager 1973, then manager January 1975-February 1978.

Honours: Wales international (1 cap); Welsh League representative.

Harry Griffiths made 424 League appearances for the Swans, scoring 71 goals. A big-hearted player with a fine shot, he started his career as a winger and, after becoming a regular at Vetch Field in 1951-52, rarely missed a game in the next 11 seasons. His fighting qualities were used at full-back later in his career. When he was manager of Swansea, they missed promotion from the Fourth Division by only one point in 1976-77, after a fine run-in. However, he left the club through ill health before the Swans went up the following season. He died at the early age of 47 whilst working in the treatment room at Vetch Field.

GRIMSDELL, Arthur

Born: Watford, 23 March 1894; Died: 13 March 1963.
Left-half   5ft 10in; 12st 9lb (1923).
Career: Watford Schools; Watford St Stephen's; Watford amateur 1909, professional November 1911; Tottenham Hotspur March 1912 (£350); Clapton Orient player-manager May 1929-March 1930; Watford director 1945-1951; sports outfitter in Watford.

Honours: England international (6 caps); England Victory international (2 caps); England Schoolboy international; Football League representative (1 cap); Division Two champions 1920; FA Cup winners 1921.

An aggressive, determined and unorthodox wing-half, Arthur Grimsdell was slightly built and light on his feet but was strong in defence as well as attack. He had a powerful long-range shot and scored twice for England in a Victory international against Scotland in 1919. Grimsdell skippered Spurs to the Division Two championship in 1919-20 (scoring 14 goals) and to the FA Cup in 1921, when they beat Wolves 1-0 at Stamford Bridge. He made 360 appearances for Spurs and scored 27 goals before moving to Homerton as player-manager of Clapton Orient.

Orient had just been relegated to the Southern Section and the board saw Grimsdell as the man to restore their club's fortunes. Sadly, things did not work out well and Grimsdell resigned after only ten months at a club riddled with financial problems and near the foot of the table. Surprisingly, he never managed again but was later a director at Watford. His brother was an England Amateur international and Arthur also kept wicket for Hertfordshire from 1922 to 1947.

GRITT, Stephen J.

Born: Bournemouth, 31 October 1957.

Defender   5ft 9in; 10st 10lb (1991).
Career: Bournemouth & Boscombe Athletic October 1975; Charlton Athletic July 1977; Walsall July 1989; Charlton Athletic February 1990, then manager July 1991 (joint with Alan Curbishley).

Charlton's Steve Gritt and Alan Curbishley just missed Division Two play-offs in 1992, despite many 'experts' expecting their joint managership not to work.

In over 300 appearances for the club, Gritt played in every position for Athletic except goalkeeper. Indeed, the appropriately named Gritt is a dedicated, determined player who thrives on hard work. After relegation in 1980, Charlton bounced back the following season, promoted in third place, and he made 11 appearances when they were runners-up in Division Two in 1985-86. He was then in and out of the side in the top division. Many felt that his Charlton career was ending with his departure to Walsall, but he soon returned and in December 1992 saw the club return to The Valley.

GURNEY, Robert

Born: Silksworth, County Durham, 13 October 1907.
Centre-forward 5ft 8in; 11st 2lb (1935).
Career: Hetton Juniors; Seaham Harbour; Bishop Auckland; Sunderland May 1925, retired in May 1946 to join training staff; Horden Colliery manager 1947; Peterborough United manager February 1950-March 1952; Darlington manager March 1952-October 1957; Leeds United scout; Horden Colliery manager 1960-1963; Hartlepools United manager April 1963-January 1964; Leeds United scout.

Honours: England international (1 cap); Football League champions 1936; FA Cup winners 1937.

Bob Gurney was an effervescent, persistent player who loved the game. He found much fame during his playing days at Roker Park after being spotted by Charlie Buchan whilst playing for Bishop Auckland. Gurney scored 228 goals in 388 appearances for Sunderland and netted one of the goals which gave the Wearsiders an FA Cup Final victory over Preston in 1937. He also helped them to runners-up spot in Division One in 1934-35 and to the League championship the following season.

Gurney scored five goals against Bolton in December 1935 and won his only England cap against Scotland in a 2-0 defeat in April 1935. He broke both his legs during his time at Roker Park. Gurney was the manager at Peterborough in their Midland League days but had little success at either Darlington or Hartlepool, although he unearthed some fine players whilst at Feethams.

HACKING, John

Born: Blackburn, 22 December 1897; Died: 31 May 1955.
Goalkeeper   6ft; 12st 7lb (1929)
Career: Grimshaw Park Co-operative (Blackburn); Blackburn Rovers Reserves; Blackpool December 1919; Fleetwood cs 1925; Oldham Athletic May 1926; Manchester United March 1934; Accrington Stanley player-manager May 1935-May 1949, retired as a player December 1935; Barrow manager May 1949-May 1955.

Honours: England international (3 caps); Football League representative (2 caps).

A goalkeeper who was alert and resourceful with a long reach, Jack

Hacking was a late developer and did not win his England caps until he joined Oldham Athletic and after Blackpool had given him a free transfer after only 33 appearances in five and a half seasons at the club. He helped Manchester United fend off relegation to the Third Division after joining them near the end of the 1933-34 season.

Hacking's two best seasons in charge at Accrington Stanley were his first — when they finished ninth in the Northern Section — and 1947-48, when they finished sixth. Stanley had to seek re-election in the last two seasons before the war but won the Third Division North, Western Region championship in 1945-46. Hacking found little success at Holker Street and he died of a heart attack shortly after being told that they were dispensing with his services. His son played for Stockport County.

HADLEY, Harold

Born: Barrow-in-Furness, 26 October 1877; Died: West Bromwich c. September 1942.
Wing-half   5ft 8in; 11st 7lb (1902).
Career: Cradley Heath & District Schools; Colley Gate United; Halesowen 1895-1896; West Bromwich Albion February 1897; Aston Villa February 1905; Nottingham Forest April 1906; Southampton April 1907; Croydon Common cs 1908; Halesowen February 1910; Merthyr Town manager May 1919-April 1922; Chesterfield manager April-August 1922; Aberdare Athletic manager November 1927-April 1928; Merthyr Town April-November 1928 and 1930-September 1931; Bangor City manager July 1935-1936; retired in April 1936.

Honours: England international (1 cap); Division Two champions 1902.

Harry Hadley was an enthusiastic player who had composure and fine judgement. A keen tackler, he was a calculated player with strong shoulders, who won his only cap against Ireland in 1905, when England won 4-0 at Wolverhampton. He helped West Brom to the Second Division championship in 1901-02 and altogether made 181 appearances for the Throstles. His brother, Ben, also played at The Hawthorns.

Harry preferred to remain a manager in the lower divisions, despite offers to manage at a higher level. He was in charge at Merthyr when they entered the Football League in 1920 and managed the club on three separate occasions. They were on the point of folding when he left in 1931. Aberdare had also given up the ghost in the summer of 1928, just after he left the club, and struggled on for a just year after losing their Football League status.

HAGAN, James

Born: Washington, County Durham, 21 January 1918.
Inside-forward 5ft 9in; 10st 4lb (1935).
Career: Intermediate School, Washington; Unsworth Colliery; Liverpool amateur January 1932; Derby County amateur May 1933, professional January 1935; Sheffield United November 1938 (£2,500), retired 1958; wartime guest for Aldershot; Peterborough United manager August 1958-October 1962; West Bromwich Albion manager April 1963-May 1967; Manchester City scout 1967-1968; Benfica (Portugal) manager March 1970-September 1973; coached in Kuwait 1974-1976; Sporting Lisbon (Portugal) manager 1976; Oporto (Portugal) manager late-1970s.

Honours: England international (1

cap); Wartime international (16 caps); 'B' international (1 cap); Schoolboy international (2 caps); Football League representative (3 caps); FA tour of Australia (3 caps); Division Two champions 1953; Division Four champions 1961; Football League Cup winners 1966, runners-up 1967.

A controversial and sometimes volatile boss, Jimmy Hagan's managerial career seems to have been a series of confrontations. His sacking at Peterborough was linked to a dispute with his players, then there was an infamous tracksuit row at West Brom and more arguments at Benfica. But in between all of this, Hagan brought success to all the clubs that he managed.

Born in County Durham towards the end of World War One, Hagan gave up the chance to go to Washington Grammar School as they did not play soccer. He played for the Durham County side for two years and for England Schoolboys against Scotland Schoolboys at St James' Park in 1932. He joined Liverpool as an amateur in January 1932, after appearing for Usworth Colliery, but moved to Derby County in the summer of 1933. He signed professional for the Rams in January 1935 on his 17th birthday.

Unable to obtain a regular place at Derby — apparently he and manager George Jobey just never got on — Hagan moved to Sheffield United in November 1938 for a fee of £2,500. That season his inspirational play led to promotion to the First Division and Hagan went on to become a legend at Bramall Lane. A man with almost magical qualities of ball control, he was an inside-forward who could baffle opponents as well as his own team-mates. His artistry led to allegations of United being a 'one-man team' and to prove the point a photographer published a team group of United with 11 Jimmy Hagan heads.

He was one of the quiet men of the game, but deep-thinking and shrewd. Despite the war years, he managed over 400 first-team appearances for United and gained a Second Division championship medal in 1953. Jimmy's father, Alf, had played for Newcastle United, Cardiff City and Tranmere Rovers but was not such a good player as his son.

Jimmy Hagan was very unlucky to reach his peak in the war years, during which he rose to the rank of major and also appeared as a guest for Aldershot.

Winning 16 wartime caps, he once scored after only 50 seconds, against Scotland at Wembley in 1942. Yet for all his artistry as an inside-forward, Hagan won only one official England cap, in an undistinguished perfor-

mance against Denmark in Copenhagen in September 1948. He also won an England 'B' cap against Switzerland in the same year and represented the Football League three times.

After he retired in March 1958 it was no surprise when he joined Peterborough United as their manager in August of that year. The Posh had been repeatedly unlucky not to be elected to the Football League but Hagan achieved this in 1960 and the club ran away with the Fourth Division title in their first season in the League, scoring an all-time League record 134 goals. Peterborough finished fifth in Division Three in 1961-62 but in October 1962 Hagan was sacked with the club near the top of the table. It later transpired that the week before, seven players had put their names on the transfer list and there was enormous friction in the club.

Hagan was out of football until April 1963, when he was appointed West Bromwich Albion's manager. Hardness, discipline and routine were built into his methods and he was soon having head-on clashes with his players, who were led by Don Howe. They claimed that his training routines were boring and unhelpful and that Hagan was unapproachable. It came to a head when the players went on strike, several of them refusing to train without tracksuit bottoms on a bitterly cold day. The strike was eventually resolved and Howe left the club. Albion did have some success on the field. They won a two-legged League Cup Final over West Ham in 1965 but lost in the 1967 Final to Third Division Queen's Park Rangers, 3-2 after being two goals up. Hagan was dismissed shortly after this in May 1967.

He was employed as a scout for Manchester City for a while but was working in a Midlands driving school when Benfica came along and employed him as their manager in March 1970.

The club was at a low ebb and Hagan's appointment was a surprise to everyone, including himself. There were many disagreements at the start and after a poor beginning there seemed to be a crisis. However, gradually an understanding grew and with harmony came a surge of success so that Benfica finished as champions. Indeed, they won the Portuguese League championship in each of his three seasons at the club and lifted the League and Cup double in 1972. He returned to the Baseball Ground that year when Benfica lost 3-0 to his old club, Derby County, in the European Cup.

Hagan left Benfica in September 1973, after an argument concerning the selection of players for Eusebio's testimonial match. He wished to return to England as a manager but when no offers were forthcoming, he moved to Kuwait as a coach from 1974. He then managed Sporting Lisbon from 1976 and was later in charge at Oporto in Portugal. He still lives in that country.

HAILS, William

Born: Nettlesworth, 19 February 1935.
Winger   5ft 8in; 10st 9lb (1964).
Career: Lincoln City March 1953; Peterborough United 1955; Northampton Town November 1962; Luton Town June 1964; Nuneaton Borough assistant manager July 1965; Peterborough United manager November 1978-January 1979; Watford physiotherapist 1983.
Honours: Division Three champions 1963; Division Four champions 1961;

Midland League champions 1956, 1957, 1958, 1959, 1960.

Billy Hails left Lincoln City after a dispute over his wages as a part-time professional. With Peterborough he won five consecutive Midland League championship medals without missing a game. He was also ever-present when they won the Fourth Division title in their first season in the Football League, 1960-61. He later helped Northampton Town to the Third Division championship in 1962-63. When he returned to manage Peterborough United, briefly, they did not win a game during his two months in charge, and were eventually relegated to Division Four. Hails is the father of Julian who broke into the Fulham side in January 1992.

HAIR, Kenneth Grenville A.

Born: Overseal, near Burton upon Trent, 16 November 1931; Died: Bradford, 7 March 1968.
Full-back   5ft 9in; 11st 2st (1962).
Career: Burton Technical High School; Newhall United; Leeds United November 1948; Wellington Town manager May 1964-February 1967; Bradford City trainer February 1967, then manager January-March 1968.
Honours: FA tours to West Indies 1955, 1958, Nigeria and Ghana 1958, New Zealand 1960.

An unassuming character, Hair was well respected by the players whilst briefly in charge at Bradford City. His infectious enthusiasm for football rubbed off on everybody around him. It was a tragedy that he died before he could prove himself as a manager. He was only 36 when he collapsed after a training session and was dead on arrival at hospital. Hair had played in Leeds' promotion side of 1955-56 and won a reputation as a nippy full-back with good positional sense. He made 474 appearances for the Elland Road club before departing to manage Wellington Town. He had been signed from Burton & District League club Newhall United by Leeds manager Frank Buckley. He was a fine, all-round sportsman.

HALE, Kenneth Oliver

Born: Blyth, 18 September 1939.
Inside-forward   5ft 6in; 10st 11lb (1964).
Career: Newcastle United October 1956; Coventry City December 1962 (£10,000); Oxford United March 1966 (£5,000); Darlington May 1968 (£5,000) and caretaker manager January-April 1972; Halifax Town player-coach January 1972 (£500); Hartlepool United manager June 1974-October 1976.
Honours: Division Three champions 1964, 1968.

A small, blond, stocky schemer who possessed good control and a fierce shot, Hale was never a regular at Newcastle but was at all his other clubs. He scored 69 goals in 366 League appearances in his career and won Third Division championship medals with Coventry City in 1963-64 and Oxford United in 1967-68. He was a favourite at Darlington where he made 173 League appearances in midfield and defence.

When he managed Hartlepool, the club achieved mid-table positions in his first two seasons but he was sacked after only one win in the first 17 games of the 1976-77 season. He had previously had experience as player-caretaker manager at Feethams.

HALL, Benjamin

Born: Ecclesfield, Sheffield, 6 March

1879; Died: 1963.
Centre-half/Inside-right
5ft 8in; 12st (1908).
Career: Grimsby Town January 1900; Derby County August 1903; Leicester Fosse August 1911; Hyde (Lancashire Combination) cs 1912; South Shields cs 1913; Grimsby Town coach; Heywood United coach; Hednesford Town trainer 1919-1920; Bristol Rovers manager July 1920-May 1921; Loughborough Corinthians manager in 1920s; Southend United scout after the war.

One of the most skilful centre-halves of his time, Ben Hall was able to link the defence and attack, being a key man of the side, especially at Derby County. Of course, this was in the days when the centre-half had a totally different role to the 'stopper'. He had immaculate ball control for a defender and was also an excellent cricketer.

Hall made 269 appearances for Derby before moving to Leicester Fosse and had begun his career as an inside-forward at Grimsby Town. Hall was Bristol Rovers' first full-time manager and they finished tenth in the newly-formed Third Division in his only season in charge, the side being greatly affected by injuries that season. His brothers Ellis, Fretwell and Harry were all professional footballers.

HALL, George William

Born: Newark, 12 March 1912; Died: Newark, 22 May 1967.
Inside-forward   5ft 7in; 12st 7lb (1935).
Career: Nottingham Schools; Ransome & Marles (Newark); Notts County November 1930; Tottenham Hotspur December 1932, retired through injury 1944; Clapton Orient manager October-December 1945; Chingford Town manager briefly December 1949.
Honours: England international (10 caps); Wartime international (1 cap); Football League representative (3 caps).

Willie Hall had creative skills and was a clever ball-player. He scored nine goals in his ten appearances for England, a healthy ratio considering he was never seen as a goalscorer and helped by five goals against Ireland in November 1938 — a feat which included three in three and a half minutes. For Spurs he managed only 29 goals in 225 games.

Hall helped Tottenham into the First Division in his first season at the club but was injured when they were relegated again and it was injury which ended his career in 1944 when thrombosis eventually led to the amputation of both legs. He faced this with great courage and spirit. Hall was forced to leave Orient due to the illness after only three months in charge. Later he ran a sports shop and also the Archers pub in Aldgate, East London.

HALLIDAY, David

Born: Dumfries, 11 December 1897; Died: January 1970.
Centre-forward   6ft; 12st (1922).
Career: Queen of the South Wanderers; St Mirren; Dundee cs 1921; Sunderland April 1925; Arsenal November 1929 (£6,000); Manchester City November 1930 (£5,700); Clapton Orient December 1933; Yeovil & Petters United manager 1935-January 1938; Aberdeen manager January 1938-July 1955; Leicester City manager July 1955-October 1958.
Honours: Scottish League representative; Scottish League champions 1955; Division Two champions 1957; Scottish Cup winners 1947, runners-up

1926, 1953, 1954; Scottish League Cup runners-up 1947.

Dave Halliday was a prolific goalscorer especially at Dundee and Sunderland. He started his career as a left winger at Queen of the South and St Mirren but was converted into a centre-forward at Dundee and scored over 100 goals in four seasons for them. At Roker Park, he hit another 162 goals before a move to Arsenal but he could not find a regular place at Highbury, although he scored four goals in his last game for the Gunners, in a 6-6 draw with Leicester City in April 1930.

Halliday had played for the Scottish League against the Football League in 1924 and for Dundee in a 2-1 defeat against Celtic in the 1925 Scottish Cup Final. He got the job as Aberdeen's manager from 100 applicants and found much success at Pittodrie, including the Scottish League championship in 1955, shortly before his move to Leicester. Aberdeen beat Hibs in the 1947 Scottish Cup Final but lost two other Finals. He steered Leicester to the Second Division championship but they struggled in the higher division and he resigned in October 1958.

HALLIDAY, Frederick John

Born: 1877.
Full-back   5ft 10in; 12st 1lb (1903).
Career: Chester; Crewe Alexandra; Everton Reserves cs 1900; Bolton Wanderers cs 1901; Bradford City June 1903; Bradford manager May 1907-May 1908; Brentford secretary-manager May 1908-November 1912, secretary only until 1915, secretary-manager until August 1921, secretary-manager again December 1924-May 1926.

Fred Halliday had an unspectacular playing career, including 30 appearances for the Trotters and 74 for the Bantams. He became the manager of Bradford at the age of 30 and was in charge during their only Southern League season, when they finished 13th. He had to turn out in goal in an emergency in March 1908 at Swindon. The regular 'keeper, Tom Badderley, missed the train for the match and his side lost 4-0.

When he moved to Brentford, he had to make financial cuts at the club. On 13 November 1912, Halliday relinquished his post as team manager to devote more time to secretarial duties. He became a virtual full-time fundraiser, organising concerts and other events to raise money for the club. Between 1915 and 1921 he was in charge of the team but concentrated on the administrative side, the signing of players being done by the directors. In December 1924, Halliday returned for

a third spell as manager. However, he left the club after the appointment of Harry Curtis as secretary-manager in 1926.

HALOM, Victor Lewis

Born: Swadlincote, 3 October 1948.
Forward   5ft 10in; 13st 13lb (1980).
Career: Burton & South Derbyshire Boys; Charlton Athletic apprentice March 1964, professional January 1966; Orient August 1967 (£5,000); Fulham November 1968 (£35,000); Luton Town September 1971 (£35,000); Sunderland February 1973 (£35,000); Oldham Athletic July 1976 (£25,000); Rotherham United player-coach February 1980 (£25,000); Fredrikstad (Norway) coach 1982; Barrow manager cs 1983; Rochdale manager May 1984-December 1986; Burton Albion manager September-October 1987, North Shields.

Honours: Division Two champions 1976; Northern Premier League champions 1984; FA Cup winners 1973.

Vic Halom was a solidly-built, aggressive and bustling striker who did the rounds as a player. Bobby Robson just beat Brian Clough for his signature when he signed Halom for Fulham and he helped the club to promotion to Division Two in 1971. He won an FA Cup winners' medal when Sunderland surprisingly beat Leeds in the 1973 Final, and also helped them to promotion as Second Division champions in 1975-76. He scored 131 goals in 452 League appearances in his career. Just before retiring he played in a central midfield role.

His first managerial experience was with non-League Barrow, who walked away with the Northern Premier League championship in 1983-84, with 97 points, 20 points clear of their next rivals. He received an offer to manage Rochdale but found little success at Spotland. His father played in Hungarian soccer. Halom fought as a Liberal Democrat candidate at Sunderland in the 1992 General Election.

HALSEY, Thomas William

Born: London 1895.
Career: Clapton Orient secretary 1935-1939, and manager January-December 1939.

During World War One, Tom Halsey served in the Royal Navy in France, Egypt, Russia and the Mediterranean. He was one of the founders and secretary of Orient's supporters' club and developed fine organisational and administrative abilities. Halsey came to the notice of the Orient board as an official of the supporters' club and was appointed club secretary in 1935. He became acting manager when Peter Proudfoot left the club and stepped down again after a short period officially in charge, to be replaced by Bill Wright. His one major signing was William McFadyen, previously with Motherwell and Huddersfield but whose Orient career was ended, almost before it had begun, by the war.

HAMILTON, Bryan

Born: Belfast, 21 December 1946
Midfield   5ft 8in; 11st 2lb (1983).
Career: Linfield; Ipswich Town August 1971 (£15,000); Everton November 1975 (£40,000); Millwall July 1977 (£12,000); Swindon Town November 1978 (£20,000); Tranmere Rovers player-manager October 1980-February 1985; retired as a player 1983; Wigan Athletic manager 1985-June 1986; Leicester City

manager June 1986-December 1987; Wigan Athletic chief executive from March 1988, manager March 1989. Wigan Athletic manager March 1989-March 1993.

Honours: Northern Ireland international (50 caps); Under-23 international (2 caps); Football League Cup runners-up 1977; Freight/Rover Trophy winners 1985.

A terrier-like midfielder in his playing days, Bryan Hamilton began his career at Linfield and as a £6 a week part-timer won his first Northern Ireland cap in 1968. After impressing during the 1971 Home International Championships, Ipswich Town signed him for £26,000 in July 1971. He moved to Everton in November 1975, for £40,000, but was not a regular at Goodison Park. In October 1980 he was transferred to Tranmere Rovers as their player-manager. He made his final appearance in November 1983, but remained in charge at Prenton Park until February 1985, when he was sacked.

He had steered the club through a number of crises before his departure. After his initial spell at Wigan, he joined Leicester City as manager in June 1986 but the club were relegated to Division Two and struggling the following season, when he was sacked in December 1987. Hamilton had a rather ambiguous role upon his return to Wigan and took full charge of team affairs only in March 1989. His best season at Wigan was 1985-86 when the club finished fourth in Division Three. He took them to a Freight Rover/ Trophy Final victory in May 1985. Wigan have struggled with very low crowds and little success on the pitch. Hamilton managed to keep the side in the Third Division for four seasons which was a miracle in itself.

Hamilton lost his job in March 1993 due to the club's poor performance as they struggled to get away from the bottom of the table. He was replaced by Dave Philpotts as caretaker manager. The one bright point of the season was Wigan reaching the Northern Final of the Autoglass Trophy where they lost at Stockport County and missed out on a trip to Wembley.

HAMILTON, James

Born: Hetton-le-Hole.
Centre-half   5ft 11in; 12st (1935).
Career: Coldstream Guards; Crystal Palace December 1922; Hartlepools United May 1931; Gateshead player-coach October 1934; Hartlepools United manager July 1935-September 1939.

Honours: FA Tour to Australia 1925 (4 caps).

Hamilton was serving in the Coldstream Guards in London when he was offered a trial by Crystal Palace in 1922. He had previously represented the Army at boxing. He made his debut against Bradford City in October 1923 and was in the Palace side relegated to the Third Division South in 1925. They were Southern Section runners-up twice, in 1928-29 and 1930-31, but were not promoted as only the champions went up. He made 196 appearances for Palace and a further 49 for Hartlepools, where he was also the captain.

Hamilton ran a sub Post Office and tobacco business whilst playing for the latter. The North-East club finished eighth in the Northern Section when he returned as manager in the 1935-36 season. Gate receipts improved and he was able to resist offers for promising youngsters, but United had to seek re-election in the last season before the outbreak of war. Some sources say he resigned in September 1939, due to the war, others that he left the club in 1943.

HAMILTON, A.John 'Jock'

Born: Ayr 1872.
Centre-half   5ft 9in; 12st 4lb (1901).
Career: Ayr United: Wolverhampton Wanderers June 1894; Loughborough cs 1895; Bristol City cs 1897; Leicester Fosse September 1900; Watford April 1901; Wellingborough cs 1902; Fulham cs 1903, assistant trainer 1904-1908, head trainer 1908-1910; Bristol City reserve-team trainer 1910, then manager May 1915-August 1919.

A serious injury, shortly after he joined Wolves, meant that Jack Hamilton played only four games for the club. He was ever-present in Loughborough's inaugural League season and was also the tough-tackling skipper of Bristol City. Hamilton was described as a player who was 'endowed with any amount of pluck and endurance and a champion tackler who feeds his forwards with wonderful tact and judgement'. He played 128 games for Bristol City and was also a regular at Leicester, Watford and Wellingborough. A very popular trainer and much liked by the players at Fulham, Hamilton was manager at Ashton Gate during the World War One, having previously been in charge of the Reserves.

HAMPSON, William

Born: Radcliffe, Lancashire, 26 August 1882; Died: Congleton, 23 February 1966.
Right-back   5ft 9in; 11st 2lb (1923).
Career: Rochdale; Bury 1906; Norwich City 1907; Newcastle United January 1914 (£1,250); guest for Leeds City in World War One; South Shields September 1927, retired cs 1928; Carlisle United manager March 1930-May 1932; Ashington manager c.1934; Leeds United manager July 1935-May 1947, then chief scout; Northumberland Schools coach.

Honours: FA Cup winners 1924.

Billy Hampson was a late developer who gave good service to all of his clubs. He did not win a regular first-team spot at St James' Park until the departure of Bill McCracken and he became the oldest person to gain an FA Cup medal, at 41 years 8 months when playing right-back in the 1924 Final, in which Newcastle beat Aston Villa 2-0.

His first managerial post was at Carlisle United where he instituted a drastic clear-out of players in the summer of 1930, leaving only nine of the previous season's squad still at Brunton Park. United scored plenty of goals but also conceded them.

At Leeds he consolidated their First Division status, signing many fine players from Ireland. They won the Central League in 1936-37, for the only time, with a fine crop of youngsters. Hampson was highly respected by the players but his last season at Elland Road was disastrous. In 1946-47, Leeds won only six games and were relegated to the Second Division. He remained at the club as chief scout for a while after losing his job as manager. His brother, Tom, played for Darlington.

HAND, Eion

Born: Dublin, 30 March 1946
Centre-half   6ft; 12st (1971).
Career: Stella Maris; Old O'Connells; Swindon Town June 1964; Dundalk; Drumcondra; Portsmouth October 1968; to South Africa March 1976; Shamrock Rovers 1977; Portsmouth December 1977; Limerick player-manager July 1979-March 1983; Republic of Ireland team manager June 1980-November 1985; St Patrick's Athletic manager June 1984-July 1985; Riyadh (Saudi Arabia) coach September 1986-November 1987; Huddersfield Town assistant manager November 1987, then manager June 1988-March 1992.

Honours: Republic of Ireland international (19 caps).

Hand failed to make the grade at Swindon and returned to Ireland to play for Dundalk and Drumcondra before Portsmouth signed him for £7,500 in October 1968. A strong, determined and forceful centre-half, Hand also appeared at full-back and midfield for Pompey, making 302/4 appearances for the club in his two spells before being given a free transfer and joining Limerick United as player-manager in July 1979.

In his first season in charge, Hand guided the unfashionable League of Ireland club to their first championship in 20 years and to the semi-finals of the FAI Cup. During the 1979-80 season he also joined Alan Kelly as the Republic of Ireland's assistant team manager and when commitments at Preston forced Kelly resignation, Hand took over as part-time team manager in June 1980, remaining as manager of Limerick United.

He stayed in charge of Ireland until the arrival of Jack Charlton but was unable to reach any finals of major competitions with the national side. As manager of Huddersfield Town, he saw the Terriers finish eighth in Division Three in 1989-90, just missing out on the play-offs after being in a good position in February.

Hand surprisingly lost his job in March 1992 with the club in fourth place in the Third Division and after two good runs in the cup, the Terriers eventually reached the play-offs after his departure.

HAPGOOD, Edris Albert

Born: Bristol, 24 September 1908; Died: Leamington Spa, 20 April 1973.
Left-back   5ft 9in; 11st (1935).
Career: Bristol Rovers trial May 1927; Kettering Town cs 1927; Arsenal October 1927 (£750); guest for Chelsea and Luton Town in World War Two; Blackburn Rovers manager January 1946-February 1947; Shrewsbury Town player-coach August 1947; Watford manager February 1948-March 1950;

Bath City manager March 1950-February 1956.

Honours: England international (30 caps); Wartime international (13 caps); Football League representative (4 caps); Football League champions 1931, 1933, 1934, 1935, 1938; FA Cup winners 1930, 1936, runners-up 1932; Football League War Cup runners-up 1941.

Eddie Hapgood, England's most capped player between the wars, rarely missed a match for Arsenal between 1929 and 1939 and would have made even more than 487 appearances had the later years of his playing career not been affected by the war. An elegant defender, calm and with a terrific positional sense, Hapgood was also an accurate passer of the ball. He won five League championship medals and two FA Cup winners' medals during his time at Highbury.

As a manager he did not have a bad record at either Watford or Blackburn Rovers, but his impulsive honesty was a handicap at times when dealing with directors. He was too straightforward and outspoken to play politics or to assuage other egos. At Ewood Park, directors signed players which he did not want and a rift developed between them, forcing Hapgood to resign his post. At Bath, he took the club to the second round proper of the FA Cup and was voted Southern League Manager of the Year in 1953. After leaving soccer he became a warden at a youth hostel.

HARDWICK, George Francis Moutry

Born: Saltburn, Yorks, 2 February 1920.
Left-back   5ft 10in; 12st 8lb (1938).
Career: South Bank East End 1934; Middlesbrough amateur October 1935, professional May 1937; guest for Chelsea in World War Two; Oldham Athletic player-manager November 1950-June 1956 (£15,000); US Army (Germany) coach August 1956; PSV Eindhoven (Holland) coach June 1957-cs 1959; Middlesbrough coach August 1961-November 1963; Sunderland manager November 1964-May 1965; Gateshead manager 1968-February 1970; chairman of a structural steel company 1970.

Honours: England international (13 caps); Wartime international (16 caps); Football League representative (3 caps); Great Britain v Europe 1947; Division Three North champions 1953; Football League South Cup runners-up 1944, winners 1945.

A cultured and immaculate defender who was one of the classiest defenders just after the war, George Hardwick played as a guest for Chelsea in two wartime Finals at Wembley and is one of the best full-backs to have played for the Middlesbrough club. He moved to Oldham Athletic as player-manager at the age of 30 and greatly improved their side. The Latics won the Third Division North title in 1952-53 but were relegated the following season as he had no money to spend on strengthening the side.

After leaving Boundary Park after a poor season in 1955-56, Hardwick did not return to management for eight years. His spell in charge of Sunderland was brief. The club struggled to avoid relegation from the First Division and eventually finished 15th. The supporters and the board expected more and he lost his job. He did not have a happy spell at Gateshead either, for they lost their Northern Premier League status in 1969-70.

HARDY, William

Born: Bedlington, 18 April 1891; Died: Newton Abbot winter 1981.
Left-half   5ft 6in; 10st 10lb (1919).
Career: Bedlington United; Heart of Midlothian 1910; Stockport County November 1911; Cardiff City December 1911, retired 1932; Bradford manager May 1934-April 1936, then chief scout.

Honours: Football League representative; FA Cup winners 1927, runners-up 1925; Welsh Cup winners 1922, 1927.

Billy Hardy made 473 Southern and Football League appearances for the Bluebirds. He cost Cardiff just £20 and stayed at Ninian Park for 21 years. They were one of the leading clubs in the 1920s and were runners-up in the First Division, missing out on goal-average, in 1923-24. Cardiff had won promotion to the First Division as runners-up in 1920-21. He also played in two FA Cup Finals for City. In 1925 they lost 1-0 to Sheffield United but two years later became the only club ever to take the trophy out of England when they beat Arsenal 1-0. The club went into decline after this and were relegated in 1928-29 and again in 1930-31 to the Third Division. Hardy was unlucky never to play for England and was probably not selected because he was with a Welsh club. He was quick in the tackle, speedy in recovery and a great distributor of the ball. Hardy was in charge of Park Avenue for two seasons in which they finished 15th and 16th in the Second Division.

HARFORD, Raymond

Born: Halifax, 1 June 1945.
Centre-half   6ft 1in; 12st 12lb.
Career: Charlton Athletic May 1964; Exeter City January 1966; Lincoln City July 1967; Mansfield Town June 1971; Port Vale December 1971; Colchester United 1973-1976, then youth-team coach. Fulham youth-team manager cs 1981, assistant manager cs 1982, then manager April 1984-1986; Luton Town assistant manager July 1986 then manager June 1987; Wimbledon assistant manager February 1990, then manager June 1990-October 1991; Blackburn Rovers assistant manager October 1991.

Honours: Football League Cup winners 1988, runners-up 1989; Simod Cup runners-up 1988.

Ray Harford was Luton Town's most successful manager ever, but still ended up getting the sack. Luton chairman Mr Robert Smith will probably always be remembered for his justification for Harford's sacking: amongst other

things he stated that Harford did not smile enough.

Certainly, Harford never had much time for the Press and would usually steer clear of journalists. But he was always willing to talk to players and other football people and although he comes across as distant and dour, he is in fact a very amiable person. He had taken Luton to two League Cup Finals at Wembley, winning the first and losing the second.

He made only three appearances for Charlton before moving to Exeter City and after a further 60 League and Cup appearances for the Grecians, he was transferred to Lincoln City, where he remained for four seasons, scoring ten goals in 161 League games for the Imps. He spent six months at Field Mill and made 20 appearances for Port Vale before moving to Colchester in January 1973. They won promotion to the Third Division in 1973-74, when they finished third. After two cartilage operations in quick succession, Harford decided to retire in 1976. He had just obtained a full FA coaching badge and became the youth-team manager at Layer Road.

In the summer of 1981, he was employed by Malcolm Macdonald as youth-team coach at Fulham and following the departure of George Armstrong 12 months later, he stepped up to be first-team coach and assistant manager.

Harford became acknowledged as one of the best coaches in the country. Fulham played neat, attractive football under his guidance and nearly won promotion to the First Division in 1982-83, but threw their chance away after looking like certainties. When Macdonald left in April 1984, Harford was given the manager's job for the rest of the season. With five wins in six games he was appointed permanently at the end of the season.

Very knowledgeable and dedicated to the game, Harford's efforts to find success at the Cottage were undermined by chairman Ernie Clay, who had a policy of selling every asset at his disposal. Ray Houghton was one of the players sold for just £125,000 to Oxford. Disillusioned with having the carpets forever pulled from under his feet, Harford resigned in June 1986 and moved to Luton Town as assistant to John Moore.

In June 1987, Moore resigned and Harford became his successor. In his first season in charge, Luton finished ninth in the First Division and also had a remarkable season in Cup competitions. In the League Cup, the Hatters reached the Final at Wembley, where they beat Arsenal 3-2 to lift their first major trophy. In the FA Cup they lost 2-1 to Wimbledon in the semi-final at White Hart Lane before a paltry crowd of 25,963. They also reached another Wembley Final in the Simod Cup but lost 4-1 to Reading. The following season they again reached the League Cup Final but lost 3-1 to Nottingham Forest.

In January 1990, with Luton lying 19th in the First Division, Harford was sacked. The following month he teamed up with Bobby Gould at Wimbledon and became caretaker manager when Gould resigned in the summer. He was permanently appointed in December 1990 but resigned, giving six months' notice, in August 1991 after Keith Curle was sold to Manchester City without his consent. Wimbledon had just moved from Plough Lane to Selhurst Park.

Harford moved to Blackburn Rovers as Kenny Dalglish's assistant in October 1991 and played a leading role in the resurgence of the club's fortune thanks to the cheque book of the club's owner, Jack Walker. Rovers gained promotion in 1991-92 to enter the newly formed Premier League and were then one of the leading club's in it's inaugural season.

HARRIS, Brian

Born: Bebbington, 16 March 1935.
Wing-half   5ft 8in; 10st 2lb (1959).
Career: Port Sunlight; Everton January 1954; Cardiff City October 1966 (£10,000); Newport County player-coach July 1971, assistant manager 1972, then player-manager January 1974-March 1975; Chepstow 1975; Cardiff City assistant manager December 1978-1980; Ipswich Town coach 1980.

Honours: Football League champions 1963; FA Cup winners 1966; England Youth international.

Harris instilled confidence in those around him. Signed by Everton as a winger, he was converted into a fine wing half who helped Everton to the League championship in 1962-63 and to the FA Cup in 1966, when Sheffield Wednesday were beaten 3-2 in an exciting Final. When he moved to Cardiff City he helped to transform a struggling side into a good Second Division outfit. He lasted 14 months as player-manager of Newport County but resigned after a disagreement over financial restraints. After leaving Somerton Park, Harris became a publican for a while.

HARRIS, John

Born: Glasgow, 30 June 1917; Died 24 July 1988.
Centre-half/Full-back
5ft 10in; 12st 8lb (1951).
Career: Swindon Town amateur; Swansea Town August 1934; Tottenham Hotspur February 1939; Wolverhampton Wanderers May 1939; Chelsea August 1945 (£8,000); Chester player-manager July 1956-April 1959; Sheffield United manager April 1959-July 1968, the general manager July 1968-August 1969, manager again August 1969-December 1973, then chief scout; Sheffield Wednesday coach late 1970s.

Honours: Scotland Wartime international (1 cap); Football League champions 1955; Division Two runners-up 1961, 1971; League Cup South winners 1945, runners-up 1944.

Like his father Neil (of Newcastle United), John Harris became a manager at the end of a distinguished playing career and they are one of the few father-and-son combinations to become managers.

John Harris started his management career at Chester in April 1956. There was not much success on the field at Sealand Road, but he did discover future Welsh international Ron Davies in a schoolboy match. Davies later found fame at Norwich City and Southampton.

Sheffield United must have been impressed with Harris' track record of producing good young talent as he was invited to take over at Bramall Lane in April 1959. There were many experienced professionals on the club's books in those days including Alan Hodgkinson, Cec Coldwell, Graham Shaw, Brian Richardson, Joe Shaw, Gerry Summers and Derek Pace. It was a good side which went on to win

promotion as runners-up in the Second Division and reached the semi-finals of the FA Cup in 1961, losing to Leicester City after three games.

When the team needed rebuilding, Harris gained a reputation for producing good young players and United had established themselves as a good mid-table First Division side when Harris made the mistake of selling two of his best players. Mick Jones went to Leeds United and Alan Birchenall to Chelsea for £100,000 each. Without them the Blades were relegated at the end of 1967-68.

For the following season Arthur Rowley took over from Harris, who became the general manager. United finished ninth the following season but Rowley was dismissed, accompanied by a strange silence from the board as to why this had happened. Harris took back his old job and it was a period where Bramall Lane was given a face-lift as a new stand was built and the sharing of the ground with Yorkshire CCC came to an end.

One of Harris' best signings came in February 1968, when he paid Watford £26,500 for Tony Currie, who later became an England international and played a big role in United's revival and eventual promotion back to Division One in 1971. The Blades were an established First Division club when Harris left in December 1973. Harris ended his career at Sheffield Wednesday in the 1970s as coach under the management of Jack Charlton.

A Glaswegian, John Harris started his playing career under his father's management at Swansea Town in 1934. Transferred to Spurs during the 1938-39 season as an inside-forward, his stay was brief. They made the mistake of giving Harris a free transfer and Wolves manager Major Buckley stepped in to sign him and converted him into a centre-half. He guested for Southampton and Chelsea during the war and played 109 wartime games for the Pensioners between 1943 and 1946, including two wartime Wembley Cup Final appearances, in 1944 and 1945. Harris was capped by Scotland against England in an unofficial international in April 1945.

Four months later he signed permanently for Chelsea, for a £5,000 fee, and went on to give them sterling service, first at centre-half and later at full-back, a position he was converted to by manager Ted Drake. Harris was a dominant figure on the field and an influential captain. He was renowned

for his hard tackling and shrewd positional sense. After missing out on two Wembley Finals, in 1950 and 1952 when Chelsea went out in the semi-finals, Harris played in the Blues' League championship side of 1954-55 at the age of 37. Greater international recognition might have come but for his lack of inches for a centre-half.

HARRIS, Neil L.

Born: Tollcross, Glasgow, 30 October 1894; Died: 3 December 1941.
Centre-forward   5ft 8in; 11st (1924).
Career: Vale of Clyde; Partick Thistle June 1913; guest for Belfast Distillery, Kilmarnock and Fulham in World War One; Newcastle United May 1920 (£3,300); Notts County November 1925 (£3,000); Oldham Athletic July 1927; Third Lanark March 1929; Burton Town player-manager July 1931; Distillery manager May 1932; Swansea Town manager July 1934-May 1939; Swindon Town manager May 1939-December 1941.

Honours: Scotland international (1 cap); FA Cup winners 1924.

Neil Harris was a daring centre-forward who was aggressive, fast and also possessed brilliant ball control. He played for Fulham as a guest in the London Victory Cup Final in 1919 and also scored in Newcastle's 2-0 FA Cup Final victory over Aston Villa in 1924. With a good shot and an eye for goal, Harris scored an outstanding total of 103 goals in his 194 appearances for the Tyneside club. His brother, Joe, played for Leeds United and Fulham and his son, John, later managed several clubs. As manager of Swansea Town, Neil Harris had a constant struggle to avoid relegation from the Second Division during his years in charge. He took over at Swindon just before the outbreak of war and died whilst in office.

HARRIS, Ronald E.

Born: Hackney, 13 November 1944.
Defender   5ft 8in; 11st 7lb (1983).
Career: Chelsea apprentice August 1960, professional November 1961; Brentford player-coach May 1980-November 1983; Aldershot manager November 1984-85.

Honours: England Under-23 international (4 caps); Schoolboy international (6 caps); Youth international (8 caps); FA Cup winners 1970, runners-up 1967; Football League Cup winners 1965, runners-up 1972; European Cup-winners' Cup winners 1971; FA Youth Cup winners 1961.

Known as 'Chopper' for his tough, uncompromising tackling, Ron Harris played 783/11 games for Chelsea over 19 seasons and holds the appearance record for the club. He was the pillar of the Blues' defence and was the youngest-ever player to captain an FA Cup Final side when Chelsea lost 2-1 to Spurs in 1967. Harris gained his winners' medal in the epic Final against Leeds three years later, and also won a European Cup-winners' Cup winners medal against Real Madrid in Athens in 1971. Ron Harris was Aldershot's manager for the 1984-85 season. The home fans had to wait until the end of October for their first League win and the Shots eventually finished 14th in Division Four. Harris lost his job when a new board took over the club.

HARRIS, William Charles

Born: Swansea, 31 October 1928; Died: Middlesbrough, December 1989.

Wing-half   6ft; 11st 6lb (1959).
Career: Swansea Town amateur; Llanelli 1949; Hull City March 1950 (£2,000); Middlesbrough March 1954 (£15,000); Bradford City player-manager March 1965-March 1966; Stockton coach November 1967-May 1969; worked in an insurance company in Middlesbrough.

Honours: Wales international (6 caps).

Harris was a lithe and lively player who had incisive passing ability. He started his career as a professional with Hull City on the right wing and made 131 League appearances before his move to Middlesbrough. He was a great favourite with the Ayresome crowd, rarely missing a game and finally scoring 72 goals in 378 appearances for the club before moving on. He made his international debut for Wales against Austria in Vienna in May 1954 and went on to gain a further five caps for his country. As manager of Bradford City he failed to find success and signed far too many players who were past their best.

HARRISON, Stephen John

Born: Blackpool, 26 December 1952.
Defender   5ft 7in; 11st 1lb (1971).
Career: Blackpool December 1970; Vancouver Whitecaps (loan) April-August 1978; Watford September 1978; Charlton Athletic July 1981; Watford youth-team coach 1983-1988, then manager January 1988-March 1990; Millwall coach July 1990-October 1991; England coach August 1990-October 1991; Crystal Palace coach November 1991.

Steve Harrison was employed by Graham Taylor at Watford, Villa and England. He has exceptional coaching ability but did not particularly enjoy being a manager. He loves a practical joke and found it difficult to adapt to the seriousness of club management. Indeed, it was a particularly revolting 'joke' which saw him sacked by Millwall and thus by England.

After the departure of Graham Taylor to Villa, Harrison soon followed. Everybody had expected Watford to offer him the manager's job when Taylor left but instead it was given to Dave Bassett. When things did not work out for Bassett, Harrison came back to Vicarage Road as manager. Watford reached the fifth round of the FA Cup in 1989-90, but could finished only 15th in Division Two and he was sacked. The previous season they had made the play-offs but lost to Blackburn in the semi-finals.

Harrison had an eventful 1990: in March he was sacked by Watford; in July he was employed as a coach by Bruce Rioch at Millwall; and in September he became an England coach under Graham Taylor. The following year, after his jape in poor taste, all this came crashing down about his ears, amidst a host of sensational newspaper headlines. He nearly moved to St Johnstone as assistant manager in December 1992 but more bad publicity made him change his mind.

HARROWER, James Swanson

Born: Crossgates, Fife, 19 June 1924.
Half-back   5ft 11in; 12st (1959).
Career: Dunfermline Athletic 1943; Third Lanark 1945; Accrington Stanley December 1954 (£1,750)-December 1961, player-manager from April 1960 until his resignation; possibly Albion Rovers manager May-November 1969.

Jimmy Harrower played 246 games for

Accrington Stanley after joining the Peel Park club from Scottish League Third Lanark. His first game as Stanley's manager ended in a 9-2 defeat at Crystal Palace on the opening day of the season but Accrington still improved on the previous season, finishing 18th in Division Four in 1960-61, thus avoiding re-election. The club was in desperate straits the following season with poor attendances and ever-increasing debts. Harrower resigned in January 1962 with Stanley on the brink of extinction. Two months later they resigned from the Football League and disbanded.

During his playing career, Harrower twice won Glasgow Cup medals with Third Lanark and was reserve for the Scottish League representative side. In 1954-55 he played for the Third Division North against the Third Division South at Reading. When he took over at Stanley he was their seventh manager since the war and their fourth in only two years.

HART, John P.

Born: Golbourne, 8 June 1928.
Inside-forward 5ft 9½in; 11st 2lb (1959).
Career: Loughton Youth Club; Manchester City December 1944, retired May 1963 to become coach, then manager May-November 1973.

Johnny Hart was a great servant to Manchester City but, largely due to a succession of injuries, in 19 years at Maine Road he made only 178 appearances, scoring 73 goals. A broken leg at Huddersfield just before City's appearances in the 1955 FA Cup Final was a particularly cruel blow for Hart. He never re-established himself after this, making only 11 more appearances before retiring.

Hart was coach for ten years but manager for only six months and had to give up the job due to ill health. He had been a surprise choice as manager after the departure of Malcolm Allison. Hart signed Denis Law on a free transfer from Manchester United during his period as manager. He was still working at Maine Road in the late-1980s, on the promotional side of the club. He is the father of Paul, Brian and Martin Hart.

HART, Leslie John

Born: Ashton-in-Makerfield, 28 February 1917.
Centre-half 5ft 11in; 12st (1951).
Career: Ashton National; Bury December 1936-1954, when he retired to become trainer, then coach and

physiotherapist from cs 1957-March 1980, except for when he was manager September 1969-September 1970.

'Mr Bury', Les Hart served the Gigg Lane club for 44 years — 18 years a player, 25 as trainer and physiotherapist and just one year as manager. He was with the club from 1936 to 1980. He made 280 League and 166 wartime appearances for the Shakers.

Hart had a thankless task as manager because there was instability in the boardroom and the club was at its lowest ebb. Bury were lucky to survive relegation in 1969-70, staying up only due to the failings of others, and they lost £47,443 on the season but sold Jimmy Kerr to Blackburn for £60,000 to cover the losses.

HART, Paul Anthony

Born: Manchester, 4 May 1953.
Centre-half 6ft 2in; 12st 8lb (1979).
Career: Manchester Boys; Stockport County apprentice June 1969, professional September 1970; Blackpool June 1973 (£25,000); Leeds United March 1978 (£300,000); Nottingham Forest May 1983 (£40,000); Sheffield Wednesday August 1985; Birmingham City December 1986; Notts County player-coach June 1987 (£15,000); Chesterfield manager November 1988-January 1991; Grantham as player 1991; Nottingham Forest coach June 1991.

A strong competitor with considerable aggression, Paul Hart was signed by Leeds United for a £300,000 fee from Blackpool as a replacement for Gordon McQueen. He had been the star of the side at the seaside club but took some time to settle at Elland Road and in his early games made simple errors and gave away own-goals. Hart made 143 League appearances for Blackpool and 223 in all for Leeds United. He had the misfortune to suffer a broken leg in his only game for Birmingham City.

Chesterfield were relegated to the Fourth Division at the end of his first season in charge. They had been rock-bottom when he took over but had made a fine recovery and were unlucky to go down. They made the Fourth Division play-offs in 1989-90 but things went badly wrong the following season and Hart lost his job.

HARTFORD, Richard Asa

Born: Clydebank, 24 October 1950.
Midfield 5ft 7in; 10st 6lb (1976).

Career: Drumchapel Amateurs; West Bromwich Albion apprentice April 1966, professional November 1967; Manchester City August 1974

(£225,000); Nottingham Forest June 1979 (£500,000); Everton August 1979 (£400,000); Manchester City October 1981 (£350,000); Fort Lauderdale (NASL) May 1984; Norwich City October 1984; Bolton Wanderers player-coach July 1985; Stockport County player-manager June 1987-April 1989; Shrewsbury Town coach July 1989, then manager January 1990-January 1991; Boston United player February 1991.

Honours: Scotland international (50 caps); Under-23 international (5 caps); Under-21 international (1 cap); Youth international; Football League Cup winners 1976, 1985, runners-up 1970; Freight/Rover Trophy runners-up 1986.

A midfield dynamo with excellent control and vision, Asa Hartford was always poised and confident. A move to Leeds in November 1971 was halted after it was discovered that he had heart problems. However, his stamina soon swept away doubts about his fitness. Indeed, he made 710 League appearances in his career including 318 in all matches for Manchester City in two spells at the club. As well as his 50 Scotland caps, Hartford also appeared in three League Cup Finals, for Albion in 1970, City in 1976 and Norwich City in 1985 when his shot was deflected in for the only goal of the game. He has not been a success as a manager. Stockport could manage no better than 20th in Division Four in his two seasons in charge and he lost his job at Shrewsbury with the club struggling near the foot of the Third Division.

HARTLEY, Trevor

Born: Doncaster, 16 March 1947.
Inside-forward 5ft 8in; 9st 13lb (1970).
Career: Holloway School; West Ham United July 1964; Bournemouth & Boscombe Athletic July 1969, coach 1971, then manager November 1973-January 1975; director of coaching in Singapore 1976; Luton Town reserve-team coach 1984-1985; Tottenham Hotspur assistant manager May 1986.

A speedy, fair-haired winger, Hartley moved from West Ham to Bournemouth as he wanted first-team football, but made only 42 League appearances for the Dean Court club. He decided to concentrate on his coaching career at the young age of 24 and three years later he took over as manager after the departure of John Bond. Hartley was later assistant manager to David Pleat at Luton Town and moved with him to White Hart Lane.

HARVEY, James Colin

Born: Liverpool, 16 November 1944.
Midfield 5ft 7½in; 11st (1976).
Career: Everton apprentice 1961, professional October 1962; Sheffield Wednesday September 1974 (£70,000), retired through hip injury March 1976; Everton youth-team coach 1976, reserve-team coach and first-team coach November 1983, then manager June 1987-November 1990 before reverting to assistant manager.

Honours: England international (1 cap); Under-23 international (5 caps); Football League representative (3 caps); Football League champions 1970; FA Cup winners 1966, runners-up 1968, 1989.

Colin Harvey had a colossal work-rate, skill on the ball, an excellent positional sense and fine passing ability. At Everton he formed a famous midfield trio with Alan Ball and Howard

Kendall and they helped the Toffees to the League championship in 1969-70. Harvey made his debut for Everton in a European Cup tie at the San Siro stadium in 1963 and won his England cap against Malta in 1971.

He replaced Kendall as manager at Everton after working as a coach for 11 years. Everton won the FA Charity Shield, against Coventry at Wembley in his first match in charge. In 1988, they lost a two-legged League Cup semi-final against Arsenal. Many problems soon developed, both on and off the field, and inconsistency fueled discontent. After winning no trophies in season 1987-88, Harvey spent £4 million on new players including Tony Cottee, Pat Nevin and Stuart McCall. Everton reached the FA Cup Final in 1989, losing 3-2 to neighbours Liverpool, but Harvey reverted to assistant manager after the return of Kendall in November 1990.

HARVEY, Joseph

Born: Edlington, Doncaster, 11 June 1918; Died: February 1989.
Wing-half 6ft; 12st 2lb (1951).
Career: Edlington Rangers; Bradford May 1936; Wolverhampton Wanderers November 1936; Bournemouth & Boscombe Athletic May 1937; Newcastle United October 1945 (£4,250), retired 1953 to become assistant trainer; Crook Town trainer 1955; Barrow manager July 1955-June 1957; Workington manager June 1957-June 1962; Newcastle United manager June 1962-June 1975, the general manager and chief scout almost up to his death.

Honours: Football League representative (3 caps); Division Two champions 1965; FA Cup winners 1951, 1952, runners-up 1974; Inter-Cities Fairs Cup winners 1969.

Joe Harvey was one of the few footballers to succeed as manager of a club where he was a star player. He was devoted to Newcastle United for almost 30 years, first as a player, then as a coach and also as manager from 1962 to 1975, and finally as the general manager and chief scout, working almost up to his death in February 1989.

He signed professional forms with Bradford but stayed for only a short while before a move to Wolves. Harvey moved on to Bournemouth in May 1937, but his career was soon to be interrupted by the war. A tough, all-round defensive player, Harvey was at his best when the contest was at its thickest.

He fell in love with the Newcastle area during his Army days, when he was stationed in the district, and Newcastle United paid £4,250 to secure his services in October 1945. Over the next eight years he was the mainstay of the half-back line at St James' Park. As captain he led United into Division One in 1948 and to two FA Cup Final victories in 1951 and 1952. His only representative honours were three appearances for the Football League. When he retired in 1953, he became club coach and held that position when United won the FA Cup again in 1955.

After a brief spell as trainer at Crook Town, he moved to Barrow as manager in July 1955. The Holker Street club needed reorganising and Harvey was not frightened to do it. His innovations included the purchase of club houses in order to attract better players, installing training floodlights, an update of the junior players set-up, and an overhaul of the club's scouting system.

When Barrow finished tenth in Division Three North in season 1956-57, it looked as though Harvey may have been on the point of producing something worthwhile for the club, but he left on 24 June 1957 to join fellow strugglers Workington. The balance sheet at Workington was his first priority and the position in the table a secondary consideration. Every season a player had to be sold to pay the summer wages of the others. Harvey was fighting a losing battle with little success on the field and as attendances plummeted, he was on the point of leaving soccer in 1962 to concentrate on his shops back in Newcastle.

In June of that year Newcastle United offered him the manager's post, an offer he could not refuse. Harvey brought the Magpies out of years of obscurity and was always willing to pay big money for players he considered were right for the club. His brand of football was fast and entertaining with star players who thrilled the crowds.

Newcastle were struggling, a very average Second Division side when he arrived, but he took them back to the First Division as champions in 1964-65. They qualified for the 1968-69 Fairs Cup and won the competition, beating Újpesti Dózsa 6-2 over two legs in the Final after some thrilling games in the earlier rounds. Harvey made some fine signings and his best was undoubtedly Malcolm Macdonald, a striker who cost £180,000 from Third Division Luton Town.

For Harvey, 'Supermac' had everything a manager was looking for in a striker: courage, speed and a sharp eye. His judgement was proved right as Macdonald became a hero of the Geordies and later the England supporters. However, Harvey was unable to complete the double of captaining and managing a club to an FA Cup Final victory, as United lost to Liverpool 3-0 in the 1974 Final.

Resignation was forced on Harvey in May 1975 by public opinion. He had taken a lot of unjustified criticism as a manager and this was the final straw. He remained at the club almost up to his death, working as either general manager or chief scout.

HARVEY, Martin

Born: Belfast, 19 September 1941.
Midfield/wing-half
5ft 10in; 11st 10lb (1964).
Career: Sunderland September 1958-1972; Carlisle United trainer-coach 1978, then manager February-September 1980, then coach for a while; Plymouth Argyle coach 1981-1989.
Honours: Northern Ireland international (33 caps); Under-23 international

(3 caps); 'B' international (1 cap); Schoolboy international.

Stylish and constructive, Martin Harvey was also a fine tackler and an excellent all-round player. He made 310/4 League appearances for Sunderland after ousting Stan Anderson from the right-half berth in 1963. He also replaced Danny Blanchflower in the Northern Ireland side and went on to make 33 appearances for his country. As manager of Carlisle United, results improved after he took over from Bobby Moncur and the club eventually finished sixth in 1979-80. However, after a very bad start to the following season, Harvey resigned. He was thus the shortest-ever serving manager of Carlisle.

HARVEY, William

Born: Grimsby, 1920.
Career: Grimsby Schools; Grimsby Town; Boston United; Peterborough United; Spalding United; Bristol City coach 1958-1962; Luton Town manager July 1962-November 1964; Swindon Town coach 1964; Bristol City coach July 1965; Grimsby Town manager January 1968-January 1969; Peterborough United physiotherapist-coach 1983.

Bill Harvey never played in the Football League, appearing only for Grimsby Town Reserves and Peterborough United during their Midland League days. After establishing a reputation as a coach at Ashton Gate, Harvey impressed the Luton directors at his interview for the manager's post and was offered the job even though he was not a front runner.

He had a difficult time at Kenilworth Road with falling attendances, lack of financial support and restrictions caused by increases in players' wages. The Hatters were relegated to Division Three with only 29 points at the close of the 1962-63 season.

Harvey was popular character who cracked jokes to try to lift morale. He nurtured Ron Davies during his spell at Luton and at Grimsby, he managed to steer the club away from relegation by the slimmest of margins at the end of his first season. He was forced to sell many of his best players and resigned with the club heading towards the bottom of the Third Division.

HARVEY, William Henry Tompkins

Born: Netley, Hants, 12 April 1896. Died: South Africa c.1970.
Outside-right   5ft 9in; 11st (1920).
Career: Yorkshire amateurs; 2nd Battalion, West Riding Regiment; Sheffield Wednesday October 1919; Birmingham July 1921, assistant secretary August 1926, then manager March 1927-May 1928; Chesterfield secretary-manager June 1932-June 1938; Gillingham manager June 1938-1939; cricket for Warwickshire and Border Province (South Africa).
Honours: England Amateur international (3 caps); FA tour to South Africa 1920; Division Three North champions 1936.

Harvey remained an amateur throughout his playing career and won an England cap against Ireland in 1920. He received a bad injury whilst on an FA tour to South Africa that year. Harvey played 20 games for the Owls and 79 for Birmingham before becoming assistant manager of the latter. The Blues finished 11th in his only full season in charge. At Chesterfield,

the club were mainly in the Second Division but struggling. They were relegated in 1933, were runners-up in 1934 and Northern Section champions in 1935-36 with 60 points, five clear of the nearest rivals. Harvey took over at Gillingham in June 1938, shortly after they had been voted out of the Football League. They finished third in the Southern League in the season before war broke out again.

HASLAM, Harold

Born: Manchester, 30 July 1921; Died: 10 September 1986.
Full-back.
Career: Manchester United during World War Two; Rochdale amateur May 1945; Oldham Athletic May 1946; Brighton & Hove Albion September 1947; Leyton Orient July 1948; Guildford City October 1949; Hastings United player-assistant manager; Eastbourne United manager; Gillingham coach; Barry Town manager 1954-1959; Tonbridge manager 1959-1968; Fulham chief scout July-November 1968; Luton Town coach and promotions manager 1969, then manager May 1972-January 1978; Sheffield United manager January 1978-May 1981; England scout 1981.
Honours: Division Two runners-up 1974.

A widely-respected manager whose cheerful demeanour and sunny personality endeared him to everyone, Harry Haslam won fame as a first-class manager after a career as a rather average full-back. In 1959, he moved to Tonbridge and gained some fame as a discoverer of young talent. He recommended David Sadler to Manchester United and also discovered John Ryan and Malcolm Macdonald for Fulham.

Fulham manager Bobby Robson made Haslam his chief scout in July 1968, but his stay at the Cottage was brief. When Robson was sacked in November of that year, Haslam went with him. Alec Stock then appointed him as coach and chief scout at Luton Town in 1969. Haslam also ran Luton's promotions department for a while and when Stock moved to Fulham, he became manager in May 1972.

Haslam, a larger-than-life character, was a natural comic, motivator, raconteur and great lover of football. He proved a popular, successful manager at Kenilworth Road, loved by the media — along with director Eric Morecambe — and between them they brought great publicity to the club. Luton won promotion to the First Division in 1974, then Haslam steered the club through

a financial collapse the following year, working miracles to keep the Hatters afloat.

In January 1978, he accepted an offer to manage Sheffield United but did not have a very happy time at Bramall Lane. The Blades were relegated to Division Three in 1979 and finished only 12th the following season. With the club sinking towards Division Four in 1980-81, Haslam was sacked in May 1981 and decided to retire from full-time soccer. He helped Bobby Robson for a while as a scout for the England team before his death in September 1986 at the age of 65. In 1993, his son, John, was involved in a take-over bid at Sheffield United.

HASTIE, John 'Jack'

Career: Barnsley manager cs 1912-April 1914.

Hastie took over Barnsley's 1912 FA Cup winning side when Arthur Fairclough moved to Huddersfield Town. They finished fourth in the Second Division at the end of his first season in charge, but lost £1,402 on the season. This was despite selling Bob Glendenning to Bolton Wanderers for £1,200. Hastie and his directors then sold George Lillicrop for £1,300 and George Utley to Sheffield United for £2,000. The fans were greatly displeased as they saw their favourite players sold off. Barnsley still managed to finish in fifth place in 1913-14.

HATTON, David H.

Born: Farnsworth, 30 October 1943.
Wing-half   5ft 8in; 11st (1964).
Career: Bolton Wanderers November 1960; Blackpool September 1969 (£40,000); Bury August 1976, then player-manager May 1978-October 1979.

Dave Hatton performed well at either right-back or right-half for the Trotters and was the club captain for many years. He made 259 appearances, scoring eight goals before his transfer to Blackpool. The Seasiders won promotion to Division One in 1969-70 but were relegated the following season. As player-manager of Bury, he failed to achieve a win in his first ten games in charge but after wholesale changes they finished 19th in Division Three. He helped Bury to clear a lot of its debts but was sacked on 30 October 1979 with the club having won only 14 games out of 62 under Hatton's control.

HAUSER, Peter B.

Born: Kimberley, South Africa, 20 April 1934.
Half-back   6ft 1in; 12st 9lb (1959).
Career: Blackpool November 1955; Cheltenham Town cs 1962; Chester manager August 1963-March 1968.

Peter Hauser worked as an underground surveyor in the gold mines of South Africa before being brought over to England to play for Blackpool in 1956. After 83 appearances and ten goals for the Seasiders, he was given a free transfer and joined Cheltenham. After a year of non-League soccer, Hauser became player-manager of Chester, playing 117/4 games for the club. Chester had to seek re-election in his first and last seasons in charge and their best season under him was 1965-66, when they finished seventh.

HAWKINS, Graham N.

Born: Darlaston, 5 March 1946.
Defender   6ft; 11st 10lb (1970).
Career: Wolverhampton Wanderers

apprentice 1961, professional June 1963; Preston North End January 1969; Blackburn Rovers June 1974; Port Vale January 1978; Shrewsbury Town assistant manager cs 1980; Wolverhampton Wanderers manager August 1982-April 1984; coaching in Saudi Arabia 1989.

Honours: Division Two runners-up 1983.

A big blond central defender, Graham Hawkins started his career in the First Division with Wolves and made his debut against West Brom in October 1964. Never a regular at Molineux, Hawkins moved to Preston where he made 245 League appearances, then appeared 109 times for Blackburn and 62 for Port Vale.

He was employed by Derek Dougan when the flamboyant Irishman became chief executive at Wolves and helped the club regain their First Division status as runners-up in 1982-83.

Hawkins made some shrewd signings including experienced players like John Burridge and Alan Dodd. Back in the First Division, though, the club hit the depths of despair, failing to win any of their first 16 games and being relegated straight back. It came as no surprise when Hawkins was sacked.

HAWORTH, John

Born: Accrington, 1876; Died: 4 December 1924 (aged 48).
Full-back.
Career: Meadow Bank FC as player and club secretary; Accrington Stanley committee member early 1897, secretary 1898; Burnley secretary-manager July 1910-December 1924.

Honours: Football League champions 1921; Division Two runners-up 1913; Lancashire Combination champions 1903, 1906; FA Cup winners 1914.

With Haworth as secretary, Accrington Stanley won the Lancashire Combination in 1902-03 and 1905-06 and he was well known in the area when he came to Turf Moor in 1910. He employed Charlie Bates as his trainer and instigated the change from green to Burnley's present-day colours. He made a major coup when he persuaded Bert Freeman to sign from Everton and Tommy Boyle from Barnsley.

In 1912-13 promotion was gained to Division One and an FA Cup semi-final was also reached. The FA Cup was won in 1914 when Liverpool were beaten 1-0 in the Final at Crystal Palace. Burnley finished as runners-up in the First Division in 1919-20 and were third two seasons later. In between they walked away with the League championship in 1920-21, finishing five points clear

of Manchester City. In 1924, Haworth caught pneumonia and died whilst still in office. He had achieved considerable success at Turf Moor. He was the nephew of George Haworth, who played for England, Accrington and Burnley.

HAYES, James Vincent

Born: Rochdale.
Full-back   5ft 8in; 10st 12lb (1909).
Career: Newton Heath 1900; Brentford cs 1907; Manchester United 1908; Bradford November 1910; Christiana (Norway) coach cs 1912; coaching in Austria 1914; coching in Madrid for 18 months; Rochdale player-manager until 1919; Preston North End manager 1919-January 1923; later a publican.

Honours: Football League representative; FA tour of South Africa; FA Cup winners 1909, runners-up 1922.

Vince Hayes made 114 appearances in his two spells at Manchester United and also won an FA Cup winners' medal when they beat Bristol City 1-0 at the Crystal Palace in the 1909 Final. After coaching abroad and managing Rochdale, Hayes arrived at Deepdale in 1919 as manager. He and his directors were very active on the transfer market in the summer of that year but his signings were mainly cautious. Preston reached the semi-finals of the FA Cup in 1921 but lost to eventual winners, Spurs.

Hayes had little power at Deepdale, for two directors really ran the club. They selected the team, worked out the tactics and bought the players. His primary role was to organise and motivate the players. After 1922 he devoted most of his time to coaching and preparing the players and he left the secretarial and financial arrangements in the hands of chartered accountants. Preston reached the FA Cup Final in 1922 but lost 1-0 to Huddersfield Town. He was presented with an inscribed medal by King Alfonso of Spain for his work with the youth of Madrid.

HAYWARD, Carl Basil

Born: Leek, 7 April 1928; Died: 1990.
Centre-half/Forward
6ft ¼in; 12st 10½lb (1959).
Career: Northwood; Port Vale May 1946; Portsmouth July 1958; Yeovil Town manager 1960-1964; Bedford Town manager 1964-January 1966; Gillingham manager January 1966-May 1971.

Honours: Division Three champions 1954; Southern League champions 1964.

Basil Hayward established himself as a centre-half at Port Vale but moved to centre-forward for the 1953-54

promotion season when he was Vale's top scorer. He was a member of Port Vale's FA Cup giantkilling side of that season, when the Third Division side reached the semi-finals before losing 2-1 to West Brom.

Indeed, Hayward was seemingly always in the thick of Cup upsets. He steered Yeovil and Bedford to notable Cup runs, Yeovil reaching the third round in 1963-64 by beating Southend United and Crystal Palace; and Bedford went one better in 1965-66, beating Exeter, Brighton and Hereford.

Yeovil were Southern League champions in 1963-64 with 63 points, scoring 93 goals. After this, his period in control of Gillingham was very undistinguished. They struggled before being finally relegated in 1970-71, finishing bottom of the Third Division. His brothers, Doug and Eric, played professional football.

HEAD, Bertram James

Born: Midsomer Norton, 8 June 1916
Centre-half   5ft 9in; 12st 1lb (1937).
Career: Midsomer Norton; Torquay United October 1936; Bury February 1952, later coach, chief scout and assistant manager; Swindon Town manager October 1955-August 1965; Bury manager August 1965-April 1966; Crystal Palace manager April 1966-March 1973, general manager March-May 1973; Bath City manager 1973.
Honours: Division Two runners-up 1969; Division Three runners-up 1963.

Bert Head spent 15 years at Torquay as a full-back and centre-half. At Bury he progressed from playing to coaching, then chief scout and assistant manager before moving to take charge at Swindon Town. He persevered with the development of his young side, which eventually paid off handsomely. He produced some fine young players including Mike Summerbee, Ernie Hunt, 'Bronco' Layne, Don Rogers and Rod Thomas.

He returned to Bury to manage the club but was forced to sell Colin Bell to Manchester City, which caused bad feeling between the Shakers and their supporters. He got Palace into Division One for the first time in their history but then experienced years of struggle. One of his signings was Don Rogers and there was a great potential at Palace but Head never achieved as much success as was expected of him. He is the father of David Head who played for Reading.

HEALD, William

Career: Rotherham United secretary-manager 1925-March 1929 & 1930-1933, also secretary from 1925-1956 and assistant secretary May 1923-1925; Sheffield United office staff.

Heald took over at Rotherham from Mr J.Briggs after the club had just been renamed and reconstituted. He had joined them as assistant secretary in May 1923 and finally retired in 1956

after 33 years. Those years at Millmoor were ones of struggle on and off the field and he had to sell promising players, such as Jackie Bestall to Grimsby Town in December 1926. His place as manager was temporarily taken by Stan Davies, but Heald was reinstated in 1930. Rotherham failed to win any away games in 1932-33 and were often close to folding, but Heald was one of the main reasons they kept going.

HEDLEY, George Albert

Born: South Bank, 20 July 1876; Died: 16 August 1942.
Centre-forward   5ft 10in; 12st (1902).
Career: South Bank; Sheffield United amateur 1897, professional May 1898; Southampton May 1903; Wolverhampton Wanderers May 1906, retired 1913; Bristol City manager April 1913-May 1915; licensee in Bristol 1918-1941; ran a boarding house in Wolverhampton from 1941.

Honours: England international (1 cap); Football League representative (1 cap); FA Cup winners 1899, 1902, 1908 runners-up 1901; Southern League champions 1904.

Hedley was a robust, aggressive player who was not a prolific scorer but a terror to defences with his rampaging rough-and-tumble style. He scored 125 goals in a career total of 385 League games and appeared in four FA Cup Finals, gaining three winners' medals. This included scoring one of the goals in Wolves' 3-1 victory over Newcastle United in 1908. His England cap came in 1901, against Ireland who were beaten 3-0 at The Dell. Hedley's two-year spell in charge of Bristol City came when they were a Second Division club. They finished 8th and 13th respectively in 1913-14 and 1914-15.

HENDERSON, Raymond

Born: Wallsend, 31 March 1937.
Outside/Inside-right
5ft 9in; 11st 6lb (1965).
Career: Wallsend Schools; Willington Quay; Howden Boys Club; Ashington; Middlesbrough May 1957; Hull City June 1961 (£2,000); Reading player-coach October 1968; Halifax Town manager August 1971-May 1972; Everton reserve-team coach July 1973-May 1976; Southport manager May 1976-March 1977.

Honours: Division Three champions 1966.

Henderson was usually a right winger but often moved inside, linking well with his fellow wingers. After only nine games for 'Boro, he moved to Hull City where he made 229 League appearances, scoring 54 goals before rounding off his playing career and coaching at Elm Park.

Halifax struggled to finish 17th in his only season in charge and also were knocked out of the FA Cup by non-League Wigan Athletic. He sold off some of the best players, which led to criticism from the fans, and had little success at Southport either. They had to seek re-election after his departure, gaining only three home wins and 25 points. On the brighter side, Henderson scored 12 goals in Hull's Third Division championship season of 1965-66.

HENDRIE, Richard

Born: Airdrie, c.1898.
Left-back   5ft 9in; 12st 2lb (1925).
Career: Royal Navy; Petershill; guest for Hearts and Grimsby Town in World War One; Airdrieonians 1918; Queens

Park 1919; Maidstone United; Gillingham June 1923-cs 1926; Brentford scout in 1927; Gillingham manager May 1929-December 1931; Tunbridge Wells Rangers manager 1932.

Hendrie made 76 appearances in his three seasons as a left-back with the Gills. He had a tough time when he returned to manage the club. With limited resources he was forced to use a make-do-and-mend policy. Gillingham had to seek re-election in 1929-30 and finished 16th, the following season. They also suffered the embarrassment of an FA Cup defeat against Kent Leaguers, Margate. Three weeks earlier Gillingham Reserves had beaten them in a league match.

HENRY, Gerald Robert

Born: Barnsley 5 October 1920.
Inside-forward 5ft 5in; 11st 4lb (1946).
Career: Yorkshire Schools; Outwood Stormcocks; Leeds United October 1937; guest for Doncaster Rovers in World War Two; Bradford November 1947; Sheffield Wednesday February 1950; Halifax Town player-coach December 1951; Halifax Town player-manager February 1952-October 1954.

Henry made 186 wartime appearances for Leeds United but only 47 in peacetime before moving to Bradford. He had a good scoring rate of 31 goals in 79 League games for the Park Avenue club but failed to find the net so regularly elsewhere. At Halifax he was upgraded from player-coach to player manager. They had a fine FA Cup run in 1952-53, beating Stoke in the fourth round but losing to Spurs in the next. Both games attracted over 35,000 to The Shay. They came down to earth the following season when they lost to Rhyl 4-3 in a replay. Henry resigned after only one win in the first 14 games of 1954-55.

HENSHALL, Horace Vincent

Born: Hednesford, 14 June 1889; Died: Nottingham, 7 December 1951.
Inside-forward 5ft 9in; 11st 9lb (1923).
Career: Bridgetown Amateurs (Walsall League); Aston Villa amateur 1905, professional May 1906; Notts County November 1912; guest for Barnsley in World War One; Sheffield Wednesday player-reserve-team coach June 1922; Chesterfield June 1923; Lincoln City manager cs 1924-cs 1927; Notts County manager cs 1927-May 1934, then secretary until April 1935; licensee of Navigation Inn, Nottingham after 1935.
Honours: Division Three South champions 1931.

Henshall was a useful utility forward, hard-running with a fine right-foot shot. Lincoln City were a mid-table Third Division side during his period in control but he found more success at Notts County. He had been a firm favourite during his playing days with the club and was popular after taking County to the Southern Section title in 1930-31, only a year after being relegated. His star was Tom Keetley, who scored 39 goals in only 34 games. Notts were eight points clear of their nearest rivals after heading the table for much of the season.

HENSON, Philip M.

Manchester, 30 March 1953.
Midfield 5ft 10in; 9st 12lb (1983).
Career: Brookdale Youth Club; Manchester City apprentice May 1969, professional July 1970; Swansea City (loan) July 1972; Sheffield Wednesday February 1975 (£50,000); Sparta Rotter-

dam April 1978; Stockport County September 1978 (£30,000); Rotherham United February 1980-cs 1984, assistant manager 1988, then manager January 1991.
Honours: Division Three champions 1981; Division Four runners-up 1992.

Henson took Rotherham United to runners-up position in Division Four at the end of his first season in charge after a late run to success. He took charge in mid-season in 1990-91 but could not prevent United dropping into Division Four. A former player, he had previously been assistant manager to Billy McEwan at Millmoor.

Henson made his Football League debut for Manchester City at Crystal Palace, as substitute, in January 1972. The Owls were relegated to Division Three shortly after he joined the club but in 1980-81 he helped Rotherham United win Division Three championship. He played 87/5 League games for United, scoring seven goals, and was Ian Porterfield's first signing as manager of Rotherham United.

Rotherham had a good season despite many critics suggesting that they would struggle in the Second Division in 1992-93.

HERD, David George

Born: Hamilton, 15 April 1934.
Centre/Inside-forward 6ft; 13st (1963).
Career: Stockport County amateur September 1949, professional April 1951; Arsenal August 1954 (£10,000); Manchester United July 1961 (£37,000); Stoke City July 1968; Waterford December 1970; Lincoln City manager March 1971-December 1972.

Honours: Scotland international (5 caps); Under-23 international (2 caps); Amateur international; Football League champions 1965, 1967; FA Cup winners 1963.

David Herd has the rare distinction of appearing in the same League side with his father, Alec, for Stockport against Hartlepools on 5 May 1951, David scoring both goals in a 2-0 victory. He took time to settle when he moved to Highbury but developed into a burly, hard-shooting marksman. He scored 107 goals in 180 appearances for the Gunners and 144 goals in 263 for Manchester United.

Herd played in many fine games for United and won two League championship medals and a FA Cup winners' medal with the club. His playing days ended at Stoke due to a troublesome knee injury. His first season in charge at Lincoln ended with the club just missing out on promotion to the Third, but he did not do so well in his second season at Sincil Bank.

HEWISON, Robert

Born: Backworth, Newcastle upon Tyne, 25 March 1889; Died: Bristol, spring 1964.
Right-half 5ft 9in; 11st 12lb (1923).
Career: East Holywell Villa; Whitley Athletic; Newcastle United March 1908; Leeds City 1914; Newcastle United December 1919; Northampton Town player-manager May 1920-1925 (£250); Queen's Park Rangers manager cs 1925-May 1931; Bristol City manager March 1932-March 1949; (suspended from October 1938-May 1939); Guildford City manager; Bristol Rovers scout until 1957; Bath City manager May 1957-1961, when he retired.
Honours: Football League representative; Southern League champions 1960.

Hewison was a steady midfield player

who was plagued by injuries throughout his career. As a manager this softly-spoken, bespectacled Geordie looked more like a bank manager than a football manager. After five seasons of mid-table mediocrity at Northampton, he moved to London to manage Queen's Park Rangers. Their best season with Hewison in charge was 1929-30, when they finished third in the Southern Section. In 1926-27, though, he forgot to enter them for the FA Cup.

Bristol City struggled under him until 1937-38, when they finished runners-up to Millwall. However, Hewison was suspended for eight months soon afterwards for illegal payments to players. He had been at Leeds City when a similar situation arose. In 1946, he received a long-service medal from the Football League. At Bath City, Hewison took the club to the Southern League title in 1959-60, 13 points clear of his nearest rivals.

HEWITT, Charles William

Born: Greatham, Cleveland, 10 April 1884; Died: Darlington, 31 December 1966.
Inside-forward 5ft 6in; 11st 4lb (1911)
Career: Middlesbrough 1904; Tottenham Hotspur May 1906; Liverpool cs 1907; West Bromwich Albion April 1908; Crystal Palace May 1910; Hartlepools United 1919; Mold manager until November 1924; Wrexham manager November 1924-December 1926; Flint manager 1927-May 1928; Connah's Quay manager May 1928-1930; Chester manager 1930-April 1936; Millwall manager April 1936-April 1940; Leyton Orient manager January 1946-April 1948; Millwall manager again August 1948-January 1956. Spennymoor United May 1910; Crystal Palace late 1910.

Honours: Division Three South champions 1938; Welsh Cup winners 1925, 1933.

A man of many words, abrasive, direct and autocratic, Charles Hewitt was probably the last of the Football League managers in the showman tradition. Either loved or hated by his players, he was a man who would not mince his words, had high ideals and expected success through his own hard work and also from those around him.

The stories of his time at Millwall are legendary. In 1940, he was sacked after being suspended for six months and by the end of his second reign in 1956, the players were so relieved at his departure that most of them went out for a celebratory drink together.

Hewitt joined Middlesbrough as an inside-forward around 1904 from local junior soccer and did the rounds during

his playing career, spending only short spells at each of his clubs except Crystal Palace. After 'Boro he went to Tottenham Hotspur, signing for the club in May 1906. A year later he was on the move again, to Liverpool, and in April 1908 he joined West Bromwich Albion. In May 1910, Hewitt signed for Palace, where he stayed until 1915.

He moved to Hartlepools United in 1919 and took his first managerial post at Mold before joining Wrexham in November 1924. The team gradually improved under his guidance but never reached higher than 16th, but they did win the Welsh Cup in 1925 beating Flint in the final.

In 1930, Hewitt joined Chester as manager, after spells in charge at Connagh's Quay and Flint, and steered them to Football League membership the following year. As well as winning the Welsh Cup in 1933, they finished in third position twice, fourth once and runners-up in 1935-36, five points behind champions Chesterfield. Hewitt probably had a job for life with Chester due to this record in his six years at the club, but accepted a lucrative offer to manage Millwall in April 1936.

A trained accountant, his football philosophy for success on the field was simple. Get the right player for the right position, don't waste his ability by using confusing tactics or giving him a role for which he has no experience, and get the team forward to score goals in as straightforward a fashion as possible. Hewitt insisted on a free rein when taking over at Millwall, something he had not had at Chester.

He revamped the club on and off the field, making sweeping changes in every department. He improved facilities for directors, players and supporters and employed his own selected staff, dispensing with previous coaches etc. Hewitt immediately strengthened the playing staff and engendered such interest that 15,334 fans turned up to see the pre-season trial match between the first team and the reserve side. At first he was rarely seen on match days and was usually off scouting somewhere. Success soon came and Millwall became the first Division Three club to reach the FA Cup semi-final, where they lost to Sunderland.

The following season the Lions won Division Three South championship and marched into Division Two, but Hewitt's first period as Millwall's manager ended in disgrace when he was suspended for six months for making illegal payments to players and he was sacked soon afterwards, in April 1940. Due to his experience in World War One — he served on a Royal Naval destroyer — he was soon called up in World War Two and put in charge of a troopship.

When the war ended, Hewitt became Leyton Orient's manager, in January 1946. However, he was soon in dispute with the directors and resigned in October, over a disagreement about signing new players. Hewitt was soon reinstated as secretary and general manager but after two poor seasons he was enticed back to Millwall in August 1948.

His second period as manager at The Den was not as successful as his first. The Lions had just been relegated from Division Two and Hewitt had a great deal of work to do to re-establish Millwall again. The 1949-50 season was one of the worst in the club's history as they finished bottom of the Southern Section. Things improved after this with the club finishing fourth in 1951-52 and just missing promotion by two points and one place the following season.

By 1954, the pressures were beginning to build up and Hewitt was often barracked from the terraces. When the end came, the club seemed to be falling apart. Half the squad were on the transfer list as they would no longer accept this autocratic style. The world had changed enormously since his first stint as Millwall's manager. He was sacked on 10 January 1956, his pride absolutely shattered by the decision. He issued a writ for breach of contract and was awarded £4,500 damages in July 1957 after a great deal of distasteful publicity. Hewitt left football for retirement at this point and died nine years later.

HIBBITT, Kenneth

Born: Bradford, 3 January 1951
Midfield   5ft 10½in; 12st 10lb (1988).

Career: Bradford apprentice November 1967, professional November 1968; Wolverhampton Wanderers November 1968 (£10,000); Coventry City August 1984; Bristol Rovers August 1986, then assistant manager 1987-1990; Walsall manager March 1990.

Honours: England Under-23 international (1 cap); Division Two champions 1977; Football League Cup winners 1974, 1980; UEFA Cup runners-up 1972.

Kenny Hibbitt, an elegant midfield player, was transferred to Wolves four days after signing professional forms for Bradford. He went on to play 526/20 League games in his career, scoring 97 goals. His brother, Terry, played for Leeds, Newcastle and Birmingham but Kenny appeared only at Under-23 level. He was on the winning side twice with Wolves in League Cup Finals. In 1974, he scored one of the goals in a 2-1 victory over Manchester City; and in 1980 Wolves beat Nottingham Forest 1-0. Hibbitt also gained promotion twice to Division One with Wolves, gaining a Second Division championship medal in 1976-77.

After retiring from playing, he became Gerry Francis' assistant at Bristol Rovers before taking up his first managerial post at Walsall. He took over too late to prevent the club from being relegated for the second successive season. Walsall moved into their new Bescot Stadium in August 1990 but their form on the pitch was poor and they struggled in the bottom half of the Fourth Division despite Hibbitt's efforts.

Walsall reached the Third Division play-offs in 1993 but were easily beaten by Crewe 9-3 on aggregate.

HIBBS, Henry Edward 'Harry'

Born: Wilnecote, Staffs, 27 May 1906;
Died: Hatfield 23 April 1984.
Goalkeeper   5ft 9in; 11st 7lb (1937).
Career: Wilnecote Holy Trinity School; Tamworth Castle 1922; Birmingham May 1924, retired May 1940; Walsall manager August 1944-June 1951; permit player for De Havilands February 1953-May 1954; Ware Town manager August 1960; Welwyn Garden City manager 1962.

Honours: England international (25 caps); Football League representative (3 caps); FA Tour of South Africa 1929 (1 cap); FA Cup runners-up 1931; Division Three South Cup runners-up 1946.

One of the finest-ever goalkeepers in English soccer, Harry Hibbs had superb aniticipation and although short, had a remarkable temperament in crisis situations. In his 16 years with Birmingham he made 388 appearances and appeared in the 1931 FA Cup Final, when the Blues lost 2-1 to West Brom. His international appearances included the famous 4-3 victory over Austria at Highbury.

Hibbs made difficult shots look easy and his hard work and superb fitness helped him to reach shots others could not. At Walsall he helped develop another England goalkeeper in Bert Williams. The Saddlers were challenging for promotion to Division Two in the two seasons after the war but struggled after that. As a manager, Hibbs was unable to find the success he found as a player.

HICKLING, John G. 'Jack'

Career: Local league player; referee in Football League list; Mansfield Mechanics FC secretary; North Nottinghamshire Football League general secretary; Mansfield Ground & Athletic Company director; Mansfield Town secretary-manager January 1928-December 1933.

Jack Hickling's position as manager of Mansfield Town and director of the company which owned their ground was occasionally compromised and he eventually left the club over a conflict of interests. Hickling wanted to have boxing and wrestling promotions at Field Mill but the club were opposed to this and felt that it would interfere with his club duties. However, a month before his sacking, he had been asked to take a pay cut which he had refused to do.

Hickling had refereed all over the world prior to his involvement at Mansfield. As the Stags' manager he

inspired them in their successful bid to join the Football League in 1931. They also had a successful FA Cup run in 1929, beating Wolves before losing to Arsenal in the fourth round.

HILDITCH, Clarence George 'Lal'

Born: Northwich, 2 June 1894.
Half-back   5ft 10in; 11st (1923).
Career: Witton Albion; Altrincham 1914; Manchester United amateur 1915, professional 1919-January 1932, and player-manager October 1926-April 1927.

Honours: England Victory international (1 cap); FA tour of South Africa 1920 (3 caps); Football League representative.

A calm and cultured half-back, Hilditch never committed an international foul in his career. He played 322 League and Cup games for United plus 81 wartime appearances, was capped for England in a Victory international in 1919 and toured South Africa the following year. He helped United gain promotion to the First Division as runners-up in 1925, three years after being relegated. They also had a run to the semi-finals of the FA Cup the following season. He became player-manager at Old Trafford when John Chapman was suspended by the FA. Hilditch was later replaced by Herbert Bamlett.

HILL, Frank Robert

Born: Forfar, 21 May 1906; Died: Luton, June 1970.
Wing-half   5ft 8in; 11st 9lb (1937).

Career: Forfar Athletic 1924; Aberdeen 1928; Arsenal May 1932 (£3,000); Blackpool June 1936; Southampton September 1937 (£2,200); Preston North End assistant trainer 1938-1939; guest for Wrexham in World War Two; Crewe Alexandra player-manager July 1944-September 1948; Burnley manager September 1948-August 1954; Preston North End manager August 1954-May 1956; Notts County manager October 1958-November 1961; Charlton Athletic manager November 1961-August 1965; Manchester City scout in 1965.

Honours: Scotland international (3 caps); Scottish League representative (1 cap); Football League champions 1933, 1934, 1935; Division Four runners-up 1960.

In his playing days, Frank Hill was a small, combative half-back who was tenacious, tough and uncompromising. He was nicknamed 'Tiger' and managed to keep playing until he was 41 years old. Hill won three League champion-

ship medals with Arsenal, although he was never a regular in their side. However, he did not receive any more caps after leaving Aberdeen.

As a manager, Hill had a reputation for being very shrewd in the transfer market. In his last three seasons at Turf Moor, the club finished sixth in the First Division each time. At Preston he produced entertaining sides rather than successful ones. He took Notts County to promotion as runners-up of the Fourth Division and discovered Tony Hateley, a prolific goalscorer. Hill had little success at The Valley, angering the fans when he got rid of one of their favourites, Stuart Leary. Hill had a reputation for running clubs well on a shoestring budget but found very little success on the field.

HILL, James William Thomas

Born: Balham, London, 22 July 1928.
Wing-half/Inside-right
6ft; 12st 4lb (1951).
Career: Fulham juniors 1943; Denmark Hill Police; Boys' Brigade; Reading amateur; Brentford May 1949; Fulham March 1952; PFA chairman; Coventry City manager November 1961-September 1967; worked for BBC TV and ITV; Fulham commercial manager March 1973; Coventry City chairman and managing director April 1975-May 1983; Charlton Athletic director November 1984-March 1987 and acting chairman December 1984-May 1985; Fulham chairman April 1987.

Honours: Division Two champions 1967; Division Three champions 1964.

Jimmy Hill seems to have tried his hand at just about everything in football and appears to be a person who needs his life to be as diverse as possible. At various times he has been a player, union leader, manager, director, television personality, businessman, soldier and even an emergency linesman.

Born in Balham, he played soccer for his two schools, Henry Cavendish and Henry Thornton, and appeared briefly for Fulham juniors during the war as well as for Denmark Hill Police and his Boys' Brigade side. Hill spent two years working as a clerk with a City insurance company.

He was spotted by Reading manager Ted Drake, playing for his regiment whilst on National Service and turned out as an amateur at Elm Park for six months. Hill also had trials for Folkestone Town and after playing mainly in Reading's third team, he moved to Brentford as a professional when he was told by Drake that he would not be offered terms. Hill signed for the Bees in May 1949 and soon made his debut at centre-forward for the club. Most of his 87 appearances at Griffin Park were at wing-half, though, before his move to Craven Cottage in March 1952. He spent the rest of his playing career at Fulham until a knee injury brought his career to a close in 1961.

Wholehearted and enthusiastic, Hill struggled to keep his place in the 1959 promotion team but appeared in an FA Cup semi-final against Manchester United in 1958, which was lost 5-3. Hill set a club record by scoring five goals in an away match, at Doncaster Rovers in March 1958. He was booked only once in his career, for dissent when asking a referee why he had made him retake a throw-in.

In 1956, Jimmy Hill had become chairman of the Professional Footballers' Association and over the next five years organised and ran the fight to rid the game of the restrictive £20 a week maximum wage. He took on employers and football bosses, organising players into a mood to assert themselves. He showed clearly that he had a feel for public relations in presenting his case.

In November 1961, Hill joined Coventry City as manager. Full of confidence and with many new ideas of his own to improve the general standards of the game, he guided City from the Third to the First Division in six years. His ability to instil confidence into those around him, probably helped to make the Coventry players better performers than they actually were. The Third Division title was clinched in the last match of the 1963-64 season and the Second Division title followed three years afterwards. They were great times at Highfield Road as the 'Sky Blue Revolution' was met with booming attendances.

Hill left Coventry in September 1968, a move which stunned the fans. Accusations were made that Hill had left because the team was not strong enough to survive in Division One. However, in truth, he had been offered a very lucrative job with London Weekend Television as their head of sport.

He had started his television career whilst at Coventry, as a regular contributor to the *World of Sport* programme, had joined a television World Cup panel in 1966 and was an advisor for the football soap opera *United*. At LWT he created *The Big Match* and for many years appeared regularly on ITV's Saturday afternoon *On the Ball* programme. His fluency, backed by his experience as a player and manager, stood him in good stead as a soccer critic.

A qualified FA coach and referee, he once made an appearance as an emergency linesman at Arsenal when the original linesman was injured. Hill was working for television that day at Highbury and when a call was made for a replacement linesman, he took up the challenge.

In October 1972, he resigned from LWT to set up his own television consultancy group to negotiate sponsorship deals in sport. Hill also became a commercial advisor to a number of clubs including Fulham. Later he joined the BBC in a similar capacity and still works for them today, although with the advent of satellite television, their football coverage is more limited than it used to be.

Over the years, Hill has been involved in negotiations between the clubs and television, discussing the cost of screening live football. He has also worked as a journalist with the *News of the World* and *Goal Magazine* and for a while in

the late 1960s was involved in a magazine called *Jimmy Hill's Football Weekly*.

Hill has many business links including some with Saudi Arabia and once organised a 'rebel' international football tour to South Africa which met with considerable opposition.

One of his less successful projects was his involvement with the NASL club, Detroit Express, where he lost a considerable amont of money when that club folded in the early 1980s. This probably accounts for his reluctance to invest in Fulham FC (1987) Ltd.

Hill got into trouble with the football authorities when working as managing director of Coventry City in 1977, for announcing over the club's public-address system the result of an Everton-Sunderland game, which affected the game still being played between Coventry and Bristol City. Both clubs needed a point to stay up and as the score was 2-2, they played out a tame finish. Later, as chairman of the club, he caused controversy and incurred fans' wrath when he made Highfield Road an all-seater stadium. Hill had to back down and allow terraces to be reintroduced, although recent legislation perhaps shows that he was right.

Hill courted more controversy as a director of Charlton Athletic when he was part of the decision which removed the club from The Valley to Selhurst Park in 1985. He later claimed that he had nothing to do with this.

In February 1987, when David Bulstrode, chairman of Fulham FC and SB Properties (later Cabra Estates), revealed his plans to merge Fulham and Queen's Park Rangers and develop the Craven Cottage site for housing, Jimmy Hill emerged with a plan to save the club. He quickly mobilised support and within weeks struck a deal with Bulstrode, despite counter-productive alternative groups also setting themselves up as Fulham 'saviours'.

He relinquished his seat on the Charlton board to form the Fulham (1987) Ltd and was made chairman by his new and inexperienced directors in April 1987.

Since then Hill has played a big role in the future of Fulham Football Club. Some of the decisions he has been involved in have angered true Fulham fans, who question where his priorities really lie. Hill has acted as a mouthpiece for the real power at Craven Cottage, Bill Muddyman, the club's vice-chairman who owns most of the shares in the club. One of his acts which the club's supporters may live to rue is Hill's and Fulham Football Club's withdrawal of support for the local council's application for a Compulsory Purchase Order on the Craven Cottage ground.

As at Coventry and Charlton, Hill claimed to have the best interests of the supporters at heart but his motives are unclear. Under his chairmanship, Fulham have lurched from one crisis to another and the main sufferers have been those loyal supporters who, despite years of decay, have stayed faithful to the club. The future of the Craven Cottage ground still hangs in the balance but, with the collapse of Cabra Estates, the club may soon be in a position to buy the ground back.

Things started to look up in March 1993 when Fulham managed to work out a deal with the Bank of Scotland in which the club could continue to play at Craven Cottage for the next ten years with an option to buy the site for £8 million.

HILL, John Henry 'Ginger'

Born: Hetton-le-Hole, County Durham 2 March 1897; Died: Scotland, April 1972.

Half-back   6ft 3in; 13st 7lb (1928).
Career: Durham City 1919; Plymouth Argyle September 1920; Burnley May 1923 (£5,450); Newcastle United October 1928 (£8,100); Bradford City June 1931 (£600); Hull City November 1931, manager March 1934-January 1936 and scout 1948-1955; Scarborough pools scheme until retirement in August 1963.

Honours: England international (11 caps); Football League representative (3 caps); Division Three North champions 1933.

A former miner, Jack Hill was a towering figure who loved to charge forward on solo runs. He had excellent distribution, was a great worker and was also dominant in the air. Hill captained Newcastle and Burnley and also skippered his country on a couple of occasions. He had been a part-timer with Durham City before joining Plymouth Argyle, for whom he made over 100 appearances. Hill played in Hull City's side which won the Northern Section in 1932-33 and then replaced the man who had bought him, Haydn Green, as manager.

He rebuilt the side and this included buying Billy Tabran for a large fee. Hill was then forced to sell players to balance the books. Resigning with Hull bottom of the Second Division, Hill was also at loggerheads with the board. He was brought back to the club after the war to supervise the scouting system.

HINDMARSH, James Lyons

Born: South Shields, spring 1885; Died: Luton, 16 March 1959.
Inside-left   5ft 11in; 12st 9st.
Career: Whitburn Colliery; Sunderland September 1905; Fulham May 1906 (£20); Watford cs 1907; Plymouth Argyle cs 1908; Stockport County cs 1910; Manchester City December 1912; Newport County September 1919 and secretary-manager May 1922-May 1935.

Hindmarsh did not find regular first-team soccer until he joined Plymouth, where he scored 24 goals in 62 games. He played in only 187 League games in his career, scoring 31 goals, but was Argyle's top scorer in 1909-10 with 16 goals. He spent 16 years at Somerton Park after joining the club as coach in charge of the Reserves just after World War One.

Hindmarsh brought about a lot of changes at Newport. A new stand was built in 1923 and the ground was generally improved. He also discovered a number of talented players during his 13 years as secretary-manager. The club were always in financial trouble and almost went bankrupt in 1928. They had to seek re-election four times during his reign and were voted out of the League in 1931 but elected back again two years later. His best season was 1924-25, when Newport finished sixth in the Southern Section.

HITCHEN, Trevor

Born: Sowerby Bridge, 25 September 1926.
Half-back   5ft 11in; 12st (1956).
Career: Sowerby Boys' Brigade; Halifax Town amateur August 1943; Notts County May 1945; Wellington Town; Southport January 1949; Oldham Athletic August 1956; Wigan Athletic manager 1957-June 1958; Southport manager June 1958-January 1959; Prescot; Formby player August 1961, manager and chairman.

A former 'Bevin Boy', Hitchin worked down the pits during the war. He became one of Southport's finest servants, making 241 League appearances and scoring 34 goals in two

spells at the club. He had initially joined Southport as a centre-forward but developed into a utility player. Hitchin was in charge at the club for only half a season and became assistant manager when Wally Fielding took over. He remained in the town after leaving the club, running a tobacconist's and newsagent's. He later spent many years involved with Formby FC.

HODDLE, Glenn

Born: Hayes, Middlesex, 27 October 1957.
Midfield   6ft; 11st 6lb (1984).
Career: Harlow Schools; Essex Schools; Tottenham Hotspur apprentice April 1974, professional April 1975; AS Monaco (France) June 1987 (£750,000), retired through injury November 1990; Chelsea Reserves March 1991; Swindon Town player-manager April 1991-June 1993. Chelsea manager June 1993.

Honours: England international (53 caps); 'B' international; Under-21 international (12 caps); Youth international; FA Cup winners 1981, 1982, runners-up 1987; Football League Cup runners-up 1982; French League champions 1988. Division One promotion 1993.

Glenn Hoddle was a naturally gifted player with great vision and ball control. A superb passer, especially 50-yard defence-splitting passes, he was also deadly from long-range and scored some spectacular goals. Hoddle was a free-kick specialist and had the ability to 'bend' a ball around a defensive wall. His talents were often wasted by England and he found himself in and out of the international side. There was always doubts about his workrate over 90 minutes, an obsession of British football in recent years.

At AS Monaco he played alongside Mark Hateley and they helped the Principality club to win the French League championship. An injury looked to have ended his career and after trying to make a come-back with Chelsea, he was chosen to replace his former Spurs teammate Ossie Ardilles as manager Swindon Town. Swindon played a refreshing brand of entertaining football under Hoddle, the team reflecting the style the manager showed as a player. They finished just outside the play-off positions in 1991-92 but had two good runs in the major cup competitions.

Swindon reached the Second Division play-offs in 1993 and beat Tranmere 5-1 on aggregate to meet Leicester City in the Final at Wembley. Hoddle scored Swindon's first goal in a scintillating match which his club eventually won 4-3 after losing a three-goal lead. Sadly for Swindon fans, it was by then an open secret that he would take over at Chelsea.

HODGE, Peter

Born: Dunfermline; **Died:** Perth, August 1934.

Career: Dunfermline Juniors manager 1890; referee in Scottish Second Division 1897-1906; Dunfermline Athletic honorary secretary; Raith Rovers manager April 1907-October 1912; Stoke manager June 1914-1915; recruitment officer at Kirkaldy in World War One; Raith Rovers manager 1916-1919; Leicester City manager May 1919-May 1926; Manchester City manager May 1926-March 1932; Leicester City manager March 1932-July 1934.

Honours: Division Two champions 1925, 1928; Southern League Division Two champions 1915.

Peter Hodge took both Leicester City and Manchester City to the Second Division championship during the 1920s, although he never played football but was a former referee in the Scottish League.

Entering football administration in his home town of Dunfermline with a local juvenile club in 1890, he was later involved with Dunfermline Juniors and Athletic, the latter as honorary secretary. He also refereed in the Scottish Second Division from 1897 to 1906.

Raith Rovers appointed Hodge as their first manager in April 1907 and he took the club into the First Division in 1910. Hodge lost his job in October 1912, ousted by an ambitious director. In June 1914, he took over at Stoke for one season, in which the club won the Southern League Second Division championship, and the Potters later replaced Glossop in the Football League after an election vote. In 1916, Hodge returned to manage Raith Rovers and was the local recruitment officer for the armed forces.

After the reconstruction of Leicester City, the new board persuaded Hodge to take control as the club's first ever secretary-manager in September 1919. He was given greater involvement in selection and tactical matters than had been previously allowed to former secretaries of the Fosse. Hodge returned to Scotland to sign many new players. These included Jock Peterson from Dundee, Adam Black and Tom and Septimus Smith, all of whom would become famous names at Filbert Street.

His best signing was Johnny Duncan, from his former club Raith Rovers, in July 1922. The Foxes just missed promotion on goal-average in 1922-23 but were Second Division champions in 1925 with Duncan scoring 30 goals.

Hodge's move to Manchester City in May 1926 came as a shock. City had just been relegated to Division Two. In his first season in charge, City just missed out on promotion, by one place in the narrowest promotion race margin ever, goal-average to the third decimal place, but were promoted as champions in 1927-28 and finished third in Division One, the following season.

During his reign at Maine Road, several notable players became established in the side including Eric Brooks and Tommy Johnson. Hodge returned to Leicester as manager in March 1932, attracted by a five-year contract. The club was in decline with a high number of ageing stars and little money to spend. However, they did reach an FA Cup semi-final in 1934, only to lose 4-1 to Portsmouth. On 30 July 1934, Peter Hodge was admitted to Perth Infirmary and died shortly afterwards.

HODGSON, Gordon

Born: Johannesburg, 16 April 1904; **Died:** Stoke-on-Trent, 14 June 1951.
Forward   6ft 1in; 13st 5lb (1935).
Career: Rustenberg FC 1921; Pretoria 1922-1923; Transvaal (South Africa) 1924-1925; Liverpool December 1925; cricket for Transvaal, Lancashire 1928-1932 and Forfarshire 1934-1936; Aston Villa January 1936 (£3,000); Leeds United March 1937 (£1,500), then youth-team coach 1942-October 1946; guest for Hartlepools United in war; retired in war; Port Vale manager October 1946-June 1951.

Honours: England international (3 caps); Football League representative (2 caps).

Gordon Hodgson was a powerfully-built player who first came to England in 1924 with the South African touring side. He held Liverpool's leading aggregate goalscoring record for many years until it was overtaken by Roger Hunt. Hodgson scored 240 goals in 378 appearances for Liverpool. This included 36 goals in 1930-31 and 32 in 1928-29. His career total of goals was 304. As well as wartime appearances for Leeds, Hodgson also coached the youth players. His best scoring performance was five goals for Leeds against Leicester in October 1938.

He was in charge at Port Vale when they moved to a new ground at Vale Park in 1950. They were usually a mid-table side during his five years in charge. It came as a great shock when he died at the early age of 47, whilst still the manager of Port Vale. Hodgson was also a fine cricketer, playing 56 matches for Lancashire.

HODGSON, John Vennor

Born: Seaham 30 September 1913; **Died:** 20 June 1970.
Full-back/Centre-half
6ft 2in; 13st 3lb (1938).
Career: Hartlepools United trial; Seaham Colliery Welfare; Grimsby Town January 1932; Doncaster Rovers January 1948, retired cs 1952, joint manager February-April 1958.

Honours: Division Three North champions 1950.

A loyal club man, John Hodgson was equally effective at left-back or centre-half, where he put his formidable physique to good purpose. He made 211 appearances for Grimsby and another 96 for Doncaster Rovers although his playing career was greatly affected by the war years. Hodgson's brother, Sam, and his son, Brian, also played for Grimsby. He was joint manager at Doncaster with S.A.Bycroft for just three months. They could not prevent the team finishing bottom of the Second Division with only 27 points.

HODGSON, Roy

Career: Malmö (Sweden) assistant manager until 1980; Bristol City assistant manager 1980, then manager January-April 1982; Malmö (Sweden) manager 1983-1990; Neuchâtel Xamax (Switzerland) manager 1990-December 1991; Switzerland national manager December 1991.

Honours: Swedish League champions 1986, 1989, 1990, Swedish Cup 1984, 1989, 1990.

Roy Hodgson was assistant manager to Bob Houghton at Malmö and Bristol City. Malmö reached the European Cup Final in 1979, when they lost 1-0 to Nottingham Forest in Hamburg. He moved with Houghton to England when he took over at Ashton Gate.

Hodgson stayed on after Houghton's sacking and was in charge from 4 January to 30 April 1982, City winning only three games out of 20 in this period. The club were in a dire financial crisis and had to release eight leading professionals from their contracts. When a new company was created at the club, Hodgson's services were dispensed with. He had many successful years at charge at Malmö in the 1980s, when they regularly appeared in European competitions. Hodgson is in charge of the national team of Switzerland who are in the same qualifying group as Scotland for the 1994 World Cup which will take place in the United States.

HOGAN, James

Born: Nelson, 16 October 1882; **Died:** Burnley, 30 January 1974.
Outside-right   5ft 7in; 10st 6lb (1907).
Career: Burnley Belvedere; Nelson; Rochdale; Burnley c.1903; Fulham cs 1905 (£100); Swindon Town cs 1908; Bolton Wanderers October 1908-1913; Holland coach 1912; Austrian national coach 1914; Young Boys (Berne) 1921; coaching in Hungary and Germany; Fulham manager May 1934-February 1935; Austria national coach 1935-1936; Aston Villa manager November 1936-September 1939; After World War Two worked for Celtic, Brentford; Aston Villa youth-team manager 1953-July 1959, when he retired.

Honours: Division Two champions 1938.

Jimmy Hogan was internationally recognised as one of the most outstanding coaches of his day. An average player, Hogan appeared in an FA Cup semi-final with Fulham in 1908, although the Cottagers were beaten 6-0 by Newcastle United. In Austria, Hogan formed a famous partnership with Hugo Meisl and these two were given much credit for the development of the game in Europe to the point where, technically, it outstripped the British game.

However, Hogan did not have much success as manager of Fulham. The players and directors did not like his unconventional training methods and tactics and he was relieved of his duties whilst recovering from illness in hospital after only 31 games in charge. He led Villa to promotion and an FA Cup semi-final in 1938. The players took more to his methods at Villa Park. In the 1950s, he returned to Villa to develop the youth scheme and produced many fine players.

HOLD, Oscar

Born: Barnsley, 19 October 1918.
Inside-forward   5ft 9½in; 11st (1947).
Career: Barnsley August 1937; Aldershot April 1939; guest for Barnsley, Bradford City, Burnley, Chelsea and Derby County in World War Two; Norwich City March 1947; Notts County October 1948 (£6,000); Cambridge City August 1949; Everton February 1950; Queen's Park Rangers February 1952; March Town player-manager; Gainsborough Trinity player-manager; Wisbech Town player-manager February 1957-February 1960; Cambridge City manager March 1961; coaching in Nigeria; Doncaster Rovers manager March 1962-1964; Fenerbahçe (Istanbul) manager 1964-1965; coaching in Ankara 1965; National Sporting Club (Jeddah) 1967.

Honours: Turkish League champions 1965; Saudi Arabian championship 1967.

A much-travelled player, Oscar Hold played regular first-team soccer only at Norwich, leaving after a dispute to play in non-League soccer for a while. He made 22 First Division appearances for Everton but otherwise played for lower division clubs. Hold managed a number of non-League clubs, then coached all over the world. He had two seasons in charge at Doncaster Rovers but achieved very little success. After taking Fenerbahçe to the Turkish League championship, he resigned immediately afterwards. Hold also took the National Sporting Club of Saudia Arabia to that country's first-ever national championship.

HOLDER, Philip

Born: Kilburn, 19 January 1952.
Midfield   5ft 3in; 11st 6lb (1971).
Career: Tottenham Hotspur February 1969; Crystal Palace February 1975; Bournemouth & Boscombe Athletic March 1979; Brentford assistant manager 1987, then manager August 1990; Brentford manager August 1990-May 1993.

Honours: England Youth international; Division Three champions 1992.

Phil Holder made his Tottenham debut at Anfield in December 1971. For Third Division Palace, he played in an FA Cup semi-final against Southampton at Stamford Bridge, which Palace lost 2-0. He made 112 appearances for them before moving to Bournemouth and made 37/1 appearances when Palace won promotion to the Second Division in 1976-77, by finishing third. He joined Brentford in 1987, as assistant to Steve Perryman, and took over from him in August 1990. The Bees made the Third Division play-offs at the end of his first season in charge, losing to Tranmere Rovers. They also reached the semi-final of the Leyland DAF Cup before going out to Birmingham City. The 1991-92 season was a great one for the Bees, who returned to the Second Division for the first time since 1954 as champions.

Phil Holder lost his job at Griffin Park when the Bees went down after losing their last game of the 1992-93 season at Bristol City 4-1. Their hopes of survival were not helped when Dean Holdsworth was sold to Wimbledon at the start of the season but Gary Blissett continued to score regularly.

HOLFORD, Thomas

Born: Hanley, 28 January 1878; **Died:** 6 April 1964.
Centre-half   5ft 6½in; 10st 8lb (1921).
Career: Granville Night School (Stoke); Colbridge; Stoke cs 1898; Manchester City April 1908; Stoke cs 1914; guest for Nottingham Forest in World War

One; Port Vale player-manager cs 1914-March 1920, trainer July 1923, retired as a player 1924, manager again June 1932-September 1935, chief scout and scout until retiring in 1950.

Honours: England international (1 cap); Division Two champions 1910.

Tom Holford filled every position except goalkeeper in his 248 League appearances for Stoke and won an England cap against Ireland in February 1903, at centre-half. He occasionally appeared at centre-forward or was pushed up front late in games. Holford made 184 appearances, scoring 38 goals, for Manchester City and helped them to promotion to Division One in 1909-10.

His overall career total was 479 games, which was remarkable considering he lost four years to the war. Holford was still playing in his 40s, at Port Vale, and also made a comeback at 48 due to a mountain of injuries at the club. Eventually he stayed with Port Vale for 36 years as player, trainer, manager and scout. When he was manager, the club remained in the Second Division, but only just.

HOLLINS,
John William MBE

Born: Guildford, 16 July 1946
Right-half   5ft 8in; 11st 7lb (1983).

Career: Guildford Schools; Chelsea apprentice July 1961, professional July 1963; Queen's Park Rangers June 1975 (£80,000); Arsenal July 1979 (£75,000); Chelsea player-coach June 1983, then manager June 1985-March 1988.

Honours: England international (1 cap); Under-23 international (12 caps); Youth international; Football League representative (3 caps); Division Two champions 1984; FA Cup winners 1970, runners-up 1967; Football League Cup winners 1965, runners-up 1972; European Cup-winners' Cup winners 1971, runners-up 1980.

John Hollins was an outstanding, attacking wing-half and midfield player whose energetic running, strong tackling and accurate passing was a key factor in the Blues' success during his time at Stamford Bridge. He won just one cap, against Spain in May 1967, shortly after playing in a losing FA Cup Final against Spurs.

Hollins was always keen to stay in the action and loved to burst through for strikes on goal. He won an FA Cup winners' medal in 1970 against Leeds and the following year Chelsea won the Euroepan Cup-winners' Cup Final against Real Madrid in Athens, Hollins missing the replay. He made a total of 887/11 appearances, scoring 77 goals in his career.

As a manager he was not very popular with the fans, due to his dull

but efficient teams. He did not endear himself to the Press and was not the best communicator, but was perhaps treated rather badly by Ken Bates before he resigned. Bobby Campbell was brought in as coach without his knowledge, putting Hollins in a very difficult position. His brother, Dave, also played professional football.

HOLLIS, Samuel W.

Born: Nottingham c.1866; Died: Bristol, 17 April 1942.
Career: Woolwich Arsenal manager 1894-1897; Bristol City manager April 1897-March 1899; Bedminster secretary-manager March 1899-1900; ran public house 1899-1909; Bristol City manager again 1901-March 1905; hotel management 1905-1911; Bristol City manager again January 1911-April 1913; Newport County manager July 1913-1917; chairman of Bristol City shareholders' association in 1921.

In his early years, Sam Hollis worked in a Probate Office and the Post Office. There are conflicting arguments about whether he was manager or trainer at Woolwich Arsenal but whatever, he had three rather mediocre seasons at the club.

Hollis became Bristol City's first manager at 31 years old. They had just been voted into the Southern League and he bought eight new players for just £40. He resigned in March 1899, after increasing interference from directors. Hollis moved to local rivals Bedminster, who later amalgamated with Bristol City and Hollis lost his job. He had two further spells at City in between running hotels and pubs. They were unlucky not to gain promotion between 1901 and 1904, but the club struggled in his last spell at Ashton Gate. Newport County were playing in the Second Division of the Southern League during his two years at the club.

HOLMES,
William M. 'The Doctor'

Born: Darley Hillside c.1875; Died: 22 February 1922.
Full-back   6ft; 13st 5lb (1904).
Career: Chesterfield Town; Manchester City July 1896; Clapton Orient August 1905, then manager March 1906-February 1922.

Honours: Football League representative; Division Two champions 1899; Lancashire Combination champions 1902.

Holmes was a big strong half-back whose biting tackles made him a feared opponent. He represented the Football League against the Irish League in November 1897, but was very disappointed to be left out of Manchester City's FA Cup Final side in 1904. He had played in the earlier rounds but lost his place to an amateur, S.B.Ashworth. When he found out, Holmes threw his boots through

the dressing-room window. He shrewdly guided Clapton Orient through their early years in the League. His teams had style and ability and came close to promotion in 1910-11 and 1911-12. Orient were rebuilt after the war, having lost a number of players during the hostilities. It came as a shock when Holmes collapsed and died at only 47.

HOOPER, Harry Reed (senior)

Born: Nelson, 16 December 1910; Died: 1970.
Right-back   5ft 10in; 11st 7lb (1937).
Career: Nelson Schools; Nelson November 1928; Sheffield United February 1930; Hartlepools United July 1947-1949; West Ham United trainer 1949-1957; Halifax Town manager October 1957-April 1962.

Honours: FA Cup runners-up 1936.

Hooper worked as a tailor's cutter when he played for Nelson. He made 269 League appearances for Sheffield United and 67 for Hartlepool after the war. Hooper skippered the Blades, who were then in the Second Division, when they lost to Arsenal in the 1936 FA Cup Final. United were promoted to Division One as runners-up in 1938-39, after narrowly missing out twice in previous seasons. After eight years as trainer at Upton Park, Hooper was appointed manager at Halifax Town. They did well under his guidance in the Third Division.

HOPKINSON, Herbert

Goalkeeper.
Career: East Ward (Rochdale & District League) as a player, then secretary 1899; secretary of the Rochdale & District League; Rochdale secretary May 1907-May 1909; referee on Football League list in 1920s and on international panel 1927-1928; Rochdale secretary-manager April 1932-January 1934.

Honours: Refereed Wales v Ireland 1928.

Hopkinson was the chairman at the meeting at which Rochdale FC were formed in May 1907, and he was secretary of the club for the first two years of its existence. He was a leading figure in local football and was one of the first secretaries of the Rochdale & District League. He resigned as secretary in May 1909 due to pressure of work, but remained as a representative of the club. Hopkinson was one of the first people to propose a new Third Division of the Football League.

He became well known as a League referee in the 1920s and joined the international panel and refereed the Wales v Ireland game in February 1928. Rochdale were struggling in the northern section when Hopkinson was appointed as manager. Even though he had a mass clearout of players he could not bring about a change in the club's fortunes and resigned in January 1934.

HORE, Kenneth John

Born: St Austell, 10 February 1947.
Defender   5ft 7in; 11st 2lb (1991).
Career: East Cornwall Schools; Plymouth Argyle December 1964; Exeter City March 1976-1979; Plymouth Argyle manager October 1983-November 1984; Bideford Town player-manager; Torrington manager in 1989.

Honours: Western League champions 1982, 1983.

This curly-haired, ruddy-faced Cornishman was a player's player, doing most of the donkey work in the side. He played in 433/7 games for Plymouth, scoring 127 goals helping Argyle regain Second Division status, before a move to Exeter. Hore missed

only two games in four seasons at St James' Park and was very consistent wherever he played.

As manager at Home Park, Hore steered the club to an FA Cup semi-final, where they lost narrowly, 1-0 to Watford at Villa Park. He was then rewarded with a two-year contract but was sacked four months later after a poor start to the season. He took Bideford Town to Western League championships in two successive seasons.

HORNER, William

Born: Cassop, 7 September 1942.
Wing-half   5ft 8in; 11st (1964).
Career: Middlesbrough amateur 1957, professional September 1959; Darlington June 1969, then player-manager 1974-cs 1975; Hartlepool United manager October 1976-March 1983; York City coach 1983; Hartlepool United manager December 1983-November 1986; Seaham Red Star manager December 1988.

A no-nonsense but stylish wing-half, Billy Horner went on to make 213/4 appearances for Middlesbrough after making his debut against Leyton Orient at Brisbane Road in March 1961. He also made over 200 appearances for Darlington after being transferred by manager Stan Anderson. Horner had two spells in charge at Hartlepool. They had to seek re-election in his first two seasons at the club and finished an improved 9th in 1980-81. His best season in charge at the Victoria Ground was when 'Pool finished seventh in the Fourth Division in 1985-86. He has recently been manager of Seaham Red Star in the Northern League.

HORTON, Brian

Born: Hednesford, 4 February 1949.
Midfield   5ft 10in; 11st 4lb (1971).
Career: Hednesford Town; Port Vale July 1970; Brighton & Hove Albion February 1976 (£30,000); Luton Town August 1981 (£100,000); Hull City player-manager June 1984-April 1988, retired as a player 1986; Oxford United assistant manager April 1988, then manager October 1988.

Honours: Division Three promotion 1985; Division Two champions 1982.

This bearded, swashbuckling player was a master of the well-timed tackle and interception. He was able to read the game well but lacked pace and acceleration. At Brighton he was synonymous with their rise from the Third to the First Division in the late

1970s. Horton also captained Luton to the Second Division championship in 1981-82 and altogether made 610 League appearances in his career.

Managerial responsibilities affected his displays at Hull but he took them to promotion to Division Two in 1984-85. A run of poor results cost him his job in April 1988. He was assistant to Mark Lawrenson at Oxford and took over when his boss resigned. United have struggled for survival whilst Horton has been in charge, especially since the death of Robert Maxwell. They had to sell most of their best players to survive after his death left the club with huge debts.

HOSKINS, Albert Hubert

Born: Tettenhall, 1883; Died: c.1955.
Career: Wolverhampton Wanderers 1900-1904, then joined office staff, secretary from 1922 and secretary-manager May 1924-March 1926; Gillingham secretary-manager May 1926-May 1929; Torquay United secretary 1929; trainer, coach and scout for several non-League clubs up to World War Two.

Hoskins worked his way up from office boy to club secretary after failing to make the grade as a player at Molineux. He efficiently combined his duties of club secretary with those of organising the playing side. Wolves finished sixth in the Second Division in 1924-25. Surprisingly he left the club for Gillingham when Fred Scotchbrook took over. After a spell at Torquay, Hoskins worked for several non-League clubs. For many years he was assistant to Jack Addenbrooke at Wolves before taking over from him.

HOUGHTON, Kenneth

Born: Rotherham, 18 October 1939.
Inside-forward   5ft 10in; 11st (1966).

Career: Silverwood Colliery; Rotherham United May 1960; Hull City January 1965 (£40,000); Scunthorpe United June 1973; Scarborough player-manager May 1974-1975; Bridlington player-coach July 1975; Hull City youth development officer May 1976; manager April 1978-December 1979.
Honours: Division Three champions 1966; Football League Cup runners-up 1961.

Ken Houghton was a stylish forward who brought out the best in those around him. His powerful left-foot shot enabled him to score 79 goals in 253/11 League appearances for Hull City and he was a great favourite with the crowd at Boothferry Park. He scored 22 goals in 1965-66, when Hull were Third Division champions.

Houghton had a lot of success as youth development officer at Boothferry Park and amongst his discoveries was Brian Marwood. Hull won the Northern Intermediate Youth League at this time. Despite spending money, he found little success when he became the manager. After a poor run and a 7-2 defeat at Brentford, he was sacked. He joined a local freight forwarding company after this and turned out for an ex-Tigers' side in charity matches.

HOUGHTON, Robert

Full-back.
Born: c.1950
Career: Stevenage Town; Fulham 1967; Brighton & Hove Albion cs 1968; Maidstone United player-manager 1971-1972; coaching in South Africa; Ipswich Town youth-team coach; Malmö (Sweden) manager 1974; Ethnikos (Greece) manager until 1980; Bristol City manager October 1980-January 1982; Toronto Blizzard (NASL) coach 1982-1984; Örgryte IS (Sweden) manager 1987.

Honours: European Cup runners-up 1979; Swedish League & Cup 4 times between 1974 and 1980.

Bob Houghton made 12 appearances for Fulham's reserve side in 1967-68. In 1974, he moved to Sweden to manage Malmö who were runners-up in the European Cup in 1979, after a dreadfully dull game against Nottingham Forest, and won the Swedish League title on four occasions. Houghton was manager of Greek club Ethnikos when he was appointed boss of Bristol City in October 1980. He had always longed to manage an English club but was sacked in January 1982 with City facing bankruptcy. Houghton then managed Toronto Blizzard from 1982 and they reached two NASL Soccer Bowl finals. He was the manager of Örgryte IS of Sweden in 1987.

HOUGHTON, William Eric 'Coog'

Born: Billingborough, Lincolnshire, 29 June 1910.
Outside-left   5ft 8in; 11st (1933).
Career: Donington Grammar School (Spalding); Boston Town 1925; Billingborough 1926; Aston Villa amateur August 1927, professional August 1928; guest for Notts County and Nottingham Forest in World War Two; Notts County December 1946, then manager April 1949-August 1953; Aston Villa manager September 1953-November 1958; Nottingham Forest chief scout July 1959-November 1960; Rugby

Town manager February 1961-March 1964; Walsall scout late 1965; Walsall director; Aston Villa director September 1972-December 1979, vice-president January 1983; also cricket for Lincolnshire and Warwickshire 2nd XI.

Honours: England international (7 caps); Football League representative; Division Two champions 1938; Division Three South champions 1950; FA Cup winners 1957; Football League North Cup winners 1944.

Eric Houghton served Aston Villa as player and then manager for a total of 24 years and won fame for his blistering shot in both feet, scoring many important goals for the club. Houghton gained six England caps in the 1930s and as manager took Aston Villa to an unlikely FA Cup Final victory over Manchester United in 1957.

Lincolnshire-born Houghton captained Donington Grammar School — one of the original entrants to the FA Cup in 1872 although they scratched before playing a game — and was their leading goalscorer. He also played for the village side, often turning out twice in a day. After more local soccer, he joined Aston Villa as an amateur upon the recommendation of his uncle and a former Villa player, Cecil Harris. Houghton signed professional forms a year later, when he gave up his baker's job, but was unable to establish himself in the first team until the departure of Arthur Dorrell to Port Vale.

Houghton was a stylish and effective player with fine ball control and became well known with his many goals from dead-ball situations. He failed to convert only seven out of 79 penalties in his career and scored direct from about 30 free-kicks. Strangely, he missed a penalty on his debut for Villa, against Leeds United in January 1930, but scored one of the greatest goals ever seen at Villa Park, with a 40-yard free-kick against Derby County in December 1931.

The previous season, as Villa finished runners-up in Division One, he scored 30 goals, despite playing on the left wing. Villa reached the semi-finals of the FA Cup in 1938 and clinched the Second Division championship that season, having been relegated two years earlier.

Houghton scored over 200 goals in his 20 years at Villa Park before moving to Notts County in December 1946, when he lost his place in the Villa side. He immediately settled down to play on the right wing for County and retired in April 1949 to become manager at Meadow Lane. Notts won the Third Division South championship in his first season in charge, with average crowds of 35,000. His side included Jackie Sewell, later to be transferred for a British record fee, and England centre-forward Tommy Lawton. After he sold the pair, the Magpies struggled and Houghton resigned in August 1953 to join his former club, Aston Villa.

Always a great favourite with the Villa crowd, his appointment was a popular move and he soon won their approval, introducing several talented young players including Bill Baxter from Wolves and Peter McParland from Ireland. Villa struggled in the First Division throughout his reign, but did pull off a shock FA Cup Final victory over the Busby Babes in 1957, Villa winning 2-1 as United goalkeeper Ray Wood went off with a fractured cheekbone early in the game after a controversial challenge from McParland, who scored both Villa's goals that day.

Houghton's days with Villa ended on a sour note, however. With the club heading for the Second Division amidst calls for his head, he was dismissed in November 1958. Houghton became Nottingham Forest's chief scout and also managed Rugby Town. In late 1965 he became a scout with Walsall and was later a director of the club. Houghton was also a excellent cricketer who played for Lincolnshire in the Minor Counties Championship and he also skippered Warwickshire's 2nd XI with great success after the war.

He returned to Villa Park as a director in the 1970s and was elected vice-president of the club in 1983.

HOWE, Donald

Born: Wolverhampton, 12 October 1935.
Full-back   5ft 11in; 11st 13lb (1959).
Career: Wolverhampton Boys; Wolverhampton Wanderers trial; West Bromwich Albion amateur December 1950, professional November 1952; Arsenal April 1964 (£42,000), after breaking his leg retired March 1966 to become coach, then chief coach November 1967, assistant manager March 1969; West Bromwich Albion manager July 1971-April 1975; Galatasaray (Turkey) coach May 1975; Leeds United coach October 1975-1977; Arsenal coach August 1977, then manager December 1983-March 1986; England assistant manager 1977-January 1982; coaching in Saudi Arabia 1986-1987; Bristol Rovers coach July 1987; Wimbledon assistant manager August 1987-July 1989; Queen's Park Rangers assistant manager July 1989, manager-coach November 1989-May 1991; Wimbledon coach May-October 1991; Coventry City manager January-July 1992; Chelsea assistant manager July 1992.

Honours: England international 23 caps; 'B' international (1 cap); Under-23 international (6 caps); Football League representative (6 caps).

Don Howe was captain at West Brom for many years where he was mainly a right-back with deft positional play. Later in his career he played at right-half and inside-right. After suffering a fractured leg with Arsenal in March 1966, he never played again. Howe was the coach when the Gunners won the double in 1970-71 and in the late 1970s he coached them to three Wembley Cup Finals and a European Cup-winners' Cup Final appearance.

He was not too successful in his period in charge of West Brom and they were relegated in 1973. But Howe became caretaker manager of Arsenal after the departure of Terry Neill and signed some useful players, although the Gunners never came close to winning anything and he asked to be released from his contract when Terry Venables was approached to manage the club.

Howe was coach of Wimbledon when they won the FA Cup in 1988 and then reluctantly took over at Queen's Park Rangers, although he was officially the chief coach. In January 1992 he replaced Terry Butcher as manager of Coventry City. He was reluctant to take over but accepted an 18-month contract. Howe was joined by Bobby Gould in May 1992 as joint manager, with City hoping they could repeat their successes from their Wimbledon days together. However, two months later Howe decided to accept an offer to become Ian Porterfield's assistant at Chelsea. He had been suffering from heart problems and had grown tired of all the travelling that he was expected to do at Coventry.

HOWIE, David

Born: Galston, near Ayr, 15 July 1886; Died: Bradford, 1 July 1930.
Centre-half   5ft 6in; 11st 7lb (1923).
Career: Galston Athletic; Kilmarnock September 1906; Bradford May 1911; player manager February-August 1925; guest for Fulham in World War One.

David Howie made 329 appearances and scored 22 goals for Bradford, who were a First Division side until 1921. Another relegation the following season put the Park Avenue side in the Third Division. Howie had been signed by Tom Maley in May 1911 from Kilmarnock, the club which also produced his brother Jimmy, who was a Scottish international. Howie had only five months in charge at Park Avenue. Bradford finished fifth in the northern section in 1924-25.

HOWIE, James

Born: Galston, Ayrshire, 19 March 1878; Died: London, January 1963.
Inside-right   5ft 10in; 12st 6lb (1908).
Career: Galston Athletic; Kilmarnock May 1898; Kettering Town 1901; Bristol Rovers May 1902; Newcastle United May 1903 (£300); Huddersfield Town December 1910 (£675); Queen's Park Rangers manager November 1913-March 1920; Middlesbrough secretary-manager May 1920-July 1923; later tobacconist in London.

Honours: Scotland international (3 caps); Scottish League representative (1 cap); Football League champions 1905, 1907, 1909; Scottish League Division Two champions 1899; FA Cup winners 1910, runners-up 1905, 1906, 1908.

Known as 'Gentleman Jim', Howie had an odd running action which concealed his speed and gave him the appearance of strolling through a game. A great maker and taker of goals, with immense flair and a great deal of stamina, he

saw his career really take off at Newcastle, where he gained three League championship medals and played in three FA Cup Finals before gaining a winners' medal in 1910. He scored 83 goals in 235 League and Cup games for United.

As manager of Queen's Park Rangers, he took them to the FA Cup quarter-finals in 1913-14, for the first time in their history. Rangers moved from ground to ground before settling at Loftus Road. Howie left the club just before they joined the Football League. At Middlesbrough he had a fine attack but a poor defence and his side struggled in the First Division. His greatest moment was probably scoring two goals against England in a 2-1 win at Hampden in 1906.

HUDSON, Geoffrey Alan

Leeds, 14 October 1931.
Full-back   5ft 7in; 10st 12lb (1964).
Career: Bradford December 1949; Bradford City February 1957; Halifax Town August 1959; Exeter City July 1961; Crewe Alexandra July 1962; Gillingham July 1963; Lincoln City May 1965; Rotherham United June 1966; Southend United manager October 1969-1970.

Honours: Division Four champions 1964.

Hudson was a good full-back who did the rounds of the lower divisions and made a total of 337 League appearances in his career. He won a Fourth Division championship medal with Gillingham in 1963-64. Hudson had one season as Southend United's manager, in which they finished 17th in Division Four and lost in the first round of the FA Cup.

HUGHES, Emlyn Walter OBE

Born: Barrow-in-Furness, 28 August 1947.
Defender   5ft 10in; 12st 6lb (1983).
Career: North Lancashire Schools; Roose (Blackpool); Barrow amateur; Blackpool September 1964; Liverpool February 1967 (£65,000); Wolverhampton Wanderers August 1979 (£90,000); Rotherham United player-manager July 1981-March 1983; Hull City March 1983; Mansfield Town August 1983; Swansea City September-October 1983; TV presenter; Hull City director 1988-1989.

Honours: England international (62 caps); Under-23 international (8 caps); Football League representative (4 caps); Football League champions 1973, 1976, 1977, 1979; FA Cup winners 1974, runners-up 1971, 1977; Football League Cup winners 1980, runners-up 1978; European Cup winners 1977, 1978;

UEFA Cup winners 1973, runners-up 1971, 1977.

Loved by the Kop, who nicknamed him 'Crazy Horse', Emlyn Hughes was a tough defender who made up for his lack of finesse with tremendous energy and enthusiasm. He captained Liverpool to many League and Cup honours, including two European Cup wins. Altogether, Hughes made 657 appearances, scoring 48 goals, for the Reds. He was awarded the OBE in the 1980 New Year's Honours List and was also voted Footballer of the Year in 1977, when Liverpool just missed a treble, lifting the League and European Cup but losing to Manchester United in the FA Cup Final.

He had a good first season in charge at Rotherham, when they finished seventh in the Second Division, but left in March 1983 with the club struggling to survive relegation. His father, Fred, was a Great Britain Rugby League international. Emlyn Hughes later gained a different kind of fame, as a captain on BBC's *Question of Sport* and ITV's *Sporting Triangles*.

HUGHES, Thomas A.

Born: Dalmuir, 11 July 1947.
Goalkeeper   6ft 1in; 12st 4lb (1971).
Career: Clydebank Juniors 1963; Chelsea July 1965; Aston Villa June 1971 (£12,500); Brighton & Hove Albion (loan) February 1973; Hereford United August 1973 (£15,000), then manager October 1982-March 1983.

Honours: Scotland Under-23 international (2 caps); Division Three champions 1976.

Tommy Hughes was unfortunate to understudy Peter Bonetti at Chelsea, making only 11 appearances for the Blues despite being a Scottish Under-23 international. He later made 240 League appearances for Hereford United and also managed that club. United won the Third Division championship in 1975-76, but the following season they were relegated straight back as the bottom club. Further relegation came in 1977-78 and Hereford had to seek re-election in 1979-80. Things did not improve much with Hughes as manager and United were bottom of the Fourth Division in 1982-83.

HULME,
Joseph Harold Anthony

Born: Stafford, 26 August 1904; Died: Winchmore Hill, 26 September 1991.
Outside-right 5ft 8in; 11st 12lb (1937).
Career: YMCA Stafford; York City 1923; Blackburn Rovers February 1924 (£250); Arsenal February 1926 (£3,500); Huddersfield Town January 1938, retired cs 1938; Tottenham Hotspur assistant secretary February 1944, manager October 1945-May 1949; sports journalist 1949-1969; also Middlesex cricketer 1929-1930.

Honours: England international (9 caps); Football League representative (5 caps); Football League champions 1931, 1933, 1935; FA Cup winners 1930, 1936, runners-up 1927, 1932, 1938.

An excellent footballer and cricketer, Joe Hulme was one of the fastest wingers of his time with great ball trickery, accurate crosses and fine shooting ability. Indeed, many considered him the complete winger. Hulme won three League championship medals with Arsenal and scored 138 goals in 403 appearances for the club. He also played cricket for Middlesex between 1929 and 1939, scoring 8,103 runs (12 centuries). Hulme scored 33

goals for Arsenal in 1932-33, a record for a winger in one season.

Retiring after playing for Huddersfield Town in the 1938 FA Cup Final, he was Spurs' manager after the war. Hulme had limited success at White Hart Lane. They lost an FA Cup semi-final in 1948, against Blackpool, but he assembled most of the side which won the League championship after he left the club. Joe Hulme suffered ill-health just before he left Spurs and was sacked when the directors ran out of patience with him. For many years he wrote for *The People* newspaper.

HUNT, Gordon

Career: Southport office boy in 1923, secretary 1936, secretary-manager April 1937-June 1958 (except 1940-1945 when just secretary), remained secretary until 1976.

Known as 'Mr Southport' as he spent 53 years with the club, Gordon Hunt arrived at Haig Avenue as an office boy in 1923, became secretary-manager in 1937 and finally retired in 1976. Essentially a background man, modest and unassuming, he worked tirelessly to keep the club going.

In the FA Cup, Southport never went further then the third round when he was in charge. When they finished fourth in the Northern Section in 1938-39, it was was easily their best season until the mid-1950s. They had to seek re-election in 1946-47, 1948-49 and 1957-58. Hunt stood down after the final one, to become secretary only.

HUNTER, Alan

Born: Sion Mills, County Tyrone, 30 June 1946.
Central-defender   6ft; 12st 7lb (1971).
Career: Coleraine amateur 1962, professional 1965; Oldham Athletic January 1967 (£5,000); Blackburn Rovers June 1969 (£30,000); Ipswich Town September 1971 (£60,000 and a player); Colchester United player-manager May 1982-January 1983; later rejoined as assistant manager August-November 1987.

Honours: Northern Ireland international (53 caps); Under-23 international (1 cap)); Youth international (4 caps); Amateur international (2 caps); FA Cup winners 1978.

A tall, long striding and cultured central defender, Hunter formed a fine partnership at Ipswich Town with Kevin Beattie in the centre of defence. Early in his career, he had played for Coleraine in the European Cup-winners' Cup and he also played in Europe for Ipswich after they won the FA Cup in 1978. Hunter made 280 League appearance for Ipswich Town.

He did not relish the managerial side of the game and resigned after only eight months in charge of Colchester United. Four years after leaving the club he was re-employed by Mike Walker as a coach. His brother, Vic, played in goal for Coleraine and Northern Ireland.

HUNTER, Norman

Born: Eighton Banks, County Durham, 24 October 1943.
Defender   5ft 11½in; 12st 8lb (1970).
Career: Birtley Juniors; Chester-le-Street; Leeds United apprentice November 1960, professional April 1961; Bristol City October 1976 (£40,000); Barnsley player-coach June 1979, then player-manager October 1980-February 1984, retired as a player 1982; Rotherham United manager June 1985-December 1987; West Bromwich

Albion coach February 1984; Leeds United coach February-October 1988; Bradford City coach February 1989-February 1990.

Honours: England international (28 caps); Under-23 international (3 caps); Football League representative (6 caps); Football League champions 1969, 1974; Division Two champions 1964; Division Three runners-up 1981; FA Cup winners 1972, runners-up 1965, 1970, 1973; Football League Cup winners 1968; European Cup runners-up 1975; Inter-Cities Fairs Cup winners 1968, 1971, runners-up 1967; 1975; European Cup-winners' Cup runners-up 1973.

Norman Hunter earned the nickname of 'bites yer leg' from the Elland Road fans for his tough-tackling style. He played for Leeds United through their greatest years, winning many honours along the way. Well-built and awkward looking, Hunter had more skill than he was given credit for. A very consistent performer, he was ever-present in five seasons for Leeds, was voted the PFA's first Player of the Year in 1973. He made 724/2 appearances in all games for United before his departure to Bristol City, where he made over 100 more appearances.

He became the player-coach under his former teammate Allan Clarke at Oakwell and took over as manager when Clarke moved back to Elland Road as boss. Hunter steered Barnsley to promotion to Division Two in 1980-81, when they finished runners-up, and also reached the fifth round of the FA Cup. The following season they finished sixth and reached the fifth round of the League Cup. Results were rather indifferent after this and he was sacked in February 1984. Hunter had two mediocre seasons at Millmoor.

HUNTER, Robert

Born: Govan; Died: Greenwich, 29 March 1933 (aged 72).
Career: Montrose trainer, secretary and manager 1888-1897; Millwall trainer 1897-1920, manager 1919-March 1933.
Honours: Division Three South champions 1928.

Bob Hunter's early career was in athletics and he won most of the events at the Highland Games. He later prepared athletes for races, including Charlie Gardner for the 1908 London Olympic marathon. As a manager, Hunter could spot a good player and kept unearthing fine talent despite having little money to spend. He produced the fine side which won the Third Division South championship in 1927-28. He was, indeed, a remarkable

manager, kind but firm, confident yet shy. In December 1932, Hunter was admitted to hospital with a serious illness and never recovered. When he died, he had been at the club for 36 years.

HURLEY, Charles

Born: Cork, 4 October 1936.
Centre-half   6ft 1in; 13st 5lb (1964).
Career: Essex Schools; West Ham United Juniors; Rainham Youth Centre; Millwall October 1953; Sunderland September 1957 (£20,000); Bolton Wanderers June 1969-1971; Reading manager January 1972-May 1977; running a business in Hertfordshire 1977.
Honours: Republic of Ireland international (40 caps); Division Four promotion 1976.

A very unorthodox and adventurous player, Charlie Hurley was snapped up by Sunderland from Millwall for a bargain £20,000. Hurley had come to England at the age of seven to live in Hornchurch and after being spotted by Bill Voisey, he signed for Millwall as a youngster. He made his international debut against England at Dalymount Park in 1957 in a World Cup qualifying game. The Irish managed a 1-1 draw and were unlucky not to win. Hurley later became player-manager of his country.

Reckoned to be one of the best pivots in Britain in the early 1960s, he helped Sunderland back into the First Division in 1964 and altogether made 400 appearances for the club, scoring 28 goals. He was appointed manager of Reading from 50 applicants and took them to promotion for the first time in 50 years when they finished third in Division Four in 1975-76. Reading were relegated the following year and Hurley resigned, saying that the players were not responding to his methods.

HURST, Geoffrey Charles

Born: Ashton-under-Lyne, 8 December 1941.
Centre-forward 5ft 11½in; 12st 9lb (1969).
Career: Chelmsford Schools; Halstead FC 1955; Chelmsford City 1956; West Ham United apprentice July 1957, professional April 1959; Stoke City August 1972 (£80,000); Cape Town (S Africa) (loan) cs 1973; West Bromwich Albion August 1975 (£20,000); Cork Celtic February 1976; Seattle Sounders (NASL) April-August 1976; Telford United player-manager March 1976-May 1979; England assistant coach August 1977-cs 1982; Chelsea coach May 1979; manager September 1979-April 1981; Al-Kuwait coach 1982-cs 1984; now director of motor insurance

company; also cricket for Essex 1962.
Honours: England international (49 caps); Under-23 international (4 caps); England Youth international; Football League representative (7 caps); World Cup winners 1966; FA Cup winners 1964; Football League Cup runners-up 1966; European Cup-winners' Cup winners 1965; FA Youth Cup runners-up 1959.

Originally a wing-half, Geoff Hurst was converted to a striker by Ron Greenwood and through hard work developed into one of the best in world soccer. Famous for his hat-trick against West Germany in the 1966 World Cup Final, Hurst also scored six goals in one game for West Ham, against Sunderland in 1968. In all games for the Hammers he netted 248 goals in 499 appearances, winning several honours along the way. He pioneered near-post goalscoring but also was unselfish and provided others with chances. Hurst had a great temperament, often being tackled from behind, but never retaliating.

He began in management with non-League Telford United before having two reasonable seasons at Stamford Bridge. The Blues finished fourth in 1979-80, missing promotion on goal-average. His father, Charles, played for Oldham Athletic, Bristol Rovers and Rochdale.

HURST, Gordon

Born: Oldham, 9 October 1924; Died: Margate, 11 June 1980.
Winger   5ft 9in; 11st 5lb.
Career: Oldham Schools; Ferranti; Oldham Athletic amateur 1941; Ramsgate; Charlton Athletic May 1946; Tunbridge Wells player-manager March 1958-May 1961; Llandudno coach June 1961-1963; Oldham Athletic reserve-team manager 1964, manager May 1965-January 1966, then assistant manager until July 1967; Rochdale trainer-coach July 1967; Bury secretary 1970-October 1976.
Honours: Football League representative (1 cap); FA touring side to Australia 1951 (5 caps); FA Cup winners 1947.

Gordon Hurst had plenty of skill and was well-known at The Valley for his excellent crosses and thunderbolt shot. He gained an FA Cup winners' medal with Charlton when they beat Burnley 1-0 in the 1947 Final and altogether made 393 appearances for the Addicks, scoring 81 goals. He travelled widely as a player, visiting Turkey and South America with Charlton and Australia with the FA in 1951.

He started as a reserve-team coach with Oldham in 1964. When he became their manager, the team struggled and after only three wins in 22 League games, he was replaced by Jimmy McIlroy. Hurst continued as assistant manager.

HUTCHISON, Thomas

Born: Cardenden, 22 September 1947.
Midfield/Outside-left
6ft 11st 2lb (1976).
Career: Dundonald Bluebell; Alloa Athletic; Blackpool February 1968 (£7,000); Coventry City October 1972 (£95,000 plus a player); Seattle Sounders (NASL) (loan) May-September 1980; Manchester City October 1980 (£47,000); Bulova (Hong Kong) (loan) February 1982, permanently July 1982; Burnley August 1983; Swansea City July 1985, player-manager December 1985-May 1986, then player-coach until 1991; Merthyr Tydfil player-coach 1991.
Honours: Scotland international (17 caps); Under-23 international (1 cap); FA Cup runners-up 1981.

Tommy Hutchison was a tricky and very talented left-sided player who was supremely fit, so much so that he was still appearing for Swansea City at the age of 43. He could be a brilliant player on his day and was a prolific supplier of chances for his colleagues. Hutchison made over 750 League appearances before his move to Merthyr Tydfil in 1991.

He helped Blackpool to promotion as runners-up in Division Two in 1970 and scored at both ends when Manchester City drew 1-1 with Spurs in the 1981 FA Cup Final. They lost the replay 3-2. Hutchison made 314 appearances for Coventry City after joining them for £95,000 plus Billy Rafferty in 1972. He made his international debut soon afterwards, against Czechoslovakia. He did not have a happy time as player-manager of Swansea City, who finished bottom of the Third Division in 1985-86, although he remained at the club as player-coach.

HYDE, Lincoln

Career: Stockport County secretary, then secretary-manager April 1926-April 1931; Preston North End manager April 1931-February 1932.

Hyde moved from secretrary to secretary-manager at Stockport County in 1926 and immediately appointed Fred Westgarth as trainer. He often had to sell players in order to pay his way but had the happy knack of finding capable men to fill the gaps.

Hyde was desperately unlucky not to get County promoted. They finished third in 1927-28 and were runners-up in the next two seasons in the Northern Section but in those days only the champions went up. In each of the last two seasons they scored over 100 goals and gained over 60 points. He was never given complete control at Deepdale. The directors decided who was bought and sold and Hyde lasted only one season as Preston struggled near the foot of the Second Division.

ILEY, James

Born: South Kirkby, 15 December 1935.
Left-half   5ft 10in; 11st 9lb (1964).
Career: Pontefract; Sheffield United June 1953; Tottenham Hotspur August 1957 (£16,000); Nottingham Forest July 1959 (£16,000); Newcastle United September 1962 (£17,000); Peterborough United player-manager January 1969-September 1972; Cambridge United scout 1972-1973; Barnsley manager April 1973-April 1978; Blackburn Rovers manager April-November 1978; Bury manager July 1980-February 1984; Exeter City manager June 1984-April 1985.
Honours: England Under-23 (1 cap); Football League representative (1 cap); Division Two champions 1965.

Jim Iley was a well-built and classy wing-half who never settled at Spurs but won a Second Division championship medal at Newcastle United. Iley was a clever, constructive player who was a fine passer of the ball.

As a manager he had a reputation as a team builder at struggling clubs. He brought about a revival of fortunes at Oakwell but after missing promotion regularly, the fans lost patience, especially as the club had a policy of selling its best players. Iley had a disastrous 172 days at Ewood Park. Everything seemed to go against him and he was unceremoniously sacked after a Press campaign against him.

Bury missed out on promotion in 1982-83, when they lost the last game of the season, and again he was sacked with the fans calling for his head. It was the reverse at Exeter, where 1,000 supporters signed a petition calling for his reinstatement after an unfair dismissal. He never had any problems finding work, despite little success on the pitch, for he was able to run clubs on a shoestring budget.

IMPEY, John E.

Born: Exeter, 11 August 1954.
Central defender 5ft 11in; 11st 12lb (1986).
Career: Cardiff City August 1972; Bournemouth July 1975; Seattle Sounders (NASL) (loan) May-August 1979; Torquay United August 1983; Exeter City July 1985; Torquay United July 1986, retired May 1988, then coach, youth development officer and became manager May-October 1991.

Honours: England Youth international; Schoolboy international.

John Impey found instant success as manager of Torquay United when he took over from Dave Smith near the end of the 1990-91 season. He steered United into the Fourth Division play-offs, where they beat Blackpool on penalties in the Final at Wembley and gained promotion to the Third Division. A year earlier, Impey had given up all hope of continuing his career in football and was working in the building trade.

As a player, Impey made 284 League appearances for Bournemouth and went on to make 461 in all during his career as a commanding central defender. He lasted only five months in charge at Torquay and was sacked after a poor start to the 1991-92 season.

INGRAM, Claude A.

Born: Bradford; Died: February 1955 (aged 66).
Career: Bradford City office staff 1908,

financial secretary 1919-1925; Bradford manager August 1925-March 1934; secretary of The Winter Garden, Morecambe July 1934.

Honours: Division Three North champions 1928.

Bradford deserved promotion under Ingram when they gained the Northern Section title in 1927-28. This included the last of a run of 25 home wins which ended in November 1927. Bradford had finished as runners-up in 1925-26 and third the following season. They went close to going straight through to the First Division, finishing third in 1928-29. Ingram continued to get good results with Park Avenue enjoying a successful period in the Second Division. He had previously held the post of financial secretary at Bradford City but had nothing to do with the playing side of things at Valley Parade.

IRWIN, George William

Born: Smethwick, 7 January 1891
Goalkeeper 6ft; 12st 6lb (1921).
Career: West Bromwich Albion Reserves August 1919; Crystal Palace June 1921; Reading June 1923-cs 1924; Southend United trainer; Sheffield Wednesday trainer 1925; Crystal Palace trainer 1937, manager July 1939-May 1947, then scout; Darlington manager April 1950-March 1952.

Honours: England Junior international.

George Irwin played just a handful of games in the Football League. He was trainer when Sheffield Wednesday won the FA Cup in 1935 and two years later moved back to his former club, Crystal Palace, as trainer. Irwin, the first former player to manage the club, had many problems to solve during the war years but Palace managed to keep going. The 1946-47 season was a disappointing one and he became a club scout at its end. In the meantime, he had sold star player Arthur Hudgell to Sunderland for £10,000. Irwin made little impact at Darlington, who had to seek re-election at the close of the 1951-52 season.

JACK, David Bone Nightingale

Born: Bolton, 3 April 1899; Died: London, 10 September 1958.
Inside-right 5ft 11in; 11st 10lb (1930).
Career: Plymouth Presbyterians; Royal Navy; guest for Chelsea in World War One; Plymouth Argyle cs 1919; Bolton Wanderers February 1921 (£3,000); Arsenal October 1928 (£10,890) Southend United manager May 1934-August 1940; Sunderland Greyhound Stadium manager in World War Two; Middlesbrough manager September 1944-April 1952; Shelbourne (Ireland) manager August 1953-April 1955.

Honours: England international (9 caps); Football League representative (5

caps); Football League champions 1931, 1933, 1934; FA Cup winners 1923, 1926, 1930, runners-up 1932.

A tall, elegant player with brilliant dribbling ability and deadly finishing, David Jack scored 301 goals in a career in which he made a total of 595 appearances. Jack scored the first goal in the first FA Cup Final to be staged at Wembley and also scored the winner three years later, when Bolton beat Manchester City 1-0. Arsenal's Herbert Chapman broke the British transfer record when he paid £10,890 for his signature in 1928.

Jack was not so successful as a manager. He found it was a constant struggle just to keep Southend in business. At Ayresome Park his best season was 1950-51, when Middlesbrough finished sixth. It was felt that he was too relaxed and lacked the forceful personality needed to motivate players. He was a publican in Islington before managing Shelbourne in Dublin. Later he took a job with the Air Ministry. His father, Bob Jack, was a manager and his brother, Rollo, also played for Bolton.

JACK, Robert

Born: Alloa, 4 April 1876; Died: Southend, 6 May 1943.
Outside-left.

Career: Alloa Athletic 1893; Bolton Wanderers 1895; Preston North End August 1901; Glossop 1902; Burslem Port Vale; Plymouth Argyle 1903, manager cs 1905-1906; Southend United player-manager 1906-cs 1910; Plymouth Argyle manager cs 1910-April 1938, when he retired; also Players' Union executive member in 1901.

Honours: Division Three South champions 1930; Southern League champions 1913; Southern League Second Division champions 1907, 1908.

Bob Jack's name is synonymous with the early history of Plymouth Argyle. He was their first professional player, appeared in their first match, took them to their first Southern League championship and into the Football League. Then after six consecutive seasons as runners-up, Jack took Argyle to their first Southern Section title, in 1929-30.

Jack first played for Alloa Athletic as a 15-year-old and became a professional for his local club in 1893. Originally destined for a legal career, the lure of soccer was too much for him to resist. He joined Bolton Wanderers in 1895 and helped them through to the semi-final of the FA Cup in 1896, where they lost 3-1 to Sheffield Wednesday.

Bob Jack was an exciting winger in the Scottish mould, who used his dribbling skills and speed to great advantage. On top of this, he possessed

excellent distribution and was a fine crosser of the ball. Jack led the Trotters' scoring charts in 1896-97 with 11 goals from the left wing. Bolton were relegated in 1898-99, but bounced back again the following season as runners-up.

In August 1901, after scoring 29 goals in 125 appearances for the Trotters, Jack moved to Preston North End. A year later he was transferred to Glossop and in the summer of 1903 he became Plymouth Argyle's first professional. He played in their first match in the Southern League, against Northampton in September 1903. At this time he was a member of the Players' Union executive.

Jack went on to appear in 106 games for Argyle in the Southern and Western Leagues and FA Cup, scoring eight goals. From the close season of 1905, Jack was player-manager at Home Park but the following summer he was lured away to become player-manager at Southend United. They won the Southern League Second Division title in 1906-07 and 1907-08, but were not elected to the First Division until 1908 when the division was extended.

In the summer of 1910, Jack returned as manager of Plymouth Argyle and stayed there for the next 28 years. He had retired from playing at the end of the 1909-10 season but was forced to make a brief comeback at Coventry City in December 1910, at inside-left in a match which was lost 6-1.

Under Jack, Argyle became the pride of the West Country. By 1911-12, they were strong enough to finish as runners-up in the Southern League and a year later they brought the championship to the far South West for the first time.

After the war, Argyle joined the Football League and entered the newly formed Third Division. In the first season they finished 11th and drew 21 out of their 42 games. They then finished as runners-up in the Southern Section in each of the next six seasons, in the days when only the champions gained promotion to Division Two. In 1922, Plymouth were locked on 61 points with Southampton when the season ended, when a point from their last game would have clinched promotion. The Saints, it was, who went up on goal-average. In 1923, Plymouth finished six points behind champions Bristol City and 1924 they were four points behind Portsmouth, who went up. Swansea Town pipped them by a single point in 1925, as did Reading a year later. And in 1927, Bristol City had a two-point advantage over Argyle.

By this time feelings were running high in Plymouth and a large number of supporters were convinced that the club were deliberately faltering in the run-in, not wanting promotion. Argyle answered that in 1929-30, when they finally took the title, winning 30 games to finish seven points clear of their nearest rivals. During the 1930s they did quite well in Division Two, finishing fourth in 1931-32 and fifth in 1936-37. However, they had a poor FA Cup record during Jack's years in charge.

Bob Jack represented England at bowls whilst at Home Park, using the sport to relax from the pressures of League management. He retired in 1938 and after his death at Southend, to where he had retired, his ashes were scattered on Home Park.

Three of his sons played for Bolton Wanderers. David, the most famous, went to play for Arsenal and England. Rollo played for the Trotters from 1923 to 1929, whilst Donald appeared in Bolton Reserves.

JACKSON, James Robert

Born: Farnworth, Lancashire, c.1896;
Died: May 1968.
Inside-forward   5ft 8in; 10st 12lb.
*Career: Sandylands Council Schools;
Caton Engineering Company FC;
Lancaster Town 1919; Darwen; White
Lund FC; Lancaster YMCA; Lancaster
Town 1922; Bury October 1922; Tran-
mere Rovers July 1924-1925 when he
retired due to injury; Bolton Wanderers
chief scout 1934-1935; Worcester City
secretary-manager 1945; Portsmouth
chief scout 1946 and manager May
1947-June 1952; Hull City manager
June 1952-March 1955.*

*Honours: Football League champions
1949, 1950.*

Robert Jackson, who steered Pompey
to two successive League championships, had scored over 400 goals in non-
League soccer before joining Tranmere
Rovers at the age of 28 but his career
was ended shortly afterwards by injury.
A pleasant, unassuming Lancas-
trian, what he achieved at Fratton Park
was as near to a miracle as could be
performed. In 1948-49 they gained the
title five points clear of Manchester
United and the following season they
pipped Wolves on goal-average. It was
a surprise when he left for Hull City
in 1952 with the club still challenging
for honours. He had a number of
running battles with the board at
Boothferry Park and after three years
of struggle was sacked. Jackson, who
sued the club for breach of contract,
left football very disillusioned.

JACKSON, John

Born: Aston, Birmingham 1861; Died:
June 1931.
*Career: Singers (Coventry); Wolver-
hampton Wanderers assistant trainer;
Loughborough manager 1893-1895;
West Bromwich Albion trainer; Liverpool trainer 1895-1896; Leicester Fosse
trainer 1896-1898; Brighton United
manager September 1898-April 1900;
Brighton & Hove Albion manager
again cs 1901-March 1905; licensee of
pub in Brighton 1900-1931; Blackpool
'manager' briefly in 1907.*

John Jackson had a chequered time as
manager of Brighton. He was in charge
of the original professional club in the
town which folded in March 1900 with
heavy debts caused by poor crowds and
accommodation. Jackson took the
revamped club into the Southern
League Division One via the Test
Match system in 1903 after finishing
runners-up in the Second Division
behind Fulham. Brighton were just
beginning to sign a better class of player

when Jackson left to concentrate on his
pub in the town. He later managed
Blackpool for a brief spell, although
the Seasiders did not appoint an official
manager until Bill Norman in 1919.

JACKSON, Richard W.

Born: Middlesbrough.
Half-back   5ft 8in; 11st 9lb (1904).
*Career: Middlesbrough; Sunderland
May 1898; Portsmouth May 1905;
Darlington manager 1912-1919; Mid-
dlesbrough assistant manager until
becoming Durham City's manager
from July 1926-1927.*

*Honours: North Eastern League
champions.*

Dicky Jackson made 168 appearances for
Sunderland, scoring nine goals, before
joining Pompey in 1905, but his playing
career took a downturn after this and
in 1912 Jackson became manager of
Darlington. They applied to join the
Football League but failed to gain
admission, despite winning the North
Eastern League with 31 victories out of
38 matches. They also reached the first
round of the FA Cup in 1914-15.
He was Durham City's manager for
one season and had to work with a
professional squad of only six players
and attendances of barely 2,000. He
raised £1,800 from selling players,
including the prolific scorer Syd Elliott
to Fulham.

JACKSON, Wilbert 'Peter'

Born: Luddenden Foot, 4 August 1904;
Died: Shipley, 9 May 1986.
Half-back   5ft 11in; 11st 10lb (1929).
*Career: Luddenden Foot; Hebden
Bridge; Stoke City April 1924; Con-
gleton Town; Southend United cs 1934;
Stoke City assistant manager 1935;
Wrexham manager November 1950-
February 1955; Bradford City manager
February 1955-March 1961; Stoke City
scout 1961; Bradford City scout 1969.*

Peter Jackson made only 71 appearances for Stoke in ten years at the club
and only three for Southend. Jackson
returned to the Victoria Ground as
assistant to the Potters' new manager
Bob McGrory in 1935. After the war,
Jackson managed Wrexham and gave
League debuts to his twin sons, Peter
and David. They followed him to
Valley Parade.
His best season at Wrexham had been
1952-53, when they finished third in the
Northern Section, three points behind
the champions. He applied a steadying
hand and brought an air of confidence
to Bradford City. They entered the
newly-formed Third Division in 1958
but after years of struggle were relegated
in 1961 and this eventually led to
Jackson's dismissal.

JAGO, Gordon Harold

Born: Poplar, 22 October 1932.
Centre-half   6ft ½in; 11st 11lb (1959).

*Career: Kent Schools; London Schools;
Dulwich Hamlet Juniors; Charlton*

*Athletic amateur February 1950, profes-
sional May 1951; Eastbourne United
player-manager July 1962; Fulham
assistant manager and coach August
1968; Baltimore Bays (NASL) manager
December 1967-1969; director of US
Soccer Federation 1969; Queen's Park
Rangers coach 1970, then manager
January 1971-October 1974; Millwall
manager October 1974-December 1977;
Tampa Bay Rowdies (NASL) coach
January 1978-1982; Queen's Park
Rangers manager May 1984 (for one
week); Dallas Sidekicks (Indoor Soccer
League); California Surf (NASL) coach.*

*Honours: England Youth international
(6 caps); Schoolboy international;
Division Two runners-up 1973; Division Three promotion 1976; NASL
Soccer Bowl winners 1978, 1979.*

Gordon Jago made his Charlton debut
against Arsenal at The Valley in March
1955, in front of a crowd of 48,084. A
reliable centre-half with leadership
qualities, Jago made 147 appearances
for the club before moving into management with Eastbourne United. He
had assisted Norman Creek in coaching
the Great Britain amateur side for the
Rome Olympics.
As a manager, he was never short of
ideas, some of which were controversial.
Jago made a name for himself in US
soccer and was especially successful at
Tampa Bay, taking them to two Soccer
Bowls. Jago was a modern coach, who
made in in-depth analysis of the
opposition. Millwall were relegated at
the end of his first season but soon
bounced back to the Second Division.
He left The Den after an upsurge in
misbehaviour by the club's fans, deciding to move back to the States.

JARMAN, Harold

Born: Bristol, 4 May 1939.
Outside-right   5ft 9in; 11st (1964).
*Career: Clifton Villa; Clifton St Vin-
cent's; Bristol Rovers August 1959;
Newport County May 1973; New York
Cosmos (NASL) May 1974; Mangots-
field United 1974; Portway (Bristol)
1976; Bristol Rovers youth and reserve-
team manager and assistant manager,
then manager January-April 1980;
Blackburn Rovers chief coach 1981-
1982; Bristol University coach 1982-
1983; Bristol Rovers coach 1984-
October 1986; Oxford United scout
October 1986-1988; Bath City manager
June-October 1988; Mangotsfield United manager 1989; also Gloucestershire
CCC 1961 until late 1970s.*

Jarman was a real entertainer and
crowd favourite during his years at
Eastville. He made 502 appearances,
scoring 143 goals for Rovers before
moving to Newport County. Later he
returned to the club to run the youth
scheme and unearthed a number of
talented youngsters including Gary
Mabbutt. Jarman was manager briefly
in 1980 and steered the club away from
the relegation zone. He was unlucky
not to remain in charge for a longer
period.
He returned for a third spell in the
mid-1980s but lost his job due to
financial cuts at the club. He was briefly
in charge at Bath City but found it
difficult working with part-time players. Jarman played 45 matches for
Gloucestershire and was a fine batsman. He captained the county 2nd XI
in the late 1970s.

JENNINGS, Samuel

Born: Cinderhill, 18 December 1898;
Died: Battle, Sussex, 26 August 1944.
Forward   5ft 11in; 11st 9lb (1924).

*Career: Coldstream Guards; guest for
Tottenham Hotspur & Notts County in
World War One; Basford United;
Norwich City May 1919; Middles-
brough April 1920 (£2,500); Reading
(loan) April 1921; West Ham United
June 1924; Brighton & Hove Albion
March 1925; Nottingham Forest May
1928; Port Vale June 1929; Stockport
County September 1931; Burnley
January-May 1932; Wisbech Town
secretary and coach; Olympic de Mar-
seilles (France) coach; Scarborough
September 1934; player-coach in Swit-
zerland; Glentoran coach June 1936-
October 1937; Rochdale manager
October 1937-September 1938.*

Sam Jennings was a regular goalscorer
at each of his eight English clubs,
although he found it difficult to break
into the Middlesbrough side despite his
£2,500 price tag. Later in his career,
whilst playing on the Continent, he met
Jimmy Hogan, who had a major
influence on his thinking about coaching. However, he had little success as
manager of Rochdale and he left the
job due to ill health. The brother of
William who played for Luton Town
and Northampton Town.

JENNINGS, William

Born: Barry, Wales, 25 February 1894;
Died: Penarth, 12 November 1968.
Half-back/Full-back
5ft 9in; 12st 8lb (1922).
*Career: Romilly School; Bethil Baptists
(Barry); Barry Town; Bolton Wanderers
August 1912-31; guest for Fulham in
World War One; Notts County coach
1933; Cardiff City chief coach 1936, then
secretary-manager April 1937-April
1939; joined Barry Town's office staff
after the war.*

*Honours: Wales international (11
caps); Schoolboy international (1 cap);
FA Cup winners 1923, 1926.*

Bill Jennings was still playing for
Bolton's reserves when he gained his
first cap for Wales in February 1914.
He went on to make 287 appearances
for the Trotters and suffered a great deal
from injuries during his career. Jennings joined the Royal Flying Corps
in World War One.
He played in the first FA Cup Final
at Wembley and also gained a medal
three years later with Bolton. He toured
Canada with the Welsh national side
in 1929.
Jennings had a difficult time as
manager of Cardiff, with little money
to spend and a fire at the ground shortly
after he took over. He bought a number
of players from his former club and
employed former England full-back
Ernie Blenkinsop as a coach in
November 1938.

JEWELL, A.James

Born: 1898; Died: 21 October 1952.
*Career: Football League referee; Nor-
wich City manager January-September
1939.*

*Honours: Referee of 1938 FA Cup
Final.*

A surprise choice when he was selected
to become Norwich's manager in
January 1939, Jimmy Jewell was a
famous referee of his era. He had
refereed the 1938 FA Cup Final between
Preston and Huddersfield Town, when
he awarded an extra-time penalty to
decide the tie. He had also refereed a
number of prestigious games including
the Football Association's 75th anniversary match between England and the
Rest of Europe at Highbury in October
1938. The Canaries were relegated from

Division Two at the end of the 1938-39 season. Jewell left the club after war was declared.

JEZZARD, Bedford A.G.

Born: Clerkenwell, 19 October 1927.
Centre-forward 5ft 10½in; 13st 4lb (1957).
Career: Croxley Green School (Herts); Croxley Boys' Club; Watford amateur; Worked on staff of Old Merchant Taylor's sports ground in mid-1940s; Fulham October 1948, retired through injury August 1957, youth coach, then manager June 1958-October 1964, then general manager October-December 1964; ran pub in Stamford Brook for many years.

Honours: England international (2 caps); 'B' international (3 caps); FA tour to South Africa 1956 (2 caps); Football League representative (3 caps); Division Two champions 1949, runners-up 1959;

After a slow start, Bedford Jezzard hit 123 goals between 1952 and 1956, when injury prematurely ended his career. At Craven Cottage, he formed a brilliant inside trio with Bobby Robson and Johnny Haynes. He revelled in heavy conditions and was about the fastest centre-forward of his day. His old-fashioned skills of speed, strength, bravery and directness, made him an ideal centre-forward.

Upon retirement he became the youth-team coach at Fulham, then manager in June 1958 with Frank Osborne as general manager. He took Fulham to the First Division in 1959, as runners-up, and maintained this status. Jezzard's easy-going style won the respect of the players. The selling of Alan Mullery to Spurs in March 1964 was done without his knowledge and this eventually led to his departure from the club. He left soccer to run his family pub in Stamford Brook near Hammersmith.

JOBEY, George

Born: Heddon-on-Tyne, July 1885;
Died: Derby, 9 March 1962.
Half-back 5ft 11in; 12st 1lb (1941).

Career: Morpeth Harriers; Newcastle United May 1906 (£10); Woolwich Arsenal May 1913 (£500); Bradford June 1914; guest for Hamilton Academical in World War One; Leicester City August 1919; Northampton Town May 1920, retired 1922; Wolverhampton Wanderers manager September 1922-May 1924; Derby County manager August 1925-May 1941, when he was suspended by the FA; Mansfield Town manager January 1952-May 1953.

Honours: Football League champions 1909; Division Two runners-up 1926; Division Three North champions 1924; FA Cup runners-up 1911.

George Jobey ruled his clubs with a rod of iron and frightened his players so much that they practically became quivering wrecks if they displeased him. He was renowned for his disciplinarian approach and although the players feared him, they remained loyal to him. He found much success as a manager at Wolves and Derby County, but was suspended in 1941 due to some rather creative accounting whilst manager at the Baseball Ground. Rams fans found out at this point how he had been able to entice and keep such fine players at Derby. It was found that he had been paying illegal bonuses since 1925.

Jobey played for Morpeth Harriers for two seasons before signing professional for Newcastle United in May 1906. A robust half-back, he also turned out at centre-forward occasionally. Jobey made only 53 appearances for United but this included an FA Cup medal in 1911, when Newcastle lost to Bradford City in the Final. He also appeared ten times in the Magpies' League championship season of 1908-09.

In May 1913, Jobey moved to Woolwich Arsenal for a £500 fee. They were just about to move to a new ground at Highbury and Jobey scored the Gunners' first goal at their new venue when he made his debut at centre-forward against Leicester City in September 1913. Later in the match he was injured and had to be wheeled home on a milk cart. In June 1914, Jobey joined Bradford and then appeared for Hamilton Acedemical during World War One. By the time he joined Leicester City in August 1919, he had lost much of his pace but made a further 34 appearances for that club.

In May 1920, Jobey turned down an offer to become player-manager of Ebbw Vale so that he could continue his league career at Northampton, where he made another 77 appearances. He retired in September 1922 to become manager-coach of Wolves.

A.H.Hoskins was appointed secretary at Molineux and George Holley as trainer with Jobey the manager. However, Wolves had a terrible season and nose-dived to the bottom of the Second Division. Terrible finishing by the forwards cost them game after game and Wolves eventually finished bottom with only 27 points, having scored just 42 goals.

It was humiliating for such a great club to play in the Third Division but Wolves stayed there for only one season. Jobey worked miracles to turn the club's fortunes around and they clinched the championship by one point from Rochdale. Their success was based on solid defence, but Jobey pulled off a masterstroke when he signed Tom Phillipson from Swindon Town. Phillipson scored some vital goals in the run-in to the title and went on to score many more for Wolves in future years, after Jobey's surprise departure in May 1924.

He ran a hotel for a year until Derby County persuaded him back into soccer as their manager in August 1925. Jobey really made a name for himself at the Baseball Ground with his shrewdness in the transfer market. He signed three of the Rams' greatest-ever players in Jack Barker, Jack Bowers and Sammy Crooks, each of whom cost next to nothing. He even managed to tame the difficult Hughie Gallacher after he signed for Derby.

Jobey took the Rams back into the First Division at the end of his first season in charge. They also finished as runners-up in Division One in 1929-30 and 1935-36. Yet Jobey rarely attended training sessions, leaving that side of things to the training staff.

In May 1941, Jobey was suspended for life when it was discovered that he had been paying illegal bonuses to his players since 1925. The suspension was lifted in 1945, but he went into the hotel business again and did not return to soccer until January 1952, when he became the manager of Mansfield Town. The Stags struggled for most of 1952-53 and he was sacked in May 1953 when the board accused him of losing interest in football. Jobey died at his home at Bangor Street, Chaddesden, Derby in March 1962.

JOHN, Robert Frederick

Born: Barry Dock, 3 February 1899;
Died: Barry Dock, 17 July 1982.
Utility 5ft 8in; 10st 6lb (1933).
Career: Barry Town; Caerphilly Town; Arsenal January 1922 (£750), retired 1938 to become West Ham United's coach; Torquay United trainer; Crystal Palace trainer May 1947-1949; Cardiff City trainer-coach 1949-1950; Torquay United manager March-November 1950.

Honours: Welsh international (15 caps); Football League champions 1931, 1933, 1934; FA Cup winners 1930, runners-up 1927, 1932; Southern League Welsh Section champions 1921.

Bob John was a quiet, thoughtful player, who was purposeful in everything he did. He was a hard-tackling half-back but also appeared at full-back and outside-left. John appeared on the left wing in the 1932 FA Cup Final for Arsenal and scored the Gunners' only goal in a 2-1 defeat against Newcastle United.

Arsenal had beaten his local club, Cardiff City, to his signature and he went on to make 467 League and FA Cup appearances for the Gunners. He was later employed by a former team-mate, Jack Butler, as trainer at Selhurst Park. John was in charge at Torquay for only eight months. They finished fifth in 1949-50 but struggled the following season.

JOHNSTON, Henry

Born: Droylesdon, 26 September 1919;
Died: 12 October 1973.
Half-back 5ft 11in; 12st 4lb (1951).
Career: Fairfield Road School, Droylesdon; Droylesden Athletic; Blackpool amateur June 1935, professional October 1936, retired November 1955; guest for Reading in World War Two; Reading manager November 1955-January 1963; Blackpool chief scout April 1967, caretaker manager April-May 1969; ran newsagent's in Blackpool.

Honours: England international (10 caps); Football League representative (4 caps); Footballer of the Year 1951; FA Cup winners 1953, runners-up 1948, 1951; Football League North Cup winners 1943, runners-up 1944.

Harry Johnston was a leading half-back of the post-war era, constructive, composed and intelligent and one of the best captains around. He made 331 League appearances for Blackpool after the war and also captained the side to three FA Cup Final appearances. The 1953 'Matthews Cup Final', in which Blackpool beat Bolton 4-3 after trailing 3-1, was probably the highlight of his career after being on two losing Final sides.

On retirement, Johnston moved south to manage Reading, for whom he had guested in the war years. He had a policy of youth development, as he had little money to spend on transfers. He had little success at Elm Park but was considered an honest, hard-working manager who provided a conveyor belt of young talent for the club.

JOHNSTON, Thomas Deans

Born: Berwick-on-Tweed, 30 December 1918.
Outside-left 5ft 9½in; 11st 7lb (1955).
Career: Kelso United; Peterborough United; Nottingham Forest amateur 1942, professional 1944; Notts County August 1948-1957; Valdokoski Harka (Finland) coach; Birmingham City coach 1957; Heanor Town player-manager 1958; Rotherham United manager November 1958-July 1962; Grimsby Town manager July 1962-October 1964; Huddersfield Town manager October 1964-May 1968; York City manager October 1968-January 1975; Huddersfield Town general manager January 1975, manager December 1975, general manager again April-September 1977, and manager again September 1977-August 1978.

Honours: Division Three South champions 1950; Football League Cup runners-up 1961; Division Three promotion 1974; Division Four promotion 1971.

Tom Johnston scored over 100 goals in his playing days for the two Nottingham clubs. Even so, he was probably more well known as a manager. After managing Central Alliance club, Heanor Town, Johnston stepped up into Football League management with Rotherham United. At Millmoor he produced a side which was challenging for promotion to the First Division and also reached a League Cup Final against Aston Villa in 1961.

He had little luck at Grimsby but steered Huddersfield to a League Cup semi-final in 1967-68. Johnston created miracles at York, taking the club from the Fourth to the Second Division. He then returned to Leeds Road, where he was highly regarded, but could not take the club to promotion. Johnston was a shrewd strategist who ruled his clubs with a rod of iron.

JONES, Allan

Career: School teacher; Blyth Spartans manager until 1972; Darlington manager April-December 1972.

Allan Jones took over from Ken Hale as manager of Darlington. Hale had been caretaker manager since January. Jones had gained a reputation as a manager in non-League soccer with Blyth Spartans, who finished runners-up in the Northern League in 1971-72. He had also been working as a school teacher.

When he took over at Feethams the club were still in danger of having to seek re-election but only one defeat in their last seven games steered them to 19th place, two points clear of trouble. When Jones lost his job at the end of December, Darlington had won only three out of 26 League and Cup games. This included first-round defeats in the League Cup and FA Cup. The final straw was a 7-0 defeat at Bradford City and with crowds barely over a thousand, the board lost their patience. Jones had lasted only seven months in charge at Feethams. Ralph Brand, who took over from Jones, lasted only six months.

JONES, Charles

Born: Troedyrhiw, 12 December 1899; Died: Merthyr Tydfil April 1966.
Outside-left   5ft 7in; 11st 9lb (1919).
Career: Cardiff City 1919; Stockport County August 1921; Oldham Athletic March 1923 (£1,000); Nottingham Forest September 1925 (£750); Arsenal May 1928 (£4,800); Notts County manager May-December 1934; Crittall's Athletic secretary-manager 1935-1939.
Honours: Wales international (7 caps); Football League champions 1931, 1933, 1934; Division Three North champions 1922; FA Cup runners-up 1932.

Charlie Jones developed as a player with Stockport County and Oldham Athletic. He was a great favourite at Forest and scored 22 goals in 100 appearances before his move to Arsenal. At Highbury, he switched to left-half after the arrival of Cliff Bastin. Small and lightweight, Jones was a tenacious and persistent type of player who was the grafter of the side. He made 214 appearances for Arsenal before joining Notts County as manager.

Arsenal were angry about Jones being poached by County, who were later given an official rap by the authorities. Ironically, though, Jones managed to alienate almost everybody at Meadow Lane. He changed the club's colours to a gory chocolate and blue halves and the team did not respond to this style, gaining only six points in 17 games before Jones was sacked after seven months in charge.

JONES, Leslie Jenkin

Born: Aberdare, 1 July 1911; Died: Llanfyrnach, Pembrokeshire, 11 January 1981.
Inside-left   5ft 8in; 11st 6lb (1935).
Career: Aberdare Athletic; Cardiff City August 1929; Coventry City January 1934; Arsenal November 1937; Swansea Town player-coach June 1946; Barry Town player-manager 1947; Brighton & Hove Albion player August 1948, then scout and coach; Scunthorpe United manager June 1950-1951; British Timken (Northampton) social club manager.
Honours: Wales international (11 caps); toured Canada with Welsh international side; Wartime international (5 caps); Football League champions 1938; Division Three South champions 1936.

Les Jones was a butcher's boy when he signed for Aberdare Athletic, his local club. He made 139 appearances

for Cardiff, scoring 31 goals, but they went from the First to the Third during his period at the club. Helped them to the Southern Section title in 1935-36 and gained a regular place in the Welsh international side after joining Arsenal in exchange for Bobby Davidson. Jones gained a League championship medal at the end of his first season at Highbury.

He played at inside-forward or wing-half with equal ability. He was a stocky, clever and constructive player who scored over 100 League goals in his career. Jones served in the RAF during the war. He took over at Scunthorpe United just as they were being elected into the Third Division North. They finished 12th in their first season of League soccer.

JONES, Michael David

Born: Sunderland 24 March 1947.
Half-back   5ft 11in; 10st 11lb (1971).

Career: Derby County November 1964; Notts County July 1969; Peterborough United August 1973-1976; Notts County trainer 1976; Kettering Town manager until 1979; Mansfield Town manager August 1979-May 1981; Bradford City coach 1981-November 1982; Derby County coach November 1982-January 1984; Halifax Town manager November 1984-December 1986; Peterborough United assistant manager 1986, then manager July 1988-August 1989; Blackpool scout 1989; Notts County coach, then assistant manager July 1990-January 1993.
Honours: Division Four champions 1970, 1974; FA Trophy runners-up 1979;

Mick Jones did not appear in Derby's first team before gaining Fourth Division championship medals at both Notts County and Peterborough United. He made a name for himself in management when he took Kettering to the 1979 FA Trophy Final, where they lost 2-0 to Stafford Rangers. They also finished runners-up in the Southern League Premier Division. Jones had certainly revived his flagging fortunes, for when he took over they were on the point of closure.

This obviously impressed Mansfield but they were relegated to Division Four at the end of his first season in charge. He worked with Roy McFarland at Bradford City and Derby County, the latter club being fined for 'poaching' the two from the former. After a constant struggle against bankruptcy at Halifax, Jones became assistant at Peterborough, where he was manager

for 1988-89 but they finished only 17th in Division Four. More recently, he struck up a fine partnership with Neil Warnock at Notts County, who gained promotion to the First Division via the play-offs in 1991. They were relegated after just one season and when County struggled near the foot of the newly-formed First Division both Jones and Warnock were sacked.

JONES, Thomas Daniel

Born: Aberaman, Glamorgan 1884; Died: Porthcawl, Glamorgan, 8 February 1958.
Career: Aberaman; Aberdare 1903-1904; Nottingham Forest 1904-1905; Aberdare 1908; Merthyr Town secretary-manager cs 1923-24; Cardiff City scout.
Honours: Welsh international 1 cap.

Jones remained an amateur throughout his career and was an important pioneer of the development of soccer in the rugby stronghold of South Wales. His father was a grocer in Aberaman and also the 'Constable of Higher Miskin', an ancient office and ceremonial post. Jones was described as a brilliant runner and a tricky dribbler, one of the stars of South Walian soccer.

He never quite made the grade at Nottingham Forest, appearing in their first team only three times before returning to Aberdare, where he was later secretary. He was also a vice-president of the FA of Wales. His one international appearance had been on his club's ground at Aberdare, a 1-0 defeat against Ireland in 1908. He had a season in charge at Merthyr Town, in which they finished 13th in the Southern Section. He became a solicitor in 1913 and practised in Aberdare after the war.

JONES, William H.

Born: Ynysddu, Wales, 26 November 1910.
Left-half   5ft 8in; 11st 2lb (1930).
Career: Ynysddu Crusaders; Newport County amateur 1929, professional 1930; Barry Town 1934-1947; Ipswich Town chief scout 1947; Barry Town manager 1951; Worcester City manager 1954; Cardiff City assistant manager & chief scout August 1957, then manager September 1958-September 1962; Worcester City manager 1962; Abergavenny Thursday manager in 1960s.
Honours: Division Two runners-up 1960.

Bill Jones made only a handful of Football League appearances before moving into non-League soccer. When manager of Barry Town, he discovered Derek Tapscott and Dai Ward. He arrived at Ninian Park in 1957 as assistant manager and chief scout to Trevor Morris, whom he succeeded a year later. Jones took Cardiff City into the First Division in 1960 and produced some exciting talents such as Graham Moore, Alan Durban, Barrie Hole and Frank Rankmore. City were relegated in 1962 and, following a bad start to the 1962-63 season, Jones was dismissed and rejoined Worcester City. The brother of David who played for Newport County.

JONES, William Lot

Born: Chirk, April 1882; Died: Chirk, 13 July 1941.
Centre-forward/Inside-left
5ft 5in; 10st 2lb (1903).
Career: Chirk 1901; Druids (Ruabon) 1902; Manchester City January 1903; Southend United August 1919-1920; Aberdare Athletic player-manager June

1920-March 1922; Wrexham March 1922; Oswestry April 1922-1923; Chirk player-manager July 1923-1926.
Honours: Wales international (20 caps); Division Two champions 1910.

A versatile forward, Billy Lot Jones was one of the stars of a Welsh side which won the Home International Championship in 1907. He scored the goal which earned Wales a 1-1 draw against England at Craven Cottage to clinch the title and altogether netted six goals in his 20 internationals. Lot Jones also played 302 games for Manchester City, scoring 74 goals, and won a Second Division championship medal in 1909-10.

He took over at Aberdare Athletic just after they had become a limited company in 1920. The club was voted into the Football League a year later and finished eighth in their first season in the Third Division South. Jones later ran green grocers shops in Oswestry and Chirk up until his death in 1941.

JORDAN, Joseph

Born: Carluke, 15 December 1951.
Centre-forward   6ft; 11st 12lb (1971).
Career: Blantyre Victoria; Morton October 1968; Leeds United October 1970 (£15,000); Manchester United January 1978 (£350,000); AC Milan July 1981 (£325,000); Verona (Italy) July 1983; Southampton August 1984 (£150,000); Bristol City February 1987, assistant manager November 1987, then player-manager March 1988-September 1990; Heart of Midlothian manager September 1990.
Honours: Scotland international (52 caps); Under-23 international (1 cap); Football League champions 1974; FA Cup runners-up 1979; European Cup runners-up 1975; European Cup-winners' Cup runners-up 1973; Freight/Rover Trophy winners 1987.

A wholehearted battler, Joe Jordan took some time to establish himself at Elland Road. He was more of a target man than a goalscorer, but he gave his all over 90 minutes of every game. A regular choice for Scotland, Jordan played in the final stages of three World Cups and scored the goal which took the Scots to the finals in West Germany in 1974. His courage brought him many injuries, and he was splendid in the air and quite unselfish.

He became player-coach at Bristol City under his old Leeds teammate Terry Cooper. After Jordan became player-manager at Ashton Gate, he took City to the Football League Cup semi-finals in 1988-89, when they lost 2-1 on aggregate to Nottingham Forest. The following season they finished runners-up in Division Three and reached the fifth round of the FA Cup. Hearts had an average season in 1990-91 with Jordan in control, but improved enormously the following season to finish as runners-up to Rangers in the

League, but nine points adrift. They also reached the semi-final of the Scottish Cup where they lost to Airdrie on penalties after two drawn games.

JOYCE, Walter
Born: Oldham, 10 September 1937.
Wing-half   5ft 10in; 11st 8lb (1959).
Career: Lancashire Schools; Burnley amateur July 1953, professional November 1954; Blackburn Rovers February 1964 (£10,000); Oldham Athletic September 1967, coach 1969-1970 and 1971-1973; Rochdale manager July 1973-May 1976; Bolton Wanderers coach and assistant manager 1978-December 1985; Preston North End coach cs 1986.

Mainly a reserve during his ten years at Turf Moor, where he made only 70 League appearances and missed out on League and Cup medals, Joyce turned down the chance to become youth-team coach at Old Trafford to take over at Rochdale. They finished bottom of Division Three with only 21 points and only two victories in 1973-74. They were also knocked out of the FA Cup by non-League Grantham. Somehow, Joyce survived and later had some fine runs in the FA Cup, but eventually lost his job.

KAY, George
Born: Manchester, 21 September 1891; Died: Liverpool, 11 April 1954.
Centre-half   5ft 10in; 12st (1926).
Career: Eccles; Bolton Wanderers 1911; Belfast Distillery; West Ham United 1919; Stockport County June 1927; Luton Town player-coach August 1928, manager December 1929-May 1931; Southampton manager May 1931-May 1936; Liverpool manager May 1936-February 1951.

Honours: Irish League representative; Football League champions 1947; Division Two runners-up 1923; FA Cup runners-up 1923, 1950.

George Kay enjoyed a long and varied career in soccer. He led West Ham to the famous 'White Horse' Wembley Final of 1923, and when he became a manager he took Liverpool to the FA Cup Final in 1950 and also to the League championship in the first season after World War Two.

As a manager, Kay was a determined man, full of ideas and also a reflective and intelligent character. His teams usually played with attacking flair. In the end, though, it brought on ill health due to all the stresses and strains of professional football.

Manchester-born Kay's early football experience was aided by his association with his local club, Eccles. He signed for Bolton Wanderers in 1911, but after three appearances in the League side he failed to agree terms and moved to Ireland to play for Belfast Distillery. He later became the first Englishman to captain the Irish League in a representative match.

In 1919, after wartime service with the Royal Garrison Artillery, Kay signed for West Ham United. At the start of the 1922-23 season, the Hammers appointed him captain and it proved a triumphant year for the Boleyn club. As well as winning promotion to the First Division, they also reached the first FA Cup Final to be staged at Wembley. His former club, Bolton Wanderers, were the opposition but the game was a near-farce. It was not an all-ticket match and nearly 200,000 people turned up on the day. Supporters ringed the pitch and Kay made his protests to the referee, but the match went ahead.

The chaos that ensued is summed up in a quote from Kay on the day: "When Bolton's second goal was scored by J.R.Smith, I was sitting among the spectators on the touch line. I had charged an opponent and fallen with him into the crowd. While I was trying to disentangle myself there was a roar. I looked up and saw the the ball in the net."

That was the extent of the scoring and the result was allowed to stand, despite the unhappy circumstances.

Kay made 259 appearances for the Hammers, scoring 17 goals, and was unlucky never to be capped by England.

He moved to Stockport County in 1927 but appeared only twice in their first team before joining Luton Town as trainer-coach under manager John McCartney. On 23 December 1929, he took over as manager and one of his first signings was a former Hammers' teammate, Tom Hodgson. Luton finished 13th and seventh respectively in the Southern Section before Kay received a more lucrative offer to manage Southampton in May 1931. At The Dell, Kay created the Saints' first nursery side and young talent soon emerged including Ted Drake, Charlie Sillett and Bill Light. Drake was later sold to Arsenal for £6,500, cash which proved a lifeline for the Southampton club. Kay managed to keep them in the Second Division, but only just, for the Saints spent much of their time in the bottom half of the table. He was forced to sell to survive and amongst the outgoing players were Johnny Arnold and Mike Keeping, sold to Fulham in 1933 for £5,000. Southampton's supporters were so angry at their departure that only 2,949 attended the next home match, against Bradford City.

Kay resigned in May 1936 and joined Liverpool as manager. The Reds did not achieve much until after the war, during which Kay had to keep the club going with the help of many guest players. At the end of the war he took the players on a tour of Canada and the USA, where they were able to eat a healthy diet and build up their strength after the deprivations of war.

The League championship was gained in 1946-47. The season was badly disrupted by the weather but after the big freeze, Liverpool dropped only one point in their last eight games to take the title. They also lost to Burnley in an FA Cup semi-final replay at Maine Road. In 1950, Kay led the Reds all the way to Wembley where they lost to Arsenal 2-0. Despite illness, he led the side out before the start of the Final. In the semi-final, Everton had been beaten with goals from Bob Paisley and Billy Liddell. Kay dropped Bob Paisley for the Final and the decision arguably cost them the match.

In February 1951, Kay was advised to retire on medical advice. Three years later he was dead.

KAYE, John
Born: Goole, 3 March 1940.
Centre-forward/Wing-half 5ft 9in; 12st 6lb (1973).
Career: Goole Schools; Goole Dockers FC; Goole United; Goole Town; Hull City amateur; Scunthorpe United September 1960 (£1,750); West Bromwich Albion May 1963 (£44,750); Hull City November 1971 (£28,000), coach August 1974, then manager September 1974-October 1977; Scunthorpe United coach and assistant manager October 1977-February 1981; then went into the hotel business; Goole Town manager 1982.

Honours: Football League representative (2 caps); FA Cup winners 1968; Football League Cup winners 1966, runners-up 1967, 1970.

In his early days, John Kaye was an inside-right and centre-forward with a bustling style which produced many goals. He moved to left-half during the late 1960s and added backbone to the defence. A wholehearted and consistent player, Kaye made 347/3 appearances for West Brom, scoring 54 goals. He played in the 1968 FA Cup Final, when Albion beat Everton, and tasted European competition the following season. A knee injury sustained playing for Hull City at Hillsborough in December 1973 ended his career which was then in the veteran stage.

The following September, Kaye took over as manager at Boothferry Park. He produced a very dour, defensive side which conceded only 40 goals in 1974-75. Although highly rated by the players, he was unable to lift the club above a mid-table Second Division spot. He lost his job at Scunthorpe due to economy measures at the Old Show Ground.

KEEGAN, Joseph Kevin OBE
Born: Armthorpe, Doncaster, 14 February 1951.
Forward   5ft 8in; 11st 7lb (1981).
Career: Lonsdale Hotel FC; Scunthorpe United apprentice December 1967, professional December 1968; Liverpool May 1971 (£35,000); SV Hamburg June 1977 (£500,000); Southampton July 1980 (£400,000); Newcastle United August 1982 (£100,000); retired May 1984; living in Spain 1984-1992; Newcastle United manager February 1992.

Honours: England international (63 caps); Under-23 international (5 caps); European Cup winners 1977, runners-up 1980; UEFA Cup winners 1973, 1976; Footballer of the Year 1976; European Footballer of the Year 1978, 1979; Bundesliga Footballer of the Year

1978; Football League champions 1973, 1976, 1977; Bundesliga champions 1979; FA Cup winners 1974, runners-up 1977; OBE 1982. Division One Champions 1993.

Sharp and creative, Kevin Keegan scored goals regularly throughout his career. Bill Shankly picked up the bargain of the decade when he paid Scunthorpe United just £35,000 for Keegan's services. Surprisingly good in the air for a small man, Keegan developed into one of the most famous players in Europe. He gained honours galore at Anfield including three League titles. Keegan also played in two European Cup Finals: in 1977 for Liverpool, who beat Borussia Mönchengladbach 3-1; and in 1980 with SV Hamburg, who lost 1-0 to Nottingham Forest. As well as two UEFA Cup winners' medals, he played for Liverpool in their losing FA Cup Final appearance in 1977.

Keegan scored 100 goals in 321 appearances for Liverpool and was also a star in West Germany before spells with Southampton and Newcastle United, whom he helped back to Division One before retiring. Keegan was a folk hero on Tyneside and he was welcomed back with open arms when he was appointed as manager to save the club from the ignominy of relegation to Division Three, a feat he achieved. He threatened to resign when money he had been promised was not made available to strengthen the side, although Newcastle were in dire financial straits. However, behind-the-scenes turmoil was forgotten when the Magpies stormed to the top of Division One in 1992-93. Keegan, with the help of his assistant Terry McDermott, turned around Newcastle United's fortunes that season. They took the First Division championship, eight points clear of runners up West Ham United. Keegan bought some excellent players including Andrew Cole from Bristol City for £1.75m. Cole scored some vital goals in the run-in to the title.

KEEN, Michael T.
Born: Wycombe, 19 March 1940.
Right-half   6ft; 11st 8lb (1964).
Career: Queens Park Rangers June 1958; Luton Town January 1969; Watford July 1972, then player-manager June 1973-April 1977, retired as a player 1975; Northampton Town manager February 1978-March 1979; Wycombe Wanderers manager April 1980-April 1984; Marlow manager 1986.

Honours: Division Three champions 1967; Football League Cup winners 1967; Isthmian League champions 1983.

A tall, imposing wing-half, Keen was an old-fashioned half-back who liked to make long passes, was skilful and perceptive and was also an excellent tackler. He made 393 League appearances and scored 41 goals for Queen's Park Rangers and skippered the side a Third Division championship and Football League Cup double in 1967. The following year Rangers went into the First Division but lasted there for only a season.

Keen also played 145 League games for Luton and 126 for Watford, where he was also the manager from June 1973. Watford were relegated to Division Four in 1975 and he was sacked after being unable to get them promoted back. He had two mediocre seasons at Northampton before being sacked in March 1979, then managed Isthmian League club Wycombe Wanderers for four years. They won the championship in 1982-83 but did not go up to the Alliance League (now Conference). They also reached the semi-finals of the FA Trophy in 1982.

KEEN, Robert

Died: October 1965
Career: Gateshead manager cs 1956-cs 1958.

Bob Keen was a little-known manager of Gateshead during their last years in the Football League. The club was already in decline when he took over. Attendances had dropped alarmingly and only 1,322 people attended a match against Rochdale in January 1957. In those days that was a quite awful figure for a League game. Gateshead made a loss of almost £6,000 during 1957-58. Whilst Keen was in charge they finished 14th and 17th respectively in the Third Division North. He made a number of signings which improved results and also brought Tommy Rigg from Gillingham to be his trainer.

KELLY, Alan J.

Born: Dublin, 5 July 1936.
Goalkeeper   6ft; 12st 3lb (1964).
Career: Drumcondra; Preston North End April 1958, retired 1974, then coach, caretaker manager December 1981, then manager December 1983-April 1985; Republic of Ireland manager briefly May 1980.

Honours: Republic of Ireland international (47 caps); Division Three champions 1971; FA Cup runners-up 1964; FA of Ireland Cup winners 1957.

A tall and commanding goalkeeper, Alan Kelly was capped three times for Ireland whilst still with Drumcondra and also won an Irish Cup winners' medal with them before going to England to join Preston. At Deepdale, he took over from Fred Else in goal and developed into a highly reliable 'keeper. Preston were relegated to Division Two in 1961, but reached the FA Cup Final in 1964, losing 3-2 to West Ham in an exciting match.

Kelly made 447 League appearances before retiring to become a coach at Deepdale in 1974. He was the Irish team manager but this interfered with his duties at Preston, so he resigned after a short spell in charge of the national side. He managed to steer Preston clear of relegation in his first season in charge, but they went down to Division Four the following year. Poor results continued and he ended his association with the club after 27 years in April 1985. His two sons have both kept goal in the Football League.

KELLY, Michael J.

Born: Northampton, 18 October 1942.

Goalkeeper   6ft; 12st 7lb (1971).
Career: Islington Boys; Chelsea Juniors 1959; Wimbledon amateur 1960; Queen's Park Rangers March 1966; Birmingham City August 1970-1974 (£18,000) and coach 1972-March 1976; Minnesota Kicks (NASL) player-coach 1975; Plymouth Argyle reserve-team manager 1976, then manager May 1977-February 1978; Fulham assistant manager February 1978-1981; Crystal Palace assistant manager 1981; Portsmouth chief coach; West Bromwich Albion chief coach September 1982-February 1984; coach at the FA School of Excellence.

Honours: England Amateur international (1 cap); Isthmian League champions 1963, 1964; FA Amateur Cup winners 1963.

Kelly enjoyed much success as a goalkeeper at Plough Lane when Wimbledon won four Isthmian League championships on the trot before joining the Southern League and turning professional. When they finished runners-up in the Southern League Division One in 1965-66, Kelly missed only two games all season. He also appeared in the Dons' FA Amateur Cup-winning side of 1963, when they beat Sutton United 4-2 at Wembley.

He made 20 First Division appearances for Queen's Park Rangers in 1968-69 and had a second spell in the top division with Birmingham City. Kelly made a total of 134 appearances for the two clubs before embarking on a coaching career. He did not have much success as a manager at Plymouth, who were 21st in the Third Division when he resigned to join Fulham in February 1978, as assistant to Bobby Campbell.

KELLY, Noel

Born: Dublin, 28 December 1921.
Inside-forward   5ft 7in; 10st 9lb.
Career: Shamrock Rovers; Glentoran; Arsenal October 1947 (£650); Crystal Palace March 1950; Nottingham Forest August 1951; Tranmere Rovers player-manager July 1955-October 1957.

Honours: Republic of Ireland international (1 cap); League of Ireland representative.

Noel Kelly made only one appearance for Arsenal, at Goodison Park in February 1950, before moving to Selhurst Park. He was a regular only at Palace and Tranmere. When Ernie Blackburn became secretary at Prenton Park, Kelly took over as manager.

He had an unspectacular period in charge and in his two seasons in charge, Tranmere finished 16th and 23rd in the Northern Section. Kelly gained his Irish cap in March 1954, against Luxembourg in a World Cup qualifying tie which was narrowly won 1-0. Today he runs a sports outfitters' shop in Bromborough. His son, John, joined Tranmere Rovers as a player in 1979.

KELLY, Robert

Born: Ashton-in-Makerfield, Lancashire, 16 November 1893; Died: Fylde, 22 September 1969.
Outside-right   5ft 7in; 9st 6lb (1933).
Career: Ashton White Star; Ashton Central; Earlestown August 1912; St Helens Town August 1913; Burnley November 1913 (£275); Sunderland December 1925 (£6,550); Huddersfield Town February 1927 (£3,500); Preston North End July 1932; Carlisle United player-manager March 1935-November 1936; Stockport County manager November 1936-January 1938; Sporting Lisbon trainer August 1946; coaching

in Switzerland and Channel Islands, Barry Town (Suffolk) manager December 1960.

Honours: England international (14 caps); Football League representative (7 caps); Football League champions 1921; Division Three North champions 1937.; FA Cup runners-up 1928, 1930

A former miner, Bob Kelly was a very skilful player who appeared in all the forward positions. He missed Burnley's FA Cup Final appearance in 1914, but won a League championship medal in 1920-21, playing in 27 of the 30 consecutive unbeaten matches they achieved that season. Kelly had a deadly shot, excellent dribbling skills and a fine body swerve. He later played in two losing Finals for Huddersfield Town. Kelly scored 154 goals in his total of 601 League appearances in his career.

When he became manager of Carlisle United in 1935, the team was in decline and the club were losing money. After Carlisle had to seek re-election in 1934-35, Kelly retained only one player for the following season, assembling a new squad for £1,000. Stockport County won the Northern Section championship at the end of his first season in charge, but were relegated straight back again the following season.

KELLY, Theo

Career: Everton manager May 1939-September 1948 and secretary 1936-1939 and 1948.

Everton were one of the last Football League clubs to appoint a manager when Theo Kelly took over in May 1939. He had previously been secretary at Goodison Park. A superb organiser with an excellent business brain, Kelly was not popular with the players, however, for they found difficulty in communicating with him. He angered Everton's fans when he sold Tommy Lawton to Chelsea in 1945, but Lawton had wanted to get away from Goodison Park for some time. Kelly rarely used the transfer market, which eventually led to stagnation at the club who were near the bottom of the First Division when he reverted to secretary in 1948.

KELSO, Philip

Born: 1871; Died: 1935.
Career: Hibernian manager; Arsenal manager March 1904-January 1908; ran hotel in Largs, Firth of Clyde 1908-1909; Fulham manager May 1909-May 1924; played for Fulham in emergency during World War One, aged 47; ran pub in West London.

A stern, abrasive Scot, Philip Kelso was a man of firm views who had a reputation as a disciplinarian. He had a

paternalistic attitude towards the players and discouraged drinking and smoking. He also demanded that they live in London when playing for Arsenal and Fulham. And he would often make them spend a week away before important games, which did not prove popular with all the players, many of whom left after clashes with Kelso.

At Woolwich Arsenal, he took the club to two FA Cup semi-finals. At both Arsenal and Fulham he took over from Harry Bradshaw and he stayed at Craven Cottage for 15 years, bringing some famous internationals to the club and adding a touch of glamour. He was just beginning to build a fine side in the early 1920s when Fulham was rocked by a bribery scandal after which the Cottagers' centre-forward Barney Travers was banned for life. Kelso lost some creditablity after this.

KEMBER, Stephen Dennis

Born: Croydon, 8 December 1948.
Midfield   5ft 8in; 11st 8lb (1971).
Career: Surrey & Croydon Schools; Crystal Palace apprentice July 1965, professional December 1965; Chelsea September 1971 (£170,000); Leicester City July 1975 (£80,000); Crystal Palace October 1977 (£50,000); Vancouver Whitecaps (loan) April 1978, permanently March 1980-July 80; Crystal Palace youth-team manager, then manager November 1981-June 1982; Whyteleafe manager.

Honours: England Under-23 international (3 caps); Youth international; Division Two champions 1979.

Steve Kember was a tireless runner in midfield and a strong tackler, and Palace received a record fee of £170,000 when they sold him to Chelsea. He had helped Palace into the First Division in 1968-69, when he was ever-present in the promotion-winning side. He made 286/5 appearances, scoring 38 goals, for Palace and a further 144/16 appearances (15 goals) for Chelsea and 126/2 (six goals) for Leicester. He had moved to Leicester when Chelsea were relegated in 1975.

After returning to Palace, Kember helped Terry Venables' side to the Second Division championship in 1978-79. Later, he coached Palace's youth team before becoming the club's manager, supposedly as the players' choice. Palace finished only 15th in the Second Division and he was dismissed in June 1982. He has been manager of Whyteleafe for many years.

KEMP, David Michael

Born: Harrow, 20 February 1953.
Forward   5ft 9in; 11st (1981).
Career: Harrow Borough; Maidenhead; Slough Town; Crystal Palace April 1975; Portsmouth November 1976; Carlisle United March 1978; Plymouth Argyle September 1979 (£75,000); Gillingham (loan) December 1981; Brentford (loan) March 1982; Edmonton Drillers (NASL) June 1982; Seattle Sounders (NASL) June-September 1983; San José Earthquakes (NASL); Vasalund (Finland) player-manager; Dulwich Hamlet; Plymouth Argyle manager March 1990-February 1992; Slough Town manager July 1992.

Dave Kemp did the rounds of the lower divisions. He was Pompey's leading scorer in 1976-77 and 1977-78, in the latter season scoring 16 goals despite the club finishing bottom of the Third Division and Kemp being sold to Carlisle United before the end of the season. He scored 24 goals for

Plymouth in 1980-81 and at the end of his Football League career had scored 106 goals in 249/7 appearances.

Kemp played in North America before moving to manage and coach in Finland. He was a surprise choice as manager of Argyle in March 1990, but he came in time to steer the club clear of relegation that season. He had little money to spend and was fired after almost two years in charge with Argyle heading for relegation from the Second Division. Kemp then took over at Conference League club, Slough Town.

KENDALL, Howard

Born: Ryton-on-Tyne, 22 May 1946.
Midfield   5ft 9in; 10st 9lb (1971).
Career: Preston North End May 1963; Everton March 1967 (£80,000); Birmingham City February 1974 (£180,000); Stoke City August 1977 (£40,000), player-coach February 1978; Blackburn Rovers player-manager June 1979-May 1981; Everton manager May 1981-June 1987; Athletic Bilbao manager June 1987-November 1989; Manchester City manager December 1989-November 1990; Everton manager again November 1990.

Honours: England Under-23 international (6 caps); Youth international; Schoolboy international; Football League representative; Little World Cup winners 1964; Football League champions 1970, 1985, 1987; Division Three promotion 1980; FA Cup winners 1984, runners-up 1964, 1968, 1985, 1986; Football League Cup runners-up 1984; European Cup-winners' Cup winners 1985; Zenith Data Systems Cup runners-up 1991.

Howard Kendall has been involved in three League championship seasons as a player and manager at Goodison Park. The first as a player came in 1969-70, then as a manager in 1984-85 and 1986-87. Kendall spent seven years as a player at Everton and has now far exceeded that as a manager.

Kendall's uncle, Harry Taylor, played for Newcastle United, but his great inspiration was his father, an enthusiastic amateur, who did everything in his power to put his only son on the road to becoming a top-class professional footballer. After winning county and area honours, Kendall was capped for England Schoolboys against Wales.

His father felt that Howard would have a better chance of making the grade if he was with a smaller club and so he joined Preston North End as an apprentice in 1961, turned professional two years later. In 1964, Kendall skippered the England youth side to victory in the Little World Cup Final and soon afterwards played for Preston in the FA Cup Final against West Ham. He got his place at Wembley because Ian Davidson, the usual right-half, was suspended by the club. At the time, Kendall was the youngest player to appear in an FA Cup Final, at 17 years 345 days. He gained a losers' medal that day as West Ham won the Final 3-2.

After 104 League appearances (13 goals) for Preston, Kendall moved to Everton for £80,000 in March 1967. He soon gained his first England Under-23 cap, against Wales that year, but must have been one of the best players never to have gained a full cap. He collected another runners-up medal when Everton lost to West Brom in the 1968 FA Cup Final, but in 1969-70 the League championship came to Goodison. Kendall formed a brilliant mid-

field partnership with Colin Harvey and Alan Ball and that season the trio played the best football of their careers.

The following season he almost went to Wembley again but the Toffees lost to Liverpool in the semi-finals of the FA Cup. Everybody expected Everton to win even more honours but, inexplicably, the club went into decline after this and in February 1974, Kendall left Everton after 272/2 appearances (27 goals) for the Toffees and moved to Birmingham City for a fee of £180,000. He was given the captaincy at St Andrew's but the Blues achieved little. They did reach the FA Cup semi-final in 1975, but lost to Second Division Fulham.

Kendall made a further 134 appearances for Birmingham before moving to Stoke City in August 1977 for a £40,000 fee. He was made player-coach in February 1978 and Stoke returned to the First Division in 1979. In June that year, Kendall became player-manager of Blackburn Rovers. In just two years in charge at Ewood Park, he steered Rovers from a mid-table Third Division position to the brink of the First Division.

Morale had been low when he joined the club after a terrible season. The team made a poor start to 1979-80 but Kendall gradually moulded a team together, spending a modest £90,000 on three new players. Success was built on defensive foundations, Kendall himself inspiring the team from midfield as they won promotion to Division Two. The following season they were pipped on goal-average by Swansea City from going straight through to the First Division. Their failure to score goals let them down.

In May 1981 Kendall retired from playing and became manager of Everton. They won no trophies in his first two years at Goodison and, indeed, he was on the point of being sacked in January 1984 when the tide turned and they eventually reached the League Cup Final, losing to Liverpool, and then won the FA Cup, beating Watford 2-0 in the Final. The following season, Everton won the European Cup-winners' Cup against Rapid Vienna in Rotterdam after beating Bayern Munich in the semi-finals. They also clinched the League championship in 1984-85, 13 points clear of runners-up Liverpool, but lost to Manchester United in the League Cup Final.

In 1985-86 they were runners-up to Liverpool in both the League championship and FA Cup, Liverpool

clinching the double in a memorable FA Cup Final at Wembley, winning 3-1 against their greatest rivals. The following season, however, Everton regained the League title, this time nine points clear of Liverpool.

In 1987 Kendall surprised everybody by deciding to move to Spain to manage Athletic Bilbao. He was not a great success in Basque country and was limited in which players he could sign. He remained in Spain, despite an offer to manage Newcastle United, but after a poor run of results was sacked in November 1989.

Within weeks of returning to England, Kendall was appointed manager of Manchester City but in November 1990, the opportunity came to return to Goodison Park as manager. City were angry at what they saw as his lack of loyalty, but the draw was too great for Kendall.

Everton's season took off after Kendall took over but they remained inconsistent in the League. They reached the sixth round of the FA Cup before losing 2-1 at West Ham and also reached the Final of the Zenith Data Systems Cup at Wembley where they were easily beaten by Crystal Palace, 4-1. After this followed two very depressing seasons at Goodison when Kendall's job was put on the line due to poor results in both the League and cup competitions.

Everton had a very poor season in 1992-93, finishing near the bottom of the Premier League and doing little in cup competitions. Kendall's hold on the job was becoming tenuous.

KENNEDY, Robert

Born: Motherwell, 23 June 1937.
Midfield   5ft 9in; 12st 5lb (1970).
Career: Coltness United May 1956; Queen of the South trailist; Clyde trialist; Kilmarnock March 1957; Manchester City July 1961 (£43,000); Grimsby Town player-manager March 1969-May 1971 (£10,000); Drogheda 1971; Bradford City youth-team manager and coach; Bradford honorary manager; Bradford City manager January 1975-January 1978; Blackburn Rovers coach January-May 1978.

Honours: Scotland Under-23 international (1 cap); Scottish League Division One runners-up 1960, 1961; Football League Division Two champions 1966; Division Four promotion 1977; Scottish Cup runners-up 1960; Scottish League Cup runners-up 1961.

Bobby Kennedy had to overcome a serious illness which kept him out of the game for eight months during his early days at Kilmarnock. He later played in two Cup Finals for them, in which Killies lost both to Rangers, 2-0. They also finished runners-up in Division One in 1959-60 and 1960-61.

He made 251/3 appearances for Manchester City, who had a rather up-and-down time after he joined the club. He helped them regain First Division status as champions in 1965-66, but made only six appearance in City's League championship season of 1967-68. When he became player-manager at Grimsby Town, he arrived too late to help the Mariners avoid re-election. Things did not improve much over the next two seasons and it came as no surprise when he was sacked in May 1971. He was controversially sacked at Bradford City, who had won promotion the previous season. Kennedy had also set up a thriving youth policy at Valley Parade.

KENT, Henry

Centre-half.
Career: Brighton & Hove Albion 1905; Middlesbrough May 1908; Watford August 1909, then player-manager 1910-1911 and manager until 1926.

Honours: Southern League champions 1915.

Harry Kent made over 100 appearances for Brighton but only six for Middlesbrough. He took over from John Goodall as manager of Watford. Goodall had been a member of Preston's 'Old Invincibles' team of 1888-89. Kent made 61 appearances for the Hornets before retiring in 1911. He did not have an easy time at Vicarage Road and had to set the pattern of economy for years to come.

He was forced to release 90 per cent of players in the close season but made a string of discoveries from works and colliery sides, whom he later sold for a profit to keep the club solvent. Amongst these were Arthur Grimsdell, who went to Spurs, and George Edmonds, who was transferred to Wolves. Kent took Watford to the Southern League championship in 1915 and into the Football League in 1920. They finished sixth in their first season in the Third Division and his departure heralded a decline at the club.

KERR, George A.M.

Born: Alexandria, Dumbarton, 9 January 1943.
Inside-forward   5ft 10in; 11st (1971).
Career: Vale of Leven; Renton Select; Barnsley May 1960; Bury March 1966 (£10,000); Oxford United September 1966; Scunthorpe United February 1968-73; Lincoln City coach and assistant manager 1973, then manager June-December 1977; Grimsby Town coach December 1977, then manager July 1979-January 1982; Rotherham United manager March 1983-May 1985; Lincoln City manager December 1985-March 1987; Boston United manager November 1987-January 1990.

Honours: Division Three champions 1980.

George Kerr scored 79 goals in 372/7 League appearances but he was better known as a manager. When he retired, Kerr joined Lincoln City's coaching staff under manager Graham Taylor. When Taylor moved to Watford, Kerr took over at Sincil Bank but was sacked after only six months. Kerr was recruited by John Newman as trainer at Grimsby. When Newman also moved on, Kerr again took over and steered the club to the Third Division championship. Kerr was respected by the players but was often at loggerheads with the directors. Later the rift widened and he was sacked.

He took Rotherham to the fifth round of the League Cup but achieved little other success at Millmoor. He returned to Lincoln but they were relegated and a year later went out of the League as the bottom club, although they seemed safe when Kerr was sacked in March 1987. He took Boston United to third place in the Conference League in 1988-89, but he was again sacked when they slumped the following year. His brother Bobby played for Sunderland.

KERR, James

Born: Annan, Scotland, November 1881; Died: Norwich, 18 February 1933.
Career: Bathgate manager 1924-1925; Coventry City manager June 1925-February 1928; Walsall manager May 1928-April 1929; Norwich City manager April 1929-February 1933.

A canny, genial and very experienced Scot, Kerr managed three Southern Section clubs. He never enjoyed any great success but managed the finances well and produced some entertaining sides. Coventry and Walsall were both in mid-table, although he took Norwich City to eighth, their best season since joining the League. However, the following season, the Canaries finished bottom of the table. Kerr entered hospital with pneumonia in January 1933 and died the following month. It came as a great shock as he had never had a serious illness before this. He was only 51 years old.

KETTLEBOROUGH, Keith Frank

Born: Rotherham, 29 June 1935.
Midfield   5ft 7in; 10st 3lb (1959).
Career: Rotherham YMCA; Rotherham United December 1955; Sheffield United December 1960; Newcastle United January 1966 (£22,500); Doncaster Rovers player-manager (£12,000) December 1966-May 1967, reverting to player again; Chesterfield November 1967 (£6,000); Matlock Town August 1969; also a professional cricketer with Rotherham Town in the Yorkshire League.

Keith Kettleborough appeared in the role of linkman during his career. He played in deep-lying positions and liked to hit long passes all over the field. Kettleborough was always in the action. He played regularly for Sheffield United in the First Division after helping them to runners-up spot in Division Two in 1960-61. United finished fifth the following season.

He also made over 100 appearances at Millmoor and Bramall Lane and cost Newcastle a large fee but stayed for only 11 months before accepting an offer to become player-manager of Doncaster Rovers. At the end of his first season, they were relegated to Division Four, having conceded 117 goals. Kettleborough then suffered the indignity of reverting back to player-only status under his successor.

KIDD, Brian

Born: Manchester, 29 May 1949.
Forward   5ft 10in; 11st 6lb (1971).
Career: St Patrick's School, Collyhurst; Manchester Schools; Manchester United apprentice August 1964, professional June 1966; Arsenal August 1974 (£110,000); Manchester City July 1976 (£100,000); Everton March 1979 (£150,000); Bolton Wanderers May 1980 (£110,000); Atlanta Chiefs (NASL) April 1981; Fort Lauderdale Strikers (NASL) January 1982; Minnesota Kicks (NASL) May-September 1984; Swindon Town assistant manager April 1985; Preston North End assistant manager 1985, then manager January-March 1986; Barrow manager; Manchester United youth development worker in 1990.

Honours: England international (2 caps); Under-23 international (10 caps); Youth international; Schoolboy international; Football League representative 1 cap; European Cup winners 1968.

Brian Kidd played for both the Manchester clubs and made a great start to his career after being spotted by United scout Joe Armstrong, whilst playing for Manchester Schools. Kidd soon established himself in United's star-studded side and scored one of the goals which beat Benfica in the 1968 European Cup Final, a victory which brought him an excellent 19th birthday present.

He was in England's squad for the 1970 World Cup finals in Mexico and

made two appearances for England, scoring in his second game against Ecuador in Quito in May 1970, before the tournament began. Altogether he scored 152 goals in 449 League appearances before retiring.

Despite sharing in United's night of European glory, he never gained any domestic honours, coming closest in 1980 when he was sent off in a losing FA Cup semi-final. He was Preston's manager for only two months, when he took over from Tommy Booth, having previously been his assistant. After just one win in 12 games and with Preston bottom of the table, Kidd was sacked.

KING, John

Born: 15 Liverpool, 1938.
Wing-half   5ft 6in; 10st (1964).
Career: Everton March 1956; Bournemouth & Boscombe Athletic July 1960; Tranmere Rovers February 1961; Port Vale July 1968; Wigan Athletic 1971; Tranmere Rovers coach 1973, then manager May 1975-September 1980; Rochdale coach 1980; Northwich Victoria manager until 1985; Caernarfon manager 1985-April 1987; Tranmere Rovers manager April 1987.

Honours: Division Three promotion 1991; Division Four runners-up 1989, promotion 1976; FA Trophy winners 1984, runners-up 1983; Leyland Daf Cup winners 1990, runners-up 1991.

John King is in his second spell as manager of Tranmere Rovers and has, to date, spent 20 years at Prenton Park as player, coach and manager.

King first joined Everton as a 15-year-old schoolboy and after 49 games for the Toffees he was transferred to Bournemouth in July 1960. Seven months later, he moved back to the Liverpool area to join Tranmere Rovers for the first time. Soon appointed captain, he made 241 League appearances and helped the club to promotion in 1967. In July 1968 he was given a free transfer and moved to Port Vale, also helping them to promotion and making a further 101 League appearances.

In 1971, King went to Wigan Athletic but returned to Prenton Park in 1973 as coach. With the departure of Ron Yeats as manager in May 1975, King was appointed his successor and at the end of his first season in charge, Rovers won promotion to Division Three. The club struggled in the higher division and crowds dropped alarmingly. King was sacked in September 1980 with Rovers struggling back in Division Four.

He coached at Rochdale for a while, then took over as manager of Northwich Victoria, taking the club to two FA Trophy Finals at Wembley. In 1983 they lost to Telford United, but the following year beat Bangor City 2-1 in a replay at Stoke. In 1985, King moved to Wales to manage Caernarfon Town, whom he steered to the third round of the FA Cup in 1986-87, beating League clubs Stockport County and York City before losing to Barnsley in a replay.

This attracted the attention of Tranmere again and he returned to Prenton Park as manager in April 1987. Tranmere finished as runners-up in Division Four in 1988-89 and the following season won the Leyland Daf Cup, beating Bristol Rovers in the Final at Wembley. A week later they returned to Wembley but lost to Notts County in the Third Division play-off Final. The club were almost promoted anyway, when Swindon Town were

initially demoted to the Third Division, but they were later reprieved much to Tranmere's disappointment. However, the following season Tranmere finally made it back to the Second Division after 52 years by beating Bolton in the Final of the play-offs at Wembley.

They reached Wembley again that season, in the Leyland Daf Cup Final, which they lost 3-2 to Birmingham City. After a season of consolidation, Tranmere were challenging for a place in the Premier League in 1992-93 and, were also the only Merseyside club left in the FA Cup by the middle of January, a very unusual occurrence. John Aldridge continued to find the net regularly and Pat Nevin was another inspired signing from Everton.

Tranmere Rovers reached the First Division play-offs in 1993 but lost to Swindon Town 5-4 on aggregate.

KING, E. Sydney

Born: Chatham, 29 July 1873; Died: February 1933.
Full-back.
Career: Northfleet; New Brompton 1897; Thames Ironworks cs 1899; West Ham United manager April 1901-November 1932.

Honours: FA Cup runners-up 1923; Division Two runners-up 1923.

Syd King formed a fine full-back partnership with Charlie Craig at West Ham. A flamboyant and charismatic character, he became club secretary in 1902 and took the Hammers into the Football League in 1919. They entered the First Division as runners-up and in 1923 also reached the first Wembley Cup Final, where they lost 2-0 to Bolton.

King was given a bonus of £300 when he sold Syd Puddefoot to Falkirk for £5,000. The Hammers' best season in the First Division came in 1926-27, when they finished sixth. But they were relegated in 1931-32 due to an ageing side, King's health deteriorated and he developed a drink problem. Things came to a head when he was rude to directors at a board meeting in November 1932 and he was suspended and replaced by Charlie Paynter. Sacked in January 1933, King committed suicide less than a month later when suffering from a mental illness.

KINGHORN, Harold McGill

Born: Midlothian 1896.
Goalkeeper   5ft 6in; 12st 1lb (1910).
Career: Leith Athletic; Sheffield Wednesday 1908-1911; Bournemouth & Boscombe Athletic manager 1920-1925, trainer 1925-39, then manager again 1939-1947.

Honours: Division Three South Cup winners 1946.

Harry Kinghorn took Bournemouth into the Football League in 1923. As Boscombe, they had finished as runners-up in the Southern League the previous season. During the summer of 1923, a new stand holding 1,600 was built at Dean Court but the club struggled in the Third Division South and Kinghorn became trainer when Leslie Knighton was appointed manager in 1925.

He remained as trainer until 1939, when he was reappointed manager. Kinghorn steered the club through the war years and they won the Third Division South Cup in 1945-46, beating Walsall 1-0 in the Final at Stamford Bridge. He left Bournemouth after they finished seventh in the first post-war season.

KINNEAR, Joseph P.

Born: Dublin, 27 December 1946.
Right-back   5ft 8½in; 11st 6lb (1971).
Career: St Albans City; Tottenham Hotspur apprentice August 1963, professional February 1965; Brighton & Hove Albion August 1975, retired through injury; Sharjah (UAE) coach; Malaysia national coach; Doncaster Rovers coach and assistant manager 1987, then caretaker manager April-June 1989; Wimbledon coach September 1989, then assistant manager, then manager January 1992.

Honours: Republic of Ireland international (26 caps); FA Cup winners 1967; Football League Cup winners 1971, 1973; UEFA Cup winners 1972.

Joe Kinnear was finally given his chance in League management after he applied for the post at Wimbledon. He had also applied when Ray Harford had departed to Blackburn Rovers. Kinnear was assistant to Peter Withe during his unhappy spell in charge. Kinnear revived the Dons' spirit and took them from the relegation zone to a mid-table position.

Kinnear had followed his former Spurs teammate Dave Mackay to Dubai and then Doncaster Rovers, where he was in charge of the club's successful youth scheme. Rovers reached the FA Youth Cup Final before losing to Arsenal, a great achievement for a struggling club. He was caretaker boss for a short period after Mackay's departure.

Kinnear played 252/7 games for Spurs and appeared in their 1967 FA Cup success over Chelsea and gained UEFA Cup and League Cup winners' medals. A quick-tackling full-back, he had his fair share of serious injuries during his playing career.

The Dons were everybody's favourites to go down in 1992-93 but surprised some of their critics with improved displays under Joe Kinnear's management, aided by the introduction of some promising youngster. Kinnear had his moments of controversy during the season but managed to do what the Dons' landlords Crystal Palace could not do. That is to stay in the Premier League.

KIRBY, George C.R.

Born: Liverpool, 20 December 1933.
Centre-forward   6ft; 12st 2lb (1964).
Career: Everton June 1952; Sheffield Wednesday March 1959; Plymouth Agyle January 1960; Southampton September 1962 (£17,000); Coventry City March 1964 (£12,000); Swansea Town October 1964; Walsall May 1965; New York Generals (NASL) 1967;

Brentford October 1968; Halifax Town manager cs 1970-August 1971; Watford manager August 1971-May 1973; Akranes (Iceland) manager; Halifax Town manager again November 1978-June 1981.

A bustling and robust forward who was strong and fearless and gave opposing defenders a tough time, George Kirby had a fine goalscoring record at all his clubs and was constantly on the move. He once scored three goals in four minutes, for the Saints against Middlesbrough in November 1962.

His best season in management came in his first with Halifax Town, who finished third in Division Three, their highest-ever position as they missed promotion by only three points. After Halifax beat Manchester United 2-1 in the Watney Cup, Kirby received a lucrative offer to manage Second Division Watford.

Alas, he had an unhappy time at Vicarage Road and the Hornets finished bottom with only 19 points at the end of his first season in charge. The following season they narrowly missed relegation again, this time on goal-difference. After managing abroad, Kirby returned to Halifax but could not work any miracles a second time and after Town had to seek re-election in 1980-81, he was sacked.

KIRKMAN, Norman

Born: Bolton, 6 June 1920.
Full-back   5ft 11in; 13st (1951).
Career: Burnley amateur 1937, professional September 1939; guest for Fulham in World War Two; Rochdale September 1946; Chesterfield December 1947; Leicester City August 1949 (£8,500); Southampton July 1950; Exeter City player-manager March 1952-March 1953; Bradford manager March 1953-January 1955; Northwich Victoria manager in 1960s.

Due to the war, Norman Kirkman did not make his League debut with Rochdale until he was 26. Chesterfield paid a record fee when he joined that club.

Kirkman was never a regular at either Leicester or Southampton and altogether made only 136 League appearances during his career. He had been a navigator in the RAF during the war. Although only at Exeter for a short spell, he managed to get the club off the foot of the table before accepting a more lucrative offer to manage Bradford. They finished in mid-table positions in his two seasons at Park Avenue.

KNIGHTON, Albert Leslie

Born: Church Gresley, near Burton upon Trent, March 1884; Died: May 1959.

Career: playing career cut short by ankle injury; Castleford Town manager 1904; Huddersfield Town assistant secretary-manager 1909; Manchester City assistant secretary-manager August 1912-1919; Arsenal manager May 1919-June 1925; Bournemouth & Boscombe Athletic manager July 1925-July 1928; Birmingham manager July 1928-August 1933; Chelsea manager August 1933-April 1939; Shrewsbury Town manager 1945-December 1948; golf club secretary in Bournemouth in 1950s. Portishead manager in 1992.
Honours: FA Cup runners-up 1931.

Leslie Knighton enjoyed a long and relatively successful career as a manager, initially working as assistant manager at Huddersfield and Manchester City and gaining a reputation for developing fine young sides.

In his first managerial post he was not in sole control at Arsenal, where the club was in debt after moving to Highbury. Sir Henry Norris, the Gunners chairman, instructed Knighton to build a successful side without spending any money. This was unrealistic and Knighton struggled to keep Arsenal in the First Division. He was rarely allowed to manage and Norris often interfered, making Knighton's task even more difficult. In the end he got fed up with these restrictions and after a couple of rows with Norris, was sacked.

Knighton soon took over at Bournemouth. He was a quiet man and rarely attended training sessions, allowing his assistants to look after team affairs, although some players took advantage of his good nature. His finest moment came at Birmingham when they appeared in an FA Cup Final in 1931 but lost to West Brom. He managed to keep the Blues in the First Division but left for Chelsea after they made him an offer he could not refuse.

Chelsea had an amazing run to avoid relegation at the end of his first season in charge. They also just avoided relegation again in 1938-39 but did reach the sixth round of the FA Cup. After managing Midland League club Shrewsbury Town, Knighton's health broke down and he retired to Bournemouth, where he took on the more gentle post of secretary of a local golf club.

KNIGHTON, Kenneth

Born: Barnsley, 20 February 1944.
Left-half   5ft 9in; 11st 5lb (1972).
Career: Barnsley Schools; Mexborough Rovers; Wath Wanderers; Wolverhampton Wanderers apprentice July 1960, professional February 1961; Oldham Athletic November 1966 (£12,000); Preston North End December 1967 (£30,000); Blackburn Rovers July 1969 (£45,000); Hull City March 1971

(£60,000); Sheffield Wednesday August 1973 (£50,000), retired January 1976 to become youth-team coach January 1976; Sunderland coach, then manager June 1979-April 1981; Manchester United scout briefly; Orient manager October 1981-May 1983; Dagenham Town manager May 1984-October 1985; Trowbridge Town manager until January 1988.
Honours: FA XI tour to New Zealand 1969; Division Two runners-up 1980.

A good all-round player who defended well and could also start attacking moves, Ken Knighton started his working life as a trainee miner before being discovered by Wolves. Never able to gain a regular first-team spot at Molineux, he moved around and commanded some respectable transfer fees in the process.

Knighton scored the vital goal which kept Sheffield Wednesday in the Second Division, against Bolton in April 1974. However, the Owls were relegated the following season. He toured New Zealand with an FA XI in 1969 and made a total of 359 League appearances in his career.

After working as a coach at Roker Park, Knighton became manager in June 1979 and took the club to runners-up spot in the Second Division in 1979-80. As a manager, he was a strict disciplinarian but often alienated his players with this approach and was considered by some as inflexibile. In his first season at Brisbane Road, Orient were relegated to the Third Division and he was sacked when they struggled again the following season.

KNOWLES, Cyril Barry

Born: Fitzwilliam, near Pontefract, 13 July 1944; Died: 31 August 1991.
Left-back   6ft; 11st 13lb (1968).
Career: South Elmsall Schools; Monkton Colliery; Manchester United amateur; Hemsworth; Blackpool trialist; Middlesbrough October 1962; Tottenham Hotspur May 1964 (£45,000), retired through injury April 1976; Hertford Town manager cs 1976; Tottenham Hotspur scout; Doncaster Rovers coach 1977-1981; Middlesbrough coach cs 1981-March 1983; Darlington manager July 1983-March 1987; Torquay United manager June 1987-October 1989; Hartlepool United manager November 1989-March 1991.

Honours: England international (4 caps); Under-23 international (6 caps); Football League representative (1 cap); Division Four promotion 1985; FA Cup winners 1967; Football League Cup winnrs 1971, 1973; UEFA Cup winners 1972.

Cyril Knowles had a sparkling career with Middlesbrough and Spurs after working down the mines at Fitzwilliam Colliery. 'Boro sold him to Tottenham for £45,000, after only 39 games for the club, and he appeared in Spurs' 1967 FA Cup Final victory against Chelsea and also in two League Cup Final victories at Wembley and in Spurs' UEFA Cup win over Wolves in 1972.

He was very popular with the fans and even had a song written about him, Nice one Cyril, which made him even more well-known. He made 507/2 appearances for Spurs, scoring 17 goals, before injury forced him to retire.

Knowles took up his first managerial post in the League with Darlington and in 1984-85 he guided them to promotion to Division Three, finishing third after leading the table in March. He lost his job at Feethams after Darlington were relegated again in 1986-87.

Torquay made the Fourth Division play-offs in 1987-88 but lost to Swansea in the Final, and the next year they reached the Sherpa Van Trophy Final at Wembley but lost 4-1 to Bolton. He lost his job the following season and moved to Hartlepool. In March 1991, Cyril Knowles became ill with a brain tumour and eventually had to step down as manager. Sadly, he died six months later. His brother, Peter, played for Wolves before giving up the game after becoming a Jehovah's Witness.

KNOWLES, James Y.

Career: Tranmere Rovers assistant secretary 1931, secretary May 1935, manager November 1936-January 1939.
Honours: Division Three North champions 1938.

Knowles, a former film extra at Elstree Studios, became assistant secretary to Bert Cooke at Tranmere in 1931 and secretary in 1935 when Cooke was sacked. When team manager Jackie Carr left the club, Knowles took on the dual role as secretary and manager. He steered Rovers to the Third Division North championship in 1937-38 and to Second Division soccer for the first time. They struggled during the following season and Knowles left just after Christmas.

KYLE, Robert Hugh

Born: Belfast; Died: Sunderland, 17 February 1841 (aged 70).
Career: Belfast Distillery secretary June 1897-August 1905; Sunderland manager August 1905-March 1928.
Honours: Football League champions 1913; FA Cup runners-up 1913.

Bob Kyle managed Sunderland for 23 years, when they were one of the most powerful clubs in English football but won very few trophies. Indeed, they could be adequately described as 'the nearly men'. Kyle spent large sums of money trying to find a winning formula at Roker Park but enjoyed major success only in 1912-13, when the Wearsiders won the League championship but missed out on the double when they lost to Aston Villa in the FA Cup Final.

Little is known about his early life except that he was the secretary of Distillery in his native Belfast, from June 1897 until he joined Sunderland as secretary-manager in August 1905. Over the next 23 years, as well as winning the championship, they finished runners-up in 1922-23 and in third place in no less than five seasons.

The first of these, in 1908-09, included an amazing 9-1 victory over Newcastle United at St James' Park. Kyle was always on the look out for good players and signed Charlie Johnson, a big powerful centre-half from Hearts to improve the defence and also winger Jackie Mordue from Woolwich Arsenal. In 1911, he bought Charlie Buchan from amateurs Leyton for £1,250. Buchan went on to become one of the greats of North-East soccer.

Sunderland were never very successful in the FA Cup, and lost 3-1 to Southern League Norwich City in 1911. The 1912-13 season started badly with only two points from the first seven games. In October, Kyle bought Joe Butler and Charlie Gladwin, who greatly improved the defence. Buchan scored five goals in a 7-0 win over Liverpool and Sunderland never looked back afterwards. They finally clinched the title four points ahead of their nearest rivals, Aston Villa. Villa got revenge in the FA Cup Final, however, winning 1-0 at the Crystal Palace before a massive crowd of 120,000.

Kyle had to rebuild the club after the war. He spent £5,250 on Michael Gilhooley, a Scottish international centre-half from Hull City, but two broken legs ruined his career. Kyle also spent £5,500 on Warney Cresswell from South Shields, who went on to be another Roker great.

Sunderland were runners-up to Liverpool in the League in 1922-23, losing their chance of another title with poor results in April. Bob Kyle made another big signing to replace the ageing Charlie Buchan, who moved to Arsenal in 1925. He paid a record £6,500 for Bob Kelly from Burnley. Another great find was David Halliday, who scored 42 goals in 1925-26 and 36 the following season. In March 1928, Kyle resigned as manager with Sunderland struggling to avoid relegation.

LAMBTON, William Ernest

Born: Nottingham, 2 December 1914; Died: Sherwood, Nottingham 16 September 1976.
Goalkeeper.
Career: Basford North End; Nottingham Forest May 1935; Exeter City April 1946; Doncaster Rovers October 1946; coaching in Denmark; Scunthorpe United coach; Leeds United trainer-coach November 1957, then manager December 1958-April 1959; Scunthorpe United manager April 1959 (for three days); Chester manager November 1961-July 1963.

Some sources say that Bill Lambton joined Nottingham Forest in 1935 but there is no record of him having played in their first team. He made three wartime appearances for Exeter City in 1945-46 and also three appearances for Doncaster Rovers. Lambton holds the record for the shortest time spent as a manager when he stayed for only three days at Scunthorpe United in April 1959.

A fitness fanatic, Lambton once helped keep British amateur boxers fit when coaching in Denmark. He devised some unusual training methods, which did not always please his employers, using trampolines to keep players fit and supple. The best thing he did whilst managing Leeds United was to sign their future guru, Don Revie.

LANE,
William Henry Charles

Born: Tottenham, 28 October 1904; Died: Chelmsford, 10 November 1985.
Centre-forward 5ft 9in; 11st 4lb (1933).
Career: London City Mission; Gnome Athletic; Park Avondale; Tottenham Hotspur amateur 1920, professional cs

1924; loaned to Barnet c.1920, and to Northfleet; Leicester City November 1926 (£2,250); Reading June 1928; Brentford May 1929; Watford May 1932; Bristol City January 1936; Clapton Orient July 1937; Brentford assistant manager 1938; guest for Brighton & Hove Albion in World War Two; Guildford City manager 1946; Brighton & Hove Albion assistant manager April 1950, then manager March 1951-May 1961; Gravesend & Northfleet manager December 1961-1963; Arsenal scout 1963; Queen's Park Rangers scout 1968; Brighton & Hove Albion scout.*
Honours: Division Three South champions 1958.

Described as a teetotaller, non-smoker and a Christian, it is said that Bill Lane had the respect of his players without having to resort to strong discipline and punitive punishments. He certainly had the right approach, enjoying ten successful seasons at the Goldstone, eventually taking Brighton into the Second Division for the first time in their history.

Quite small for a centre-forward, Lane joined Tottenham Hotspur as an amateur in 1920 and was farmed out to Spurs' nursery clubs, Barnet and Northfleet. He scored seven goals in 26 appearances for Spurs before moving to Leicester City, where he understudied Arthur Chandler and suffered a frustrating period in which he made only five first-team appearances, scoring two goals. In June 1928, Lane was on the move again, this time to Reading.

But his career did not take off until he joined Brentford in May 1929, where he scored 84 goals in 114 games for the Bees. He scored a further 72 goals for Watford, before moving to Bristol City and then Clapton Orient in July 1937. Altogether, he scored 208 goals in 344 League appearances before retiring to become assistant manager to Harry Curtis (his former manager at Gnomes) at Griffin Park.

Lane made a brief comeback for Brighton in the war years and in 1946 became the manager of Guildford City. They finished runners-up in the Southern League in 1946-47, but struggled after this.

In April 1950, Lane moved to the Goldstone as assistant manager to Don Welsh. When Welsh left the club in March 1951, Bill Lane took control and steered Brighton to fifth place in the Southern Section in his first full season.

The Seagulls were unfortunate to finish as runners-up in 1953-54 and 1955-56. In the first of these they finished three points behind Ipswich Town. In the second they were a point behind Leyton Orient after a close fought finish. They scored 112 goals that season and the average crowd was 16,000. The title finally came in 1957-58, when they won their last game 6-0 to enter the Second Division.

Lane resigned in May 1961, after three seasons of struggle in the higher division. He publicly stated that he had resigned due to the abolition of the maximum wage, describing it as the most retrogressive step in the history of the game. In reality, if he had not resigned he would probably been sacked due to poor results. Albion were relegated the season after he left.

His spell at Gravesend & Northfleet ended unhappily with relegation to the lower division of the Southern League. Lane then became a scout for Arsenal. In 1968 he joined Queen's Park Rangers in a similar capacity and worked for Brighton again as a scout in the 1970s. He was still scouting when he was 75 years old.

LANGLEY, Ambrose

Born: Horncastle, 10 March 1870; Died: Sheffield, 29 January 1937.
Right-back   5ft 11in; 14st 7lb (1903).
Career: Horncastle; Boston; Grimsby Town March 1889; Middlesbrough Ironopolis 1891; Sheffield Wednesday 1893, office duties & scouting 1903; Hull City player-manager April 1905-April 1913, retired as a player 1906; Sheffield Wednesday assistant secretary 1913; Huddersfield Town manager December 1919-March 1921.

Honours: Football League representative (1 cap); Football League champions 1903, 1904; Division Two champions 1900, runners-up 1920; Northern League champions 1892, 1893; FA Cup winners 1896, runners-up 1920.

A tough, uncompromising full-back who was a loyal and consistent performer for the Owls, Ambrose Langley was a great fighter with lots of determination which sometimes led to trouble with referees. He gained two League championship medals and made an FA Cup Final appearance for Wednesday before a bad injury at Sunderland in 1903 led to his early retirement after 317 appearances for the Owls.

He made a comeback when he joined Hull City as player-manager but lasted only to Christmas 1905. Langley discovered some fine players at Anlaby Road. He once rowed across the Humber to sign a player to beat the opposition to his signature. He came close to leading the Tigers in the First Division in 1910, but was then forced to sell his best players. Langley laid the foundations for future success at Huddersfield Town and also led the team to runners-up position in Division Two and to an FA Cup Final, which they lost 1-0 to Aston Villa in 1920.

LAWRENCE, James

Born: Glasgow, 16 February 1885; Died: November 1934.
Goalkeeper   5ft 10in; 11st (1904).
Career: Partick Athletic; Glasgow Perthshire; Hibernian; Newcastle United July 1904; chairman of Players' Union in September 1921; retired May 1922; South Shields manager May 1922-January 1923; Preston North End manager January 1923-May 1925; Karlsruhe (Germany) coach August 1925; Stranraer chairman 1933-1934.

Honours: Scotland international (1 cap); Football League champions 1905, 1907, 1909; FA Cup winners 1910, runners-up 1905, 1906, 1908, 1911.

Lawrence was probably the finest goalkeeper to play for Newcastle United, for whom he holds the appearance record of 432 games. A fine, consistent 'keeper, who was sometimes criticised for the way he handled high crosses, he did not miss a game for six seasons until temporarily dropped in November 1910. He gained three League championship medals and five FA Cup Final medals for United, with one winners' medal against Barnsley in 1910. He won his Scottish cap against England in a 1-1 draw at Liverpool in April 1911.

Lawrence did not complete a season as manager of South Shields before moving to Preston. There was a financial crisis at Deepdale in 1924 and he was forced to sell his leading goalscorer, Tommy Roberts, to Burnley. Preston were relegated to Division Two in 1924-25, gaining a meagre 26 points. Lawrence resigned shortly afterwards.

LAWRENCE,
Robin Michael 'Lennie'

Born: Brighton, 14 December 1947.
Career: Croydon; Carshalton Athletic; Sutton United; Plymouth assiatant manager then caretaker manager February-May 1978; Lincoln City assistant manager 1981-82; Charlton Athletic reserve-team manager December 1982, then manager November 1983-June 1991; Middlesbrough manager June 1991.

Honours: Division Two runners-up 1986, 1992.

Lennie Lawrence experienced just about everything in his eight years as manager of Charlton Athletic. As well as promotion and relegation, they also nearly went bankrupt, lost their Valley ground, shared with Crystal Palace and won an exciting play-off match to avoid relegation. Lawrence never played League soccer. He was Malcolm Allison's assistant at Plymouth and filled in as caretaker manager between the appointments of Mike Kelly and Allison. Joined Charlton as reserve-team manager and was promoted to manager after the sacking of Ken Craggs. The club almost went under in 1984 then lost the Valley in September 1985. There were many squabbles with their new landlords, Crystal Palace. Promotion was achieved in 1985-86 when they finished as runners-up, they survived in the First Division by the skin of their teeth. Winning a sensational play-off game with Leeds United with two extra-time goals by Shirtliff in 1987. They were relegated back in 1990 and with Charlton on the point of returning to the Valley a year later, Lawrence resigned to take a job at Ayresome Park. It is questionable how long he would have lasted at Charlton if he had remained though.

Lawrence took Middlesbrough to promotion to the newly-formed Premier League at the end of his first season in charge. They finished as runners-up and also reached the semifinal of the League Cup where they lost, over two legs, to Manchester United.

Lawrence could not work his usual trick and save Middlesbrough from relegation. They looked doomed well before the end of the 1992-93 season.

LAWRENSON, Mark

Born: Preston, 2 June 1957.
Defender   5ft 10in; 10st 10lb (1981).
Career: Preston Schools; Preston North End August 1974; Brighton & Hove Albion July 1977 (£100,000); Liverpool August 1981 (£900,000), retired through injury March 1988; Thame United 1988; Barnet 1988; Oxford United manager April-October 1988; Tampa Bay Rowdies (NASL) 1989; Peterborough United manager September 1989-November 1990; Corby Town player 1991; Chesham United player 1992.

Honours: Republic of Ireland international (38 caps); Football League champions 1982, 1983, 1984, 1986; FA Cup winners 1986; Football League Cup winners 1982, 1983, 1984; European Cup winners 1985, runners-up 1985.

Mark Lawrenson signed for his local club, Preston North End, as a 14-year-old schoolboy. His father had also played for the club. Lawrenson helped Brighton to runners-up position in Division Two in 1978-79 and Liverpool broke their club transfer record when they paid £900,000 for him in August 1981.

It was money well spent, for Lawrenson developed into one of the finest defenders in British soccer in the 1980s. Elegant, unruffled and with a fine turn of speed, he could tackle with perfect timing. He made 240 appearances for the Reds before an Achilles tendon injury ended his Football League career in May 1988. He had helped Liverpool to four League championships, including the FA Cup and League double in 1986 and the Football League Cup and League double on three occasions. He played in four Wembley Finals and also won a European Cup winners' medal in 1984, when the Reds beat AS Roma in Rome, 4-2 on penalties after a 1-1 draw. He also played in the tragic match against Juventus at the Heysel Stadium the following year.

Lawrenson played for the Republic of Ireland 38 times and gained qualification through his mother. After retirement, he made a comeback with Thame United in the South Midlands League and also appeared for Barnet and Tampa Bay Rowdies.

His first managerial post was at Oxford United, in a brief and traumatic spell from April to October 1988. Oxford were already on their way to the Second Division, eventually finishing bottom of the table. Lawrenson threatened to resign when Dean Saunders was sold to Derby County for £1 million without his knowledge. The deal had been struck between Derby's chairman Robert Maxwell and his son, Kevin, the Oxford chairman. Lawrenson was sacked the following day.

He did not last very long at Peterborough either and was surprisingly sacked, despite the Posh getting off to a good start to the 1990-91 season. Lawrenson later returned to just playing with Corby Town and Chesham United.

LAWSON, James

Born: Middlesbrough, 11 December 1947.
Midfield   5ft 8in; 10st 10lb (1970).
Career: Middlesbrough December 1964; Huddersfield Town August 1968 (£6,000); Halifax Town June 1976 (£6,000), then player-manager November 1977-October 1978, player only October 1978-May 1979.

Honours: Division Two champions 1970.

A midfield tactician, Jimmy Lawson played a key role in Huddersfield's Second Division title success in 1970. Soon afterwards he was sacked and transfer-listed for breach of contract. In November 1971, Lawson was reinstated but Town slid from the First to the Fourth Division and he appeared in all four divisions. He scored 46 goals in 254/12 appearances before moving to Halifax Town.

When he took over as manager at The Shay, he created a near miracle, steering Town clear of the re-election zone in 1977-78. After only one win from the first 15 games the following season, Lawson was sacked but remained as a player at the club. Attendances had dropped alarmingly to under the 1,000-mark. He made 93 League appearances and scored nine goals for Halifax before leaving the club.

LAWTON, Thomas

Born: Bolton 6 October 1919.
Centre-forward 5ft 10½in; 12st 4lb (1937).

Career: Lancashire Schools; Hayes Athletic; Rossendale United; Burnley amateur May 1935, professional October 1936; Everton January 1937 (£6,500); guest for Aldershot, Tranmere Rovers and Morton in World War Two; Chelsea November 1945 (£14,000); Notts County November 1947 (£20,000); Brentford March 1952 (£12,000), then player-manager January-September 1953; Arsenal September 1953 (£109,000); Kettering Town player-manager February 1956-April 1957 (£1,000); Notts County manager May 1957-July 1958; Kettering Town manager November 1963-April 1964, later a director; Notts County coach and chief scout October 1968-April 1970; in recent years has written a column in the Nottingham Evening Post.

Honours: England international (23 caps); Wartime international (15 caps); Football League representative (3 caps); Football League champions 1939; Division Three South champions 1950; Southern League champions 1957.

One of the best-ever centre-forwards, Tommy Lawton was great in the air, with a powerful shot and natural goalscoring ability. He replaced the immortal Dixie Dean at Everton and scored 38 goals in the Toffees' League title season of 1938-39. Lawton scored almost 250 goals in wartime soccer plus 282 in League, Cup and international matches. He is also the youngest player to score a League hat-trick, four days after his 17th birthday.

Notts County paid £20,000 for his signature in 1947, an amazing sum for a Third Division club, and Lawton was capped for England from that division. He had a disastrous spell as player-manager of Brentford, with relegation followed by a poor start to the 1953-54 season, when he experienced booing and jeering from a crowd for the first time.

But he took Kettering to the Southern League title in 1956-57, eight points clear of their nearest rivals. He was not so successful in his second spell with the club as they were relegated. Lawton moved to Notts County as manager but at the end of his season in charge they were relegated with only 30 points. He wanted to play again but his former club required a transfer fee, so he decided to retire.

LEA, Cyril

Born: Moss, near Wrexham, 5 August 1934.
Wing-half   5ft 9½in; 11st 2lb (1959).
Career: Bradley Rangers; Leyton Orient July 1957; Ipswich Town November 1964 (£20,000), coach 1968-1979; Stoke City assistant manager August 1979-1980; Hull City assistant manager 1980-1981; Wales national coach; Colchester United coach, then manager February 1983-April 1986; Leicester City youth-development officer May 1987-May 1989; West Bromwich Albion youth coach cs 1989.

Honours: Wales international (2 caps); Amateur international.

A rugged wing-half with plenty of skill, Cyril Lea was strong in the tackle and had excellent distribution. Originally a full-back, his career blossomed after he converted to wing-half. Capped as a full-back by the Welsh amateur side, Lea established himself in Orient's team from 1960-61 and went on to make 228 appearances for the club. He helped the O's into the First Division in 1962, but did not gain a full Welsh cap until he joined Ipswich Town, for whom he made a further 123 appearances.

After retirement Lea joined the training staff and also coached the Welsh national side. Assistant to Alan Durban at Stoke, Lea also had three good seasons at Colchester United when they just missed promotion in each of the seasons he was in charge. He was surprisingly sacked, along with coach Stewart Houston, despite his relative success.

LEE, Colin

Born: Torquay, 12 June 1956.
Forward   6ft 1in; 11st 9lb (1987).
Career: Bristol City July 1974; Hereford United (loan) November 1974; Torquay United January 1977; Tottenham Hotspur October 1977 (£60,000); Chelsea January 1980 (£200,000); Brentford July 1987, and youth development

officer, retired from playing summer 1989; Watford manager March-November 1990; Reading youth-team manager 1991.

Honours: Division Two champions 1984; Full Members' Cup winners 1986.

Colin Lee started his career as a striker and Torquay received a record fee of £60,000 when he signed for Spurs. He helped Spurs to promotion to Division One in 1977-78 and scored 21 goals in 65/6 games for the club. Lee later helped Chelsea to the Second Division title, when he had developed into a sound and solid full-back. He scored twice in the Full Members' Cup Final when Chelsea beat Manchester City 5-4 in a highly entertaining match.

He played over 200 games for the Blues and finished his playing career at Brentford, where he also became the youth development officer. The Bees reached the FA Youth Cup semi-final, where they were beaten by Watford. Lee became manager at Vicarage Road the following year but was sacked after a dreadful start to the 1990-91 season.

LEE, Gordon

Born: Hednesford, 13 July 1934.
Defender   5ft 9½in; 11st 2lb (1959).

Career: Littleworth School; Girton Road Gasworks; Hednesford Town 1951; Aston Villa October 1955; Shrewsbury Town player-coach July 1966; Port Vale manager May 1968-January 1974; Blackburn Rovers manager January 1974-June 1975; Newcastle United manager June 1975-February 1977; Everton manager February 1977-May 1981; Preston North End manager December 1981-December 1983; KR Reykjavik (Iceland) coach; coached in Middle East; Leicester City coach January 1988, then assistant manager, then caretaker manager January-May 1991.

Honours: Third Division champions 1975; Fourth Division promotion 1970; Football League Cup winners 1961, runners-up 1963, 1976, 1977.

Gordon Lee won a hard-earned reputation as a soccer troubleshooter at Port Vale and Blackburn Rovers before being enticed to manage bigger clubs, Newcastle United and Everton.

A resourceful defender, Lee attended the local Littleworth School and played in non-League soccer before joining Aston Villa, being recommended by former player and Hednesford manager Jack Martin.

He appeared in two League Cup Finals for Aston Villa, at left-back against Rotherham United in the first-ever Final, which Villa won 3-2 on aggregate, and at left-half against local rivals Birmingham City in 1963, when Villa lost 3-1 on aggregate. Lee made 142 appearances for Villa before moving to Shrewsbury Town as player-coach, but played in only two League games for the Shrews before concentrating on his coaching duties under manager Arthur Rowley.

Lee accepted his first managerial post with Port Vale in May 1968 and Vale finished fourth in the Fourth Division to gain promotion in 1969-70. They struggled the following season but avoided relegation by three points. In 1972-73, Vale were in with a chance of promotion but eventually finished sixth. Lee never paid more than £5,000 for a player and developed an excellent youth scheme at Vale Park.

In January 1974, he received an offer to manage Blackburn Rovers. Lee had established a simple philosophy — hard work and dedication. He had the ability to motivate average players and soon began a rebuilding programme at Ewood Park to raise money for future investments, selling Tony Field and Terry Garbett to Sheffield United for a joint fee of over £100,000. After winning the Third Division title in May 1975, Lee became a central figure in a controversial tug-of-war with Newcastle United for his services and Blackburn were forced to let him move on, despite Lee being under contract.

He took the Geordies to the League Cup Final in his first season in charge, where they lost to a spectacular goal from Manchester City's Dennis Tueart. But Tyneside soccer was rocked by the sale of Malcolm Macdonald to Arsenal. Apparently the two just hadn't got on. The fans were outraged and Lee was fast gaining a reputation for producing dull sides with no star names.

Everton, though, were sufficiently impressed with his record to offer him their manager's job in February 1977, on a wage of £20,000 per annum. The Goodison club reached the League Cup Final in 1977, but lost to Aston Villa 3-2 after extra-time in a second replay. They also reached the semi-final of the FA Cup before losing to Liverpool in a replay. The Toffees finished third in 1977-78 and were unbeaten in their first 14 games the following season but eventually finished fourth.

Lee found it difficult to handle star players and results now went from bad to worse. A dedicated and hard-working man, he did not bring enough success to Goodison Park to satisfy the board and was sacked in May 1981 after a poor season. The following December he became the manager of Preston North End. After two mediocre seasons in the Third Division he was sacked again in December 1983.

Lee now worked abroad as a coach with KR Reykjavik of Iceland and then coached in the Middle East. He returned to England in January 1988 to coach with Leicester City and was later assistant manager to David Pleat. When Pleat was sacked in January 1991, Gordon Lee became the caretaker manager. However, he was sacked in May 1991, even though he steered Leicester clear of relegation.

LEIVERS, William E.

Born: Bolsover, 29 January 1932.
Full-back   6ft 2in; 13st (1959).
Career: Chesterfield February 1950; Manchester City November 1953 (£10,000); Doncaster Rovers player-manager July 1964-February 1966; Workington manager November 1966-

December 1967; Cambridge United manager December 1967-October 1974; Chelmsford City manager in 1970s; Cambridge City manager early 1980s until 1987, when he became general manager before retiring in 1989.
Honours: FA XI v Army 1956; Division Four promotion 1973; Southern League Premier Division champions 1969, 1970, Southern League Southern Section champions 1986; FA Cup winners 1956.

Bill Leivers could play equally well at right-back or centre-half. He gained an FA Cup winners' medal in 1956, when Manchester City beat Birmingham City 3-1 in the Final, and made 250 League appearances for City. It would have been more but for a succession of injuries including five broken noses.

On the brink of taking Doncaster Rovers to the Fourth Division championship, he surprisingly resigned, supposedly after a row with his board of directors. A tough-talking but scrupulously fair manager, Leivers found a great deal of success at Cambridge United. They won the Southern League championship by one point in both 1968-69 and 1969-70 and then gained entry into the Football League. United struggled at first but won promotion to the Third Division in 1972-73, when they finished in third place. However, they were immediately relegated and he was sacked with United struggling in the Fourth Division. Leivers continued his link with Cambridge, managing the other club, City, for a number of years.

LEVER, John Edward

Born: Burnopfield, County Durham, 5 April 1911.

Inside-left   5ft 11in; 10st 4lb (1929).
Career: White-le-Head Rangers; Portsmouth Reserves May 1929; teacher in

Alton; Portsmouth reserve-team coach, then manager August 1952-April 1958.
Eddie Lever never played in Portsmouth's first team and was teaching in nearby Alton when he was appointed reserve-team coach at Fratton Park in the late 1940s. He discovered Jimmy Dickinson whilst teaching and was later his manager at Pompey. When Lever replaced Bob Jackson, who had accepted a lucrative offer to manage Hull City, one of the first things he did was to appoint Dickinson captain.

Pompey were often struggling near the foot of the First Division when Lever was in charge, but they did finish third, four points behind champions Chelsea, in 1954-55. After narrowly avoiding relegation in 1957-58, Lever left the club, ending a link of almost 30 years. One of his best signings had been Derek Dougan from Belfast club, Distillery.

LEWIN, Ronald Dennis

Born: Edmonton, 21 June 1920; Died: 1986.
Full-back   5ft 8½in; 11st 10lb (1947).
Career: Edmonton Schools; Middlesex Boys; Enfield 1936; Bradford City September 1943; Fulham June 1946; Gillingham June 1950; Chatham May 1955; Skied (Norway), coach; Cheltenham Town manager 1962; Wellington Town manager 1963; Everton assistant coach 1963; Newcastle United coach August 1966-1968; Walsall manager July 1968-February 1969; Newcastle United coach & assistant manager cs 1974-July 1976; also coaching in Kuwait, Greece, Iceland; Brandon United manager 1981; Workington coach in 1986.
An accomplished full-back, Ron Lewin made 42 appearances for Fulham including some in their Second Division championship season of 1948-49. He played almost 200 games for Gillingham and later had a long and varied coaching and management career which took him all over Europe and to all levels of football in this country. He tried management, initially in the Southern League with Cheltenham Town and Wellington Town, and had a brief period in charge of Walsall, who finished 12th in the Third Division in 1969-70. He was also in charge of coaching and the training at Fellows Park. He was coaching with former League club, Workington, at the time of his death.

LEWINGTON, Raymond

Born: Lambeth, 7 September 1956.
Midfield   5ft 6in; 10st 5lb (1980).
Career: Chelsea February 1974; Vancouver Whitecaps (NASL) March 1979 (£40,000); Wimbledon September 1979; Fulham March 1980 (£50,000); Sheffield United cs 1985; Fulham player-manager July 1986-June 1990 (£20,000), then chief coach and caretaker manager again November-December 1991.
Honours: NASL Soccer Bowl winners 1979.

A forceful ball-winning midfielder who was often to be found at the centre of the action, either breaking up an attack or starting one, Ray Lewington helped Chelsea to promotion to Division One in 1976-77, when he was ever-present.

'Lewie' began his association with Fulham in March 1980 but was signed too late to prevent their relegation to the Third Division. However, he was a central figure in their return to the Second in 1981-82. Fulham narrowly missed further promotion the following season.

After a season at Sheffield United,

Lewington returned to the Cottage as player-manager but had a tough spell in charge. Fulham nearly went out of existence in February 1987, with a proposed merger with Queen's Park Rangers on the cards. He managed to get them into the Third Division play-offs in 1988-89, but Fulham played badly and lost to Bristol Rovers. He was demoted to coach in June 1990, working under Alan Dicks, then took over as caretaker manager after the sacking of Dicks. Lewington reverted to coach again when new manager, Don Mackay was appointed.

LEWIS, Harry 'Percy'

Born: Rotherham.
Career: Rotherham Town player; member of Sheffield & Hallamshire FA, also referee and licensee; Stockport County manager June 1911-April 1914; Barnsley manager April 1914-April 1919; Hull City manager July 1921-January 1923.

A genial and unassuming man, Percy Lewis had limited success at Stockport County. War broke out just after he became manager of Barnsley, who finished in their highest-ever position in 1914-15, third in Division Two. During the latter war years, Lewis had a tough time even fielding 11 players.

He got the Hull job from 80 applicants and in 1921-22, they just missed promotion. But things became strained at Anlaby Road when the Hull board instituted a selection committee to pick the team for him. Lewis resigned after a poor season in 1922-23. He quit management due to business commitments but advised Rotherham County in their early years in the Football League. As a referee, Lewis once sent off the legendary Billy Meredith in an FA Cup tie.

LEWIS, John

Born: Tredegar, 15 October 1955.
Midfield   5ft 9in; 11st 3lb (1980).
Career: Aberbargoed Buds; Pontllanfraith; Cardiff City August 1978; Newport County September 1983, then player-manager February-October 1987; Swansea City player October 1987-1988; Abergavenny Thursday 1989; Newport AFC July 1990.
Honours: Wales Under-21 international (1 cap).
John Lewis was spotted when playing against Cardiff City for Pontllanfraith in a Welsh League match. He gave up a clerical job with British Steel to join the Bluebirds and rarely missed a game, helping City to promotion as runners-up in Division Three. He was involved in a five-player deal when he moved to Newport County. Lewis had a tough time as the Somerton Park club's player-manager. After finishing bottom of Division Three in 1986-87, County nearly went bankrupt in the summer of 1987. Confidence at the club ebbed and he was sacked in October 1987.

LIDDLE, Edward 'Ned'

Born: Whitburn, near Sunderland, April 1877; Died: 22 November 1969.
Half-back   6ft; 12st (1914).
Career: East Bank Black Watch 1901; Whitburn 1903; Southampton December 1905; Gainsborough Trinity cs 1906; Clapton Orient cs 1907; Southend United October 1913; Arsenal September 1914; Southend United manager April 1919-April 1920; Queen's Park Rangers manager April 1920-1924; Fulham scout 1925, then manager May 1929-April 1931; West Ham United scout 1931-1936; Luton

Town manager August 1936-February 1938; scouted for Chelsea 1938, Portsmouth 1938, Brentford 1939 and Tottenham Hotspur 1946-January 1968.

Honours: Division Three South champions 1937.

A consistent performer for Orient, where he made 201 appearances, Ned Liddell could play at centre-half or left-half. Described as 'tall and slim with long legs and a gaunt face', Liddell enjoyed a long career as a manager but won only one honour, the Third Division South championship in 1936-37 with Luton Town.

After a season at Southend United, he took over at Queen's Park Rangers. Liddell became adept at producing a good teams from an average set of players. Rangers reached the quarter-final of the FA Cup in 1923, but Liddell left after they had to seek re-election in 1924. Initially, he joined Fulham as a scout but when he took over as manager the Cottagers played open, attractive football, albeit never making a serious promotion challenge. He always had an uneasy relationship with chairman John Dean and was sacked in 1931.

LIDDELL, George M.

Born: Muirton, County Durham, 14 July 1895.
Right-back   5ft 9in; 12st (1922).
Career: Johnston Grammar School; City of Leeds Training College; The Honorable Artillery; Duke of Wellington FC; Yorkshire Amateurs; South Shields 1915; Birmingham May 1920-April 1932, manager July 1933-September 1939; later became headmaster at Handsworth Secondary Modern School, eventually retiring to Hampshire.

Honours: FA Cup runners-up 1931.

A strong tackler who used the ball well, Liddell was cool under pressure. Originally a right-half, he converted to right-back in 1928 and this was a turning point in his career and he went on to play 345 games for Birmingham.

He always wanted to manage the club and his wish was granted by Blues' chairman Harry Morris in 1933. Liddell always struggled to find success, despite some excellent players including Harry Hibbs. His youth policy produced a string of stars but after a few near-misses, Birmingham were relegated to Division Two in 1938-39.

LILLYCROP, George Beanland

Born: Gosport, 7 December 1886; Died: South Shields, 21 January 1962.
Centre-forward 5ft 8½in; 11st 7lb (1914).
Career: Shields Albion; North Shields Athletic; Barnsley cs 1907; Bolton Wanderers July 1913 (£1,300); South Shields 1919, retired 1921, then trainer-coach cs 1922-May 1934; Bradford City trainer in 1936; Crewe Alexandra manager 1938-July 1944.

Honours: FA Cup winners 1912, runners-up 1910.

Usually top goalscorer at Barnsley, where he scored 104 goals in 224 League and FA Cup appearances, George Lillycrop then scored 32 goals in 55 games for Bolton. He played in all the games in Barnsley's Cup run of 1910, but they were beaten 2-0 by Newcastle United in a replayed Final. Two years later, he scored some important goals on the way to another FA Cup Final, including two against Bradford City in a marathon tie which was won 3-2 at Bramall Lane after three goalless draws. This time Lillycrop

collected a winners' medal when Barnsley beat West Brom in another replay, with a goal two minutes from the end of extra-time.

He coached at South Shields/Gateshead for 12 years but left after a series of poor results. Crewe finished eighth in the Northern Section in 1938-39, but had a poor record in the war years as they struggled to keep going.

LINDLEY, Maurice William

Born: Keighley, 5 December 1915.
Centre-half   6ft ¼in; 11st 2lb (1951).
Career: Keighley Town; Everton March 1936; Swindon Town coach 1951. then manager; May 1953-May 1955; Crewe Alexandra manager 1955-1958; Leeds United coach in 1960s; Bradford City scout in 1989.

Maurice Lindley did not make his League debut until he was 30 years old, due to the war in which he served in the Royal Artillery. Skilful for a defender, Lindley made 54 League and FA Cup appearances for Everton before moving to Swindon Town as coach in 1951.

He was not a great success as a manager. Swindon finished 19th in the Southern Section in 1953-4 and lost at Southern League Hastings United in the second round of the FA Cup. Lindley was given £3,000 to spend on new players, £2,250 of which went on Pompey's Matthew Gemmell, whose signing proved a disaster, the player making only eight appearances. Swindon finished 21st in 1954-55 and won just one away game. Lindley worked out three-months notice.

He had a terrible time at Crewe, where he was virtually an odd-job man, trying his hand at secretary, team boss, scout, stand-in trainer and even cleaning the boots. Crewe finished bottom of the Northern Section in each of his three seasons in charge. He undoubtedly enjoyed his time much better at Elland Road as a member of Don Revie's coaching staff during their rise to prominence in the 1960s.

LINDON, Albert Edward

Born: Aston, Birmingham, 24 January 1891; Died: Dowlais, Wales, 1 October 1976.
Goalkeeper   6ft; 14st (1923).
Career: Birmingham Fruiterers; Delta Metal Works 1907; Birmingham June 1910; Aston Villa August 1911; Barnsley September 1912; Coventry City March 1918; Merthyr Town August 1920, then player-manager August 1924-January 1928; Charlton Athletic player-manager January-May 1928, assistant manager May 1928-December 1932, manager December 1932-May 1933, assistant manager again May 1933-March 1934, retired from playing cs 1931; Arsenal scout 1947-December 1949; Cardiff City scout January 1950, later assistant manager; Merthyr Tydfil manager June 1957-May 1959; Swindon Town scout cs 1960; Newport County scout October 1961 until his death.

Honours: Division Three South champions 1929; Welsh Cup runners-up 1924; Birmingham League & Senior Cup medals with Aston Villa.

Merthyr took advantage of a technical oversight in the matter of retaining players by Coventry City to secure Lindon's transfer. It was a good move because he went on to make a club record of 254 appearances for the Welsh side. His first League appearance had been back in March 1912, for Villa against Tottenham Hotspur.

Lindon had a tough time as player-manager of Merthyr, where he ran only the playing side. They had to seek re-

election twice, in his first and last season. The 1924-25 season was awful, Merthyr finishing bottom of the League with 29 defeats. There was a great deal of unemployment in the pits and this affected the club's attendances. When he moved to Charlton Athletic, he took Dai Astley with him and Astley later became a regular Welsh international. When Alex MacFarlane returned after a period at Dundee, Lindon reverted to assistant manager. After he took control again, Athletic were relegated to Division Three in 1933 and he was sacked.

LITTLE, Alan

Born: Horden, 5 February 1955.
Midfield   5ft 11½in; 12st 12lb (1983).
Career: Horden Schools; Durham County Boys; Aston Villa apprentice June 1971, professional January 1973; Southend United December 1974 (£10,000); Barnsley August 1977 (£6,000); Doncaster Rovers December 1979 (£30,000); Torquay United October 1982; Halifax Town November 1983; Hartlepool United July 1985; retired to become coach May 1986; York City assistant manager & coach then manager March 1993.

Honours: FA Youth Cup winners 1972. Division Three promotion 1993.

Alan Little made 410 League appearances in his career, scoring 48 goals. He played in the same side as his brother Brian which won the FA Youth Cup in 1972 when Liverpool were beaten in the Final. Little made only 4/1 appearances for Villa before moving to Southend United. He played over a hundred games at both Southend and Barnsley. He helped Barnsley to promotion from Division Four in 1979. Alan moved to Doncaster Rovers for a club record £30,000 after losing his place the following season. He also helped Rovers to promotion from the Fourth Division in 1981 and he was also voted the club's 'Player of the Year' that season. Little was an experienced coach by the time he took charge at York City in March 1993 when John Ward moved to Bristol Rovers to become manager. They reached the Third Division play-offs after finishing fourth in the table at the end of the season and narrowly beat Bury on aggregate to play Crewe Alexandra at Wembley in the Final. York eventually beat Crewe on penalties after the match finished in a 1-1 draw after extra time. Alan's brother, Brian, the manager of Leicester City, also reached Wembley via the play-offs in 1993.

LITTLE, Brian

Born: Peterlee, County Durham, 25 November 1953.

Forward   5ft 8in; 11st 2lb (1975).
Career: County Durham Schools; Durham Youth; East Durham Boys; Aston Villa apprentice July 1969, professional March 1971, promotions department from 1981 and retired through injury in May 1982; Aston Villa coach 1985-January 1986; Wolverhampton Wanderers coach January 1986, caretaker manager August-October 1986; Middlesbrough coach; Darlington manager February 1989-May 1991; Leicester City manager May 1991.

Honours: England international (1 cap); Division Four champions 1991; Vauxhall Conference League champions 1990; Football League Cup winners 1975, 1977; World Youth Cup winners; FA Youth Cup winners 1972.

Brian Little, who had a ten-minute England career after coming on as substitute against Wales at Wembley in May 1975, gave Aston Villa fine service before injury ended his career. He made over 300 appearances, scoring 82 goals for Villa. A proposed £610,000 transfer to Birmingham City broke down on medical grounds in 1979 and he was unlucky not to be offered the manager's post at Molineux after a period as caretaker manager.

Little made a name for himself at Darlington, whom he steered back into the Football League after a season in the Conference League. They also reached the third round of the FA Cup and then won the Fourth Division championship before his departure to Leicester City. Leicester reached the Second Division play-offs at the end of Little's first season in charge, where they lost to Blackburn Rovers 1-0 in the Final at Wembley. He is the brother of Alan Little.

Leicester finished seventh in the First Division and Portsmouth were their opponents in the play-offs. They brought off a surprise victory when they beat Pompey 3-2 on aggregate to play Swindon Town in the Final at Wembley. Leicester lost the game 4-3 after pulling back to equalise after being three goals down in a superb match. For the second season in succession, City lost to a controversial penalty when Swindon scored the winning fourth goal.

LIVERMORE, Douglas Ernest

Born: Liverpool, 27 December 1947.
Midfield   5ft 8½in; 10st 5lb (1974).
Career: Liverpool November 1965; Norwich City November 1970 (£22,000); Bournemouth & Boscombe Athletic, loan March 1975; Cardiff City August 1975 (£15,000); Chester City October 1977; Cardiff City coach 1978-1980; Swansea City coach 1980-1984; Norwich City coach; Wales national assistant manager; Tottenham Hotspur coach 1986, caretaker manager October-November 1987, then team manager-chief coach May 1992.

Honours: Division Two champions 1972; Football League Cup runners-up 1973; Welsh Cup winners 1976, runners-up 1977.

Doug Livermore started his career at Anfield but after only 17 appearances for the club he moved to Norwich City. He was an important member of the Canaries' promotion sides of 1972 but rarely played when they were promoted to Division One again three years later.

In 1975-76, Livermore helped Cardiff City to runners-up spot in Division Three and when they won the Welsh Cup also played in European competition. Livermore had appeared at Wembley in 1973 when Norwich lost 1-0 to Spurs in the League Cup Final. He was coach at Swansea City under John Toshack in their glory days when they reached the First Division. He was also assistant to Mike England when he was in charge of the Welsh national side.

Livermore was placed in charge of team affairs at Spurs with Ray Clemence, although after Peter Shreeve's departure in May 1992, Terry Venables played a more active role in team matters at White Hart Lane until his much publicised departure in May 1993. Spurs had a disappointing season under Livermore in 1992-93. They lost to their great rivals Arsenal in the FA Cup semi-finals, finished only 11th in the Premier League and then the shock sacking of Venables by his business partner Alan Sugar rocked Spurs. Clemence eventually left, too, casting doubts over Livermore's future.

LIVINGSTONE, Dugald

Born: Alexandra, near Dumbarton, 25 February 1898. Died: Marlow, 15 January 1981.
Full-back   5ft 7in, 11st (1922).
Career: Glasgow Celtic; Everton April 1921; Plymouth Argyle February 1926; Aberdeen August 1927; Tranmere Rovers June 1930, retired 1933; Exeter City trainer 1935; Sheffield United trainer 1936; Sparta Rotterdam manager 1949. Republic of Ireland national manager 1951; Belgium national manager 1953; Newcastle United manager December 1954-January 1956; Fulham manager January 1956-May 1958; Chesterfield manager May 1958.
Honours: FA Cup winners 1955.

An unflappable, happy-go-lucky character, Duggie Livingstone's main claim to fame as a manager was taking Newcastle United to an FA Cup Final victory in 1955, but he had a long and varied career in football and managed two national sides and three League clubs along the way.

Livingstone joined Glasgow Celtic as a youngster, but overall he had an undistinguished playing career. Being unable to break into the Celtic side regularly, he moved south to join Everton. He was a cool, calculating full-back but his lack of speed let him down. He played over 100 games for Everton before disillusionment set in and he moved to Plymouth Argyle. In and out of the side at Home Park, Livingstone returned to Scotland with Aberdeen and after 81 appearances for the Dons, he moved back to the Liverpool area to play for Tranmere Rovers. He retired in 1933 after another 88 League appearances with Rovers.

Two years later he became trainer at Exeter City under manager Jack English, then a year later moved to Sheffield United in a similar capacity. He stayed at Bramall Lane for 13 years until becoming manager of Sparta of Rotterdam in 1949. Two years later and he was on the move again, this time to become the national team manager of the Republic of Ireland.

In 1953 he took a similar post in Belgium, where he gained a reputation for his modern coaching methods and took Belgium to the 1954 World Cup finals. They finished bottom of their group but managed to draw 4-4 with England.

In December 1954, Livingstone was appointed manager of Newcastle United. By May 1955 they had reached the FA Cup Final, where they beat Manchester City, but his reward was to have his team selection powers taken away from him by the board. After a furious row, Livingstone left the club in January 1956 and became manager of Fulham.

The players at St James' Park had not liked his use of modern training techniques but the players at Craven Cottage proved more amenable to his coaching. Livingstone made some critical changes, especially in defence, which laid the foundations for future success after he had left the club. Fulham lost to Manchester United in the 1958 FA Cup semi-final and also missed out on promotion to Division One, due to pressure of Cup matches.

In May 1958 he was offered a new contract but chose to move to Chesterfield as manager instead, due to his wife having failed to settle in the south. Chesterfield finished bottom of the Third Division in 1960-61 and after they also struggled the next season, Livingstone left the club in May 1962. He watched football regularly right up to his death.

LLOYD, Barry D.

Born: Hillingdon, 19 February 1949.
Midfield   5ft 7in; 10st 5lb (1971).
Career: Middlesex Schools; Chelsea February 1966; Fulham December 1968; Hereford United October 1976; Brentford June 1977; Houston Hurricane (NASL) June-August 1978; Yeovil Town manager 1978-1981; Worthing manager 1981-1986; Brighton & Hove Albion assistant manager cs 1986, then manager January 1987.
Honours: England Youth international; Division Three runners-up 1988; Isthmian League Premier Division champions 1984, 1985; Isthmian League Division One champions 1983; Isthmian League Division Two champions 1982; FA Cup runners-up 1975 (sub).

After 14 First Division appearances for Chelsea, Barry Lloyd joined Fulham in exchange for John Dempsey plus £35,000. He was later made club captain

and helped Fulham to promotion to Division Two in 1970-71. A team player rather than an individualist, Lloyd was substitute when the Cottagers reached the FA Cup Final in 1975. He played under the management of Bill Dodgin at Fulham and Brentford, and later employed Dodgin as a scout at Brighton.

He was very successful as manager of Worthing, whom he took from the Isthmian League Second Division to runners-up position in the Premier Division in seasons 1983-84 and 1984-85. He moved to the Goldstone Ground as assistant to Alan Mullery, taking over on his departure. Brighton were relegated in 1986-87 but bounced straight back as runners-up the following season. After two seasons of struggle, they reached the Second Division play-off Final at Wembley in 1991 but lost to Notts County.

With the club hit by huge financial restraints, due to their massive debts, Lloyd was unable to strengthen their squad. Their form slumped alarmingly, eventually leading to their relegation to the Third Division. The fans were calling for Lloyd's sacking, but the board continued to give him their backing.

The fans were calling for Barry Lloyd's head at one stage of the 1992-93 season but he survived and went close to taking the club to the play-offs. Brighton were hampered by big debts and a search for a new ground to help them pay them off.

LLOYD, Clifford

Born: Brymbo, 14 November 1916; Died: Brymbo, 3 June 1973.
Outside-right   5ft 7in; 11st 8lb (1938).
Career: Brymbo Sports Club; Liverpool trialist; Wrexham amateur 1932, part-time professional 1936; Wrexham assistant secretary 1946, later secretary until cs 1973, also secretary-manager February 1955-October 1957, October 1959-May 1960, caretaker manager October 1965-January 1966 and April 1967; also cricket for Denbighshire.
Honours: Welsh Cup winners 1957.

Cliff Lloyd served Wrexham as player, secretary and manager for 41 years. He was mainly a reserve but played 12 games, scoring two goals. Lloyd had an excellent business acumen and was able to deal with all sorts of problems which arise at a lower division club. He was secretary-manager on four separate occasions, his longest period being from February 1955 to October 1957.

In 1957, Wrexham won the Welsh Cup for the first time in 26 years and that season they also reached the fourth round of the FA Cup, losing to Manchester United before a record crowd of 34,445 at the Racecourse. Lloyd discovered many fine players including Wyn Davies, Don Weston and Arfon Griffiths. His sons, John and Geoff, also played for Wrexham. Cliff Lloyd was an excellent cricketer who represented Denbighshire in Minor Counties competitions.

LLOYD, Laurence Valentine

Born: Bristol, 6 October 1948.
Central defender 6ft 2in; 14st 3lb (1975).
Career: Bristol Schools; Bristol Rovers July 1967; Liverpool April 1969 (£50,000); Coventry City August 1974 (£240,000); Nottingham Forest October 1976 (£60,000); Wigan Athletic player-manager March 1981-April 1983, retired as a player 1983; Notts County manager July 1983-October 1984.
Honours: England international (4

caps); Under-23 international (8 caps); Youth international; Football League champions 1973, 1978; Division Four promotion 1982; FA Cup runners-up 1971; Football League Cup winners 1978, 1979; European Cup winners 1979, 1980; UEFA Cup winners 1973.

Very tall with great physical presence, Larry Lloyd was a dominant figure in defence. His spells at Liverpool and Nottingham Forest coincided with some vintage years at both clubs. He scored one of the goals in Liverpool's UEFA Cup Final win over Borussia Mönchengladbach in 1973 and appeared in two European Cup successes for Forest. Lloyd also won many other domestic honours including League championship medals at Anfield and the City Ground.

He was not so successful as a manager and although he took Wigan to promotion to Division Three in 1981-82, he was sacked the following season. Notts County were relegated to Division Two in 1983-84 and he was sacked with the club again at the bottom of the table. His signings did not prove a success, although they included Martin O'Neill, Justin Fashanu and John Chedozie.

LOCHHEAD, Arthur William

Born: Busby, Renfrewshire, 8 December 1897.
Inside-right   5ft 11in; 10st 8lb (1933).
Career: Heart of Midlothian March 1919; Manchester United June 1921; Leicester City October 1925 (£3,300), then manager August 1934-October 1936.
Honours: Scotland international trailist.

Arthur Lochhead showed a lot of early promise and played in a Scottish international trial, for Home Scots v Anglo Scots in March 1920. He joined Manchester United after only six Scottish League appearances for Hearts and went on to average almost a goal every three games for United, finishing with 50 in 153 League and FA Cup appearances. The Old Trafford club were relegated at the end of his first season, but he was top scorer when they won promotion in 1924-25.

Lochhead made only five more First Division appearances before his place came under threat from Chat Rennox and just after the start of the season he was transferred to Leicester City. Whilst playing for Leicester, he also worked as a school teacher. He scored 114 goals in 320 appearances for City and helped them to third in the First Division in 1927-28 and runners-up position in 1928-29.

In 1934, he was persuaded to give up playing and become the club's manager. He immediately made two important signings in Tony Carroll, from Clyde, and Welsh international Taffy O'Callaghan, from Spurs. Leicester had problems with the centre-forward position and Lochhead tried five different players there in his first season. City were relegated at the end of it and after finishing sixth in Division Two in 1935-36, Lochhead resigned. He had been unlucky to take over an ageing side and the rebuilding process took too long for him to find success at Filbert Street.

LOCHHEAD, Dougald

Born: Partick, 16 December 1904; Died: Leeds, 29 August 1968.
Left-half   5ft 11in; 10st 9lb (1933).
Career: St Anthony's; St Johnstone 1926; Walsall June 1928; Norwich City July 1929, training staff on retirement, assistant manager February 1937, then manager 1945-June 1946 and December 1947-March 1950; Galatasaray (Turkey) October 1950-October 1952; Almelo (Turkey) coach December 1953; Merthyr Tydfil manager June 1956.

Honours: Division Three South champions 1934.

Doug Lochhead served Norwich City in various capacities for 20 years. He made 222 appearances for the Canaries after joining them from Walsall in 1929, scoring the first League goal at Carrow Road although he scored only another four for the Norfolk club. He was a member of City's side which won the Third Division South title in 1933-34.

After spells as coach and assistant manager, Lochhead became manager just after World War Two. He was appointed too late to prevent City having to apply for re-election in his first season but his drive and shrewdness soon began to achieve modest success on the field and they finished tenth in 1947-48. Lochhead's health was ruined after an accident in August 1949 and after a long illness he left the club in March 1950.

LOCKIE, Thomas

Born: Duns, Berwickshire, 13 January 1906; Died: New Earswick, Yorkshire, July 1977.
Centre-half   6ft 1in; 12st (1933).
Career: Duns; Glasgow Rangers cs 1927; Leith Athletic 1931; Barnsley August 1932; York City May 1933; Accrington Stanley July 1934; Mansfield Town May 1935; York City reserve-team trainer August 1936, senior trainer September 1937-1960, then manager July 1960-October 1967.

Honours: Division Four promotion 1965.

A big bustling centre-half, Tom Lockie was a useful team man with a sound grasp of the game. He made his first-team debut for Rangers in 1929-30 but played mainly in the Reserves at Ibrox. Lockie had one season each at Barnsley (14 appearances), York City (29), Accrington Stanley (36) and Mansfield Town (14).

He married a woman from York and, when his playing career ended, accepted a trainer's job at Bootham Crescent. Lockie stayed at York for 31 years, 24 of them as trainer and seven as manager. He was involved in the York side which reached the quarter-finals of the FA Cup in 1938 and he shared managerial duties with Bill Sherrington for a while from September 1954.

In his first two seasons in charge, York went close to promotion but had to seek re-election in 1963-64. In

1964-65 they finished third and gained promotion to Division Three with 62 points. The following season they won only nine games, conceded over 100 goals and were relegated again. He was eventually sacked with York bottom of the Football League.

LOFTHOUSE, Nathaniel

Born: Bolton, 27 August 1925.
Centre-forward 5ft 9½in; 11st 13lb (1959).
Career: Brentwood & Castle Hill Schools; Lomax's; Bolton Boys' Federation; Bolton Wanderers amateur September 1939, professional August 1942, retired July 1961, assistant coach March 1960-1968, caretaker manager August 1968, manager December 1968-November 1970 and April-May 1971, general manager November 1970-April 1971, chief scout August 1971-June 1972; Arsenal scout August 1973; Burnden Executive Club manager 1978; Bolton Wanderers caretaker manager December 1985 (one game); club president October 1986.

Honours: England international (33 caps); 'B' international (1 cap); Footballer League representative; Footballer of the Year 1953; FA Cup winners 1958, runners-up 1953; Football League North Cup winners 1945.

One of the finest post-war centre-forwards and probably Bolton's greatest-ever player, Nat Lofthouse scored 285 goals in 503 games for the Trotters as well as many wartime appearances. He made his debut aged 15 years 207 days, against Bury in a 5-1 win in March 1941, when he scored twice, and once scored six goals for the Football League against the Irish League in September 1953.

Lofthouse became known as the 'Lion of Vienna' after a particularly brave goal for England against Austria. In all he scored 30 goals for England in 33 internationals, breaking the long-standing record of the great Steve Bloomer.

Lofthouse also played in two FA Cup Finals. In the famous 'Matthews' Cup Final of 1953, Bolton lost 4-3 to Blackpool, but in 1958 they beat Manchester United. Lofthouse is remembered for his shoulder-charge on United 'keeper Harry Gregg which led to one of the goals. Surprisingly, he did not play for England from 1955 to 1959, but was recalled at the age of 35.

A nagging injury finally ended his carer. He then served Wanderers as a coach until becoming temporary manager in August 1968 after the departure of Bill Ridding. The post was made permanent from December but he had little money to spend on new players

and, despite buying Roger Hunt in 1969, he failed to find success. Lofthouse became general manager when Jimmy McIlroy was appointed in November 1970, but returned as care-taker five months later, as Bolton sunk into the Third Division. He was then appointed chief scout by new manager Jimmy Armfield. Lofthouse became caretaker manager for a third time in December 1985, for one game only. He has given almost a lifetime's service to Bolton Wanderers.

LOGAN, James Henry 'Captain'

Born: Dunbar, Scotland, 11 October 1885.
Centre-half/Forward
6ft 1in; 13st (1910).
Career: St Bernards; Bradford City April 1905; Chesterfield August 1906; Bradford 1909-1912; Raith Rovers; joined the Army 1916; Raith Rovers manager 1918-1928 and December 1930; ran pub in Kerriemuir; Wrexham manager December 1936-May 1938. Raith Rovers 1912

Honours: Scottish Junior international (1 cap).

Jimmy Logan gained his junior international cap with St Bernards in March 1905, against Ireland in Belfast. He played only five games for Bradford City, although his brother, Peter, appeared in over 300 games for the club between 1908 and 1925. Jimmy Logan then made 94 appearances (nine goals) for Chesterfield and 59 for Bradford (three goals) before returning to Scotland to play for, and later manage, Raith Rovers.

The period just after World War One was perhaps the club's greatest years with Logan in charge. They finished third behind Celtic and Rangers in 1921-22 and produced their best-ever forward line of Bell, Miller, Jennings, James and Archibald. The star performer was Alex James, who was sold to Preston for £3,250 in September 1925. Logan did quite well at Wrexham. They reached the third round of the FA Cup and finished eighth in the Northern Section in 1936-37 and tenth the following season. He resigned with one game of the 1937-38 season still to play but agreed to take charge for the last match, against Hartlepools United, which was lost 2-0.

His title came from his wartime days. Logan enlisted as a private in the so-called Sportsmen's Battalion of the Royal Scots and rose to the rank of captain before being demobbed.

LORD, Frank

Born: Chadderton, 13 March 1936.
Centre-forward   6ft; 12st 4lb (1963).
Career: Chadderton Secondary Modern School; Royton Amateurs; Rochdale October 1953; Crewe Alexandra July 1961 (£3,000); Plymouth Argyle November 1963 (£12,000); Stockport County February 1966; Blackburn Rovers December 1966; Chesterfield August 1967; Plymouth Argyle player-coach October 1967; Preston North End caretaker manager February-March 1973; Crystal Palace coach 1973-July 1975; Cape Town (South Africa) manager in late 1970s; Hereford United manager December 1979-September 1982; Penang State (Malaysia) manager January 1983.

A big, bustling forward who was ideally suited as a target man, Frank Lord had lots of injury problems, including two broken legs. Early in his career, Lord

was converted from centre-half to centre-forward by Rochdale manager Harry Catterick. When he moved to Crewe, he broke their club record for goals in a season, when he scored 31 in 1961-62. Lord played Second Division football at Plymouth but otherwise appeared in the lower divisions.

He was caretaker manager at Preston between Alan Ball senior and Bobby Charlton and did not have a particularly happy time as manager of Hereford United. They had to seek re-election in 1979-80 and 1980-81 and also lost to non-League Enfield in the FA Cup in the latter season. They improved to finish tenth in 1981-82 and reached the fourth round of the FA Cup, but Lord was the first managerial casualty of the new season after a poor start to 1982-83.

LOVE, John DFC

Born: Edinburgh, 18 March 1924.
Inside-forward.
Career: Leith Athletic 1941; Hibernian; Leith Athletic 1947; Albion Rovers 1948; Nottingham Forest February 1949 (£7,000); Llanelli player-manager 1952-1953; Walsall March 1953, player-assistant manager March 1955, then manager September 1955-December 1957; Wrexham manager December 1957-October 1959.

Honours: Scottish League Division Two runners-up 1948; Division Three South champions 1951.

John Love helped Nottingham Forest to the Southern Section title in 1950-51 and scored 21 goals in 59 League games for the Reds before surprisingly moving out of League soccer to play for Southern League Llanelli, whom he also managed. Love returned to the League scene with Walsall, where he was appointed player-assistant under Major Frank Buckley. Three weeks later, Buckley resigned and Love took over. He scored 11 goals in 39 League appearances but arrived too late to help Walsall clear of the re-election zone. In the next two seasons they finished 20th and 15th before he moved to Wrexham as manager. The Robins just managed to get into the newly-formed Third Division in 1958 and finished 18th in 1958-59. He resigned on 2 November that season, with Wrexham lying in 21st place having won only five of their first 20 games.

His DFC was awarded after he was wounded by shrapnel during the crossing of the Rhine in 1944. Love had served as a flight-lieutenant with Bomber Command and then as a glider pilot.

LOW, Norman Harvey

Born: Newcastle upon Tyne, 23 March 1914.
Centre-half   6ft; 12st (1935).
Career: Newcastle Boys; Rosehill Villa (Newcastle); Newcastle United amateur; Liverpool October 1933; Newport County November 1936 (£2,000); guest for Bristol City, Everton, Lovells Athletic, Liverpool and Swindon Town in World War Two; Norwich City October 1946, manager May 1950-April 1955; Workington manager January 1956-February 1957; Port Vale manager February 1957-October 1962; Liverpool chief scout 1965-1967, then emigrated to North America; Cleveland Stokers coach.

Honours: Division Three champions 1939; Division Four champions 1959.

Norman Low, like his father Wilf, was dominant in the air and a very difficult opponent but although they were similar in style, Norman never reached the standards set by his father. After only 13 appearances for Liverpool, he made 265 peacetime appearances for Newport County and Norwich City.

He was certainly better-known as a manager. Norwich were runners-up to Nottingham Forest in the Southern Section in 1950-51 and Low spent heavily in the transfer market, including paying £19,500 for Fulham's Bobby Brennan, but he was unable to gain promotion for the Canaries, although they did beat Arsenal at Highbury in the FA Cup in 1953-54. He was surprised to be sacked, for he had been Norwich's most successful manager up until that time.

Low was unable to prevent Port Vale's relegation to Division Three in 1956-57, but after entering the Fourth Division in 1958 they bounced back a year later as champions. They also had good FA Cup runs in 1960 and 1962.

LOWE, Edward

Born: Halesowen, 11 July 1925.
Wing-half   5ft 11in; 11st 3lb (1949).
Career: Halesowen & Stourbridge Schools; Napier Aircaft Company; Millwall amateur; Finchley; Kynoch's (Birmingham works side); Aston Villa September 1945; Fulham May 1950 (£10,000); Notts County player-manager July 1963-April 1965; in 1965 he became purchasing manager for a central heating company in Nottingham; Plymouth Argyle scout September 1965.
Honours: England international (3 caps).

Eddie Lowe was a very fit player who thrived on hard work. He was a tenacious tackler and an excellent defender and has the second-highest appearances total for Fulham with 511 games for the Cottagers. Lowe won his three caps whilst at Villa, including a 10-0 win over Portugal, and was unlucky never to be capped whilst at the Cottage. Lowe moved to Fulham with his brother, Reg, after 117 appearances for Villa, and in his last season at Fulham he was voted fourth in the Footballer of the Year poll.

At Notts County, Lowe had a disastrous first season in charge. Soon after he took over, he made an unpopular move by selling top scorer Tony Hateley to Villa for £20,000 and his replacement, Terry Bly, was a flop. The Magpies finished bottom of the Third Division with only 27 points In desperation, Lowe made a comeback as a player, just before his 40th birthday. He was sacked after a mediocre season in 1964-65.

LOWE, Harold

Born: Northwich, 10 August 1886;
Died: Camden Town, London, 15 July 1966.
Centre-half   5ft 9in; 11st 4lb (1914).
Career: Northwich Victoria; Brighton & Hove Albion 1913; Tottenham Hotspur 1914; Fulham May 1927-cs 1928; Tottenham Hotspur coach early 1930s; Deportivo Espanol (Barcelona) manager in 1935; Bournemouth & Boscombe Athletic manager 1947-February 1950; Yeovil Town manager 1951-1953.

In his 13 years at White Hart Lane, Harry Lowe made only 72 League and FA Cup appearances for Spurs. He made his debut in a 7-5 defeat at Middlesbrough in February 1915 and his best season was 1923-24, when he appeared 22 times.

Lowe was past his best by the time he arrived at Craven Cottage. He returned to Spurs as a coach in the early 1930s and managed in Spain after this.

After the war he came back to England and took over at Bournemouth. They were runners-up in the Southern Section in 1947-48, four points behind champions Queen's Park Rangers, and third the following season. He did not have much success at Yeovil.

LOWES, Thomas

Born: Walker, Newcastle, spring 1902.
Inside-forward   5ft 8in; 11st (1922).
Career: Wallsend Park Villa; Newcastle United September 1910 (£25); Coventry City July 1919 (£50); Caerphilly August 1920; Newport County July 1922; Yeovil Town player-coach 1926, then manager; Barrow trainer, then manager 1932-April 1937; Walsall manager April 1937-September 1939; Arsenal scout 1945; Norwich City scout 1961.

Tommy Lowes did not have a distinguished playing career and was better known as a manager and he discovered a number of talented players, including Bert Williams and Johnny Hancocks of Wolves, and John Barnwell of Arsenal.

Lowes' best season at Barrow was 1933-34, when they finished eighth in the Northern Section. He made a shrewd signing whilst at Barrow by signing Thomas Shankly from Southend United and Shankly scored a record 38 goals that season. Barrow also beat Gateshead by a record 12-1. In 1937 he moved on to Walsall, who had to seek re-election in both of the seasons before the outbreak of war.

LOXLEY, Herbert

Born: Bonsall, Derbyshire, 3 February 1934.
Wing-half   6ft; 12st 7lb (1959).
Career: Bonsall; Notts County March 1952; Mansfield Town July 1964; Lochhead Leamington; Lincoln City October 1966, then manager July 1970-March 1971, then coach-physiotherapist 1971-1987.

Bert Loxley started his career at his local club, Bonsall, and later played 245 League games for Notts County. Ending his career at Lincoln City, Loxley stayed at the club for 21 years as player, trainer, manager and physiotherapist. His son, Tony, made one appearance for City in the late 1970s. Loxley's best season at Notts County was 1959-60, when they finished runners-up in Division Four and scored 107 goals. In 1970-71, when Loxley was in charge, he was replaced by David Herd with the club heading towards the re-election zone. He was a great club servant.

LUCAS, William Henry

Born: Newport, 15 January 1918.
Inside-forward.

Career: Brookside Athletic; Treeharris; Newport County 1933; Wolverhampton Wanderers amateur 1935, professional May 1936; Swindon Town May 1937; guest for Mansfield Town, Lovells Athletic, Chesterfield, Hull City, Chester, Blackburn Rovers, Aldershot and Swansea Town in World War Two; Swansea Town March 1948 (£11,000); Newport County player-manager December 1953-April 1961, retired as a player 1958, manager March 1962-February 1967; Swansea Town manager February 1967-cs 1969; Newport County manager November 1970-January 1974, then general manager until 1975.

Honours: Wales international (7 caps); Wartime international (8 caps); Welsh League representative (2 caps); Division Three South champions 1949.

Billy Lucas played for Wales in wartime internationals whilst with Swindon Town. He was a regular first-teamer at Swansea Town until appointed player-manager of Newport County in 1953. Lucas appeared in 366 peacetime League games and gained a Third Division South championship medal in 1948-49.

At Newport, Lucas was in charge of one of the smallest professional squads in the League. He had to sell to survive and County rarely set the football world alight. Lucas ran the club in three separate periods. He resigned the managership in 1961 but was re-appointed less than a year later, when Bobby Evans was sacked. County were heading for Division Four by then. In the first six months of his third period at Somerton Park, Lucas worked without wages. In 1972-73 they missed out on promotion on goal average. He also kept a pub in Newport called The Talisman.

LUMSDEN, James

Born: Kinning Park, Glasgow, 7 November 1947.
Inside-forward   5ft 5in; 12st 7lb (1970).
Career: Glasgow Schools; Leeds United November 1964; Southend United September 1970; Morton 1971; St Mirren December 1972; Cork Hibernian 1973; Morton 1973; Clydebank cs 1975; Glasgow Celtic youth-team manager until July 1982; Leeds United assistant manager July 1982-October 1985; Rochdale assistant manager December 1986-December 1987; Bristol City assistant manager, then manager September 1990-February 1992.
Honours: Scottish Division Two champions 1976.

Jimmy Lumsden made only four appearances for Leeds in his six years at Elland Road but he won a Scottish Second Division championship medal with Clydebank in 1975-76 and promotion to the Premier Division the following season. A great friend of Eddie Gray, Lumsden was appointed Gray's assistant at Leeds United in 1982. Sacked with Gray three years later, he worked with another former Leeds player, Joe Jordan, as his assistant manager at Bristol City and took over at Ashton Gate when Jordan moved to Scotland to manage Hearts. The 1990-91 season was one of consolidation for City. Lumsden was sacked after City dropped to 20th in the Second Division, with only one win in 14 games.

LYALL, John

Born: Ilford, February 24th 1940.
Full-back   5ft 10in; 12st 8lb (1970).
Career: Ilford Boys; West Ham United May 1957-1963, retired through injury,

office work at Upton Park and coaching, assistant manager 1971, team manager August 1974, then manager December 1977-May 1989; Tottenham Hotspur technical co-ordinator November 1989; Ipswich Town manager May 1990-August 1992, general manager.

Honours: England Youth international; Second Division champions 1981, 1992; FA Cup winners 1975, 1980; Football League Cup runners-up 1981; European Cup-winners' Cup runners-up 1976; FA Youth Cup runners-up 1957.

John Lyall was the longest-surviving manager in the Football League when he was dismissed by West Ham in May 1989. Lyall had a great deal of success as manager at Upton Park, the Hammers winning the FA Cup twice, reaching a European Final and League Cup Final and also gaining the Second Division championship.

Lyall won an England Youth cap against Luxembourg at Upton Park in 1957 and also appeared in an FA Youth Cup Final against Manchester United. He made his League debut against Chelsea in February 1960 — the Hammers won 4-2 — but his playing career was plagued by injury and he was forced to retire in 1963 after only 35 senior appearances.

He worked in the offices at Upton Park for a while before taking up coaching at the club. In 1971 he became assistant manager to Ron Greenwood and then team manager with Greenwood as general manager in August 1974. Lyall was given full mangerial responsibilities when Greenwood became the England manager in 1977.

West Ham won the FA Cup twice during Lyall's management. In 1975 they beat Fulham 2-0, and in 1980 beat Arsenal 1-0 in the Final. The Hammers also reached the European Cup-winners' Cup Final in 1976, where they lost 4-2 to Anderlecht in the Heysel Stadium. West Ham were relegated in 1978 but in 1980-81 they won the Second Division title. Also that year they reached the League Cup Final but lost to Liverpool in a replay.

The Hammers were relegated again in 1988-89 and Lyall was sacked, despite reaching a League Cup semi-final and the sixth round of the FA Cup that season. In November 1989 he became a technical co-ordinator with Tottenham Hotspur and in May 1990 he took over as manager at Ipswich Town. Lyall quickly rebuilt the team and they took the Second Division title in 1991-92. He managed to get the best out of prospects like Chris Kiwomya and Jason Dozzell, and Ipswich's good form continued in the newly-formed Premier League.

Lyall remained in overall charge at Portman Road but Mick McGiven was appointed team manager of Ipswich Town in August 1992. At the turn of the year Ipswich were fourth in the table but in the end just missed relegation from the Premier League.

LYONS, Barry

Born: Shirebrook, Notts, 14 March 1945.
Outside-right 5ft 7in; 10st 8lb (1971).
Career: Shirebrook Miners' Welfare; Rotherham United September 1962; Nottingham Forest November 1966; York City September 1973; Darlington July 1976; York City youth coach 1978, then manager March 1980-December 1981, then youth coach again until July 1982.

Barry Lyons made his reputation at Rotherham United, where he scored 24 League goals in 125 games. He helped Forest to runners-up spot in the First Division in 1966-67, four points behind champions Manchester United. Lyons eventually made 203 League appearances for Forest, scoring 28 goals. A tricky winger, he gained a reputation for his fine crosses to supply Forest's target men. Most of his games were in Division One but Forest were relegated in 1972.

He played a major part in York City's promotion drive to the Second Division in the mid-1970s. Lyons, a youth-team coach, was appointed caretaker manager at York in March 1980 and after steering them from the re-election zone he was officially appointed two months later. After a good start to the 1980-81 season, they slumped badly and finished 92nd in the League. After his sacking, he reverted back to youth-team coach.

LYONS, Michael C.

Born: Liverpool, 8 December 1951.
Defender 6ft; 12st 2lb (1983).
Career: Everton amateur August 1968, professional July 1969; Sheffield Wednesday August 1982 (£100,000); Grimsby Town player-manager November 1985-June 1987; Everton coach 1987.

Honours: England Under-23 international (5 caps); 'B' international; Football League Cup runners-up 1977.

Mick Lyons joined Everton as a striker

but reverted to centre-half after the emergence of David Johnson. A steady and reliable defender, Lyons made 434/26 appearances for the Toffees, scoring 59 goals. He appeared in all three games of the 1977 Football League Cup Final, which Everton eventually lost 3-2 to Aston Villa, and was also unfortunate to appear in three losing FA Cup semi-finals for Everton and Sheffield Wednesday, in 1977, 1980 and 1983. He made a further 164 appearances (16 goals) for the Owls and was ever-present when they reached the First Division as runners-up in 1983-84.

More at home as a coach at Everton than he was as a manager at Grimsby Town, Lyons was sacked after the Mariners were relegated to Division Three. He lacked the experience to turn things around at Blundell Park and, as things went wrong, his relationship with the players deteriorated.

McANEARNEY, James

Born: Dundee, 20 March 1935.
Inside-forward 5ft 8in; 10st 9lb (1964).
Career: Dundee St Stephen's; Sheffield Wednesday March 1952; Plymouth Argyle January 1960; Watford November 1963; Bradford City September 1966; Rotherham United coach May 1968, manager December 1968-May 1973; Sheffield Wednesday coach 1973-1975 and caretaker manager 1975; Scarborough manager 1981-April 1982; Hallam manager 1989.

Jimmy McAnearney found it difficult to break into Wednesday's side due a glut of good inside-forwards at the club in the 1950s. He moved to Plymouth Argyle, where he helped them to promotion to Division Two and scored 37 goals in 147 games. Slightly built, McAnearney was good at bringing his colleagues into the game with excellent passes.

He was employed by Tommy Docherty as a coach at Millmoor and when the Doc departed, McAnearney took over as manager. His first job was to sort out the mess left by Docherty, who had given the players very lucrative contracts which nearly crippled the club. The new manager had to sell some players, including Dave Watson to Sunderland for £100,000, to pay the rest. His best season was 1971-72, when his signing, Carl Gilbert, scored 28 goals and United finished fifth in Division Three. The following season, though, they were relegated. After a period as caretaker manager at Hillsborough, he left the game in 1975 to work in industry. He is the brother of Tom and John McAnearney.

McANEARNEY, Thomas

Born: Dundee, 6 January 1933
Wing-half 5ft 9in; 12st (1964).
Career: Dundee St Stephen's; Sheffield Wednesday October 1951; Peterborough United November 1965; Aldershot March 1966, player-manager April 1967-October 1968, retired 1968; Sheffield Wednesday assistant manager October 1968-1970; Bury manager November 1970-May 1972; Aldershot manager again May 1972-March 1981.

Honours: Division Two champions 1956, 1959; Division Four promotion 1973.

A tall, thoughtful and perceptive wing-half, Tom McAnearney gave Sheffield Wednesday excellent service. He appeared 382 times, scoring 22 goals, for the Yorkshire club. Not always appreciated by the crowd but admired by his colleagues, he helped the Owls to two Second Division titles as the club led a yo-yo existence in the 1950s.

McAnearney had two spells in charge at Aldershot. In 1972-73 they were promoted to Division Three on goal-average but were relegated two seasons later. They just missed promotion in 1977-78 and reached the fifth round of the FA Cup the following year. At Bury, McAnearney gambled heavily by signing a number of players in an effort to avoid relegation to the Fourth Division. But the Shakers finally went down in 1971 and with the club losing £800 a week, this meant there was no money for new players. He is the brother of Jimmy and John McAnearney.

MACARI, Luigi 'Lou'

Born: Edinburgh, 7 June 1949.
Midfield 5ft 5½in; 10st 9lb (1976).
Career: St Michael's Academy; Kilwinning; Kilmarnock Amateurs; Kilwinning Rangers; Glasgow Celtic 1966; Manchester United January 1973 (£200,000); Swindon Town player-manager July 1984-July 1989, retired as a player 1986; West Ham United manager July 1989-February 1990; Birmingham City manager February-May 1991; Stoke City manager May 1991.

Honours: Scotland international (24 caps); Under23 international (2 caps); Youth international; Schoolboy international; Scottish League champions 1970, 1972; Football League Division Two champions 1975; Division Three promotion 1987; Division Four champions 1986; Scottish Cup winners 1971, 1972; Scottish League Cup winners 1972, 1973; FA Cup winners 1977, runners-up 1976, 1979; Leyland DAF Cup winners 1991, 1992.

A busy little player who buzzed around the penalty area inspiring others around him, Lou Macari found it all too easy to win honours with Celtic and so moved south of the border for a fresh challenge at Old Trafford. He helped United back into the First Division and appeared in three Cup Finals for them, collecting a winners' medal when United beat Liverpool 2-1 in 1977. Macari made 365/26 appearances, scoring 88 goals, for United before joining Swindon Town as player-manager.

He was sacked in April 1985 after a row with his assistant Harry Gregg, but was reinstated six days later. Macari steered the club from the Fourth to the Second Division in two seasons. Swindon clinched the Fourth Division championship with an enormous 102 points, 18 clear of their nearest rivals. They beat Gillingham 2-0 in the 1987 Third Division play-off Final at Sel-

hurst Park and two years later reached the Second Division play-offs but lost to Crystal Palace.

When he took over at West Ham, Macari was only the club's sixth manager in their history, but he lasted just seven months. In January 1990, the FA charged Macari, along with Swindon chairman Brian Hillier, of unauthorised betting on a Swindon match. After a 6-0 defeat by Oldham Athletic in the League Cup semi-final, the strain became too much for Macari and he resigned five days later. He returned to management a year later, at St Andrew's, and took Birmingham to the Leyland DAF Final at Wembley but resigned shortly afterwards, saying that the club lacked ambition.

Macari was soon offered the Stoke City job and took them to the Third Division play-offs at the end of his first season in charge but they lost to Stockport County on aggregate. Three days later they got some sort of revenge when they beat the same opponents in the Final of the Autoglass Trophy (previously the Leyland DAF Trophy) 1-0 at Wembley, thanks to a goal from Mark Stein.

Stoke comfortably took the Second Division title wth 93 points after only seven defeats during 1992-93. Large crowds came back to the Victoria Ground as Macari's men ended the club's period in the wilderness.

MACAULAY, Archibald Renwick

Born: Falkirk, 30 July 1915; Died: June 1993.
Right-half/Inside-right
5ft 10½in; 12st 4lb (1937).
Career: Sawyer; Camelon Juniors; Glasgow Rangers March 1933; West Ham United June 1937 (£6,000); guest for Falkirk, Northampton Town, Aldershot and Doncaster Rovers in World War Two; Brentford November 1946; Arsenal July 1947; Fulham May 1950 (£10,000); Guildford City player-manager June 1953-November 1955; Dundee trainer-coach 1955-1957; Norwich City manager April 1957-October 1961; West Bromwich Albion manager October 1961-April 1963; Brighton & Hove Albion manager April 1963-October 1968.

Honours: Scotland international (7 caps); Wartime international (5 caps); Great Britain representative; Scottish League champions 1935, 1937; Football League champions 1948; Football League Cup winners 1962; Division Three runners-up 1960; Division Four champions 1965; Football League War Cup winners 1940.

Archie Macaulay found success as a player and a manager. He was one of the most cultured footballers of his day. Competitive, calm and with great ball control, Macaulay was also a fierce tackler and possessed a powerful shot. He began and ended his career as an inside-right but developed into a right-half during the war years. As a manager he was innovative, being one of the first to adopt the 4-3-3 system, and he was generally regarded as a tactician ahead of his time.

Macaulay won Scottish League championship medals with Rangers in 1934-35 and 1936-37. He made his debut for West Ham in the first match of the 1937-38 season, against Aston Villa, but the war soon interrupted his career, although in 1940 he played at Wembley when West Ham beat Blackburn Rovers 1-0 in the League War Cup Final. Macaulay served in the Essex Regiment

Territorials, eventually becoming a sergeant-major PT instructor. When the war ended, he found it difficult to settle at Upton Park and was transferred to Brentford early in the first post-war League season.

Macaulay, who had been capped in wartime, gained his first full cap whilst at Griffin Park, against England at Wembley in 1947. A month later he represented Great Britain against the Rest of Europe. He made another six appearances for Scotland after he moved to Arsenal in July 1947 for £10,000. The Gunners won the League championship in his first season at Highbury, a remarkable achievement for a club with such an ageing side. Macaulay missed Arsenal's 1950 FA Cup Final appearance due to a knee injury and shortly afterwards he moved to Fulham for £10,000, ending his playing career at Craven Cottage.

In June 1953, Macaulay gave up his restaurant business to go into management with Guildford City. He did an excellent rebuilding job at the club but left before he could see his work completed. In November 1955 he moved to Dundee as trainer-coach but hankered for a managerial job in English soccer. The opportunity came when he accepted an offer to manage Norwich City in April 1957.

Macaulay took the Canaries from the re-election zone to the semi-final of the FA Cup in 1959, despite having little cash to spend on players. They entered the newly-formed Third Division in 1958 and the following season had their great Cup run. It started in the first round against non-League amateurs Ilford and ended in bitter defeat in a semi-final second replay against Luton Town. On the way they had outstanding victories over mighty Manchester United and Spurs. In 1959-60, Norwich finished runners-up to Southampton and gained promotion to Division Two. Then they surprised most people by finishing fourth in the Second Division the following season.

Macaulay had many offers to manage at a higher level and decided to accept West Bromwich Albion's offer of £3,000 per annum to manage them. That was in October 1961 but he stayed only 18 months at The Hawthorns and left complaining of not being given a free hand at the club.

In April 1963, Macaulay moved to the south coast to manage Brighton, who were then in the Third Division. Brighton were an ambitious club but he was unable to stop them sinking into the Fourth Division soon after he joined the club. However, they were soon back as champions of Division Four in 1964-65, scoring 102 goals and gaining 63 points. Macaulay had paid Spurs £5,000 for Bobby Smith, who gave him one good season then suffered from weight problems and also admitted to being a compulsive gambler. After a few mediocre seasons, Macaulay decided to resign in October 1968. This did not come as a surprise. He left football and worked in many different jobs, including that of a traffic warden in the Chelsea area in the 1970s.

McBAIN, Neil

Born: Campbelltown, Argyllshire, 15 November 1895; Died: 13 May 1974.
Wing-half   5ft 8in; 12st 3lb (1925).
Career: Campbelltown Academical; Ayr United cs 1914; Manchester United November 1921 (£4,600); Everton January 1923 (£4,200); St Johnstone July 1926 (£1,100); Liverpool March 1928; Watford November 1928, then player-

manager 1929-August 1937; Ayr United manager 1937-1938; Luton Town manager June 1938-June 1939; New Brighton manager June 1946-February 1948 (played in an emergency); Leyton Orient assistant manager February 1948, then manager April 1948-August 1949; Estudiantes De La Plata (Argentina) coach August 1949; Ayr United manager 1955-1956; Watford manager August 1956-February 1959; Ayr United manager 1962-1963; also scouted for Watford, Mansfield Town, Everton, Chelsea.

Honours: Scotland international (3 caps); Scottish League Divison Two runners-up 1956.

Neil McBain is the oldest player to appear in the Football League when he kept goal in an emergency for New Brighton against Hartlepool at the age of 52 years 4 months. McBain had been an elegant wing-half with an adventurous approach and he had excellent heading ability.

McBain had very little success as a manager. He took Ayr United to promotion from Division Two as runners-up in 1955-56 and Watford to fourth in the Southern Section. However, McBain had a reputation for spotting young talent and developed a good network of contacts and scouts all over the country. He is one of the few Englishmen to have managed in Argentina. Sacked at New Brighton with the club bottom of the League, McBain then worked as Charles Hewitt's assistant at Leyton Orient before taking over.

McCAFFREY, Aiden

Born: Newcastle, 30 August 1957.
Central defender 5ft 11in; 11st 5lb (1984).
Career: Newcastle United January 1974; Derby County August 1978 (£60,000); Bristol Rovers August 1980 (£70,000); Bristol City (loan) February 1982; Torquay United (loan) March 1985; Exeter City July 1985; Hartlepool United February 1987; Whitley Bay cs 1987; Carlisle United player-coach January 1988, then manager April 1991-September 1992.

Honours: England Youth international; Texaco Cup winners 1974, 1975.

McCaffrey left his first club, Newcastle United, after a series of rows with the management. He had brief spells at most of his clubs but did make over 150 appearances for Bristol Rovers. He almost moved permanently to Bristol City in 1982, but the club almost went bankrupt at this time and he had to return to Eastville. He was coach at Carlisle United for three years under Clive Middlemass and took over when he was sacked. Carlisle finished 22nd in Division Four in McCaffrey's only full season in charge, and he was replaced as manager by the club's new owner, Michael Knighton, with his own man, David McCreery. He made his League debut for Newcastle against Ipswich in March 1975 and played his last game for Carlisle in April 1988.

McCALLIOG, James

Born: Glasgow, 23 September 1946.
Midfield   5ft 9in; 10st 5lb (1976).
Career: Glasgow Schools; Leeds United amateur; Chelsea September 1963; Sheffield Wednesday October 1965 (£37,500); Wolverhampton Wanderers August 1969 (£70,000); Manchester United March 1974 (£60,000); Southampton February 1975 (£40,000); Chicago Sting (NASL) April-August 1977; coaching in Nigeria in 1977; Lincoln City player-coach September 1978; played in Norway 1978; Runcorn player-manager cs 1979; Halifax Town

manager April 1990-October 1991.

Honours: Scotland international (5 caps); Under-23 international (2 caps); Youth international; Schoolboy international; Division Two champions 1975; FA Cup winners 1976, runners-up 1966; UEFA Cup runners-up 1972.

A gifted and skilful midfield player, Jim McCalliog was the game's costliest teenager when he moved from Chelsea to the Owls for £37,500 in 1965. He played in their disappointing FA Cup Final defeat against Everton in 1966 and a year later appeared for Scotland against England at Wembley, the Scots inflicting the first defeat on their old enemy since England became world champions. McCalliog appeared in a UEFA Cup Final, for Wolves against Spurs in 1972, and later helped Manchester United back to the First Division. He made the winning goal in Southampton's surprise victory over his former club in the 1976 FA Cup Final. McCalliog had one season in charge at The Shay.

McCalliog went the way of many Halifax managers when he failed to lift the club off the foot of the Fourth Division. This was despite signing Steve Norris from Carlisle United for a bargain £20,000. He scored 35 goals in 1990-91, but the Shaymen still finished in 22nd position.

McCALMAN, Donald S.

Born: Greenock, 18 October 1935.
Centre-half   6ft; 12st (1959).
Career: Glasgow Rangers; Armadale; Hibernian 1956; Bradford June 1959; Barrow July 1966; Bradford manager October-December 1968 & October 1969-February 1970, then became assistant manager.

Don McCalman was one of the best pivots in the Fourth Division and was a regular first-team choice at Bradford, where he made 317 appearances including 150 consecutive games. He was on Rangers' books as a youngster and had three seasons at Hibs. His first spell in charge at Bradford was brief, lasting only 12 games. He then reverted to assistant manager under Laurie Brown, although on the same salary. When he took over again, McCalman was constantly undermined by director Herbert Metcalfe, who even took over team selections.

McCANDLESS, William 'Billy'

Born: Kingseat, Belfast, 1894; Died: Corkett, Swansea, 18 July 1955 (aged 62).
Career: Ligoniel; Barn Athletic (Carrisfergus); Linfield 1914; Glasgow Rangers November 1920 (£2,500); Ballymena United player-manager cs 1930; Dundee manager 1934-May 1937; Newport County manager September 1937-April 1946; Cardiff City manager June 1946-November 1947; Swansea Town manager November 1947-July 1955.

Honours: Ireland international (9 caps); Scottish League champions 1921, 1923, 1924, 1925, 1927, 1928, 1929; Division Three South champions 1939, 1947, 1949 (three different clubs); Scottish Cup runners-up 1921, 1922; Irish Cup Winners 1916, runners-up 1918; Welsh Cup winners 1950, runners-up 1949.

One of the great characters of the game, Billy McCandless has a unique record, having taken three separate South Wales sides to the Third Division South championship. He gained honours galore at Linfield and Glasgow Rangers during his playing career and carried on in the same vein when he became a manager.

McCandless played in three Irish Cup Finals for Linfield. In 1916 they beat their great rivals, Glentoran, 1-0; In 1918 they lost 3-2 to Belfast Celtic; and a year later beat Glentoran again, 2-1 after two draws. Shortly afterwards, McCandless moved to Ibrox, where he gained seven League championship medals in Rangers' great side of that time. They did not do so well in the Cup and lost two Finals they should have won to lesser opposition. Partick Thistle beat them in 1921 and a year later Morton shocked everybody when they beat Rangers 1-0.

McCandless gained nine caps for Ireland. He made his international debut against England in 1-1 draw in Belfast in October 1919. His last appearance came near the end of his career, in February 1929 against Wales at Wrexham. He often partnered Bill McCracken at full-back but never played in a winning Irish side.

He left Scotland in the close season of 1930 to become the player-manager of Ballymena United. In 1934, he became the manager of Dundee who held their own in the Scottish League Division One without ever looking like winning anything. McCandless lost his job at Dens Park on 3 May 1937.

In September 1937, he became the manager of Newport County. McCandless knew football inside out and other managers often sought his advice. A popular and jovial character, he was soon to create a miracle at the South Wales club. He inherited some excellent players from his predecessor, Louis Page, and his astute and inspiring leadership soon developed them into an outstanding combination. He rarely made team changes and used only 13 players in the championship season.

Newport leapt to the top of the table in early October and were never seriously challenged after that. Apart from Norman Low, signed from Liverpool for £2,000, the team was built on a shoestring budget. Sadly the war years decimated the Newport side. Somerton Park was requisitioned by the Army during the hostilities and the club closed down. McCandless resigned in April 1946. Two months later, he took charge at Cardiff City.

In the first season after the war they ran away with the Southern Section title, finishing seven points clear of their nearest rivals Queen's Park Rangers. This included 30 wins and they scored 93 goals.

On 13 November 1947, McCandless moved to Swansea Town to become secretary-manager and reverted to manager only from May 1952. Swansea also took the Southern Section title in 1948-49. The side was built around a magnificent half-back line of Paul, Weston and Burns. McCandless discovered a wealth of talent at Vetch Field, including the Allchurch brothers, Cliff Jones, Mel Charles and Terry Medwin. There followed some unspectacular seasons in the Second Division up until his death.

McCARTHY, Michael

Born: Barnsley, 17 February 1959.
Central Defender 6ft 2in; 12st 12lb (1991).
Career: Barnsley Schools; Worsbrough Bridge MW Athletic; Barnsley apprentice December 1975, professional July 1977; Manchester City December 1983; Glasgow Celtic May 1987; Olympic Lyonnais (France) cs 1989; Millwall March 1990, then player-manager March 1992.

Honours: Republic of Ireland international (57 caps); Scottish Premier champions 1988; Scottish Cup winners 1988, 1989.

A dominating centre-half, McCarthy has a good attitude and dedication for the game. A very determined player who hates to lose, he has two good feet, is calm under pressure, uses the ball well and is exceptional in the air. McCarthy replaced Bruce Rioch as the Millwall manager. He helped Barnsley rise from the Fourth to the Second Division and was the backbone of their defence. When he was at Manchester City, they gained promotion into the First Division in 1985, but he left when they were relegated.

McCarthy helped to steer Celtic to the Premier League title in 1987-88 but missed the start of the season through injury. They also had two Scottish Cup success in 1988, beating Dundee United 2-1 and in 1989 beating Rangers 1-0 with McCarthy in the side. He helped Millwall reach the Second Division play-offs in 1991, where they lost to Brighton, but their form slumped the following season.

In their last season at the Den before their move to a new stadium at Senegal Fields, Millwall were unlucky to miss out on a place in the play-offs as they were one of the most entertaining sides in the First Division. McCarthy is adroit on the transfer market signing a number of useful players for small fees.

McCARTNEY, W.John

Born: Glasgow c.1866; Died: Edinburgh, 18 January 1933.
Full-back.
Career: Cartwell 1884; Glasgow Rangers 1887; Cowlairs (Glasgow) 1889; Newton Heath 1893; Luton Town 1894; Barnsley cs 1898, secretary-manager April 1901-cs 1904; St Mirren manager 1904-1910; Heart of Midlothian manager 1910-1920; Portsmouth manager May 1920-May 1927; Luton Town manager September 1927-December 1929.

Honours: Division Two runners-up 1927; Division Three South champions 1924; Scottish Cup runners-up 1908.

An authoritive Scot with plenty of individuality, McCarthy started his managerial career at Barnsley where he had complete control of team affairs, which was unusual at this time. He did a tremendous team building job and improved the club's financial position but became unpopular when he sold Benny Green to Birmingham for £500 and the team's form slumped.

He took St Mirren to a Scottish Cup Final, which they lost 5-1 to Celtic. Hearts were runners-up twice in the First Division, in 1914-15 and 1918-19, and also reached the Cup semi-finals in 1912 and 1913. He moved south to manage Portsmouth in 1920 and developed the 'Pompey style' to lift the Third Division South title in 1924. Three years later, Pompey were in the First Division. McCartney resigned through ill health in May 1927, but four months later he took over at Luton where he was a former player. Again he was dogged by ill health and this finally forced his resignation and he retired from football.

McCLELLAND, Joseph

Career: Halifax & District Association secretary until 1912; Halifax Town secretary-manager May 1911-July 1930; Lincoln City secretary manager May 1936-1946.

Joe McClelland attended the meeting at which Halifax Town was formed in 1911 and soon afterwards he was appointed secretary-manager, the club winning the Yorkshire Combination in their first season. Halifax then joined the Midland League and McClelland strengthened the playing staff by signing former England international Fred Pentland. Halifax moved to The Shay in December 1920 and joined the Football League the following year. Under him their best position was fourth in the Northern Section in 1926-27.

He was replaced by Alex Raisbeck in 1930, after 19 years' service, and took Lincoln to runners-up position in the Northern Section but they missed out on promotion by three points. He had a good season in 1941-42, in wartime competitions.

McCOLL, John Miller 'Ian'

Born: Alexandria, Dumbartonshire, 7 June 1927.
Right-half   5ft 11in; 11st 6lb (1955).
Career: Vale of Leven Academy; Boys' Brigade; Vale of Leven Juniors; Queen's Park 1943; Glasgow Rangers June 1945, retired cs 1961; Scotland national team manager November 1960-May 1965; Sunderland manager June 1965-February 1968.

Honours: Scotland international (14 caps); Scottish League representative (7 caps); Scottish League champions 1947, 1949, 1950, 1953, 1956, 1957; Scottish Cup winners 1948, 1949, 1950, 1953, 1960; Scottish League Cup winners 1947, 1949, runners-up 1952, 58.

Ian McColl was a qualified engineer who gained his BSc at Edinburgh University. He developed into one of Scotland's finest right-halves and made over 400 post-war appearances for Rangers. McColl had a brilliant game in the 1960 Scottish Cup Final after being recalled following a long absence. Tireless, very committed and an excellent passer, he was the grandson of William McColl, who also played for Scotland.

Ian McColl did not have sole charge of the Scottish national side when he became the manager. The Scottish FA picked the teams and also had a great say in tactics. They had lots of good players but results were indifferent, the best result being a 6-2 win in Spain in June 1963.

At Sunderland, McColl spent £340,000 on nine new players, but with little success. These included Jim Baxter — from Rangers for £75,000 — who rarely showed good form and Neil Martin, from Hibs for £80,000. Sunderland usually struggled near the foot of the First Division.

McCORMICK, James

Born: Rotherham, 26 April 1912; Died: Marbella, Spain, 3 January 1968.
Inside-right   5ft 6in; 11st (1933).
Career: Yorkshire Schools; Rotherham YMCA; Rotherham United April 1931; Chesterfield August 1932; Tottenham Hotspur March 1933; guest for Birmingham, Chelmsford City, Chester, Crewe Alexandra, Derby County, Fulham, Leicester City, Lincoln City, Liverpool, Rochdale, Southend United, Tranmere Rovers, Walsall and West Bromwich Albion in World War Two; Fulham May 1946; Lincoln City August 1947 and trainer; Crystal Palace February 1949; Sliema Wanderers (Malta) coach cs 1949; Turkey national coach May 1950; Wycombe Wanderers coach; Lincoln City coach; Walton & Hersham manager-coach; Sheffield United coach until 1953; York City manager June 1953-September 1954; publican in Lemsford, Herefordshire.

Jimmy McCormick was employed at the local steelworks when he signed for Rotherham United. A goalscoring inside-forward, he was fairly successful at Spurs where he scored 28 goals in 150 appearances before war interrupted his career. Spurs were relegated to Division Two in 1935 and he rarely appeared in the first team after September 1937.

Soon after taking over as manager of York City, he sold Dave Dunmore to Spurs for £10,750 and recruited five new players with this cash in the summer of 1954. He resigned after a dispute with the board over team selection, although the side he largely built went on to an FA Cup semi-final after he left the club. He was a Hertfordshire publican at the time of his death in a motoring accident in Spain, where he was on holiday.

McCRACKEN, William R.

Born: Belfast, 29 January 1883; Died: Hull, 20 January 1979.
Left-back   5ft 10in; 12st (1904).
Career: Belfast Distillery December 1900; Newcastle United May 1904, retired 1922; Hull City manager February 1923-May 1931; Gateshead manager September 1932-May 1933; Millwall manager May 1933-March 1936; Aldershot manager February 1937-November 1949; Newcastle United scout until cs 1958; Watford scout until January 1979.

Honours: Ireland international (15 caps); Victory international (1 cap); Irish League representative (5 caps); Football League champions 1905, 1907, 1909; FA Cup winners 1910, runners-up 1908, 1911; Irish Cup winners 1903, runners-up 1902.

Billy McCracken was famous for his mastery of tactics, perfecting the ploy of the offside trap which many others copied. This ultimately led to a change in the law in 1925 and also made McCracken an unpopular figure throughout the country as his teams frustrated opposing supporters. He made only 15 appearances for Ireland due to his clashes with authorities over cash. He retired from playing at the age of 40, after 432 games for Newcastle United.

As a manager he also had a reputation for fielding boring sides with their repeated use of the offside trap. At Hull he managed to gain control of team affairs after a struggle with the board and he took the Tigers to an FA Cup semi-final in 1930, where they lost 1-0 to Arsenal in a replay. They also lost their Second Division status that year and he was sacked after failing to get them promoted straightaway.

Millwall achieved little in his three seasons at The Den and he resigned after an argument with the disillusioned board. At Aldershot it was a constant struggle against having to seek re-election. The Shots enjoyed some marvellous times during the war years, though, being able to call upon some of the finest players in the country due to the club's close proximity to several military headquarters, where many good players were stationed.

McCREADIE, Edward Graham

Born: Glasgow, 15 April 1940.
Left-back   5ft 9in; 11st 3lb (1971).
Career: Drumchapel Amateurs; Clydebank Juniors; East Stirling 1959; Chelsea April 1962 (£6,000), coach November 1974, then manager April 1975-July 1977; Memphis Rogues (NASL) coach February 1978-79.

Honours: Scotland international (23 caps); Division Two promotion 1977; FA Cup winners 1970, runners-up 1967; Football League Cup winners 1965.

A superb buy for Chelsea for just £5,000 from East Stirlingshire, Eddie McCreadie formed a formidable full-back partnership with Ken Shellito and they helped the Blues to promotion to Division One in 1963 as runners-up. Aggressive, adventurous and flamboyant, McCreadie scored a great goal when Chelsea beat Leicester City in the League Cup Final second leg to win the trophy. He played in two FA Cup Finals for Chelsea, losing the first (2-1 to Spurs) and winning the second (2-1 against Leeds in a replay). He made 410 appearances for Chelsea, despite the later part of his career being plagued by injuries.

In 1977, he guided Chelsea to the First Division as manager, then had a dispute over a new contract and left the club. Some sources say the pressures of management had been too much for him.

McCREERY, David

Born: Belfast, 16 September 1957.
Midfield   5ft 7in; 9st 7lb (1978).
Career: Manchester United apprentice 1972, professional October 1974; Queen's Park Rangers August 1979 (£200,000); Tulsa Roughnecks (NASL) March 1981; Newcastle United October 1982 (£75,000); Heart of Midlothian cs 1989-91; Hartlepool United August 1991; Coleraine 1992; Hartlepool United assistant manager 1992; Carlisle United manager September 1992.

Honours: Northern Ireland international (67 caps); Under-21 international (1 cap); Schoolboy international; Youth international; FA Cup winners 1977, runners-up 1976.

A very committed midfield player, David McCreery was used mainly as cover at Old Trafford. He did appear as substitute in two FA Cup Finals for Manchester United and picked up a winners' medal in 1977 when the Reds beat Liverpool 2-1 in the Final.

McCrery appeared regularly for Newcastle United and helped them back into Division One in 1984. A good ball-winner, and always in the thick of the action, McCreery also did well when covering at full-back for the Magpies. He appeared 237/6 times in their

League side before joining Hearts. McCreery played in the 1982 and 1986 World Cup finals for Northern Ireland.

He was assistant manager to Alan Murray, at Hartlepool before being offered the manager's job at Carlisle United. McCreery was the choice of Carlisle's new owner, Michael Knighton, who had previously been a director at McCreery's first club, Manchester United. The Cumbrians struggled in the Third Division in 1992-93 and went out at Wigan in the first round of the FA Cup.

McDEVITT, William

Born: Belfast, 5 January 1898; Died: 10 January 1966.
Centre-half/Inside-left
5ft 11½in; 11st 10lb (1926).
Career: Swansea Town 1920; Belfast United 1922; Liverpool cs 1923; Exeter City May 1925, then player-manager February 1929-September 1935, retired 1931.

McDevitt was a shrewd Irishman who had a happy knack of obtaining good players for practically no fees, and welding successful combinations. Exeter had a great run to the sixth round of the FA Cup with a team which cost only £1,000. They were runners-up in the Southern Section in 1933 and at this time McDevitt turned down a good offer to manage Queen's Park Rangers. He left the club after a poor start to the 1935-36 season. He had captained Exeter City, appearing 139 times (and scoring 11 goals) after just four games for Liverpool. A slow but intelligent inside-forward, he switched to centre-half later in his career.

McDONALD, Colin Agnew

Born: Summerseat, Lancashire, 15 October 1930.
Goalkeeper   6ft; 12st (1958).
Career: Bury Technical College; Hawkshaw St Mary's; Burnley amateur August 1948, professional October 1948; Headington United (loan) 1950, retired through injury cs 1961; Wycombe Wanderers coach August-September 1961; Bury chief scout October 1961-January 1965; Altrincham January 1965-cs 1967 (comeback); Bury chief scout May 1967-October 1968; Bolton Wanderers chief scout October 1968-August 1969; Bury administrative manager August 1969, then general manager May 1970-1972, then manager September-November 1970; Oldham Athletic coach; Tranmere Rovers coach until February 1987.

Honours: England international (8 caps); Football League representative (3 caps).

Safe, reliable and often brilliant, MacDonald was a great favourite with the crowd. He made 186 League appearances for Burnley before a broken leg received whilst playing for the Football League in March 1959, ultimately led to his early retirement in 1961. Earlier he had played for Headington United whilst on National Service. He made a comeback with Altrincham, four years after retiring. McDonald had two periods as Bury's chief scout, then becoming administration and general manager before a three-month spell as team manager in which they won only two games.

MacDONALD, Ian Clifford

Born: Barrow, 10 May 1953.
Midfield   5ft 9in; 11st 9lb (1991).
Career: Barrow May 1971; Workington February 1973 (£3,000); Liverpool January 1974 (£35,000); Colchester

United (loan) February 1975; Mansfield Town July 1975 (£19,000); York City November 1977; Aldershot November 1981, later player-coach, then player-manager November 1991-March 1992; Millwall reserve-team coach May 1992.
Honours: Division Three champions 1977.

Ian MacDonald was in charge at Aldershot when they were forced to drop out of the Football League due to huge unpaid debts. He had great difficulties in keeping the club going in the final weeks. Players had not been paid for months and many drifted away to other clubs as the club lurched towards bankruptcy.

MacDonald has been involved in four clubs who have left the League: Barrow, Workington, Colchester United (recently returned) and Aldershot. He played in Barrow's last-ever season in the League in 1971-72 and did not make the grade when he moved to Liverpool. Transferred to Mansfield Town, he had happier days at Field Mill when they won the Third Division title in 1976-77. He played over 350 games for Aldershot and scored over 50 goals, helping them to rare success in 1986-87 when they beat Wolves in the Fourth Division play-off Final. After finishing bottom of Division Three in 1988-89, they struggled for survival until their demise on 25 March 1992.

McDONALD, Malcolm

Born: Glasgow, 26 October 1913.
Half-back   5ft 9in; 11st 3lb (1935).
Career: St Anthony's; Glasgow Celtic April 1932; Kilmarnock (loan) May 1940, permanently October 1945; Brentford October 1946 (£1,500), then coach June 1948; Kilmarnock manager May 1950-May 1957; Brentford manager May 1957-January 1965; Kilmarnock manager June 1965-April 1968; Tottenham Hotspur scout 1969; Glasgow Celtic scout July 1975.

Honours: Scotland Wartime international (3 caps); Junior international (1 cap); Schoolboy international (1 cap); Scottish League representative (1 cap); Scottish League Division Two runners-up 1954; Division Four champions 1963; Scottish Cup runners-up 1957; Scottish League Cup runners-up 1953.

'Malky' was a classy player with silky skills who was versatile, filling every position except goalkeeper. As well as his wartime caps, he also won a schoolboy cap against England in 1928 and a junior international cap against Ireland in 1931. He played for and managed both Kilmarnock and Brentford.

A qualified physiotherapist, 'Malky' enjoyed great successes in his first spell as the Killies' manager. They lost 2-0 to Dundee in the 1953 Scottish League Cup Final, after beating Rangers in the semi-final, and won promotion the following season as runners-up. He kept the club up with a series of astute purchases on the transfer market. They also reached a Scottish Cup Final in 1957, losing to Falkirk, and finished third in First Division.

Moderately successful in his second spell at Rugby Park, he took the Killies to a Fairs Cup semi-final, where they lost to Leeds in 1967. He was sacked after a big home defeat by Celtic. At Brentford, McDonald took them close to promotion in 1957-58 and 1958-59. The Bees were relegated to Division Four in 1962 but bounced back the following season as champions with 62 points.

MACDONALD, Malcolm Ian

Born: Fulham, 7 January 1950.
Centre-forward 5ft 10½in; 13st 4lb (1974).
Career: Knowle Juniors; Tonbridge July 1967; Fulham August 1968; Luton Town July 1969 (£17,500); Newcastle United May 1971 (£180,000); Arsenal August 1976 (£333,000); Djorgarden (Sweden) summer 1979, retired August 1979 due to injury; Fulham commercial manager September 1979, then manager November 1980-April 1984 and director November 1981-April 1984; Worthing licensee 1984-1987; Huddersfield Town manager October 1987-April 1988.

Honours: England international (14 caps); Under-23 international (4 caps); Football League representative (1 cap); Division Three promotion 1982; FA Cup runners-up 1974, 1978; Football League Cup runners-up 1976.

A brash and arrogant centre-forward, Malcolm Macdonald became a cult figue on Tyneside as he scored 95 goals in 187 appearances for Newcastle United. He was never given a proper chance at Fulham, the club he supported as a boy. He joined them as a left-back and was converted to centre-forward by manager Bobby Robson. Macdonald made a name for himself at Luton, and Newcastle paid a large fee for him. The Magpies fans were shocked when he was sold to Arsenal for £333,333. Macdonald played in losing Finals at both clubs and once scored five goals in a match for England.

Forced to retire through injury, after scoring 191 goals in 339 League games, he returned to Fulham as commercial manager and replaced Bobby Campbell as manager in 1980. Thoughtful and articulate, Macdonald was comfortable with the Press, honest with the supporters and respected by the players. He took Fulham into Division Two in 1982 and almost to the First a year later with a team of flair and style. He resigned after publicity about his private life, did not enjoy his period at Huddersfield Town and left football a disillusioned man.

McDONOUGH, Roy

Born: Solihull, 16 October 1958.
Forward   6ft 1in; 11st 11lb (1983).
Career: Warwickshire Schools; Birmingham City apprentice October 1974, professional October 1976; Walsall September 1978 (£15,000); Chelsea October 1980 (£15,000); Colchester United February 1981 (£15,000); Southend United August 1983 (£5,000); Exeter City January 1984 (£2,000); Cambridge United October 1984; Southend United August 1985; Colchester United 1990, then player-manager July 1991.

Honours: Conference League champions 1992; FA Trophy winners 1992.

Roy McDonough is a tall, hard-

working forward. He has played in three Fourth Division promotion sides, with Walsall in 1980 and with Southend United in 1987 and 1990. He appeared in over 200 games in his two spells for Southend United and also played regularly for Walsall and Colchester United.

McDonough took over from Ian Atkins at Layer Road and guided United back into the Football League as Conference League champions in 1991-92. They also won the FA Trophy Final at Wembley, beating Witton Albion in a tough game. McDonough played an important role in this game when he made the first goal for Mike Masters.

Colchester edged out Wycombe Wanderers on goal-average to take the League title with 94 points — a new record and McDonagh scored 29 goals in 1991-92. Attendance have improved enormously at Layer Road and Colchester consolidated their position on their return to the Leauge, finishing in tenth position in 1992-1993.

McDOWALL, Leslie J.

Born: India, 25 October 1912; Died: 18 August 1991.
Wing-half   5ft 10in; 11st 4lb (1933).
Career: Glenryan Thistle; Sunderland December 1932; Manchester City March 1938, retired 1950; Wrexham player-manager May 1949-May 1950; Manchester City manager June 1950-May 1963; Oldham Athletic manager June 1963-March 1965.

Honours: Division Two champions 1947, runners-up 1951; FA Cup winners 1956, runners-up 1955.

Les McDowall took Manchester City to consecutive FA Cup Finals in the mid-1950s. The first one was lost to Newcastle United but the 1956 game is particularly memorable for the fact that City goalkeeper Bert Trautmann played part of the game with a broken neck and also for the famous 'Revie Plan' which helped bring the trophy to Maine Road as Birmingham City were beaten.

Born in India, McDowall was the son of a Scottish missionary. He trained as a draughtsman but was made unemployed from his shipyard in the early 1930s. Along with a number of others in the same position, he helped form a football team, Glenryan Thistle, and whilst playing for this side he was spotted by Sunderland. McDowall signed for the Wearsiders on Christmas Eve 1932, but it was almost two years before he got a chance in the first team. He made his debut in November 1934, at left-half in a 1-0 First Division defeat by West Brom at Roker Park.

This was a highly successful period for the Wearsiders, however. They won the League championship and the FA Cup in consecutive seasons, although McDowall played little part in either. In over five years at Roker, he was restricted to an occasional outing as deputy to either skipper Alex Hastings or Scottish international centre-half Bert Johnstone. Although he made only 13 appearances for Sunderland, Manchester City were persuaded to pay £7,000 for his services in March 1938.

McDowall arrived at Maine Road at a difficult time. League champions the previous season, City were then faced with the prospect of relegation, but McDowall — who went straight into the first team at centre-half, taking over from Bobby Marshall — could not help them beat the drop. He took over the captaincy in 1938-39, but the war then disrupted his career. He returned to his draughtsman's job on the outbreak of hostilities, this time in an aircraft factory, and played in wartime competitions for City.

When League football was resumed in 1946, McDowall was still a regular in the half-back line and, although no longer capable, he helped City to the Second Division title in 1946-47. After two more First Division seasons, McDowall left Maine Road. His final appearance was in a 5-1 defeat at Bolton in November 1948, and the following May he took over as player-manager of Wrexham. At the Racecourse Ground, he selected himself only three times before hanging up his boots to concentrate on management.

As a player, McDowall was respected for his hard work and organisational skills rather than any natural gifts as a wing-half. These qualities had made an impression on the Maine Road board, who earmarked him as a potential manager. The opportunity arose sooner than expected. After less than a year at Wrexham, he was offered a return to City when manager Jock Thomson decided to leave football and run a hotel in his native Dundee.

Just as his arrival as a player at Maine Road coincided with relegation to Division Two, so his introduction to management in Manchester came as City dropped out of Division One. These were difficult times for City, living in the shadow of Matt Busby's hugely successful Manchester United, but in his first season, he got them back to the top flight as runners-up and they remained there until the last of his 13 years at the helm. Relegation in 1963 precipitated McDowall's resignation and the end of his long association with Manchester City.

Although his League record as a manager was, at best modest and certainly paled in comparison with Matt Busby's across the city at Old Trafford, he enjoyed a measure of success in the Cup and won a deserved reputation for tactical boldness and innovation. City reached Wembley in consecutive seasons, losing to Newcastle in 1955 and beating Birmingham in 1956 (repeating the pattern the club had recorded in 1933 and 1934, against Everton and Portsmouth). McDowall's teams always contained their share of exciting individual talent, such as Ivor Broadis in his early days and Denis Law towards the end of his tenure.

As a tactician, his major contribution was the so called 'Revie Plan' — which, according to Revie, could easily have been called the McDowall Plan. Based on the formation used to such devastating effect by the Hungarians, Revie

adopted the deep-lying centre-forward role assumed by the great Hidegkuti for the wonderful Magyars side.

Although it started shakily, McDowall kept faith with the idea and it eventually paid off. In those days of more naive thinking it caught a lot of sides by surprise and much of the credit was due to the manager.

In their autobiographies, City players of this era, such as Roy Paul, Bert Trautmann and Don Revie, make the point that McDowall was a quiet man, who did not say much — but when he did speak, the players listened and did as he suggested. He was not a self-publicist in the way of many modern managers, and he had the respect of both the players and the board. To have lasted so long at Maine Road with little to show in terms of League honours (when neighbours United were doing so well) suggests the confidence the club had in him.

Alas, in the early 1960s it started to go wrong for McDowall, as the nucleus of the Cup team broke up and were not adequately replaced. The lower half of the table was City's regular position from 1958 onwards and relegation, threatened earlier, became a reality in 1963. McDowall had left Wrexham to take charge at Maine Road in June 1950 and resigned in May 1963.

The following month he became manager of Oldham Athletic, taking over a newly-promoted side. After a good start in the Third Division they fell away to finish ninth. When he was sacked in March 1965, Oldham were struggling against relegation. McDowall left football at this point and died in August 1991.

McEVOY, Donald W.

Born: Golcar, 3 December 1928.
Centre-half   5ft 9in; 12st 8lb (1959).
Career: Kirkheaton Rovers; Bradley Rangers; Huddersfield Town September 1947; Sheffield Wednesday December 1954 (£15,000); Lincoln City player-coach January 1959; Barrow player-coach July 1960; Halifax Town manager May 1962-August 1964; Barrow manager August 1964-July 1967; Grimsby Town manager July 1967-January 1968; Southport manager March 1968-January 1970; Barrow manager February 1970-November 1971; publican in Brighouse from 1971.
Honours: Division Two champions 1957; Division Four promotion 1967.

Don McEvoy made his debut at Huddersfield Town at centre-forward but later converted to centre-half. A regular until he lost his place through injury, he made up a formidable half-back line with Bill McGarry and Len Quested and the Town bounced straight back after relegation in 1952 as runners-up in Division Two in 1952-53. After 155 appearances for Town, McEvoy moved to Hillsborough and captained the Owls to the Second Division title in 1956-57. Altogether, he made a further 112 appearances for Wednesday.

Halifax were relegated to Division Four in 1963 and he moved to Barrow as manager a year later. They sought re-election in his first season at the club but got into Division Three in 1967, the club's first-ever promotion. His second spell at Barrow was a nightmare as they finished bottom of Division Three in 1969-70 and then 23rd in Division Four in 1970-71.

McEWAN, James 'Punch'

Born: Liverpool 1875; Died: Leeds, 28 May 1942.

Full-back   5ft 6in; 11st (1904).
Career: Lansdowne; Bootle South End; Liverpool Reserves 1892; Everton Reserves 1893; Luton Town cs 1894; Glossop cs 1898; Bury cs 1900; Luton Town cs 1903; Norwich City cs 1905, then player-manager July 1907-September 1908 when he retired; Fulham coach 1909; Glossop manager March 1911-February 1914; Arsenal coach 1914-1930s.
Honours: FA Cup winners 1903; North v South international trial; Manchester Cup and Lancashire Cup winners' medals (with Bury).

McEwan made 388 League appearances in his career including over 100 games each for Bury and Norwich City. He played in Bury's record 6-0 victory over Derby County in the 1903 FA Cup Final and won a reputation as a fearless defender and later as an excellent trainer. He was captain of Norwich City and was appointed manager after the departure of John Bowman. McEwan did not have full managerial control and lost his job after a poor season for the club in September 1908.

He became something of an institution at Arsenal. Tom Whittaker in his book *Tom Whittaker's Arsenal Story* tells an amusing story about 'Punch'. He was in charge of the dressing-room for Arsenal's 1927 FA Cup Final appearance against Cardiff. A case of champagne was delivered but when the Gunners embarrassingly lost, McEwan drank the lot before the players got back to the changing-room.

McEWAN, William J.M.

Born: Clelland, 20 June 1951.
Midfield   5ft 10in; 11st 2lb (1974).
Career: Hibernian; Blackpool May 1973; Brighton & Hove Albion February 1974; Chesterfield November 1974; Mansfield Town January 1977; Peterborough United November 1977; Rotherham United July 1979; Sheffield United manager March 1986-January 1988; Rotherham United manager April 1988-January 1991.

Honours: Division Four champions 1989.

Billy McEwan steered Rotherham United to the Fourth Division championship in 1988-89, his first full season in charge at Millmoor. He had taken over too late to save them from relegation the previous season but made a number of useful signings, including Bobby Williamson, who scored 27 goals in the championship season. Rotherham performed well in 1989-90 and finished ninth in the Third Division

but were relegated the following season and McEwan was sacked.

McEwan had previously been in charge at Sheffield United whom he joined in 1984 as youth-team manager. The Blades were heading towards the play-offs and relegation in 1987-88 and McEwan resigned after a disastrous 5-0 home defeat against Oldham Athletic in January 1988. His chairman, Reg Bradley, described him as a committed manager, honest and hard working, but things did not work out for him on the pitch.

McEwan had made 61 League appearances for Hibs but did not play in their 1972 Scottish Cup Final. He moved south in May 1973 and then moved around from one club to another without really establishing roots. In January 1977, McEwan signed for Mansfield Town and helped them to promotion to Division Two. He missed over a year due to a serious injury in the early 1980s.

MacFARLAND, Alex 'Sandy'

Born: Dundee, c.1878.
Inside-forward   5ft 8½in; 12st (1914).
Career: Bailleston Juniors; Airdrieonions; Newcastle United October 1898 (£30); Dundee November 1901; Chelsea cs 1913-1914; Dundee manager March 1919-May 1925; Charlton Athletic manager May 1925-December 1927; Dundee manager December 1927-June 1928; Charlton Athletic manager May 1928-December 1932; Blackpool manager July 1933-July 1935.

Honours: Scotland international (5 caps); Scottish League representative (3 caps); Division Three South champions 1929; Scottish Cup winners 1910, runners-up 1925.

A sturdy, hardworking player, Sandy McFarland served Dundee and Charlton Athletic twice as a manager. He played his best soccer in Scotland, where he won a Scottish Cup winners' medal in 1910, and made 87 appearances for Newcastle and only four for Chelsea. In his spell at Dens Park, MacFarland took the club to a Scottish Cup Final in 1925, but they lost 2-1 to Celtic. Dundee were usually challenging at the top of the League during his time with them.

A relentless perfectionist, this was he strength and his weakness. After seeking re-election in his first season at The Valley, he took the club to the Southern Section title in 1929 after his surprising return to Charlton a year earlier. He performed a near-miracle as he had little money to spend on players. McFarland resigned midway through a disastrous 1932-33 season. He had a couple of good seasons at Blackpool, where he used his skill as a quick and accurate judge of a player to build a good side at Bloomfield Road.

McFARLAND, Roy Leslie

Born: Liverpool, 5 April 1948.
Centre-half   5ft 11in; 11st 11lb (1970).
Career: Edge Hill Boys' Club; Tranmere Rovers July 1966; Derby County August 1967 (£24,000); Bradford City player-manager May 1981-November 1982; Derby County assistant manager November 1982, registered as a player August 1983 caretaker manager April-June 1984.

Honours: England international (28 caps); Under-23 international (5 caps); Football League representative (6 caps); Football League champions 1972; Division Two champions 1969; Division Four promotion 1982.

A bargain buy by Brian Clough, Roy

McFarland formed an excellent partnership with Dave Mackay, helping Derby to the Second Division title in 1969. He made his England debut against Malta in February 1971 and was an inspirational captain as Derby won their first League championship the following season. October 1973 was a bad month for McFarland. He played in the England side which failed to beat Poland and thus missed out on the 1974 World Cup finals, and Brian Clough left the Baseball Ground amidst huge controversy. McFarland missed almost all Derby's championship season of 1974-75 due to an Achilles tendon injury sustained whilst playing for England.

Skilful, consistent and uncompromising, McFarland made 530 appearances for Derby, scoring 48 goals. He played in a European Cup semi-final against Juventus in 1973 and his overall tally includes some games in an emergency after he rejoined the club.

McFarland took Bradford City to promotion to Division Three in 1982 but shortly afterward he was enticed to leave Valley Parade and rejoin Derby as assistant manager. Derby later had to pay a large fine and compensation to City for allegedly poaching him and his assistant Mick Jones. McFarland took over as caretaker boss when Peter Taylor was sacked but was appointed far too late to save the Rams from relegation to Division Three. He remained at the Baseball Ground as Arthur Cox's assistant and has seen Derby climb from the Third to the top flight and drop back to the First Division. In all his service at the Baseball Ground totals over 25 years.

McFARLANE, Ian

Born: Lanark, 26 January 1933.
Full-back   6ft 1in; 12st 7lb.
Career: Aberdeen 1955; Chelsea August 1956; Leicester City May 1958 (£9,000); Bath City July 1959; Middlesbrough assistant manager; Manchester City assistant manager; Carlisle United manager January 1970-July 1972; Sunderland assistant manager, caretaker manager October-November 1976; Leicester City assistant manager-coach 1977-1982 and caretaker manager April-June 1978; Leeds United chief scout 1990.

Honours: Southern League champions 1960.

A hefty full-back, McFarlane had a limited career as a player and appeared only 17 times for Aberdeen, once for Leicester and 43 times for Chelsea. As a manager and coach he tended to be associated with highly motivated but dull, dour sides. As Carlisle's manager he almost steered the club into the First Division in 1971, when they finished

fourth, but was sacked after a poor start the following season. His biggest coup was signing Stan Bowles for £13,000 from Crewe; Bowles was later sold for £115,000 to Queen's Park Rangers. McFarlane was caretaker for only one month at Roker Park and was also caretaker at Filbert Street between Frank McLintock and Jock Wallace. He was known as the 'Big Man'.

McFAUL, William Stewart

Born: Coleraine 1 October 1943.
Goalkeeper   5ft 9½in; 12st (1971).
Career: Coleraine 1960; Linfield cs 1963; Newcastle United November 1966 (£7,000), retired in 1975 to become assistant coach, then manager September 1985-October 1988.

Honours: Northern Ireland international (6 caps); Inter-Cities Fairs Cup winners 1969; FA Cup runners-up 1974.

A safe and agile 'keeper, McFaul was a regular at Newcastle United despite his lack of inches. He played 354 games for the Magpies and kept goal in the Fairs Cup triumph against Újpesti Dózsa in 1969 and in United's FA Cup Final defeat against Liverpool in 1974. His brilliant performance against Burnley in the semi-final at Hillsborough probably got them to Wembley.

McFaul endured years of frustration as deputy to Pat Jennings in the Northern Ireland side, gaining only six caps. After ten years as coach at St James' Park, he was offered the chance to manage the club. The fans expected a lot and when honours did not materialise, they vented their frustration on the manager. He was sacked with the club next to bottom in the First Division.

McGARRY, William Harry 'Bill'

Born: Stoke-on-Trent, 10 June 1927.
Wing-half   5ft 8in; 11st (1957).
Career: Northwood Mission (Hanley); Port Vale June 1945; Huddersfield Town March 1951 (£10,000); Bournemouth & Boscombe Athletic player-manager March 1961-July 1963 (£2,000); Watford manager July 1963-October 1964; Ipswich Town manager October 1964-November 1968; Wolverhampton Wanderers manager November 1968-May 1976; Saudi Arabia coach June 1976-October 1977; Newcastle United manager November 1977-August 1980; Brighton & Hove Albion scout; Power Dynamo (Zambia) coach; Zambian national team coach; Wolverhampton Wanderers manager September-November 1985; coaching in Bophuthatswana in 1993.

Honours: England international (4 caps); 'B' international (1 cap); FA tour of South Africa in 1956; Football League representative (1 cap); Division Two champions 1968; Football League

Cup winners 1974; UEFA Cup runners-up 1972.

A strong disciplinarian, Bill McGarry was most successful in his first spell with Wolves and a great career in management was predicted. But it all seemed to go wrong for him around 1975 and he never really recovered. From that point, his career seemed to go into a steady decline.

He joined Port Vale just after the war and in March 1951 moved to Huddersfield Town for a £10,000 fee after making 146 League appearances and scoring five goals for Vale. McGarry went on to make another 381 League and Cup appearances for the Town, scoring 26 goals. He gained four full England caps, appearing in the 1954 World Cup.

A dependable wing-half and a sound and solid tackler, McGarry was very competitive and an effective passer. He was a member of the Huddersfield side which gained promotion from the Second Division in 1952-53, the entire Town's defence — goalkeeper, two full-backs and three half-backs — being ever-present that season.

In March 1961, Bill McGarry became the player-manager of Bournemouth, who just missed promotion to Division Two in 1961-62 when they finished third. From July 1963 he was the manager of Watford and in October 1964 moved to Ipswich Town as manager. McGarry took them to the Second Division championship in 1967-68.

In November 1968, McGarry moved to Wolves and led them into Europe, where they reached the UEFA Cup Final before losing to Spurs, 3-2 on aggregate. Wolves had earned their European entry by finishing fourth in the First Division in 1970-71 and also lifted the Texaco Cup that season. In 1973 they reached the semi-finals of the League Cup and a year later took the trophy by beating Manchester City 2-1 in the Final at Wembley. Relegation came in 1975-76, mainly due to the loss through retirement of experienced players like Derek Dougan, and David Wagstaffe through injury.

McGarry handed in his resignation at the end of the season and moved abroad to coach the national team of Saudi Arabia, then returning to England to manage Newcastle United. Even though he spent big money on new players, McGarry was unable to get the Magpies back into the First Division after their relegation in 1978. He tried to completely rebuild the club that summer and there were many new arrivals, including Peter Withe and Terry Hibbitt, but Newcastle had a poor season in 1978-79. McGarry continued to spend money on players like Stuart Boam, but after another poor season he was sacked in August 1980.

He scouted for Brighton for a while, then went to work in Zambia. In September 1985 he returned to Wolves as manager again. They had just been relegated to the Third Division and made a disastrous start to the season. McGarry stayed for only 61 days, resigning in despair on 4 November. He returned to Africa to coach in Bophuthatswana.

McGHEE, Mark Edward

Born: Glasgow, 25 May 1957.
Striker   5ft 10in; 12st 2lb (1978).
Career: Stirling junior football; Bristol City apprentice 1973; Morton 1975; Newcastle United December 1977 (£150,000); Aberdeen March 1979

(£80,000); SV Hamburg May 1984 (£285,000); Glasgow Celtic November 1985 (£200,000); Newcastle United August 1989; Reading player-manager May 1991.

Honours: Scotland international (4 caps); Under-21 international (1 cap); Scottish League champions 1980, 1984, 1986, 1988; Scottish Cup winners 1982, 1983, 1984, 1988, 1989; Scottish League Cup runners-up 1980, 1987; European Cup-winners' Cup winners 1983.

A clever forward who was a good dribbler with plenty of ball skills, Mark McGhee was released by Bristol City and moved to Morton, where his 37 goals in 64 games attracted the attention of Newcastle United. McGhee became a star forward in Aberdeen's successful side in the early 1980s, which won the European Cup-winners' Cup in 1983, when they beat Real Madrid in the Final in Gothenburg. He played in three Scottish Cup Final victories for Aberdeen, plus two for Celtic, and scored vital goals in the 1982 victory over Rangers and the 1984 victory over Celtic.

Altogether, McGhee netted 63 goals in 164 League appearances for Aberdeen before trying his luck in the Bundesliga with SV Hamburg. He later found more success at Celtic and Newcastle United, in a second spell at Gallowgate. He took over at Reading in the summer of 1991, but the team had a poor season in 1991-92 and finished just above the relegated clubs.

Reading came close to the play-offs and had a good run in the FA Cup in 1992-93.

McGOVERN, John Prescott

Born: Montrose, 28 October 1949.
Midfield   5ft 8in; 9st 13lb (1971).

Career: Hartlepools United apprentice 1965, professional May 1967; Derby County September 1968 (£7,500); Leeds United August 1974 (£125,000); Nottingham Forest February 1975 (£60,000); Bolton Wanderers player-manager June 1982-January 1985, retired 1984; Horwich RMI manager 1985; living in Tenerife; Chorley manager February 1990; Plymouth Argyle assistant manager March 1992.

Honours: Scottish Under-23 international (2 caps); Schoolboy international; Football League champions 1972, 1978; Division Two champions 1969; Football League Cup winners 1978, 1979; European Cup winners 1979, 1980.

John McGovern was a modest player who seems to have been appreciated more by his colleagues than the crowd. He had considerable skill, was good at closing down the opposition and kept his side ticking.

McGovern followed Brian Clough around from club to club and captained

around from club to club and captained

Forest to two European Cup Final successes. He made his debut for Hartlepool as a 16-year-old and after he helped Derby into the First Division in 1969 he was the youngest player to have appeared in all four divisions. McGovern made over 200 appearances at both Derby County and Nottingham Forest, winning League championship medals with both clubs.

He had little success and a lot of bad luck as manager of Bolton Wanderers, who were relegated to Division Three at the end of his first season in charge. The club had financial problems and McGovern worked very hard at alleviating these problems. He even took a drop in wages to help the club and sold lottery tickets. He returned to League management as Peter Shilton's assistant at Home Park.

McGRATH, John Thomas

Born: Manchester, 23 August 1938.
Centre-half   6ft; 12st 6lb (1963).
Career: Bolton Wanderers amateur; Miles Platting Swifts; Bury October 1955; Newcastle United February 1961 (£24,000 and a player); Southampton February 1968 (£30,000); Brighton & Hove Albion (loan) December 1972; Southampton trainer and youth-team coach 1975-1979; Port Vale manager December 1979-December 1983; Chester City manager January 1984-May 1985; Preston North End manager May 1986-January 1990; Halifax Town manager October 1991-November 1992.
Honours: England Under-23 international (1 cap); Football League representative; Division Three champions 1961; Division Four runners-up 1987, promotion 1983.

A tough muscular centre-half who never shirked a challenge, McGrath gained a reputation for his fierce tackling, although he was the archetypal gentle giant off the field. He moved to Newcastle in a deal which took Bob Stokoe the other way and left Bury just before they clinched the Third Division championship. McGrath made 489 League appearances during his career, including over 150 at both Newcastle and Southampton.

When he retired, McGrath concentrated on coaching the youth team at The Dell. He took his first managerial post at Port Vale and was fortunate to retain the job after a poor season in 1980-81, which included an FA Cup defeat against Enfield. Vale won promotion to Division Three at the end of 1982-83, but McGrath was sacked the following season with the club at the bottom of the table.

Chester finished bottom of the League when he moved to Sealand

Road but the damage had been done before his arrival. He took Preston to promotion to the Third Division in 1986-87 and to the play-offs two years later. Under McGrath Halifax finished 20th in Division Four in 1991-92 and struggled to score goals, hitting just 34 all season.

McGrath lost his job shortly after Halifax lost 4-1 at Marine in the first round of the FA Cup. They eventually lost their league status in May 1993. He is now becoming well-known on the after-dinner speakers circuit.

McGRORY, Robert

Born: Bishopton, Scotland, 17 October 1894; Died: 23 May 1954.
Wing-half/Right-back
6ft; 12st 8lb (1921).
Career: Dumbarton 1914; Burnley August 1920 (£3,000); Stoke April 1921, player-coach 1930, later reserve-team manager and assistant manager, then retired from playing to become manager June 1935-May 1952.

A dour and fearless full-back, McGrory earned a reputation with Dumbarton before Burnley paid £3,000 for his services. He could not gain a regular place in their side and moved to Stoke, where he made 511 appearances. He is possibly the oldest player to be ever-present in a season, when he made a comeback for Stoke in 1934-35.

As a manager, McGrory's loyalty, perseverance, tenacity and judgement were legendary. He took over at Stoke in June 1935 and the Potters finished fourth in the First Division in his first season in charge. He had many disputes with star player, Stanley Matthews, who tried to leave the club on a number of occasions. Stoke just missed the League championship in the last game of the 1946-47 season, when they were pipped by Liverpool. McGrory resigned in May 1952 after 31 years service with the club.

McGUIGAN, James

Born: Glasgow, 1 March 1924; Died: Walton, Chesterfield, 30 March 1988.
Wing-half/Outside-right.
Career: Hamilton Academical; Sunderland June 1947; Stockport County June 1949; Crewe Alexandra August 1950; Rochdale August 1956-1958; Crewe Alexandra trainer 1958, then manager June 1960-November 1964; Grimsby Town manager November 1964-July 1967; Chesterfield manager July 1967-May 1973; Rotherham United manager May 1973-November 1979; Stockport County manager November 1979-April 1982; Sheffield United coach November 1983-1987.

Honours: Division Four champions 1970, promotion 1963, 1975.

Jimmy McGuigan was one of the finest wingers in the Third Division with Stockport and Crewe and was a great favourite with the Gresty Road fans. He made 207 League appearances for Crewe, scoring 32 goals, and also managed both those clubs. McGuigan took Crewe to promotion for the first time in their history in 1963 but they were relegated straight away. At Grimsby he was hindered by the reserve side being scrapped as an economy measure, but managed to keep the club in respectable League positions despite a lack of adequate reserves. Players were later sold without his knowledge and this untenable position led to his resignation. He took Chesterfield into Division Three in 1970 and almost to promotion again the following year. He rounded off his managerial career with two mediocre seasons at Stockport County.

McGUINNESS, Wilfred

Born: Manchester, 25 October 1937.
Left-half   5ft 8in; 11st 10lb (1959).

Career: Mount Carmel School; Manchester & Lancashire Schools; Blackley; Manchester United amateur June 1953, professional November 1954, retired through injury December 1961 to become assistant trainer, brief comeback 1967; England youth trainer 1963-1969; Manchester United manager June 1969-December 1970, then assistant trainer until February 1971; Aris Salonika (Greece) manager-coach July 1971-1973; Panaraiki Patras (Greece) 1973-1974; Everton scout late 1974; York City manager February 1975-October 1977; Hull City coach July 1978-December 1979; Everton scout 1979; Bury coach August 1980, later assistant manager-physiotherapist, caretaker manager March-April 1989, retired July 1991.
Honours: England international (2 caps); Under-23 international (4 caps); Youth international; Schoolboy international (5 caps); Football League representative.

Wilf McGuinness was Sir Matt Busby's choice as his successor at Old Trafford. McGuinness was 31 years old at the time and was sacked after only 18 months in charge. But he had an awesome task to carry on in the shadow of the great man and, even then, with a little more luck the story might have been different. United reached three semi-finals in his time in charge but lost them all. The most humiliating was against Third Division Aston Villa in the 1970-71 League Cup semi-final, shortly after which McGuinness lost his job. He did not appear to know how to handle star players and then lost their respect.

McGuinness had been a thrustful, skilled wing-half with United but did

not break regularly into the side until the death of Duncan Edwards. He made 81 League appearances for United before his career was ended when he suffered a broken leg in a reserve match. He played twice for England, against Northern Ireland and Mexico in 1959. McGuinness is now a popular after-dinner speaker on the northern circuit.

McHALE, Raymond

Born: Sheffield, 12 August 1950.
Midfield   5ft 8in; 12st 6lb (1983).
Career: Chesterfield May 1970; Halifax Town October 1974; Swindon Town September 1976 (£8,000); Brighton & Hove Albion May 1980 (£100,000); Barnsley March 1981 (£60,000); Sheffield United August 1982-1984 (£20,000); Bury (loan) February 1983; Swansea City January 1985; Rochdale August 1986; Scarborough December 1987, player-assistant manager 1988, then manager November 1989. Scarborough manager November 1989-April 1993.

Ray McHale enjoyed a long and varied career in which he made 513/7 League appearances, improving with experience. McHale played for Brighton in the First Division after they paid £100,000 for his services but lost his place after only 11 appearances.

At Swindon, he played in their run to the semi-finals of the League Cup in 1979-80, when they lost to Wolves, 4-3 on aggregate. And he appeared in the last 13 games of the 1980-81 season to help Barnsley to runners-up spot in Division Three. McHale then made 42 appearances for Sheffield United, who clinched promotion by finishing third in Division Three in 1983-84.

McHale struggled with financial problems at Scarborough, who were finding the transition from non-League to League status a difficult one. They had some disastrous results in the FA Cup losing at home to Whitley Bay in November 1989 and Leek Town a year later. However, they did well in the League Cup, reaching the fourth round in 1992-93 before losing to Arsenal.

McHale was replaced by Phil Chambers in April 1993 after Scarborough had an average season in the Third Division.

MACHIN, Melvyn

Born: Newcastle under Lyme 16 April 1945.
Midfield   5ft 10in; 11st 6lb (1973).
Career: Stoke on Trent Schools; Port Vale July 1962; Gillingham July 1966; Bournemouth & Boscombe Athletic December 1970 (£9,000); Norwich City December 1973; Seattle Sounders (NASL) (loan) May-August 1977; Norwich City chief scout 1983; Manchester City manager May 1987-November 1989; Barnsley manager November 1989-May 1993.
Honours: Division Two runners-up 1989; NASL Super Bowl runners-up 1977.

Mel Machin started his career as a striker but later appeared in midfield and at full-back. A cultured player, Machin was appreciated by his fellow professionals. He formed an effective and successful partnership with John Bond and followed him from Bournemouth to Norwich City. Machin helped the Canaries back into the First Division in 1975 and spent 14 years at Carrow Road before taking charge at Manchester City. After promotion in 1989, City struggled in the First Division and Machin was sacked. He gained a reputation at

Barnsley for developing good young players but struggled to find success on the field.

Machin steered Barnsley clear of the relegation zone in 1989-90 and they improved to finish eighth the following season. The departures of Steve Agnew to Blackburn Rovers and Carl Tiler to Nottingham Forest brought much-needed funds to the club but also led to a downturn in form. In May 1993 he surprisingly resigned after Barnsley had finished 13th in the new First Division.

McILROY, James

Born: Lambeg, Northern Ireland, 25 October 1931.
Inside-forward 5ft 9in; 12st 2lb (1963).
Career: Glentoran; Burnley March 1950 (£7,000); Stoke City March 1963; Oldham Athletic (£5,000) player-manager January 1966-August 1968; Stoke City chief coach August 1968; Bolton Wanderers chief coach August-November 1970, then manager November 1970 (for 18 days).
Honours: Northern Ireland international (55 caps); Youth international; Great Britain representative 1955; Football League representative (2 caps); Football League champions 1960; Division Two champions 1963; FA Cup runners-up 1962; Football League Cup runners-up 1964.

Jimmy McIlroy had a superb playing career, scoring 131 goals in 568/6 League appearances. He won League championship and FA Cup runners-up medals with Burnley, where he made over 400 appearances. A marvellously gifted inside-forward with tantalising footwork, McIlroy formed an amazing understanding with Danny Blanchflower in the Northern Ireland side. His 55 caps include 34 in consecutive matches. He also represented Great Britain against the Rest of Europe in August 1955 and played for the Football League against the Italian League in 1961.

Recruited on a five-year contract by Oldham chairman Ken Bates, McIlroy made huge changes to the playing staff. He did not achieve anything spectacular on the pitch but the Latics did win the Lancashire Senior Cup in 1967, for the first time in 60 years. He had a very brief spell at Bolton and resigned after refusing to sell players as directed by the board. He is now a sports journalist with the weekly *Burnley Express*.

McINTOSH, Thomas Herbert

Born: Scotland, 24 February 1879; Died: 29 October 1935.
Right-half.
Career: Darlington 1895, player-secretary July 1902-August 1911, retired as a player in 1908; Middlesbrough manager August 1911-December 1919;
Everton secretary December 1919-October 1935.
Honours: Durham County representative.

Tom McIntosh joined Darlington as a right-half and was offered the secretary's job at Feethams in July 1902. They turned professional in 1908 and had an excellent Cup run in 1910-11, when they started in the first qualifying round and reached the third round proper before losing 9-3 at home to Swindon Town. They had beaten League clubs Sheffield United and Bradford in the previous rounds.

McIntosh became Middlesbrough's secretary on 1 August 1911 after the previous incumbent had been suspended for bribery. 'Boro achieved their highest-ever League position in 1913-14, when they finished third in Division One, but the war brought an end to a successful period when the club closed down.

McIntosh joined the Teesside Pioneers in August 1914 and saw service as a sergeant in France. He guided 'Boro to the Northern Victory League title in 1919, then accepted an offer to join Everton as secretary without team responsibilities and remained there until his death. In March 1925 McIntosh signed 18-year-old 'Dixie' Dean, who went on to become one of the great names in the Toffees' history.

McINTYRE, James Alfred

Born: Walsall, 1881.
Forward 5ft 10in; 11st 4lb (1903).
Career: Witton; Darlaston Town; Wednesbury Old Athletic; Walsall 1901; Notts County 1902; Northampton Town 1903; Reading 1904, retired 1906; Coventry City assistant trainer 1907, then chief trainer 1908-1912; Southampton trainer April 1912-1915, then manager August 1919-December 1924; ran a hotel in Scotland from 1925; Coventry City manager June 1928-February 1931; Fulham manager April 1931-February 1934; worked for Follands (Southampton) company from 1934.
Honours: Division Three South champions 1922, 1932.

Jimmy McIntyre, who had a reputation for being outspoken and effective, was the first manager to take two different clubs to the Third Division South championship. He was an average forward and appeared for several clubs. For Notts County, Northampton Town and Reading he made a total of only 44 first-team appearances but scored 12 goals. After McIntyre retired he worked in the Humber car factory and refereed in the North Warwickshire League for a while.

After a spell on Coventry's training staff, he moved to Southampton as their trainer. The Saints' fortunes gradually improved but after war came, McIntyre returned to Coventry to work in a munitions factory for the duration. In August 1919 he returned to The Dell as manager and the Saints entered the Football League in 1920, narrowly missing promotion in their first season. In 1921-22 they won the Third Division South championship to gain promotion but two years later McIntyre left football to run an hotel in Scotland.

Coventry persuaded him back to became their manager but he achieved little success at Highfield Road before taking over at Fulham. In his first full season the Cottagers clinched the Southern Section title and their leading scorer was Frank Newton with 43 goals. McIntyre had signed him from Stock-

port County at the start of the season. The following season Fulham just missed further promotion but McIntyre turned the board and the fans against him when he sold Newton to Reading for a paltry sum and replaced him with Jack Lambert who cost £2,500 and was a flop at the Cottage.

After a run of poor results, McIntyre was sacked in February 1934. He left football to live in Southampton and work for a local firm.

MACKAY, David Craig

Born: Edinburgh, 14 November 1934.
Left-half 5ft 8in; 11st 6lb (1963).
Career: Slateford Athletic; Newton-range Star; Heart of Midlothian April 1952; Tottenham Hotspur March 1959 (£32,000); Derby County July 1968 (£5,000); Swindon Town player-manager May 1971-November 1972; Nottingham Forest manager November 1972-October 1973; Derby County manager October 1973-November 1976; Walsall manager March 1977-May 1978; Al-Arabi Sporting Club (Kuwait) manager August 1978; Alba Shabab (Dubai) manager 1986; Doncaster Rovers manager December 1987-March 1989; Birmingham City manager April 1989-January 1991; Zamalek (Egypt) coach September 1991.
Honours: Scotland international (22 caps); Under-23 international (4 caps); Schoolboy international; Scottish League representative (3 caps); Football League representative (2 caps); Footballer of the Year 1969 (joint); Scottish League champions 1958; Football League champions 1961, 1975; Second Division champions 1969; Scottish Cup winners 1956; Scottish League Cup winners 1955, 1959; FA Cup winners 1961, 1962, 1967.

One of the great players of his era, Dave Mackay has won just about every honour in the game during his long and distinguished career. A driving force during his playing days, this barrel-chested player was renowned for his scathing tackles, his tough, no-nonsense approach, his inspirational leadership and his all-round ability as a wing-half, for as well as being tough he was a magnificent footballer with lots of skill.

With Hearts, Mackay won every major honour in the Scottish game before Bill Nicholson signed him for Spurs. He became one of Tottenham's greatest-ever players, helping the club to the League and FA Cup double in 1961 and retaining the Cup the following year. He won a third FA Cup winners' medal in 1967, when he skippered the side to victory over Chelsea. Mackay broke his leg twice whilst at White Hart Lane but recovered to full fitness on both occasions, although a stomach injury ruled him out of Spurs' 1963 Cup-winners' Cup success.

When he signed Mackay for only £5,000 in July 1968, Brian Clough described it as 'the best day's work of my life'. Mackay inspired Derby County to the Second Division championship in his first season and was elected joint Footballer of the Year (with Tony Book) in 1969.

His management career began at Swindon Town and he left them for Nottingham Forest after selling Swindon's star player, Don Rogers, to Crystal Palace for £147,000. Mackay had most success at Derby County, where he succeeded Clough and took the side to the League Championship in 1974-75 and an FA Cup semi-final the following year.

He had stepped into a hornet's nest at the Baseball Ground. The players and the fans wanted Clough reinstated and Derby skipper Roy McFarland pleaded with Mackay to turn down Derby's offer. But the Scotsman rose to the challenge, won over both the team and its supporters and Derby marched on. Then came rumours of a lack of discipline in the team. Mackay asked the board for a vote of confidence and when it was not forthcoming, he was sacked. After he left in November 1976, Derby County went steadily downhill.

He took over at Walsall, steering the club clear of relegation and to sixth in the Third Division and the fifth round of the FA Cup the following year. Mackay then received an offer to manage the Al-Arabi Sporting Club in Kuwait and later moved to Dubai to manage Alba Shabab.

In December 1987 he returned to England to take over at Doncaster Rovers and built a successful youth side but resigned in March 1988 when young players were sold over his head. Mackay joined Birmingham City as general manager in April 1989 and had a number of run-ins with the club's owners. He was sacked in January 1991 with impoverished Birmingham struggling in the Third Division.

MACKAY, Donald S.

Born: Partick, 19 March 1940.
Goalkeeper 5ft 10in; 11st 6lb (1973).
Career: Forfar Athletic; Dundee United c.1962; Southend United July 1972, retired 1974; Bristol City coach; Dundee manager 1980-December 1983; Norlesundby (Denmark) coach; Coventry City assistant manager, then manager December 1984-April 1986; Glasgow Rangers caretaker manager April 1986, then youth and reserve-team manager; Blackburn Rovers manager February 1987-September 1991; Fulham manager January 1992.

Honours: Scottish League Division One promotion 1981; Scottish League

Cup runners-up 1981; Full Members' Cup winners 1987.

Donald Mackay is a quietly-spoken Scotsman who is a much-respected figure in the game. He started his managerial career at Dundee and had a very successful season in 1980-81, taking the club to promotion to the Premier League and to a League Cup Final with local rivals, Dundee United, who won 3-0 at Dens Park.

Dundee struggled to beat the drop before Mackay moved to Coventry City as assistant manager to Bobby Gould. When Gould left, Mackay took over with Frank Upton as his assistant but Coventry struggled to stay in the First Division. He was briefly caretaker boss at Rangers whilst Graeme Souness ended his commitments with Sampdoria before taking over as manager at Ibrox. Mackay took Blackburn to three successive Second Division play-offs but on each occasion they failed to win through. He made some audacious signings at Ewood Park including on-loan players Steve Archibald and Ossie Ardiles.

Mackay was very unfortunate to be sacked after just three games of the 1991-92 season by Rovers' new owner, Jack Walker. Walker clearly wanted a big name in charge of the club and later appointed Kenny Dalglish as the manager. Mackay took over at Fulham at the beginning of 1992 and results greatly improved. They eventually just missed the play-offs after a good finish to the season.

Most of the interesting things were happening off the pitch at Fulham in 1992-93. A ten-year lease on Craven Cottage ground with an option to buy was worked out in March 1993 much to the delight of the fans. Mackay said that a winning team was more important than keeping an historic ground, which was out of step with most supporters wishes for the club.

McKENNA, John

Born: Ireland c.1850; Died: 23 March 1932 (age 82).

Career: Liverpool secretary 1892-August 1896, chairman 1909-1914 and 1917-1919; Football League management committee 1902, vice-president 1908, president 1910; Football Association vice-president.

Honours: Division Two champions 1894, 1896; Lancashire League champions 1893.

John McKenna is one of the most famous names in the early history of the Football League as well as Liverpool Football Club. A deep-thinking man with sound judgement, McKenna was one of the game's great personalities in the early years of football.

Strictly speaking, McKenna should

not be included here because he was secretary of Liverpool, not the manager. However, he performed many functions of the manager's job. A self-made man, McKenna was born in Ireland and came to Liverpool from Ulster as a nine-year-old.

He later became a successful businessman and was invited to join the Liverpool committee by John Houlding. When Houlding stepped down, McKenna became the power at Anfield and saw the club into the Football League after they had won the Lancashire League championship in 1892-93. He had a liking for Scottish players and brought many to the club. Indeed, there were so many that Liverpool became known as 'the team of Macs'.

The Reds won the Second Division championship in 1893-94 and were unbeaten all season with a 100 per cent home record before beating Newton Heath 2-0 in the Test Match to enter the First Division. The following season Liverpool were relegated after finishing 16th and losing the Test Match to Bury, 1-0. However, they bounced straight back as Second Division champions again, dropping only one point at Anfield. They won their series of Test Matches and again moved up.

McKenna stepped down at this point. He had been the main influence at the club, despite the official secretary-manager being W.E.Barclay, and he made a great move in bringing Tom Watson from Sunderland to manage the club. McKenna was chairman of Liverpool between 1909 and 1914 and 1917 to 1919 and was also connected with the Football League administration for 34 years.

Elected to the League Management Committee in 1902, he became a vice-president in 1908 and president in 1910, remaining in that post until his death 22 years later at the age of 82. He was also a vice-president of the Football Association. A shrewd, assertive and outspoken member of the League Management Committee, McKenna could be gruff and could also bluff. He was severe on colleagues who did not pull their weight. He was feared, yet admired and his bark was usually worse than his bite.

McKENNA, Thomas

Born: Stewarton, Ayrshire, 27 September 1900.
Goalkeeper   5ft 10½in; 11st 4lb (1926).
Career: Arteer Thistle; Glasgow Celtic Reserves; Dalry Thistle; Fulham March 1925; South Shields August 1926; Charlton Athletic cs 1927; Merthyr Town cs 1928, player-manager November 1928-May 1929; Southend United June 1929; Portadown cs 1930.

Honours: Scotland Junior international; Ayrshire Cup winners.

Tom McKenna worked on the Clyde as an apprentice boilermaker as a youngster. He made 102 League appearances in his five-year career. He was reserve to Ernie Beecham at Craven Cottage and lost his place at The Valley when Albert Lindon was appointed player-manager. McKenna was a surprise choice as player-manager of Merthyr Town. He lasted for only six months in charge and Merthyr finished 20th in the Southern Section, conceding 103 goals including an 8-0 thrashing by Queen's Park Rangers. A season after he left the club they lost their League status.

MACKIE, Alex

Born: Auchterless, Banffshire, 1870.

Career: Aberdeen; Victoria United; The Heatherley; Inverness Thistle; Glasgow Association; Sunderland manger cs 1899-June 1905; Middlesbrough manager June 1905-November 1906; publican in Middlesbrough from June 1906.

Honours: Football League champions 1902.

Alex Mackie was involved in two illegal payments scandals and allegations of failing to keep proper books at both Sunderland and Middlesbrough. He was suspended at both clubs.

An administrator who never played professional football, Mackie was associated with several Scottish clubs before becoming Sunderland's manager in the summer of 1899. In 1901-02, Sunderland won the League championship with consistent but unspectacular football and a defence which conceded only 35 goals. The following season they were third, a point behind Sheffield Wednesday.

The FA investigated the club's books after a player called Andy McCombie claimed that Sunderland had made him a gift of £100 to start a business. The club said it had been a loan but when the books were examined, irregularities were found. Mackie was banned for three months. When he returned he sold Alf Common to Middlesbrough for £1,000, the first four-figure transfer fee in football history. Shortly afterwards, Mackie followed Common to Ayresome Park when he obtained the post of 'Boro's manager from 70 applicants.

It was Mackie's swoop into the transfer market which saved Middlesbrough from relegation. He signed the legendary Steve Bloomer and fellow international Billy Brawn in March 1906. But again accusations began to fly and again the FA looked into the matter. Illegal payments had been paid and yet again the books had not been kept properly. Mackie was suspended for a second time. Disillusioned with football, he left the game to run a pub in Middlesbrough.

McKINNON, Angus

Born: Paisley, 6 December 1885; Died: May 1968.
Left-half   5ft 8in; 11st 10lb (1923).
Career: Hearts trialist; Petershill (Glasgow); Woolwich Arsenal May 1908; Charlton Athletic July 1922-1924; Wigan Borough trainer 1925, then manager May 1926-January 1930; Connah's Quay manager cs 1930; New Brighton trainer-coach August 1931-1939; Rhyl Athletic trainer post-war.

A strongly-built half-back, McKinnon served Arsenal for 14 years, making 217 League and Cup appearances. He made

his debut in December 1908 but was unable to gain a regular place until the 1911-12 season. He moved with the club from Plumstead to Highbury and during World War One was a driver with the Royal Field Artillery in France.

His best season was the first full season after the war when he missed only one game for the Gunners. His best season in charge of Wigan Borough was 1927-28, when they finished fourth and scored 82 goals. He endured many years of struggle at New Brighton.

MACKRILL, Percy A.

Born: Wyneburg, South Africa, 19 October c.1894.
Full-back   5ft 8in; 12st 4lb (1919).
Career: Bradford cs 1913; Rotherham County 1915-1919; Coventry City cs 1919; Halifax Town 1919; Pontypridd cs 1923; Torquay United 1925, player-manager 1927-March 1929.

Honours: Southern League champions 1927.

Mackrill played only two games for Coventry City and 57 for Halifax Town in League soccer. He helped Torquay to the Southern League title in 1926-27, on goal average from Bristol City Reserves. United were voted into the Football League in the summer of 1927, in place of Aberdare Athletic and Mackrill was appointed player-manager soon afterwards. They finished bottom of the Southern Section in 1927-28, with only 30 points and conceding 103 goals on the way. They improved the following season to finish 18th.

McLEAN, Angus

Born: Queensferry, 20 September 1925; Died: 1979.
Centre-half.
Career: Aberystwyth Town; Hilton Main; Wolverhampton Wanderers amateur 1939, professional November 1942-May 1951; Aberystwyth Town player-manager 1951; Bromsgrove Rovers; Bury player-coach May 1953; Crewe Alexandra June 1954; Hartlepool United manager May 1967-April 1970; Bromsgrove Rovers manager 1973-1975; scout after 1975.

Honours: Division Four promotion 1968.

A solidly built centre-half, Gus McLean had legs like tree trunks. He made 144 post-war League appearances for Wolves, helping them to third place in Division One in 1946-47, fifth in 1947-48 and sixth 1948-49. He was not selected to play in the 1949 FA Cup Final, when Wolves beat Leicester. He lost his regular place during that season.

After years of coaching at League and non-League level, he was selected to take over from Brian Clough as manager at Hartlepool. McLean took advantage of the foundations left by Clough and steered the club to their first-ever promotion in 1967-68, when they finished third in Division Four. However, United were relegated the following season and he was sacked when they had to seek re-election in 1969-70.

McLEAN, David

Born: Forfar, 13 December 1887.
Centre-forward 5ft 8in; 11st 12lb (1914).
Career: Forfar Athletic; Glasgow Celtic; Preston North End 1909; Sheffield Wednesday February 1911 (£1,000); guest for Rangers and Third Lanark in World War One; Bradford October 1919 (£2,000); Forfar Athletic; Dundee cs 1922; Forfar Athletic; East Fife secretary-manager until May 1929; Bristol Rovers manager May 1929-October 1930.

Honours: Scotland international (1 cap); Scottish Cup runners-up 1925.

A prolific scorer, McLean scored almost 500 goals in his playing career which included three spells with Forfar Athletic. The peak of his career was reached during his time at Hillsborough. He set a club record in 1912-13, when he scored 30 League goals plus eight in the FA Cup. In the summer of 1913, he could not agree terms and had a spell in Scottish junior football. A brilliant player on his day, McLean twice scored four goals in a game for the Owls.

He played for Scotland against England in 1913 and scored 100 goals in 147 appearances for Wednesday before moving to Bradford. He also appeared in the 1925 Scottish Cup Final for Dundee against Celtic, scoring Dundee's goal in a 2-1 defeat. He had little success as manager of Bristol Rovers. His brother, George, played for Bradford and Huddersfield Town.

McLENNAN, Daniel

Career: Glasgow Rangers; Stirling Albion (loan); East Fife; Dundee; Berwick Rangers player-manager 1957; Oldham Athletic manager May-June 1960; Stirling Albion manager June 1960-1964; Worcester City manager in 1960s; Iran national coach 1973; coaching in Bahrain 1974; Iraq director of coaching 1975-1977; Jordan director of coaching 1977; Phillipines national coach; Zimbabwe national coach for five years; coaching in Iran; Mauritius; FA coach in 1980s.

Honours: Scottish League Division Two champions 1961.

A qualified FA Coach, Danny McLennan could also have made a career as a professional golfer. As a manager, he kept Berwick Rangers going despite poor attendances and spent only one month in charge at Boundary Park before resigning after receiving a better offer from Stirling Albion. McLennan took Albion to the Second Division title in 1960-61 and to the quarter-finals of the Scottish Cup in 1962. However, they were relegated that season and he left when they hit the bottom of the Second Division in 1963-64. After a brief spell in charge of Worcester City, McLennan coached all over the World including Iraq and Iran.

McLINTOCK, Francis MBE

Born: Gorbals, Glasgow, 28 December 1939.
Right-half 5ft 10in; 11st 4lb (1963).
Career: Shawfield Juniors 1955; Leicester City December 1956; Arsenal October 1964 (£80,000); Queen's Park Rangers April 1973 (£25,000), retired May 1977; Leicester City manager June

1977-April 1978; Football radio commentator; Queen's Park Rangers coach December 1982-February 1984; Brentford manager February 1984-January 1987; Millwall assistant manager 1988-February 1990; Worked in broadcasting and newspapers.

Honours: Scotland international (9 caps); Under-23 international (1 cap); Football League champions 1971; FA Cup winners 1971, runners-up 1961, 1963, 1972; Football League Cup runners-up 1968, 1969; Inter-Cities Fairs Cup winners 1970.

Frank McLintock had a superb playing career in which he made 609 League appearances. Resolute, very skilled and a natural leader, he led Arsenal to the double in 1971, although he had played in four Wembley Cup Finals before gaining a winners' medal that year. These were two losing FA Cup Finals for Leicester in 1961 and 1963 and two losing League Cup Finals for Arsenal. Originally a wing-half, he converted very successfully into a central defender in 1969. McLintock won a Fairs Cup winners' medal in 1970, when Arsenal beat Anderlecht in an exciting Final. He also helped QPR to runners-up position in Division One in 1975-76.

Inexperience proved his undoing as manager at Filbert Street. He made some poor signings, including Roger Davies who proved a big disappointment after costing £250,000. Leicester were relegated in 1977-78, scoring only 26 goals on the way, and this led to the sack for McLintock. He was very articulate when talking about the game but never seemed able to motivate his sides to any great degree. He had little success at Griffin Park.

McMENEMY, Christopher

Born: Gateshead, 1 August 1961
Midfield 6ft 1in; 12st 7lb (1978).
Career: Southampton apprentice June 1977, professional June 1979-November 1979 when his contract was cancelled due to injury; Salisbury 1981; Romsey Town; Sunderland coach 1985-1989; Chesterfield assistant manager and coach 1989, then manager April 1991-February 1993. Chesterfield manager April 1991-February 1993.

Chris McMenemey played under his father, Lawrie, at Southampton but his career was blighted by injury. After nearly two years out of the game, he turned out for Salisbury in the Southern League and Romsey Town in the Hampshire League. He also coached many junior and non-League sides.

After passing his advanced coaching

badge in 1986, he joined his father at Sunderland as coach when Lawrie became manager at Roker Park. Chris remained at the club after the departure of his father and Sunderland took the Third Division title in 1987-88.

He was assistant manager to Paul Hart at Chesterfield and took over from him in April 1991, making him the youngest manager in the Football League at 29 years old. Chesterfield had reached the Fourth Division play-offs in 1990. In February 1993, Chris McMenemy was sacked, despite the Derbyshire club holding Premier League giants Liverpool to a 4-4 draw at Anfield in the Coca-Cola Cup earlier in the season.

McMENEMY, Laurence 'Lawrie'

Born: Gateshead, 1936.
Centre-half.
Career: Newcastle United juniors; Gateshead player (retired due to injury in 1961), then caretaker manager and trainer-coach; Bishop Auckland manager; Sheffield Wednesday coach; Doncaster Rovers manager December 1968-May 1971; Grimsby Town manager May 1971-July 1973; Southampton assistant manager July 1973, then manager December 1973-June 1985; Sunderland manager June 1985-April 1987; England assistant manager July 1990.

Honours: Division Two runners-up 1978; Division Four champions 1969, 1972; FA Cup winners 1976; Football League Cup runners-up 1979.

Lawrie McMenemy rocketed to fame as the manager of Southampton. He turned one of the provincial clubs into a force to be reckoned with and his

strong personality and ability to communicate with players and fans has made him admired by many. He is a strong disciplinarian, a legacy of his days in the Guards, and behind a warm veneer there is a man ready to make difficult decisions.

McMenemy failed to make the grade at Newcastle United and joined his local club, Gateshead, in the late 1950s. An injury ended his career in 1961 but he became trainer-coach at the club for the next three years. In 1964 he became manager of Bishop Auckland and transformed them from a struggling side into Northern League champions and also took them to the third round of the FA Cup.

McMenemy spent two years as coach at Sheffield Wednesday under manager Alan Brown, then got his first break when he became manager of Doncaster Rovers. After his appointment they lost only two games up until the end of the season and finished as Fourth Division champions after a run of 21 games without defeat. Doncaster struggled in the higher division and when they were relegated, McMenemy was sacked in May 1971.

He was out of work for about a week when he was offered the manager's post at Grimsby Town. McMenemy quickly transformed the side here as well, and the Mariners became Fourth Division champions at the end of his first season in charge.

In July 1973, McMenemy accepted an offer to become assistant manager under Ted Bates at The Dell. Bates planned to groom McMenemy as his successor and he became Southampton's manager in December 1973, although the Saints were relegated at the end of the season. McMenemy came in for a lot of criticism when they did not go straight back up but he did take the Saints to a shock FA Cup Final victory over Manchester United in 1976.

McMenemy advocated that the club should be part of the community and that players should attend all club functions. He had once assembled a surprised Grimsby squad at the crack of dawn on a fish pontoon as he felt that the players should know how supporters earned their money and he wanted to show his team how lucky they were to make a living from football.

One of McMenemy's trademarks was to revitalise senior players' careers. These included Mel Blyth, Jim McCalliog, Peter Rodrigues and Kevin Keegan. It was a great coup getting Keegan, who was still at his peak, to join Southampton. In 1977-78 the Saints won promotion to the First Division and a year later reached the League Cup Final, where they lost 3-2 to Nottingham Forest. The Saints lost to Everton in the 1984 FA Cup semi-final, to a last-gasp effort.

The disappointment made McMenemy restless, although Southampton enjoyed their best-ever season in the First Division in 1983-84, when they finished runners-up.

In June 1985, McMenemy moved to Sunderland but had a tough time at Roker Park. He was earning very good money but could not deliver success. The problems at the club were probably too deep-rooted for McMenemy to do anything about and he was sacked in April 1987 with Sunderland sliding towards the Third Division. McMenemy and the club received a lot of adverse publicity over how much he was being paid. The fans, sick of the club's lack of success, vented their feelings on the easy target, the manager.

After three years out of the game, McMenemy returned as assistant manager to England boss Graham Taylor.

McMILLAN, John Stuart

Born: Port Glasgow, 16 February 1871; Died: Derby, 4 November 1941.
Inside-left   5ft 6in; 11st 10lb (1907).
Career: Port Glasgow Athletic; St Bernards cs 1890; Derby County December 1890; Leicester Fosse May 1896; Small Heath January 1901; Bradford City May 1903; Glossop May 1906, then trainer to 1908; Birmingham trainer August 1909; Gillingham manager July 1920-August 1922; then Derby licensee.

Johnny McMillan was an agile player with excellent command of the ball, was very fast and possessed a superb shot. He left St Bernards after only one game, following a row over professionalism. McMillan scored 50 goals in 126 games for Derby, where he added class to the attack. In January 1891, he scored five goals in a 9-0 win over Wolves at the Rams' old home, the County Ground. At Leicester Fosse, he developed a great creative flair as well as scoring goals.

McMillan helped Small Heath to two runners-up spots in Division Two, in 1901 and 1903, and was captain of Bradford City when they entered the Football League. He was offered £7 a week plus bonuses when he took charge at Gillingham. McMillan created a family atmosphere at the club and all the players and staff mixed together, although Gillingham ran up huge debts whilst he was in charge.

McMILLAN, Stuart Thomas

Born: Leicester, 17 September 1896; Died: Ashbourne, Derbyshire, 27 September 1963.
Outside-right   5ft 7½in; 11st (1923).
Career: Derby County December 1914; Chelsea cs 1919; Gillingham March 1921; Wolves June 1922; Bradford City May 1924; Nottingham Forest June 1927; Clapton Orient August 1928; Derby County advisor 1942, then manager January 1946-November 1953; Derby licensee; also cricket for Derbyshire.

Honours: FA Cup winners 1946.

Stuart McMillan played only once for Derby County, in their Second Division championship season of 1914-15, but he has a great claim to fame as the only manager to take Derby to an FA Cup Final victory, when they beat Charlton Athletic in the first Final after World War Two.

He was born in Leicester, the son of Johnny McMillan who played for Leicester Fosse and Derby County and managed Gillingham from 1920 to 1922. Stuart McMillan moved around as an honest run-of-the-mill professional. He joined the Rams in December 1914 but his career was soon interrupted by the war and he played only one game in the first team, standing in for regular Billy Grimes in January 1915. After the war, McMillan signed for Chelsea in the summer of 1919 but never played for their first team.

He joined his father at Gillingham, where he played in 30 League games before leaving for Wolves just before his father lost his job as manager of the Gills. At Molineux, McMillan scored his first League goal in 22 games for the club before yet another move to Bradford City, after a disastrous season which saw Wolves relegated to the Third Division for the first time in their history.

At Valley Parade he scored seven goals in 73 appearances but left the club after relegation to the Third Division in 1926-27. That summer, McMillan moved to Nottingham Forest but was unable to find a regular place in their side and, after only seven League games for Forest, moved to Clapton Orient. He ended his playing days in 1930, after 24 games for Orient. He had also played four first-class cricket matches for Derbyshire in the early 1920s.

McMillan was out of football for some time and took over the Nag's Head pub at Mickleover on the outskirts of Derby, scouting for the Rams in his spare time. In 1942, Derby County started up again in wartime football and McMillan was appointed advisor to the club. When manager Ted Magner left in January 1946, McMillan inherited a team destined to reach the FA Cup Final. On a humid spring day at Wembley, the Rams beat Charlton Athletic 4-1 after extra-time in an entertaining Final in which Jack Stamps, a brave centre-forward, scored twice.

After this McMillan entered the transfer market and twice broke the British record, paying £15,000 for Billy Steel from Morton and £24,500 for Johnny Morris from Manchester United.

Derby finished fourth in Division One 1947-48 — and also reached the FA Cup semi-final, and third the following season. His trainer was Jack Poole, who had played alongside him at Bradford City.

But the Derby side was breaking up. Peter Doherty had left soon after the Cup Final, after falling out with the directors. Raich Carter, now in the veteran stage, was allowed to leave for Hull City in 1948. And a number of other players, including the brilliant centre-half Leon Leuty, left when resentment grew in the dressing-room.

The signing of Billy Steel had worked against McMillan as other players became annoyed at the Scotsman's attitude — saving himself for internationals or big games in London — and the fact that he had several 'jobs' to supplement his income in the days of the maximum wage for footballers.

Ageing stars were not replaced by players of the same calibre and although some talented local youngsters were coming through, Derby's directors adopted a 'make-do-and-mend' policy. Derby were relegated in 1953 and then struggled near the foot of the Second Division. In November that year, McMillan left to run the Station Hotel in Ashbourne, where he died ten years later. His funeral was attended by many former stars including Raich Carter.

McMULLAN, James

Born: Denny, Stirlingshire, 26 March 1895; Died: Sheffield, 28 November 1964.
Left-half   5ft 5in; 11st (1926).
Career: Denny Hibernian; Third Lanark; Partick Thistle November 1913; Maidstone United player-manager cs 1921; Partick Thistle cs 1923; Manchester City February 1926 (£4,700), retired May 1933; Oldham Athletic manager May 1933-May 1934; Aston Villa manager May 1934-October 1936; Notts County manager November 1936-December 1937; Sheffield Wednesday manager December 1937-April 1942.

Honours: Scotland international (16 caps); Victory international (4 caps); Scottish League representative (4 caps); Division Two champions 1928; FA Cup runners-up 1926, 1933.

Jimmy McMullan was a small, intelligent half-back who played an excellent close-passing game and was also a great captain for both club and country. He missed the Jags' Scottish Cup Final appearance in 1921 through injury but they turned down a £5,000 offer from Newcastle for his transfer.

But McMullan was desperate to move south and joined non-League Maidstone United as player-manager. Manchester City paid a large fee for him and he made 242 appearances for the Maine Road club, gaining two FA Cup losers' medals, in 1926 and 1933, and a Second Division championship medal in 1928. He captained the 'Wembley Wizards' who beat England 5-1 in 1928.

McMullan took Oldham to a commendable ninth position in 1933-34 and they also reached the Lancashire Senior Cup Final that season before losing to Bolton. Villa were relegated in 1935-36, despite spending £35,000 on new players. He later dragged Sheffield Wednesday clear of relegation to Division Three but they missed out on promotion back to Divsion One in the last game of the 1938-39 season. His contract was not renewed in 1942.

McNALLY, Harold

Career: Skelmersdale United player and coach; Altrincham manager; Southport manager until September 1979; Wigan Athletic assistant manager and chief scout, then manager July 1983-March 1985; Chester manager June 1985-October 1992.

Honours: Division Four runners-up 1986.

Harry McNally never appeared in the Football League and spent most of his playing career with Skelmersdale, where he was also a coach in his latter days there. He was manager at non-League Altrincham and Southport before joining Wigan Athletic. They struggled against relegation in his two seasons in charge but he took Chester to runners-up spot in Division Four in 1985-86 and to eighth in Division Three in 1988-89.

In 1990, Chester lost their Sealand Road ground, sold to pay off massive debts. Attendances dropped off alarmingly but he managed to keep Chester in the Third Division despite this and was awarded a four-year contract. He had to sell high-scoring forward Stuart Rimmer to Watford for a large fee in 1988 but found many useful players in non-League soccer. Chester had a constant struggle to avoid relgation from the Third Division and McNally was sacked after a poor start to the 1992-93 season. They had just returned to Chester to play at their new Deva Stadium after two seasons playing at Macclesfield's Moss Rose ground.

McNAMEE, John

Born: Coatbridge, Glasgow, 24 February 1932.
Centre-half   6ft; 13st 6lb (1971).
Career: Bellshill Athletic; Glasgow Celtic 1959; Hibernian June 1964; Newcastle United December 1966 (£26,000); Blackburn Rovers November 1971 (£15,000); Morton 1973; Hartlepool United (loan) December 1973; Lancaster City; Workington player-manager June-December 1975.

Honours: Scotland Schoolboy international.

A tall, strong centre-half, McNamee was unable to break into the Celtic side and moved to Hibs. He attracted the scouts whilst with the Edinburgh club

and was signed by Newcastle United. He was popular with the crowd, but not with opponents as he gained a reputation for rough play. He made 129 appearances for Newcastle, after making his debut against Spurs in December 1966, and 57 for Blackburn Rovers.

McNamee played two games for Workington as a non-contract player whilst manager of the club. He was replaced by Alan Ashman and they finished bottom of the Football League at the end of the 1975-76 season with crowds barely above 1,000.

McNEILL, Ian McKeand

Born: Baillieston, Glasgow, 24 February 1932.
Inside-forward   5ft 8in; 10st 8lb (1963).
Career: Bridgetown Waverley; Aberdeen 1950; Leicester City March 1956; Brighton & Hove Albion March 1959; Southend United July 1962 (£3,000); Ross County manager in mid-1960s; Wigan Athletic manager May 1968-January 1970; Northwich Victoria manager in 1970s; Wigan Athletic manager May 1976-February 1981; Chelsea assistant manager 1981-1987; Shrewsbury Town manager December 1987-January 1990; Millwall assistant manager 1991.

Honours: Division Two champions 1957.

Ian McNeill soon made an impact at Filbert Street after being signed by his former manager at Aberdeen, David Halliday. He scored 18 goals in Leicester's Second Division championship season of 1956-57 but found it more difficult to gain a regular place in the higher division, although he netted the goal which kept Leicester in the First Division in 1958. McNeill made over 100 appearances for Brighton but did not score so regularly as he had done at Filbert Street.

He had two spells in charge at non-League Wigan Athletic. They finished runners-up in the Northern Premier League in 1969-70 and 1977-78 before being elected to the Football League in place of Southport and finishing sixth in their first season. McNeill had six years as assistant manager of Chelsea. McNeill did not have much success as manager of Shrewsbury Town who were relegated to Division Three in 1989 and, he was sacked when they struggled the following season.

McNEIL, John Law

Born: Inverkeithing, Scotland.
Centre-half   5ft 11in; 12st 12lb (1935).
Career: Musselburgh Brutonians; Portsmouth December 1928; Reading January 1930; Guildford City; Inverness Caledonians; Plymouth Argyle August 1934; Clapton Orient cs 1939; Torquay United manager June 1947-March 1950; Bury manager March 1950-November 1953.

McNeil was a regular at Home Park, where he made 143 appearances, scoring 13 goals. He was also a regular at Elm Park and had three good seasons as manager of Torquay United. He took them to fifth in the Southern Section in 1949-50 and then left for a bigger salary at Second Division Bury.

McNeil took over at Gigg Lane four months after the departure of Norman Bullock. Bury avoided relegation only in the last game of 1950-51, despite spending large amounts on players including £13,000 for Jimmy Greenhalgh. McNeil resigned with the club still struggling in the Second Division.

McNEIL, Richard 'Dixie'

Born: Melton Mowbray, 16 Janaury 1947.
Strikcr   5ft 10in; 11st 12lb (1971).
Career: Holwell Works; Leicester City November 1964; Exeter City June 1966; Corby Town; Northampton Town May 1969; Lincoln City January 1972 (£8,000); Hereford United August 1974 (£20,000); Wrexham September 1977 (£60,000); Hereford United October 1982, retired January 1983; Wrexham manager April 1985-October 1989; Coventry City coach January 1990.

Honours: Division Three champions 1976, 1978.

A much-travelled, bustling goalscorer, Dixie McNeil dropped down to the Southern League with Corby Town in the mid-1960s, but Northampton Town saw his potential and he responded with plenty of goals. Indeed, McNeil scored 277 goals in 594/4 League and Cup games in his career and won two Third Division championship medals, with Hereford United in 1975-76, when he scored 34 goals, and with Wrexham in 1977-78. He scored 11 goals in Wrexham's excellent run in the FA Cup in 1978, when they lost 3-2 to Arsenal at The Racecourse in the quarter-finals.

His best season in charge at Wrexham was 1988-89, when they finished fourth and entered the Fourth Division play-offs. They lost 2-1 on aggregate to Leyton Orient in the Final and McNeil was sacked as they slumped the following season.

McNEILL, William MBE

Born: Bellshill, Lanarkshire, 2 March 1940.
Centre-half   6ft 1in; 13st 2lb (1963).

Career: Blantyre Victoria; Glasgow Celtic August 1957 (£250), retired May 1975; Clyde manager April-June 1977; Aberdeen manager June 1977-May 1978; Glasgow Celtic manager May 1978-June 1983; Manchester City manager June 1983-September 1986; Aston Villa manager September 1986-May 1987; Glasgow Celtic manager May 1987-May 1991.

Honours: Scotland international (29 caps); Under-23 international (5 caps); Scottish League representative (9 caps); Scottish League Division One champions 1966 to 1974 inclusive; Premier League champions 1979, 1981, 1982, 1988; Football League Division Two promotion 1985; Scottish Cup winners 1965, 1967, 1969, 1971 1972, 1974, 1975, 1980, 1988, 1989, runners-up 1961, 1963, 1966, 1970, 1973, 1978, 1990; Scottish League Cup winners 1966 to 1970

inclusive, 1974, 1975, 1983, runners-up 1971, 1973; European Cup winners 1967, runners-up 1970; Full Members' Cup runners-up 1986.

Billy McNeill could do no wrong in Scottish soccer as his honours list shows, but he had little success when managing in the Football League. A commanding centre-half, McNeill was a born leader. He made a traumatic debut for Scotland in the 9-3 defeat against England in 1961 but played in 831 games for Celtic which included their 1967 European Cup success. McNeill won League title medals nine seasons on the trot for Celtic.

Whilst at Aberdeen he signed Gordon Strachan and Steve Archibald and also had two excellent spells with Celtic before the talent dried up and the club struggled. He lost his job after a poor season in 1990-91. McNeill took Manchester City to promotion to Division One in 1985 and to a Full Members' Cup Final appearance at Wembley, where they lost 5-4 to Chelsea. He had a terrible season at Villa Park and they were relegated to Division Two as the bottom club. After his sacking he moved back to Celtic Park.

McPHEE, George Magnus 'Tony'

Born: Edinburgh, 30 April 1914; Died: 1960.
Centre-forward   6ft; 12st 3lb (1938).
Career: Belfast Celtic; Workington; Bradford October 1936; Coventry City June 1937; Reading May 1938 (£2,750), retired cs 1949 and joined administrative staff; Walsall manager July-December 1951.

Tony McPhee was an instant hit when he joined Second Division Bradford from non-League Workington at the age of 22. He scored 17 goals in 30 League appearances in 1936-37 before being transferred to Coventry City. He had difficulties breaking into the City side but scored six goals in only 12 League games, including a hat-trick in a 4-3 victory at Fulham.

Reading saw his potential and paid a large fee for his services. A prolific goalscorer, McPhee netted 217 in 226 wartime games for the club and also 63 goals in 90 peacetime League games. His best season was 1940-41, when he poached 45 goals in 30 games. He helped Reading to runners-up spot in the Southern Section in 1948-49, then retired.

He had a very brief period in charge of Walsall. They had a terrible start to the 1951-52 season and also lost 1-0 to his former club, Reading, in the first round of the FA Cup. McPhee left Fellows Park soon afterwards. He was awarded a benefit match by Reading, against Arsenal, which attracted a crowd of 15,996.

McQUEEN, Matthew

Born: Harthill, Lancashire, 18 May 1863; Died: 29 September 1944.
Right-half.
Career: Leith Athletic; Heart of Midlothian 1887; Leith Athletic 1889; Liverpool October 1892-1899; Football League linesman in 1904; Liverpool director in World War One and manager February 1923-February 1928.

Honours: Scotland international (2 caps); Football League champions 1923; Division Two champions 1894, 1896.

Matt McQueen was a utility player with Liverpool and although his main position was right-half, he played in goal for half the 1895-96 season when they won the League championship.

McQueen lost his regular first-team spot after this season. His two Scottish caps came in March 1890, in a 5-0 win over Wales, and a year later, also against Wales, when the Scots won 4-3. He made 87 appearances for Liverpool.

McQueen had a short spell as a League linesman after retiring from playing. He took Liverpool to their second successive League title in 1923-24 but lost a leg in a road accident that year. McQueen was astute in the transfer market and his signings included the prolific South African goalscorer Gordon Hodgson. He retired in 1928, due to continued illness. His brother, Hugh, played for Liverpool and Derby County.

McROBERTS, Robert

Born: Coatbridge, July 1874; Died: Birkenhead, 27 February 1959.
Centre-half/Forward   5ft 9in; 12st (1904).
Career: Coatbridge 1892; Airdrieonions; Albion Rovers; Gainsborough Trinity August 1896; Small Heath August 1898 (£150); Chelsea August 1905-May 1909 (£100); Birmingham manager July 1910-May 1915.

Honours: Division Two champions 1901.

Birmingham's first full-time manager, Bobby McRoberts had been a great favourite with the crowd when he played for the club. He had sound positional sense and was a fine header of the ball. McRoberts played in Chelsea's first-ever League match and was captain of the club from 1907, making 114 appearances for them overall. He was equally at home at centre-half or centre-forward, where he used his cannon-like shot to good effect. When he became manager at St Andrew's, McRoberts engaged former England and Villa player Billy George as his assistant. Things gradually improved on the field and they finished third in 1912-13 and fifth two seasons later.

McSEVENEY, John Haddon

Born: Shotts, Lanarkshire, 8 February 1931.
Forward   5ft 8in; 10st 4lb (1963).
Career: Carluke Rovers; Hamilton Academical 1948; Sunderland October 1951 (£5,000); Cardiff City May 1955; Newport County July 1957; Hull City July 1961 (£1,000), retired as a player June 1965, coach June 1965; Barnsley manager September 1971-November 1972; Home Farm (Dublin) coach February-December 1973; Nottingham Forest chief coach and assistant manager December 1973-January 1975; Waterford manager late 1975-December 1977; Guyana national coach 1978; Oman Sports Club (United Arab Emirates) 1979; Rotherham United coach 1980; Sheffield United assistant manager and coach 1984-1987.

Honours: Welsh Cup winners 1956.

John McSeveney was never a regular at Roker Park and on moving to Cardiff City scored twice against his former club — and on his debut, too. He scored the winning goal in the 1956 Welsh Cup Final, when the Bluebirds beat Swansea Town 3-2, and altogether netted 18 goals in 75 games for Cardiff before moving to Newport County, where he scored a further 51 in 172 games. Many thought he was past his best when he signed for Hull but McSeveney scored over 20 goals in 1962-63 and 60 in his 161 appearances for the Tigers.

A firm believer in a good youth policy, McSeveney had an unhappy time in charge at Oakwell, where he

was eventually sacked after a string of poor results. Chief coach at Forest under Allan Brown, he left after the arrival of Brian Clough. McSeveney took Guyana to their first win in 29 years when they beat Surinam 2-0. He was assistant manager to Ian Porterfield at both Rotherham United and Sheffield United.

McSHANE, Anthony

Born: Belfast, 28 February 1927.
Wing-half   5ft 8in; 11st 4lb (1951).
Career: Belfast Celtic; Brantwood; Plymouth Argyle December 1948; Swindon Town June 1955; Goole Town manager 1957-1958; Scunthorpe United manager cs 1958-April 1959; Chesterfield manager May 1962-May 1967.

Honours: Division Three South champions 1952; Division Three North champions 1958.

Tony McShane started his career in Irish soccer before moving to England to join Plymouth Argyle. An attacking half-back, McShane was a good passer but often let himself down when defending. Never a regular at Home Park, where he made 91 appearances, he played a further 41 times for Swindon Town. He once scored a hat-trick of penalties for Plymouth Reserves.

McShane resigned at the end of his one season in charge at Scunthorpe, who finished 18th in Division Two. He had five seasons at Chesterfield but was unable to lift them out of the Fourth Division. His best season was 1964-65, when they finished 12th.

McWILLIAM, Peter

Born: Inveravon, Banffshire, 22 September 1878; Died: Redcar, 1 October 1951.
Left-half   5ft 8½in; 11st 8lb (1906).
Career: Heatherley (Inverness); Inverness Thistle; Newcastle United August 1902, retired through injury 1911; Tottenham Hotspur manager May 1913-January 1927; Middlesbrough manager January 1927-March 1934; Arsenal scout cs 1934-1938; Tottenham Hotspur manager May 1938-June 1942.

Honours: Scotland international (8 caps); Football League champions 1905, 1907, 1909; Division Two champions 1920, 1927, 1929; FA Cup winners 1910, 1921, runners-up 1905, 1906, 1908; Football League long-service medal June 1939.

Peter McWilliam excelled as a player and as a manager, one of the few to do so. He played in Newcastle United's great sides between 1905 and 1910 and also became a much-respected and successful manager with Tottenham Hotspur and Middlesbrough.

As a player, McWilliam could dribble as well as any forward, was an excellent tackler and a precise passer. He possessed a famous body wriggle which fooled opponents and characterised his play. Football folklore records that he was so relaxed before a game that he would occasionally take a half-hour nap before kick-off. As a manager there was a complete contrast, for he was often so nervous that he could not bear to watch his team in action.

As a manager, McWilliam was a quiet man, astute and canny but also an idealist. His method was simple and he never held tactical talks or discussed strategy. McWilliam left footballers to play the game their way. He was extremely popular with the players and when he selected them for his club, he could make them feel like great players. He knew how to deal with a player who was off his game. He would pick his moment to get the player on to one side away, from his colleagues. No one was ever admonished in front of the others. McWilliam would begin to work on them, probing their weaknesses and gradually restoring their self-confidence so that they could find their best form again.

He played for local clubs before joining Newcastle United and with the Magpies he gained three League championship medals and also won an FA Cup winners' medal, against Barnsley in 1910 after picking up three runners-up medals. He made his Scotland debut against England at the Crystal Palace in April 1905 but received a knee injury against Wales in March 1911 which ultimately ended his playing career. McWilliam made 198 appearances, scoring 11 goals for Newcastle United.

In May 1913, McWilliam was selected as the new Tottenham Hotspur manager. Spurs were relegated in 1914-15 and had to wait four years before they could seek to restore their place in the top division. They ran away with the Second Division title in 1919-20, gaining 70 points. Unbeaten all season at home, they won their first seven games of the season and never looked back.

McWilliam had assembled a great team before and during the war years. In 1921 they won the FA Cup at Stamford Bridge, beating Wolves 1-0 in the Final. Spurs also finished runners-up in the First Division in 1921-22 but went into decline after this.

McWilliam would go to any lengths to get his player. When signing Jimmy Seed from Mid-Rhondda, the local supporters felt so strongly about losing their idol that they threatened to lynch the Spurs manager if they found him anywhere near the ground. He watched Seed from the stands, heavily disguised with spectacles and false beard, to appraise the young inside-forward. He signed Seed immediately after the game.

McWilliam was in the process of rebuilding the team at White Hart Lane when he was approached by Middlesbrough, then top of the Second Division. They offered him £1,500 per annum to become their manager. This was £200 more than Spurs were paying him. After asking for a rise and being refused, he handed in his notice at White Hart Lane and joined 'Boro as manager in January 1927. Spurs later regretted his loss and tried to entice him back in later years, but did not succeed until 1938.

At Ayresome Park, McWilliam was given complete control of team selection without interference from the board. It was an up-and-down period for the club and he never won the hearts of the fans. 'Boro went on to clinch the title that season but were relegated the following term. They again took the Division Two title in 1928-29 and stayed in the top division whilst he was manager.

McWilliam was sacked in March 1934 and then scouted in the North-East for Arsenal until he returned to London to manage Spurs in May 1938. They had a mediocre season in 1938-39, then war was declared. McWilliam retired in June 1942 and he returned to the North-East, to his wife's home town. He died at his home at Corporation Road, Redcar, and was buried at nearby Kirkleatham cemetery.

MADDEN, Peter

Born: Bradford, 31 October 1934.
Centre-half 6ft 2in; 14st (1963).
Career: Thornton Juniors; Rotherham United October 1955; Bradford July 1966; Aldershot July 1967; Skegness Town player-manager 1968-1970; Rochdale coach 1970-1973; Darlington coach July 1973, then manager cs 1975-October 1978; Rochdale caretaker manager December 1978-January 1979, then manager June 1980-November 1983.

Honours: Football League Cup runners-up 1961; Lincolnshire County Cup medals (with Skegness Town).

Peter Madden helped to keep Rotherham in the Second Division and appeared 308/2 times for the club in League matches. A tall, well-built centre-half, he later took his honesty, strong principles and hard work into management. He played for United in the first-ever Football League Cup Final and was unlucky to finish on the losing side. Winning the first leg 2-0, they lost the second 3-0 in a dramatic match. He could not have managed two more difficult clubs but did well at Darlington and Rochdale, using his knowledge of lower division players to find some success. Madden had the ability to motivate average players.

MADDREN, William D.

Born: Billingham, 11 January 1951.
Defender 5ft 11in; 12st (1971).
Career: Port Clarence Juniors: Middlesbrough June 1968, retired through injury; Hartlepool United coach 1977; Middlesbrough coach and physiotherapist 1978, then manager June 1984-February 1986.

Honours: England Under-23 international (5 caps); Division Two champions 1974; Anglo-Scottish Cup winners 1975.

A defender of high quality, Willie Maddren developed a superb partnership in defence at Ayresome Park with Stuart Boam. They had a marvellous understanding on the field. Maddren made 341 appearances for 'Boro before a serious knee injury ended his career. He had a tough time as manager of Middlesbrough. They were £1.2 million in debt, which meant that he could buy very few players, and were relegated to Division Three in 1986.

Back in 1973-74, Maddren had helped the club into the First Division as champions. After his sacking at Ayresome, he left the club with some bitterness and today runs two sports outfitter shops in the area.

MAGNER, Edward

Born: Newcastle upon Tyne; Died: Derby, July 1948.
Centre-forward 5ft 8½in; 11st 8lb (1910).
Career: Expansion FC; Gainsborough Trinity 1909; Everton 1910; St Mirren January 1912; coaching in Amsterdam; Metz (France) coach; Corinthians and Casuals coach; FA scheme of coaching; Huddersfield Town coach December 1938, then manager June 1942-September 1943; Derby County manager March 1944-January 1946; then coaching in Europe.

Honours: Football League North champions 1945; Midlands Cup winners 1945.

Ted Magner made very few Football League appearances during his playing career — five for Gainsborough and six League and three FA Cup with Everton — although he once created a Scottish League Division One record by scoring five goals for St Mirren against Queen's Park. Magner served in the Northumberland Fusilliers in World War One and afterwards coached in Amsterdam before returning to England to take FA coaching refresher courses at Leeds and Loughborough. He replaced Clem Stephenson as manager of Huddersfield Town and later in the war moved to Derby County.

Magner managed to find some excellent guest players for Derby in the war years and persuaded both Raich Carter and Peter Doherty to sign officially for the Rams. Derby won the Football League North championship and Midland Cup double in 1944-45 and Magner set them on the road to the 1946 FA Cup Final before leaving to work abroad. Peter Doherty said that he would never have left Derby County had Magner still been his manager. Said Doherty, "His man management was superb and he had an excellent knowledge of the game. And he would take us out on to the pitch and hit the crossbar six times out of six from the 18-yard line, just to show us that he could play."

MALEY, Alexander S.

Career: Clydebank manager 1919-cs 1921; Hibernian manager cs 1921-1925; Crystal Palace manager November 1925-October 1927; Clydebank manager again October 1927; Hibernian director.

Honours: Scottish Cup runners-up 1923, 1924.

Alex Maley's brothers, Tom and Willie, were also managers. Willie was probably the most famous when managing Celtic. Alex was in charge twice at the original Clydebank club, which folded in 1931. He took them to their best-ever position, fifth in Division One in 1919-20. Also took Hibs to two Scottish Cup Finals. In 1923, they lost 1-0 to Celtic and a year later they lost 2-0 to Airdrie. He introduced a number of Scottish players to Crystal Palace but they had mixed success.

MALEY, Thomas E.

Born: Portsmouth, 8 November *c.*1865; Died: 1935.
Career: Partick Thistle; London Scottish Hibernians; Third Lanark Rifle Volunteers; Glasgow Celtic; Manchester City manager July 1902-July 1906; Bradford manager February 1911-February 1924; Southport manager May-October 1925.

Honours: Division Two champions 1903, runners-up 1914; FA Cup winners 1904.

Tom Maley came from a footballing family of players, secretaries and managers. The most famous was Willie Maley, who was the manager of Celtic for many years. Tom was secretary-manager of Manchester City, Bradford and Southport. Alex was manager at Hibernian and Crystal Palace and Tom's son, Charles, was secretary at Leicester City and Bradford City.

Tom played alongside his older brother, Willie, at Celtic and also appeared for Partick Thistle, London Scottish Hibernian and Third Lanark. He also worked in an official capacity for Celtic and Third Lanark. He became secretary-manager at Hyde Road, the home of Manchester City, in July 1902 and in his first season in charge he steered the club to the Second Division title.

In 1903-04, City beat Bolton in the FA Cup Final and also finished runners-up in the First Division. Maley liked the Scottish style of play, which was a skilful, close-passing game. He signed a couple of useful players to enhance a squad which already included Billy Meredith and Sandy Turnbull.

Alas, in 1906 Maley became embroiled in a scandal over illegal payments at the club and was suspended *sine die* along with City chairman Mr W.Forrest. Many of the players were also fined and suspended for shorter periods in an episode which almost brought about the demise of Manchester City.

In 1911, the FA decided to end Maley's suspension and in February of that year he became the manager of Bradford. He immediately strengthened the Park Avenue club's team with a contingent of Scottish players — and he was given full charge of team affairs by the board, which was rare in those days. Bradford reached the quarter-finals of the FA Cup in 1913 but struggled in the Second Division. However, the following season they gained promotion to the top flight, going up on goal-average as runners-up. When they finished ninth in the First Division in 1914-15, it was to be the highest position the club ever achieved in the Football League.

The club was greatly hit by the war and went into a sharp decline in the post-war years. They finished bottom of the First Division in 1920-21 and were also relegated again the following season, when they finished 21st. Bradford were struggling in the Third Division North when Maley left the club in February 1924. The only trophy that he brought to Park Avenue was the West Riding Cup which was won in 1911 and 1924.

Maley had a very short period in charge of Southport before leaving football for good.

MALLETT, Joseph

Born: Gateshead, 8 January 1916.
Wing-half 5ft 8in; 11st (1936).
Career: Dunston Colliery Welfare; Charlton Athletic November 1935; Queen's Park Rangers (loan) May 1937-May 1938; Queen's Park Rangers February 1939 (£800); guest for Fulham and West Ham United in 1944-45; Southampton February 1947 (£5,000); Leyton Orient July 1953; Nottingham Forest coach August 1954; Birmingham City coach June 1964, manager July 1964-December 1965, then assistant manager until March 1970; Panionios (Athens) manager 1970-1973 and 1973-July 1974; Appollon (Greece) coach 1973 for six months; New York Cosmos (NASL) coach August 1975; Southampton scout; San Jose Earthquakes (NASL) coach 1982; Southampton scout again in the Midlands.

Joe Mallett's playing days were restricted by the war but he made up for the lost years by playing until he was almost 40. He made most of his League appearances for Southampton, 215 in all.

A shrewd unflappable man, nothing went right for Mallett whilst he was in charge at St Andrew's. Birmingham went down to the Second Division and there was a lot of discontent inside the club and, despite making a number of good signings, he was unable to turn things around. He did a fine job at Greek club, Panionios, turning a poor side into a good one, although he had a lot of problems when the military junta was overthrown in Greece. The colonels appointed managers at all Greek clubs and Mallett was given a hard time after their downfall and was even under arrest for a while.

MALLOY, Daniel

Born: Dennyloan, 6 November 1930.
Centre-half   5ft 11in; 12st 6lb (1959).
Career: Dundee; Cardiff City October 1953 (£17,500); Doncaster Rovers player-manager August 1961-March 1962 (£10,000).

Honours: Scotland 'B' international (2 caps); Scottish League representative.

Danny Malloy was signed from Dundee by Cardiff manager Trevor Morris to solve a problem position at Ninian Park. He proved to be an inspired signing and rarely missed a game, being one of the main reasons why Cardiff managed to stay in the First Division for so long. After failing to agree terms following the abolition of the maximum wage, Malloy moved to Doncaster Rovers as player-manager.

He had conceded the remarkable total of 14 own-goals for Cardiff, his one goal for the club coming from the penalty spot, in December 1956 against Manchester United. A pillar of strength, Malloy was unfortunate never to win a full Scottish cap. He played 42 League games for Doncaster but was unable to prevent them from seeking re-election in 1961-62.

MANGNALL, David

Born: Wigan, 21 September 1905; Died: Penzance, 10 April 1962.
Centre-forward; 5ft 10in; 11st 10lb (1935).
Career: Maltby Colliery; Maltby New Church; Huddersfield Town trialist; Doncaster Rovers amateur 1926; Rotherham United trailist; Leeds United November 1927; Huddersfield Town December 1929 (£3,000); Birmingham February 1934; West Ham United March 1935; Millwall May 1936-June 1938; Queen's Park Rangers May 1939, then manager April 1944-May 1952; guest for Southend, Millwall and Fulham in World War Two.

Honours: Division Three South champions 1938, 1948.

A prolific goalscorer, Dave Mangnall was a bustling centre-forward with a deceptive body swerve which confounded defenders. He once scored ten goals in a reserve match for Leeds against Stockport County, but could not find a regular first-team spot and moved to Huddersfield Town. Mangnall scored 42 goals in 1931-32 and netted 73 goals in only 90 games for the Town overall. The highlight of his career was appearing in Millwall's side which reached the 1937 FA Cup semi-finals. The following season they won the Southern Section title. As manager of Queen's Park Rangers, Mangnall took them into the Second Division as champions in 1947-48, but when they were relegated four seasons later he was sacked.

MANGNALL, J. Ernest

Born: Bolton; Died: early 1932.
Career: Lancashire local football; Burnley secretary January 1900-

September 1903; Manchester United manager September 1903-August 1912; Manchester City manager August 1912-July 1924; Bolton Wanderers director.*

Honours: Football League champions 1908, 1911; Division Two runners-up 1906; FA Cup winners 1909; Football League long-service medal 1921.

Ernest Mangnall was the first great manager of Manchester United, the second was Matt Busby. Mangnall helped transform a poverty-stricken club playing on a poor ground with mediocre results into a wealthy club with triumphs in major competitions and a new stadium.

Mangnall kept goal for the Lancashire County side in his early days. He also played rugby and soccer for Bolton Grammar School and many other minor clubs. He won road races as a cyclist and was a good cross-country runner who represented Bolton Harriers.

Mangnall became the secretary of Burnley in January 1900, with responsibilities for team affairs. He inherited a struggling side and despite a number of new signings, including former England international Edgar Chadwick, they were relegated in 1900. Burnley finished bottom of the Second Division in 1902-03.

Despite this poor record, Manchester United made him their secretary-manager in September 1903. Mangnall developed the ability to motivate players and was also able to spot talent and develop it. He also had an unquenchable thirst for success. Along with chairman J.H.Davies, he developed United into one of the giants of the League. He brought many famous players to Clayton, including such names as Charlie Roberts, Dick Duckworth and Harry Moger. He also signed Sandy Turnbull and Billy Meredith from neighbours Manchester City when that club was hit by an illegal payments scandal.

In 1905-06, United finished runners-up in the Second Division. They then went on to win the League championship twice, in 1907-08 and 1910-11, and lifted the FA Cup in 1909, beating Bristol City 1-0 in the Final at Crystal Palace. In February 1910 the club moved to Old Trafford.

In August 1912, Mangnall surprisingly left United to manage neighbours Manchester City. It was a difficult period for the Hyde Road club but he managed to keep them in the First Division, then helped keep them going during the rigours of wartime football. City finished fifth in 1914-15 and runners-up in 1920-21. They also reached the semi-finals of the FA Cup in 1924 but lost 2-0 to Newcastle United. In May 1924, his contract was not renewed and he left the club two months later, eventually joining the board of directors at Bolton.

Mangnall was also one of the founders of the Central League in 1911 and helped with the formation of the Football Managers' Association. He was awarded a long-service medal by the FA in 1921 after 21 years service to football and was awarded a testimonial in 1924, when a combined Manchester side played Liverpool.

MANNERS, John Albert 'Jack'

Born: Morpeth, March 1878; Died: May 1946.
Half-back   5ft 8in; 12st (1911).
Career: Morpeth YMCA: Morpeth Harriers; West Bromwich Albion May 1904; Hartlepools United player-manager July 1919-May 1920, manager June 1924-July 1927.

Honours: Division Two champions 1911.

Jack Manners had a biting tackle, good distribution and was a very consistent player for West Brom, for whom he made 209 appearances. He was one of the most important members of the side. Manners played in a losing FA Cup semi-final in 1907, against Everton, and won a Second Division championship medal in 1911 despite only appearing 12 times. His best season as manager of Hartlepools was 1925-26, when they finished sixth, scoring lots of goals including a 9-3 victory over Walsall.

MANSELL, John 'Jack'

Born: Manchester, 22 August 1927.
Full-back   5ft 9in; 12st (1953).

Career: Manchester United amateur; Brighton & Hove Albion March 1949; Cardiff City October 1952; Portsmouth November 1953, retired cs 1957; Telstar (Holland) coach; Eastbourne United coach February 1958; FA staff coach; Sheffield Wednesday coach; Ajax Amsterdam (Holland) coach; Rotherham United manager cs 1965-cs 1967; Boston Beacons (USA) manager 1967-1968; Reading manager April 1969-January 1972; West Ham United scout; Queen's Park Rangers assistant manager March-April 1974; then coached in Turkey and Bahrain.

Honours: England 'B' international (2 caps); Football League representative.

Jackie Mansell's combination of public relations and advanced coaching techniques bought him deserved national recognition. He had a reputation for producing sides which tried to play with First Division style in the lower divisions. However, he did not prove to be a good motivator. At Reading, he made lots of changes and there was a great turnover of players which made results unpredictable. After going close to promotion in 1969-70, playing excellent soccer, Reading's defence suddenly became brittle and began leaking goals. After relegation, Mansell was sacked.

MARCHI, Anthony Vittorio

Born: Edmonton, 21 January 1933.
Left-half   5ft 11in; 12st 6lb (1963).
Career: Edmonton, London and Middlesex Schools; Tottenham Hotspur amateur July 1948, professional June 1950; Lanerossi (Italy) cs 1957 (£40,000); Torino (Italy) cs 1958; Tottenham Hotspur July 1959; also Cambridge University coach 1961; Cambridge City player-manager August 1965-March 1967; Northampton Town manager September 1967-May 1968.

Honours: England 'B' international (1 cap); Youth international; Schoolboy international; European Cup-winners' Cup winners 1963.

A solid reliable defender, Tony Marchi was captain during his first spell at Spurs but was the League's most expensive reserve when he returned from Italy and was unable to gain a regular place in their side. His only honour with Tottenham was when he gave a magnificent performance in their Cup-winners' Cup victory over Atlético Madrid in 1963. He appeared in the second leg of the European Cup semi-final against Benfica a year earlier. Marchi, who made 260 appearances for Spurs, was tall, composed and essentially a defensive midfield player. He spent only eight months in charge of the Cobblers, who finished 18th in the Third Division in 1967-68.

MARSDEN, William

Born: Silksworth, County Durham, 10 November 1901; Died: Sheffield, summer 1983.
Inside-right/Left-half
5ft 8in; 10st 6lb (1923).
Career: Silksworth Colliery; Sunderland October 1920; Sheffield Wednesday May 1924, retired due to a spinal injury and broken neck received playing for England in Germany; Gateshead trainer cs 1934; Dutch FA coach; Be Quick FC (Holland) coach; Hermes DWS (Holland) coach 1938; then licensee in Sheffield early 1940s; Doncaster Rovers manager April 1944-January 1946; Worksop Town manager May 1953.

Honours: England international (3 caps); Football League champions 1929, 1930; Division Two champions 1926.

A shrewd tackler and clever passer, Billy Marsden understudied Charles Buchan at Roker Park. He joined the Owls as an inside-forward but switched to wing-half with great success. Marsden made 221 appearances for Wednesday, scoring nine goals before receiving a spinal injury which ended his career. This happened playing for England against Germany in Berlin in May 1930, when he was accidentally injured by his teammate Ray Goodall. He was part-time manager of Doncaster Rovers and then only during wartime soccer. After the war he became a publican.

MARSHALL, John Gilmore

Born: Bolton, 29 May 1917.
Full-back.
Career: Burnley November 1936, retired through injury 1946; Bury coach 1949; Stoke City coach; Sheffield Wednesday trainer-coach 1954; England trainer late 1950s; Rochdale manager October 1958-June 1960; Blackburn Rovers manager September 1960-February 1967; Sheffield Wednesday assistant manager, then manager February 1968-June 1969; Bury manager May-September 1969; Blackburn Rovers physiotherapist July 1970-1979.

Jack Marshall was a popular football

personality who was known to his friends as 'Jolly Jack'. After his playing career was cut short by injury, he turned to coaching. His first managerial job was at Rochdale, who finished bottom of the Third Division at the end of his first season in charge. But he signed one of Dale's best-ever players in Stan Milburn from Leicester City. Milburn made over 250 appearances for the club.

At Blackburn, Marshall converted Fred Pickering into a centre-forward with great success and Rovers achieved good results by playing entertaining football in his early days there. After Marshall sold Pickering to Everton, the side began to break up and was relegated in 1966 after a disastrous campaign. He assisted Alan Brown at Hillsborough and took over when he left. Marshall lasted only seven games in charge at Bury and was sacked, along with his assistant Jimmy Meadows, for financial reasons.

MARSHALL, Robert Samuel

Born: Hucknall, 3 April 1903.
Inside-right/Centre-half
5ft 9in; 11st (1921).
Career: Hucknall Olympic; Sunderland 1920; Manchester City March 1928; Stockport County manager March 1939-February 1949; Chesterfield manager February 1949-July 1952.

Honours: Football League champions 1937; FA Cup winners 1934, runners-up 1933.

Bobby Marshall was a brilliant ball-playing inside-forward who scored regularly for all his sides. He played in two FA Cup Finals and gained a League championship medal with City. Marshall made 205 appearances, scoring 71 goals, for Sunderland and played in 355 games, scoring 80 goals, for Manchester City. He managed Stockport through the war years and they finished fourth in the Northern Section in the first season after the war. Under him Chesterfield finished sixth in the Second Division in 1948-49 but were relegated two seasons later.

MARTIN, George Scott

Born: Bothwell, Lanarkshire, 14 July 1899; Died: 1972.
Inside-forward 5ft 9in; 11st 6lb (1925).
Career: Cadzow St Anne's (Motherwell); Boness; Hamilton Acedemical 1920-1921; Bathgate on loan; Hull City October 1922; Everton March 1928; Middlesbrough May 1932; Luton Town August 1933, retired 1937, coach 1937, then manager August 1939-May 1947; Newcastle United manager May 1947-December 1950; Aston Villa manager December 1950-August 1953; Luton

Town chief scout 1960 and caretaker manager February 1965-November 1966.
Honours: Division Two champions 1931, runners-up 1948.

A fast, powerful and versatile player at Hull, George Martin played in five different positions and appeared 204 times, scoring 56 goals. He helped Everton win the Second Division championship in 1930-31.

In his first spell at Kenilworth Road, Martin found many good young players and built the club up again after World War Two. A very smart and elegant man in an old-fashioned way, he took Newcastle back to Division One in 1948 and did well in the higher league. At Villa, he had a difficult relationship with the board and left in controversial circumstances when he was forced to resign. He moved into business in Liverpool in 1953 but returned to soccer again at Luton Town. His second spell in charge was an unhappy experience as the club went down to Division Four and were at their lowest ebb. He was a talented sculptor and a fine singer who made several records in the early 1940s.

MARTIN, Henry

Born: Selston, Notts, 5 December 1891.
Outside-left 5ft 11in; 11st 7lb (1923).
Career: Sutton Junction 1909; Sunderland January 1912; Nottingham Forest May 1922; Rochdale June 1925, then caretaker manager July-August 1930; York City coach; Mansfield Town trainer-coach November 1933, then manager December 1933-March 1935; Swindon Town trainer cs 1936-1950s.

Honours: England international (1 cap); Victory international (2 caps); Football League representative (3 caps); Football League champions 1913; FA Cup runners-up 1913.

Henry Martin was a daunting proposition for any defence with his excellent speed and accurate crosses. He was nearly involved in a League and Cup double with Sunderland in 1913, when they were League champions but lost to Aston Villa in the FA Cup Final. His only England cap came against Ireland at Middlesbrough in 1914, when he played poorly and his country lost 3-0. He also gained two Victory international caps.

Martin was the caretaker manager at Rochdale between Jack Peart and William Cameron and was initially caretaker boss at Mansfield. He was permanently appointed in January 1934 but was sacked, despite a good season in 1934-35, with the Stags finishing ninth and having a good FA Cup run. He was with Swindon Town for many years as the club's trainer.

MARTIN, Neil

Born: Alloa, 20 December 1940.
Centre-forward 6ft; 11st 3lb (1972).
Career: Trament Juniors; Alloa Athletic 1959; Queen of the South 1961 (£2,000); Hibernian July 1963 (£6,000); Sunderland October 1965 (£45,000); Coventry City February 1968 (£90,000); Nottingham Forest February 1971 (£65,000); Brighton & Hove Albion July 1975; Crystal Palace March 1976; St Patrick's Athletic 1976; Al-Arabi Sporting Club (Kuwait), assistant manager 1978; Walsall youth-team coach, then manager July 1981-June 1982 (briefly joint with Alan Buckley).

Honours: Scotland international (3 caps); Under-23 international (1 cap); Scottish League representative (2 caps).

Neil Martin served an apprenticeship

as a mining engineer whilst at Alloa. Very good in the air, he became a prolific goalscorer at Hibernian, scoring 40 goals in 1964-65. He also scored 20 goals for Sunderland two seasons later. Martin gained his first two Scottish caps whilst at Hibs. He scored 78 goals in Scottish football and 115 in 331/8 in the Football League. He was joint manager with Alan Buckley at Walsall for a while, having previously been the youth-team coach. Walsall just missed relegation by one place on goal difference at the end of his only season in charge at Fellows Park.

MASSIE, Alex C.

Born: Possilpark, Glasgow, 13 March 1906; Died: Welwyn Garden City, 20 September 1977.
Right-half 5ft 10in; 11st 7lb (1936).
Career: Shawfield Juniors; Partick Thistle; Petershill; Glasgow Benburb; Glasgow Ashfield; Ayr United; Bury January 1927 (£1,000); Bethlehem (USA) cs 1928; Dolphins (Dublin) 1930; Heart of Midlothian 1930; Aston Villa December 1935 (£6,000); guest for Solihull Town, Birmingham, Nottingham Forest, Notts County and Portsmouth in World War Two, retired cs 1945; Aston Villa manager August 1945-August 1950; Torquay United manager November 1950-September 1951; Hereford United manager 1951-November 1952; coached local amateur sides in Welwyn Garden City area.

Honours: Scotland international (18 caps); Scottish League representative (6 caps); Division Two champions 1938; Wartime League North Cup 1944.

One of the greatest Scottish players in the inter-war period, Alex Massie skippered club and country. He helped Villa to the Second Division title and an FA Cup semi-final in 1937-38 and to the Football League North War Cup in 1944. He played 337 League games on either side of the border before the war broke out and he made a further 108 appearances for Villa in wartime games.

Massie was not a success in his early days at Bury and moved to the USA to work and play for the Bethlehem Steel Corporation for a while. When he was manager at Villa after the war, Massie was not given complete control of the playing side. Villa finished sixth in 1947-48, their best season under Massie. He wanted footballing sides at Villa Park but was barracked by the fans when there was no success on the field.

MATHER, Thomas

Born: Chorley, 1888; Died: Stoke on Trent, March 1957.
Career: Manchester City assistant secretary; Bolton Wanderers assistant secretary, manager summer 1915-July 1919; Southend United manager cs 1920-1921; Stoke manager October 1923-May 1935; Newcastle United manager June 1935-September 1939; Leicester City manager June 1945-March 1946; Kilmarnock manager June 1947-March 1948.

Honours: Division Two champions 1933; Division Three North champions 1927.

Over a period of 40 years, Tom Mather had wide experience as a secretary and manager with Manchester City, Bolton Wanderers, Southend United, Stoke City, Newcastle United, Leicester City and Kilmarnock. He worked as assistant secretary at Manchester City before moving to Bolton Wanderers in a similar capacity. Later he became

secretary at Burnden Park and then secretary-manager in the summer of 1915. All the games played under his charge were played during wartime.

He remained as manager in name only until July 1919, as he had been called up by the Royal Navy. Ted Vizard took over team affairs temporarily in February 1919 and Charles Foweraker had covered for Mather before this.

In the summer of 1920, Mather became the secretary-manager at Southend United. They had just moved to the Kursaal ground. He stayed for only one season, in which they had a good Cup run to the third round. In October 1923, Mather took over as manager of Stoke. They finished sixth in the Second Division in 1923-24 but due to financial problems, a number of players were not re-signed at the end of the season and others were asked to take a pay cut. Some of these players arrived at the ground in a taxi, and started to smash up the offices and dressing-rooms.

There was a mass clear out after this. Things went rapidly downhill and Stoke were relegated in 1926. They bounced straight back as Northern Section champions in 1926-27 and narrowly missed promotion to the First Division in 1932 before going up as champions a year later. In 1934, the Potters reached the quarter-finals of the FA Cup but lost to Manchester City before 84,569 spectators at Maine Road, a record crowd. Tom Mather had become a fine manager who, with little resources, had built a team to challenge at a higher level.

In May 1935, Mather left Stoke and a month later took over at Newcastle United. However, he had little control over which players were bought and sold and United had little success. He left the club when war was declared.

In June 1945, he returned to football as the manager of Leicester City. He was given full control of the players by the board but resigned on 19 March 1946. From June 1947 to March 1948, Mather was in charge at Kilmarnock but things did not work out for him.

MATHIAS, Raymond

Born: Liverpool, 13 December 1946.
Defender 5ft 9in; 11st 4lb (1971).
Career: Tranmere Rovers December 1964-1985, and player-assistant manager 1983-1985; Wigan Athletic assistant manager 1985, then manager June 1986-March 1989; Tranmere Rovers coach 1989.

Ray Mathias was assistant to Bryan Hamilton at Prenton Park and followed him to Wigan Athetic before taking over as manager in 1986. After a dreadful start to the 1986-87 season, Wigan finished fourth but lost to Swindon Town in the play-offs. After a poor season with Wigan in 1988-89, Mathias returned to Tranmere as coach. Only Harold Bell has made more appearances for Tranmere Rovers than Mathias, who played 636 games in over 21 years at the club.

MATTHEWS, Harold J.

Career: Thames FC; Reading secretary-manager May 1902-November 1922 (team duties from 1904), connected with club since 1887.

Honours: Southern League Division Two champions 1911.

An energetic administrator, Harry Matthews was in charge of the Reading team from 1904. They finished runners-up in the Southern League at the end of his first season in charge. Reading were runners-up again in 1914-15, when they finished three points behind Watford, but the club was in financial difficulties after their relegation into the Second Division in 1910. Matthews helped them weather the crisis and they won the Southern League Division Two title on goal-average from Stoke in 1910-11. He took Reading into the Football League, where they struggled in their initial seasons.

MATTHEWS, Sir Stanley

Born: Hanley, 1 February 1915.
Outside-right   5ft 9in; 11st (1963).
Career: Stoke St Peter's; Stoke City amateur September 1930, professional February 1932; guest for Morton, Blackpool and many other clubs in World War Two; Blackpool May 1947 (£11,500); Stoke City October 1961 (£2,500), retired 1965; Port Vale general manager July 1965, then manager May 1967-April 1968; Hibernian (Malta) manager April 1970; also coached in Canada and Soweto (South Africa).

Honours: England international (54 caps); Wartime international (29 caps); Schoolboy international; Great Britain representative; Football League representative (13 caps); Division Two champions 1933, 1963; FA Cup winners 1953, runners-up 1948, 1953; Football League North Cup winners 1943, runners-up 1944.

Sir Stanley Matthews — who became soccer's first knight in 1965 — is one of the greatest names in British soccer history, who played in the Football League for an incredible 33 years. He made his debut in March 1932 and played his final game against Fulham in 1965. He made over 700 League and Cup appearances in his career, despite losing seven years to the war, and there were 22 years between his international debut and last match for England. Perhaps his most memorable international appearance was when he scored a hat-trick in England's 5-4 victory over Czechoslovakia in December 1937.

He also had a brilliant game for Blackpool in the 1953 Cup Final, when they beat Bolton in a pulsating game which was later dubbed the 'Matthews Final', although Stan Mortensen had scored a hat-trick as Blackpool fought back from 3-1 down to win 4-3. When he left Stoke for Blackpool in 1947, Stoke fans were so angry that they held a public protest meeting. But there was great delight when he returned to the Potteries in October 1961 and revived Stoke's fortunes to help them back to Division One.

His career as a manager was far less auspicious. As general manager of Port Vale he had an unhappy time. In 1968, the Vale club was fined £4,000 and were expelled from the League for making illegal payments to players. They were immediately re-elected but Matthews was distressed by the affair and resigned.

MAVEN, Frederick

Born: Newcastle upon Tyne, 1885; Died: Bradford, May 1957.
Centre-half   5ft 10in; 12st 2lb (1914).
Career: Newcastle United Reserves; New Brompton 1905; Fulham cs 1909; Bradford December 1913; Reading 1919; Boscombe cs 1921; Exeter City manager January 1923-November 1927; Crystal Palace manager November 1927-October 1930; Gillingham manager January 1932-May 1937.

Fred Maven was the mainstay of the

side at New Brompton, where he made 115 appearances. An attacking centre-half, Mavin scored ten goals in one season for Fulham, a record which stood for 70 years. Altogether he netted 27 goals in 147 games for the Cottagers. A serious injury brought an end to his career in 1922. At Exeter, the club was at a low ebb when he took over but he left with the Grecians in better shape. He discovered some excellent players at Exeter including Cliff Bastin, Harold Blackmore and Wilf Lowton. He was offered a better salary by Palace, who just missed promotion to Division Two in 1928-29 when they finished runners-up behind Charlton on goal-average. His best season at Gillingham was his first when they finished seventh in the Southern Section.

MAY, Edward C.

Born: Epping, Essex, 19 May 1943.
Defender   6ft 1½in; 13st 3lb (1971).
Career: Dagenham; Southend United January 1965; Wrexham June 1968; Swansea City August 1976; Leicester City coach 1978-1983; Charlton Athletic assistant manager 1983-1986; Al Hahda (Saudi Arabia) coach 1986; coaching in Kenya; KS (Iceland) manager May 1988; Newport County manager July-August 1988; Lincoln City assistant manager; IFK Ravdeberg (Norway) coach 1989; Cardiff City chief coach-manager July 1991.

Honours: Welsh Cup winners 1972, 1974. Division Three Champions 1993.

A solid and useful defender, May made over 500 League appearances in his career including 330/3 for Wrexham in which he scored 34 goals. He helped Wrexham to promotion to Division Three in 1969-70 and to two Welsh Cup successes which gave them entry into Europe, Wrexham reaching the quarter-finals of the European Cup-winners' Cup in 1975-76. In eight seasons, May missed only 35 League games for Wrexham.

He was a coach at Leicester City when they gained the Second Division title in 1979-80 and for three years was assistant manager under Lennie Lawrence at Charlton. After coaching in Saudi Arabia and Iceland May was manager at Newport County for just a month. Officially chief coach in charge of team affairs at Cardiff City, he saw them narrowly miss the Fourth Division play-offs in 1991-2, but with a large increase in support.

Big crowds returned to Ninian Park as Cardiff City took the Third Division title with 83 points. Eddie May signed Phil Stant midway through the 1992-93 season to help boost the Bluebirds' goal power. They also won the Welsh Cup beating Rhyl 5-0 in the Final at Cardiff Arms Park to gain entry into the European Cup Winners Cup. The only blight on the season was a first round FA Cup defeat against non-League Bath City.

MEADOWS, James

Born: Bolton, 21 July 1931.
Full-back   6ft; 12st 1lb (1957).
Career: Bolton YMCA; Southport amateur October 1948, professional February 1949; Manchester City March 1951, retired October 1957, then training staff late 1959, trainer-coach August 1960-April 1965; Stockport County trainer-coach January 1966, then manager October 1966-April 1969; Bury assistant manager July-September 1969; Blackpool training staff September 1969, caretaker manager October-December 1970, assistant man-

ager December 1970 (and two other periods in 1970s); Bolton Wanderers manager January-April 1971; Southport manager May 1971-December 1973; Stockport County manager May 1974-August 1975; Blackpool caretaker manager February-May 1978; Kuwait Sporting Club assistant manager; coaching in Sweden.

Honours: England international (1 cap); Football League representative (1 cap); Division Four champions 1967, 1973; FA Cup runners-up 1955.

Jimmy Meadows had to retire from playing at 26 after a bad knee injury received in the 1956 FA Cup Final. Meadows was a winger in his early years but converted to full-back at Maine Road. A direct, enthusiatic player who was very fast, Meadows gained his one England cap, in the 7-2 win over Scotland in April 1955.

In charge for only 11 weeks at Bolton, he left with the team bottom of Division Two. Meadows liked to use wingers in his sides. He took Southport to the Fourth Division championship in 1972-73 but they were relegated the following season and he lost his job. He had two spells in charge at Stockport. They were Fourth Division champions in 1966-67 but he was sacked for fielding a player against his chairman's instructions. He enjoyed little luck in his second spell there and also could not prevent Blackpool's relegation to Division Three, when he was caretaker manager in 1978.

MEE, N.Bertram OBE

Born: Bulwell, Notts, 25 December 1920.
Career: Derby County Reserves 1937-1939; Mansfield Town, retired through injury; guest for Southampton in World War Two; RAMC for six years; Rehabilitation Officer for 12 years; Arsenal physiotherapist and trainer August 1960, then manager June 1966-July 1976; Watford general manager until he retired in 1986 to become director.

Honours: Football League champions 1971; FA Cup winners 1971; runners up 1972; Football League Cup runners-up 1968, 1969; Inter-Cities Fairs Cup winners 1970.

Along with Kenny Dalglish and Bill Nicholson, Bertie Mee has taken a club to the League and Cup double in the 20th century, but he is probably the least famous of the three. A modest man, thoroughly efficient and knowledgeable in the arts of person-management and motivation, Mee gradually steered Arsenal from strength to strength. He gained a reputation for his organisational skills and built a highly successful 'method' team within a disciplined framework.

Mee had a spell as a winger on

Derby's books before the war — his brother George was with Derby and Blackpool — but did not play in the first team before joining Mansfield Town just before the outbreak of hostilities. He made some guest appearances for Southampton during the war and appeared in a representative Army Wanderers side in the Middle East.

Mee was forced to retire at the age of 27, due to injury. He spent six years as a sergeant in the RAMC, when he qualified as a physiotherapist, and then spent 12 years as a rehabilitation officer for disabled servicemen. Mee also organised FA treatment of injury courses at Carnegie College, Leeds, and Lilleshall and worked in the Health Service, running remedial centres in London.

In August 1960 he became Arsenal's trainer and physiotherapist, replacing Billy Milne who had retired. A coaching badge and his physiotherapy qualification seemed hardly enough for the challenge of managing Arsenal when he was appointed to succeed Billy Wright. Mee agreed to manage the club for a trial period from June 1966 and was officially appointed in March 1967.

Quiet, precise, a little formal in manner and very neat in mind and appearance, Mee was not given to excessive enthusiasm. His ability to communicate his own passion for order and excellence was to revive Arsenal. He gave star players like Charlie George no special treatment. The team was more important than the individual and Mee steered away from the media and avoided self publicity. He was well-known for his dislike of swearing and bad conduct by players.

Much of the football planning and most of the coaching was done by Don Howe in Arsenal's best years during Bertie Mee's period as manager. It was probably the freedom which Mee gave to Howe, and his relationship with his chief lieutenant, that made their partnership tick.

After he took control, Mee was soon in action on the transfer market and in his first season bought future Gunners manager George Graham as well as Colin Addison and Bob McNab to Highbury. In 1967-68 Arsenal lost to Leeds United in the Football League Cup Final, to a controversial goal, and the following season again reached the Final but suffered the indignity of losing 3-1 to Third Division Swindon Town. In April 1970, the Gunners won their first major trophy for 17 years when they beat Anderlecht 4-3 on aggregate in the Inter-Cities Fairs Cup Final. They lost 3-1 in Belgium but won an exciting second leg 3-0 at Highbury to take the trophy.

The following season was the greatest in their history when Mee, along with Don Howe, guided the Gunners to a League and FA Cup double. This was an achievement even the great Herbert Chapman could not manage. Not surprisingly, Mee was voted Manager of the Year.

Arsenal clinched the League title at great rivals Spurs on the Monday before the Cup Final, then went out and beat Liverpool at Wembley, partially thanks to a great goal from Charlie George.

In 1972, Arsenal reached the FA Cup Final again but lost to Leeds United in a dull game. In 1972-73 they were runners-up in Division One and were knocked out of the FA Cup at the semi-final stage. After this, their fortunes went into decline and after two particularly difficult seasons the pressure began to tell and Mee announced his retirement in March 1976 and worked on until his replacement, Terry Neill, took over. He left Highbury four months later and after a short break from football became a director at Watford until September 1991.

MEGSON, Donald H.

Born: Sale, 12 June 1936.
Left-back   5ft 10in; 12st (1963).

Career: Mossley October 1952; Sheffield Wednesday May 1953; Bristol Rovers player-coach March 1970, then manager July 1972-November 1977; Portland Timbers (NASL) coach November 1977-1979; Bournemouth manager March-October 1983.

Honours: Football League representative 1 cap; Division Three runners-up 1974; FA Cup runners-up 1966; Watney Cup winners 1972.

A quick and determined left-back, Don Megson soon established himself as a regular in the Owls line-up after making his debut in November 1959 at the age of 23. He skippered the side to a losing FA Cup Final in 1966 and Wednesday also finished runners-up in the First Division in 1960-61. Megson played for the Football League against the Italian League in 1961.

Later, after a spell as player-coach at Eastville, Megson took over as manager. Almost immediately, Rovers won the Watney Cup. In 1974 they gained promotion to Division Two. His teams were built on strong defence and quick counter-attacking but were usually dull and boring. Megson was only in charge at Dean Court for seven months and resigned after a string of poor results.

MELDRUM, Colin

Born: Galsgow, 26 November 1941.
Left-back   5ft 11in; 12st 4lb (1963).
Career: Arsenal December 1958; Watford December 1960; Reading April 1963; Cambridge United October 1969; York City chief coach 1973; Workington player-manager July 1974-April 1975; Stafford Rangers manager September 1975-May 1976; Workington manager February-May 1977; Scarborough assistant manager 1979-1980; Frickley Athletic assistant manager 1980-1981; Barnet coach 1981-1982; York City assistant manager 1982-1983; Hull City chief scout 1983-1984; Swansea City assistant manager 1984-1985; coaching in Saudia Arabia 1986; Wealdstone manager February 1987.

Honours: FA Trophy runners-up 1976.

Meldrum had limited chances at Vicarage Road after failing to make the grade at Highbury and was just about to move back to Scotland when he was signed by Reading. It was a good move because he made 266 League appearances, scoring eight goals, for the Berkshire club. He later helped Cambridge United gain League status and appeared in their first season in the Fourth Division.

He had two spells in charge at Workington. They finished second-to-bottom of the League in 1974-75 and bottom in 1976-77. In his second spell at the club, Workington gained only one win in 22 games and lost their League status. Meldrum took Stafford Rangers to runners-up position in the Northern Premier League and to the FA Trophy Final at Wembley, where they lost 3-2 to Scarborough before a 21,000 crowd.

MELIA, James

Born: Liverpool, 1 November 1937.
Inside-right   5ft 8in; 10st 12lb (1963).
Career: Liverpool Schools; Liverpool apprentice 1953; professional November 1954; Wolverhampton Wanderers March 1964 (£55,000); Southampton November 1964 (£30,000); Aldershot player-coach November 1968 (£10,000), then player-manager April 1969-January 1972; Crewe Alexandra February 1972, then player-manager May 1972-December 1974; coaching in the Middle East late 1975; Southport manager July-September 1975; California Lasers (USA) scout; Brighton & Hove Albion scout, then manager January-October 1983; Beleneses (Portugal) manager October 1983-November 1985; Stockport County manager July-November 1986; coaching in Texas (USA) 1992.

Honours: England international (2 caps); Youth international; Schoolboy international; Football League representative (1 cap); Division Two champions 1962; FA Cup runners-up 1983.

Jimmy Melia was a fine playmaker and an excellent passer. He was in the shadow of Johnny Haynes as far as

England were concerned and had to wait until Haynes was involved a car crash before breaking into the England side. Melia helped Liverpool to the Second Division title and also Saints to the top sphere for the first time in 1966. He scored 78 goals in 287 appearances for the Reds, including 21 goals in 1958-59. He cost Saints a club record £30,000 and played 139 League games, scoring 11 goals for the club.

A flamboyant manager, Melia began his career at Aldershot, who reached the fourth round of the FA Cup in 1969-70. He was sacked midway through the 1971-72 season, however, with the Shots in a lowly positiion. Crewe had to seek re-election twice with Melia in charge and he lasted only three months at Southport and nine months at Brighton, who also reached the FA Cup Final in his spell there. Melia resigned when, against his wishes, Chris Cattlin was appointed coach. Melia was in charge at Stockport County for only four months.

MELLOR, Robert

Born: Bottom o'th'Moor, 16 December 1877; Died: May 1967.
Career: Oldham Athletic 1906, secretary January 1910-1949 and secretary-manager July 1924-July 1927, July 1932-May 1933 and May 1934-February 1945.

Honours: Football League long-service medal 1936.

Bob Mellor spent 39 years as secretary at Boundary Park which included three spells as secretary-manager. He served in the RAMC in World War One. He returned to Oldham after the war and was officially put in charge of the team in 1924, although club trainer Jimmy Hanson had a big say in decisions about tactics and training methods. Oldham were relegated to the Third Division North in 1935, but on a number of occasions they went close to re-establishing their Second Division status. Mellor then guided the Latics through the difficult war years.

MENZIES, David Lister

Born; Kirkcaldy, 23 June; Died: Hull, 11 October 1936.
Career: Raith Rovers player and later chairman; Bradford City Reserves 1903, steward 1906-1908, then assistant trainer 1908-1914; Hull City trainer 1914, manager July 1916-June 1921; Bradford City manager July 1921-June 1926; Doncaster Rovers manager July 1927-March 1936; Hull City manager February-October 1936.

Honours: Division Three North champions 1935.

As a player, Menzies appeared for Raith Rovers, where his father was chairman. He did not make the first team at Bradford City but worked there as a

steward and trainer before becoming trainer at Hull City in 1914 and manager two years later. He returned to Valley Parade as manager before moving on to Doncaster Rovers, who won the Third Division North championship in 1934-35 after many mediocre seasons. Menzies brought £20,000 into the club through selling players he had discovered and developed. He had a second spell at Hull and got off to an unbeaten start to the 1936-37 season when tragedy struck and he suffered a fatal heart attack.

MERCER, Joseph OBE

Born: Ellesmere Port, 9 August 1914; Died: Merseyside, August 1990.
Left-half   5ft 9in; 11st (1939).

Career: Ellesmere Port & Cheshire Schools; Elton Green; Shell Mex; Runcorn; Ellesmere Port Town; Everton amateur 1931, professional September 1932; Arsenal November 1946 (£7,000); guest for Aldershot in World War Two; retired through injury cs 1954; Sheffield United manager August 1955-December 1958; Aston Villa manager December 1958-July 1964; Manchester City manager July 1965-October 1971, then general manager until June 1972; Coventry City general manager June 1972-1974 and director April 1975-July 1981; England caretaker manager May 1977.

Honours: England international (5 caps); Wartime international (27 caps); Football League representative (1 cap); Football League champions 1939, 1948, 1953, 1968; Division Two champions 1960, 1966; FA Cup winners 1950, 1969, runners-up 1952; Football League Cup winners 1961, 1970, runners-up 1963; European Cup-winners' Cup winners 1970, runners-up 1971.

Joe Mercer had a great career as a player and a manager. He gained three League championship medals, appeared in two FA Cup Finals for Arsenal and played for his country. As a manager Mercer won honours galore, especially at Manchester City who won the League title, FA Cup, League Cup and European Cup-winners' Cup under him.

Mercer had spirit, courage, determination and a never-say-die attitude as a player and was able to instil this into his players when he became a manager.

Mercer played for Cheshire Schools in the same side as Frank Soo and Stanley Cullis, who later played alongside him in the England team. He soon made his first team debut for Everton and was developing into one of the finest wing-halves in the country and had helped the Toffees to the League championship in 1938-39 when war came. He lost seven seasons of top-class soccer but played regularly in wartime soccer, being part of a famous England half-back line with Cullis and Cliff Britton.

Mercer was suffering from a knee injury and was out of favour at Goodison Park when he signed for Arsenal in November 1946 for a £7,000 fee. Many felt that his career was coming to an end but he proved them all wrong. He had made 184 League and FA Cup appearances for the Toffees and over the next eight seasons made another 293 appearances for the Gunners. Mercer developed into one of the game's most popular personalities. An outstanding wing-half with a biting tackle, he could read the game well and loved to make runs up the field to feed his forwards. He was a distinguished figure on the pitch with his spindly legs and huge famous smile.

His career was rejuvenated at Highbury as he led Arsenal first clear of relegation, then to the League championship in 1947-48 as captain. He played in his first FA Cup Final for the Gunners in 1950, when they beat Liverpool; two seasons later they lost to Newcastle United in the Final. Mercer was voted Footballer of the Year in 1950 and he gained another League championship medal in 1952-53. He announced his retirement in 1953 but came back to play one more season. His illustrious career came to an end when he broke his leg in April 1954, against Blackpool at Highbury, just before his 40th birthday.

For a year after that he ran a wholesale grocery in the Wirral before seeking the vacant manager's post at Sheffield United. At Bramall Lane he had to function on a shoestring budget and the fans were angry when he sold favourites Colin Grainger and Jim Iley, but he raised £65,000 to rebuild the side.

Mercer left to become manager at Aston Villa in December 1958. He could not save them from relegation that season but soon changed the club's fortunes around and they took the Second Division championship in 1959-60. Villa also reached two FA Cup semi-finals, in 1959 and 1960, but lost by a single goal on each occasion. The club's debts inhibited Mercer from buying many new players and they struggled in the top division. Villa did win the first-ever Football League Cup in 1961, beating Rotherham United in a two legged Final.

Mercer developed then sold star centre-forward Gerry Hitchins to Internazionale for £85,000 and signed Derek Dougan and later Tony Hateley as replacements. After an FA Cup defeat against Aldershot, there were rumblings of discontent and in 1964, Mercer suffered a stroke due to over work. The directors of a struggling club waited until he was over the worst effects, then sacked him in July 1964.

He was out of the game for a year before making a comeback as manager of Manchester City. His wife and friends felt that the job might kill him, but they were wrong. Along with his assistant Malcolm Allison, Mercer revitalised a club that had been in the doldrums for many years. City won the Second Division title in 1965-66, then the League championship two years later, usurping their great rivals, United.

More trophies soon followed and City beat Leicester City to take the 1969 FA Cup Final, then the European Cup-winners' Cup the following year, beating Gornik of Poland 2-1 in the

Final in Vienna. City possessed some excellent players, including Colin Bell, Mike Summerbee, Francis Lee, Neil Young, Tony Book, Tommy Booth and Alan Oakes. There was a great contrast in Mercer's and Allison's temperaments but they worked very well as a partnership.

In June 1972, Joe Mercer moved to become general manager at Coventry City with Gordon Milne as team manager. The partnership was not so successful as his one with Malcolm Allison and Coventry struggled to stay in the First Division. Mercer's role gradually diminished and Milne took complete control in 1974. In April 1975, Mercer joined the board of directors and stayed until 1981.

In May 1974, Joe Mercer made a comeback as the caretaker manager of England, bringing a smile to the players faces between Sir Alf Ramsays last days and before Don Revies traumatic reign. After this, Mercer lived in retirement in the Merseyside area until his death in August 1990.

MERCER, Stanley

Born: Tranmere, 11 September 1919.
Forward   5ft 8in; 11st 7lb (1947).
Career: guest for Accrington Stanley and Manchester United in World War Two; Blackpool amateur January 1944; Leicester City amateur July 1944, professional November 1944; Accrington Stanley January 1947 (£750); Mansfield Town October 1948, retired through injury 1949, then trainer and manager August 1953-January 1956; administrator in Lytham St Annes until his retirement in 1989.

Stan Mercer lost most of his playing days to the war and then injury ended his career. Mercer had served in the RAF as a PT instructor during the war. He was Accrington Stanley's top scorer in 1947-48 and netted 36 goals in 68 League games before moving to Mansfield Town. In 15 games for the Stags, Mercer scored ten goals including two hat-tricks before a knee injury put him out of the game and he became the club's trainer.

His teams scored plenty of goals when he became the manager. Mercer resigned in early 1956 on principle after rejecting a call from the directors to undertake secretarial duties in addition to looking after the players, in an attempt to save money.

MERRICK, Gilbert Harold

Born: Sparkhill, Birmingham, 26 January 1922.
Goalkeeper   6ft 1in; 13st (1951).
Career: Fenton Rovers; Olten Sports; Shirley Juniors; Solihull Town July 1939; Birmingham professional August 1939-May 1960; guest for Northampton Town, Nottingham Forest and West

Bromwich Albion in World War Two; served in Army Physical Training Corps; Birmingham City manager June 1960-April 1964; personnel manager for Midlands sales firm from 1964; Bromsgrove Rovers manager cs 1967; Atherstone Town manager 1970.

Honours: England international (23 caps); Football League representative (11 caps); Division Two champions 1948, 1955; Football League Cup winners 1963; FA Cup runners-up 1956; Football League South champions 1946; Inter-Cities Fairs Cup runners-up 1961.

Gil Merrick modelled himself on his childhood favourite, Harry Hibbs, and later succeeded him in goal for Birmingham. Calm and unspectacular Merrick's excellent positioning, great handling and superb anticipation soon brought England honours. He played in 170 wartime games and 551 peacetime games for Birmingham City. They twice won promotion to the First Division and Merrick also played in the 1956 FA Cup Final for the Blues.

When he became the manager, City lost to AS Roma in the Fairs Cup Final at the start of the 1961-62 season. They were constantly fighting against relegation but did beat Aston Villa 3-1 on aggregate in the 1963 Football League Cup Final. He was sacked a year later, after another season of struggle.

METCALFE, Victor

Born: Barrow-in-Furness, 3 February 1922.
Outsdie-left   5ft 9in; 11st 4lb (1959).
Career: West Riding Schools; Raventhorpe Albion; Huddersfield Town amateur January 1940, professional December 1945; Hull City June 1958, retired February 1960; Huddersfield Town youth coach 1961-October 1964; Halifax Town coach/scout December 1964, then manager June 1966-November 1967.

Honours: England international (2 caps); Football League representative (2 caps).

Vic Metcalfe was a tricky winger with excellent ball control who went on to make 459 appearances for Huddersfield Town. He was their penalty-taker for many seasons and scored 90 goals for the Town. He made two appearances for England in 1951, against Argentina and Portugal, and also played twice for the Football League, against the Irish League in 1950 and the League of Ireland in 1954.

After spells as youth coach at Huddersfield and Halifax, Metcalfe became manager at The Shay. They finished 12th in 1966-67, after a poor start, and reached the third round of the FA Cup for the first time since 1953, including a 7-0 victory over Bishop Auckland. He resigned after a disagreement with the chairman. Metcalfe had helped Huddersfield to promotion to Division One in 1952-53 and Hull City to Division Two in 1958-59.

METHVEN, James

Born: Perth, 7 December 1868; Died: Derby, 25 March 1953.
Right-back   5ft 8in; 12st (1904).
Career: Leith Athletic; Heart of Midlothian; St Bernards (Edinburgh); Derby County May 1891, retired 1906 then manager August 1906-June 1922.
Honours: Division Two champions 1912, 1915; FA Cup runners-up 1898, 1899, 1903.

Jimmy Methven served Derby County as player and manager for 31 years. He

appeared in three losing FA Cup Finals for the club and also steered them to two Second Division championships in the up-and-down period in which he was manager of the club.

A clever tackler who was wonderfully cool, Methven was a regular in the Rams side for 15 seasons. He played a few games for Leith and Heart of Midlothian before becoming a regular first-teamer at St Bernards (Edinburgh) at the age of 17. He was also named as reserve when Scotland played England in 1890 but never made the full side, probably because he was playing for an English club.

Methven turned down a contract with Burton Swifts because it included a hotel managership which his wife did not want. A former St Bernard's teammate, Johnny McMillan, persuaded him to join Derby and Methven was ever-present in five seasons after he joined the club in May 1891. He also played in three losing FA Cup Finals for Derby, along with John Boag and Jack Fryer. The Rams lost quite easily in each of these Finals: to Nottingham Forest, 3-1 in 1898; to Sheffield United, 4-1 in 1899; and a record 6-0 defeat by Bury in 1903.

Methven slowed down considerably as his career reached its end in 1906. He was appointed as manager in August 1906 but did not have any secretarial duties, unlike his predecessors. He was in charge until June 1922, except during World War One when he worked for Rolls-Royce in the town.

Methven never had full control of the team at the Baseball Ground and the directors also bought the players, although usually after a recommendation from Methven. The club went into decline after they sold Steve Bloomer to Middlesbrough in 1906 and were relegated at the end of Methven's first season in charge. Things picked up again after Bloomer rejoined Derby in 1910. They won the Second Division championship in 1911-12 and 1914-15, but were relegated in 1914 and 1921. In 1922, Methven entered hospital with eye problems and lost his job soon afterwards. He left football altogether.

MIDDLEMASS, Clive

Born: Wortley, 25 August 1944.
Defender.
Career: Leeds United Reserves August 1962; Workington November 1963-1970; Bristol City coach 1983, assistant manager 1985-1987; Carlisle United manager November 1987-March 1991.

Middlemass appeared for Workington in 170 League games, scoring six goals, after failing to make the grade at Elland Road. In the 1980s he was assistant manager to Terry Cooper at Bristol City before joining Carlisle United as manager. They came close to dropping out of the Football League in 1987-88, when they finished 91st in the League. Newport County dropped out instead and within a year were defunct. However, Carlisle were 19 points clear of them.

Things improved the following season and they finished 12th and reached the third round of the FA Cup, where they lost to Liverpool. The following season Carlisle missed the play-offs on goal-difference but when they slumped in the 1990-91 season, Middlemass lost his job.

MIDDLETON, Raymond

Born: Bolden, 6 September 1919; Died: Boston, 12 April 1977.
Goalkeeper.
Career: Washington Church; North Shields; Chesterfield amateur August 1937, professional October 1937; Derby County June 1951; Boston United player-manager April 1954-May 1957; Hartlepools United manager May 1957-November 1959; Boston United manager again 1959 and later secretary, pools promoter and director.
Honours: England 'B' international (4 caps).
A former miner and a model of consistency, Ray Middleton was one of the many fine goalkeepers discovered by Chesterfield. Middleton played 210 League games for the club before moving to the Derby to make another 120 appearances for the Rams.

In December 1955 he returned to the Baseball Ground as player-manager of Boston United to meet Derby County in an FA Cup tie. Boston, with six former Derby players in their ranks, came away with an amazing 6-1 victory over the Third Division North side.

When he became the manager of Hartlepools United, they had a good start to the 1957-58 season and were third in January. However, a poor run meant they finished 17th and dropped into the newly-formed Fourth Division. Middleton had to try to revitalise an ageing side. They beat Barrow 10-1 the following season but he resigned after a poor start to the 1959-60 season. He had been a Justice of the Peace in Chesterfield. His brother, Matt, kept goal for Plymouth, Bradford City, York and Southport.

MILBURN, John

Born: Ashington, 18 March 1908; Died: Leeds, 21 August 1979.
Right-back   5ft 10in; 12st 2lb (1935).
Career: Spen Black & White; Leeds United November 1928 (£100); Norwich City February 1939 (£2,000); guest for Bolton Wanderers, Bradford City, Darlington and Leeds United in World War Two; Bradford City player-coach October 1946, then player-manager January 1947-July 1948, assistant manager until May 1949.

Famed for his bone-jarring shoulder charges, Jack Milburn was a strong and steady full-back who missed only 19 games in an 11-year period at Elland Road. He made a total of 408 appearances for Leeds and scored 30 goals, many of which came from the penalty-spot. These included nine in 1935-36, a club record.

Milburn was also ever-present when United finished runners-up in Division Two in 1931-32. He was the oldest of the Milburn clan and partnered his brother George at full-back at Elland Road. Bradford City finished fifth and 14th respectively with Milburn as manager. He worked as assistant manager to David Steel after stepping down from the manager's chair.

MILBURN, John Edward Thompson

Born: Ashington, 11 May 1924; Died: 9 October 1988.
Centre-forward 5ft 11½in; 12st 9lb (1951).
Career: Ashington; Newcastle United August 1943; Linfield player-manager June 1957-October 1960; Yiewsley player-manager November 1960-1962; coaching in Reading area in 1962; Ashington for a brief spell; Ipswich Town manager January 1963-September 1964; Football journalist in Newcastle after 1964; Gateshead manager November 1965.

Honours: England international (13 caps); Football League representative (8 caps); Irish League representative (2 caps); Ulster Footballer of the Year 1958; FA Cup winners 1951, 1952, 1955; Irish Cup winners 1960, runners-up 1958.

'Wor Jackie' was an idol of the Geordies for over a decade and was one of the best centre-forwards after the war. He was very fast with a lethal shot and scored many spectacular goals, cracking two great ones in Newcastle's 1951 Cup Final success and scoring one of the quickest-ever Wembley goals in the 1955 Final after just 45 seconds. Milburn scored 199 goals in 395 games for United before moving to Linfield, where he led the side to two Irish Cup Finals.

He returned to England as player-coach at Southern League Yiewsley under Bill Dodgin before succeeding Alf Ramsey as manager of Ipswich Town. He had a difficult time at Portman Road and the club was relegated to Division Two in 1963-64, finishing bottom with only 25 points and nine wins. When Jackie died of cancer in 1988, the whole of Newcastle city centre ground to a halt for his funeral. He was the cousin of Jack and George Milburn of Leeds United.

MILLER, Brian George

Born: Hapton, near Burnley, 19 January 1937.
Wing-half   6ft; 13st (1963).
Career: Blackburn Schools; St Mary's College, Blackburn; Burnley February 1954, retired through injury April 1968, coach, manager October 1979-January 1983, chief scout 1983-1986, manager again July 1986-January 1989.
Honours: England international (1 cap); Under-23 international (5 caps); Football League representative (2 caps); Football League champions 1960; Division Three champions 1982; FA Cup runners-up 1962.
Miller was a solid hard tackling wing-half who was excellent at backing up the attack. He was at Turf Moor for 35 years as player, trainer, chief scout and manager on two occasions. Miller won a League championship medal with unfashionable Burnley in 1959-60 and played in the European Cup the following season. He also played in their losing FA Cup Final side against Spurs in 1962. His England cap came in Vienna in May 1961, when the Austrians won 3-1.

Injury ended his playing career in April 1968, when he took to coaching at Turf Moor. He could not prevent Burnley's relegation in 1979-80 but two seasons later they won the Third Division championship on goal-difference. Miller was sacked the following season with the club heading towards relegation again. In his second spell in charge, Burnley went close to dropping out of the League altogether

and stayed in only after beating Orient in the final game of the 1986-87 season, before 15,781 at Turf Moor. With the club struggling again, he was sacked for a second time in January 1989.

MILLER, Thomas

Born: Motherwell, 29 June 1890; Died: 3 September 1958.
Centre/Inside-forward
5ft 9in; 11st (1921).
Career: Larkhall Hearts; Gleniven; Lanark United; Third Lanark; Hamilton Academical; Liverpool February 1912 (£400); Manchester United September 1920; Heart of Midlothian cs 1921 (£2,300); Torquay United 1922-1923; Hamilton Academical 1923 (£100); Raith Rovers December 1926-1927; Barrow manager cs-November 1930.
Honours: Scotland international (1 cap); FA Cup runners-up 1914.
Although small for a centre-forward, Miller had lots of pace, excellent shooting powers and possessed good distribution. Four members of his family played for Hamilton Academical and Tom played for Liverpool in the 1914 FA Cup Final which they lost to Burnley. He had been top scorer that season with 20 goals in League and FA Cup competitions. He scored twice on his debut for Scotland, against England in April 1920, but ended on the losing side, the Scots going down 5-4.

Miller had served a suspension for helping to fix a match between Liverpool and Manchester United in 1915 and was fortunate to be allowed to play again. He scored 58 goals in 146 games for Liverpool before moving to Old Trafford. After an period in Scottish football, Miller returned south of the border to manage Barrow but lasted only half a season and left with the club struggling near the foot of the Northern Section. His brother John played for Liverpool.

MILLS, Michael Denis MBE

Born: Godalming, 4 January 1949.
Left-back   5ft 6in; 10st 8lb (1971).
Career: Portsmouth apprentice; Ipswich Town apprentice August 1965, professional February 1966; Southampton November 1982 (£50,000); Stoke City player-manager May 1985-November 1989; Colchester United manager January-May 1990; Coventry City assistant manager November 1990-November 1991.
Honours: England international (42 caps); Under-23 international (5 caps); Youth international; Football League representative (2 caps); FA Cup winners 1978; UEFA Cup winners 1981.
A stocky, naturally left-footed player, Mick Mills joined Ipswich after being released when Portsmouth abandoned their youth policy. He captained Ipswich and England and played 591 games for the Suffolk club, scoring 22 goals. The highlights were Ipswich's 1978 FA Cup Final victory over Arsenal and the winning of the UEFA Cup. Mills also played over 100 games for the Saints, including an FA Cup semi-final defeat against Everton in 1984. He moved to Stoke as player-manager.

There was no cash to spare at the Victoria Ground and the supporters were deserting in droves. After a number of mediocre seasons, Mills was being given a rough time by the fans and was replaced by Alan Ball, whom he had recently appointed as his assistant. Things were also tough at Colchester, who finished bottom of the

Fourth Division, thus losing their League status.

MILNE, Gordon

Born: Preston, 29 March 1937.
Right-half   5ft 8in; 11st (1963).
Career: Preston Amateurs; Morecambe; Preston North End January 1956; Liverpool September 1960 (£16,000); Blackpool May 1967 (£30,000); Wigan Atheltic player-manager January 1970-1972; England Youth team manager August 1971; Coventry City manager June 1972-May 1981, then executive manager until August 1982; Leicester City manager August 1982-June 1986, general manager June 1986-May 1987; Besiktas manager (Turkey) 1987.

Honours: England international (14 caps); Football League representative (2 caps); Football League champions 1964, 1966; Division Two champions 1962; promotion 1983; Northern Premier League champions 1971; Turkish League champions 1990, 1991, 1992; European Cup-winners Cup runners-up 1966; Turkish Cup winners 1989, 1990.

A polished wing-half, Gordon Milne was an integral part of the Liverpool side which won the Second Division title in 1961-62. Altogether he played 279 games for Liverpool before moving to Blackpool and also gained two League championship medals at Anfield and played in the European Cup-Winners Cup Final against Borussia Dortmund in Glasgow in May 1966, which Liverpool lost 2-1.

Milne has enjoyed a long career in management. He started with Wigan Athletic, who won the Northern Premier League title in 1970-71 and had a good run in the FA Cup that year. At Coventry, Milne produced some fine players through the youth scheme but his sides never fulfilled their potential and the directors and fans eventually lost patience with him. Initially, he had worked with Joe Mercer at Highfield Road.

He took Leicester into the First Division in 1983, after a late run saw them squeeze home. It was difficult to fathom how he felt about football, as he appeared to have an unemotional attitude to the game. Eventually sacked at Leicester, Milne enjoyed great success with Besiktas in Turkey, winning the double in 1990. He is the son of Jimmy Milne, (see below)

MILNE, James

Born: 11 October 1911.
Left-half   5ft 11in; 12st (1935).
Career: Dundee Violet; Dundee United; Preston North End 1932-1939; Wigan Athletic   manager   1946-1947;

191

Morecambe player-manager late 1940s; Doncaster Rovers trainer; Preston North End trainer, then manager April 1961-November 1967 to become general manager, chief scout May 1968.

Honours: FA Cup runners-up 1937, 1964.

Jimmy Milne was one of the best uncapped wing-halves of the inter-war period. He was working as a porter at Lochee West Station, near Dundee, when he signed for the local club, United. Milne was soon attracting scouts from England and was signed by Preston. Milne was a regular up to the outbreak of war and made 272 League appearances for the club.

A very consistent player who attacked well and was reliable in defence, he played in the 1937 FA Cup Final, when Preston lost to Sunderland, but missed their winning Final the following year due to injury.

He returned to Preston as trainer in the 1950s. When he was manager at Deepdale, Preston surprised everybody when they reached the FA Cup Final in 1964, losing 3-2 to West Ham at Wembley. They also went close to promotion to the First Division that season. He became general manager when replaced by Bobby Seith in late 1967 and was appointed chief scout at the end of the season. He sold his son, Gordon, to Liverpool's Bill Shankly, a former teammate of Jimmy's at Deepdale.

MINTER, William J.

Born: Woolwich, 16 April 1888; Died: 21 May 1940.
Inside-right   5ft 9½in; 12st 7lb (1914).

Career: Norwich City amateur November 1905; Woolwich Arsenal Reserves February 1906; Reading June 1906; Tottenham Hotspur cs 1908, retired June 1920 to become trainer, then manager February 1927-November 1929, then assistant secretary until May 1940.

Honours: Division Two champions 1920.

Billy Minter had a fine goalscoring record at White Hart Lane, scoring 101 in 268 League and FA Cup games for the club. He was attracted to Spurs after two good seasons with Norwich City, in which he had finished as top scorer. He rarely played in the war years but returned afterwards to help Spurs to the Second Division title in 1919-20. He lost his place halfway through the season and retired to become trainer under Peter McWilliam.

Minter replaced him as manager in 1927 but was not a success. He let things get on top of him and Spurs were relegated in 1927-28. Minter worked hard to get them back into the top flight again, but the strain made him ill and he resigned to become assistant secretary, a post he held until his death.

MITCHELL, Archibald P.

Born: Birmingham, 15 December 1885; Died: April 1949.
Centre-half   5ft 8in; 12st (1920).
Career: Aston Villa Reserves 1905; Queen's Park Rangers May 1907-cs 1921; Brentford player-manager August 1921-December 1924; (left club April 1925); coaching abroad in 1926; Dartford manager until 1930; Queen's Park Rangers Reserves coach 1930, then manager November 1931-May 1933.

Honours: Southern League champions 1908, 1912; Southern League representative (6 apps); Birmingham FA representative.

A great club servant for Queen's Park Rangers, Mitchell was brought to West London by new Rangers manager Jimmy Cowan who, like Mitchell, also played for Aston Villa. Mitchell went on to make 308 appearances (12 goals) for Rangers before moving to Brentford. He gained Southern League championship medals in 1907-08 and 1911-12.

Mitchell played in his first season at Griffin Park before retiring in the summer of 1922 to concentrate on his managerial duties. The Bees did not do very well under him and were heading for re-election when he resigned to concentrate on searching for new players. He returned to QPR as manager just as they were moving to play at the White City. This did not prove a success and attendances dropped alarmingly in the two seasons in which Mitchell was in charge. With little success on the field, he was relieved of his duties and Rangers moved back to Loftus Road

MITCHELL, Thomas Brown

Died: August 1921.
Career: Blackburn Rovers secretary 1884-1896; Woolwich Arsenal manager 1897-March 1898.

Mitchell was the secretary at Ewood Park for 12 years in a period in which Blackburn won the FA Cup five times, but he cannot be directly attributed with this as he was not in charge of the playing side, only the administration. He stayed less than a year at Arsenal. They finished fifth in Division Two in 1897-98 and reached the first round of the FA Cup. Despite improved performances, support fell away and the financial position at the club became acute. He resigned in March 1898.

MITCHELL, Thomas Morris

Born: Spennymoor, 30 September 1899; Died: November 1984.
Outside-left   5ft 8in; 10st 7lb (1923).

Career: Parkside United; Spennymoor United; Newcastle United May 1920 (£100); Leeds United October 1926 (£785); York City September 1931, then manager March 1937-February 1950; Yorkshire Schools coach; publican in Leeds; coaching in Norway; York City director.

Tommy Mitchell competed for the left-wing berth with Stan Seymour at Newcastle United. An artistic winger, he was mainly a reserve at St James' Park, playing only 61 games in six seasons. Mitchell found more success at Elland Road, where he used his pace and skill to good effect. He was ever-present in their Second Division promotion season of 1927-28 and played 152 games for the club, scoring 21 goals.

He scored the first goal at Bootham Crescent in 1932 and later took York City to the quarter-finals of the FA Cup when he was the manager in 1937-38. He often coached in Norway in the summer months and was later stationed in that country with the RAF during the war. Mitchell set up a sports outfitting shop in York after resigning from the manager's job. He was later a director of York City but ill health forced him to leave the board.

MITTEN, Charles

Born: Rangoon, Burma, 17 January 1921.
Outside-left   5ft 8in; 11st (1955).

Career: Dunblane Rovers; Strathalen Hawthorne; Manchester United amateur August 1936, professional January 1938; guest for Tranmere Rovers, Southampton, Aston Villa and Chelsea in World War Two; Sante Fé (Bogota) 1950; Fulham December 1951 after FA suspension; Mansfield Town player-manager February 1956-June 1958; Newcastle United manager June 1958-October 1961; White City (Manchester) greyhound stadium manager; Altrincham manager in 1960s; ran sports promotions firm.

Honours: England Wartime international (1 cap); FA Cup winners 1948; Football League South Cup winners 1944.

A colourful and controversial figure, Charlie Mitten was born in Rangoon where his father was serving in the Royal Scots Guards. He helped Chelsea win a Cup Final during wartime and was a key figure in Manchester United's resurgence after the war. Mitten made 161 appearances for the Reds including their 1948 FA Cup winning side. He is only the second player ever to score a hat-trick of penalties in the First Division.

Mitten was one of a number of players who left British football in 1950 to play in Colombia, which led to his suspension from the game. He returned to make 160 appearances for Fulham, scoring 33 goals, and delighted the Craven Cottage crowd with his superb skills. Mitten took Mansfield to sixth in the Northern Section in 1957-58 but left for Newcastle United when he received a better offer after making over 100 appearances as player-manager at Field Mill. He had little success at St James' Park and the Mapgies were relegated in 1961. Mitten was sacked soon afterwards. He is the father of John and Charles Mitten.

MOIR, William

Born: Bucksburn, Aberdeenshire, 19 April 1922; Died: 9 May 1988.
Inside-right   5ft 7½in; 9st 13lb (1950).
Career: 25th Old Boys FC; Bucksburn Juniors; RAF Kirkham; Bolton Wanderers April 1943; guest for Dundee and Aberdeen in 1945-46; Stockport County September 1955 (£4,500), then player-manager June 1956-July 1960, retired May 1958; Nelson manager March 1961; Bolton Wanderers coach November 1969, then helped on the commerical side until his death.

Honours: Scotland international (1 cap); 'B' international (2 caps); FA Cup runners-up 1953; Football League War Cup, North v South winners 1945.

Willie Moir was a small, lightweight but skilful player who developed a fine partnership with Nat Lofthouse in the Bolton side. He went on to score 134 goals in 358 appearances for the Trotters, many of his games being as skipper. Moir was discovered playing for RAF Kirkham by Bolton's chief scout Bob Jackson. He appeared in every position in the forward line but as he was a naturally right-footed player, he was most successful at inside-right.

Moir topped the First Division goalscoring charts in 1948-49 with 25 goals. He gained his Scottish cap against England at Hampden Park in April 1950, finishing on the losing side. He captained the Trotters to the 1953 FA Cup Final in which they lost 4-3 to Blackpool after leading 3-1 but being reduced to virtually ten men when full-back Eric Bell was injured. Moir scored 26 goals in 69 League games for Stockport County but he had little success as manager of the club. They were relegated to Division Four in 1959 and he lost his job after failing to get them promoted straight away.

MONCUR, Robert

Born: Perth, 19 January 1945.
Centre-half   5ft 10in; 10st 9lb (1976).
Career: West Lothian Schools; Newcastle United apprentice October 1960, professional April 1962; Sunderland June 1974 (£30,000), Carlisle United player-manager November 1976-February 1980; retired from playing September 1977; Heart of Midlothian manager February 1980-1981; Plymouth Argyle manager June 1981-September 1983; Whitley Bay coach; Hartlepool United manager October 1988-November 1989.

Honours: Scotland international (16 caps); Under-23 international (1 cap); Schoolboy international; Division Two champions 1965, 1976; Scottish League Division One champions 1980; FA Cup runners-up 1974; UEFA Cup winners 1969; FA Youth Cup winners 1962.

A hard and uncompromising defender, Bobby Moncur was captain of Newcastle United and Scotland and, indeed, his best playing days were at St James' Park. He scored three goals in the Magpies' two-legged Fairs Cup Final victory in 1969, against Újpesti Dózsa, and also played in their FA Cup Final defeat by Liverpool in 1974. Altogether, Moncur played 342 times for Newcastle.

He had a tough time in his first managerial job at Carlisle United. They were relegated to Division Three in 1977, then struggled in the lower division. Moncur, who 'discovered' Peter Beardsley whilst at Carlisle, was the surprise choice to take over at Hearts in 1980. He took Hearts into the Premier League at the end of his first season in charge but lost his job when they struggled in 1980-81. He also had an unhappy spell at Plymouth and was sacked after a poor start to the 1983-84 season. At Hartlepool, he had a near-impossible task but did take them to the fourth round of the FA Cup before being sacked in November 1989 with the club bottom of the Football League.

MONEY, Richard

Born: Lowestoft, 13 October 1955.
Utility   5ft 11in; 11st 5lb (1978).
Career: Lowestoft Town; Scunthorpe United July 1973; Fulham December 1977 (£50,000); Liverpool April 1980 (£330,000); Derby County, loan December 1981-February 1982; Luton Town April 1982 (£100,000); Portsmouth August 1983 (£55,000); Scunthorpe United October 1985, later coach and caretaker March-April 1987; Aston Villa youth-team coach in 1991; Scunthorpe United manager January 1993.
Honours: England 'B' international (1 cap); Division Two champions 1982.

Richard Money was a utility player who was an exciting all-action midfielder in his early days at Craven Cottage and later played at right-back and in the centre of defence. Money was sold to Liverpool by Fulham for a club record £330,000 after joining the Cottagers for only £50,000 from Scunthorpe United.

He gained an England 'B' cap against New Zealand at Brisbane Road in October 1979 and looked like achieving even more honours at Liverpool. Alas, Money lost his form at Anfield and played only 16 times before joining Luton Town after a loan period at Derby County, who also wanted to buy him. He began and ended his playing career with Scunthorpe United and played over 300 games for the club and a total of 527 in his career. Money was caretaker manager at Scunthorpe between Frank Barlow and Mick Bux-

ton assumed full control in early 1993 after working at Villa Park as youth-team coach.

MONTGOMERY, Archibald

Born: Chryston, Lanark, 1875; Died: 5 January 1922.
Goalkeeper; 5ft 6½in; 11st (1903).
Career: Local football; Glasgow Rangers; Bury March 1895, retired 1905, manager February 1907-April 1915; Albion Rovers manager June 1920-January 1922.

Archie Montgomery made all but two of his 210 League appearances for Bury in the First Division. He missed both their FA Cup Final appearances, in 1900 and 1903. The first time he was injured, the second he was in the Reserves at the time. His team-manager role at Bury was more as a scout/trainer with team selection still firmly in the hands of the directors.

Because of debts of £3,000, Montgomery was forced to sell centre-forward Billy Hibbert to Newcastle United in October 1911, for £1,950. After years of struggle, Bury were relegated to Division Two in 1911. The club dispensed with the manager in April 1915, as an economic measure due to the war. His brother, Tom, played for Notts County.

MOORE, John

Born: Harthill, 21 December 1943.
Wing-half   5ft 11in; 12st 4lb (1971).
Career: Motherwell; Luton Town May 1965; Brighton & Hove Albion October 1972; Northampton Town August 1974; Dunstable Town until 1978; Luton Town coach 1978, then manager May 1986-June 1987; Leicester City coach May 1989; Luton Town Reserve-team coach 1992.
Honours: Division Four champions 1968.

A reliable and dedicated player, John Moore's enthusiasm and enjoyment of the game won him the affection of the Luton crowd. Tall, slim and fair, Moore started as a left-half but later converted into a central defender. He played prominent roles in Luton's two promotion seasons. In 1968, they won the Fourth Division championship and two years later they were runners-up in the Third Division. He scored some spectacular own-goals during his playing career. Moore made 276 appearances for Luton before moving to Brighton. His playing career went into decline after this.

He lost his job as manager after a good season in Division One, when Luton finished seventh in 1986-87. His former assistant, Ray Harford, took over from him and Moore accused him of 'stabbing him in the back' to get the job. Harford denied this.

MOORE, Robert Frederick Chelsea OBE

Born: Barking, Essex, 12 April 1941; Died: London, 24 February 1993.
Left-half   6ft; 12st 13lb (1968).
Career: Barking & Leyton Schools; Woodford Youth Club; West Ham United June 1958; Fulham March 1974-May 1977 (£20,000); San Antonio Thunder (NASL) April-August 1976; Seattle Sounders (NASL) July-August 1978; Herning (Denmark) player-coach February 1978; Oxford City manager December 1979-May 1981; Eastern AA (Hong Kong) manager in August 1982; Southend United chief executive August 1983, then manager February 1984-April 1986 and director in 1989.
Honours: England international (108

caps); Under-23 international (8 caps); Youth international; Football League representative (12 caps); World Cup winners 1966; Footballer of the Year 1964; FA Cup winners 1964; Football League Cup winners 1966; European Cup-winners' Cup winners 1965; FA Youth Cup runners-up 1959.

Everybody expected Bobby Moore to be a good manager as he was such a fine player, but it was not to be. Southend United were relegated to Division Four in 1984 and then struggled near the bottom of the League with attendances under 2,000. He resigned on 25 April 1986.

Moore had captained England to a World Cup triumph at Wembley in 1966 and gained a record 108 caps for his country. He led West Ham to two Cup Final triumphs at Wembley, winning the FA Cup in 1964 and the European Cup-winners' Cup against Munich 1860 the following year. Moore made 642 appearances for the Hammers before moving to Fulham, where he made another 150 appearances including an FA Cup Final appearance at Wembley in 1975 against his former club. Moore was a calm, unhurried player who always seemed to have control over the ball and his emotions. He was also an excellent reader of the game and had many great moments in his playing career. In February 1993 Moore announced that he was suffering from cancer and sadly died a few days later.

MOORE, Ronald David

Born: Liverpool, 29 January 1953.
Forward   6ft; 12st 9lb (1971).
Career: Liverpool & Cheshire Schools; Tranmere Rovers May 1971; Cardiff City February 1979 (£120,000); Rotherham United August 1980 (£100,000); Charlton Athletic September 1983 (£30,000); Rochdale July 1985; Tranmere Rovers July 1986, then player-manager February-April 1987, then coach (retired from playing cs 1989).
Honours: Division Three champions 1981.

Moore was a central defender in his early days at Tranmere but later played as a striker and sometimes even in midfield. He appeared in 249 League games in his first spell at Prenton Park and made 610 League appearances altogether before retiring. He scored 157 goals in his career.

Moore always gave his all and was a great favourite with the crowd because

of this. The goals dried up when he moved to Ninian Park but he later helped Rotherham United to promotion to Division Two in 1980-81. He was player-manager at Tranmere for only two months and was replaced by John King after failing to agree terms for a new contract.

MOORE, William

Born: New Washington, spring 1916.
Right-half   5ft 8in; 10st 4lb (1938).
Career: Walker Celtic; Stoke City August 1935 (after a month's trial); trainer with Notts County and Aston Villa; Walsall manager December 1957-November 1963 and February 1969-October 1972.
Honours: Division Three runners-up 1961; Division Four champions 1960.

Billy Moore appeared only four times for Stoke City and made more of a name for himself as a manager. He was trainer to the Villa team which won the FA Cup in 1957, as assistant to Eric Houghton. Moore was an honest, straight-talking man who brought his parade-ground discipline into the dressing-room. He was a hard taskmaster and his teams never lacked strength and stamina.

Walsall won the Fourth Division championship in 1959-60 and were runners-up in Division Three the following season to move from the Fourth to the Second in consecutive seasons. They were a little unlucky to be relegated in 1962-63. Needing a point to stay up from the final game against Charlton, who needed to win, two bad injuries meant they were down to nine men and lost 2-1 to be relegated. Walsall had a good season in 1971-72, during his second spell in charge.

MORDUE, John 'Jackie'

Born: Edmondsley, County Durham, winter 1887; Died: Sunderland, March 1938.
Outside-right   5ft 8in; 11st 2lb (1923).
Career: Sacriston; Spennymoor United; Barnsley October 1906; Woolwich Arsenal April 1907; Sunderland May 1908; guest for Fulham in World War One; Middlesbrough May 1920; Hartlepools United cs 1922; Durham City player-manager February 1923-February 1924.
Honours: England international (2 caps); Football League representative (3 caps); Football League champions 1913; FA Cup runners-up 1913.

Jackie Mordue formed a great partnership with Charlie Buchan at Sunderland, for whom he played 299 games and scored 83 goals in the League. Mordue had great pace and accurate distribution. He played in the Sunderland side which narrowly missed gaining the League and Cup double in 1913 and he also won two England caps, both against Ireland. In 1912 England won 6-1 in Dublin and a year later they lost 2-1 in Belfast, where he partnered his Roker teammate Buchan.

Mordue had a tough time as player-manager of Third Division North Durham City, who had to play in the first qualifying round of the FA Cup in 1923-24, as they forgot to apply for exemption. After Durham beat local rivals, Darlington, 3-2 in February 1924, Mordue was sacked as he was considered 'unsuitable for the post' by the club's directors.

MORGAN, Lawrence 'Lol'

Born: Rotherham, 5 May 1931.
Full-back/Left-half   5ft 9in; 12st (1963).

Career: Sheffield United amateur; Huddersfield Town March 1949; Rotherham United August 1954; Darlington player-manager July 1964-June 1966; Norwich City manager June 1966-May 1969.

Honours: Division Four runners-up 1966.

A sturdy defender, Lol Morgan was unable to break into the Huddersfield Town side on a regular basis and made only seven appearances at wing-half before moving to Rotherham United. At Millmoor, he became a full-back and made 290 League appearances for the club before moving to Darlington as player-manager.

The 1965-66 season was the club's most successful one for 41 years. A crowd of 16,469 attended the last match of the season against Torquay United, which they won to finish runners-up to Doncaster Rovers in Division Four. Morgan was wooed away to Norwich at the end of that season.

Morgan immediately lost his star striker when Ron Davies was sold to Southampton. He made a number of signings, including Lawrie Brown and Laurie Sheffield. The Canaries beat mighty Manchester United at Old Trafford in the FA Cup in February 1967, but Morgan was unable to produce a consistent side and was asked to resign after a poor run. He had spent lots of money on new players but found little success.

MORGAN, Richard L.

Born: Cardiff, 3 October 1946.
Half-back   5ft 11in; 12st 6lb (1971).
Career: Cardiff Corries; Cardiff City February 1966, retired 1976 and joined administrative staff, then manager November 1978-November 1981, general manager until February 1982; Barry Town manager in 1980s.

Honours: Wales Under-23 international (1 cap); Schoolboy international.

Richie Morgan made only 69 appearances in Cardiff City's first team in his ten-years at Ninian Park, where he was deputy to Don Murray. He was the surprise choice as manager in November 1978 but surrounded himself with an excellent backroom staff of Brian Harris, Dave Elliott and Doug Livermore. Morgan spent large amounts of money on players like Ronnie Moore, Colin Sullivan, Peter Kitchen and Dave Bennett but found little success.

City plunged down the table after they brought in Graham Williams as team manager, with Morgan as general manager. Both were eventually sacked. He had outstanding success as manager of Barry Town, who won the Welsh League championship on a number of occasions in the 1980s.

MORGAN, Stuart E.

Born: Swansea, 23 September 1949.
Defender   5ft 11in; 12st 6lb (1975).
Career: West Ham United March 1967; Torquay United February 1969; Reading November 1969; Colchester United August 1972; Bournemouth March 1975; Weymouth manager November 1978-November 1983; Bournemouth assistant manager November 1983-September 1985; Torquay United manager September 1985-May 1987; Weymouth manager June 1987-1989.

Honours: Bob Lord Trophy winners 1982; GMAC Cup runners-up 1988.

Stuart Morgan moved around the lower divisions after failing to make the grade at Upton Park. He made a total of 222 League appearances at his other four clubs and had two spells as manager of Weymouth. In the first, they finished as runners-up of the Alliance Premier League in 1979-80 and won the League Cup in 1982. In the second spell they made the GMAC Cup Final but lost then plummeted into the Southern League in 1989.

He had been assistant manager to Harry Redknapp at Bournemouth. Torquay United won only 19 League games in his two seasons in charge and just missed dropping out of the League in 1986-87, staying up on goal-difference whilst Lincoln City went into the Conference League.

MORGAN, Thomas M.

Right winger.
Career: Port Vale player, scout, assistant secretary and reserve-team manager, manager October 1929-June 1932, assistant secretary again, manager again December 1937-April 1939; Wrexham manager April 1939-April 1942.

Honours: Division Three North champions 1930.

After many years as assistant secretary of Port Vale, Tom Morgan was appointed manager in succession to Joe Schofield, who died in September 1929. The side he inherited won the Division Three North title that season, with 67 points and scoring 103 goals. To bolster the attack he signed Stewart Littlewood from Oldham for the biggest-ever fee paid by Port Vale, who finished fifth in the Second Division in 1930-31 but just avoided relegation on goal-average the following season.

Morgan was replaced by Tom Holford. He was not promoted to manager again immediately in April 1937, when Warney Cresswell left the club, and Vale had nobody in charge until December of that year, when Morgan again became manager. Just before the war, he left for Wrexham, much to most people's surprise. All the club's records were destroyed in a fire at his home.

MORRELL, George

Born: Glasgow, c.1873.
Career: Glenure Athletic (Glasgow) manager; qualified referee; Glasgow Rangers staff; Greenock Morton manager 1905-1908; Woolwich Arsenal manager February 1908-May 1915.

George Morrell was committee man, secretary, treasurer, president and occasional player with Glenure Athletic, a Glasgow junior club. He joined the staff of Glasgow Rangers and helped to revive their fortunes. Morrell

got the Morton job from 85 applicants. The club were heavily in debt but Morrell soon made them solvent and they were voted into the Scottish First Division.

Woolwich Arsenal were experiencing poor support and were in financial difficulties when he took over. He was forced to sell a number of excellent players such as Andy Ducat, Jimmy Sharp, Tim Coleman, Jimmy Ashcroft and Bert Freeman, and relegation inevitably came in 1912-13. Arsenal then moved across London, from Plumstead to Highbury, in search of better support. Morrell was forced to resign when the club reduced operations due to the war. 'Punch' McEwan ran the teams during the war at Arsenal.

MORRIS, Colin

Born: Blyth, 22 August 1953.
Winger   5ft 7in; 11st 5lb (1984).
Career: Burnley September 1971; Southend United January 1977; Blackpool December 1979 (£111,000); Sheffield United February 1982 (£100,000); Scarborough player-coach June 1988, then player-manager January-November 1989.

Honours: Division Four champions 1982.

Colin Morris was one of the best wingers outside the First Division. After only 11 appearances for Burnley, he moved to Southend United, where he played 156 games, scoring 30 goals. Southend had finished runners-up in Division Four in 1977-78 with Morris in the side. After another 100 appearances (33 goals) for Blackpool, Morris moved to Sheffield United.

He was made club captain at Bramall Lane and helped Sheffield United to the Fourth Division championship in 1981-82 and to promotion to Division Two, two seasons later. A penalty expert, Morris scored 68 goals in his 240 League appearances for United before joining Scarborough as player-coach and later manager. They made the Fourth Division play-offs when they finished fifth in 1988-89, but lost to Leyton Orient. He was sacked after four successive defeats just a month after Scarborough had beaten First Division Chelsea in a League Cup second-round tie.

MORRIS, Peter John

Born: New Houghton, Derbyshire, 8 November 1943.
Midfield   5ft 8in; 11st (1963).

Career: New Houghton; Ladybrook Colts; Mansfield Town November 1960; Ipswich Town March 1968 (£12,000); Norwich City June 1974 (£60,000), later reserve-team coach;

Mansfield Town player-manager July 1976-February 1978 (£20,000); Newcastle United assistant manager February 1978-February 1979; Peterborough United manager February 1979-May 1982; Crewe Alexandra manager November 1982-June 1983; Southend United manager July 1983-February 1984; Nuneaton Borough manager June 1985; coaching in Saudi Arabia; Leicester City coach May 1987; Kettering manager June 1988-May 1992; Boston United manager May 1992.

Honours: Division Two champions 1968, 1972; Division Three champions 1977; Football League Cup runners-up 1975.

A non-stop runner who was a hard-tackler and also possessed fine passing ability, Morris made over 600 appearances during his career. He helped Ipswich and Norwich City to the Second Division championships, in 1968 and 1972 respectively, and also played in Norwich's Football League Cup Final appearance against Aston Villa in 1975. He made his debut for Mansfield Town at 17 and made a total of 365 appearances for the club in his two spells there.

Morris took the Stags to the Third Division championship in 1976-77, but they lasted only one season in the higher grade. He almost took Peterborough to promotion and had a fine run in the FA Cup with Kettering in 1988-89, when they reached the fourth round before losing to Charlton Athletic. They beat Bristol Rovers and Halifax Town on the way. They also just missed moving into the Football League, finishing runners-up in the Conference that season.

MORRIS, Trevor OBE, DFM

Born: Gorslas, near Llanelli, autumn 1920.
Wing-half.

Career: West Bromwich Albion amateur; Caerphilly; Ipswich Town August 1938; Cardiff City May 1939, retired through injury 1942, then assistant secretary 1946, secretary from 1949, manager April 1954-August 1958; Swansea Town manager August 1958-May 1965; Newport County general manager March 1967-January 1968; Welsh FA assistant secretary June 1970, secretary March 1971-1982.

Trevor Morris' playing career was ended by a broken leg in a wartime cup game against Bristol City in 1942. He piloted the lead aircraft of a squadron of Lancaster bombers on D-Day and flew more than 40 missions over enemy territory, being awarded the Distinquished Flying Medal.

Cardiff were relegated from the First Division in 1957, with Morris in charge, but he took Swansea Town to an FA Cup semi-final in 1964, where they lost 2-1 to fellow Second Division club, Preston. They had beaten Liverpool 2-1 on the way to the last four. Morris left after the Swans were relegated a year later. He received a lucrative severence payment when he left the club and was secretary of the Welsh FA for 11 years but left because of a heart complaint.

MORRIS, William

Born: Llandulas, near Colwyn Bay, 30 July 1918.
Inside-forward   5ft 6in; 10st 11lb (1950).
Career: Abergale County School; Old Colwyn Youth; Llandudno Town 1938-1939; Burnley January 1939, then 'A' team trainer 1952, retired to become trainer-coach cs 1954-60; guest for Wrexham in World War Two; Wrexham manager June 1960-May 1961 and March-October 1965; ran guest house in Llandudno 1960-1965; worked for Isle of Man Steamship Company.
Honours: Wales international (5 caps); Wartime international (1 cap); FA Cup runners-up 1947.

Morris went straight into Burnley's first team in Janary 1939, against Norwich City, after he joined the club from Llandudno Town. After the war, he went on to make 230 appearances, scoring 53 goals, for the club. He was a sergeant in the Army during the war, serving in India and Burma. A very small, lightweight inside-right, Morris was an elusive player, difficult to mark, and had the knack of being in the right place at the right time to score opportunist goals.

He gained his first cap for Wales in April 1947, against Scotland, and appeared in the 1947 FA Cup Final, for Burnley in their 1-0 defeat by Charlton.

Wrexham finished 16th in Division Four in his only full season in charge and he had his nephew, Elfed, in his squad of players at this time. Morris had been lucky to survive the war after being shot through the neck by the Japanese in Burma.

MORTENSEN, Stanley Harding

Born: South Shields, 26 May 1921; Died: Blackpool, 22 May 1991.
Centre-forward   5ft 9½in; 11st 7lb (1950).
Career: South Shields Schoolboys; Blackpool amateur April 1937, professional May 1938; guest for Aberdeen in World War Two; Hull City November 1955 (£2,000); Southport February 1957; Bath City July 1958, retired May 1959; comeback with Lancaster City November 1960, retired March 1962; Blackpool manager February 1967-April 1969; member of pools promoters panel.
Honours: England international (25 caps); 'B' international (1 cap); Wartime international (3 caps); Football League representative (5 caps); played once for Wales in wartime (sub); FA Cup winners 1953, runners-up 1948, 1951.

Stan Mortensen was one of the most lethal strikers after the war, scoring 197 goals in 317 League games for Blackpool and 24 goals in 25 internationals for England, including four goals against Portugal on his debut in May 1947.

He was involved in an air crash when flying for the RAF during the war but

recovered from head injuries to make many wartime appearances for many different clubs. He played in three FA Cup Finals for Blackpool between 1948 and 1953, losing the first two but gaining a winners' medal in the memorable 'Matthews Final', when he scored a hat-trick in Blackpool's 4-3 win over Bolton. Mortensen had electrifying speed and was a great header of the ball.

When he became the club's manager he arrived too late to save Blackpool from relegation to Division Two but was very upset when he was sacked at the end of the 1968-69 season, only a year after the Seasiders missed promotion by 0.21 of a goal despite winning last seven matches. His most important signings were Tony Green and Tommy Hutchinson.

MORTIMORE, John H.

Born: Farnborough, 23 September 1934.
Centre-half   6ft 1in; 12st (1959).
Career: Woking; Aldershot amateur; Chelsea April 1956; Queen's Park Rangers September 1965 (£8,000); Sunderland Reserves March 1966, then player-coach; manager in Greece until May 1973; Portsmouth manager May 1973-September 1974; Southampton assistant manager June 1979-1984; Benfica (Portugal) manager until June 1987; Betis (Seville) manager June 1987-February 1988; Belenenses (Portugal) manager 1988-February 1989.
Honours: England Amateur international; Youth international; Portuguese League champions 1987; Football League Cup winners 1965; Portuguese Cup winners 1985, 1986, 1987.

A commanding centre-half, who was powerful in the air. John Mortimore was still an amateur with Woking when he made his debut for Chelsea. He lost his place to Bobby Evans and then Mel Scott, although probably a better player, but still made 279 appearances for the Blues and was ever present in Chelsea's promotion side of 1962-63, where he was an experienced head amongst many youngsters.

Mortimore spent heavily on the transfer market as manager of Pompey. He paid £155,000 for Fulham defender Paul Went, but there was a financial crisis at Fratton Park and he had to make 11 players available for transfer to offset the debts. He was sacked and then worked abroad. He was Lawrie McMenemy's assistant manager at The Dell. He also took Benfica to the Portuguese League and Cup double in 1986-87, then surprisingly left for Betis.

MOYSE, R.S.

Career: Crystal Palace director and manager July-December 1936, chief scout, banned for 12 months over illegal payments in 1939.

Moyse spent only five months in charge of team affairs at Selhurst Park. A director of the club, he took over from Tom Bromilow, who in turn returned to the club to replace Moyse. In December 1939, it came to light that illegal payments had been made involving the transfer dealings of players Vince Blore and Jack Palethorpe. Moyse was banned for 12 months for his part in this, as he had been manager at the time.

MUDIE, John Knight

Born: Dundee, 10 April 1930; Died: 2 March 1992.
Inside-forward 5ft 6¾in; 11st 2lb (1961).
Career: Dunkeld Amateurs; Dundee

Stobswell; Dundee; Blackpool amateur September 1946, professional May 1947; Stoke City March 1961 (£7,500); Port Vale November 1963 (£12,000 and a player), then player-manager March 1965-May 1967; Oswestry Town player-manager July 1967; Crewe Alexandra assistant manager-coach September 1967; Eastwood Town trainer-coach 1968-February 1971; Northwich Victoria manager 1973; Johannesburg Rangers (South Africa) scout.
Honours: Scotland international (17 caps); Division Two champions 1963; FA Cup winners 1953, runners-up 1951.

A lively and clever forward who was an excellent centre-forward despite his small build, Jackie Mudie combined with Stanley Matthews to give many defenders a tough time with their clever play. Mudie appeared in the memorable 'Matthews' Cup Final of 1953, when Bolton were beaten 4-3, after picking up a runners-up medal in 1951, when Blackpool lost to Newcastle. He won 17 consecutive caps for Scotland and scored a hat-trick against Spain at Hampden Park in May 1957, in a World Cup tie.

Mudie helped Stoke to the Second Division championship in 1962-63, having teamed up again with Matthews, and altogether he scored 184 goals in 463 League appearances before retiring. The two were together again at Port Vale, with Mudie as team manager and Matthews as general manager. Vale struggled in the Fourth Division at this time and, a year after he left the club, they were fined £4,000 and expelled from the League for paying illegal bonuses and making payments to schoolboy players. Fortunately, they were re-elected immediately.

MUIRHEAD, Thomas Allan

Born: Cowdenbeath, 31 January 1897; Died: June 1979.
Wing half/Inside-right
5ft 8½in; 11st 2lb (1925).
Career: Fife junior soccer; Hibernian cs 1914; Glasgow Rangers May 1917 (£20); Boston (USA) player-manager briefly in mid-1920s; retired 1930; St Johnstone manager June 1931-April 1936; Preston North End manager April 1936-May 1937; sports journalist.
Honours: Scottish international (8 caps); Scottish League representative (6 caps); Scottish League champions 1920, 1921, 1923, 1924, 1927, 1928, 1929, 1930; Scottish Second Division runners-up 1932; Scottish Cup winners 1928, runners-up 1922, 1929. FA Cup runners-up 1937.

A fine utility player, Tommy Muirhead was at his best at wing-half. He was a fine passer and keen tackler who went on to make 352 appearances for Rangers, scoring 49 goals in his 13 years at Ibrox. He gained eight Scottish League championship medals but his only Scottish Cup winners' medal was awarded to him in 1928, even though he did not play in the Final.

Muirhead took St Johnstone into the First Division as runners-up in 1931-32 when he became the club's manager. They held their own in the higher grade and also reached a Scottish Cup semi-finals in 1934. At Preston, he surprisingly resigned after only one season. They had just lost to Sunderland in the 1937 FA Cup Final.

MULHALL, George

Born: Falkirk, 8 May 1936.
Outside-left   5ft 8in; 10st 9lb (1963).

Career: Denny YMCA: Kilsyth Rangers; Aberdeen 1953; Sunderland September 1962 (£23,000); Cape Town City (South Africa) player-coach June 1969, retired 1971; Halifax Town trainer-coach October 1971, then manager June 1972-September 1974; Bolton Wanderers assistant manager October 1974; Bradford City manager November 1978-March 1981; Bolton Wanderers assistant manager March 1981, then manager June 1981-June 1982; Ipswich Town scout; Tranmere Rovers assistant manager July 1985-February 1987; Huddersfield Town chief scout and youth development officer in 1990. Huddersfield Town assistant manager in 1992.
Honours: Scotland international (3 caps); Scottish League representative (3 caps); Scottish League Cup winners 1959.

A fast direct left-winger with an eye for goal, George Mulhall hit the target 42 times in 150 games for Aberdeen and 66 times in 284 appearances for Sunderland. He came from a footballing family, his two brothers appearing for Falkirk and Albion Rovers. Mulhall scored on his international debut, in a 4-0 victory over Ireland in October 1959. He helped Sunderland to promotion to Division One in 1963-64 and also gained League and Cup medals with Cape Town City in South Africa.

Mulhall improved the playing squad when in charge at The Shay, even though he sold Alan Waddle to Liverpool for £46,000, and all-in-all made over £40,000 from transfer dealings for Halifax Town. He was assistant to Ian Greaves in his first spell at Bolton, then just missed out on promotion with Bradford City in 1980. Bolton were in turmoil when he became manager at Burnden Park. Despite many problems, he saved the Trotters from relegation, but then resigned after a row with directors over the sale of Paul Jones. He was assistant to Frank Worthington at Tranmere.

MULLEN, James

Born: Jarrow, 8 November 1952.

Defender   5ft 10in; 9st 6lb (1977).
Career: Sheffield Wednesday October 1970; Rotherham United August 1980 (£25,000); Preston North End, (loan) November 1981; Cardiff City March 1982 (£10,000), assistant manager 1984; Newport County player-manager June-October 1986 (£1,500); Cardiff City assistant manager October 1986-1987; Aberdeen assistant manager February 1987; Blackpool manager May 1989-April 1990; Burnley manager October 1991.

A loyal, dependable and popular

defender, Jimmy Mullen was a whole-hearted player who was a good reader of the game. He captained Sheffield Wednesday to promotion from the Third Division in 1980, after years of decline, and also led both Rotherham, in 1980-81, and Cardiff, in 1982-83, to promotion from the same division to complete a rare treble. He made 254/8 appearances for the Owls in all.

Cardiff City had a disastrous season in 1985-86, when Mullen was assistant to Alan Durban. He spent only five months in charge at Somerton Park before leaving for Aberdeen to become Ian Porterfield's assistant. Mullen had an up-and-down season in charge at Blackpool. They reached the fifth round of the FA Cup before losing to Queen's Park Rangers in a second replay but were relegated to the Fourth Division. Burnley lost only five of their last 35 games of the 1991-92 season to take the Fourth Division title under the management of Mullen. This included nine wins on the trot, an amazing record for a new manager.

MULLERY, Alan Patrick MBE

Born: Notting Hill, 23 November 1941.
Right-half   5ft 9in; 12st 4lb (1971).
Career: West London, London & Middlesex Schools; Fulham amateur June 1957, professional December 1958; Tottenham Hotspur March 1964 (£72,500); Fulham (loan) March-April 1972, permanently August 1972 (£65,000), retired May 1976; Brighton & Hove Albion manager July 1976-June 1981; Charlton Athletic manager July 1981-June 1982; Crystal Palace manager June 1982-May 1984; Queen's Park Rangers manager June-December 1984; Brighton & Hove Albion manager May 1986-January 1987; Southwick manager August-November 1987; ran a sports shop in Banstead; worked for BSkyB Sport.

Honours: England international (35 caps); Under-23 international (3 caps); Football League representative (2 caps); Footballer of the Year 1975; Division Two runners-up 1979; Division Three runners-up 1977; FA Cup winners 1967, runners-up 1975; Football League Cup winners 1971; UEFA Cup winners 1972.

An accomplished and aggressive wing-half, Alan Mullery established himself in Fulham's promotion side of 1958-59. He moved to White Hart Lane for a record fee but took some time to settle before winning over the Spurs fans. Mullery played in two all-London FA Cup Finals, in 1967 when Spurs beat Chelsea 2-1 and in 1975 when he was the driving force in Fulham's great run

to Wembley where they lost 2-0 to West Ham. Before moving back to Craven Cottage he scored the clincher when Spurs beat Wolves in the 1972 UEFA Cup Final. Mullery made 785/1 appearances, scoring 72 goals, in his career and also played in the 1970 World Cup finals.

In 1979, he took Brighton into the First Division for the first time as runners-up, but had little success at his other clubs. He resigned at Charlton when chairman Michael Gliksten stood down but was sacked at Crystal Palace, at Queen's Park Rangers and at the end of his second spell at the Goldstone.

MURDOCH, Robert White

Born: Bothwell, Lanarkshire, 17 August 1944.
Right-half   5ft 10in; 12st 8lb (1975).
Career: Cambuslang Rangers; Glasgow Celtic August 1959; Middlesbrough September 1973-1976, then youth-team coach, then manager May 1981-September 1982.
Honours: Scotland international (12 caps); Under-23 international (1 cap); Scottish League representative (5 caps); Scottish League champions 1966 to 1973 inclusive; Football League Division Two champions 1974; Scottish Cup winners 1965, 1967, 1969, 1972, runners-up 1963, 1966, 1970, 1973; Scottish League Cup winners 1966 to 1970 inclusive, runners-up 1965, 1971, 1972; European Cup winners 1967, runners-up 1970.

The controlled power of Bobby Murdoch was an integral cog in the Celtic team machine of the 1960s. He helped them to eight consecutive League championships and also appeared in eight Scottish Cup Finals and another eight Scottish League Cup Finals. Their greatest achievement, though, was as the first British team to win the European Cup in 1967, when Internazionale were beaten 2-1 in Lisbon. Three years later they lost in the Final to Feyenoord, 2-1 in Milan, with Murdoch again in the side.

After 288/3 League appearances and 61 goals for Celtic, Murdoch moved south to join Middlesbrough and in his first season helped them back into the First Division. After 113/2 appearances and seven goals for 'Boro, he retired to become youth-team coach. When he was appointed manager at Ayresome Park, the loss of star players like Craig Johnston and David Armstrong greatly weakened the side and relegation to Division Two was the result. He was sacked soon afterwards.

MURPHY, Colin

Born: Croydon, Surrey, 21 January 1944.
Career: Cork Hibernian; Wimbledon; Hastings United player-manager; Crystal Palace Reserves, retired through injury; Charlton Athletic coach 1971-1972; Nottingham Forest youth-team manager November 1972; Derby County coach October 1973, then manager November 1976-September 1977; Notts County coach and assistant manager October 1977; Lincoln City manager November 1978-May 1985; Stockport County manager August-October 1985; Saudi Arabia coaching October 1985; Stockport County manager again November 1986-May 1987; Lincoln City manager May 1987-May 1990; Leicester City youth coach 1990-1991; Luton Town assistant manager 1991-1992; Southend United manager May 1992-April 1993.

Honours: Division Four runners-up 1981; Conference League champions 1988.

Colin Murphy never played League soccer but enjoyed a career as a respected coach and manager. He was reserve-team manager under Dave Mackay at both Forest and Derby but had a tough time as manager at the Baseball Ground. He was nearly replaced by Clough and Taylor in February 1977 but they turned down the offer of a return to Derby. Murphy spent £300,000 on Derek Hales, but he never settled in the Midlands, and also paid £175,000 for Gerry Daly from Manchester United.

Eventually Murphy was sacked, although the circumstances of his going reflected no credit on Derby. Six games into the season he took charge of the team to meet Leeds, knowing that Tommy Docherty had replaced him. He became assistant to Jimmy Sirrel at Notts County and had two spells at Stockport, the first ending when Murphy received a good offer to coach in Saudi Arabia. In his first spell at Lincoln City, Murphy got the club promoted from the Fourth Division in 1981, as runners-up. On his return they had just dropped out of the League but he led them back as champions of the Conference. Murphy has a good reputation for developing young players. Murphy returned to League management at Southend United who were struggling in the newly-formed First Division.

Southend were near the bottom of the First Division when Murphy lost his job in April 1993. His replacement, Barry Fry, successfully saved the club from relegation.

MURRAY, Alan

Born: Newcastle upon Tyne, 5 December 1949.
Midfield   5ft 8in; 10st 8lb (1975).
Career: Middlesbrough September 1967; York City (loan) January 1972; Brentford June 1972; Doncaster Rovers July 1973-1977; Middlesbrough commercial manager 1988-1990; Hartlepool United commercial manager 1990, manager March 1991-February 1992; Hartlepool manager March 1991-February 1993.

Honours: Division Four promotion 1991.

Alan Murray, an average player, was a youngster at Ayresome Park at the same time as Graeme Souness. After only ten appearances for 'Boro, Murray moved south to play for Brentford and after 45 League games for them he was transferred to Doncaster Rovers, where he made another 133/13 appearances, scoring 21 goals. He became caretaker manager at Hartlepool, when Cyril Knowles became ill with a brain tumour, and took over permanently in May 1991. Sadly, Knowles died three months later. Murray is one of the few commercial managers to become a team manager.

United finished third in 1990-91 to gain entry into Division Three. Joe Allon scored 35 League and cup goals and was transferred to Chelsea for a big fee. They challenged in 1992-93 for further promotion. United also beat Crystal Palace 1-0 at home in the third round of the FA Cup. Despite a mid-table position in the new Second Division Murray was sacked in February 1993 following six consecutive defeats and replaced by Viv Busby.

MURRAY, William

Born: Aberdeen, 10 March 1901; Died: 14 December 1961.
Right-back   5ft 9in; 11st 6lb (1935).

Career: Hall Russells (Aberdeen); Cowdenbeath 1924; Sunderland April 1927; St Mirren January 1937; Sunderland manager April 1939-June 1957.
Honours: Football League champions 1936.

Bill Murray was studying engineering with a view to taking up a position with a shipping firm in Shanghai when he was approached by a number of clubs to become a professional footballer. He chose Cowdenbeath so that he could carry on with his studies and developed into steady, stylish right-back who was very dependable and consistent. He served in the Highlanders during World War One, being demobbed in December 1919.

Murray captained Cowdenbeath into the Scottish First Division in 1924 and had made 111 appearances for them before moving to Sunderland, where he made a further 328 appearances. Murray helped the Wearsiders to the League championship in 1935-36 before moving back to Scotland to play for St Mirren. He returned to Roker Park as manager just before the outbreak of World War Two and produced a very skilful side with plenty of personalities, including Len Shackleton. Sunderland finished third in 1949-50 and reached two FA Cup semi-finals, in 1955 and 1956. Murray resigned after an illegal payment scandal at the club.

MUSGROVE, Malcolm

Born: Lynemouth, 8 July 1933.
Outside-left   5ft 8in; 10st 5lb (1959).

Career: Lynemouth Colliery; West Ham United December 1953; Leyton Orient player-coach December 1962 (£11,000), retired 1966; chairman of PFA 1963; Aston Villa coach-November 1968; Leicester City assistant manager and coach; Manchester United coach 1971-1973; Torquay United manager January 1973-November 1976; Connecticut Bicentennials (NASL) coach 1977;

Chicago Sting (NASL) coach 1978; Charlton Athletic coach; Exeter City coach and scout 1981-1984; Plymouth Argyle coach and physiotherapist 1987.

Honours: Division Two champions 1958.

A direct, high-scoring winger who rarely missed a match for West Ham, Malcolm Musgrove scored 89 goals in his 301 games for the club, winning a Second Division championship medal in 1957-58. Leyton Orient sunk from the First to the Third Division during Musgrove's time at the club. As well as playing 91 games for Orient, he was also coach under Dave Sexton.

Musgrove was assistant to Frank O'Farrell at Leicester City and Manchester United but had little success as manager of Torquay United. He coached, scouted and worked as a physiotherapist at the other West Country clubs, Exeter City and Plymouth Argyle, and is still at Home Park. Musgrove was one of several members of the West Ham team that went on to do well as managers, including Sexton, O'Farrell, Malcolm Allison and John Bond.

NAPIER, Robert John

Born: Lurgan, Northern Ireland, 23 September 1946.
Centre-half   6ft 2in; 12st 2lb (1970).
Career: Lurgan Schools; Bolton Wanderers September 1963; Brighton & Hove Albion August 1967 (£25,000); Bradford City October 1972 (£10,000); Baltimore Comets (NASL) (loan) May-August 1975; Mossley 1976; Bradford City player-coach 1976; San Diego Jaws (NASL) March 1976; Bradford City manager February-October 1978; Philadelphia Fury (NASL) 1978; coach to soccer schools in USA.

Honours: Northern Ireland international (1 cap); Under-23 international (2 caps); Youth international (11 caps); Schoolboy international.

John Napier chose Bolton Wanderers rather than Everton so that he could live near relatives in the area and was a regular in the Trotters' side until he lost his place to John Hulme early in 1967. Napier asked for a transfer and moved to Brighton. He was a firm favourite at the Goldstone, where he made 219 League appearances before moving to Valley Parade. He had joined both Brighton and Bradford City for club record fees.

Napier made one appearance for Northern Ireland, against West Germany in May 1966, he would have gained more caps but for the presence of Terry Neill. He made over 100 appearances for Bradford City before trying his luck in the USA. He was in charge at Valley Parade for only eight months. Napier was hampered by his lack of experience and City were relegated to Division Four at the end of 1977-78.

NEAL, John

Born: Silksworth, County Durham, 3 April 1932.
Full-back   5ft 8in; 10st 10lb (1963).
Career: Silksworth Colliery Welfare Juniors; Hull City August 1949; King's Lynn July 1956; Swindon Town July 1957; Aston Villa July 1959 (£6,000); Southend United November 1962, retired June 1967; worked at Fords, Dagenham 1967-1968; Wrexham coach, then manager September 1968-May 1977; Middlesbrough manager May 1977-May 1981; Chelsea manager May 1981-June 1985, then advisor.

Honours: Division Two champions

1960, 1984; Division Four runners-up 1970; Football League Cup winners 1960; Welsh Cup winners 1972, 1975; Division Three South representative.

John Neal gained a reputation as a keen tackling full-back who could make a quick recovery. After 60 League appearances for Hull City he moved to King's Lynn but his Football League career was resurrected by Swindon Town. Joe Mercer signed him for Aston Villa, where he made over 100 appearances, gained a Second Division championship medal in 1959-60 and played in the first League Cup Final, when Villa beat Rotherham. Neal also made over 100 appearances for Southend.

He enjoyed success as Wrexham's manager, taking them to promotion to Division Three in 1970 and to the quarter-finals of the European Cup-winners' Cup in 1976. He left a strong side when he moved to Middlesbrough and Wrexham were soon in the Second Division. Neal instilled attacking flair in 'Boro's side, but sold some excellent players including Graeme Souness to Liverpool and David Mills to West Brom. He left the club after a disagreement over the sale of Craig Johnston to Liverpool. Neal took Chelsea to the Second Division championship in 1983-84 but after undergoing heart surgery in 1985 he was replaced by John Hollins.

NEAL, Philip George

Born: Irchester, 29 February 1951.
Right-back   5ft 11in; 12st 2lb (1980).
Career: Irchester FC; Northampton Town apprentice July 1967, professional December 1968; Liverpool October 1974 (£65,000); Bolton Wanderers player-manager December 1985-May 1992, retired as a player 1989. Coventry City assistant manager 1992.

Honours: England international (50 caps); Football League champions 1976, 1977, 1979, 1980, 1982, 1983, 1984; Division Four promotion 1988; FA Cup runners-up 1977; Football League Cup winners 1981, 1982, 1983, 1984, runners-up 1978; European Cup winners 1977, 1978, 1981, 1984, runners-up 1985; UEFA Cup winners 1976; European Super Cup winners 1977, runners-up 1978, 1985; World Club championship runners-up 1981, 1984; Freight/Rover Trophy runners-up 1986.

Like several Liverpool players of his era, Phil Neal won just about every honour in the game but never gained an FA Cup winners' medal. A penalty expert, Neal was also remarkably consistent and skilful and had excellent positional sense. He loved to attack and scored 60 goals in 633/2 appearances for Liverpool. Neal reached double-figures twice in a season, in 1976-77 and 1982-83. He scored from the spot when the Reds beat Borussia Mönchengladbach in the 1977 European Cup Final and also one of the penalties in the shoot-out against AS Roma. He also played 50 times for his country and in two World Club Championship matches.

Alas, after all that Neal left Liverpool rather bitterly for Bolton. He wrote a controversial book about life at the club and came under fire for the bad publicity he allegedly gave the game. Neal took Bolton to the Final of the Freight/Rover Trophy at Wembley in his first season in charge, when they lost to 3-0 Bristol City. After relegation in 1987, the Trotters bounced straight back, then made the Third Division play-offs in 1990 and 1991. In 1991 they came closest to promotion but lost to

Tranmere Rovers in the Wembley Final. Neal lost his job after six and a half years in charge, despite Wanderers reaching the fifth round of the FA Cup in 1992.

NEILL, William John Terence

Born: Belfast, 8 May 1942.
Centre-half   5ft 10½in; 12st 8lb (1971).
Career: Belfast Schoolboys; Bangor (Irish League); Arsenal December 1959 (£2,500); Hull City player-manager June 1970-September 1974 (£44,000), retired as a player 1973; also PFA chairman; Northern Ireland player-manager, then manager until March 1975; Tottenham Hotspur manager September 1974-July 1976; Arsenal manager July 1976-December 1983.

Honours: Northern Ireland international (59 caps); Under-23 international (4 caps); 'B' international; Schoolboy international; FA Cup winners 1979, runners-up 1978, 1980; Football League Cup runners-up 1968; European Cup-winners' Cup runners-up 1980.

Terry Neill served Arsenal as a player for 11 years, as a manager for seven and had most of his success at Highbury. In the late 1970s and early '80s he took Arsenal to three successive FA Cup Finals and as well as other success in Cup competitions.

Neill was a strong tackler who was stubborn and uncompromising but always slow on the turn and susceptible to a player with quick acceleration. He could also be quick-tempered and had his fair share of bookings and sendings off, but his natural optimism left him unmoved if he had a poor match.

As a manager he was often in the public eye and was eloquent and charming with the media. However, his teams had a negative playing style which some people claim led to the drop in attendances at Highbury.

Neill joined Arsenal as a wing-half. He made his debut at Sheffield Wednesday in December 1960 and was later switched to centre-half by manager Billy Wright. Neill made his international debut for Northern Ireland against Italy in Bologna in April 1961 and went on to play 59 games for his country. He did not win any domestic honours as a player except in picking up a losers' medal when the Gunners went down to Leeds United in the 1968 League Cup Final. And then he was only substitute, despite appearing in all the previous rounds. He missed the following year's débâcle against Third Division Swindon Town in the League Cup Final.

Neill was only 28 when he was became player-manager of Hull City in June 1970, costing the Tigers a £44,000 fee. He was also chairman of the PFA at the time. City finished fifth in his first season in charge but then struggled to maintain their Second Division status. He also took on the responsibility of being player-manager of Northern Ireland at this time until March 1975, when pressures at White Hart Lane forced him to quit the job. He celebrated his final appearance for his country by scoring the goal which beat England at Wembley in May 1972. When he signed Steve Deere in May 1973, Neill decided to call it a day as a player and retired. He had played in 267/3 games for Arsenal, scoring ten goals, and 103 for Hull City, scoring four goals.

When his contract expired in May 1974 he worked on without one until, in September of that year, he was offered the managership of Tottenham Hotspur.

Succeeding the great Bill Nicholson was never going to be an easy task and Neill was certainly not the choice of the fans, who could not take to him due to his long association with Arsenal. Neill was never really given a chance by the White Hart Lane crowd and by his own admission, his spell in charge at Hull had been undistinguished, so his appointment at Tottenham seems strange in hindsight.

At Spurs, Neill drastically pruned the playing staff, which was far too large, and cleared the decks for the emergence of players like Glenn Hoddle. Spurs only just avoided relegation in 1974-75, with a good run at the end of the season, but improved to finish ninth the following season. Neill had appointed Keith Burkinshaw as his coach in 1975 and it was Burkinshaw who got most of the credit for this improvement. Spurs reached the semi-finals of the League Cup but lost 3-2 on aggregate to Newcastle United.

Neill resigned in July 1976 to take up the manager's post at Arsenal and in his seven years in charge, the Gunners never finished below tenth in the First Division. He immediately signed Malcolm Macdonald from Newcastle United for £333,000. Initially, Neill had experienced difficulties in managing old playing colleagues and made the mistake of making public his disagreements and criticisms of players. His sense of humour often camouflaged his serious attitude and philosophical approach to the game.

Arsenal reached the FA Cup Final in 1978, 1979 and 1980, their only victory coming in an exciting finish to the 1979 Final when they beat Manchester United 3-2. They lost 1-0 to Ipswich Town in 1978 and to West Ham in 1980, by the same score. The Gunners' best season in the First Division came in 1980-81 when they finished third. In 1980 they beat Valencia in the European Cup-winners' Cup Final in Brussels, 5-4 on penalties. Neill took Arsenal to two semi-finals in 1982-83, losing both to Manchester United in the FA and League Cups. He was sacked in December 1983, a month after a League Cup defeat against Walsall and after mounting pressure from the Press and fans. Neill had never been able to replace players such as Liam Brady and Frank Stapleton. He left football after this to work for charitable organisations.

NELSON, Andrew Nesbitt

Born: Custom House, London, 5 July 1935.

Centre-half   6ft 2in; 13st (1963). *Career: Custom House Youth Club; West Ham United December 1953; Ipswich Town June 1959 (£8,000); Leyton Orient September 1964; Plymouth Argyle October 1965 (£4,000); Millwall coach cs 1969; Gillingham manager June 1971-May 1974; Charlton Athletic manager May 1974-March 1980, commercial manager 1981-November 1982.*

Honours: Football League champions 1962, Division Two champions 1961; Division Three promotion 1975; Division Four runners-up 1974; Army Cup winners.

Andy Nelson captained Ipswich Town to great success. Second Division champions under Alf Ramsey in 1960-61, they surprised everybody by clinching the League championship the following season. Nelson made 193 League appearances for Ipswich before moving to Leyton Orient. He took his first coaching post at Millwall under Benny Fenton.

Nelson's tough approach was tempered by his desire to create a happy atmosphere at clubs he managed. He took Gillingham to runners-up spot in Division Four in 1973-74 and greatly improved the fund-raising activities at the club. Shortly afterwards he moved to Charlton Athletic. They finished third in Division Three in 1974-75, then struggled in the higher division, losing several players to the North American Soccer League at the beginning and end of seasons which affected performances. Nelson was sacked in March 1980, when there were rumours of friction between the manager and the coach, Mike Bailey. Nelson later returned to Charlton as commercial manager but the fans never really forgave him for selling their two best forwards, Derek Hales and Mike Flanagan. Nelson's brother, Bill, played for West Ham.

NEWBOULD, Harry J.

Born: Everton; Died: 1929.
Outside-right.
Career: Derby St Luke's; noted sprinter; qualified accountant; Derby County assistant secretary 1896, then secretary, secretary-manager 1900-July 1906; Manchester City secretary-manager July 1906-July 1912; secretary of Players' Union. Acedemicals (Copenhagen) coach & advisor August 1912.

Honours: Division Two champions 1910; FA Cup runners-up 1903.

Harry Newbould was secretary-manager of Derby County and Manchester City in the early years of the century. He found success at both clubs but ended his career as the secretary of the Players' Union, forerunner of today's PFA.

Newbould was born in the Everton district of Liverpool and never played professional football. Instead he appeared for Derby St Luke's, a leading local side, and made a name for himself as a sprinter, a skill he used to great effect on the right wing. A qualified accountant, Newbould was appointed as assistant secretary at Derby in 1896 and later promoted to secretary.

In 1900 he was appointed as Derby County's first secretary-manager but was not solely responsible for team affairs.

Many fine players joined the club during his six years in charge, including Ben Warren and Ben Hall. He was instructed by the board to sell star player Steve Bloomer, which was a great blow to the club and ultimately led to relegation soon after Newbould had left the club. Derby reached an FA Cup Final in 1903 but lost by a record 6-0 to Bury. They also reached two semi-finals, in 1902 losing 1-0 to Sheffield United in a second replay after two 1-1 draws, and in 1904 losing 1-0 to Bolton at Molineux.

In July 1906, Newbould surprised and disappointed the Derby board by becoming secretary-manager of Manchester City. Maybe he could see the writing on the wall after the departure of Steve Bloomer, but the prospects at Manchester City looked very bleak. They had just lost most of their playing staff after a financial scandal at the club over illegal payments to players had led to a number of suspensions. Newbould had to completely rebuild the team from scratch. This took time and City had a disastrous start to the season, including a 9-1 defeat at Everton.

But after a number of shrewd signings, Newbould ended the season with a forward line which included four internationals. City finished third in Division One in 1907-08 but were relegated the following season. They immediately bounced back as champions of the Second Division. Newbould left the club in July 1912, City having narrowly avoided relegation again the previous season. After working for the Players' Union, Newbould retired from football and died in 1929.

NEWCOMB, Leamon Robinson

Born: Stillington, 28 November 1903; Died: 3 July 1964.
Right-half   6ft 1in; 11st 10lb (1928). *Career: Stillington Juniors; Middlesbrough amateur; Stockton-on-Tees; Darlington amateur 1926, professional 1927; Sittingbourne January 1928; Millwall April 1928; Southport cs 1936-1942; worked as an engineer; Marine Crosby manager; Southport 'A' team coach, then manager July 1960-March 1964.*

'Lem' Newcomb is probably the oldest person to start a football man-

agement career in the Football League, when he took over at Southport in 1960, aged 56. Newcomb had been a well-known figure at Haig Avenue before the war and made 82 League appearances for the club. He had also played 197 times for Millwall. A clever player who concentrated on getting his wing moving, Newcomb had been an amateur working as an engineer when he made his League debut with Darlington.

He had gained a local reputation as manager of Marine before taking over the 'A' team at Haig Avenue. Southport's form greatly improved when he took over and they reached the third round of the FA Cup in his first season. They conceded 106 goals in 1962-63 but staved off re-election until 1964. He left Southport soon afterwards, with the club in something of a mess.

NEWMAN, John Henry George

Born: Hereford, 13 December 1933.
Wing-half   5ft 11in; 12st 4lb (1963). *Career: Herefordshire County youth; Hereford United; St Andrew's Athletic; Birmingham City amateur July 1949, professional March 1951; Leicester City November 1957; Plymouth Argyle January 1960; Exeter City November 1967 (£8,000), then player-manager April 1969-December 1976, retired as a player June 1972; Grimsby Town manager December 1976-July 1979; Derby County assistant manager July 1979, then manager January-November 1982; Hereford United manager November 1983-September 1987; Notts County assistant manager July 1988; York City assistant manager 1988; Mansfield Town coach and chief scout in 1991.*

Honours: Wales Junior international; Football League representative; Division Two champions 1955; Division Four runners-up 1979; FA Cup runners-up 1956.

John Newman played over 600 games in his career and appeared for Birmingham City in the 1956 FA Cup Final as a replacement for an injured regular. He had played for Wales at junior level, despite being English, as he had attended a school in Wales. Newman had a tough time at Leicester but enjoyed more luck at Plymouth, where he was made the skipper. He once passed a penalty a few feet for a colleague to score at Home Park.

Newman became player-manager at Exeter City and nearly resigned in October 1971 — he changed his mind — but could not get them out of the Fourth Division, despite a successful period in charge. But Newman did lead Grimsby out of that division in 1978-79, as runners-up to Reading. Good public relations became the hallmark of his management and he became assistant to Colin Addison at Derby, then inherited a struggling team — and a struggling club — when he took over. Newman almost took Hereford to promotion in 1985 and was then assistant to John Barnwell at Notts County, becoming caretaker manager briefly when Barnwell left the club.

NICHOLL, Christopher J.

Born: Wilmslow, 12 October 1946.
Central defender   6ft 2in; 12st 7lb (1970).
Career: Macclesfield Schools; Burnley apprentice June 1963, professional April 1965; Witton Albion 1966; Halifax Town June 1968 (£1,000);

Luton Town August 1969 (£30,000); Aston Villa March 1972 (£90,000); Southampton June 1977 (£90,000); Grimsby Town player-assistant manager August 1983, retired as a player July 1985; Southampton manager July 1985-May 1991.*

Honours: Northern Ireland international (51 caps); Division Three champions 1972; Football League Cup winners 1975, 1977 runners-up, 1979.

A tall, commanding defender who was very powerful in the air, Chris Nicholl failed to make the grade at Burnley but quickly made a name for himself after his Football League career was rescued by Halifax Town. He signed for Luton for a record fee and quickly became the cornerstone of their defence.

Honest, direct and hardworking, Nicholl was sold to Villa to help clear the Hatters' debts. He played for Northern Ireland in the 1982 World Cup finals and made 51 appearances for his country. He helped Villa to the Third Division championship, promotion to Division One and League Cup Final wins in 1975, and 1977.

Nicholl once scored all four goals in a game — a 2-2 draw against Arsenal, thus becoming the only person to have done this with two for each side. He helped Southampton regain their First Division status in 1978 and as manager kept them there but gained little other success. The Saints reached the semi-finals of the League Cup in 1986-87 but lost to Liverpool. He was sacked at the end of the 1990-91 campaign. His is the brother of Terry Nicholl of Gillingham.

NICHOLSON, John

Born: Sheffield; Died: Sheffield, 23 April 1932.
Career: Attercliffe secretary; executive of Sheffield FA 1893-1899; Sheffield United secretary-manager May 1899-April 1932.

Honours: FA Cup winners 1902, 1915, 1925, runners-up 1901.

John Nicholson was secretary-manager of Sheffield United for 33 years, during which the Blades had an excellent record in the FA Cup. They won the trophy three times, in 1902, 1915 and 1925, and were Finalists in 1901. They also reached the semi-finals in 1914, 1923 and 1928 and played continuously in the First Division during this period, much to Nicholson's credit.

Nicholson was born and bred in Sheffield and the only club with which he was connected prior to joining the Blades was Attercliffe, whom he served for a long period. He also represented the club on the executive of the Sheffield FA and worked as a clerk at a local deputy coroner's office. However on 1 May 1899, when Sheffield United became a limited company, he was asked to take over as secretary-manager of the club.

United came close to relegation only once during Nicholson's years in charge, in 1920-21 when they finished 20th. Their best seasons in Division One were 1902-03 and 1906-07, when they finished fourth, and 1923-24 and 1925-26, when they were fifth.

United's first real cup success under Nicholson came in 1901, when they lost 3-1 to Southern League Spurs in a replayed Final after a 2-2 draw at Crystal Palace. They made amends the following year, when another Southern League club, Southampton, were beaten 2-1 at the Palace in another replayed Final.

United also won the only Final to be played in wartime, in 1915 when they beat Chelsea 3-0 in what became known as the 'Khaki Cup Final' as most of the crowd was made up of servicemen. Ten years later, in 1925, they won the FA Cup again, beating Cardiff City 1-0 at Wembley.

Nicholson discovered a number of excellent players including Wally Hardinge, Billy Gillespie and Fred Tunstall, all of whom helped United to coast along in Division One, always guaranteeing attractive, enterprising play for the club.

It came as a great shock when he died. A much-loved and irreplaceable figure, John Nicholson passed away on 23 April 1932. He went to Sheffield Midland Station to catch a train to Birmingham for United's game at Villa Park that day. In the forecourt of the station he was knocked down by a lorry and killed. His life's work had been to maintain the highest standards in football both on and off the field.

NICHOLSON, William Edward OBE

Born: Scarborough, 26 January 1919.
Wing-half 5ft 9in; 11st 7lb (1951).
Career: Scarborough Working Men's Club; Tottenham Hotspur amateur March 1936, professional August 1938; Northfleet (loan); guest for Sunderland, Middlesbrough and Newcastle United in World War Two; retired 1955; Cambridge University coach; England Under-23 coach/scout; Tottenham Hotspur coach 1955, assistant manager August 1957, then manager October 1958-August 1974; West Ham United consultant August 1975; Tottenham Hotspur chief advisor and scout July 1976.

Honours: England international (1 cap); 'B' international (3 caps); Football League representative (1 cap); Football League champions 1951, 1961; Division Two champions 1950; FA Cup winners 1961, 1962, 1967; Football League Cup winners 1971, 1973; European Cup-winners' Cup winners 1963; UEFA Cup winners 1971, runners-up 1974.

Bill Nicholson was one of the greatest managers of British soccer. Despite his apparently dour nature and gruff exterior, he produced some of the most stylish and exciting sides ever seen in English football. He was never afraid to pay large fees for the players he wanted and had very few failures in the transfer market. Some say that he 'bought' success, but Nicholson turned very skilful individual players into important cogs of his exciting sides.

Spurs won the League and FA Cup double in 1960-61, the first club to do so in the 20th century, and they achieved this with a side which is still remembered today with great affection. This remarkable triumph was followed by a steady stream of Cup successes as Spurs went marching on.

Nicholson was playing for Scarborough Working Men's Club when he was spotted by Tottenham Hotspur. He joined the club as a groundstaff boy in March 1936 and was farmed out to their nursery club, Northfleet, where he developed over the next two years. In August 1938 he signed professional forms and made his League debut at left-back at Blackburn two months later. His career was soon interrupted by the outbreak of war, during which he rarely played, although after joining the Durham Light Infantry he stayed mainly in England. He was initially an infantry training instructor, then

became a physical training instructor and made occasional guest appearances for clubs in the North-East.

After the war, Nicholson returned to White Hart Lane and now turned out at centre-half before, in 1947-48, establishing himself at right-half. He was an ultra-reliable performer, hard but fair in the tackle. He played in Arthur Rowe's 'push and run' side which took the Second Division championship in 1949-50 and the Football League title the following season.

His one appearance for England, against Portugal at Goodison Park in May 1951, saw him score from long range with his first kick of the game, after only seconds. He also gained three 'B' caps, two against Switzerland and the other against Italy, and also represented the Football League against League of Ireland.

Nicholson made 345 League and Cup appearances and scored six goals for Spurs before retiring to take up a coaching post at the club in 1954. He had taken an interest in coaching whilst still a player and had gained his FA badge at the first attempt. He had taken charge of the Cambridge University side in the early 1950s and became first-team coach at Spurs in 1955, when Jimmy Anderson succeeded Arthur Rowe as manager.

In August 1957 he became assistant manager, then took over from Anderson in October 1958. Under Walter Winterbottom, Nicholson had been a coach of England's 1958 World Cup squad in Sweden. In his first season in charge, Spurs were struggling near the bottom of the First Division but achieved an astonishing victory in their first game under Nicholson, 10-4 against Everton.

A perfectionist, Nicholson developed sides with great style and allowed his players to show off their skills and entertain the crowds. He was meticulous in his preparation and care for detail and almost all his time and thoughts were devoted to the club. He was never frightened to pay big sums of money for players and rarely made a poor deal, achieving a blend of attacking soccer which delighted the crowds and won trophies.

Success soon came on the field and the 1960-61 double-winning side was one of the greatest-ever club line-ups in English soccer. They took the League title with ease after winning their first 11 matches of the season, then beat Leicester City 2-0 in the FA Cup Final. The following season they won the FA Cup again, beating Burnley 3-1 in the Final. Spurs also reached the semi-finals of the European Cup before

losing an epic struggle with Benfica, 4-3 on aggregate after two exciting games. In 1963, Spurs won their first European trophy when they beat Atlético Madrid 5-1 in Rotterdam in the European Cup-winners' Cup Final. Tragedy struck in 1964, when the mercurial schemer John White was killed by lightning whilst out playing golf.

Nicholson was in the process of rebuilding the side which reached another FA Cup Final in 1967, when they beat London rivals, Chelsea, 2-1. Tottenham reached four Cup Finals between 1971 and 1974. They won the League Cup in 1971 and 1973, beating Aston Villa and Norwich City respectively, and in 1972 and 1974 reached the UEFA Cup Final. In 1972 they beat Wolves over two legs and in 1974 lost to Feyenoord 4-2 on aggregate with crowd trouble marring the second leg in Rotterdam.

Over the years Nicholson made a number of excellent signings. To help create the double-winning side of 1960-61 he signed Dave Mackay, Bill Brown, John White and Les Allen and later Jimmy Greaves from Italy. After 1963, when he rebuilt the side, he signed Alan Mullery, Pat Jennings, Cyril Knowles, Alan Gilzean and Terry Venables and in the late 1960s signed Martin Peters and Martin Chivers. He had very few failures on the transfer market and only Tony Marchi and Ralph Coates never really fulfilled their promise.

Nicholson was apparently never a great communicator with his players or the Press and he found it difficult to trust either. He was often hostile to journalists but was said to be most animated and responsive when his teams lost.

After a poor start to the 1974-75 season, Nicholson surprised most people by resigning his post as Spurs' manager after 16 years in charge. The players and directors tried to persuade him to change his mind but to no avail. Nicholson took a deserved rest from football but returned to work as a consultant at West Ham from August 1975. Since July 1976, when re-appointed by Keith Burkinshaw at Spurs, Bill Nicholson has worked as chief advisor and scout at White Hart Lane and can be seen regularly today scouting at matches throughout London.

NIXON, Ernest

Career: Rochdale secretary possibly from November 1928, caretaker manager December 1931-April 1932 and January-July 1934, then secretary-manager November 1935-October 1937.

Ernie Nixon had two periods as caretaker manager of Rochdale whilst also acting as secretary before becoming the official secretary-manager in 1935.

Nixon initially took control after the departure of Billy Cameron in December 1931. He made many team changes as well as recalling former players who were now playing in non-League soccer. On 19 March 1932, Rochdale drew 1-1 at New Brighton to end a run of 21 consecutive away defeats in the League and FA Cup.

In his second spell in charge, Nixon could not prevent the club finishing bottom of the Northern Section in 1934 with only 24 points. In November 1935, he took over from the sacked Billy Smith and Rochdale finished 18th in 1936-37 but Nixon was forced to sell his best players to stave off financial disaster. After a poor start to the season, he was replaced by Glentoran manager Sam Jennings on 6 October 1937.

NORMAN, William

Career: Barnsley trainer January 1904-1913; Huddersfield Town trainer cs 1914; Blackpool manager cs 1919-cs 1923; Leeds United assistant manager June 1923-1927; Hartlepools United manager August 1927-April 1932. Barnsley coach again 1912-13.

Bill Norman was the trainer at Barnsley when they won the FA Cup in 1912. His waxed moustache and the spartan training routines that he organised earned him the nickname 'Sergeant Major'. His teams were notable for their speed and fitness, not their tactical ability. Norman worked with Arthur Fairclough at both Barnsley and Leeds United. When he became Blackpool's first full-time manager, his son-in-law, Allan Ure, became the trainer.

Blackpool had a good season in 1919-20, finishing fourth in the Second Division and winning the Central League championship for the first time. He then raised £10,200 by selling three players and performances deteriorated. He and Fairclough took Leeds to promotion to Division One in 1924 but both resigned when the club was relegated three years later. He had a constant struggle at Hartlepools but did unearth W.G.Richardson, who was sold to West Brom. One story sums up Norman: on bitterly cold day, the players hesitated to strip for training. Norman showed them he was not worried by the weather by taking off his clothes and rolling naked in the snow.

OAKES, Alan

Born: Winsford, 1 September 1942.
Midfield 5ft 11in; 12st 2lb (1963).
Career: Manchester and Cheshire Boys; Manchester City apprentice April 1958, professional July 1959; Chester July 1976 (£15,000), then player-manager September 1976-March 1982; Port Vale player-coach 1982-December 1983 and coach 1985-1987.

Honours: Football League representative (1 cap); Football League champions 1968; Division Two champions 1966; FA Cup winners 1969; Football League Cup winners 1970, 1976; European Cup-winners' Cup winners 1970.

Alan Oakes was a quiet, unassuming and gentlemanly player who did a thoroughly professional job without fuss. He made surging runs and penetrating passes and was one of the most consistent performers at Maine Road. Oakes had a great record for City. He made 665/3 appearances, scoring 33 goals, and won many medals in the process, including Second Division and League championship medals. He also gained an FA Cup winners' medal when City beat West Brom in the 1969 Final, a European Cup-winners' Cup medal against Gornik the following year plus two League Cup winners' medals. He gained only one representative honour, for the Football League against Scottish League in March 1969.

Oakes made 211 League appearances for Chester as player-manager. His best season there was when they finished fifth in Division Three in 1977-78. They also reached the fifth round of the FA Cup in 1977 and 1980. Oakes was sacked with Chester bottom of Division Three in March 1982. He had two spells as coach at Port Vale but was finally sacked for economic reasons, after turning out in one League match in an emergency in 1983-84, aged 42.

O'BRIEN, Michael Terence

Born: Kilcock, County Down, 10 August 1893; Died: Uxbridge, 21 September 1940.
Centre-half 6ft 2in; 13st 7lb (1925).
Career: Walker Celtic; Wallsend; Blyth Spartans; Newcastle North End; Glasgow Celtic; Alloa Athletic two months trial; Brentford 1919; Norwich City August 1919; South Shields December 1919; Queen's Park Rangers May 1920; Leicester City March 1922; Hull City June 1924 (£750); Brooklyn Wanderers (USA) May 1926; Derby County December 1926; Walsall June 1928; Norwich City May 1929; Watford June 1931-April 1933, then retired; Queen's Park Rangers manager May 1933-April 1935; Brentford assistant manager 1935-1936; Ipswich Town manager May 1936-August 1937.
Honours: Ireland international 10 caps; Republic of Ireland international 4 caps; Football League representative v Army 1921; Southern League champions 1937.

A much travelled player, Mick O'Brien was a genuinely talented player and a classical centre-half. He served in the Army before World War One, then in the Navy and the Royal Flying Corps during hostilities. He claimed that he did not play football until he was 18 years old, when his family moved to South Shields from Ireland. He had two spells at Norwich City, in the second also running a confectionary and tobacconist's shop. He also had a brief and unhappy spell in the United States and his registration was held up by the FA when he returned to England to sign for Derby County.

When O'Brien took over at Queen's Park Rangers they had just returned to Loftus Road after a costly spell at White City. The club had massive debts, so O'Brien had little money to spend on new players. QPR managed to finish fourth in the Southern Section in 1933-34 but he left after a poor season in the next campiagn. He took Ipswich Town to the Southern League title in 1936-37. In 1937 personal problems, including the death of his wife, began to overwhelm him and he died a few years later.

O'CONNELL, Patrick

Born: Dublin c.887.
Half-back 5ft 10in; 12st (1909).
Career: Belfast Celtic; Sheffield Wednesday cs 1909; Hull City May 1912; Manchester United May 1914; Dumbarton August 1919; Ashington player-manager cs 1921-1922; coaching in Spain in 1920s.
Honours: Ireland international (5 caps).

Pat O'Connell was skipper of the first Irish side to win the Home Championship in 1913-14. Ireland beat England 3-0 at Middlesbrough, Wales 2-1 at Wrexham and drew 1-1 with Scotland in Belfast to take the title. After moving to Sheffield Wednesday from Belfast Celtic, he made 21 appearances for the Owls before being transferred to Hull City. He played 58 times for the Tigers and 51 times for Manchester United in peacetime and wartime games.

Appointed Ashington's manager when they entered the Football League, O'Connell made 19 appearances for the club. He retired in 1922 and also seemed to have left Ashington at this time. Attendances were poor, often numbering little more than 1,000, and the club was always going to struggle to survive.

O'FARRELL, Frank

Born: Cork, 9 October 1927.
Wing-half 5ft 8½in; 12st (1959).
Career: Cork United; West Ham United January 1948; Preston North End November 1956, retired due to injury 1961; Weymouth player-manager May 1961-1965; Torquay United manager May 1965-December 1968; Leicester City manager December 1968-June 1971; Manchester United manager June 1971-December 1972; Cardiff City manager November 1973-April 1974; Iran national team manager April 1974; Torquay United manager November 1976-March 1977 and June 1981-June 1982, then general manager until 1983.
Honours: Republic of Ireland international (9 caps); Division Two champions 1971; Division Four promotion 1966; FA Cup runners-up 1969; Southern League champions 1965; Southern League Cup runners-up 1964, 1965.

Frank O'Farrell will probably be best remembered for his 18-month spell in charge of Manchester United and the shabby way he was treated by the club. O'Farrell walked into a minefield at Old Trafford, with the great side of the 1960s beginning to break up, having to live in the shadow of the great Matt Busby and having to deal with the crazy antics of George Best, who was in the process of destroying his own career. O'Farrell must have wished that he had not left Leicester City, who he had just taken to the Second Division championship when he accepted the lucrative offer to manage the Reds.

O'Farrell played for his local side, Cork United, before moving to West Ham in January 1948. He made his League debut in December 1950, against Notts County, and soon established himself in the first team. A polished wing-half, O'Farrell was to become part of the West Ham 'academy' which produced a generation of managers including Malcolm Allison, Dave Sexton, John Bond, Noel Cantwell, Jimmy Andrews, Ken Brown and Malcolm Musgrove, who later worked with O'Farrell at Leicester and Manchester United.

O'Farrell gained a representative honour for the Football Combination against the Brussels League and later made nine appearances for the Republic of Ireland. He played 210 League and FA Cup games for the Hammers before moving to Preston in a straight exchange for Eddie Lewis in November 1956. O'Farrell made a further 118 League appearances for Preston before moving to Weymouth as player-manager in May 1961.

He proved a success at the South Coast club, steering them to the Southern League championship in 1964-65 and to two League Cup Finals in 1964 and 1965, both of which were lost on

aggregate. They also reached the fourth round of the FA Cup in his first season in charge before losing to his previous club, 2-0 at Deepdale.

Obviously impressed by this record, Torquay United asked O'Farrell to become their manager in May 1965. They gained promotion at the end of his first season in charge when they finished third in the Fourth Division. In the next two seasons they finished seventh and fourth respectively in the Third Division. Attendances remained small at Plainmoor, however, and O'Farrell had to find success with little money to spend. He spent a total of £30,000 on seven players including many from West Ham United. These included John Bond, Ken Brown and Bill Kitchener. He also brought some much-needed discipline to the club and returned to manage Torquay for two further spells, but took over a different club from his first spell in charge. Torquay were hard up and having to survive by playing part-time players. At the end of his third spell, he was happy to retire and let his coach, Bruce Rioch, take over. He remained at the club as general manager until 1983.

Back in December 1968, O'Farrell was enticed away to become manager of Leicester City. He narrowly won the board's vote over Allan Brown of Luton Town to replace Matt Gillies as the manager. Leicester were relegation-bound but reached an FA Cup Final where they lost 1-0 to Manchester City at Wembley. The softly spoken Irishman then remoulded the club for a rapid return to the top flight after only two seasons.

Just after Leicester became Second Division champions, he was invited to take over at Old Trafford in June 1971. O'Farrell found it difficult to follow in the footsteps of Matt Busby. The board wanted instant success from a team which was going through a transitional period but after leading the table at Christmas, United finished eighth at the end of his first season. O'Farrell and his assistant Malcolm Musgrove were sacked in December 1972, with United struggling in the First Division. He had spent a considerable amount of money in this short time, including fees of over £200,000 each for Ian Storey-Moore and Ted MacDougall and £125,000 for Martin Buchan, only the latter proving a real success.

George Best was doing his disappearing act and O'Farrell left Old Trafford a bitter man. He took over at Cardiff City in November 1973, but lasted only 158 days in office before accepting a lucrative offer to coach in Iran from April 1974. Today, Frank O'Farrell lives in retirement in Torquay.

O'HAGAN, Charles

Born: Buncruna, County Donegal, 1882.
Inside-forward 5ft 9in; 10st 7lb (1904).
Career: Derry Celtic; Old Xaverians (Liverpool); Everton Reserves cs 1903; Tottenham Hotspur cs 1904; Middlesbrough July 1906; Aberdeen December 1906 (£175); Morton cs 1910 (£185); Norwich City manager July 1920-January 1921; coaching in Berlin in 1924.
Honours: Ireland international (11 caps).

A born entertainer, O'Hagan thrived on the popularity he received at Pittodrie. Never a regular at both Tottenham or Middlesbrough, O'Hagan scored eight goals in 37 appearances for Spurs and played only five times for 'Boro. Things

changed at Aberdeen, where he formed an excellent partnership with Willie Lennie. Often the target of the opposing hard men, O'Hagan scored 24 goals in his 112 appearances for the club and was their first player to be capped at international level, for Ireland.

In World War One he served in France for over three years with the Highland Light Infantry and was fortunate to survive. He was manager of Norwich City when they entered the Football League but did not last very long. The home fans had to wait until November for their first victory and he resigned after the Canaries won only four games in their first 22.

O'ROURKE, Peter

Born: 22 September 1874; Died: Odsal, Bradford, 10 January 1956
Centre-half.
Career: Glasgow Celtic 1894; New Brighton Tower; Burnley May 1897; Lincoln City July 1899; Chesterfield Town 1901-1902; Bradford City June 1903, reserve-team manager 1904, club coach March 1905, then player-manager November 1905-June 1921; Pontypridd manager 1921 (for five months); Dundee Hibernian manager 1922-April 1924; Bradford manager April 1924-February 1925; Bradford City manager May 1928-May 1930; Walsall manager October 1930-December 1931; Llanelli coach 1932-July 1933.
Honours: Division Two champions 1898, 1908; Division Three North champions 1929; FA Cup winners 1911.

Peter O'Rourke is Bradford City's most successful manager in their history. He was in charge of the club when they won the FA Cup in 1911 and he also kept them in the First Division for most of the years that he was in charge at Valley Parade. He also managed Bradford's other club, Park Avenue, for a ten-month spell in the 1920s.

He played junior soccer in the Glasgow area as a youngster. In 1894 he joined Celtic but was unable to break into their successful side on a regular basis, making only nine appearances before moving south to join New Brighton. In May 1897, O'Rourke moved to Burnley and gained a Second Division championship medal in his first season at Turf Moor after making 15 appearances. He played in only two games the following season in the First Division and moved to Lincoln City in July 1899, but they quickly lost their Football League status. He re-emerged as captain of Chesterfield Town in 1901-02.

O'Rourke joined Bradford City as a player in June 1903, appearing mainly at centre-half. He became player-coach for the 1904-05 season, then club coach from March 1905. In November of that year O'Rourke was appointed player-manager but played his last game the following month, in an FA Cup tie at Darlington.

O'Rourke shrewdly built the team up in 1907-08 when they won the Second Division title to enter the top flight only five years after their formation. He was given a five-year contract, which helped to bring stability to the club and City reached the pinnacle of their success in 1911, when they beat Newcastle United in a replayed FA Cup Final. They also finished fifth in the First Division that season, their highest-ever position. Jimmy Spiers scored the only goal of the Cup Final replay at Old Trafford, playing in a side which contained eight Scotsmen. City had conceded only one goal in their Cup run of seven matches.

Peter was deeply affected by the death of his son, Francis, in Newfoundland in 1919 and took some time to recover. He resigned from the manager's job at Valley Parade in June 1921 and moved to Wales to manage Pontypridd for five months. In 1922, O'Rourke returned to Scotland to take charge at Dundee Hibernian, who had just lost their Scottish League status. In 1923 they changed their name to Dundee United and rejoined the Second Division to finish seventh in their first season back. O'Rourke left the club in April 1924 to join Bradford as manager but stayed at Park Avenue for only ten months, in which time they scored freely and challenged, ultimately unsuccessfully, for Third Division North honours.

In May 1928, O'Rourke was persuaded to come out of retirement to manage Bradford City again. They had dropped from the First to the Third Division and had hit hard times. They had just avoided being liquidated when O'Rourke took over. He soon turned things around and City marched away with the Northern Section title in 1928-29. After an poor season, when they finished 18th in the Second Division, just avoiding relegation, O'Rourke resigned in May 1930.

Soon afterwards he took over at Walsall but could not get the club out of the doldrums and left in December 1931. Early the following year, O'Rourke moved back to Wales to manage Llanelli until his retirement in July 1933. He returned to live in the Bradford area and died in the Odsal district of the city in 1956.

ORMEROD, Samuel

Born: Accrington; Died: 1906.
Career: Referee in local Lancashire football in 1880s; Manchester City manager 1895-July 1902; Stockport County manager 1903-1905; Clapton Orient manager April 1905 January 1906.

Honours: Division Two champions 1899, runners-up 1896.

Sam Ormerod was Manchester City's first secretary-manager but he did not have sole charge in his seven years at the club, during which City were promoted and relegated. He had little success at Stockport County and Clapton Orient, where he was in sole charge.

Ormerod hailed from Accrington and gained a reputation as a player and referee in local Lancashire soccer in the 1880s. He officially became Manchester City's manager in 1895, as part of a three-man committee which included his predecessor Joshua Parlby. Ormerod exerted the most influence on this committee and helped spot many fine players for the club.

He used over 50 players in three seasons and with so many new faces coming and going, forming a team plan must have proved very difficult. Ormerod had little tactical awareness and many of the problems that he encountered were because of this. His main role was to select the team. City finished runners-up in Division Two in 1895-96 and qualified for the play-offs. They did not do very well in these, losing 6-1 at West Brom and 8-0 at Small Heath.

They finished sixth and third in the next two seasons, then became champions of Division Two in 1898-99 with a team built around a strong defence and the attacking skills of Billy Meredith, who scored 29 goals that season.

City found the going tough in Division One and were relegated at the end of 1901-02. Ormerod resigned in July 1902, after receiving a lot of criticism on how the club was being run financially by those attending a shareholders' meeting. They were especially critical of the amounts spent on travelling expenses, bonuses and wages.

Ormerod followed this with a two-year spell in charge at Stockport County from 1903. They were not re-elected at the end of the 1903-04 season after finishing third from bottom of Division Two.

In April 1905, Ormerod became the first full-time manager of Clapton Orient when they joined the Football League. He did not last the season, though, resigning in January 1906 after a crisis meeting to discuss the club's financial situation. Little of this had been caused by Ormerod but Orient eventually finished bottom of Division Two and were re-elected by just one vote. His best signing for the club had been Billy Holmes from Manchester City, who eventually succeeded Ormerod as Orient's manager. Ormerod died a couple of months after leaving Orient.

ORR, William

Born: Shotts, Lanarkshire, 20 June 1873; Died: 26 February 1946.
Wing-half   5ft 9in; 12st 2lb (1899).
Career: Airdrie Fruitfield; Airdrieonians; Preston North End February 1894; Glasgow Celtic May 1897, retired cs 1907; Airdrieonions director 1909-1921, then secretary-manager 1921-1926; Leicester City secretary-manager July 1926-January 1932; Falkirk secretary-manager June 1932-April 1935.

Honours: Scotland international (3 caps); Scottish League champions 1898, 1905, 1906, 1907; Football League runners-up 1929; Scottish Cup winners 1900, 1904, 1907, 1924, runners-up 1901, 1902.

Willie Orr enjoyed ten great years as a defender with Celtic, picking up four League championship and three Cup winners' medals as well as appearing in another two Finals and winning three Scottish caps.

He also had a great record as manager of Airdrie, who finished First Division runners-up three seasons on the trot between 1922 and 1925 and also won the Scottish Cup in 1924 when they beat Hibernian 2-0 at Ibrox to clinch the trophy for the only time in their history.

In 1926, Orr moved to Leicester City and found much success in his early years at Filbert Street. Leicester finished third in Division One in 1927-28 and runners-up to Sheffield Wednesday the following season, although after this they struggled to maintain their First Division status.

His time at Falkirk was far less happy. Not only were the club relegated in 1934-35 but Orr was banned for life in April 1935 after being found guilty of bribery and also paying £3 to Ayr United player Robert Russell as an inducement to miss a crucial game.

OSBORNE, Frank Raymond

Born: Wynberg, South Africa, 14 October 1896; Died: 8 March 1988.
Outside-right/Centre-forward
5ft 11½in; 10st 7lb (1925).
Career: Bromley 1919; Fulham November 1921; Tottenham Hotspur January 1924; Southampton June 1931, retired cs 1933; sales representative for Deans Blinds 1933-1935; Fulham director March 1935, general manager

September 1948-October 1964, and team manager September 1948-June 1949 and October 1953-January 1956.
Honours: England international (4 caps); Division Two champions 1949.

Frank Osborne was equally effective as a right-winger or a centre-forward. His slim physique helped his mobility and he was a graceful, stylish player. He came to England in 1911 and he and his brother, Reg, both represented his adopted country. He gained his first cap against Ireland at West Bromwich in October 1922 and also scored a hat-trick against Belgium in Antwerp. He was the first Fulham player to be capped for England.

Osborne scored 82 goals in 220 appearances for Spurs before ending his playing career at The Dell. As Osborne was a director at Fulham he had to be given special permission to become the club's general manager. He created high-scoring teams and also encouraged a family atmosphere at the Cottage. The players were given freedom to express themselves and entertain the crowds. Osborne was a nervous character who was unable to watch the closing minutes of a match. Poorly treated by the club at the end, despite helping them to two FA Cup semi-finals and into Division One, he left football a disillusioned man. He died in a Surrey nursing home at the age of 91.

OSMAN, Russell Charles

Born: Repton, Derbyshire, 14 February 1959.
Central Defender   6ft; 12st (1991)
Career: Ipswich Town apprentice 1974, professional March 1976; Leicester City July 1985 (£240,000); Southampton June 1988 (£325,000); Bristol City October 1991, player-assistant manager March 1992, then player-manager January 1993.

Honours: England International 11 caps; Under 21 International 7 caps; 'B' International; Youth International; FA Youth Cup Winners 1975; UEFA Cup Winners 1981.

Russell Osman's father, Rex was a half-back with Derby County Reserves in the 1950s. A two-footed defender, Osman formed an excellent partnership with Terry Butcher at Ipswich under the managership of Bobby Robson. Osman was cool under pressure and assured on the ball. He gained an FA Youth Cup winners' medal in 1975, when Ipswich beat West Ham 5-1 on aggregate over two legs, and twice went close to a League Championship medal in 1981 and 1982, when Town finished as runners-up in the First Division. Osman helped Ipswich gain the UEFA Cup in 1981, when they beat AZ67 Alkmaar in the Final. They won the first leg 3-0 at Portman Road and scraped home in Holland after a 4-2 defeat. Osman gained his first England cap in Australia in May 1980 and made his final appearance for his country when they lost 1-0 to Denmark in the European Championship in September 1983 to miss out on qualification. His first managerial appointment came with Bristol City where he was initially the caretaker manager for seven weeks. He steered the club clear of relegation despite selling star striker Andrew Cole to Newcastle United for £1.75m.

OWEN, Sydney William

Born: Birmingham, 29 February 1922.
Centre-half   6ft; 11st 10lb (1957).
Career: YMCA; Birmingham City

October 1945; Luton Town June 1947 (£1,500), player-coach 1955, then manager May 1959-April 1960; Leeds United chief coach May 1960-October 1975; Birmingham City assistant manager October 1975-September 1977; Hull City coach December 1977-February 1978; Manchester United youth coach May 1978-April 1981, then scout until August 1982.*

Honours: England international (3 caps); Football League representative (2 caps); FA XI tours of South Africa, West Indies and Australia; Footballer of the Year 1959; FA Cup runners-up 1959.

Syd Owen was one of Luton Town's greatest-ever players. A dominant centre-half, he is fondly remembered by his fellow players and was considered a great captain. Tall, slender, almost ungainly, Owen had a slight frame and long legs. He was very fit and had good self discipline. Owen was Footballer of the Year in 1959, the year Luton reached the FA Cup Final where they lost 2-1 to Nottingham Forest.

He did not have a very happy spell as Luton's manager, however. He was usually at loggerheads with directors over the signing of new players and the Hatters were relegated to Division Two. Owen became a first-class coach, working with Don Revie for many years at Elland Road during their great days of the 1960s and early '70s.

PAGE, Louis Antonio

Born: Kirkdale, 27 March 1899; Died: Birkenhead, 12 October 1959.
Outside-left   5ft 9in; 11st 8lb (1923).
Career: St Alexander School; Liverpool Schools; Sudley Juniors; South Liverpool; Stoke cs 1919; Northampton Town cs 1922; Burnley May 1925; Manchester United March 1932; Port Vale October 1932; Yeovil & Petters United player-manager July 1933-May 1935; Newport County manager June 1935-September 1937; Glentoran trainer-coach December 1938; Carlton (Liverpool) manager in war; Swindon Town manager July 1945-May 1953; Chester manager June 1953-June 1956; Leicester City scout late 1950s.

Honours: England international (7 caps); Southern League Western Section champions 1935; Southern League Cup runners-up 1935.

A flying winger who was an elusive, fast and powerful marksman, Page once scored six goals in a match, for Burnley at Birmingham in April 1926. His three brothers all played professional football — John (Merthyr Town), Bill (Northampton Town) and Tommy (Port Vale) — and all represented their country at baseball. Louis scored 115 goals in 259 games for Burnley. He had served in the Royal Navy in World War One and was torpedoed whilst on HMS Virginian.

His first managerial job was with

Yeovil, who in 1934-35 had a good run to the third round of the FA Cup. They also did well in the Southern League that season. Page had an unhappy spell as Newport's manager and after a row over team selection he was suspended in September 1937, then sacked. He won damages for wrongful dismissal. During World War Two, Page worked at Liverpool docks and managed a local side called Carlton. Swindon went close to promotion in 1946-47 and 1948-49 but under Page, Chester finished bottom of the Northern Section two seasons running from 1953 to 1955. He later scouted for Leicester City.

PAGHAM, Frederick

Born: Poulton-le-Fylde near Blackpool, 4 September 1891; Died: 7 March 1962.
Centre-forward 5ft 8½in; 11st 4lb (1914).
Career: Poulton Grammar School; Lytham; Blackpool Wednesday; Huddersfield Town 1910; Southport Central cs 1912; Blackpool February 1913; Liverpool October 1914; Arsenal October 1919 (£1,500); Cardiff City March 1921 (£1,500); Watford December 1921 (£1,000), then manager 1926-1929; licensee in Rickmansworth from 1924; Turkey national coach; coaching in Holland for eight years.

A robust centre-forward who also appeared on the right wing and at inside-right, Fred Pagham was the son of a Blackpool bank manager. He played for his local club before moving to Anfield and scored 30 goals in 39 games for Liverpool before playing in wartime soccer, when he scored another 42 goals in 48 wartime appearances for the Reds. He then had a successful period with Arsenal, where he scored another 29 goals. Pagham then moved to Cardiff City, who went on to win promotion to the First Division.

Alas, the goals dried up for Pagham in the higher sphere but his scoring touch returned when he moved to Watford, where he scored a further 72 goals in 144 appearances. This included a game as manager in an emergency after he had officially retired. Watford had to seek re-election at the end of his first season in control but improved to finish eighth in 1928-29, when he left to concentrate on his pub at nearby Rickmansworth.

PAINE, Arthur

Died: October 1954.
Career: Lancaster Town secretary; Bury secretary June 1923, secretary-manager January 1930-cs 1934, then financial secretary until his death.

Arthur Paine had a long association with Bury, from 1923 until his death in October 1954, when he was the financial secretary of the club. When Paine was secretary-manager he did not have full control. The directors picked the side and decided which new players to sign. Paine also relied a great deal on team captain Norman Bullock for advice about the players and organising them in training. However, Bury did well at this time finishing fourth in 1932-33 and fifth in 1929-30 and 1931-32. In the latter they also reached the quarter-finals of the FA Cup where they lost 4-3 to Manchester City at home. The team was beginning to grow old together and there was an obvious need for a change and an influx of new blood, so Bullock took over from Paine in 1934.

PAISLEY, Robert OBE

Born: Hetton-le-Hole, 23 January 1919.
Wing-half 5ft 7in; 11st 4lb (1947).
Career: Bishop Auckland 1938; Liver-

pool May 1939; guest for Bristol City in World War Two; retired July 1954; Liverpool assistant trainer, chief trainer 1957, assistant manager then manager July 1974-June 1983, when he retired to become a director.
Honours: Football League champions 1947, 1976, 1977, 1979, 1980, 1982, 1983; FA Cup runners-up 1977; Football League Cup winners 1981, 1982, 1983, runners-up 1978; European Cup winners 1977, 1978, 1981; UEFA Cup winners 1976; FA Amateur Cup winners 1939.

Bob Paisley is one of the most successful managers in the history of English soccer. He continued on the great work done by his predecessor Bill Shankly in maintaining Liverpool as one of the great clubs sides in the world. They won many honours under Paisley including six League championships, three European Cup victories, three League Cup successes and a UEFA Cup victory. The FA Cup eluded him as a player and a manager but he was voted Manager of the Year a record six times.

Paisley's managerial career dwarfed his playing accomplishments, but he was no mean performer on the field. He began his playing career at Bishop Auckland and in 1939 gained an FA Amateur Cup winners' medal when Willington were beaten 3-0 in the Final after extra-time at Roker Park.

Soon after the Final, Paisley joined Liverpool but his early years at the club were lost to the war. He developed into a gritty, tenacious wing-half who was a dour tackler with indefatigable spirit. His powerful throws helped Liverpool to several goals and he gained a League championship medal in 1946-47 when he made 33 appearances. Paisley scored the vital goal in the 1950 FA Cup semi-final victory against Everton but much to his disappointment he was left out of the Wembley side. He retired in July 1954, after 278 League and Cup games for Liverpool, in which he scored 13 goals.

Paisley joined the backroom staff and gradually worked his way through the ranks. Starting as assistant trainer, he became chief trainer in 1957 and was assistant manager to Bill Shankly for many years before being appointed as manager in July 1974, when Shankly retired. Unlike Shankly, Paisley always preferred to keep a low profile and when he became manager he, rather predictably, said that the team would do his talking for him.

Paisley had a deep understanding of football and his first master-stroke was to convert Ray Kennedy from a striker

into an invaluable and authoritative midfield player.

In 1977 he signed Kenny Dalglish from Celtic to replace Kevin Keegan, who had moved to Hamburg. He also signed Graeme Souness from Middlesbrough and both men later managed the club.

There were no trophies in 1974-75 but the following season Liverpool won the League championship and the UEFA Cup, beating Bruges 4-3 on aggregate in the Final. They needed victory from their final match at Molineux to clinch the title and Paisley probably cast his mind back to 1947 when Liverpool also needed to win the last game at Molineux to win the Championship. This time the Reds won 3-1 to take the title.

They retained the championship in 1976-77 but missed out on the double when they lost 2-1 to Manchester United in the FA Cup Final, although four days later they beat Borussia Mönchengladbach 3-1 in the European Cup Final to take that trophy for the first time in their history. In 1977-78 the European Cup was lifted again, this time with a dull 1-0 victory over Bruges at Wembley, thanks to a fine goal from Dalglish. The 1978-79 League championship success was probably their greatest when they conceded only 16 goals all season including just four at Anfield. They took a record 68 points with 30 wins and only four defeats. Ray Clemence kept 28 clean sheets, another record.

Liverpool also took the League title in 1979-80, 1981-82 and 1982-83 and the European Cup for the third time in 1981, beating Real Madrid 1-0 in Paris with a goal from Alan Kennedy. The Reds played in four League Cup Finals under Paisley, winning in 1981, 1982 and 1983 but losing to Nottingham Forest in the 1978 Final replay at Old Trafford. Liverpool also played in a disappointing World Cup championship match in Tokyo when they lost 3-0 to Flamengo in December 1981.

In June 1983 Paisley decided to retire but remained at the club as an advisor to his successors, Joe Fagan and Kenny Dalglish, and also served on the board of directors. By this time he had served Liverpool for 44 years as player, trainer and manager. Paisley retired from the Liverpool board of directors in February 1992 due to ill health.

PALMER, Joseph

Career: Bristol City trainer 1913-1914; gymnastic staff in the Army at Aldershot in World War One; Bristol City manager August 1919-December 1921; Bradford trainer 1923-1926; Bristol Rovers manager May 1926-May 1929.

Joe Palmer was a strong disciplinarian and demanded that players under his control should be utterly dedicated and very fit. A former Army sergeant, Palmer took Bristol City to an FA Cup semi-final in 1920, where they lost to Huddersfield Town, and they also finished third in Division Two in 1920-21, thus just missing promotion.

Things went wrong the following season and Palmer resigned after disagreements with the directors. City were relegated at the end of the season. Palmer had an unspectacular stay at neighbours Bristol Rovers. They finished tenth, 19th and 19th respectively in the Southern Section during his three years in charge.

PARKER, Alex Hershaw

Born: Irvine, Ayrshire, 2 August 1935.
Right-back 5ft 8in; 11st 2lb (1955).

Career: Kello Rovers (Kirkconnel) c.1950; Falkirk August 1952; Everton May 1958 (£18,000); Southport September 1965 (£2,000); Ballymena United player-manager January 1968-December 1969; Drumcondra January 1970; Southport trainer-coach March 1970, then manager May 1970-May 1971; licensee in Runcorn.
Honours: Scotland international (15 caps); Under-23 international (6 caps); Scottish League representative (8 caps); Scottish Player of the Year 1957; Football League champions 1963; Scottish Cup winners 1957.

A classic right-back, Alex Parker was thoughtful, methodical, fast and adventurous. He possessed accurate distribution and was very strong in the tackle. He won a Scottish Cup winners' medal with Falkirk, when they beat Kilmarnock 2-1, in the 1957 Final after a replay, and was also playing for Falkirk when he won his first Scottish cap, against Portugal in May 1955. He played in the 1958 World Cup finals, against Paraguay, his last appearance for his country.

When he joined Everton, Parker was still doing his National Service and was immediately posted to Cyprus. He still managed to make 219 appearances for the Toffees before moving to Southport. After a spell in Northern Ireland as player-manager at Ballymena United and in Dublin with Drumcondra, Parker moved back to Southport as trainer-coach and then became manager. They had a good season under Parker and finished eighth in Division Four in 1970-71.

PARKER, Charles

Career: accountant in Civil Service in World War One; worked for Poultry Fanciers' Utility Association; Preston North End secretary 1906-1915; Southport manager May 1926-January 1929; Manchester Central secretary-manager in 1930s.

In March 1924, Parker announced that he would become secretary-manager of Bradford. He said that he would take up the post at the end of the month but this never happened and he withdrew from the appointment ten days later without beginning his duties at Park Avenue.

In 1926, Parker took over at Southport. They finished 12th, eighth and 12th in the Northern Section in his three seasons in charge and had an excellent FA Cup run in 1926-27, knocking out First Division Blackburn Rovers 2-0 and reaching the fourth round where they lost 3-1 to Liverpool before 51,600 spectators, a great pay day for the club. They had beaten Tranmere Rovers, Crook Town and Blackburn Rovers on the way. They also reached the fourth round in 1927-28, where they lost 3-0 to Middlesbrough at Ayresome Park. This run included victories over Denaby United, Bradford and Second Division Fulham, who were beaten 3-0.

PARKER, Thomas Robert

Born: Woolston, Hants, 19 November 1897; Died: near Southampton 1 November 1987.
Full-back 5ft 10in; 12st (1923).
Career: Sholing Rangers; Sholing Athletic; Woolston St Marks; Southampton amateur 1918, professional May 1919; Arsenal March 1926 (£3,250); Norwich City manager March 1933-February 1937; Southampton manager March 1937-June 1943; surveyor with Lloyds' Registry June 1943; Ministry of Transport (Marine Division) 1946;

Norwich City manager May 1955-March 1957; Southampton chief scout 1963-1973.

Honours: England international (1 cap); Football League champions, 1931; 1933 Division Three South champions 1922, 1934; FA Cup winners 1930, runners-up 1927, 1932.

An excellent full-back whose positional sense and natural leadership more than made up for a certain slowness, Tom Parker gained his England cap against France in 1925, before his transfer to Arsenal for a large fee. He missed only two games for Arsenal between 1926 and 1931, including 155 consecutive appearances. An expert penalty-taker, Parker took over the Gunners' captaincy in 1928 and led the club to an FA Cup Final victory in 1930 and two other Finals and also to two League championships.

He retired to take over at Norwich City in 1933 and guided City to the Third Division South championship in his first season, and also supervised the club's move from The Nest to Carrow Road in 1935. In 1937 he asked to be released from his contract to take over at The Dell, where he got the job from 120 applicants. Over the next two seasons, Parker spent £9,000 on new players including signing two future managers, Bill Dodgin and Ted Bates. After a series of disagreements he left the club in 1943 and had a second spell at Norwich, but his contract was terminated after a series of boardroom changes.

PARKES, Harry Arnold

Born: Gorstey Hill, Halesowen, September 1888; Died: Basford, March 1947.
Outside-right 5ft 8in; 9st 2lb (1906).
Career: Halesowen Grammar School; Halesowen; West Bromwich Albion February 1906; Coventry City May 1908; West Bromwich Albion May 1914; Newport County manager June 1919-May 1922; Chesterfield manager August 1922-April 1927; Lincoln City manager May 1927-May 1936; Mansfield Town manager May 1936-January 1938; Notts County manager January 1938-July 1939.

Honours: Division Three North champions 1932.

Harry Parkes never managed at a high level, being mainly in charge in the Third Division and then with only limited success. His one title came with Lincoln City in 1931-32, when they clinched the Northern Section title. He had a reputation for keeping struggling clubs solvent and his sides usually entertained the crowds without finding major success in the League or Cup.

Parkes was captain of both football and cricket at Halesowen Grammar School and played for local clubs Coombes Wood and Halesowen before signing for West Bromwich Albion in February 1906. He made his debut against Notts County in an FA Cup tie in March 1907 and then played in a semi-final at the tender age of 17, against Everton in a game which was lost 2-1. Later he fell out with the management over terms and moved to Coventry City in May 1908, after 31 appearances and four goals for Albion.

Parkes was not a regular at Coventry City until 1910-11, when he switched from the right wing to inside-right. Nicknamed 'Tickle', Parkes was a dashing player, quick on the ball and an accurate crosser. He was popular with his teammates and was noted for his dry sense of humour. Parkes went on to score 38 goals in 170 League and Cup games for City.

After they finished bottom of the First Division of the Southern League, he left Coventry and rejoined West Bromwich Albion in May 1914, during the war acting as player-assistant manager of the Throstles as well as working in munitions. Eventually he was forced to give up playing due to cartilage problems.

In June 1919 he became secretary-manager of Newport County and had only two months to prepare the club for their first season in the First Division of the Southern League. They joined the Football League in the summer of 1920 but struggled to make their mark in the Third Division. In April 1920, Parkes was forced to play in goal in an emergency and he also turned out for Lincoln City Reserves in the early 1930s.

In May 1922, he left Newport to join Chesterfield as manager. In his five seasons in charge they were usually challenging for promotion in the Northern Section but could not finish any higher than third, although they were no lower than seventh. In the summer of 1927 he became boss at Lincoln City. They finished runners-up to Bradford in Division Three North in 1927-28, albeit seven points behind, but were only one point behind Chesterfield when runners-up again in 1930-31. That season they also lost 6-4 to non-League Scarborough in the FA Cup.

Lincoln City finally gained promotion when they were champions of the Northern Section in 1931-32, on goal-average from Gateshead and scoring 106 goals. Two seasons later Lincoln were relegated back again. In May 1936, Parkes moved to Mansfield Town as manager. He was anxious for a change and the directors at Field Mill heard about this and interviewed him, offering Parkes the job at £10 a week plus bonuses on a three-year contract.

In January 1938 he asked to be released from his contract so that he could take up a similar post at Notts County. This was granted reluctantly. He signed Dixie Dean but by this time the former Everton striker was a shadow of his former self as an injury to his leg limited his effectiveness. There was a lot of chopping and changing of personnel as Parkes unsuccessfully sought a winning combination. He resigned in July 1939 and retired from football.

PARLBY, Joshua

Career: Stoke player and on club committee; Ardwick and Manchester City secretary 1893-1995, director 1895-1905 and April 1909-1912, then retired.

Josh Parlby played for Stoke before becoming a member of that club's committee. He was Ardwick's first paid secretary but those were traumatic days for the club. Bankruptcy and a crippling defection of first-team players in September 1894 nearly finished them off. The club re-emerged as Manchester City and managed to retain their place in the Football League, thanks largely to the work of Parlby. A gifted amateur, Parlby knew very little about football tactics but, a burly, boisterous man, he excelled in the art of wrangling. He signed Billy Meredith before taking over a public house in Bolton in 1895 and also joining City's board.

PARRY, Maurice Pryce

Born: Trefonen, near Oswestry, 1878; Died: Bolton, 24 March 1935.

Right-half 5ft 6in; 11st 7lb (1904).
Career: Newtown; Long Eaton Rangers; Oswestry United 1895; Leicester Fosse August 1898; Loughborough February 1899; Brighton United May 1899; Liverpool March 1900; Partick Thistle May 1909; coaching in South Africa 1911; Oswestry United September 1913-1914; Rotherham County manager October 1921-1923; coached in Barcelona, Frankfurt, Cologne and Jersey; Liverpool coach.

Honours: Wales international (16 caps); Football League champions 1906; Division Two champions 1905.

Parry went to Leicester to find work in the engineering trade and was persuaded to become a professional footballer with Leicester Fosse. He appeared only once in their first team before moving to Southern League Brighton United and was a regular before their demise. He made 221 appearances for Liverpool as a ball-winning half-back who was very consistent and also an excellent passer of the ball.

He gained 16 caps for Wales and his brother, Tom, was also capped by Wales whilst with Oswestry. His son, Frank, was a winger for Everton in the early 1920s. Parry was badly gassed during World War One but recovered to take over as Rotherham County's manager in October 1921. They scored only 32 goals in 1921-22 and lost Second Division status in April 1923 after a series of blunders, throwing away vital points.

PATON, John Aloysius

Born: Glasgow, 2 April 1923.
Outside-left 5ft 8in; 11st (1947).
Career: St Mungo's Academy; Dennistown Waverley; Glasgow Celtic; Chelsea November 1946 (£7,000); Glasgow Celtic cs 1947; Brentford September 1949; Watford July 1952, then manager October 1955-February 1956; Press photographer; Arsenal scout and coach.

Honours: Scotland Schoolboy international.

A clever winger with good footwork and the ability to cross accurately, Paton often produced goals for his fellow forwards. Was mainly a reserve at Chelsea, where he made 23 League and FA Cup appearances, scoring three goals, in between two spells at Celtic. He scored 14 goals in 90 League games for Brentford and 16 goals in 84 games for Watford. A former amateur boxer, Paton combined his job in football with that of a Press photographer.

He had a four-month spell in charge at Watford who experienced an FA Cup defeat against Bedford Town shortly after he took control. Results were poor and, due to financial problems at the club, Paton's contract was terminated. He later scouted and coached for Arsenal.

PATTERSON, George

Died: 8 May 1955.
Career: Marine as player; Liverpool assistant manager 1908-1928, secretary 1915, then manager February 1928-May 1936.

Patterson started a long association with Liverpool when he became assistant manager to Tom Watson at Anfield in 1908. He was secretary from 1915 and secretary-manager from February 1928. Thus, promotion from within is not a new thing at Liverpool. The Reds were mainly a mid-table side during Patterson's reign although they were nearly relegated in 1935-36.

He made some shrewd signings and developed many useful youngsters including Matt Busby, Tommy Cooper and Tom Bradshaw. He was forced to resign in 1936 due to ill health but remained as club secretary for a while. Patterson was awarded the Football League long-service medal for 21 years' service to Liverpool. Despite ill health, he continued to attend matches at Anfield after his retirement.

PAYNTER, Charles William

Born: Swindon, 29 July 1879; Died: Barking, 1 December 1970.
Outside-left.
Career: Grange Road School, Plaistow; Victoria Swifts; South West Ham; West Ham United November 1901, retired due to injury in 1903 to become assistant trainer, trainer 1912-1932, then manager November 1932-August 1950.

Honours: Football League War Cup winners 1940.

Paynter was an apprentice electrician but had his apprenticeship cancelled due to playing too much sport. He joined West Ham as an outside-left but was forced to retire after only two years. Gradually he worked his way through the ranks to end up as the club's manager. This took him over 30 years to achieve.

Paynter was looked upon as a father figure at Upton Park and a link between the players and the manager Syd King. He was appointed trainer to the England team in 1924, for the first international played at Wembley. After taking over as manager after the sad demise of King, he developed a style of his own. His dealings with players were part psychology, part paternalistic and part authoritarian. West Ham were developing into an excellent side when the war came. They reached a wartime Cup Final at Wembley in 1940 when they beat Blackburn Rovers 1-0. Paynter retired in 1950 having failed to get the Hammers back in Division One. But he had spent 49 happy years at Upton Park.

PEACOCK, Keith

Born: Barnhurst, 2 May 1945.
Midfield 5ft 6½in; 10st 7lb (1970).
Career: ROFSA Colts; Witton (Metropolitan Sunday League) 1961-62; Erith & Belvedere Reserves 1962; Charlton Athletic amateur May 1961, professional July 1962, contract cancelled May 1979; Tampa Bay Rowdies (NASL) assistant manager November 1979; Columbus (Ohio) player-coach; Gillingham manager July 1981-January 1988; Queen's Park Rangers reserve-team coach March 1988; Maidstone United manager May 1989-January 1991; Charlton Athletic youth-team coach 1991.

Peacock was a splendid club man with an exemplary disciplinary record who scored 107 goals in 567/24 appearances for Charlton Athletic over 17 seasons. One of the most popular and respected footballers in the country, he was a complete professional who was highly dedicated. In August 1965, he became the first substitute to be used in a League game when he came on for an injured goalkeeper against Bolton.

When he was manager of Gillingham, he signed his son, Gavin, to play for the club. The Gills were nearly always challenging for promotion when he was manager and lost to Swindon Town in the finals of the 1987 Third Division play-offs. He also took Maidstone United to the Fourth Division play-offs in 1990, when they lost to Cambridge United in the semi-finals. United's form slumped the following season and Peacock was sacked just after the turn of the year.

PEARSON, Stanley C.

Born: Salford, 15 January 1919.
Inside-forward 5ft 9in; 10st 8lb (1938).
Career: Frederick Road School, Salford; Aldephi Boys' Club; Manchester United amateur 1935, professional May 1936; Bury February 1954; Chester October 1957, then manager April 1959-November 1961; Prestbury FC coach and ran a local newsagent's until 1980s.

Honours: England international (8 caps); Football League representative (1 cap); Football League champions 1952; FA Cup winners 1948; Welsh Cup winners 1958.

Stan Pearson was an opportunist with good distribution who was also a good forager. He made his debut for Manchester United in November 1937, against Chesterfield in a 7-1 victory at Saltergate. His lethal shot helped him to 149 goals in 345 games for United, despite the lost war years and he gained his first England cap against Scotland in 1948 and also scored in United's FA Cup Final triumph over Blackpool that year. Pearson scored a hat-trick in United's semi-final victory over Derby to get them there.

The highlight of his international career was probably scoring both goals in England's 2-1 victory over Scotland at Hampden in April 1952, in a 2-1 victory. Pearson left Old Trafford for Bury and scored 56 goals in 122 League games and then made 56 appearances (16 goals) for Chester, where he was also player-manager after 1959. In his first season in charge they just missed having to seek re-election but in the 1960-61 season they finished bottom of the League, conceding 104 goals. He left after another poor start to a season.

PEART, John George

Born: South Shields, 3 October 1888; Died: Paddington, 3 September 1948.
Centre-forward 5ft 10in; 12st (1907).
Career: South Shields Adelaide 1905; Sheffield United May 1907; Stoke July 1910; Newcastle United March 1912 (£600); Notts County February 1913; guest for Leeds City and Rochdale in World War One; Birmingham November 1919; Derby County January 1920; Ebbw Vale player-manager cs 1920-1922; Port Vale January 1922; Norwich City July 1922; Rochdale player-manager February 1923-July 1930, retired as a player May 1924; Bradford City manager July 1930-March 1935; Fulham manager May 1935-September 1948.

Honours: Football League representative (1 cap); Southern League representative (3 caps); Division Two champions 1914.

One of the great travellers in football, Jack Peart was known as the most injured man in football. He played in every division of the Football League plus the Southern and Welsh Leagues. A broken leg kept him out of football for two years from 1910. Peart scored 28 goals for Notts County in 1913-14, when they clinched the Second Division title.

As a manager he was safe and conventional. A quiet but knowledgable man, Peart was an administrator rather than a tactician. When player-manager of Ebbw Vale, he negotiated his own transfer to Port Vale. He later brought Second Division respectability to Valley Parade when manager of Bradford City. At Fulham, he lacked ambition and vision but brought stability to the Cottage. In his first season in charge they reached the semi-finals of the FA Cup but lost 2-1 to Sheffield United. Peart died after a brief illness whilst still in office. Fulham went on to clinch the Second Division title with the team that he built. He had created a sound basis for the future of the club.

PEAT, William Arthur

Born: Liverpool, 1 September 1940.
Wing-half 5ft 8in; 11st 4lb (1963).
Career: Everton April 1959; Southport July 1961, then player-manager February-April 1970; Crewe Alexandra July 1972.

Peat never played in Everton's first team and made his League debut for Southport. He went on to play 401 League games for them, a club record, and scored 27 goals. A dedicated professional and clubman, Peat showed Southport great loyalty but was not happy when he was transferred to Crewe where he ended his playing career. He could fill in anywhere in the side if required.

He enjoyed playing under Lem Newcomb at Haig Avenue but after Newcomb left, some of the fun went out of playing for the club. He was player-manager of Southport for a while and they were relegated to Division Four, after which he reverted to just being a player.

PELHAM, Bertram

Born: c.1884; Died: 1 April 1977.
Career: New Brighton secretary August 1922 and secretary-manager August 1927-April 1931; Southport secretary-manager April 1931-March 1933 and honorary manager September 1940-1945.
Honours: Liverpool Senior Cup 1931, 1932.

Pelham unearthed some fine players at New Brighton including Jimmy Dunne, a prolific goalscoring centre-forward

who later gained Irish international caps. During his period of office, New Brighton beat the Corinthians and Sheffield Wednesday in the FA Cup. When he became the secretary-manager of Southport, they reached the fourth round of the FA Cup in 1932. They drew 1-1 at Newcastle, then drew 1-1 again at Haig Avenue before a record 20,010 crowd. In the third match at Hillsborough they were crushed 9-0.

They also finished seventh in the Third Division North that season but he was surprisingly dismissed in March 1933, although returning as honorary manager during the war years. He retained his interest in the club until his death at the age of 93.

PENTLAND, Frederick Beaconsfield

Born: Wolverhampton, summer 1883; Died: Poole, 16 March 1962.
Outside-right 5ft 9in; 11st 11lb (1909).
Career: Willenhall Swifts; Avondale Juniors; Small Heath August 1900; Blackpool June 1903; Blackburn Rovers October 1903; Brentford May 1906; Queen's Park Rangers May 1907; Middlesbrough cs 1908; Halifax Town February 1913; Stoke May 1913; coaching in Europe; interned during the war; coaching in France in 1920; Atheltic Bilbao manager 1921; Spanish national coach; Athletic Bilbao manager again May 1933-1936; Brentford staff and assistant manager 1936; Barrow manager February 1938-September 1939.

Honours: England international (5 caps); Southern League champions 1908.

A speedy winger who possessed excellent ball skills and could cross a ball well, Fred Pentland's one drawback was that he tended to over-elaborate. The son of a Lord Mayor of Birmingham, he was unable to break permanently into his local side but later developed into an international class winger. He helped Queen's Park Rangers to the Southern League championship in 1907-08, then played almost 100 games for Middlesbrough. He made his international debut against Wales in March 1909 and then played in two eight-goal victories against Austria and Hungary that summer.

During World War One, Pentland was interned along with Steve Bloomer and Sam Wolstenholme as he was coaching in Germany at the outbreak. After the war, he played a major role in the development of soccer in Spain and took Bilbao to five Spanish championships in seven seasons. He was very proud when Spain became the first foreign country to beat England in a full international. Pentland returned to England to be assistant manager to Harry Curtis at Brentford, then managed Barrow for a season.

PENDREY, Gary James Sidney

Born: Winson Green, Birmingham, 9 February 1949.
Defender 5ft 9in; 11st (1970).
Career: Aston Schools; Stanley Star; Harbourne Lynwood; Birmingham City apprentice July 1965, professional October 1966; West Bromwich Albion August 1979 (£30,000); Torquay United August 1981; Bristol Rovers December 1981; Walsall player-coach August 1982, assistant manager 1983-August 1986; Wolverhampton Wanderers assistant manager August 1986-May 1987; Birmingham City manager May 1987-April 1989; Wolverhampton Wanderers coach July 1989; West Bromwich All Stars 1982-1988.

Honours: FA Youth Cup runners-up 1967.

A tenacious tackler and a whole-hearted grafter, Pendrey played at full-back, wing-half, sweeper and midfield in his 337/23 games for Birmingham City. He helped the Blues to an FA Youth Cup Final against Sunderland in 1967, which was lost, and became the club's youngest captain at 20. Pendrey was often in trouble with referees and was once charged with bringing the game into dispute.

He helped City return to the First Division in 1972 and came close to an FA Cup Final appearance but City lost to Fulham in the last seconds of a semi-final replay. He was assistant manager to Alan Buckley at Walsall and Graham Turner at Wolves. He was not a great success as manager at St Andrew's and City were relegated to Division Three at the end of 1988-89 with only eight wins all season.

PERRY, Edwin

Born: Rhymney, 19 Janaury 1909.
Centre-forward 6ft; 12st (1938).
Career: Tredomen Engineering Works; Rhymney; Swansea Town trialist; Merthyr Town; Bournemouth & Boscombe Athletic April 1928 (£200); Thames Association June 1930; Fulham May 1931; Doncaster Rovers November 1936 (£1,500); Fulham cs 1939, later coach and scout, then chief coach September 1948-June 1949; Southend United manager cs 1956-May 1960.

Honours: Wales international (3 caps); Wartime international (1 cap); London War Cup Final (Brentford) 1942.

A go-getting, dashing centre-forward with an eye for goal, Eddie Perry was a Welsh schoolboy international trialist who left school to become a mining engineer. He gained local fame as a vocalist and violinist before stumbling into the world of professional football.

Although officially a Rhymney player, Perry played for Merthyr Town in an FA Cup tie against Bournemouth and so impressed the opposition that they signed him.

After he had scored 16 goals in the struggling Thames side in 1930-31, Fulham saw his potential and signed him. Injury-prone, he spent a great deal of time in the Reserves but had a long run in the first team in 1935-36 and helped Fulham to the semi-finals of the FA Cup that season.

He had most success at Doncaster Rovers, where he gained his three Welsh caps. Perry returned to Fulham at the outbreak of the war and gained a wartime cap in 1940. He also played for Brentford in a wartime Final in 1942. He joined Fulham's coaching staff in 1946 and was team coach under Frank Osborne when Fulham won the Second Division championship in 1948-49. He later had a frustrating spell as manager of Southend United, the highspot being when they beat Liverpool 2-1 in the FA Cup in 1956-7.

PERRYMAN, Stephen John MBE

Born: Ealing, 21 December 1951.
Midfield   5ft 8in; 10st 10lb (1980).
Career: Middlesex and London Schools; Ealing Schoolboys; Tottenham Hotspur apprentice July 1967, professional January 1969; Oxford United player-coach March 1986; Brentford player-assistant manager November 1986, then player-manager January 1987-August 1990; Watford manager November 1990-July 1993; Tottenham Hotspur assistant manager July 1993.

Honours: England international (1 cap); Under-23 international (17 caps); Youth international; Schoolboy international; Footballer of the Year 1982; FA Cup winners 1981, 1982; Football League Cup winners 1971, 1973, runners-up 1982; UEFA Cup winners 1972, 1984, runners-up 1974; FA Youth Cup winners 1970.

Steve Perryman had a superb playing career with Spurs, for whom he rarely missed a game. He made a total of 853/1 appearances (39 goals) for the club and was unfortunate to gain only one cap for England, against Iceland in June 1982. Originally a midfield player, Perryman dropped into the back-four from 1977. He gained many honours for Spurs and also captained them to two FA Cup triumphs and a UEFA Cup success. Voted the Footballer of the Year in 1982, he was awarded the MBE in the Queen's birthday honours list of 1986.

At Brentford, he came close to getting them promoted to Division Two but they always fell away in the run-in. In 1988-89 they just missed the play-offs after an excellent FA Cup run, beating Manchester City and Blackburn before losing 4-0 to Liverpool in the sixth round. Perryman resigned in August 1990 and later succeeded his former youth development officer, Colin Lee, as Watford manager. He steered them clear of relegation in 1990-91 when it looked inevitable, to tenth in 1991-92 and kept his job despite a 4-1 FA Cup defeat at lowly Shrewsbury. He joined Ardiles at Spurs in July 1993.

PETCHEY, George W.

Born: Whitechapel, London, 24 June 1931.
Wing-half   5ft 10in; 12st 8lb (1963).
Career: West Ham United August 1948; Queen's Park Rangers July 1953; Crystal Palace June 1960, retired through injury 1963, coach 1963-1969, youth-team manager and assistant manager 1969-1971; Orient manager July 1971-August 1977; Millwall manager January 1978-November 1980; Brighton & Hove Albion juniors coach and assistant manager 1984-1985.

Honours: Anglo-Scottish Cup runners-up 1977.

George Petchey spent his entire football career with London clubs. After a chequered early career with West Ham and Queen's Park Rangers, he played 153 games for Palace before an eye injury ended his playing days. He had helped Palace from the Fourth to the Second Division by 1964.

Petchey was then appointed youth-team manager and then assistant manager at Selhurst Park. In 1971 he became the manager of Orient. They reached the sixth round of the FA Cup in 1972 and were unlucky not to gain promotion to Division One in 1973-74. They also reached the Anglo-Scottish Cup Final in 1976-77. Petchey brought some excellent talent to Brisbane Road, including Laurie Cunningham, Glenn Roeder and Tony Grealish, and also bought some excellent players from his former club Palace.

He was finally sacked but was soon back in football as manager of Millwall. He had a unhappy spell at The Den and the Lions were relegated to Division Three. They did win the FA Youth Cup in 1979, but mainly thanks to the work of chief scout Bob Pearson and youth coach David Payne. Petchey was sacked with the club in a poor financial state.

PETTS, John William Frederick James

Born: Edmonton, 2 October 1938.
Wing-half   5ft 8in; 11st (1963).
Career: Arsenal May 1956; Reading October 1962; Bristol Rovers July 1965; Northampton Town manager January 1977-January 1978.

Honours: England Youth international.

Petts had a fairly undistinguished playing career after showing a lot of potential in his early days at Highbury. He made his League debut in February 1958, in a 2-1 home defeat against Bolton, and played in two other exciting games that season, in a 5-4 victory over Chelsea at Highbury and a 5-4 defeat at Portsmouth. Petts only played when Tommy Docherty was not available.

After 32 League appearances for the Gunners, Petts moved to Reading. He

played another 34 League games for them before finishing his League career at Bristol Rovers where he made another 88/4 appearances (five goals). He took over from Pat Crerand at Northampton Town. The Cobblers had a revival in March 1977, but were still relegated and were struggling in 15th place in the Fourth Division when he resigned in January 1978.

PICKERING, John

Born: Stockton, 7 November 1944.
Half-back   5ft 11½in; 12st 7lb (1970).
Career: Newcastle United July 1963; Halifax Town September 1965 (£1,250); Barnsley July 1974; Blackburn Rovers coach June 1975, then manager November 1978-May 1979; Carlisle United coach 1980-81; Lincoln City assistant manager and coach 1982, then manager July-December 1985; Newcastle United coach 1988; Lincoln City assistant manager 1990; Middlesbrough coach cs 1991.

Pickering set a new appearance record for Halifax Town, playing 364/3 League games (five goals) for the club before ending his career at Barnsley. He was ever-present in Halifax's promotion season of 1968-69, when they entered the Third Division. Club captain, Pickering gave Halifax excellent service as a rugged centre-half.

He was in charge of Blackburn Rovers Reserves under manager Jim Smith and was later assistant manager to Jim Iley, stumbling into the manager's job by default when Iley left. He broke Rovers' record transfer fee when he paid £75,000 for Duncan McKenzie from Chelsea, but despite gallant efforts he was unable to steer Blackburn away from relegation and lost his job. He also had a short spell as Lincoln City's manager. He was sacked when they lost ten out of 11 games and were 21st in Division Four.

PICKLES, Albert

Career: Burnley Belvedere as player; Burnley director 1918, secretary-manager January 1925-September 1932.

Elected to Burnley's board of directors in 1918, Pickles had been an outstanding schoolboy athlete. He played for local side Burnley Belvedere and was once offered a trial by Aston Villa but his parents would not give him permission to go.

The prospects were not good when he took over at Burnley. The team was ageing and attendances falling. The Clarets made a terrible start to the 1925-26 season when they lost 10-0 to Aston Villa. He was forced to sell star player Bob Kelly and relegation inevitably came in 1930. After further struggles in the Second Division, Pickles offered his resignation after a heavy defeat. It was accepted by the board of directors.

PILKINGTON, Samuel Turneil

Born: Accrington 1890; Died: 29 June 1970.
Outside-right   5ft 7in; 10st (1911).
Career: Accrington Stanley October 1906; Haslingden; Oldham Athletic February 1911; Haslingden June 1912; Accrington Stanley July 1913, then secretary-manager cs 1919-June 1923 and May-October 1924, later director and chairman from 1946-July 1953; Lancashire Football Combination president 1946-1968; town councillor in Accrington; cotton merchant business; also cricket for Accrington CC (Lancashire League).

Pilkington was instrumental in reviving Accrington Stanley's flagging fortunes. Although officially the secretary, he also dealt with team affairs. He helped steer Stanley into the Football League in 1921 and was responsible for the day-to-day running of the club and the signing of new players until Matthew Bruton was appointed as trainer-coach in the summer of 1921, allowing Pilkington more time to devote to looking for new players.

In June 1923, Curtis Booth was appointed player-manager and Pilkington's role became purely administrative. When Booth left in May 1924, Pilkington again took on full managerial responsibilities but resigned in October 1924. He was invited to join the board at this stage. In 1953 he became honorary vice-president of Stanley. He was only 16 when he made his debut for Stanley and he also played five games for Oldham Athletic in the First Division. Pilkington served as an independent on the local council for 14 years and also gave Accrington Cricket Club over 50 years' service.

PLEAT, David John

Born: Nottingham, 15 January 1945.
Winger   5ft 8in; 11st 9lb (1970).
Career: Nottingham Forest March 1962; Luton Town August 1964 (£8,000); Shrewsbury Town July 1967; Exeter City July 1968; Peterborough United July 1970; Nuneaton Borough player-manager 1971-72; Luton Town coach 1972, chief coach December 1977, then manager January 1978-May 1986; Tottenham Hotspur manager May 1986-October 1987; Leicester City manager December 1987-January 1991; Luton Town manager June 1991.

Honours: England Schoolboy international; Youth international; Division Two champions 1982; FA Cup runners-up 1987.

A highly-respected manager, David Pleat is articulate, honest and very popular with his staff and directors as well as the media. Pleat helped establish Luton Town as a First Division club, then almost tasted success at Tottenham Hotspur before his unfortunate departure.

Pleat joined his local side, Nottingham Forest, as an apprentice and showed great potential, gaining England Schoolboy and Youth honours. But after only six appearances for Forest, he was signed for Luton Town, for a £8,000 fee by Bill Harvey. Alas, Pleat joined Luton at a bad time as they had just been relegated to Division Four. He broke his leg in training during his first season and returned to the team prematurely which caused chronic back problems. This effected his natural speed which he had used well, combined with his polished control and accomplished trickery. After the injury he became a more studious and constructive player.

Pleat then moved around the lower divisions, his best spell coming at Exeter City, where he scored 13 goals in 66/2 League appearances.

In 1971 Pleat joined Nuneaton Borough as player-manager, then the following year rejoined Luton as a coach after a period of umemployment. He had also tried his hand at freelance journalism. His initial role at Kenilworth Road involved coaching the juniors, visiting local schools to coach, and selling lottery tickets.

Harry Haslam, the Luton manager, promoted him to chief coach in December 1978 and Pleat replaced Haslam when he moved to Sheffield United as manager. Luton struggled against relegation to the Third Division in 1978-79 but thereafter challenged for promotion and finally clinched the Second Division championship in 1981-82 with 88 points, eight clear of runners-up Watford.

Pleat then established the Hatters as a First Division club, although they would usually struggle against relegation. He became known as an innovative manager who was receptive to new ideas. Luton avoided the drop in 1982-83 only by winning their last game at Manchester City, with a goal four minutes from time by Raddi Antic, thus sending down the opposition instead. Many probably remember the image of Pleat galloping across the pitch to hug his players in delight.

Luton were unlucky to lose 2-1 to Everton the 1985 FA Cup semi-finals. They reached the quarter-finals of the League Cup in 1985-86, again losing to Everton. That season Pleat also took Luton to ninth in the First Division, one of their best-ever positions, and was then offered the manager's job at Tottenham Hotspur which he accepted in May 1986.

Pleat introduced an attractive style of play, using five midfield players and one front-runner. This was highly entertaining for the fans but just failed to bring trophies to the club. In 1987, Spurs lost in an FA Cup Final for the first time in their history, to Coventry City 3-2, finished third in the League and also reached the semi-final of the League Cup but lost to their great rivals, Arsenal.

In October 1987, Pleat lost his job at White Hart Lane following newspaper disclosures about his private life, but he was not out of football for long and two months later became the manager of Leicester City. Despite spending £4m on 25 players, Pleat was unable to find a winning combination and the fans became disillusioned. He was sacked in January 1991 with Leicester on the brink of relegation to the Third Division. In June 1991, he returned to Luton Town as manager but despite playing attractive soccer, the club were relegated to Division Two after ten years of struggling against the drop.

Luton were nearly relegated for the second season in succession. This was caused by the club's poor financial state which meant that Pleat had to sell players to survive.

POLLITT, Harry

Career: Coventry City manager November 1919-May 1920.

Little is known about Harry Pollitt before and after he joined Coventry City as manager. They were bottom of Division Two, without a win, when he

took over. Given a then astronomical sum of £5,000 to spend on new players, he managed to steer Coventry clear of the relegation zone but lost his job anyway. Later it transpired that he had helped set up a 'fix' in the last game of the season, against Bury when Coventry needed to win to avoid having to apply for re-election. This was not unearthed for three years. Pollitt was banned *sine die* at this time.

POOLE, John Smith

Born: Codnor, Derbyshire, autumn 1892; Died: Mansfield, 21 March 1967.
Wing-half   5ft 11in; 12st 4lb (1923).
Career: Sutton Junction; Nottingham Forest 1914; guest for Sheffield United in World War One; Sunderland May 1919; Bradford City May 1924, player-coach from cs 1927, retired 1928 and coach until August 1935; Mansfield Town trainer August 1935, then manager May 1938-August 1944; Notts County trainer August 1944; Derby County trainer after war until 1956; Sutton Town trainer-coach August 1956.

Due to World War One, Jack Poole did not make his League debut for Sunderland until the age of 27. He went on to play 152 times in League and Cup games for the Wearsiders, plus 101 appearances for Bradford City. He made 39 appearances when Sunderland finished as runners-up in the First Division in 1922-23 and played his last match for City at Wigan Borough in December 1927.

Poole was reserve-team player-coach for a while at Valley Parade, then assistant trainer to George Livingstone until both left in 1935. At Mansfield, Poole was trainer, being given overall control of the players. When Harry Parkes left the club in January 1938, Poole was initially caretaker manager. This position was not confirmed until May 1938. He managed to find a steady stream of guest players in the war years but left to become trainer at Notts County in 1944. He ended his football career as trainer-coach of Central Alliance club Sutton Town.

PORTEOUS, Trevor

Born: Hull, 9 October 1933.
Wing-half   5ft 10in; 11st 10lb (1950).
Career: Hull City amateur 1949, professional October 1950; Stockport County June 1956, then player-manager September 1963-October 1965, retired as a player July 1965.

Porteous was a professional with a lot of grit, plenty of vision and ability. He became first-choice only in 1955-56, for Hull City, but played 336 League games for Stockport County. He qualified as a coach and later in his career he switched from wing-half to full-back.

Porteous helped Stockport County to fifth in the Northern Section in 1956-57, but they were relegated to the Fourth Division in 1959. Had two seasons as player-manager, when they finished 17th and 24th, having to seek re-election in 1964-65. That season they managed to hold Liverpool to a 1-1 draw in the FA Cup, despite being bottom of the Football League. He left football after his sacking by Stockport County.

PORTER, James

Born: Hamilton, Lanarkshire, 31 July 1901.
Right-back   5ft 11in; 11st 2lb (1925).
Career: Wishaw YMCA: Bury August 1922, then chief scout 1935-1938; Manchester United trainer in charge of team affairs November 1938-March 1944; Bury manager March 1944-July 1945 and assistant manager from 1945; Accrington Stanley manager June 1949-March 1951.

Porter made over 500 appearances for the Shakers in League and FA Cup games before being appointed assistant manager and chief scout. He left in 1938 to become trainer-manager at Manchester United. During the war, he also had an important administration position in the Air Ministry. After the war, Porter became assistant manager to Norman Bullock, after a brief spell as manager of Bury.

The Accrington board negotiated Porter's release from his contract at Bury so that he could become manager of that club in 1949. Porter had a great ability to spot young talent and also had a wide knowledge of the game. He was given a free hand but by Christmas 1949 the club was in severe financial difficulties. Porter had to rely on a young side but they did well in the second half of the 1949-50 season. He had to sell Stan Lynn to Aston Villa to keep Stanley alive. In November 1950, Porter was offered the Wrexham managership but turned it down. He must have regretted this decision as he was soon sacked when Stanley hit a bad patch.

PORTERFIELD, Ian John

Born: Dunfermline, 11 February 1946.
Midfield   5ft 11in; 11st 6lb (1970).

Career: Leeds United trailist 1963; Heart of Midlothian juniors; Glasgow Rangers juniors; Raith Rovers; Sunderland December 1967 (£38,000); Reading November 1976 (£20,000); Sheffield Wednesday July 1977; Rotherham United manager December 1979-June 81; Sheffield United manager June 1981-March 1986; Aberdeen manager November 1986-May 1988; Chelsea

assistant manager early November 1989; Reading manager November 1989-April 1991; Chelsea manager June 1991-February 1993. Chelsea manager June 1991-February 1993.

Honours: Division Three champions 1981; Division Four champions 1982; FA Cup winners 1973; Scottish League Cup runners-up 1988.

Ian Porterfield scored the goal which won Second Division Sunderland a sensational FA Cup Final victory in 1973, when they beat Leeds United 1-0. He made 117 appearances (17 goals) for Raith Rovers before moving to Roker Park and made his debut against fierce rivals Newcastle United in December 1967. Porterfield went on to make 250 appearances (19 goals) for Sunderland before his move to Reading, a club he later managed.

He began his managerial career at Rotherham United and took them to the Third Division championship in 1980-81, then left to manage Fourth Division Sheffield United. The Blades won the title at the end of his first season in charge and in 1983-84 they were promoted again to the Second Division. Sacked despite a good record at United, Porterfield was the surprise choice as Alex Ferguson's successor at Aberdeen. They reached the semi-finals of the Scottish Cup and the League Cup Final in 1987-88, where they lost to Rangers on penalties. He had little success at Reading and was again a surprise choice, this time to succeed Bobby Campbell as manager of Chelsea.

Chelsea finished in a respectable 14th place in the First Division in 1991-92 and also reached the semi-final of the League Cup, where they lost 5-1 on aggregate to Sheffield Wednesday. Soon afterwards, Porterfield sold his leading goalscorer, Gordon Durie, to Spurs for a large fee. Porterfield was sacked in February 1993 after fading dramatically following a promising start.

Porterfield lost his job at Chelsea after a poor run in which Chelsea went without a win in 12 games.

POTTER, Cecil Bertram

Born: West Hoathley, Sussex, 14 November 1888; Died: 17 October 1975.
Inside-forward   5ft 8in; 11st 13lb (1914).
Career: Melton; Ipswich Town July 1910; Norwich City 1911-1915; guest for Hull City and Tottenham Hotspur in World War One; Hull City cs 1919; Hartlepools United player-manager May 1920-July 1922; Derby County manager July 1922-July 1925; Huddersfield Town manager July 1925-August 1926; Norwich City manager December 1926-January 1929.

Honours: Football League champions 1926.

Cecil Potter had the unenviable task of following in the footsteps of the legendary Herbert Chapman at Huddersfield Town. He inherited a team of immense talent and achieved success when Huddersfield took the League championship for a third successive season. The pressures of managing at the highest level were too much for Potter, though, and he resigned for health and family reasons. It was the only honour that he won in football, but it is probably the ultimate prize in English football.

The son of a Congregational minister, he was born in Sussex but moved to Suffolk as a child. As a youngster he joined his local club, Melton, then progressed to sign for Ipswich Town in July 1910. Ipswich were then playing in the Southern Amateur League.

Potter signed as a professional with Norwich City in 1911 and made 131 League and FA Cup appearances, scoring 31 goals, before the war came. An adaptable player, Potter had filled most forward positions. During the war he guested for Hull City and Spurs and signed for the Tigers permanently in the summer of 1919.

He made only ten appearances for Hull before moving to Hartlepools United as player-manager in the close season of 1920. In March 1921, United were accepted into the newly-formed Third Division North and finished fourth in their first season but 14 points behind the leaders. The club lost a great deal of money in this first season and when Potter received a lucrative offer to manage Derby County, he departed in July 1922.

Potter was only 33 years old when he took charge at the Baseball Ground. He brought two players with him from Hartlepools, Tom Crilly and Harry Thoms but success did not come to Derby until the season after he left the club. Derby finished 14th in Division Two in his first season in charge but Potter soon developed a more successful side which narrowly missed promotion in 1924 and 1925 and reached the FA Cup semi-final in 1923 but missed appearing in the first Wembley Final when they lost 5-2 to fellow Second Division side, West Ham, at Stamford Bridge. In 1924, Derby failed to gain promotion on the narrowest of goal averages.

Potter left Derby in July 1925 and originally intended to take a dairy business in Sussex but was approached by Huddersfield Town within a week of his departure from Derby and led them to the completion their hat-trick of League championships which had been started by Herbert Chapman. He had to re-adapt the Huddersfield style of play due to a comprehensive change in the offside law in the summer of 1925. The stress of keeping Huddersfield at the top took its toll and Potter resigned in August 1926.

He had plans again to leave the game but four months later took over as manager at his former club, Norwich City. His best signing was Percy Varco, who scored 32 goals in 1927-28, but the club finished in a lowly position. The 1928-29 season was another poor one and Potter resigned in January 1929 with the club at the bottom of the Southern Section. This came close on the heels of an 5-0 FA Cup defeat at the hands of the amateurs Corinthians.

POTTS, Harold J.

Born: Hetton-le-Hole, 22 October 1920.
Inside-forward 5ft 10in; 10st 4lb (1951).
Career: Hetton; Burnley November 1937; guest for Sunderland and Fulham in World War Two; Everton October 1950 (£20,000); Wolverhampton Wanderers coach July 1956; Shrewsbury Town manager summer 1957-February 1958; Burnley manager February 1958-February 1970, general manager February 1970-July 1972; Blackpool manager 1973-May 1976; Burnley chief scout July 1976, then manager February 1977-October 1979; Colne Dynamos chief scout late 1980s.

Honours: Football League champions 1960; FA Cup runners-up 1947, 1962; Anglo-Scottish Cup winners 1979.

Harry Potts was Burnley's most successful manager and his first spell in charge was a golden era for the club. They were Football League champions in 1959-60 and reached the FA Cup Final in 1962, where they lost to Spurs. The Burnley youth scheme was famous throughout football for its excellence which produced a steady stream of young talent during Potts' reign.

Potts was one of the first products of the Burnley youth policy which he was later to use to his best advantage. He became a professional with Burnley in November 1937 but war broke out just as he looked likely to make a big impact in English football. He spent a large part of the war with the RAF in the Far East and in 1945 was a member of Denis Compton's star-studded team which toured India. He also made an impact with Sunderland and Fulham as a wartime guest, scoring 11 goals in only ten games for Fulham.

Potts made his League debut in the first match of the 1946-47 season, at the age of 25, and by the end of the season had helped Burnley to promotion to Division One as runners-up and to the FA Cup Final. Burnley lost 1-0 to Charlton Athletic after extra-time but Potts came close to scoring the winner in normal time when his stinging shot hit a crossbar.

Later in his career Potts became a more defensive-minded midfield player who was the engine-room of the side. In 1950 he became unsettled at Turf Moor and asked for a move. He joined Everton in October 1950 for a £20,000 fee, but they were relegated at the end of his first season at Goodison Park and he was never a regular afterwards.

Potts retired in July 1956 and became a coach at Wolves. The following year he took over as manager of Shrewsbury Town who could only finish 17th in the Southern Section in 1957-58. In February 1958, Potts returned to Burnley as manager. He inherited the nucleus of a side which was soon to bring much success to Turf Moor. The team included established players such as Tommy Cummings, Jimmy Adamson, Jimmy McIlroy and Ray Pointer, who were mixed with up-and-coming stars such as Jimmy Robson, Gordon Harris, Brian Miller and Alex Elder. Burnley took the League championship in 1959-60 with 56 points, two ahead of Wolves. They were runners-up in 1961-2, three points behind champions Ipswich Town.

Burnley also reached the FA Cup Final in 1962, only to lose 3-1 to Spurs. The previous season they had lost to Spurs in a semi-final. They entered European competition for the first time and gave a good account of themselves in the European Cup. Burnley also reached the semi-final of the very first League Cup, but lost to Aston Villa in a third game.

Many saw the rot beginning to set in when Potts sold Jimmy McIlroy for a paltry £25,000 to Stoke. Many of the fans were so angry that they refused to attend future games at Turf Moor. The club gradually went into decline and Potts was forced to sell promising young players due to the low attendances that the club now attracted despite their success on the field.

The heart was ripped out of the club and amongst those who left were: John Connelly to Manchester United for £56,000 in 1964; John Talbot to West Brom for £35,000 in 1966; Alex Elder to Stoke for £55,000; Willie Irvine to Preston for £40,000 in 1967; Andy Lochhead to Leicester and Gordon Harris to Sunderland for £70,000 each; and Willie Morgan to Manchester United for £117,000 in 1968.

In February 1970, Potts became the general manager of Burnley ending 12 years of probably the most successful period in the club's history. He left Burnley in July 1972. The following year he made a comeback as manager of Blackpool, who were always challenging for promotion to Division One but never quite made it. He lost his job in May 1976 but two months later returned to Turf Moor as chief scout. In February 1977, Potts was again appointed as Burnley's manager. They won the Anglo-Scottish Cup in 1978-79 beating Oldham in the Final, having previously beaten Celtic in an earlier round. After a poor start to the season, Potts was sacked in October 1979. In the '80s he served the now-defunct Colne Dynamos as chief scout.

POWELL, Ivor Verdun

Born: Gilfach, Bargoed, South Wales, 5 July 1916.
Wing-half 5ft 8in; 11st 6lb (1951).
Career: Bargoed 1933; Queen's Park Rangers amateur 1935, professional August 1937; Aston Villa December 1948 (£17,000); Port Vale player-manager June-December 1951; Bradford City player-manager May 1952-February 1955, retired through injury November 1954; Leeds United trainer-coach July 1956; Carlisle United manager May 1960-February 1963; Bath City manager June 1964-February 1967; retired in 1967 to run a pub in Manningham.

Honours: Wales international (8 caps); Division Three South champions 1948; Division Four promotion 1962.

Ivor Powell was a PE instructor in the RAF during the war and toured India and Burma, playing soccer. He won his first Welsh cap whilst with Queen's Park Rangers and also helped them to the Southern Section title in 1947-48. When he moved to Aston Villa for £17,000, it was a record for both clubs.

He had a brief period as player-manager of Port Vale in 1951 but his contract was terminated when the club hit the bottom of the League. He also had a tough time as player-manager of Bradford City and a knee injury forced him to retire in September 1954. The club was in financial difficulties and Powell was forced to sell some of their better players. This turned the fans against him. At Carlisle United, Powell had a disastrous first season, then the team clinched promotion to Division Three in 1961-62. Powell lost his job when United were beaten by Gravesend & Northfleet in the FA Cup and they were relegated at the end of that season.

POYSER, George Henry

Born: Mansfield, 6 February 1910.
Full-back 6ft; 12st 7lb (1936).
Career: Nottingham Schoolboys; Tieversal Colliery; Wolverhampton Wanderers 1927; Stourbridge late 1928; Mansfield Town 1928-1929; Port Vale 1931; Brentford cs 1934; Plymouth Argyle 1945; Dover Town player-manager 1947; Wolverhampton Wanderers chief coach until 1953; Notts County manager October 1953-Janaury 1957; Manchester City assistant manager 1957, then manager May 1963-April 1965.

Honours: Division Two champions 1935.

Strong with a surprising turn of speed, George Poyser made a name for himself as a full-back with Port Vale. He moved to Brentford in 1934 and was ever-present when they clinched the Second Division championship in his first season at the club, for whom he went on to make 150 appearances.

His first managerial job was at Dover and after this he was out of football for a while but returned as coach at Wolves in 1953. Under Poyser, Notts County reached the quarter-finals of the FA Cup in 1954-55 but lost to York City. The Magpies were lucky to avoid relegation after this and Poyser was sacked after they lost to Rhyl Athletic in the FA Cup. He was not out of work for very long and became assistant manager to Les McDowell at Maine Road. Later he was promoted as McDowell's successor but could do little to stop City's slide. They reached the semi-finals of the League Cup in 1963-64 but lost to Stoke. After two poor seasons, Poyser resigned as neighbours Manchester United clinched the League championship.

PRATT, David

Born: Lochore, Fife, 5 March 1896.
Left-half 5ft 11in; 12st 6lb. (1926).
Career: Hill O'Beath (Fife); Glasgow Celtic June 1919; Bradford City November 1921; Liverpool January 1923; Bury November 1927; Yeovil & Petters United player-manager June 1929-May 1933; Clapton Orient manager May 1933-December 1934; Notts County manager April-June 1935; Heart of Midlothian manager July 1935-February 1937; Bangor City manager July-October 1937; Port Vale manager December 1944-July 1945.

Honours: Southern League (Western Section) champions 1932.

A highly efficient half-back who played 55 games for Bradford City and 85 for Liverpool, Pratt was never a regular at Anfield and missed out on a League championship medal in 1922-23, when he appeared only seven times. He had some success at Yeovil before taking over at Clapton Orient. Pratt had no players when he first joined the club, as they had all been released for financial reasons.

He signed 26 new players in the summer of 1933 and Orient then played some sparkling football for their long-suffering fans' delight. Pratt was very popular with the fans, who were disappointed when he resigned for a job at Notts County. However, he quit after only eight weeks with Notts bottom of the Second Division. He then had two seasons at Hearts, in which they finished fifth both seasons. Pratt worked as a sports commentator for the BBC. Port Vale wanted him as their manager in 1944, but they could not get his release from the RAF and although he was officially in charge for seven months, he was rarely seen at the ground.

PRICE, Ioan Haydn

Born: Pontypridd, spring 1883; Died: Portsmouth, 7 March 1964.
Left-half 5ft 8in; 11st 6lb (1909).
Career: Mardy Corinthian; Aberdare

1902; *Aston Villa Reserves December 1904-1905; Burton United 1907; Wrexham 1908; Leeds City May 1909; Shrewsbury Town June 1910; Walsall secretary 1914-1919; Mid-Rhondda manager 1919-1920; Grimsby Town manager July-November 1920; Walsall secretary November 1920-1921; Mid-Rhondda secretary-manager 1921-1922; schoolmaster by profession.*

Honours: Wales international (5 caps); Welsh Cup winners 1909, runners-up 1904.

Price was a semi-professional throughout his career whilst he pursued his full-time employment in teaching. He was capped for Wales against Scotland in March 1907 whilst in Villa's third team. Indeed, he never played in Villa's first team and made only one appearance for Burton United and eight for Leeds City before ending his playing career at Birmingham & District League club Shrewsbury Town.

Price was the Walsall secretary before and after his time in charge of Grimsby Town. When he took over at Blundell Park, he signed five players from his former club, Mid-Rhondda. He was given full control by the board after pressure from the fans. Results were poor and the team struggled. The directors blamed Price for not strengthening his squad, Price blamed them for interference in team selection and for not allowing him to go on scouting trips. After only four months he resigned publicly in the *Grimsby Evening Telegraph* and returned to Walsall.

PRINCE-COX, Captain Albert

Born: Southsea, 8 August 1890.
Career: Playing days cut short by knee injury; Royal Flying Corps; Fellow of the Royal Meterological Society; international referee; professional boxing and wrestling promoter in Plymouth; Bristol Rovers manager November 1930-October 1936.

A merry and whimsical character, Albert Prince-Cox did things with style. His first job was as a boy impressionist in the theatre. He served in the Royal Flying Corps in World War One before 'a flying accident curtailed this'. Prince-Cox became an assistant meterologist and was later a Fellow of the Royal Meterological Society.

His own playing career was cut short by a knee injury. He got the job of Bristol Rovers manager from 200 applicants, despite having no background in football. He signed a lot of experienced players and in 1932-33 had five full internationals on the books. He tried a few stunts to get the club the maximum amount of publicity. Once he flew an amateur player to a match in an aircraft, in order to get him from his normal work to a midweek match. When he resigned, Prince-Cox took up boxing promotions and later worked for the British Boxing Board of Control. He is undoubtedly the only Football League manager whose job it once was to deliver the weather forecast to Buckingham Palace.

PROUDFOOT, Peter

Born: Wishaw, 25 November; Died: 4 March 1941.
Half-back.
Career: St Mirren; Lincoln City 1900; Millwall October 1904; Clapton Orient cs 1905; Chelsea April 1906; Manchester United Reserves; Stockport County cs 1908-1909; Clapton Orient manager April 1922-April 1929, April 1930-April 1931 and January 1935-January 1939, when he retired due to ill health.

A terrier-type of defender, Proudfoot was energetic and constructive but, despite his many clubs, he was a regular first-teamer only at Clapton Orient, Stockport County and Lincoln City, where he scored 20 goals in 79 League appearances.

He had three spells as boss of Clapton Orient and managed the club at three different grounds — Homerton, Lea Bridge and Brisbane Road. In 1925-26, Orient reached the quarter-finals of the FA Cup, beating Newcastle United and Middlesbrough on the way before losing heavily to Manchester United. When Orient were relegated in 1929, Proudfoot stood down but remained at the club in an administrative post whilst Arthur Grimsdell ran the team. He took over again after Grimsdell, until Jimmy Seed was appointed as manager in April 1931. Proudfoot started his third spell in 1935 when financial problems dogged the club again. He did well to keep them off the bottom of the League. Proudfoot retired due to ill health in 1939.

PUDAN, Albert Ernest 'Dick'

Born: West Ham
Left-back   5ft 9†in; 11st 10lb (1910).
Career: Clapton Orient; West Ham United cs 1900; Bristol Rovers cs 1902; Newcastle United July 1906 (£150); Leicester Fosse May 1909; Huddersfield Town secretary-manager September 1910-April 1912; Leicester Fosse player November 1912, retired 1914; Leicester City director 1919-39, chairman 1929; successful businessman in the Midlands.

Honours: Southern League champions 1905; FA Cup runners-up 1908.

Dick Pudan was the first former professional footballer permitted to serve as a director of a League club and he later became chairman of Leicester City. A cultured full-back, Pudan was thoughtful and constructive in his approach to the game. He made 116 appearances for Bristol Rovers and gained a Southern League championship medal with the club in 1904-05. Although never a regular at Newcastle, Pudan appeared in their 1908 FA Cup Final defeat against Wolves.

He took over at Huddersfield Town when they entered the Football League and in 1912 he resigned so that the club could find a more experienced manager as they were enduring great financial problems. He formed a successful hosiery manufacturing business and was one of the new directors of the reconstituted Leicester City in 1919. This role was not sanctioned by the FA until March 1921.

PUDDEFOOT, Sydney Charles

Born: West Ham, 17 October 1894.
Died: Rochford, 2 October 1972.
Inside-right/Centre-forward
5ft 10½in; 12st (1926).
Career: Condor Athletic; Limehouse Town; West Ham United March 1913; guest for Falkirk in World War One; Falkirk February 1922 (£5,000); Blackburn Rovers February 1925 (£4,000); West Ham United February 1932; Fenerbahçe (Turkey) March 1933, retired cs 1933; Galatasaray (Turkey) coach 1934-1935; Northampton Town manager March 1935-March 1937; coaching in Istanbul 1937-1940; also Essex cricketer 1922-1923; worked in the Civil Service until 1963; Southend United scout 1963.

Honours: England international (2 caps); Victory international (3 caps); Football League representative (2 caps); Southern League representative (1 cap); FA Cup winners 1928.

A prolific goalscorer for West Ham, Syd Puddefoot was involved in a sensational transfer when he moved to Falkirk for £5,000 in 1922. He scored 107 goals in 186 games in his two spells at Upton Park and also scored prolifically for the Hammers in wartime games. He once scored seven goals against Crystal Palace in November 1918.

After his unlikely move to Falkirk, Puddefoot moved back to England with Blackburn Rovers and appeared in their surprise victory over Huddersfield Town in the 1928 FA Cup Final. He made over 230 appearances for Blackburn before returning to West Ham at the age of 36. He had a tough time out in Turkey and was beaten up by spectators at the end of his first spell in the country. He spent two years as manager of Northampton Town, in which they finished 15th and 7th respectively in the Southern Section. Puddefoot was also an accomplished cricketer who played eight first-class matches for Essex.

PULIS, Anthony R.

Born: Newport, Gwent, 16 January 1958.
Defender   5ft 10in; 11st 8lb (1983).
Career: Bristol Rovers September 1975; Happy Valley (Hong Kong) 1981; Bristol Rovers June 1982; Newport County June 1984 (£8,000); Bournemouth & Boscombe Athletic July 1986; Gillingham August 1989; Bournemouth & Boscombe Athletic player-assistant manager August 1990, then manager June 1992.

Honours: Wales Youth international; Division Three champions 1987.

Tony Pulis was a very cool and polished defender who played under the lower divisions. Of Maltese extraction, Pulis won Youth international honours for Wales. He enjoyed his most successful period at Dean Court, where he made 80/10 appearances and won a Third Division championship medal in 1986-87. Pulis played 122/8 games for Bristol Rovers and also had a year playing in Hong Kong.

He was assistant manager to Harry Redknapp and retired from playing in 1991. He was appointed as Redknapp's replacement in June 1992, when Harry moved to West Ham as assistant manager to Billy Bonds. Pulis' brother, Ray, played one game for Newport County and his father-in-law, Bill Stroud, played for Southampton, Leyton Orient and Newport County.

Bournemouth struggled against relegation in 1992-93. This was mainly

due to the sale of leading scorer Jimmy Quinn to Reading and Efan Ekoku to Norwich City for £750,000.

QUIGLEY, Edward

Born: Bury, 13 July 1921.
Inside-forward 5ft 7½in; 11st 7lb (1951).
Career: Bury September 1941; Sheffield Wednesday October 1947 (£12,000); Preston North End December 1949 (£26,000); Blackburn Rovers November 1951; Bury August 1956; Mossley manager (for six years); Bury juniors coach, later chief scout; Stockport County manager April-October 1966; Blackburn Rovers assistant manager November 1966, manager February 1967-October 1970, then chief scout and in charge of youth team until June 1971; Stockport County manager May 1976-April 1977; Blackburn Rovers chief scout 1979-May 1981; Blackpool scout.

Honours: England 'B' international (2 caps); Division Two champions 1951.

Eddie Quigley began as a full-back but early in his career he scored five goals on the first occasion he played at centre-forward, for Bury at Millwall. Quigley was a deceptive player due to his big build and casual manner, but if a chance occured he would pounce quickly. He also had great positional play and scored four goals twice in a match for the Owls before moving to Preston for a British record fee of £26,500.

He had scored 50 goals in only 74 games for Wednesday but struggled at Deepdale, where he never hit it off with Tom Finney. Quigley, who was perhaps unlucky never to gain a full England cap, later scored 92 goals in 159 League appearances for Blackburn Rovers.

His first managerial post was with Mossley, where he stayed six years. Quigley then moved to Bury and on to Stockport County, where he became manager. They were Fourth Division champions soon after he left in October 1966. He became assistant manager at his old club, Blackburn Rovers, but was in sole charge of the coaching when Jack Mansell resigned, Quigley was made caretaker manager and was formally appointed two months later after going close to promotion.

But money was tight, he was unable to buy quality players and with the club at the bottom of Division Two, he was replaced by general manager Johnny Carey and took charge of scouting and the youth team. He had been criticised by the Press for being too much of a blackboard theorist. When the club was relegated, both he and Carey were sacked. He later returned to both Stockport and Blackburn.

QUINN, John David

Born: St Helens, 30 May 1938.
Inside-forward 5ft 6in; 10st 10lb (1963).
Career: Prescot Cables; Sheffield Wednesday May 1959; Rotherham United November 1967; Halifax Town player-coach July 1972, then player-manager September 1974-February 1976, retired as a player 1975.

Honours: FA Cup runners-up 1966.

Quinn had the strength and ability to adapt to any role that was required of him as a player and for this he was greatly respected by his colleagues. He scored 24 goals in 186/9 appearances for the Owls, for whom he played in the 1966 FA Cup Final against Everton, which Wednesday lost 3-2 after being two goals up.

Quinn was a hero at Millmoor where he was called the 'Mighty Quinn' — a pop song of the time. He ended his playing career at Halifax Town, where he became player-manager. In his first season in charge they lost to non-League Stafford Rangers in the FA Cup. He was a likeable and hardworking manager and the fans at The Shay were angry when he was sacked for poor results.

RAE, James Clarkson

Born: Blackmill, Argylshire; Died: Shirley, Warwickshire, 4 July 1958.
Left-back 5ft 11in; 12st 7lb (1933).
Career: King's Park 1928; Partick Thistle 1929; Plymouth Argyle May 1932, retired 1946 to become assistant manager, then manager September 1948-January 1955; ran pub in Solihull from 1955.

Honours: Scottish Junior international; Division Three South champions 1952.

A stylish full-back who was never flurried, Rae preferred to play himself out of trouble rather than punt the ball up the field. He played 259 games for Argyle before the war but did not appear for them in wartime soccer between 1940 and 1945. Rae played his last match for the club against Charlton Athletic in December 1945.

He retired soon afterwards to become assistant manager to Jack Tresadern. When he became manager, Rae guided Plymouth Argyle to the Third Division South championship in 1951-52. This was aided by the inspired signing of Jack Chisholm in 1949. Plymouth finished fourth in the Second Division the following season but the team was gradually ageing and when they struggled against relegation, Rae was sacked.

RAISBECK, Alexander Galloway

Born: Wallacestone, near Polmont, 26 December 1878; Died: Liverpool, 12 March 1949.
Centre-half 5ft 10in; 12st 9lb (1900).
Career: Blantyre Boys' Brigade; Larkhill Thistle; Royal Albert; Hibernian 1896; Stoke March 1898; Liverpool May 1898 (£350); Partick Thistle 1909 (£500); Hamilton Academical secretary-manager April 1914-1917, director 1917; Bristol City manager December 1921-June 1929; Halifax Town secretary-manager July 1930-May 1936; Chester manager May 1936-April 1938; Bath City manager; Liverpool scout.

Honours: Scotland international (8 caps); Scottish League representative (3 caps); Football League champions 1901, 1906; Division Two champions 1905; Division Three South champions 1923, 1927.

Alex Raisbeck was a superb centre-half who won two League championship medals with Liverpool around the turn of the century. As a manager he found success at Bristol City, the club he twice took to promotion to Division Two. He was one of seven brothers, one of whom, William, was a half-back with Derby County and Sunderland. Alex Raisbeck played for several junior clubs before joining Hibernian in 1896 and at 18 years of age he played for the Scottish League against the Irish League.

In March 1898, Raisbeck moved south to join Stoke and helped them stay in the First Division. He then attracted the attention of Liverpool chairman John McKenna, who sent his manager Tom Watson to sign him. Raisbeck joined Liverpool in May 1898, for a £350 fee, and went on to play 340 League and FA Cup games for the Anfield club, scoring 21 goals. His League championship medals came in 1900-01 and 1905-06 and a Second Division championship medal in 1904-05. Liverpool went close to the double in 1898-99 but failed with both, losing to Sheffield United in a third replay of an FA Cup semi-final and finishing runners-up in the League.

With his fair hair, Raisbeck stood out on the field and although well under 6ft he could outjump much taller opponents. A hard-tackling and very quick player, he was superb at heading the ball and breaking up attacks. Seven of his eight Scottish caps were against England and he also represented the Scottish League on three occasions, the last coming in 1913 when they met the Irish League.

In 1909, Raisbeck returned to Scotland to join Partick Thistle for a £500 fee. In April 1914 he became secretary-manager of Hamilton Academical, until 1917 when he became a director of the club. In December 1921, Raisbeck was appointed manager of Bristol City. He came too late to prevent their relegation from Division Two but the following season they bounced straight back as champions of the Southern Section, six points ahead of runners-up Plymouth Argyle. Unfortunately, they finished bottom of the Second Division the following season and also suffered their worst-ever home defeat, losing 8-0 to Derby County on 29 September 1923.

Tommy Walsh signed from Bolton for £2,000 and City were third in 1924-25 and fourth in 1925-26. Raisbeck then sacked former Liverpool centre-half Walter Wadsworth and appointed him as skipper. Wadsworth helped City win the Southern Section title again, two points ahead of Plymouth again, and they also scored 104 goals. To avoid instant relegation this time Raisbeck strengthened the squad by signing Cecil Blakemore and Percy Cherrett from Crystal Palace. However, he also sold the promising youngster Clarrie Bourton to Blackburn Rovers, for the large fee of £3,650 and after a disappointing season, Raisbeck was sacked in June 1929

Just over a year later, he became the manager of Halifax Town, steering them away from their usual re-election spot to finish 17th at the end of his first season in charge. Halifax had an excellent run in the FA Cup in 1932-33, when they reached the fifth round before losing at home to Luton Town before a then record crowd of 29,235. Despite selling leading scorer William Chambers to Blackburn for £2,600 in 1934, Halifax finished runners-up in the Northern Section in 1934-35.

Raisbeck resigned in May 1936 and joined Chester as manager. They finished third and ninth in his two seasons in charge. He left the club in April 1938 and later managed Bath City and was scouting for Liverpool when he died in that city.

RAMSEY, Sir Alfred Ernest

Born: Dagenham, 22 January 1920.
Full-back 5ft 8½in; 12st 8lb (1951).
Career: Essex Schools; Beacontree High School; Five Elms; Portsmouth amateur c.1942; Southampton amateur 1943, professional August 1944; Tottenham Hotspur May 1949 (£21,000), retired May 1955; Ipswich Town manager August 1955-January 1963; England manager January 1963-May 1974; Birmingham City director January 1976, until he became manager September 1977-March 1978.

Honours: England international (32 caps); 'B' international (1 cap); Football League representative (5 caps); World Cup winners 1966; Football League champions 1951, 1962; Division Two champions 1950, 1961; Division Three South champions 1957

Not only was Alf Ramsey a fine international full-back who helped Spurs to successive titles, culminating in the League championship, he also became one of the most famous managers of all time. He took England to their World Cup triumph over West Germany in 1966 and had earlier guided Ipswich Town from the Third Division to the League championship in little over five years.

As a player Ramsey was a strong, polished and distinguished defender who was a precise passer of the ball and his slowness on the turn was countered by his intelligent positional sense. He joined Portsmouth as an amateur in 1942 and a year later moved to The Dell after playing against them for the Army, signing professional forms in August 1944.

Ramsey made his England debut in December 1948, in a 6-0 victory over Switzerland at Highbury, and went on to play in 28 consecutive games for his country, captaining England when Billy Wright was absent. He won 32 caps for England in all and also represented the Football League on five occasions and gained one 'B' cap. Ramsey played in all of England's three games in the 1950 World Cup finals including the humiliating 1-0 defeat by the USA at Belo Horizonte. His last game for his country came in the infamous 6-3 defeat against the Hungarians in 1953.

Ramsey scored eight goals in 90

League appearances for the Saints before moving to Tottenham Hotspur for a record £21,000 in May 1949, the only one of the famous 'push and run' side to cost a large fee. He missed only three games as Spurs clinched the Second Division title in 1949-50 and the First Division title the following season. Ramsey was very accurate with free-kicks and penalties and developed into a great strategist and reader of the game. He sometimes appeared at centre-half for the Saints and Spurs. Ramsey retired in May 1955, after 250 League and FA Cup games for Spurs in which he scored 24 goals. The nearest he came to playing in an FA Cup Final came in 1953, but it was his poorly-hit back-pass which led to Blackpool's winning goal in the semi-final.

In August 1955, Ramsey accepted the offer of the manager's post at Ipswich Town. He found turmoil in his early days at the club and threatened to resign after experiencing an uneasy relationship with his predecessor Scott Duncan, who had been appointed secretary when Ramsey became manager. The highest fee paid by Ramsey was a mere £12,500 and he rehabilitated the careers of players like Jimmy Leadbetter, Andy Nelson and Ray Crawford, who achieved wonders for him in return. Ipswich won the Third Division South title in 1956-57, the Second Division championship in 1960-61, then the First Division title in 1961-62. So Ramsey had taken the club from the Third Division to the League championship in only five years, a fantastic achievement.

His tactics changed English football for all time. Gifted individuals did not necessarily fit into Ramsey's plans. He required complete commitment from all his players and absolute acceptance of his authority. In return he gave unstinting support to his players. His tactics were innovative and by the time the opposition had worked them out, Ipswich had gained the League championship. The club was in decline when he became the England manager in January 1963.

He was the first full-time manager of England, given full control of selection as well as preparation. Ramsey was often seen as a reserved, colourless character who was wary and cautious, but he had a driving determination and strength of character to trust his own judgement. He did not like journalists and had his moments of anger, like when England beat Argentina 1-0 in the quarter-finals of the 1966 World Cup. He told his players not to exchange shirts with the opposition and later described the Argentinians as playing 'like animals'. These indiscretions were rare but made him seem more human. As at Ipswich, he sacrificed the specialist winger in favour of more versatile forwards with higher work-rate and more involvement, which was not very pretty but very effective.

His greatest triumph came in 1966 when England, playing on home territory, took the World Cup for the first and only time. He preferred the efficiency of Geoff Hurst to the genius of Jimmy Greaves and in the process perhaps contributed unwittingly to Greaves' downfall as he never fully recovered from losing his place in England's World Cup-winning side. There were some memorable victories for England. Their semi-final win over Portugal was a superb match and in the Final, England were a couple of minutes away from victory when West

Germany equalised to put the game into extra-time. Ramsey managed to raise the morale of his side and Geoff Hurst went on to complete his hat-trick in England's 4-2 victory at Wembley. Ramsey was knighted in 1967 for his services to football.

Ramsey always liked to have 'hard-men' in his sides. They included Nobby Stiles, Norman Hunter and Peter Storey, but it never stopped him criticising the opposition for rough play. In later years he failed to use a number of very talented players properly in his England side but was not as guilty of this as the man who took his place, Don Revie. Sir Alf remained cautious and uneasy with everybody but his players and he was often prickly, intransigent and unyielding, and was much hurt by criticism but endlessly defiant.

England reached the semi-finals of the European championships in 1968, losing to Yugoslavia in an ill-tempered game. They reached the quarter-finals of the World Cup in Mexico in 1970 but lost to great rivals West Germany, 3-2 after being two goals up. Ramsey was greatly criticised for his substitutions which included taking the great Bobby Charlton off when England led 2-0. It was Charlton's last appearance for his country.

In the 1972 European championships, England qualified for the quarter-finals by winning their group. In those days the quarter-final was played over two legs, home and away. Ramsey was accused of being tactically naive and out-of-date when, in the first leg, England lost 3-1 at Wembley. They could only draw the return in Germany, 0-0, so went out of the competition.

Ramsey's days were numbered when England failed to qualify for the finals of the 1974 World Cup. They needed to beat Poland in their last group match but managed only a 1-1 draw. How they did not win this match remains a mystery today. They had so many chances to score that, on the law of averages, they should have netted three at least. With seconds to go, Ramsey gave Derby's prolific striker Kevin Hector his international debut and Hector almost became a national hero when he went agonisingly close to scoring. He might also have saved Ramsey's job.

As it was, the England manager was rather shabbily treated when he was sacked in May 1974 after such an unfortunate match. His successor, Don Revie, was an utter disaster as a national manager. Under Ramsey, England had lost only 17 out of 113 games and had won 69 of these. However, his tactics had become outdated when compared with the 'total football' of Holland and West Germany.

In January 1976, Sir Alf joined the board at Birmingham City and in September 1977, at the age of 57, was appointed the Blues' manager, becoming the first knight to manage a Football League club. He held office for only six months before being forced to relinquish the position due to ill health. The team played with style and were in a respectable position in the First Division. He retired from football after this and continues to live in the Ipswich area.

RANDALL, Kevin

Born: Ashton-under-Lyne, 20 August 1945.
Forward 5ft 10½in; 12st 9lb (1970).
Career: Droylesden; Bury October 1965; Chesterfield July 1966; Notts County August 1972; Mansfield Town November 1975; York City October 1977 (£8,000), youth-team coach 1980-1981, caretaker manager December 1981-March 1982; Chesterfield assistant manager 1984-1987, then manager June 1987-October 1988; Mansfield Town youth development officer 1991. Goole Town manager 1982; Chesterfield assistant manager February 1993.

Honours: Division Three champions 1977; Division Four champions 1970.

Kevin Randall was a late starter in League soccer, being 20 years old when he signed for Bury from Droylesden. At Chesterfield he developed an excellent partnership with Ernie Moss and they scored many goals between them. Randall netted 97 in 258 League games for the Spireites and was top scorer with 18 goals when they were Fourth Division champions in 1969-70. He also helped Notts County to promotion to Division Two in 1972-73, as runners-up, and was again top scorer with 19 goals.

Randall renewed his partnership with Moss at Mansfield and was top scorer again when they were Third Division champions in 1976-77. He lost his place mainly due to a pelvic injury and moved to York City, for whom he was caretaker manager between Barry Lyons and Denis Smith. Randall took over as manager from John Duncan at Saltergate, when Duncan moved to Ipswich Town. The team struggled and Randall lost his job in October 1988, after eight defeats in ten games.

RATHBONE, Michael John

Born: Sheldon, Birmingham, 6 November 1958.
Left back 5ft 10in; 11st 3lb (1982).
Career: Sheldon High School; Villa Boys; Birmingham City apprentice December 1974, professional November 1976; Blackburn Rovers February 1979 (£40,000); Preston North End July 1987-May 1991 (£20,000); Darwen FC commercial manager August 1991; Halifax Town manager December 1992.

Honours: England Youth international 2 caps.

Mick Rathbone was a solid, reliable defender who also liked to attack down the flanks. He never established himself at St Andrews but was a regular at Blackburn Rovers for whom he played 299/3 League and Cup games but scored only two goals in these games. In 1979-80, he helped Rovers to promotion to Division Two and also to the fifth round of the FA Cup. Rovers came close to further promotion the following season when they finished fourth. Rathbone broke his leg in 1983 and missed almost a season out injured as a consequence. In his last season at Ewood Park, he played in midfield before moving to Preston, where he played 82/9 League appearances. He was commercial manager at Darwen before taking charge at The Shay. It was a tough baptism into League management with Halifax Town struggling not only for their League status but also for their very existence. They finished at the bottom of the table and thus lost their League membership. Many felt that Town's final game of the season, against Hereford United, would be their last ever.

RAY, Richard

Born: Newcastle-under-Lyme, 4 February 1876; Died: Leeds, 28 December 1952.
Full-back.
Career: Macclesfield Town 1893; Burslem Port Vale 1894; Manchester City May 1896; Macclesfield Town cs 1900; Manchester City September 1902; Stockport County cs 1903; Chesterfield Town cs 1904; Leeds City July 1905; non- League soccer 1908, retired 1912; Leeds United manager October 1919-February 1920, then assistant secretary until 1923; Doncaster Rovers manager 1923-July 1927; Leeds United manager again July 1927-March 1935; Bradford City manager April 1935-February 1938; Millwall chief scout 1938.

Honours: Division Two champions 1899, runners-up 1928, 1932.

Dick Ray achieved success with Leeds United in the 1920s and '30s, twice taking them to promotion to Division One. An outspoken character who liked to do things his own way, he had never reached the heights as a player, plying his trade mainly with Second Division clubs.

After non-League soccer with Macclesfield Town, he appeared regularly at full-back for Burslem Port Vale. A dependable player, Ray was transferred to Manchester City in May 1896 and played 89 League and FA Cup games, scoring three goals, for the club. This included helping the club to the Second Division title in 1898-89. Ray lost his place soon after City joined the First Division. He moved into non-League soccer in the summer of 1900 but returned for the second spell with Manchester City in September 1902, although he did not appear for the first team.

In the close season of 1903 Ray moved to Stockport County, playing 34 League games before another move to Chesterfield Town in the summer of 1904. Here he made a further 34 appearances. Ray joined Leeds City in July 1905 and was made skipper of the side with a further 39 appearances for that club. In 1908 he moved into non-League football again and retired in 1912. An all-round sportsman, he played cricket in the Bradford League with Laisterdyke, and he also served in the RASC during World War One.

Leeds City were disbanded by the FA in October 1919, due to illegal payments to players during the war years. Dick Ray joined the committee of the newly-formed Leeds United and was manager from October 1919 until February 1920, when Arthur Fairclough was appointed manager. He then worked as assistant secretary and ran the reserve side in the Midland League with considerable skill and on a shoestring budget.

In 1923, Dick Ray became manager of Doncaster Rovers, who finished mainly in mid-table positions during his four seasons in charge. He signed four Keetley brothers at Doncaster, Tom, Harry, Joe and Frank.

When Fairclough resigned as manager of Leeds United, Ray replaced him in July 1927. He was responsible for team selection and playing policy and developed many fine players at Elland Road including Bert Sproston and Wilf Copping. Ray took Leeds back into the First Division in 1927-28, as runners-up, and they finished fifth in Division One in 1929-30 but were relegated the following season. They bounced straight back as runners-up in 1931-32.

In February 1934 Dick Ray was put in charge of the Football League representative side which drew 2-2 with the Scottish League side. He resigned in March 1935, with Leeds United not doing too well in the First Division.

The following month he took charge at Bradford City but achieved very little at Valley Parade and they were relegated to Division Three at the end of 1936-37. Ray had already been relieved of team selection when his contract was not renewed in February 1938. Soon afterwards he became chief scout at Millwall but by 1940 he was out of football and running a garage business in Leeds, where he died in 1952.

RAYNOR, George S.

Born: Hoyland, near Wombwell, 13 January 1907.
Outside-right 5ft 6in; 10st 6lb (1930).
Career: Barnsley Grammar School; Elsecar Bible Class; Wombwell; Mexborough Athletic trial; Sheffield United Reserves cs 1930; Mansfield Town June 1932; Rotherham United July 1933; Bury February 1935; Aldershot July 1938, retired in World War Two; Aldershot reserve-team trainer 1945-46; Sweden national team coach 1946-1954; manager of Juventus (Italy) and Lazio (Italy) 1954-1956; Coventry City coach June 1955, then manager January-June 1956; Lincolnshire Education Committee coach 1956-1957; Sweden national team coach 1957-1960; Skegness Town manager c.1960 and stores job at Butlin's; Doncaster Rovers manager May 1967-December 1968. Coach at AIK Stockholm & Atviaaberg.

Honours: World Cup runners-up 1958; Olympic Gold Medal 1948, Bronze Medal 1952; Knight of the order of Vasa (Sweden).

George Raynor was on the small side but was a speedy, clever winger who had an average playing career before winning fame as the coach of the Swedish national side which won the Olympic Games in 1948 and reached the 1958 World Cup Final, which they lost 5-2 to Brazil.

During the war he had served in the Middle East and organised football in Baghdad. When he was unable to find a coaching job in England, he was recommended to the Swedish FA by Sir Stanley Rous. In Sweden many of his best players departed to the major European sides but he did well there. When he was manager of Juventus, Raynor was loaned to Lazio, where he found corruption and bribery. Disillusioned with Italian football and craving for a job in England, he returned to work with Jesse Carver at Coventry City and took over when Carver returned to Italy.

There was plenty of interference from directors at Highfield Road and he resigned soon after being demoted to accommodate general manager Harry Warren. He later managed Doncaster Rovers, who went on to win the Fourth Division title after his departure.

RAYNOR, Walter Jesse

Born: Wanstead, 10 April 1882.
Left-back/Left-half
5ft 11½in; 12st 4lb (1913).
Career: Leytonstone 1904; South Weald 1906; Norwich City August 1907; Luton Town May 1909; Peterborough City

April 1910; Croydon Common August 1912-1914; Arsenal player-coach 1916; Tottenham Hotspur player-coach; Charlton Athletic manager June 1920-May 1925; Wigan Borough manager cs 1925-February 1926; suspended sine die from football in October 1926.

Raynor was mainly a reserve-team player and appeared only 16 times for Norwich City, three for Croydon Common and none for Arsenal and Spurs. He was Charlton's first professional manager and steered them through their first season in the Southern League after the club turned professional. Charlton almost went bankrupt after a disastrous move to Catford and due to financial restraints, Raynor became dependent on good amateur players.

They had a great FA Cup run in 1922-23, beating three First Division opponents before losing to eventual winners Bolton Wanderers in the quarter-finals. He was sacked on 13 May 1925 and quickly took over at Wigan Borough but was suspended in February 1926 after a row with the referee and opposition players. However, worse followed eight months later when he was suspended *sine die* after enquiries into the affairs of Charlton Athletic, where financial irregularities were found. He later ran a hardware store in Croydon and possibly emigrated to the USA.

REDKNAPP, Harold James

Born: Poplar, London, 2 March 1947.
Outside-right 5ft 10in; 11st 4lb (1971).
Career: West Ham United March 1964; AFC Bournemouth August 1972; Brentford September 1976; Seattle Sounders (NASL) player-coach 1976-1979; Oxford City assistant manager 1979-1981; AFC Bournemouth player-coach October 1982, then manager November 1983-June 1992; West Ham United assistant manager July 1992.

Honours: England Youth international 6 caps; Division Three champions 1987; FA Youth Cup winners 1963; London Youth Cup winners 1963; Associate Members' Cup winners 1984.

Harry Redknapp was an 'old-fashioned' winger who was popular with the Upton Park fans. He was a regular in the Hammers' side only from 1967-68, but still made 170/5 appearances (8 goals) for the club. The nearest he came to a major honour was in 1970-71, when West Ham reached the semi-final of the League Cup but lost to Stoke City in a dramatic second replay at Old Trafford.

He was assistant to Bobby Moore at Oxford City and made a brief comeback for Bournemouth against Manchester United for a League Cup tie in 1982. In his first season in charge at Dean

Court, the club won the Associate Members' Cup, beating Hull City in the Final, and also had a fantastic 2-0 victory over Manchester United in the FA Cup. Bournemouth won the Third Division championship in 1986-87 to enter the Second Division for the first time in their history. They spent three seasons in the higher sphere before being controversially relegated in 1990 before disgraceful scenes at Dean Court where the visiting Leeds fans went on the rampage after their team had won the last game of the season to win promotion. In June 1990 Redknapp was injured in a car crash whilst in Italy watching the World Cup. Former Aston Villa defender Brian Tiler was killed in the accident. More recently, Redknapp transferred his son Jamie for a good fee to Liverpool.

After narrowly missing the Third Division play-offs in 1991-92, Redknapp decided to resign the managership at Bournemouth and moved to Upton Park as assistant manager to Billy Bonds.

REID, Peter

Born: Huyton, Liverpool, 20 June 1956.
Midfield 5ft 8in; 10st 7lb (1986).
Career: Huyton Schools; Bolton Wanderers apprentice July 1971, professional May 1974; Everton December 1982 (£60,000), player-coach 1987-1989; Queen's Park Rangers February 1989; Manchester City player-coach December 1989, then player-manager November 1990.

Honours: England international (13 caps); Under-21 international (6 caps); Football League champions 1985, 1987; Division Two champions 1978; FA Cup winners 1984, runners-up 1985, 1986; Football League Cup runners-up 1984; European Cup-winners' Cup winners 1985.

Peter Reid had to make a brave recovery from a series of serious injuries to resurrect his career. In a three-year spell he suffered a broken leg and knee cap, torn ligaments and cartilage problems. He scored 25 goals in 251/4 appearances for Bolton and missed only four games between December 1974 and April 1978 before being hit by his injury jinx.

Everton bought him for a bargain £60,000, as it was felt that his playing career was almost over, but Reid helped the Toffees to two League titles, three FA Cup Finals, a League Cup Final and the European Cup-winners' Cup Final. Reid was on the winning side twice in five Finals. In 1984, Everton beat Watford 2-0 in the FA Cup Final, then the following year beat Rapid Vienna in the Cup-winners' Cup Final. He made his England debut against Mexico in Mexico City in 1985. Reid still plays regularly for Manchester City, where as manager he has taken the club to two excellent seasons in Division One, without yet winning any trophies.

Reid continued to do a useful job at Maine Road, but City have not yet won any honours. They reached the quarter finals of the FA Cup but lost to Spurs. Some fans marred a fine game by running on the pitch and looking for a confrontation with the opposition fans.

REID, William

Born: Scotland, c.1917; Died: Troon, mid-1970.
Career: St Mirren 1944, later trainer, then manager 1959-1961; Norwich City manager December 1961-May 1962.
Honours: Football League Cup winners 1962.

Reid was one of eight different managers at St Mirren between 1959 and

1972. He was trainer when they won the Scottish Cup against Aberdeen in 1959 and also took the club to the semi-final as manager in 1961. Reid got the job at Norwich City from 100 applicants. His broad Scottish accent made it difficult for his new players to understand him and City finished 17th in the Second Division in 1961-62 but did reach the League Cup Final, where they beat Rochdale easily over two legs. After a 3-0 victory at Spotland, the second leg was an anticlimax which was won 1-0. Just eight days after the Final, Reid decided to return to Scotland and left the club.

RELISH, John Derek

Born: Huyton, Liverpool, 5 October 1953.
Defender 5ft 8in; 12st (1980).
Career: Cardiff City trialist 1969; Chester apprentice 1969, professional October 1971; Bury (loan) September 1983; Newport County June 1974-October 1986 and player-coach 1983-1986, then player-manager March-May 1986; PFA staff May 1986; Forest Green Rovers October 1986; Newport AFC player-manager June 1989, retired 1990.

Honours: Hellenic League champions 1990.

Relish was a wholehearted player and an excellent clubman. He joined Chester straight from school and made 13/1 appearances before moving to Newport County. Despite a broken leg which prevented him from playing for a year, he had made 338 League appearances for Newport by the time he left in October 1986.

Relish helped Newport into Division Three in 1979-80 and they also reached the quarter-finals of the European Cup-winners' Cup where they lost on aggregate to Carl Zeiss Jena. They went down 1-0 at Somerton Park and managed a 2-2 draw in East Germany. Relish had missed the previous season's Welsh Cup triumph through injury. He spent just two months as player-manager in 1986, then departed to work for the PFA. After the demise of County, Relish was appointed the first manager of the newly-formed Newport AFC. He helped them win the Hellenic League title, playing all their home games at Moreton Town in England. They returned to Somerton Park in 1990 and joined the Southern League Midland Division.

REVIE, Donald George OBE.

Born: Middlesbrough, 10 July 1927; Died: Edinburgh, 26 May 1989.
Centre-forward 6ft; 12st (1950).
Career: Archibald School (Middlesbrough); Newport Boys' Club; Middlesbrough Swifts; Leicester City August 1944; Hull City November 1949 (£20,000); Manchester City October 1951 (£13,000 and a player); Sunderland November 1956 (£23,000); Leeds United December 1958 (£14,000), player-manager March 1961-July 1974, retired as a player May 1963; England manager July 1974-July 1977; United Arab Emirates coach July 1977-May 1980; then coaching in Egypt.

Honours: England international (6 caps); 'B' international (1 cap); Football League representative (2 caps); Footballer of the Year 1955; Football League champions 1969, 1974; Division Two champions 1964; FA Cup winners 1956, 1972, runners-up 1955, 1965, 1970, 1973; Football League Cup winners 1968; Inter-Cities Fairs Cup winners 1968, 1971, runners-up 1967; European Cup-winners' Cup runners-up 1973.

Don Revie was one of the great man-

agers of his era, transforming a struggling Second Division side into one of the most powerful and successful teams in Europe, although Leeds were often the 'nearly men', missing out on honours at the last hurdle. However, Revie was successful enough to become a legend at Elland Road, the club going into decline after his departure. As the England boss he was not cut out for the very different role of international manager and left under something of a cloud to coach in the Middle East.

Revie joined Leicester City towards the end of the war but took some time to be appreciated by the Filbert Street crowd. He turned the corner with his performances in City's run to the 1949 FA Cup Final, culminating with his two goals in the semi-final victory over Portsmouth. He missed the Wembley game due to broken blood vessels in his nose.

Hull City signed him for a £20,000 fee in November 1949, over competition from Arsenal and Manchester City. They were pushing strongly for a First Division place when he joined the club but Revie lost his form and eventually switched to wing-half to recover some confidence. Hull missed out on promotion and the team's form slumped.

After the departure of player-manager Raich Carter from Boothferry Park, Revie requested a transfer, moving to Manchester City in October 1951 for a £13,000 fee plus full-back Ernie Phillips who was valued at £12,000. At Maine Road, Revie hit the headlines as the tactical architect of the 'Revie Plan', a domestic response to the style of the Hungarians. Revie played as a deep-lying centre-forward who prompted his inside men, rather than playing in the traditional style of out-and-out striker. The plan bore his name but City boss Les McDowall must take a lot of the credit.

By 1954-55, City were one of the top sides in the First Division. Revie was capped for England and was also voted Footballer of the Year in 1955. He made his international debut in Belfast, scoring one of the goals in a 2-0 victory over Northern Ireland. He also helped his country to a 7-2 win over Scotland and scored two goals in a 5-1 victory over Denmark in Copenhagen in October 1955. He gained six caps in all, as well as one 'B' cap and two appearances for the Football League.

Revie appeared for Manchester City in the 1955 FA Cup Final, which they lost 3-1 to Newcastle United. However, the following year, they beat Birmingham City 3-1 in the Final. Revie played only because first-choice Billy Spurdle developed boils on his knee on the morning of the match and could not play. Revie was the star of the Wembley game and set up the first goal for Joe Hayes. His career had appeared to be faltering before this and in November 1956, he was on the move again, this time joining Sunderland for £23,000.

In December 1958 he moved to Leeds United, where he was later to make a name for himself as one of the most successful managers of all time. He became player-manager of the club in March 1961 and retired from playing in May 1963 after a career in which he made 515 League and Cup appearances and scored 110 goals. He had taken over as manager when Jack Taylor resigned and was to turn the club into one of the finest in Europe.

His managerial career got off to a slow start as Leeds narrowly avoided relegation in 1962. Revie, though, developed a youth policy and produced the likes of Gary Sprake, Paul Reaney and Norman Hunter. They powered their way to the Second Division title in 1963-64 under the midfield generalship of Bobby Collins, an inspired signing from Everton. Revie was much criticised for his safety-first approach and later for his legendary dossiers on the opposition.

Leeds made an immediate impact on the First Division as Revie bought wisely on the transfer market. One of the great bargains of all time was the £35,000 signing of Johnny Giles from Manchester United. Giles was to play a crucial part in Leeds' success over the next decade. Revie built his side around the midfield genius of Giles and over the next few years was never afraid to pay large fees for players including Allan Clarke, Trevor Cherry and Mick Jones. To the players he became the father figure of the Leeds family. He made every player feel an important part of the club and was also an astute tactician who used his excellent backrooom staff of Les Cocker, Syd Owen and Maurice Lindley to his best advantage. Revie had the happy knack of keeping all of his squad happy even when out of the side. But the belligerent attitude of the team and their gamesmanship were widely criticised and few neutrals spoke of Leeds with affection. In the early days of Revie's reign, the football was often dull and defensive. Later his sides were more entertaining and able to turn on the skills.

In the First Division, Leeds came close to the championship on a number of occasions, only to blow it in the last couple of games of the season. They were League champions in 1968-69 and 1973-74, but were runners-up on no less than four occasions during Revie's period of control. The 1968-69 season was a record-breaking one with 67 points gained and only two defeats recorded during the entire season.

They reached four FA Cup Finals, winning only one, in 1972 when Arsenal were beaten in a poor Final. They lost 2-1 to Liverpool after extra-time in 1965, to Ian St John's goal; to Chelsea after a replay in 1970, after they should have won the first match; and, worst of all, to Second Division Sunderland in 1973. Revie nearly moved to Everton after this defeat.

Leeds also won the Football League Cup in 1968, when they beat Arsenal 1-0 in the Final. They had an excellent record in European competitions. They won the Inter-Cities Fairs Cup in 1968, when they beat Ferencváros, and in 1971 when they beat Juventus over two legs on the away-goals rule. They also reached the Final in 1967, but lost to

Dinamo Zagreb. Leeds reached the European Cup-winners' Cup Final in 1973, losing to AC Milan 1-0, and also reached the semi-finals of the European Cup in 1970 before losing to Celtic.

There were also some low moments, like the FA Cup defeat against Colchester United in 1970-71, but as a mark of all this success, Revie was awarded the OBE in 1970.

In July 1974, he was appointed England manager but was a complete disaster in the role and missed the constant involvement with players. He chopped and changed the side around and any players with imagination and skill never stayed long in his team. England missed the 1976 European championships and looked like failing to qualify for the 1978 World Cup finals when Revie secretly negotiated a massively-paid coaching job in the United Arab Emirates, worth £60,000 a year. He was bitterly criticised by the FA and Press — although he sold the story of his going to a national paper before telling the FA — and was later suspended from British soccer until he was willing to face a charge of bringing the game into disrepute.

He was later banned for ten years from English soccer but later won a High Court case against the FA and was guaranteed an injunction quashing the ban. It was a hollow victory, although he later took up an consultancy post at Elland Road. Don Revie was later accused in a newspaper of being involved in the fixing of results in matches involving Leeds, although these allegations were never proved.

Revie held his post in the UAE from July 1977 until May 1980, after which he coached in Egypt for a short time. In the late 1980s he was struck down by motor neurone desease and in his last years was confined to a wheelchair. He died in Edinburgh, much mourned by everybody at Elland Road.

RICHARDS, Frank H.

Career: Birmingham secretary-manager May 1915-May 1923 and cs 1927-July 1928, also secretary 1911-1912 and 1923-1925; Preston North End secretary-manager May 1925-cs 1927; Bournemouth & Boscombe Athletic secretary-manager July 1928-1930.

Honours: Division Two champions 1921.

Although Frank Richards was officially in charge of team affairs in two spells at Birmingham, he was mainly regarded as an administrative secretary of the club. He left most of the day-to-day running of the team to his trainers and had very little say in who was bought and sold, this being undertaken by the directors. Richards forgot to enter Birmingham for the 1921-22 FA Cup, which today would probably have meant the sack.

After going close to promotion in the first season after the war, the Blues clinched the Second Division championship in 1920-21. Bournemouth did reasonably well when Richards spent two seasons as their secretary-manager and reached the fifth round of the FA Cup in 1928-29.

RICHARDSON, Damien John

Born: Dublin, 2 August 1947.
Forward 6ft; 12st (1980).
Career: Home Farm; Shamrock Rovers 1965; Gillingham October 1972; Gravesend & Northfleet August 1981; Folkestone April 1982; Chatham Town; Faversham Town; Gillingham youth-

team manager, then manager May 1989-September 1992.

Honours: Republic of Ireland international (3 caps).

Richardson was not a prolific goalscorer but managed 91 goals in his 323 League appearances for the Gills. He helped them to runners-up spot in Division Four in 1973-74 and then fourth in the Third Division in 1978-79, when they missed promotion by a point. He gained three caps for the Republic of Ireland but was only in the starting line-up once, in his last appearance, against Czechoslovakia in September 1979. The Irish lost 4-1 with Richardson at centre-forward.

He did a good job as youth-team manager at Priestfield and was then offered the manager's job. He appointed Ron Hillyard as his assistant manager but although he has developed some fine young players, he was still waiting for success when he was sacked after a terrible start to 1992-93.

RICHLEY, Lionel

Born: Gateshead, 2 July 1924.
Half-back.
Career: Sunderland amateur; Crystal Palace; Tonbridge player-secretary; Hartlepools United June 1951; King's Lynn player-manager 1953-1960s; Bury assistant manager in 1960s; Rochdale assistant manager, then manager October 1968-February 1970; Darlington manager cs 1970-July 1971; Newcastle United chief scout 1971.

Honours: Division Four promotion 1969; Eastern Counties League champions 1954.

Len Richley never appeared in Palace's first team but played 72 League games for Hartlepools United. He had almost ten years as manager at King's Lynn and discovered a number of players who went on to play League soccer. These included John Neal, who signed for Swindon Town. Lynn had some good FA Cup runs and beat Coventry City 2-1 at Highfield Road in 1961-62.

He took Rochdale to promotion in 1968-69, but resigned after a 'conflict of views' in February 1970. Richley had a great start to the following season with Darlington but they fell away to finish 12th. He proved a useful chief scout at St James' Park in the 1970s.

RIDDING, William

Born: Heswall, Cheshire, 4 April 1911;
Died: Heaton, Bolton, 20 September 1981.
Inside-forward 5ft 10in; 12st 5lb (1933).
Career: Tranmere Rovers August 1928; Manchester City March 1930; Manchester United December 1931; Northampton Town August 1934; Tranmere Rovers August 1935; Oldham Athletic October 1935, retired through injury 1936; Tranmere Rovers manager May 1939-1945; Bolton Wanderers trainer 1946, then manager February 1951-August 1968; England team trainer 1950, from 1968 started his own physiotherapy business; Lancashire CCC physiotherapist.

Honours: FA Cup winners 1958, runners-up 1953.

Percy Young, in his history of Bolton Wanderers, described Bill Ridding as 'a man of Cheshire and a countryman at heart, who has never sought nor achieved the more strident headlines. With a supremely good appreciation of football talent, a professional knowledge of human physiology, a sympathetic talent for seeing the hidden virtues of players and an economic

acumen that prevents misdirection by cheque-book speculation, Ridding is the ideal manager for Bolton as perhaps his length of service shows.'

Ridding was born a farmer's son on the Wirral. He developed into a centre-forward with a go-ahead style, whose earnestness brought him goals and popularity. In 17 games for Tranmere he scored 12 goals before Manchester City paid a four-figure fee for his services in March 1930.

Sadly, a very promising career was to be blighted by injury. He scored four goals in only nine appearances for City before moving to neighbours United in December 1931. Manchester United were in one of the worst spells in their history and Ridding scored 14 goals in 44 games for the club before moving to Northampton Town in August 1934. He does not appear to have played any games for the Cobblers before returning to Tranmere Rovers in August 1935 and going on to Oldham Athletic two months later. The following year he was forced to retire due to a double cartilage injury.

Ridding returned to Prenton Park, initially as 'A' team trainer, having qualified as a physiotherapist and chiropodist. He was appointed trainer after the death of Jimmy Morton and also managed the club from May 1939 to 1945. Officially titled the club's trainer, due to the war Ridding was in fact incorporating the task of secretary, manager, kit washer and even groundsman.

He joined Bolton Wanderers as trainer in 1946 and when manager Walter Rowley resigned, Ridding became the caretaker manager in October 1950. In February 1951, he was officially appointed manager and was also the club's trainer for a while until the appointment of Bert Sproston. Ridding was also coach to the England team for the 1950 World Cup finals in Brazil. The Trotters reached the FA Cup Final in 1953, only to lose to Blackpool in one of the most exciting Wembley games. They were 3-1 up with 20 minutes to go but lost 4-3 after a great fightback by the Seasiders.

The 1958 FA Cup success over Manchester United was marred by the fact that most of the country wanted United to win due to the recent Munich air disaster which wiped out most of their side. Nat Lofthouse scored both goals in the Trotters' 2-0 victory, one of them a controversial effort after he bundled United goalkeeper Harry Gregg over the line. In 1955, the Reserves won the Central League for the first time and the Youth team reached the semi-final of the FA Youth Cup in 1956. Ridding discovered many fine players at Bolton including Eddie

Hopkinson, Francis Lee, Bryan Edwards, Dennis Stevens and Doug Holden.

The abolition of the maximum wage proved disastrous for small-town clubs and Ridding had to fight to hold on to his better players. Performances deteriorated and from finishing fourth in the First Division in 1958-59, the Trotters were relegated in 1963-64 with only 28 points. They finished third the following season but missed promotion by six points. In August 1968, he left Burnden Park to run his own physiotherapy business and later helped Lancashire CCC in that capacity.

RIGBY, Norman
Born: Newark, 23 May 1923.
Centre-half.
Career: Notts County September 1944; Peterborough United 1952-1962, manager September 1967-January 1969.

Honours: Division Four champions 1961; Midland League champions 1956, 1957, 1958, 1959, 1960.

Rigby was the stalwart centre-half and captain of the Peterborough United side of the 1950s and was considered one of the finest pivots outside the Football League. He helped the Posh to five successive Midland League championships and also in many excellent FA Cup runs. In 1954-55 they reached the fourth round and in 1958-59 reached the third round where they held Second Division Fulham to a goalless draw at Craven Cottage before losing 1-0 in the replay.

He played for the Posh for their first two seasons in the Football League and was prominent in Peterborough walking away with the Fourth Division title in their first season. When he became manager of the club they were demoted after finishing ninth in Division Three in 1967-68, when an inquiry found that the club had been making illegal payments to their players. This seemed to knock the stuffing out of the Posh. Manchester United were found guilty of a similar offence but were only fined £5,000. Talk about one law for the rich and one for the poor!

RIMMER, Warwick Robert
Born: Birkenhead, 1 March 1941
Defender   5ft 8in; 10st 6lb (1963).
Career: Cheshire Boys; Bolton Wanderers March 1958; Crewe Alexandra March 1975, then manager 1978-May 1979; coaching in Sierra Leone in 1980s; Bolton Wanderers commercial staff 1981; Tranmere Rovers commercial manager 1983.

Honours: England Schoolboy international (5 caps); Youth international; Division Three champions 1973.

Rimmer was a strong tackler with a no-nonsense approach to the game. He was the nephew of Ellis Rimmer of Sheffield Wednesday and England fame. His son, Syd, also played for Tranmere Rovers. Warwick made his debut in Bolton's first-ever League Cup tie, at Hull City in October 1960. He was ever-present in four seasons at Burnden Park and made 521/7 appearances, scoring 17 goals. Bolton sunk from the First to Third Division in the 1960s and early '70s.

Rimmer captained the side to the Third Division championship in 1972-73 as the Trotters staged a revival. After this he made 114/14 League appearances for Crewe and was coach under Harry Gregg until he succeeded him as manager at Gresty Road. Crewe finished bottom of the Football League in 1978-79 and Rimmer then left the club.

RIOCH, Bruce David
Born: Aldershot, 6 September 1947.
Midfield   5ft 11in; 12st 5lb (1970).
Career: Luton Town apprentice July 1963, professional September 1964; Aston Villa July 1969 (£100,000); Derby County February 1974 (£200,000); Everton December 1976 (£180,000); Derby County November 1977 (£150,000); Birmingham City (loan) December 1978; Sheffield United (loan) March 1979; Torquay United player-coach October 1980; Seattle Sounders (NASL) (loan) March-June 1981; Torquay United player-manager July 1982-January 1984; Seattle Sounders (NASL) coach July 1985-January 1986; Middlesbrough assistant manager January 1986, then manager March 1986-March 1990; Millwall manager April 1990-March 1992; Bolton Wanderers manager May 1992.

Honours: Scotland international (24 caps); Football League champions 1975; Division Two promotion 1988; Division Three champions 1972, runners-up 1987; Division Four champions 1968; Football League Cup runners-up 1971. Division Two runners-up 1993.

Rioch possessed power, pace and a lethal shot. He also had great competitiveness and a ruthless streak. He could play for Scotland through parental qualification. His father was a regimental sergeant major in Aldershot, where Bruce was born. Bruce's brother, Neil, played alongside him at Luton Town and Aston Villa. Bruce Rioch played in three divisional championship sides. He gained a Fourth Division medal with Luton in 1967-68, a Third Division medal with Villa in 1971-72 and a League championship medal with Derby County in 1974-75. He also played in Villa's losing League Cup Final side in 1971. He captained Scotland in their ill-fated 1978 World Cup in Argentina. He once scored four goals in a match for Derby, against Spurs in October 1976.

Rioch made a name for himself in management at Torquay United, where he got his first break. He found success at Middlesbrough, a club he took from the brink of liquidation to promotion to Division Two in 1986-87 and into the First Division via the play-offs the following season. They were relegated immediately and Rioch was eventually sacked.

Millwall reached the Second Division play-offs in 1991, under Rioch, after finishing fifth but they lost easily to Brighton. The Lions also won the FA Youth Cup that season beating Sheffield Wednesday in the Final. The Lions' form slumped the following season after Rioch sold Jimmy Carter to Liverpool for £800,000 and Teddy Sherringham to Nottingham Forest for £2 million. Rioch resigned in March

1992 but two months later took charge at Bolton Wanderers. After a poor start the Trotters were challenging for a promotion spot and also had an excellent FA Cup run. They beat Liverpool at Anfield and Wolves at Molineux, before losing 3-1 to Derby County at the Baseball Ground. Eventually, they came with a late run to clinch the runners-up spot in the Second Division in what was a great season for the club under Rioch. The stars of the team were Andy Walker, John McGinlay and Dave Lee as 20,000 plus attendances were seen once more at Burnden Park.

ROBERTS, Charles
Born: Rise Carr, Darlington, 6 April 1883; Died: Manchester, 7 August 1939.
Centre-half   5ft 11½in; 12st 7lb (1909).
Career: Darlington St Augustine; Bishop Auckland; Grimsby Town May 1903; Manchester United April 1904 (£600); Oldham Athletic August 1913 (£1,750), retired through injury January 1919, manager July 1921-December 1922; founder of Players' Union, chairman until September 1921; owner of stationery and newsagent's shop in Manchester area.

Honours: England international (3 caps); Football League representative (9 caps); Football League champions 1908, 1911; FA Cup winners 1909.

Charlie Roberts gained just three England caps, fewer than his talents deserved. He felt that he was victimised due to his involvement with the Players' Union. A brilliant pivot, he was strong in the air and tackle as well as a fine reader of the game. He twice played in League championship sides with Manchester United and picked up a winners' medal in the 1909 FA Cup Final against Bristol City. He built his stamina up in the summer months by working on East Coast trawlers as a fisherman.

Roberts played 299 games for United, scoring 23 goals. He then led Oldham to fourth and runners-up in Division One between 1913 and 1915. When he managed the club, they just missed relegation in 1921-22 with a late run. After another terrible slump he resigned in December 1922, confessing that he could not stand the strain of watching his club.

ROBERTS, Kenneth Owen
Born: Rhosmedre, Cefn Mawr, near Wrexham 27 March 1936.
Outside-right/winger.

Career: Wrexham amateur April 1951; Aston Villa May 1953, retired through

injury cs 1958; Oswestry Town trainer-coach 1958-1961; Wrexham coach 1961, later assistant manager; Bradford assistant manager; Chester manager March 1968-September 1976, then administrator and assistant manager for a while.

Honours: Wales Youth international; Division Four promotion 1975.

A ball-playing winger who was fast and elusive, Roberts had shown great promise at Villa but his career was ended by a knee injury. He was 32 when he became manager of Chester and lasted in the job for over eight years. Roberts had considerable success at the club. They almost reached the League Cup Final in 1974-75 but were knocked out in the semi-finals, 5-4 on aggregate by Aston Villa. They had some great results on the way, the best being their 3-0 home victory over Leeds United in the fourth round and a 1-0 replay success over Newcastle United at Sealand Road in the quarter-finals.

Chester had just missed promotion to the Third Division in 1970-71 but slumped in the following seasons. They finished fourth in 1974-75 and gained promotion on goal-average from Lincoln City. Roberts resigned on 2 September 1976 and Alan Oakes took over.

ROBERTS, Robert
Born: Edinburgh, 2 September 1940.
Wing-half   5ft 10½in; 11st 3lb (1963).

Career: Motherwell 1958; Leicester City September 1963 (£41,000); Mansfield Town September 1970; Coventry City coach; Colchester United player-coach July 1973, then manager June 1975-April 1982; Wrexham manager June 1982-March 1985; El Shabar (Kuwait) coach 1985-1987; Grimsby Town manager July 1987-May 1988; Leicester City coach June 1988.

Honours: Scotland Under-23 international (1 cap); Scottish League representative (1 cap); Division Four promotion 1977; FA Cup runners-up 1969.

An attacking linkman, Roberts initially struggled at Filbert Street but was often played out of position. He missed the 1964 League Cup Final, despite scoring in both legs of the semi-final. A midfield anchorman, he always tried his hardest. He played 275/6 games for Leicester City, scoring 36 goals before moving to Mansfield Town. He did an excellent job on a shoestring budget at Colchester United. They were relegated to the Fourth Division in 1976 but bounced straight back in third place the following season.

In 1979 they reached the fifth round of the FA Cup before losing narrowly to Manchester United. Colchester were relegated again in 1981 and when he failed to get them straight back up, he was sacked. Roberts had a tough time at Wrexham and was lucky to hold on to his job for so long. Things did not improve much at Grimsby Town either. Roberts' one major honour was achieved when he appeared in the FA Cup Final for Leicester City against Manchester City in 1969, although he ended up on the losing side.

ROBERTSON, John Tait

Born: Dumbarton, 25 February 1877; Died: 24 January 1935.
Left-half   5ft 8in; 11st 7lb (1902).
Career: Dumbarton junior football; Morton 1896; Everton; Southampton May 1898; Glasgow Rangers August 1899 (£300); Chelsea player-manager April 1905-October 1906; Glossop player-manager October 1906-1909; coached on the Continent; Coventry City trainer-coach cs 1927.

Honours: Scotland international (16 caps); Scottish League representative (6 caps); Southern League champions 1899; Scottish League champions 1900, 1901, 1902; Scottish Cup winners 1903, runners-up 1904, 1905.

One of the best wing-halves of his time, Jackie Robertson was powerful in the tackle with an excellent shot and great heading ability and he liked to run with the ball. He spent only one season at The Dell but the Saints won the Southern League championship. He then moved back to Scotland to join Rangers and had even more success. They were League champions three seasons on the trot and he also picked up a Scottish Cup winners' medal in 1903, when they beat Hearts 2-0 in a second replayed Final.

A football strategist of the classical Scottish school, Robertson became Chelsea's first manager shortly after they were formed in 1905. He quickly put together an excellent squad of players through his contacts in English and Scottish football. Chelsea finished third in their first season, narrowly missing promotion. He played 39 games for the club before moving to manage Glossop. The highspot of his stay there was reaching the quarter-finals of the FA Cup in 1908-09, which included victory at Sheffield Wednesday.

ROBINSON, William

Born: Whitburn, County Durham, 4 April 1919.
Centre-forward   5ft 10in; 12st (1938).
Career: Hylton Juniors; Sunderland April 1936; guest for Charlton, Barnsley, Hamilton Academical, Luton Town and Stockport County in World War Two; Charlton Athletic May 1946 (£1,000); West Ham United January 1949 (£7,000), retired to become youth-team manager May 1953-November 1957, then assistant manager until 1959; Hartlepools United manager November 1959-June 1962.

Honours: FA Cup winners 1947; Football League South Cup winners 1944; England Schools Shield winners 1935 (with Durham Boys).

Robinson had just become a regular in the Sunderland side when war broke out and he lost many of his best years as a player. He scored four goals for Sunderland against Manchester United in March 1939 and joined Charlton Athletic after the war, appearing at

centre-forward when they beat Burnley in the 1947 FA Cup Final. He scored 18 goals in 60 appearances for the Valiants before moving to West Ham and netted another 61 goals in 195 appearances for the Hammers before retiring to run the club's excellent youth scheme with Wally St Pier.

Robertson was then assistant manager to Benny Fenton for the season that West Ham won the Second Division championship in 1957-58. He could well have had a job for life at Upton Park, but in 1959 he moved north to manage Hartlepools United. They had to apply for re-election in all three seasons that he was in charge in what was probably the most difficult job in the Football League.

ROBSON, Bryan Stanley 'Pop'

Born: Sunderland, 11 November 1945.
Striker   5ft 7in; 11st 8lb (1983).
Career: Newcastle United November 1962; West Ham United February 1971 (£120,000); Sunderland July 1974 (£145,000); West Ham United October 1976 (£80,000); Sunderland June 1979 (£40,000); Carlisle United player-coach March 1981 (£10,000); Chelsea player-coach August 1982; Carlisle United (loan) March 1983; Sunderland player-coach August 1983; Gateshead as player 1985; Carlisle United assistant manager 1985, then manager August-October 1985; Gateshead coach 1986; Hartlepool United coach and assistant manager 1988-1991; Manchester United Reserve-team manager.

Honours: England Under-23 international (2 caps); Football League representative (1 cap); Division Two champions 1965, 1976; Inter-Cities Fairs Cup winners 1969.

Bryan Robson had an outstanding playing career in which he scored almost 300 goals in just under 700 appearances. A small, stocky striker, he was extremely quick on the turn and very difficult to mark. Robson gained Second Division championship medals and shared in Newcastle's Fairs Cup success over Újpesti Dózsa in 1969. He scored over 100 goals in his two spells at Upton Park.

A prolific goalscorer, Robson was acrobatic, strong, sharp in the penalty area and had a powerful shot. At Chelsea, 'Pop', as he was universally known, was in charge of the juniors and occasionally played in the first team. He had a three-month spell as manager of Carlisle United but resigned to allow Bob Stokoe to take over again. He had proved happier as a coach than a manager.

ROBSON, John R.

Born: Gainford, County Durham (or Chester-le-Street), spring 1854; Died: Hull, 11 January 1922.
Goalkeeper.
Career: Middlesbrough Swifts; Middlesbrough, connected with club from 1892, then manager May 1899-May 1905; Crystal Palace manager cs 1905-April 1907; Brighton & Hove Albion manager March 1908-December 1914; Manchester United manager December 1914-October 1921, then assistant manager until his death.

Honours: Division Two runners-up 1902; Southern League champions 1910.

Jack Robson was connected with Middlesbrough for many years and become their first manager. He had previously played in goal in their

reserve side, Middlesbrough Swifts. Initially, Robson was assistant secretary when 'Boro reverted to amateur status. He took over the manager's job when they joined the Football League and moulded a Northern League club into a side ready for Second Division soccer in just three months. 'Boro gained promotion to Division One in 1902. Robson was absolved of any responsibility when there was an irregular payments scandal at the club in 1905.

He was also Palace's first manager and at Brighton he drove the players hard but looked after their welfare and recreational activities. Brighton finished third in the Southern League in 1906-07 and 1910-11 and won the title in 1909-10 with 59 points, conceding only 29 goals. They then surprisingly beat Aston Villa 1-0 in the FA Charity Shield match. Initially team manager at Manchester United, he also took over secretarial duties when J.J.Bentley resigned in 1916. Ill health led to him stepping down to assistant in 1921 and shortly afterwards he died of pneumonia.

ROBSON, Robert William

Born: Sacriston, County Durham, 18 February 1933.
Inside-forward/Wing-half
5ft 9½in; 11st 10lb (1960).
Career: Westhouses Secondary Modern School; Middlesbrough amateur; Chester-le Street; Langley Park Juniors; Fulham May 1950; West Bromwich Albion March 1956 (£25,000); Fulham August 1962 (£20,000), retired May 1967; Oxford University coach 1965-1966; Vancouver Royals manager May 1967-January 1968; Fulham manager January-November 1968; Chelsea scout briefly in 1968; Ipswich Town manager January 1969-July 1982; England 'B' manager January 1978-July 1982, then national manager July 1982-July 1990; PSV Eindhoven manager August 1990-May 1992; Sporting Lisbon manager May 1992.

Honours: England international (20 caps); Under-23 international (1 cap); Football League representative (5 caps); 'B' international (1 cap); FA tour to South Africa 1956; FA Cup winners 1978; UEFA Cup winners 1981; Texaco Cup winners 1973.

Bobby Robson has been one of the most successful managers for the last two decades, not only finding success at unfashionable Ipswich Town but also taking England to the semi-final of the 1990 World Cup where they narrowly lost to West Germany. He took Ipswich close to the League title on many occasions and also to an FA Cup Final

triumph in 1978. Robson was also an excellent player for both Fulham, West Brom and England.

Middlesbrough never pursued their interest in him and after playing for Chester-le-Street and Langley Park Juniors, Robson joined Fulham in 1950. Fulham's manager, Bill Dodgin, pipped Newcastle United for his signature and Robson left his mining job to move to London. He later formed a brilliant inside trio with Bedford Jezzard and Johnny Haynes, all of whom played for England. Robson began his career as an inside-right but later played at wing-half for West Brom. As an inside-forward he was a dangerous raider who was always on the lookout for goals and at half-back he was tireless and confident, a constructive, sound and stylish player.

In March 1956, West Brom's manager Vic Buckingham paid £25,000 for his services and Robson renewed his partnership with Johnny Haynes in the England side. He made his international debut in November 1957, at Wembley, and scored two goals in a 4-0 victory over France. Robson went on to gain 20 caps as well as an Under-23 cap, five appearances for the Football League and one 'B' cap. He toured South Africa with the FA in 1956 and played in the final stages of the 1958 and 1962 World Cups.

He lost his England place after the World Cup in Chile and in August 1962 returned to Craven Cottage for a second spell for a fee of £20,000. Robson brought an air of calm authority to the shaking Fulham defence and when he retired in May 1967, he had played 370 games for the Cottagers in his two spells on top of the 61 goals in 257 games for West Brom. He was also a good cricketer and played for Sacriston, Worcester Park (London) and West Bromwich Dartmouth.

Robson was encouraged to take up coaching by England manager Walter Winterbottom, when he was playing for his country. He became an FA staff coach and coached the Oxford University team from 1965 to 1966. After leaving Fulham he moved to North America to manage Vancouver Royals but in January 1968 returned to Fulham for a third spell at Craven Cottage, this time as the club's manager.

When he took over, relegation to the Second Division looked a strong possibility. He unsuccessfully used short-term measures to stop the decline but had little success in the transfer market, buying players who were past their best or not good enough for the First Division. He sold his greatest asset, Allan Clarke, to Leicester City and replaced him with Frank Large, who proved a big disappointment. Robson found difficulties in handling his former colleagues. During the close season of 1968 he re-organised the backroom staff but things did not improve and with Fulham near the foot of the Second Division, he was sacked in November 1968 after only ten months in charge.

After a short spell scouting for Chelsea, Robson was appointed as manager of Ipswich Town in January 1969. It was the start of a highly successful 13 years in charge at Portman Road. He was articulate and up-to-date with the latest coaching techniques but the first few years in charge proved tough. He paid large fees for Jimmy Robertson and Frank Clarke, in a successful attempt to keep Ipswich in the First Division in 1969-70.

Robson was beginning to put a useful side together. The new players included Colin Viljoen and Mick Mills. However, his strong personality led him into frequent clashes with established players. The most unsavoury was the Baxter/Carroll affair caused by a dispute over wives using the players' guest room. Reserve-team players' wives were not allowed to use the room and Baxter and Carroll disputed this rule which led to a furious row with Robson and eventually to the departure of the players from the club.

Ipswich finished fourth in the First Division in both the 1972-73 and 1973-74 seasons. They also finished third in seasons 1974-75, 1976-77 and 1979-80 and runners-up in 1980-81 and 1981-82. In 1980-81 they should have won the League title but were pipped by Aston Villa. Ipswich were victims of their own success, as an overcrowded fixture list cost them valuable points at a vital time. They had a seemingly unassailable lead in the League but missed out after winning only one of their last five games. That season they were also chasing the FA Cup, but lost in the semi-finals to Manchester City, and they won the UEFA Cup, beating AZ Alkmaar over two legs in an exciting Final. Ipswich won the first leg 3-0 at Portman Road and lifted the trophy, despite losing the away leg 4-2. In 1981-82 they were runners-up to Liverpool, finishing four points behind the Reds.

Robson's greatest triumph came in the 1978 FA Cup Final when Ipswich beat Arsenal 1-0, thanks to a goal from unlikely hero Roger Osborne. They also reached the semi-finals of the League Cup in 1982 but lost to Liverpool, 4-2 on aggregate. The club's other triumph came in the Texaco Cup in 1973, when they beat local rivals, Norwich City, 2-1 both home and away in the Final.

In July 1982 Robson succeeded another former Fulham player, Ron Greenwood, as the England manager. He had previously been manager of the England 'B' side from January 1978. Robson now had to put up with a lot of stick from the British Press, most of it completely unjustified as he became the most successful England manager since Alf Ramsey. The highlight came after he announced that he would be relinquishing the role after the 1990 World Cup finals. He took England to the semi-final , where they were unfortunate to lose to West Germany on penalties after a 1-1 draw. They had qualifed as runners-up to Sweden in their group, then won their section in the finals in Italy. They beat Belgium 1-0 with a goal in the last seconds of extra-time, then beat the Cameroons 3-2 in an exciting quarter-final.

England had failed to qualify for the European championships in 1984, when they lost 1-0 to Denmark at Wembley, but in 1986 they qualified for the World Cup finals in Mexico and reached the quarter-finals. Here they lost 2-1 to Argentina with both goals coming from Maradona, one of which he clearly fisted into Shilton's net. England had made a terrible start to the finals but important goals from Gary Lineker saw them to the last eight. The 1988 European championship were disastrous for England. After qualifying with ease they lost all of their games in the finals.

By August 1990, Robson had had enough of the limelight as England's manager and accepted the manager's job at PSV Eindhoven. They took the Dutch title in both 1990-91 and 1991-

92 but could not find success in Europe. In May 1992 he moved to Portugal to manage Sporting Lisbon.

ROEDER, Glenn V.

Born: Woodford, Essex, 13 December 1955.
Central defender 6ft 2in; 12st 8lb (1990).
Career: Orient December 1973; Queen's Park Rangers August 1978 (£250,000); Notts County (loan) November 1983; Newcastle United December 1983 (£150,000); Watford July 1989; Leyton Orient player-coach January 1991; Gillingham player-manager October 1992.

Honours: England 'B' international (6 caps); Division Two champions 1983; FA Cup runners-up 1982.

A cool, stylish and elegant player, Glenn Roeder started his career as a midfield player but was later converted to a central defender. He helped Orient to the semi-finals of the FA Cup in 1978 and toured New Zealand with an FA party. After scoring four goals in 128/8 games for Orient, Roeder moved to Queen's Park Rangers and played in their 1982 FA Cup Final side which lost to Tottenham Hotspur.

Roeder played only nine times in Rangers' Second Division championship side in 1982-83 and, after a loan spell with Notts County, moved to Newcastle United after scoring 17 goals in 157 League games for Rangers. Roeder went on to play over 200 games for Newcastle and helped them back into Division One in 1984. He could have gone to Italy as Paul Gascoigne's 'minder' in 1992 but decided to stay in England and manage Gillingham who were at the bottom of the Football League.

The Gills were bottom when Roeder took over but eventually avoided the drop into the Conference League finishing second to bottom of the Third Division.

ROFE, Dennis

Born: Fulham, London, 1 June 1950.
Left-back 5ft 7in; 10st 11lb (1981).
Career: East London Schools; Orient February 1968; Leicester City August 1972 (£112,000); Chelsea February 1980; Southampton July 1982, retired to become youth-team coach in 1984, first-team coach February 1987-1991; Bristol Rovers coach cs 1991, then manager October 1991-November 1992.

Honours: England Under-23 international (1 cap); Division Two champions 1980; Division Three champions 1970.

A sturdy, fast defender who was known for his tough tackling, Dennis Rofe also

liked to attack when he could. He was a key member of the O's Third Division championship side in 1969-70 and was snapped up by Leicester manager Jimmy Bloomfield as a replacement for David Nish.

The dressing-room joker, Rofe scored six goals in his 324 appearances for City, added to his 188/1 games for Orient in which he also scored six goals. He came close to playing in a Wembley Final in 1974, but Leicester lost 3-1 to Liverpool in a semi-final replay. Rofe also gained a Second Division championship medal with Leicester in 1979-80, but moved to Chelsea in mid-season where he was club captain. Under Rofe, Bristol Rovers looked a team with potential in Division Two. They had a good FA Cup run in season 1991-92, but Rofe lost his job after a poor start to the following season.

ROOKE, Ronald Leslie

Born: Guildford, 7 December 1911;
Died: July 1985.
Centre-forward 5ft 9in; 12st 4lb (1938).
Career: Guildford City; Crystal Palace March 1933; Fulham October 1936; Arsenal December 1946 (£1,000); Crystal Palace player-manager June 1949-November 1950; Bedford Town player-manager February 1951-May 1955 and 1959-October 1961, with occasional games for reserve team in early 1960s.

Honours: England wartime international (1 cap); Football League champions 1948; Southern League (South East zone) champions 1959.

Ronnie Rooke was an unmistakeable figure with his bandy legs, shirt sleeves flapping and black wavy hair on top of a craggy face dominated by a 'Roman' nose. Lethal with either foot and a clinical and ruthless finisher, Rooke deserved more than just one wartime cap for England. After failing to establish himself at Selhurst Park, it was a major coup when Fulham signed him and he made an immediate impact with a hat-trick on his debut, against West Ham.

Top scorer in all of his 11 seasons at the Cottage, he netted 77 goals in 110 League and FA Cup games for Fulham, plus 212 goals in 199 wartime games. He also scored all six in an FA Cup victory over Bury in January 1939. Rooke joined Arsenal when he was 35 and took the First Division by storm. He scored 35 goals as the Gunners took the League championship in 1947-48 and altogether netted 67 in his 93 games for Arsenal. He then scored another 26 in 46 games as player-manager of Crystal Palace.

Rooke was possibly the first manager ever to be sent off, when he was dismissed during a tough game at Millwall. At Selhurst Park he had £20,000 to spend on new players, but had little success. Rooke had many years as manager of Bedford Town, who had some fine FA Cup runs and did well in the Southern League. He was still playing for Bedford Reserves in his 50s.

ROOKS, Richard

Born: Sunderland, 29 May 1940.
Centre-half 5ft 10in; 12st 7lb (1959).
Career: Sunderland Schools; Sunderland June 1957; Middlesbrough August 1965 (£20,000); Bristol City June 1969 (£17,000); Willington player-coach; Scunthorpe United manager November 1974-January 1976.

Rooks was understudy to Charlie Hurley at Roker Park became frustrated with reserve-team football and moved

to Middlesbrough. It was a good move because he made 150 appearances for 'Boro and once scored a hat-trick for the club, when he played at centre-forward at Cardiff in May 1966. 'Boro were relegated to Division Three after this game but they soon returned to the Second as runners-up in 1966-67.

Rooks was unhappy when he was dropped by manager Stan Anderson just before completing what would have been ever-present season for 'Boro. He left Ayresome Park soon afterwards, transferred to Bristol City, which upset the fans. He played 97 League games for City before becoming player-coach at Willington. Rooks had a tough time as manager of Scunthorpe United, who had to seek re-election in 1974-75.

ROSS, Ian

Born: Glasgow, 26 November 1947.
Defender 5ft 9½in; 11st 9lb (1973).
Career: Glasgow Schools; Liverpool apprentice 1963, professional August 1965; Aston Villa February 1972 (£60,000); Notts County (loan) October 1976; Northampton Town (loan) November 1976; Peterborough United December 1976; Santa Barbara FC (USA); Wolverhampton Wanderers August 1979; Hereford United October 1982; Wolves coach; coaching in Oman 1982-1983; Birmingham City reserve-team coach; Valur (Iceland) coach-manager 1984-1988; also coached in South Africa and Australia in the 1980s; Huddersfield Town manager March 1992.

Honours: Division Three champions 1972; Football League Cup winners 1975. Iceland League champions 1985.

A fine professional who always tried his hardest, Ian Ross had lots of skill and commitment. Mainly a reserve at Anfield, he was considered a very useful squad member by manager Bill Shankly. He made 202 appearances for Aston Villa, which included a League Cup winners' medal in 1975, when Villa beat Norwich 1-0, and a Third Division title medal in 1971-72.

He helped Villa from the Third to the First Division and also played over 100 games for Peterborough United. By the time he became manager at Huddersfield Town, Ross was a very experienced coach. having worked all over the world and guiding Valur to an Icelandic League Championship. At Huddersfield, he took over from Eoin Hand late in the 1991-92 season and steered Town to the Third Division play-offs where they lost to Peterborough United.

The Terriers made a great recovery to avoid relegation in 1992-93. They were bottom at the turn of the year but they fought their way to survival with some gutsy performances and also enjoyed a good run in the FA Cup competition. The turning point to the season seemed to be the return, as coach, of their former manager Mick Buxton and his presence helped the Huddersfield club avoid the drop after all.

ROUGHTON, William George

Born: Manchester, 11 May 1909; Died: Southampton, 7 June 1989.
Left-back 5ft 11in; 12st (1935).
Career: Lancashire & Manchester Schools; Droylesden; Huddersfield Town November 1928; Manchester United September 1936-1945; Exeter City manager October 1945-March 1952; Southampton manager March 1952-September 1955.

Honours: Football League representative (1 cap); FA tour of Canada 1931.

Roughton was an apprentice engineer when he signed for Huddersfield Town. An authoritative player, he was unlucky to miss the 1930 FA Cup Final but toured Canada with the FA that summer and played for the Football League against the Irish League in 1934. An instant success at Manchester United, Roughton was a key figure in United's side after they returned to the First Division.

Initially player-manager at Exeter City, he made 14 appearances in 1945-46 before retiring at the end of the season to concentrate on management. Exeter were an average Third Division side and maintained this position under Roughton. Southampton were relegated from Division Two in 1952-53 but he failed to get them back. Disillusionment and failing health led to his resignation and he left the club £60,000 in debt, due to his savage team-building policy.

ROWE, Arthur Sydney

Born: Tottenham, 1 September 1906.
Centre-half   5ft 9in; 12st 8lb (1935).
Career: Parkhurst School, Cheshunt; Cheshunt; Northfleet; Tottenham Hotspur May 1929, retired due to injury May 1939; coaching in Hungary; Chelmsford City manager July 1945; Tottenham Hotspur manager May 1949-May 1955; West Bromwich Albion coach cs 1957; Crystal Palace assistant manager October 1958 and manager April 1960-November 1962, general manager March 1963, caretaker manager January-April 1966, later assistant manager until May 1971, secretary of the Football Hall of Fame May-December 1971; Orient general advisor January 1972-cs 1978; Crystal Palace director; Millwall consultant June 1978.

Honours: England international (1 cap); Football League champions 1951; Division Two champions 1950; Division Four runners-up 1961.

Arthur Rowe will remain an important part of English soccer history as the man who invented a style of play called the 'push and run' method which helped Spurs win the League title for the first time in their history. He will also be remembered as a white-haired, softly-spoken man with a gentle manner. Rowe was a brilliant tactician who would have had even more success in soccer management but for a number of bouts of ill health. And during his playing career he would have gained more than one cap for England had he not suffered from so many injuries.

Born a stone's throw away from the home of Tottenham Hotspur, Arthur Rowe attended Parkhurst School in Cheshunt and before joining Spurs in May 1929 he played for his local club. Rowe enjoyed great success as a schoolboy footballer and in his early days at White Hart Lane he appeared for Tottenham's nursery club at Northfleet in Kent. He made his League debut against Burnley in October 1931 and quickly established himself as first-choice centre-half. Spurs finished runners-up in Division Two in 1932-33 and third in the First Division the following season.

A constructive player, Rowe was a centre-half of the thoughtful kind, cleverly turning defence into attack with his accurate distribution. The highlight of his playing career was his England cap, which came against France at White Hart Lane in December

1933. Shortly afterwards he sustained an injury which greatly restricted his appearances for his club and his absence at the end of 1934-35 proved costly for Spurs, who were relegated to Division Two. Rowe made 201 League and FA Cup appearances for Tottenham before being released in May 1939, having failed to recover fully from cartilage problems.

He was soon appointed by the Hungarian government as a national coach but this ended with the outbreak of war and he returned to England to serve in the Army as a PTI and took charge of the Army football team. On demobilisation, Rowe took over as secretary-manager of Chelmsford City and quickly found success. They were runners-up in the Southern League in 1948-49 and he was in control at the Essex club from July 1945 until May 1949, when he became manager of Tottenham Hotspur.

He had been favourite to take over, due mostly to having played for the club and also due to the excellent reputation he had gained at Chelmsford. Rowe was the architect of the celebrated 'push and run' style which was to take Spurs to successive titles in Divisions Two and One in seasons 1949-50 and 1950-51. This entailed a player quickly passing the ball along the ground and running into open space to receive a return pass, or decoy an opposing player.

This was the first time that Tottenham had won the League championship in their history and massive crowds rolled into White Hart Lane to watch the triumphant Spurs. His only new signing had been Alf Ramsey from Southampton, otherwise all the players helped win successive titles were already at the club. Spurs finished runners-up in 1951-52 and reached the FA Cup semi-finals in 1953. The club then went into decline and this affected Rowe's health. He suffered a nervous breakdown in 1954 and had a complete rest from football for six months.

Alas, in April 1955 his health broke down again and his assistant, Jimmy Anderson, became caretaker manager in June 1955 until Rowe's contract expired in January 1956, when Anderson took full control.

Initially, Rowe retired but his love of football brought him back. In the summer of 1957 he accepted a coaching post at West Bromwich Albion and in October 1958 he became assistant manager at Crystal Palace. In April 1960, Rowe became the manager at Selhurst Park and guided Palace to promotion to Division Three in 1960-61. But a poor start to the 1962-63 saw him again suffer ill health and he resigned in November 1962. He

returned to Selhurst as general manager in March 1963 and was caretaker manager from January to April 1966, between managers Dick Graham and Bert Head. He was later assistant manager until May 1971, when he left the club. In November 1969, Palace organised a testimonial match for him to celebrate his 40 years in the game and the guest of honour was the England manager and his former player, Sir Alf Ramsey.

From May to December 1971, Rowe was the secretary of the short-lived Football Hall of Fame, a museum about the game. At the age of 66 he had still not finished with football, however, and in January 1972 he became the general advisor at Orient and remained there until June 1978, when he joined Millwall as a consultant. Rowe was also on the board of directors at Crystal Palace for a while. Today he lives in retirement at Norbury, South London.

ROWLEY, George Arthur

Born: Wolverhampton, 21 April 1926.
Centre-forward   5ft 11in; 14st (1959).
Career: Wolverhampton Schools; Wolverhampton Gas Works; Blackenhall St Luke's; Wolverhampton Wanderers amateur 1942; West Bromwich Albion amateur March 1944, professional May 1944; guest for Manchester United, Middlesbrough, Brighton & Hove Albion and Lincoln City in World War Two; Fulham December 1948; Leicester City July 1950 (£12,000); Shrewsbury Town player-manager June 1958-July 1968 (£7,000), retired 1965; Sheffield United manager July 1968-August 1969; Southend United manager March 1970-May 1976, then scout; Oswestry Town manager July 1979-October 1980.

Honours: England 'B' international (1 cap); Football League representative (1 cap); Division Two champions 1949, 1954, 1957; Division Four runners-up 1972, promotion 1959.

The most prolific goalscorer in the history of the Football League, Arthur Rowley scored 434 goals in his career. He was only 15 years old when he made his debut for Manchester United in a wartime fixture alongside brother, Jack. Arthur first gained a reputation with Fulham and his goals were crucial as they sped into Division One in 1949. He also gained two Second Division championship medals with Leicester City and his best season was 1956-57, when he scored 44 goals for City.

A big, burly player Rowley was powerful in the air and lethal on the ground. He took Shrewsbury to promotion to Division Three in 1958-59 and they also came close to promotion the following season. They beat Everton in the 1960-61 League Cup and also reached the semi-finals. Rowley played

his last game for the club in April 1965, at the age of 39.

He never hit it off with John Harris at Sheffield United and lost his job at the end of the 1968-69 season. Rowley took Southend United to promotion in 1971-72, for the first time in their history, but was sacked when they were relegated in 1976. His teams were often defensive, despite the way he played.

ROWLEY, John Frederick

Born: Wolverhampton, 7 October 1920.
Centre-forward 5ft 9in; 11st 7lb (1936).
Career: Dudley Old Boys; Wolverhampton Wanderers November 1935; Cradley Heath (loan) 1936; Bournemouth & Boscombe Athletic (loan) February 1937; Manchester United October 1937 (£3,500); guest for Tottenham Hotspur, Wolverhampton Wanderers and Distillery in World War Two; Plymouth Argyle player-manager February 1955-March 1960, retired as a player cs 1957; Oldham Athletic manager July 1960-May 1963; Ajax Amsterdam coach August 1963-July 1964; Wrexham manager January 1966-April 1967; Bradford manager March 1967-October 1968; Oldham Athletic manager October 1968-December 1969.

Honours: England international (6 caps); Wartime international (1 cap); 'B' internaional (1 cap); Football League representative; Football League champions 1952; Division Three champions 1959; Division Four runners-up 1963; FA Cup winners 1948; Football League War Cup winners 1942.

One of the finest centre-forwards of the post-war era, Jack Rowley scored 208 goals in 422 games for Manchester United. He had a deadly left-foot and was excellent in the air. Rowley scored prolifically in the war years and once netted eight goals in one game for Wolves and seven for Spurs whilst guesting for those clubs. He scored twice in United's 4-2 victory over Blackpool in the 1948 FA Cup Final and hit the target 30 times in their 1951-52 League championship season.

Rowley had a varied career in management. He took some time to rebuild Plymouth Argyle but the boards' patience was rewarded in 1959 when Plymouth returned to the Second Division. He left the club suddenly but was soon back as manager of Oldham Athletic. Rowley was very active in the transfer market but three days after Oldham achieved promotion, he was asked to resign after an internal row.

He brought about a recovery at Wrexham, then moved to Bradford. The club was in decline and Rowley could not stop it. They won only eight games in the 69 played whilst he was in charge. Things continued to be tough when he moved back to Oldham for a second spell in charge. After relegation and more poor results, he was sacked.

ROWLEY, Walter James

Born: Little Hulton, 14 April 1891.
Died: Shrewsbury, 22 March 1976.
Left-half/Right-back
5ft 10in; 11st 12lb (1922).
Career: Farnworth Wednesday; Walkden Wednesday; Little Hulton Wednesday; Oldham Athletic Reserves cs 1910; Bolton Wanderers August 1912, retired May 1925 to become reserve-team coach, later first-team coach, then manager August 1944-October 1950; Middlesbrough manager June 1952-February 1954; Shrewsbury Town manager July 1954-June 1957.

Honours: Football League North Cup winners 1945.

Rowley gave Bolton 38 years' service as player, coach and manager before resigning due to ill health. He played 191 games for the Trotters, making his debut in February 1913 against West Brom. Rowley was 12th man in their 1923 FA Cup Final success, the first big Wembley game. He missed the Final as he had just finished a suspension after being sent off in the fifth round at Huddersfield.

After 19 years as coach, Rowley succeeded Charles Foweraker as manager at Burnden Park. Bolton soon had some success when they beat Manchester United 3-2 on aggregate to take the League North Cup in May 1945. Wanderers also reached the FA Cup semi-finals in 1946, although there had been a disaster at the Burnden Park ground earlier in the year when many spectators died during a Cup tie against Stoke City.

The Trotters continued to make steady progress under Rowley but did not win anything. He had little success at Middlesbrough and resigned whilst in hospital. Then followed three years of struggle at Shrewsbury Town.

ROYLE, Joseph

Born: Norris Green, Liverpool 8 April 1949.
Centre-forward 6ft 1in; 13st 8lb (1975).
Career: Liverpool Schools; Everton apprentice July 1964, professional August 1966; Manchester City December 1974; Bristol City November 1977; Norwich City August 1980 (£60,000), retired through knee injury April 1982; Oldham Athletic manager July 1982.

Honours: England international (6 caps); Under-23 international (10 caps); Youth international; Football League representative (1 cap); Football League champions 1970; Division Two champions 1991; FA Cup runners-up 1968; Football League Cup winners 1976, runners-up 1990.

Joe Royle was a tremendous header of the ball and enjoyed a rapid rise to stardom after making his debut as a 16-year-old. He utilised his huge physique to maximum advantage and scored 119 goals in 272/3 appearances for Everton. Royle appeared in their losing FA Cup Final of 1968 and later played in Manchester City's winning League Cup Final side in 1976. He gained his first England cap against Malta in 1971.

Royle produced miracles at Oldham, despite the club's small attendances. He took Latics back to the First Division in 1990-91 as champions, after a break of 68 years. They also reached the League Cup Final in 1990, losing to

Nottingham Forest 1-0 after beating Arsenal on the way. Oldham then reached the semi-finals of the FA Cup, where they lost 2-1 to Manchester United in a replay after an exciting 3-3 draw. Up until 1989-90, Oldham had often promised success but never achieved it. The turning point possibly came in December 1989, when Royle rejected an offer to manage Manchester City.

Oldham avoided relegation by winning their last three games of 1992-93, against Villa, Liverpool and Southampton. Their 63 goals scored was in marked contrast to their defensive record where most of the problems seemed to be. Royle is now the longest-serving League manager.

RUDGE, John Robert

Born: Wolverhampton, 21 January 1948.
Forward 5ft 10in; 11st 1lb (1970).
Career: Wolverhampton Wanderers Juniors; Huddersfield Town apprentice April 1960, professional November 1961; Carlisle United December 1966; Torquay United January 1969; Bristol Rovers February 1972; AFC Bournemouth March 1975-1976; Port Vale coach, chief coach 1981, then manager December 1983.

Honours: Division Three promotion 1989; Division Four promotion 1986. Autoglass Trophy Winners 1993.

Rudge was a reserve striker at all of his clubs except Torquay United. He helped Bristol Rovers to runners-up spot in Division Three in 1973-74 with 13/6 appearances. Better known as a manager, he initially took over at Port Vale as caretaker and was offered the job permanently in March 1984. Rudge suffered an immediate blow when he lost Mark Bright to Leicester City, as the player was out of contract.

After he took Port Vale to promotion to Division Three in 1986, Rudge turned down an offer to manage Preston. Vale beat Spurs 2-1 in the FA Cup in January 1988 and then qualified for the Third Division play-offs after finishing third in 1988-89. They proceeded to beat Bristol Rovers in the Final and entered the Second Division. Rudge kept his job despite Port Vale's relegation back to Division Three in 1992. The club recently enjoyed an FA Cup thriller against neighbours Stoke City.

Port Vale were desperately unlucky not to gain instant promotion from Division Two in 1992-93 after gaining 89 points during the season but only finishing third. They beat Stockport County in the play-offs to reach Wembley where they were disappointed

to lose 3-0 to West Bromwich Albion and miss out on promotion. However, they beat Stockport County 2-1 in the Final of the Autoglass Trophy at Wembley a week earlier.

RUSSELL, David W.

Born: Methil.
Wing-half 5ft 9in; 11st 7lb (1938).
Career: Dundee; East Fife; Sheffield Wednesday cs 1938, retired near end of war and became trainer of Odense FC (Denmark) c.1946; Denmark national coach for three years; Bury coach 1950, then manager November 1953-December 1961; Tranmere Rovers manager December 1961-December 1969, then general manager until 1978.

Honours: All-British XI representative v Football League XI 1941; Division Three champions 1961; Division Four promotion 1967; Scottish Cup winners 1938; Olympic Games Bronze Medal 1948.

Dave Russell's career was wrecked by the war. Having helped East Fife to the Scottish Cup in 1938, he moved to Sheffield Wednesday and was ever-present in 1938-39. Russell joined the RAF, which limited his footballing activities, and after the war he coached Denmark to a Bronze Medal in the 1948 Olympic Games in London.

Russell was an astute manager and an excellent coach, although under him Bury had a constant struggle against relegation and finally went down in 1957, after 63 years of membership of the two top divisions. There was a large turnover of players at Gigg Lane before a comeback in 1960-61 when the Shakers finished as Third Division champions.

Russell then surprised everybody by dropping two divisions to manage Tranmere Rovers. At Prenton Park he had five years of frustration and near-misses before producing a promotion side in 1967. A canny and shrewd businessman with an eye for a bargain, Russell became general manager of Tranmere in 1969, letting his right-hand man, Jackie Wright, take over as team manager.

RUTHERFORD, John

Born: Percy Main, Newcastle upon Tyne, 12 October 1884; Died: 21 April 1963.
Outside-right 5ft 8½in; 11st 7lb (1923).
Career: Percy Main School; Willington Athletic 1900; Newcastle United January 1902 (£75); Woolwich Arsenal October 1913 (£800); guest for Fulham and Chelsea in World War One; Stoke player-manager March-August 1923; Arsenal September 1923, retired January 1926; made comeback with Clapton Orient August 1926, retired again cs 1927; Tufnell Park coach late 1920s; ran an off-license in Neasden, London, in the 1930s.

Honours: England international (11 caps); Football League representative (1 cap); Football League champions 1905, 1907, 1909; FA Cup winners 1910, runners-up 1905, 1906, 1908, 1911; Victory Cup winners 1919.

Jock Rutherford had tremendous speed and ball control and was a precise crosser. One of Newcastle's greatest-ever forwards, he gained three League championship medals and played in five FA Cup Finals for the Magpies. Rutherford scored 90 goals in 336 games for Newcastle and 31 in 255 appearances for Arsenal. He worked in munitions in World War One but continued to turn out for the Gunners.

He had a brief stay as player-manager

at Stoke but left after a row with a director, probably over interference in team affairs. He had been unable to play at the start of the 1923-24 season due to a motor accident. Rutherford rejoined Arsenal after his spell at Stoke and was persuaded to come out of retirement to play for Clapton Orient in 1926. He was brother of Sep Rutherford, who played for Portsmouth.

RYAN, James

Born: Stirling, 12 May 1945.
Forward 5ft 9in; 11st 11lb (1974).
Career: Corrie Hearts; Manchester United apprentice 1962, professional January 1963; Luton Town April 1970-1977, Dallas Tornado (NASL) April 1976-August 1979 and non-League soccer from 1977; Luton Town youth-team manager, then manager January 1990-May 1991; Manchester United Reserve-team coach 1991.

Originally a right-winger who later played in midfield with Luton Town, Ryan was unable to win a regular first-team place at Old Trafford, where he made 24/3 appearances, scoring four goals. He was involved in a four-player move from United to Luton Town, which also included Don Givens, at a price of £35,000.

Ryan helped Luton to runners-up spot in Division Two in 1973-74 but they lasted for only one season in the higher grade. He made 172/12 League appearances for the Hatters, scoring 21 goals, and returned to Kenilworth Road in the early 1980s as youth-team coach. Ryan was rather harshly treated as Luton's manager after twice steering them clear of relegation from Division One. He was sacked in May 1991, to be replaced by David Pleat.

RYAN, John Gilbert

Born: Lewisham, 20 July 1947.
Full-back 5ft 11in; 11st 8lb (1980).
Career: Maidstone United; Arsenal October 1964; Fulham July 1965; Luton Town July 1969; Norwich City August 1976; (£60,000); Seattle Sounders (NASL) March 1979 (£70,000); Sheffield United September 1980 (£70,000); Manchester City January 1982, then youth-team coach until July 1983; Stockport County August 1983; Chester City player-coach September 1983; Cambridge United player-manager January 1984-January 1985; Maidstone United player-coach 1985, then assistant manager 1986; Sittingbourne manager 1991.

Honours: Division Four champions 1982.

John Ryan started his career as an inside-forward but was converted to a central defender at Fulham and then to left-back by Luton Town. Surprisingly given a free transfer after Fulham were relegated to Division Three in 1969, he moved to Luton Town with Malcolm Macdonald. Luton finished runners-up in Division Three in 1969-70 and runners-up in Division Two in 1973-74, giving Ryan another taste of First Division football.

However, they were relegated in 1975 and Ryan moved to Norwich a year later after 295/2 appearances for the Hatters. He made 128/4 appearances for Norwich, scoring 29 goals, before being transferred to Sheffield United. The Blades were Fourth Division champions in 1981-82. He also did well in the United States with Seattle Sounders, scoring 18 goals from full-back in 59 appearances.

Ryan had a brief and unsuccessful spell as manager of Cambridge United. They had only five wins in 41 games under him and were relegated to the

Third Division and heading straight through to the Fourth. His career had gone full circle when he returned to his first club, Maidstone United, in 1985.

ST JOHN, Ian

Born: Motherwell, 7 June 1938.
Centre-forward   5ft 7½in; 11st 6lb (1963).

Career: Motherwell Bridge Works; Douglas Water Thistle; Motherwell August 1956; Liverpool May 1961 (£37,500); Coventry City August 1971, assistant manager December 1971-March 1972; Tranmere Rovers player October 1972; Motherwell manager July 1973-September 1974; Portsmouth manager September 1974-May 1977; Sheffield Wednesday coach July 1978-cs 1979; television presenter working for many years on the 'Saint & Greavsie Show'.

Honours: Scotland international (21 caps); Under-23 international (2 caps); Scottish League representative (4 caps); Football League champions 1964, 1966; Division Two champions 1962; FA Cup winners 1965; European Cup-winners' Cup runners-up 1966.

Ian St John built up a reputation with Motherwell, for whom he once scored a hat-trick in two and a half minutes. Small in stature, St John could still outjump most defenders and also possessed good close control. He gained his first Scottish cap whilst at Motherwell before signing for Liverpool for £37,500. He scored a superb headed goal when the Reds beat Leeds United in the 1965 FA Cup Final and also scored 41 goals in 40 appearances when they won the Second Division championship in 1961-62. St John went on to score 118 goals in 419/5 appearances for Liverpool. Near the end of his playing career he switched to midfield.

Motherwell finished seventh in Division One in St John's first season in charge. He then moved to south to manage Portsmouth but had little money to spend at Fratton Park as Pompey had enormous debts of £300,000. Things became so desperate that he had to pitch youth-team players straight into first team. The entire board resigned and St John was sacked with Portsmouth close to relegation to the Third Division.

SAINTY, John

Born: Poplar, London, 24 March 1946.
Centre-forward 5ft 10in; 13st 4lb (1970).

Career: Tottenham Hotspur July 1963; Reading August 1967; Bournemouth & Boscombe Athletic February 1970; Mansfield Town (loan) November 1972; Aldershot August 1974; AFC Bournemouth coach; Norwich City coach; Manchester City coach 1980-November 1982; Chester coach, then manager November 1982-December 1983; Burnley coach January 1984; Armthorpe Welfare manager 1986; Mossley manager 1987; Stockport County assistant manager 1990.

Honours: England Schoolboy international.

Sainty never made the grade at White Hart Lane and moved to Reading, where he made 64/8 appearances, scoring 20 goals. He started his career as an inside-right, later adapting to become an attacking midfielder. He first teamed up with John Bond at Bournemouth, where Sainty played 111/7 League games, scoring 21 goals. He missed only one game in 1970-71, when Bournemouth finished runners-

up in the Fourth Division. They narrowly missed promotion again the following season but by this time Sainty was not a first-team regular.

He was only 30 when he decided to give up playing and concentrate on coaching. He worked under John Bond at Norwich, Manchester City and Burnley, and had a year in charge at Chester City, who reached the semi-finals of the Football League Trophy in 1983 before losing to Lincoln City. Sainty was sacked in December 1983, after a terrible start to the season with only two wins in the first 20 games.

SANT, Peter (or Percy)

Born: Oldham; Died: c.1935.
Career: Midland League referee, on Football League list from 1911, supplementary list season 1912-13 and Southern League list; Barnsley Association Football Union; Barnsley Referee's Society; member of the Sheffield & Hallamshire FA.; Midland Section Executive of Referee's Union; Barnsley manager April 1919-cs 1926.

Sant had a reputation as an administrator when he became manager of Barnsley in his early 30s. A former referee, Sant had been on the Football League list in 1911-12 and was involved with many local FAs and referee's organisations. Whilst at Oakwell, he was forced by his directors to sell players to keep the club financially solvent.

He realised £2,700 by transferring popular centre-half Frank Barson to Aston Villa but the fans became disillusioned with the club's policy of selling their best players and attendances dropped alarmingly. Sant had enough and resigned at the end of the 1925-26 season. His best season had been 1923-24, when Barnsley finished third and missed promotion to Division One on goal-average.

SAUNDERS, Ronald

Born: Birkenhead, 6 November 1932.
Centre-forward 5ft 10in; 12st 8lb (1963).
Career: Birkenhead & Liverpool Schools; Everton February 1951; Tonbridge July 1956; Gillingham May 1957 (£800); Portsmouth September 1958 (£8,000); Watford September 1964 (£10,000); Charlton Athletic August 1965; Yeovil Town general manager May 1967-1968; Oxford United manager March-June 1969; Norwich City manager July 1969-November 1973; Manchester City manager November 1973-April 1974; Aston Villa manager June 1974-February 1982; Birmingham City manager February 1982-January 1986; West Bromwich Albion manager February 1986-September 1987.

Honours: England Youth international; Football League champions 1981; Division Two champions 1972, runners-up 1975, 1985; Football League Cup winners 1975, 1977, runners-up 1973, 1974.

Unyielding, blunt and a strict disciplinarian, Ron Saunders took Aston Villa to the League championship in 1980-81 and in successive seasons in the 1970s also took three different clubs to the League Cup Final. His teams often played dull and unimaginative football and his dour image did not endear him to the football public, but he knew his job inside out and was greatly respected by the players in his charge.

Saunders played for Birkenhead and Liverpool Schools before signing for Everton in February 1951. Much was expected when he gained Youth international honours but he never established himself at the top level. He made

his League debut in a 4-3 defeat at Cardiff City, but after only three appearances for the Toffees, he moved to non-League Tonbridge. His League career was resurrected by Gillingham, who signed him in May 1957 for an £800 fee. After 20 goals in 49 League appearances for the Gills, Portsmouth saw his potential and signed him for £8,000 in September 1958.

Portsmouth were still a First Division club when Saunders made his debut and he went on to make 258 League and Cup appearances for Pompey, scoring 156 goals, before a move to Watford in September 1964 for a £10,000 fee. He was transferred to Charlton Athletic in August 1965.

Saunders started on the road to management with Southern League Yeovil Town in May 1968 and saved them from relegation in 1967-68. In March 1969, he got the manager's job at Oxford United and did a remarkably good job in a short period. Oxford were fighting against relegation to Division Three and were bottom of the table when he took over. They gained 15 points from their last 12 games to avoid relegation.

Obviously impressed, Norwich City offered Saunders their manager's post and he accepted in July 1969. He had a tough job on his hands and little money to spend. His players were highly trained but their style of play was often negative. He signed some fine players, though, including Graham Paddon, David Cross and Jim Bone, and in 1971-72 Norwich City took the championship, one point ahead of Birmingham City to enter the First Division for the first time in their history. They just escaped relegation the following season and lost to Ipswich Town in the Texaco Cup Final.

However, they also reached the Football League Cup Final before losing 1-0 to Spurs in a dreary game at Wembley. After a poor start to the 1973-74 season, Saunders resigned in November, following a bitter row in the boardroom.

He was employed as Manchester City's manager the same month but lasted only five months in charge at Maine Road before being sacked, despite taking City to the League Cup Final, where they lost 2-1 to Wolves.

In June 1974, Saunders took control at Aston Villa and transformed a disappointing team into League Cup winners and runners-up in the Second Division in his first season in charge. Villa beat his former club, Norwich City, 1-0 at Wembley, so at last he gained a winners' medal after taking

three different clubs to three successive League Cup Finals.

In 1980-81, Villa won their first League championship since 1910, when a late spurt pushed them ahead of long-time leaders, Ipswich Town. It was a fine achievement by Saunders and this qualified Villa for the following season's European Cup. They had reached the quarter-finals when Saunders surprisingly resigned in February 1982 to take up the manager's post at neighbours Birmingham City. Villa went on to win the European Cup under his former assistant, Tony Barton.

Birmingham City, meanwhile, made a miraculous recovery to avoid relegation that season with 16 points from their last six games but the drop came two seasons later. The Blues made an immediate return as Second Division runners-up in 1984-85, but after gaining only two points from 16 games and suffering an FA Cup defeat at the hands of non-League Altrincham at St Andrew's, Saunders resigned on 16 January 1986. The following month he took over at West Brom but could not prevent the Throstles being relegated to Division Two that season. After being sacked in September, Ron Saunders left football, apparently for good.

SAWARD, Patrick

Born: Cork, Ireland, 17 August 1928.
Wing-half 6ft; 13st 3lb (1959).

Career: Cork and Cobh County Schools; Beckenham 1945; Crystal Palace amateur; Millwall July 1951; Aston Villa August 1955 (£7,000); Huddersfield Town March 1961; Coventry City October 1963, then player-coach, then assistant manager July 1967; Brighton & Hove Albion manager July 1970-October 1973; in business in Minorca; NASR Al (Saudi Arabia) general manager and coach 1973-1975.

Honours: Republic of Ireland international (18 caps); Division Two champions 1960; Division Three runners-up 1972; FA Cup winners 1957.

As a manager, Pat Saward was an extrovert and used his good humour to create a happy dressing-room. He had a good eye for a player and had a lot of success with the youth team at Coventry City, who reached the FA Youth Cup Final. City also entered European competitions under his and manager Noel Cantwell's guidance.

Saward's first job in full charge was at Brighton, who finished runners-up in Division Three in 1971-72, but he really needed a number of new signings to boost an average squad and Brighton were instantly relegated. His sides played attacking football but after a poor start to the 1973-74 season, he was sacked by the board as they felt he could no longer motivate the side.

As a player, he was best at wing-half and was badly missed by Millwall after his departure to Aston Villa. He helped Villa to an FA Cup Final victory over Manchester United in 1957 and to the Second Division championship in 1959-60.

SAWYER, William James

Born: Liverpool; Died: Wallasey, 27 June 1940 (aged 69).
Career: Everton honorary secretary 1918-1919 and director for 12 years; Wigan Borough founder; originator of South Liverpool Football League and secretary for ten years; New Brighton secretary-manager March 1933-June 1940.

After two years without a manager, New Brighton appointed Bill Sawyer, who was formerly a director and honorary secretary with Everton and played a part in the formation of South Liverpool and Wigan Borough. A shrewd judge of player, Sawyer put together an excellent side in 1937-38 for less than £100. They had an excellent run in the FA Cup before losing to Spurs in the fourth round. Sawyer was awarded a benefit match against Everton in April 1938.

SAXTON, Robert

Born: Bagby, Doncaster, 6 September 1943.
Defender   5ft 10in; 11st 4lb (1970).
Career: Denaby United; Derby County February 1962; Plymouth Argyle February 1968 (£12,000); Exeter City September 1975, then player-manager January 1977-January 1979; Plymouth Argyle manager January 1979-May 1981; Blackburn Rovers manager May 1981-December 1986; Preston North End advisor January 1987; York City manager June 1987-September 1988; Blackpool coach September 1988; Newcastle United assistant manager 1989, then caretaker manager March-April 1991; Manchester City chief scout October 1991.
Honours: Division Four runners-up 1977.

A sound centre-half, Bobby Saxton had a respectable if unspectacular playing career. A wholehearted and enthusiastic player, he made 246/10 appearances for Plymouth Argyle and altogether played over 400 games in his career. Saxton, one of the Derby players eventually moved on when Brian Clough arrived at the Baseball Ground, played in Plymouth's promotion side of 1974-75.

He was beginning to make things happen at Exeter when he received a better offer to manage the Pilgrims, his former club. Saxton took them to seventh in the Third Division in

1980-81, when he was offered the Blackburn Rovers job. He consolidated Rovers' position in Division Two and inspired great loyalty from his players, but was sacked as things began to stagnate at Ewood Park with Blackburn unable to make the final push for promotion to Division One. Things did not go well at York City, who slipped to the bottom of the Fourth Division. Saxton was Jim Smith's assistant at Newcastle United before taking over temporarily when Smith was sacked.

SCHOFIELD, Joseph Arthur

Born: Hanley, 1 January 1871; Died: 28 September 1929.
Outside-left.
Career: Hanley Hope Sunday School; Stoke 1890, retired through injury 1899; then schoolmaster and Poor Law official; Stoke secretary 1915-1919 and director 1908; Port Vale secretary-manager March 1920-September 1929.
Honours: England international (3 caps); Football League representative (2 caps).

Schofield made his debut for Stoke in October 1891 and established himself as a left winger with a good turn of speed and clever play, known as a perfect gentleman on and off the pitch. As Port Vale's manager he had well-balanced judgement and discovered many promising players. He sold Bob Blood, the fans' idol, to West Brom £4,000 in February 1921 with the club on the point of folding due to financial problems. Schofield did not have complete control of Vale's affairs until March 1927, when he also dropped the secretarial aspects of the job. Port Vale were relegated to the Third Division North in 1928-29 and Schofield died at the age of 48, before they could bounce back again.

SCHOLEY, Sidney

Born: Walsall.
Career: Walsall trainer 1908-1911; Stockport County trainer 1911-1914; served in RAMC in World War One; Birmingham trainer 1920-1928; Walsall trainer April 1928, then manager April 1929-October 1930; worked for Marine Hydro as a masseur from 1930.

Sid Scholey never played professional football but spent 20 years in the game as a trainer and masseur. He was not a great success as a manager and never really got to grips with the job. In his only full season in charge Walsall finished 17th in the Third Division South although they had a good FA Cup run, reaching the fourth round before losing in front of a 74,000 crowd at Villa Park.

Birmingham had won promotion to the First Division at the end of his first season at St Andrew's in 1921. Scholey was caretaker manager of the Blues for a short period in the 1928 close season. He later treated many famous players as a masseur at the Marine Hydro in Rhyl.

SCOTCHBROOK, Alfred

Born: Horwich, Lancashire, 1886.
Career: Gymnasium FC (Horwich); Horwich FC; Bolton Wanderers, then coach and assistant secretary until 1924; Stockport County manager November 1924-February 1926; Wolverhampton Wanderers manager March 1926-May 1927.

Fred Scotchbrook joined Bolton just before war was declared in 1914 but failed to make the grade as a player and appeared only five times in their first

team. He retired to concentrate on coaching and was later assistant secretary at the club. He was never given full control at Molineux and became disheartened when directors would make decisions at a whim, which he could do nothing to prevent. Their financial strategy also meant that he could not sign any players.

Wolves reached the FA Cup sixth round in 1927 but lost to Arsenal. Scotchbrook blamed the directors for the club's lack of success and left soon after criticising club policy at the annual meeting in the summer of 1927. He was replaced Major Frank Buckley. Scotchbrook lost his job at Stockport County with the club heading for relegation.

SCOTT, Laurence

Born: Sheffield, 23 April 1917.
Full-back   5ft 9½in; 11st 8lb (1951).
Career: Bradford City amateur 1933, professional May 1935; Arsenal February 1937; Crystal Palace player-manager October 1951-October 1954, retired as a player August 1953; Hendon manager late 1954-cs 1957; Hitchin Town coach August 1957-1960s; sales representative in late 1950s.
Honours: England international (17 caps); Wartime international (16 caps); 'B' international (4 caps); Football League representative (5 caps); Football League champions 1948; FA Cup winners 1950; Football League South Cup winners 1943; Football League War Cup runners-up 1941.

Laurie Scott was one of the fastest full-backs of his era. He tackled powerfully, had good positional sense and made accurate clearances. Scott did not make his League debut for Arsenal until August 1946, nine years after joining the club. Before the war, George Male and Eddie Hapgood kept him out of the side, then war brought an end to League soccer.

Scott gained two London Combination medals before the war and played in both of Arsenal's wartime Cup Final appearances. He gained a League championship and FA Cup winners medal with the Gunners and played in 17 consecutive internationals for England between September 1946 and November 1948.

Scott had a poor record as manager of Crystal Palace. He bolstered the defence until 1953, but then Palace had a terrible season, just avoiding having to seek re-election in 1953-54. They also lost to Great Yarmouth and Finchley in the FA Cup. Scott was one of several fine footballers who was unable to make a successful transition from player to manager.

SCOTT, William

Born: Willington Quay, Northumberland 1893.
Inside-forward   5ft 10in; 12st 7lb (1921).
Career: South Shields amateur 1910s, assistant trainer, masseur and player from 1920, when he turned professional; guest for Crystal Palace in World War One; Preston North End trainer January 1923, then secretary March 1941-April 1947; Blackburn Rovers manager April-December 1947; Preston North End manager June 1949-March 1953; Sunderland assistant manager in 1960.
Honours: Division Two champions 1951.

Will Scott did not become a manager until he was 54, but he found success at Deepdale, taking Preston to the

Second Division title and almost to the First Division championship, missing out on goal-average.

Born on Tyneside, he signed amateur forms for South Shields before the war but joined the Navy in 1914. After he guested for Crystal Palace, the club tried to sign him as a professional in 1919, but he chose instead to return to South Shields as an amateur. When he finally signed professional forms in 1920, Scott continued to appear at centre-half and was also assistant trainer and masseur. He made only three first-team appearances for South Shields, these all coming in season 1921-22. He moved to Preston in January 1923 as trainer, going to Deepdale with the man who had been his boss at Horsley Hill, Jimmy Lawrence, who had been appointed manager of North End.

Scott spent the next 24 years at Deepdale, as trainer, coach and often in charge of team affairs. He was appointed the club's secretary in March 1941 and remained in that post until April 1947, when he became the manager of Blackburn Rovers. Scott stayed just eight months at Ewood Park before ill health forced his resignation, although he remained with the club as a scout.

Recovered, he returned to Preston in June 1949 as manager. The first player that he recruited was Willie Cunningham, from Airdrie, and soon afterwards he signed another tough-tackling Scot in Tommy Docherty. In December 1949, Preston broke the British transfer record when Eddie Quigley was signed from Sheffield Wednesday for £26,500. Scott appointed Jimmy Milne as trainer in 1950 and Milne later managed the club.

The 1950-51 season was an excellent one for Preston as they walked away with the Second Division title and they were unbeaten from late November until April, going 20 games without defeat. They also achieved 14 consecutive League victories, equalling the record set by Burnley in 1946-47. Tom Finney was the star of the side and was probably playing at his best that season.

Scott left Preston in March 1953, just as they were in hot pursuit of Arsenal and Wolves at the top of the First Division. They eventually finished as runners-up on goal-average behind the Gunners. Scott was assistant manager to Allan Brown at Sunderland in 1960.

SCOTT-WALFORD, Frank

Born: Perry Barr, Birmingham.
Goalkeeper.
Career: Tottenham Hotspur amateur;

London Caledonian; Brighton & Hove Albion manager March 1905-March 1908; Leeds City manager March 1908-May 1912; Southern league referee; Coventry City secretary-manager 1914-1915.

Scott-Walford was an amateur goalkeeper with Spurs and Isthmian League club London Caledonian before becoming a referee. He officiated in the Southern League and also helped set up the Enfield & District League. At Brighton, he was suspended for three months in April 1906 for illegal approaches to players. He had to completely rebuild the club's playing staff after the departure of most of the players in 1905.

Scott-Walford took many of his former players to Leeds City, but few made a lasting impact. His best signing was Billy Gillespie from Derry Celtic, who later became a star at Sheffield United. Scott-Walford left Leeds after they had to seek re-election in 1912. Coventry had just dropped into the Second Division of the Southern League when he took over there. They made a huge loss in 1914-15, due to the increased travelling costs and lack of spectators due to the war. When the club was wound up in 1915, Scott-Walford was still owed £100 in wages.

SCOULAR, James

Born: Livingston, 11 January 1925.
Wing-half   5ft 7in; 11st 6lb (1955).
Career: Livingston Station; Edinburgh Waverley; Gosport Borough in World War Two; Portsmouth December 1945; Newcastle United June 1953 (£22,250); Bradford player-manager (£1,300) January 1961-May 1964; Cardiff City manager June 1964-November 1973; Aston Villa scout 1973; Wolverhampton Wanderers scout; Newport County manager February 1976-January 1977; Swansea City and Newcastle United scout 1978.

Honours: Scotland international (9 caps); Football League champions 1949, 1950; Division Four promotion 1961; FA Cup winners 1955; Welsh Cup winners 1965, 1967, 1968, 1969, 1970, 1971, 1973.

An inspiring captain, Jimmy Scoular was a well-built half-back who was renowned for his hard and relentless tackling, although he was also an intelligent distributor and could produce delicate touches when needed. Scoular helped Pompey to successive League championships between 1948 and 1950 and captained Newcastle to success in the 1955 FA Cup Final. He played the same number of games for Portsmouth and Newcastle United —

247 — and appeared over 100 times for Bradford as player-manager at Park Avenue. At Bradford, Scoular discovered such talents as Ian Gibson, Kevin Hector and Jim Fryatt, but was sacked in May 1964.

He was unlucky never to win anything other than seven Welsh Cup Finals at Cardiff City. They reached the semi-finals of the European Cup-winners' Cup in 1967-68, losing 4-3 on aggregate to SV Hamburg, and Scoular turned the Bluebirds into one of the best sides in Division Two before being sacked following boardroom changes at Ninian Park. His father, Alec, played for Alloa Athletic, Stenhousemuir and Leith Athletic before the war.

SEAR, Clifford Reginald

Born: Rhostyllen, near Wrexham, 22 September 1936.
Full-back   5ft 10in; 10st 8lb (1963).
Career: Rhostyllen Sports Club FC; Oswestry Town; Manchester City amateur June 1955, professional January 1957; Chester April 1968, retired 1969 to become youth-team coach, then assistant manager 1980, manager June-November 1982 and youth-team coach 1982-1986; Wrexham youth development officer in 1991.

Honours: Wales international (1 cap); Under-23 international (2 caps).

Cliff Sear worked as a miner at Bershaw Colliery before turning professional with Manchester City. A stylish left-back, Sear, who captained the Welsh Under-23 side in the late 1950s, made his League debut against Birmingham in April 1957. He gave the Maine Road club's defence much-needed stability and played in the semi-final of the League Cup in 1962-63, when City lost 2-1 on aggregate to Stoke. He was ever-present in their 12 games in that competition that season.

Despite not appearing in the first team after 1966, Sear played 279 games for Manchester City, scoring one goal. At Chester, he linked up with former City colleague, Alan Oakes, and played a large part in the development of the young Ian Rush. Sear was manager of Chester for only five months.

SEED, Angus Cameron MM

Born: Lanchester, County Durham, 6 February 1893; Died: Barnsley, 7 February 1953.
Centre-half/Full-back
5ft 11½in; 12st (1914).
Career: Seaham Harbour; Everton trialist December 1913; Leicester Fosse January 1914; Reading July 1914; St Bernards (Edinburgh) November 1916; Mid-Rhondda December 1919; Workington cs 1921, later trainer and manager; Aldershot manager 1927-February 1937; Barnsley manager February 1937-February 1953.

Honours: Division Three North champions 1939; Southern League champions 1930; London Combination champions 1931.

Never more than an average player, Angus Seed played mainly reserve-team soccer. He suffered a hip injury in the war, whilst serving in the Footballers' Battalion, and was awarded the Military Medal after actions at Vimy Ridge.

After the war, Seed played for, trained and managed Workington, then spent ten years as manager of Aldershot. They were Southern League champions in 1929-30 and joined the London Combination, which was mainly for League clubs' reserve sides. The Shots joined the Football League in 1932, despite a

poor season, and had an excellent FA Cup run in 1932-33, beating Accrington, Bristol Rovers and Millwall before losing to First Division Derby.

In 1937, Seed moved to Barnsley as manager and was responsible for bringing many fine players to Oakwell including Danny Blanchflower, George Robledo and Johnny Kelly. Barnsley were relegated in his first season but bounced straight back as Northern Section champions, 11 points clear of runners-up Doncaster Rovers. Seed, who suffered a great deal of ill health from 1951, was a great advocate of youth football and helped in the development of the Northern Intermediate League. He was the brother of Jimmy Seed.

SEED, James Marshall

Born: Blackhill, County Durham, 25 March 1895; Died: 16 July 1966.
Inside-right   5ft 10½in; 11st 9lb (1925).

Career: Whitburn; Sunderland April 1914; Mid-Rhondda 1919; Tottenham Hotspur February 1920 (£350); Sheffield Wednesday August 1927, retired early 1931; Clapton Orient secretary-manager April 1931-May 1933; Charlton Athletic manager May 1933-September 1956; Bristol City advisor January 1957, caretaker manager January 1958; Millwall manager January 1958-July 1959, advisor and director January 1960-July 1966.

Honours: England international (5 caps); FA tour to South Africa 1929; Football League champions 1929, 1930; Division Three South champions 1935; Division Two runners-up 1936; FA Cup winners 1921, 1947, runners-up 1946.

Jimmy Seed was the greatest manager in Charlton Athletic's history. Not only did he take them from the Third to the First Division in consecutive seasons, he also kept them there for over 20 years. Charlton also played in two FA Cup Finals, winning one, and came close to taking the League championship in 1936-37. Sadly, his departure from the club he served so well left him a bitter man.

Seed played for Whitburn before joining Sunderland in April 1914, but the war soon intervened and he served with the West Yorkshire Regiment in France for three years. Seed was badly gassed during his time in the trenches and was released by Sunderland after the war. He recuperated with the Mid-Rhondda club in South Wales from 1919 and in February 1920, Tottenham Hotspur signed him for £350.

Now fully recovered from his wartime experiences, Seed gained an FA Cup winners' medal in 1921, when Spurs beat Wolves 1-0 in the Final at Stamford Bridge. An inside-right with excellent

vision, he went on to score 77 goals in 254 appearances for Tottenham. He was a tireless, thrustful player who was a subtle and excellent schemer with lots of stamina. A clever football caricaturist, his work appeared widely in the 1920s' sports pages but ceased when he took up management.

In August 1927, Spurs allowed Seed to move to Sheffield Wednesday, considering that his best days were over. They could not have been more wrong and after helping the Owls avoid relegation in 1927-28, Seed then played in successive League championship sides for Wednesday, in seasons 1928-29 and 1929-30. In 1929 he also toured South Africa with the Football Association. Seed had gained five England caps, the first coming in May 1921, against Belgium in Brussels.

His brother, Angus, was manager at Aldershot when Jimmy started his managerial career at Clapton Orient in April 1931. He retired from playing earlier in the year, after scoring 37 goals in 146 appearances for the Owls. At Orient, he was employed as secretary-manager at £12 per week and had to face enormous financial problems at the club which was on the verge of bankruptcy. Things became so bad that at one stage an Official Receiver was appointed. After two seasons of struggle, Seed was relieved when the Gliksten brothers asked him to manage Charlton Athletic in May 1933.

Although the Gliksten brothers, who owned Charlton, put restrictions on his spending, he now had some money to invest in new players but retained a cautious, economic approach and rebuilt the club without resorting to big spending. Indeed, during his 23 years in charge at The Valley, Seed spent £55,000 on new players and made £170,000 from the sale of others. He made many excellent signings over the years, including Sam Bartram, probably the club's greatest servant.

In 1934, he appointed his former teammate at Hillsborough, Jimmy Trotter, as his assistant. Huge crowds, some over 60,000, attended matches at The Valley but little was spent on the ground, a policy that would later have dire consequences for the club. Before the start of the 1934-35 season, Seed spent £650 on striker Ralph Allen from Brentford. Allen went on to score 32 goals in only 29 appearances as Charlton won the Third Division South championship that season.

They went straight up into the First Division the following season, as runners-up, and Seed had thus created a miracle at the club. Charlton finished runners-up in the First Division in 1936-37, just three points behind champions Manchester City. In the two seasons up until World War Two, the Valiants also finished fourth and third in the First Division.

Seed continued to bring success to the club during the war years. In 1943, Charlton reached a Wembley Final but lost 7-1 to Arsenal. But the following year they beat Chelsea 3-1 at the same venue in a Southern Cup Final. The match was watched by future US president, General Eisenhower. As well as running Charlton Athletic practically on his own during the war, Seed also organised physical training schemes for the public as well as serving in the Observer Corps.

After the war, Seed took Charlton to two FA Cup Finals. In 1946 they were well-beaten by Derby County, 4-1 after extra-time, but the following year they beat Burnley 1-0 in a dull Final, in which Chris Duffy at last broke the Burnley barrier in extra-time with a tremendous volley.

There were also lots of struggles against relegation in the post-war years at The Valley and in 1950-51, only the signing of Hans Jeppson saved Charlton from the drop. His goals proved vital and he later found much fame in Italy.

Seed also had an extensive scouting system in South Africa and uncovered a number of stars such as John Hewie and Eddie Firmani. In July 1955, Firmani was sold for a record £35,000 to Italian club, Sampdoria. This proved a great loss to Charlton as their goal power rapidly diminished after Firmani's departure. Attendances dropped due to the lack of success and worse followed when goalkeeper Sam Bartram retired in 1956. Seed was sacked rather acrimoniously in September 1956, after five successive defeats and an 8-1 humiliation at Sunderland. The Valiants were relegated to Division Two at the end of the season.

Seed was out of the game for a while, but in January 1957 he was appointed as an advisor to manager Pat Beasley at Bristol City and was caretaker manager for two weeks in January 1958, when Beasley left the club. Shortly afterwards, Seed left Ashton Gate to manage Millwall. The Lions did not reach the top half of the Southern Section that season in fact they finished next to bottom and had to seek re-election and so had to join the newly-formed Fourth Division for 1958-59. They made a good start that season, but after an FA Cup defeat at the hands of non-league Worcester City, their form went into decline.

It was no surprise when Seed resigned in July 1959, as he was now over 60 years old and his long service to football had taken its toll on his health and strength. The following January, he joined the Millwall board and also acted as an advisor to the club.

Just after his departure from The Valley, an autobiography appeared called *The Jimmy Seed Story* (published by Phoenix Sports Books) which gave a lot of insights into his time in charge at Charlton. After a short retirement, Jimmy Seed died on 16 July 1966, the day that England beat Mexico at Wembley on their way to winning the World Cup.

SEITH, Robert

Born: Coatbridge, 9 March 1932.
Wing-half   5ft 11in; 12st (1963).
Career: Monfieth Tayside Juniors; Burnley amateur 1948, professional March 1949-1960; Dundee 1960, retired 1965 to become coach; Glasgow Rangers coach; Preston North End manager November 1967-cs 1970; Heart of Midlothian manager November 1970-October 1974.

Honours: Football League champions 1960; Scottish League champions 1962.

A cultured, strong tackling wing-half, who was an accurate passer, Bobby Seith made 238 appearances for Burnley, scoring six goals. Despite playing 27 games in their 1959-60 League championship side, he was denied his medal after a row with chairman Bob Lord. Seith requested a transfer and moved to Dundee, with whom he gained a Scottish League championship medal in 1961-62.

He did not gain full control at Preston until the departure of Jimmy Milne in May 1968 and left the club

after they finished bottom of Division Two in 1969-70. However, Preston did see the emergence of Archie Gemmill in this period. Hearts struggled to compete with the leading clubs with Seith in control. The highest they finished was sixth in Division One in 1971-72. They also reached the semi-final of the Scottish Cup in 1974 but Seith resigned after a terrible start to the 1974-75 season.

SETTERS, Maurice Edgar

Born: Honiton, Devon 16 December 1936.
Wing-half   5ft 10in; 13st (1970).
Career: Honiton & Cullompton Schools; Exeter City amateur June 1952, professional January 1954; West Bromwich Albion January 1955 (£3,000); Manchester United January 1960 (£30,000); Stoke City November 1964 (£30,000); Coventry City November 1967 (£25,000); Charlton Athletic February 1970; Doncaster Rovers manager May 1971-November 1974; Sheffield Wednesday coach August 1980; Rotherham United assistant manager-coach 1983; Newcastle United chief scout 1984; Republic of Ireland assistant manager 1986.

Honours: England Under-23 international (16 caps); Youth international; Schoolboy international; FA Cup winners 1963.

A fierce competitor, Setters frightened many opposing forwards with his bone-crunching tackles and his fearsome appearance — all crew-cut and scowls. He played regular First Division soccer throughout the 1960s and appeared in the 1963 FA Cup Final, when Manchester United beat Leicester City 3-1.

He was not a great success as manager of Doncaster Rovers, who were struggling near the foot of Division Four when Setters was in charge. He was awarded £1,340 for unfair dismissal after his sacking. He worked with Jack Charlton at Sheffield Wednesday, Newcastle United and with the Republic of Ireland national side. Charlton and Setters took the Irish to the European championship in 1988 and the World Cup finals in 1990. Setters was assistant manager to George Kerr at Rotherham United.

SETTLE, William

Born: c.1868; Died: Caernarfon, September 1941.
Career: Bolton Wanderers director 1899, then manager January 1910-1915; engaged in coal trade; moved to Caernarfon in 1918.

Honours: Division Two runners-up 1911.

Will Settle's father, Miles Settle JP,

joined Bolton Wanderers' board in 1895 and Will took his place four years later, until January 1910 when he was appointed the Trotters' manager. Both men were coal merchants of the firm Settle, Speakman & Co.

Will was unable to prevent their relegation that season but appointed George Eccles and Peter Bullough as his trainers and between them they steered the Trotters to runners-up spot in the Second Division in 1910-11. Settle also developed the great left-wing partnership of Joe Smith and Ted Vizard and brought many other fine players to Burnden Park, managing also to keep the club in a good financial position. The Trotters finished fouth in Division One in 1911-12, sixth in 1913-14 and reached the semi-final of the FA Cup in 1915. He left under a cloud after some responsibilities had been taken away from him shortly after this.

SEXTON, David James

Born: Islington, London, 6 April 1930.
Inside-forward   5ft 9in; 11st 9lb (1959).
Career: Newmarket Town; Chelmsford City 1950; Luton Town June 1951; West Ham United April 1952; Leyton Orient June 1956 (£2,000); Brighton & Hove Albion October 1957; Crystal Palace May 1959, retired January 1962 due to cartilage problems; Chelsea assistant coach February 1962; Leyton Orient manager January-December 1965; Fulham coach February 1966; Arsenal assistant manager and coach August 1966; Chelsea manager October 1967-October 1974; Queen's Park Rangers manager October 1974-July 1977; Manchester United manager July 1977-April 1981; Coventry City manager May 1981-May 1983; England assistant manager July 1983.

Honours: Division Three South representative; Division Three South champions 1958; FA Cup winners 1970, runners-up 1979; football League Cup runners-up 1972; European Cup-winners' Cup winners 1971.

Dave Sexton was an excellent coach but was sometimes criticised for his apparent aloofness and lack of skills in dealing with the Press. He had a flexible tactical approach, which was dependent on the quality of players at his disposal, and was a master at exploiting dead-ball situations, never being afraid to try out new ideas. He had a shy, reserved manner which kept him remote from the public and had the traditional image of a staid manager. He found major success at both Chelsea and Manchester United but is not remembered with any great affection by either set of supporters.

Sexton was the son of Archie Sexton, a well-known boxer who fought Jock McAulay for the British middleweight

title in 1933. Dave played for Newmarket Town before joining Chelmsford City in 1950. In June 1951, he moved to Luton Town but played only nine games for the Hatters before being transferred to West Ham United in April 1952. At Upton Park, Sexton developed into a useful inside-forward and scored 26 goals in 77 appearances for the Hammers before another move, to Leyton Orient in June 1956 for a £2,000 fee. He had a chequered playing career but could often be a useful striker. At Brighton, whom he joined in October 1957, he scored 26 goals in 47 League games before moving to Crystal Palace in May 1959. Sexton retired from the game in January 1962, due to cartilage problems, but he had played his last game at Workington in February 1960. His only honours during his playing career were representative ones: he played for the FA against the RAF in October 1953 and represented the Third Division South against the Northern Section.

Sexton became an assistant coach at Chelsea in February 1962, under Tommy Docherty, and remained there until he was appointed manager of Leyton Orient in January 1965. He did not endear himself to the Orient fans when he released many of their old favourites in the summer of 1965. Amongst the players who left the club were Sid Bishop, Stan Charlton and Dave Dunmore. He replaced these with untried youngsters and it was not a surprise when Orient had a disastrous start to the season. Sexton even gave Paul Went his debut at the age of 15 years and 10 months, still the youngest player to appear for the club. Sexton resigned in December 1965, after 11 months in charge and with Orient at the bottom of the table.

In February 1966, he arrived at Craven Cottage as coach and helped transform a side struggling at the bottom of the First Division. Most of the players at the club at this time admitted that it was the inspiration of Sexton which led Fulham to their 'great escape' that season which ensured another year of First Division soccer. He did not stay long at the Cottage, though, and in August 1966 became assistant manager and coach at Arsenal.

In October 1967, Sexton was appointed manager of Chelsea, replacing Tommy Docherty. He later replaced Docherty at Old Trafford. At Stamford Bridge, Sexton paid large fees for defenders Dave Webb and John Dempsey, but could also find bargains such as the £5,000 signing of Ian Hutchinson from Cambridge United. Chelsea won the FA Cup in 1970. After beating Watford 5-1 in the semi-final they met the mighty Leeds United in an unforgettable Final. Fortunate to get a 2-2 draw in the first game at Wembley, Chelsea won the replay at Old Trafford in extra-time with Webb scoring the vital goal.

The following year, Sexton took Chelsea to a European Cup-winners' Cup victory over Real Madrid in Athens, in another replayed Final. In 1972 they lost to Stoke City in the Football League Cup Final and at this point Chelsea decided to build a new three-tiered and very expensive stand at Stamford Bridge, which almost bankrupted the club and greatly inhibited Sexton's ability to spend money on new players. A number of fine players left Chelsea after rows with the manager, the most important being the crowd's favourites, Peter Osgood and Alan Hudson. Sexton soon lost popularity with the Chelsea fans and was sacked in October 1974.

Thirteen days later, he became manager at Queen's Park Rangers and one of his first moves was to buy Don Masson for £300,000. Rangers had a patchy first season under Sexton and finished 11th in the First Division. In 1975-76, however, they were runners-up to Liverpool the clubs best ever placing, only one point behind the Merseysiders after a superb run in which brought 15 wins in their last 17 matches. QPR entered Europe for the first time and reached the quarter-finals of the UEFA Cup. In 1976-77, they also reached the semi-finals of the League Cup before losing to Aston Villa in a third game.

Sexton felt that he had achieved all he could at Loftus Road and in July 1977 accepted a lucrative offer to take charge at Manchester United. Despite spending £1m on new players Gordon McQueen and Joe Jordan, United had a poor first season under Sexton. In 1979 they reached the FA Cup Final, but lost 3-2 to a late Arsenal goal. Sexton paid £825,000 for Ray Wilkins from Chelsea in 1979-80 and that season United finished runners-up to Liverpool. Sexton then paid £1m for Garry Birtles, but he was not a great success and United's League form slumped. Sexton was sacked in April 1981, despite United winning their previous seven games.

The following month he became manager of Coventry City but the club struggled against relegation and when they just missed the drop at the end of his second season in charge, Sexton was sacked in May 1983, much to the disgust of his loyal players. In July 1983 he became assistant manager of the England team under Bobby Robson and also played a leading role in the newly-formed soccer school of excellence.

SEYMOUR, George Stanley

Born: Kelloe, County Durham, 16 May 1893; Died: Newcastle upon Tyne, 24 December 1978.
Outside-left   5ft 6½in; 10st 2lb (1925).
Career: Newcastle United amateur; Shildon Town; Coxhoe; Bradford City September 1911 (£150); Morton February 1913; Newcastle United May 1920 (£2,500), retired May 1929; Newcastle United director June 1938-April 1976, and manager September 1939-March 1947 and December 1950-December 1954, chairman 1954-1956, vice-president to death; sports journalist and sports outfitter.
Honours: FA XI tour of Australia (2 caps); Football League representative (2 caps); Football League champions 1927; FA Cup winners 1924, 1951, 1952.

Stan Seymour was associated with Newcastle United for well over 50 years. He gained FA Cup winners' and League championship medals as a player and guided the club to two FA Cup Finals as manager, although he never had full managerial responsibilities at the club and was more of a front man for the rest of the directors.

Seymour had a trial with Newcastle United but was considered too small to become a footballer and played for local clubs, Shildon Town and Coxhoe, before joining Bradford City in September 1911 for a £150 fee. He first made his name when he moved to Scotland to join Morton in February 1913. A small but ever-improving left winger, Seymour was nicknamed 'the little Englishman' by the Morton fans.

English scouts flocked to Greenock to see him play and in May 1920, Newcastle United, the club that had earlier turned him down, signed him for £2,500.

Seymour became a key member of the Newcastle side and scored the second goal in their FA Cup winning side of 1924. He also scored 19 goals in the season in which the Magpies won the League championship in 1926-27. He formed excellent partnerships on the left wing with Tom MacDonald and Hughie Gallacher at St James' Park and altogether scored 84 goals in 244 appearances for the club before falling out with them over unpaid benefits when he retired in the summer of 1929. He had made up his differences by June 1938, when he joined United's board. By this time he was a sports journalist and sports outfitter.

In September 1939, Seymour took over as manager of Newcastle United and was in charge until March 1947. United reached the semi-finals of the League War Cup in 1940, but lost to Blackburn Rovers. After the war, huge crowds attended matches at Gallowgate and Seymour signed Joe Harvey, Frank Brennan and Roy Bentley in the transitional season of 1945-6. The following season saw an average home crowd of 49,336, but a run to the FA Cup semi-finals distracted from the Magpies' main aim, a quick return to the First Division. In the end they finished fifth and lost their semi-final against Charlton Athletic, 4-0 at Elland Road.

Seymour signed Len Shackleton in September 1946 and he scored six goals in his debut, in a 13-0 victory over Newport County. Seymour stepped down as manager and United gained promotion to the First Division the following season.

He returned as manager in December 1950 and United won the FA Cup two years in succession, but were fairly average in the League. In 1951 they beat Blackpool 2-0 in the Cup Final with two excellent goals from Jackie Milburn. The following year they were lucky to beat an injury-hit Arsenal side, 1-0 with a goal from George Robledo.

In December 1954, Stan Seymour stepped down as manager to be replaced by Duggie Livingstone. Soon afterwards, Seymour became the club's chairman, a position he held for nearly two years. He remained a director and vice-president of the club until April 1976. His son, Stan junior, was later chairman of the club. Stan Seymour died on Christmas Eve 1978.

SHALLCROSS, Arthur J.

Born: Leek.
Career: Leek player; Football League referee 1895; Stoke secretary-manager cs 1919-April 1923.
Honours: Division Two promotion 1922.

Shallcross hardly endeared himself to the Stoke supporters when he sold star player Charlie Parker to Sunderland in October 1920. This caused a shortage of goals and Stoke scrambled around the lower reaches of the Second Division and avoided relegation only by the narrowest of margins in 1920-21 when they finished 20th.

But he signed future manager Bob McGrory and with a new chairman in John Slater, Shallcross was able to strengthen his squad with an influx of new money. The Potters finished runners-up in 1921-22 to gain promotion to Division One, but were instantly

relegated despite Shallcross signing a number of new players. He lost his job just as Stoke were being relegated.

SHANKLY, William OBE

Born: Glenbuck, 2 September 1913; Died: Liverpool, 29 September 1981.
Wing-half   5ft 7in; 11st 3lb (1937).
Career: Cronberry; Glenbuck Cherrypickers; Carlisle United July 1932; Preston North End July 1933 (£500); guest for Northampton Town, Liverpool, Arsenal, Cardiff City, Bolton Wanderers, Luton Town and Partick Thistle in World War Two; retired March 1949; Carlisle United manager March 1949-July 1951; Grimsby Town manager July 1951-January 1954; Workington manager January 1954-November 1955; Huddersfield Town assistant manager December 1955, then manager November 1956-November 1959; Liverpool manager December 1959-July 1974.
Honours: Scotland international (5 caps); Wartime international (7 caps); Football League champions 1964, 1966, 1973; Division Two champions 1962; FA Cup winners 1938, 1965, 1974, runners-up 1971; UEFA Cup winners 1973; European Cup-winners' Cup runners-up 1966.

Bill Shankly had the great ability to instill his own brand of confidence into players. Shankly hated defeat with a blind, consuming rage and, much loved by his players and the fans, he remains a legend at Anfield, not only for his great abilities as a manager but also for his famous sense of humour.

Shankly hated having to stop playing and never completely replaced the thrill he got on the field with those as a manager. However, he transformed Liverpool into one of the great club sides in the world. They won many more honours than he ever achieved as a player and his legacy remains today as Liverpool continue to be one of the leading clubs in British soccer, albeit that tradition creaking uneasily under Graeme Souness in 1992-93.

Shankly's uncle, Bob Blythe, had been manager and chairman of Portsmouth Football Club and Bill came from a family of ten, four of his brothers going on to play professional football. His brother Bob also became well-known as a manager in Scotland.

Shankly played for Cronberry and Glenbuck Cherrypickers before signing for Carlisle United in July 1932. He quickly made his debut and after only 16 appearances for Carlisle moved to Preston North End in July 1933 for a £500 fee. At Deepdale his skills were

honed to perfection. Always fiercely competitive, his brash, ebullient nature made him a key figure in Preston's promotion side of 1933-34. He also played in two FA Cup Finals for Preston, in 1937 and 1938. They lost the first, 3-1 to Sunderland, but Shankly gained a winners' medal the following year when his side beat Huddersfield Town with a penalty goal in the last minute of extra-time.

Shankly made his international debut for Scotland against England at Wembley in April 1938, when the Scots won 1-0, thanks to a goal from Tommy Walker. He made four other appearances for his country, plus seven in wartime internationals. His playing career was, like most others of his generation, greatly affected by the war. Shankly guested for a number of clubs including King's Park, Northampton Town, Liverpool, Arsenal, Cardiff City, Bolton Wanderers, Luton Town and Partick Thistle. In 1941, he helped Preston beat Arsenal in a Wartime Cup Final at Wembley. When he retired in March 1949, Shankly had played 300 League games for Preston, plus 87 wartime games.

Coinciding with his retirement, he took his first job in management with Carlisle United. Shankly endeared himself to the fans by speaking to them before every match over the public-address system regarding the progress of the club. He gradually improved things at Brunton Park and in his final season in charge, Carlisle finished third in the Northern Section. In July 1951, he became the boss at Grimsby Town, where he felt there was more chance of success. A fitness fanatic, a disciplinarian and, above all, a football fanatic, Shankly was a 'player's manager'.

When he arrived at Blundell Park, he found a depleted and demoralized squad but soon brought in some experienced players and results began to improve. They finished runners-up in the Northern Section in 1951-52, three points behind champions Lincoln City. Only the champions went up in those days. The following season he again looked like achieving promotion but a poor late run meant they missed out again.

In January 1954, Shankly surprised everyone by moving to manage lowly Workington. They were struggling for their very existence, having only joined the League in 1951. Shankly changed them from a team of no-hopers to one challenging for promotion and in November 1955 he was invited by Huddersfield Town manager Andy Beattie to become his assistant manager at Leeds Road. Huddersfield were relegated at the end of the season and in November 1956, Shankly replaced Beattie as manager. He was unable to get Town back into the First Division and left the club in November 1959. Shankly gave youth a chance at Leeds Road and introduced the teenage Denis Law to the Football League.

The following month, Shankly was appointed manager of Liverpool, who were then in the Second Division. A man of outstanding vision, he transformed Liverpool into one of the most consistently successful clubs in British soccer. 'Shanks' decided at an early stage that he wanted to change a lot of the players at the club, but retained the backroom staff which included future managers Bob Paisley and Joe Fagan. Two of his early signings were Ian St John, from Motherwell for £37,000, and Ron Yeats, from Dundee United for £30,000. After going close to promotion twice, Liverpool won the Second Division title in 1961-62. They were unbeaten at home for the first time since 1905 and Roger Hunt hit a new club record 41 goals in the season.

The Reds reached the semi-finals of the FA Cup in 1963 but lost to Leicester City and before the start of the next season, Shankly signed Peter Thompson from Preston for £40,000. That season Liverpool won the League championship after an average start. The three victories they achieved over Easter virtually clinched the title from their nearest rivals, Manchester United. In 1965, they won the FA Cup for the first time in their history when they beat Leeds United 2-1 after extra-time, thanks to St John's headed winning goal. They also reached the semi-finals of the European Cup but lost to Internazionale in suspicious circumstances in Italy, to two controversial goals. In 1965-66 Liverpool were champions again, losing only two of their last 19 games and conceding only 34 goals. They also reached the European Cup-winners' Cup Final but lost 2-1 to Borussia Dortmund at Hampden Park.

At this point the club went into a period of transition in which Shankly decided to completely rebuild the side. Some criticised him for loyally hanging on to some players longer than he should. However, he always regarded continuity as one of the most important factors in his success at Anfield. One criticism which could be made of Shankly is that he rarely produced top-class players through the club's youth system and had to rely on buying talent. But he usually chose well and only occasionally bought a dud. One of his few failures was Alun Evans, who he bought as an 18-year-old for £100,000 from Wolves. Evans never lived up to his promise.

On the other hand, Shankly bought two players from Scunthorpe United who were to become leading figures in English soccer in the next decade. These were Kevin Keegan and Ray Clemence and both cost very moderate fees. Liverpool finished runners-up in 1968-69 but it was the end of the road for a lot of the old guard when the Reds lost at Watford in the quarter-finals of the FA Cup the following season.

Goals were becoming hard to come by and Shankly decided to buy John Toshack from Cardiff City for a £110,000 fee. Toshack teamed up well with Keegan in later years. In 1971, Liverpool reached the FA Cup Final but lost to double-winners, Arsenal. 1972-73 saw the Reds take the League championship again and also win the UEFA Cup when they beat Borussia Mönchengladbach in a two-legged final. Keegan scored two of the goals in their first leg 3-0 victory at Anfield. In 1974 they beat Newcastle United 3-0 in the FA Cup Final with goals from Keegan and Heighway.

Shortly after this, in July 1974, Shankly surprised everybody by announcing his retirement from football. Around this time he was awarded the OBE for his services to the game. In 1976, a biography about his life was published called simply *Shankly*. He died in Liverpool on 29 September 1981.

There are many stories about Bill, many of which are probably apocryphal. He always denied the story that he took his new wife to watch Rochdale Reserves instead of going on their honeymoon as completely fabricated. He claimed that he would never have got married during the season anyway as football took up all of his time!

SHANNON, Leslie

Born: Liverpool, 12 March 1926.
Wing-half   5ft 8in; 11st 2lb (1959).
Career: Liverpool amateur 1943, professional November 1944; Burnley November 1949 (£6,000); Everton coach August 1959; Arsenal chief coach and assistant manager 1963-1966; Bury manager July 1966-May 1969; Blackpool manager May 1969-October 1970; POAK Salonika (Greece) trainer-coach January 1971-April 1974; Iraklis (Greece) manager; Olympiakos Piraeus (Greece) manager 1976; Luton Town coach 1990.

Honours: England 'B' international (3 caps); Division Two runners-up 1970; Division Three runners-up 1968.

Les Shannon made his League debut in a Merseyside derby and scored in a 3-1 defeat at the hands of Everton. He scored 44 goals in 281 appearances for Burnley before moving to Everton as coach and his first managerial post was with Bury.

The club was going into decline when he was appointed as manager and although he was sacked in the summer of 1967, he was reinstated after boardroom changes at Gigg Lane.

Shannon sold Colin Waldron to Chelsea for £30,000 to cover enormous debts accumulated the previous season and took the Shakers to promotion in 1968, although they were relegated straight back again to Division Three. He took Blackpool to runners-up spot in Division Two in 1969-70, signing Mickey Burns and Fred Pickering, but he kept most of the side inherited from Stan Mortensen and it was his successor, Bob Stokoe, who changed the team. Shannon resigned after Blackpool lost 4-3 to Chelsea after being three goals up. Recently he was an advisor to the Channel 4 TV series *The Manageress*.

SHAW, Joseph

Born: Murton, County Durham, 23 June 1928.
Centre-half   5ft 8in; 11st 8lb (1963).

Career: Upton Colliery; Sheffield United amateur 1944, professional July 1945, from 1965 player-reserve team coach; York City manager November 1967-August 1968; Fulham chief scout 1972; Chesterfield manager September 1973-October 1976.

Honours: Football League representative (2 caps); FA XI tour to Australia 1952; Division Two champions 1953.

Joe Shaw was a great stalwart for

Sheffield United, for whom he made 629 League appearances. Not tall for a centre-half, he made up for his lack of inches with his terrific recuperative powers, excellent positional sense and his dependability. Shaw gained a Second Division championship medal in 1952-53 and again helped United to promotion in 1962. He toured Australia with the FA in 1952 and also represented the Football League against the Scottish League and Irish league in 1959.

When he was appointed manager of York City, he signed Billy Hodgson, a former teammate at Bramall Lane, as player-coach. Another signing was Phil Boyer from Derby. York had to seek re-election at the close of the 1967-68 season and Shaw surprised everybody by resigning just before the start of the following season. He went close to promotion from Division Three with Chesterfield in his first season in charge but could not lift them beyond the mediocre after this and he was sacked after a poor start in 1976-77.

SHAW, Raymond

Born: Walsall, 18 May 1913; Died: Kirby Muxloe, Leicestershire, 29 April 1980.
Wing-half.
Career: Walsall amateur; Streetly Works; Darlaston; Birmingham May 1937, retired May 1947 to become club coach; Aston Villa trainer-physiotherapist until July 1964; Walsall trainer-physiotherapist July 1964, then manager October 1964-March 1968; Leicester City scout in early 1970s.

A constructive player who spent much of his time in the reserves at Birmingham, Shaw played 13 games in League and FA Cup ties plus 111 appearances in wartime competitions. He turned into a top-class coach at St Andrew's and Villa Park before becoming manager at Walsall.

Much respected by the players, he guided Walsall to two good FA Cup runs, in 1966 and 1968, and to seventh place in Division Three in 1967-68. Shaw had a good understanding with his players and was given money to spend on established, experienced footballers. In his first season he signed Trevor Smith and Howard Riley but neither paid dividends and he relied on young players produced by the club after this. Shaw sold one of these, Allan Clarke, to Fulham for £35,000 to help balance the books.

SHELLITO, Kenneth J.

Born: East Ham, London, 18 April 1940.
Right-back   5ft 10in; 11st 2lb (1959).
Career: Sutton School (Hornchurch); Hornchurch, London & Essex Schools; Chelsea junior March 1956, professional April 1957, retired through injury January 1969, youth-team coach cs 1969, youth-team manager December 1969, then manager July 1977-December 1978; Queen's Park Rangers coach-assistant manager May 1979-1980; Crystal Palace coach 1980-81; Preston North End assistant manager July-December 1981; Crystal Palace assistant manager June 1982-November 1983; Wolverhampton Wanderers coach January 1985; Cambridge United manager March-December 1985; Tonbridge general manager in 1990.

Honours: England international (1 cap); Under-23 international (3 caps); FA Youth Cup runners-up 1958.

Ken Shellito had a promising career wrecked by injury. His appearance in the FA Youth Cup Final of 1958 proved

to be the first disappointment of his career. Chelsea beat Wolves 5-1 in the first leg, then sensationally lost the return 6-1 at Molineux, to go down on aggregate. He formed a marvellous partnership at full-back with Eddie McCreadie and helped Chelsea back to the First Division in 1963.

Shellito gained his England cap against Czechoslovakia in Bratislava in 1964. He fought back to fitness a number of times before giving up the game after only 123 appearances for Chelsea. For many years he ran the youth team at Stamford Bridge before taking over as manager in 1977. Chelsea struggled and were bottom of Division One when he resigned. He also had a tough time at Cambridge United and was clearly more successful as a coach.

SHEPHERD, Ernest

Born: Wombwell, 14 August 1919.
Outside-left   5ft 6½in; 10st 12lb (1949).
Career: Dearne Valley Schools; Bradford City amateur 1934; Bradford Rovers; Fulham amateur August 1935, professional August 1936; guest for Huddersfield Town, Brentford and Bradford City in World War Two; West Bromwich Albion December 1948; Hull City March 1949 (£4,500); Queen's Park Rangers August 1950; coached in Iceland 1953-1954; Hastings United July 1956; Bradford coach 1957-1958; Southend United trainer 1959, later assistant manager 1966, manager April 1967-October 1969, then general manager until 1972; Orient trainer-assistant manager 1973-1976; coaching in Dubai 1977-1979; retired 1980.

A forceful, goalscoring winger with great speed, Shepherd has the distinction of playing for three promoted clubs in one season but failed to make enough appearances with any of them to win medals. This happened in 1948-49 when he played for Fulham, WBA and Hull City. He scored 51 goals in 219 appearances League for Queen's Park Rangers, where he finished his League career.

Shepherd started his career at Craven Cottage and played in Fulham's last match before the outbreak of the war, against Luton Town in August 1939. He was Bradford's top scorer in 1944-45 with 26 goals. Trainer and assistant manager at Southend for eight years before becoming manager, he bought Phil Chisnall from Manchester United and Eddie Clayton from Spurs, but neither were a success. Southend twice came close to promotion and Shepherd worked his way to the edge of a nervous breakdown in his efforts to find success at Roots Hall.

SHERRINGTON, George W. 'Bill'

Career: York City secretary 1924-1960, including secretary in charge of team affairs May 1930-May 1933 and September 1954-March 1956.

Sherrington was twice in charge of team affairs at York City, usually because the club was short of funds and unable to pay a full-time manager. He was really a financial secretary who knew little about the tactical side of soccer. The highlight of his two spells in charge came in 1955, when York City became the third Division Three side to reach the semi-finals of the FA Cup. They beat the 1953 Cup winners' Blackpool, 2-0 at Bloomfield Road. They then beat Bishop Auckland, Spurs (3-1 at home in the fifth round) and Notts County in the sixth. In the semi-finals, York lost to Newcastle United after a replay and must rate as one of the best-ever giantkilling sides.

SHILTON, Peter Leslie MBE

Born: Leicester, 18 September 1949.
Goalkeeper   6ft; 12st 10lb (1979).
Career: Leicester Schools; Leicester City apprentice June 1965, professional September 1966; Stoke City November 1974 (£325,000); Nottingham Forest September 1977 (£270,000); Southampton August 1982 (£300,000); Derby County June 1987 (£90,000); Plymouth Argyle player-manager March 1992.

Honours: England international (125 caps); Under-23 international (13 caps); Youth international; Schoolboy international; Football League representative (3 caps); Footballer of the Year 1978; Football League champions 1978; Division Two champions 1971; FA Cup runners-up 1969; Football League Cup winners 1979, runners-up 1980; European Cup winners 1979, 1980.

Peter Shilton was still playing at the age of 43 having played well over 1,000 games in his career, including a record 125 caps for England. A dedicated and strict trainer, Shilton has been a brilliantly consistent goalkeeper. A solid shot-stopper, fine aerial ability, great sense of positioning and command of his area have all gone to make Shilton one of the greatest 'keepers of all time.

He is Leicester's youngest debutant at 16 and dislodged England's regular 'keeper Gordon Banks, who moved to Stoke City. Shilton has won many honours in the game but the ones he is probably most proud of are his European Cup medals and the League championship medal he gained under Brian Clough at Nottingham Forest.

Shilton has played in three World Cup finals for England. He was unable to prevent Derby being relegated to Division Two, nor Plymouth's drop to Division Three after taking over as manager at Home Park near the end of the 1991-92 season. An injury to

Shilton hardly helped the club's cause, although he bided his time to give the club's regular 'keeper a chance.

Shilton survived a crisis board meeting in February 1993 when chairman Dan McCauley was critical as, even though Shilton had spent £1m on new players, the club was still near the bottom of Division Two. There was much criticism of the club that apparently paid Shilton £125,000 a year but were suffering from financial difficulties.

SHREEVE, Peter

Born: Neath, Wales, 30 November 1940.
Inside-forward   5ft 8½in; 11st 7lb (1959).

Career: Finchley; Reading January 1959; Chelmsford City 1966; Wimbledon cs 1969; Charlton Athletic coach 1974; Tottenham Hotspur youth-team manager 1974, reserve-team manager 1977, assistant manager 1980-1984, manager June 1984-March 1986; Queen's Park Rangers coach August 1986, assistant manager December 1988; Watford assistant manager; Tottenham Hotspur manager again July 1991-May 1992; Wales assistant manager in 1990s.

Peter Shreeve was born in South Wales, where his mother was evacuated during World War Two, but was brought up in Islington. He began his career at Finchley before moving to Reading, where he made 112/1 League appearances, scoring 15 goals. Shreeve then played for Southern League Chelmsford City and Wimbledon before starting his coaching career at The Valley.

Quickly moving to White Hart Lane, he gradually worked his way through the ranks to eventually take over from Keith Burkinshaw as manager in 1984. Spurs finished third in his first season but otherwise had little success. At Loftus Road, Shreeve was hoping to get the manager's job but it went to Trevor Francis instead. He was assistant to Steve Perryman at Watford before returning Spurs as team manager when Terry Venables moved upstairs to become chief executive. Shreeve lasted only one season and was sacked after Spurs could only finish 15th. They had reached the League Cup semi-final, though, but lost Nottingham Forest on aggregate.

SIBLEY, Frank Philip

Born: London, 4 December 1947.
Wing-half   5ft 10in; 12st 4lb (1970).
Career: Queen's Park Rangers February 1965-1970, coach 1974, manager July 1977-July 1978, then coach again; Walsall manager February-April 1979; Hounslow coach 1983; Queen's Park Rangers reserve-team manager February 1984, caretaker manager December

1984-June 1985, coach August 1986; assistant manager December 1988; Millwall assistant manager 1990; Queen's Park Rangers coach 1991.
Honours: England Youth international; Division Three champions 1967; Football League Cup winners 1967.
Frank Sibley, who made his League debut for QPR at the age of 16, was originally an inside-forward but was later converted to half-back. He captained the England Youth side and was chosen for an Under-23 touring party in 1967 but did not play. Sibley was a member of Rangers' Third Division championship and League Cup winning side in 1967, a unique double. Due to cartilage problems he missed much of the 1968-69 season as Rangers won promotion again, although they struggled in the First Division and were immediately relegated. Sibley was forced to retire through injury in 1970.

He had two spells in charge at Loftus Road. In the first, QPR just missed relegation but Sibley was not given enough time to rebuild. In the second spell he was acting manager and lost his job to Jim Smith. Sibley could not prevent Walsall's relegation to the Fourth Division and lost his job at Fellows Park.

SILLETT, John Charles

Born: Southampton, 20 July 1936.
Right-back   6ft; 12st 6in (1963).
Career: Southampton amateur; Chelsea April 1954; Coventry City April 1962 (£3,000); Plymouth Argyle July 1966-1967; Bristol City coach late 1960s; Hereford United manager July 1974-January 1978; Coventry City coach 1983-1984 and 1985; chief coach May 1986, then manager May 1987-November 1990; Hereford United manager again May 1991-May 1992.
Honours: Football League representative (1 cap); Division Three champions 1964, 1976; FA Cup winners 1987.
John Sillett came to Stamford Bridge with his brother Peter. A strong, hardtackling full-back, he made 102 appearances for Chelsea before losing his place to Ken Shellito. Sillett was almost ever-present in Coventry's Third Division title side of 1963-64, then suffered a slipped disc and was transferred to Plymouth Argyle. His father, Charles, had played for Southampton before the war.

John Sillett took Hereford to the Third Division championship in 1975-76 and was brought to Highfield Road as coach by former teammate Bobby Gould. From 1986, he formed a successful managerial partnership with George Curtis. They brought a fun-

loving attitude and an expressive type of football to the club, who lifted their first major trophy by beating Spurs 3-2 in the 1987 FA Cup Final. However, Coventry later suffered two terrible Cup defeats, against Sutton United and Northampton Town, although they were rarely out of the top half of the First Division. Sillett was upset when relieved of his duties to be replaced by Terry Butcher. Hereford had a good FA Cup run in 1991-92 under Sillett, before losing to Nottingham Forest in the fourth round, but finished only 17th in Division Four.

SIMPSON, John

Born: Hull, 27 October 1918.
Full-back   5ft 10in; 11st 12lb (1951).
Career: Hull Schools; Bridlington Town; Hull City Reserves; Huddersfield Town March 1939; York City March 1948 (£1,000), retired 1954 to become trainer-physiotherapist until 1963; Hartlepool United coach 1963, manager May 1970-March 1971; Cambridge United coach-physiotherapist 1971; York City physiotherapist 1977-1983.

Simpson did not make his debut for Huddersfield Town until after the war. In those days Huddersfield were a First Division side. He served in the Army Physical Training Corps in the war and guested for several clubs as well as captaining a Southern Command side.

York City paid a club record £1,000 fee for his services and Simpson, a hardtackling, no-nonsense player with great fitness and speed, made 220 League and FA Cup appearances for York. He gave the club great service in various capacities and in May 1983 was awarded a testimonial match against Leeds United which attracted a crowd of over 3,000. Shortly afterwards he retired to live in Market Weighton. Simpson took over from Gus McLean as manager of Hartlepool after seven years as coach. They lost to Rhyl in the first round of the FA Cup and Simpson resigned when the team slumped in the League.

SIMS, John

Born: Belper, 4 August 1952.
Forward   6ft; 12st (1980).
Career: Derby County August 1970; Luton Town (loan) November 1973; Oxford United (loan) September 1974; Colchester United (loan) January 1975; Notts County December 1975; Exeter City December 1978; Plymouth Argyle October 1979 (£22,000); Torquay United August 1983; Exeter City February 1984; Torquay United player-coach November 1984, then manager August-September 1985 (for 33 days); Saltash United 1985; Waldon Athletic player-manager and licensee in Torquay.

Sims played for all three Devonian sides and although he appeared in only three League games for Derby County, he came on as substitute against Juventus in a European Cup semi-final. Sims, who gained a Central League championship medal at the Baseball Ground, was an automatic choice at Plymouth where he made 180/2 appearances, scoring 48 goals. He played under Bobby Saxton at Exeter and Plymouth and was in charge at Torquay United for just 33 days.

SIRREL, Jimmy

Born: Glasgow, 2 February 1922.
Inside-forward   5ft 8½in; 11st 2lb (1955).
Career: Glasgow Celtic 1945; Bradford May 1949; Brighton & Hove Albion August 1951; Aldershot August 1954, later trainer; Brentford manager Sep-

tember 1967-November 1969; Notts County manager November 1969-September 1975; Sheffield United manager October 1975-September 1977; Notts County manager October 1977-1982, general manager 1982-June 1984, then director, manager again May 1985-May 1987; Derby County chief scout 1990.

Honours: Division Two runners-up 1981; Division Three runners-up 1973; Division Four champions 1971.

Jimmy Sirrel's toothy grin and dry sense of humour became synonymous with Notts County, where he was manager on three separate occasions. Sirrell took the club from the Fourth to the Second Division and was a good communicator about the game. He would often say that he could handle players and knew what makes the game work. He always talked good sense and expected great loyalty and effort from all of his players.

Sirrel made a late start in football due to the war. An inside-forward, he joined Celtic in 1945 and moved south to Bradford in May 1949. After only 12 appearances and two goals for the Park Avenue club, Sirrel moved to Brighton in August 1951. At the Goldstone he was again in and out of the side, playing a further 55 League games and scoring 13 goals before moving to Aldershot in August 1954. After 33 games and two goals for the club, Sirrel retired to become a trainer at the Recreation Ground.

He took his first managerial post with Brentford in September 1967 and it proved a tough baptism with the club heavily in debt and having just avoided folding altogether. Sirrel worked 100 hours a week to get the Bees going again. He was manager, chief scout, coach, trainer, baggage man and tidy-up man. There was no money for new players but by the time he left in November 1969, Sirrel had reduced the overdraft from £100,000 to £20,000.

He moved to Notts County as manager and teamed up with chairman Jack Dunnett MP. They had to fight apathy at Meadow Lane and destroy the legacy of failure, but Sirrell made an immediate impact and Notts County became Fourth Division champions in 1970-71. They set the pace from the start and went on to score 89 goals. The signing of Tony Hateley was inspirational and he scored 22 goals in 29 games for Notts. Sirrel was voted the Fourth Division Manager of the Year and County finished fourth in 1971-72, then were runners-up in Division Three the following season. This was the first time they had been in the Second Division since 1958. Their last 21 games of that season produced 33 points and, with them, promotion. The team was built around Don Masson, Dave Needham and Les Bradd, and Sirrel had

produced success with little outlay in the transfer market.

After two fairly good seasons in the Second Division, Sirrel left to manage Sheffield United from October 1975, but the move proved a disaster for him as the Blades finished bottom of the First Division with only 22 points. He was sacked in September 1977 after another poor start to the season.

Sirrell was out of work for only two weeks and returned to Notts County as manager in October 1977. Again he brought in many fine players and after finishing sixth in 1978-79, the Magpies entered the First Division for the first time in 55 years at the end of the 1980-81, as runners-up. After a season of consolidation, Sirrel became general manager in July 1982, a post he held until June 1984 when he joined the club's board of directors. In May 1985, Sirrel returned to the manager's chair for a third time and had moderate success in the Third Division before retiring in May 1987. He keeps involved with football as Derby's chief scout under Arthur Cox.

SLADE, Howard Charles

Born: Bath, 29 January 1891; Died: Doncaster, April 1971.
Left-half/Centre-forward
5ft 7in; 10st 3lb (1923).
Career: Bath City 1910; Stourbridge 1912; Aston Villa June 1913; Huddersfield Town March 1914; Middlesbrough October 1922; Darlington September 1925, retired 1927; coached in Europe, Turkey, Venezuela, Mexico, Scandinavia; Rotherham United trainer cs 1929; Aldershot coach; Middlesex Schools instructor October 1934; Crystal Palace chief scout, then manager November 1950-October 1951, then chief scout again until June 1955.
Honours: FA Cup winners 1922, runners-up 1920.

Slade had a varied career in football. He started his career as an inside-right but was converted to right-half at Huddersfield Town. He made only three appearances for Villa before moving to Huddersfield. He was a reservist in a cavalry regiment when he broke his leg playing football in November 1916.

Slade went on to make 129 appearances for Town and played in two FA Cup Finals for them, losing 1-0 to his former club, Aston Villa, in 1920 and beating Preston 1-0 in the 1922 Final. He also helped Huddersfield to promotion to Division One in 1919-20, as runners-up, and later made 70 appearances for Middlesbrough and helped Darlington to consolidate a place in Division Two (promoted 1924-25).

Slade then coached all over the world in the 1920s and '30s. At Crystal Palace, he was joint manager with Fred Dawes. Palace had to seek re-election in 1950-51 but they did sign Cam Burgess, who went on to score many goals for the club.

SLADE, William G.

Born: Walsall, c.1898.
Career: St John's School (Walsall); Coventry City director 1922-1932 and caretaker manager February-June 1931; Walsall manager February 1932-October 1934.

Bill Slade played in local soccer until he was 24, when he became a director of Coventry City. When he took over as manager of Walsall, many of his new signings were from his former club. These included Bill Coward, Chris Ball, Bill Sheppard and Freddie Lee.

Slade was in charge of the Walsall team which pulled off one of the biggest shocks in FA Cup history, when they beat mighty Arsenal 2-0 in January 1933. The Gunners, the great team of the era, had reached the Final the previous season.

Walsall also did well in the League, finishing fifth in the Northern Section in 1932-33 and fourth the following season. He lost his job after a poor start to the 1934-35 season, when Walsall won only one of their first 16 games.

SMAILES, Andrew

Born: Ratcliffe, near Amble, 21 May 1896; Died: Mendip, autumn 1978.
Inside-right/Centre-half
5ft 10in; 12st (1925).
Career: Blyth Spartans; Newcastle United October 1919 (£300); Sheffield Wednesday October 1922 (£1,500); Bristol City October 1923; Rotherham United August 1929, retired 1932; Rotherham United trainer 1934, then manager August 1952-October 1958; Scarborough manager February 1959-1961.
Honours: Division Three South champions 1927.

A prolific goalscorer until he was converted to centre-half in his latter days at Bristol City, Smailes was a weighty but fast forward, who scored over 100 goals for City. He could not prevent their relegation in 1924 but helped them win the Third Division South championship in 1926-27.

After he retired, Smailes spent 18 years as trainer under manager Reg Freeman and took over when Freeman left the club in 1952. In 1952-53, Rotherham beat the FA Cup holders, Newcastle United, 3-1 in the fourth round. In November 1958, with Rotherham bottom of their division, he resigned, thus ending nearly 30 years with the club.

SMITH, Arthur John

Born: Aberaman, Wales, 27 October 1911; Died: Weymouth, 7 June 1975.
Left-back   5ft 10in; 11st 7lb (1936).
Career: Aberaman; Aberdare Athletic; Merthyr Town; West Bromwich Albion; Wolverhampton Wanderers May 1930; Bristol Rovers cs 1934; Swindon Town May 1935; Chelsea March 1938 (£4,000); guest for West Bromwich Albion in World War Two; career ended by road accident and he retired 1945; Wolverhampton Wanderers trainer; West Bromwich Albion manager July 1948-April 1952; Reading manager June 1952-October 1955; ran a pub in Weymouth after 1955.
Honours: Wales Wartime international (1 cap); Division Two runners-up 1949.

A capable, wholehearted player, Smith was an excellent passer of the ball. He

started his professional career at Wolves, where he made 30 appearances, and he made another 114 for Swindon and 49 for Chelsea. His playing career was truncated by the war, in which he served as a flight-sergeant in the RAF. A car accident at the end of the war ended his playing career.

Smith took West Brom to promotion as Second Division runners-up in 1948-49 and the Throstles held their own in the top division. He put Reading on a sounder financial footing but sold a number of star players to enable him to do this. These included Gordon Brice, Johnny Brook and Stan Wicks, and the standard of play soon fell sharply. In October 1955, Smith was given a month's leave of absence and he resigned three weeks later.

SMITH, David

Born: South Shields, 12 October 1915.
Outside/Inside-right
5ft 7in; 10st 5lbs (1951).
Career: Middle Docks; Reyrolles; Newcastle United October 1935 (£35); South Shields May 1936; guest for Derby County, Glasgow Rangers and Northampton Town in World War Two; Northampton Town September 1943, secretary 1951, manager July 1954-July 1959; Aldershot secretary-manager July 1959-March 1967, then secretary-general manager August 1971.

David Smith made only one appearance for Newcastle United before joining non-League South Shields. He was a first-team regular for Northampton Town, for whom he scored 30 goals in 128 League games. In 1951, he was appointed the Cobblers' secretary and then manager three years later. They reached the fourth round of the FA Cup in 1957-58 but when they could finish only 13th in the Third South that season, entered the newly-formed Division Four.

The FA Cup run included a great 3-1 victory over Arsenal at the County Ground. In 1960-61, Aldershot reached the same stage, losing to Stoke in a second replay. Their best season under Smith was 1961-62, when they finished seventh. Smith became general manager in March 1967 with Tom McAvenney as team manager. He was sacked in August 1971.

SMITH, David B.

Born: Dundee, 22 September 1933.
Full-back   5ft 10in; 11st 2lb (1959).

Career: East Craigie; Burnley September 1950; Brighton & Hove Albion July 1961; Bristol City July 1962-63; Burnley assistant trainer; coaching in Lybia; Sheffield Wednesday assistant trainer and coach 1965-1967; Newcastle United coach cs 1967, senior coach

1968-1971; Arsenal assistant trainer cs 1971-1974; Mansfield Town manager April 1974-April 1976; Southend United manager May 1976-June 1983; Plymouth Argyle manager November 1984-June 1988; Dundee manager June 1988-January 1989; Torquay United manager October 1989-April 1991.

Honours: Division Three runners-up 1986; Division Four champions 1975, 1981, runners-up 1978.

Smith broke his leg five times and was never a first-team regular at Turf Moor where he made 108 appearances before moving to Brighton. He was more famous as a manager. Mansfield Town were Fourth Division champions under Smith in 1974-75, gaining 68 points and losing only six games. The following season they reached the semi-finals of the Anglo-Scottish Cup and the fifth round of the League Cup. He was controversially sacked at the end of the season after, steering the club clear of relegation.

He was soon employed again, however, and took Southend United into the Third Division in 1977-78 and to the Fourth Division championship in 1980-81. They just missed promotion again the following season. Smith carried on his good record when Plymouth gained promotion to Division Two in 1985-86, as runners-up. Smith then had a seven-month spell in charge of Dundee, then joined Torquay United. In January 1990, they beat West Ham 1-0 in the FA Cup third round and the following season were on their way to the Fourth Division play-offs when he surprisingly left the club.

SMITH, Denis

Born: Stoke, 19 November 1947.
Defender   5ft 11in; 12st (1970).
Career: Stoke City September 1966; York City March 1982, then player-manager May 1982-June 1987; Sunderland manager June 1987-December 1991; Bristol City manager March 1992-January 1993.

Honours: Division Two promotion 1990; Division Three champions 1988; Division Four champions 1984; Football League Cup winners 1972.

Smith was a tough, no-nonsense central defender who was the linchpin of the Stoke side for many years. He made 462/1 appearances, scoring 38 goals, for the Potteries club before moving to York City, where he made another 43 appearances. Smith was outstanding in Stoke's run to take the Football League Cup in 1972, when Chelsea were beaten 2-1 in the Final. He helped Stoke to promotion to Division One in 1978-79.

When he was manager at York and Sunderland, his right-hand man was Viv Busby, whom he had met up with during his time at Stoke. They took York to their first major trophy in the club's history when they finished Fourth Division champions in 1983-84 with a massive 101 points. They reached the fifth round of the FA Cup in the next two seasons, each time losing to Liverpool. Sunderland paid York £20,000 when Smith and Busby moved to Roker Park. They clinched the Third Division title in their first season there, then made the Second Division play-offs in 1990. They lost to Swindon in the Final but were promoted when Swindon were demoted after an illegal betting scandal.

They lasted only one season in the top flight and when they then struggled in the Second Division, Smith was sacked. He lasted ten months in charge

at Bristol City and despite having many talented players, City struggled at the wrong end of the table.

Smith was sacked in January 1993 and replaced by Russell Osman as manager. Despite selling Andrew Cole to Newcastle United for £1.75m, City managed to avoid relegation that season.

SMITH, Edward John William

Born: Grays, 3 September 1914; Died: abroad, possibly in Portugal, early 1989.
Full-back   6ft 12st (1938).
Career: Grays Albion; Grays Athletic; Barking Town; Tilbury; Millwall August 1935-May 1948; guest for Reading and Fulham in World War Two; Benfica coach October 1948, later Portugal national team manager; Workington manager June 1952-September 1953; manager of the Labour Club in Keswick October 1955.

Honours: Division Three South champions 1938; Portuguese League champions 1950, Portuguese Cup winners 1949.

Ted Smith gave Millwall great service as a player and was a firm favourite of the crowd. He had played at centre-half at Barking but when he joined Millwall, he appeared mainly at right-back. He made 142 League appearances for the Lions before the outbreak of war. This included being ever-present in the season in which they won the Third Division South championship in 1937-38. He appeared in 191 wartime games for Millwall, scoring the only goal of his career in 1939-40. He made only one appearance after the war, in a 7-1 defeat at Bury in which the opposing forwards took full advantage of his lack of fitness and speed.

He took Benfica to a League title and national cup before returning to England to manage Workington. He preferred to concentrate on reorganising the club than talking to the media. They had to seek re-election again in 1952-53 and after a poor start the following season in which only 4 points were gained in the first 11 games, Smith was sacked. His trainer, Tommy Jones, took over as caretaker manager.

SMITH, George Casper

Born: Bromley-by-Bow, London, 23 April 1915; Died: Bodmin, 31 October 1983.
Centre-half.

Career: Hackney Schools; Bexleyheath & Welling 1937-1938; Charlton Athletic

May 1938; guest for Tottenham Hotspur in World War Two; Brentford November 1945 (£3,000); Queen's Park Rangers May 1947; Ipswich Town September 1949, later assistant manager until January 1950; Chelmsford City manager August 1950; Redhill manager July 1951; Eastbourne United manager 1952-55; manager of FA Youth squad; Sheffield United coach September 1955-February 1956; Sutton United manager May 1956-July 1958; Crystal Palace manager July 1958-April 1960; Sheffield United coach April 1960-April 1961; Portsmouth manager April 1961-April 1970, then general manager.

Honours: England Wartime international (1 cap); Division Three South champions 1948; Division Three champions 1962; Football League South Cup winners 1944.

Smith played for Charlton Athletic in the war and appeared in an FA Cup final against Chelsea at Wembley in 1944, which was won 3-1. He also gained a wartime cap for England against Wales in May 1945 and gained a Third Division South medal with Queen's Park Rangers in 1947-48. Smith spent many years managing non-League clubs before being offered the Crystal Palace job.

He said that he would resign in two years if he did not get them promoted, and kept his promise when he failed to do so, although he left a good team for his successor. He took Portsmouth to the Third Division championship in 1961-62, at the end of his first season in charge. They were nearly relegated in 1964-65, but a late equaliser by Jimmy Dickinson saved them in the last match of the season. Smith made some radical changes in the summer of 1965, when he scrapped the reserve side and had only 16 professionals in an attempt to save money. He became the general manager in 1970 but lost his job three years later when new chairman John Deacon restructured the management.

SMITH, James Christopher Reginald 'JR'

Born: Battersea, 20 Janaury 1912.
Inside/Outside-left   5ft 9in; 11st 8lb (1937).
Career: Hitchin Town: Crystal Palace trial; Tottenham Hotspur amateur cs 1932; St Albans City August 1933; Millwall August 1935; guest for West Ham, Luton, Partick Thistle, Watford, Chelsea and Spurs in World War Two; Dundee March 1946; Corby Town player-manager 1948-1949; Dundee trainer-coach 1949; Dundee United manager September 1954-December 1956; Falkirk manager January 1956-May 1959; Millwall manager July 1959-January 1961; Addington (South Africa) coach March 1961; Durban City manager 1961; Bedford Town manager late 1961-September 1963; Addington manager 1963; Cape Town manager; Bedford Town manager November 1971-June 1972; Stevenage Town manager.

Honours: England international (2 caps), Wartime international (3 caps); Division Three South champions 1938; Scottish Cup winners 1957; Herts FA and Spartan League representative.

Reg Smith was an incisive winger who was strong and fast with a lethal shot in both feet. His surname was actually Schmidt and he was the son of a South African rugby international who came to England with the first Springbok touring side. Smith worked as an electrician when he played non-League

football and later converted The Den from gas to electricity after he joined the club. He helped the Lions to the Third Division South championship in 1937-38 and gained two England caps, scoring two goals against Norway and helped his country to 7-0 victory over Ireland in November 1938.

He spent the last year of the war in Scotland and was persuaded to join Dundee in 1946. He was later trainer-coach at Dens Park and they had success in the Scottish FA Cup and League Cup. He took Falkirk to the Scottish Cup in 1957, beating Kilmarnock 2-1 in the Final but they were to relegated in 1958-59 and he left the club to take over at The Den. Here, he concentrated solely on the players, tactics and coaching, leaving the media to Jimmy Seed. Smith attempted a new style of play which he called 'Funnel Football' which made Millwall very difficult to beat. They started the 1959-60 season with a run of 19 unbeaten games but won only eight of them. They lost to Bath City, 4-1 in the FA Cup but narrowly missed out on promotion. Reg Smith was fired, inexplicably, with the club heading for promotion. No reason was ever given for his sacking. Smith decided to try his luck in South Africa for a while.

SMITH, James M.

Born: Sheffield, 17 October 1940.
Left-back   5ft 8in; 11st (1959).

Career: Sheffield United amateur 1957, professional January 1959; Aldershot July 1961; Halifax Town July 1965; Lincoln City March 1968; Boston United player-manager 1968-1972; Colchester United player-manager October 1972-June 1975, retired as a player 1973; Blackburn Rovers manager June 1975-March 1978; Birmingham City manager March 1978-February 1982; Oxford United manager March 1982-June 1985; Queen's Park Rangers manager June 1985-December 1988; Newcastle United manager December 1988-March 1991; Middlesbrough coach March-June 1991; Portsmouth manager June 1991.

Honours: Division Two champions 1985, promotion 1980; Division Three champions 1984; Division Four promotion 1974; Football League Cup runners-up 1986.

Known as the 'Bald Eagle', Jim Smith is a typical tough Yorkshireman who has found success at nearly every club that he has managed. An extrovert character, he is popular with the media for his outspoken views about soccer. His greatest achievement has been taking Oxford United to successive divisional titles and promotion to the First Division for the first time in their history.

Smith played all his football in the Fourth Division. A useful hard-tackling left-back, he was unable to break into Sheffield United's first team but after moving to Aldershot appeared in 74 League games, scoring one goal. He was a first-team regular at Halifax Town, with 112/1 League appearances, and he played 54 times for Lincoln City.

From 1969, Smith became player-manager of non-League Boston United and gained a reputation with the club as a shrewd manager. Colchester United, attracted by Smith's deeds at Boston, appointed him their manager and he made a brief comeback in their League side before retiring at the end of 1972-73. Colchester had to seek re-election at the end of that season but good times were just around the corner. The following season they finished third in the Fourth Division and thus gained promotion. They consolidated their position the following season and also had a good run in the League Cup, reaching the quarter-finals without conceding a goal before losing to eventual winners Aston Villa.

At this stage in his career, Blackburn Rovers came in with a lucrative offer for Smith to take over at Ewood Park, where he inherited a winning team and a crowd with high expectations that he would bring more success. It was a great struggle for Smith to win those fans over and Blackburn just missed relegation at the end of his first season in charge. After this he began to build a team which reflected his own approach to the game. His sides were capable of exciting, attacking football but inconsistency meant that they never challenged for promotion to Division One during Smith's time in charge.

In March 1978 he accepted an offer to move to St Andrew's, with his assistant Norman Bodell. The Birmingham board saw him as the man to motivate a team which lacked confidence. City were relegated to the Second Division at the end of his first full season in charge but bounced straight back again after finishing third in 1979-80. Smith bought many experienced players including Colin Todd, Frank Worthington, Don Givens, Archie Gemmill and Willie Johnston. He also paid large fees for Argentinian international Alberto Tarantini and Alan Buckley, both of whom flopped at St Andrew's. After two mediocre seasons in the top flight, Smith was sacked to make way for Ron Saunders.

He was not out of work for long, however, and the following month he was appointed manager of Oxford United. They came close to promotion twice before achieving their goal as champions in 1983-84, with 95 points, eight clear of their nearest rivals. Oxford then amazed everybody by taking the Second Division title the following season, two points clear of Smith's previous club, Birmingham City. Smith had made some marvellous entries into the transfer market with signings such as John Aldridge, Billy Hamilton, David Langan and John Trewick. He surprised everybody when he chose to move to Queen's Park Rangers as manager in June 1985, rather than enjoying his triumph at Oxford.

Within a year, he had taken Rangers to a League Cup Final at Wembley and the opposition was none other than Oxford United. It did not prove to be the happiest day in Rangers' history as they were well beaten, 3-0. QPR had eliminated Liverpool in an epic semi-final, thanks to two own-goals and a penalty save at Anfield. Smith made a killing when he signed David Seaman from Birmingham for only £225,000, as the goalkeeper was later sold for a huge fee.

Early 1987 was an uncertain time for QPR with news of a possible merger with Fulham. Thankfully this came to nothing but part of the deal which created the new Fulham '1987' club was the arrival at Loftus Road of Paul Parker and Dean Coney from Craven Cottage. Four years later, Parker moved to Old Trafford for over £2m. Rangers' best season under Smith came in 1987-88 when they finished fifth in the First Division.

In December 1988, Smith became the manager of troubled Newcastle United. It was not the greatest move that he could have made as he walked into a minefield of politics at St James' Park. The Magpies were relegated to the Second Division at the end of the 1988-89 season but came very close to bouncing straight back the following year before failing to negotiate the play-offs. Smith became tired of the behind-the-scenes in-fighting and resigned in March 1991, taking up a coaching post at Middlesbrough under manager Colin Todd.

In June 1991, he took over at Portsmouth and had an excellent first season, taking the club to the semi-finals of the FA Cup, where they were unlucky to lose to Liverpool in a penalty shoot-out after two drawn games. He inherited a very useful young side but has been forced to sell many of his promising youngsters as the players wished to further their careers in the newly-formed Premier League.

Pompey's luck deserted them again in 1992-1993. They were very unfortunate to miss instant promotion to the Premier League with a great late run which almost displaced West Ham. Then they lost to seventh-placed Leicester City in the play-offs to miss out.

SMITH, John

Born: Shoreditch, London, 4 January 1939; Died: 1988.

Inside-forward 5ft 7in; 11st 2lb (1963).

Career: East London, Middlesex and London Schools; West Ham United amateur 1954, professional January 1956; Tottenham Hotspur March 1960; Coventry City March 1964; Leyton Orient October 1965; Torquay United October 1966; Swindon Town June 1968; Walsall June 1971, manager October 1972-March 1973.

Honours: England Under-23 international (1 cap); Youth international; Division Two champions 1958; Football League Cup winners 1969.

In his younger days, John Smith looked good enough to play for his country but his career went into decline when he left West Ham. He had an excellent season when the Hammers took the Second Division championship in 1957-58 and moved to Spurs in an exchange deal which took Dave Dunmore the opposite way. Smith scored 22 goals in 132 appearances for the Hammers but made only 21 League appearances in four years at White Hart Lane.

He later found success at Swindon Town who, as a Third Division side, beat Arsenal 3-1 in the 1969 League Cup Final and also finished runners-up in the Third Division. Smith gained his one Under-23 cap, against France in 1960, and also appeared in a European Cup-winners' Cup semi-final for Spurs against OFK Belgrade in 1963. Walsall finished 17th in the Third Division in the season in which he was in charge at the club.

SMITH, Joseph

Born: Dudley Port, Staffs, 25 June 1889; Died: Blackpool 12 August 1971.

Inside-left 5ft 8in; 11st 5lb (1925).

Career: Newcastle St Luke's; Bolton Wanderers May 1908 (£10); guest for Chelsea in World War One; Stockport County March 1927 (£1,000); Darwen cs 1929 player-coach; Manchester Central cs 1930; Hyde United September 1930; Reading manager July 1931-August 1935; Blackpool manager August 1935-April 1958.

Honours: England international (5 caps); Victory international (3 caps); FA tours to South Africa and Canada; Division Two runners up 1937; FA Cup winners 1923, 1926, 1953, runners-up 1948, 1951.

A bluff, down-to-earth character, Joe Smith was manager of Blackpool for almost 23 years. These were by far the most successful in their history and included three appearances at Wembley in FA Cup Finals.

A frank character, Smith did not mince his words. A tremendous judge of footballer, he also bought well on the transfer market as well as developing his own players. If his sides were playing well he would never tinker with them. Smith possessed warmth and humanity beneath his blunt surface and was a great character with a very original sense of humour and a wonderful way with people. His team talks were legendary and, depending on how the team had played in the first half, Smith could be either encouraging or caustic.

One afternoon his key inside-forward was making no impact on the game.

"What time did you go to bed last night?" Joe asked.

The player replied, "I was in bed by ten."

Smith retorted, "Yes, but whose bloody bed?"

Staffordshire-born Smith started his playing career at a Potteries club called Newcastle St Luke's. He signed for Bolton Wanderers in May 1908, for a £10 fee, and made his League debut at West Brom in April 1909. He guested for Chelsea during World War One and after the war scored 38 goals in 1920-21, which is still Bolton's club record for a season. At Burnden Park, he developed an excellent left-wing partnership with Ted Vizard and both played major roles in the Trotters' success. Smith scored 227 goals in 492 appearances for Bolton, plus 48 goals in 51 wartime games for the club. This included six goals against Stoke in September 1916.

In 1920, he toured South Africa with the FA. In 1923, he was the first skipper to receive the FA Cup at Wembley, when the Trotters beat West Ham 2-0 in the first Final at that venue. Three years later they were back at Wembley and this time beat Manchester City 1-0. Smith also gained five caps for England, the first coming in a 2-1 defeat by Ireland in Belfast in February 1913. After moving to Stockport County in March 1927, Smith scored 61 goals in only 69 appearances, despite being 38 years old. Almost 20,000 came to see his debut but the club were later fined £100 as his registration was not in order.

In the summer of 1929, Smith joined Darwen as player-coach and a year later moved to Manchester Central. His final club was Hyde United, whom he joined in September 1930. In July 1931, Joe retired to take over as manager at Reading. He was selected from 100 applicants. At the end of his first season in charge, Reading finished runners-up behind Fulham in the old Southern Section of the Third Division. He may have found success at Elm Park but was often forced to sell his best players to keep the club solvent. Reading were unbeaten at home from 8 April 1933 until 15 January 1936 but could still not gain promotion to Division Two. They also reached the fifth round of the FA Cup in 1935 before losing narrowly to Arsenal at Elm Park before 30,621 spectators.

After being offered a three-year contract by Blackpool, Smith moved to the Seasiders as manager in August 1935. Before the war he bought good players like Jock Dodds from Sheffield United, Alec Munro from Hearts and William Buchan from Celtic, but was forced to sell promising inside-forward Peter Doherty due to financial circumstances. Doherty, of course, later went on to great things.

Blackpool won promotion to Division One as runners-up in 1936-37 and stayed there through the rest of Smith's reign. Stan Mortensen emerged as a star during the war and Blackpool won the League North Cup in 1942-43, beating Sheffield Wednesday 4-3 over two legs. They followed this by beating Arsenal, the League War South Cup winners, 4-2 at Stamford Bridge in the Cup-winners match. In the 1944 League North Cup Final, the Seasiders lost 5-4 to Aston Villa on aggregate.

After the war, Blackpool appeared in three FA Cup Finals in five years. In 1948 they lost 4-2 to Manchester United and in 1951 they lost 2-0 to Newcastle United. They finally took the trophy in 1953, in the famous 'Matthews' Cup Final in which they beat Bolton Wanderes 4-3 after being 3-1 down with 20 minutes remaining.

Smith's major coup was the signing of Stanley Matthews from Stoke City in 1947, for a meagre £11,500. Many critics felt that Matthews was past his best but were soon proved wrong as he was still playing in the First Division at the age of 50 in 1965. Smith later said that he did not buy Matthews, he 'stole' him at that price. Blackpool finished third in the First Division in 1950-51 and were runners-up in 1955-56. In April 1958, Joe Smith decided to call it a day at the age of 68. He remained in the town and died there in August 1971.

SMITH, Michael John

Born: Hendon, London 1936.
Career: Corinthian Casuals; British Universities; schoolteacher by profession; coaching in Sussex for nine years; team manager and coach of Conference of Grammar Schools; FA of Wales director of coaching, managed Welsh amateur and youth sides, then national manager 1974-1979; Hull City manager January 1980-March 1982; worked in sports promotions in Nottingham in 1982; Egypt national team manager 1985-1988; Wales youth-team manager autumn 1988 and national team assistant manager in 1989; Newtown FC consultant 1991.

Honours: Great Britain Olympic team 1960; England Amateur international; British Universities representative; Middlesex, Leicestershire and Cornwall County sides.

Mike Smith never played in professional soccer, instead he turned out for Corinthian Casuals and also played for Great Britain in the 1960 Olympic Games. Trained as a teacher at Loughborough College of Education, he spent many years coaching in schools and youth soccer. Being English, he was the surprise choice as Welsh national team manager in 1974, but he took Wales to the European championship finals in 1976, the only British side to qualify. Wales also did very well in the Home International Championships.

Smith later laid the foundations for Egypt's good showing in the 1990 World Cup. When he took over at Hull City, Smith took Cyril Lea and Bobby Brown, who had helped him with the Welsh side, with him to Boothferry Park. There was a high turnover of players but things did not improve and the Tigers were relegated to Division Four in 1981. When there was a financial collapse at the club, Smith and Lea were axed by the Official Receiver.

SMITH, Norman

Born: Newburn, Newcastle upon Tyne, 15 December 1897; Died: Newcastle upon Tyne May 1978.
Left-half   5ft 8in; 10st 9lb (1927).
Career: Mickley; Ryton United; Huddersfield Town April 1923; Sheffield Wednesday December 1927; Queen's Park Rangers August 1930, retired 1932; Kreuzlingen (Switzerland) player-coach; St Gallen (Switzerland) coach; Newcastle United trainer July 1938-December 1962 and caretaker manager October 1961-June 1962; England and Football League representative trainer.

Norman Smith had a very average playing career, mainly being a reserve-team player. He played only 24 games for Huddersfield Town, 23 for Sheffield Wednesday and 27 for Queen's

Rangers before retiring to start a career in coaching.

Smith was trainer at Newcastle United for 24 years before taking over from Charlie Mitten as caretaker manager in 1961, when he was 63. Newcastle won the FA Cup three times in the 1950s. In 1961-62, Smith steered the club clear of relegation but they lost at home to Peterborough United in the FA Cup. He was replaced by Joe Harvey after eight months in charge.

SMITH, Percy James

Born: Burbage Spring 1880; Died: Watford, 18 April 1959.
Centre-forward/Half-back   5ft 11in; 12st 3lb (1919).
Career: Hinckley Town; Preston North End cs 1902; Blackburn Rovers cs 1910; Fleetwood Town player-manager cs 1920; Nelson secretary-manager cs 1925-May 1927; Bury manager May 1927-January 1930; Tottenham Hotspur manager January 1930-April 1935; Notts County manager June 1935-October 1936; Bristol Rovers manager November 1936-November 1937.

Honours: Football League champions 1912, 1914; Division Two champions 1904, runners-up 1933.

Percy Smith played centre-forward for Preston, scoring 90 goals in 239 League appearances. He then made 172 appearances for Blackburn Rovers as a half-back before beginning his managerial career at Fleetwood Town and then taking over at Third Division North club Nelson. At Bury he sold Tiny Bradshaw to Liverpool for a staggering fee of £8,250 but found only limited success on the field. At Spurs he spent heavily on reconstructing the side and under him, Tottenham played an attractive, short-passing game with emphasis on attack.

Smith was a stern man with a tactical brain which probed the weaknesses of the opposition. Promotion to Division One was gained as runners-up in 1932-33 and Spurs finished third the following season before an injury crisis in 1934-35 led to disastrous results and relegation. He made an acrimonious departure. Smith signed Hughie Gallagher at Notts County and lasted only one year at Eastville before being sacked after an 8-1 home defeat by Queen's Park Rangers in the FA Cup.

SMITH, Robert William

Born: Prestbury, Manchester, 14 March 1944.
Inside-forward   5ft 7in; 10st 12lb (1970).
Career: Manchester United April 1961; Scunthorpe United March 1965; Grimsby Town January 1967 (£8,000);

Brighton & Hove Albion June 1968; Chester June 1971; Hartlepool United October 1971; Bury player-coach August 1973, manager November 1973-October 1977; Port Vale manager October 1977-May 1978; Swindon Town manager May 1978-October 1980; Blackpool coach 1981; Newport County coach July 1982, then manager June 1985-March 1986; Cardiff City coach 1989-July 1990; Hereford United assistant manager 1990; Swansea City coach March 1991. Swansea City assistant manager in 1992.

Honours: England Youth international; Schoolboy international (6 caps); Division Four promotion 1974.

Smith made a name for himself as a manager after an unspectacular playing career drifting around the lower divisions. He made over 200 reserve-team appearances at Old Trafford but had to wait for a move to Scunthorpe United for his League debut.

He was only 29 when he took over as manager at Bury and steered the club to promotion from Division Four in 1973-74. He was sacked after a poor start to the 1977-78 season but was out of work for only one day before being offered the Port Vale job. Smith took Swindon Town to the semi-finals of the League Cup in 1979-80, beating Arsenal on the way. They lost narrowly to Wolves in the semi-final, 4-3 on aggregate. Smith has moved around from one club to another in the 1980s.

SMITH, Stephen

Born: Huddersfield, 28 April 1946.
Midfield   5ft 9in; 10st 3lb (1970).
Career: Huddersfield Town October 1963; Bolton Wanderers (loan) December 1974; Halifax Town August 1977; Huddersfield Town chief scout and youth coach September 1979, then manager January-October 1987, coach again until July 1988; Bradford City youth development officer April 1989. Bradford City youth team coach in 1992.

Honours: Division Two champions 1970.

Described by Ian Greaves as the 'perfect professional', Steve Smith made his name as a right winger and helped Huddersfield into Division One in 1970, although they later went all the way down to the Fourth Division with Smith in the side. He made 368/13 appearances for the Terriers, scoring 33 goals, before departing to Halifax Town.

Smith made a brief comeback in November 1981, in an FA Cup tie against Workington, due to a massive injury crisis at Leeds Road. He was happiest as a coach and had a difficult time as the club's manager. He was sacked and reverted to coach but was

then axed by the club as an economy measure in July 1988.

SMITH, Thomas George

Born: Whitburn, County Durham, 1900.
Inside-right   5ft 8in; 12st (1927).
Career: Marsden Villa; Whitburn; South Shields cs 1919; Leicester City December 1919; Manchester United January 1924; Northampton Town June 1927; Norwich City May 1930; Whitburn February 1931; Northampton Town September 1939-March 1949.

Tom Smith played for, and managed Northampton Town. He joined South Shields from his local side just after World War One but was soon to move to Leicester City where he scored 15 goals in 82 appearances. He helped Manchester United to an FA Cup semi-final in 1926 where they lost to local rivals Manchester City, 3-0, at Bramall Lane.

Smith moved to Northampton after losing his first-team place at Old Trafford. He scored 22 goals in 112 games for the Cobblers before moving to Norwich City where he made just one first-team appearance. After his appointment as manager of Northampton Town just after the start of World War Two, Smith steered the Cobblers through the difficult war years and brought many famous names to the County Ground. After the war they did reasonably well in the Third Division South before Smith resigned after a row with the directors.

SMITH, William Henry

Born: Tantobie County Durham, 23 May 1895; Died: 13 April 1951.
Outside-left   5ft 10in; 11st 4lb (1925).
Career: West Stanley Seniors; Hobson Wanderers; Tantobie; Huddersfield Town October 1913; Rochdale player-manager July 1934-November 1935, retired as a player cs 1935.

Honours: England international (3 caps); Football League representative (3 caps); Football League champions 1924, 1925, 1926; FA Cup winners 1922, runners-up 1928, 1930.

A legend at Huddersfield Town, where he scored 126 goals in 574 appearances, Billy Smith played a major role in Huddersfield's halcyon days of the 1920s, when they won the League championship three seasons on the trot and played in three FA Cup Finals. An automatic choice on the left wing after serving in the Royal Navy in World War One, he missed the 1920 FA Cup Final due to a sending off at Stoke over Easter.

Two years later he played when a controversial penalty gave Town the only FA Cup victory in their history. One of the fastest players of his days, Smith was the first player to score direct from a corner, against Arsenal in October 1924. He had little success as manager of Rochdale, where he was forced to sell his best players. He signed Gwyn Jones from his former club but had to sell him to Stockport, where he proved a great asset. He was the father of Conway Smith of Huddersfield, Queen's Park Rangers and Halifax.

SOMERVILLE, John

Born: Ayr.
Right-back   5ft 9in; 12st (1898).
Career: Ayr Parkhouse; Bolton Wanderers March 1890, player-secretary 1898, retired as a player 1901, secretary-manager cs 1908-January 1910, secretary until July 1910; Football League linesman.

Honours: Division Two champions 1909; FA Cup runners-up 1894.

Known as 'Johnny Surefoot', due to his reliable displays for Bolton Wanderers at right-back, Somerville made 293 appearances for the Trotters, scoring just two goals. He was a fine player and steady personality who was admired for his judicious and generous qualities both on and off the field. Along with Jones and Sutcliffe, they formed a most formidable trio in defence. Somerville played in the 1894 FA Cup Final, which was lost 4-1 to Notts County.

The Trotters had a yo-yo existance with Somerville in charge. They were promoted to Division One in 1900, 1905 and 1909 but were relegated in 1899, 1903 and 1908. He left the club after they were relegated again in 1910, after he had spent over £3,000 in transfer fees, all to no avail. He was only in charge of team affairs after 1908, having previously been responsible for the administration of the club.

SOO, Hong Y 'Frank'

Born: Buston, Liverpool, 8 March 1914; Died: February 1991.
Wing-half/Inside-forward
5ft 7½in; 10st 12lb (1935).
Career: Liverpool Schoolboys; Prescot Cables; Stoke City January 1933; guest for Everton, Chelsea and Brentford in World War Two; Leicester City September 1945 (£4,600); Luton Town July 1946 (£5,000); Chelmsford City cs 1948; St Albans City manager in 1950s, coaching in Sweden; Scunthorpe United manager June 1959-May 1960. S.C.Padua (Italy) coach April 1950-June 1952; IF City of Eskiltuna (Sweden) coach 1952; Orebro (SW) coach 1953; Djurgaarden IF (Sw) coach 1954; Oddevold 1956; Scunthopre United manager June 1959-May 1960; Koping IS (Sw) coach 1962; IFK Stockholm coach 1963; AB Copenhagen coach 1965; various clubs in Copenhagen & Malmo 1966-71; Hoganas BK coach 1972.

Honours: England Wartime international (9 caps); Staffordshire Senior Cup winners 1934. Swedish League champions 1955.

A wonderfully clever ball player whose style was very modern for its time, Frank Soo was widely respected by his fellow professionals and fans alike. A polished player, Soo was both crafty and skilful with great ball trickery. He was on the verge of England recognition when war was declared in 1939.

Soo, who was of Chinese extraction, started his career at Cheshire County League side, Prescot Cables. He played under Tom Mather at Stoke and Leicester City and made a total of 244 peacetime appearances, scoring nine goals. He had one season in charge at Scunthorpe United, who finished 15th in the Second Division.

SOUNESS, Graeme James

Born: Edinburgh, 6 May 1953.
Midfield   5ft 11in; 12st 13lb (1982).
Career: Edinburgh Schools; Tottenham Hotspur apprentice April 1969, professional May 1970; Middlesbrough January 1973; Liverpool January 1978 (£352,000); Sampdoria (Italy) June 1984 (£650,000); Glasgow Rangers player-manager May 1986-April 1991; Liverpool manager April 1991.

Honours: Scotland international (54 caps); Under-23 international (2 caps); Youth international; Schoolboy international; Football League champions

1979, 1980, 1982, 1983, 1984; Division Two champions 1974; Scottish Premier League champions 1987, 1989, 1990; FA Cup winners 1992; Football League Cup winners 1981, 1982, 1983, 1984; European Cup winners 1978, 1981, 1984; Scottish Cup runners-up 1989; Scottish League Cup winners 1987, 1988, 1989, 1991.

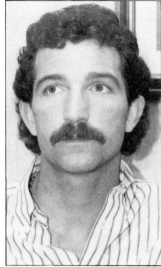

A fearsome, hard-tackling player, Graeme Souness started his career at Spurs, where he gained an FA Youth Cup winners' medal but became homesick and returned to Scotland without appearing in the first team. He proved a great capture for Middlesbrough and helped them to the Second Division championship in 1973-74. Souness had a marvellous career at Anfield and was badly missed when he moved to Italy. He played in three European Cup Finals and won five League championship medals with the Reds. Souness also played in four Football League Cup Finals, all won.

He was a great success in Italian soccer as well and later resurrected a flagging Glasgow Rangers side when he took over as manager and brought a number of English internationals to Ibrox. They won the Scottish League championship on three occasions and lifted the Scottish League Cup four times. He took over from Kenny Dalglish as Liverpool manager in April 1991. The 1991-92 season was not a vintage one in the First Division, Liiverpool finishing sixth, but they won the FA Cup, beating Second Division Sunderland in the Final. In April 1992 Souness underwent a triple heart bypass operation and Ronnie Moran took over for a while. Liverpool struggled for the first time in years the following season and Souness' job was on the line.

Souness survived a boardroom bid to oust him in May 1993 at the end of one of Liverpool's least successful seasons in 30 years. With no trophies in the boardroom cabinet and the team in great need of rebuilding, Souness was lucky to survive.

SOWERBY, J.W.

Career: Durham City manager 1919-February 1923, February 1924-1926 and cs 1927-1928.

Sowerby's main job at Durham City was club secretary but he was put in charge of team affairs on three occasions. His best season was 1921-22 when City finished 11th in the Third Division North. They had been elected into the Football League in 1921, despite a poor season in the North-Eastern League.

Sowerby signed 13 new players for

the start of their first Football League campaign but attendances were always poor and it was a constant struggle to survive. He relied heavily on amateurs to make up the side and sold three players who went on to greater things — George Camsell, a prolific goalscorer at Middlesbrough, Jack Hill, to Plymouth Argyle, and Sammy Crooks to Derby County. Durham City lost their League status after a disastrous season in 1927-28, finishing next to bottom of the Northern section.

SPENCER, Charles William

Born: Washington, County Durham, 4 December 1899; Died: York, 9 February 1953.
Centre-half   5ft 10in; 11st 11lb (1925).
Career: Glebe Rovers; Washington Chemicals; Newcastle United October 1921; Manchester United July 1928 (£3,250); Tunbridge Wells Rangers player-manager May 1930; Wigan Athletic player-manager August 1932-March 1937; Grimsby Town manager March 1937-May 1951; Hastings United manager 1951-1952; York City manager November 1952-February 1953.

Honours: England international (2 caps); tour to Australia with FA XI 1925 (5 caps); Football League representative (2 caps); Football League champions 1927; FA Cup winners 1924.

Charlie Spencer had to change his role as a centre-half after the alteration to the offside law in 1925. Originally an attacking pivot, Spencer had to play in a more defensive role after the change in rules. He made 178 appearances for Newcastle United and 48 for Manchester United. He toured Australia with the FA party in 1925 and gained two England caps, against Scotland in April 1924, in a 1-1 draw at Wembley, and in a 2-1 win over Wales at Swansea in February 1925.

He signed many established League players for Tunbridge Wells before taking over at newly-formed Wigan Athletic. At Grimsby, it was a constant struggle against relegation. The Mariners finished bottom of Division One in 1947-48, with only 22 points, and bottom of Division Two in 1950-51. At one time during the war he had found himself the only full-time employee at Blundell Park. Spencer was dogged by serious illness late in his life.

SPIERS, Cyril Henry

Born: Witton, Birmingham, 4 April 1902; Died: 21 May 1967.
Goalkeeper   6ft 1in; 12st (1935).
Career: Brookvale United; Handsworth Central; Halesowen; Aston Villa December 1920; Tottenham Hotspur December 1927; Wolverhampton Wanderers September 1933, later coach; Cardiff City manager April 1939-June 1946; Norwich City manager June 1946-1947; Cardiff City manager April 1948-April 1954; Crystal Palace manager October 1954-June 1958; Leicester City chief scout; Exeter City manager May 1962-February 1963; Leicester City chief scout February 1963.

Honours: Division Two runners-up 1952.

An agile and alert goalkeeper, Spiers found himself in competition with Tommy Jackson for the first-team spot at Aston Villa. He made 112 appearances for Villa but was a reserve when they reached the FA Cup Final in 1924. He played 169 League and FA Cup games for Spurs and did not miss a game from November 1928 until October 1931, a run of 124 consecutive matches.

He was mainly a reserve at Wolves before joining their training staff under Major Buckley. When he became Cardiff's manager, Spiers set up a network to bring many fine young players to the club. He took Cardiff City into Division One as runners-up in 1952, in his second spell at the club, but eventually left after a disagreement over money. Norwich City had to seek re-election in 1946-47 but again he brought many fine young players to the club. At Crystal Palace, he discovered Johnny Byrne, one of their greatest-ever players, but they languished near the bottom of the Southern Section with Spiers in charge.

SPROSON, Roy

Born: Stoke, 23 September 1930.
Full-back   6ft; 12st 8lb (1963).
Career: Stoke City amateur; Port Vale July 1949-1971, then manager January 1974-October 1977.

Honours: Division Three North champions 1954; Division Four champions 1959.

Roy Sproson made a massive 756/5 League appearances for Port Vale, scoring 29 goals, before hanging up his boots. He played in two divisional championship sides. In 1953-54, Vale took the Third Division North title and in 1958-59 lifted the Fourth Division title. They also reached the semi-finals of the FA Cup in 1954 before losing 2-1 to a Ronnie Allen penalty against West Brom. Known as 'Mr Loyalty', Sproson started his career as a wing-half before settling down at full-back. He came close to Jimmy Dickinson's record of 764 appearances for one club.

Sproson was initially caretaker manager at Port Vale as he was unsure whether he wanted the job permanently. Surprisingly, Vale had a poor disciplinary record, despite Sproson's excellent personal record during his playing days. Eventually the board lost confidence in his abilities as a manager and he was sacked, ending a long association with the club. He is the uncle of Phil Sproson of Port Vale.

SPUHLER, John Oswald

Born: Sunderland, 18 September 1917.
Centre-forward 5ft 8in; 10st 11lb (1938).
Career: Redby School; Sunderland Schools; Sunderland September 1934; Middlesbrough October 1945-1953 (£1,750) and guest in World War Two; Darlington June 1954 (£1,000); Spennymoor United player-manager 1956; Stockton manager; Shrewsbury Town manager February-June 1958; ran a sub Post Office at Yarm for eight years.

Honours: England Schoolboys international.

Nicknamed 'Sulphur' by his team-mates, Johnny Spuhler was a brave player who once played in a number of matches despite a broken nose. He liked to sprint into good positions and use his fine heading ability. He played 35 games for Sunderland and scored 81 goals in 241 appearances for Middlesbrough. Spuhler left 'Boro after relegation in 1954. He managed North-East clubs Spennymoor United and Stockton before a short spell as manager of Shrewsbury Town. They finished 17th in the Southern Section in 1957-58.

STANIFORTH, Ronald

Born: Newton Heath, 13 April 1924.
Right-back 5ft 11in; 11st (1959).
Career: Hague Street School (Newton Heath); Manchester Schools; Newton Albion; Stockport County October 1946; Huddersfield Town May 1952 (£1,000); Sheffield Wednesday July 1955; Barrow player-manager October 1959-July 1964 (£1,000), retired as a player 1961; Sheffield Wednesday assistant coach July 1970, chief coach March 1971, youth-team coach to January 1976.

Honours: England international (8 caps), 'B' international (3 caps); Division Two champions 1956, 1959.

A tall, stylish and cultured full-back, Ron Staniforth served in the Royal Navy during the war. He then worked as a milkman before signing for Stockport County at the age of 21. Staniforth gave some brilliant displays in his 223 League appearances for County and then became one of the best right-backs in the country under Andy Beattie at Huddersfield Town.

He made 118 appearances for Huddersfield and 107 for the Owls, helping Huddersfield to promotion and to third in Division One and gaining a Second Division championship medal with Wednesday. He made his England debut in a 4-2 victory at Hampden and also played in the 1954 World Cup finals. He made another 38 League appearances as player-manager of Barrow. They had to seek re-election in 1960-61 and 1963-64, after which he resigned, complaining about not being given enough control by the board.

STANSFIELD, Frederick

Born: Cardiff, 12 December 1917.
Centre-half 6ft; 13st (1948).
Career: Moorland Road School; Whitchurch Schools; D.Morgan and Rees Co Ltd, c.1934; Grange Albion; Cardiff City August 1943; Newport County September 1949, then player-manager March 1950-December 1953; Bedford Town assistant manager.

Honours: Wales international (1 cap); Division Three South champions 1947.

Due to the war, Stansfield did not turn professional with Cardiff City until he was 24. He appeared at right-back and centre-half for the South Wales club and missed only one game in the first two seasons after the war. He lost his place after breaking his leg against Barnsley in January 1949 and was unable to break back into the side. Stansfield gained his Welsh cap against Scotland in October 1948, finishing on the losing side as the Welsh went down 3-1. His aerial dominance and tenacity were an important factor in Cardiff's successful Division Three South campaign of 1946-47. His best season in charge at Newport County was 1951-52, when they finished sixth in the Southern Section.

STANSFIELD, James Brown 'Bertie'

Born: Bolton, Spring 1869; Died: Newcastle upon Tyne, 5 January 1938.
Career: Rossendale United secretary; vice-president of Rossendale Association; one of the promoters of the Stacksteads club (Central Lancashire League); Carlisle United manager until 1910; Norwich City manager March 1910-1915 and March-November 1926; proprietor of Crown Hotel in Lowestoft; Poole Town manager late 1920s.

Bertie Stansfield failed to achieve more than mid-table mediocrity at Norwich City in his first spell as manager. He signed several players from his former clubs, Rossendale United and Carlisle United. The best of these was Jock McKenzie, who played over 200 games for the club.

He also signed future Canaries manager, Cecil Potter, in 1911. He left the club at the outbreak of war and had been running a Lowestoft hotel for some years when he returned to The Nest for a second spell. Stansfield found the job too demanding and left soon after a 3-1 FA Cup defeat against non-League Clapton.

STAPLETON, Francis Anthony

Born: Dublin, 10 July 1956.
Forward 6ftin; 13st 1lb (1990).
Career: Arsenal apprentice June 1972, professional September 1973; Manchester United August 1981 (£1.1m); Ajax (Amsterdam) July 1987; Derby County (loan) March 1988; Le Havre (France) cs 1988; Blackburn Rovers July 1989-cs 1991; Aldershot September 1991; Huddersfield Town coach October-December 1991; Bradford City player-manager December 1991.

Honours: Republic of Ireland international (70 caps); Youth international; FA Cup winners 1979, 1983, 1985, runners-up 1978, 1980; Football League Cup runners-up 1983; European Cup-winners' Cup runners-up 1980.

Frank Stapleton enjoyed many successful years at Arsenal and Manchester United and played an important attacking role for both clubs. He always had great heading ability and also worked very hard to improve his ball control and mobility. Stapleton blossomed at Highbury with the arrival of Malcolm Macdonald and they formed a fine partnership. He played in three successive FA Cup Finals and five in all. He gained a winners' medal in 1979, when Arsenal beat the club he would later join, Manchester United, 3-2 in an exciting finale. Stapleton also gained two winners' medals with United.

In 1983, they beat Brighton 4-0 after a 2-2 draw, in which he scored, then two years later beat Everton 1-0. Stapleton captained the Republic of Ireland in the 1988 European championship finals. He scored 108 goals in his 297/3 appearances for Arsenal and 69 goals in 234/12 games for United.

Stapleton took over as Bradford City's manager in December 1991 and since then results have steadily improved and the side have played with more attacking flair which has been more entertaining for the fans to watch. City were challenging for promotion in 1992-93 but just missed out on the play-offs after a good start to the season.

STEELE, David Morton

Born: Carluke, Lanarkshire, 26 July 1894; Died: 25 May 1964.
Wing-half 5ft 9in; 11st 2lb (1925).
Career: Armadale; St Mirren; Douglas Water Thistle; Bristol Rovers November 1919; Huddersfield Town May 1922 (£2,500); Preston North End May 1929, retired July 1930; Bury coach July 1930; Ashton National coach October 1930; Bold Klubben (Denmark) coach late 1930-August 1934; Sheffield United coach August 1934-1936; Bradford manager May 1936-September 1943; Huddersfield Town manager September 1943-June 1947; Bradford City manager July 1948-February 1952; Huddersfield Town scout 1950s and ran a public house in Stanningley.

Honours: Scotland international (3 caps); Football League champions 1924, 1925, 1926; FA Cup runners-up 1928.

A member of a famous half-back line at Huddersfield Town — Steele, Wilson and Watson — which took the club to three successive League titles in the mid-1920s, David Steele also played in the 1928 FA Cup Final defeat against Blackburn Rovers. His broad Scottish accent was so strong that many of his colleagues could not understand him. A former miner, Steele had great endeavour and skill as well as marvellous stamina.

Signed by Huddersfield manager Herbert Chapman, with Joe Walter, for a joint fee of £2,500, he made over 200 appearances for the club and also gained three Scottish caps. Steele made a comeback in an emergency, for Bradford against Sheffield Wednesday in October 1942 when he was 48. His best season as manager at Park Avenue was 1937-38, when the club finished seventh in Division Two.

Huddersfield Town just missed relegation in 1946-47 and Steele resigned soon afterwards. At Valley Parade, he helped to develop Len Shackleton. He had been working at the family's fruit farm when enticed back into management with City.

STEELE, Frederick Charles

Born: Hanley, Stoke, 6 May 1916; Died: 23 April 1976.
Inside-right 5ft 8½in; 10st 8lb (1935).
Career: Downings FC (Tileries); Stoke City amateur 1931, professional August 1933; Mansfield Town player-manager (£750) August 1949-December 1951; Port Vale player-manager December 1951-January 1957, retired as a player May 1953; licensee 1957-1962; Port Vale manager again October 1962-February 1965.

Honours: England international (6 caps); Football League representative (2 caps); Division Three North champions 1954.

Freddie Steele is one of the few managers to have taken a Third Division side to the FA Cup semi-finals and in Vale's case they were also Northern Section champions the same season. True, his sides were dull and boring but they were defensively very efficient and, in a sense, Steele was ahead of his time as truly defensive sides did not really come into vogue until the 1970s.

Steele was born in the Potteries during World War One and his first club was Downings, a local works side. He joined Stoke City in 1931 and developed into an excellent inside or centre-forward. A marvellous header of the ball, especially from the crosses of Stanley Matthews, Steele was robbed of ultimate greatness by an injury which ended his international career and made him a far less effective player. In October 1937 he injured his knee in a collision with Sam Bartram, the Charlton goalkeeper. The injury led to a great loss in confidence and then his career was blighted by the outbreak of war in 1939.

Steele still holds Stoke records for most goals in a season, 33 scored in only 35 appearances in 1936-37, and he hit a career total of 161 goals in League and FA Cup games for City, also a record. He once scored five goals in a match against Derby County in September 1937. Steele netted 150 goals in wartime soccer and represented his country on six occasions and the Football League twice.

In August 1951, Steele moved to Mansfield Town for a fee of £750 and was appointed player-manager at Field Mill. He scored 19 goals in only 20 games in 1949-50 and the following season the Stags finished runners-up to Rotherham United in the Third Division North. They also reached the fifth round of the FA Cup but this proved a diversion to their main aim of promotion.

In December 1951, Steele moved to Port Vale as player-manager. Here he produced a very dour and defensive side which was generally disliked by the English football public who wanted to see entertaining soccer. They finished runners-up in the Northern Section in 1952-53, just one point behind Oldham Athletic and conceded only 35 goals, the second fewest in the League. Steele retired from playing in May 1953.

The following season brought enormous success to the club, when they clinched the Division Three North championship, conceding only 21 goals in 46 games including only five at Vale Park. They also reached the semi-finals of the FA Cup before losing to West Brom, to two late goals before a 68,221 crowd at Villa Park. Yet their style of play alienated the public, despite the unusual success of a Third Division side. Vale played to a set pattern which was aimed at preventing the opposition from scoring, a style of play devised by Steele.

As a manager he seemed to understand the workings of a player's mind and was able to get the best out of his side. He was very superstitious and, if a game was tight, he had to hide in the toilet for the last few minutes.

Steele resigned in January 1957, with Vale at the bottom of Division Two and the manager having been unable to adequately replace an ageing side. He ran a pub for five years before his surprise return to Vale Park as manager in October 1962. The chairman, Joe Machin, was hoping that Steele would rekindle his old successes. There was a large turnover of players and Steele paid £15,000 for both Billy Bingham from Everton and Albert Cheeseborough from Leicester City. Vale finished third in the Third Division in 1962-63 but only the top two went up in those days. The 1964-65 season proved a disaster and Vale were eventually relegated. Freddie Steele left the club by 'mutual consent' in February 1965. He was an uncle of David Steele, the Northants, Derbyshire and England cricketer.

STEELE, John

Born: Glasgow, 24 November 1916.
Inside-left   5ft 9in; 12st 2lb (1937).
Career: Lesmahngow Juniors; East fife; Ayr United; Barnsley June 1938 (£2,500), coach 1951, then manager March 1960-September 1971 and November 1972-April 1973, general manager September 1971-1982, director 1982-1984.

Honours: Division Four runners-up 1968; Division Three North champions 1939; Scottish League Division Two champions 1937.

Johnny Steele helped Ayr United to the Scottish League Division Two championship in 1936-37. He scored 17 goals in 39 games as Barnsley took the Third Division North title in 1938-39 and netted 53 in 80 wartime games for the Oakwell club. He was one of the last Barnsley players to return after the war, in which he served in the RAF in India. He lost his prime years due to the war and played only nine post-war games for the club.

Steele became a coach at Oakwell in 1951 and manager nine years later. The Colliers reached the quarter-finals of the FA Cup in 1961, losing to Leicester in a replay, and finished bottom of Division Three in 1964-65 but returned in 1967-68 as runners-up, five points behind champions Luton Town. Barnsley then rather unspectacularly consolidated their position until Steele became general manager in the early 1970s.

STEIN, Edwin

Born: Cape Town, South Africa, 28 September 1955.
Midfield   5ft 10in; 11st (1987).
Career: Edgware Town 1977; Luton Town 1978; Harrow Borough 1979; Dagenham 1981 (£20,000), Barnet July 1982; retired in 1991 to become assistant manager, then manager April-June 1993. Southend United assistant manager June 1993.

Honours: Division Three promotion 1993; England Youth international; Conference League Champions 1991; FA Representative.

Stein was offered a three-year contract in May 1993 after initially deciding to stay at Underhill rather than moving with his former boss, Barry Fry, to Southend United as his assistant. He therefore became the first black person to become a Football League manager. The 1992-93 season had been a traumatic one for Barnet. Amongst other things they were fined £50,000 for the way the club had kept its books. Barnet then faced an FA

inquiry into illegal payments to players and the non-payment of the fine. When Fry resigned with the departure of chairman Stan Flashman, Stein took over and steered the team to promotion to the Second Division at the end of only their second season in the League, despite players not always being paid on time. Stein had spent virtually all his playing career in non-League soccer. He did not make the grade at Luton, unlike his brother Brian who went on to play for England. Another brother, Mark, plays for Stoke. Dagenham paid a large fee for a non-League player of £20,000 when Eddie joined them. Stein played 493 games for Barnet, scoring 33 goals. His only Football League appearance came in Barnet's first-ever game in the League when they lost 7-4 at home to Crewe in August 1991, when Stein was almost 36. In the summer of 1993, with Barnet's future uncertain, he joined Fry at Southend after all.

STEIN, John CBE

Born: September 1923; Died: Cardiff, 10 September 1985.
Defender.

Career: Blantyre Victoria; Albion Rovers 1942; Llanelli 1950; Glasgow Celtic December 1951 (£1,200), player-coach 1955, retired as a player through injury 1956; Dunfermline manager 1960; Hibernian manager 1964-March 1965; Glasgow Celtic manager March 1965-May 1978; Leeds United manager August-October 1978; Scotland national team manager October 1978-September 1985.

Honours: Scottish League champions 1954, 1966, 1967, 1968, 1969, 1970, 1971, 1972, 1973, 1974; Premier League champions 1977; Scottish Cup winners 1954, 1961, 1965, 1967, 1969, 1971, 1972, 1974, 1977, runners-up 1966, 1970, 1973; Scottish League Cup winners 1966, 1967, 1968, 1969, 1970, 1975; runners-up 1971, 1972, 1973, 1976, 1977, 1978; European Cup winners 1967, runners-up 1970.

Jock Stein was one of the greatest managers in the history of Scottish football but stayed for just 44 days with a Football League club. That was Leeds United, whom he left to manage the Scottish national side. Stein did not become a full-time professional until he was 27, when he joined Celtic. He had worked as a miner whilst with Llanelli but led Celtic to the League and Cup double in 1954 before injury ended his playing career.

Stein took Dunfermline to the Scottish Cup in 1961 and after a brief period in charge at Hibs, he took over at Celtic Park. Stein took Celtic to the European Cup in 1967, when they defeated Internazionale 2-1 in Lisbon in the Final to become the first British club to lift the trophy. They also gained ten League titles, nine Scottish Cups and

six League Cups during his period in charge. In May 1978 he was offered the general manager's job after suffering a heart attack but chose to manage Leeds instead. Stein took Scotland to the 1982 World Cup finals but collapsed and died shortly after the Scots had beaten Wales in a dramatic game at Cardiff in 1985.

STEPHENSON, Clement

Born: New Delaval, County Durham, 6 February 1890; Died: 24 October 1961.
Inside-left   5ft 8in; 11st 3lb (1925).
Career: New Delaval Villa; West Stanley; Blyth Spartans; Durham City; Aston Villa March 1910 (£165); Stourbridge (loan) August 1910-February 1911; guest for Leeds City in World War One; Huddersfield Town March 1921 (£3,000), retired to become manager May 1929-May 1942.

Honours: England international (1 cap); Football League representative (3 caps); Football League champions 1924, 1925, 1926; FA Cup winners 1913, 1920, 1922, runners-up 1928, 1930, 1938.

Stephenson was involved in six FA Cup Finals, four as a player and two as a manager. He gained three winners' medals as a player, two of these coming in his days at Aston Villa. He also helped Huddersfield Town to three consecutive League titles in the 1920s and spent 21 years at Leeds Road as a player and manager.

Clem Stephenson was the brother of George and Jim, both of whom played for Aston Villa, and he, too, joined Villa in March 1910 after playing for New Delaval Villa, Blyth Spartans, West Stanley and Durham City. From August 1910 until February 1911, Villa sent him on loan to Stourbridge to develop as a player. He returned to Villa Park and made his debut the same month, scoring a goal against Tottenham Hotspur. He developed into a player who was a fine schemer, a brilliant strategist and an excellent marksman with a powerful shot in both feet. Stephenson went on to score 96 goals in 216 appearances for Villa and this included two appearances in the FA Cup Final. The first in 1913 was won 1-0, against Sunderland at Crystal Palace. Villa should have scored a second goal when Stephenson was brought down in the area but Charlie Wallace missed the spot-kick. The following season Villa finished runners-up in the First Division and also reached the semi-finals of the FA Cup. He played on the winning side again when Villa beat Huddersfield Town 1-0 in the 1920 FA Cup Final at Stamford Bridge.

Stephenson played as a guest for Leeds City during World War One and moved to Huddersfield Town in March 1921 for a £3,000 fee. He was not fast but a classical player who was shrewd,

poised and accurate. He weighted and judged his passes to perfection and was an unselfish player. Surprisingly, Stephenson gained only one cap against Wales in March 1924 when England lost 2-1 to Wales at Ewood Park. He also represented the Football League on three occasions.

Huddersfield were just about to embark on a hat-trick of League championships, from 1923 to 1926. They were lucky to win the title in 1923-24 on goal average from Cardiff City. The following season they conceded only 28 goals when taking the title, and in 1925-26 were undefeated for the first ten games and finished the season five points clear of Arsenal. Stephenson went on to score 50 goals in 275 appearances for Huddersfield. He played in his first losing FA Cup Final side in 1928, when Town lost 3-1 to Blackburn Rovers.

In May 1929, Stephenson retired to take over as manager of Huddersfield Town. A year later they were back at Wembley in the FA Cup Final, but lost 2-0 to Arsenal. His luck was still out in 1938 when Huddersfield lost 1-0 to Preston in the FA Cup Final, thanks to a penalty from George Mutch in the last minute of extra-time. Stephenson kept the club amongst the game's elite with a series of shrewd acquisitions, the most notable being George McLean and David Mangnall. He was very much his own man and displayed exceptional organising skills as a manager. The Town finished runners-up in the First Division to Arsenal in 1933-34, and also finished fourth in 1931-32 and third in 1935-36. Clem's brother, George, later managed Huddersfield Town from 1947 to 1952 and had been his assistant manager during the 1930s. Clem Stephenson resigned as manager in May 1942 and left football for good.

STEPHENSON, George Ternent

Born: New Delaval, County Durham, 3 September 1900; Died: Derby, 18 August 1971.
Inside-left   5ft 10in; 11st (1935).
Career: Northumberland Schools; New Delaval Villa; Leeds City August 1919; Aston Villa November 1919 (£250); Stourbridge (loan) August 1920-May 1921; Derby County November 1927; Sheffield Wednesday February 1931; Preston North End July 1933; Charlton Athletic May 1934 (£660), retired through injury and joined coaching staff in May 1937, assistant manager 1938; Huddersfield Town assistant manager, then manager August 1947-March 1952; licensee of Sportsman Inn, near Huddersfield, in 1954; Rolls-Royce factory worker 1957; Derby County 'A' team coach early 1960s.

Honours: England international (3 caps); English Junior international (1 cap); Division Three South champions 1935.

A brainy, cultured inside-forward, Stephenson scored 120 goals in 319 League appearances in his career. He twice scored four goals in a match for Derby and helped them to runners-up spot in Division One in 1930. Small in stature, Stephenson had an eye for goal. He scored a hat-trick for England in a 5-4 win against Belgium in May 1928 and helped Preston to runners-up position in the Second Division in 1933-34 with 16 goals. He was also in the Charlton team which climbed from the Third to the First Division in the 1930s.

As manager of Huddersfield Town, Stephenson had a constant struggle against relegation. He finally resigned in 1952 with the club heading for the Second Division. His son, Bob, played for Derby County, Shrewsbury and Rochdale and for Derbyshire and Hampshire as a wicketkeeper.

STEWARD, Alfred

Born: Manchester.
Goalkeeper 5ft 11½in; 11st 13lb (1927).
Career: Stalybridge Celtic; Manchester United 1919; Manchester North End June 1932; Altrincham manager in 1930s; Torquay United manager May 1938-May 1940.

As well as being a steady and reliable goalkeeper for Manchester United, Steward was also a fine cricketer who was on Lancashire's books for a while. He made his debut in October 1920, for United versus Preston in a 1-0 victory at Old Trafford, but did not become a regular until 1923-24.

He did not win a single honour during his time with the Reds but was ever-present when they won promotion, as runners-up, to the First Division in 1925. He let in 93 goals in 38 games when United were relegated again in 1931. Steward managed Altrincham for a period in the 1930s before taking over at Torquay United. The club finished 19th in the Southern Section in 1938-39, then played in the first wartime season before closing down in 1940.

STEWART, Fred

Died: Cardiff 1954.
Career: Stockport County manager August 1900-May 1911; Cardiff City manager May 1911-May 1933.

Honours: Division Two runners-up 1921; Southern League Division Two champions 1913; FA Cup winners 1927, runners-up 1925.

Fred Stewart took Cardiff City to two FA Cup Finals, in 1925 and 1927, and they also went very close to winning the League championship in 1923-24, blowing their chances in the last game of the season. He had taken the club from humble beginnings in the Second Division of the Southern League to the pinnacle of English soccer. However, just as quickly as they had risen to become a leading power in the country did they rapidly fall in to decline by the early 1930s.

Stewart was appointed secretary-manager of Stockport County just after they had been elected to the Football League in August 1900 and remained in that post until May 1911, when he moved to Cardiff City in a similar post. Sam Ormerod was in charge of team affairs from 1903 and 1905, otherwise Stewart had full control of the club. County struggled just to stay in the League and finally lost their place in 1904, when they were not re-elected and went to play in the Lancashire Combination. A year later they returned to the League but continued on with their struggles. Their best position in the Second Division was tenth in 1905-06.

Stewart was Cardiff City's first-ever secretary-manager and brought a wealth of experience and knowledge with him to Ninian Park. He appointed George Latham as trainer. His greatest capture was Billy Hardy from his former club. Hardy was to stay with the Bluebirds until 1932 and was one of the greatest players in their history. Cardiff entered the Southern League Division Two in 1911 and were champions in 1912-13, sustaining only one defeat. They did well in the top division and finished third in 1914-15 and fourth in 1919-20.

Cardiff entered the Football League in 1920 and went straight into Division Two. Stewart signed players from all over the country and had a number of internationals playing for him throughout the 1920s. In their first season they gained promotion to the First Division as runners-up on goal-average to Birmingham City. They also reached the semi-finals of the FA Cup, but lost to Wolves, 3-1 after a 0-0 draw. City finished fourth in the First Division in their first season in the top flight and were desperately unlucky not to clinch the League title in 1923-24. Needing to win the last game of the season to take the title, they were drawing 0-0 at Birmingham with minutes to go. Suddenly, they were awarded a penalty but Len Davies missed the spot-kick and they finished the season as runners-up to Huddersfield Town on goal-average.

Cardiff reached the FA Cup Final in 1925 but lost 1-0 to Sheffield United. Two years later they won the Cup and became the first and only club to take the trophy out of England. Arsenal were the favourites but, thanks to a goal from Hugh Ferguson, City won 1-0. This was the height of Stewart's success at Ninian Park, for within four years they found themselves in the Third Division South. They were relegated to the Second Division in 1928-29 and to the third in 1930-31. These were dark days for the club and Stewart retired in May 1933 after Cardiff could finish only 19th in the Southern Section. He concentrated on his other business interests after this and remained living in Cardiff until his death in 1954.

STILES, Norbert Peter

Born: Manchester, 18 May 1942.
Wing-half 5ft 6in; 11st 3lb (1963).

Career: Manchester & Lancashire Schools; Manchester United apprentice September 1957, professional June 1959; Middlesbrough May 1971 (£20,000); Preston North End August 1973 (£20,000), chief coach August 1975, then manager July 1977-June 1981; Vancouver Whitecaps (NASL) coach 1981-1984; West Bromwich Albion youth-team manager February 1984-June 1989 except when manager October 1985-February 1986; Manchester United youth-team coach 1989.

Honours: England international (28 caps); Under-23 international (3 caps); Youth international (6 caps); Schoolboy international (5 caps); Football League representative (3 caps); World Cup winners 1966; Football League champions 1965, 1967; Division Three promotion 1978; European Cup winners 1968.

A great competitor, Nobby Stiles became famous throughout the nation for his toothless grin after England took the World Cup in 1966. He made almost 400 appearances for Manchester United, in which he gained two League championship medals and also played in the club's European Cup triumph over Benfica at Wembley in 1968. United also reached the semi-final twice with Stiles in the side, in 1966 and 1969. He made his England debut against Scotland at Wembley in 1965.

Stiles was made captain when he joined Middlesbrough, but he was affected by injuries and loss of form. He was not so successful in management and was unable to put across his burning desire to win over to his players. He took Preston to promotion to Division Two in 1977-78 but lost his job when they were relegated in 1981. Stiles joined his brother-in-law, Johnny Giles, at The Hawthorns and succeeded him when he left but could not prevent their relegation in 1986.

STOCK,
Alexander William Alfred

Born: Peasedown St John, Somerset, 30 March 1917.
Inside-forward 5ft 9⅝in; 10st 10lb (1939).
Career: Wilmington Village; Redhill; Tottenham Hotspur amateur; Charlton Athletic 1936; Queen's Park Rangers February 1938; wartime guest for several clubs including Clapton Orient; Yeovil Town player-manager 1946-May 1949; Leyton Orient manager August 1949-February 1956; Arsenal assistant manager February-April 1956; Leyton Orient manager again April 1956-August 1957; AS Roma manager August-November 1957; Leyton Orient manager again February 1958-February 1959; Queen's Park Rangers manager August 1959-August 1968; Luton Town manager December 1968-April 1972; Fulham manager June 1972-December 1976; Queen's Park Rangers director April 1977, caretaker manager July 1978; AFC Bournemouth manager January 1979-December 1980, general manager until October 1981, director October 1981-1986.

Honours: Division Two runners-up 1968; Division Three South champions 1956; Division Three champions 1967, runners-up 1970; FA Cup runners-up 1975; Football League Cup winners 1967.

Dapper, smart, fastidious and much loved by his players, Alec Stock was always happiest managing smaller clubs. A master in the transfer market, Stock helped keep Leyton Orient solvent and also took them to the Third Division South title. He also took Queen's Park Rangers from the Third to the First Division and to a famous League Cup Final victory, Luton to promotion, and Fulham to their first-ever FA Cup Final in 1975.

Stock was born in Somerset on 30 March 1917. He attended a rugby-playing school and was later a trainee bank clerk before becoming a professional footballer. He played for Wilmington Village and Redhill before signing amateur forms for Tottenham Hotspur and then becoming a professional with Charlton Athletic, although he did not appear in the first team. In February 1938 he moved to Queen's Park Rangers, where he scored four goals in 16 appearances before war was declared in the summer of 1939. During the war, Stock played occasionally for QPR and guested for a number of clubs including Clapton Orient. At the start of the war he joined the Royal

Armoured Corps and eventually rose to the rank of major.

At the age of only 29, Stock was appointed player-manager of Yeovil Town in 1946 and took them to the fifth round of the FA Cup in 1949, when they beat star-studded Sunderland 2-1 in a famous victory on their sloping pitch at The Huish. This achievement pushed Stock into the limelight and Leyton Orient persuaded him to become their boss in August 1949.

Stock brought some great times to Brisbane Road. In 1951-52, they had a fine FA Cup run beating Everton 3-1 and Birmingham City 1-0 before losing at home to Arsenal, 3-0 in front of a 30,000 crowd. They reached the quarter-final in 1953-54 and were very disappointed when they lost 1-0 to Port Vale at Leyton Stadium. The Os finished runners-up the following season and champions of the Third Division South in 1956, when they scored 106 goals during an eventful season. In February 1956, with Orient top of the table, Stock had left for Highbury to become Arsenal's assistant manager under Tom Whittaker. He lasted only 53 days before returning to Orient to see them to promotion. Stock missed being in total charge too much to feel happy at Highbury.

In August 1957, Stock accepted a lucrative offer to become manager of Italian club AS Roma, but he stayed in Italy just three months before returning to Orient for a third spell in charge in February 1957. Les Gore, his assistant manager for many years, had been caretaker manager on both occasions when Alec had been away. Stock stayed another year at the East London club.

After six months out of football, Stock was appointed manager of QPR in August 1959. Rangers finished third in Division Three in 1960-61 and fourth the following season, scoring 111 goals but conceding 73. In October 1962 the club moved from their cosy but run-down ground at Loftus Road to the massive White City Stadium which was capable of holding 60,000 fans. It was a terrible move for the club as the attendances were poor and in such a large ground there was little atmosphere. Rangers moved back to Loftus Road at the end of the season.

Things began to look up after the arrival of Jim Gregory in late 1964. He became QPR's chairman in March 1965 and Stock was given money to spend on new blood. The manager had also developed an excellent youth scheme and some exciting players were beginning to break into the first team, such as Dave Clement, Frank Sibley and the Morgan twins. On top of this, Stock bought Les Allen from Spurs, Ian Watson from Chelsea, Keith Sanderson from Plymouth and Jim Langley from Fulham during the summer of 1965. In March 1966, Stock signed a future star of the Bush, Rodney Marsh, for the giveaway fee of £15,000, from Fulham. Marsh helped in a good late run that season but Rangers just missed out on promotion. The 1966-67 season was to be a great one for QPR and Stock. They took the Third Division title with ease, 12 points clear of Middlesbrough, and also won the first League Cup Final to be played at Wembley. They beat First Division West Brom 3-2 after being two goals down. As near neighbours Fulham plummeted from the First to the Third Division, Rangers went in the opposite direction. They finished runners-up to Ipswich Town in 1967-68 to enter the top flight for the first time in their history.

He never selected a First Division team for QPR, however, because he resigned before the start of the season after pressures built up behind the scenes at Loftus Road. He was also suffering from ill health caused by a wartime injury when a bazooka blew up near him, injuring his back.

Stock was not out of work for long. Five months later he became manager of Luton Town and soon had the Hatters heading for promotion. In 1969-70 they finished runners-up in the Third Division behind his former club, Orient. Stock had made another steal from Fulham when he signed Malcolm Macdonald for just £17,000 in the summer of 1969. 'Super Mac' developed into a prolific scorer who was later sold to Newcastle United for £180,000. Luton consolidated their position in Division Two and might have gone up again, but for financial problems at the club. In April 1972 Stock resigned, stating that he had become tired of the travelling from his Epsom home.

Two months later Stock took over as boss at Craven Cottage. He soon entered the transfer market, signing Alan Mullery from Spurs and Paul Went from Charlton for large fees. But in December 1973, he was forced to sell Went and Steve Earle to balance the books. The financial problems at Fulham were caused by the huge outlay on a new stand which almost crippled the club. His greatest achievement at Fulham was taking the Cottagers to their first FA Cup Final, at Wembley in 1975. It took 11 matches to reach the Final, where Fulham lost 2-0 to West Ham. Their side was a mix of youth and experience. Bobby Moore had come to the Cottage near the end his career and was an inspiration that season.

More financial problems and the ousting of the old board of directors at the club ultimately led to Stock's departure in December 1976. His old-world manners were in marked contrast to the aggressive, financially motivated approach of the new regime and his services were dispensed with.

In April 1977, Stock became a director at Queen's Park Rangers and also acted as caretaker manager in July 1978 after the departure of Frank Sibley. The following January, he returned to management as the boss of Bournemouth and stayed in charge until December 1980, when moved upstairs to become general manager until October 1981. Stock was also a director of the club after this until 1986, when he retired. He retains an interest in football today through his local club, Swanage Town & Herston.

STOKOE, Robert

Born: Mickley, 21 September 1930.
Centre-half   6ft; 12st 2lb (1959).
Career: Spen Juniors; Newcastle United

September 1947; Bury player-manager December 1961-August 1965, retired as a player May 1964; Charlton Athletic manager August 1965-September 1967; Rochdale manager October 1967-October 1968; Carlisle United manager October 1968-January 1970; Blackpool manager December 1970-November 1972; Sunderland manager November 1972-October 1976; Bury manager again November 1977-May 1978; Blackpool manager again May 1978-August 1979; Rochdale manager again November 1979-June 1980; Carlisle United manager August-November 1979, then manager again September 1980-August 1985 and October 1985-May 1986; Sunderland caretaker manager April-June 1987; Chelsea scout in 1991.
Honours: Division Two champions 1976; Division Three promotion 1982; FA Cup winners 1955, 1973.

Bob Stokoe is one of the few managers to play for and manage an FA Cup winning side. He appeared for Newcastle United in their 1955 Final success and managed Sunderland to their shock victory over mighty Leeds United in 1973. Stokoe played most of his career with the Magpies but managed six different clubs in 12 separate spells. He was in charge at Carlisle on three separate occasions and also in charge at Bury, Blackpool, Sunderland and Rochdale twice but never managed his great love, Newcastle United.

Stokoe made his League debut for Newcastle on Christmas Day 1950, at centre-forward against Middlesbrough, and scored a goal. He became a regular when he switched to centre-half and went on to play 287 games for the club, scoring five goals. He gained an FA Cup winners' medal when Newcastle beat Manchester City 3-1 in the 1955 Final.

In December 1961, he was appointed player-manager of Bury, moving to the club in part exchange for John McGrath. A dedicated professional, Stokoe had plenty of self-discipline who was strong in the tackle and a good passer of the ball. He played 81 League games for Bury before retiring in May 1964. As player-manager he took the Shakers to the semi-finals of the League Cup in 1962-63, where they lost to Birmingham City. They also finished eighth in the Second Division that season. Stokoe signed the young Colin Bell in July 1963, but debts of over £30,000 forced him to sell players such as George Jones to Blackburn for £30,000.

Stokoe resigned in August 1965 and immediately took over at Charlton Athletic. They struggled against relegation under him and when he sold Mike Bailey to Wolves for £40,000, the

struggle became even more uphill. Charlton were so short of players that Stokoe made a comeback in the Reserves in 1966. He then angered the fans when he sold Billy Bonds to West Ham United for £49,500 in May 1967. Stokoe was sacked in September 1967 and was paid compensation by the club after he departed.

The following month he became manager of Rochdale and in 1967-68, they just avoided re-election for the third season running, by two points. He had a mass clear out of players in the summer of 1968, but with the club getting off to a fine start the following season, Stokoe resigned and took over at Carlisle United, who were then in the Second Division. He took them to the semi-final of the League Cup in 1969-70, beating Chelsea 1-0 on the way before they lost 4-2 on aggregate to West Brom.

With Carlisle riding high in the Second Division in December 1970, he was offered the manager's post at Blackpool. Stokoe could not prevent the Seasiders' relegation from the First Division at the end of that season, when they finished bottom with only four wins, whilst Carlisle finished fourth. Blackpool won the Anglo-Italian trophy at the beginning of the 1970-71 season but Bob was unable to get the Seasiders back into the top flight. He also sold star player Tony Green to Newcastle United for £140,000, part of a mass clear-out.

In November 1972, Stokoe became manager of Sunderland. It was to be a great move for him. They fought their way to the FA Cup Final that season and beat Leeds United 1-0 at Wembley, thanks to a goal from Ian Porterfield. Jim Montgomery made some great saves and few will forget Stokoe charging across the pitch to hug his 'keeper at the final whistle. It was a great achievement by the Wearsiders and their manager. Sunderland entered European competiton for the first time but lost to Sporting Lisbon in the second round of the Cup-winners' Cup.

Stokoe was busy on the transfer market and sold many of his star players such as Dave Watson, Dennis Tueart and Tony Towers. It took him longer than it should have done to get Sunderland back into the First Division, mainly due to the sale of so many fine players. He finally achieved promotion in 1975-76, when they won the Second Division championship. They also reached the quarter-finals of the FA Cup but lost to Crystal Palace at Roker Park. It all went wrong the following season and after only four points from nine games, Stokoe resigned in October 1976, a decision he later regretted.

It was over a year before he returned to management for a second spell in charge of Bury in November 1977. It was not a happy time for Stokoe, Bury struggled in Division Three and he resigned in May 1978 to take over again at Blackpool. He did not set the world alight at Bloomfield Road either and in August 1979 was sacked.

In November 1979, Stokoe returned to Rochdale for another spell as manager but they finished 92nd in the League. He left, saying the job was too big for him. At this point it looked as though Stokoe's career in football had come to an end, but another of his former clubs, Carlisle United, gave him a scouting job. In September 1980 he was appointed manager at Brunton Park and was back doing what he loved best. He took United back to the Second Division in 1981-82, as runners-up to

Burnley on goal-average, and consolidated their position there.

In August 1985, Stokoe decided that it was time to retire and appointed his assistant 'Pop' Robson as his successor. This arrangement did not last long and within two months Stokoe was back in charge again. However, Carlisle were relegated that season and Bob finally resigned in May 1986. He returned to Roker Park briefly as caretaker manager from April to June 1987 and in recent years scouted for his former player and Chelsea manager, Ian Porterfield.

STOLLERY, Arthur

Died: February 1955.
Career: Chelsea trainer 1939-1946; RAF commission in war; Notts County manager June 1946-February 1949.

Stollery was appointed as first-team trainer at Chelsea in 1939, by manager Billy Birrell in succession to Jack Whitley. He made his name as a PE expert in the RAF and returned to Stamford Bridge after the war. He soon made the headlines after taking over at Notts County, when he flew to Canada to sign forward Fred Whittaker. He also caused a sensation when he signed England's regular centre-forward, Tommy Lawton, as the striker dropped from the First to the Third Division. Attendances boomed at Meadow Lane but success came only after Stollery's departure due to ill health.

STORER, Harry

Born: West Derby, Liverpool, 2 February 1898; Died: Derby, 1 September 1967.
Inside-forward/Wing-half/Utility
5ft 9in; 11st 10lb (1925).
Career: Heanor Secondary School; Heanor Wesleyans; Marehay; Codnor Park; Riddings St James; Eastwood Bible Class; Ripley Town; Eastwood Town; Notts County amateur 1918; Grimsby Town February 1919; Derby County March 1921 (£2,500); Burnley February 1929 (£4,250), retired May 1931; Coventry City manager June 1931-June 1945; Birmingham City manager June 1945-November 1948; Coventry City manager November 1948-December 1953; Derby County manager June 1955-May 1962; Everton scout; also cricket for Derbyshire 1920-1936.
Honours: England international (2 caps); Division Two champions 1948; Division Three South champions 1936; Division Three North champions 1957; Football League South champions 1946.

Harry Storer never won any major club honours but he took each side that he managed to promotion and was unlucky never to be given a job with any of the leading clubs in the country. A no-nonsense, forthright character

who had no time for players who did not give their all, Storer was hard and aggressive but players always knew where they stood with him. Some could not stand him, but many others did not mind his bullying, domineering style. They also found him knowledgeable about soccer and very fair, with an inborn sense of humour.

Blunt, often to the point of rudeness, Storer had a tendency to frighten people when he first met them. Today, he is still remembered as the sharp-tongued football man with a heart of gold and he is regarded by Forest manager Brian Clough as his greatest teacher of the game. Stories about Storer are legendary. Once Sheffield United boss Joe Mercer complained about five Derby players 'clogging'. The Rams manager asked for their names and Mercer inquired, "Are you going to discipline them?" Harry's response was typical. He answered: "No, I'm going to give the other six a rollicking for not trying hard enough."

Storer was born in the West Derby district of Liverpool and came from a sporting family. His father kept goal for Woolwich Arsenal and Liverpool as well as playing cricket for Derbyshire. His uncle, William, played football for Derby County and cricket for Derbyshire and England. Harry junior also played cricket for Derbyshire and scored 13,513 runs, including 18 centuries, at an average of 27.63 between 1920 and 1936. He also took over 200 wickets and was in their 1936 County Championship winning side.

Storer played local football in Derbyshire and Nottinghamshire before signing amateur forms for Notts County in 1918 at the age of 20. After the war he became a professional with Grimsby Town. He made his debut in August 1919 against Stockport County. Storer was a hard player, a grafter and a tough tackler. When playing in the attack he was an unselfish and intelligent player who possessed an excellent shot.

After scoring 20 goals in 68 appearances for Grimsby, he moved to Derby County in March 1921, for a large fee of £4,500. Most of his games for the Rams were at wing-half but he had an outstanding season in 1923-24 when he appeared at inside-left and scored 27 goals including four in an 8-0 win over Bristol City. He gained two England caps, the first coming in Paris against France in 1924. Storer played 274 games for the Rams, scoring 63 goals, before moving to Burnley in February 1929 for a fee of £4,250. When he retired in May 1931, Storer had made a total of 396 appearances and scored 88 goals.

Storer was 33 when he became manager of Coventry City in June 1931 and had given up a regular place in Burnley's First Division line-up for his chance. Clarrie Bourton, a reliable goalscorer, was signed from Bristol City and Coventry were soon going for promotion to Division Two. They finished runners-up in 1934 and Third in 1935 and finally won the Southern Section title and promotion in 1936. The following season Coventry finished eighth, and then fourth in the two seasons before the outbreak of war in 1939.

Many were surprised when Harry Storer decided to move to Birmingham City as manager in June 1945. His tactical knowledge and astuteness transformed a side without stars into one with strength and purpose which developed an impregnable defence. Storer took the Blues to promotion in 1947-48, as Second Division cham-

pions, when they conceded only 24 goals. In his first season in charge, Birmingham had been champions of the League South in the last season of wartime football and had also reached the semi-final of the FA Cup, where they lost to Derby County.

In November 1948, Storer returned to Highfield Road, saying he had greatly missed the club. His second spell in charge at Coventry was not as successful as he was unable to find a winning combination. Coventry were relegated to Division Three in 1952. Overwork had made him ill and when he was sacked in December 1953, it was a very acrimonious departure. He was out of the game for 18 months and did some scouting and worked in holiday camps in the summer, organising sports events.

He hankered to get back into management and in June 1955 got his wish when Derby County, who he had played for in the 1920s, invited him to return to the Baseball Ground as manager. The Rams were in the doldrums as they had just been relegated to the Third Division North. Storer signed Reg Ryan from West Brom and the veteran Irish international travelled to Derby each day from Coventry in Storer's car as the two men plotted Derby's return. Ryan proved an influential skipper of a Derby side which was a blend of skill and cold steel. They finished runners-up to Grimsby Town in 1955-56 and the following season won the championship to return to the Second Division. Storer reduced the club's overdraft from £60,000 to £23,000 by the time he left the Baseball Ground. His biggest signing was Brighton centre-forward Bill Curry, for £12,000. Storer always liked players with skill, guts and character and Curry fitted this mould. After leaving Derby County in May 1962, Storer did some scouting for Everton and was still scouting when he died in Derby in September 1967, just after Brian Clough had taken over Derby County.

STRAWSON, John Henry

Born: East Firsby Grange, Lincolnshire.
Career: Referee 1882, Football League lists 1888-1905; Midland League honorary secretary for many years, president in 1904; member of Football League management committee; Lincoln City honorary secretary 1888-1907, chairman from 1899, then secretary-manager August 1907-1914.

Strawson played a leading role at Lincoln City at the turn of the century. Originally he was the club's honorary secretary, then became chairman and finally he also ran the team. He had many years of experience as a referee and was on the League's lists from its formation. Lincoln City lost their Football League status twice under Strawson's control, in 1908 and 1911, but on both occasions they regained it within a year.

The Imps usually struggled near the foot of the table but did finish in eighth place in 1912-13. They also reached the second round of the FA Cup in 1911-12, when playing in the Midland League, before losing 2-1 at Wolves. Strawson had taken over as manager when his predecessor David Calderhead moved to Chelsea to become their manager.

STRINGER, David Ronald

Born: Great Yarmouth, 15 October 1944.
Defender 5ft 10in; 11st 6lb (1970).
Career: Alderman Leach School; Arse-

nal Juniors; Crystal Palace trailist; Gorleston juniors; Norwich City May 1963; Cambridge United September 1976; Norwich City youth-team manager 1980, then manager December 1987-May 1992.
Honours: England Youth international.

A superbly balanced player, Dave Stringer has proved a great club servant, both on and off the field for Norwich City. He is third in the all-time appearance list for the club with 497/2 games in which he scored 22 goals. Stringer was one of the strong men of the defence and excellent in the air.

As manager, he took the Canaries to the semi-finals of the FA Cup in 1989, where they lost 1-0 to Everton at Villa Park. That season they also finished fourth in the First Division after leading the table up to December. They reached the quarter-finals of the FA Cup in 1991, losing to Forest. There was much talk that Stringer's job was on the line in 1992, as Norwich struggled against relegation and he moved upstairs at Carrow Road, being replaced as manager by Mike Walker in the summer of 1992, after Norwich had narrowly avoided relegation. This was despite reaching the semi-final of the FA Cup where they lost to Sunderland 1-0 at Hillsborough. In 1992-93 they were Premier League championship contenders.

STRINGER, Frederick George

Born: 1875; Died: January 1940 (aged 64).
Career: Hull City manager September 1914-July 1916; president of East Riding County FA.
Honours: East Riding representative.

Stringer was a club director when he took over as manager at Hull City after the outbreak of World War One. Attendances at Anlaby Road slumped and players left the club to join up. Hull had a good run in the FA Cup in 1915 and although Stringer stood down in July 1916, he continued to be involved in the running of the club until the end of the war. He had been an enthusiastic player and represented East Riding. After the war he devoted much of his time to the administration of the East Riding County FA, eventually becoming its president.

STUTTARD, John Ellis

Born: Burnley, 24 April 1920; Died: Burnley 1984.
Wing-half 5ft 9in; 11st (1951).
Career: Burnley Reserves; Plymouth Argyle September 1938; Torquay United September 1947-1951; Swindon

assistant trainer and chief scout early 1960s; Plymouth Argyle assistant trainer, manager November 1961-October 1963, then assistant manager; Exeter City chief scout December 1964, then manager February 1965-June 1966; Plymouth Argyle chief scout 1968, then manager March 1970-October 1972 and chief scout again until 1982.

As a manager, Stuttard was cool, calm and relaxed despite the pressures of the job. In his first season in charge at Plymouth, they looked like going for promotion at Easter but after only one win in the last six games, their chance disappeared. Stuttard stepped down to assistant manager after a disastrous start to the 1963-64 season, with only one win in the first 16 games.

He was not a success at Exeter City and for the last three months was in charge in name only, with trainer Jock Basford running the club. Studdard's resignation came as no surprise and he was brought back to Plymouth by Billy Bingham, as chief scout. He was given money to spend in his second spell as manager but could not find success. Stuttard lost much of his playing career to the war. After leaving Home Park he made 82 League appearances for Torquay United.

SUART, Ronald

Born: Kendal, 18 November 1920.
Full-back/Centre-half
5ft 11½in; 12st 6lb (1951).

Career: Netherfield; Blackpool January 1939; Blackburn Rovers September 1949; Wigan Athletic player-manager September 1955-1956; Scunthorpe United manager cs 1956-May 1958; Blackpool manager May 1958-February 1967;

Chelsea assistant manager April 1967, caretaker manager October 1967 and manager October 1974-April 1975, general manager April 1975-1978 and chief coach until February 1983; Wimbledon chief scout in 1992.

Honours: Division Three North champions 1958.

Suart made 280 appearances for Blackpool and Blackburn, mostly at full-back although his favourite position was centre-half. As a manager, he was a sincere and quietly-spoken man with a keen eye for young talent. He steered Scunthorpe United into Division Two as Northern Section champions in 1957-58, then moved to Blackpool.

They finished eighth in the First Division and reached the quarter-finals of the FA Cup in 1958-59. Suart fought a constant battle against relegation after this and lost his job after relegation in 1967. Shortly afterwards he started a 16-year period in various capacities at Stamford Bridge. He was initially assistant to Tommy Docherty and succeeded Dave Sexton as manager in 1974. Chelsea were relegated to Division Two at the end of the 1974-75 season and Suart became general manager.

SUMMERBEE, Michael George

Born: Cheltenham, 15 December 1942.
Outside-right 5ft 10in; 11st 9lb (1963).
Career: Naunton Park School, Gloucester; Cheltenham Schools; Baker Street Youth Club (Cheltenham); Swindon Town apprentice August 1959, professional March 1960; Manchester City August 1965 (£30,000); Burnley June 1975 (£25,000); Blackpool December 1976; Stockport County August 1977 and player-manager March 1978-October 1979; Mossley November 1980.

Honours: England international (8 caps); Under-23 international (1 cap); Football League representative (1 cap); Football League champions 1968; Division Two champions 1966; FA Cup winners 1969; Football League Cup winners 1970, runners-up 1974; European Cup-winners' Cup winners 1970 (awarded medal despite missing Final through injury).

In his younger days, Mike Summerbee was a traditional right winger but eventually began to assume a more versatile role as a midfielder and created many chances for his colleagues. Summerbee was Joe Mercer's first signing when he became manager of Manchester City. Mercer had played alongside Mike's father, George, whilst with Aldershot during the war. Summerbee won many honours with City after helping them out of Division Two. He gained a League championship medal, helped City win the FA Cup and League Cup and also the European Cup-winners' Cup in 1970.

He had made his League debut for Swindon at 16 years of age and helped them gain promotion to Division Two in 1963. Summerbee made his England debut against Scotland in February 1968. He moved to Burnley after making 441/2 appearances for City in which he scored 67 goals. He had little success as manager of Stockport County and resigned after a poor start to the 1979-80 season. Father of Nicky Summerbee of Swindon Town.

SUMMERS, Gerald Thomas F.

Born: Small Heath, Birmingham, 4 October 1933.
Wing-half 5ft 9in; 11st 4lb (1963).

Career: Erdington Albion 1948; West Bromwich Albion amateur April 1950, professional August 1951; Sheffield United May 1957 (£3,000); Hull City April 1964 (£11,000); Walsall October 1965 (£10,000), retired May 1967, then coach from February 1967; Wolverhampton Wanderers coach August 1967; Oxford United manager July 1969-September 1975; Gillingham manager October 1975-May 1981; Southampton scout 1981; West Bromwich Albion chief coach October 1981-April 1982; Leicester City assistant manager and coach October 1982-December 1986; Derby County chief scout and youth-team manager December 1986.

Honours: FA tour of Far East and USA 1962.

A cool and collected wing-half with great stamina, who was usually unruffled and precise in his passing, Gerry Summers made 260 appearances for Sheffield United and helped them regain First Division status in 1961. He made his League debut for West Brom against Manchester United on Christmas Eve 1955.

After coaching at Walsall and Wolves, Summers took his first managerial position with Oxford United. He kept them in the Second Division and they had a good run in the League Cup in his first season in charge but he was sacked in September 1975 with Oxford bottom of Division Two. Gillingham went close to promotion in 1979 but otherwise he did not set the soccer world alight at the Priestfield Stadium and was finally sacked.

SUTTON, David W.

Born: Tarleton, Lancashire, 21 January 1957.
Defender 6ft 1in; 12st 7lb (1989).
Career: Plymouth Argyle apprentice October 1973, professional July 1974; Reading (loan) November 1977; Huddersfield Town March 1978 (£15,000); Bolton Wanderers June 1985-cs 1987 (£12,000); Rochdale August 1988, caretaker manager March 1989 and then assistant manager, retired through injury May 1989, appointed manager February 1991.

Honours: Division Four champions 1980.

Sutton formed an excellent central defensive partnership with Keith Hanvey at Huddersfield Town, for whom he made 284 appearances, scoring 15 goals. The Terriers moved from the Fourth to the Second Division between 1980 and 1983. Sutton made 65/2 appearances for Plymouth, mainly in

the Second Division. He was ever-present when the Terriers won the Fourth Division championship in 1979-80 but suffered from long periods out through injury and missed the entire 1984-85 season due to this.

He appeared in relegation and promotion sides for Bolton before his playing career ended prematurely due to injury. At Rochdale, Sutton was initially caretaker manager between Danny Bergera and Terry Dolan before becoming the latter's assistant. Later, he was given full control after Dolan's departure to Hull City. Rochdale just missed out on the Fourth Division play-offs in 1992 after losing their last two games of the season.

SUTTON, Melvyn Charles

Born: Birmingham, 13 February 1946.
Half-back 5ft 10in; 11st 10lb (1970).
Career: Aston Villa amateur; Cardiff City December 1967; Wrexham July 1972 (£15,000), player-assistant manager cs 1978, then player-manager June 1981-May 1982; Crewe Alexandra August 1982; King's Heath manager in 1989; Ipswich Town scout.

Honours: Division Three champions 1978; Welsh Cup winners 1975, 1978, runners-up 1979.

Sutton's appearance, all-round shoulders and hunched, belied his footballing ability. He also seemed to have plenty of rows with referees during his career. Sutton made 135/3 appearances for Cardiff City before being surprisingly sold to Wrexham for £15,000. At the Racecourse, he proved a great bargain and made 355/5 League appearances for Wrexham, scoring 21 goals. He helped Wrexham to the Third Division championship in 1977-78 and they also reached the sixth round of the FA Cup that season. Sutton played in two winning Welsh Cup Final sides for Wrexham and regularly in European competition. Wrexham were relegated to Division Three at the end of Sutton's season in charge.

SWIFT, George Harold

Born: St George's, Wellington, c.1875.
Left-back 5ft 9in; 13st (1906).
Career: St George's Swifts; Wellington Town 1885; Stoke trialist 1886; Wellington St George's; Crewe Alexandra 1888; Wolverhampton Wanderers cs 1891; Loughborough cs 1894; Leicester Fosse August 1896; Notts County June 1902; Leeds City trainer cs 1904 (1 app in March 1906); Chesterfield secretary 1907-1910; Southampton manager April 1911-April 1912.

Honours: Football League representative; FA Cup winners 1893.

Swift, who appeared in the Football Alliance for Crewe, played in the 1893 FA Cup Final with Wolves, who beat Everton 1-0. He was the only Loughborough player ever to win a senior representative honour when he appeared for the Football League against the Irish League in 1895. An inspirationally consistent captain for Fosse, he was ever-present in four of his six seasons with the club.

Swift had one game for Leeds City, in an emergency on the left wing against Chelsea in March 1906. Chesterfield had to seek re-election in his first two seasons in charge but were voted out of the League in 1909. All his new recruits at Southampton proved failures and they had their poorest season ever in 1911-12, finishing in a lowly 16th place with Swift resigning.

SWINDIN, George Hedley

Born: Campsall, near Doncaster, 4 December 1914.
Goalkeeper 5ft 10in; 10st 10lb (1937).
Career: Rotherham YMCA; Rotherham United amateur; Bradford City February 1933; Arsenal April 1936 (£4,000); Peterborough United player-manager February 1954-June 1958; Arsenal manager July 1958-May 1962; Norwich City manager May-October 1962; Cardiff City manager October 1962-April 1964; Kettering Town manager July 1965; Corby Town until October 1970 and managed a garage business in the town.

Honours: Football League champions 1938, 1948, 1953; FA Cup winners 1950, runners-up 1952; London Combination champions 1938, 1939; Midland League champions three times; Welsh Cup winners 1963.

A coolly efficient, brave and agile goalkeeper, George Swindin was one of Arsenal's best-ever 'keepers. He moved to Highbury after only 26 League games for Bradford City and gained a League championship medal in 1937-38, despite only 17 games for the club. Unlucky not to win international honours, he was ever-present when Arsenal were again champions in 1947-48 and played 14 games when they won it again in 1952-53. Swindin played in two FA Cup Finals for the Gunners, picking up a winners' medal in 1950 when they beat Liverpool 2-0.

He took Peterborough United to three Midlands League titles before returning to Highbury as manager but was unable to find much success there, in contrast to neighbours Spurs who were winning just about everything in sight. Swindin was in charge for only 20 games at Norwich City when he received a more lucrative offer from Cardiff City. John Charles was signed from Roma, against Swindin's wishes, and he was sacked after 18 months of struggle. They did win the Welsh Cup, though, entering Europe for the first time.

SYMON, James Scotland

Born: Errol near Perth, 9 May 1911; Died: 30 April 1985.
Wing-half 5ft 11in; 13st 4lb (1933).
Career: Perth North End; Dundee Violet; Dundee 1930; Portsmouth August 1935 (£7,000); Glasgow Rangers August 1938, retired 1947; East Fife manager 1947-1953; Preston North End manager March 1953-August 1954; Glasgow Rangers manager June 1954-

November 1967; Partick Thistle manager September 1968-April 1970, then general manager; also a qualified architect and played cricket for Perthshire.

Honours: Scotland international (1 cap); Junior international (1 cap); Scottish League champions 1939, 1956, 1957, 1959, 1961, 1963, 1964; Scottish League Division Two champions 1948; Scottish Cup winners 1960, 1962, 1963, 1964, 1966, runners-up 1950; Scottish League Cup winners 1948, 1950, 1961, 1962, 1964, 1965, runners-up 1946, 1958, 1966, 1967; FA Cup runners-up 1954; European Cup-winners' Cup runners-up 1967.

Scott Symon made his name as a wing-half with Dundee in the 1930s before moving south to join Pompey, who paid £7,000 for him plus Lewis Morgan. He gained a Scottish League championship medal with Rangers in 1938-39 and steered East Fife into Division One when he became manager of that club. They reached the semi-final of the Scottish Cup in 1949 and lost 3-0 in the Final to Rangers in 1950. They also finished third in Division One in 1951-52 and 1952-53. Symon took Preston to an FA Cup Final in 1954 but they lost 3-2 to West Brom at Wembley.

He moved to Ibrox after this and took Rangers to six League titles, five Scottish Cups and four League Cup victories. They also reached two European Cup-winners' Cup Final, losing 4-1 on aggregate to Fiorentina in 1961 and 1-0 to Bayern Munich in Nurenberg in 1967. He came in for a lot of criticism after this and left the club soon afterwards. Symon represented Scotland at both football and cricket.

TAGG, Ernest

Born: Crewe, 15 September 1917.
Inside-right.
Career: Crewe Alexandra October 1937; Wolverhampton Wanderers May 1938 (£1,200); Bournemouth & Boscombe Athletic May 1939; Carlisle United November 1948; Crewe Alexandra trainer 1951, assistant manager, manager November 1964-cs 1971, secretary until 1972, then caretaker manager December 1974-January 1975, director 1976-83.

Honours: Division Four promotion 1968.

Ernie Tagg's playing career, like those of many of his generation, was ruined by the war. After scoring seven goals in 19 games for Crewe, he moved to Wolves where he made just one appearance. After the war Tagg signed for Bournemouth and made another 80 appearances, scoring eight goals, then went to Carlisle United, where he rarely played in the first team.

He worked as a milkman when part-time trainer of Crewe Alexandra in the 1950s and took Crewe to promotion to Division Three in 1967-68, when they

finished fourth but were immediately relegated the following season. Shortly after he rejoined the club in 1965, the Football League put a ban on incoming transfers because Crewe owed money to Port Vale and Northampton. In 1967, he sold John Mahony to Stoke, for a club record £19,500, and with the money the club bought the lease on their Gresty Road ground. Crewe won £30,000 as runners-up of the Ford Sporting League in 1970. Tagg was on the board of directors until 1983.

TALBOT, Brian Ernest

Born: Ipswich, 21 July 1953.
Midfield   5ft 10in; 12st (1975).
Career: Ipswich & Suffolk Schoolboys; Ipswich Town apprentice July 1970, professional August 1972; Toronto Metros (Canada) (loan) in early 1970s; Arsenal January 1979 (£450,000); Watford June 1985 (£25,000); Stoke City October 1986 (£25,000); PFA chairman until November 1988; West Bromwich Albion January 1988, then manager November 1988-January 1991; sports reporter for Capital Radio January 1991; Fulham as player March 1991; Aldershot player-manager March-November 1991; Sudbury Town player 1992; Joint owner of Kettering Town 1992.

Honours: England international (6 caps); Under-21 international (1 cap); 'B' international (6 caps); FA Cup winners 1978, 1979, runners-up 1980; European Cup-winners' Cup runners-up 1980.

Talbot was a tireless worker with skill and determination, whose driving enthusiasm and rugged committment did not diminish over a career in which he played almost 700 games. Talbot has the unique distinction of winning FA Cup medals with two different clubs in successive years. Ipswich beat Arsenal 1-0 in the 1978 Final and the following year he played in the Gunners' side which beat Manchester United.

Talbot played 315/11 games for the Gunners, scoring 61 goals. He played in the 1980 European Cup-winners' Cup Final, which they lost to Valencia, 5-4 on penalties. He qualified as an FA coach in 1980, probably one of the youngest players ever to do so. Initially, Talbot took over at The Hawthorns as caretaker manager but was soon appointed permanently. They were top of Division Two in January 1989, but slumped to finish ninth. Talbot was sacked after an FA Cup defeat against Woking at the Hawthorns, a great humiliation for a once great club. He did not last very long in charge at Aldershot, leaving when the club looked on the point of folding.

Talbot almost played in a Wembley Final in 1992 but Sudbury Town lost to Guiseley in the semi-final of the FA Vase. He was part of a consortium which owned Kettering Town for a short period from March 1992.

TANN, Bertram James

Born: Plaistow, London, 4 May 1914;
Died: Bristol, 7 July 1972.
Right-half/Inside-right   6ft; 11st 5lb (1935).
Career: East Ham Schools; Essex County FA; Clapton Orient amateur; Romford 1933; Charlton Athletic February 1934, career ended by injury in 1939; Erith & Belvedere coach, then manager September 1945; Bristol Rovers coach February 1948, then manager January 1950-April 1968, then general manager-secretary until July 1972.

Honours: Division Three South cham-

pions 1953; Football League long-service medal.

Ernie Tann spent over 18 years as manager of Bristol Rovers. One of 11 children, he started his working life as a painter at the Dorchester Hotel. He joined Charlton Athletic and played only 19 games for the club before his career was ended by injury. A shrewd tactician, Rovers reached the sixth round of the FA Cup in 1951 before losing to Newcastle and in 1958 they again reached the quarter-finals. Tann turned a team of local recruits and free transfer signings into one of the leading sides in the Second Division. Rovers won the Third Division South championship in 1952-53, which included a run of 27 games without defeat, and just missed promotion to Division One in 1955-56, being four points behind runners-up Leeds United. Tann and Rovers were badly hit by the abolition of the maximum wage, as many of the better players left the club for bigger wages. Rovers were relegated to Division Three in 1962, although Tann was still held with great affection due to the club's attractive style of play.

TAYLOR, David

Born: Bannockburn; Died: Bridge of Allan, near Stirling, 6 August 1949.
Right-back   5ft 10½in; 13st 4lb (1920).
Career: Motherwell; Glasgow Rangers; Bradford City October 1910; Burnley December 1911; guest for Chelsea in World War One; Glasgow Celtic 1919; Burnley 1920, retired May 1924; St Johnstone manager May 1924-c.1930; Blackburn Rovers coach early 1930s; Dunfermline Athletic manager 1936-April 1938; Carlisle United manager April 1938-1939.

Honours: FA Cup winners 1911, 1914.

Dave Taylor was one of the fastest full-backs of his era and made 250 appearances for Burnley, scoring five goals. Taylor had made 51 appearances for Bradford City, which included their great FA Cup Final victory over Newcastle United in the 1911 Final. He made only 11 appearances when Burnley took the League championship in 1920-21 and played in a losing semi-final for the club against Aston Villa in 1924 as well as picking up a winners medal in 1914, when they beat Liverpool in the Final.

St Johnstone had just won the Second Division title when Taylor became their manager. They maintained their First Division status until 1930 and Taylor left at this time. Dunfermline were relegated to Division Two in 1936-37 and he moved on to Carlisle United after being unable to get them promoted straight away. At Brunton Park, Taylor went for tall, well-built players and Carlisle finished the 1938-39 season with the top scorer in the Northern Section Sam Hunt netting 33 goals. However, they conceded a massive 111 goals, 78 of them on away grounds.

TAYLOR, Eric

Born: Birtley Carr, 1912; Died: September 1974.
Career: Sheffield Wednesday office boy late 1920s, manager April 1942-July 1958, then general manager and secretary until 1973; trustee of Football League pension scheme in 1970; working committee of HM Department of Education and Science looking at hooliganism; vice-president of Sheffield and Hallam FA; chairman of Football League Secretaries' and Managers' Association.

Honours: Division Two champions 1952, 1956, runners-up 1950; Football League long-service medal.

Eric Taylor spent nearly 45 years at Hillsborough and was the man behind the ambitious plans to make the ground into one of the best stadiums in the country. Unfortunately, the team rarely matched their surroundings. He joined the Owls as an office boy in 1929, became assistant secretary and then secretary. For 16 years, Taylor was in charge of team affairs but left the day-to-day coaching, training and tactics to coaches Bill Knox, Allan Brown and Jack Marshall.

The 1950s were yo-yo years for the club. They won promotion from the Second Division in 1950, 1952 and 1956, but were relegated in 1951 and 1958. He relinquished team management responsibilities after the second relegation and concentrated on the administrative side of the club. Taylor had not been afraid to enter the transfer market and paid a British record £35,000 for Jackie Sewell in 1951. He nearly died in a car crash in 1967 and never fully recovered from his injuries.

TAYLOR, Frank

Born: Hemsworth, 30 April 1916; Died: Chapletown, Sheffield, January 1970.
Right-back   5ft 8¾in; 10st 9lb (1939).
Career: Barnsley Grammar School; Wolverhampton Wanderers 1936, retired through injury 1944; guest for Aldershot, Millwall, Darlington, St Mirren in World War Two; Wolverhampton Wanderers training staff 1947; Scarborough manager June 1948-1950; Leeds United assistant manager 1950-1952; Stoke City manager June 1952-May 1960.

Honours: England wartime international (1 cap); FA Cup runners-up 1939.

Frank Taylor made 56 appearances for Wolves before the outbreak of the war. He played in their surprise 4-1 drubbing by Portsmouth in the 1939 FA Cup Final. Taylor gained a wartime cap for England against Scotland at Hampden Park, in April 1944 when England won 3-2 before a massive crowd of 133,000.

Forced to retire at 28, Taylor was invalided out of the Army. He was a new breed of manager who set great store by fitness. Stoke City were relegated to Division Two at the end of his first season in charge and remained a mid-table Second Division side throughout the 1950s. He was shocked when he was sacked but the Stoke board had shown a great deal of patience with his management. His brother Jack managed Leeds United and Queen's Park Rangers.

TAYLOR, George Alexander

Born: King Edward, Aberdeen, 9 June 1913; Died: Plymouth, June 1982.
Left-half.
Career: Hall Russell's; Aberdeen 1937; Plymouth Argyle August 1948, trainer

1950, then manager March 1960-November 1961 (joint with Neil Dougall).

Honours: Scottish Cup winners 1947.

Originally a forward, George Taylor converted to left-half. A solid, hard-working and tough-tackling wing-half, Taylor made six appearances for Aberdeen before the outbreak of war and played regularly for the club during hostilities. He skippered the Dons to a Scottish Cup success in 1947, when they beat Hibernian 2-1 in the Final, and played another 82 games (scoring six goals) for Aberdeen before moving south to join Plymouth Argyle.

Taylor was trainer at the club for ten years before being appointed joint manager with Neil Dougall in 1960. He was officially called the 'chief trainer'. Dual control proved difficult to implement and, after two five-goal defeats, they were replaced by Ellis Stuttard. Argyle finished 11th in Division Two in 1960-61 and reached the quarter-finals of the League Cup, losing 5-3 to Aston Villa in a second replay.

TAYLOR, Graham

Born: Worksop, 15 September 1944.
Full-back   5ft 8in; 11st 4lb (1972).
Career: Scunthorpe United amateur; Grimsby Town apprentice August 1961, professional July 1962; Lincoln City player-coach July 1968-December 1972, retired due to hip injury in 1972, then manager December 1972-June 1977; Watford manager June 1977-July 1987; Aston Villa manager July 1987-July 1990; England Youth, Under-21 and 'B' team manager from November 1982, then national manager July 1990.

Honours: Division One runners-up 1983, 1990; Division Two runners-up 1982, 1988; Division Three runners-up 1979; Division Four champions 1976, 1978; FA Cup runners-up 1984.

Graham Taylor pursued success at Watford with great single-mindedness, taking the club from the depths of the Fourth Division to runners-up spot in the First within six years of taking over at the club. He also took them to their first FA Cup Final in 1984, where they lost to Everton. During his time in charge at Vicarage Road, the club became an integral part of the community rather than just an extension of it. As a coach he was innovative and persuasive but also a pragmatist who did not set his sights above the level of his players' ability. Taylor earned the respect of his men and demanded discipline and character from them.

With Grimsby Town he developed into a good full-back who was a fine reader of the game. He usually remained calm under pressure and was a very fair player. Taylor appeared in 215 games for Grimsby and later played 150/2 for Lincoln City but scored only three goals during his career. He joined Lincoln in July 1968 and later became a coach under David Herd, taking over as manager at Lincoln in December 1972, when Herd was sacked. This came shortly after Taylor was forced to retire from playing due to a hip injury.

He developed into a first-class judge of a player and a splendid administrator at Sincil Bank. It took until his 11th game in charge for Taylor to experience a victory as a manager, but he rebuilt the side and they just missed promotion on goal-average in 1974-75 when they lost 3-2 to Southport in the last game of the season. The following season the Imps swept all before them, taking the Fourth Division title with a record 74 points and scoring over 100 goals.

After establishing them in the Third Division, Taylor received a good offer to take over at Watford in June 1977. He was to stay for ten years in charge at Vicarage Road, working alongside chairman and rock star Elton John in revitalising the fortunes of the club. When Taylor arrived, Watford had been going nowhere but within six years they finished as runners-up in the First Division. The rise was rapid: Watford won the Fourth Division title in 1978; runners-up in the Third in 1979; runners-up of the Second in 1982; and runners-up of the First, behind Liverpool, in 1983 with Luther Blissett scoring 27 goals. Taylor produced some great players at the club including John Barnes and Blissett, both of whom later moved for huge fees.

Watford also had some excellent Cup runs. In 1978-79 they reached the semi-finals of the League Cup after beating Newcastle United and Manchester United. In the semi-finals they lost on aggregate to Nottingham Forest. In 1984 the Hornets reached their first FA Cup Final, which they lost 2-0 to Everton.

Watford reached their peak that day and thereafter Taylor had his work cut out to keep them at the top, although they were still a First Division club when he decided that a fresh challenge was needed. In July 1987 he became boss at Aston Villa, who were then in the Second Division. At the end of his first season in charge, Villa were back in the top flight after finishing runners-up to Millwall. After just missing relegation by one point in 1988-89, they finished as runners-up to Liverpool the following season after leading the table for a while in March.

With the England manager Bobby Robson deciding to leave the job after the 1990 World Cup finals, Graham Taylor was lined up as his replacement. His first move was to make Laurie McMenemy, the former Southampton manager, his assistant. Taylor had previously been in charge of England's Youth, Under-21 and 'B' sides. England reached the 1992 European Championships finals but had a poor tournament. That and problems in qualifying for the 1994 World Cup finals led to Taylor being much criticised for his team selection and style of play.

TAYLOR, John

Born: Barnsley, 15 February 1914; Died: Barnsley, 22 February 1978.
Full-back   5ft 9in; 11st (1938).
Career: Worsborough Bridge (Barnsley); Wolverhampton Wanderers ama-

teur 1931, professional January 1934; Norwich City June 1938; guest for Barnsley and Watford in World War Two; Hull City July 1947; Weymouth player-manager May 1950-June 1952; Queen's Park Rangers manager June 1952-May 1959; Leeds United manager May 1959-March 1961.

Honours: Division Three North champions 1949.

Jack Taylor played in the same side as his brother, Frank, with Wolves for a couple of seasons before moving to Norwich City. A classically built full-back, Jack Taylor made 56 appearances for the Canaries in peacetime football and 215 games in wartime soccer. At Loftus Road, Taylor was a solid if unspectacular manager, often picking up useful players from the Leeds area.

But attendances gradually dropped due to lack of success in the Southern Section. Rangers also experienced two humiliating defeats to non-League opposition. In 1954-55, they lost 4-0 to Walthamstow Avenue at Highbury in the FA Cup and in 1957-58 lost to Hereford United 6-1. Leeds United were relegated to Division Two at the end of his first season in charge and after another season of struggle, Taylor left full-time football.

TAYLOR, Paul

Born: Sheffield, 3 December 1949.
Midfield.
Career: Sheffield Wednesday June 1971; York City July 1973; Hereford United (loan) January 1974; Colchester United (loan) March 1974; Southport July 1974-April 1977; Gillingham assistant manager 1982, then manager December 1987-October 1988; Walsall caretaker manager March-May 1990.

Paul Taylor was unable to find regular first-team football until he joined Southport, for whom he scored 16 goals in 95 League games. He had made his League debut for Sheffield Wednesday against Queen's Park Rangers in August 1971.

At Gillingham, Taylor was assistant manager to Keith Peacock and they came close to Second Division football but lost to Swindon Town in a Third Division play-off Final replay at Selhurst Park in 1987. Taylor took over as manager on Peacock's departure but had no success. After a mediocre first season in charge, the Gills had a terrible start to 1988-89 and Taylor was sacked after a 5-0 defeat at Preston. They were eventually relegated. Taylor was caretaker manager at Walsall between John Barnwell and Kenny Hibbitt.

TAYLOR, Peter T.

Born: Nottingham, 2 July 1928; Died: Majorca, 4 October 1990.
Goalkeeper.
Career: Nottingham Forest amateur in war; Coventry City May 1946; Middlesbrough August 1955; Port Vale June 1961; Burton Albion player-manager 1962-1965; Hartlepools United assistant manager 1965; Derby County assistant manager May 1967-October 1973; Brighton & Hove Albion assistant manager November 1973, then manager August 1974-July 1976; Nottingham Forest assistant manager July 1976-81; Derby County manager November 1982-April 1984.

Peter Taylor found fame as Brian Clough's assistant at Derby County and Nottingham Forest. Clough claimed they were equal managerial partners but the media did not see things this way. Whatever the secret, together they won honours galore.

Taylor started his career as a goal-keeper, making 90 appearances for Coventry and 146 for Middlesbrough, where he played in the same team as Clough. He was managing Southern League Burton Albion when Clough asked him to join him at Hartlepool. After moving to Derby, they took the Second Division title in 1968-69, followed by the Rams' first League championship in 1971-72.

At Forest they took the League championship in 1977-78, won the League Cup in 1978 and 1979 and the European Cup in 1979 and 1980. In 1981, came an acrimonious split which was never healed before Taylor's death in 1990. Some of it centered around a book *With Clough by Taylor*. Peter Taylor was in sole charge at Brighton after Clough's departure to Leeds, but was unable to achieve promotion at the Goldstone. He was later persuaded out of retirement to manage Derby County. He helped them out of trouble with a remarkable run-in to the season but left the club again just before they were relegated to Division Three a year later.

TAYLOR, Philip Henry

Born: Bristol, 18 September 1917.
Wing-half/Inside-right 5ft 11in; 11st 2lb (1949).
Career: Greenback School, Bristol; Bristol Schools; Bristol Rovers amateur cs 1932, professional March 1935; Liverpool March 1936 (£5,000); guest for Bristol Rovers, Brighton & Hove Albion, Newcastle United and Leeds United in World War Two; retired July 1954 to become coach, then manger May 1956-November 1959; later sales representative; also cricket for Gloucestershire (one match in 1938).

Honours: England international (3 caps); 'B' international (2 caps); Schoolboy international; Football League representative; Football League champions 1947; FA Cup runners-up 1950.

Phil Taylor was an adaptable player who was composed, polished, a great reader of the game and an excellent skipper at Anfield. He scored 34 goals in 345 appearances for Liverpool and gained a League championship medal in 1946-47, making 35 appearances, and also played in Liverpool's FA Cup Final defeat against Arsenal in 1950. He had come close to an appearance at Wembley in 1947 but Burnley won a replayed semi-final 1-0.

Taylor gained three caps for England, against Wales, Northern Ireland and Sweden. He was unlucky not to get Liverpool back into the First Division when he became the club's manager. They finished third, fourth and fourth respectively during his three seasons in charge. But they were also knocked out of the FA Cup by non-League Worcester City. His health suffered due to the strain of the job and he resigned in November 1959.

TAYLOR, Reginald

Born: *c*.1873.

Career: Preston North End assistant secretary 1922; Blackburn Rovers secretary April 1936, then secretary-manager October 1936-April 1938.

When Arthur Barritt resigned as manager of Blackburn Rovers, Reg Taylor left Preston to become secretary at Ewood Park, with the directors in charge of team affairs. This arrangement did not last long and when the team struggled in the Second Division, Taylor was also put in charge of team affairs.

In 1936-37 he pulled the club off the bottom of the table to finish 12th but they lost to lowly neighbours Accrington Stanley in the FA Cup. After another battle against relegation the following season, old favourite Bob Crompton returned to manage the club with Taylor again becoming the secretary.

TAYLOR, Richard Eric

Born: Wolverhampton, 9 April 1918.
Centre-half 5ft 10in; 11st (1935).

Career: Grimsby Town May 1935; Scunthorpe United April 1948, then reserve-team manager and trainer-coach from 1954; Sheffield United coach and assistant manager 1956; Aston Villa coach and assistant manager December 1958, then manager July 1964-May 1967.

An old-fashioned centre-half who was dedicated and hard working, with a pragmatic approach to the game, Taylor saw his 35 games for Grimsby Town separated by the war. He was a regular at Scunthorpe United, where he made 131 League appearances plus many more in the Midland League. After retiring Taylor became trainer-coach at the club, then worked with Joe Mercer at Sheffield United and Aston Villa.

He took over as manager of Villa when Mercer left the club and sold Tony Hateley to Chelsea for £100,000, but spent £140,000 on new players. He could not avoid relegation, though, which came in 1966-67 when he was sacked, along with his assistant manager Jimmy Easson and trainer Johnny Dixon. He became a successful businessman after leaving Villa and ran a sports shop at Witton, 600 yards from Villa Park.

TERNENT, Francis Stanley

Born: Gateshead, 16 June 1946.
Right-half 5ft 8in; 11st 6lb (1972).

Career: Burnley June 1963; Carlisle United May 1968; Sunderland May 1974-1976; Blackpool coach 1979, then manager August 1979-February 1980; Bradford City assistant manager in 1988; Crystal Palace assistant manager February-November 1989; Hull City manager November 1989-January 1991; Chelsea assistant manager 1991-cs 1992.

Stan Ternent played at Burnley with his brother Ray, but being unable to obtain a regular first-team place he moved to Carlisle United, for whom he made 186/2 League appearances, scoring five goals. United finished fourth in Division Two in 1970-71 and three seasons later gained promotion to Division One, but Ternent made only 13 appearances that season and was then signed by Sunderland, although he never played for their first team.

Ternent had a tough time in his first manager's job, at Blackpool, and was sacked when the club slumped to 20th in the Third Division. He was assistant to Terry Dolan at Valley Parade and to Steve Coppell at Selhurst Park before taking over from Dolan at Hull City. He steered the Tigers away from what looked like certain relegation to finish 14th after they won six of their last eight games. Hull had a dreadful season in 1990-91, however, and were bottom of Division Two when he was sacked in January 1991.

THICKETT, Henry

Born: Hexthorpe near Doncaster, 1873; Died: Trowbridge, 15 November 1920.
Right-back 5ft 10in; 14st (1903).

Career: Hexthorpe; Sheffield United 1890; Rotherham Town 1892; Sheffield United December 1893; Bristol City May 1904, then player-manager March 1905-October 1910, retired as a player cs 1905; licensee in Trowbridge 1910-until his death.

Honours: England international (2 caps); Football League representative (2 caps); Football League champions 1898; Division Two champions 1906; FA Cup winners 1899, 1902, runners-up 1901, 1909.

Harry Thickett found a good deal of success as manager of Bristol City but was not appreciated by the board of directors who unceremoniously sacked him after he took the club to an FA Cup Final and to runners-up in the First Division.

He also had an excellent playing career with Sheffield United, playing for them in three FA Cup Finals and picking up a League championship medal, as well as playing for his country.

Thickett played for his local side before joining Sheffield United in 1890. In 1892 he moved to Rotherham Town but returned to the Blades in December 1893. He went on to play 261 League games for United. A swift moving defender, despite his bulk, he had a strong clearance kick and was usually fearless in the tackle. In the 1899 FA Cup Final, he appeared at right-back against Derby County when United won 4-1. Thickett had been injured in the semi-final and was heavily bandaged for the Final. Indeed, the Blades had endured an epic struggle with Liverpool in the semis, when it took four games before they scraped home 1-0.

In 1901, United lost 3-1 to Southern League Spurs in a replayed Final at Bolton. And the following year they beat Southampton 2-1 in another replayed Final. United had also won the League championship medal with Harry in the side in 1897-8, five points ahead of runners-up Sunderland. Thickett gained two caps for England, against Wales in a 4-0 victory at Bristol in March 1899 and the following month against Scotland, in a 2-1 victory at Birmingham. He also played for the Sheffield FA in many inter-city games.

In May 1904, he moved to Bristol City and played for one season before retiring in the summer of 1905. In March 1905, he had been appointed the club's manager and he had a spectacular first season in charge as Bristol City who clinched the Second Division title with ease. Many club records were set that season, records which still stand today. They won 30 games in the League that season, had 14 consecutive wins, went 24 League games without defeat and won six consecutive away matches.

In 1906-07, they finished runners-up in the First Division and blew their chances of the title over Easter, otherwise they may have won the championship. In 1909, Thickett took Bristol City to an FA Cup Final in which they gave a spirited performance before losing 1-0 to Manchester United, to a goal from Sandy Turnbull after 22 minutes. It came as a surprise when Thickett was sacked in October 1910, in a season in which the club was eventually relegated to Division Two. He probably lost his job due to internal strife rather than the performance of the team. Thickett left the game after this and moved to Trowbridge to run a pub. In his later life his weight rose to 26 stone and this may have had a bearing on his early death in Trowbridge in November 1920, at the age of 47.

THOMPSON, Alan William

Born: Liverpool, 20 January 1952.
Defender 5ft 10in; 11st 9lb (1972).

Career: Sheffield Wednesday apprentice July 1967, professional January 1969; Stockport County August 1976, then player-manager April 1977-March 1978; Portland Timbers (NASL) April 1979; Bradford City January 1980; Scunthorpe United March-May 1982.

Alan Thompson played for Sheffield Wednesday during a period of decline at the club. He made 167/6 appearances for the club which had sunk into the Third Division by the time he joined Stockport County. Thompson scored 17 goals in 94 League appearances for Stockport, after which his playing career seemed to tail off. He was surprisingly appointed player-manager at Edgeley Park and strangely lost his job after the club's best run of an otherwise mediocre season. He carried on playing for the club after his dismissal. After a spell in the United States with Portland Timbers, he played 31/4 League games for Bradford City and 11 for Scunthorpe United.

THOMPSON, George Alexander

Born: South Shields, 23 March 1884.
Outside-right 5ft 6in; 10st 6lb (1907).

Career: South Shields Bertram 1904-1905; South Shields Adelaide 1905; North Shields; Sheffield United October 1906; Derby County September 1908-1911; Newcastle United Reserves; Luton Town manager February-October 1925.

Honours: Tyneside League and Shield 1906; Durham County representative.

At Derby County, Thompson played in the same side as the great Steve Bloomer. He had to compete for the right-wing spot with Billy Grimes and Ron Trueman and played 55 games for the Rams, scoring six goals, before moving to Newcastle United. He played for Derby in an FA Cup semi-final against Bristol City in 1909, but finished on the losing side, 2-1 after a replay.

In his early days with South Shields Adelaide, Thompson won Tyneside League and Shield medals and also represented Durham. He was employed as a boilermaker at this time. Thompson was the first manager of Luton Town but lasted only eight months in the job. He tried to introduce weight and height to the team but his new signings were no better than the players they had replaced.

THOMPSON, James Hunter

Born: Shetland Isles 1884.
Right-back 5ft 7½in; 11st 3lb (1914).

Career: Heart of Midlothian; Leith Athletic; Portsmouth cs 1906; Coventry City June 1911; Bury cs 1913, retired during the war, later coach and assistant manager, then manager May 1923-February 1927; Swansea Town manager February 1927-1931; Halifax Town manager May 1936-May 1947.

Honours: Anglo Scots v Home Scots trial match; Division Two runners-up 1924.

A reliable and steady full-back, Thompson moved south to play for Pompey in the Southern League after Scottish League experience with Hearts and Leith Athletic. He made 158 appearances (two goals) for Pompey before moving to Coventry, for whom he made another 73 appearances. Thompson ended his career at Bury, where he played 61 games.

After the war he became coach and trainer at Gigg Lane and succeeded William Cameron as manager when his boss was suspended after a bribery scandal. Bury clinched promotion to Division One in 1923-24, by 0.02 of a goal in a very close finish. Rivals Derby needed to win their last game 5-0 but could only score four. Bury then finished fourth in Division One with Norman Bullock scoring 31 goals, in 1925-26.

Thompson resigned to join Swansea Town but they struggled against relegation to the Third Division during his spell in charge. When he was at The Shay, Halifax had one of their best seasons in 1936-37, when they finished seventh in Division Three North. He steered the club through the war years and then resigned at the end of the first peacetime season. His brother played for Hearts and Portsmouth.

THOMPSON, Stephen P.

Born: Sheffield, 28 July 1955.
Central defender 6ft 1in; 14st 4lb (1991).

Career: Boston United; Lincoln City April 1980 (£15,000); Charlton Athletic August 1985; Leicester City July 1988 (£40,000); Sheffield United November 1988 (£20,000); Lincoln City August 1989, then manager November 1990-May 1993.

A tough-tackling defender who could operate in midfield or defence, Thompson soon established himself at Lincoln City after his £15,000 move from Boston United. City went close to promotion to Division Two in 1981-82, but needing to beat rivals Fulham in the last game to go up in their place, they could only manage a 1-1 draw. After scoring eight goals in 154 League games for Lincoln, Thompson moved to Charlton and helped them to promotion to Division One in 1986.

He probably regretted leaving The Valley, because he could not win a first-team place at Leicester and soon moved on to Sheffield United. He finished his playing career back at Lincoln City, then became manager at Sincil Bank. The Imps were 23rd in the Fourth Division when he took over, but after a run in of only three defeats in the last 18 games, finished in a comfortable 14th place.

Thompson surprisingly resigned in May 1993 despite Lincoln finishing in eighth place in the Third Division. But they did lose to Stafford Rangers in the first round of the FA Cup earlier in the season.

THOMPSON, William Gordon

Born: Glasgow, 10 August 1921.
Full-back 5ft 10in; 11st 2lb (1951).
Career: Carnoustie; Portsmouth March 1946; Bournemouth & Boscombe Athletic January 1953; Guildford City manager 1955-1957; Exeter City manager May 1957-January 1958; Worcester City manager January 1958; Portsmouth caretaker manager February-April 1961.

Honours: Southern League champions 1956.

Bill Thompson was mainly a reserve through Portsmouth's golden era of the late 1940s. He played only 41 times for Pompey and in 45 League games for Bournemouth before moving to Guildford City as manager. They won the Southern League championship in his first season but he made little impression at Exeter City, where chairman Mr A.S.Line wanted to change Thompson's role at the club, taking away his secretarial duties. Thompson was not happy with this and left to join Worcester City as manager. He was caretaker manager at Portsmouth between Freddie Cox and George Smith and bought a couple of players but could not halt Pompey's slide down the table.

THOMSON, John Ross

Born: Thornton, Fifeshire, 6 July 1906;
Died: 1979.
Left-half 6ft; 12st 3lb (1935).
Career: Thornton Rangers (Fife); Dundee 1925; Everton March 1930, retired December 1939; Carnoustie Panmuir in World War Two; guest for Aldershot and Fulham in World War Two; Manchester City manager July 1947-February 1950; ran pub in Carnoustie until November 1974.

Honours: Scotland international (1 cap); Scottish League representative; Football League champions 1932, 1939; Division Two champions 1931; FA Cup winners 1933.

A heftily-built wing-half who played a powerful and commanding game, Jock Thomson appeared in 294 matches for Everton, scoring five goals. He gained his only cap for Scotland against Wales at Tynecastle in October 1932 and had an amazing first two years at Goodison Park, experiencing relegation, following by winning the Second Division and the First Division championships.

Thompson lost his place to Joe Mercer but made a comeback in 1938-39, playing 26 games in another League championship season for the Toffees. He won his FA Cup medal in 1933, when Everton beat Manchester City 3-0. Alas, he did not have a happy time as manager at Maine Road. City finished seventh in 1948-49 but were relegated to Division Two the following season and Thomson left the club.

TINDALL, Ronald Albert Ernest

Born: Streatham, London, 23 September 1935.
Centre-forward/Full-back
5ft 11in; 12st 10lb (1963).
Career: Camberley Wanderers; Chelsea professional April 1953; West Ham United November 1961; Reading October 1962; Portsmouth September 1964, coach, manager April 1970-May 1973, then general manager until 1974 and caretaker manager September 1974; also Surrey CCC 1956-1966; director of cricket coaching in Western Australia in the 1970s.

Honours: Football League representative (1 cap).

A tall and speedy centre-forward, Tindall was industrious and strong in the air. Later in his career he converted to full-back at Portsmouth and he was also an excellent cricketer, playing 172 games for Surrey between 1956 and 1966. An all-rounder, he could bat and was a useful off spinner.

Tindall played 172 games for Chelsea, scoring 70 goals, before moving to Upton Park in an exchange deal which took Andy Malcolm in the opposite direction. Unable to find regular first-team soccer at West Ham, Tindall moved to Reading and later played 176/2 games for Portsmouth, scoring nine goals.

When he took over as manager at Fratton Park, Tindall soon entered the transfer market and bought Norman Piper from Plymouth for £40,000 and Jim Standen from his old club, West Ham. As Pompey did not have a reserve side, Tindall 'adopted' Southern League club Waterlooville as a nursery side. Portsmouth developed large debts during his management as he was allowed to spend more and more on new players. He became the general manager in 1973.

TINN, John William

Born: South Shields, 20 January 1878;
Died: Aylesbury, 13 March 1971.
Career: South Shields manager 1920-July 1927; Portsmouth manager July 1927-May 1947.

Honours: FA Cup winners 1939, runners-up 1929, 1934.

Jack Tinn was a colourful character who realised the value of publicity and psychology in getting his teams into the correct mood for matches. He was a shrewd and indestructible manager, a kind of forerunner to Bill Shankly. He was also famous for wearing his lucky spats, which were religiously put on by the same player before every match. Tinn managed to keep Pompey in the First Division, although they often came close to relegation, and also took them to three FA Cup Finals.

Born in South Shields, he did not play professional football and, indeed, very little is known about his early life. He was 42 before becoming involved in top-class soccer, when he became manager of South Shields, who were playing in the Second Division of the Football League. Support was low and Tinn was often forced to sell his better players so that the club could survive financially. Attendances were poor, but after he sold Warney Cresswell to

Sunderland and Alf Maitland to Middlesbrough, each for £5,000, the crowds dropped even lower.

Despite this, South Shields — who later became Gateshead — were usually to be found in the top half of the Second Division whilst Tinn was manager at Horsley Hill. But the club went into decline after he moved to Portsmouth as manager in July 1927.

Pompey had just been promoted to the First Division when Tinn took control. They narrowly escaped relegation in 1927-28 and 1928-29, finishing 20th in both seasons. In 1929, Tinn took Pompey to the FA Cup Final and they held out for 78 minutes against the favourites Bolton Wanderers before conceding two goals. He introduced some better players to the club and they finished fourth in 1930-31.

In 1934, Portsmouth again reached the FA Cup Final but this time lost to Manchester City. Pompey took the lead through Rutherford after 26 minutes and seemed to be on their way to victory until centre-half Jimmy Allen was injured and City equalised as he received treatment on the touch line. City scored a late winner to take the trophy.

Tinn finally took Pompey to a winning Final in 1939. Their opponents, Wolves, were the biggest favourites for many years but Tinn used his experience of two losing Finals to plot their opponents' downfall. He employed a noted comedian to keep the players in good heart and they ran out very relaxed to beat Wolves 4-1 at Wembley.

Although he managed to keep Pompey in the First Division, they usually struggled at the wrong end of the table and Tinn was heavily criticised near the end of his time as manager for sometimes being amateurish in his approach and also not having a great knowledge of the game. However, this was a little unfair as he had brought much success to Fratton Park especially in the Cup. He resigned in May 1947.

TODD, Colin

Born: Chester-le-Street, 12 December 1948.
Defender 5ft 9in; 11st 5lb (1972).
Career: Chester-le-Street Boys; Sunderland apprentice July 1964, professional December 1966; Derby County February 1971 (£180,000); Everton September 1978 (£330,000); Birmingham City September 1979 (£300,000); Nottingham Forest August 1982 (£70,000); Oxford United February 1984; Vancouver Whitecaps (NASL) May-September 1984; Luton Town October 1984; Whitley Bay manager 1985; Middlesbrough reserve-team coach May 1986, chief coach September 1986, then manager March 1990-May 1991; Bolton Wanderers assistant manager May 1992.

Honours: England international (27 caps); Under-23 international (14 caps); England Youth international; Football League representative (3 caps); Football League champions 1972, 1975; FA Youth Cup winners 1967.

Colin Todd was that rarity — a defender who excited crowds. He was an elegant and poised player who was always comfortable on the ball. He developed a great partnership with Roy McFarland at Derby, which was later transferred into the England team. Todd cost the Rams a record £180,000 for a defender but won two League championship medals at the Baseball Ground, under Brian Clough and later Dave Mackay. The second, in 1974-75, was probably his greatest season in

which he rarely made an error. At the end of it he was voted the PFA's Footballer of the Year.

He helped Birmingham City gain promotion to the First Division and Oxford United to the Third Division title in 1983-84, playing 12 games after his transfer that season. Altogether, Todd played 747 games in his career before managing Whitley Bay for a while. He was assistant manager to former Derby colleague Bruce Rioch at Middlesbrough, eventually succeeding him as manager. 'Boro made the Second Division play-offs in 1991, after finishing seventh, but lost to Notts County in the semi-final. Todd had been employed too late to save the club from relegation the previous season. In May 1991 he surprisingly resigned and a year later became assistant manager to Bruce Rioch again, this time at Bolton, who were promoted to Division One in 1992-93.

TOMLINSON, Francis

Born: Manchester, 23 October 1925.
Winger 5ft 8in; 10st 10lb (1948).
Career: Bolton Wanderers amateur; Goslings FC; Oldham Athletic November 1946; Rochdale November 1951; Chester August 1952; Ashton National 1953-1954; Hawker Siddeley, Manchester, where he was in charge of sports acitivities; Bradford manager February-December 1970.

Tomlinson must be one of the most unusual choices to become manager of a Football League club when, after over 15 years out of the game, he was selected to take over at struggling Bradford. He had previously been in charge of sports activities and the bar at Hawker Siddely workers' club in Manchester.

Appointed by Bradford chairman Herbert Metcalfe, who was trying his hardest to save the Park Avenue club from folding, his cause was not helped when Bradford were voted out of the Football League at the end of 1969-70, after seeking re-election in the three previous seasons. Nineteen players immediately made transfer requests when Tomlinson was appointed. When Bradford also struggled in the Northern Premier League, Tomlinson left the club. In his playing days he had been an enterprising winger with speed, good control and an excellent body swerve. He played 115 games, scoring 27 goals, for Oldham, but was never the same player after he fractured his leg against York City in September 1950.

TORRANCE, James

Born: Coatbridge, 28 July 1889; Died: Frien Barnet, North London, 2 July 1949.

Utility   5ft 9in; 12st 2lb (1923).
Career: Rob Roy (Coatbridge) 1908; Glasgow Ashfield July 1910; Fulham September 1910; Walsall cs 1926, then player-manager February 1927-May 1928.

A boiler-maker by trade, Torrance played 490 games for Fulham in peacetime and wartime football and was one of the great names of the club's early history. A marvellous one-club man, Torrance did not establish himself in the side until he switched from a forward to a half-back in 1913. He had a curious build for a footballer and seemed to be all body and no legs. He loved to attack when he appeared at centre-half and scored 50 goals for the Cottagers.

He was past his best when he joined Walsall but when he became player-manager he usually selected himself. Not a great success as a manager, after Walsall he left football for good and worked for a telephone company. He was very unfortunate in later life. He had an unhappy marriage, his only child died in his teens and illness led to his own demise at the age of 60, from lung cancer.

TOSHACK, John Benjamin MBE

Born: Cardiff, 22 March 1949.
Centre-forward   6ft; 11st 7lb (1972).
Career: Cardiff Schools; Cardiff City apprentice June 1965, professional March 1966; Liverpool November 1970 (£110,000); Swansea City player-manager February 1978-March 1984, retired as a player 1980; Sporting Lisbon manager July 1984-May 1985; Real Sociedad manager June 1985-May 1989; Real Madrid manager May 1989-November 1990; Real Sociedad manager again May 1991.

Honours: Wales international (40 caps); Under-23 international (3 caps); Schoolboy international; Football League champions 1973, 1976, 1977; Division Two promotion 1981; Division Three promotion 1979; Division Four promotion 1978; FA Cup winners 1974, runners-up 1971; UEFA Cup winners 1973, 1976; Welsh Cup winners 1968, 1969, 1970, 1981, 1982, 1983; Spanish League champions 1990; Spanish Cup winners 1987, runners-up 1990.

A tall, powerful centre-forward, John Toshack cost Liverpool £110,000 when he joined the club from Cardiff City. He had nearly signed for Fulham in 1968 but went on to score 95 goals in 236/9 games for Liverpool. He played in two FA Cup Finals, Liverpool losing 2-1 to double winners Arsenal in 1971 and beating Newcastle United in 1974. He also helped the Reds to two UEFA Cup successes and three League championships, forging a great partnership with Kevin Keegan at Anfield.

Toshack took Swansea from the Fourth to the First Division but the club was virtually bankrupted in the process, when attendances did not cover the players' large wages. In each of the promotion seasons, Swansea had to win their last game to clinch their place in the higher division and succeeded each time. Toshack later took Real Sociedad to their first Spanish Cup success and also took Real Madrid to a Spanish League championship.

TRAUTMANN, Bernhard Carl 'Bert'

Born: Bremen, Germany, 22 October 1923.

Goalkeeper   6ft 1½in; 13st 5lb (1959).
Career: St Helens March 1948; Manchester City November 1949, retired May 1964; Stockport County general manager October 1964, then team manager October 1965-April 1966 and general manager again; Wellington Town manager; Burma national team manager February 1972; since then working for German government coaching all over the world.
Honours: Football League representative; FA Cup winners 1956, runners-up 1955; Footballer of the Year 1956.

Bert Trautmann had to overcome considerable hostility from supporters in Manchester, a city with a significant Jewish population, because he had been a German PoW and the war was still fresh in people's minds. Trautmann had served in the German Army as a paratrooper before being captured after D-Day. An excellent decathlete, he had been selected for Germany's Olympic training squad for the abandoned 1940 Olympics.

After joining Manchester City, he went on to make 545 appearnaces for them and gained an FA Cup winners' medal in 1956, when he played with a broken neck for much of the Final against Birmingham City. Trautmann is the only German to have represented the Football League, when he played against the Irish League at Blackpool in October 1960.

He had arrived in England as a PoW in April 1945, at Ashton-in-Makerfield, worked on a farm and played for St Helens on his release almost three years later. He was not a great success as a manager. Stockport County finished 13th in Division Four in his only season in charge of team affairs at the club.

TRESADERN, John

Born: Leytonstone, 26 September 1890;
Died: Tonbridge, 26 December 1959.
Left-half   5ft 6in; 10st (1921).
Career: Wanstead; Barking Town; West Ham United July 1913; Burnley October 1924, retired due to broken leg December 1926; Northampton Town player-manager May 1925-October 1930; Crystal Palace manager October 1930-June 1935; Tottenham Hotspur manager June 1935-April 1938; Plymouth Argyle manager April 1938-November 1947; Aston Villa scout 1948-1949; Chelmsford City manager June 1949-November 1950; Hastings United manager December 1951; Tonbridge manager April 1958-December 1959.
Honours: England international (2 cap); FA Cup runners-up 1923.

Jack Tresadern was a small, dapper, terrier-like wing-half, who played 165 times for the Hammers and appeared for the club in the first Wembley FA Cup Final, attended by almost 200,000 people. He gained his England caps against Scotland and Sweden.

Tresadern did well in charge of Northampton, who were third in the Southern Section in 1928-29 and fourth the following season. Palace were runners-up to Notts County in 1930-31 but only the champions won promotion in those days. He was not a success at White Hart Lane. Results were poor and Tresadern was unpopular with supporters and club officials. Things were not helped by constant rumours of a return for Peter McWilliam as manager of the club. Tresadern moved to Plymouth when he knew the sack was imminent but the Pilgrims had a tough time in the war and their Home Park ground was badly damaged in the blitz. Tresadern struggled on after the war for a while before losing his job.

TROLLOPE, Norman John

Born: Wroughton, 14 June 1943.
Left-back   5ft 10in; 11st 13lb (1972).
Career: Swindon Boys; Swindon Town amateur 1958, professional July 1960, player-assistant manager April 1975, player-youth-team manager from 1979, then player-manager November 1980-March 1983, retired as a player 1981, later youth-team coach.
Honours: Football League Cup winners 1969.

John Trollope beat Jimmy Dickinson's appearance record for one club when he appeared 767/3 times for Swindon Town. This included a run of 368 consecutive League and Cup games between 1961 and August 1968, which ended when he broke his arm against Hartlepools. Trollope was a tall, well-built full-back and a fine sportsman.

He helped Swindon to promotion to Division Two in 1963 and 1969. The highlight of his career, though, was playing in Third Division Swindon's League Cup Final success against Arsenal in 1969. He made his debut in opening game of the 1960-61 season, against Halifax, and his last appearance was at Blackpool in May 1979. He was not a success as manager of the club and they were relegated to Division Four in 1982.

TROTTER, James W.

Born: Easington, 25 November 1899;
Died: St Albans, 17 April 1984.
Centre-forward   5ft 9in; 12st 3lb (1926).
Career: Bury 1919; Sheffield Wednesday February 1922; Torquay United cs 1930; Watford 1932-1933, retired due to cartilage injury; Charlton Athletic trainer 1935, then manager September 1956-October 1961; also England trainer.
Honours: Division Two champions 1927.

A prolific goalscorer, Jimmy Trotter twice scored five goals in a game for Sheffield Wednesday. In December 1924, he got five against Portsmouth and the following September scored five against Stockport County. His overall goal tally for the Owls was 114 in 160 appearances. He scored 37 goals in the 1926-27 season and netted 26 for Torquay United in 1930-31. Late in his career, Trotter was troubled by injuries.

In 1935, he became Jimmy Seed's right-hand man at The Valley. They had met during their time at Hillsborough. Trotter was also trainer to the England team under Walter Winterbottom.

Seed and Trotter's relationship gradually deteriorated over the years and was on the point of ending when Seed was sacked and Trotter became his successor. Trotter was dour, determined, forthright and a man of few words, in contrast to Seed. Charlton finished bottom of Division One in 1956-57 with only 22 points. They were third in 1957-58, missing promotion by one point, and he was eventually sacked when he could not get Athletic back into the First Division.

TULIP, William R.

Born: c.1879; Died: September 1961.
Career: Gateshead director 1930, honorary manager and secretary May 1933-cs 1956, also chairman and president.

In 23 years, Bill Tulip never received wages for managing Gateshead. A wealthy businessman, he ruled the roost at Redheugh Park but his efforts held the club together and as his strength weakened with age, then so did the club. Tulip became a director when South Shield metamorphosised into Gateshead in 1930 and found, developed and sold many players and negotiated the club through the continuing bad years.

He left his trainer Bob Keen in charge of the players and tactics but carried out many of the administrative duties at the club. In 1934, Tulip had to sell Jack Wesley and Joe Meek to guarantee the survival of the club but just before the war, he signed the ageing Hughie Gallacher for £500. Gateshead finished runners-up of the Northern Section in 1949-50 and reached the fourth round of the FA Cup in 1948-49 and 1951-52.

They reached the quarter-finals in 1953 before losing 2-1 at home to Bolton. Tulip was 77 when he gave up the manager's chair and allowed his deputy, Bob Keen, to take charge. It came as a terrible shock to him when Gateshead were voted out of Football League in 1960.

An extrovert, he was not everybody's favourite man but was regarded as faultlessly fair by many. In 1959, five directors resigned out of frustration, claiming, "Old Tulip turns down all our ideas and we can't do a thing about it." It was said that when he chaired some meetings he intentionally left his hearing-aid at home. He died soon after Gateshead were thrown out of the League.

TURNER, Arthur Owen

Born: Chesterton, Staffs, 1 April 1909.
Centre-half   5ft 11in; 12st 10lb (1935).
Career: Wolstanton PSA; Downing's Tilleries; West Bromwich Albion trailist; Stoke City amateur November 1930, professional November 1930; Birmingham January 1939 (£6,000); Southport February 1948; Crewe Alexandra player-manager October 1948-December 1951, retired as a player May 1949; Stoke City assistant manager 1952-November 1954; Birmingham City manager November 1954-September 1958; Oxford United manager January 1959-February 1969, then general manager until 1972; Rotherham United chief scout in 1970s; Sheffield United chief scout 1980-July 1981.

Honours: Division Two champions 1933, 1955; Division Three champions 1968; Division Four promotion 1965; Football League South champions 1946; Southern League champions 1961, 1962; FA Cup runners-up 1956.

Arthur Turner's name became synonymous with Oxford United after he took the club from the Southern League to the Second Division of the Football League. His successes at the Manor Ground included two Southern League titles, a run to the quarter-finals of the FA Cup and the Third Division championship.

Before joining Stoke City as a professional in November 1930, he played for Wolstanton PSA, Downing's Tilleries and had a trial with West Brom. He went on to make over 300 appearances for the Potters, playing alongside the likes of Stanley Matthews and Freddie Steele. He gained a Second Division championship medal in 1932-33, as a resolute, no-nonsense defender. In January 1939, Turner moved to Birmingham for the large fee of £6,000, but the war soon interrupted his playing career, although he did manage 186 wartime games for the club.

He joined the Blues too late to help prevent relegation from Division One in 1938-39, but in 1945-46 he skippered the side to the semi-finals of the FA Cup and also to the League South title in the last season of wartime soccer. Turner joined Southport in February 1948 but after only 28 League appear-ances moved to Crewe Alexandra as manager in October 1948, retiring from the playing side in May 1949 after a career total of 361 League games.

It was always a struggle for survival at Gresty Road, but Crewe reached the third round of the FA Cup in 1948-49 before losing to Sunderland. His best season at Crewe was 1949-50, when they finished seventh, and his worst was his last at the club, leaving in December 1951. The following year he returned to Stoke City as assistant manager.

In November 1954, Turner was offered the manager's job at another former club, Birmingham City. He took them to the Second Division title at the end of his first season in charge, when they clinched the championship with a last-gasp winner at Doncaster to take the title on goal-average. Turner took City to the FA Cup Final in 1956 but they did not rise to the occasion and lost 3-1 to Manchester City at Wembley. The following season they reached the semi-finals before losing to Manchester United.

Turner did well in the transfer market, signing many good players, and he also developed some fine youngsters like Terry Hennessey and Colin Withers. Arthur Turner was the first person to manage an English club in European competition when Birmingham reached the semi-finals of the Inter-Cities Fairs Cup.

Alas, an unsavoury episode led to his resignation at St Andrew's. Turner was made to believe that the appointment of Pat Beasley in January 1958 was to be as his assistant in charge of the reserve side and to deal with some of his more routine chores. In reality, Beasley was appointed as joint manager and, to make matters worse, Turner was not told by the club but by the Press. He threatened to leave but stuck it out until September 1958, when he resigned.

Turner was not out of work for long. In January 1959, he was appointed manager of Headington United of the Southern League. One of the first things he did was to persuade the board to change the name of the club to Oxford United. Leeds United tried to entice him back into League management but Oxford matched their offer and Turner decided to stay at the Manor Ground.

He soon set about making the club a full-time outfit and signed many fine players such as Ron and Graham Atkinson, Maurice Kyle and Cyril Beavon. Oxford took the Southern League titles in 1960-61 and 1961-62 and were elected into the Football League in 1962 as a replacement for the defunct Accrington Stanley. United reached the quarter-finals of the FA Cup in 1963-64, becoming the first Fourth Division club to achieve this. The following season they gained promotion and in 1967-68 clinched the Third Division title with a team which cost only £14,500.

Turner was something of a wizard on the transfer market and made a steady profit for the club over the years. When Oxford struggled near the foot of the Second Division in 1968-69, he decided to step down as manager in February 1969 to become general manager of the club.

In 1972, Oxford decided they could not afford the luxury of a general manager and sacked Turner. He left the Manor Ground a very disillusioned man. During the 1970s, Turner worked as chief scout for Rotherham United and from 1980 until July 1981 he was the chief scout at Sheffield United.

TURNER, Christopher J.

Born: St Neots, 3 April 1951.
Defender   6ft 1in; 11st 5lb (1972).

Career: Peterborough United November 1969; Luton Town July 1978 (£100,000); New England Teamen (NASL) May 1978 (£90,000); Cambridge United September 1979; New England Teamen (NASL) April 1980; Swindon Town September 1980; Cambridge United October 1980; Southend United October 1983-1984; Cambridge United manager January 1986-January 1990; Peterborough United manager January 1991-December 1992, then chairman.

Honours: Division Three promotion 1992; Division Four champions 1974, promotion 1991.

Chris Turner was an accomplished defender who was the mainstay at Peterborough United for nine years before being bought by Luton's David Pleat for £100,000. Turner had made 357/5 appearances, scoring 43 goals, for the Posh, but played only 39 matches for Luton before moving to Cambridge United. He also had three summers in the North American Soccer League with New England Teamen, for whom he appeared 86 times, scoring 9 goals.

He helped the Posh to the Fourth Division title in 1973-74 and they went close to further promotion four seasons later. In January 1986 he became manager of Cambridge United, recently relegated to Division Four. They struggled to get back again but just missed the play-offs in 1989 and, when it looked as though they would miss out again, Turner resigned. However, after he left the club they reached the sixth round of the FA Cup and achieved promotion under his successor, John Beck. Turner took Peterborough to promotion in 1990-91, when they lost only one home game as they finished fourth. They were promoted again the following season after beating Stockport County 3-1 in the play-off Final at Wembley. Turner was part of a consortium which bought the club in December 1992. He was appointed chairman and his assistant, Lil Fuccillo, became the manager.

TURNER, Graham James

Born: Ellesmere Port, 5 October 1947.
Defender   6ft; 11st 5lb (1972).
Career: Wrexham July 1965; Chester January 1968; Shrewsbury Town January 1973 (£30,000), then player-manager November 1978-July 1984, retired as a player 1984; Aston Villa manager July 1984-September 1986; Wolverhampton Wanderers manager October 1986.

*Honours: England Youth interna-*tional; Division Three champions 1979, 1989; Division Four champions 1988; Sherpa Van Trophy winners 1988.

The revival of Molineux over the last six years has been mainly thanks to the shrewd management of Graham Turner. He took over with Wolves at their lowest ebb, having just been relegated to Division Four, but discovered some outstanding players like Steve Bull, whom he bought for a small fee from West Brom, and transformed him into one of the most lethal strikers in British soccer. At present, Turner has taken Wolves back to the Second Division (now the new First) and Molineux fans are hoping that he can bring even more success to the club.

Turner, a former England youth international, signed professional forms for Wrexham in July 1965 and made 77 League appearances before moving to Chester in January 1968. He was a hard-working player who was tenacious in the tackle and equally effective in defence or midfield. He scored five goals in 215/3 League appearances for Chester before being transferred to Shrewsbury Town for a club record fee of £30,000 in January 1973. The Shews were relegated to Division Four in 1973-74 but promoted as runners-up the following season.

In November 1978, Turner became player-manager at Gay Meadow and went on to make 342/13 League appear-ances for the club before retiring in 1984. under him, Shrewsbury were Third Division champions in 1978-79, with 61 points. Their success was based around a strong defence and they remained unbeaten at home that sea-son. Shrewsbury also reached the semi-finals of the FA Cup that season before losing 2-0 at Highbury in a replay. This run included an excellent 2-0 home win over Manchester City in the fourth round. They reached the quarter-finals in 1982 before losing 5-2 at Leicester.

Shrewsbury maintained a mid-table position in the Second Division during his time in charge at the club and only in 1981-82 were they threatened with relegation.

In July 1984, Turner received a lucrative offer to take control at Aston Villa and accepted the challenge. He had a tough time at Villa Park, though, and after two mediocre seasons and a poor start to 1986-87 he was sacked in September 1986. They did reach the semi-finals of the League Cup in 1986, but lost 4-3 on aggregate to Oxford United.

In October 1986, Turner was offered the manager's job at Wolves. The club was in dire straits in the Fourth Division and heavily in debt. Early on he was given a tough time by the fans as he gradually began the difficult task of rebuilding their club from scratch. Wolves had a big setback in November 1986, when they crashed out of the FA Cup to non-League Chorley. Turner, though, quickly put this disaster behind him and soon made some inspired signings including future England international Steve Bull and Andy Thompson. Bull became a prolific goalscorer for Wolves and played a major role in their rise back to the Second Division.

At the end of the 1986-87 they got to the Fourth Division play-offs but surprisingly lost to Aldershot. The following season, however, Wolves walked away with the Fourth Division championship. It became a double celebration when they beat Burnley in the Sherpa Van Trophy Final at Wembley before an 80,000 crowd. Bull scored over 50 goals that season.

Wolves won the Third Division title in style in 1988-89, in style with an eight points margin over Sheffield United. They have since consolidated their position in the Second Division without setting the world alight. Their Molineux ground was gradually being transformed, which hampered Turner's chances to spend money on the transfer market. After a poor start to the 1991-92 season there was talk that Turner may be sacked but when results improved the rumours died out.

Wolves had a very average 1992-93 season and one of the main reasons was the loss of form of their star striker Steve Bull. With the ground in the process of being rebuilt and Turner finally having some money to spend, Wolves could soon be returning to the big time.

TWENTYMAN, Geoffrey

Born: Carlisle, 19 January 1930.
Centre-half   5ft 11in; 12st 9lb (1963).
Career: Swifts Rovers (Carlisle); Carlisle United amateur 1945, professional February 1947; Liverpool December 1953 (£10,000); Ballymena United player-manager March 1959; Carlisle United June 1963; Morecambe player-manager May 1964; Hartlepools United manager June-October 1965; Penrith manager-coach cs 1966; Liverpool chief scout August 1967.

Honours: Irish League representative (9 caps).

Geoff Twentyman was one of Carlisle's finest discoveries and there was a lot of speculation about who would sign him before he moved to Anfield. A commanding centre-half with enormous spirit, if lacking in pace, Twentyman possessed an unexpectedly powerful shot.

He made 149 appearances for Carlisle and then 184 for Liverpool, for whom he scored 19 goals. Liverpool were unlucky not to win promotion back to Division One during Twentyman's time at the club. He spent three seasons as player-manager of Ballymena United, where he also captained the Irish League representative side on several occasions. He lasted only four months in charge at Hartlepool and was replaced by Brian Clough.

UFTON, Derek Gilbert

Born: Crayford, Kent, 31 May 1928.
Centre-half   5ft 11½in; 12st 4lb (1957).
Career: Dartford Grammar School; Borough United (Kent); Dulwich Hamlet 1945; Cardiff City amateur; Bexleyheath & Welling United; Charlton Athletic September 1948, retired through injury cs 1960; Tooting & Mitcham United coach January 1962; Plymouth Argyle coach September 1964, then manager May 1965-February 1968; worked as a photographic model and was the manager of the Sporting Club (London) in 1972; also cricket for Kent 1949-1962; Charlton Athletic

director August 1984; chairman of the Lords Taverners April 1990.

Honours: England international (1 cap).

A cultured footballing centre-half, Ufton was also a strong tackler. He made 277 appearances for Charlton Athletic and he dislocated his shoulder 20 times during his career. He gained his England cap against the Rest of Europe in a 4-4 draw and was given a tough time by the FIFA team's forwards.

Ufton also played 148 matches for Kent between 1949 and 1962, scoring 3,919 runs and taking 314 dismissals as a wicketkeeper.   Initially, he joined Plymouth Argyle as coach to Malcolm Allison and when Allison left for Manchester City, Ufton became the manager. He set about transforming the side against mounting criticism from the fans and, although he made a profit on the transfer market, he sold some of the best players, replacing them with inferior ones. In 1967-68, Argyle made early Cup exits in both competitions and after only three wins in 25 games, Ufton was sacked. The club was eventually relegated. Ufton played an important role in Charlton Athletic's return to The Valley in December 1992.

UPTON, Frank

Born: Ainsley Hill, 18 October 1934.
Wing-half   5ft 11in; 11st 9lb (1959).
Career: Nuneaton Borough; Northampton Town March 1953; Derby County June 1954; Chelsea August 1961 (£15,000); Derby County September 1965; Notts County September 1966; Worcester City July 1967; Workington player-manager January-July 1968; Northampton Town coach October 1969; Aston Villa coach January 1970; Chelsea coach August 1977, caretaker manager December 1978; Randers Freja coach February 1979-February 1980; Dundee coach August 1980; Al-Arabi coach 1981; Wolverhampton Wanderers coach 1982-October 1984; Bedworth United manager October 1984; Coventry City coach and assistant manager December 1985-April 1987, IBK Keflavik (Iceland) coach May 1987; Borneo national coach May 1989; Burton Albion caretaker manager January-February 1990; Northwich Victoria youth development officer April 1990; Cheltenham Town YTS officer to November 1990; Leicester City coaching staff in 1992; also runs treatment of injury clinic in Derby.

Honours: Division Three North champions 1957.

A strongly built, hard tackling wing-half, Frank Upton made 272 appearances in his two spells with Derby County. He played a crucial role in Chelsea's promotion side of 1962-63, in

which he occasionally played at centre-forward. Known as 'The Tank' for his brave runs at opposing defences, not to mention some bone-jarring tackles, Upton later developed into a coach with a good reputation for working with young players.

He was player-manager of Workington for six months but they finished 23rd in Division Four and had to seek re-election, whereupon Upton's employment was terminated. Since then he has had a long and varied career in football, working mainly as youth-team coach and manager at his various Football League clubs. In 1991 he opened a treatment of injuries clinic at a Derby sports centre and continues this with his work in football.

URE, Allan R.

Born: 12 January c.1892.
Career: Blackpool Reserves, then trainer 1919-1923; Leeds United trainer cs 1923-cs 1928; Blackpool trainer cs 1928; Barnsley trainer; Gillingham manager May 1937-May 1938; Millwall trainer 1938; Bradford trainer in 1947; Halifax Town trainer and physiotherapist 1952-cs 1962, then continued as masseur.

Ure never made it as a player, instead gaining a reputation as a trainer, physiotherapist and masseur and becoming known throughout the game as 'the man with the magic in his fingers'. This was because he seemed to have just the right touch when looking after players' injuries. He worked at Blackpool and Leeds United with his father-in-law, Bill Norman, and was trainer when Leeds gained promotion to Division One in 1924 and when Blackpool won the Second Division title in 1929-30.

He had a disastrous time as manager of Gillingham, who lost their League status at the end of his season in charge, after they finished 22nd in the Southern Section and had to seek re-election. Ipswich Town were voted into the League instead, mainly due to them boasting average attendances of 20,000 in the Southern League. For ten years after the war, Ure worked at Halifax before eventually retiring at the age of 70 due to his wife's ill health.

VEITCH, Colin Campbell McKechnie

Born: Newcastle upon Tyne, 22 May 1881; Died: Berne, Switzerland, 26 August 1938.
Half-back   5ft 9in; 11st (1904).
Career: Newcastle Schools; Rutherford College; Newcastle United amateur April 1899, professional 1903, retired in World War One; Newcastle United coach 1918; Newcastle Swifts (United's nursery side) coach 1924-August 1926; Bradford City secretary-manager August 1926-January 1928; also chairman of PFA; journalist with the Newcastle Chronicle from 1928; chairman, producer and actor for Newcastle People's Theatre.

Honours: England international (6 caps); Football League representative (4 caps); Football League champions 1905, 1907, 1909; FA Cup winners 1910, runners-up 1905, 1906, 1908, 1911.

Colin Veitch was one of the greatest-ever utility players, who could play equally well in most positions. He appeared in five FA Cup Finals for Newcastle United, in four different positions. Veitch had immaculate control and always seemed to have plenty of time when on the ball. He

was unlucky to win only six England caps, but played 321 games, scoring 49 goals for Newcastle. Veitch was also a musician, scholar, actor, playwright, producer, conductor and composer and was a key figure of the Newcastle People's Theatre.

He looked after and developed Newcastle United's youth policy but was shoddily treated after 27 years service, when he was sacked and given just one week's notice. He did not find much success as manager of Bradford City, who were from relegated from Division Two in 1926-27. Halfway through the following season, Veitch resigned, saying that he 'did not like management much'. He worked as a journalist for many years and was once banned from United's press box for his sometimes critical views on the club. He became ill with pneumonia and went to the Swiss Alps to recuperate but died suddenly in a Berne Hospital at the early age of 57.

VENABLES, Terence Frederick

Born: Bethnal Green, London, 6 January 1943.
Inside-forward   5ft 9in; 11st 6lb (1972).
Career: Dagenham Schools; Chelsea apprentice July 1958, professional August 1960; Tottenham Hotspur May 1966 (£80,000); Queen's Park Rangers June 1969 (£70,000); Crystal Palace September 1974, coach February 1975, then manager June 1976-October 1980; Queen's Park Rangers manager October 1980-May 1984; Barcelona manager May 1984-September 1987; Tottenham Hotspur manager November 1987-July 1991, then chief executive until May 1993.

Honours: England international (2 caps); Under-23 international (4 caps); Youth international; Amateur international; Schoolboy international; Football League representative; Division Two champions 1979, 1983; Division Three promotion 1977; FA Cup winners 1967, 1991, runners-up 1982; Football League Cup winners 1965; FA Youth Cup winners 1961; Spanish League champions 1985; European Cup runners-up 1986.

A charismatic and knowledgeable football man, Terry Venables was a stylish player with four London clubs and won an FA Cup and a League Cup winners' medal during his playing career. As a manager, he is well-known for his abilities as a coach and man management. He took Palace from the Third to the First Division, and Queen's Park Rangers and Spurs to FA Cup Finals. Then he became part-owner of Spurs, playing a major role in all aspects of the running of the club, financially and on the football field, until his controversial sacking.

London-born Venables represented Dagenham and England Schoolboys before joining Chelsea and winning an FA Youth Cup winners' medal in 1961. Initially an inside-left, Venables later appeared in midfield. He became the first player to represent England at five different levels: Schoolboy, Amateur, Youth, Under-23 and full. His two full caps came when he was a Chelsea player. He made his debut against Belgium in a 2-2 draw at Wembley in October 1964 and the following month played against Holland. He was at his best at Stamford Bridge and his career never hit the heights again after his £80,000 move to Tottenham. Venables scored 31 goals in 237 appearances for Chelsea and gained a League Cup winners' medal in 1965, when the

Blues beat Leicester City in a two-legged Final.

At Spurs he never won over the critical White Hart Lane fans but did pick up a FA Cup medal in 1967, when they beat his former club, Chelsea, 2-1 in the Final. In a side with many stars including Jimmy Greaves, Alan Gilzean, Dave Mackay and Alan Mullery, he failed to shine and made 139/2 appearances for Spurs, scoring nine goals before his departures to Queen's Park Rangers for £70,000. He helped Rangers back into the First Division in 1972-73.

About this time Venables was joint author, with Gordon Williams, of a book *They Used To Play On Grass*. It was a prophetic title because, a decade later when he was manager of QPR, they became the first club to dispense with their grass pitch and replace it with an artificial one. Venables also co-wrote the television detective series *Hazell*.

After another 178 appearances and nine goals for Rangers, Venables was on the move again, this time joining Crystal Palace. His playing career was near its end and he played only another 16 games before retiring to become a coach at Selhurst Park under Malcolm Allison.

When Allison left in June 1976, Venables took over as manager and at the end of his first season in charge had taken Palace to promotion from Division Three. In a tight finish they just edged out rivals, Wrexham and on goal-average Rotherham. The march under Venables continued. In 1978-79, Palace were Second Division champions, conceding only 24 goals. A huge record crowd of 51,482 saw them clinch promotion at Selhurst Park by beating Burnley. Palace also won the FA Youth Cup in 1977 and 1978. These sides produced many fine players including Kenny Sansom and Terry Fenwick.

On entering the top flight, Venables went into the transfer market and signed Gerry Francis, from QPR for £450,000, and Mike Flanagan, from Charlton for £650,000. Palace were dubbed by the Press as 'The Team of the Eighties', but they never fulfilled their promise.

In their second season back in the top flight, Palace began badly and Venables resigned in October 1980, after a boardroom row, and immediately joined QPR as manager. Their form was patchy in the Second Division and Venables signed a number of players who helped Rangers gain higher status. In 1982, they lost 1-0 to Spurs in dull FA Cup Final replay. The following

year, Rangers took the Second Division championship, ten points clear of their nearest rivals, Wolves, and the following season finished fifth in Division One.

In May 1984, Venables received a huge offer to manage Barcelona and left with his assistant, Allan Harris, for sunnier climes. With former Spurs striker Steve Archibald leading the attack, Barcelona took the Spanish League title at the end of his first season in charge. They also reached the European Cup Final the following year but surprisingly lost to Steaua Bucharest on penalties after a 0-0 draw. Barcelona finished runners-up to Real Madrid in the League in 1986-87 and after only four games of the next season, Venables resigned.

By now, a wealthy man, due to his many business ventures. he returned to England to manage Tottenham Hotspur. He soon bought a large interest in the club and has increased his holdings to an even greater extent over the last couple of years. Financial problems have dogged Spurs in recent years. The problems began when they became a public company and it was not the football club which was causing the headaches but the subsidiary companies attached to the club.

Spurs became financially dependent on the sale of Paul Gascoigne to Italy and Gascoigne was on the point of leaving for £8m, when a serious injury — self-inflicted during the 1991 FA Cup Final — meant that Tottenham's prize asset was out of the game for over a year. By the time he moved to Lazio, the fee had been reduced to £5.5m. It had helped the club's finances when Venables took them to the 1991 FA Cup Final. The semi-final against Arsenal was the first to be played at Wembley and Spurs beat their great rivals 3-1, thanks to a marvellous display and goal from Gascoigne. Spurs beat Nottingham Forest 2-1 in the Final.

Tottenham had been under the threat of a takeover from Robert Maxwell — later dubbed 'the world's biggest crook' — and this worried the fans. But Venables and computer millionaire Alan Sugar masterminded a takeover at Spurs, since when Venables has worked hard in an attempt to clear the club's debts. In May 1991, he become chief executive as Peter Shreeve returned to White Hart Lane as team manager. When Shreeve was sacked in May 1992 it became unclear who was actually in charge at Spurs. Officially Doug Livermore and Ray Clemence were the coaches in charge of team affairs but Venables obviously still had a big say in club policy and planning. In May 1993, came the sensational news that Sugar had effectively sacked him. Venables took his case to court and the saga looked set to run.

VENGLOS, Josef

Born: Czechoslovakia, 12 December 1936.
Left-half.
Career: Slovan Bratislava for ten years; Doctor of Philosphy & Physical Education; Head of the Physical Education Department at Bratislava University; player-coach in Australia; Australia national team manager late 1960s; Slovan Bratislava manager early 1970s; Czechoslovakia aide 1976, manager 1978-1982; FIFA consultant; Sporting Lisbon manager early 1980s; coaching in Malaysia & Indonesia; Czechoslovakia manager 1988-July 1990; Aston Villa manager July 1990-May 1991; Fenerbahçe (Turkey) manager 1992.

Honours: European champions 1976; Czechoslovakian League champions 1974, 1975, Czechoslovakian Cup winners 1974.

Venglos played for Slovan Bratislava for ten years but was never able to get into the national side due to the dominance of the great Josef Masopust. After retiring he completed his studies to become a Doctor of Philosophy. Venglos was national manager of Australia for a while in the late 1960s before returning to Czechoslovakia to manage his former club. He took them to two League titles and a Cup success.

This earned him an appointment as aide to the national side which won the European Championships in 1976. The Czechs beat West Germany in the Final, on penalties after an exciting match. Venglos took over as national manager in 1978, after the departure of Vaciav Jezek, and in 1980 took them to third place in the European Championships in Italy, but after a poor World Cup in Spain in 1982, Venglos left the job. In FIFA circles he was widely admired as a coach and lecturer, but his cool, educated approach to the game was not appreciated in Lisbon, Sporting wanting instant success.

During his second spell in charge of the Czech national side he took them to the 1990 World Cup finals in Italy, where they reached the quarter-finals, being unlucky to lose there to West Germany. Venglos was doing well at Aston Villa until they played Internazionale in the UEFA Cup. After winning the first leg 2-0, Villa lost the return 3-0 to go out of the competition. Their form in the League slumped after this and he lost his job after they could finish only 17th. His was, though, an imaginative appointment for an English League club.

VIOLETT, Dennis S.

Born: Manchester, 20 September 1933.
Inside-forward 5ft 8in; 11st 8lb (1963).
Career: St Margaret's Central School, Whalley; Manchester Schools; Manchester United amateur cs 1949, professional September 1950; Stoke City January 1962 (£25,000); Baltimore Bays (USA) May 1967-September 1968 (£10,000); Witton Albion January 1969; Linfield player-coach July 1969; Preston North End coach 1970; Crewe Alexandra coach February 1971, then manager cs-November 1971; Washington Diplomats (NASL) coach 1974-June 1977.

Honours: England international (2 caps); Schoolboy international (5 caps); Football League representative (3 caps); Football League champions 1956, 1957; Division Two champions 1963; FA Cup runners-up 1958; Football League Cup runners-up 1964; Irish Cup winners 1970; .

Dennis Violett's frail appearance belied his skill and stamina, for he was an accurate passer with a delicate body swerve. Violett scored 178 goals in 291 games for Manchester United with 20 goals in their 1955-56 championship season and 16 in the following title season. He survived the Munich air crash with relatively minor head injuries and soon recovered to play in United's European Cup semi-final defeat against Real Madrid. He had missed the 1957 FA Cup Final but appeared the following season when United lost 2-0 to Bolton.

Viollett helped Stoke to the Second Division title in 1962-63 and scored 59 goals in 182 League games for the

Potters. He made his England debut in Budapest in May 1960 and scored in his other game for his country, against Luxembourg. He also gained an Irish Cup winners' medal with Linfield in 1970.

Violett had a short spell in charge of Crewe but was sacked after an FA Cup defeat against non-League Blyth Spartans. Crewe had managed only five wins in their first 17 games. He was coach of NASL club Washington Diplomats for three years but they won no trophies.

VIZARD, Edward Thomas

Born: Cogan, Wales, 7 June 1889; Died: Wolverhampton, 25 December 1973.
Outside-left 5ft 10in; 10st 6lb (1926).
Career: Cogan Old Boys'; Penarth Rugby Club; Barry Town; Bolton Wanderers December 1910-1931, then scout and coach of 'A' team 1931-1933; guest for Chelsea in World War One; Swindon Town manager April 1933-May 1939; Queen's Park Rangers manager May 1939-April 1944; Wolverhampton Wanderers manager April 1944-June 1948; Cradley Heath manager February 1949; licensee at a Tattenhall hotel in 1950.

Honours: Wales international (22 caps); FA Cup winners 1923, 1926.

Ted Vizard was one of the greatest players to appear for Bolton Wanderers, playing 512 games and scoring 70 goals in his 21 years at the club. As a youth he divided his time between playing soccer for Cogan Old Boys' and rugby for Penarth. He joined the Trotters when 21 years old and enjoyed a meteoric rise to fame, making his debut two months after signing and his international debut two months after that. He became the mainstay of the Welsh side and was caretaker manager of Bolton from February to August 1919.

Vizard played in two winning FA Cup Final sides for the club. In 1923, he appeared in the first Wembley Final, against West Ham, and three years later, again picked up a winners' medal against Manchester City. He played his last game in March 1931, at the age of 41 years 287 days, the oldest player to appear for Bolton.

Vizard obtained a BA degree whilst playing football. In 1933 he became manager of Swindon Town after they had sought re-election the previous season and was their first full-time manager. He was unable to lift them above mid-table mediocrity, though, and took over at Queen's Park Rangers just before the outbreak of war. QPR won the 'B' South League in the first half of the 1939-40 season and were runners-up in the Supplementary 'D' League later in the season. In 1941 they joined the 'breakaway' London League and then finished third in 1942-43 and 1943-44, in the League South. In 1944, Vizard moved to Wolves to replace Major Buckley. He got the job from 100 applicants and laid the foundations for future success at the club. Unfortunately, Vizard was not a great motivator and was replaced by Stan Cullis, despite taking Wolves to third place in Division One in 1946-47.

VOISEY, William T. MM, DCM, C de G.

Born: Millwall, 1891; Died: Wanstead, 19 October 1964.
Right-half 5ft 7in; 11st (1914).
Career: Glengall Road School; Glengall Rovers; Millwall St John's; Millwall cs 1908; Bournemouth & Boscombe

Athletic July 1923-24; Leytonstone trainer-coach; Fulham assistant trainer cs 1930, head trainer April 1934; Millwall trainer 1939, then trainer-manager April 1940-November 1944 and trainer again until retirement in 1962.

Honours: England Victory international (1 cap); FA tour of South Africa 1920 (3 caps); FA XI v Army February 1921.

'Banger' Voisey was a tenacious, skilful wing-half who played 231 League and FA Cup games for Millwall before departing late in his career to Bournemouth. He first worked for Millwall as a programme seller and joined them as a player when they still played on the Isle of Dogs. During World War One, Voisey rose through the ranks of the Royal Field Artillery, winning the Distinguished Conduct Medal, the Military Medal and the Belgian Croix de Guerre for bravery.

He played in a Victory international for England against Wales in 1919 and toured South Africa in 1920 with the FA. After retiring from playing, Voisey became a well-known coach and, as well as coaching Leytonstone, Fulham and Millwall, also trained the Isthmian League, London FA and London Combination representative sides as well as the England Amateur international side.

He was in charge at Millwall during the war and experienced only wartime competitions during his term of office. Voisey suffered ill health after being caught in an air-raid at The Den, which suffered a direct hit.

WADDINGTON, Anthony

Born: Manchester, 9 November 1924.
Wing-half/Full-back
5ft 11in; 11st 6lb (1951).
Career: Manchester Boys; Manchester United amateur 1941; Crewe Alexandra January 1946, retired through knee injury 1952; Stoke City coach 1952, assistant manager 1957, then manager June 1960-March 1977; Crewe Alexandra manager June 1979-July 1981.

Honours: Division Two champions 1963; Football League Cup winners 1972, runners-up 1964.

A much-respected manager, Tony Waddington brought many good times to the success-starved fans at Stoke City. He gained a reputation for giving ageing stars an 'Indian summer' to their careers at the Victoria Ground and Stoke remained a First Division side for most of his 17 years in charge and also won their first major trophy in 1972,

when they took the League Cup against Chelsea at Wembley.

Manchester-born Waddington joined Manchester United as an amateur in 1941, whilst serving in the Royal Navy. Playing at either wing-half or full-back, he moved to Crewe Alexandra in 1946 and six years later was forced to retire from the game through a knee injury, after scoring seven goals in 179 League appearances for Crewe.

In 1952 he became a third-team trainer and coach at Stoke City under manager Frank Taylor and gradually worked his way up to assistant manager by September 1957. Stoke had just finished in the bottom half of the Second Division when he became the manager in June 1960. There was a resurgence at the club after the return of 46-year-old Stanley Matthews from Blackpool for a small fee of £3,000. Another masterstroke by Waddington was the signing of Jimmy McIlroy from Burnley, for £25,000, a move which angered the Turf Moor fans. Stoke finished as Second Division champions in 1962-63 after a close-fought tussle with Chelsea and Sunderland. Waddington's sides gained a reputation as a 'veterans team' as he signed many players who were nearing the ends of their careers. These included Dennis Viollett, Roy Vernon, David Herd, Eddie Clamp and Alex Elder. He also signed England's regular goalkeeper, Gordon Banks, from Leicester City.

Waddington stabilised Stoke City, kept them on a sound financial footing and later brought them a reputation for entertaining and successful football. In 1964, Stoke reached the Final of the League Cup but lost to Leicester City, 4-3 on aggregate. They were often struggling at the wrong end of the First Division but managed to maintain their place until 1977. They also reached the semi-finals of the FA Cup in 1971 and 1972, losing to Arsenal on both occasions after a replay.

Waddington's major triumph came in 1972, when Stoke reached the the League Cup Final, where they beat Chelsea 2-1 at Wembley, veteran George Eastham scoring the winning goal. This was Stoke's first major trophy and the following season they played in Europe for the first time. They finished fifth in the First Division in 1973-74 and 1974-75, but then went into decline with the exodus of most of their star players during 1976-77, which ultimately led to their relegation and Waddington's departure in March 1977.

In June 1979, Waddington returned to management, taking charge of Crewe Alexandra, where he remained in control until July 1981. In his first season they had to seek re-election and were also knocked out of the FA Cup by non-League Altrincham, who won 3-0. The following season, Crewe's position in the League improved a little and they finished 18th. But again they were knocked out of the Cup by non-League opposition, this time losing 1-0 at Mossley. Waddington left football after this.

WADE, Amos

Born: c.1885; Died: 15 December 1961 (aged 76).
Career: ran confectionary business in Nelson 1907; Accrington Stanley director 1922-1929; running a boarding house in Morecambe in 1929; Accrington Stanley secretary-manager January 1932-May 1935; Liberal councillor in Accrington 1932-1939 & 1955-1961; Mayor of Accrington 1941; Alderman 1952-1955.

Amos Wade was persuaded out of retirement to become the secretary-manager of Accrington Stanley. He knew little about players or tactics, but was an administrator and secretary. This was useful as the club was in severe financial difficulties. He managed to keep them afloat and left training and tactics in the hands of Fred Brennan after the long-serving full-back was appointed player-coach in December 1933. Results were disappointing and Joe Clemmell was appointed coach in 1934. The team was still selected by committee. Wade stood down in May 1935, but continued as secretary until the start of the war.

WAITERS, Anthony Keith

Born: Southport, 1 February 1937.
Goalkeeper   6ft 2in; 14st (1963).
Career: King George V Grammar (Southport); Redcar Albion; RAF football; Loughborough Colleges; Bishop Auckland; Macclesfield; Blackpool amateur July 1959, professional October 1959, retired May 1967; FA North-West regional coach May 1967; Liverpool coach January 1969; Burnley player-coach July 1970-71; Coventry City director of coaching December 1971-March 1972; England Youth-team manager July 1972; Plymouth Argyle manager October 1972-April 1977; Vancouver Whitecaps (NASL) coach 1977-1979 & 1980-1985; Canadian national team coach 1984; Tranmere Rovers coach; Chelsea scout.

Honours: England international (5 caps); Amateur international (1 cap); Football League representative (5 caps); Division Three runners-up 1975.

A heftily-built but agile goalkeeper, Tony Waiters had great reflexes with shots from close range. He gained his England amateur cap in May 1959 whilst at Loughborough Colleges, where he was studying to be a PE teacher. He succeeded George Farm in the Blackpool goal but did not become a regular until the departure of Gordon West to Everton.

Waiters won his first England cap in May 1964, in a 3-1 win against Ireland in Dublin. He appeared in 257 League games for Blackpool before giving up playing at the age of 30 to concentrate on coaching, although he returned three years later to play for Burnley.

Waiters did well as manager of Plymouth Argyle. They reached the semi-finals of the League Cup in 1974, before losing to Manchester City, and then he took them to promotion to Division Two in 1974-75. He left after a dispute with some directors and with the club heading towards relegation. Waiters took Vancouver Whitecaps to the NASL Soccer Bowl in 1979 and stayed with the club in various capacities until 1985, when the League collapsed. He led Canada to the 1986 World Cup finals.

WALKER, Andrew D.

Career: Airdrieonians manager until 1910; Middlesbrough manager June 1910-January 1911; Barrow manager 1929-cs 1930, when he became secretary.

Andy Walker did not get off to a good start at Middlesbrough, being suspended for four weeks for an illegal approach to one of his former Airdrie players. There was even more trouble when 'Boro chairman Thomas Gibson-Poole, a local Tory parliamentary candidate, wanted the club to beat local rivals Sunderland in an attempt to

enhance his chances of being elected at the forthcoming election. Walker was used to offer Sunderland's captain, Charlie Thomson, £30 to draw the match. He reported the incident to his own chairman and an FA Commission was set up to investigate.

In January 1911, Gibson-Poole and Walker were permanently suspended from football. Despite a big petition, the FA refused to review Walker's case. Many felt that he had been used by his chairman and the ban was eventually lifted and Walker returned to manage Barrow 18 years later. They had to seek re-election at the end of his only season in charge.

WALKER, David Clive Allan

Born: Watford, 24 October 1945.
Left-back   5ft 10in; 11st (1970).
Career: Leicester City October 1962; Northampton Town October 1966; Mansfield Town July 1969-1974; Chelmsford City cs 1975; Gravesend & Northfleet; Northampton Town manager May 1979-October 1980, coach 1980-1982 and manager again May 1982-May 1984, then assistant manager 1984-July 1990; Maidstone United assistant manager February 1991, then manager February-August 1992.

Honours: England Schoolboy international; Football League Cup runners-up 1965.

Despite playing only 18 games for Leicester City, Dave Walker appeared in the second leg of the 1965 League Cup Final, against Chelsea which Leicester lost 3-2 on aggregate. A quick-tackling defender, Walker went all the way down to the Fourth Division with Northampton Town. He then played 253/6 games, scoring ten goals, for Mansfield Town. He was pacey with the ability to support his forwards with dangerous breaks down the flanks.

Walker had two spells in charge at Northampton, achieving little in either with the Cobblers finishing in lowly positions in Division Four. In 1983-84 they lost to non-League Telford United in the FA Cup. Walker worked with Graham Carr at Northampton and Maidstone United. He took over at Maidstone in 1992, with the club struggling for survival. He lost his job when the club went in to liquidation in 1992.

WALKER, Leonard

Born: Darlington, 4 March 1944.
Defender   5ft 11in; 12st 4lb (1970).

Career: Spennymoor & District Boys; Middlesbrough amateur 1959; Spennymoor United 1962; Newcastle United May 1963 (£250); Aldershot July 1964;

Darlington player-coach August 1976; Charterhouse part-time coach 1976; Darlington coach 1977, then manager October 1978-June 1979; Aldershot coach 1980, then manager April 1981-November 1984 and 1985-March 1991, when he became general manager.

Honours: Division Four promotion 1987.

Len Walker made only one appearance for Newcastle United, at Leyton Orient in August 1963, but played 440/10 League games, scoring 23 goals, for Aldershot. They gained promotion to Division Three in 1972-73 and finished eighth the following season. It was too good to last, though, and the Shots were relegated in 1976.

Darlington had to seek re-election in 1978-79 with Walker in charge. He moved back to his old club as manager and Aldershot went close to promotion in 1983-84 and three years later surprisingly beat Wolves over two legs in the Fourth Division play-off Final after finishing sixth. When the bubble burst, they plummeted back to the bottom of Division Four with the club on the verge of bunkruptcy and Walker was sacked.

WALKER, Michael Stewart Gordon

Born: Colwyn Bay, 28 September 1945.
Goalkeeper 6ft 1in; 13st 4lb (1977).
Career: Caversham Secondary Modern School; Berks & Bucks and Oxfordshire Schools; Reading January 1963; Shrewsbury Town June 1964; York City June 1966; Watford September 1968; Charlton Athletic (loan) March 1973; Colchester United June 1973-1982 (£5,000), then coach and assistant manager, and manager April 1986-November 1987; Norwich City reserve-team coach 1988, then manager June 1992.

Honours: Wales Under-23 international (4 caps); Division Three champions 1969.

A reliable and consistent goalkeeper, Mike Walker gave especially great service to Colchester United, where he made 451 League appearances including 310 consecutive games between February 1977 and January 1983. He also served the club as coach, assistant manager and manager.

Walker's father was English but was stationed in Wales when Mike was born, thus his qualification to play for the Welsh national team. Mike's son, Ian, also a goalkeeper, is on Spurs' books and has won England Under-21 honours. Mike Walker also made 60 appearances for York City and 137 for Watford. He helped the Hornets to the Third Division title in 1968-69 and to an FA Cup semi-final appearance in 1970, in which they lost 5-1 to Chelsea. He gained promotion to Division Three with Colchester United in 1973-74 and took Colchester to the Fourth Division play-offs in 1987 as their manager, but they lost to Wolves. Mike Walker and his assistant Allan Hunter resigned on a matter of principle in November 1987.

Mike Walker replaced Dave Stringer as manager of Norwich City in June 1992. Norwich were the pace-setters in the new Premier League but not many people felt that they would actually take the championship.

The Canaries' challenge did not fade until the closing weeks of the season and they finished in a very creditable third place in the Premier League. When Arsenal won both domestic cup trophies, the Canaries were assured of a UEFA Cup place for season 1993-94.

WALKER, William Henry

Born: Wednesbury, Staffs, 29 October 1897; Died: Sheffield, 28 November 1964.
Centre-forward 6ft; 12st 5lb (1926).
Career: King's Hill School (Wednesbury); Hednesford Town; Darlaston; Wednesbury Old Park; Wednesbury Old Athletic; Aston Villa amateur March 1915, professional May 1919, retired November 1933; guest for Birmingham in World War One; Sheffield Wednesday manager December 1933-November 1937; Chelmsford City manager January-October 1938; Nottingham Forest manager March 1939-July 1960, when he joined Forest's committee until his death; also cricket for Warwickshire Club & Ground.

Honours: England international (18 caps); Division two runners-up 1957; Division Three South champions 1951; FA Cup winners 1920, 1935, 1959, runners-up 1924.

Billy Walker was not only a great footballer for Aston Villa and England, he was also an excellent manager for Sheffield Wednesday and Nottingham Forest. He played in two FA Cup Finals for Villa and took both Wednesday and Forest to FA Cup Final victories, in 1935 and 1959 respectively. He remained in charge at Forest for 21 years, in which time he brought the club back to the First Division from the depths of the Third. One of England's greatest-ever inside-forwards, he remains Villa's record goalscorer.

Walker, born at Wednesbury in Staffordshire in 1897, was the son of Wolves player, George Walker. His father had discouraged him from becoming a professional footballer and had sent him off to work in an engineering firm. Walker attended King's Hill School in Wednesbury and after leaving school played for Hednesford Town, Darlaston, Wednesbury Old Park and Wednesbury Old Athletic before signing amateur forms with Aston Villa in March 1915. Due to the war he did not sign professional forms until he was 21, in May 1919, and he played as a guest for Birmingham during World War One.

He scored two goals on his debut for Villa, against Queen's Park Rangers in the FA Cup in January 1920, and was soon playing in an FA Cup Final. That season Walker helped Villa reach the Final, where they beat Huddersfield Town 1-0 at Stamford Bridge just four months after his debut. He initially made his mark as a centre-forward but later played mainly at inside-left. He had fine ball control and was an excellent header on the ball.

A clever inside-forward, Walker was a fine tactician and a lethal marksman. In August 1920, he scored four goals in a game against Arsenal and in November 1921 netted a hat-trick of penalties against Bradford City. He was also a good deputy goalkeeper and once played in goal for England in an emergency.

This happened in 1925, when England played France in Paris and goalkeeper Fred Fox was carried off injured in his only international. Walker played 18 times for his country. This included a gap of five years before he was recalled to captain the side in an important game against Austria in December 1932, when England narrowly won 3-2 in one of the greatest international matches ever staged in this country.

Walker played in another FA Cup Final in 1924 and this time Villa lost 2-0 to Newcastle United at Wembley. He scored 244 goals in 531 games for Aston Villa, still the most goals scored for Villa in aggregate over a player's career. Villa were twice runners-up to Arsenal in the First Division. In 1930-31 they finished seven points behind the Gunners, but scored 128 goals in the League, and in 1932-33 they finished four points behind Arsenal. They also reached the semi-finals of the FA Cup in 1929 but lost 1-0 to Portsmouth. Walker retired from playing in November 1933, having shown great loyalty to Aston Villa. He had also been a fine cricketer and had appeared for Warwickshire's junior sides.

The following month, Walker was appointed manager of Sheffield Wednesday. When he arrived at Hillsborough the Owls were struggling near the foot of the First Division but immediately embarked on an unbeaten 12-match run and finished the season in mid-table. Some of his decisions upset people, especially some of his opinions about the players that he had inherited and soon parted with. But Walker was a man of ideas and vision and he soon found some success when the Owls reached the 1935 FA Cup Final and beat West Brom 4-2 at Wembley. Two late goals from Ellis Rimmer brought the Cup back to Sheffield.

Wednesday narrowly escaped relegation in 1935-36 but went down the following season. After 14 games of 1937-38 they were second from bottom of Division Two and Walker resigned after a stormy meeting of shareholders in November 1937.

He soon became bored with being out of football and was persuaded to return as manager of non-League Chelmsford City in January 1938. They were in the process of moving up from amateur to semi-professional status and he took them to the third round of the FA Cup in 1938-39.

In March 1939, Walker became manager of Nottingham Forest and remained in charge at the club for the next 21 years. The war soon intervened and he appeared eight times for Forest in wartime soccer. Forest were badly affected by the war and struggled in the Second Division when League soccer resumed in 1946. They were relegated to the Third Division South in 1949.

At this point Walker made some crucial signings, including Wally Ardron and Horace Gager, and Forest clinched the Southern Section title in 1950-51. In 1956-57, Forest were runners-up in the Second Division and returned to the top flight for the first time in 32 years.

At the start of their 1959 run to the FA Cup Final, Forest nearly lost in the third round at non-League Tooting & Mitcham United, coming from 2-0 down to draw 2-2 before winning the replay 3-0 at the City Ground. They beat Luton Town 2-1 in the Final, despite losing Roy Dwight with a broken leg. By the following year, management was becoming too much for Billy Walker and he resigned in July 1960 at the age of 62. He remained on the club's committee until his death in Sheffield in November 1964. Walker had often suffered from ill health and suffered a stroke in October 1963.

WALLACE, John Martin Bokas

Born: Wallyford, Edinburgh, 6 September 1935.
Goalkeeper 6ft 1in; 13st (1960).
Career: South of Scotland Schools; Wallyford Boys' Club; Blackpool trialist August 1960; Workington amateur July 1951, professional September 1952; Ashton United August 1953; Berwick Rangers 1955; Airdrie September 1956; West Bromwich Albion October 1959 (£10,000); Bedford Town June 1962; Hereford United August 1964; Berwick Rangers player-manager December 1966-cs 1969; Heart of Midlothian coach and assistant manager January 1969-April 1970; Glasgow Rangers coach June 1970-cs 1972, then manager June 1972-May 1978; Leicester City manager May 1978-July 1982; Motherwell manager July 1982-November 1983; Glasgow Rangers manager November 1983-April 1986; Seville (Spain) coach May 1986-August 1987; Colchester United manager January-December 1989, then director.

Honours: Division Two champions 1980; Scottish League champions 1975, 1976. 1978; Scottish Cup winners 1973, 1976, 1978, runners-up 1977; Scottish League Cup winners 1976, 1978, 1984, 1985.

A hard man as a manager, Jock Wallace always wanted very committed players in his teams and he built sides on the foundation of hard work and guts. After a fairly undistinguished playing career, he took over as player-manager at Berwick Rangers and the high spot of his term of office there was beating Rangers 1-0 in the Scottish Cup in 1967. Wallace gained honours galore at Rangers, with three League titles, three Scottish Cup winners' medals and four Scottish League Cup winners' medals.

After gaining the treble in 1977-78, Wallace surprisingly left to manage Leicester City. There was a great turnaround in the playing staff at Filbert Street, after they just missed relegation in his first season in charge, and City won the Second Division title in 1979-80. They were relegated in 1981 and he left after failing to take them straight up again. They did reach the semi-finals of the FA Cup in 1982, but lost to Spurs. Wallace returned to Ibrox but had only limited success before moving to Spain. He was unable to lift Colchester United off the bottom of Division Four. He is the son of Blackpool goalkeeper Jock Wallace.

WALSH, Michael Thomas

Born: Manchester, 20 June 1956.
Defender 6ft; 12st (1990).
Career: Bolton Wanderers July 1974; Everton August 1981 (£90,000 & player); Norwich City (loan) October 1982; Burnley (loan) December 1982; Fort Lauderdale Strikers (NASL) July 1983; Manchester City October 1983; Blackpool February 1984 (£6,000); Bury July 1989, then manager December 1990.

Honours: Republic of Ireland international (5 caps); Division Two champions 1978.

A product of Bolton's youth policy, Walsh started his career as a left-back but later played in the centre of the defence and in midfield. He made his League debut in February 1975, as substitute at Nottingham Forest, and played in the Trotters' League Cup semi-final defeat by Everton in 1976-77, in front of over 50,000 at Burnden Park. He also helped them to the Second Division title the following season and was ever-present in Bolton's First Division seasons of 1978-80, a run of 126 consecutive games coming to an end with injury in December 1980.

Walsh moved to Everton for £90,000 plus Jim McDonagh, who returned to Burnden Park. After only 22 appearances for the Toffees, Walsh later won back a regular first-team place at Blackpool, where he made 153 League appearances. He helped the Seasiders to promotion from Division Four in 1984-85. Bury were relegated to Division Four in 1991-92, with Walsh in charge, and looked an outfit lacking in self-confidence and class up front. Bury reached the Third Division play-offs but lost narrowly to York City over two legs.

WALSH, William

Born: Dublin, 31 May 1921.
Half-back.
Career: Manchester United amateur 1935; Manchester City amateur May 1936, professional June 1938-April 1951; Chelmsford City player-manager April-August 1951; Canterbury City player-manager August 1951-February 1954; Grimsby Town manager February 1954-March 1955.

Honours: Republic of Ireland international (9 caps); Northern Ireland international (5 caps).

Due to the war, Walsh did not make his League debut until he was 25, against Arsenal in August 1946. He appeared in 242 wartime games and 118 peacetime ones for City but missed a Second Division championship medal in 1946-47 as he played in only 13 games. He was capped by both Northern Ireland and the Republic as Eire-born players could appear in the Home International Championship.

Walsh turned down the chance to remain in the Football League, with either Lincoln City or Port Vale, to become player-manager of Canterbury City. His only season in charge of Grimsby Town was one of the worst in the club's history and he was sacked before the end of 1954-55, when they sought re-election.

WARD, John P.

Born: Lincoln, 7 April 1951.
Forward   5ft 8in; 10st 7lb (1981).
Career: Adelaide Park (Lincoln); Lincoln City apprentice September 1970, professional March 1971; Workington (loan) September 1972; Watford July 1979 (£15,000); Grimsby Town June 1981; Lincoln City March-cs 1982; Aston Villa assistant manager 1988-1991; York City manager October 1991; York City manager October 1991-March 1993; Bristol Rovers manager March 1993.

Honours: Division Four champions 1976.

John Ward was a regular goalscorer at Lincoln City, where his goal tally was 91 in 223/17 League appearances. He first linked up with Graham Taylor at Lincoln and was later signed by him at Watford. Ward then worked as assistant manager to Taylor at Aston Villa. Lincoln were Fourth Division champions in 1975-76 and Ward was top scorer with 24 goals plus five in Cup competitions.

When they were relegated in 1979, he moved to Watford but never established himself in the first team at Vicarage Road and also suffered cartilage problems. Upon his return from injury, he played in midfield. Ward managed six goals in 22/5 games for Watford and his career seemed to go into decline after this. His first season in charge at York City was an unspectacular one. However, they got off to a great start in 1992-93 until they lost form in December.

York faded after a cracking start to the season and Ward was offered the manager's post at Bristol Rovers in March 1993 but could not prevent their relegation.

WARD, Ralph Arthur

Born: Oadby, near Leicester, 5 February 1911.
Full-back   5ft 8½in; 12st 8½lb (1935).
Career: Leicester City trailist; Kettering Town; Hinckley United; Bradford November 1929; Tottenham Hotspur March 1936; Crewe Alexandra August 1946, then manager June 1953-1955.

Honours: England Schoolboy international (2 caps).

A former butcher, Ward got his big break with Bradford. A good kicker and a tenacious tackler, he was a fine exponent of the shoulder-charge. He played 133 League and Cup games for Bradford and was awarded a benefit match which took place shortly after he moved to Spurs.

He scored 11 goals in his 135 appearances for Tottenham before the outbreak of the war, then played in another 243 games in wartime competitions, scoring 17 goals. Ward joined Crewe just before the start of the first post-war season and played 89 games, scoring seven goals for the club. Crewe achieved little success in his two seasons in charge, finishing 17th and 22nd in the Northern Section.

WARD, Timothy Victor

Born: Cheltenham, 17 October 1917; Died: Barton-under-Needwood, Staffs, 28 January 1993.
Wing-half   5ft 9in; 11st 9lb (1951).
Career: Cheltenham Schools; Cheltenham Town; Derby County April 1937 (£100); guest for Hamilton Academical in World War Two; Barnsley March 1951-1952, then 'A' team coach; Exeter City manager March 1953 (for eight days); Barnsley manager March 1953-February 1960; Grimsby Town manager February 1960-June 1962; Derby County manager June 1962-May 1967; Carlisle United manager September

1967-September 1968; Nottingham Forest scout August 1969; representative for a concrete firm from 1970.

Honours: England international (2 caps); FA tour of Canada 1950; FA Canadian Touring XI v England World Cup XI (FA Charity Shield game) 1950; Division Three North champions 1955; Division Three runners-up 1962.

Tim Ward had a long career in management and found success at Barnsley, who he took to the Third Division North title, and Grimsby Town, who he also guided to promotion to Division Two. There then followed a less happy spell as manager of Derby County, although Ward had enjoyed a fine playing career at the Baseball Ground and had been twice capped for England.

Cheltenham-born Ward was signed by Derby County manager George Jobey after a successful trial in which he scored with his first kick. He made his debut at left-half at Sunderland in January 1938 and, after replacing Ike Keen, missed only two games for the Rams up to the outbreak of war. He served in the Army during the war and found it difficult to get back to Derby to play many games. He was slightly wounded in the D-Day landings but played in the Rams' first game of the 1945-46 FA Cup campaign, at Luton. Army duties then took him back to Germany, where he played for the BAOR side, and he had no chance of winning back his place for the 1946 Cup Final, when Derby lifted the trophy for the only time in their history.

He switched to right-half after the war and was a stylish player with pace, who liked to join the attack. Arsenal offered £10,000 for him but he decided to stay at the Baseball Ground and played for the Rams in their 1948 FA Cup semi-final defeat by Manchester United. In 1950, Ward toured Canada with the FA and he had also played twice for England. In September 1947 he helped them to a 5-2 victory over Belgium in Brussels and in November that year they beat Wales 1-0 at Villa Park with Ward in the side.

After scoring five goals in 260 appearances for the Rams, Ward moved to Barnsley in 1951. It was a move which disappointed Derby fans and was another sign that their club was on the wane. Barnsley signed him as a replacement for Danny Blanchflower, who had been sold to Aston Villa, and he played 33 League games for the Colliers before

retiring to run the 'A' team at Oakwell. In March 1953, Ward was appointed manager of Exeter City, but stayed for only eight days before returning to Oakwell after being offered the manager's job after the death of Angus Seed.

Ward was 34 when he took over, the youngest manager in the League at that time. Barnsley were relegated to the Third Division North at the end of 1952-53 but two seasons later they bounced back as champions. They were relegated again in 1958-59. Ward could be rigid in his approach and would not tolerate foul play or bad language from his players. He was a good public relations man and allowed his players to take the limelight when they found success.

In February 1960, he moved to Grimsby Town as manager and took them to runners-up in Division Three in 1961-62, then received a very good offer to take over at Derby County, which he accepted in June 1962.

Ward was delighted to return to Derby, for the club were his first love in football, but at the Baseball Ground his gentlemanly approach went against him and he was accused of not being ruthless enough. One of his best signings was Eddie Thomas, who cost less than £10,000 from Swansea and scored plenty of goals. After this, the Derby board expected all his signings to be successful bargains but, of course, this was impossible to achieve.

However, Ward also signed future stars such as Alan Durban, Peter Daniel and Colin Boulton and his one major signing was Kevin Hector, from Bradford for £40,000. It was a lot of money for a Fourth Division player — and a remarkable fee for Derby to find. Ward had pursued Hector for months but he had to fight long and hard before he could sign him. Hector, of course, went on to become one of the greatest players in Derby County's history.

With the club a mid-table Second Division side, his contract was not renewed and Ward left Derby in May 1967. He said that his five years in charge at the Baseball Ground had been the unhappiest time of his football career. "I had to ask the directors' permission to stick a twopenny stamp on a letter," he said. He also told of having to wait outside the boardroom for hours before being summoned in to meetings.

Ward was not out of football for long, however, and returned to manage Carlisle United in September 1967. After they finished 11th in the Second Division in 1967-68, he resigned in September 1968 after a poor start to the new season. From August 1969, he became a scout for Nottingham Forest and then worked as a representative for the Douglas Concrete firm near Burton-upon-Trent.

Tim Ward was still playing in his 70s, turning out for the Ex-Rams All Stars team, and was the first chairman of the Derby County Former Players' Association when it was formed in 1991. He became ill the following year and died in hospital near his Staffordshire home in 1993. A service of thanksgiving for his life was held in Derby Cathedral.

WARE, Harry

Born: Birmingham, 22 October 1911; Died: Stoke, 28 October 1970.
Inside-right   5ft 10in; 12st 5lb (1935).
Career: Stoke St Peter's; Hanley St Luke's; Stoke City amateur December 1927, professional December 1929; Newcastle United September 1935

(£2,400); Sheffield Wednesday May 1937 (£1,700); Norwich City November 1937; Northwich Victoria player-coach in World War Two and manager 1946-1948; Haarlem (Holland) trainer-coach August 1948; Northwich Victoria coach 1950; Port Vale coach 1956; Crewe Alexandra manager 1958-May 1960; Stoke City assistant trainer 1960, then scout until death.

Honours: Division Two champions 1933.

A former potter, Ware helped Stoke City to the Second Division title in 1932-33, in the same side as Stanley Matthews, and scored 16 goals in 53 League games for Stoke before moving to Newcastle United. But he never made the impact that was expected of him and left after only nine goals in 49 games.

After 12 games for the Owls, he moved to Norwich City where he scored 14 goals in 45 appearances before the outbreak of war. Due to a chest wound received in the Normandy landings, Ware was forced to retire and, after coaching in Holland, in non-League soccer and at Vale Park, he took over as manager at Gresty Road. Crewe finished 18th and 14th respectively in Division Four in his two seasons in charge. They reached the fourth round of the FA Cup in 1960, but lost 13-2 to Spurs in a replay. He was the son of a famous boxer.

WARNER, John

Born: Tonyrefail, 21 September 1911.
Wing-half   5ft 7in; 10st 7lb (1951).
Career: Trealaw FC; Treorchy Juniors; Aberaman 1932-1934; Swansea Town January 1934; Manchester United June 1938; Oldham Athletic player-coach June 1951; Rochdale player-manager July 1952-May 1953; ran a betting shop in Stretford, Manchester.

Honours: Wales international (2 caps).

Jack Warner created openings for his forwards and was a steadying influence on his defence. A tenacious tackler and calmly assured, he played over 100 games each for Swansea Town and Manchester United, plus over 150 in wartime competitions for the Reds. He lost his first-team place before United's appearance in the 1948 FA Cup Final but turned out until his early 40s, priding himself on his physical fitness.

When he was player-manager of Rochdale, the club avoided having to apply for re-election by one point and Warner was not a great success in management. He had been appointed by George Hardwick as player-coach at Oldham Athletic.

WARNOCK, Neil

Born: Sheffield, 1 December 1948.
Forward   5ft 9½in; 10st 10lb (1973).
Career: Chesterfield July 1968; Rotherham United June 1969; Hartlepool United July 1971; Scunthorpe United February 1972 (£3,000); Aldershot March 1975; Barnsley October 1976; York City May 1978; Crewe Alexandra December 1978; Burton Albion August 1979; Gainsborough Trinity manager cs 1980; Burton Albion manager February 1981; Scarborough manager 1986-January 1989; Notts County manager January 1989-January 1993; Torquay United consultant January 1993, caretaker manager March-May 1993.

Honours: Division Two promotion 1991; Division Three promotion 1990; Vauxhall Conference League champions 1987.

Neil Warnock had a varied career, playing around the lower divisions, and scored 36 goals in a total of

295/30 League appearances in his career. Whilst playing, he qualified as a chiropodist and ran his own practice in Sheffield. As boss of Burton Albion, he took the club to the third round of the FA Cup in 1985, where they lost to Leicester City.

Warnock joined Scarborough and took them to the Conference League championship and into the Football League as the first club to be automatically elected. They finished 12th in their first season in the Fourth Division and seemed to heading for promotion again when Warnock was enticed away by Notts County.

He took County from the Third to the First Division. They finished third in Division Three in 1989-90 and were promoted via the play-offs, beating Tranmere Rovers 2-0 at Wembley. The following season they beat Brighton 3-1 in the final of the Second Division play-offs, also at Wembley, to enter the First Division. They also reached the quarter-finals of the FA Cup. However, Notts were relegated in 1992 and as they struggled in the new First Division, Warnock was sacked.

Warnock was sacked by Notts County in January 1993 with the club near the bottom of the table. He was then employed as a management consultant by Torquay United and became caretaker manager (replacing Paul Compton) from March to May 1993. He stepped down after steering United clear of relegation.

WARREN, Harry

Born: Newhall, Derbyshire Spring 1902; Died: Leigh on Sea, 4 April 1968 (aged 65).
Centre half   5ft 11½in; 11st 10lb (1926).
Career: Gresley Rovers; Blackpool cs 1924; Exeter City cs 1927; Merthyr Town cs 1928; Sheffield United April 1929; Folkestone secretary-manager 1931-39; Chelmsford City secretary-manager 1939-40; Southend United secretary-manager August 1940-June 1956; Coventry City manager June 1956-September 1957.

Never as good a player as his England international father, Harry Warren played only 33 League appearances for his four League clubs before taking over as player-manager at Folkestone at the age of 29. He liked to give young men a chance and produced players like Jack Vinall, Jack Acquroff, Viv Woodward, Alex McIntosh and Bob Iverson, all of whom went on to play League soccer.

He managed both Chelmsford and Southend United during the war, as they played at the same ground at

Chelmsford, and regretted leaving Southend after 16 years in charge. His best season in the League was 1955-56, when they finished fourth in the Southern Section. They also reached the fifth round of the FA Cup in 1952.

He left a secure job at Southend for a minefield of a task at Coventry. A rift soon developed between Warren and the players over wages. Morale sagged, some of the players seeing Warren as too soft. He was given little money to spend on players and when things went from bad to worse he was sacked. His father, Ben, played for Derby County, Chelsea and England.

WATSON, Thomas

Born: Newcastle upon Tyne, 9 April 1859; Died: 11 May 1915.
Career: connected as manager with Rosehill, Willington Quay, Newcastle West End & East End; Sunderland manager 1889-August 1896; Liverpool manager August 1896-May 1915.

Honours: Football League champions 1892, 1893, 1895, 1901, 1906; Division Two champions 1905; FA Cup runners-up 1914.

Tom Watson was one of football's first great managers. He brought in a lot of players from Scotland, especially at Sunderland, most of whom were individually brilliant. Watson then managed to harness these players into wonderful teams at both Roker and Anfield. As manager, he guided his clubs to five League championships, a Second Division title and an FA Cup Final appearance as well as to countless semi-final appearances.

At Sunderland, Watson produced the 'Team of all the Talents' which won the League championship three times, taking the title in 1891-92, 1892-93 and 1894-95. He had been appointed match secretary and manager before the start of the 1889-90 season and brought together an excellent side, then expertly guided them.

Sunderland had joined the Football League as recently as in 1890 but in their first season, Watson took them to the semi-final of the FA Cup, where they lost to Notts County after a replay. They also reached the semi-final in 1892, when they lost 4-1 to Aston Villa and then went down to Villa again at the same stage in 1895, this time 2-1.

In 1891-92, Sunderland confirmed themselves as champions when they beat Blackburn Rovers 6-1 with two games still to go. They won all their home games, had 13 wins on the trot and scored a massive 93 goals. The following season they finished 11 points clear of runners-up Preston and scored 100 goals, 28 more than anyone

else. In 1893-94, Sunderland were runners-up to Aston Villa and the following season won the League championship again, five points clear of Everton.

In August 1896, Watson accepted a higher pay offer from Liverpool and became their manager. He had also run his own tobacconist shop opposite Monkwearmouth Station since 1894. One of his best signings was Alex Raisbeck, who had first been spotted by the Reds chairman John McKenna. It took Watson a little time to build Liverpool up to be a force to be reckoned with. They lost to Aston Villa in an FA Cup semi-final at Bramall Lane in 1897 and also reached the same stage in 1899, but lost to Sheffield United in a fourth match. They also went very close to the League title that season. It was decided in the last match of the season. Both Villa and Liverpool had 43 points before they met in the last game of the season. Villa won the game 5-0 and the Reds probably let themselves down due to fatigue after having to play 16 matches in the previous 43 days.

Liverpool took the League championship in 1900-01, for the first time. This was mainly due to their run-in, which produced nine wins and three draws in their last 12 games. They were relegated to Division Two in 1903-04, but bounced straight back as champions the following season. They had ten consecutive victories and won 27 of their League games. The following year, they became the first side to take the Second and First Division titles in consecutive seasons . They also reached the semi-final of the FA Cup again but lost to neighbours Everton, 2-0 at Villa Park.

Liverpool finished runners-up in 1909-10 but then languished near the foot of Division One until the outbreak of World War One. They did reach the FA Cup Final in 1914, but lost to Burnley 1-0 at Crystal Palace, despite dominating most of the match. Watson signed a number of outstanding players during his period in charge including goalkeepers Elisha Scott, Sam Hardy, Ted Doig and goalscorers Jack Parkinson and Sam Raybould. Watson was a great character and much liked by the players. He was still in office when he died in May 1915 and many of his players attended his funeral.

WATSON, William

Born: Bolton-on-Dearne, Yorkshire, 7 March 1920.
Inside-forward   5ft 8½in; 11st 4lb (1950).
Career: Huddersfield Schools; Huddersfield Town October 1937; Sunderland April 1946 (£8,000); Halifax Town player-manager November 1954-April 1956 (£4,000), retired as a player 1956, manager September 1964-April 1966; Bradford City manager April 1966-January 1968; Wanderers (Johannesburg) manager April 1968-1972; also Yorkshire, Leicestershire and England cricketer.

Honours: England international (4 caps); 'B' international (3 caps); Wartime international (1 cap).

One of the few people to be capped by England at both football and cricket, Willie Watson made his debut for his country at soccer against Northern Ireland in a 9-2 win at Maine Road in November 1949. He also played in 22 Tests for England, having joined Yorkshire in 1939 and being awarded his county cap in 1947.

Watson made only 11 appearances for Huddersfield before the war but played in 223 League games for Sunderland, scoring 16 goals, after it. He gained no domestic club honours.

He had two spells in charge at The Shay but did not achieve much success. Halifax were also knocked out of the FA Cup by Birmingham League side Burton Albion during his time there. He produced some good footballers, but the club was always in financial difficulties and were forced to sell their better players. At Bradford City, he laid the foundations for a future promotion side.

His cricket career was of a higher profile. Besides his Test appearances he captained Leicestershire and was assistant secretary at Grace Road from December 1957. He was also an England cricket selector and was player-manager of the MCC tour party to East Africa in 1963. His father, William, also played for Huddersfield Town.

WATTS-JONES, Benjamin

Born: Swansea.
Career: Cardiff City manager February 1934-April 1937, director 1934-1939; also Southern League committee; director and chairman of Swansea Town for 21 years; FA committee of Wales; chairman of Welsh League.

Watts-Jones spent 21 years at Swansea Town prior to joining Cardiff City as a director. He helped them gain admission to the Football League in 1921 and also served on the selection committee of the Welsh FA. He took over at Ninian Park with the club at its lowest ebb after years of success.

He replaced Bart Wilson as secretary-manager and released all but five of the existing playing staff to bring in 17 new players. He had a constant battle with low attendances and little cash to spend. In 1937, when William Jennings took over as manager, Watts-Jones reverted to his place on the board of directors.

WEAVER, Samuel

Born: Pilsley, Derbyshire, 8 February 1909; Died: 15 April 1985.
Wing-half   5ft 10in; 11st 5lb (1932).

Career: Pilsley Red Rose; Sutton Junction trialist; Sutton Town 1926; Hull City March 1928 (£100); Newcastle United November 1929 (£2,500); Chelsea August 1936 (£4,160); guest for Leeds United in World War One; Stockport County December 1945, retired cs 1947; Leeds United trainer 1947-1949; Millwall trainer June 1949-January 1954; steward of Oxo Sports Club (Bromley) January 1954; Mansfield Town coach September 1955, then manager June 1958-January 1960, coach 1960, chief scout 1967 and caretaker manager November 1971; also Derbyshire and Somerset cricketer and Derbyshire CCC masseur.

Honours: England international (3 caps); Football League representative (2 caps); FA Cup winners 1932.

A polished and stylish left-half who was a good tackler and distributor, Sam Weaver was famous for his long throws. He scored 42 goals in 229 League appearances for Newcastle United before moving south to join Chelsea, where he was an automatic choice and captain from 1938. He played 120 games, scoring nine goals, for the Blues. Weaver gained an FA Cup winners' medal against Arsenal with the Magpies in 1932 and made his international debut against Scotland in April that year, in a 3-0 victory at Wembley.

He worked for many years at Field Mill, becoming trainer-coach in 1956 under Charlie Mitten and being caretaker manager on a number of occasions over the next 20 years. Mansfield Town were heading towards relegation to Division Four when he reverted to coach in 1960. When Weaver died, his ashes were scattered at Field Mill.

WEBB, Charles Graham

Born: The Curragh, near Kildare, Ireland, 1887; Died: Hove, 13 June 1975.
Inside-left   5ft 8½in; 12st (1909).
Career: Worthing 1902; Essex Regiment June 1904; Bohemians (Dublin) 1907; Worthing 1908; Brighton & Hove Albion amateur 1909-1919, then manager cs 1919-May 1947.

Honours: Ireland international (3 caps); Amateur international; Irish League representative; West Sussex Senior League champions; Southern League champions 1910; Sussex Senior Cup.

Charlie Webb was one of a family of seven, his father being a quartermaster in the Black Watch, serving with the British Army in Ireland when he was born. Webb joined the Essex Regiment in June 1904 and whilst serving in Ireland he played for an Irish Army XI v the English Army at Aldershot in 1907, scoring both goals in a 2-0 win.

Webb played for Ireland against England when he was with Bohemians and also represented the Irish League and Leinster. He bought himself out of the Army in February 1909 and was invited to join Brighton. He packed a deadly shot in each foot and helped the Seagulls to the Southern League title and an FA Charity Shield victory over Aston Villa in 1910. He wrote regularly about his club for the *Sussex Daily News*.

Webb managed the club for 30 years but was unable to get them into Division Two, although they went close on a number of occasions. They reached the fifth round of the FA Cup in 1932-33, after having to play from the first qualifying round. He was awarded a testimonial match in September 1949, when Arsenal and Portsmouth attracted 13,000 spectators to the Goldstone Ground.

WEBB, David James

Born: East Ham, 9 April 1946.
Centre-half   5ft 10in; 12st 11lb (1972).
Career: West Ham United amateur; Leyton Orient May 1963; Southampton March 1966; Chelsea February 1968 (£40,000 and a player); Queen's Park Rangers June 1974 (£100,000); Leicester City September 1977; Derby County December 1978; AFC Bournemouth player-coach May 1980, then manager December 1980-December 1982; Torquay United manager February 1984-August 1985, then managing director until June 1986; Southend United manager June 1986-March 1987 and general manager November 1988-July 1992. Chelsea manager February 1993-May 1993; Brentford manager May 1993.

With Chelsea he gained an FA Cup winners' medal after scoring the winner against Leeds in the 1970 replayed Final. He also gained a European Cup-winners' Cup winners' medal against Real Madrid in Athens in 1971 and played in the Blues' losing League Cup Final appearance against Stoke City in 1972. Webb made a total of 298 appearances for Chelsea, scoring 33 goals.

He began his managerial career with Bournemouth in 1980 and took them to promotion in 1981-82 but was sacked after a 9-0 defeat at Lincoln the following season. He took the club to court for unfair dismissal. Webb was not popular at Torquay, where he had to make tough financial decisions to keep the club alive. In 1984-85 they were bottom of Division Four and a stand at Plainmoor burned down.

At Southend, Webb became general manager but in charge of team affairs. He had taken the club from Division Four to the brink of Division One. Relegated to Division Four in 1988-89, they were promoted in third place the following season. Southend were then runners-up in 1990-91, one point behind Cambridge United after being top for most of the season. Webb had not only taken the club to the brink of Division One but was also party to plans to take the club away from Southend and move to Basildon. Webb's relationship with chairman Vic Jobson began to deteriorate and he resigned in March 1992, leaving the club at the end of the season. In February 1993 he was appointed manager of Chelsea following the dismissal of Ian Porterfield.

Dave Webb ended Chelsea's poor run when he took over as manager in February 1993 but he did not do enough to please chairman Ken Bates and his contract was not extended at the end of the season. Webb was not out of work for very long and soon afterwards became the manager of Brentford.

WEBBER, Eric Victor

Born: Portslade, 22 December 1919.
Centre-half   6ft; 12st 12lb (1991).
Career: Southampton amateur 1938, professional 1946; guest for Mansfield Town in World War Two; Torquay United player-manager October 1951-May 1965, retired as a player 1955; publican in Southampton until 1986.

Honours: Division Four promotion 1960.

An effective stopper centre-half, Webber played 182 League games for Southampton and 149 for Torquay United after six years in the RAF. He lasted almost 14 years as manager of Torquay United, who came close to winning Division Three South championship in 1956-57. They could only manage to draw their last game of the season, with Crystal Palace, and when Ipswich Town won their last game, it was the Suffolk club who went up to Division Two instead of Torquay.

With limited resources and poor attendances, Webber still achieved success at Plainmoor. Torquay entered Division Four in 1958 and finished third in 1959-60 to gain promotion. Two seasons later, though, they were relegated. Webber brought many fine players to the club including star forward Robin Stubbs for just £6,000 from Birmingham City. He was shocked when he was sacked after an average season in 1964-65. Webber survived open-heart surgery in 1979.

WEBSTER, Eric

Born: Manchester, 24 June 1931.
Half-back.
Career: Manchester City February 1952-June 1953; Ashton United; Hyde United; Macclesfield Town; Nantlle Vale; Pwllheli; Stalybridge Celtic manager; Hyde United manager; Runcorn manager; Stockport County groundsman, assistant manager, then manager May 1982-May 1985, then groundsman again.

Webster made only one appearance for Manchester City, in a 6-0 defeat at Cardiff City in February 1953. He then did the rounds in non-League soccer, initially staying in local soccer with Ashton United, Hyde United and Macclesfield before moving to Wales to play for Nantlle Vale and Pwllheli.

Webster was groundsman at Edgeley Park, then assistant manager to Jimmy McGuigan before taking over. He had previous managerial experience at Stalybridge Celtic, Hyde United and Runcorn. Stockport County struggled near the foot of Division Four during his three seasons in charge. They lost 3-0 to Telford United in the FA Cup in 1983-84 and had to seek re-election the following season. Webster is still the groundsman at Edgeley Park.

WEIR, David

Born: Aldershot, c.1863; Died: Bolton November 1933 (aged 70).
Centre-forward/Inside-left.
Career: Maybole (Ayrshire); Glasgow Thistle; Halliwell; Bolton Wanderers cs 1888; Ardwick May 1890; Bolton Wanderers January 1893, retired cs 1895; Maybole coach 1895; Glossop manager late 1909-April 1911; Stuttgart coach April 1911.

Honours: England international (2 caps).

A utility player, Weir made his two appearances for England in different positions: at centre-half against Ireland, in which he scored a goal in a 6-1 victory at Goodison Park; and at inside-left against Scotland in a 3-2 defeat at The Oval in April 1889.

A forceful attacker, Weir was not

liked by his fellow players being described as 'individualistic'. The son of an officer's batman, which probably explains his birthplace, Weir was brought up in Scotland from the age of 12. He played in Bolton's first Football League match, against Derby at Pike's Lane on 8 September 1888. He missed the 1894 FA Cup Final due to his unpopularity with the other players. He scored 41 goals in 92 games for the Trotters.

WELSH, Donald

Born: Manchester, 25 February 1911; Died: Stevenage, 2 February 1990.
Utility   5ft 11½in; 12st 4lb (1938).
Career: Manchester & Lancashire Schools; Royal Navy; Torquay United amateur early 1933, professional July 1934; Charlton Athletic February 1935 (£3,250); guest for Valetta (Malta), Southend United, Aldershot, Brighton & Hove Albion, Chester, Liverpool, Manchester City and Millwall in World War Two; retired November 1947; Brighton & Hove Albion manager November 1947-March 1951; Liverpool manager March 1951-May 1956; licensee in Devon 1956; Bournemouth & Boscombe Athletic manager July 1958-February 1961; manager of Clubland, Camberwell Youth Centre May 1961; Wycombe Wanderers manager July 1963-November 1964; Charlton Athletic administrative staff December 1964.
Honours: England international (3 caps); Wartime international (9 caps); Football League representative (1 cap); Division Three South champions 1935; FA Cup winners 1947, runners-up 1946; Football League South Cup winners 1944, runners-up 1943.

A 'complete' and inspirational player, Don Welsh captained Charlton to two FA Cup Final appearances. In 1946 they lost 4-1 to Derby County but the following year beat Burnley 1-0, probably the highlight of Welsh's career, although he had captained Charlton from the Third to the First Division, where they were runners-up in 1936-37. They also reached two Wembley Cup Finals in the war years. He scored 50 goals in 216 League and FA Cup games for the club as well as netting 100 goals in 118 wartime appearances. Welsh guested for Liverpool in the war years, a club he later managed. He scored six goals in a 12-1 victory over Stockport County in December 1940 and 43 goals in 40 games for the club overall.

Welsh retired to start his managerial career at Brighton and although he could not prevent the club finishing bottom of the Southern Section in 1947-48, he was the surprise choice to take over at Liverpool in March 1951. He spent heavily on the transfer market but could not halt Liverpool's slide into Division Two. Despite taking them to third place in 1955-56, Welsh was sacked. After two years spent running a public house in Devon, he was persuaded to take charge at Bournemouth but again had little success and was sacked during a poor 1960-61 season.

WENT, Paul Francis

Born: Bromley-by-Bow, 12 October 1949.
Centre-half   6ft; 12st 10lb (1972).
Career: East London Schools; Leyton Orient apprentice August 1965, professional October 1966; Charlton Athletic June 1967 (£24,250); Fulham July 1972 (£80,000); Portsmouth December 1973 (£155,000); Cardiff City October 1976

(£30,000); Orient September 1978, retired 1980, scout October 1980, coach July 1981, caretaker manager August 1981, then manager September-October 1981 (19 days); ran guest house in Portsmouth; tenant at Whalebone Inn, West Roding (Essex); played for Orient Supporters' Club in 1981-1982.*
Honours: England Youth international (10 caps); Schoolboy international (6 caps).

Paul Went is probably the most expensive player (in real terms) never to have played in the First Division. He made his debut for Orient against Preston in September 1965, at the age of 15 years 11 months. A fine, commanding central defender, Went gave Charlton great service, making 174/1 appearances before moving to Fulham for a £80,000 fee. He was soon on the move again, when sold to Portsmouth for a massive £155,000 in an attempt to ease the Cottagers' debts. Hard-up Pompey sold him to Cardiff City for much the same reason.

Went was once booked at Fulham in an Anglo-Italian match for backchatting to an Italian referee. His mother was Italian, thus his command of the language. He did not last very long as manager of Orient and was sacked after only 19 days officially in charge.

WESTGARTH, Frederick

Born: South Shields July 1887; Died: 4 February 1957.
Career: South Shields assistant trainer until cs 1926; Stockport County trainer cs 1926; Ebbw Vale coach; Workington coach; Luton Town coach; Stockport County manager May 1934-September 1936; Carlisle United manager December 1936-March 1938; Bradford City manager March 1938-July 1943; Hartlepools United manager August 1943-February 1957, then chief scout.
Honours: Division Three North Cup winners 1939.

Fred Westgarth never played League soccer and worked for many years as a coach before breaking into club management with Stockport County, who gained promotion to Division Two shortly after he left the club. A forthright man, Westgarth was a shrewd judge of player. He took Bradford City to the Division Three North Cup in 1939 and it was a surprise when he left for Hartlepools United, where he found great success, moulding together a team which gave the club its finest years. After finishing fifth in 1954-55 and fourth in 1955-56, they probably would have won the Northern Section title but for his death the following season, in which they finished runners-up.

WHEELER, James

Born: Reading, 21 December 1933.
Inside-forward   5ft 6½in; 10st 12lb (1963).
Career: Huntley & Palmers 1950; Reading August 1952; Bradford City manager June 1968-September 1971.
Honours: Division Four promotion 1969.

Wheeler gave Reading fine service after joining the club from local Spartan League side, Huntley & Palmers, the works team of the biscuit makers. He went on to make 406 League appearances, scoring 147 goals, for Reading. His best season was 1960-61 when he scored 31 goals. A broken leg at Barnsley in September 1964 effectively ended his career but he appeared

regularly for Reading Reserves after this and was also assistant manager to Roy Bentley.

He moved to Valley Parade as manager in 1968 and Bradford City won promotion at the end of his first season in charge, going up in fourth place. This included a run of 21 games without defeat. The supporters turned against him after a season of struggle against relegation and Wheeler resigned after a poor start to 1971-72.

WHITTAKER, Spence

Died: April 1910
Career: Local football in Accrington; Burnley manager September 1903-April 1910.

Spen Whittaker was full-time team manager at Turf Moor with director W.R.Thornton carrying out secretarial duties. He introduced many new players to Burnley, including Hugh Moffat, Terry Dawson and Alec Leake. The club's fortunes steadily improved. Sadly, whilst on his way to London by train to register a player in April 1910, he fell from the carriage and died instantly near Crewe. A benefit match was arranged with the proceeds going to his family.

WHITTAKER, Thomas James

Born: Aldershot, 21 July 1898; Died: London, W1, 24 October 1956.
Left-back/Left-half
5ft 8½in; 12st 2lb (1923).
Career: Worth View Technical College; Arsenal November 1919, retired due to injury to become assistant trainer cs 1925, trainer February 1927, assistant manager 1946, then manager June 1947-October 1956, also England and FA XI trainer; chairman of Football League Secretaries' and Managers' Association.
Honours: Football League champions 1948, 1953; FA Cup winners 1950, runners-up 1952.

The son of a regular soldier, a sergeant-major in the 12th Lancers, Tom Whittaker was born at East Cavalry Barracks, Aldershot, on 21 July 1898. He grew up in the Newcastle area from the age of three and attended Worth View Technical College. Whittaker initially wanted a career in engineering and later became a fully-trained marine engineer working for Hawthorn Leslie & Co of Tyneside. He joined the Army in 1917 and later moved to the Navy, playing football for the Royal Garrison Artillery.

After his demob, Whittaker joined Arsenal in November 1919 as a promising centre-forward. He made his debut at West Brom on Easter Monday 1920, in a 1-0 defeat. His best season as a player came in 1921-22, in which he made 42 League and FA Cup appearances for the Gunners, appear-

ing at left-back, right and left-half and on the right wing. He gained two London Challenge Cup winners' medals and had made 70 appearances for the club when he was selected to tour Australia with the Football Association in 1925. Whilst playing in a game in Wollongong, a small township near Sydney, he broke his knee cap in June 1925 and was unable to play again.

Sir Robert Jones, the surgeon who told him he would have to retire, later arranged a year's course in anatomy, massage and electrical treatment of injuries particularly associated with muscles. Whittaker built up a reputation as one of the finest trainers in the game, working for Arsenal, England and the FA touring sides and travelling all over the world. He was the first modern physiotherapist-coach and had all the latest equipment to help look after players' injuries, encouraged by his manager Herbert Chapman.

Whittaker joined the RAF in World War Two and on demob in 1946 became assistant manager at Arsenal to George Allison. Between them they saved Arsenal from relegation with the inspired signings of Joe Mercer and Ronnie Rooke. In June 1947, Whittaker succeeded Allison as manager and added Don Roper and Archie Macauley to his squad. He also signed Alex Forbes, for £13,000 from Sheffield United, and Doug Lishman, from Walsall for £10,000, and the Gunners ran away with the League championship that season with Rooke scoring 33 goals.

Whittaker did not seek personal publicity and liked to keep a low profile, but further honours were not far away and it became more difficult for him to achieve this. Arsenal won the FA Cup in 1950, beating Liverpool 2-0 in the Final. Two years later they reached the FA Cup Final again but, down to ten men due to a serious injury to Wally Barnes, they fought a gallant losing battle against Newcastle United.

In 1952-33 the Gunners won their last game of the season to take the League title again, but an ageing side was beginning to break up and the club entered a transitional period. The lack of success caused Whittaker added strain and he became ill with nervous exhaustion. Tom Whittaker died of a heart attack at the University College Hospital, London, in October 1956, at the age of 58. A fine book about his life was published just after his death, called *Tom Whittaker's Arsenal Story*, edited by Roy Peskett.

WIGHTMAN, Harold

Born: Sutton-in-Ashfield, 19 June 1894; Died: Nottingham, 5 April 1945.
Centre-half/Half-back
5ft 11in; 11st 10lb (1924).
Career: Sutton Town 1908; Mansfield Mechanics; Eastwood Rangers; Chesterfield cs 1913; Nottingham Forest guest September 1915-May 1919; Derby County May 1919 and assistant manager 1928-1929; Chesterfield May 1929; Notts County player-coach and assistant manager May 1930-June 1931; Luton Town manager June 1931-October 1935; Derby County scout October 1935; Mansfield Town manager January-May 1936; Nottingham Forest manager May 1936-March 1939.
Honours: Division Three South champions 1931.

Wightman was a steady centre-half who played at right-back later in his career. He made 189 appearances for the Rams, scoring nine goals, and was George Jobey's assistant manager in his last 18 months at the club. When he was assistant manager at Notts County, they took the Third Division South championship in 1930-31, eight points clear of Crystal Palace. He had helped Derby County to promotion in 1925-26 as a player and had also gained FA honours against France and Combined Universities.

At Luton, Wightman laid the foundations for future success and his resignation in 1935 came as a shock, after he had had a difference of opinion with his directors. During this period, he signed Joe Payne. Wightman was very briefly with Mansfield Town but soon left to take up the manager's post at Nottingham Forest. He was their first-ever manager, the team having previously been run by the club's committee. They went close to relegation in each of his three seasons in charge.

WILD, Wilfred

Died: December 1950.
Career: Manchester City assistant secretary 1920-1924, secretary 1924-1932, secretary-manager March 1932-November 1946, then secretary again until December 1950.
Honours: Football League champions 1937; FA Cup winners 1934, runners-up 1933.
Wilf Wild worked for Manchester City for 30 years, as assistant secretary, secretary and secretary-manager. When he was in charge of team affairs, he took City to a League title and two FA Cup Finals and was also in control throughout the war years.

Wild initially joined the club as assistant secretary in 1920 and four years later became secretary. In March 1932, he took over both team manager and secretarial duties and pushed hard for his role to be uncluttered by administrative duties but never succeeded in achieving this. Many fine players arrived at Maine Road during Wild's period in control. They included Peter Doherty, whom he bought for £10,000, and Alec Herd, Frank Swift and Sam Barkas. City reached the 1933 FA Cup Final but lost 3-0 to Everton.

They included in their ranks the sturdy centre-half Sam Cowan, future Manchester United boss Matt Busby, Jimmy McMullen, who captained the Scottish 'Wembley Wizards' that tamed England in 1928, and Alec Herd, father of David. The following year, City returned to Wembley and this time they won the FA Cup, beating Portsmouth 2-1 thanks to two goals from Fred Tilson. Their run to the Final included a 6-1 victory over Aston Villa in the semi-final.

When City won the League championship in 1937-38, their success came in remarkable fashion. At Christmas, they had only 20 points from 20 games but in the last 22 games they won 15 and drew the other seven to take the title. Doherty scored 18 goals in these last 22 games. Incredibly, City were relegated the following season, despite scoring more goals than anybody else in the First Division — and with virtually the same team from the previous season.

They finished fifth in the Second Division in 1938-39, then the war came along and Wild had to fight just to keep the club going. In November 1946, he stepped down to be replaced by Sam Cowan, who took the club to the Second Division title later that season.

Wilf Wild became club secretary again and died whilst still in office in December 1950. His wife Betty worked in the club offices up until the early 1960s.

WILE, John David

Born: Sherburn, County Durham, 9 March 1947.
Centre-half   6ft 1½in; 12st (1980).
Career: Eppleton Juniors (Hetton); Hetton Juniors; Durham City; Sunderland apprentice June 1964, professional June 1966; Peterborough United July 1967; West Bromwich Albion December 1970 (£32,000), caretaker manager December 1977 and player-coach 1981; Vancouver Whitecaps (NASL) May-August 1982; Rotherham United non-contract 1983; Peterborough United player-manager May 1983-November 1986; Sutton United August 1987; Solihull Cricket School manager in 1989.

An astute, reliable, commanding and powerful centre-half, Wile managed to instill his will to win in others around him. He rarely missed a game and played 831 times in his career, including 618/1 for West Brom. He played in three losing semi-finals for Albion. He is remembered for his brave display in the 1978 FA Cup semi-final, against Ipswich when he played on despite a nasty head injury but could not prevent a 3-1 defeat. Albion also lost to QPR in an FA Cup semi-final, again at Highbury, in 1982, and also lost to Spurs in the League Cup semi-final that season. He helped Albion to promotion to Division One in 1975-76.

Wile had three and a half seasons in charge of Peterborough United but could not get them out of Division Four. They suffered a humiliating defeat against Dagenham in the FA Cup in 1984, then reached the fifth round in 1985-86 before losing to Brighton in a replay. They had beaten Leeds United in the third round. In November 1986, Wile was sacked with the club in a lowly 19th position.

WILKINSON, Howard

Born: Sheffield, 13 November 1943.
Forward   5ft 9in; 11st 12lb (1970).
Career: Sheffield United amateur; Sheffield Wednesday June 1962; Brighton & Hove Albion July 1966-1970; Boston United player-manager 1970; England semi-professional team manager; England Under-21 assistant manager, later manager November 1982; Notts County assistant manager, then manager July 1982-June 1983; England coach November 1982; Sheffield Wednesday manager June 1983-October 1988; Leeds United manager October 1988.

Honours: England Youth international; Football League champions 1992; Division Two champions 1990, runners-up 1984; Four-Nations championship (semi-professional) winners 1979.
In a steady if unspectacular playing career, Howard Wilkinson played 22 games for the Owls before moving to Brighton, where he appeared in 116/13 League games, scoring 19 goals.

Wilkinson started his managerial career at Boston United and gained a degree in physical education at Sheffield University. He was a teacher for a while and was later an FA regional coach in Sheffield and managed England's semi-professional international team. He became an England Under-21 coach in November 1982.
Wilkinson took Notts County to 15th in Division One in his only season in charge and his efforts were hampered by poor attendances. He took Sheffield Wednesday back into Division One at the end of his first season in charge and, despite having little money to spend, was very successful at Hillsborough. In 1985-86, they reached an FA Cup semi-final before losing to Everton and finished fifth in Division One.
He took Leeds United to the Second Division championship in 1989-90 and to fourth place the following season. Then in 1991-92, Leeds went all the way to lift the League Championship, pipping Manchester United in a thrilling run-in. The signing of Eric Cantona probably made the difference between the two sides. After an early departure from the European Cup against Rangers, their form in the League also deteriorated.
Leeds slumped badly after their championship season and eventually just missed relegation. His ageing defence did not help and a series of injuries to key players meant that Wilkinson needed to bring in some younger players near the end of the season.

WILKINSON, Martin

Career: Rotherham United apprentice; sales representative; Barnsley coach; Leeds United coach and assistant manager 1981-June 1982; Peterborough United manager June 1982-February 1983.
Wilkinson failed to make the grade after an apprenticeship at Millmoor and drifted out of football, working as a sales representative. He coached at Oakwell and Elland Road and was assistant manager to Allan Clarke at

Leeds for a while. He was the surprise choice to take over at Peterborough United in June 1982, but lasted only eight months and was relieved of his duties with the club in a mid-table position in Division Four.

WILLIAMS, Albert

Career: Stockport County manager December 1919-November 1924.
Honours: Division Three North champions 1922.
Williams managed Stockport County for almost five years. They were relegated in 1920-21 with only 30 points, finishing bottom of Division Two. This was the season in which Edgeley Park was closed due to crowd trouble. Stockport were forced to play a home game at Old Trafford after a United home fixture. It is claimed that only 13 spectators paid to watch this game.
Williams signed proven goalscorer Ernie Simms, winger Benny Boardman and another goalscorer in Bob Blood. Stockport won the Third Division North championship at their first attempt, conceding only 21 goals all season. The following season, though, they missed relegation by one place.

WILLIAMS, Alvan

Born: Penmon, 21 November 1932.
Half-back   5ft 10in; 14st (1959).
Career: Stalybridge Celtic; Bury December 1954; Wrexham June 1956; Bradford June 1957; Exeter City August 1960; Hartlepools United manager February 1964-May 1965; Southend United manager May 1965-March 1967; Wrexham manager April 1967-September 1968.

Alvan Williams enjoyed regular first-team football only at Bradford, where he scored 21 goals in 92 games for the Park Avenue club. He also had little success as a manager. Under him, Hartlepools finished 15th in Division Four in 1964-65, Southend were relegated to Division Four in 1965-66 and he lost his job the following season despite being in the promotion pack. Wrexham finished eighth in 1967-68, his only full season in charge.
He appointed future Wrexham manager, John Neal, as his trainer. Williams also set up a youth policy which was to produce a wealth of talent in the next decade but, he resigned after a dispute with the directors and later ran a pub in Bala, North Wales.

WILLIAMS, Daniel T.

Born: Rotherham, 20 November 1924.
Wing-half   5ft 8in; 12st 6lb (1959).
Career: Silverwood Colliery; Rotherham United October 1942-1960, later trainer & coach, then manager July 1962-February 1965; Swindon Town manager August 1965-July 1969; Sheffield Wednesday manager July 1969-January 1971; Mansfield Town manager November 1971-March 1974; Swindon Town manager March 1974-May 1978, then assistant manager 1978.

Honours: Division Three North champions 1951; Division Three runners-up 1969; Football League Cup winners 1969.

A great club man with Rotherham United, where he made 459 League appearances, scoring 19 goals, Danny Williams started as an inside-forward but later played at wing-half. He had worked as a miner during the war. Rotherham were Northern Section champions in 1950-51 and went close to promotion to Division One in 1954-55, when they finished third.

When he left Millmoor, Williams intended to run his sports outfitter's shop in Rotherham but was persuaded to join Swindon Town as manager. He had great success at the club, taking them to promotion to Division Two and to a League Cup Final success over Arsenal in 1969, when they were still a Third Division club. But he had a disastrous spell in charge at Hillsborough, when Sheffield Wednesday were a club in decline and where internal strife and fading spirits led to relegation to Division Two in 1970. He lacked experience at the top grade.

Williams could not prevent Mansfield's relegation in 1971-72 and moved back to Swindon for a second spell in charge. Again he experienced relegation when Swindon went down in 1973-74. They came very close to instant promotion but after another three mediocre seasons he retired to South Yorkshire.

WILLIAMS, David Michael

Born: Cardiff, 11 March 1955.
Midfield   5ft 10in; 11st 8lb (1988).
Career: Clifton Athletic; Bristol Rovers August 1975, then player-manager May 1983-May 1985; Norwich City player-assistant manager July 1985 (£40,000).
Honours: Wales international (5 caps); Under-23 international (1 cap); Under-21 international (1 cap); Youth international; Division Two champions 1986.

A stylish midfielder with a footballing brain, Dave Williams had fine distribution skills. At 28, he was the youngest manager in the League, when he became player-manager of Bristol Rovers. Williams, who worked as a schoolteacher throughout most of his career, scored 79 goals in 400 appearances for Rovers. He was the first amateur to play League football for Rovers since Allen Wood in 1962. Indeed, in his first full season, when he missed only one game, he was an amateur throughout.

He gave up the manager's job at Rovers to become player-assistant manager at Norwich City under Dave Stringer and scored another 11 goals in 60 League appearances for the Canaries. He helped them to the Second Division title in 1985-86 and won his first Welsh cap against Saudi Arabia as late as February 1986. He is still assistant manager at Carrow Road.

WILLIAMS, Graham Evan

Born: Henllan, near Rhyl, Wales, 2 April 1938.
Left-back   5ft 8in; 12st (1963).
Career: Flintshire Boys; Rhyl Athletic; Burnley trialist 1953; West Bromwich Albion amateur September 1954, professional April 1955, retired April 1972; Weymouth player-manager May 1972-June 1975; Sport Club (Kuwait), coach 1975-1976; OFI (Greece) coach 1976-1977; Poole Town manager September 1979-June 1981; Cardiff City coach June 1981, then manager-chief coach November 1981-February 1982; Newport County scout 1983-1984; Leopards (Nigeria) coach; Rovaniemen (Norway) manager 1987-1989.
Honours: Wales international (26 caps); Under-23 international (2 caps); FA Cup winners 1968; Football League Cup winners 1966, runners-up 1967, 1970.

Graham Williams joined West Brom as a left winger but soon converted to left-back. A regular first-teamer from 1962-63, this stout-hearted defender went on to make 354/6 appearances for Albion, scoring 11 goals. He played in two League Cup Finals for the club. In 1966 Albion beat West Ham in a two-legged Final, 5-3 on aggregate. The following season they lost the first League Cup Final to be played at Wembley, going down 3-2 to Third Division QPR after being 2-0 ahead.

In 1968, Williams skippered Albion to an FA Cup Final success against Everton. During the 1970s he managed non-League sides and coached abroad in Kuwait and Greece. He was in charge at Cardiff City for only three months and his official title was chief coach, not manager. They won just one game in this period and was sacked along with colleague, Richie Morgan.

WILLIAMS, Thomas Watson

Born: Rhyl 1897; Died: 8 August 1961 (aged 64).
Career: scout for Burnley, Blackburn Rovers and Wrexham; Wrexham assistant manager September 1939, then secretary-manager April 1942-February 1949; Liverpool scout; ran sports shop in Wrexham; president of Wrexham Supporters' Club.

Despite never playing the game at any reasonable level, Tom Williams had an eye for spotting football talent. He took over as manager of Wrexham in the war years and built up a star-studed side with guest players such as Stan Cullis, Johnny Hancocks and Jackie Milburn, so that Wrexham were able to compete on an equal footing with the likes of Liverpool.

He had to rebuild the side when the war was over and Wrexham finished third in the Northern Section 1947-48 but were ten points behind the champions, Lincoln City. Many felt that he was hard done by when asked to resign after a board meeting following an internal dispute. He refused and was sacked.

Williams bought a sports shop in Wrexham and scouted for Liverpool. But he loved the Racecourse club and remained popular with players and supporters. His name was often put forward when the manager's job became available but he had enemies on the board of directors and was probably never reconsidered.

WILLIAMS, William Thomas

Born: Esher, Surrey, 23 August 1942.
Centre-half   6ft 1in; 13st (1970).

Career: Esher Schools; Surrey County; Portsmouth apprentice June 1957, professional June 1960; Queen's Park Rangers July 1961; West Bromwich Albion June 1963 (£10,500); Mansfield Town January 1966 (£10,000); Gillingham September 1967 (£7,000); Maidstone United cs 1972; Durban United (South Africa) August 1973 (£7,000); Durban City (South Africa) 1974; Sacramento Gold (USA) coach 1979; Atlanta Chiefs (NASL) coach 1980-1981; Maidstone United manager November 1981-December 1984; coaching in South Africa December 1984; Maidstone United manager again July 1986-1987 and October 1991-January 1992, also general manager and secretary 1987-January 1992; Gillingham manager January 1992.
Honours: England Youth international; Schoolboy international; Conference League champions 1984.

Although he had won his Schoolboy and Youth caps as a right-back, Williams developed into a steady centre-half who was signed by West Brom as cover for Stan Jones but who made only one appearance for the Throstles. He found most success at Gillingham, where he made 169/2 League appearances, scoring eight goals.

Williams had three spells in charge of team affairs at Maidstone United and also worked there as a general manager and club secretary. Maidstone won the Conference League in 1983-84 but there was no automatic promotion to the Football League in those days. They finished third in 1986-87 and Williams was general manager when they won it again in 1988-89 to enter the League at last. The club were continually dogged by financial worries ever since and in January 1992 Williams said that he had had enough and moved to Gillingham in a similar job.

WILSON, Andrew

Born: Irvine, Ayrshire, 10 December 1880; Died: 13 March 1945.
Centre-forward/Inside-left
5ft 10in; 13st 6lb (1913).
Career: Irvine Meadow 1897-1898; Clyde 1899; Sheffield Wednesday cs 1900, retired 1920; Bristol Rovers manager June 1921-May 1926; Oldham Athletic manager July 1927-July 1932; Stockport County manager July 1932-May 1933.
Honours: Scotland international (6 caps); Anglo Scots v Scottish XI 1903; Football League champions 1903, 1904; FA Cup winners 1907.

A big, powerful forward, Andy Wilson had a great career at Sheffield Wednesday, for whom he scored 216 goals in 546 appearances. He was leading scorer in eight of his 16 seasons at Hillsborough and was a great hero of the crowd. He played a key role in the Owls' League championship successes in the early years of the century and also appeared in Wednesday's FA Cup Final victory over Everton in 1907. He gained six Scottish caps, making his debut against England in April 1907 at Newcastle.

As a manager, he was a quiet, deep-thinking man whose team talks were always concise and brief. He brought several former Owls players to Eastville but resigned when Rovers just missed re-election in 1925-26. Oldham should have gained promotion to Division One in 1929-30, but lost their last game at Barnsley to finish third. The team broke up after this and he sold players to keep the club going including Fred Worrall to Portsmouth.

Wilson took Stockport County to third position in the Northern Section in 1932-33. His brother, David, was manager at Nelson and Exeter City and his other brother, James, played for St Mirren and represented the Scottish League.

WILSON, Andrew Nesbit

Born: New Mains, Lanarkshire, 15 February 1896; Died: 15 October 1973.
Centre-forward 5ft 8in; 12st 6lb (1930).
Career: Cambuslang Rangers; Middlesbrough February 1914; guest for Heart of Midlothian and Hamilton Academical in World War One; Dunfermline Athletic 1919-1921; Middlesbrough cs 1921; Chelsea November 1922 (£6,500); Queen's Park Rangers October 1931; Nimes (France) May 1932-1934; Clacton Town manager 1934; Walsall manager October 1934-April 1937; Gravesend & Northfleet manager late 1930s; Chelsea coach.
Honours: Scotland international (12 caps); Victory international (2 caps).

A thoughtful player who kept his forward line together, Andy Wilson also possessed an excellent shot. He overcame the handicap of a shattered arm sustained in the war in 1918 and scored 57 goals in 90 games for Middlesbrough. This total would have been greater but for the fact that he played for breakaway Scottish club, Dunfermline, between 1919 and 1921.

Wilson cost Chelsea a large fee and repaid them with 62 goals in 253 games, usually playing at inside-forward at Stamford Bridge. Strangely, he never capped for Scotland after joining Chelsea. He had scored 13 goals in 12 internationals after his debut in February 1920 in Wales.

Wilson played in France before becoming manager of Clacton Town. Walsall were a mid-table Third Division side during his three years in charge. Their best season was tenth in 1935-36 and they reached the fourth round of the FA Cup the following season. His son, Jimmy, was on Chelsea's books in the 1950s.

WILSON, Bartley

Born: Bristol.
Career: founder of Cardiff City, secretary 1910-1933, Cardiff City manager May 1933-February 1934; backroom staff from 1934; also lithographic artist.

Bart Wilson helped form Cardiff City and was appointed their secretary in 1910. Wilson, who had to get about on crutches, had a great knowledge of soccer. A sound judge of a player and of tactics, he saw the Cardiff club grow from its pioneering amateur days as Riverside Cricket Club to a First Division side. With the retirement of manager Fred Stewart, he stepped into the breach but it proved a disastrous period for a club anchored to the foot of Division Three South. Wilson was relieved to give up the manager's post to Ben Watt-Jones.

WILSON, David

Born: Irvine, Ayrshire, 14 January 1884.
Left-half   5ft 8in; 12st 6lb (1911).
Career: St Mirren 1901; Hamilton Academical 1902-1903; Bradford City November 1904; Oldham Athletic May 1906 (£90); Nelson player-manager May 1921-May 1925, retired as a player cs 1924; Exeter City manager March 1928-February 1929.
Honours: Scotland international (1 cap); Division Three North champions 1923.

Originally a half-back with lots of energy, enthusiasm and skill, Dave Wilson was a canny tactician and an excellent passer who played until his 40th year. He appeared in 264 consecutive League games for Oldham, until injury ended his run in January 1912. Bradford City had certainly made an error of judgement when they allowed him to move to Boundary Park.

Under him, Nelson clinched the Third Division North title in 1922-23 with two games still to play. Their reward was a tour of Spain that summer but they were relegated the following season. He gained his Scottish cap against England at Stamford Bridge in April 1913. Wilson, who conducted a stocks and shares business in Blackpool between 1925 and 1928, got the Exeter job from 100 applicants. He did not endear himself to the fans by selling favourites Stan Charlton and Billy Compton and was sacked after six successive defeats. He was the brother of Andrew and James Wilson.

WILSON, Glen E.

Born: Newcastle upon Tyne, 2 July 1929.
Wing-half   5ft 9in; 11st 10lb (1959).
Career: Newcastle United amateur; Brighton & Hove Albion September 1949; Exeter City player-manager June 1960-April 1962; publican in Brighton 1962; later rejoined Brighton & Hove Albion staff.
Honours: Division Three South champions 1958.

Known as Albion's 'iron man', Glen Wilson gave the club great service, playing 433 League and Cup games, scoring 25 goals, in 11 seasons at the Goldstone. He was club captain in his last five years there and helped the Seagulls to the Third Division South title in 1957-58.

Wilson had a difficult period as manager of Exeter City with the abolition of the maximum wage hitting the club hard and they had to apply for re-election in 1960-61. He had been offered the job despite not having applied for it but was sacked after Exeter finished 18th in 1961-62. He had made 37 appearances for the Grecians. His brother, Joe, played for Newcastle United and Brighton.

WILSON, Thomas Carter

Born: Preston, 20 October 1877.
Outside-left   5ft 6in; 11st 6lb (1906).
Career: Kensal Rise; Swindon Town 1897; Millwall 1898; Aston Villa April 1901; Queen's Park Rangers 1901; Bolton Wanderers 1904; Leeds City December 1906; Manchester United February 1908; Rochdale manager July 1922-February 1923.
Honours: England international trialist 1901.

An amateur for most of his career, Tom Wilson did the rounds of clubs. He made his League debut for Swindon Town against Southampton in 1897, skippered Queen's Park Rangers and was selected for an international match for the South versus the North in 1901. He was a publican in Bolton in 1907. A first-team regular only at QPR, he made 59 appearances for them, easily the most games he played for any of his clubs. In his only season in management, Rochdale struggled near the bottom of their division.

WITHE, Peter

Born: Liverpool, 30 August 1951.
Forward   6ft 2in; 12st (1983).
Career: All Hallow's School (Speke);

Smiths Coggins (Liverpool); Skelmersdale; Southport amateur cs 1970, professional August 1971; Barrow, trialist December 1971; Port Elizabeth City (South Africa) early 1972; Arcadia Shepherds (South Africa); Wolverhampton Wanderers (loan) October 1973, signed February 1974 (£13,500); Portland Timbers (NASL) May 1975; Birmingham City August 1975 (£50,000); Nottingham Forest September 1976 (£42,000); Newcastle United August 1978 (£200,000); Aston Villa May 1980 (£500,000); Sheffield United June 1985; Birmingham City (loan) September-November 1987; Huddersfield Town assistant manager and player-coach July 1988; Aston Villa assistant manager and coach January-October 1991; Wimbledon manager October 1991-January 1992.
Honours: England international (11 caps); Football League champions 1978, 1981; Football League Cup winners 1978; European Cup winners 1982; European Super Cup winners 1982.

Withe's career took some time to take off. Strong and tall, he became an expert at shielding the ball. He was a great trier and a very unselfish player. He played for several League clubs but had his greatest days at Nottingham Forest and Aston Villa.

Under Brian Clough, Withe developed into an excellent target man and at Villa he formed a great partnership with Gary Shaw. He won two League championship medals. In 1977-78, he was top scorer — with only 12 goals — when Forest took the title, and in 1980-81 he scored 21 when Villa became champions. He also netted the winner in Villa's European Cup success over Bayern Munich in 1982. Withe made his international debut against Brazil at Wembley in May 1981 and went on to win 11 caps.

After spells as assistant manager at Huddersfield and Villa, he applied for the Wimbledon job and got it. However, Withe experienced a terrible run of results and was sacked after only three months. His brother Chris played for Bradford City.

WOMACK, Francis

Born: Wortley, near Sheffield, 16 September 1888; Died: Caistor, Lincolnshire, 8 October 1968.
Full-back   5ft 8½in; 11st (1923).
Career: Lapham Street; Rawmarsh Albion; Birmingham July 1908-May 1928; Worcester City player-manager May 1928-1930; Torquay United manager July 1930-May 1932; Grimsby Town manager May 1932-October 1936; Leicester City manager October 1936-May 1939; Notts County manager July 1942-1943; Oldham Athletic manager February 1945-April 1947;

Grimsby Town caretaker manager January-May 1951.
Honours: Football League representative (2 caps); Division Two champions 1921, 1934, 1937; Birmingham League champions 1929.

Frank Womack gained three Second Division championship medals during his career, one as a player with Birmingham and one each as manager of Grimsby Town and Leicester City. He

gave Birmingham excellent service and was later a well-known figure as a manager, taking charge of six different clubs at one time or another. He was a 'systems' manager who tailored the abilities of his players to fit his concept of the game. He made a careful analysis of opponents and was a great theorist who worked out strategies to beat the opposition.

Womack, who was born near Sheffield in 1888, made his League debut for Birmingham at Gainsborough Trinity in September 1908. A full-back, Womack never scored a goal during his career, despite making 515 League and FA Cup appearances for Birmingham. Indeed, he holds the club record for appearances and, at 39 years and 207 days, is also the oldest player to appear for the Blues. He was unlucky never to be capped for his country, but did appear twice for the Football League and also helped Birmingham to the Second Division championship in 1920-21. He was one of the club's greatest-ever players and skippered the side for 17 consecutive seasons. He had the strange habit of always clapping his hands before heading a ball.

In 1913, Womack became unwittingly involved in a bribery scandal. He was offered 55 guineas to 'fix' a Blues match against Grimsby Town to end in a draw. He reported the incident to officials and a trap was set, the culprit being arrested in the act of passing money over to Womack.

In May 1928, he became player-manager of Worcester City and led them to the Birmingham League title in 1928-29, a season in which they also reached the first round of the FA Cup. In July 1930, he accepted an offer to manage Torquay United. They had an inconsistent season in 1931-32, losing 10-2 to Fulham and 7-0 to Crystal Palace. However, they also beat Bristol Rovers 8-1. Seeing his chances limited at Torquay, he applied for the vacant job at Grimsby Town and was appointed as boss there in May 1932.

Womack proved to be the most successful manager in the Mariners' history. When he took over at Blundell Park, morale was low as Grimsby had just been relegated from the First Division. Relegation again looked a strong possibility in his first season in

charge, but an unbeaten run in their last 11 games took the Mariners to safety.

Then Grimsby swept all before them in 1933-34. Playing some superb football, they took the Second Division title and then finished fifth in Division One the following season. In 1936 they reached the semi-final of the FA Cup before losing 1-0 to Arsenal. It was a great blow to Grimsby Town, when Womack decided to move to Leicester City in October 1936.

Leicester were 21st in the Division Two when he took over but results improved after he paid £6,000 for Derby County centre-forward Jack Bowers, who went on to score 33 goals in 27 games as City ended the season as Second Division champions. However, after they were relegated, Womack resigned in May 1939.

In 1940 he was suspended for a year after being implicated in a financial irregularities scandal whilst in charge at Filbert Street. Womack did not return to management until July 1942 when he took control at Notts County, where he introduced a policy of developing young players. Amongst the players he groomed was Jackie Sewell, who later commanded large fees on the transfer market. Womack left Meadow Lane in 1943 but in February 1945 became manager of Oldham Athletic, getting the job ahead of 60 other applicants. They just missed having to seek re-election in the first season after the end of the war and Womack resigned in April 1947.

He returned to manage Grimsby Town as caretaker boss in January 1951, taking over from Charlie Spencer who had become ill. But Womack could not prevent their relegation at the end of that season and left football for good in May 1951.

WOOD, Alfred R.

Born: Aldridge, near Walsall, 14 May 1915.
Goalkeeper.
Career: Sutton Town; Nuneaton Borough; Coventry City 1935; guest for Northampton Town in World War Two; Northampton Town December 1951 (£2,100); Coventry City player-trainer July 1955, retired as a player 1958, left club November 1961; Walsall manager November 1963-1964.

Wood made only two appearances for Coventry City before the outbreak of war. He was called up into the Army and near the end of the war contracted spinal meningitis and was told that he would never play again. Happily, he made a complete recovery and re-signed for Coventry, going on to make 225 consecutive appearances over the next six years. Wood was consistently brave, giving many memorable performances before losing his place to Peter Taylor in 1951.

He made 98 consecutive appearances for Northampton Town before returning to Highfield Road as a trainer, but was forced into a comeback at the age of 43 when regular goalkeeper Jim Sanders broke a leg. Wood played ten games in City's promotion side of 1958-59. He was sacked, along with the rest of the managerial and training staff, after a purge at Highfield Road in 1961.

Wood discovered Allan Clarke at Walsall but stayed only one season as manager at Fellows Park. He left the professional game after this and ran the works side at Massey Ferguson (Coventry) with a side which included many former professionals.

WOODS, Maurice

Born: Skelmersdale, 1 November 1931.
Centre-half 6ft; 12st 6lb (1959).
Career: Burscough; Everton amateur 1947, professional November 1949; Blackburn Rovers November 1956; Hakoah (Australia) cs 1963; Luton Town July 1965; Stockport County July 1966, later trainer, then manager April 1970-December 1971; Southport coach 1974.
Honours: Football League representative (1 cap); Australia international.

A dominating centre-half, who in the 1950s made up an excellent half-back line with Ronnie Clayton and Mick McGrath at Ewood Park, Matt Woods had his early professional career suspended while he did his National Service. When he returned to England he was unable to break into the Everton side. Blackburn manager Johnny Carey signed Woods for a bargain £6,000 and the pivot soon established himself in Rovers' side, making 307 appearances and scoring three goals before emigrating to Australia after losing his place to the young Mike England. Woods had missed only two League games from November 1956 until August 1961.

A born leader and organiser, it was not a surprise when he went into training and management but he was not very successful as manager of Stockport County, who finished 11th in Division Four at the end of his first season in charge. He was sacked midway through his second season after a defeat by Blyth Spartans in the FA Cup. Stockport were also near the foot of the table.

WOOTON, William

Born: Longton, Staffs, 27 August 1904.
Left-back 5ft 8in; 11st 3lb (1925).
Career: Congleton Town; Stoke amateur 1924; Port Vale cs 1925; Southend United August 1932, retired through injury 1933; Northwich Victoria player-manager; Oldham Athletic manager June 1947-September 1950; Halifax Town manager November 1950-February 1952.
Honours: Division Three North champions 1930.

Wooton had a very average playing career with 54 appearances for Port Vale and only two for Southend. His best season was 1929-30, when Vale won the Northern Section title and Wooton appeared 20 times. He helped win the Cheshire League Challenge Cup and the Cheshire Senior Cup whilst manager of Northwich Victoria.

Wooton had a dreadful start at Oldham but they recovered to finish 11th with only one defeat in their last 17 games. His best season was 1948-49, when they finished sixth. He resigned after another poor start to the 1950-51 season. At Halifax, Wooton recruited a number of useful players and helped clear large debts at the club.

WORTHINGTON, Frank Stewart

Born: Halifax, 23 November 1948.
Centre-forward 6ft; 12st (1975).
Career: Huddersfield Town apprentice April 1963, professional November 1966; Leicester City August 1972 (£80,000); Bolton Wanderers September 1977 (£90,000); Philadelphia Fury (NASL) (loan) May-August 1979; Birmingham City November 1979 (£150,000); Tampa Bay Rowdies (NASL) March 1981 (£100,000); Leeds United March 1982 (£100,000); Sunderland December 1982 (£50,000); Southampton June 1983

(£20,000); Brighton & Hove Albion May 1984; Tranmere Rovers player-manager July 1985-February 1987; Preston North End player-coach February 1987; Stockport County November 1987; Cape Town Spurs April 1988; Chorley October 1988; Stalybridge Celtic December 1988; Galway United October 1989; Preston North End coach February 1990; Weymouth; Radcliffe Borough; Guiseley 1990; Hinckley Town manager September 1990-April 1991; Halifax Town coach October 1991.
Honours: England international (8 caps); Under-23 international (2 caps); Football League representative (1 cap); Division Two champions 1970, 1978.

Frank Worthington's skill stood out in an era of mediocre football. A great character, Worthington was flamboyant, very elegant, had subtle and spectacular skills and possessed many flicks and volleys. He should have won more than eight caps for England. His best record was with Leicester City, for whom he scored 78 goals in 237/1 appearances. Worthington helped Huddersfield Town to the Second Division title in 1969-70 and did the same with Bolton in 1977-78. He was the First Division top scorer with 24 goals in 1978-79.

He took over at Tranmere Rovers in a blaze of publicity but was not perhaps a great motivator, nor able to communicate well with his players. He left this to his assistant George Mulhall. Worthington was never given any money to spend and was sacked with the club at their lowest ebb. However, he discovered some useful players for Tranmere.

He was still playing in non-League soccer, well into his forties. One brother, Bob, played for Halifax, Middlesbrough, Southend and Notts County and another brother, David, played for Halifax, Barrow, Grimsby and Southend.

WRIGHT, Charles George

Born: Glasgow, 11 December 1938.
Goalkeeper 6ft; 12st 2lb (1959).
Career: Glasgow Schools; East Kilbride YMCA; New Hill (Paisley); Glentyre Thistle; Morton; Glasgow Rangers 1956; Workington June 1958; Grimsby Town February 1963 (£6,500); Charlton Athletic March 1966 (£10,000); Bolton Wanderers June 1971, retired through injury April 1974 to become coach; York City manager November 1977-March 1980; Bolton Wanderers reserve-team manager August 1981, chief coach November 1983, manager February-December 1985; running a transport cafe in South London.
Honours: Division Three champions 1973; Scottish Juvenile Cup winners; Hong Kong international (3 caps whilst on National Service).

Charlie Wright gained his Hong Kong caps when stationed in the colony during his National Service. Against Peru he saved a penalty and was later voted Hong Kong Player of the Year. Wright had a great sense of humour and continually chatted to spectators behind his goal. He helped Bolton to the Third Division title in 1972-73 and when he retired due to a spinal injury he had made 535 League appearances in his career.

He enjoyed little success as manager of York City and was sacked by the club. Wright returned to Burnden Park as reserve-team manager. The club struggled when he took over as manager, although he signed some useful and experienced players before leaving

Bolton by mutual consent. Very outspoken, he was perhaps not always able to communicate as well with the players or fans as a manager.

WRIGHT, John

Born; Tyldesley, Lancashire, 11 August 1926.
Left-back 5ft 7in; 11st 5lb (1958).
Career: Atherton Colliery; Mossley; Blackpool June 1946, retired through injury August 1959 and joined the training staff; Tranmere Rovers trainer June 1961, then manager December 1969-April 1972.
Honours: England 'B' international (1 cap).

Jackie Wright missed all Blackpool's FA Cup successes but played 158 League games for the club, despite rarely being first choice. He also gained England 'B' honours. Wright was Dave Russell's assistant at Tranmere and stepped up to become boss when Russell became general manager. Wright steered Tranmere away from relegation in 1969-70, but they again came close to relegation in 1971-72, missing the drop on goal-average. Eventually Wright was sacked and left football for good.

WRIGHT, Robert Cooper Allen

Born: Glasgow, 20 February 1915.
Defender.
Career: Horden Colliery Welfare; Charlton Athletic May 1937 (£100); guest for Middlesbrough in World War Two; captain in Royal Armoured Brigade in World War Two; Charlton Athletic assistant manager September 1947-June 1949; Bristol City manager April 1949-June 1950; licensee in Bristol from 1950; Bristol Rovers assistant manager July 1951-July 1952; licensee at White Hart, Lower Maudlin Street, Bristol.

Wright's playing career was wrecked by the war. After his debut for Charlton at Portsmouth in October 1938, he made 28 appearances before the outbreak of war and spent much of it abroad. He made 47 wartime appearances for Charlton and 19 for Middlesbrough, but retired 1947. Wright was Jimmy Seed's assistant at The Valley, then took over at Bristol City in 1949. He complained that he was not given a free hand and, after an ordinary season, resigned because of this. He was assistant to Bert Tann at Eastville.

WRIGHT, William

Born: Sheffield, 1903; Died: October 1983.
Centre-half/Left-half.
Career: Clapton Orient amateur in 1920s, professional 1930, trainer 1935, then manager December 1939-August 1945, masseur from 1946; Chingford Town manager.

Wright made only one appearance for Clapton Orient, at centre-half in a 3-1 home defeat against Torquay United in October 1931, although he was associated with Orient for almost 20 years. He was never in charge during peacetime but guided the club through the war years and even played in goal in emergencies. He became the club's masseur in 1946 and then managed new semi-professional club Chingford Town. Wright was still playing at 65, in the Birmingham Sunday Alliance in a team with three generations of Wrights in their ranks.

WRIGHT, William Ambrose CBE

Born: Ironbridge, Salop, 6 February 1924.
Centre-half 5ft 8in; 11st 6lb (1950).

Career: Staffordshire Schools; Wolverhampton Wanderers amateur 1938, professional February 1941, retired August 1959; guest for Leicester City in World War Two; England youth-team manager October 1960; Arsenal manager May 1962-June 1966; worked in television for many years.
Honours: England international (105 caps); 'B' international (1 cap); Football League representative (21 caps); Footballer of the Year 1952; Football League champions 1954, 1958, 1959; FA Cup winners 1949.

An inspiring captain for club and country, Billy Wright was an excellent tackler and passer. A model professional who was never sent off or booked in his career, Wright was the first player to make 100 appearances for England and was voted Footballer of the Year in 1952. He made his debut at 15½, just after the outbreak of war, and went on to make over 500 peacetime appearances for Wolves, plus many wartime games. He gained his first cap in a Victory international against Belgium in January 1946.

Wright captained Wolves to three League titles and an FA Cup Final victory over Leicester City in 1949. He skippered England 90 times and played in the 1950, 1954 and 1958 World Cup finals. He had no previous managerial experience when he took over at Arsenal.

Wright bought centre-forward Joe Baker from Italian soccer and later signed centre-half Ian Ure from Dundee to boost the Gunners' defence. But he had little success as a manager and was considered 'too soft'. He was sacked after another poor season at Highbury but he did produce some good young players. One of his last acts as manager was to sign Charlie George from schoolboy soccer in May 1966. Wright later worked for Midlands television franchise ATV as an anchorman and was later head of sport for that company and its successor, Central TV.

WYLIE, Andrew

Born: c.1887.
Career: Boness manager until 1926; Reading manager cs 1926-June 1931; Guildford City manager; Glenavon manager; Hamilton Academical manager.

Reading won the Third Division South

title without a manager but, upon entering the Second Division, appointed 'Angus' Wylie, who kept them in that division for five years. In his first season they had a good run in the FA Cup, beating Manchester United 2-1 at Villa Park in a third-round second replay. They reached the semi-final before losing to Cardiff City, 3-0 at Molineux. In 1931 he resigned when they were relegated, ironically with Cardiff, to the Third Division. He also managed in Scottish League soccer with Boness and Hamilton Academical.

WYLIE, Ronald M.

Born: Glasgow, 6 August 1933.
Inside-forward 5ft 9in; 11st 3lb (1963).
Career: Clydesdale Juniors 1946-1947; Notts County amateur April 1949, professional September 1950; Aston Villa November 1958 (£8,250); Birmingham City June 1965, retired June 1970; Aston Villa coach June 1970-1972; Coventry City coach 1975, then assistant manager 1978-1981; Cyprus coach; Bulova (Hong Kong) player-coach 1982; West Bromwich Albion manager July 1982-February 1984; Aston Villa reserve-team coach February 1984-May 1987; then scouting for several clubs; Football in the Community Officer at Villa Park August 1990.

Honours: Scotland Schoolboy international (3 caps); Division Two champions 1960; Football League Cup winners 1961.

A cultured footballer with skill and determination, Ron Wylie made over 700 appearances, scoring 71 goals in his career. He helped Villa to success over Rotherham United in the first League Cup Final, in 1961, and also to the Second Division title in 1959-60. He also played in two losing semi-finals for Birmingham, in the League Cup in 1967 and the FA Cup in 1968.

After being turned down by Burnley as being too small to make the grade, he was twice signed by Eric Houghton, for Notts County and Aston Villa. After many years in coaching, Wylie was appointed as West Brom's manager in 1982. His teams looked good on paper but gave mediocre performances on the field and he resigned with his coach, Mike Kelly, midway through a poor season in 1983-84.

YEATS, Ronald

Born: Aberdeen, 15 November 1937.
Centre-half 6ft 2in; 13st 12lb (1963).
Career: Aberdeen Boys Club; Dundee United 1957; Liverpool July 1961 (£22,000); Tranmere Rovers December 1971 player-assistant manager, then player-manager April 1972-April 1975,

retired as a player April 1974) Stalybridge Celtic player 1975; Barrow player-manager 1976; Liverpool chief scout 1986-1987.

Honours: Scotland international (2 caps); Schoolboy international; Football League champions 1964, 1966; Division Two champions 1962; FA Cup winners 1965; European Cup-winners' Cup runners-up 1966.

Ron Yeats was described by Bill Shankly, his manager at Liverpool, as 'the colossus of the defence'. Dominant in the air, he rarely played a bad game for Liverpool and made 450/1 appearances, scoring 15 goals for the club. He gained two League championship medals, a Second Division medal and helped his club beat Leeds United in the 1965 FA Cup Final. Yeats probably has unhappy memories of the 1966 European Cup-winners' Cup Final, in which his own-goal won the game for Borussia Dortmund.

At Tranmere he became player-assistant manager under Jackie Wright and took over as manager in 1972. Yeats took many former Anfield men to Prenton Park, including Ian St John, Tommy Lawrence, Willie Stevenson and Bobby Graham. He also had some up-and-coming youngsters like Steve Coppell and Ronnie Moore. Attendances rocketed as interest in the club was revitalised. However, with relegation looming after a down turn in the club's fortunes, Yeats was sacked in 1975.

YEOMAN, Raymond I.

Born: Perth, Scotland, 13 May 1934.
Inside-forward 5ft 8in; 12st 6lb (1963).
Career: St Johnstone; Northampton Town September 1963; Middlesbrough November 1958 (£3,740); Darlington June 1964, then manager March 1968-cs 1970; Sunderland youth-team manager 1970; Everton scout in the 1980s.

Yeoman had an honest style and was a player with integrity, dedication and determination. He was twice signed by Bob Dennison, at Northampton and Middlesbrough, and made 168 League appearances for the Cobblers, 227 for 'Boro and 103 for Darlington. This included 207 consecutive games for Middlesbrough, a run which ended when he was dropped in August 1963. He did not score many goals in his career, only nine.

When he took over at Darlington, they looked like promotion certainties in 1968-69, but requiring a victory in the last match over promotion rivals Bradford City, they crashed to a 3-1 defeat at Feethams and Bradford were promoted. The following season they slumped to third from bottom of Division Four and were relegated. Yeoman lost his job soon afterwards.

YORATH, Terence Charles

Born: Cardiff, 27 March 1950.
Midfield 5ft 10in; 10st 12lb (1975).
Career: Cardiff Schools; Leeds United apprentice 1965, professional April 1967; Coventry City August 1976 (£125,000); Tottenham Hotspur August 1979 (£300,000); Vancouver Whitecaps (NASL) (£140,000) March 1981; Bradford City December 1982, coach 1983 and assistant manager 1984-1985; Swansea City manager July 1986-February 1989; Bradford City manager February 1989-March 1990; Swansea City manager again March 1990-March 1991; also Wales national manager April 1988.

Honours: Wales international (59

caps); Under-23 international (7 caps); Schoolboy international (4 caps); Football League champions 1974; Division Four promotion 1988; FA Cup runners-up 1973; European Cup runners-up 1975; European Cup-winners' Cup runners-up 1973.

Tenacious, tough-tackling and an aggressive competitor, Terry Yorath had the ability to motivate others around him. He was nearly always on the fringe of the first team at Leeds United but eventually played 162/32 games for the club. He appeared as substitute in the 1973 FA Cup Final, when Leeds lost 1-0 to Second Division Sunderland, and played in the European Cup-winners' Cup Final defeat against AC Milan and the 1975 European Cup Final defeat against Bayern Munich in Paris. Yorath captained Wales 42 times in his 59 games for his country.

He played a pivotal role at the centre of Coventry's midfield and also did well for Spurs before losing his first-team place and moving to Vancouver Whitecaps. He was assistant to Trevor Cherry at Valley Parade and was then appointed Swansea's manager. He took them to promotion to Division Three in 1988 but left the club in controversial circumstances to return to Bradford City. He paid £18,000 out of his own pocket to honour his contract at Swansea.

However, he did not last long at Valley Parade and was sacked after a string of poor results. In a bizarre turn of events, he returned to Swansea but was later sacked. Yorath took Wales very close to qualification to the 1992 European championships. He suffered a personal tragedy in 1992, when his teenage son, who had just signed for Leeds, died from a hitherto undiagnosed heart complaint.

YOUNG, Alfred

Born: Sunderland, 4 November 1905; Died: 30 August 1977.
Centre-half 5ft 11in; 12st 11lb (1938).
Career: Durham City amateur 1926; Huddersfield Town January 1927; York City November 1945; Koge Boldclub (Copenhagen) coach 1946-1948; Huddersfield Town coach August 1948-May 1952; Bradford manager December 1957-November 1958; Esjberg (Denmark) coach November 1958; Huddersfield Town coach December 1960, chief scout 1964-July 1965.

Honours: England international (9 caps); Football League representative (3 caps); FA Cup runners-up 1938.

A former colliery worker, Young played

309 games, scoring six goals, for Huddersfield Town. A regular first-teamer throughout the 1930s, Young was appointed skipper in February 1935. An outstanding pivot who adapted the 'policeman' role that many centre-halves of this period took on, Young was also strong and dominating in the air. He gained his first England cap against Wales in November 1932, in a 0-0 draw at Wrexham, and played in England's famous 6-3 victory over Germany in Berlin in May 1938, when the players were issued with orders to give the Nazi salute to Adolf Hitler.

Young gave away the penalty in the last minute of extra-time which allowed Preston to beat Huddersfield 1-0 in the 1938 FA Cup Final. When he became Bradford manager in 1957, he was their fifth manager in six years. He was unable to stop the rot as the club entered the Fourth Division in 1958.

YOUNG, Richard

Born: Gateshead, 17 April 1918; Died: 31 January 1989.
Centre-half 6ft; 12st 7lb (1951).
Career: Bolden Colliery; Sheffield United November 1935; RAF in World War Two; Lincoln City player-coach March 1949, retired 1954; Carlisle United trainer-coach from 1955, then manager November 1975-November 1976, assistant manager November 1976-1977, manager again 1980-1982, when he retired.

A six-footer, Dick Young could play at right-back or centre-half. He helped Sheffield United to promotion from Division Two in 1938-39 but lost much of his playing career to the war. He served under Fred Emery when he first joined Carlisle United and succeeded Alan Ashman as manager at the age of 57, after having been trainer at the club for 20 years.

He paid £50,000 for Ian MacDonald from St Johnstone and £30,000 from Billy Rafferty from Plymouth to bolster the attack. But with the club near the bottom of Division Two, Young stepped down to be replaced by Bobby Moncur. By his own admission he loved the club and must have been sad when the day came for him to move on.

YOUNG, Robert Thornton MM

Born: Brandon, 5 September 1893; Died: Norwich, 8 September 1960.
Left-back 5ft 8in; 12st (1919).
Career: Esh Winning; Sunderland March 1913; Norwich City trainer May 1926, then manager February 1937-January 1939 and 1940-1946. Brancepeth School; Brancepeth Villa; Esh Winning Rangers.

Bob Young was never a first-team regular at Roker Park and played only 56 games for the club before hanging up his boots. Young was wounded in World War One, during which he received the Military Medal. He spent 20 years at Norwich City as trainer and manager, steering the club clear of relegation in 1936-37.

Due to the development of the Carrow Road ground, cash was in short supply and he had no money for new players. The 'A' team was abandoned in 1937, as a cost-cutting exercise, and Barry Town were adopted as a nursery club. With Norwich heading for relegation in 1938-39, Young was replaced by Jimmy Jewell, although he returned to steer the club through the difficult war years.

Bibliography

We have managed to find histories for most Football League clubs and Dave Twydell's book on clubs that have gone out of the League has been an especially useful source of information. There is much conflicting information in these sources and we have had to make a personal judgement as to which is likely to have been correct. This is split into six sections: Club Histories; Annuals/Yearbooks; Autobiographies; Magazines/Programmes; Who's Whos; and Statistics and Others.

Club Histories

Appleton, Arthur *Hotbed of Soccer.*
Attaway, Pete *Nottingham Forest: A Complete Record 1865-1991.*
Batters, Dave *York City: A Complete Record 1922-1990.*
Bell, Ted *On the Ball City (Norwich City).*
Berry, Harry & Allman Geoff *100 years at Deepdale 1881-1981.*
Binns, George *75 years on — Huddersfield Town.*
Bishop, Peter *The A-Z of Tranmere Rovers.*
Chalk, Gary & Holley, Duncan *Southampton: A Complete Record 1885-1987.*
Cheshire, Scott & Hockings, Ron *Chelsea: A Complete Record 1905-1991.*
Childerhouse, Tim *Aldershot-Sixty Years of . . .*
Clough, Brian *Forward with the Dale (Rochdale).*
Collings, Timothy *The Luton Town Story 1885-1985.*
Cowing, Ronald *The Carlisle United Story.*
Crewe Alexandra *100 years up (Brochure).*
Cullen, Peter *Bury F.C. 1885-1985.*
Dean, Rod *Coventry City: A Complete Record 1883-1991.*
Downs, David *Biscuits and Royals — History of Reading F.C.*
Dykes, Garth *Oldham Athletic: A Complete Record 1899-1988.*
Dykes, Garth *New Brighton: A Complete Record in the F.L.*
Eastwood, John & Davage, Mike *Canary Citizens — History of Norwich City.*
Eastwood, John & Moyse, Tony *The Men Who Made The Town — (Ipswich Town history).*
Elton, Chris *Hull City: A Complete Record 1904-1989.*
Farnsworth, Keith *Sheffield Wednesday: A Complete Record 1867-1986.*
Finn, Ralph *Chelsea F.C. Official History.*
Finney, Richard *History of Rotherham United.*
Frost, Terry *Bradford City: A Complete Record 1903-1988.*
Frost, Terry *Huddersfield Town: A Complete Record 1910-1990.*
Futter, Alan *History of Croydon Common 1897-1917 — Who Killed the Cock Robins?*
Glanville, Brian *Arsenal.*
Glasper, Harry *Middlesbrough: A Complete Record 1876-1989.*
Goble, Ray *Manchester City: A Complete record 1887-1987.*
Godsiff, Peter *Bristol City.*
Golesworthy, Maurice, Dykes, Garth & Wilson, Alex *Exeter City: A Complete Record 1904-1990.*
Goodwin, Bob *Spurs: A Complete Record 1882-1988.*
Goodyear, David & Matthews, Tony *Aston Villa: A Complete Record 1874-1988.*
Grande, Frank *The Cobblers — The Story of Northampton F.C.*
Hartley, Malcolm & Clapham, Tim *Bradford Park Avenue.*
Hodgson, Derek *Manchester United Story.*
Holland, Julian *Spurs.*
Howland, Andy & Roger *Oxford United: A Complete Record 1893-1989.*
Jackman, Mike *Blackburn Rovers: A Complete Record 1875-1990.*
Jackman, Mike & Dykes, Garth *Accrington Stanley: A Complete Record 1894-1962.*
Jarred, Martin & MacDonald, Malcolm *Leeds United: A Complete Record 1919-1989.*
Jay, Mike *Bristol Rovers: A Complete Record 1883-1987.*
Joannou, Paul *History of Newcastle United.*
Joannou, Paul *Newcastle United: A Complete Record 1882-1986.*
Johnson, Ian *Aston Villa.*
Joint, Laura *Torquay United — the first 70 years.*
Jones, Peter *Wrexham: A Complete Record 1872-1992.*
Joy, Bernard *Forward Arsenal.*
Kaufman, Neil & Ravenhill, Alan *Orient F.C.*
Kaufman, Neil & Ravenhill, Alan *Leyton Orient: A Complete Record 1881-1990.*
Kent, Jeff *The Valiants' Years — The Story of Port Vale.*

Knight, Brian *Plymouth Argyle: A Complete Record 1903-1989.*
Korr, Charles *West Ham United.*
Law, Ed *Hartlepool United: A History.*
Lawson, John *Nottingham Forest 1865-1978.*
Lee, Edward & Simpson, Ray *Burnley: A Complete Record 1882-1991.*
Lindsay, Richard *Millwall: A Complete Record 1885-1991.*
Marland, Simon *Bolton Wanderers: A Complete Record 1877-1989.*
Martin, Wade — *The Potter's Tale (Stoke).*
Matthews, Tony *Birmingham City: A Complete Record 1875-1989.*
Matthews, Tony *Albion! A Complete Record 1879-1987.*
Matthews, Tony & Allman, Geoff *The History of Walsall F.C. 1888-1992.*
Matthews, Tony & Smith, Les *The Wolves — History 1877-1989.*
Mattick, Dick *The Robins: The Story of Swindon Town F.C.*
Morris, Peter *Aston Villa. The First 100 Years.*
Morris, Peter *West Bromwich Albion.*
Morrison, Ian & Shury, Alan *Manchester United: A Complete Record 1878-1986.*
Mortimer, Gerald *Derby County: A Complete Record 1884-1988.*
Moynihan, John *Chelsea Story.*
Murray, James *Millwall — Lions of the South.*
Neasom, Mike, Cooper, Mike and Robinson, Doug *Pompey — The History of Portsmouth F.C.*
Northcutt, John & Shoesmith, Roy *West Ham United: A Complete Record 1900-1987.*
Ollier, Fred *Arsenal: A Complete Record 1886-1988.*
Pead, Brian *Liverpool: A Complete Record 1892-1986.*
Peskett, Roy *Crystal Palace.*
Phillips, Oliver *The Official Centenary of Watford F.C. 1881-1991.*
Phillips, Stephen *The Survivors — History of Rochdale F.C.*
Prole, David *Football In London.*
Purkiss, Mike *Crystal Palace: A Complete Record 1905-1989.*
Redden, Richard *Charlton Athletic 1905-1990 - The Story of. . .*
Rickaby, Jim *Aberdeen: A Complete Record 1903-1987.*
Rippon, Anton *Great Soccer Clubs of the North East.*
Rippon, Anton *The Tottenham Hotspur Story.*
Searl, Stan *Mansfield Town: A Complete Record 1910-1990-*
Shaoul, Mark *The History of Queen's Park Rangers.*
Shorrocks, Alec *Manchester United — Winners & Champions.*
Shrewsbury Town F.C. *Shrewsbury Town Centenery Souvenir.*
Signy, Dennis *Queen's Park Rangers.*
Simmons, Bill and Graham, Bob *Sunderland.*
Smailes, Gordon *Everton: A Complete Record 1878-1985.*
Smith, Dave and Taylor, Paul *Of Fossils and Foxes (Leicester).*
Soar, Phil *Tottenham Hotspur — Spurs Go Marching On.*
Soar, Phil *Arsenal 1886-1986 — The Official History.*
Sutton United *Sutton United 1898-1973.*
Taylor, Hugh *Glasgow Rangers — We Will Follow Rangers.*
Thornton, Eric *Manchester City.*
Thwaites, Tony *From Sandhall to the Shay (Halifax Town History).*
Triggs, Roger *Gillingham, A Chronology 1893-1984.*
Triggs, Les *Grimsby Town: A Complete Record 1878-1989.*
Turner, Dennis *Fulham Centenary 1879-1979.*
Turner, Dennis & White, Alex *Fulham: A Complete Record 1879-1987.*
Turton, Tom *Stockport County Centenary 1883-1983.*
Tweddle, Frank *Darlington 1883-1983.*
Twydell, Dave *Rejected F.C. Volume 1.*
Twydell, Dave *Rejected F.C.Volume 2.*
Twydell, Dave *Football League — Grounds for a change.*
Vinicombe, John *Albion — An Illustrated history of Brighton & Hove Albion.*
Warsop, Keith *Notts County.*
White, Eric & Haynes, Graham et al *100 Years of Brentford.*

Wild, K.A. *Carlisle United 50 seasons 1928-84.*
Willmore, G.A. *West Bromwich Albion.*
Wilson, Brian *Celtic — A century with honour.*
Wingfield, Martin (Ed) *The League History of Workington.*
Woods, David & Crabtree, Andrew *Bristol City: A Complete Record 1894-1987.*
Young, Percy *Football on Merseyside.*
Young, Percy *Bolton Wanderers.*
Young, Percy *Football in Sheffield.*
Young, Percy *Manchester United.*
Young, Percy *Centenary Wolves (Wolves History).*

Annuals/Yearbooks

Daily Telegraph *Football Yearbook.*
F.A. *F.A. Official Year Books.*
Granville, Brian (Ed) *World Football Handbook.*
Hammond, Mike (Ed) *The European Football Yearbook 1988-89.*
Johnston, W.M. *The Football League 1932-39.*
Panini *Football Yearbook.*
Rothmans *Football Yearbook Vol 1-23.*
Williams, Tony (Ed) *Non-League Directory 1982-93.*
Williams, Tony (Ed) *Football League Club Directories.*

Biographies

Buchan, Charles *A lifetime in Soccer.*
Busby, Matt *Soccer At The Top.*
Busby, Matt *My Story.*
Clarke, Allan *Goals are my business.*
Cullis, Stanley *All for the Wolves.*
Docherty, Tommy *Soccer from the Shoulder.*
Dunphy, Eamon *Only a game.*
Firmani, Eddie *Football with the Millionaires.*
Greenwood, Ron *Yours Sincerely.*
Harding, John *Football Wizard — The Story of Billy Meredith.*
Hill, Jimmy *Striking for Soccer.*
Peskett, Roy *Tom Whittaker's Arsenal Story.*
Raynor, George *Football Ambassador at Large.*
Seed, Jimmy *The Jimmy Seed Story.*
Shankly, Bill *Shankly.*
Stock, Alec *A Little Thing Called Pride.*
Walker, Billy *Soccer in the blood.*

Magazines/Programmes

A.F.S. *Football Recollections.*
A.F.S. *A.F.S.Bulletins.*
Around Football *Magazine (early 1980s).*
Book of Football Magazine *Book of Football (early 1970s).*
Football Monthly *Magazine 1951-73.*
Football Today *Magazine (late 1980s).*
Football Weekly News *Magazine (early 1980s).*
Goal *Magazine (1970s).*
Jimmy Hill's Football Weekly *Magazine (late 1960s).*
Non-League Football *Magazine January 1989-February 1992.*
Pyramid *Non-League Football Magazine.*
Programme *Newport County v Rochdale 7 May 1988.*
Programme *Southport v Huddersfield Town 22 April 1978.*
Robinson & Rippon et al *The Footballer Magazine.*
Soccer Star *Magazine (1960s).*
Team Talk *Magazine August 1991-present.*
World Soccer *Magazine.*

Who's Who

A.F.S. *Football Who's Who 1902, 1903, 1907 & 1909.*
Ambrosen, Tony *Ironsides — A Lifetime in the League (Newport County).*
Brown, Harry (Ed) *Soccer Who's Who 1970.*
Brown, H.R. *1907-1908 Football Who's Who.*
Cameron, Colin *The Valiant 500: Biographies of Charlton Athletic Players Past & Present.*
Cheshire, Scott & Hockings, Ron *Chelsea Players Who's Who.*
Clipper Annual *Who's Who in Football 1970, 1971, 1975.*
Crooks, John *A Who's Who of Cardiff City's F.L. Players.*
Davies, Gareth *Who's Who of Welsh International Soccer Players.*
Donnachie, Bill *Who's Who of Kilmarnock.*
Empire News *Footballer's Who's Who 1955.*
Farror, Morley & Lamming, Douglas *English Internationals Who's Who 1872-1972.*

Football Weekly *Book of 650 Football Stars 1936.*
Glanville, Brian *Who's Who in Football 1951.*
Golesworthy, Maurice *Soccer Who's Who.*
Green, Benny (Ed) *The Wisden Book of Obituaries.*
Hogg, Tony & Hellier, Jack *Who's Who of West Ham 1900-1986.*
Jeffrey, Gordon *International Football Who's Who.*
Joannou, Paul *A Complete Who's Who of Newcastle Utd.*
Johnston, Frank (Ed.) *The Football's Who's Who 1935.*
Lamming, Doug *Scottish Internationalist Who's Who 1872-1986.*
Lamming, Doug *A Who's Who of Grimsby Town 1890-1985.*
Lamming, Doug *A Who's Who of Liverpool 1892-1989.*
Lamming, Doug *A Who's Who of Hull City 1904-1984.*
Lamming, Douglas *An English Football Internationals' Who's Who.*
Matthews, Tony *Aston Villa Who's Who 1874-1989.*
Matthews, Tony *West Bromwich Albion — Who's Who.*
Matthews, Tony *Manchester United Who's Who 1945-1985.*
Matthews, Tony & Baker, Roger *Birmingham City Who's Who 1875-1991.*
Noble, Graham *Oakwell Heroes — Who's Who of Barnsley.*
Oakes, Peter & Spiers, Graham *Who's Who in F.L. Division One.*
Price, E.C. (Ed) *Men Famous in Football 1903, 1904, 1905.*
Rollin, Jack *Who's Who in Soccer 1980s & 1990s.*
Sports Budget *Who's Who 1925.*
Sports Fun *Footballer's Who's Who 1922.*
Topical Times *New Who's Who of 2,000 Football Stars (1933).*
Topical Times *Who's Who 1938.*
Triggs, Roger *Priestfield Profiles — A Who's Who of Gillingham 1950-88.*
Williams, Tony (Ed) *Non League Footballers Who's Who.*

Other

Athletic News *Pre-Season lists 1914-1930.*
Barrett, Norman *World Soccer from A-Z.*
Barrett, Norman *The Book of Football.*
Barton, Bob *The History of the F.A.Amateur Cup.*
Fabian, A.H. & Green G *Association Football (4 Volumes).*
Francis, Lionel *75 Years of the Southern League.*
Gibson, John *Soccer's Golden Nursery.*
Gibson A. & Pickford W. *Association Football and the men who made it.*
Golesworthy, Maurice *Encyclopædia of Association Football.*
Harrison, Paul *Southern League Football — The First fifty years.*
Hill, Jimmy *Great Soccer Stars.*
James, Brian *England v Scotland.*
Johnston, Frank (Ed) *The Football Encyclopædia 1934.*
Jose, Colin *NASL-A Complete Record of North American Soccer League.*
McMenemy, Lawrie *The Diary of a Season.*
Meek, David *Manchester United Football Books.*
Morris, Peter *The Team Makers.*
Pawson, Tony *The Football Managers.*
Rollin, Jack *Soccer at War.*
Taylor, Hugh *Great Masters of Scottish Football.*
Tyler, Martin *Cup Final Extra.*
Yorkshire Sports and Football Argus *Transfer Lists 1926-1933.*